DYNAMICS *of* DEMOCRACY

DYNAMICS *of* DEMOCRACY

Second Edition

PEVERILL SQUIRE
University of Iowa

JAMES M. LINDSAY
University of Iowa

CARY R. COVINGTON
University of Iowa

ERIC R.A.N. SMITH
University of California–Santa Barbara

Madison, WI Dubuque Guilford, CT Chicago Toronto London
Mexico City Caracas Buenos Aires Madrid Bogotá Sydney

Book Team

Acquisitions Editor *Scott Spoolman*
Developmental Editor *Marsena Konkle*
Editorial Assistant *Kari Geltemeyer*
Production Editor *Ann Fuerste*
Proofreading Coordinator *Carrie Barker*
Art Editor *Miriam Hoffman*
Photo Editor *Rose Deluhery*
Permissions Coordinator *Karen L. Storlie*
Production Manager *Beth Kundert*
Production/Costing Manager *Sherry Padden*
Design and New Media Development Manager *Linda Meehan Avenarius*
Visuals/Design Freelance Specialist *Mary L. Christianson*
Marketing Manager *Kirk Moen*

Basal Text *10/12 Times Roman*
Display Type *Times Roman*
Typesetting System *Macintosh™ Quark™XPress*
Paper Stock *45# Recycled Courtland*

Executive Vice President and General Manager *Bob McLaughlin*
Vice President, Business Manager *Russ Domeyer*
Vice President of Production and New Media Development *Victoria Putman*
National Sales Manager *Phil Rudder*
National Telesales Director *John Finn*

The credits section for this book begins on page 716 and is considered an extension of the copyright page.

Cover and interior designs by Maureen McCutcheon Design

Cover image © Chris Hamilton/The Stock Market

Photo research by Shirley Lanners

Copyedited by Anne Caylor Cody; proofread by Rose R. Kramer

Freelance Permissions Editor Karen Dorman

Library of Congress Catalog Card Number: 96–86062

ISBN 0–697–32752–3

Printed in the United States of America

10 9 8 7 6 5 4 3 2 1

To
Russell and Emma
Ian, Cameron, and Flora
Sarah, Michael, and David
Katharine and Stephanie

Brief Contents

List of Boxes *xviii*
Preface *xix*
About the Authors *xxiv*

1 Studying the Dynamics of Democracy: Conflict, Rules, and Change *3*
2 The Constitution *19*
3 The Social Context of American Politics *67*
4 Civil Liberties *93*
5 Civil Rights *125*
6 Public Opinion *169*
7 Voting and Participation *201*
8 The News Media *231*
9 Political Parties *267*
10 Interest Groups *295*
11 Congress *331*
12 The Presidency *381*
13 The Federal Bureaucracy *425*
14 The Courts *461*
15 The Federal System and State Government *493*
16 The Federal Budget *527*
17 Domestic Policy *563*
18 Foreign Policy *603*

Appendixes

A The Declaration of Independence *637*
B The Articles of Confederation and Perpetual Union *639*
C Federalist No. 10 *643*
D Federalist No. 51 *646*
E Antifederalists and the Constitution *648*
F Letter from Birmingham Jail *650*
G Race and the U.S. Constitution *656*
H The Presidents and Vice Presidents of the United States *661*
I Presidential Election Results, 1789–1996 *662*
J Party Control of the Presidency, Senate, and House of Representatives, 1901–1997 *665*
K Twentieth-Century Justices of the Supreme Court *666*
L Presidential General Election Returns by State, 1996 *668*
M Portrait of the Electorate, 1984–1996 *670*
N American Political Parties Since 1789 *671*
O Contract With America *672*

Notes *673*
Glossary *710*
Credits *716*
Name Index *718*
Subject Index *725*

Contents

List of Boxes *xviii*
Preface *xix*
About the Authors *xxiv*

Part One

The Context of American Politics

1

Chapter 1

Studying the Dynamics of Democracy: Conflict, Rules, and Change

3

Politics and Conflict *8*
- *The Roots of Conflict* *8*
- *The Role of Government in Managing Conflict* *9*

Government as Rule Maker *11*
- *Structural Rules* *11*
- *Policy Rules* *12*
- *The Biased Character of Rules* *14*
- *The Changing Rules of Government* *15*

Putting It All Together: Context, Participants, Institutions, and Processes *16*
- *The Context of American Politics* *16*
- *Individuals and Groups in American Politics* *16*
- *The Institutions of American Politics* *17*
- *The Policy Process in American Politics* *17*

Summary *18*

Key Terms *18*

Readings for Further Study *18*

Chapter 2

The Constitution

19

The Constitution as a Reflection of Political Conflict *20*
- *The Colonial Experience* *21*
- *The Articles of Confederation* *22*
- *The Politics of the Constitutional Convention* *23*
- *The Politics of Ratification* *28*

The Constitution as a Reflection of the Founders' Philosophy *31*
- *Individual Rights and Democratic Rule* *32*
- *Majority Tyranny: The Paradox of Majority Rule* *32*
- *Preventing Majority Tyranny* *33*

The Core Provisions of the Constitution *38*
- *Congress* *38*
- *The Presidency and the Executive Branch* *39*
- *The Federal Judiciary* *40*
- *Interstate Relations* *41*
- *Other Provisions* *41*

Three Consequences of the Constitution *42*
- *The Protection of Individual Rights* *42*
- *A Bias in Favor of the Status Quo* *43*
- *Political Flexibility* *44*

Federalism: The Vertical Dimension to the Constitution *46*
Confederal, Unitary, and Federal Governments 47
Establishing National Supremacy 47
The Assertion of States' Rights 49
The Civil War and the Reassertion of National Supremacy 50
Dual Federalism 51
The Present Era—National Supremacy as Fiscal Federalism 51
Summary *53*
Key Terms *54*
Readings for Further Study *54*
The Constitution of the United States *55*

CHAPTER 3

THE SOCIAL CONTEXT OF AMERICAN POLITICS

67

Who Are Americans? *68*
A Growing and Changing Population 69
Race and Ethnicity 72
Immigration 76
Language 77
Age 78
Family Households 78
Sexual Orientation 79
Social and Economic Characteristics *80*
Religion 80
Education 81
Wealth and Income 82
Home Ownership 86
Occupation 86
Diversity and Social Harmony *88*
Political Power in the United States *89*
Summary *91*
Key Terms *92*
Readings for Further Study *92*

CHAPTER 4

CIVIL LIBERTIES

93

Interpreting the Constitution *94*
The Bill of Rights and State Government *96*
The First Amendment: Freedom of Speech, Assembly, Press, and Religion *97*
Freedom of Speech 97
Freedom of Assembly and Association 104
Freedom of the Press 105
Freedom of Religion 108
The Second Amendment: The Right to Bear Arms? *112*
State Militias 113
Supreme Court Rulings 113
Gun Control Laws 115
Government and the Rights of Criminal Suspects *116*
The Fourth Amendment: Search and Seizure 117
The Fifth Amendment: Criminal Procedure for a Person Accused 118
The Sixth Amendment: Procedures for People Charged with a Crime 119
The Eighth Amendment: Cruel and Unusual Punishment 120
Privacy as a Constitutional Right *121*
Summary *123*
Key Terms *124*
Readings for Further Study *124*

CHAPTER 5

CIVIL RIGHTS

125

Civil Liberties and Civil Rights *127*
Discrimination Against African Americans *128*
From Slavery to Emancipation 128
Jim Crow 130
The First Civil Rights Organizations 133
The Brown Decision 135
The Civil Rights Movement 138
Congress Responds 139
The Continuing Fight Against Discrimination 141
Discrimination Against Asian Americans, Hispanic Americans, American Indians, and Others *143*
Asian Americans 143
Hispanic Americans 146
American Indians 146
Other Minorities 148
Discrimination Against Women *148*
Campaigning for the Right to Vote 149
The Fight for Equal Rights on Capitol Hill 150
The Fight for Equal Rights in the Courts 153
The Continuing Struggle Against Sex Discrimination 154
Extending Civil Rights *156*
People with Disabilities 156
People with Age Claims 157
Gays and Lesbians 157
The Burden of Proof 160
Affirmative Action: Equal Opportunity or Equal Outcomes? *160*
Summary *164*
Key Terms *165*
Readings for Further Study *165*

Part Two

Individuals and Groups in American Politics

167

Chapter 6

Public Opinion

169

The People's Limited Knowledge of Politics *170*
- *The Distribution of Knowledge 174*
- *Sources of Knowledge 176*
- *People with Knowledge: Issue Publics 176*

The Nature and Acquisition of Opinions and Values *177*
- *Family and Friends 177*
- *School 178*
- *The Media 179*
- *Lifetime Learning 180*

Ideologies *180*
- *Liberalism 181*
- *Conservatism 183*
- *Changes Over Time 183*
- *Sources of Ideologies 185*
- *The Process of Molding Ideologies 186*

Public Opinion on the Issues *187*
- *Ideological Thinking by the Public 187*
- *Abstract Symbols Versus Concrete Policies 188*
- *Public Opinion on Clusters of Related Issues 190*
- *Change in Opinion Over Time 195*
- *Causes of Change 196*

Summary *197*

Key Terms *198*

Readings for Further Study *198*

Chapter 7

Voting and Participation

201

Who Votes? *202*
- *The Effect of Individual Voter Characteristics 202*
- *The Effect of Registration Laws 206*
- *The Effect of Campaign Contacts 208*
- *The Puzzling Decline of Voter Turnout 212*
- *Does Turnout Matter? 214*

Political Activists *215*
- *Who Becomes an Activist? 215*
- *Types of Activists 216*

How Voters Make Choices *217*
- *Party Identification 217*
- *Candidate Characteristics 220*
- *Issues 221*
- *Changes Over Time 225*
- *Voting and Social Groups 226*

Summary *228*

Key Terms *229*

Readings for Further Study *230*

Chapter

8

The News Media

231

Do the News Media Matter? *233*
- *The News Media and Public Opinion 233*
- *The News Media and the Political Agenda 234*
- *The News Media and Government 235*

The Changing Face of the News Media *236*
- *Changes in Journalistic Conventions 236*
- *Changes in Readership and Viewership 238*
- *Changes in Media Ownership 243*

Freedom of the Press *245*
- *Limits to Press Freedom 246*
- *The Electronic Media 247*

Reporting the News *249*
- *What Is News? 249*
- *Telling the Story 251*

Evaluating the News Media *254*
- *Ideological Bias 254*
- *Cynicism 256*
- *News as Entertainment 257*
- *On the Campaign Trail 258*
- *Reporting Leaks 262*

The News Media and Democracy *263*

Summary *263*

Key Terms *264*

Readings for Further Study *265*

Chapter 9

Political Parties
267

What Is a Political Party? *268*
- *Party Functions* *269*

Characteristics of U.S. Political Parties *271*
- *The Spatial Theory of Elections* *272*
- *The U.S. Two-Party System Versus Multiparty Systems* *275*
- *The Spatial Model Applied to Real Politics* *276*

The History of U.S. Parties and Elections *279*
- *The First Party System (1796–1824)* *279*
- *The Second Party System (1828–1856)* *279*
- *The Third Party System (1860–1892)* *280*
- *The Fourth Party System (1896–1928)* *280*
- *The Fifth Party System (1932–?)* *281*
- *Critical Elections and Party Realignment Theory* *281*
- *From Realignment to Dealignment?* *282*
- *The Uncertain Future* *283*

Modern Party Organization *284*
- *Local Organizations* *285*
- *State Organizations* *290*
- *National Organizations* *291*
- *Relationships Among Party Organizations* *292*

Summary *292*

Key Terms *293*

Readings for Further Study *293*

Chapter 10

Interest Groups
295

Defining Interest Groups *296*
- *Interest Groups Versus Political Parties* *297*
- *The Roles of Interest Groups* *297*

The Growth of Interest Groups *299*

The Diversity of Organized Interests *300*
- *Economic Interest Groups* *300*
- *Citizen Groups* *301*
- *Government Interest Groups* *302*
- *Coalitions and Divisions* *303*

Interest Group Formation and Maintenance *304*
- *Obstacles to Interest Group Formation* *304*
- *Overcoming Obstacles to Interest Group Formation* *305*
- *Interest Group Maintenance* *307*
- *Interest Group Bias* *307*

Interest Group Strategies *308*
- *Creating Political Action Committees* *308*
- *Lobbying the Government* *312*
- *Mobilizing Public Opinion* *316*
- *Litigating* *320*

Interest Group Influence *320*
- *External Factors* *321*
- *Internal Factors* *322*

The Balance Sheet on Interest Groups *323*
- *A Love/Hate Relationship* *323*
- *Calls for Reform* *325*
- *The Contributions of Interest Groups* *327*

Summary *327*

Key Terms *328*

Readings for Further Study *328*

Part Three

The Institutions of American Politics
329

Chapter 11

Congress
331

The Structure of Congress *332*
- *Bicameralism* *332*
- *The House of Representatives* *333*
- *The Senate* *334*

The Evolution of Congress *334*
- *Changing Attitudes Toward Service in Congress* *335*
- *Change in the House* *337*
- *Change in the Senate* *340*

Getting There and Staying There—Congressional Elections *341*
- *Incumbents and Reelection* *341*

The Election Setting *342*
The Incumbents' Advantages *346*
The Challengers' Disadvantages *351*
Voters and Election Outcomes *352*
Serving in Congress *353*
Who Serves? *353*
Congress as a Job *355*
Congress and Ethics *358*
Congress as an Organization *360*
Political Parties in Congress *360*
Party Leadership in Congress *361*
Committees *364*
Staff *367*
The Business of Congress *367*
The Legislative Process *368*
Decision Making *372*
Policy Oversight *376*
Congress and the Idea of Representation *377*
Summary *378*
Key Terms *379*
Readings for Further Study *380*

CHAPTER 12

THE PRESIDENCY

381

The Development of the Presidency *382*
The Presidency on Paper: Constitutional Rules *382*
The Presidency in Practice: Applying the Rules *386*
The Advent of the "Modern" Presidency *388*
Selecting a President *389*
The Nomination Process *390*
The General Election *396*
The Electoral College *400*
Consequences for Governing *402*
The Presidency as an Institution *402*
The Powers of the Presidency *402*
The Organizational Structure of the Presidency *405*
The Workings of the Presidency *409*
Assessing the Presidency as an Institution *415*
The Presidency in American Politics *415*
The Political Context: Permanent Crisis *416*
Presidential Strategies *418*
Presidential Relationships *419*
Summary *422*
Key Terms *423*
Readings for Further Study *424*

CHAPTER 13

THE FEDERAL BUREAUCRACY

425

What Is Bureaucracy? *427*
The Structure and Tasks of the Federal Bureaucracy *428*
Types of Federal Agencies *428*
The Tasks of the Federal Bureaucracy *432*
Development of the Federal Bureaucracy *434*
Constitutional Foundations *434*
The Growth of the Federal Bureaucracy *435*
The Expanding Functions of the Federal Bureaucracy *436*
Changes in the Federal Bureaucracy's Personnel System *439*
The Politics of the Federal Bureaucracy *441*
The Political Character of the Federal Bureaucracy *442*
The Goals of the Federal Bureaucracy *445*
The Political Resources of the Federal Bureaucracy *446*
Political Constraints on the Federal Bureaucracy *449*
Iron Triangles and the Federal Bureaucracy *454*
The Evolving Role of the Bureaucracy *456*
Reinventing the Federal Bureaucracy *457*
Summary *459*
Key Terms *460*
Readings for Further Study *460*

CHAPTER 14

THE COURTS

461

The Federal Courts *462*
The Constitution and the Federal Courts *462*
Congress and the Federal Courts *463*
The Federal Court System *464*
The Federal Courts as Policy Makers *466*
Judicial Review, Judicial Activism, and Policy Making *466*
Limitations on the Courts *468*
The Supreme Court as a Political Institution *469*
The Characteristics of the Court *470*
The Politics of Nomination and Confirmation *473*
Presidential Legacies on the Supreme Court *475*
Decision Making at the Supreme Court *475*
Hearing a Case *475*
Individual Decision Making *477*
Supreme Court Opinions *480*
Voting Patterns *481*
Who Wins Before the Supreme Court? *482*
The Lower Federal Courts *483*
District Courts *483*
Courts of Appeal *483*
Nomination and Confirmation *483*

State Courts 485
Organization 485
Judicial Selection 485
Length of Service 486
State Laws 486
Summary 487
Key Terms 488
Readings for Further Study 489

PART FOUR

THE POLICY PROCESS IN AMERICAN POLITICS
491

CHAPTER 15

THE FEDERAL SYSTEM AND STATE GOVERNMENT
493

Relations Between Federal, State, and Local Government 494
Federal Aid to State and Local Governments 494
Other Forms of Federal Influence 499
The Changing Nature of Federalism 500
State Government and Politics 502
State Constitutions 503
Governors 503
State Legislatures 507
Interest Groups in State Politics 511
The Public and Direct Democracy 514
Summing Up 516
State Budgets 517
Raising Revenues 517
Budgeting 520
Spending 521
Local Government 521
Forms of Local Government 521
Local Government Structures 522
Local Government and Representation 522
The Costs of Local Government 523
Privatization of Government Services 523
Who Delivers? Public Opinion and Level of Government 524
Summary 525
Key Terms 526
Readings for Further Study 526

CHAPTER 16

THE FEDERAL BUDGET
527

Budgets, Deficit Spending, and the National Debt 528
The Growing Federal Budget 529
The Rise of Deficit Spending 530
The Exploding National Debt 532
The Consequences of an Exploding National Debt 533
Where Does Government Revenue Come From? 534
Government Revenue in Historical Perspective 534
Income and Payroll Taxes 535
Where Does Government Spending Go? 538
The Changing Nature of Government Spending 538
The Growth of Entitlement Programs 539
Limiting Entitlement Programs 543
What About Pork? 544
Why Do Budget Deficits Persist? 546
Congress and the President 546
The American Public 546
The Budgetary Process 548
The Budgetary Process from George Washington to Richard Nixon 548
Budgetary Reform in the 1970s 549
Budgetary Reform in the 1980s 551
Budgetary Reform in the 1990s 553
A Balanced Budget by 2002? 553
More Reforms? 556
Is the Budget Process Irrational? 560
Summary 561
Key Terms 562
Readings for Further Study 562

Chapter 17

Domestic Policy

563

Managing the Economy *564*
- *From Government Restraint to Government Intervention 565*
- *Managing the Economy by Taxing and Spending 566*
- *Managing the Economy by Controlling the Money Supply 567*
- *Can the Government Manage the Economy? 569*
- *The Current Status of Economic Stewardship 570*

Regulating Business *574*
- *Basic Concepts and Categories 575*
- *The Objectives of Economic Regulation 575*
- *The Evolution of Economic Regulation 576*
- *Social Regulation 579*
- *Protecting Worker Safety and Health 579*
- *Protecting the Environment 581*

Promoting Social Welfare *586*
- *Basic Concepts and Categories 586*
- *The Evolution of Social Welfare Policy 587*
- *The Current Status of Social Welfare Policy 593*
- *The Future of Social Welfare Policy 595*

Summary *600*

Key Terms *601*

Readings for Further Study *601*

Chapter 18

Foreign Policy

603

A Brief History of U.S. Foreign Policy *604*
- *The Era of Isolationism 604*
- *The Era of Globalism 607*
- *After the Cold War 610*

Foreign Policy Versus Domestic Policy *611*
- *The Constitution and Foreign Policy 612*
- *The President's Inherent Advantages 612*
- *Precedent 613*
- *Supreme Court Rulings 613*
- *The Behavior of Congress 615*

Who Makes U.S. Foreign Policy? *617*
- *The White House 618*
- *The Foreign Policy Bureaucracy 618*
- *Congress 624*
- *The Public 625*

Challenges to the United States in the Post–Cold War Era *627*
- *Economic and Budgetary Constraints 627*
- *A Changing Foreign Policy Agenda 629*
- *Unilateralism Versus Multilateralism 631*

Summary *634*

Key Terms *635*

Readings for Further Study *635*

Appendixes

A The Declaration of Independence *637*

B The Articles of Confederation and Perpetual Union *639*

C Federalist No. 10 *643*

D Federalist No. 51 *646*

E Antifederalists and the Constitution *648*

F Letter from Birmingham Jail *650*

G Race and the U.S. Constitution *656*

H The Presidents and Vice Presidents of the United States *661*

I Presidential Election Results, 1789–1996 *662*

J Party Control of the Presidency, Senate, and House of Representatives, 1901–1997 *665*

K Twentieth-Century Justices of the Supreme Court *666*

L Presidential General Election Returns by State, 1996 *668*

M Portrait of the Electorate, 1984–1996 *670*

N American Political Parties Since 1789 *671*

O Contract With America *672*

Notes 673

Glossary 710

Credits 716

Name Index 718

Subject Index 725

List of Boxes

The People Behind the Rules

1.1 The Pros and Cons of Congressional Term Limits: Reps. Bob Inglis (R-S.C.) and Henry Hyde (R-Ill.) *6*

2.1 Antifederalists Versus Federalists: Patrick Henry and James Madison *28*

2.3 The Impact of Individuals on the Meaning of Federalism: Chief Justices John Marshall and Roger Taney *48*

3.1 The Average American, 1900 and 1995 *70*

4.1 Margaret Gilleo's Signs and the Right to Free Speech *102*

5.1 Who Were Plessy and Brown? *132*

5.2 The Women's Movement Then and Now *150*

6.2 The Liberals: Sen. Edward M. Kennedy and the Rev. Jesse Jackson *182*

6.3 The Conservatives: Sen. Phil Gramm and Patrick J. Buchanan *184*

7.2 The Politics of Voter Turnout: William Marcy "Boss" Tweed and Willie Velasquez *210*

8.1 William Randolph Hearst and Ted Turner *238*

9.2 The Mayor and the Reformer: Richard J. Daley and Michael Shakman *286*

10.1 Tommy Boggs and Marian Wright Edelman *314*

11.1 The Political Careers of Henry Clay and Newt Gingrich *336*

11.2 Changing Paths to the Senate: The Careers of Margaret Chase Smith and Olympia Snowe *356*

12.2 Martin Van Buren: Living and Dying by the Two-Thirds Rule *392*

12.3 Contrasting Management Styles: Reagan and Clinton *412*

13.2 Managing Public Lands: James Watt and Bruce Babbitt *444*

14.1 The Career Paths of William Rehnquist and Sandra Day O'Connor *472*

15.1 An Independent in the Governor's Mansion: Angus King of Maine *506*

16.2 Estimating the Numbers: June E. O'Neill, Alice Rivlin, and the 1996 Budget Battle *554*

17.2 Who Receives Welfare? Image Versus Reality *600*

18.3 The (Slowly) Changing Face of the Foreign Service *622*

Point of Order

1.2 Presidential Term Limits: The Twenty-second Amendment *13*

2.2 Obstacles to Amending the Constitution *45*

3.2 Figuring the Poverty Rate *85*

4.2 The Ninth Amendment: What Does It Mean? *122*

5.3 Standards of Judicial Scrutiny: Who Is Protected Under Civil Rights Laws? *161*

6.1 Public Opinion Polling Methods *172*

7.1 The Voting Rights Act of 1965 *209*

8.2 The Changing Rules of News Coverage *259*

9.1 The Politics of Getting on the Ballot: Sen. Robert Dole and the New York Republican Presidential Primary *272*

10.2 Limiting the Influence of Interest Groups: The Lobbying Disclosure Act of 1995 *326*

11.3 The Byrd Rule and Senate Voting on the Budget *373*

12.1 Alternative Arrangements for the Presidency Considered at the Constitutional Convention *384*

13.1 Who Gets the Job? The Effects of Veteran's Preference and Affirmative Action Rules on Government Hiring *442*

14.2 Precedent, Public Opinion, and the Supreme Court's Legitimacy *478*

15.2 Changing the Rules: The Effects of Legislative Term Limits on the California Assembly *512*

16.1 Measuring Inflation and Its Consequences for the Budget *540*

17.1 The Demise of the Interstate Commerce Commission *580*

18.1 The War Power *616*

18.2 Executive Agreements *618*

Preface

American politics can often seem a confusing swirl of personalities and issues: Bill Clinton and the complexities of Welfare reform, Newt Gingrich and the Contract With America, Marian Wright Edelman and the tragedy of children living in poverty. Such a list could go on and on, as we each add people and issues we find important and compelling, as well as those we don't understand or care about.

Without question, politics and the political system touch the lives of every American every day in a myriad of ways. But how can we make sense of it all? This book is our attempt to help college students understand the political structures and forces that shape their lives.

Approach

We address the issue of government and politics by emphasizing two lessons that appear in virtually every chapter. First, *politics arises from conflict.* The variety of interests in society makes conflicts virtually inevitable. Government seeks to manage (though not necessarily resolve) some of those conflicts by creating procedures and institutions. The Constitution, for instance, establishes many of the fundamental rules that structure politics in the United States. The second lesson we emphasize is that *the rules that stipulate how the government makes its decisions help determine the winners and losers in particular conflicts.* Rules are not neutral. Inevitably, the rules that structure the political process help some participants and harm others. That is why the rules themselves are often the target of vociferous debate and why changing the rules can change the outcome of a conflict. Thus, throughout *Dynamics of Democracy,* we show how the rules of politics and government reflect and shape conflicts in society.

Pedagogical Features

You will find a number of features within the text of each chapter to facilitate learning. First, each chapter is previewed with an outline of the main points covered in the text. These outlines provide an overview to the chapter and help you see how the various topics fit together. Second, each chapter opens with a brief story that highlights the key themes of the chapter and shows in concrete terms why they matter. Third, especially important concepts appear in the text in bold-faced print, with a definition provided in the margin. This "point of contact" approach to learning makes it easier for you to understand key points in the text because it puts the definitions where they are easy to find. The bold-faced terms also serve as a list of core concepts for study and review. Fourth, we have placed the text of the Constitution at the end of the chapter 2 discussion of the Constitution, so you can refer to it as needed. To ease your exploration of the Constitution, we have supplied marginal annotations that summarize the key points of each section.

In addition to these in-text features, you will find two types of boxes in each chapter. The first type of box, called "Point of Order," focuses on rules in government. You will read about how rules were adopted, how they changed over time, and how those changes affect the workings of the government. The second type of box, called "The People Behind the Rules," focuses on the people in government and politics. It, too, emphasizes change, showing how changes in the people involved in politics can affect the outcomes of political conflicts. Thus, each chapter contains in-depth examples that illustrate how rules and participants shape the political process.

Finally, at the end of each chapter, you will find an alphabetized list of key terms used in the chapter, as well as an annotated list of suggested readings for further study. By its very nature, an introductory textbook can only introduce the many important subjects of American politics. The readings at the end of each chapter suggest ways to explore further those topics that you find particularly interesting.

Finally, at the end of the book, you will find a rich array of supplemental readings and historical materials. They provide an important resource for independent study and research. How did the *Federalist Papers* explain the Constitution's solution to the threat of majority tyranny? Find the answer in Federalist No. 10 in appendix C. How frequently have we experienced periods of "divided" government (when Congress is controlled by one party and the presidency by the other)? Analyze appendix J for the answer. Thus, in a variety of ways, we have tried to ensure that reading the book will be a rewarding and enjoyable experience.

Ancillary Materials

Instructor's Manual by authors Peverill Squire, James M. Lindsay, Cary R. Covington, and Eric R. A. N. Smith. For every test chapter, the *Instructor's Manual* provides learning objectives; chapter outline; chapter summary; list of key terms; lecture outlines; a set of additional lecture topics, discussion questions and activities, and further readings; and a list of movies, videotapes, and documentaries.

Test Item File, prepared by Edward Weber of Washington State University, and Craig Coleman of the University of Wisconsin–Madison, consists of more than 2,500 quality test items, many of them class-tested. Page-referenced to the text, the test items identify each question as knowledge, conceptual, or applied, based on the first three levels of Benjamin Bloom's Taxonomy of Educational Objectives.

MicroTest III is a powerful but easy-to-use test generating program by Chariot Software Group that is available to users of *Dynamics of Democracy* in DOS, Windows, or Macintosh versions. With MicroTest III, you can easily select questions from the book's test item file; customize questions, headings, and instructions; add or import questions of your own; and print a test and answer key in a choice of fonts if your printer supports them. To obtain a copy of MicroTest III, contact your Brown & Benchmark Sales Representative or call Educational Resources at 1-800–338–5371.

Computerized and **Softcover Student Study Guides,** authored by Brian L. Fife of Ball State University, enhance student learning. The student guides contain chapter summaries, learning objectives, and chapter outlines. In addition, the guides provide a variety of review exercises for each chapter of the text, including a Review of Key Terms, Concepts, Events and People, a Practice Test (with answers) and Critical Thinking Exercises.

World Wide Web Guide for American Government, by Robert Bradley of Illinois State University, includes an introduction to the Internet and World Wide Web, information on browsers and search engines, lists of governmental web sites and political information sites, and tips on how to navigate the Web and make the best use of all the information available.

The **American Government Interactive Videodisc,** developed by Mark Triebwasser of Central Connecticut State University, was selected as "Best Instructional Software of 1994" by the Computers and Multimedia Section of the American Political Science Association. Available to qualified adopters, the videodisc and accompanying Instructor's Guide help you supplement lectures and illustrate points in the introductory American government course as well as upper-level political science courses. The two-sided videodisc, which may be used by itself and accessed with a remote control or barcode reader, consists primarily of C-SPAN footage as well as forty descriptive charts and figures. The videodisc is accompanied by HyperCard stacks that provide interactive commentary and video and search options, allowing you to use the videodisc with the HyperCard program and any Macintosh computer—perfect for computer labs and research projects.

American Government Interactive Simulation Software, developed by Steven E. Frantzich of the U.S. Naval Academy, gives your students the opportunity to actively experience American politics through simulation exercises that explore campaigning, the judicial process, and congressional coalition building. An interactive student polling simulation tabulates and compares user responses to classroom and national averages. For more information, contact your Brown & Benchmark Sales Representative.

Congressional Database, 104th Congress Version, is an analytical computer program for the IBM PC and compatibles which contains detailed biographical information, Capital Hill and district office addresses and phone numbers, committee and subcommittee assignments, personal financial assets, and ten interest group voting record ratings for each member of the 104th Congress. An accompanying workbook, developed by Steven E. Frantzich, serves as an introduction and guide, including six interesting exercises, for using the Database.

Color Transparencies provide you with forty-five important charts, graphs, and figures presented in the text to help with classroom presentation and student comprehension. **Customized Transparencies** are available to qualified adopters of *Dynamics of Democracy.* For details, contact your Brown & Benchmark Sales Representatives.

Videos, CD-ROMS, and videodiscs exploring a wide array of topics in American government and politics are available through Brown & Benchmark to qualified adopters of *Dynamics of Democracy.* The newest offering, *Campaign '96,* is a 30-minute videotape (from the creators of *Changing of the Guard: A Video Guide to the 1994 Elections,* also available from B&B) that covers the 1996 election season from the Iowa caucuses through the campaigns and conventions to the election. It includes interviews with key players from the major political parties and analysis by political scientists, as well as illustrative graphics and a chronicle of the key events leading up to the election night results. (Available January 1997)

Dynamics of Democracy adopters may have notes, handouts, or other classroom materials printed and bound inexpensively for classroom use through Brown & Benchmark's Custom Publishing Service. Talk to your Brown & Benchmark Sales Representative for details.

You may also complement *Dynamics of Democracy* with any of the following popular Dushkin Publishing Group supplements now available through Brown & Benchmark:

- *Annual Editions: American Government* 96/97 (97/98 edition available March 1997)
- *Taking Sides: Clashing Views on Controversial Political Issues,* 10th edition
- *Sources: Notable Selections in American Government*
- *ELITE Reader in American Government* (a menu of readings from a fascinating variety of sources from which you can construct your own custom-built reader)

Finally, the Brown & Benchmark **Course Integrator** provides you with a detailed guide for incorporating the ancillaries and readers into your course, showing section-by-section lists of ancillary contents correlated to the chapters in the textbook.

Instructors who wish to devote more coverage to gender and ethnicity issues should consider using *Dynamics of Democracy* in combination with *Voices of Diversity: Perspectives on American Political Ideals and Instructions* by Pat Andrews of West Valley College in California. This innovative and reasonably priced supplement from the Dushkin Publishing Group combines writings and speeches by American women and minority-group members with key public documents. Finally, your students can get a thorough and multifaceted analysis of the 1996 election in a new reader, with contributed articles from 12 respected experts, compiled by William Crotty of Northeastern University, entitled *America's Choice: The Election of 1996*. Combine any of these supplemental texts with *Dynamics of Democracy* at a discount for students under the Brown & Benchmark CourseKits™ program.

Acknowledgments

We wish to thank the many editors we have worked with at Brown & Benchmark: Dorian Ring, Ed Laube, Sue Alt-Pulvermacher, Roger Wolkoff, Michael Lange, Irv Rockwood, and Scott Spoolman.

We owe a special debt of gratitude to our developmental editor, Anne Caylor Cody. She is the best. None of us will forget her repeated injunction that students will follow our arguments only if the chapters "preview, discuss, and review" the material.

We also wish to thank our many colleagues around the country who read and commented on our draft chapters. *Dynamics of Democracy* second edition, became a much better book because of the care and thought our readers put into their reviews. We thank:

Alan Balboni
Community College of Southern Nevada

Donald Downs
University of Wisconsin-Madison

Richard Frese
Bentley College

John G. Geer
Vanderbilt University

Sara A. Grove
Shippensburg University of Pennsylvania

Samuel B. Hoff
Delaware State University

John S. Klemanski
Oakland University

Nancy Bolin Kral
Tomball College

Jay C. Mumford
Pennsylvania State University at Harrisburg

Doug Parrott
Sheridan College

Christopher Rhines
Essex Community College

Kevin H. Smith
The University of Memphis

Larry Wight
Sierra College

The following individuals reviewed the first edition of *Dynamics of Democracy,* and their helpful suggestions have been carried forward to the second edition:

Sheldon Appleton
Oakland University

Vincent Auger
Hamilton College

Ryan C. Barilleaux
Miami University (Ohio)

Gayle Berardi
University of Southern Colorado

Frederic Bergerson
Whittier College

Thad Beyle
University of North Carolina—Chapel Hill

William T. Bianco
Duke University

Barbara C. Burrell
University of Wisconsin—Extension

Robert Carp
University of Houston

John Clark
University of Georgia

Dennis Daley
North Carolina State University

Richard Davis
Brigham Young University

Thomas Dickson
Auburn University

Leon Epstein
University of Wisconsin—Madison

Brian Fife
Ball State University

Terri Fine
University of Central Florida

Dana Glencross
Oklahoma City Community College

George J. Gordon
Illinois State University

Doris Graber
University of Illinois—Chicago

Mark A. Graber
University of Maryland—College Park

Laura Greyson
Rollins College

Justin P. Halpern
Northeastern State University

Beth Henschen
Loyola University of Chicago

Paul Herrnson
University of Maryland—College Park

Joseph Ignagni
University of Texas—Arlington

Calvin C. Jillson
University of Colorado—Boulder

Laurence Jones
Angelo State University

Lyman Kellstedt
Wheaton College

Matthew Kerbel
Villanova University

Bert Kritzer
University of Wisconsin—Madison

Nancy S. Lind
Illinois State University

Brad Lockerbie
University of Georgia

H. R. Mahood
Memphis State University

Steven J. Mazurana
University of Northern Colorado

Don McCabe
Southern Illinois University—Edwardsville

David Menefee-Libey
Pomona College

Calvin Mouw
University of Missouri—St. Louis

Philip A. Mundo
Drew University

Albert J. Nelson
University of Wisconsin—LaCrosse

Michael Nelson
Rhodes College

Robert O'Connor
Pennsylvania State University

James Pfiffner
George Mason University

John Price
Louisiana Tech University

Diane Schmidt
Southern Illinois University—Carbondale

David F. Schwartz
Southern Illinois University—Edwardsville

Morton Sipress
University of Wisconsin—Eau Claire

Steven Stehr
Washington State University

Robert Smith Thompson
University of South Carolina—Columbia

Clyde Wilcox
Georgetown University

Christopher Wlezien
University of Houston

Robert A. Wood
North Dakota State University

Norman Zucker
University of Rhode Island

Tim Hagle of the University of Iowa deserves special thanks because we repeatedly barged into his office demanding that he explain the finer point of constitutional law, help us track down Supreme Court decisions, and make our computers run properly. He did all three with his usual elegance and good grace.

Finally, we would like to thank our families. They supported and encouraged us throughout the many ups and downs that attended the writing of *Dynamics of Democracy*. We deeply appreciate their love and understanding.

Peverill Squire

Peverill Squire is professor of political science at the University of Iowa, where he has served as chair of the department. Professor Squire received his A.B., M.A., and Ph.D. from the University of California, Berkeley. He was a visiting professor at Meiji University in Tokyo, Japan, where he taught a course on American politics. Professor Squire is the co-author of *The Politics of California Coastal Legislation* (Institute of Governmental Studies) and editor of *The Iowa Caucuses and the Presidential Nominating Process* (Westview Press). His articles on legislatures and elections at both the state and national levels, and on other aspects of American politics, have appeared in *American Political Science Review, American Politics Quarterly, British Journal of Political Science, Legislative Studies Quarterly, Journal of Politics, Political Behavior, Political Research Quarterly, Polity, Public Opinion Quarterly, State and Local Government Review,* and other leading journals. He has served on the planning committees for the 1992 National Election Study, Senate Election Study, and the 1994 National Election Study, and on the editorial boards for *Congress and the Presidency, Legislative Studies Quarterly, and Political Research Quarterly.* Professor Squire regularly teaches Introduction to American Politics, Legislative Process, The Presidency, and American State Politics.

James M. Lindsay

James M. Lindsay is professor of political science at the University of Iowa. He received his A.B. from the University of Michigan and his M.A., M.Phil., and Ph.D. from Yale University. He has been a guest scholar at the Center for International Affairs at Harvard University, the Center for Science and International Affairs at Harvard University, and the Brookings Institution. He is a recipient of a John D. and Catherine T. MacArthur Foundation Fellowship in International Peace and Security and of an Advanced Research Fellowship in Foreign Policy Studies, both from the Social Science Research Council, and a recipient of an International Affairs Fellowship from the Council on Foreign Relations. In addition to numerous articles in scholarly journals, Professor Lindsay is the author of *Congress and Nuclear Weapons* (Johns Hopkins University Press) and *Congress and the Politics of U.S. Foreign Policy* (Johns Hopkins University Press), and the co-editor of *Congress Resurgent* (University of Michigan Press) and *Change in U.S. Foreign Policy After the Cold War* (University of Pittsburg Press). An acclaimed teacher for his courses on U.S. foreign policy, he has received the Collegiate Teaching Award from the University of Iowa, the James N. Murray Faculty Teaching Award from the Finkbine Society, and a Pew Faculty Fellowship in International Affairs. In 1996–97, Professor Lindsay served as Director for Global Issues and Multilateral Affairs at the National Security Council, the White House.

Cary R. Covington

Cary R. Covington is associate professor of political science at the University of Iowa. He received his B.A. from Whittier College and his A.M. and Ph.D. from the University of Illinois at Urbana-Champaign. He is co-author of *The Coalitional Presidency* (Brooks/Cole Publishing Company), and his research on the institution of the presidency and on presidential-congressional relations has been published in such journals as *American Journal of Political Science, Journal of Politics, Political Research Quarterly, Legislative Studies Quarterly,* and *American Politics Quarterly.* Professor Covington has had a long and abiding interest in teaching, both in and out of the classroom. Before becoming a member of the faculty at the University of Iowa, he taught at Texas A&M University. He has worked as a consultant for the Educational Testing Service (ETS) as a member of its Test Development Committee for the College Level Examination Program (CLEP) in American government. At the University of Iowa, Professor Covington regularly teaches both large and small-enrollment courses on introductory American politics, as well as courses on the American presidency and bureaucratic politics. In addition to his activities in the classroom, he has assisted many students by serving at various times as the political science department's Director of Undergraduate Studies, Director of Graduate Studies, and Director of Government Internships.

Eric R. A. N. Smith

Eric R. A. N. Smith is associate professor of political science at the University of California, Santa Barbara. He received his A.B., M.A., and Ph.D. degrees from the University of California, Berkeley. He taught at Brandeis University and then at Columbia University from 1982 to 1986, before moving to U.C. Santa Barbara. He is the author of *The Unchanging American Voter* (University of California Press) and numerous articles in journals such as *American Political Science Review, Journal of Politics, Legislative Studies Quarterly,* and *Public Opinion Quarterly.* Professor Smith enjoys teaching and has taught a wide range of classes—including introduction to American government and politics, public opinion and elections, political parties, and Congress. He believes that to understand and appreciate politics, students should both study academic theories about politics and be exposed to real politics and politicians. Toward that end, Professor Smith teaches his Congress course based on a simulation of the U.S. House of Representatives; he regularly brings politicians into his classes to talk with his students; and he sponsors dozens of internships in local, state, and national politics. Smith is not only a scholar who studies politics, he is also an active participant in politics. He sponsors one of the political clubs on his campus and has worked in campaigns ranging from local to national office.

Part One

The Context of American Politics

1
Studying the Dynamics of Democracy: Conflict, Rules, and Change

2
The Constitution

3
The Social Context of American Politics

4
Civil Liberties

5
Civil Rights

CHAPTER

1

STUDYING THE DYNAMICS OF DEMOCRACY: CONFLICT, RULES, AND CHANGE

Politics and Conflict
- *The Roots of Conflict*
- *The Role of Government in Managing Conflict*

Government as Rule Maker
- *Structural Rules*
- *Policy Rules*
- *The Biased Character of Rules*
- *The Changing Rules of Government*

Putting It All Together: Context, Participants, Institutions, and Processes
- *The Context of American Politics*
- *Individuals and Groups in American Politics*
- *The Institutions of American Politics*
- *The Policy Process in American Politics*

Summary

Key Terms

Readings for Further Study

Contract With America
The ten-point platform that Republican candidates for the House of Representatives campaigned on in 1994.

Term limits
Laws that limit the number of terms a person may serve in an elected, and in some cases, an appointed office.

In the 1994 congressional elections, Republican candidates for the House of Representatives committed themselves as part of their campaign platform, the **Contract With America,** to seek a constitutional amendment limiting the number of terms anyone could serve in Congress. In calling for **term limits,** Republicans argued that Congress had strayed from the founders' vision of a "citizen legislature" and become an institution populated by professional politicians. The demise of the citizen legislature had hurt the country because "an entrenched body of politicians erodes Congress's accountability and responsiveness. An enormous national debt, deficit spending, and political scandals are but a few of the results." The solution, stated the Contract With America, was to send "the professional politicians a message—that politics shouldn't be a lifetime job."[1]

By any measure, term limits enjoyed widespread support among the American public. In 1990 and 1992, voters in fourteen states had approved initiatives limiting how many terms representatives and senators from their states could serve in Congress, and eight more states would do so in 1994.[2] Polls showed that an overwhelming majority of Americans favored term limits, making it one of the most popular provisions in the Contract With America.[3] When the voting booths closed on Election Day, Republicans had won a stunning victory. For the first time in forty years, they and not the Democrats were the majority party in the House.

Congressional candidates make a campaign promise, and, when their party captures control of Congress, they take steps to carry out their pledge. That sounds like an ideal description of how democracy ought to work. A conflict emerges; the people speak; the conflict is resolved. But the workings of the American political system are not quite that simple. What if elected officials disagree on an issue? What if elected officials disagree with the voters? Who decides who will resolve the dispute, and how?

House Republicans faced a problem when the 104th Congress convened in January 1995: not everyone favored term limits. Most Democratic members of Congress as well as interest groups such as the League of Women Voters opposed them. They argued that term limits would deny people the right to vote for whomever they pleased, substitute inexperienced legislators for experienced ones, and give more power to unelected government officials who can serve without limits. Indeed, opponents argued, term limits were unnecessary; as the 1994 elections proved, if voters disapprove of Congress's performance, they have an opportunity every two years to elect new members.

In addition to encountering opposition from most congressional Democrats, term limit proponents also faced opposition from some Republicans. Senate Republicans had campaigned on a seven-point platform, known as "Seven More in '94," that made no mention of term limits, and many leading Republican senators dismissed term limits as a bad idea.[4] Nor were House Republicans united in their support for term limits. Many senior House Republicans openly criticized the proposed constitutional amendment even though they had signed the Contract With America.[5] Rep. Henry Hyde (R-Ill.), the chair of the House committee that had to write a term limits bill, described term limits as "a terrible mistake, a kick in the stomach of democracy."[6]

The push for term limits also foundered over disagreements among its supporters. Although the Contract With America pledged that the House of Representatives would vote on term limits, it did not specify what a term limits bill would look like. In keeping with the old adage that "the devil is in the details," supporters disagreed over the length and scope of the limits. As a result, at least twelve different bills were introduced to limit service in Congress.[7] These bills differed along several dimensions. Should service in the House be limited to three two-year terms (six years), four terms (eight years) or six terms (twelve years)? (Almost all the bills limited service in the Senate to two six-year terms, or twelve years.) Should term limits apply to con-

In 1995, when House Republicans sought to pass a constitutional amendment imposing term limits on members of Congress, they discovered the idea was much more popular among first-term members than more senior members.

Brian Duffy/*Des Moines Register*. Reprinted by permission.

secutive years of service in Congress or to service over a lifetime? Should the term limit clock start with the next election or apply to past service in Congress? The infighting over these and other issues became so bitter that U.S. Term Limits, an interest group that favored a six-year limit on House service, ran television ads attacking Speaker of the House Newt Gingrich (R-Ga.) and other senior Republicans for supporting a twelve-year limit.[8] The opposition of many Democrats and senior Republicans and the disagreements among term limit supporters were critical because constitutional amendments, unlike ordinary legislation, require the support of two-thirds of the House to pass.

After much wrangling and infighting, the House Republican leadership brought four different term limit bills to the floor in late March 1995 for a vote.[9] The debate over the bills was emotional, with proponents and opponents delivering passionate speeches to the packed galleries (see box 1.1). When the speeches were finished and the votes tallied, term limits had been defeated. Three of the bills failed to secure a simple majority, and the fourth, which would have imposed twelve-year limits on both representatives and senators, won a majority but fell sixty-one votes short of the necessary two-thirds. Republicans were quick to blame Democrats for the defeat. Yet the generational split among House Republicans was also to blame; thirty of the forty Republicans who voted against term limits were senior members who chaired either a committee or a subcommittee.[10]

Despite the outcome of the House vote, supporters of term limits held out hope that eventually all states would decide to limit the number of years that members of their congressional delegations could serve in Congress. That hope was dashed in May

The People Behind the Rules

BOX 1.1

The Pros and Cons of Congressional Term Limits: Reps. Bob Inglis (R-S.C.) and Henry Hyde (R-Ill.)

The House debate in March 1995 over term limits stirred passions on both sides of the issue. Proponents hailed the virtues of citizen legislators, whereas critics emphasized the need to retain experienced professionals. To some extent, the debate followed party lines, with Republicans in favor and Democrats opposed. But it also pitted junior Republicans against some of their senior Republican colleagues, as the speeches of Reps. Bob Inglis (R-S.C.) and Henry Hyde (R-Ill.) illustrate.

Rep. Bob Inglis (R-S.C.)

Rep. Bob Inglis (R-S.C.)

Bob Inglis was elected to Congress in 1992 on a simple pledge: he would work to make congressional term limits the law. He made good on his pledge; he quickly became one of the most vocal supporters of a bill to limit members of the House of Representatives to no more than six years in office. To drive home his claim that he was a citizen legislator and not a professional politician, Inglis left his family behind in South Carolina when he moved to Washington. And rather than rent or buy a home in Washington, he slept in his office on an air mattress.

When the House voted on term limits in March 1995, Representative Inglis explained why the country needed to limit service in Congress:

> I rise today . . . to point out the basic case for term limits. . . .
>
> First, the basic case: The average American . . . keeps his or her job six years. The average member of Congress keeps his or her job eight years. That is not terribly long, and a lot of speakers will point out that some 200 members [of the current House of Representatives] are relatively new.
>
> But here is the critical statistic: The average members of the leadership who we all know run this place have kept their jobs for an average of twenty-two years. This tells the story of why we need term limits.
>
> Let me point out another . . . story of why we need term limits. . . . We will hear plenty . . . from opponents of term limits, about the fact that we have had such a massive turnover in this body [in recent years]. But let us ask where the turnover came from. The turnover came from open seat elections. Relatively few members have lost their attempts to be elected. . . .
>
> In 1990, 96 percent of those who wanted to come back came back. In 1992, it went down a little bit. Eighty-eight percent of those who wanted to come back came back. In 1994, . . . 90 percent of those of us who wanted to come back were reelected. That I think tells the story of a permanent Congress, a Congress that becomes out of touch with the people back home.

Although the House voted down term limits in 1995, Representative Inglis's own service in the House will be limited. In 1996, he reaffirmed his pledge to serve no more than three terms in the House.

Continued

1995. In a historic decision, the U.S. Supreme Court voted 5 to 4 to strike down an Arkansas law banning incumbents who had served six years in the House or twelve years in the Senate from appearing on the state ballot. In a broadly worded opinion, the Court ruled that "Such a state-imposed restriction is contrary to the 'fundamental principle of our representative democracy,' embodied in our Constitution, that 'the people should choose whom they please to govern them'. . . . If the qualifications [for election to Congress] set forth in the text of the Constitution are to be changed, that text must be amended."[11] By deciding that term limits could be imposed only through a constitutional amendment, the Court invalidated every state law limiting service in Congress. (The Court's ruling did not affect laws limiting service in state legislatures; the constitutions of individual states, and not the U.S. Constitution, govern the validity of these laws.)[12]

The People Behind the Rules

BOX 1.1 CONTINUED

Rep. Henry Hyde (R-Ill.)

Rep. Henry Hyde (R-Ill.)

Henry Hyde was first elected to Congress in 1974, when Representative Inglis was a sophomore in high school. He gained national fame as a staunch opponent of abortion; since 1978, the so-called Hyde Amendment has banned federal funding of abortion in most circumstances. Through his many years of service, Representative Hyde slowly gained seniority in the House. When the Republicans regained control of the House in 1995, he was named chair of the Judiciary Committee.

During the floor debate over term limits, Representative Hyde gave an impassioned speech denouncing term limits as "the dumbing down of democracy":

> George Orwell . . . said it has become the task of the intellectual to defend the obvious. I make no pretense at being an intellectual, but defending experience against ignorance is obvious.
>
> Have you ever been in a storm at sea? I have, and I knew real terror until I looked up on the bridge and the old Norwegian skipper, who had been to sea for forty-five years, was up there sucking on his pipe. And I can tell you that was reassuring.
>
> When that dentist bends over with the drill whirring, do you not hope he has done that work for a few years?
>
> And when the neurosurgeon has shaved your head and they have made the pencil mark on your skull where they are going to have the incision and he approaches with the electric saw, ask him one question, are you a careerist?
>
> Is running a modern complex society of 250 million people and a $6 trillion economy all that easy? To do your job . . . you have to know something about the environment, health care, banking and finance and tax policy, farm problems, weapons systems, Bosnia and Herzegovina and North Korea, not to mention Nagorno-Karabakh, foreign policy, the administration of justice, crime and punishment, education and welfare, budgeting in the trillions of dollars and immigration. And I have not scratched the surface.
>
> We need our best people to deal with these issues. . . . With a revolving door Congress, where will we get our Everett Dirksens, our Scoop Jacksons, our Arthur Vandenbergs, our Hubert Humphreys, our Barry Goldwaters, our Sam Ervins? You do not get them out of the phone book. Where did Shimon Peres and Yitzak Rabin get the self-confidence to negotiate peace for their people with the PLO? I will tell you where: experience, bloody, bloody experience.

When Representative Hyde concluded his speech, his colleagues gave him a standing ovation.

Sources: Jennifer Babson, "House Rejects Term Limits; GOP Blames Democrats," *Congressional Quarterly Weekly Report,* 1 April 1995, p. 918; *Congressional Record,* 29 March 1995, pp. 3892, 3905; Michael Barone and Grant Ujifusa, *The Almanac of American Politics, 1996* (Washington, D.C.: National Journal, 1995), pp. 432–33, 1209–10.

The Supreme Court's decision forced term limit supporters to seek a strategy for amending the Constitution. Some supporters argued for persuading two-thirds of the states (thirty-four in all) to call for a constitutional convention on term limits. The prospects for such a strategy were uncertain, however; although the Constitution had been amended twenty-seven times since it was ratified in 1789, none of the amendments came about through a constitutional convention. The traditional route for amending the Constitution had instead been through winning the approval of two-thirds of the members in both houses of Congress. But would senators and representatives vote to limit their service in Congress? On this score, some supporters of term limits were skeptical. As Rep. Bob Inglis (R-S.C.) put it: "Asking an incumbent member of Congress to vote for term limits is a bit like asking the chicken to vote for Colonel Sanders."[13]

The fight over term limits illustrates two important lessons about politics and government in the United States. First, politics arises from conflict. A long-standing conflict over an issue (in this case, What kind of Congress best serves the interests of the American public?) erupts into a specific policy question (Should the terms of members of Congress be limited?). As the public, interest groups, and government officials express their opinions and pressure the government to adopt the policy they favor, government must respond by making some decision to resolve the issue—or at least, to keep the conflict within manageable boundaries. (In the case of term limits, the House refused to approve a constitutional amendment mandating term limits.)

A second lesson the term limits issue highlights is that the rules of government help determine who wins the political battle. In the United States, the rules allow politicians, political activists, and individual Americans to express their opinions on an issue. The rules also govern how political decisions are made by allocating power among the three branches of the federal government—the executive, the legislature, and the judiciary—and between the federal and state governments. In the 1995 conflict over term limits, the effort failed because the rules of government (as the Supreme Court interpreted them) held that only an amendment to the Constitution could limit service in Congress. The effect of this rule was to make it much more difficult for term limit supporters to translate their policy proposal into the law of the land. If the rules of government had been different—if, for example, the Supreme Court had decided that the states could limit the terms their members of Congress serve—then the outcome of the battle over term limits would have been different as well.

Politics and Conflict

The wide variety of activities that constitute politics all have one important characteristic in common: they arise from conflict. We conduct elections because we disagree about who should represent us in Congress and the White House. We have a set of rules for turning bills into laws because we disagree on which pieces of legislation will best serve the public interest, and we need a way to determine whether a bill's supporters or opponents have more public support. We write letters of complaint to elected officials and demonstrate against government policies because we disagree with the government's actions. In short, politics arises from conflict over both resources—that is, who will get what—and values—that is, over how we will govern ourselves, what rules we will follow to make our decisions, and what sort of society we hope to have. In turn, government provides the primary means for managing, if not always resolving, conflict in society.

The Roots of Conflict

Material scarcity
The inability of a society to provide its citizens with all the goods and services they may want or need.

Conflict is an inherent feature of all societies because it springs from two roots that cannot be eradicated: material scarcity and disagreement over values. **Material scarcity** simply means that no country can provide its citizens with everything they may need or desire. To be sure, nations vary greatly in the relative scarcity they experience. For instance, we have all seen photographs of the famines that killed tens of thousands of Ethiopians, Somalis, and Sudanese in recent years. The lack of adequate quantities of food, water, and medicine in these countries represents an extreme example of scarce resources. But even in a wealthy country such as the United States, many citizens are underfed, underemployed, ill-housed, and poorly educated. Because societies cannot meet the physical needs and wants of all their citizens, conflict inevitably arises over who should get how much of the resources that are available.

Scarcity, and thus conflict, are also found in government itself. If Congress had enough seats to accommodate every candidate who might wish to serve, there would be no conflict and therefore no need for elections. If the federal budget were based on an unlimited number of dollars, then interest groups, government agencies, and committees in Congress would not compete over taxpayer dollars. Thus, in both its private

Material scarcity, a feature of all societies, is a source of much political conflict.

and public spheres, society is unable to provide resources adequate to satisfy the wishes of all its members. As a result, those members inevitably compete with one another over the distribution of resources.

The second reason political conflict is inevitable is that people disagree over the kind of society they want for themselves and their fellow citizens. Put another way, civilization has yet to produce a political community whose members all share the same values, principles, and beliefs. The conflicts that have arisen when large numbers of U.S. citizens have held sharply different ideas about what constitutes good public policy have profoundly affected the political history of the United States. The Civil War was fought in large part because northern and southern states disagreed over the morality of slavery. In the early 1900s, Americans disagreed over whether women should be allowed to vote. In the 1950s and 1960s, Americans disagreed over whether private businesses and state and local governments should be allowed to discriminate against African Americans and other minorities. In the late 1960s and early 1970s, Americans disagreed over U.S. involvement in the Vietnam War. And in the 1990s, Americans disagree over issues ranging from term limits to a woman's right to an abortion to whether everyone has a right to medical care.

Because material resources are scarce and because people often subscribe to very different values, principles, and beliefs, political conflict typically produces outcomes that create winners and losers. For example, service in Congress will either be limited or not. Both sides cannot win, though at times compromise may make it possible for each side to achieve at least some of its goals.

As you might imagine, the hope in a democracy usually is that the outcome of a political conflict will create many more winners than losers. (As we shall see in chapter 2, in some circumstances, the goals of democratic government are served only when the rights of the minority triumph over the preferences of the majority.) But nothing guarantees that winners will outnumber losers. Indeed, politicians and the public alike frequently complain that special interests dominate government. This raises the possibility that political conflict may create more losers than winners.

The Role of Government in Managing Conflict

If conflict is an enduring feature of society, what prevents conflict from degenerating into political violence and civil war? The answer is government. A government provides a society with a way to manage and sometimes solve its internal conflicts. In societies where the government collapses entirely, chaos and warfare typically erupt. This happened in the early 1990s in Somalia and in several of the republics in the former Soviet Union and Yugoslavia.

Governments are uniquely empowered to manage conflict because they can authoritatively allocate values in society; that is, they can decide who wins, who loses, and by how much.[14] The decisions of government are authoritative in the sense that

One way government can exercise authority: using coercive force to make citizens comply with its rules. Several states revived the chain gang practice in the 1990s.

government is the only institution in society that can enforce its decisions on the participants in a conflict. No other institution possesses such power. The authority of a government derives from both its legitimacy and its ability to control the use of coercive force in society.[15]

Legitimacy
A self-imposed willingness of citizens to respect and obey the decisions of their government.

Legitimacy refers to the willingness of citizens to obey the decisions of their government. In essence, then, legitimacy is a self-imposed obligation on the part of the people to obey their government. Legitimacy can derive from a variety of sources. In fifteenth- through eighteenth-century Europe, for example, monarchs ruled because their subjects accepted the doctrine of divine right, the idea that God had ordained that the royal family would rule. In Germany under Adolf Hitler, the legitimacy of the government was based on its promotion of German nationalism, the belief that the German people had special traits that set them apart from other people. And in communist countries such as the People's Republic of China, the legitimacy of the government rests on the public's acceptance of the principles of communism.

In the United States, as in all democracies, the legitimacy of the government is based on the consent of the governed, that is, the people. Since Americans choose who will lead their country by voting in elections, they believe they can hold the government accountable for its actions. In theory, they can influence the work of the government by writing to their elected officials, donating money to an interest group, participating in a protest march, or engaging in a host of other activities. If the government fails to respond to their concerns, the people can vote to elect new officials. Thus, most Americans believe their government is legitimate because they believe it usually responds to their wishes.

Coercive force
The ability of a government to compel its citizens to obey its decisions.

If legitimacy provides one source of government authority, the other stems from the government's usual monopoly on the use of **coercive force** against the members of society. Through its police, judicial, and military institutions, a government can force its citizens to comply with its decisions and punish those who refuse to obey. For example, the government can arrest and jail criminals, force people to pay taxes, and deny people the right to enter or leave the country. Although many individuals or organizations in society may use force, as when a mugger robs someone or a drug gang shoots at its rivals, typically no group or institution in society can successfully challenge the government's dominance in the use of force on a national scale.

To succeed in managing conflict in society, a government needs to possess both legitimacy and coercive force. Legitimacy in the absence of the threat of coercion cannot ensure that people will obey the decisions of government. For example, many people would refuse to pay taxes if they knew the government was unable or unwilling to

Nelson Mandela's 1994 election to the presidency in South Africa's first all-race elections signaled the end of apartheid, a system that oppressed the nation's non-white citizens. The demise of apartheid came about largely because the white-run government recognized it could no longer forcibly control the non-white majority.

enforce the tax laws. Likewise, more people would be inclined to steal if they knew their crimes would go unpunished. Only the threat of penalties and imprisonment ensures that most people will comply with government directions.

By the same token, no government can endure for long if it possesses coercive force but lacks legitimacy. A government may be able to frighten its citizens into submission for a time, but eventually they will challenge its authority and demand a more legitimate basis for governing. One example of this challenge to authority was the collapse of the communist governments in Eastern Europe and the Soviet Union in the late 1980s and early 1990s. Their threats to use physical violence finally failed to compensate for their growing lack of legitimacy. Likewise, the system of apartheid, or white rule, in South Africa came to an end in the early 1990s because white South Africans finally recognized that they could not compel the obedience of non-white South Africans indefinitely. Thus, government must possess both legitimacy and coercive force to manage conflict in society successfully.

Government as Rule Maker

How does a government manage conflict and make choices about how society will function? The answer is by devising rules that structure how political decisions will be made and then by issuing rules that determine the winners and losers on specific issues. As we shall see time and time again in this book, the rules that a government adopts and follows are not neutral; rather, they create winners and losers by helping some groups and hurting others.

Structural Rules

The rules of government consist of two types: structural rules and policy rules. **Structural rules** establish the organization, procedures, and powers of government. These rules tell us how we are to choose government officials, what steps government officials must follow when they make policy decisions, and what actions government officials can and cannot take. In the United States, the most important structural rules come from the Constitution. But structural rules also stem from the constitutions of the fifty states, from the laws passed by Congress and the state legislatures, and from the decisions of both state and federal courts.

Structural rules
Rules that establish the organization, procedures, and powers of government.

The debate over term limits illustrates the idea of a structural rule. Ever since the Constitution was ratified in 1789, the structural rules of American government

Rules matter—they benefit some and disadvantage others.
PEANUTS © 1996. United Features Syndicate. Reprinted by permission.

have allowed members of Congress to serve as long as their constituents are willing to reelect them. The same was true until 1951 for the presidency, though presidents traditionally declined to serve for more than two terms. After Franklin Roosevelt was elected president four times between 1932 and 1944, Congress passed and the states ratified a constitutional amendment barring anyone from being elected president more than twice (see box 1.2). If congressional term limits become a reality in the future, new structural rules will govern how long members can serve in Congress.

Another way to make the idea of structural rules concrete is to think for a moment about a presidential election campaign. How do we know when someone has been elected president? The answer lies in the Constitution. It clearly states that the president shall be the candidate who wins a majority of the votes in the electoral college. In the (unlikely) event that no candidate receives a majority of the electoral college votes, then the newly elected members of the House of Representatives must decide who will be the next president. The Constitution stipulates that the House must choose from among the three presidential candidates who won the most electoral votes, with the delegation from each state casting one vote. (Although most state delegations in the House consist of more than one member, the Constitution says nothing about the rules representatives must follow in deciding how their state delegation will vote.)

As the procedure for selecting presidents attests, the structural rules of American government can be quite complicated. Despite their occasional complexity, however, these rules tell us how government is to be organized and operated, and they tell us what powers government can and cannot exercise. Because these structural rules exist, we know how to choose government officials, we know what rules government officials must follow when they decide public policy issues, and we know which actions government officials can and cannot take. In short, structural rules give government stability and continuity.

Policy Rules

Policy rule
A decision a government institution reaches on a specific political question within its jurisdiction.

The second type of government rule is the **policy rule,** which is simply the decision that a government institution reaches on a specific political question within its jurisdiction. For example, how much money shall the government spend on defense? At what rate shall it tax incomes? By what means and to what extent shall the government act to improve the quality of the environment? Shall American citizens be allowed to

Point of Order

BOX 1.2

Presidential Term Limits: The Twenty-second Amendment

President Franklin Delano Roosevelt

The congressional debate in 1995 over whether to limit service in Congress was not the first time Congress debated term limits for elected federal officials. In 1947, Congress passed a proposed constitutional amendment that read in part:

> No person shall be elected to the office of the President more than twice, and no person who has held the office of President, or acted as President, for more than two years of a term to which some other person was elected President shall be elected to the office of the President more than once.

Over the next four years, the required thirty-six states ratified the proposal, and in 1951 the Twenty-second Amendment, which barred anyone from being elected president more than twice, became part of the Constitution.

The question of whether to limit presidential service was one the founders grappled with at the Constitutional Convention in 1787. The issue was inextricably mixed up with the questions of how the president would be elected and how long presidential terms would be. After much debate, the founders decided on four-year terms with no limits on service. In deciding against term limits, many of the founders agreed with George Washington that it made no sense at all "in precluding ourselves from the services of any man who on some emergency shall be deemed universally most capable of serving the public."

Although the Constitution did not limit the number of terms a president might serve, the early presidents established a custom that no president should serve more than two terms. George Washington rejected suggestions that he seek a third term, telling the country in his Farewell Address that he preferred "the shade of retirement." Thomas Jefferson elevated Washington's pragmatic decision to the level of principle: "If some termination of the services of the Chief Magistrate be not fixed by the Constitution, or supplied by practice, his office, nominally four years, will in fact become for life." Although the two-term tradition was deeply rooted for more than one hundred years, Congress often revisited the issue of presidential term limits. Between 1789 and 1947, members of Congress introduced 270 resolutions seeking to limit the president's eligibility for reelection.

The two-term tradition ended with the presidency of Franklin Delano Roosevelt (FDR). First elected in 1932 and then reelected in 1936, Roosevelt was in his seventh year as president when World War II began in Europe. Faced with a perilous threat to U.S. national interests, and despite substantial public support for the two-term tradition, he announced in July 1940 that he would seek a third term. Reelected by a wide margin (though smaller than his first two victories), he ran again and won in 1944. Less than three months after his inauguration as president for the fourth time, Roosevelt died.

The congressional elections of 1946 saw Republicans win control of Congress for the first time in fourteen years. The new majority, determined to see that no future president would match Roosevelt's four terms in office, passed a proposed constitutional amendment in less than three months. Proponents of presidential term limits spoke eloquently of the need to protect the country from an unscrupulous president who would use his powers to secure repeated reelection to the detriment of the country's best interests. Thus, limiting the freedom of Americans to vote for whomever they wanted for president would in the long run prevent "autocracy" and "the destruction of the real freedom of the people."

Despite the claims of principle, it is difficult to escape the conclusion that the Twenty-second Amendment passed largely because of a Republican desire to inflict posthumous revenge on FDR. No public hearings were held on the proposed amendment, debate in the House lasted only two hours, and no Republican in either the House or the Senate voted against it. Moreover, when a motion was offered in the Senate to protect the American public from unscrupulous representatives and senators by limiting the terms of members of Congress as well, senators voted down the motion 82 to 1.

The Twenty-second Amendment carries with it one great irony. Since it was ratified in 1951, it has affected only two presidents—Dwight Eisenhower and Ronald Reagan. Both were Republicans.

Sources: Calvin C. Jillson, *Constitution Making: Conflict and Consensus in the Federal Convention of 1787* (New York: Agathon Press, 1988), pp. 104–20; Sidney M. Milkis and Michael Nelson, *The American Presidency: Origins and Development*, 2d ed. (Washington, D.C.: CQ Press, 1994), pp. 303–5; Clinton Rossiter, *The American Presidency*, rev. ed. (New York: Mentor Books, 1960), pp. 220–27; and Paul G. Willis and George L. Willis, "The Politics of the Twenty-second Amendment," *Western Political Quarterly* 5 (September 1952): 469–82.

travel to communist countries such as Cuba, North Korea, and Vietnam? The answer to each of these questions, and many more as well, constitutes a policy rule of government, or what we can more simply call a policy. (Throughout the remainder of the book we will use the shorter term *policy* when referring to a policy rule. We are using the full term here because we want to emphasize that all government policies are rules that allocate costs and benefits among citizens.) All of a government's policy rules taken together constitute what we call public policy.

Unlike structural rules, policy rules generally do not spring from the U.S. Constitution or from the constitutions of the fifty states. Instead, the government makes policy rules whenever an institution of government decides a question about public policy. Thus, when Congress or a state legislature passes a law, when a president issues an executive order, when a government agency writes a new regulation, or when a state or federal court hands down a decision, another policy rule is created. As you might imagine, federal, state, and local governments in the United States produce tens of thousands of policy rules each year. Despite the large number of policy rules, each must be developed according to the relevant procedures called for by the structural rules of government. But policy rules, because they address specific issues at specific times, give government flexibility to meet society's changing desires and needs.

The Biased Character of Rules

Governments have the responsibility to devise structural and policy rules that will manage conflict in society. Yet rules are not neutral in their effect. They inevitably create winners and losers because, compared to other possible rules, they benefit the interests of some parties and harm the interests of others. The inescapable fact that different rules have different effects means that structural rules and policy rules are inherently biased. Of course, recognizing that all rules are biased does not mean that rules are bad or unfair or that they inevitably serve the interests of one group (say, the wealthy) over another (say, the poor). The point is that any rule, even one adopted for the best of reasons, inevitably will help some citizens and hurt others.

The biased character of rules applies to both structural and policy rules. To see the biased nature of structural rules, consider the consequences that flow from the provision in the U.S. Constitution that "the Senate of the United States shall be composed of two Senators from each State." As a result of this structural rule, the 14 million people living in the eight Mountain states (Arizona, Colorado, Idaho, Montana, Nevada, New Mexico, Utah, and Wyoming) send sixteen senators to Washington, D.C. In contrast, the 31 million people who live in California send only two senators to Washington, D.C. Because the people living in the Mountain states have Senate representation disproportionate to their share of the American population, they also wield disproportionate influence in Senate decisions and, as a result, over which laws are passed. If representation in the Senate were instead based on the size of each state's population, as is the case with the House of Representatives, people living in the Mountain states would see their representation in Congress shrink and, along with it, their influence over public policy. Thus, the structural rule that stipulates that two senators will represent each state benefits states with small populations and hurts those with large ones.

The fact that rules are not neutral explains why structural rules, as well as policy rules, often become the target of vociferous debate. Moreover, the biased character of rules reveals a critical lesson about politics that we will return to time and again in the pages that follow: changing either structural or policy rules can alter which groups win and which groups lose in a political conflict. The political history of the United States would look much different if the structural rules dictated that the state legislatures are to elect the U.S. president, that Congress can pass laws without submitting them to the president, or that representation in the Senate is based on population. Likewise, the

The structural rules of American politics have changed over the past two hundred years. In 1920, for example, American women won the right to vote.

composition of the U.S. military would look very different today if the Defense Department's policy rules segregated African-American and white soldiers and denied women the right to serve in the armed forces. In short, different rules benefit different groups in society. That is why groups compete with such great intensity over the decisions government makes.

The Changing Rules of Government

If the rules of government are inherently biased, they also are subject to great change. Indeed, the rules of American government have changed frequently, and often dramatically, over the past two hundred years. It is easy to fall prey to the erroneous assumption that today's policies and governmental arrangements resemble yesterday's and that tomorrow's will look much like those we have today. Yet governmental institutions, procedures, and policies are not handed down unchanged by past generations, nor are they etched in stone for future generations. A review of our nation's history reveals that change is the one constant of American politics.

Take, for example, the structural rules that determine who can vote in the United States. Although today virtually every American citizen over the age of eighteen is entitled to vote, this was not always the case. The Constitution originally stipulated that "the Electors in each State shall have the Qualifications requisite for Electors of the most numerous Branch of the State Legislature." Given the common practice of the time, this meant only white men over the age of twenty-one were allowed to vote. With the passage of the Fifteenth Amendment to the Constitution after the Civil War, the right to vote was extended to all male citizens regardless of race or color. In 1920, with the ratification of the Nineteenth Amendment, the right to vote was extended to all women. And in 1971, with the ratification of the Twenty-sixth Amendment, the right to vote was extended to all Americans from ages eighteen through twenty.

The rules of government change not by magic but because the American people and government officials make choices. When they make choices, by definition, they reject other alternatives. For example, the Constitution assigns the president important powers and responsibilities because two hundred years ago some delegates to the Constitutional Convention sought to create an independent presidency. If those delegates had been less persuasive and less adept at manipulating the rules of parliamentary debate in their favor, the office of the presidency might look very different today. Their opponents wanted to fill the office of the president with a committee of presidents, each elected by Congress, and without the power to appoint judges and make foreign treaties.[16] Thus, governmental institutions, procedures, and policies that might appear inevitable in hindsight turn out on closer examination to be only one of a number of possible outcomes.

Putting It All Together: Context, Participants, Institutions, and Processes

The overall objective of this book is to describe and explain how the rules of politics operate in the United States. Although we will talk from time to time about state and local government, our focus is primarily on the rules that govern the operation of our national government, or, as it is more commonly called, the federal government. To accomplish our goal of explaining how the rules of American politics operate, we have divided the chapters that follow into four distinct categories: the context of American politics, the participants in American politics, the institutions of American politics, and the policy process in American politics.

The Context of American Politics

In the first section, we examine the context of American politics. We begin in chapter 2 by discussing the origins of the Constitution and the reasoning behind the basic structural rules that define the political system in the United States. Here we explore issues such as the division of power among the legislative, executive, and judicial branches of government and the federal relationship between the national and state governments. We continue in chapter 3 by describing the social context of American politics—that is, the people who make up our nation. We profile the changing demographic and social characteristics of the United States so you can better understand what sorts of political conflicts arise and what sorts of demands people make on the government. In chapter 4, we review the structural rules that specify the civil liberties of the American people. Although the words of the Constitution and Bill of Rights—which set forth many of the basic rules about civil liberties—have not changed since their adoption, their interpretation has changed a good deal. We conclude our discussion of the context of American politics in chapter 5 by examining the civil rights movement and the structural rules that specify the civil rights of the American people. We carefully trace the evolving nature of civil rights over the course of our nation's history.

Individuals and Groups in American Politics

In the second section of the book, we look at the "input" side of American politics, the individuals and groups that place demands on government and influence its decisions. We begin in chapter 6 with a discussion of public opinion—what people want from government, why they want it, and how their opinions and desires fit together to form ideologies. We continue our focus on individuals in chapter 7 by examining individual political participation. Of special importance is the act of voting, so we discuss who does or does not vote and why, and we analyze how voters make up their minds once they step into the voting booth. We also consider other forms of participation, such as writing letters to members of Congress and joining marches to protest government policy.

In chapters 8, 9, and 10, we shift our focus from individuals to groups as we examine the political roles the news media, political parties, and interest groups play. All three of these groups act as intermediaries in American politics; they help people to make demands of the government and they help the government to explain itself to the people. Chapter 8 examines the role of the media, the principal source of information about government and politics for most people. We look at the relationship between the media and the government, and we discuss how a robust media is essential to a healthy democracy. In chapters 9 and 10, we discuss the history and current behavior of political parties and interest groups—the two primary forms of organized mass political participation in the United States. In each case, we explain how people use these groups to influence the government, and we explore the limits each group faces on its ability to shape government policy.

The Institutions of American Politics

After setting the context for American national government and describing the individuals and groups who seek to influence the government, we next turn to the core institutions of the federal government: Congress, the presidency, the bureaucracy, and the courts. These institutions handle the "output" side of the system—they make the decisions, or policy rules, of the federal government.

We begin in chapter 11 with what has been called the first branch of government—Congress. We describe the institution, its history, and its policy-making processes. We also discuss congressional elections because the unique aspects of these elections strongly influence how members of Congress behave once they are in office. We move on to the presidency in chapter 12, discussing its historical development and the ways in which the Constitution and the actions of past presidents have defined the nature of the office. We examine the organization, methods of operation, powers, and functions of the modern presidency. In this chapter, we also discuss how the United States chooses its presidents because changes in the rules governing presidential selection have significantly affected how presidents relate to the rest of government. Throughout both chapters 11 and 12, we devote special attention to how Congress and the president respond to the pressures the American people, the news media, political parties, and interest groups place on them.

In chapter 13, we turn to a key set of government officials who are *not* elected—the bureaucrats in the executive branch of government. Although government agencies are sometimes considered politically neutral, we show that because part of their job is to make rules and to resolve conflicts, they are inherently political institutions. We conclude our discussion of the institutions of the federal government in chapter 14 by examining the court system in the United States. We both describe the judicial system and explain the unique role the courts play as an undemocratic institution operating within a larger democratic political system.

The Policy Process in American Politics

In the final section of the book, we examine different processes the national government is involved in and some of the policies it produces. We begin in chapter 15 by discussing state governments, the roles they play in domestic policy formation, and how they relate to the federal government. In chapter 16, we turn to the federal budget process—a process that has grown in importance along with our budget deficits and national debt. We examine the conflicts over whether the government should tax more or spend less, and we explain how the rules of the budgetary process operate. In chapter 17, we examine the federal government's role in domestic policy. We examine how the federal government has become responsible for managing the economy, regulating the business practices of private firms, and providing a social safety net for the American people. We complete our tour of American politics in chapter 18 with a look at foreign policy. After briefly reviewing the history of U.S. foreign policy, we discuss how foreign policy decisions are made in the United States as well as how the distribution of political power pertaining to foreign policy differs from what we are accustomed to seeing in domestic policy.

Summary

In this chapter, we have learned two lessons about American politics and government: politics arises from conflict, and the rules of government help determine the winners and losers in particular conflicts. The debate over congressional term limits illustrates both lessons. When House Republicans tried to make good on their pledge in the Contract With America to pass a constitutional amendment limiting service in Congress, they met with considerable opposition. In the end, the proposed constitutional amendment failed as Republicans were unable to muster the necessary two-thirds support in the House. Although proponents of term limits argued that individual states could impose term limits on members of their congressional delegations, the Supreme Court ruled that such state laws were unconstitutional. The only way to impose term limits on members of Congress is through a constitutional amendment.

Throughout the next seventeen chapters, we try to emphasize that the rules and institutions of government provide society with a way to cope with its internal conflicts. Moreover, because the rules help determine who wins and who loses, the rules themselves often become the subject of intense political conflict. Indeed, the rules—and government itself—are continually undergoing dynamic change. These three factors—conflict, rules, and change—underlie the dynamics of democracy.

Key Terms

Coercive force
Contract With America
Legitimacy
Material scarcity
Policy rule
Structural rules
Term limits

Readings for Further Study

Benjamin, Gerald, and Michael J. Malbin, eds. *Limiting Legislative Terms.* Washington, D.C.: CQ Press, 1992. A collection of essays on various issues surrounding the question of limiting legislative terms.

Contract With America: The Bold Plan by Rep. Newt Gingrich, Rep. Dick Armey and the House Republicans to Change the Nation, ed. Ed Gillespie and Bob Schellhas. New York: Times Books/Random House, 1994. This expanded version of the platform that Republican candidates for the House of Representatives campaigned on in 1994 outlines the ten policy proposals that became the focal point of American politics during the 104th Congress (1995–97).

Dahl, Robert A. *Modern Political Analysis,* 2d ed. Englewood Cliffs, N.J.: Prentice-Hall, 1970. A concise introduction to the fundamental concepts of political science by a man many consider the most influential political scientist of the past fifty years.

Dionne, E. J. *Why Americans Hate Politics.* New York: Simon & Schuster, 1992. A prominent journalist explores why so many Americans dislike politics and politicians.

The Encyclopedic Dictionary of American Government. Guilford, Conn.: Dushkin, 1991. An informative and useful guide to the terms, institutions, and practices of government in the United States.

Lasswell, Harold. *Politics: Who Gets What, When, How.* New York: Whittlesey House, 1936. A classic study of the nature of politics by a scholar who helped found the modern discipline of political science.

Plano, Jack C., and Milton Greenberg. *The American Political Dictionary,* 8th ed. Fort Worth: Holt, Rinehart, and Winston, 1989. A rich and helpful guide to the language of politics and political science, with terms organized by major topic.

Safire, William. *Safire's New Political Dictionary.* New York: Random House, 1993. One of the country's leading newspaper columnists provides an engaging tour of the American political lexicon, with entries ranging from Abolitionist to Zulu.

Schattschneider, E. E. *The Semi-Sovereign People.* New York: Holt, 1960. A classic study that provides simple yet powerful concepts for understanding politics in the United States.

Tocqueville, Alexis de. *Democracy in America,* ed. J. P. Mayer. New York: Anchor Books, 1969. One of the most insightful studies ever made of American democracy, written by a French aristocrat who traveled around the United States in the 1830s.

Chapter

2

The Constitution

The Constitution as a Reflection of Political Conflict

The Colonial Experience

The Articles of Confederation

The Politics of the Constitutional Convention

The Politics of Ratification

The Constitution as a Reflection of the Founders' Philosophy

Individual Rights and Democratic Rule

Majority Tyranny: The Paradox of Majority Rule

Preventing Majority Tyranny

The Core Provisions of the Constitution

Congress

The Presidency and the Executive Branch

The Federal Judiciary

Interstate Relations

Other Provisions

Three Consequences of the Constitution

The Protection of Individual Rights

A Bias in Favor of the Status Quo

Political Flexibility

Federalism: The Vertical Dimension to the Constitution

Confederal, Unitary, and Federal Governments

Establishing National Supremacy

The Assertion of States' Rights

The Civil War and the Reassertion of National Supremacy

Dual Federalism

The Present Era—National Supremacy as Fiscal Federalism

Summary

Key Terms

Readings for Further Study

The Constitution of the United States

In November 1994, Republicans won control of both houses of Congress for the first time in forty years. They immediately argued that their victory gave them a mandate to make revolutionary changes in government policy. First-term House Republicans were particularly insistent on the need to start a revolution. They had campaigned vigorously on the basis of their Contract With America, which clearly proposed rewriting much of the legislation Congress had passed over the previous four decades. By the end of 1995, though, relatively few Republican proposals had become law. Perhaps most striking, Congress had enacted only one of the ten provisions of the Contract With America, and a relatively minor one at that. The other bills Congress passed were generally far less revolutionary than those the Republicans had contemplated in the heady days following their victory in the 1994 congressional elections.[1]

What happened? Why wasn't the "Republican Revolution" more successful? The answer, as one astute political analyst has observed, is that "the conservative Republican tidal wave . . . crashed against a formidable and perhaps insurmountable seawall: the United States Constitution."[2] The rules of government the Constitution sets forth are designed to prevent intense majorities, such as the Republicans in 1995, from sweeping into government and making drastic changes in policy. For example, the Constitution requires that both houses of Congress approve all bills. Because its consent was necessary to pass laws, and because many of its members doubted the need for revolutionary change, the Senate was able to ignore, water down, or reject many bills the House had supported. Similarly, the Constitution empowers the president to veto legislation he dislikes. President Bill Clinton made frequent use of the veto power, and Republicans lacked the votes needed to override him. Thus, while the Republican Congress made many changes to government policy in 1995, those changes were made more modest in scope by virtue of the rules of government contained in the Constitution.

The limited success of the "Republican Revolution" in 1995 reminds us that the United States is a nation of laws and that our most fundamental laws are set forth in the Constitution. Written more than two hundred years ago, the Constitution provides the basic structural rules of American politics. These rules tell us how the federal government is to be organized, and they specify many of the procedures that federal officials must follow in performing their duties. By stipulating the most fundamental rules of American politics, the Constitution helps to determine who wins and loses in the political arena. Therefore, to understand government in the United States, we must first know something about the Constitution, the rules it sets forth, and how those rules are interpreted in practice.

In this chapter, we will examine the Constitution. We begin by considering why the founders wrote the document they did. As we shall see, the Constitution—and thus the structure of our government—was shaped by both the political experiences and objectives of those who wrote it and by the underlying philosophical values they believed in. We will also discuss the core provisions of the Constitution: the rules that govern the operation of Congress, the presidency, and the judiciary, as well as the relations between the federal and state governments. We will show how these rules have affected the way politics operates in the United States. Finally, we will review the changing relationship between the federal and state governments to illustrate how the interpretation of the Constitution changes over time and how its rules have shaped our nation's history.

The Constitution as a Reflection of Political Conflict

The Constitution reflects the political values and choices of the people who wrote it. To understand why, we need to recognize that the delegates to the Constitutional Convention, like politicians of today, represented states with competing political interests. The years as English colonies left each of the thirteen states jealously protective of its independence and fearful of conceding power to a national government. Previous

An increasing number of colonists throughout the 1760s and 1770s viewed British rule as illegitimate. They often expressed their frustration through protests and acts of disobedience.

efforts "to build one government out of thirteen" had foundered as individual states refused to surrender supreme power over events within their borders.[3] The need to reconcile the states' competing political interests profoundly affected the rules the founders set down in the Constitution. As a result, our constitutional rules of government are rooted not only in high-minded philosophical concepts such as democracy and liberty, but also in the political maneuverings of eighteenth-century politicians.

The Colonial Experience

The relationship between England and the colonies shaped the political outlook of the founders. England had created each of the original thirteen colonies, and the King of England appointed most colonial governors to govern on his behalf. Because the governors owed their jobs to the King, they put England's interests ahead of the interests of the colonists. Nonetheless, most of the colonies had relatively powerful legislatures. For almost a century and a half, these elected bodies exercised considerable authority, and many colonists grew accustomed to substantial independence from England.

This freedom began to diminish in the middle of the eighteenth century. Under the leadership of King George III, England began to exert more direct control over the colonies. During the 1760s, England imposed a number of taxes on the colonies to help pay for the French and Indian War. The colonists deeply resented the taxes, but quickly discovered that the English government felt no obligation to heed the colonial legislatures' requests that the taxes be repealed. The fact that the colonists had no voice in the decisions to impose the taxes they were required to pay gave rise to the famous claim of "no taxation without representation."

As a result of the lack of representation in decision making that affected their lives, many colonists became disillusioned with the English government. To use the terms introduced in chapter 1, the English government was losing *legitimacy* in the eyes of the colonists. As more and more colonists began to regard the English government as illegitimate, England increasingly relied on *coercive force* to compel the colonies to obey. The resulting conflicts culminated, of course, in the American Revolutionary War, which, as one eminent historian has observed, "was not fought to *obtain* freedom, but to *preserve* the liberties that Americans already had as colonials."[4] With the defeat of the British at Yorktown in 1781 and the signing of the Treaty of Paris in 1783, the American colonies achieved their independence.

The leaders of the newly independent states drew two important lessons from their years under English rule. The first was that a political system that put political power in the hands of state government would better guarantee liberty and representation than a system that concentrated power in a national government. Having thrown off what they viewed as English tyranny, the leaders of the newly independent colonies wanted nothing to do with another distant and unresponsive national government. The fact that many colonists had a strong sense of identity and loyalty to their own states reinforced their preference for state government. They saw themselves not as "Britons" or "Americans," but as Pennsylvanians, Virginians, and New Yorkers. The combination of a negative experience with a powerful national government and a strong identification with their individual states led the colonists to place their confidence in governments at the state rather than national level.

The second important lesson the leaders of the newly independent colonies drew from their colonial experience was that a new national government should have a strong legislature but not a strong executive leader. The years under English rule left many colonists with a deep distrust of executive authority. The new states would not give leaders of the new nation the powers that King George had. At the same time, the leaders of the newly independent states had an abiding respect for elected legislatures. Many had served in the colonial legislatures, which had forcefully expressed the views of the colonies in their disputes with the colonial governors and the King of England. In sum, the colonial era "ended with the belief prevalent that 'the executive magistry' was the natural enemy, the legislative assembly the natural friend of liberty."[5]

The Articles of Confederation

Articles of Confederation The document written by the states following their declaration of independence from England and adopted in 1781. It established a system of strong states and a weak national government with a legislative branch but no separate executive or judicial branches and few powers beyond the sphere of foreign relations.

The preference the leaders of the newly independent colonies had for strong state government and their aversion to creating a powerful national executive guided the writing of the **Articles of Confederation,** which represented the first attempt to create a political system for the newly independent country. Written in 1777 and ratified in 1781, the Articles of Confederation contained the rules that governed our nation until the Constitution was adopted in 1789.

Because the colonial experience left many colonists with a deep distrust of powerful national government, the authors of the Articles of Confederation chose to create a *confederal government.* In this form of government, the states retain their sovereignty, that is, supreme power over events within their borders. In turn, the national government exercises only those powers the states choose to give it. The one major task the state governments gave the national government under the Articles of Confederation was responsibility for managing most of the country's foreign relations. Beyond this, however, the national government received few powers. For example, it was not allowed to impose taxes or regulate economic relations among the states or between individual states and foreign countries. Moreover, to prevent any possible tyranny by the national government, the Articles provided for no executive branch. Instead, all the powers of the national government were vested in Congress. As a result of the decision to erect a confederal government lacking an executive branch, the Articles of Confederation established a very weak national government.

The confederal government the Articles of Confederation created quickly proved inadequate to meet the needs of the new country. The national government could not represent itself effectively in foreign affairs because Congress was unable to respond quickly and decisively to other governments. Individual states negotiated their own trading relationships with Europe, which undermined efforts to construct a national economic policy. States sought to protect their own industries by imposing tariffs

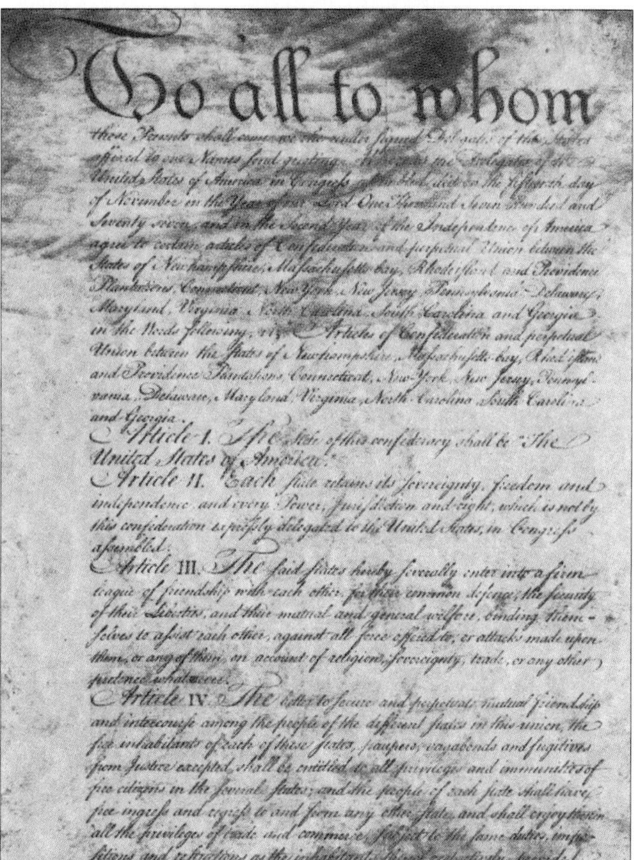

To all to whom

these Presents shall come we the under signed Delegates of the States affixed to our Names send greeting. [illegible] the Delegates of the United States of America in Congress assembled did on the fifteenth day of November in the Year of our Lord One Thousand Seven Hundred and Seventy seven, and in the Second Year of the Independence of America agree to certain articles of Confederation and perpetual Union between the States of Newhampshire, Massachusetts-bay, Rhode island and Providence Plantations, Connecticut, New York, New Jersey, Pennsylvania, Delaware, Maryland, Virginia, North Carolina, South Carolina and Georgia in the Words following, viz. "Articles of Confederation and perpetual Union between the States of Newhampshire, Massachusetts-bay, Rhode island and Providence Plantations, Connecticut, New-York, New Jersey, Pennsylvania, Delaware, Maryland, Virginia, North Carolina, South Carolina and Georgia.

Article I. The Stile of this confederacy shall be "The United States of America."

Article II. Each state retains its sovereignty, freedom and independence, and every Power, Jurisdiction and right, which is not by this confederation expressly delegated to the United States, in Congress assembled.

Article III. The said states hereby severally enter into a firm league of friendship with each other, for their common defence, the security of their Liberties, and their mutual and general welfare, binding themselves to assist each other, against all force offered to, or attacks made upon them, or any of them, on account of religion, sovereignty, trade, or any other pretence whatever.

Article IV. The better to secure and perpetuate mutual friendship and intercourse among the people of the different states in this union, the free inhabitants of each of these states, paupers, vagabonds and fugitives from Justice excepted, shall be entitled to all privileges and immunities of free citizens in the several states; and the people of each state shall have free ingress and regress to and from any other state, and shall enjoy therein all the privileges of trade and commerce, subject to the same duties, impositions and restrictions as the inhabitants thereof respectively, provided

The Articles of Confederation made no provision for an independent executive. It also withheld many important powers from the national government, including the powers to tax and regulate interstate commerce.

(or taxes) on goods from other states, which in turn hurt economic growth throughout the country. Wealthy citizens complained when state legislatures passed laws that enhanced the interests of the working and debtor classes at the expense of the wealthy.

Several efforts were made to revise the Articles of Confederation. The most important was the Annapolis Convention, held in 1786, which produced a resolution calling for another convention in Philadelphia to discuss proposed revisions. The call for another convention took on special urgency when farmers in western Massachusetts took up arms in what became known as **Shays's Rebellion** to protest the state's economic policies. The governor of Massachusetts asked the national government for help in putting down the revolt, but none came. Massachusetts eventually contained the revolt, but Shays's Rebellion heightened concerns that the national government could not govern effectively. In light of growing dissatisfaction with the status quo, delegates from every state but Rhode Island met in Philadelphia in the summer of 1787. The convention began as a discussion of how best to revise the Articles of Confederation, but it quickly became the forum for drafting what would become the U.S. Constitution.

Shays's Rebellion
A protest, staged by small farmers from western Massachusetts and led by Daniel Shays, an officer in the American Revolutionary War, against the state's taxes and policy of foreclosing on debtor farmers.

The Politics of the Constitutional Convention

The colonial experience led many Americans to prefer a weak, decentralized national government and to place considerable political power in the state legislatures. But a few years experience with the Articles of Confederation showed that the country needed a national government that could act on behalf of the entire nation and settle disputes between the states. Those two lessons came to the forefront as the founders met in Philadelphia in 1787 to discuss revisions in the Articles of Confederation. When James Madison and Edmund Randolph immediately proposed, on behalf of the Virginia delegation, an entirely new plan of government, the convention quickly abandoned the Articles of Confederation and began to write a new constitution.

In 1786, Daniel Shays led a band of debtor farmers in western Massachusetts to try to block the state's foreclosure on bankrupt farms. Massachusetts's inability to enlist national aid in suppressing the uprising helped build support for a stronger national government, laying the foundation for the Constitutional Convention.

How should we understand the weeks of debate that ultimately produced the Constitution? A review of the proceedings shows that the delegates held very strong beliefs about the principles that should form the basis of a new government. We would be greatly mistaken, however, to think of the writing of the Constitution as simply the process of great minds debating the merits of various forms of government. The delegates to the Constitutional Convention were self-interested politicians who understood that the decisions they made would have enormous consequences. Some of them were even prepared to let the Convention fail if delegates could not reach acceptable compromises.[6] Yet in the end, the delegates produced a document that they accepted as an improvement over the Articles of Confederation.

What were some of the critical political disputes at the Constitutional Convention? Three issues were especially divisive: how to allocate representation in the new Congress, how to deal with the question of slavery, and how to define the powers of the new office of the presidency. The founders managed to resolve these disputes through a mix of compromise and calculated ambiguity. Let's consider each dispute in turn.

Representation in the National Legislature

Virginia Plan
A plan for a new national government that the Virginia delegation proposed at the Constitutional Convention in 1787. It called for a strong, essentially unitary national government, with separate executive and judicial branches, and a two-house legislative branch with representation based on each state's population.

The plan that James Madison and Edmund Randolph introduced is known as the **Virginia Plan.** The main elements of the plan appear in table 2.1. As originally proposed, it called for dividing the powers of government among three separate branches: a legislative branch for making laws; an executive branch for enforcing laws; and a judicial branch for interpreting laws. The Virginia Plan called for the national legislature to consist of two houses. Seats in each house would be allocated among the states in proportion to each state's population. The voters would directly elect the members of the lower chamber, and the lower chamber would in turn elect the members of the upper chamber from a slate of nominees each state legislature would submit. The Virginia Plan had a simple appeal: every voter in the United States would be represented equally in the national legislature. What could be more fair?

Delegates to the Constitutional Convention debated the provisions of the new Constitution.

TABLE 2.1 The Virginia Plan, the New Jersey Plan, and the Constitution

The Constitutional Convention considered substantially different plans for structuring the new government.

Characteristic	Virginia Plan	New Jersey Plan	Constitution
Congress	Two houses	One house	Two houses
Representation in Congress	Both houses based on population	Equal representation for each state	One house based on population; other house two seats per state
Decision Rule	Simple majority	Extraordinary majority	Concurrent majority
Executive	Single, elected by Congress	More than one person	Single, elected by electoral college
Removal of Executive	By Congress	By a majority of states	By Congress
Courts	National judiciary, elected by Congress	Judiciary, appointed by executive to hear appeals on violations of national laws in state courts	National judiciary, nominated by president and confirmed by Senate
Ratification	By the people	By the states	By state conventions
State Laws	Congress can override	National supremacy	National supremacy

As it turned out, many delegates thought the Virginia Plan was unfair. In what became known as the **New Jersey Plan,** whose main elements appear in table 2.1, critics of the Virginia Plan proposed that rather than representing each *citizen* equally, the new national legislature should represent each *state* equally. Proponents of the New Jersey Plan argued for treating states equally on the grounds of both precedent and principle. In terms of precedent, they argued that the states were equally represented in the national legislature under the Articles of Confederation. As for principle, proponents of the New Jersey Plan pointed out that the states, and not the people, were writing and ratifying the new government, so the states should have equal voices in the legislature.

New Jersey Plan
A plan for a new national government that the New Jersey delegation proposed at the Constitutional Convention in 1787. Its key feature consisted of giving each state equal representation in the national legislature, regardless of its population.

Although both sides in the debate over the Virginia and New Jersey plans invoked principle, the debate involved much more than simply deciding which principle held greater merit. Also at stake was the political power some states would gain and some would lose under the new national government. The more populous states such as Massachusetts, Pennsylvania, and Virginia favored the Virginia Plan because it would give them the most seats in the new Congress. Conversely, less populous states such as New Jersey, Connecticut, and Delaware favored the "one state-one vote" principle embodied in the New Jersey Plan because it preserved their political power. The small states feared that if representation in the new national government were based solely on population, their interests would become secondary to those of the more populous states. The small states felt strongly about this issue and threatened to leave the Convention if it did not address their concerns.

Connecticut Compromise
A plan the Connecticut delegation proposed at the Constitutional Convention. This plan sought to manage the dispute between large- and small-population states by creating a two-house legislature with representation in one house based on population and representation in the second house set at two seats per state.

The dispute between large and small states was resolved by the **Connecticut Compromise** (also known as the Great Compromise), which combined elements of both the Virginia and New Jersey plans and formed the basis for the Constitution (see table 2.1). In the House of Representatives, seats would be allocated on the basis of population, thereby satisfying the concerns of the more populous states. In contrast, in the Senate, two seats would be allocated to each state, thereby satisfying the concerns of the less populous states. The Connecticut Compromise also required that both the House of Representatives and the Senate had to pass a bill before it could become law. This provision gave both large and small states further assurance that the new Congress would not disregard their interests. Thus, in the end, both large and small states gained some, but not all, of what they had wanted.

Slavery and the Three-Fifths Compromise

The second divisive issue the delegates at the Constitutional Convention faced was how the new government should deal with the question of slavery. This time, geography rather than population divided the states. Southern delegates staunchly defended slavery, while northern delegates favored limiting and eventually terminating the practice. Southern delegates made it clear they would desert the Convention rather than accept rules that would outlaw slavery.

The debate over slavery quickly became tied to the debate over representation. Southern delegates recognized that because the northern states outnumbered the southern states, and because more white people lived in the North than the South, northern states would have more representation in Congress, which might enable them to limit or even outlaw slavery. Southern delegates could not simply create new states to strengthen the South's position in the Senate, so they proposed counting slaves as part of a state's population when seats were allocated in the House of Representatives. Northern delegates, however, opposed counting people that Southerners themselves considered property. In a clear example of compromising to accomplish a larger purpose, the northern states agreed to count each slave as three-fifths of a person. The Constitution also extended other protections to slave owners. Article I prevented the government from ending the importation of slaves until 1808, and Article IV required that the states respect the rights of slave owners from other states by returning escaped slaves to their masters.

Northern delegates found the three-fifths compromise easier to accept when southern delegates agreed that slaves would also be counted on a three-fifths basis if the national government imposed a per capita tax on each state. Under such a tax system, states with larger populations would carry a higher tax burden than smaller states. Southern states were willing to pay higher taxes in return for the political advantage of inflating the size of their populations.

Defining the Powers of the President

In addition to struggling with the issues of representation and slavery, the founders struggled with the question of how much power to give the president of the new national government, or what is more commonly called the federal government. The dismal experience with the Articles of Confederation convinced the founders that they needed to create an executive branch of government headed by a president. The delegates agreed that the president should have the power to veto legislation Congress had passed as well as powers to appoint officials in the executive branch, to negotiate treaties on behalf of the United States, and to grant pardons. Beyond this

Slavery was a recurring source of conflict in the new nation. Northern and southern delegates clashed at the Constitutional Convention over whether to count slaves as part of the population when allocating seats in the House of Representatives. The contending factions sidestepped the issue by counting each slave as three-fifths of a person.

point, however, the delegates disagreed. Some wanted to bestow substantial powers on the president, whereas others feared that creating a powerful presidency would promote tyranny.

Although the founders disagreed on the powers to be given to the presidency, they all believed its first occupant would be George Washington. Widely admired and trusted, Washington was expected to serve with integrity and balance. Because of their immense respect for Washington, the founders agreed to finesse their differences over the presidency by being ambiguous about the precise boundaries of presidential power; thus, the Constitution discusses the powers of the presidency in fairly vague terms. The founders were willing to use ambiguity to settle their differences because they trusted President Washington to give acceptable concrete meaning to the abstract language of the Constitution.

The assurance that Washington would be elected as the first president enabled the founders to leave the powers of the presidency ambiguous.

Gilbert Stuart, *George Washington* (Vaughn portrait) 1795, detail, oil on canvas, 735 × 605 (29 × 23¾). Andrew W. Mellon Collection, National Gallery of Art, Washington.

To see how reluctant the founders were to define the powers of the presidency, compare Articles I and II of the Constitution. Article I lays out the structure, operation, and powers of Congress. It begins: "All legislative Powers *herein granted* shall be vested in a Congress of the United States" (emphasis added). The remainder of Article I enumerates the many powers of Congress. Article II of the Constitution lays out the structure, operation, and powers of the presidency, but it looks quite different from Article I. It begins with the simple statement: "The executive Power shall be vested in a President of the United States of America." Nothing in Article II defines what is meant by the term *executive power,* and Article II avoids enumerating the powers of the presidency as Article I does for Congress.

The founders resorted to ambiguity because it enabled them to disguise their differences on the question of presidential power. But as is true any time people resort to ambiguity to mask their differences, the underlying conflict remains. In the case of the Constitution, the founders' failure to define the precise limits of presidential power sowed the seeds of much future conflict. For more than two hundred years, presidents and Congresses have struggled to define the proper limits of presidential power on issues ranging from who can send U.S. troops into combat to when the president can disregard the directives of Congress. Historically, presidents argue for expansive readings of their constitutional powers, while members of Congress usually prefer restrictive interpretations.

As the debates over representation, slavery, and the powers of the presidency all show, both principle and self-interest greatly influenced the content of the Constitution. By the end of the summer of 1787, after weeks of debate, compromise, and

The People Behind the Rules

BOX 2.1

Antifederalists Versus Federalists: Patrick Henry and James Madison

The success the American political system has enjoyed for more than two centuries makes the wisdom of the Constitution and its authors seem obvious. Yet when it was written, the Constitution was a controversial document that divided the American people. The leading voices in the Antifederalist and Federalist camps included two of the most important political figures in eighteenth-century America: Patrick Henry and James Madison.

Patrick Henry

Patrick Henry

Patrick Henry was born in Virginia in 1736. First as a lawyer and then as a member of Virginia's colonial legislature, Henry made a name for himself as a brilliant orator. He frequently used his oratorical gifts to criticize British rule. By the mid-1770s, Henry had become convinced that the colonies had no choice but to rebel against Great Britain. In a speech in 1775, he urged his fellow Virginians to arm the state militia for the inevitable fight against the British. Henry ended the speech with a line that galvanized his compatriots and that remains well known to American school children more than two centuries later: "I know not what course others may take, but as for me, give me liberty or give me death."

During the American Revolutionary War, Henry served three one-year terms as the governor of Virginia. In 1786, he was selected as a delegate to what would become the Constitutional Convention. However, he declined the offer to go to Philadelphia. When the Convention produced a new political blueprint for the United States, Henry became a leading Antifederalist. He denounced the Constitution for reasons involving both political philosophy and practical politics. He believed the document was grievously flawed because it failed to guarantee the rights of either states or individuals, and he worried that in the new political system the northern states would cede navigation rights on the lower Mississippi to Spain. (Navigation on the lower reaches of the Mississippi was an issue of great concern to Americans then living on the western frontier.)

Although Henry opposed ratification of the Constitution, he is largely responsible for the passage of the Bill of Rights. To blunt his criticisms and those of other Antifederalists, the Federalists promised to attach a list of individual rights and liberties to the Constitution once the new Congress met. When the states ratified the Constitution, Henry turned his energies toward seeing that the Federalists kept their promise. With the eventual adoption of the Bill of Rights, Henry dropped his opposition to the new federal government.

Despite Henry's efforts to block ratification of the Constitution, he retained the respect of Federalist leaders. George Washington offered to appoint him as secretary of state or as chief justice of the Supreme Court. He declined both offers, citing poor health and family duties. Henry gave his last public speech during an election campaign in 1799 for a seat in the Virginia state legislature. The topic of his speech: a call for American unity.

Continued

appeals to ambiguity, the Constitutional Convention approved the final draft of the Constitution. The Constitutional Convention had ended, but the struggle to create a new federal government had just begun, for the states had to ratify, or approve, the Constitution before it could replace the Articles of Confederation.

Federalists
The label describing those who supported adoption of the Constitution. They believed in the need for a national government stronger than the one provided under the Articles of Confederation.

The Politics of Ratification

The fight to ratify the Constitution pitted two groups against each other. People who supported ratification, known as **Federalists,** had as their most vocal leaders James Madison and Alexander Hamilton. Federalists argued that the new Constitution was needed to remedy the problems the new nation had experienced under the Articles of Confederation. People who opposed ratification, including such leading figures in the American Revolution as Samuel Adams and Patrick Henry, were known as

The People Behind the Rules

BOX 2.1 CONTINUED

James Madison

James Madison

Like Patrick Henry, James Madison was a son of Virginia. Born in 1751, he was elected to Virginia's Revolutionary Convention at the age of twenty-five. There he helped to draft legislation that guaranteed religious freedom to all Virginians as well as legislation that effectively abolished Virginia's state church. Madison ran for reelection to what had become the Virginia state legislature, but he was defeated when he refused to follow the customary practice of wooing voters with free whiskey.

In 1780, Madison became one of Virginia's delegates to the Continental Congress. He soon established himself as a leading proponent of a strong national government. Following the passage of the Articles of Confederation, which concentrated power in the hands of the states, Madison searched unsuccessfully for ways to strengthen the national government. In 1784, he rejoined the Virginia state legislature, where, among other things, he helped defeat a bill sponsored by Patrick Henry that would have directed the state of Virginia to provide financial support to "teachers of the Christian religion."

Despite his return to Virginia, Madison remained deeply involved in national affairs. When the states refused to cede power to the national government despite the obvious failings of the Articles of Confederation, he helped lead the calls for holding the Annapolis Convention and, eventually, the Constitutional Convention. In Philadelphia, Virginia Gov. Edmund Randolph introduced Madison's vision of a new political system for the thirteen states. Although the Connecticut Compromise and other changes modified the Virginia Plan in many of its particulars, Madison, more than anyone else, deserves the title of architect of the Constitution.

Madison continued his efforts on behalf of the Constitution once the Constitutional Convention adjourned. When ratification appeared in doubt in New York, he joined with Alexander Hamilton and John Jay to write the *Federalist Papers*. (Madison wrote twenty-nine of the eighty-five essays in the series.) He also played a key role in convincing the Virginia state convention to ratify the Constitution, despite Patrick Henry's impassioned pleas to reject it. Madison subsequently won election to the first Congress, and he used his seat in the House of Representatives to push passage of the Bill of Rights. He later served as secretary of state under Thomas Jefferson and then as president of the United States from 1809 to 1817.

Sources: Robert Douthat Meade, *Patrick Henry: Practical Revolutionary* (Philadelphia: J. B. Lippincott, 1969); and Ralph Ketcham, *James Madison: A Biography* (New York: Macmillan, 1971).

Antifederalists (see box 2.1). Fearful that the Constitution gave too much power to the national government, Antifederalists denounced the document as a "political monster," a "*Colossus of Despotism*," and the "most daring attempt to establish a despotic aristocracy among freemen, that the world has ever witnessed."[7] Because the Antifederalists were well represented in the state legislatures, the Federalists took two steps to increase the chances of ratification: they wrote rules of ratification that favored the supporters of the Constitution, and they sought to undercut support for the Antifederalists by agreeing to amend the Constitution to include a specific list of guarantees for individual rights.

Antifederalists
The label describing those who opposed adoption of the Constitution. While opponents gave a variety of reasons for rejecting the Constitution, their main concern was that a strong national government would jeopardize individual rights.

The Rules for Ratification

For the Constitution to replace the Articles of Confederation, the states first had to give their approval. But who in each state had the authority to approve or reject the Constitution? And how many states would need to ratify the Constitution before it could take effect? The founders answered these two questions in Article VII of the Constitution: "The Ratification of the Conventions of nine States, shall be sufficient for the Establishment of this Constitution between the States so ratifying the Same."

The founders chose to make the Constitution subject to ratification by conventions in nine states because this was the one rule that was both politically acceptable and likely to lead to ratification.[8] The founders could have put the Constitution to a vote among the state legislatures, but many Antifederalists served as state legislators. Thus, to minimize any organizational advantage the Antifederalists might have, the founders opted to rely on special state conventions. (This decision had some precedent. In 1780, Massachusetts had put its new constitution to the vote of a special state convention rather than to a vote of the state legislature.) Because they were already well organized and the Antifederalists were not, the Federalists calculated that they could gain the upper hand in the state conventions. At the same time, the reliance on state conventions made the Constitution seem more democratic; the people of each state would elect delegates to the conventions.

Like the decision to make the Constitution subject to the approval of special state conventions, the decision to require the approval of nine states reflected shrewd political calculation. The founders could have made the Constitution subject to unanimous approval. After all, such a rule had precedent; the Articles of Confederation, for example, required that every state approve all amendments. Adoption of a unanimity rule, however, would have doomed the Constitution to defeat. Rhode Island had refused even to send delegates to the Convention, and it would have blocked adoption of the Constitution if it had the chance to do so. Given that the Antifederalists opposed the Constitution, it is not surprising they criticized the abandonment of the unanimity rule as an illegitimate change in the rules governing the relations among the thirteen states.

At the other extreme, the founders might have made ratification of the Constitution subject to a simple majority vote. But they recognized that ratification by a majority vote was simply not politically acceptable to most of the voting public. While in principle the Constitution applied only to the states that ratified it, in practice its adoption would effectively end the national government created by the Articles of Confederation. The decision to dissolve one union and initiate a second would have lacked legitimacy with the American electorate if only seven of the thirteen states had endorsed the new system of government.

Since the founders deemed both ratification by unanimous consent and by simple majority unacceptable, they settled on the rule of nine. A precedent for requiring a majority of nine states existed in the Articles of Confederation, which required that nine states had to approve a bill before it became law. Additional support for the rule of nine came from Article V of the Constitution, which states that three-fourths of the states must ratify amendments to the Constitution. Because Rhode Island was virtually certain to reject the Constitution, only twelve states were seriously willing to entertain the notion of adopting it. Thus, by requiring the approval of nine of twelve states, the founders, in essence, were subjecting the Constitution to a three-fourths majority standard similar to the one proposed for adopting amendments.

The Bill of Rights

The founders wrote the rules of ratification in response to prevailing political realities and their desire to maximize the chances the Constitution would be ratified. But once the text of the Constitution became public, the Federalists found themselves on the defensive. Antifederalists began to complain that the Constitution failed to protect the rights of individual citizens. To undercut these criticisms, the Federalists promised to amend the Constitution to include a list of provisions guaranteeing certain individual rights. These amendments would eventually become known as the **Bill of Rights.**

Bill of Rights
The name given to the first ten amendments of the Constitution. They outline a large number of important individual rights.

At the Constitutional Convention, delegates such as Madison and Hamilton had strongly opposed incorporating an explicit statement of rights into the Constitution for a number of reasons. They argued that such a list could never be complete and that, if the statement enumerated only some rights, the government could use the existence of such a list to deny the people other rights. Moreover, they claimed that since the government had not been given the power to regulate these rights, there was no need to protect against abusive uses of such powers. Finally, Madison and Hamilton preferred a system of structural protections. They persuaded the other delegates to structure the new government so that groups and individuals could defend their own interests. As we shall see in the next section, the belief that a properly structured government could promote individual rights was part of the philosophical justification for the doctrines of separation of powers and checks and balances.

Antifederalists put little stock in the structural protections Madison and Hamilton favored. They instead called for a second convention that would revise the Constitution to include a statement of rights. Not surprisingly, Federalists reacted to such a proposal with alarm. They knew the delegates to a second constitutional convention might scrap the proposed Constitution, just as they had scrapped the Articles of Confederation. To defeat calls for a new convention, the Federalists promised the new government's first task would be to amend the Constitution to include a list specifying a wide variety of individual rights. The willingness of the Federalists to provide explicit guarantees of individual rights persuaded some Antifederalists, including Samuel Adams, to drop their opposition to the Constitution. As a result, the bid to convene a second constitutional convention failed.

Ratification of the Constitution

The Federalists' strategy of writing favorable rules of ratification and offering to add a Bill of Rights to the Constitution succeeded in blunting the challenge the Antifederalists posed. In December 1787, Delaware became the first state to ratify the Constitution, and eight months later, New Hampshire became the ninth. (Three other states ratified the Constitution before the end of 1788, and Rhode Island withheld its approval until May 1790, after the first Congress convened, George Washington was inaugurated, and the Supreme Court was established.) But while the Federalists had triumphed, their victory had depended on narrow margins in several states. New York, for example, approved the Constitution by a vote of 30 to 27, while in Rhode Island the vote was 34 to 32.

The new Congress of the United States met for the first time in March 1789. The Federalists quickly made good their pledge to formulate a list of individual rights to append to the Constitution. By September, Congress had approved twelve amendments for consideration by the states. The states ratified ten of the twelve in short order, and these ten amendments make up what we know as the Bill of Rights. (One of the two remaining amendments, which requires members of Congress to stand for reelection before receiving a pay raise, was ratified in 1992.) Thus, the Bill of Rights was created not to correct a philosophical oversight in the Constitution, but as a political tactic designed to strip the Constitution's critics of their most potent weapon.

THE CONSTITUTION AS A REFLECTION OF THE FOUNDERS' PHILOSOPHY

Although many sharp political conflicts influenced the writing of the Constitution, the document is not the product of politics alone. The philosophical principles the founders shared also profoundly influenced the Constitution. These philosophical principles led the founders to create rules of government that seek to protect individual rights and prevent the majority from unfairly imposing its will on the minority. We use the term *minority* here not to denote racial or ethnic minorities such as African Americans or Arab Americans, but rather to refer to any group in society whose numbers fall short of a majority. Indeed, many of the founders felt that they, as members of the wealthier classes, were a minority threatened by the more numerous poor. The root beliefs of the founders, then, provide the Constitution with its essential structuring principles.

Individual Rights and Democratic Rule

Classical liberalism
A political philosophy, particularly strong in the eighteenth century, that claims that the rights of the individual predate the existence of government and take priority over government policy. This philosophy advocates the protection of individual freedoms from the government.

The principle that stood first and foremost in the thinking of the founders was the need to protect the rights of the individual. In strongly emphasizing individual rights, the founders leaned heavily on the **classical liberalism** of philosophers such as John Locke. (Classical liberalism, which emphasizes the rights of individuals, should not be confused with modern liberalism, which emphasizes using government to solve problems in society.) The willingness of the founders to embrace the arguments of classical liberalism had roots in and was reinforced by the Judeo-Christian beliefs prominent among the colonies at the time. These beliefs contended that people are created in the image of God and thus possess an intrinsic value deserving of protection.

Classical liberals believed in the doctrine of *natural rights,* the idea that individuals possess certain rights that are inherent and inalienable—that is, that cannot be taken away. In his *Two Treatises of Government,* Locke argued that all humans possess the rights to life, liberty, and property.[9] The influence of the doctrine of natural rights is evident in the Declaration of Independence (1776), which declares that people are "endowed by their Creator with certain unalienable rights, that among these are Life, Liberty, and the pursuit of Happiness."

The writings of John Locke (1632–1704), a leading proponent of classical liberalism, profoundly influenced the founders at the Constitutional Convention.

Although Locke and other classical liberals claimed that these individual rights were self-evident and could not be denied, they nonetheless recognized that these rights could be suppressed. Locke argued that in a society without any government, or what he called the "state of nature," the strong in all likelihood would suppress the rights of the weak. According to classical liberals, then, government was needed to ensure liberty for everyone so that all could enjoy the freedom to fully exercise their rights. Beyond this duty, the responsibilities of government were extremely limited. Indeed, Locke argued that even the government itself was subordinate to these rights, because God had given the people the right to revolt against unjust governments that violated their rights. Thomas Jefferson drew on precisely this argument when he wrote in the Declaration of Independence that citizens have the right to rebel when their government "becomes destructive of" the free exercise of the rights of citizens.

The twin beliefs in individual rights and the need for a government that would protect them led the founders to favor a way of making government decisions that was quite radical for the eighteenth century: majority rule. If everyone possesses the same rights and possesses them to the same degree, then claims that kings have a divine right to rule or that only aristocrats can govern are fundamentally illegitimate. Instead, all citizens (which to the founders meant all white males who owned property) should have a voice in government. At the same time, if every citizen has an equal voice in government, it follows that government should act on the basis of what the most citizens desire. A minority should not be allowed to impose its wishes on the majority. Yet as appealing as the founders found the argument for majority rule, it posed a potential paradox. What if the majority's wishes conflicted with an individual's rights? Who should prevail—the majority or the individual?

Majority Tyranny: The Paradox of Majority Rule

Majority tyranny
A situation in which the majority uses its advantage in numbers to suppress the rights of the minority.

The great disadvantage of government by majority rule is that it may produce **majority tyranny:** a situation in which the majority uses its advantage in numbers to suppress the rights of the minority. The problem of majority tyranny is not simply that a majority prevails on a given issue. By definition, majority rule always produces minorities because every decision has a losing side. Since the existence of a losing side is unavoidable, the fact that some people find themselves in a minority on any given decision does not mean that majority tyranny exists. Rather, majority tyranny arises, threatening individual rights, when the same groups repeatedly find themselves in the majority and minority. Under these conditions, the majority has little reason to constrain its behavior, and the minority has few means to protect itself.

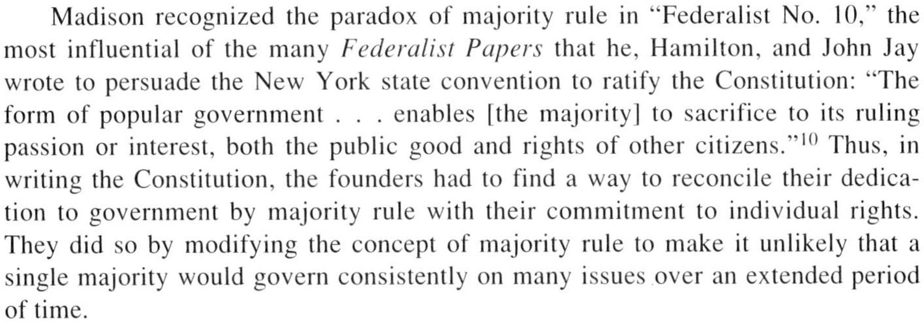

The FŒDERALIST, No. 10.

To the People of the State of New-York.

AMONG the numerous advantages promiſed by a well conſtructed Union, none deſerves to be more accurately developed than its tendency to break and control the violence of faction. The friend of popular governments, never finds himſelf ſo much alarmed for their character and fate, as when he contemplates their propenſity to this dangerous vice. He will not fail therefore to ſet a due value on any plan which, without violating the principles to which he is attached, provides a proper cure for it. The inſtability, injuſtice and confuſion introduced into the public councils, have in truth been the mortal diſeaſes under which popular governments have every where periſhed; as they continue to be the favorite and fruitful topics from which the adverſaries to liberty derive their moſt ſpecious declamations. The valuable improvements made by the American Conſtitutions on the popular models, both ancient and modern, cannot certainly

Alexander Hamilton

James Madison

John Jay

Alexander Hamilton, James Madison, and John Jay combined to author the Federalist Papers *in 1787 and 1788. They wrote the* Papers *to justify ratification of the Constitution and to defend it from attacks by Antifederalists.*

Madison recognized the paradox of majority rule in "Federalist No. 10," the most influential of the many *Federalist Papers* that he, Hamilton, and John Jay wrote to persuade the New York state convention to ratify the Constitution: "The form of popular government . . . enables [the majority] to sacrifice to its ruling passion or interest, both the public good and rights of other citizens."[10] Thus, in writing the Constitution, the founders had to find a way to reconcile their dedication to government by majority rule with their commitment to individual rights. They did so by modifying the concept of majority rule to make it unlikely that a single majority would govern consistently on many issues over an extended period of time.

Preventing Majority Tyranny

To prevent the emergence of a permanent majority that could suppress the rights of the minority, the founders took three important steps: (1) they wrote electoral rules into the Constitution that make it difficult for permanent electoral majorities to form; (2) they divided authority among government institutions as well as between the federal and state governments; and (3) they placed formal boundaries on what the government may do. Each of these three steps created a barrier to majority tyranny.

FIGURE 2.1
The Use of Indirect Elections in the Constitution

The founders wrote the Constitution so that only members of the House of Representatives were directly elected by the people.

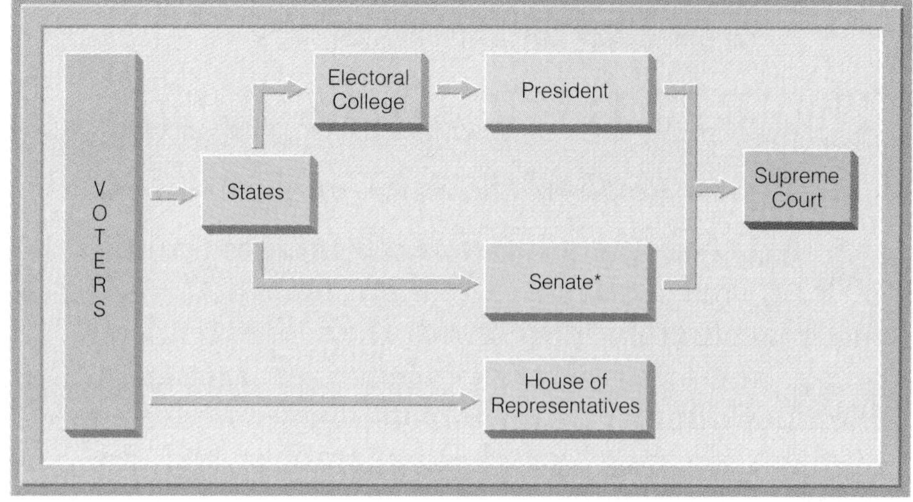

*The Seventeenth Amendment, which provided for direct election of senators by the people, eliminated the state legislature's role in choosing senators in 1913.

Electoral Rules

The founders settled on elections as the mechanism for choosing most government leaders because of their commitment to the principles of democracy and republicanism. **Democracy** recognizes that the authority to create and run a government rests with the people. As we saw earlier, the doctrine of classical liberalism justifies a democratic system of government. **Republicanism** is a specific form of government run by representatives of the people. Elections thus make the American political system a democratic republic because the people run the government through their chosen representatives. (Note that a democracy need not be republic. In a so-called pure, or participatory, democracy, the people govern themselves directly rather than through elected representatives.)

Democracy
A form of government in which the people (defined broadly to include all adults or narrowly to exclude women or slaves, for example) are the ultimate political authority.

Republicanism
A system of government in which the people's selected representatives run the government.

While elections make American politics democratic, the founders chose to subject elections to rules that inhibit the formation of permanent electoral majorities. These rules include indirect elections, fixed terms of office, and geographically defined representation.

Indirect elections Under the original provisions of the Constitution, only members of the House of Representatives were to be elected directly by the people. All other government officials were to be elected indirectly or appointed by the president and Congress. Although today the people directly elect senators, the Constitution originally stipulated that state legislatures were to elect the members of the Senate. The nation moved to direct election of senators only with the passage of the Seventeenth Amendment in 1913. Even today, the president is elected not by the people but by an electoral college (see chapter 12). Members of the electoral college are chosen in each state according to rules that state establishes, and electoral college members are free to exercise their own judgment in electing a president. (As a practical matter, members of the electoral college almost always cast their votes according to the popular vote in their state.) The president (who is not directly elected) in turn nominates, and the Senate (which originally was not directly elected) confirms, all federal court judges, who serve life terms. Figure 2.1 depicts how the electoral system the founders created works.

The founders resorted to indirect elections because they feared having government officials who were too responsive to the wishes of the majority. The founders believed that if government officials were somewhat insulated from the passions of the public, they would find it easier to protect the rights of the minority and to promote the common good.

Fixed terms of office The second set of electoral rules that helps prevent the creation of a permanent electoral majority is fixed terms of office. In the United States, unlike most other industrial democracies, elections are set on fixed dates. The president and members of Congress cannot reschedule an election to take advantage of favorable circumstances or avoid unfavorable ones. At the same time, the founders varied the length of the different fixed terms. Representatives are elected every two years, presidents every four years, and senators every six years, with only one-third up for election every two years. The founders calculated that staggering elections would make it impossible for a passionate majority to seize control of both Congress and the White House in a single election.

Geographically defined representation The third set of electoral rules that helps deter the formation of permanent electoral majorities is the geographically defined system of representation. Whereas in some countries people vote for the national legislature in nationwide elections, in the United States elections to Congress are tied to where we live; each state elects its own senators and representatives. (In the case of elections to the House of Representatives, each state is divided into a number of districts based on its population, with each district electing a single representative. Although a district is another example of a geographically defined system of representation, a federal law passed in 1842, rather than the Constitution, mandates districts.) Because each district and state contains a different mix of economic, social, and political interests, the founders doubted that the same groups could win a majority of congressional elections. At the same time, while presidents are elected in a nationwide election, they must win a majority of the electoral college votes rather than a majority of the popular vote. Again, because each state contains such a different mix of interests, candidates for president are discouraged from attending exclusively to the interests of any one group.

Divided Authority

The founders created a second line of defense against majority tyranny by dividing authority among government institutions as well as between the federal government and state governments. Thus, even if voters elect a permanent majority, the fact that authority is dispersed among government institutions makes it difficult for that majority to govern because minorities have many opportunities to protect their own interests. In dividing authority among government institutions, the founders embraced the doctrines of separation of powers, checks and balances, bicameralism, and federalism.

Separation of powers One way the founders sought to block majority tyranny was to divide the power to govern among three separate branches of government. This doctrine of **separation of powers,** which the founders took from the work of French philosopher Montesquieu, holds that separate branches of government should exercise the legislative, executive, and judicial powers of government.[11] Thus, in the United States, unlike many other countries, Congress, the president, and the judiciary are independent of each other, meaning that none of the three can control the decisions of the others. The separation of powers seeks to prevent majority tyranny by making it impossible for any majority to control government simply by gaining control of one or even two sources of political power.

Separation of powers
The principle that each of the three powers of government—legislative, executive, and judicial—should be held by a separate branch of government.

Checks and balances Closely aligned with the doctrine of separation of powers is the principle of **checks and balances.** Checks and balances are negative powers each branch of government can use to block the actions of another branch. For example, only Congress can pass laws, but the president can use the veto power to cancel them. In turn, if two-thirds of both the House and Senate wish to, Congress can override a presidential veto. Checks and balances put teeth into the separation of powers by allowing a group that controls one branch of government to protect itself from groups

Checks and balances
The powers each branch of government can use to block the actions of other branches.

FIGURE 2.2
Separation of Powers and Checks and Balances

To protect against majority tyranny, the founders created a system based on two principles: separation of powers, and checks and balances. Separation of powers divides the federal government into three equal branches, and the principle of checks and balances gives each branch powers that enable it to prevent the other branches from taking actions that it opposes.

Separation of Powers	**Legislature**	**Executive**	**Judiciary**
Establishes each branch of government and defines the powers of each	The Legislature can make laws. 	The Executive can enforce laws. 	The Judiciary can interpret laws. 
Checks and Balances Gives each branch power to override the actions of other branches	• Confirm executive appointments (Senate) • Override executive veto • Impeach executive and judicial officials	• Veto legislation • Recommend legislation • Grant pardons	• Review legislative acts • Review executive acts • Issue injunctions

controlling the other branches of government. Figure 2.2 illustrates the relationship between the doctrine of separation of powers and the system of checks and balances.

By combining checks and balances with the principle of the separation of powers, the founders actually created a political system in which the separation of powers is incomplete. The practice of checks and balances means that more than one branch of government is involved in exercising a particular power. For example, as we just mentioned, the structural rules of American politics give Congress the power to write laws, but these rules also give the president the power to veto any law Congress passes. Thus, both the legislative and executive branches of government participate in the law-making process. Because some political powers belong to more than one branch of government, we can most accurately describe the federal government as "separated institutions *sharing* powers."[12]

Bicameral legislature
A legislature with two houses—such as the House and the Senate.

Bicameralism The third step the founders took to make it difficult for permanent majorities to govern was to create a **bicameral legislature,** which divides law-making authority between two legislative houses. Thus, in most circumstances, no proposal can become law unless *concurrent majorities*—that is, majority votes in both the House and Senate—approve it. This means that if a majority of the members of the House favor a bill to cut income taxes but a majority of the Senate opposes it (or vice versa), the bill does not become law. In the few circumstances in which the founders did not require a majority vote in both House and Senate, they required that a *supermajority* of one house approve legislation, or some number greater than a simple majority. For example, no treaty can go into effect unless two-thirds of the members of the Senate give their consent.

In some circumstances, the founders combined the requirements of concurrent and supermajorities to make it especially difficult for a single majority to impose its will. For example, Congress can propose an amendment to the Constitution only if two-thirds of the members of the House *and* two-thirds of the members of the Senate vote to do so. Likewise, to override a presidential veto, two-thirds of both the House and the Senate must vote to reverse the president's decision. In today's Congress, the combination of concurrent and supermajorities means that thirty-four senators who agree with the president can frustrate the will of 501 members of Congress who do not. Because the combination of concurrent and supermajorities poses such a formidable barrier, Congress has overridden only 7 percent of all presidential vetoes.[13]

Federalism With the separation of powers, the Constitution divides political power among the three branches of the federal government. To further deter the operation of permanent majorities, the founders developed the doctrine of **federalism**, the idea that a country should have different levels of government, each with its own set of sovereign or independent political powers. In the United States, the Constitution divides power between the federal and state governments. Federalism initially emerged at the Constitutional Convention as an imaginative compromise between those who wanted a more powerful national government and those who feared that a strong national government might tyrannize small states and other minorities. By reserving powers to the states, the founders established a basis for groups that are a majority within a state but a minority within the nation to exercise some degree of local self-government.

Federalism
A two-tiered form of government in which governments on both levels are sovereign and share authority over the same geographic jurisdiction.

Formal Boundaries on Government Action

The final barrier the founders erected to prevent a permanent majority from suppressing the rights of the minority was to place formal boundaries on the powers of the national government. In general, leading supporters of the Constitution such as James Madison were not sympathetic to this approach. They argued that a determined majority could easily ignore any formal rules protecting minority rights. Moreover, they argued that a failure to mention some rights might later allow others to argue that those rights did not exist or did not need protection. In deference to other delegates at the Constitutional Convention, the Constitution does include several specific limitations on government power. As we have seen, the founders also agreed to add a Bill of Rights to the Constitution in order to win ratification.

Limits in the original Constitution One specific limitation the Constitution places on the powers of government is that government officials cannot suspend an individual's right to *habeas corpus,* that is, an individual's right not to be imprisoned unless charged with a crime, except in time of "rebellion or invasion." Thus, in normal circumstances, the government cannot imprison people unless it can produce credible evidence that they may have committed a crime. The Constitution further forbids the government from passing *bills of attainder,* which means Congress cannot punish an individual for a crime without first providing a trial in court. Finally, the Constitution forbids Congress from passing *ex post facto* laws, laws that declare an act criminal after the act was committed. More recently, the courts have interpreted the prohibition against ex post facto laws to mean that the government cannot impose a punishment greater than the punishment in effect when the crime was committed.[14] Thus, if a state reinstated the death penalty, officials could not apply it to prisoners who had been convicted of committing murder before the law was changed.

Limits in the Bill of Rights The Bill of Rights adds an extensive list of prohibitions to government actions (see chapter 4). As we learned earlier, Antifederalists feared that a strong national government would suppress individual rights. Thus, they insisted on, and the Federalists ultimately agreed to, the inclusion of a list of rights that individuals possess and that limit the government's jurisdiction. These serve as a final defense of individual rights by proclaiming that, even if all parts of the government wish to act, the government cannot take an action if it violates the rights of an individual.

In erecting the three barriers we have just discussed to prevent majority tyranny, the founders placed a higher value on preventing "bad" government decisions (the suppression of the rights of the minority) than on encouraging "good" government decisions (achieving the wishes of the majority). In a practical sense, this means it is easier to block than to accomplish action in our system of government; this causes the wheels of government to lumber along slowly. Although today's politicians decry gridlock, the Constitution clearly sets forth rules that are designed to prevent the government from making hasty, unilateral decisions that might harm the rights of the minority.

The Capitol—home to the U.S. Congress.

The Core Provisions of the Constitution

We have seen that a combination of political imperatives and philosophical beliefs influenced the writing of the Constitution. But exactly what does the Constitution say? Its core provisions set forth the rules governing Congress, the presidency, and the judiciary, as well as the rules governing relations between the federal and state governments.

Congress

Although the Constitution discusses Congress in several places, the most thorough discussion of the rules, structures, and powers of Congress appears in Article I. The ten sections that make up Article I specify the rules for electing members of Congress, the procedures for turning bills into laws, and the powers of Congress.

We already have discussed some of the details of Article I that regulate congressional elections. For example, Article I stipulates that Congress shall consist of two chambers, the House of Representatives and the Senate. Each state is represented in the House of Representatives in proportion to its population, and all representatives are elected to two-year terms. Every state has two seats in the Senate, and senators serve six-year terms. Other election rules Article I lays out are less well known. For instance, each state sets its own rules for electing members of Congress, subject to the provision that it must permit every person it allows to vote in the election for the most numerous branch of the state legislature to vote in the election for the House. The responsibility for resolving any disputes that arise over the outcome or validity of an election lies with the chamber in which the dispute occurs, and no member of Congress may hold a position in another branch of government during his or her congressional service.

Besides establishing the rules for electing people to Congress, Article I also specifies the rules that Congress must follow to turn a bill into a law. Under Article I, the House and Senate must first approve identical versions of a bill. Then, the bill goes to the president. If the president signs the bill, it becomes law; if the president vetoes the bill, it returns to Congress. Members of Congress have the option of trying to override the president's veto, but, as we already have mentioned, two-thirds of each house must vote to override the veto. If members of Congress decide not to override the veto or fail in their attempt to do so, the bill does not become law. Finally, if the president neither signs the bill nor vetoes it, the bill becomes law after ten days, provided Congress does not adjourn during that time. If Congress does adjourn within that ten-day period, however, the bill does not become law. Allowing a bill to die when Congress adjourns is known as the *pocket veto*.

The White House—where the president of the United States lives and works.

The Constitution lays out other powers of Congress (many of which are subject to a presidential veto). Congress controls the finances of government because it has the power to write tax laws, appropriate money, and borrow and coin money. Congress is centrally involved in establishing the structure of the government through its power to create, fund, and set the jurisdictions of agencies in the executive branch and courts in the judicial branch. Congress influences the state of the economy through its powers to regulate foreign and interstate commerce. It is integrally involved in the nation's defense and foreign policies through its power to declare war; raise, support, and establish rules of conduct for the army and navy; and through the Senate's responsibility to approve treaties and confirm ambassadors.

The Constitution also empowers Congress "To make all Laws which shall be necessary and proper for carrying into Execution the foregoing Powers." Often referred to as the **necessary and proper clause** (or the *elastic clause*), this provision enables Congress to act in ways the Constitution does not specify, provided Congress can show that such acts are appropriate in fulfilling its duties. As we shall see later in this chapter, the Supreme Court's decision in *McCulloch v. Maryland* (1819) gave Congress wide latitude to define the realm of the elastic clause.

Necessary and proper clause The provision in Article I of the Constitution that states that Congress possesses whatever additional and unspecified powers it needs to fulfill its responsibilities.

Still, the powers of Congress are not infinite. As we saw in our discussion of habeas corpus, bills of attainder, and ex post facto laws, the Constitution withholds some powers from Congress. Likewise, the Constitution requires Congress to give a public accounting of all public expenditures. But in general, the Constitution assigns Congress a great deal of power, consistent with the founders' belief in empowering the legislative rather than the executive branch of government.

The Presidency and the Executive Branch

As with Congress, the Constitution specifies the rules for electing presidents as well as the powers of the presidency. Most of the discussion of the presidency and the executive branch is in Article II.

As we have already discussed, presidents are elected by the vote of the electoral college rather than by the direct vote of the people. Article II sets the number of electoral votes assigned to each state at a figure equal to the number of senators and representatives that state has in Congress. The Constitution authorizes each individual state to decide how to select its electors. Article II also requires that the president be a natural born citizen of the United States. Thus, the Constitution bars immigrants who become naturalized citizens from becoming president. (No constitutional provisions bar naturalized citizens from holding other government offices.)

The Supreme Court—where the highest judicial body in the land interprets the law.

In keeping with the founders' wariness about giving too much power to any one branch of government, the Constitution gives the president powers it denies Congress. Perhaps the most important presidential power is the executive power. As we discussed earlier, the founders so disagreed over the proper boundaries of presidential power that they refused to define the exact meaning of the executive power. At a minimum, it was meant to give presidents the authority they would need to implement congressional directives and to fulfill the other duties of the executive branch. Over the past two hundred years, however, presidents have successfully argued that the executive power confers a very broad range of additional powers. Presidents have also expanded their political power by expanding the meaning of the so-called commander-in-chief clause, which designates the president as the commander in chief of American military forces. The founders intended the position of commander in chief to be simply an office rather than an independent source of political power. For much of U.S. history, however, and especially since World War II, presidents have argued that the commander-in-chief clause gives them wide powers in foreign policy.[15]

In addition to the broad grant of power the executive power gives and the special foreign policy powers that successive presidents have read into the commander-in-chief clause, Article II of the Constitution gives the president several specific powers. These presidential powers include the right to negotiate treaties with other countries (provided that two-thirds of the Senate concurs), the right to appoint people to positions in the executive and judicial branches of government (provided that a majority of the Senate concurs), the right to grant pardons and reprieves to people convicted of crimes, and the right to receive foreign ambassadors. Article II also grants the president special powers relative to Congress. Presidents are required to inform Congress of the state of the union, and they may recommend legislation for its consideration. Presidents also have the authority to call Congress into session and to adjourn Congress if the House and Senate fail to agree on those dates. As you can see, the Constitution creates an executive whose powers are checked and balanced by the other branches, and who can in turn check and balance the powers of those branches.

The Federal Judiciary

The Constitution specifies the rules and powers of the federal judiciary in Article III. (The constitution of each state sets forth rules governing that state's courts.) As a quick glance at Article III shows, the Constitution only briefly discusses the federal courts. Article III creates the Supreme Court and gives Congress the power to create all lower federal courts. Federal court judges are appointed for life, so long as they remain on "good Behaviour." If federal judges act unethically or illegally, Congress can

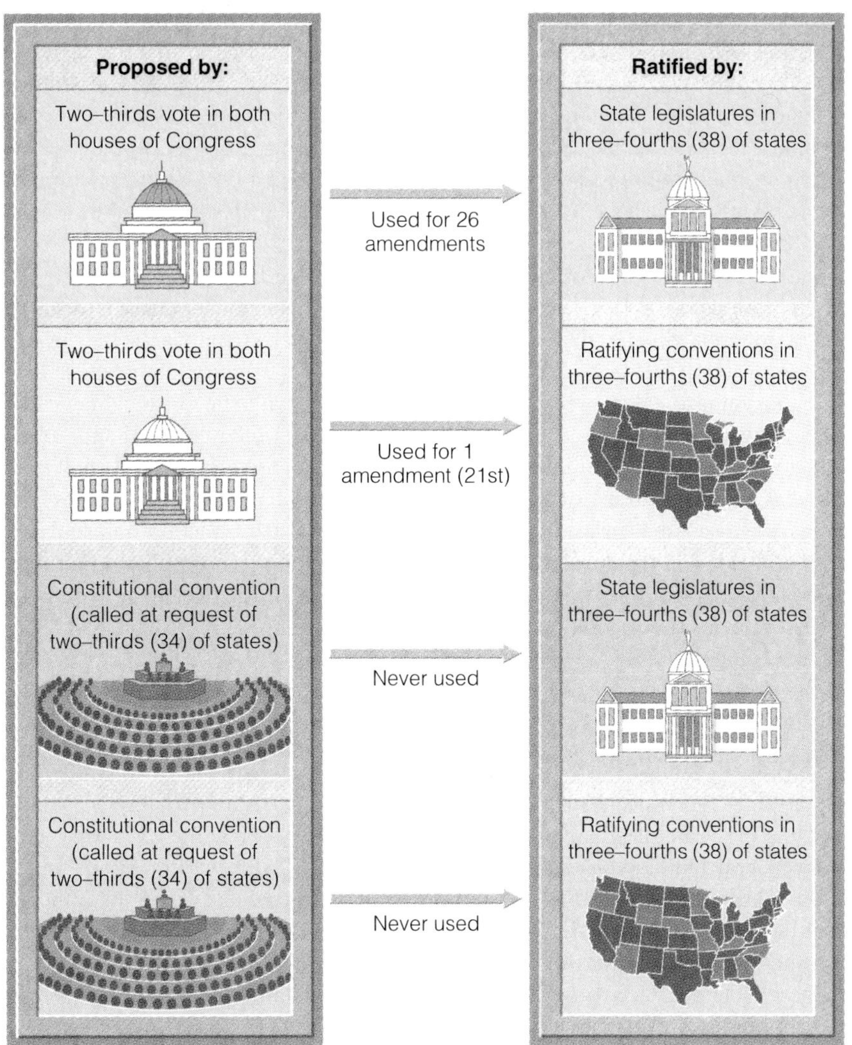

FIGURE 2.3
Amending the Constitution

The founders provided four different methods to amend the Constitution, but twenty-six of twenty-seven amendments were proposed by Congress and ratified by three-fourths of the states' legislatures.

remove them from office. The Constitution requires the federal courts to hear all cases under the Constitution, and it specifies that in some special circumstances the Supreme Court must be the first court to hear a case.

Interstate Relations

Article IV of the Constitution sets forth the rules that govern interstate relations, that is, the relationship between the national and state governments and the relationship among the states themselves. Article IV requires each state to respect, honor, and cooperate with the decisions of other states. For example, the Constitution requires the state of New York to respect a divorce granted in the state of California. Article IV also bars states from discriminating against citizens of other states. Finally, Article IV lays out the rules governing the admission of new states to the Union, and it guarantees that the national government will come to the aid of the states in the event of a foreign invasion or domestic violence.

Other Provisions

The remaining three articles in the Constitution establish rules for amending the Constitution, for resolving conflicts between the states and the federal government, and for ratifying the Constitution. Article V prescribes four methods for amending the Constitution. Figure 2.3 describes how each method works. In practice, amendments are almost always enacted through the first route in the figure; twenty-six of the first twenty-seven amendments to the Constitution were approved by two-thirds vote of both houses of Congress and then ratified by state legislatures in three-fourths of the states. The other successful amendment, the Twenty-first, originated in Congress, which then sent it to state conventions for ratification by three-fourths of the states. Most amendments are enacted within a few years of being proposed to the states, and in recent years, most proposed amendments have included a time limit for ratification. The exception was the Twenty-seventh Amendment, which was proposed by Congress in 1789 but not ratified by the states until 1992.[16]

The key provision of Article VI establishes that the laws of the federal government are the "supreme law of the land" and that the states must adhere to them. The practical import of this provision is that federal law, which encompasses the entire text of the Constitution, all laws Congress passes, and all legal obligations that duly ratified treaties impose, takes precedence when it conflicts with state or local law. Article VI also requires all federal and state officials, whether elected or appointed, to swear an oath to support the Constitution, and it stipulates that "no religious test shall ever be required as a qualification" for any government office. Finally, Article VII lays out the rules that we discussed earlier in the chapter for ratifying the Constitution itself.

As you can see, the core provisions of the Constitution set out the basic rules for each branch of government as well as for the relationship between the national and state governments. Let's look now at what consequences these rules have had for politics in the United States.

Three Consequences of the Constitution

The Constitution is more than a quaint relic kept under glass at the National Archives. It contains the principles and rules that have guided Congress, the executive branch, and the federal judiciary over the past two centuries. These principles and rules, in turn, have had significant effects on politics in the United States. The three most important effects warrant specific consideration. First, the rights of the individual enjoy such strong legal protection that at times they frustrate the will of the majority. Second, the obstacles placed in the way of passing legislation create a strong bias in American politics in favor of the existing state of affairs, or status quo, even when a majority of Americans would prefer otherwise. Third, even though the Constitution makes it difficult to pass new laws, it has created a political system that is sufficiently flexible to meet the country's changing needs.

The Protection of Individual Rights

As the statement of the rules of politics in the United States, the Constitution clearly favors protecting the rights of the individual over respecting the wishes of the majority. We have already seen how ideas such as the separation of powers, checks and balances, and federalism had their roots in the founders' desire to prevent majorities in the federal government from suppressing the rights and interests of individuals and minorities. The intention to protect individuals became even more pronounced once the Bill of Rights and other amendments were adopted. Amendments protect the rights of individuals to express and inform themselves (the First Amendment), ensure they receive fair treatment in the criminal and civil justice system (the Fourth through Eighth Amendments), prevent states from violating rights protected by the Constitution (the Fourteenth Amendment), expand the rights of citizenship in general (the Thirteenth Amendment), and extend the right to vote (the Fifteenth, Nineteenth, Twenty-fourth, and Twenty-sixth Amendments).

The most important consequence of the Constitution's protection of individual rights is that the power of government is limited. Initially, however, the Constitution was understood only to limit the power of the *federal government*. As chapter 4 discusses at greater length, the protections afforded to individuals by the Constitution in general and the Bill of Rights in particular did not extend to the actions of *state and*

TABLE 2.2 Public Opinion on Banning School Prayer

Although sizable majorities of the American public support prayer in public school, the Supreme Court has held since 1962 that government-sponsored prayer in public school violates the establishment clause of the First Amendment.

	Percentage of Respondents*		
Year	**Favor**	**Oppose**	**Don't Know or No Opinion**
1963	24	70	6
1971	28	67	6
1974	31	66	3
1975	35	62	3
1977	33	64	2
1981	31	66	3
1982	37	60	3
1983	40	57	4
1985 (March)	43	54	3
1985 (September)	37	62	1
1986	37	61	2
1988	37	59	4
1989	41	56	3
1990	40	56	5
1991	38	58	4

*Numbers may not add to 100 percent because of rounding.

Note: Question posed: "The U.S. Supreme Court has ruled that no state or local government may require the reading of the Lord's Prayer or Bible verses in public schools. What are your views on this—do you approve or disapprove of the court ruling?"

Source: Data from Harold W. Stanley and Richard G. Niemi, *Vital Statistics on American Politics*, 5th ed. (Washington, D.C.: Congressional Quarterly, 1995), p. 21.

local government for more than one hundred years. Only in 1897 did the Supreme Court begin to use the due process clause of the Fourteenth Amendment to argue that the Bill of Rights limited the ability of state and local government to infringe on the rights of individuals.

Because the Supreme Court's interpretation of how to apply the Bill of Rights has changed, federal, state, and local governments are limited today in their ability to pass laws that infringe on an individual's rights under the Constitution. Take, for example, the controversy over prayer in public schools. In two landmark cases in 1962 and 1963, the Supreme Court ruled that government-sponsored prayer in public schools violates the **establishment clause** of the First Amendment, which states that "Congress shall make no law respecting an establishment of religion." (Although the First Amendment literally bars only Congress from making such laws, for half a century the courts have interpreted the Amendment to apply to state and local governments as well.) As table 2.2 shows, public opinion surveys consistently show that a majority of Americans wants to reinstate the practice of official school prayer. Despite strong public support for school prayer, the Constitution protects dissenting minorities from the majority's preference for public prayer. (Of course, to say that the Constitution protects individual rights is not to say that these rights are absolute or never violated. As chapters 4 and 14 both discuss, sometimes the courts rule that compelling reasons justify a governmental decision to suppress individual rights, and sometimes federal, state, and local governments refuse to abide by court rulings.)

Establishment clause
The provision in the First Amendment of the Constitution that "Congress shall make no law respecting an establishment of religion."

A Bias in Favor of the Status Quo

The obstacles the Constitution places in the way of passing legislation make it difficult to change the political status quo in the United States. As we have discussed, bills seldom become law unless the House of Representatives, the Senate, and the president all agree. And, as with the Republican Revolution in 1995, the three often do not agree on the best course of action for the country. Thus it should not be surprising that most bills never become law. For example, the House of Representatives introduced more than 6,600 bills and the Senate introduced more than 3,000 during the 103d Congress

For nearly two hundred years, organized prayer in public schools was a common event. In 1962, the Supreme Court ruled in Engel v. Vitale *that the practice violated the establishment clause of the First Amendment. The issue of prayer in public schools has raised controversy ever since.*

(1993–94), but only 465 became law.[17] The founders constructed a political system that favors the status quo because they believed that the status quo embodies important values that merit protection from the momentary passions of politics.

The bias in American politics toward the status quo persists even when a majority of Americans would prefer to make changes. Take, for instance, the failed effort to pass the Equal Rights Amendment (ERA), which would have amended the Constitution to guarantee equal rights to men and women. In 1972, Congress passed the ERA and gave the states seven years to ratify it. Over the next decade, public opinion surveys consistently showed that more than 50 percent of the American public supported ratification of ERA. In 1979, the last year in which the amendment could be ratified under the terms Congress originally laid out, public support stood at 58 percent, but only thirty-five states had ratified it—three short of the required three-fourths. Congress then voted to extend the ratification deadline until 1982, but even though public support for the ERA continued to exceed 50 percent, the measure failed to secure support from three additional states. (As box 2.2 shows, this experience is not unique.) The example of the ERA shows once again how the rules that govern the political decision-making process can determine the eventual outcome.

By favoring the status quo, the Constitution helps some Americans and hurts others. Some Americans benefit from existing laws. To protect their interests, they need only to block changes in the status quo. In contrast, Americans who dislike existing laws face the more difficult task of steering new legislation through Congress and winning the president's approval, a task made all the more difficult by the need to assemble supermajorities in some circumstances. In short, defenders and critics of the status quo face dramatically different tasks. Defenders of the status quo usually need to win only once at some point in the process. If they defeat a proposal to change existing law at any point in the policy-making process, they win. Critics of the status quo, on the other hand, face exactly the opposite task: they must win at every point in the policy-making process if they want to see their proposal become law. Once again, the rules of American politics shape the outcome of political debates.

Political Flexibility

Although efforts to write new laws must overcome many obstacles, the Constitution nonetheless created a political system capable of considerable flexibility. Americans' understanding of the Constitution has changed greatly over the past two hundred years. The flexibility of the Constitution and, in turn, the American political system stems partly from the provisions that allow the Constitution to be amended, partly from the general nature of the text, and partly from the Constitution's silence on many of the practical aspects of government.

POINT OF ORDER

BOX 2.2

Obstacles to Amending the Constitution

Although various groups sometimes attempt to change the rules of government by calling for a constitutional amendment, the Constitution itself makes it difficult to pass one.

Imagine the confusion that would result if you were playing a game in which players could change the rules as they went to help them win. No one could ever be sure what the rules are or whether they have been broken. Eventually, most people would probably decide not to play. The founders wanted to protect the Constitution from this kind of easy manipulation. Public confidence in the stability of the rules encourages confidence in the fairness of the government itself.

The rules the founders put in place for amending the Constitution reflect this desire for stability. These rules require extraordinary support to pass an amendment (see figure 2.3). As a result, while many amendments have been proposed, few have been adopted. Over the past two centuries, members of Congress have proposed nearly 11,000 amendments, but only twenty-seven have made their way into the Constitution.

This degree of stability is unusual, as we can see when we compare the experience of state constitutions. Twenty-two states have had three or more constitutions. Twenty-three states have amended their constitutions more than a hundred times, with Alabama leading the way with 556 amendments. Only five states have amended their constitutions fewer than the twenty-seven times the U.S. Constitution has been amended.

While many people take comfort in the stability of the Constitution, others find its resistance to change frustrating. For several decades, for example, conservatives have called for the adoption of amendments to require a balanced budget, give the president a line-item veto, permit organized school prayer, impose term limits on members of Congress, and prohibit abortions. Yet none of these proposals has found its way into the Constitution.

Proponents of constitutional change criticize Congress for failing to approve their favored amendments, and some of them seek alternative ways to bring constitutional amendments before the states. One possibility is for Congress to convene a constitutional convention in which state delegations could propose amendments. Congress can by a simple majority vote convene such a convention whenever two-thirds (or thirty-four) of the states request it. By one count, as many as fourty-five states have formally called for a constitutional convention over the past two hundred years. Yet we have had no constitutional convention. Why?

The answer involves both legal and political concerns. While at least thirty-four states may have formally called for a constitutional convention—the number the Constitution requires—not all thirty-four requests for a convention may be legally *valid.* Some states requested a constitutional convention more than a hundred years ago, and many legal scholars argue that such requests are too old to count. At the same time, states have specified a wide range of reasons for calling a constitutional convention, from passing a balanced budget amendment to banning the burning of the American flag. Legal scholars argue over whether all requests must agree on the reason for seeking a convention, and the courts have never settled the matter.

As for the political concerns involved, the questionable validity of state requests for a constitutional convention makes it easy for Congress to avoid convening a convention. As you might imagine, members of Congress have a self-interest in keeping the power to propose amendments to themselves. Once a constitutional convention is convened, they would no longer monopolize that power. Thus, until and unless Congress is forced to call for a convention, say, because of a Supreme Court ruling, the prospects for one are virtually nil.

What would happen if a constitutional convention were convened is anyone's guess. Some observers fear that it would result in a "runaway" convention that would rewrite the Constitution, thereby tampering with our basic rights and government procedures. Such an outcome is not totally out of the realm of possibility. After all, this is precisely what the founders did to the Articles of Confederation when they met in Philadelphia in the summer of 1787.

So we are left with a situation that the founders no doubt intended. Passionate groups, even majorities, come and go, seeking to embed their preferences into the fundamental rules that structure our nation's government. But unless those preferences enjoy the consensus support of the public, they stand little chance of surmounting the difficult challenges the Constitution lays down.

Sources: Terry Eastland "To Amend or Not to Amend?" *Wall Street Journal,* 23 November 1994; Michael Stokes Paulsen, "The Case for a Constitutional Convention," *Wall Street Journal,* 3 May 1995; Harold W. Stanley and Richard G. Niemi, *Vital Statistics on American Politics,* 5th ed. (Washington, D.C.: CQ Press, 1995), pp. 13–15.

The founders recognized when they wrote the Constitution that they could not foresee what the future would hold for the new nation. To ensure that the new political system could meet the needs of future generations, the founders provided that the Constitution could be amended and that the amendments would be as binding as the original text. However, to prevent the Constitution from constant revision to reflect every majority whim, they imposed stringent requirements on the passage of amendments (see figure 2.3). As a result, only twenty-seven amendments have been added to the Constitution over the past two hundred years, and ten of those—the Bill of Rights—were adopted as part of the political agreement that made the ratification of the Constitution itself possible. The flexibility that the amending process provides applies even to correcting mistakes made in previous amendments. In 1933, for example, the country decided that it had erred with Prohibition and passed the Twenty-first Amendment, which repealed the Eighteenth Amendment's ban on the manufacture and sale of intoxicating liquors.

In addition to the flexibility the amending process provides, the American political system gains flexibility from the very ambiguity of the Constitution. A quick glance at the Constitution shows that the founders did not specify their plan for a new government in great detail. They instead wrote in general language. For example, the necessary and proper clause in Article I empowers Congress "to make all Laws which shall be necessary and proper," but it says nothing about what constitutes necessity or propriety. Likewise, Article II directs the president to make treaties with the "Advice and Consent" of the Senate, but it fails to explain precisely how senators are to give their advice. As we mentioned earlier, sometimes the founders resorted to ambiguity as a way of disguising their differences on key issues. Elsewhere, however, the ambiguity reflects the founders' recognition that much of the effort to apply the principles of the Constitution would inevitably depend on the good judgment of elected officials rather than on a lengthy explanation of the rules of the political system.

The final source of flexibility in the Constitution is its silence on many of the practical aspects of government. Although Article II vests the executive power in the president, it says nothing about what the structure of the executive branch should look like. Nor does the Constitution say anything about political parties and their role in government. Although the omission of these and other aspects of government might seem strange, it has contributed to the strength of the American political system by enabling the government to adapt more easily to changes in the nation and in public expectations.

As this discussion shows, certain broad features of the Constitution—protecting individual rights and making it difficult to change existing laws—have stood the test of time and continue to shape our government today. Yet amendments, as well as the ambiguity and silences of the Constitution, allow the operational specifics of government to change as our needs as a nation evolve. One of the areas in which the flexibility of the Constitution is most evident is in the so-called vertical dimension of the Constitution—the way in which the federal and state governments interact.

Federalism: The Vertical Dimension to the Constitution

Federalism
A two-tiered form of government in which governments on both levels are sovereign and share authority over the same geographic jurisdiction.

Any discussion of the Constitution would be incomplete without a discussion of the principle of **federalism** and how it has changed over time. You may recall that federalism is the idea that a country should have different levels of government, each with its own set of sovereign political powers. The founders settled on a federal political system because they wanted to avoid the problems that had undermined the Articles of Confederation without creating a national government that could impose its will on the states. Exactly how the new federal political system was meant to work, however, has been the subject of bitter political debate. For most of U.S. history, federal law has been interpreted to be superior to state law. At other times, however, some people have forcefully challenged the claim that the federal government is the dominant partner in its relationship with the states.

	State Governments	National Government	Both Governments
Powers Denied to:	• Cannot refuse to abide by lawful acts of other states • Cannot enter into treaties or alliances with foreign governments	• Cannot challenge state power to govern • Cannot return indictments without grand jury • Cannot tax goods transported from state to state	• Cannot pass bills of attainder or ex post facto laws • Cannot deprive individuals of rights guaranteed in Constitution
Powers Granted to:	• Can supervise elections within state • Can provide local government, public health, and public safety	• Can declare war and raise and support an army and a navy • Can establish post office and coin money	• Can tax and can spend funds for general welfare

FIGURE 2.4
Examples of the Constitution's Distribution of Powers Between State and National Governments

To create a federal system of government with sovereign states and a sovereign national government, the founders granted and withheld a variety of powers to each level of government. They allocated powers in an attempt to create a strong national government without seriously weakening the states.

Confederal, Unitary, and Federal Governments

As we discussed earlier, one of the most important decisions the delegates to the Constitutional Convention had to make was how to structure the relationship between the national and state governments. Neither of the two most likely options had much political appeal. On the one hand, the confederal government the Articles of Confederation had created had proved inadequate to meet the needs of the new country. On the other hand, the fear many Americans had of a tyrannical national government ruled out the possibility of creating a *unitary* government in which political power was concentrated in the hands of a national government. Faced with two unpalatable options, the founders created a third: the federal form of government in which the national and state governments share political power.

In a confederal government, authority rests fundamentally with the members of the union; as a result, political power essentially flows from the bottom up. A contemporary example of a confederal government is the United Nations, which can exercise only the powers its member states choose to give it. In contrast, in a unitary government, power is centralized in the national government. State governments are subsidiary entities that can exercise only the powers the national government delegates to them. In short, instead of flowing from the bottom up, power in a unitary government flows from the top down.

Federalism represents a mix of both the confederal and unitary forms of government. In a federal system, the national government and member states share some political powers and possess other powers independent of each other. Figure 2.4 illustrates how the American federal system allocates political powers between the federal and state governments.

As you might imagine, a federal system can work in practice only as long as both the national and state governments agree on policies in the areas where their powers overlap. But what happens when the federal government and the state governments prefer different policies? Which level should prevail? A review of U.S. history shows that the answers to these questions have changed over the years. Federalism in the United States has meant different things at different times, and as these meanings change, so does the relative balance of power between the federal government and the state governments.

Establishing National Supremacy

The Supreme Court provided its first (but not last) definitive interpretation of federalism in the case of *McCulloch v. Maryland* (1819). Chief Justice John Marshall, a proponent of a strong national government, wrote the opinion for the Court (see box 2.3). The genesis for the case lay in a law Congress passed creating a national bank.

THE PEOPLE BEHIND THE RULES

BOX 2.3

The Impact of Individuals on the Meaning of Federalism: Chief Justices John Marshall and Roger Taney

John Marshall

Roger Taney

John Marshall and Roger Taney are two of the acknowledged great Chief Justices of the U.S. Supreme Court. Both believed in a strong national judiciary. Yet differences in their views on the respective roles of the national and state governments created major shifts in the nature of federalism during the first half of the nineteenth century.

President John Adams appointed John Marshall as Chief Justice in 1801. Marshall was a dedicated Federalist, committed to the principle of a strong national government. He served thirty-four years (longer than all but three other justices) and authored 519 of the 1,215 decisions his court rendered. In those cases, he established the principle of national supremacy over the states, most clearly in the case *McCulloch v. Maryland* (1819). For a unanimous Court, he wrote: "the constitution and the laws made in pursuance thereof are supreme; . . . they control the constitution and laws of the respective states, and cannot be controlled by them."

President Andrew Jackson appointed Roger Taney as Chief Justice in 1836 to fill the vacancy created by John Marshall's death. While he shared Marshall's belief in a strong and independent judiciary, Taney repeatedly sought to "enhance the role of the states as governmental and philosophical entities." Although he is held in high esteem by scholars, Taney's decision in the *Dred Scott* case (1857) is widely acknowledged to be one of the "most disastrous" decisions the Court ever rendered. In it, he held that the Missouri Compromise was unconstitutional because the national government lacked the authority to outlaw slavery in the territories. He argued further that blacks were "of an inferior order" and that no black was a part of "the American people."

The *Dred Scott* decision was Taney's effort to avert civil war over slavery by redefining Marshall's interpretation of federalism. Taney's ultimately unsuccessful attempt to uphold the rights of the states and slaveowners against the authority of the national government and the rights of black Americans confused the meaning of federalism in the tumultuous period leading up to the Civil War. The roles of the national and state governments were not to be clearly reestablished until the Union defeated the South in the Civil War.

Source: Henry J. Abraham, *Justices and Presidents,* 2d ed. (New York: Oxford University Press, 1985).

National supremacy
An interpretation of federalism that holds that the national government's laws should take precedence over state law. This idea is based on the provision in Article VI of the Constitution that the national government's laws are the "supreme law of the land."

Federalists favored the law, arguing that it would help integrate the economies of the individual states into a single national economy. Many states, however, opposed what they saw as an unwarranted federal intrusion into their affairs. Maryland sought to limit the bank's operations within its borders by taxing the bank's transactions. The federal government argued that Maryland's tax was improper on the grounds that states could not adopt policies that contradicted national goals. In ruling that Maryland's tax was unconstitutional, the Supreme Court set forth the doctrine of **national supremacy,** the argument that federal law is superior to state law.

In deciding *McCulloch v. Maryland,* the Supreme Court had to answer two important questions. First, did the federal government have the authority to create such a bank? Maryland argued that the Constitution did not specifically authorize the federal government to do so. It reasoned that the federal government must show that a national bank was the only or best means of accomplishing its goal of integrating the states' economies. The federal government argued that the "necessary and proper" clause of Article I implied the power to create a national bank. At issue was the meaning of that clause. The Supreme Court agreed with the federal government, thereby greatly expanding the scope of federal power.

The second question dealt more directly with federalism. Given that the bank was constitutional, could Maryland tax its operations? Maryland had the power to tax, so shouldn't it tax the national bank? The federal government argued that such a tax would effectively allow the states to negate federal laws, contrary to the provision in Article VI of the Constitution that federal laws "shall be the supreme Law of the Land." Again, the Supreme Court sided with the federal government, striking down the Maryland tax on the grounds that "the States have no power, by taxation or otherwise, to retard, impede, burden, or in any manner control, the operations of the constitutional laws enacted by Congress to carry into execution the powers vested in the general government."[18] The Court's decision established the first authoritative interpretation of federalism—the federal government ruled supreme. The victory, however, would not go unchallenged.

The Assertion of States' Rights

The Supreme Court's decision in *McCulloch v. Maryland* angered people who opposed the emergence of a dominant federal government. These opponents argued for a different interpretation of the proper relationship between the federal and state governments. In the years before the Civil War, the most prominent challenge to the doctrine of national supremacy was the doctrine of **states' rights.** Advocates of states' rights turned the argument for national supremacy on its head; they claimed that properly interpreted federalism made the states, not the federal government, supreme.

States' rights
An interpretation of federalism that claimed that states possessed the right to accept or reject federal laws.

Advocates of states' rights based their argument on two principles: the *doctrine of interposition* and the *doctrine of nullification.* According to the doctrine of interposition, states are placed between the people and the federal government; hence, states have the right to intervene on behalf of their citizens to evaluate federal policies. The doctrine of nullification held that states have the right to block the application of federal policies that affect their citizens. The interposition and nullification doctrines both dated back to the 1790s, and they both enjoyed broad support. In 1798, for example, Madison and Jefferson argued that states could nullify federal laws that punished newspaper editors for writing stories criticizing the federal government. Andrew Jackson was a strong supporter of states' rights, and as president he sought to protect the states from the federal government by forcing the 1832 collapse of the national bank that had spawned the Supreme Court's ruling in *McCulloch v. Maryland.*

Dred Scott brought the issue of national supremacy back before the Supreme Court when he sought his freedom in 1857. He claimed that because he had lived in a federal territory where slavery was outlawed, he was no longer bound by the Missouri law that had made him a slave. The Supreme Court ruled, however, that the national government lacked the authority to outlaw slavery, and so Missouri's law prevailed.

The doctrine of states' rights took on special urgency in the 1830s and 1840s as southern states came to fear that the federal government would use its supremacy to outlaw slavery. Those fears were mollified when the Supreme Court strengthened the cause of states' rights in the *Dred Scott* case (1857). In this case, Scott, a slave, was taken from Missouri, a slave state, to a federal territory in which slavery was illegal. A dispute then arose over whether Scott had gained his freedom or remained a slave. The case eventually reached the Supreme Court, where Chief Justice Roger Taney wrote the majority opinion (see box 2.3). Taney, whom Jackson had appointed to succeed John Marshall, the author of *McCulloch v. Maryland,* was widely known to be a supporter of states' rights. Taney held that Scott had lost whatever freedom he had gained when he returned to Missouri to file his lawsuit. Taney went further to rule that the federal ban on slavery in the territories was unconstitutional because it violated the right of slaveowners to own property (that is, slaves). In short, the *Dred Scott* case placed state law above federal law.

The inability of the northern and southern states to reach a compromise over the relative authorities of the national and state governments contributed to the start of the Civil War. Only through its superior military and industrial might could the North force the South to accept its national supremacy doctrine of federalism.

As a result of the *Dred Scott* case, the meaning of federalism was in great dispute during the years leading up to the Civil War. To a large extent, the dispute fell along geographic lines. Northern states generally supported the doctrine of national supremacy; southern states supported the doctrine of states' rights. The dispute between northern and southern states grew increasingly bitter, so much so that the southern states eventually sought to secede. It was only with the North's victory in the Civil War that the doctrine of national supremacy triumphed over the doctrine of states' rights.

The Civil War and the Reassertion of National Supremacy

In one sense, the Civil War was a dispute over the meaning of federalism. The southern states, embracing the logic of the states' rights doctrine, claimed they were free to secede from the Union. The federal government, which insisted on the doctrine of national supremacy, argued that the citizens of the southern states were also citizens of the United States and could not be stripped of their national citizenship without the permission of the federal government. Since the federal government rejected secession, the southern states could not leave the Union.

The dispute over the legality of secession had important implications for the behavior of other countries. If they accepted the argument the southern states made, then the Civil War was a conflict between independent nations and the norms of international relations would allow other countries to aid the Confederacy. If other countries accepted the argument the federal government made, however, the Civil War was a domestic insurrection and the norms of international relations would discourage other nations from becoming entangled in the internal affairs of the United States. The Confederacy desperately sought support from European countries in general and Britain in particular, but President Lincoln convinced Europe that the Civil War was a domestic matter. Unable to obtain outside help, Confederate forces slowly wore down against the superior military and industrial might of the Union.

Once the southern states surrendered at Appomattox, the federal government tried to drive the last nail in the coffin of the states' rights doctrine. The "nail" was the Fourteenth Amendment. Enacted along with the Thirteenth and Fifteenth Amendments, which outlawed slavery and guaranteed former male slaves the right to vote, the Fourteenth Amendment provided that "No State shall make or enforce any law which shall abridge the privileges or immunities of citizens of the United States; nor shall any State deprive any person of life, liberty, or property, without due process of

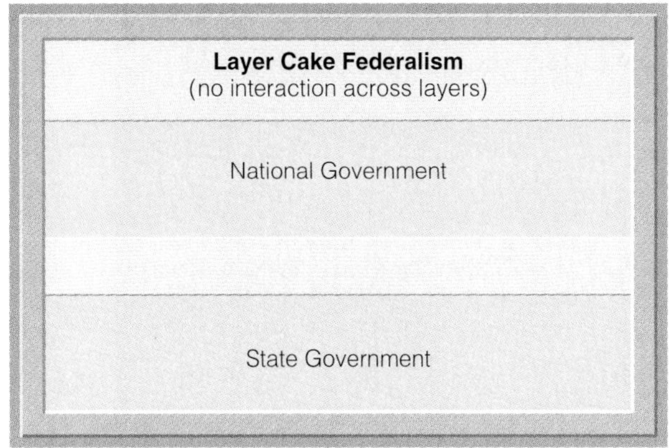

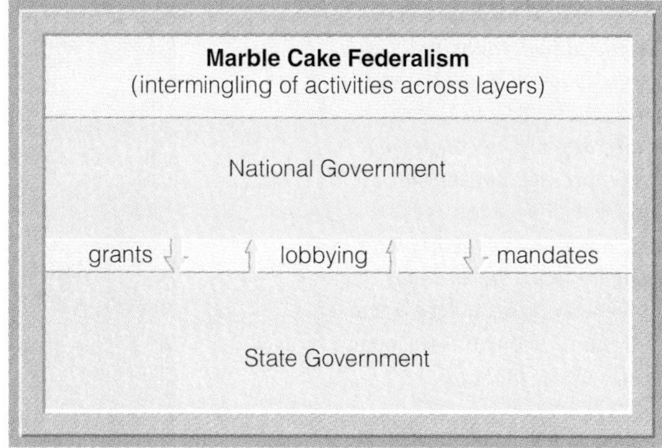

law; nor deny to any person within its jurisdiction the equal protection of the laws." In other words, no state could violate or abridge the rights the Constitution accorded to citizens of the United States. With the passage of the Fourteenth Amendment, the federal government again reigned supreme.

FIGURE 2.5
"Layer Cake" versus "Marble Cake": Two Versions of Federalism

Prior to the New Deal, the "layer cake" model of federalism described a system in which states and the national government performed their respective duties with little interaction. In the 1930s, New Deal programs gave the national government a key role in funding services that the states handle. In turn, the states now try to influence national government decisions about the forms federal aid takes. The resulting intermingling of state and national government activities describes the "marble cake" model of federalism.

Dual Federalism

Although the Civil War marked the eclipse of the doctrine of states' rights, it did not mark the end of challenges to national supremacy. American political culture continued to reflect the long-standing mistrust of a strong national government. These fears surfaced in the decades after the Civil War in a second challenge to the claims of national supremacy: the doctrine of **dual federalism.**

Dual federalism
An interpretation of federalism that held that the national government was supreme within the areas the Constitution specifically enumerated and that the states were supreme in other areas of public policy.

The doctrine of dual federalism held that the federal and state governments possessed complementary spheres of influence, within which each was supreme. According to this view, the federal government was supreme when it came to conducting those tasks that the Constitution explicitly assigned to it. For example, the Constitution made it clear that only the federal government could manage foreign affairs, impose tariffs on foreign goods, coin the country's money, and create a postal system. On the other hand, the doctrine of dual federalism argued that state governments were supreme in conducting tasks the Constitution did not explicitly give to the federal government. Proponents of dual federalism argued that the states were supreme when it came to education, fire and police protection, and welfare programs.

The doctrine of dual federalism, then, held that the federal and state governments would each exercise responsibility within their own sphere of activity without interference from the other. Because of the idea of non-interference, dual federalism is sometimes called the "layer cake" model of federalism.[19] As figure 2.5 illustrates, in this model, the two levels of government operate like separate layers of a cake. Each possesses its own independent character. The two layers are joined as a single entity, but they retain their respective roles within that union. Because advocates of dual federalism were able to tap American's long-standing distrust of a powerful national government, the doctrine of dual federalism held sway in the half century after 1880. In the 1930s, however, the doctrine of national supremacy would once again become ascendant.

The Present Era—National Supremacy as Fiscal Federalism

The 1930s gave rise to yet another interpretation of the meaning of federalism, an interpretation that prevails to this day. Under this new version of federalism, not only are federal laws superior to state laws, but the federal government has a responsibility for providing financial assistance to state governments. Because federal aid has emerged as a major source of state revenue over the past sixty years, this newest form of federalism is known as **fiscal federalism.**

Fiscal federalism
The principle that the federal government should play a major role in financing some of the activities of state and local governments.

The Great Depression forced people to look to their states for assistance. When the states were unable to deliver, the national government stepped in, initiating a new era of national supremacy characterized by the financial bond between the national government as a source of aid and the state governments as recipients of that aid.

Great Depression
The worst economic crisis in U.S. history, with unemployment rates reaching 25 percent. It began in 1929 and lasted until the start of World War II.

New Deal
The economic and social programs Congress enacted during Franklin Roosevelt's presidency before World War II.

Great Society
The economic and social programs Congress enacted during Lyndon Johnson's presidency, from 1963 to 1969.

Interstate commerce clause
The provision in Article I of the Constitution granting Congress the power to "regulate commerce . . . among the several states."

The **Great Depression** triggered the shift away from dual federalism toward fiscal federalism. During the early 1930s, unemployment reached 25 percent in the United States, national income fell by 50 percent, and the people turned to their state governments for relief. The states, however, could not cope with the demand. The Great Depression had reduced their tax revenues, and most state constitutions barred the states from spending more than they took in. With the states unable to get the economy going again, all eyes turned to the federal government.

In Washington, D.C., President Franklin Roosevelt was quick to respond. During Roosevelt's presidency, the federal government assumed a new role as a provider of services to states and individuals. Together with Congress, the Roosevelt administration created a number of federal programs, known collectively as the **New Deal,** which were designed to provide federal assistance to the states and unemployment compensation and retirement insurance to individuals. The federal role in providing services to states and individuals would grow even larger three decades later. In the 1960s, President Lyndon Johnson persuaded Congress to launch the **Great Society,** federal programs designed to end poverty in the United States, make health care accessible to more people, and revitalize America's cities. With the creation of these programs, federal aid emerged as a primary source of revenue for state and local governments.

As federal aid to the states has grown, federal involvement in activities once thought to be the domain of the states has grown as well. Because many government services today represent a mix of federal and state activities, fiscal federalism is sometimes called "marble cake" federalism (see figure 2.5).[20] In many instances, the federal government stipulates what sorts of services should be provided and gives the states the money they need to carry out its mandates. In turn, the states accept the money, meet the requirements, and provide the services.

The shift to fiscal federalism in some ways represents the most profound change in our understanding of federalism. Before the 1930s, the relationship between the federal and state governments was highly conflictual. Washington and the state capitols frequently jockeyed for legal authority and for dominance over one another. Since the 1930s, however, the focus has shifted from legal to fiscal concerns, as the states have accepted federal preeminence in exchange for needed financial support. (We will discuss fiscal federalism more fully in chapter 15 when we discuss state government.)

In 1995, the Supreme Court handed down a decision that may ultimately limit the range of activities subject to national supremacy. The case involved the scope of the **interstate commerce clause** of the Constitution, which gives Congress the authority to "regulate commerce . . . among the several states." Beginning in the 1930s, the Court interpreted this power to include not only the regulation of interstate commerce, but also activities that merely affect interstate commerce. With this broad mandate, the federal government enacted laws giving itself power over a growing range of activities traditionally reserved to the states. One such law, the Gun-Free School Zones Act, prohibited the possession of guns within one thousand feet of a school. The Court ruled the law unconstitutional because possession of a gun at school was not sufficiently related to interstate commerce.[21] If the Court follows this line of reasoning in future rulings, it will place important limits on the authority of the federal government.

The continually changing interpretations of the meaning of federalism remind us that the Constitution is not a rigid document. Although it sets forth the basic rules structuring the American political system, our understanding of what those rules mean has changed over time. As our interpretations of the rules change, so do the sorts of policies the government pursues. It is this flexibility of the Constitution that has enabled the federal government to meet the changing needs of the country.

Summary

The need for the U.S. Constitution grew out of the failure of the confederal government established by the Articles of Confederation. The founders brought conflicting political ambitions and objectives to the Constitutional Convention, and as a result, politics greatly influenced the content of the Constitution. Three issues were especially divisive: how to allocate representation in the new Congress, how to deal with the question of slavery, and how to define the powers of the new office of the presidency. The founders managed to settle their differences through a mix of compromise and ambiguity. The states eventually ratified the Constitution after its proponents agreed to add a series of amendments, now known as the Bill of Rights, that would guarantee individual rights.

As they wrote the Constitution, the founders were influenced by their philosophical principles as well as by politics. The principle that stood first and foremost in their thinking was the need to protect individual rights. The importance the founders attached to individual rights led them to favor democratic government by majority rule. The founders recognized, however, that if left unchecked, a majority could use its advantage in numbers to suppress individual rights. To limit the potential for majority tyranny, the founders modified the principle of majority rule in three important ways. First, they wrote electoral rules into the Constitution that make it difficult for permanent majorities to form. Second, they divided authority among branches of government as well as between the federal government and state governments. Third, they placed formal boundaries on government action.

The Constitution specifies the fundamental structural rules that govern how the federal government is organized, how its officials are selected, the procedures by which it makes decisions, and how it relates to the state governments. Article I of the Constitution discusses the structure and powers of the legislative branch of government. Among other things, it stipulates that Congress shall consist of two chambers, the House and Senate, both of which must approve identical versions of a bill before it can become law. Article II discusses the powers of the presidency. Among other things, it assigns the president the power to run the executive branch as well as the right to veto legislation Congress has passed. The Constitution says little about either the federal court system or relations between the states. Article III creates a Supreme Court and authorizes Congress to create other federal courts as needed. Article IV requires each state to respect, honor, and cooperate with other states, and it guarantees that the federal government will protect the states in time of foreign and domestic violence. Articles V, VI, and VII establish rules for amending the Constitution, for resolving conflicts between the states and the federal government, and for ratifying the Constitution.

The principles and rules contained in the Constitution have had three important consequences for politics in the United States. First, the rights of the individual enjoy such strong legal protection that the will of the majority may be frustrated at times. Second, the obstacles placed in the way of passing legislation create a strong bias in American politics in favor of the status quo, or the existing state of affairs, even when a majority of Americans would prefer change. Third, even though the Constitution makes it difficult to pass new laws, it has created a political system sufficiently flexible to meet the country's changing needs.

The flexibility of the Constitution shows clearly in the changing nature of federalism, the rules governing the relationship between the federal and state governments. The founders chose to construct a federal political system because they wanted to remedy the problems that had undermined the Articles of Confederation without creating a national government that could impose its will on the states. Exactly how they meant the new federal political system to work, however, has stirred bitter political debate. For most of U.S. history, federal law has been interpreted to be superior to state law. At other times, however, states have challenged the claim that the federal government is the dominant partner in the relationship between Washington, D.C., and the states. The continually changing meaning of federalism reminds us that the Constitution is not a rigid document, but a flexible set of rules still relevant to a dynamic society and political system.

Key Terms

Antifederalists
Articles of Confederation
Bicameral legislature
Bill of Rights
Checks and balances
Classical liberalism
Connecticut Compromise
Democracy
Dual federalism
Establishment clause
Federalism
Federalists
Fiscal federalism
Great Depression
Great Society
Interstate commerce clause
Majority tyranny
National supremacy
Necessary and proper clause
New Deal
New Jersey Plan
Republicanism
Separation of powers
Shays's Rebellion
States' rights
Virginia Plan

Readings for Further Study

Bailyn, Bernard, ed. *The Debate on the Constitution: Federalist and Antifederalist Speeches, Articles, and Letters During the Struggle over Ratification.* New York: Library of America, 1993. A collection of speeches, articles, and letters by both supporters and critics of the Constitution as they debated its ratification.

Bailyn, Bernard. *The Ideological Origins of the American Revolution.* Cambridge: Harvard University Press, 1967. The most widely accepted account of the development of support for independence in the American colonies.

Beard, Charles. *An Economic Interpretation of the Constitution of the United States.* New York: Macmillan, 1913. The classic treatment of how the Constitution reflects the economic self-interest of the founders.

Grodzins, Morton. *The American System.* New Brunswick, N.J.: Transaction Books, 1984. A comprehensive discussion of the federal relationship in the United States.

Hamilton, Alexander, James Madison, and John Jay. *The Federalist Papers.* New York: Penguin Books, 1987. The collection of articles these three Federalists wrote. The papers contain the essential arguments used to justify adoption of the Constitution.

Storing, Herbert J. *What the Antifederalists Were For.* Chicago: University of Chicago Press, 1981. A well-documented presentation of the arguments the losers made in the constitutional debate.

Wills, Gary. *Explaining America.* New York: Doubleday & Company, 1981. An interesting exploration of the themes of the *Federalist Papers.*

The Constitution of the United States

We the People of the United States, in Order to form a more perfect Union, establish Justice, insure domestic Tranquility, provide for the common defence, promote the general Welfare, and secure the Blessings of Liberty to ourselves and our Posterity, do ordain and establish this Constitution for the United States of America.

Preamble

Article I.

Section 1. All legislative Powers herein granted shall be vested in a Congress of the United States, which shall consist of a Senate and House of Representatives.

Bicameral Congress

Section 2. The House of Representatives shall be composed of Members chosen every second Year by the People of the several States, and the Electors in each State shall have the Qualifications requisite for Electors of the most numerous Branch of the State Legislature.

Membership of the House

No Person shall be a Representative who shall not have attained to the age of twenty-five Years, and been seven Years a Citizen of the United States, and who shall not, when elected, be an Inhabitant of that State in which he shall be chosen.

Representatives and direct Taxes shall be apportioned among the several States which may be included within this Union, according to their respective Numbers, which shall be determined by adding to the whole Number of free Persons, including those bound to Service for a Term of Years, and excluding Indians not taxed, three fifths of all other Persons.[1] The actual Enumeration shall be made within three Years after the first Meeting of the Congress of the United States, and within every subsequent Term of ten Years, in such Manner as they shall by Law direct. The Number of Representatives shall not exceed one for every thirty Thousand, but each State shall have at Least one Representative; and until such enumeration shall be made, the State of New Hampshire shall be entitled to chuse three, Massachusetts eight, Rhode-Island and Providence Plantations one, Connecticut five, New-York six, New Jersey four, Pennsylvania eight, Delaware one, Maryland six, Virginia ten, North Carolina five, South Carolina five, and Georgia three.

When vacancies happen in the Representation from any State, the Executive Authority thereof shall issue Writs of Election to fill such Vacancies.

The House of Representatives shall chuse their Speaker and other Officers; and shall have the sole Power of Impeachment.

Power to impeach

Section 3. The Senate of the United States shall be composed of two Senators from each State, *chosen by the Legislature thereof,*[2] for six Years; and each Senator shall have one Vote.

Membership of the Senate

Immediately after they shall be assembled in Consequence of the first Election, they shall be divided as equally as may be into three Classes. The Seats of the Senators of the first class shall be vacated at the Expiration of the second Year, of the second Class at the Expiration of the fourth Year, and of the third Class at the Expiration of the sixth Year, so that one third may be chosen every second Year; *and if Vacancies happen by Resignation, or otherwise, during the Recess of the Legislature of any State, the Executive thereof may make temporary Appointments until the next Meeting of the Legislature, which shall then fill such Vacancies.*[3]

No Person shall be a Senator who shall not have attained to the Age of thirty Years, and been nine Years a Citizen of the United States, and who shall not, when elected, be an Inhabitant of that State for which he shall be chosen.

Note: The topical headings are not part of the original Constitution. Excluding the Preamble and Closing, those portions set in italic type have been superseded or changed by later amendments.

[1]Changed by the Fourteenth Amendment, section 2.

[2]Changed by the Seventeenth Amendment.

[3]Changed by the Seventeenth Amendment.

The Vice President of the United States shall be President of the Senate, but shall have no Vote, unless they be equally divided.

The Senate shall chuse their other Officers, and also a President pro tempore, in the Absence of the Vice President, or when he shall exercise the Office of President of the United States.

Power to try impeachments

The Senate shall have the sole Power to try all Impeachments. When sitting for that Purpose, they shall be on Oath or Affirmation. When the President of the United States is tried the Chief Justice shall preside: and no Person shall be convicted without the Concurrence of two thirds of the Members present.

Judgment in Cases of Impeachment shall not extend further than to removal from Office, and disqualification to hold and enjoy any Office of honor, Trust or Profit under the United States: but the Party convicted shall nevertheless be liable and subject to Indictment, Trial, Judgment and Punishment, according to Law.

Laws governing elections

Section 4. The Times, Places and Manner of holding elections for Senators and Representatives, shall be prescribed in each State by the Legislature thereof; but the Congress may at any time by Law make or alter such Regulations, except as to the Places of chusing Senators.

The Congress shall assemble at least once in every Year, and such Meeting shall be on the *first Monday in December, unless they shall by Law appoint a different Day.*[4]

Rules of Congress

Section 5. Each House shall be the Judge of the Elections, Returns and Qualifications of its own Members, and a Majority of each shall constitute a Quorum to do Business; but a smaller Number may adjourn from day to day, and may be authorized to compel the Attendance of absent Members, in such Manner, and under such Penalties as each House may provide.

Each House may determine the Rules of its Proceedings, punish its Members for disorderly Behaviour, and, with the Concurrence of two thirds, expel a Member.

Each House shall keep a Journal of its Proceedings, and from time to time publish the same, excepting such Parts as may in their Judgment require Secrecy; and the Yeas and Nays of the Members of either House on any question shall, at the Desire of one fifth of those Present, be entered on the Journal.

Neither House, during the Session of Congress, shall, without the Consent of the other, adjourn for more than three days, nor to any other Place than that in which the two Houses shall be sitting.

Salaries and immunities of members

Section 6. The Senators and Representatives shall receive a Compensation for their Services, to be ascertained by Law, and paid out of the Treasury of the United States. They shall in all Cases, except Treason, Felony and Breach of the Peace, be privileged from Arrest during their Attendance at the Session of their respective Houses, and in going to and returning from the same; and for any Speech or Debate in either House, they shall not be questioned in any other Place.

Ban on members of Congress holding federal appointive office

No Senator or Representative shall, during the Time for which he was elected, be appointed to any civil Office under the Authority of the United States, which shall have been created, or the Emoluments whereof shall have been encreased during such time; and no Person holding any Office under the United States, shall be a Member of either House during his Continuance in Office.

Money bills originate in House

Section 7. All Bills for raising Revenue shall originate in the House of Representatives; but the Senate may propose or concur with Amendments as on other Bills.

Procedure for enacting laws; veto power

Every Bill which shall have passed the House of Representatives and the Senate, shall, before it become a Law, be presented to the President of the United States; If he approve he shall sign it, but if not he shall return it, with his Objections to that House in which it shall have originated, who shall enter the Objections at large on their Journal, and proceed to reconsider it. If after such Reconsideration two thirds of that House shall agree to pass the Bill, it shall be sent, together with the Objections, to the other House, by which it shall likewise be reconsidered, and if approved by two thirds of that House, it shall become a Law. But in all such Cases the Votes of both Houses shall be determined by Yeas and Nays, and the Names of the Persons voting for and against the Bill shall be entered on the Journal of each House respectively. If any Bill shall not be returned by the President within ten Days (Sundays excepted) after it shall have been

[4]Changed by the Twentieth Amendment, section 2.

presented to him, the Same shall be a Law, in like Manner as if he had signed it, unless the Congress by their Adjournment prevent its Return, in which Case it shall not be a Law.

Every Order, Resolution, or Vote to which the concurrence of the Senate and House of Representatives may be necessary (except on a question of Adjournment) shall be presented to the President of the United States; and before the Same shall take Effect, shall be approved by him, or being disapproved by him, shall be repassed by two thirds of the Senate and House of Representatives, according to the Rules and Limitations prescribed in the Case of a Bill.

Powers of Congress

raise taxes

Section 8. The Congress shall have Power To lay and collect Taxes, Duties, Imposts and Excises, to pay the Debts and provide for the common Defence and general Welfare of the United States; but all Duties, Imposts and Excises shall be uniform throughout the United States;

borrow money

To borrow Money on the credit of the United States;

regulate foreign commerce

To regulate Commerce with foreign Nations, and among the several States, and with the Indian Tribes;

write naturalization and bankruptcy laws

To establish an uniform Rule of Naturalization, and uniform Laws on the subject of Bankruptcies throughout the United States;

coin money

To coin Money, regulate the Value thereof, and of foreign Coin, and fix the Standard of Weights and Measures;

punish counterfeiting

To provide for the Punishment of counterfeiting the Securities and current Coin of the United States;

establish post offices

To establish Post Offices and post Roads;

provide for patents and copyrights

To promote the Progress of Science and useful Arts, by securing for limited Times to Authors and Inventors the exclusive Right to their respective Writings and Discoveries;

create courts

To constitute Tribunals inferior to the Supreme Court;

punish piracies

To define and punish Piracies and Felonies committed on the high Seas, and Offences against the Law of Nations;

declare war

To declare War, grant Letters of Marque and Reprisal, and make Rules concerning Captures on Land and Water;

create army and navy

To raise and support Armies, but no Appropriation of Money to that Use shall be for a longer Term than two Years;

To provide and maintain a Navy;

To make Rules for the Government and Regulation of the land and naval Forces;

call forth the militia

To provide for calling forth the Militia to execute the Laws of the Union, suppress Insurrections and repel Invasions;

To provide for organizing, arming, and disciplining, the Militia, and for governing such Part of them as may be employed in the Service of the United States, reserving to the States respectively, the Appointment of the Officers, and the Authority of training the Militia according to the discipline prescribed by Congress;

govern District of Columbia

To exercise exclusive Legislation in all Cases whatsoever, over such District (not exceeding ten Miles square) as may, by Cession of particular States, and the Acceptance of Congress, become the Seat of the Government of the United States, and to exercise like Authority over all Places purchased by the Consent of the Legislature of the State in which the Same shall be, for the Erection of Forts, Magazines, Arsenals, dock-Yards and other needful Buildings;—And

necessary and proper clause

To make all Laws which shall be necessary and proper for carrying into Execution the foregoing Powers, and all other Powers vested by this Constitution in the Government of the United States, or in any Department or Officer thereof.

Restrictions on powers of Congress

slave trade

Section 9. The Migration or Importation of such Persons as any of the States now existing shall think proper to admit, shall not be prohibited by the Congress prior to the Year one thousand eight hundred and eight, but a Tax or duty may be imposed on such Importation, not exceeding ten dollars for each Person.

habeas corpus

The Privilege of the Writ of Habeas Corpus shall not be suspended, unless when in Cases of Rebellion or Invasion the public Safety may require it.

no bill of attainder or ex post facto law

No bill of Attainder or ex post facto Law shall be passed.

No Capitation, or other direct, Tax shall be laid, *unless in Proportion to the Census or Enumeration herein before directed to be taken.*[5]

no interstate tariffs

No Tax or Duty shall be laid on Articles exported from any State.

[5]Changed by the Sixteenth Amendment.

no preferential treatment for some states

No Preference shall be given by any Regulation of Commerce or Revenue to the Ports of one State over those of another; nor shall Vessels bound to, or from, one State, be obliged to enter, clear or pay Duties in another.

no spending without appropriations

No Money shall be drawn from the Treasury, but in Consequence of Appropriations made by Law; and a regular Statement and Account of the Receipts and Expenditures of all public Money shall be published from time to time.

no titles of nobility

No Title of Nobility shall be granted by the United States: And no person holding any Office of Profit or Trust under them, shall, without the Consent of the Congress, accept of any present, Emolument, Office, or Title, of any kind whatever, from any King, Prince, or foreign State.

Restrictions on powers of states

Section 10. No State shall enter into any Treaty, Alliance, or Confederation; grant Letters of Marque and Reprisal; coin Money; emit Bills of Credit; make any Thing but gold and silver Coin a Tender in Payment of Debts; pass any Bill of Attainder, ex post facto Law, or Law impairing the Obligation of Contracts, or grant any Title of Nobility.

No State shall, without the Consent of the Congress, lay any Imposts or Duties on Imports or Exports, except what may be absolutely necessary for executing its inspection Laws: and the net Produce of all Duties and Imposts, laid by any State on Imports or Exports, shall be for the Use of the Treasury of the United States; and all such Laws shall be subject to the Revision and Controul of the Congress.

No State shall, without the Consent of Congress, lay any Duty of Tonnage, keep Troops, or Ships of War in time of Peace, enter into any Agreement or Compact with another State, or with a foreign Power, or engage in War, unless actually invaded, or in such imminent Danger as will not admit of delay.

Article II.

Office of President

the executive power

Section 1. The executive Power shall be vested in a President of the United States of America. He shall hold his Office during the Term of four Years, and, together with the Vice President, chosen for the same Term, be elected, as follows

Election of President

Each State shall appoint, in such Manner as the Legislature thereof may direct, a Number of Electors, equal to the whole Number of Senators and Representatives to which the State may be entitled in the Congress: but no Senator or Representative, or Person holding an Office of Trust or Profit under the United States, shall be appointed an Elector.

The Electors shall meet in their respective States, and vote by Ballot for two Persons, of whom one at least shall not be an Inhabitant of the same State with themselves. And they shall make a List of all the Persons voted for, and of the Number of Votes for each; which List they shall sign and certify, and transmit sealed to the Seat of the Government of the United States, directed to the President of the Senate. The President of the Senate shall, in the Presence of the Senate and House of Representatives, open all the Certificates, and the Votes shall then be counted. The Person having the greatest Number of Votes shall be the President, if such Number be a Majority of the whole Number of Electors appointed; and if there be more than one who have such Majority, and have an equal Number of Votes, then the House of Representatives shall immediately chuse by Ballot one of them for President; and if no Person have a Majority, then from the five highest on the List the said House shall in like Manner chuse the President. But in chusing the President, the Votes shall be taken by States, the Representation from each State having one Vote; a quorum for this Purpose shall consist of a Member or Members from two thirds of the States, and a Majority of all the States shall be necessary to a Choice. In every Case, after the Choice of the President, the Person having the greatest Number of Votes of the Electors shall be the Vice President. But if there should remain two or more who have equal Votes, the Senate shall chuse from them by Ballot the Vice President.[6]

The Congress may determine the Time of chusing the Electors, and the Day on which they shall give their Votes; which Day shall be the same throughout the United States.

Requirements to be President

No Person except a natural born Citizen, or a Citizen of the United States, at the time of the Adoption of this Constitution, shall be eligible to the Office of President; neither shall any person be eligible to that Office who shall not have attained to the Age of thirty five Years, and been fourteen Years a Resident within the United States.

In Case of the Removal of the President from Office, or of his Death, Resignation, or Inability to discharge the Powers and Duties of the said Office, the Same shall devolve on the Vice

[6]Superseded by the Twelfth Amendment.

President, and the Congress may by Law provide for the Case of Removal, Death, Resignation or Inability, both of the President and Vice President, declaring what Officer shall then act as President, and such Officer shall act accordingly, until the Disability be removed, or a President shall be elected.[7]

Pay of President

The President shall, at stated Times, receive for his Services, a Compensation, which shall neither be encreased nor diminished during the Period for which he shall have been elected, and he shall not receive within that Period any other Emolument from the United States, or any of them.

Before he enter on the Execution of his Office, he shall take the following Oath or Affirmation:—"I do solemnly swear (or affirm) that I will faithfully execute the Office of President of the United States, and will to the best of my Ability, preserve, protect and defend the Constitution of the United States."

Powers of President
commander in chief clause
require opinion of departmental officers
grant pardons

Section 2. The President shall be Commander in Chief of the Army and Navy of the United States, and of the Militia of the several States, when called into the actual Service of the United States; he may require the Opinion, in writing, of the principal Officer in each of the executive Departments, upon any Subject relating to the Duties of their respective Offices, and he shall have Power to grant Reprieves and Pardons for Offences against the United States, except in Cases of Impeachment.

make treaties and appointments

He shall have Power, by and with the Advice and Consent of the Senate, to make Treaties, provided two thirds of the Senators present concur; and he shall nominate, and by and with the Advice and Consent of the Senate, shall appoint Ambassadors, other public Ministers and Consuls, Judges of the supreme Court, and all other Officers of the United States, whose Appointments are not herein otherwise provided for, and which shall be established by Law: but the Congress may by Law vest the Appointment of such inferior Officers, as they think proper, in the President alone, in the Courts of Law, or in the Heads of Departments.

The President shall have Power to fill up all Vacancies that may happen during the Recess of the Senate, by granting Commissions which shall expire at the End of their next Session.

Relations of President with Congress

Section 3. He shall from time to time give to the Congress Information of the State of the Union, and recommend to their Consideration such Measures as he shall judge necessary and expedient; he may, on extraordinary Occasions, convene both Houses, or either of them, and in Case of Disagreement between them, with Respect to the Time of Adjournment, he may adjourn them to such Time as he shall think proper; he shall receive Ambassadors and other public Ministers; he shall take Care that the Laws be faithfully executed, and shall Commission all the Officers of the United States.

Impeachment

Section 4. The President, Vice President and all civil Officers of the United States, shall be removed from Office on Impeachment for, and Conviction of, Treason, Bribery, or other high Crimes and Misdemeanors.

Article III.

Federal courts

Section 1. The judicial Power of the United States, shall be vested in one supreme Court, and in such inferior Courts as the Congress may from time to time ordain and establish. The Judges, both of the supreme and inferior Courts, shall hold their Offices during good Behaviour, and shall, at stated Times, receive for their Services, a Compensation, which shall not be diminished during their Continuance in Office.

Jurisdiction of courts

Section 2. The judicial Power shall extend to all Cases, in Law and Equity, arising under this Constitution, the Laws of the United States, and Treaties made, or which shall be made, under their Authority;—to all Cases affecting Ambassadors, other public Ministers and Consuls;—to all Cases of admiralty and maritime Jurisdiction;—to Controversies to which the United States shall be a Party;—to Controversies between two or more States;—*between a State and Citizens of another State;*[8]—between Citizens of different States;—between Citizens of the same State claiming Lands under Grants of different States, and between a State, or the Citizens thereof, and foreign States, Citizens or Subjects.

[7]Modified by the Twenty-fifth Amendment.

[8]Modified by the Eleventh Amendment.

original

appellate

In all Cases affecting Ambassadors, other public Ministers and Consuls, and those in which a State shall be Party, the supreme Court shall have original Jurisdiction. In all the other Cases before mentioned, the supreme Court shall have appellate Jurisdiction, both as to Law and Fact, with such Exceptions, and under such Regulations as the Congress shall make.

The Trial of all Crimes, except in Cases of Impeachment, shall be by Jury; and such Trial shall be held in the State where the said Crimes shall have been committed; but when not committed within any State, the Trial shall be at such Place or Places as the Congress may by Law have directed.

Treason

Section 3. Treason against the United States, shall consist only in levying War against them, or in adhering to their Enemies, giving them Aid and Comfort. No Person shall be convicted of Treason unless on the Testimony of two Witnesses to the same overt Act, or on Confession in open Court.

The Congress shall have Power to declare the Punishment of Treason, but no Attainder of Treason shall work Corruption of Blood, or Forfeiture except during the Life of the Person attainted.

Article IV.

Full faith and credit

Section 1. Full Faith and Credit shall be given in each State to the public Acts, Records, and judicial Proceedings of every other State. And the Congress may by general Laws prescribe the Manner in which such Acts, Records and Proceedings shall be proved, and the Effect thereof.

Privileges and immunities

Section 2. The Citizens of each State shall be entitled to all Privileges and Immunities of Citizens in the several States.

Extradition

A person charged in any State with Treason, Felony, or other Crime, who shall flee from Justice, and be found in another State, shall on Demand of the executive Authority of the State from which he fled, be delivered up, to be removed to the State having Jurisdiction of the Crime.

No Person held to Service or Labour in one State, under the Laws thereof, escaping into another, shall, in Consequence of any Law or Regulation therein, be discharged from such Service or Labour, but shall be delivered up on Claim of the Party to whom such Service or Labour may be due.[9]

Creation of new states

Section 3. New States may be admitted by the Congress into this Union; but no new State shall be formed or erected within the Jurisdiction of any other State; nor any State be formed by the Junction of two or more States, or Parts of States, without the consent of the Legislatures of the States concerned as well as of the Congress.

Governing territories

The Congress shall have Power to dispose of and make all needful Rules and Regulations respecting the Territory or other Property belonging to the United States; and nothing in this Constitution shall be so construed as to Prejudice any Claims of the United States, or of any particular State.

Protection of states

Section 4. The United States shall guarantee to every State in this Union a Republican Form of Government, and shall protect each of them against Invasion; and on Application of the Legislature, or of the Executive (when the Legislature cannot be convened) against domestic Violence.

Article V.

Amending the Constitution

The Congress, whenever two thirds of both Houses shall deem it necessary, shall propose Amendments to this Constitution, or, on the Application of the Legislatures of two thirds of the several States, shall call a Convention for proposing Amendments, which, in either Case, shall be valid to all Intents and Purposes, as Part of this Constitution, when ratified by the Legislatures of three fourths of the several States, or by Conventions in three fourths thereof, as the one or the other Mode of Ratification may be proposed by the Congress; Provided that no Amendment which may be made prior to the Year One Thousand eight hundred and eight shall in any Manner affect the first and fourth Clauses in the Ninth Section of the first Article; and that no State, without its Consent, shall be deprived of its equal Suffrage in the Senate.

[9]Changed by the Thirteenth Amendment.

Article VI.

All Debts contracted and Engagements entered into, before the Adoption of this Constitution, shall be as valid against the United States under this Constitution, as under the Confederation.

Assumption of debts of Confederation

This Constitution, and the Laws of the United States which shall be made in Pursuance thereof; and all Treaties made, or which shall be made, under the Authority of the United States, shall be the supreme Law of the Land; and the Judges in every State shall be bound thereby, any Thing in the Constitution or Laws of any State to the Contrary notwithstanding.

Supremacy of federal laws and treaties

The Senators and Representatives before mentioned, and the Members of the several State Legislatures, and all executive and judicial Officers, both of the United States and of the several States, shall be bound by Oath or Affirmation, to support this Constitution; but no religious Test shall ever be required as a Qualification to any Office or public Trust under the United States.

No religious test

Article VII.

The Ratification of the Conventions of nine States, shall be sufficient for the Establishment of this Constitution between the States so ratifying the Same.

Ratification procedure

Done in Convention by the Unanimous Consent of the States present the Seventeenth Day of September in the Year of our Lord one thousand seven hundred and Eighty seven and of the Independence of the United States of America the Twelfth In witness whereof We have hereunto subscribed our Names,

---

G[o] WASHINGTON—*Presid[t] and deputy from Virginia*

New Hampshire	JOHN LANGDON NICHOLAS GILMAN	*Delaware*	GEO: READ GUNNING BEDFORD jun JOHN DICKINSON RICHARD BASSETT JACO: BROOM
Massachusetts	NATHANIEL GORHAM RUFUS KING	*Maryland*	JAMES M[C]HENRY DAN OF S[T] THO[S] JENIFER DAN[L] CARROLL
Connecticut	W[M] SAM[L] JOHNSON ROGER SHERMAN	*Virginia*	JOHN BLAIR— JAMES MADISON Jr.
New York	ALEXANDER HAMILTON	*North Carolina*	W[M] BLOUNT RICH[D] DOBBS SPAIGHT HU WILLIAMSON
New Jersey	WIL: LIVINGSTON DAVID BREARLEY W[M] PATERSON JONA: DAYTON	*South Carolina*	J. RUTLEDGE CHARLES COTESWORTH PINCKNEY CHARLES PINCKNEY PIERCE BUTLER
Pennsylvania	B FRANKLIN THOMAS MIFFLIN ROB[T] MORRIS GEO. CLYMER THO[S] FITZSIMONS JARED INGERSOLL JAMES WILSON GOUV MORRIS	*Georgia*	WILLIAM FEW ABR BALDWIN

[The first ten amendments, known as the "Bill of Rights," were ratified in 1791.]

Amendment I.

Congress shall make no law respecting an establishment of religion, or prohibiting the free exercise thereof; or abridging the freedom of speech, or of the press; or the right of the people peaceably to assemble, and to petition the Government for a redress of grievances.

Freedom of religion, speech, press, assembly

Amendment II.

A well regulated Militia, being necessary to the security of a free State, the right of the people to keep and bear Arms, shall not be infringed.

Right to bear arms

Amendment III.

No Soldier shall, in time of peace be quartered in any house, without the consent of the Owner, nor in time of war, but in a manner prescribed by law.

No quartering of troops in private homes

Amendment IV.

Unreasonable searches and seizures prohibited

The right of the people to be secure in their persons, houses, papers, and effects, against unreasonable searches and seizures, shall not be violated, and no Warrants shall issue, but upon probable cause, supported by Oath or affirmation, and particularly describing the place to be searched, and the persons or things to be seized.

Amendment V.

Rights when accused; due process clause

No person shall be held to answer for a capital, or otherwise infamous crime, unless on a presentment or indictment of a Grand Jury, except in cases arising in the land or naval forces, or in the Militia, when in actual service in time of War or public danger; nor shall any person be subject for the same offence to be twice put in jeopardy of life or limb; nor shall be compelled in any criminal case to be a witness against himself, nor be deprived of life, liberty, or property, without due process of law, nor shall private property be taken for public use, without just compensation.

Amendment VI.

Rights when on trial

In all criminal prosecutions, the accused shall enjoy the right to a speedy and public trial, by an impartial jury of the State and district wherein the crime shall have been committed, which district shall have been previously ascertained by law, and to be informed of the nature and cause of the accusation; to be confronted with the witnesses against him; to have compulsory process for obtaining witnesses in his favor, and to have Assistance of Counsel for his defence.

Amendment VII.

Common-law suits

In Suits at common law, where the value in controversy shall exceed twenty dollars, the right of trial by jury shall be preserved, and no fact tried by a jury, shall be otherwise reexamined in any Court of the United States, than according to the rules of the common law.

Amendment VIII.

Bail; no cruel and unusual punishments

Excessive bail shall not be required, nor excessive fines imposed, nor cruel and unusual punishments inflicted.

Amendment IX.

Unenumerated rights protected

The enumeration in the Constitution, of certain rights, shall not be construed to deny or disparage others retained by the people.

Amendment X.

Powers reserved for states

The powers not delegated to the United States by the Constitution, nor prohibited by it to the States, are reserved to the States respectively, or to the people.

Amendment XI.
[*Ratified in 1795.*]

Limits on suits against states

The Judicial power of the United States shall not be construed to extend to any suit in law or equity, commenced or prosecuted against one of the United States by Citizens of another State, or by Citizens or Subjects of any Foreign State.

Amendment XII.
[*Ratified in 1804.*]

Revision of electoral college procedure

The Electors shall meet in their respective states and vote by ballot for President and Vice President, one of whom, at least, shall not be an inhabitant of the same state with themselves; they shall name in their ballots the person voted for as President, and in distinct ballots the person voted for as Vice President, and they shall make distinct lists of all persons voted for as President, and of all persons voted for as Vice President, and of the number of votes for each, which lists they shall sign and certify, and transmit sealed to the seat of the government of the United States, directed to the President of the Senate;—The President of the Senate shall, in the presence of the Senate and House of Representatives, open all the certificates and the votes shall then be counted;—The person having the greatest number of votes for President, shall be the President, if such number be a majority of the whole number of Electors appointed; and if no person have such majority, then from the persons having the highest numbers not exceeding three on the list of those voted for as President, the House of Representatives shall choose immediately, by ballot, the President. But in choosing the President, the votes shall be taken by states, the representation from each state having one vote; a quorum for this purpose shall consist of a member or members from two-thirds of the states, and a majority of all the states shall be necessary to a choice. *And if the House of Representatives shall not choose a President whenever the right of choice shall devolve upon them, before the fourth day of March next following, then the Vice President shall act as President, as in the case of the death or other constitutional disability of the President.*—[10] The person having the greatest number of votes as Vice President, shall be the Vice President, if such number be a majority of the whole number of Electors appointed, and if no person have a majority, then from the two highest numbers on the list, the Senate shall choose the Vice President; a quorum for the purpose shall consist of two-thirds of the whole number of Senators, and a majority of the whole number shall be necessary to a choice. But no person constitutionally ineligible to the office of President shall be eligible to that of Vice President of the United States.

Amendment XIII.
[*Ratified in 1865.*]

Slavery prohibited

Section 1. Neither slavery nor involuntary servitude, except as a punishment for crime whereof the party shall have been duly convicted, shall exist within the United States, or any place subject to their jurisdiction.

Section 2. Congress shall have power to enforce this article by appropriate legislation.

Amendment XIV.
[*Ratified in 1868.*]

Ex-slaves made citizens

Due process clause

Equal protection clause

Section 1. All persons born or naturalized in the United States and subject to the jurisdiction thereof, are citizens of the United States and of the State wherein they reside. No State shall make or enforce any law which shall abridge the privileges or immunities of citizens of the United States; nor shall any State deprive any person of life, liberty, or property, without due process of law; nor deny to any person within its jurisdiction the equal protection of the laws.

Rules for reducing congressional representation for states that deny adult males the right to vote

Section 2. Representatives shall be apportioned among the several States according to their respective numbers, counting the whole number of persons in each State, excluding Indians not taxed. But when the right to vote at any election for the choice of electors for President and Vice President of the United States, Representatives in Congress, the Executive and Judicial officers of a State, or the members of the Legislature thereof, is denied to any of the male inhabitants of such State, being *twenty-one*[11] years of age, and citizens of the United States, or in any way abridged, except for participation in rebellion, or other crime, the basis of representation therein shall be reduced in the proportion which the number of such male citizens shall bear to the whole number of male citizens twenty-one years of age in such State.

Southern rebels denied federal office

Section 3. No person shall be a Senator or Representative in Congress, or elector of President and Vice President, or hold any office, civil or military, under the United States, or under any State, who, having previously taken an oath, as a member of Congress, or as an officer of the United States, or as a member of any State legislature, or as an executive or judicial officer of any State, to support the Constitution of the United States, shall have engaged in insurrection or rebellion against the same, or given aid or comfort to the enemies thereof. But Congress may by a vote of two-thirds of each House, remove such disability.

Rebel debts repudiated

Section 4. The validity of the public debt of the United States, authorized by law, including debts incurred for payment of pensions and bounties for services in suppressing insurrection or rebellion, shall not be questioned. But neither the United States nor any State shall assume or pay any debt or obligation incurred in aid of insurrection or rebellion against the United States, or any claim for the loss or emancipation of any slave; but all such debts, obligations and claims shall be held illegal and void.

[10]Changed by the Twentieth Amendment, section 3.

[11]Changed by the Twenty-sixth Amendment.

Section 5. The Congress shall have power to enforce, by appropriate legislation, the provisions of this article.

Amendment XV.
[*Ratified in 1870.*]

African American males given right to vote

Section 1. The right of citizens of the United States to vote shall not be denied or abridged by the United States or by any State on account of race, color, or previous condition of servitude.

Section 2. The Congress shall have power to enforce this article by appropriate legislation.

Amendment XVI.
[*Ratified in 1913.*]

Federal income tax authorized

The Congress shall have power to lay and collect taxes on incomes, from whatever source derived, without apportionment among the several States, and without regard to any census or enumeration.

Amendment XVII.
[*Ratified in 1913.*]

Popular election of senators required

The Senate of the United States shall be composed of two Senators from each State, elected by the people thereof, for six years; and each Senator shall have one vote. The electors in each State shall have the qualifications requisite for electors of the most numerous branch of the State legislatures.

When vacancies happen in the representation of any State in the Senate, the executive authority of such State shall issue writs of election to fill such vacancies: *Provided,* That the legislature of any State may empower the executive thereof to make temporary appointments until the people fill the vacancies by election as the legislature may direct.

This amendment shall not be so construed as to affect the election or term of any Senator chosen before it becomes valid as part of the Constitution.

Amendment XVIII.
[*Ratified in 1919.*]

Manufacture and sale of liquor prohibited (Prohibition)

Section 1. *After one year from the ratification of this article the manufacture, sale, or transportation of intoxicating liquors within, the importation thereof into, or the exportation thereof from the United States and all territory subject to the jurisdiction thereof for beverage purposes is hereby prohibited.*

Section 2. *The Congress and the several States shall have concurrent power to enforce this article by appropriate legislation.*

Section 3. *This article shall be inoperative unless it shall have been ratified as an amendment to the Constitution by the legislatures of the several States, as provided in the Constitution, within seven years from the date of the submission hereof to the States by the Congress.*[12]

Amendment XIX.
[*Ratified in 1920.*]

Women given right to vote

The right of citizens of the United States to vote shall not be denied or abridged by the United States or by any State on account of sex.

Congress shall have power to enforce this article by appropriate legislation.

Amendment XX.
[*Ratified in 1933.*]

Federal terms of office to begin in January

Section 1. The terms of the President and Vice President shall end at noon on the 20th day of January, and the terms of Senators and Representatives at noon on the 3d day of January, of the years in which such terms would have ended if this article had not been ratified; and the terms of their successors shall then begin.

Section 2. The Congress shall assemble at least once in every year, and such meeting shall begin at noon on the 3d day of January, unless they shall by law appoint a different day.

[12]Repealed by the Twenty-first Amendment.

Section 3. If, at the time fixed for the beginning of the term of the President, the President elect shall have died, the Vice President elect shall become President. If a President shall not have been chosen before the time fixed for the beginning of his term, or if the President elect shall have failed to qualify, then the Vice President elect shall act as President until a President shall have qualified; and the Congress may by law provide for the case wherein neither a President elect nor a Vice President elect shall have qualified, declaring who shall then act as President, or the manner in which one who is to act shall be selected, and such person shall act accordingly until a President or Vice President shall have qualified.

Emergency presidential succession

Section 4. The Congress may by law provide for the case of the death of any of the persons from whom the House of Representatives may choose a President whenever the right of choice shall have devolved upon them, and for the case of the death of any of the persons from whom the Senate may choose a Vice President whenever the right of choice shall have devolved upon them.

Section 5. Sections 1 and 2 shall take effect on the 15th day of October following the ratification of this article.

Section 6. This article shall be inoperative unless it shall have been ratified as an amendment to the Constitution by the legislatures of three-fourths of the several States within seven years from the date of its submission.

Amendment XXI.
[*Ratified in 1933.*]

Section 1. The eighteenth article of amendment to the Constitution of the United States is hereby repealed.

Ban on manufacture and sale of liquor (Prohibition) repealed

Section 2. The transportation or importation into any State, Territory, or possession of the United States for delivery or use therein of intoxicating liquors, in violation of the laws thereof, is hereby prohibited.

Section 3. This article shall be inoperative unless it shall have been ratified as an amendment to the Constitution by conventions in the several States, as provided in the Constitution, within seven years from the date of the submission hereof to the States by the Congress.

Amendment XXII.
[*Ratified in 1951.*]

Section 1. No person shall be elected to the office of the President more than twice, and no person who has held the office of President, or acted as President, for more than two years of a term to which some other person was elected President shall be elected to the office of the President more than once. But this Article shall not apply to any person holding the office of President when this Article was proposed by the Congress, and shall not prevent any person who may be holding the office of President, or acting as President, during the term within which this Article becomes operative from holding the office of President or acting as President during the remainder of such term.

Two-term limit for President

Section 2. This article shall be inoperative unless it shall have been ratified as an amendment to the Constitution by the legislatures of three-fourths of the several States within seven years from the date of its submission to the States by the Congress.

Amendment XXIII.
[*Ratified in 1961.*]

Section 1. The District constituting the seat of Government of the United States shall appoint in such manner as the Congress may direct:

A number of electors of President and Vice President equal to the whole number of Senators and Representatives in Congress to which the District would be entitled if it were a State, but in no event more than the least populous State; they shall be in addition to those appointed by the States, but they shall be considered, for the purposes of the election of President and Vice President, to be electors appointed by a State; and they shall meet in the District and perform such duties as provided by the twelfth article of amendment.

Residents of the District of Columbia given right to vote for President

Section 2. The Congress shall have power to enforce this article by appropriate legislation.

Amendment XXIV.
[*Ratified in 1964.*]

Poll taxes in federal elections prohibited

Section 1. The right of citizens of the United States to vote in any primary or other election for President or Vice President, for electors for President or Vice President, or for Senator or Representative in Congress, shall not be denied or abridged by the United States or any State by reason of failure to pay any poll tax or other tax.

Section 2. The Congress shall have power to enforce this article by appropriate legislation.

Amendment XXV.
[*Ratified in 1967.*]

Presidential disability and succession

Section 1. In case of the removal of the President from office or of his death or resignation, the Vice President shall become President.

Section 2. Whenever there is a vacancy in the office of the Vice President, the President shall nominate a Vice President who shall take office upon confirmation by a majority vote of both Houses of Congress.

Section 3. Whenever the President transmits to the president pro tempore of the Senate and the Speaker of the House of Representatives his written declaration that he is unable to discharge the powers and duties of his office, and until he transmits to them a written declaration to the contrary, such powers and duties shall be discharged by the Vice President as Acting President.

Section 4. Whenever the Vice President and a majority of either the principal officers of the executive departments or of such other body as Congress may by law provide, transmit to the President pro tempore of the Senate and the Speaker of the House of Representatives their written declaration that the President is unable to discharge the powers and duties of his office, the Vice President shall immediately assume the powers and duties of the office as Acting President.

Thereafter, when the President transmits to the President pro tempore of the Senate and the Speaker of the House of Representatives his written declaration that no inability exists, he shall resume the powers and duties of his office unless the Vice President and a majority of either the principal officers of the executive department[s] or of such other body as Congress may by law provide, transmit within four days to the President pro tempore of the Senate and the Speaker of the House of Representatives their written declaration that the President is unable to discharge the powers and duties of his office. Thereupon Congress shall decide the issue, assembling within forty-eight hours for that purpose if not in session. If the Congress, within twenty-one days after receipt of the latter written declaration, or, if Congress is not in session, within twenty-one days after Congress is required to assemble, determines by two-thirds vote of both Houses that the President is unable to discharge the powers and duties of his office, the Vice President shall continue to discharge the same as Acting President; otherwise, the President shall resume the powers and duties of his office.

Amendment XXVI.
[*Ratified in 1971.*]

Voting age lowered to eighteen

Section 1. The right of citizens of the United States, who are 18 years of age or older, to vote shall not be denied or abridged by the United States or by any State on account of age.

Section 2. The Congress shall have power to enforce this article by appropriate legislation.

Amendment XXVII.
[*Ratified in 1992.*]

No congressional pay increase within a term

Section 1. No law, varying the compensation for the services of the senators and representatives, shall take effect until an election of representatives shall have intervened.

Chapter

3

The Social Context of American Politics

Who Are Americans?
- *A Growing and Changing Population*
- *Race and Ethnicity*
- *Immigration*
- *Language*
- *Age*
- *Family Households*
- *Sexual Orientation*

Social and Economic Characteristics
- *Religion*
- *Education*
- *Wealth and Income*
- *Home Ownership*
- *Occupation*

Diversity and Social Harmony

Political Power in the United States

Summary

Key Terms

Readings for Further Study

A *Washington Post* survey conducted in 1995 found that the average white American thinks that America is 50 percent white, 24 percent African American, 16 percent Hispanic American, and 12 percent Asian American.[1] In truth, however, whites constitute an overwhelming majority of the American population. According to the U.S. Census Bureau, roughly 75 percent of all Americans describe themselves as white, while 12 percent describe themselves as African American, 9 percent as Hispanic American, and 3 percent as Asian American. White Americans are not alone in believing that the United States has more minorities than it does. African Americans, Hispanic Americans, and Asian Americans also greatly underestimate the number of white Americans and exaggerate their own numbers.

The findings of the *Washington Post* survey are by no means unusual, nor are they confined just to racial and ethnic identity. Public opinion polls repeatedly find that many Americans do not have an accurate idea of the demographic, economic, or social composition of the country. This lack of awareness is particularly prevalent among the young, the less educated, and those who live in areas with large concentrations of minorities. More important, these misconceptions are not innocuous; for example, people who think more Americans are minority members than is really the case also feel more threatened by minorities.[2]

Is it necessary to know the makeup of the American population to understand politics in the United States? In a word, yes. The preamble to the Constitution makes it clear that governing authority in the United States rests ultimately in the hands of "We the People." And for more than two hundred years, observers have lauded the American commitment to, in Abraham Lincoln's immortal words, "government of the people, by the people, for the people." In short, the founders sought to create a representative government.

But representative of what or whom? The United States is an extraordinarily diverse society. Whether Americans identify themselves in terms of race, ethnicity, religion, or some other characteristic determines how they see their political interests and, in turn, shapes the demands they make on government and the kind of political rules they favor. At the same time, many voters now doubt that the American political system lives up to Lincoln's lofty vision of a government by the people. Callers to radio talk shows frequently complain that the average American has no effective voice in politics, and some scholars argue that a power elite dominates American politics. So to evaluate whether American government in the 1990s fulfills the founders' vision of representative government, we need to understand the diverse nature of American society.

In this chapter, we look at who the American people are and at which groups wield political power in the United States. We begin by examining the basic demographic characteristics of American society, such as the size of the population, its racial and ethnic makeup, proportion of immigrants, and how these characteristics have changed over the past two centuries. We then explore some of the current social and economic characteristics of American society, including religion, education, and wealth. We go on to discuss why the United States, unlike so many other countries, has dampened social conflict and succeeded in combining social diversity with political stability. We show that the answer lies in the overlapping memberships of groups in the United States, a phenomenon that enables the government to respond to at least some of the needs of nearly all groups or individuals. We argue that our political system is pluralistic—that is, responsive to many groups, although these groups neither wield equal political power nor share equally in government benefits. These two characteristics—group overlap and pluralism—enable our political system to manage the inevitable conflicts that arise among different groups.

Who Are Americans?

Political commentators like to speak about the average American, usually using colorful terms such as Joe SixPack or Jane Q. Public. And it is a relatively simple matter to generate a statistical profile of the average American (see box 3.1). Yet focusing

More than half of all Americans think that the population is about 25 percent African American. In fact, only 12 percent of the population is African American.

solely on statistical averages can obscure more than it reveals. Because American society is extraordinarily diverse, most Americans look anything but average. To begin to draw a more accurate picture of who Americans are as a people, we look first at the growth of the American population over the past two hundred years and at the shift the population made from rural to urban life. We will then examine American society along several key demographic dimensions: race, ethnicity, immigration, language, age, family households, and sexual orientation.

A Growing and Changing Population

In 1995, the U.S. Census Bureau estimated that 263,814,000 people lived in the United States, making it the third most populous country in the world, following China and India.[3] Although this figure may not be precisely accurate—in 1990, census takers apparently missed some people, particularly among the poor and minorities—it represents incredible growth since the first census was taken in 1790. When George Washington was president, fewer than 4 million people lived in the United States, a figure roughly equal to 10 percent of California's population today. As figure 3.1 shows, population growth exploded over the next half century, as America grew westward and new immigrants arrived; the rate of population growth was actually higher during the nineteenth century than it is today. Nonetheless, in the last few decades, the United States has added more than 20 million people every ten years. (Of course, because the United States is so large today, even a small percentage increase adds millions of people to our population.) This increase has outstripped our geographic growth: in 1795, an average of 4.5 people populated each square mile, and in 1990 this had grown to 74.6 people per square mile. A growing population affects the political system because it usually entails more demands on government and more problems for government to solve.

The dramatic growth in the population of the United States over the past two hundred years has been accompanied by equally dramatic changes in where Americans live. As figure 3.2 shows, the United States has changed from being a predominantly rural country to a predominantly urban one. (An urban area encompasses both a central or inner city and the surrounding suburbs.) For much of U.S. history, rural-urban migration meant that people moved to a central city. In recent decades, however, both rural areas and cities have seen their residents migrate to the suburbs. In 1930, only 14 percent of Americans lived in suburbs, whereas by 1990, more than 46 percent did.[4] Indeed, more people now live in the suburbs than live in central cities (31 percent) or rural areas (22 percent).

The People Behind the Rules

BOX 3.1

The Average American, 1900 and 1995

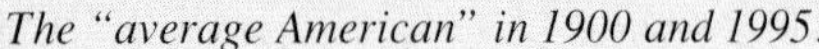

The "average American" in 1900 and 1995.

A look at the statistically average American is enlightening because it reveals some of the general ways our society is changing.

Characteristic	**1900**	**1995**
Race and Ethnicity	White	White
Sex	Male	Female
Age	22.9	34.0
Marital Status	Unmarried	Married
Education	8.2 years	High School Graduate
Household Income	$651	$34,076
Home Ownership	Renter	Owner

The average American has changed in significant ways since 1900. Over the last ninety-five years, the population has, on average, grown older, but the majority of the population is still white. Since 1950, women have outnumbered men. In large part this is because women live longer than men do. The number of men and women is virtually the same in most age groups, with the only major difference occurring among people over sixty-five years of age.

In 1900, the average American was a twenty-three-year-old man, three years away from marriage. In 1995, the average American was a thirty-four-year-old woman, married and with children. In 1900, a slight majority of Americans were renters, while in 1995, the average American owned his or her home.

Finally, the average American household in 1900 earned $651 dollars a year, while in 1995, the average household income exceeded $34,000 a year. Comparing the relative buying power is, of course, difficult, because so many things we take for granted as routine expenses—such as cars, televisions (98 percent of homes own one or more, and 97 percent have color televisions), radios (98 percent), telephones (96 percent, with 52 percent having a cordless phone and 54 percent of all phones connected to answering machines), VCRs (85 percent), microwave ovens (88 percent), smoke alarms (79 percent), automatic coffee makers (67 percent) and other items—were either not invented or not generally available in 1900. Indeed, more changes are in the offing; in 1995, only 33 percent of homes had a personal computer, and 6 percent had a home fax machine, figures that are likely to increase dramatically in the next few years. All of these technological advances change the way we live, and in many cases, the way we interact with each other and conduct politics. During the 1996 presidential campaign, for example, almost every candidate had a home page on the World Wide Web, introducing a new way to transmit information about the candidates and to try to win votes.

Sources: Historical Statistics of the United States: Colonial Times to 1979 (Washington, D.C.: U.S. Bureau of the Census, 1975), pp. 14, 19, 20, 381; *Statistical Abstract of the United States, 1995,* 115th ed., (Washington, D.C.: U.S. Bureau of the Census, 1995); "People, Opinions & Polls," *The Public Perspective 6* (August/September 1995): 45; "This Is Your Life, Generally Speaking," *New York Times,* 26 July 1992; "What America Plugs Into," *San Francisco Chronicle,* 6 January 1995; *U.S. Census Bureau,* "Income and Poverty Status of Americans Improve, Health Insurance Coverage Stable, Census Bureau Reports," 22 September 1996.

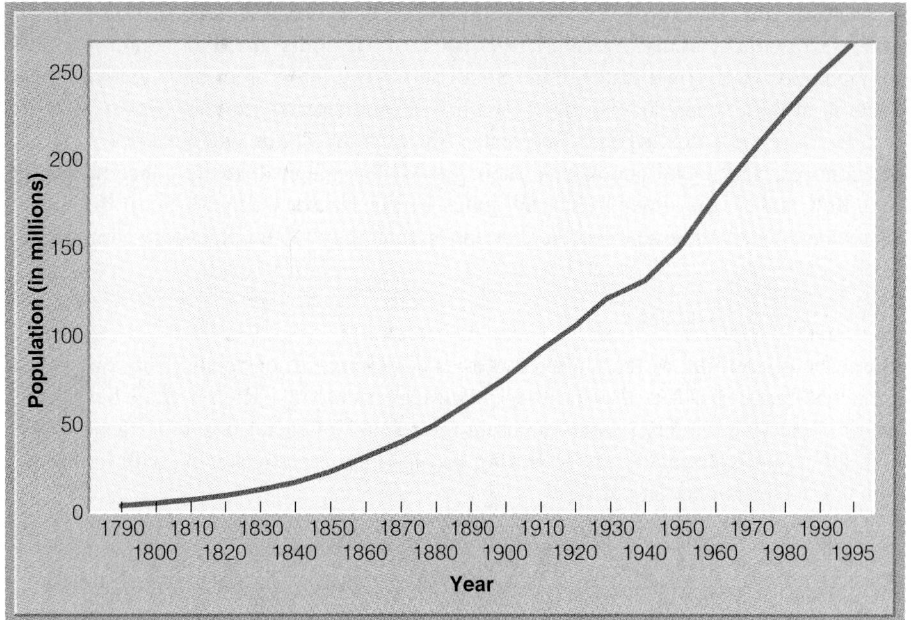

FIGURE 3.1
Population of the United States, 1790–1995

From 1950 to 1995, the population increased from 150 million to more than 260 million people.

Source: Data from *Statistical Abstract of the United States, 1995,* 115th ed. (Washington, D.C.: U.S. Bureau of the Census, 1995), p. 8.

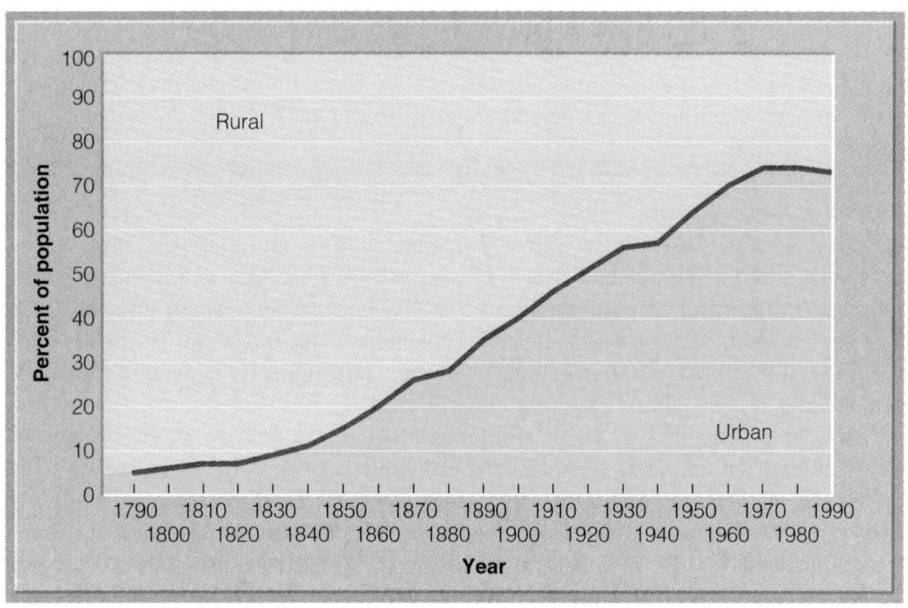

FIGURE 3.2
Rural and Urban Population, 1790–1990

The United States has changed from a rural country to one with an overwhelmingly urban population.

Source: Data from *Statistical Abstract of the United States, 1992,* 112th ed. (Washington, D.C.: U.S. Bureau of the Census, 1992), p. 16.

The movement of Americans from towns to cities and from cities to suburbs has had important political consequences. City dwellers, suburbanites, and rural voters have different interests on many issues. Take, for example, government spending on transportation. City dwellers may wish to spend their tax dollars on mass transit, suburbanites may prefer to build more freeways for the commute to work, and rural voters may want better county roads. Because American legislatures are designed to be representative and because they usually cannot satisfy every group, they generally are most responsive to whichever group commands the most votes. Thus, as the U.S. population has become more suburban, the interests of rural areas and inner cities have become secondary.

In addition to moving from towns to cities, the population has shifted away from the Eastern seaboard (and the original thirteen colonies) to other areas of the country. The country's mean center of population—the point on an imaginary flat map of the United States where the country would balance if an equal weight sat on the spot where each American lived—has moved from twenty-three miles east of Baltimore in 1790 to Crawford County, Missouri, southwest of St. Louis, in 1990. Again, because the population has grown faster in the South and West, these areas have gained representation at the expense of the more established (and slower growing) East and Midwest. Because the so-called **Sun Belt** states (those in the South and West) have different economic and social conditions, their growth has meant that the concerns of the **Rust Belt** states (the older industrial states in the Northeast and around the Great Lakes) have received less government attention than they would otherwise command.

Sun Belt
The Sun Belt states are the states in the South, Southwest, and West Coast—areas that have experienced tremendous population and economic growth since 1950.

Rust Belt
The Rust Belt states are the major industrial states of the Northeast and Midwest. For the most part, they have not enjoyed great population or economic growth in the second half of the twentieth century.

Race and Ethnicity

Americans often think of the United States as a melting pot of people from many different backgrounds. Yet the melting pot image misleads. Rather than becoming generic Americans, many people maintain their sense of racial or ethnic identity. Indeed, the nation's population is becoming increasingly heterogeneous, with important implications for American politics.

White Americans

White Americans continue to be the country's largest racial group. The original white colonists came from northern Europe. (Keep in mind, of course, that American Indians lived here long before Europeans arrived.) Although the United States saw large-scale immigration from southern Europe at the beginning of the twentieth century, northern Europeans remain the largest ethnic groups in the United States. Germany claims the honor of providing the largest contribution to the U.S. population; 23 percent of all Americans say they are of German descent. Other major European ethnic groups are Irish (16 percent), English (13 percent), Italian (6 percent), French (4 percent), and Polish (4 percent).

African Americans

African Americans currently constitute the largest minority group in the United States at 12 percent of the population. (Surveys disagree over what African Americans prefer to be called. One poll found a preference for *African American,* another a preference for *black,* and a third suggested both are acceptable.)[5] Indeed, African Americans have always been the country's largest minority group, constituting 19 percent of the population in 1790.

African Americans are a significant group in American politics not just because of their numbers, but because their social and economic heritage forged a common political orientation. From the end of the Civil War to the New Deal era, African Americans who were able to vote overwhelmingly supported Republican candidates because Lincoln, who issued the Emancipation Proclamation, was a Republican and because the Democrats were linked to segregationist policies in the South. African Americans began to shift their allegiance to the Democratic Party in the 1930s when northern Democrats began to push civil rights legislation over the opposition of many Republicans and southern Democrats. The African-American identification with the Democratic Party was cemented in 1964, when the Republicans ran Sen. Barry Goldwater, an ardent foe of the Civil Rights Act of 1964, for president against the incumbent, Lyndon Johnson, who had pushed hard for the legislation.[6] Now, because of their political cohesiveness, African Americans form a significant component of the Democratic Party.[7] But some evidence suggests that political differences are starting to appear between middle- and lower-class African Americans, though these differences have yet to shift any substantial number of African Americans away from their liberal leanings and toward the more conservative Republican Party.[8]

The political influence of African Americans is concentrated in the South and in large cities. A majority of African Americans lives in the South. They constitute more than 30 percent of the voting age population in Mississippi, more than 25 percent in Louisiana and South Carolina, and more than 20 percent in Georgia, Maryland,

Although we label people of Mexican and Central or South American ancestry Hispanics *or* Latinos, *the cultures and political beliefs of people whose ancestors came from different Hispanic nations differ greatly. For instance, most Americans of Mexican descent are Democrats, while most Americans of Cuban descent are Republicans.*

Alabama, and North Carolina.[9] As chapter 5 discusses in greater detail, the civil rights movement succeeded in ending the discriminatory practices that prevented African Americans from exercising their right to vote, and, as a result, they have become an important political force in the South. African Americans also have enjoyed great electoral success in cities where they form a significant portion of the population. Over the past two decades, for example, most major cities, including Atlanta, Chicago, Cleveland, Detroit, Los Angeles, New York, Philadelphia, San Francisco, Seattle, and Washington, D.C., have elected African-American mayors.

Outside of the South and large cities, African Americans exercise much less political clout. In twenty states, most of which are in the North and West, African Americans constitute less than 5 percent of the population. Likewise, only 25 percent of African Americans live in the suburbs. Where African Americans are few in number, they have a harder time achieving their political goals—not necessarily because of racism, but because they lack the votes needed to command the attention of elected officials. Simply put, elected officials respond to voters.[10]

Hispanic Americans

Although African Americans constitute the largest minority group in the United States, demographic projections predict that people of Hispanic origin will become the nation's largest minority group within the next two decades. (The U.S. Bureau of the Census defines Hispanic Americans as people of Spanish background, who may be of any race. Many Hispanic Americans also call themselves white; thus, in census figures some whites are also Hispanic Americans.) In 1995, Hispanic Americans were estimated to constitute more than 9 percent of the nation's population, a sharp rise from 6 percent in 1980. Indeed, Hispanic Americans now outnumber African Americans in four of the nation's largest cities: Houston, Los Angeles, Phoenix, and San Antonio. And by the late 1990s, more Hispanic Americans than African Americans will live in New York City.[11]

Almost two-thirds of Hispanic Americans trace their heritage to Mexico. The rest come from South America (14 percent), Puerto Rico (11 percent), Cuba (5 percent), and other Latin countries. The fact that Hispanic Americans trace their roots to so many different countries carries a crucial lesson: Hispanic Americans cannot be treated as a monolithic group. They hold a wide variety of political attitudes and concerns. Indeed, Americans of Latin descent even disagree over whether they should be called Hispanics, Latinos, or a more country-specific term such as *Chicanos* for Mexican Americans. (A survey the U.S. Department of Labor conducted in 1995 found that roughly 60 percent of Hispanic households preferred the term *Hispanic,* while 12 percent preferred *of Spanish origin,* and another 12 percent liked *Latino.* The rest chose other labels or no label.)[12]

Hispanic Americans of Mexican origin have tended to settle in states bordering Mexico. More than half of the nation's Hispanic Americans live in California and

FIGURE 3.3
Asian American Population, 1990

Asian Americans have remarkably diverse backgrounds.

Source: Data from U.S. Bureau of the Census.

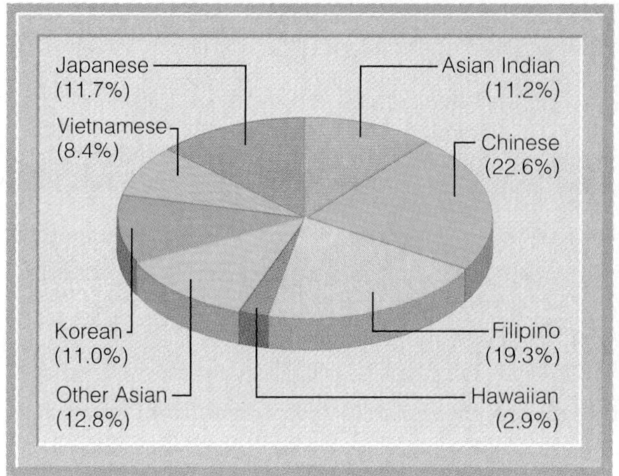

Texas, where they make up one-quarter of the total population. As we discuss in chapter 5, Mexican Americans living in California and Texas endured substantial economic, political, and social discrimination for decades. Only over the last two decades have they begun to move toward gaining political clout that mirrors their numbers in the population. In both California and Texas, the majority of Mexican Americans vote for Democratic candidates.[13] But, although their attachment to Democratic candidates has increased over time, Mexican Americans remain less devoted to the Democratic Party and to liberal political causes than African Americans.[14]

In contrast to the political experience of Mexican Americans in California and Texas, Mexican Americans in New Mexico have long been integrated into that state's political (but not economic) elite. With almost 40 percent of New Mexico's population, Mexican Americans have been elected to every political office, including governor and both houses of Congress. As is true of Mexican Americans living in Texas and California, Mexican Americans in New Mexico favor the Democratic Party.

Most Hispanic Americans of Cuban descent live in Florida. Many Cuban Americans fled their homeland during the 1960s to escape Fidel Castro and communist rule. Because of their strong anti-communist beliefs, most Cuban Americans identify themselves as Republicans; relatively few belong to the Democratic Party.[15]

Asian Americans

Like Hispanic Americans, Asian Americans are a fast-growing and diverse community. Between 1980 and 1995, the number of Asians living in the United States more than doubled, rising from 3.7 million to 9.7 million. Asian Americans now constitute almost 4 percent of all Americans. More than 40 percent of Asian Americans live in California, making them the second largest minority group in the state (behind Hispanic Americans and ahead of African Americans). The state where Asian Americans constitute the largest share of the population is Hawaii, and Asian Americans have enjoyed the most political success there, electing governors and members of Congress.

Although earlier immigrants hailed primarily from China, Japan, and the Philippines, figure 3.3 shows that many Asian immigrants now come from India, Korea, and Vietnam.[16] Like Cuban Americans, Asian Americans from China, Vietnam, and Korea—nations that are partly or entirely communist-ruled—have favored the Republican Party because of its hard-line anti-communist policies. Other Asian Americans, however, do not exhibit any strong partisan preferences.[17] Obviously, Asian Americans do not always share common political interests. In Hawaii, for example, people of Hawaiian heritage often spar with Japanese Americans over political offices and other issues.

Ten thousand high school students took to the streets of Los Angeles in 1994 to protest Proposition 187. Members of some minority groups supported the measure, which was designed to limit public services to illegal immigrants, while members of other minority groups opposed it. California voters passed the measure.

American Indians

American Indians, Eskimos, and Aleuts together constitute less than 1 percent of the nation's population. (A strong plurality of American Indians prefer that label over the name *Native American.*)[18] From 1980 to 1990, their numbers grew from 1.4 million to just under 2 million. Most American Indians live in the western and southern states; very few live in the Northeast. Almost 55 percent of American Indians reside in "federally identified areas" such as reservations. Thus, many American Indians, Eskimos, and Aleuts have a relationship with the federal government that differs greatly from that of the rest of the population, as we discuss in chapter 5. Voter turnout rates are low among American Indians. Most of those who do vote favor the Democrats.[19]

A Multicultural America

The United States is becoming an increasingly multicultural society. Minorities now constitute 25 percent of the population. Given current population trends, the Census Bureau estimates that the number will reach 37 percent by 2020 and 50 percent by 2099.[20] Such massive changes may, of course, alter the political landscape in important ways. But three things suggest that the changes are more likely to be subtle than startling.

First, as we have noted several times in this chapter, ethnic and racial groups in the United States are not monolithic—their members do not always think and act alike. Each group harbors a wide variety of opinions on political, social, and economic issues. Moreover, differences within groups appear to be widening, not narrowing. Second, different minority groups that might be thought to share common ground do not always make common cause. For example, the African-American and Hispanic-American communities in Los Angeles often compete rather than cooperate, even though (or perhaps because) both can claim to be a disadvantaged minority community.[21] Thus, African-American labor leaders in Los Angeles have complained that affirmative action programs benefit Hispanic Americans rather than African Americans.[22] And in 1994, when Californians voted on Proposition 187, a controversial measure to cut off most public services to illegal immigrants, African Americans generally supported it, while a majority of Hispanic Americans strongly opposed it.[23]

In addition to divisions within and between minority communities, a third reason that the increasingly multicultural nature of American society may not bring about dramatic change is that increased multiculturalism is blurring the lines between different ethnic and racial groups. In recent years, the United States has witnessed a sharp rise in the number of interracial couples—some 1.2 million in 1992—and their children belong to multiple racial and ethnic groups. As pollsters have discovered, many of these people and others no longer know how to categorize themselves in terms of race, and many have requested

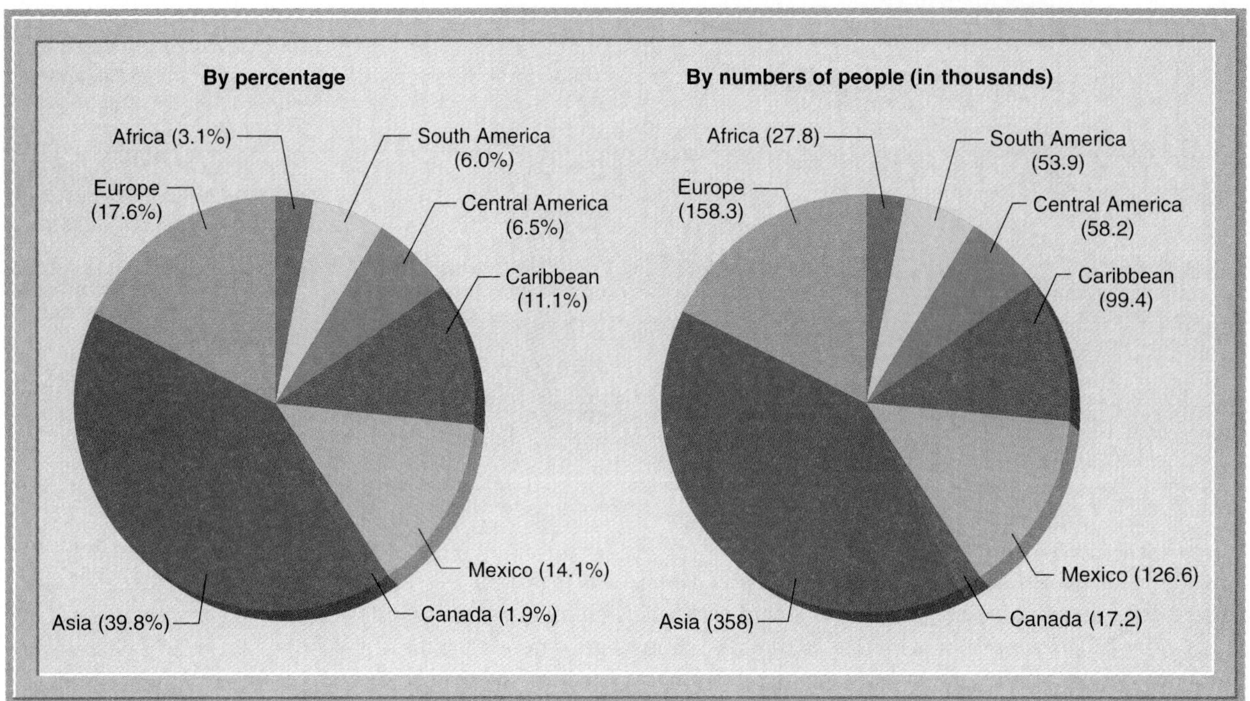

FIGURE 3.4
U.S. Immigration by World Region, 1993
Immigrants come to the United States from around the world.
Source: Data from *Statistical Abstract of the United States, 1995*, 115th ed. (Washington, D.C.: U.S. Bureau of the Census, 1995), p. 11.

the inclusion of a "multiracial" category in surveys and on public forms.[24] Indeed, a third of African Americans consider themselves multiracial.[25] And among whites, intermarriage rates among various ethnic groups are extremely high—in 1990, only one out of five white married couples had spouses of the same ethnic background.[26]

The rise of interracial marriage and the growing number of multiracial children has led to calls for the federal government to rethink its racial and ethnic categories. The Census Bureau has discussed using different categories when it conducts the next census in 2000, but the idea of changing the current racial and ethnic categories stirs up considerable political controversy. Some civil rights groups oppose adding a "multiracial" category to the census because they believe it will reduce the number of people counted as belonging to their group and thereby diminish their community's political clout. In a similar vein, the National Congress of American Indians opposes efforts by Sen. Daniel Akaka (D-Hawaii) to reclassify native Hawaiians as Native Americans because the move would entitle native Hawaiians to certain privileges currently restricted to American Indians.[27]

Immigration

It is trite but true to say that America is a country of immigrants. The rate of immigration, however, has fluctuated over time. Between 1901 and 1910, for example, almost 9 million people came to the United States as immigrants, a rate of 10 immigrants per 1,000 people in the U.S. population. The number of immigrants then declined, fluctuating between 500,000 to 4.5 million immigrants per decade from 1930 to 1980. Since then, the number of immigrants has increased dramatically, numbering 11 million from 1981 to 1993. Even with that increased number, however, the proportion of immigrants to the rest of the population is much lower than it was at the turn of the century.

Immigrants come to the United States from around the world. As figure 3.4 shows, of the 904,300 people legally admitted to the country in 1993, about 18 percent came from Europe, 40 percent from Asia, 6 percent from South America, and 3 percent from

America is a nation of immigrants and their descendents.

Steve Kelley/Copley News Service. Reprinted by permission.

Africa. The rest came from North America, particularly Mexico and countries in the Caribbean. More than 60 percent of the people admitted in 1993 were close family members of people who were already U.S. citizens or legal permanent residents. Another 15 percent were allowed in for employment purposes because they possessed special or unusual skills. The rest fell under other special circumstances, including fleeing political persecution in their homeland.[28]

Immigration has long been an explosive political issue. As chapter 5 discusses in greater detail, Congress has over the years responded to political pressures to limit immigration by establishing quotas designating how many people from a particular country may come to this country, or in some cases, by passing laws preventing any people from a particular country from immigrating. Currently, the political debate over immigration breaks down into two main issues. The first involves the appropriate level of legal immigration. Congress has addressed that issue several times in the last few decades. The most recent legislation, the Immigration Act of 1990, established a limit of about 700,000 new arrivals each year, but loopholes have allowed far more people to enter the country.

The second issue involves how best to stem illegal immigration. Estimates of the number of illegal immigrants in this country are imprecise, because people in such a predicament are unlikely to volunteer information about themselves to government agents such as census takers. In 1994, the Census Bureau estimated that between 3.5 million and 4 million people lived in the United States illegally, numbers reasonably consistent with the Immigration and Naturalization Service's 1992 estimate of 3.4 million. A third of the illegal immigrants are thought to come from Mexico, the rest from all other parts of the world. But the image of illegal immigrants scurrying across the border may be greatly exaggerated. The Immigration and Naturalization Service estimates that more than half of all illegal immigrants are visa overstays, that is, people who enter the country with a legal visa but then fail to leave when the visa expires.[29] About a third of illegal immigrants reside in California, with most of the rest living in New York, Texas, Florida, and Illinois. Each of those states has felt the financial burden of providing social services to illegal immigrants, and California and five other states went so far as to sue the federal government to cover those costs. In 1994, California voters also approved Proposition 187, which greatly limits the public services provided to illegal immigrants. (Federal judges have barred most of Proposition 187's provisions from going into effect while they consider lawsuits that challenge its constitutionality.)

Language

One source of great conflict in many countries with diverse populations is language. Predominantly English-speaking Canada, for example, has struggled with the problem of accommodating the interests of its French-speaking citizens in Quebec. Other countries, including Belgium and India, have struggled with ongoing problems between citizens of different language groups.

America's changing social composition has pushed language concerns onto the U.S. political agenda. The 1990 census found that 14 percent of Americans speak a language other than English at home. In California, the percentage was a great deal higher: 32 percent. New Mexico had the highest percentage at 36 percent. The most commonly spoken language, after English, was Spanish. The other most commonly spoken languages were (in order) French, German, Italian, Chinese, and Tagalog, a language spoken in the Philippines.

Recent immigrants to the United States do not appear less likely to learn English than their predecessors were. Almost all Hispanic Americans, for example, believe that everyone should learn to speak English.[30] Nonetheless, language has become a political issue in the United States. Groups such as U.S. English have lobbied to make English the official language, thereby abolishing multilingual ballots, forms, and educational programs.[31] By 1996, twenty-two states had adopted some version of an English-only amendment to their state constitutions, and the Supreme Court was poised to render a decision on the constitutionality of such laws.[32]

Age

Over the course of American history, the average age of the population has increased dramatically. In 1820, the median age was less than seventeen; by 1994, it was thirty-four. (The median age means that half of all people are older and half are younger.) The median age has risen in part because improvements in nutrition and medical care are cutting infant mortality rates and enabling adult Americans to live longer. It also has risen because Americans are marrying at later ages and having fewer children.

Changes in the age of the population have important political consequences. As figure 3.5 shows, the proportion of the nation's population that is sixty-five years of age or older has increased significantly during the twentieth century. Moreover, that trend is expected to continue well into the future as the **baby boomers**—usually defined as the large number of people born between the end of World War II and 1964—start to gray. As the population becomes older, more demands are made on the health care system and Social Security. Moreover, there are (and will be) fewer people in the work force in proportion to the number who are retired. This means fewer workers will be available to pay the taxes needed to finance these programs. In 1950, for instance, there were fifteen workers for every retiree; in 1990, there were only five; and experts predict that by 2030 there will be fewer than three.[33] (Other countries are facing similar aging in their populations. For example, when roughly 25 percent of Americans are over sixty-five years old in 2025, the proportion in Germany will be 30 percent and in Japan, 31 percent.[34]) On the flip side, when the proportion of younger people grows, governmental attention is directed toward other problems, notably education (because the young are the primary consumers) and crime (because the young are much more likely to commit crimes).

Baby boomers
The generation of Americans born between 1946 and 1964.

Family Households

The social units in which Americans live their lives have changed in recent decades. About 81 percent of Americans still live in a family—that is, with people they are related to by birth, marriage, or adoption. But the size of the typical family household has declined from 3.7 people in 1960 to 3.2 in 1994. The declining size of the American household stems in part from the sharp rise in the number of people living in nonfamily households, many of whom live alone. Moreover, many people now delay marrying and starting families, and once couples marry, they have fewer children than their parents and grandparents did.

Perhaps the most significant change in the family has been in the number of children living with one parent, a figure that more than doubled from 13 percent in 1970

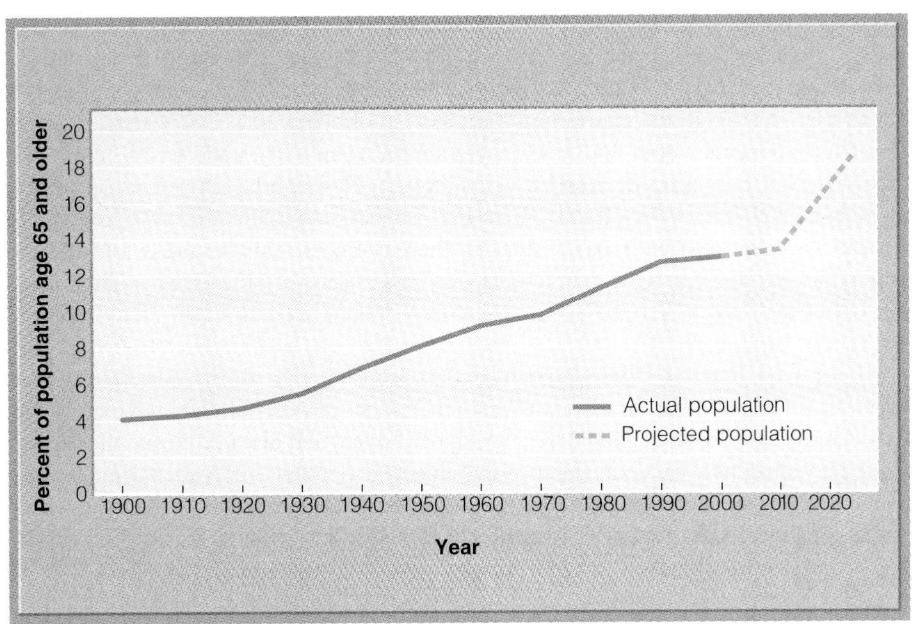

FIGURE 3.5
Percent of U.S. Population Age 65 and Older, 1900–2025

The number of elderly people in the United States has been steadily increasing for decades and will continue to increase, a situation that creates serious economic risks as the ratio of workers to retirees shrinks.

Source: Data from *Statistical Abstract of the United States, 1995*, 115th ed. (Washington, D.C.: U.S. Bureau of the Census, 1995), p. 25.

to 31 percent in 1994. Mothers head most single-parent homes. This trend has been particularly pronounced in African-American and Hispanic-American families: in 1994, 65 percent and 36 percent, respectively, were single-parent households. Divorce and abandonment account for part of the rise in single-family households. A third reason is that single women are increasingly choosing to have children. For example, in 1994, 30 percent of African-American children under the age of eighteen lived with a mother who had never been married, up steeply from 4 percent in 1970. The comparable figures for white and Hispanic-American children were 4 percent and 11 percent, respectively, both up from negligible percentages in 1970.

Although African-American women have a higher rate of out-of-wedlock births, far more children are born to unwed white mothers than to African-American mothers every year. (Keep in mind that whites far outnumber African Americans in the general population.) Moreover, only around 30 percent of out-of-wedlock births are to teenage mothers; the vast majority are to women in their twenties. And while the rising number of children born to unwed mothers is a significant social problem in the United States (30 percent of all births in 1992), the rate of such births is actually much higher in several other industrialized countries, including Sweden (50 percent of all births), Denmark (46 percent), France (33 percent), and the United Kingdom (31 percent).[35]

The rising number of single-parent households is important because it places greater demands on government. Single-parent households are much more likely to be poor and, as a result, to require welfare or other government assistance. At the same time, a working parent in a single-parent household needs greater access to affordable child care.

Sexual Orientation

Since the early 1970s, the gay rights movement has actively sought to extend civil rights protections to gay and lesbian Americans, as chapter 5 discusses. Yet the number of people considered gay or lesbian is in question. For several decades, the most widely accepted estimate was that 10 percent of the population was gay or lesbian. In the 1990s, however, several studies suggested that the percentage of gays and lesbians in the population is smaller, probably under 3 percent.[36]

Does it matter if gays and lesbians constitute only 3 percent of the population rather than 10 percent? In politics, the answer is usually yes. Groups on both sides of the gay rights battle have fought over which estimates to use because they believe that public acceptance of the gay rights cause depends on perceptions of the size of the gay and lesbian community. As a representative of the National Gay and Lesbian Task Force said about the conflicting estimates: "Politically, it's a very sensitive subject. Our opponents would like to say there are thirty-nine of us and we all live in the Castro in San Francisco or Greenwich Village in New York." In the same vein, a member of the conservative Family Research Council complained that the 10 percent figure "has been used with great effect by the gay rights lobby to press for political power and extra civil rights protections. It's been used to tell businessmen that 10 percent of their work force is gay and that they should accommodate them like they do African Americans."[37]

Politically, gays, lesbians, and bisexuals lean heavily toward the Democratic Party. In 1990 and 1992, for example, more than three-quarters of the gay vote went to Democratic congressional candidates. But gay, lesbian, and bisexual ties to the Democratic Party may be weakening. In the 1994 midterm elections, 40 percent of gays, lesbians, and bisexuals voted for Republican congressional candidates.[38] As a leader of the Log Cabin Republicans—a group of gay Republicans—observed, "Among all minority groups, the gay vote showed the greatest shift toward the GOP in 1994."[39]

Social and Economic Characteristics

Race, ethnicity, immigration, language, age, household makeup, and sexual orientation tell only one part of the story of who Americans are as a people. Another way to tell the story is to examine the social and economic makeup of the United States. In this section, we explore five social and economic characteristics that have great political relevance: religion, education, wealth, home ownership, and occupation.

Religion

A cursory glance around the world is all it takes to understand the importance of religion in politics. Different religious beliefs continue to fuel conflict between countries (for example, predominantly Hindu India and Moslem Pakistan) and within countries (for example, Protestants and Catholics in Northern Ireland). But religion has generated little civil strife in the United States.

America is based, in theory if not always in practice, on a strong belief in religious freedom. Religious activity of all sorts abounds. The number of active religious denominations is difficult to pin down, but credible estimates put it somewhere between two hundred and one thousand. Roughly 70 percent of Americans say they belong to an organized denomination (although only a bit more than 40 percent say they regularly attend services), and a much higher percentage say they hold religious beliefs.[40] Of Americans who identify with a denomination, 94 percent are Christian, 2 percent are Jewish, and just under 2 percent are Muslim.

Christians in the United States represent a staggering number of different churches. Roman Catholics form the single largest group, with more than 59 million members. Catholics are found in the largest numbers in the Northeast and industrial Midwest, and, with the influx of Hispanic immigrants, in the Southwest. Baptists are the second largest denomination, with almost 30 million members. About half are Southern Baptists, with the rest scattered among some twenty other Baptist denominations. Baptists are concentrated in the southern states. About 20 percent of all Americans belong to one of the so-called mainline Protestant denominations—Episcopalians, Lutherans, Methodists, and Presbyterians. Most other denominations are small, and only the Mormons are geographically concentrated in significant enough numbers to dominate politics in a state (Utah, and, to a lesser extent, Idaho).

Jews represent a very small percentage of the U.S. population: about 2 percent. But as with minority groups, people often greatly overestimate the number of Jews.

Roughly half of all Americans think that more than 20 percent of Americans are Jewish.[41] But New York is the only state where Jews constitute even 10 percent of the population. Although the Jewish population in the United States is just slightly larger than the Muslim population, Jewish organizations are much more active and widely thought to influence politics, particularly American policy toward Israel.[42]

Religion matters because religious beliefs influence the political behavior of many Americans. But the ability of religious leaders to influence the political beliefs of their followers varies. Catholics, for example, are split on the issue of abortion rights despite their church's unequivocal opposition to abortion.[43] Similarly, the liberal policy preferences of mainline Protestant church leaders diverge from the thinking of many of their members.[44] Indeed, an important point to remember about religion in American politics is that important political differences exist not only *among* religious groups, but also *within* them.[45] Only a few denominations—predominantly, but not exclusively, fundamentalist churches aligned with the Republican Party—possess the social characteristics necessary to produce political conformity among their members.[46] Otherwise, religious groups do not form cohesive political blocs.

Education

Education is a critical issue in American politics. For the individual, education is usually the key to getting a better job and earning more money over a lifetime. For the nation, education is an important factor in making the country competitive in the world economy. Not surprisingly, education is one of the most important activities the government undertakes. Roughly 90 percent of all primary and secondary students are enrolled in public schools, and public colleges and universities account for about 80 percent of all college students. Federal, state, and local governments spend more than $360 billion on education each year.

Americans today have completed far more schooling than their parents and grandparents did. As recently as 1940, only about 25 percent of American adults had finished four years of high school. Now that figure stands at more than 80 percent. The percentage of the population with at least four years of college also has gone up dramatically, from less than 5 percent in 1940 to 22 percent in 1994. Education levels are higher in the West than in the rest of the county, and higher in metropolitan areas than rural areas.

Educational attainment also varies by race and sex. Whites graduate from high school at a higher rate than African Americans and Hispanic Americans, although over the last decade, African Americans have virtually closed that gap. In 1993, almost 75 percent of African American adults had graduated from high school—up from 67 percent in 1973—while 83 percent of whites and 61 percent of Hispanic Americans had high school degrees.[47] (The most recent data on American Indians, from 1990, show that 66 percent are high school graduates.) At the college level, whites graduate at a higher rate than African Americans, Hispanic Americans, and American Indians. But Asian-American graduation rates surpass those of whites. (Among all ethnic groups in the United States, the best educated is people of Egyptian heritage; some 60 percent have at least a bachelor's degree. Other highly educated American ethnic groups are Iranians, Nigerians, Taiwanese, and Pakistanis.)[48]

Over the last fifty years, women, like men, have increased their average educational level. Until 1980, women were more likely than men to graduate from high school. Now the balance has tilted slightly the other way. Men have always been more likely than women to graduate from college, and in 1994, 25 percent of men over the age of twenty-five had at least a bachelor's degree, compared to almost 20 percent of women. But this, too, may be changing. Among people who graduated from high school in 1980, a slightly higher percentage of women than men had earned an undergraduate degree by 1986.

Although movies and television often portray Americans as rich, the median household income in 1995 was only $30,076—and even less for most minority households—hardly lending itself to the life-style of the rich and famous.

Wealth and Income

The distribution of wealth and income in a country often reflects social class. Many critics of capitalism, for example, argue that the upper class benefits by exploiting the labor of the lower class. Indeed, in many countries, politics is organized around class conflict.

Yet class rarely has been an important political issue in the United States. Despite objective evidence to suggest that lower, middle, and upper classes do exist in this country, Americans generally do not think in class terms. Using Census Bureau definitions, 63 percent of Americans could be classified as middle class in 1990, down from the high point of 71 percent in 1969. Almost 15 percent qualified as high income.[49] But in one recent survey, 94 percent of Americans identified themselves as middle class![50] Exploiting class distinctions holds little political payoff when most people see themselves as members of the same group. Nor does knowing that someone is middle class tell us anything about his or her politics because in the United States social class usually has not been an important basis for beliefs or action.

Still, *middle class* is a term loaded with political meaning. Because most Americans think of themselves as middle class, elected officials usually try to pitch their pet programs as good for the middle class. In 1995, for example, both President Clinton and congressional Republicans offered tax cut proposals that they said would benefit the middle class. For many Republican members of Congress, that definition extended to people earning up to $200,000 a year, while Democrats tended to peg the top figure at $75,000. When asked how he defined middle class, Speaker of the House Newt Gingrich (R-Ga.) said, "I think it's a state of mind . . . It's a psychological, not an economic figure, and I think the minute you start putting numbers in there it gets pretty weird."[51] As if to demonstrate the Speaker's point, first term Rep. Frederick Heineman (R-N.C.) claimed that the fact that he receives a $133,600 salary as a member of Congress and a $50,000-a-year pension from his days as a police officer "does not make me rich. That does not make me middle class. In my opinion that makes me lower middle class. When I see someone who is making anywhere from $300,000 to $750,000 a year, that's middle class."[52] Using Representative Heineman's definition, less than one percent of the country is middle class.

Wealth and income are distributed unevenly in the United States. The share of national income the highest-paid 20 percent of the American public receives actually has increased in recent years, from 44 percent in 1967 to 49 percent in 1995. The income share of the lowest-paid 20 percent of the public declined during that same period from 4 percent to 3.7 percent. Figure 3.6 shows another way to look at income distribution in the United States. The median household income in 1993 was $31,241. Fewer than 13 percent of the households in the country earned more than $75,000, while more than 23 percent made less than $15,000.

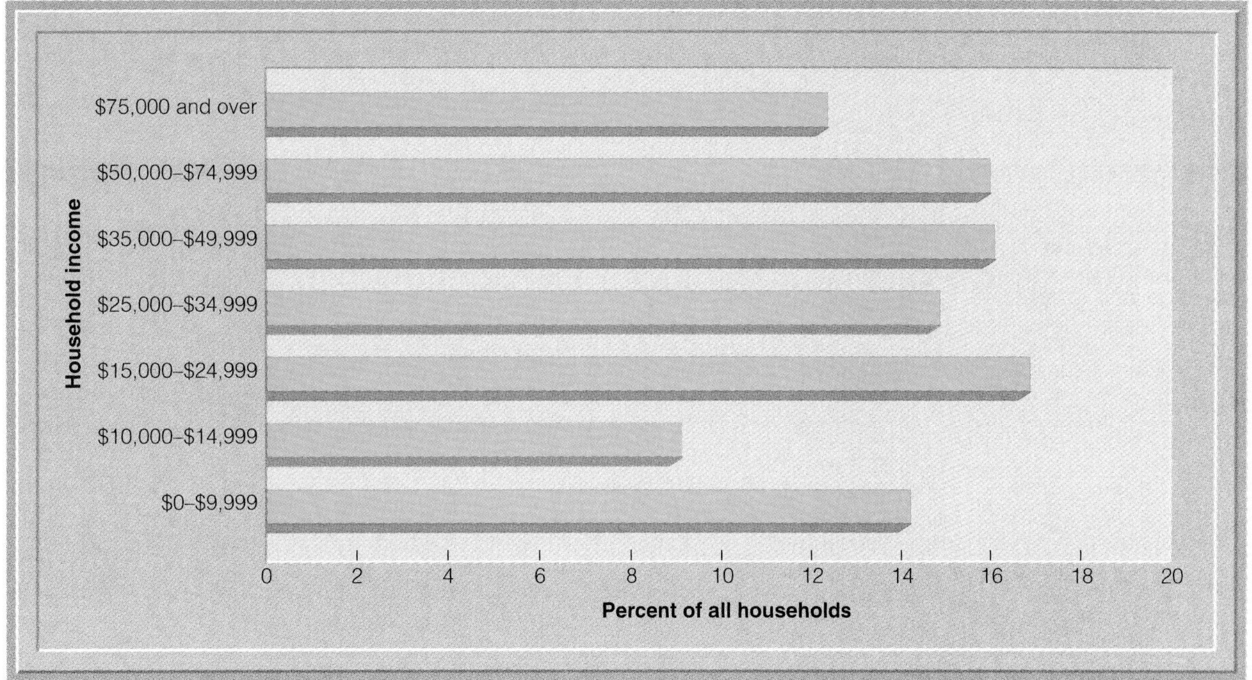

FIGURE 3.6
U.S. Household Income, 1993

Most Americans are middle class; relatively few are very poor or very rich.

Source: Data from *Statistical Abstract of the United States, 1995*, 115th ed. (Washington, D.C.: U.S. Bureau of the Census, 1995), p. 469.

Income in the United States is strongly linked to race and education. The median income for white households in 1995 was $35,766, while Hispanic-American households averaged $22,860 and African-American households just $22,393. Asian-American households earned the most: $40,614. The impact of education on income is even more striking. In 1995, a college graduate earned an average of $37,224, while a person who failed to complete high school earned just $13,697.

The income figures in figure 3.6 show that many Americans are poor. In 1995, the Census Bureau considered a family of four earning less than $15,569 a year to live below the poverty line. Figure 3.7 shows the percentage of all Americans living in poverty since 1960 (based on the yearly poverty line the Census Bureau establishes, as box 3.2 discusses). From 1960 to 1970, the percentage of poor people dropped almost in half, in large part because of the success of the federal government's concerted attack on the problem, including many of the Great Society programs President Lyndon Johnson initiated.[53] Since 1970, the percentage of Americans living below the poverty line has fluctuated between 10 and 15 percent of the population, standing at 13.8 percent in 1995.

Figure 3.8a shows that African Americans and Hispanic Americans are roughly three times more likely than whites to live in poverty. (The most impoverished group in America comprises American Indians who live on reservations, where more than 20 percent of the households live on annual incomes of less than $5,000.)[54] But while minorities do not fare as well as whites, the problem of poverty is not limited to minorities. As figure 3.8b shows, *far more poor people are white than African American or Hispanic American.* The reason that whites constitute the single largest group of poor Americans is that they are by far the largest group in the country, so even a small percentage of whites in poverty translates into a large number. Moreover, poverty does

Figure 3.7
U.S. Poverty Rate, 1960–1994

After declining during the 1960s, the poverty rate has stabilized at between 10 and 15 percent of the public.

Sources: Data from Dana Milbank, "Poverty Measure Declined in 1994: Income Stagnated," *Wall Street Journal,* 6 October 1995; Harold W. Stanley and Richard G. Niemi, *Vital Statistics on American Politics,* 5th ed. (Washington, D.C.: CQ Press, 1995), p. 351.

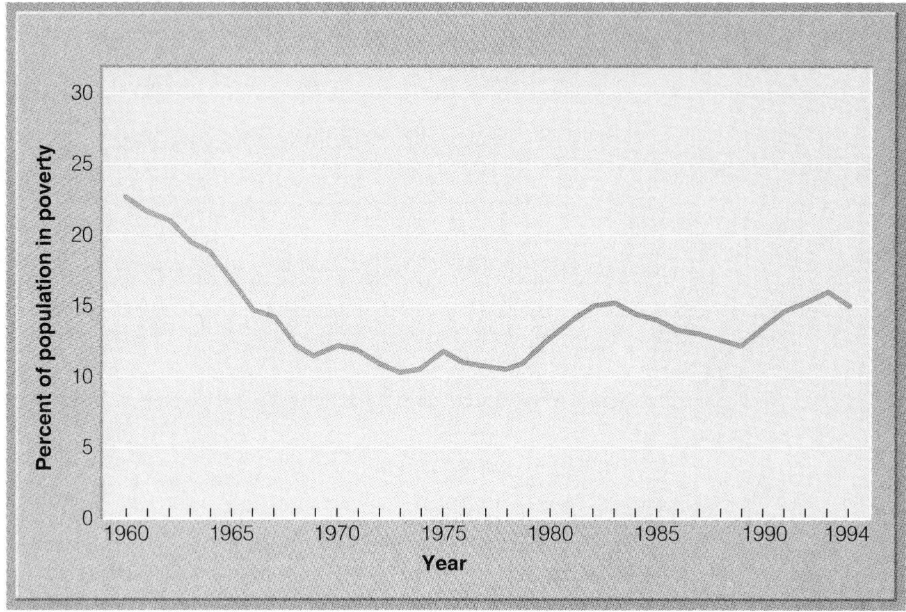

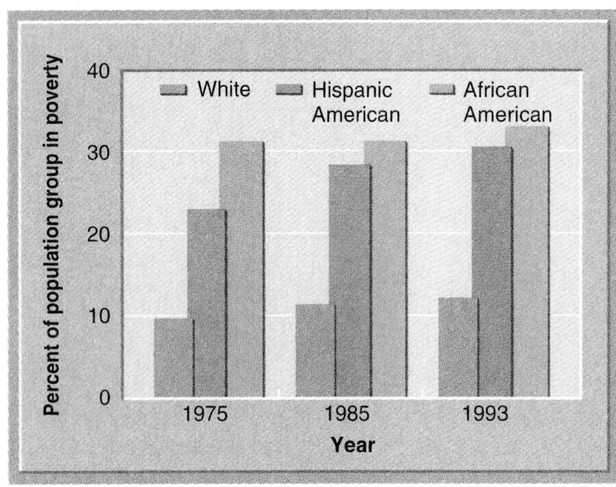

(a)

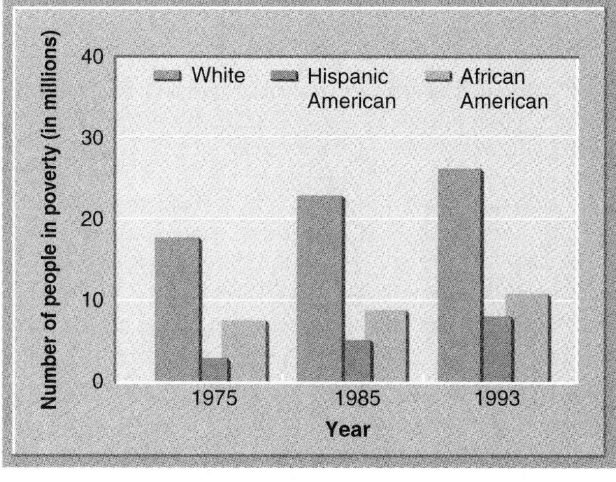

(b)

Figure 3.8

(a) Percentage of U.S. Poor by Race and Ethnicity, 1975–1993

A smaller percentage of white Americans is poor than African and Hispanic Americans.

(b) Number of U.S. Poor by Race and Ethnicity, 1975–1993

The number of poor white Americans is much larger than the number of poor African and Hispanic Americans.

Source: Data from *Statistical Abstract of the United States, 1995,* 115th ed. (Washington, D.C.: U.S. Bureau of the Census, 1995), p. 480.

not limit itself to the inner cities, but affects rural areas and even the suburbs as well. Politically, these figures suggest that characterizations of poverty as a problem facing minorities alone are dead wrong.

Poverty in the United States is associated with age as well as with race. Children are much more likely to be poor than older people. In 1993, 22 percent of children under the age of eighteen lived in poverty—the highest figure among industrialized nations. African-American and Hispanic-American children were particularly hard pressed, with 46 percent and 40 percent of them, respectively, living in poverty. In contrast, the poverty rate for people over sixty-five years of age is lower than the

POINT OF ORDER

BOX 3.2

Figuring the Poverty Rate

Mollie Orshansky developed the basic measure the federal government uses to calculate the poverty line in the United States.

In 1963, Mollie Orshansky, an employee of the U.S. Department of Health, Education, and Welfare (the predecessor to today's Department of Health and Human Services) developed a crude measure of poverty to assess how many older Americans lived in dire financial conditions. The poverty index she created was relatively simple. It took the Agriculture Department's estimate of how much money an individual needed for food each year, and multiplied that number by three to account for all other basic living expenses. The final figure was then adjusted to take different family sizes into account.

The measure might have languished in obscurity had President Lyndon Johnson not needed a national measure of poverty as part of his War on Poverty. Johnson seized on Orshansky's measure, and ever since, each October brings the Census Bureau's announcement of the poverty figure for the previous year, triggering a debate about the improving or deteriorating financial well-being of the American public. But more hangs on the poverty figure than just the image of how well Americans are faring. The numbers are used to help determine eligibility standards for some twenty-seven federal programs, including the Food Stamps program, Head Start, Medicaid, and school lunches.

But does this simple measure really capture the level of poverty in America? Surprisingly, given the figure's long history and political importance, no one argues that it does. One liberal critic asserts the measure is "completely outdated, with a technique that makes no sense." A conservative economist exclaims, "The Census Bureau stuff isn't even on the right planet." Even the Census Bureau official in charge of compiling data on poverty admits, "the current measure is flawed." But that does not mean people agree on a replacement measure, or even on how much poverty exists in the United States. Some people think the real poverty figure is higher than what is currently reported, while others think fewer people live in poverty than the official figure suggests.

People who think that Orshansky's measure for calculating the poverty line understates poverty note that it does not take into account regional differences in the cost of living. As a result, it probably underestimates the number of poor people residing in more expensive urban areas and overestimates the number of poor people living in lower-cost rural areas. Similarly, the measure does not assess the rising costs of child care, medical coverage, and transportation. Many economists think families now spend only one-quarter of their income on food, not the one-third that Orshansky's measure assumes. Including better estimates of such expenses might swell the ranks of the poor by several percentage points.

People who think that Orshansky's measure overstates poverty point out that it fails to take into account "in-kind" benefits the government provides, such as food stamps, subsidized housing, school lunches, and home energy assistance. The measure also fails to take into account the effect of tax credits such as the Earned Income Tax Credit that help boost the incomes of the working poor. If these benefits were counted, then the number of people thought to live in poverty would fall. The Census Bureau estimates that including in-kind and credit benefits would have reduced the poverty level in 1993 from 15.1 percent to 12.1 percent.

In May 1995, a committee of thirteen professors, charged by the government with studying the issue, produced a five-hundred-page report suggesting changes to the way the government measures poverty. The report responded to many of the criticisms leveled against the current measure. It proposed a new poverty measure that would take into account in-kind benefits as well as expenses such as child care and medical care that are not incorporated in the current measure. The report concluded that the new measure would create a slight increase in the number of poor people in the United States. Although the authors of the report were highly respected for their expertise, the federal government did not adopt their proposed measure. Orshansky's measure remains basically unaltered because changing the method of calculating the poverty line is a politically charged undertaking.

Sources: Neela Banerjee, "Debate Over Measuring the Poverty Line Will Come to a Head in Senate Hearing," *Wall Street Journal,* 12 May 1994; Dana Milbank, "Old Flaws Undermine New Poverty-Level Data," *Wall Street Journal,* 5 October 1995; Robert Pear, "Experts' Concept of Poverty Makes More People Poor," *Des Moines Register,* 30 April 1995; *Statistical Abstract of the United States, 1995,* 115th ed. (Washington, D.C.: U.S. Bureau of the Census, 1995), pp. 450, 485.

national average, at just over 12 percent in 1993. As recently as 1970, almost 25 percent of older Americans lived in poverty. Social Security, Medicare, and other government programs have, in large part, lifted senior citizens out of poverty.[55]

Another important characteristic of poverty is its strong association with sex and family status. Women are more likely than men to be poor, particularly women heading a single-parent household. In 1979, 35 percent of households headed by single women fell under the poverty line. By 1992, that number had risen to 39 percent. Even more striking, 53 percent of households headed by single African-American or Hispanic-American women were poor.[56] The fact that families headed by women account for a growing share of the people who live below the poverty line is often referred to as the **feminization of poverty.**

Feminization of poverty
The trend in the United States in which families headed by women account for a growing share of the people who live below the poverty line.

Income figures have obvious political implications. For example, although millions of Americans live in poverty, they form too small a percentage of the population to influence policy making except when they can form coalitions with other groups in society. For example, the poor are too few in number to account for the creation and continuation of the Food Stamps program, a very expensive but successful federal government program designed to limit hunger in America. But those promoting the interests of the poor aligned with agricultural and food processing interests to develop and support a program that benefits each group.

Home Ownership

A big part of the American Dream has always been to own one's own home. In 1994, 64 percent of households lived in homes they owned. The percentage of married couples owning their own home was even higher—79 percent. But both figures represent a slight drop in home ownership over the last decade, the first such decline since the Depression years of the 1930s. Not surprisingly, given the income figures we just discussed, a higher percentage of whites own their own homes than do African Americans or Hispanic Americans. Also, a much higher percentage of older people are homeowners: 34 percent of those twenty-five to twenty-nine years old own homes, compared to 80 percent of those sixty to sixty-four years old.

Not all Americans have a place to live. The number of homeless people is difficult to pin down, but credible estimates range from fifty thousand to 3 million, and almost all observers agree that the number has grown since 1980.[57] One 1994 study claimed some 13.5 million Americans have experienced homelessness for at least a few days during their lives. The chronic homeless were likely to be men and minorities. Other studies suggest that many of the homeless suffer from mental illness and addictions.[58] A 1994 survey of thirty city governments found that they had spent more than $230 million on programs to provide shelter and services for the homeless.[59]

Home ownership and homelessness have important political consequences. For example, tax policy favors homeowners because of the generous tax deduction for interest paid on mortgages. Renters do not get a similar break. But property taxes, the main source of revenue for local governments and school districts, fall directly on landowners. Homeowners also differ politically from renters in that homeowners are more likely to vote, and ownership may make people more conservative in their political outlook.[60]

Occupation

The most important change in the American economic landscape over the last century has been in what Americans do for a living. In 1880, 44 percent of the population lived and worked on farms. By 1990, that number had dwindled to less than 2 percent. The number of farms has declined from four million in 1880 to just 1.9 million in 1992.[61] At first, Americans left the farm to work in manufacturing industries such as steel and automobiles. In recent years, however, jobs in the service industries, which may be as simple as flipping hamburgers and as complex as working in the health care, computer, and education fields, have eclipsed manufacturing jobs. By some estimates, service industries now employ upward of 70 percent of Americans.

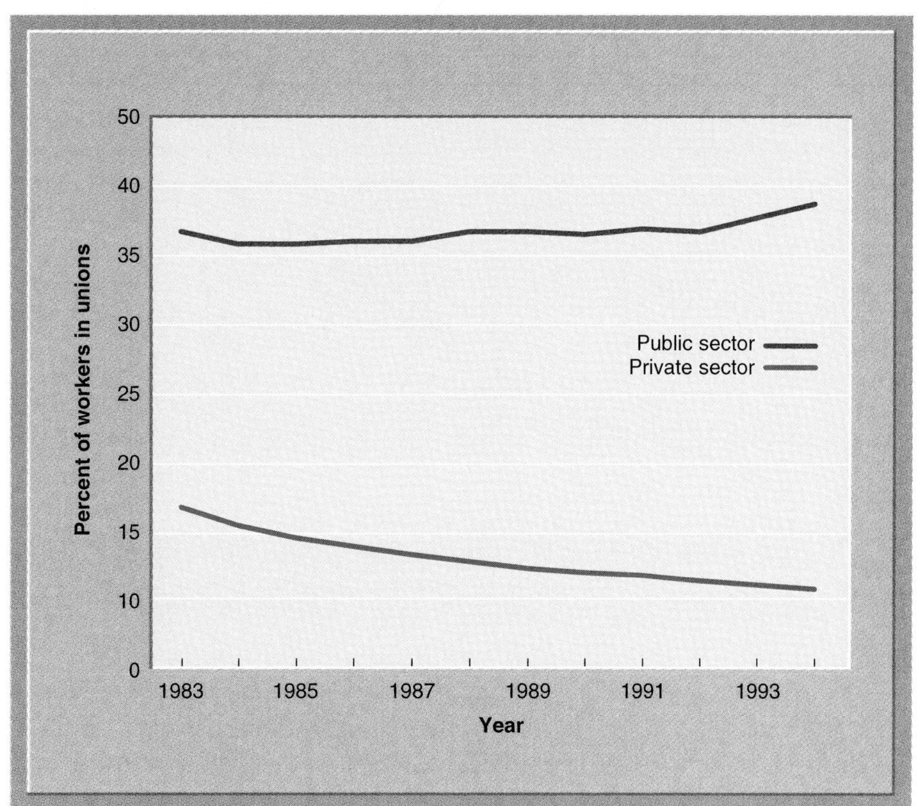

FIGURE 3.9
Unionization Trends, Public vs. Private Sector, 1983–1994

Since 1983, unionization in the private sector has continued to drop, but public sector unionization remains strong.

Source: Data from "Uncle Sam Gompers," *Wall Street Journal,* 25 November 1995.

The shift from a manufacturing economy to a service economy has been accompanied by a change in where Americans work. Fewer Americans work for large companies today than in years past. Indeed, the percentage of the work force that Fortune 500 companies (the five hundred largest companies in the country) employ has fallen by half over the last two decades.[62] The growing importance of small business to the American economy has many implications for politics. For example, small firms are less able to provide health benefits than large ones, which puts more pressure on the government to do so.[63] Indeed, when President Clinton took office in 1993, one of his top priorities was to find a way to provide health insurance and benefits for all Americans, and one of his most controversial proposals was to require small businesses to contribute to health care coverage for their employees.

Along with the shift from manufacturing to services and the increased importance of small businesses, a third major change in the American work force has been the declining importance of unions. In 1955, the percentage of all nonagricultural workers belonging to unions stood at 32 percent, but this figure has fallen steadily since then, dropping to 14.9 percent in 1995.[64] As figure 3.9 shows, in recent years union membership has been strong and even growing slightly in the public sector, but weak and getting weaker in the private sector. Overall membership in labor unions fell in part because highly organized manufacturing industries such as automobiles and steel laid off many workers, and in part because government policies favored management at the expense of unions. The decline in union membership, in turn, has diminished the ability of organized labor to influence government policy. And because most unions favor Democratic candidates, dwindling union membership has weakened the Democratic Party.

A fourth major change in the American labor force is the increasing number of working women. As figure 3.10 shows, the percentage of women either working outside the home or actively seeking such employment almost doubled between 1950 and 1994. Sixty-one percent of married women now work outside the home. Perhaps even more striking, the percentage of women with children under the age of six who work outside the home rose from 19 percent in 1960 to 62 percent in 1994. On average,

FIGURE 3.10

Percent of Women in U.S. Work Force, 1950–1994

Far more women are in the work force now than forty years ago, bringing new issues to the political agenda.

Sources: Data from Harold W. Stanley and Richard G. Niemi, *Vital Statistics on American Politics,* 4th ed. (Washington, D.C.: CQ Press, 1994), p. 430; *Statistical Abstract of the United States, 1995,* 115th ed. (Washington D.C.: U.S. Bureau of the Census, 1995), p. 400.

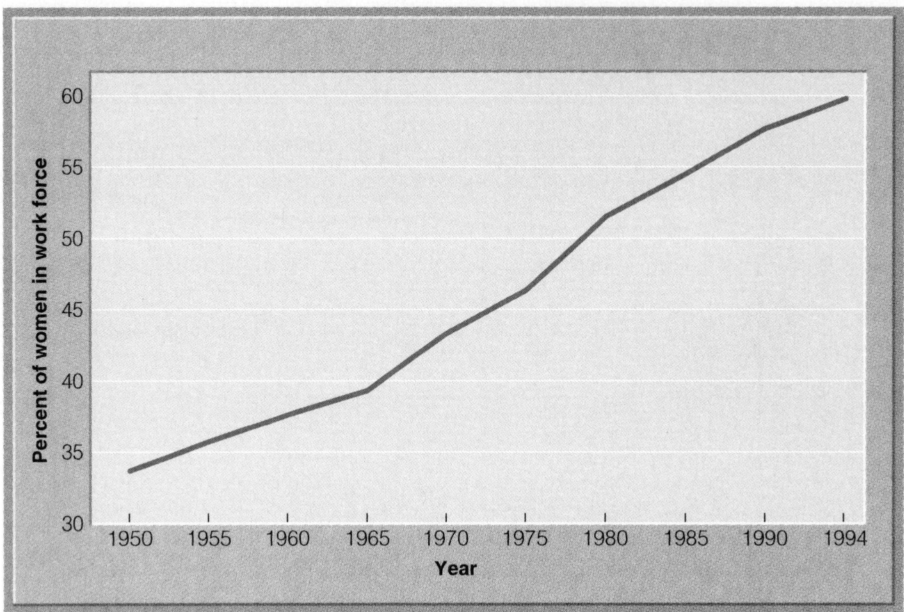

women still do not make as much money as men, but that gap has narrowed in recent years. In 1977, women made 59 percent of what men earned; in 1994, they made 76 percent of what men made. Among younger age cohorts, where women and men have more comparable educational and work experience, the gap narrows significantly. For example, according to one study, "Among people age twenty-seven to thirty-three who have never had a child, the earnings of women are close to 98 percent of men's."[65] Indeed, some have argued that the widening income gap in the United States stems in large part from the increase in two-income families, particularly those with two high-income earners.[66] The influx of women into the labor force has forced a host of new issues such as child care, sexual harassment in the workplace, and comparable pay onto the political agenda.

Finally, over the last three decades, unemployment rates have fluctuated between 3 and 10 percent. Unemployment rates are higher for minorities than for whites, and higher for younger people than for older people. Typically, the highest rate is among African-American males between the ages of sixteen and nineteen. Unemployment is, of course, a politically sensitive issue. Presidents and members of Congress often see their political fortunes tied to the unemployment rate. Unemployment has budgetary costs as well. People out of work may draw unemployment compensation, and they do not pay many taxes.

DIVERSITY AND SOCIAL HARMONY

The diversity of American society is unparalleled in the world. Yet in many other countries, diversity is a source of political conflict and instability. While America's murder rate shows it to be a violent society, and while civil disorders such as the 1992 Los Angeles riots occasionally occur, perhaps the most exceptional fact about American society is that, with the tragic exception of the Civil War, its diverse population has managed to avoid widespread social unrest. One reason for this stability is that, for the most part, the social and economic cleavages or divisions that might threaten American society do not coincide to create sharply distinct, homogeneous groups. That is, differences between rich and poor, white and non-white, Protestant and Catholic, and labor and management are not the same.

Cross-cutting cleavages
Divisions that split society into small groups so that people have different allies and opponents in different policy areas and no group forms a majority on all issues.

We call these divisions **cross-cutting cleavages,** because the lines that divide, for example, rich and poor, may cut across a variety of social, racial, and ethnic groups. Cross-cutting cleavages tend to dampen social conflict. Thus, not all African

Unemployment is generally higher now than a generation ago. Fears about job loss have increased Americans' sense of economic insecurity.

Americans or Catholics are poor, not all Protestants and whites are wealthy, and not all Hispanic Americans and Muslims hold blue-collar jobs. Every racial, ethnic, and religious group is represented (though not necessarily equally) in management and labor. Indeed, most members of every major social group in the United States (and group membership is overlapping) are likely to be middle class.

The tremendous diversity of American society, then, is in many ways its strength. It prevents the government from catering to the interests of one group of Americans to the exclusion of others, thereby lessening the chances for political violence. Instead, the government must respond to a number of different, often competing, concerns. In turn, both political parties are forced to seek political support in the same social, religious, and economic groups. In 1996, for example, both the Democratic and Republican candidates for president gained substantial support from almost every social and economic group in the United States. Conflict does exist in the United States, but cross-cutting cleavages help dampen it. If cleavages begin to reinforce one another, as some recent commentators worry, social unrest may increase and threaten America's social and political stability.

Political Power in the United States

Regardless of background, many Americans share the belief that the government does not take their interests into account. One does not have to look too hard to find complaints that government by the people has become government by an elite. (Whether Big Business, Big Labor, or some other group plays the villain in such complaints depends on who is doing the complaining.) Who, then, wields political power in the United States? Is political power distributed equally, or do some groups of people have more than others? We argue that **pluralism** characterizes our political system—that is, different groups tend to exercise power on different issues.

Pluralism
The theory that political power is spread widely and that different groups of people exercise power on different issues.

Defining and measuring power is a difficult and controversial task that lies well beyond the scope of this book. For our purposes here, however, power can be defined simply as the ability of person A to get person B to do something person B would not otherwise do. For instance, if the National Rifle Association persuades a senator to drop her support for gun control, or if the National Association of Manufacturers convinces the president to push for lower corporate taxes, we normally say that these groups have exercised power.

Comparing two landmark studies of power in American cities is a useful way to examine the distribution of political influence because the basics of what we learn at the local level can apply to the national level. Although these studies are now dated and other researchers have since done much more work on these questions, we discuss them because they draw a simple and stark distinction between competing notions of how American politics works.[67] One study found that power is concentrated in the hands of a few elite leaders, whereas the other found power distributed among different groups—a finding consistent with the idea of pluralism.

The first study, Floyd Hunter's investigation of Atlanta in the early 1950s, argued that a power elite composed of a small group of powerful white men who interacted socially at country clubs and churches dominated the city.[68] Most of the members of the power elite were business leaders; very few were politicians. Hunter claimed these men acted behind the scenes to enact policies that benefited their economic interests and protected the city's political and social status quo.

Hunter's findings are consistent with a belief many Americans express, that they are politically powerless because a small elite dominates politics. Before accepting Hunter's conclusions as fact, however, it is important to understand how he reached them. Hunter identified Atlanta's power elite by first asking community leaders (the chamber of commerce, League of Women Voters, and newspaper editors, for example) to provide names of people they thought were powerful. Using these names, he then asked other community observers to develop a list of the forty people he would examine as the power elite. One might question why Hunter settled on forty people and not twenty or one hundred or one thousand, but an even more important objection arises. By asking people who they thought composed Atlanta's power elite, Hunter assumed that such an elite group existed; yet he never showed that this elite actually influenced city government. Because reputations often bear little relation to reality, Hunter's findings should be treated with skepticism.

One of the many studies to follow Hunter's was Robert Dahl's examination of political power in New Haven, Connecticut.[69] As Hunter had done in Atlanta, Dahl tried to determine who belonged to New Haven's power elite. But he went further to see if the elite actually exercised power across a broad range of issues in the city. He found that no single power elite controlled New Haven. The people and groups that influenced urban renewal differed from those who influenced educational issues, who in turn differed from those who influenced nominations for political office. Dahl found that New Haven's business leaders exercised power on relatively few issues.

Dahl's findings are consistent with the idea of pluralism, which holds that political power is widely dispersed in the United States and that different groups of people exercise power on different issues. *Although pluralism rejects the claim that a single political elite wields power in the United States, it recognizes that Americans do not share political or economic power equally.* No one would argue, for example, that the homeless have as much influence as corporate executives on government policy, or that politicians pay as much attention to the views of college students as to those of senior citizens. Yet, while it acknowledges that political inequalities exist in the United States, pluralism holds that American politics can be best understood as the result of bargaining among competing groups rather than the outcome of decisions made by some small political elite.

In the context of national politics, then, pluralism tells us that the voices heard on gun control differ from those heard on farm subsidies, which in turn differ from those that influence welfare policies or defense spending. As we will show in later chapters, especially in the discussion of interest group politics in chapter 10, American society has produced a dizzying array of groups designed to promote the political, economic, and social interests of their members. These so-called interest groups tend to focus their attention on their narrow area of concern and generally try to influence government policy only within that limited area. Thus, only a small number of interest groups are active on most issues that come before government. And those groups, regardless of the interests they represent, tend to be dominated by wealthier and better educated people.

The distribution of political power in Atlanta has changed over the years. In the 1950s William Hartsfield was finishing his long run as mayor of Atlanta. In 1993, Atlantans elected Bill Campbell mayor.

Because the wealthy and well educated tend to dominate interest groups, pluralism can be thought of as a system of competing elites. Yet, the membership of these elite groups varies across policy issues, and the identity and composition of the elite on any policy issue is likely to change over time. Consider the situation in Atlanta, for example. In many important respects, Atlanta in the 1990s looks nothing like the Atlanta Hunter described in the early 1950s. Although Atlanta's African-American community still does not share equally in the city's economic wealth, it does dominate city politics. Indeed, since the 1970s, African Americans have held every major elected position in Atlanta, including the office of mayor, and in 1993, all three major candidates for mayor were African American.

American politics is pluralist because it involves competition and bargaining among groups. But it is important to remember that not all groups are equal; some groups have more resources than other groups, and some groups win more often than other groups. When groups tend to see themselves losing most of the time or when cleavages reinforce rather than overlap, political conflict or even violence may result, as the civil unrest in many urban areas over the last few years shows. Although American politics does respond to the country's changing population, the changes tend to lag, and they may never produce a society that achieves equality on every social, economic, or political dimension.

Summary

America has changed dramatically over its two-hundred-year history. The population has grown and become incredibly diverse on almost every social dimension. What was once a country of immigrants from a handful of northern European countries now draws citizens of every race from every country in the world. The basis of the American economy has shifted from agriculture to industry to services. As it stands today, great social and economic differences exist in American society, including differences in religion, education, and wealth. These and other economic characteristics, such as the numbers of Americans who own homes and who work, have important political implications.

Despite the tremendous diversity of American society, Americans for the most part have avoided the political violence that has ripped apart many other multicultural countries. The reason for America's success is that social and economic divisions in the United States tend to be cross-cutting cleavages in which the "have nots" on one issue are the "haves" on another. In addition, the American political process is pluralistic. It gives access to unlimited numbers of people and groups, although they do not enjoy equal success in getting what they want from government.

Key Terms

Baby boomers
Cross-cutting cleavages
Feminization of poverty
Pluralism
Rust Belt
Sun Belt

Readings for Further Study

Dawson, Michael C. *Behind the Mule: Race and Class in African-American Politics*. Princeton, N.J.: Princeton University Press, 1994. An exhaustive look at the political consequences of the development of an African-American middle class.

de la Garza, Rodolfo O., Louis DeSipio, F. Chris Garcia, John Garcia, and Angelo Falcon. *Latino Voices*. Boulder, Colo.: Westview, 1992. An informative analysis of the political attitudes of Latinos in America, based on a large survey.

Hero, Rodney. *Latinos and the U.S. Political System*. Philadelphia: Temple University Press, 1992. An examination of the gap between the extension of legal rights and the persistence of racism.

Hochschild, Jennifer L. *Facing Up to the American Dream: Race, Class, and the Soul of a Nation*. Princeton, N.J.: Princeton University Press, 1995. A political scientist contrasts and compares lower- and middle-class African Americans, finding that the former are more optimistic about attaining the American Dream.

Horton, John. *The Politics of Diversity: Immigration, Resistance, and Change in Monterey Park, California*. Philadelphia: Temple University Press, 1995. A study of the change brought on by the influx of Asian immigrants in a Southern California community.

Phillips, Kevin. *The Politics of Rich and Poor*. New York: Random House, 1990. An important Republican adviser examines the increasingly inequitable distribution of wealth in American society and the policies of the 1980s that caused it.

Schlesinger, Arthur M., Jr. *The Disuniting of America*. New York: Norton, 1992. One of the country's leading historians discusses the political problems posed by an emphasis on social diversity.

Stanley, Harold W., and Richard G. Niemi. *Vital Statistics on American Politics*. 5th ed. Washington, D.C.: CQ Press, 1995. A compendium of statistics dealing with many aspects of American life and politics.

Takaki, Ronald T. *A Different Mirror: A History of Multicultural America*. Boston: Little, Brown, 1993. A reexamination of American history and race relations from a multicultural perspective.

Chapter

4

Civil Liberties

Interpreting the Constitution

The Bill of Rights and State Government

The First Amendment: Freedom of Speech, Assembly, Press, and Religion

Freedom of Speech

Freedom of Assembly and Association

Freedom of the Press

Freedom of Religion

The Second Amendment: The Right to Bear Arms?

State Militias

Supreme Court Rulings

Gun Control Laws

Government and the Rights of Criminal Suspects

The Fourth Amendment: Search and Seizure

The Fifth Amendment: Criminal Procedure for a Person Accused

The Sixth Amendment: Procedures for People Charged with a Crime

The Eighth Amendment: Cruel and Unusual Punishment

Privacy as a Constitutional Right

Summary

Key Terms

Readings for Further Study

In the fall of 1991, a group of University of Virginia students published the first issue of *Wide Awake,* a magazine designed to give the campus a "Christian perspective on both personal and community issues."[1] The magazine's editors asked the university for a $5,900 subsidy from a student fund used to support campus activities. That fund, generated from a $14 per semester student fee, doled out some $450,000 to 118 student groups.[2] The funded groups represented a wide variety of interests and viewpoints, among them the Muslim Student Association and the Jewish Law Students. The university, however, decided not to subsidize *Wide Awake,* claiming that, as a state agency, it could not fund an avowedly religious group without violating the constitutional separation of church and state. Without the university's financial support, the magazine folded.

The editors of *Wide Awake* challenged the university's decision in federal court, claiming violations of their rights to free speech, free exercise of religion, and equal protection under the law. The federal district court upheld the university's position, a decision the court of appeals affirmed. The students then appealed to the Supreme Court. High-powered attorneys represented both the students and the university. Ultimately, the Supreme Court sided with the students by a narrow 5 to 4 margin. The Court's majority opinion in *Rosenberger v. University of Virginia* required the university to treat student religious magazines as it would any other student publication, arguing that to do otherwise would risk suppressing free speech.[3] One of the justices in the majority, Justice Sandra Day O'Connor, concurred, but she stated that such judgments would have to be made on a case-by-case basis, thereby potentially limiting the implications of this decision for similar cases in the future.

The questions the *Rosenberger* case raises are complex. For more than two hundred years, Americans have struggled to define what the freedoms set forth in the Constitution mean in practice. Disagreements have frequently arisen over how to interpret these structural rules of American politics, and many of these disputes have led to bitter political conflict. Moreover, the way the government and the public have interpreted phrases such as "freedom of religion," "freedom of speech," and "freedom of the press" has changed over time.

Civil liberties
The freedoms guaranteed to all Americans in the Bill of Rights (although some are in the body of the Constitution). These liberties include freedom of speech, freedom of religion, and the right to assemble peaceably.

Although we like to think that the Constitution guarantees certain absolute **civil liberties,** the truth is that our interpretations of these freedoms constantly change. The question of how to settle conflicts between competing liberties is a tricky one, akin to achieving a delicate balance between two items on a scale. On one side of the scale are individual liberties, on the other, societal rights—in the case of *Wide Awake,* the rights of religious students rested on one side, the rights of a public university on the other. The balance constantly shifts, and politics often dictates the final results. In other words, the rules governing our liberties change, and politics helps to determine the changes.

In this chapter, we examine the evolution of civil liberties in the United States and the role politics plays in defining them. We look at how the founders introduced the concept of individual rights in the Bill of Rights, which forms the foundation for the civil liberties we enjoy today. We then discuss specific changes in the way our political system has interpreted the Bill of Rights over the past two centuries, tracing its relationship to state government and to the still-evolving rules that mediate conflict in areas such as First Amendment rights, the right to bear arms, government treatment of criminal suspects, and the right to privacy.

Interpreting the Constitution

As we saw in chapter 2, the vague, ambiguous language of the Constitution allows a flexible interpretation of its provisions. Most of the ten amendments in the Bill of Rights are short in length and broad in scope. A few, particularly the Ninth and Tenth Amendments, are so vague that we still have not reached a consensus about what they mean. How, then, are we to interpret the meaning of the Constitution and its amendments? How can we apply it to resolve or manage conflicts over rights—to balance, as in the *Wide Awake* case, the rights of the individual against the rights of the larger society?

Ron Rosenberger and Erick Sierra, editor of a revived Wide Awake *at the University of Virginia, celebrate the Supreme Court's favorable decision in* Rosenberger v. University of Virginia.

Some people believe in interpreting the Constitution in light of **original intent**—in other words, according to what its writers originally had in mind.[4] This approach requires a judge to comb the historical record to learn what the founders or the sponsors of constitutional amendments intended when they adopted the specific words in the Constitution. For example, in the famous *Dred Scott* case, in which the Supreme Court ruled that short of a constitutional amendment the federal government lacked the authority to outlaw slavery (see chapter 2), Chief Justice Roger Taney wrote:

Original intent
The theory that judges should interpret the Constitution by determining what the founders intended when they wrote it.

> No one, we presume, supposes that any change in public opinion or feeling . . . should induce the court to give to the words of the Constitution a more liberal construction . . . than they were intended to bear when the instrument was framed and adopted. . . . [I]t must be construed now as it was understood at the time of its adoption. It is not only the same in words, but the same in meaning.[5]

As you can see, using original intent as a rule limits a judge's discretion in deciding what the Constitution means. It requires the judge to settle legal challenges on the basis of what the founders meant, not what the judge might think is reasonable or justified.[6] The idea of original intent promises a stable interpretation of the Constitution, with decisions about whether to change the law left to legislators rather than judges.

Although original intent offers one way to interpret the Constitution, by necessity it cannot be the only way. Determining original intent raises a host of thorny questions. One problem involves the question of whose original intent one should examine. Should it be the people who wrote the applicable clause in the Constitution, or the people in the state conventions or legislatures that ratified it? Many people believe that the intent of the people who wrote the language is crucial. But several of the founders believed that to determine the meaning of the Constitution, one should look not to their views, but to the views of the ratifying conventions. Albert Gallatin, a key ally of Thomas Jefferson and a major political figure in the early years of the Republic, argued that "the gentlemen who formed the general [Constitutional] Convention . . . only drew it and proposed it. The people and the State Conventions who ratified and who adopted the instrument, are alone parties to it, and their intentions alone might, with any degree of propriety, be resorted to."[7] James Madison, who is generally considered the main architect of the Constitution, agreed with Gallatin: "If we were to look . . . for the [Constitution's] meaning beyond the face of the instrument, we must look for it, not in the General Convention which proposed, but in the State Conventions which accepted and ratified the Constitution."[8]

Even when one decides whose intent to examine, it is not always possible to determine what their intent was. Ferreting out the intent of the founders can be arduous work. After all, their deliberations were conducted in secret; thus, we have limited

"The Constitution is what the judges say it is"—Charles Evans Hughes.

information about their discussions. Moreover, when it came to applying the text of the Constitution to concrete issues, the founders frequently disagreed over what the document they had drafted meant. In a similar vein, determining the intent of the delegates attending state ratifying conventions or the members of the state legislatures is easier said than done. Disagreements about what those who wrote and ratified the Constitution intended by their handiwork can leave Supreme Court justices scratching their heads. For example, in the famous case of *Brown v. Board of Education* (see chapter 5), which found that laws requiring segregated public schools are unconstitutional, Chief Justice Earl Warren wrote that he and his fellow justices heard extensive arguments about the meaning of the equal protection clause of the Fourteenth Amendment. These arguments

> covered exhaustively consideration of the Amendment in Congress, ratification by the states, then existing practices in racial segregation, and the view of the proponents and opponents of the Amendment. This discussion and our own investigation convince us that, although these sources cast some light, it is not enough to resolve the problem with which we are faced. At best, they are inconclusive.[9]

As a result of their inability to determine original intent, Warren and his fellow Supreme Court justices had to look elsewhere when deciding how to rule.

Beyond the problems of whose intent to examine and how to determine that intent, the idea of original intent may run into another obstacle: the precise meanings of many of the words used in the Constitution and the Bill of Rights are open to debate. When, for instance, does a police search become *unreasonable* in the eyes of the Fourth Amendment? When do punishments become *cruel and unusual* under the Eighth Amendment? No dictionary will help here.

A final problem with original intent is the fact that American society in the 1990s faces many issues that no one envisioned two hundred years ago. Do the free speech protections the founders instituted for the print press extend to electronic media such as radio, television, and the Internet? What does the Fourth Amendment's prohibition against unreasonable search and seizure mean in a world with electronic eavesdropping and DNA testing? With the world having changed so much over two centuries, the founders' thinking may not be relevant, even when we know what they thought. As a result, many people agree with Justice Oliver Wendell Holmes that the Constitution must be interpreted "in light of our whole experience and not merely in the light of what was said a hundred years ago."[10]

In the end, decisions about the extent of our civil liberties rest with our governmental institutions. Congress, the president, and state governments have, over time, taken a number of important steps to protect and extend civil liberties. But the members of the Supreme Court have an especially important role in defining civil liberties. As Charles Evans Hughes said in 1907, a few years before he joined the Supreme Court, "The Constitution is what the judges say it is." In making their decisions, individual justices are free to rely on their own judgments, whatever the thoughts of the founders or other justices may be. Thus, the meanings of the words in the Constitution can and do change as the membership of the Court and other governmental institutions and society at large change.

This constant redefinition of our civil liberties helps our government to respond to the needs and desires of a changing, increasingly diverse population. What Americans take civil liberties to mean in the 1990s differs markedly from what most people took them to mean in 1789. This very flexibility, as we discussed in chapter 2, may be a major reason the Constitution is still relevant (and relatively unchanged by amendments) after two centuries; it may become even more important as a diverse American society enters the next century. As society changes, the rules of American politics change as well.

The Bill of Rights and State Government

Recall that the Bill of Rights encompasses the first ten amendments to the Constitution and guarantees some of our most treasured individual rights, including freedom of speech, freedom of religion, and the right to legal protections when charged with a crime. When the Bill of Rights was adopted, it applied only to the relations between the federal government and the people, not to those between the states and their citizens (although many states incorporated similar rights into their own constitutions). During congressional deliberations on the Bill of Rights, some members of the House of Representatives wanted to protect some individual rights against intrusion by the state governments, but the Senate rebuffed the effort.

In 1833, the Supreme Court was asked to extend the Bill of Rights to relations between state governments and the people by applying the "just compensation" clause in the Fifth Amendment to a dispute between a wharf owner and the city of Baltimore. (This clause says simply that the government may not seize private property without providing "just compensation," or fair payment, for it.) The Court refused to apply the clause to the Baltimore case. The Court's reasoning was that each state had adopted its own constitution, and that document determined the mix of restrictions on government powers it thought appropriate. The Bill of Rights applied only to the relationship between the federal government and the citizenry. The Court's ruling set a precedent that stood for more than sixty years.[11]

Over time, however, the courts gradually began to extend the Bill of Rights to the states, although after two hundred years the application remains incomplete. The ratification of the Fourteenth Amendment in 1868 prompted the change. That Amendment, one of three passed in the immediate aftermath of the Civil War, declares that no state shall "deprive any person of life, liberty, or property, without due process of law." As early as 1873, justices argued in dissenting opinions that these words meant that the Bill of Rights should apply to the states.[12] In 1897, the Court first applied part of the Bill of Rights to the states, overturning its 1833 ruling that the just compensation clause did not apply to the states.[13] A few years later, the Court began assuming that states had to protect free speech rights, finally explicitly applying the First Amendment's guarantee of free speech to the states in 1925.[14] As table 4.1 shows, other rights have been extended to the state level since then, although a few still have not.

The First Amendment: Freedom of Speech, Assembly, Press, and Religion

Interpretations of First Amendment rights have also changed over the years. Many of our political and religious rights flow directly from the First Amendment. Yet it has never been taken to mean an absolute guarantee of political or religious freedom. In determining whether a law violates the First Amendment, the Supreme Court usually balances what it sees as the rights of the individual against the interests of society. Moreover, as the political and societal climate changes with time, the Supreme Court changes its interpretation of what the First Amendment means in practice.

The First Amendment guarantees Americans freedom of speech, freedom to assemble peaceably, freedom of the press, and freedom of religion. Let's look at each in turn, focusing on past and present interpretations and how they affect our rights in a practical sense today.

Freedom of Speech

The founders believed that the health of a democracy rested on the ability of its citizens to speak their minds without fear of government reprisal. Yet Congress has passed laws outlawing or limiting certain speech, and the Supreme Court has upheld many of these limitations. For example, truth-in-advertising laws limit what advertisers can say about their products, and truth-in-lending laws limit what banks can say about their services. As we move away from commercial speech and toward political and symbolic speech, however, the Court in the last fifty years has looked more and more skeptically on laws that infringe on the freedom of speech.

Not all parts of the Bill of Rights have been applied to the states.

TABLE 4.1 Application of the Bill of Rights to the States

Amendment Right	Supreme Court Case (Year)
First	
Speech	*Gitlow v. New York* (1925)
Press	*Near v. Minnesota* (1931)
Assembly	*De Jonge v. Oregon* (1937)
Free exercise of religion	*Cantwell v. Connecticut* (1940)
Establishment of religion	*Everson v. Board of Education* (1947)
Second	Not applied
Third	Not applied
Fourth	
Search and seizure	*Wolf v. Colorado* (1949)
Exclusionary rule	*Mapp v. Ohio* (1961)
Fifth	
Grand jury	Not applied
Just compensation	*Chicago, Burlington & Quincy Railroad Co. v. Chicago* (1897)
Self-incrimination	*Malloy v. Hogan* (1964)
Double jeopardy	*Benton v. Maryland* (1969)
Sixth	
Public trial	*in re Oliver* (1948)
Assistance of counsel	*Gideon v. Wainwright* (1963) *Argersinger v. Hamlin* (1972)
Confrontation	*Pointer v. Texas* (1965)
Impartial jury	*Parker v. Gladden* (1966)
Speedy trial	*Klopfer v. North Carolina* (1967)
Jury trial	*Duncan v. Louisiana* (1968)
Seventh	Not applied
Eighth	
Excessive bail and fines	Not expressly applied (see *Shilb v. Kuebel*, 1971)
Cruel and unusual punishment	*Robinson v. California* (1962)
Ninth	Not applicable
Tenth	Not applicable

Political Speech

One civil liberty that amply demonstrates the effects of changes in rules and policies is the freedom of political speech. The balance between the individual right to freely criticize the U.S. government and society's right to ensure political stability has shifted back and forth as circumstances have changed over the past two centuries.

To the founders, the freedom of speech the First Amendment provides for meant first and foremost freedom of *political* speech. But whether Americans actually had a right to speak their minds on the major political matters of the day became an issue early in U.S. history. In 1798, Congress passed the Alien and Sedition Acts, which made it illegal for anyone to write, speak, or publish defamatory statements about the federal government. One motive behind the passage of the acts was political: the Federalists, the party in control of the government, wanted to destroy the opposition Democrat-Republican Party.[15]

The first person convicted under the Alien and Sedition Acts was Matthew Lyon, a Democrat-Republican representative from Vermont. He was sentenced to four months in jail and fined $1,000 (a huge sum in 1798) for having written a letter to the editor criticizing President John Adams for his "unbounded thirst for ridiculous pomp,

In 1918, Congress passed the Sedition Act, making it a crime to "say, print, write, or publish anything intended to cause contempt or scorn for the federal government." The Supreme Court upheld the law in 1919, but later decisions gave citizens the right to express contempt and scorn for the government.

foolish adulation and selfish avarice."[16] Nine other people were eventually convicted under the act. As a practical matter, the Alien and Sedition Acts backfired on the Federalists. The convictions caused great popular concern and helped to derail Adams's bid for reelection. The laws expired in 1801, and one of Thomas Jefferson's first decisions as president was to pardon all those convicted under them.

Although the Alien and Sedition Acts clearly conflicted with the First Amendment, the lower federal courts upheld them, and the Supreme Court never heard a direct challenge to their legality. (In a 1964 case the Court did, in passing, finally call the acts unconstitutional!)[17] Indeed, the Court did not rule on the extent to which the First Amendment protects political speech until the early twentieth century, when it ruled on the constitutionality of the Espionage Act of 1917 and the Sedition Act of 1918. Written amidst the heated political atmosphere of World War I and the communist revolution in Russia, the Espionage Act made it illegal to interfere with any military activity, including recruitment and induction, or to advocate insubordination or mutiny. The Sedition Act was even more sweeping. It made it "a federal crime to . . . say, print, write, or publish anything intended to cause contempt or scorn for the federal government, the Constitution, the flag, or the uniform of the armed forces, or to say or write anything that interfered with defense production."[18] These two laws outlawed some political speech because of its supposed subversive content.

Almost one thousand people were convicted under the Espionage and Sedition Acts, and several appealed to the Supreme Court. The first case to reach the Court involved Carl Schenck, the general secretary of the Socialist Party. Schenck had mailed leaflets urging American men to resist the draft, and as a result, he was convicted of violating the Espionage Act. The Supreme Court upheld the conviction even though Schenck had failed to obstruct the induction of draftees. Writing for a unanimous Court in *Schenck v. United States,* Justice Oliver Wendell Holmes set forth the **clear and present danger standard,** which allows Congress to impose restrictions on political speech when it thinks such speech threatens the interests of the country. Holmes wrote that

Clear and present danger standard
The doctrine that Congress may limit speech if it causes a clear and present danger to the interests of the country.

> in many places and in ordinary times the defendants in saying all that was said in the circular would have been within their constitutional rights. But the character of every act depends upon the circumstances in which it is done. . . . The question in every case is whether the words used are used in such circumstances and are of such a nature as to create a clear and present danger that they will bring about the substantive evils that Congress has a right to prevent.[19]

Thus, with the *Schenck* decision, the Supreme Court established that freedom of speech is not an absolute right. They removed some weight from the individual side of the scale, deciding that in some circumstances, government can restrict or punish some kinds of political speech.

A few months after the *Schenck* decision, the Supreme Court placed conditions on political speech even more restrictive than the clear and present danger standard. In *Abrams v. United States,* the Court upheld the conviction of five Russian immigrants for violating the Espionage Act.[20] The accused, all of whom had lived in the United States for at least five years, were prosecuted for writing political pamphlets that criticized U.S. interference in the Russian revolution and claimed, among other things, that President Wilson was a coward and a hypocrite. The Court's majority opinion set forth the **bad tendency doctrine.** This doctrine held that the clear and present danger standard required the government to show only that certain speech was likely to lead to the negative consequences Congress thought must be avoided. The government was not obligated to demonstrate that danger was imminent.

Bad tendency doctrine
The doctrine that speech need only be likely to lead to negative consequences, in Congress's judgment, for it to be illegal.

Justice Holmes disagreed with the bad tendency doctrine. In his written dissent, he argued that Abrams and his associates did not pose the sort of imminent danger that had led him to propose the clear and present danger standard:

> It is only the present danger of immediate evil or an intent to bring it about that warrants Congress in setting a limit to the expression of opinion where private rights are not concerned. . . . Now nobody can suppose that the surreptitious publishing of a silly leaflet by an unknown man, without more, would present any immediate danger that its opinions would hinder the success of government arms or have any appreciable tendency to do so.[21]

One of the most influential justices ever to serve on the Supreme Court was Oliver Wendell Holmes. His opinions and dissents on free speech cases still help frame our understanding of First Amendment rights.

Holmes went on to argue that in most circumstances, speech is constitutionally protected because facts ultimately will triumph over falsehoods in the marketplace of ideas. But a majority of the Supreme Court would not heed Holmes's call for a return to a strict interpretation of clear and present danger for many years.

The Supreme Court again shifted the balance, giving individual rights more weight in the late 1930s, when it developed a standard that gave preferred status to the liberties granted by the Bill of Rights.[22] In the context of the First Amendment, this preferred status meant that free speech was so fundamental to the health of a democracy that the Court would assume any measure that limited it was unconstitutional unless the government could prove otherwise.

The government's chance to test the preferred status of free speech came quickly. World War II and the perceived resurgence of the communist threat to the United States led to legislation restricting political speech similar to that passed during World War I. In 1940, Congress passed the Alien Registration Act (also known as the Smith Act, after its main congressional sponsor). The act made it illegal to advocate the overthrow of the government through force or violence or to organize or even be a member of any group that espoused such ideas. The McCarran Act, passed in 1950, required communist organizations to register with the federal government and to disclose the names of their members. The Communist Control Act of 1954 barred all communist party organizations from participating in elections.

In deciding the cases these laws prompted, the Supreme Court weighed the rights of the individual against the interests of society. Given the immense concern at the time over the threat that communism posed to the United States, it is perhaps not surprising that the Court placed less value on individual rights in favor of protecting society as a whole. In *Dennis v. United States* (1951), the Court upheld the conviction of top members of the Communist Party of the United States for violating several provisions of the Smith Act. The majority opinion again employed the clear and present danger standard, but defined it in a way that brought it very close to the bad tendency doctrine. The application of the clear and present danger standard in *Dennis* has sometimes been called the "sliding scale rule." Chief Justice Vinson wrote that academic discussions of revolution were protected. But he went on to state that the government did not have to "wait until the *putsch* [overthrow] is about to be executed, the plans have been laid and the signal is awaited" to prohibit speech. "In each case [courts] must ask whether the gravity of the 'evil,' discounted by its improbability, justifies such invasion of free speech as is necessary to avoid the danger."[23] In this case, the

Court believed that an organized group's threat to overthrow the government was sufficient to override the group's right to free speech, even if justices did not think the group actually had the ability to overthrow the government.

In the two decades after the *Dennis* case, the Supreme Court moved toward a less restrictive interpretation of the clear and present danger standard, granting more weight to the individual right to freedom of speech. In the early 1960s, it found several provisions of the McCarran Act unconstitutional, and Congress subsequently repealed the act's registration requirement. In the 1969 case *Brandenburg v. Ohio,* which involved a top Ku Klux Klan official, the Court returned to a rule close to Holmes's original clear and present danger standard, rejecting the more restrictive bad tendency doctrine. In *Brandenburg,* the Court erected the **incitement standard.** Under this test, the government has to prove the speech in question is likely to produce immediate illegal activity. The Court judged that the law under which the Klan leader had been convicted was unconstitutional because it "purports to punish mere advocacy."[24] In other words, the Court held that it is acceptable to express opinions as long as the speaker does not incite listeners to commit illegal acts.

Incitement standard
The doctrine that speech must cause listeners to be likely to commit immediate illegal acts for the speech itself to be illegal.

Over time, the Supreme Court's views on how to balance the rights of individuals and the interests of society have changed. In general, the Court has moved to reduce restrictions on the exercise of free speech (see box 4.1). This movement has not occurred in a vacuum; it has often paralleled changes in public opinion about free speech and other civil liberties.[25] For example, as Congress and the courts have removed restrictions on the free speech of avowed communists, the public has also become more tolerant of such speech. As figure 4.1 shows, over the last four decades, the public has become more willing to allow admitted communists to speak, teach college, and have their books remain on library bookshelves. As perceptions of a communist threat receded, people (and judges and legislators) became more willing to allow unpopular political speech. Our understanding of what our liberties are changes over time.

Symbolic Speech

Not all questions about free speech revolve around spoken or written words. Some "speech" takes the form of symbols or actions instead of words, and important questions have arisen about how far the right to free speech extends to protect symbolic speech. The Supreme Court generally has sought to draw a distinction (sometimes quite murky) between acts that constitute speech, and thus are constitutionally protected, and acts that constitute conduct, and thus are not.

The Supreme Court first tackled symbolic speech in a 1931 case in which the state of California had made it illegal to use a red flag "as a sign, symbol, or emblem of opposition to organized government." Again, communists were the target of the law. The Court threw out their convictions, claiming the law was too vague and denied people "the opportunity for a free political discussion."[26]

During the Vietnam War, the Supreme Court decided several more cases involving symbolic speech. In *United States v. O'Brien,* the Court upheld the conviction of a man who burned his draft registration card to protest the war. The Court decided that the government's interest in seeing that draft-age men had continual access to the information on their draft card outweighed the individual's right to burn the card as an act of political protest.[27] Thus, the Court recognized some restrictions on symbolic speech. But one year later in *Tinker v. Des Moines School District,* the Court ruled that students could not be suspended for wearing black armbands to protest the Vietnam War because their actions were not disruptive and they were entitled to express their political opinions.

The most heated symbolic speech case in recent years was *Texas v. Johnson,* decided in 1989. Johnson, a member of a radical left-wing organization, burned an American flag outside the 1984 Republican National Convention in Dallas. Texas (and forty-seven other states) had made it illegal to deface an American flag. But, in a

The People Behind the Rules

BOX 4.1

Margaret Gilleo's Signs and the Right to Free Speech

One of Margaret Gilleo's signs.

As U.S. military personnel poured into the Persian Gulf in the fall of 1990, Margaret Gilleo wanted to express her opposition to going to war. On December 8, Gilleo, a resident of Ladue, Missouri, an upscale suburb of St. Louis, placed a 24-by-30-inch sign reading "Say No to War in the Persian Gulf, Call Congress Now" on her front lawn. The sign soon disappeared, and she replaced it with another. When that sign was knocked down, Gilleo reported the apparent vandalism to the police. The police, in turn, told her that the signs violated a Ladue city ordinance against posting signs in residential neighborhoods. When Gilleo asked the city council for a waiver to allow her to post a sign on her lawn, the council denied her request. At that point, Gilleo took her case to court, claiming that the city's ordinance violated her First Amendment right to free speech.

The federal district court—the initial court to hear most federal cases—sided with Gilleo and issued a preliminary injunction against enforcement of the city ordinance. Following that ruling, Gilleo placed an 8 1/2-by-11-inch sign reading "For Peace in the Gulf" in an upstairs window in her home. The Ladue City Council responded to the injunction and Gilleo's new sign by repealing the old ordinance and writing a new one to take its place. The new ordinance enacted a general prohibition against any signs, with a few exceptions for commercial signs such as the "for sale" signs real estate agents place in front of homes on the market. The city council justified the new rule by claiming that a proliferation of signs would lead to ugliness, visual blight, and clutter which would tarnish the beauty of the landscape and damage property values. The new ordinance explicitly outlawed window signs.

Gilleo again went to court, claiming the new ordinance violated her constitutional right to free speech. Again the district court agreed with her, and when the city appealed the decision, the Court of Appeals affirmed the decision. The city then appealed to the U.S. Supreme Court.

The Supreme Court rendered its decision in June 1994. In a unanimous decision, the Court reaffirmed the lower court rulings and held in Gilleo's favor. Its reasoning, however, differed from that of the district and appeals courts. The lower courts had said that the Ladue ordinance was unconstitutional because it favored commercial speech over political speech. That suggested that a complete ban on both commercial and political signs would be acceptable. The Supreme Court, in a decision written by Justice John Paul Stevens, asserted that the Ladue city rule was unconstitutional because it inhibited political speech. Justice Stevens wrote,

> A special respect for individual liberty in our home has long been part of our culture and our law. That principle has a special resonance when the government seeks to constrain a person's ability to *speak* there. Most Americans would be understandably dismayed, given that tradition, to learn that it is illegal to display from their window an 8-by-11-inch sign expressing their political views.

The Court did not rule out all regulation of signs, stating that municipalities might, for example, be able to limit political advertisements placed on residential property for a fee. But the Court's decision stated that no regulation could interfere with First Amendment rights.

Margaret Gilleo, who by the time of the Supreme Court's decision was running to be the Democratic nominee for the U.S. House of Representatives in her district, responded to the Court's decision by saying she would display a "Gilleo for Congress" sign at home. Although she did not win her race for office, Margaret Gilleo did win her right to free speech.

Sources: City of Ladue v. Gilleo, 114 S.Ct. 2038 (1994); Linda Greenhouse, "In Broad Ruling, Court Prohibits Banning of Homeowners' Signs," *New York Times,* 14 June 1994.

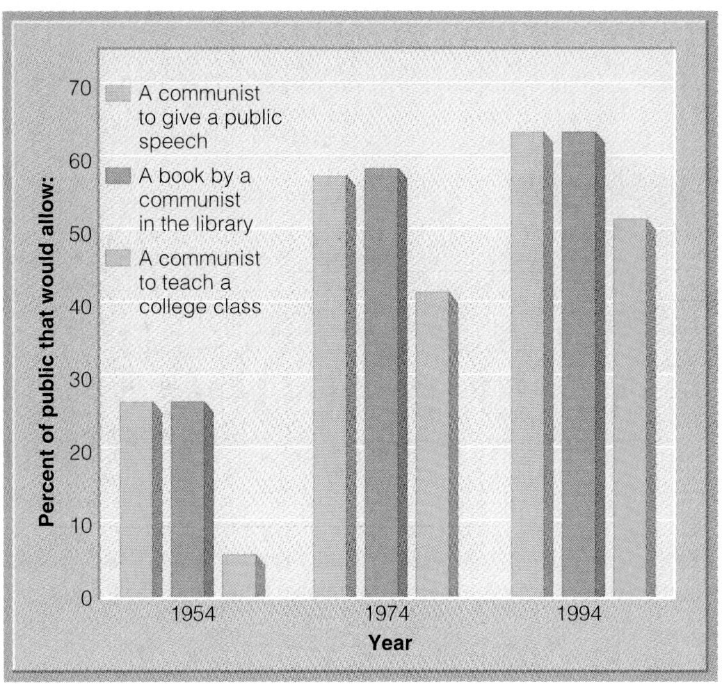

Figure 4.1
Public Tolerance of Communists, 1954–1994

Americans are much more tolerant of communists in public life now than they were forty or more years ago.

Source: Data from Harold W. Stanley and Richard G. Niemi, *Vital Statistics on American Politics*, 4th ed. (Washington, D.C.: CQ Press, 1994), pp. 28–29.

5 to 4 decision, the Supreme Court overturned Johnson's conviction, supporting his right to burn the flag. The majority opinion harkened back to Justice Holmes's marketplace argument of seven decades before:

> We can imagine no more appropriate response to burning a flag than waving one's own, no better way to counter a flag burner's message than by saluting the flag that burns. . . . We do not consecrate the flag by punishing its desecration, for in doing so we dilute the freedom that this cherished emblem represents.[28]

The Court's decision to overturn Johnson's conviction was deeply unpopular with the American public, but efforts to amend the Constitution to ban flag burning have failed, albeit by the narrowest of margins in recent years.

So-called hate crimes are at the core of another controversial issue that touches on symbolic speech. In recent years, many state and local governments have outlawed the use of symbols thought to be deeply offensive to minorities. The first Supreme Court ruling on these laws involved an ordinance in St. Paul, Minnesota, that made it illegal to burn crosses or place swastikas on public or private property. In *R.A.V. v. City of St. Paul* (1992), the Court overturned the conviction of several teenagers for burning a cross in the yard of an African-American family. The Court noted that St. Paul could have punished the conduct of the cross burners by charging them with an offense such as trespassing or arson, but that the city instead sought to punish the teenagers for the words and thoughts behind their actions. Because the ordinance forbade only certain offensive words and symbols and not others, the Court ruled that the city had "no such authority to license one side of a debate to fight freestyle, while requiring the other to follow Marquis of Queensbury Rules."[29]

Although the Supreme Court overturned the St. Paul ordinance on First Amendment grounds, the following year it upheld a Wisconsin law that imposed harsher penalties for violent crimes in which the victims were selected because of their race, religion, color, disability, sexual orientation, national origin, or ancestry. The Court

Although the U.S. government has not always tolerated anti-government protests, our strong traditions of free speech and the rule of law set this country apart from many others in the world, as the crushing of the democracy movement in China in 1989 demonstrates.

noted in its opinion that whereas the St. Paul ordinance was explicitly directed at speech, the Wisconsin law was "aimed at conduct unprotected by the First Amendment."[30] Thus, the Court ruled that the cross burning qualified as legitimate symbolic speech, but violent offenses did not.

Freedom of Assembly and Association

The First Amendment establishes "the right of the people peaceably to assemble, and to petition the Government for the redress of grievances." The Supreme Court first upheld the constitutional right to assemble peaceably in 1875.[31] In *Hague v. Committee of Industrial Organization* (1939), the Court ruled that the government cannot limit the right to assemble in public places in ways that favor one group over another. The government can, however, control the time, place, and manner of the assembly so long as the rules apply to all groups equally.[32] As one justice wrote in a later decision, the government can prevent "a street meeting in the middle of Times Square during rush hour."[33]

A critical test of the right to assemble peaceably came in 1978 when a group of American Nazis proposed to march in Skokie, Illinois.[34] After being denied an opportunity to march in nearby Chicago, the Nazis chose Skokie, a town in which many people had family members who had survived the Jewish Holocaust of World War II. Most residents of Skokie vehemently opposed the proposed march, even though the Nazis posed no threat to the community. As a result, town officials demanded that the Nazis post a $350,000 bond before holding their rally, an amount everyone knew the Nazis could not raise. The Nazis responded by announcing that they would hold a quiet gathering outside Skokie Village Hall to protest what they saw as the town's violation of their rights of assembly and free speech. City officials asked the courts to bar the proposed demonstration.

The legal battle dragged on for months, and a federal district court eventually sided with the Nazis. It ruled that the bond requirement and other impediments Skokie had imposed were unconstitutional because they infringed on free speech. After their legal victory, the Nazis held two marches in Chicago, their original target. On both occasions, the handful of Nazis who marched were greatly outnumbered by the people who came to protest against them.

In recent decades, the Supreme Court has also read the First Amendment to include an implicit right of political association.[35] In 1958, the Court decided a case challenging an Alabama law that required the National Association for the Advancement of Colored People (NAACP) to disclose its membership lists. In its ruling, the Court noted the importance of group membership in promoting and protecting the political interests of different groups, and it noted that previous disclosures of the NAACP's membership lists had exposed its members to various kinds of harassment.

As a result, the Court concluded that forced disclosure was unconstitutional since it would hinder the ability of the NAACP and its members "to pursue their collective effort to foster beliefs which they admittedly have a right to advocate."[36] With this ruling, the Court expanded our understanding of what the right to "peaceably assemble" means as well as our understanding of the right of an individual to associate with the group of his or her choice.

Freedom of the Press

The First Amendment not only protects the rights of individual citizens to speak freely and assemble peaceably, it also stipulates that "Congress shall make no law . . . abridging the freedom . . . of the press." In the more than two hundred years since these words were penned, the Supreme Court has extended the freedom of the press to include the modern media of television, radio, and film as well as the printed media so familiar to the founders. Regardless of the medium used to convey information, three potential checks can restrict the freedom of the press: prior restraint, libel law, and obscenity law.

Prior Restraint

One of the central questions in the debate over freedom of the press is whether the government has the right to suppress a story before it has been published or broadcast. The Supreme Court first addressed the constitutionality of **prior restraint** in *Near v. Minnesota,* a 1931 case in which the Court used the due process clause of the Fourteenth Amendment to apply the First Amendment's freedom of the press guarantee to state governments for the first time. Jay Near was the publisher of a small-circulation newspaper convicted of violating a Minnesota law that prohibited malicious and scandalous publications. Although the Court showed no admiration for Near's anti-Semitic scandal sheet, it overturned his conviction on the grounds that the First Amendment gives enormous leeway to the press in deciding what to publish: "The fact that liberty of the press may be used by miscreant purveyors of scandal does not make any the less necessary the immunity of the press from previous restraint in dealing with official misconduct."[37] Using logic similar to the clear and present danger doctrine presented in the *Schenck* case, the Court indicated that prior restraint was constitutional only in exceptional cases. The Court weighed the right to freedom of the press against society's right to suppress offensive publications, and the justices favored freedom of the press in their decision.

Prior restraint 
An act of government preventing publication or broadcast of a story or document.

During the Vietnam War, the Supreme Court had an opportunity to specify exactly when the government's interest in suppressing a story is strong enough to override the press's freedom to publish it. In June 1971, the *New York Times* began publishing a series of secret government documents known as the **Pentagon Papers.** The documents, which showed that Presidents Kennedy and Johnson had misled the American public about U.S. policy in Vietnam, were leaked to the *Times* by a former Defense Department official who opposed the war. Although the Papers dealt with historical material and did not jeopardize existing diplomatic or military plans, the Nixon administration asked a federal court to bar the *Times* from publishing any more of the documents on the grounds that their publication violated the Espionage Act of 1917. The lower court granted the request, marking the first time in U.S. history that a newspaper had been barred from printing a specific article. Two weeks later, however, the Supreme Court ruled that the government had failed to prove its claim that the threat to national security justified prior restraint. The Court lifted the ban and the *Times* was free to resume publishing the documents.[38]

Pentagon Papers
A set of secret government documents—leaked to the press in 1971—showing that Presidents Kennedy and Johnson misled the public about U.S. involvement in Vietnam.

Despite the political importance of the Pentagon Papers case, it broke no new ground on the circumstances under which prior restraint is constitutional. Indeed, the *New York Times* did not claim that the First Amendment made prior restraint unconstitutional. Instead, the paper chose to defend itself by arguing that the government had failed to prove that publication of the Pentagon Papers would harm national security.

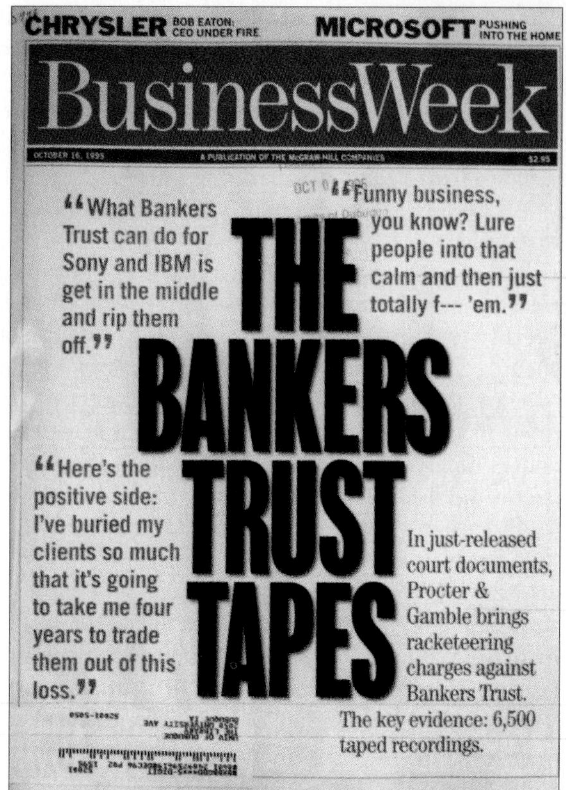
CHRYSLER BOB EATON: CEO UNDER FIRE MICROSOFT PUSHING INTO THE HOME

BusinessWeek

OCTOBER 16, 1995 A PUBLICATION OF THE McGRAW-HILL COMPANIES $2.95

THE BANKERS TRUST TAPES

"What Bankers Trust can do for Sony and IBM is get in the middle and rip them off."

"Funny business, you know? Lure people into that calm and then just totally f--- 'em."

"Here's the positive side: I've buried my clients so much that it's going to take me four years to trade them out of this loss."

In just-released court documents, Procter & Gamble brings racketeering charges against Bankers Trust. The key evidence: 6,500 taped recordings.

In 1995, a federal judge issued a prior restraint order that barred Business Week *from publishing an article based on legal documents involving corporate giants Procter & Gamble and Bankers Trust. Three weeks later, the judge made the documents public, thereby allowing* Business Week *to publish its article.*

The justices disagreed so strongly over the merits of the government's case and the propriety of prior restraint that they wrote nine separate opinions. While some justices argued that freedom of the press is absolute, others held that some circumstances justify prior restraint. As a result, it remains unclear exactly when the government can obtain an order for prior restraint.

A recent case highlights the uncertainty surrounding prior restraint. On September 13, 1995, just hours before *Business Week* was about to go to press, a federal court directed it to withhold publication of a particular article or be held in contempt of court. The article in question discussed a lawsuit involving corporate giants Procter & Gamble and Bankers Trust Company. Because of a mistake by a lawyer for one of the law firms involved in the case, reporters for *Business Week* had received confidential documents from the lawsuit. This happened despite the fact that a federal district judge had ordered the documents sealed—that is, made a court secret not to be shared with anyone other than the parties to the case. Even though it had obtained the documents legally, *Business Week* feared what would happen if it disobeyed the judge's order. As a result, it pulled the story and appealed this rare instance of court-ordered prior restraint. For procedural reasons, no higher federal court rushed to the magazine's rescue. Three weeks later, the federal judge who had imposed the prior restraint order unsealed the files in question, allowing *Business Week* to publish a story based on the documents it had obtained. In unsealing the files, however, the judge did not change the legal logic that had led him to issue a prior restraint order.[39] (Several months later a federal appeals court threw out the lower court's ruling and criticized the judge in the case for failing to realize that he "was engaging in a practice that, under all but the most exceptional circumstances, violates the Constitution.")[40]

Libel

Libel law
Laws governing written or visual publications that unjustly injure a person's reputation.

A more common check on the freedom of the press than prior restraint is **libel law,** which governs any written or visual publication that unjustly injures a person's reputation. (Slander applies to spoken words that unjustly injure a person's reputation.) Simply

Heed Their Rising Voices

"As the whole world knows by now, thousands of Southern Negro students are engaged in widespread non-violent demonstrations in positive affirmation of the right to live in human dignity as guaranteed by the U.S. Constitution and the Bill of Rights. In their efforts to uphold these guarantees, they are being met by an unprecedented wave of terror by those who would deny and negate that document which the whole world looks upon as setting the pattern for modern freedom. . . .

"In Montgomery, Alabama, after students sang 'My Country, Tis of Thee' on the State Capitol steps, their leaders were expelled from school, and truckloads of police armed with shotguns and tear-gas ringed the Alabama State College Campus. When the entire student body protested to state authorities by refusing to re-register, their dining hall was padlocked in an attempt to starve them into submission. . . .

"Small wonder that the Southern violators of the Constitution fear this new, non-violent brand of freedom fighter. . . even as they fear the upswelling right-to-vote movement. Small wonder that they are determined to destroy the one man who, more than any other, symbolizes the new spirit now sweeping the South—the Rev. Dr. Martin Luther King, Jr., world-famous leader of the Montgomery Bus Protest. . . .

"Again and again the Southern violators have answered Dr. King's peaceful protests with intimidation and violence. They have bombed his home almost killing his wife and child. They have assaulted his person. They have arrested him seven times—for 'speeding,' 'loitering,' and similar 'offenses.' And now they have charged him with 'perjury'—a felony under which they could imprison him for ten years. . . .

"We urge you to join hands with our fellow Americans in the South by supporting, with your dollars, this Combined Appeal for all three needs—the defense of Martin Luther King—the support of the embattled students—and the struggle for the right-to-vote."

FIGURE 4.2 *New York Times Co. v. Sullivan*

In *New York Times Co. v. Sullivan,* the Supreme Court ruled that this ad was not libelous.

Committee to Defend Martin Luther King, as appeared in the *New York Times,* 29 March 1960.

stated, these laws prohibit the press as well as individuals from writing (or uttering) false and damaging statements about people. Because it usually is impractical to prevent people from speaking, writing, or broadcasting offensive words, legal action comes only after someone believes those words have injured his or her reputation.

The landmark case in libel law is *New York Times Co. v. Sullivan* (1964).[41] L. B. Sullivan, a city commissioner in Montgomery, Alabama, sued the *Times* for printing an advertisement that condemned the way the police in Montgomery had treated civil rights protesters. (Figure 4.2 reproduces the text of the disputed advertisement.) When a state court awarded Sullivan $500,000 in damages because of factual errors in the ad, other officials filed lawsuits of their own. Suddenly it looked as if segregationists would be able to use libel laws to discourage the press from covering the civil rights movement.

The Supreme Court, however, overturned the Alabama court's ruling. For the first time in its history, the Court held that a libel judgment violated the First Amendment. The Court ruled that robust political debate will suffer unless public officials carry a higher burden of proof than ordinary citizens do in libel cases. The Court ruled that public officials must not only prove that a news report contained a damaging error—the standard for a private citizen—but that the falsehood "was made with 'actual malice'—that is, with knowledge that it was false or with reckless disregard of whether it was false or not."[42] In later rulings, the Court extended its requirement that certain plaintiffs suing for libel prove the press acted with actual malice. These plaintiffs include all government officials who have substantial control over public policy making, candidates for public

Controversy surrounded the 1990 exhibit of the work of photographer Robert Mapplethorpe. In Cincinnati, the director of the museum that showed the exhibit was charged with obscenity, but a jury found him not guilty on the basis of the city's community-based obscenity standards.

office, and people whose prominence places them in the public eye. In general, public figures, whether they are members of Congress, heads of foreign governments, or entertainers, have a harder time establishing libel than do private citizens, because freedom of the press is a civil liberty given considerable weight by Supreme Court rulings.

Obscenity

Obscenity law
Laws governing materials whose predominant appeal is to a prurient interest in nudity, sex, or excretion.

No issue has proved more vexing for members of the Supreme Court than **obscenity law,** which forbids materials whose predominant appeal is to a prurient interest in nudity, sex, or excretion. Again, the Court usually tries to balance society's interests against personal liberties. Although Congress first passed legislation on obscenity in 1842, and the Court upheld later obscenity legislation in 1878, it was not until 1942 that the Court held that obscenity did not enjoy First Amendment protection.[43] Since then, the Court has had great difficulty, however, establishing standards by which to judge material obscene. For example, in *Roth v. the United States* (1957), the Court held that the appropriate test was "whether to the average person, applying contemporary community standards, the dominant theme of the material taken as a whole appeals to prurient interest."[44] But determining who qualifies as an "average" person or what prevailing "community standards" are proved difficult. Other standards have since been offered, but none have gained wide acceptance.[45] So difficult is the definition problem that Justice Potter Stewart was reduced in one 1964 case to stating that although he could not define obscenity, he knew it when he saw it.[46]

In a 1973 case, *Miller v. California,* the Supreme Court established a three-part test to determine whether material is obscene, a standard that is still in place. The first part of the test is the "average person applying community standards" rule from *Roth.* The second component is "whether the work depicts or describes, in a patently offensive way, sexual conduct specifically defined by the applicable law." The third part of the test is "whether the work, taken as a whole, lacks serious literary, artistic, political, or scientific value."[47] In essence, with the *Miller* decision, the Court turned the question of defining obscenity back to the states. The Court continues to hear obscenity cases—although the number has declined dramatically since the early 1970s—and it has overturned some community-based obscenity standards as too strict or too vague.[48] In obscenity cases, as in prior restraint and libel cases, the Court has generally favored press freedom over restraint.

Establishment clause
The provision in the First Amendment of the Constitution that "Congress shall make no law respecting an establishment of religion."

Free exercise clause
The provision in the First Amendment of the Constitution that "Congress shall make no law . . . prohibiting the free exercise" of religion.

Freedom of Religion

The First Amendment states that "Congress shall make no law respecting an establishment of religion, or prohibiting the free exercise thereof." These two clauses—referred to as the **establishment clause** and the **free exercise clause**—were intended to keep the government separate from religion and to allow Americans to practice whatever religion they choose. But, as is often the case with civil liberties, the Supreme Court's attitude toward the separation of church and state and the free exercise of religion has changed with the times.

The Establishment Clause

The establishment clause has always been taken to mean that the federal government cannot create an official state church such as the Church of England in England. This interpretation reflects political reality as much as grand theories about individual rights; even when the Constitution was adopted, Americans adhered to a wide array of religious practices, and as chapter 3 shows, the diversity of religious beliefs has only increased. But the establishment clause did represent something of a breakthrough in political thought. Even after the federal Constitution was enacted, five states continued to have state churches, with Massachusetts having an official church (Congregational) until 1833.[49]

Although there has never been much doubt that the government cannot establish a state religion, considerable debate surrounds the government's treatment of religion. The Supreme Court has never taken the position that the federal government must adopt a pure hands-off approach. We still print "IN GOD WE TRUST" on our money, swear presidents into office using a Bible, and ask chaplains to open sessions of Congress with prayer. But beyond these symbolic acts lie a host of complex constitutional issues. Can the government assist, promote, or hinder the practice of any religion? Must the government treat all religions alike? What happens if a religious practice runs contrary to other public policy goals? Just precisely where do we draw the line between church and state?

In recent decades, many of the cases dealing with separation of church and state have involved the constitutionality of public assistance to religious schools. The Supreme Court has allowed the expenditure of some public money on students attending religious schools for books, lunch programs, transportation, and even the provision of an interpreter for a deaf student. The Court approves such expenditures when the aid is deemed to benefit the student and not the religious entity that operates the school.[50] The Court has declared many other expenditures, however, such as loans of instructional materials and equipment, unconstitutional.[51] The Court generally has ruled that public aid to religious *colleges* is constitutional, in part because "college students are less impressionable and less susceptible to religious indoctrination."[52]

More controversial than public assistance for religious schools has been the issue of religious activities in the public schools. In 1962, the Supreme Court ruled that a school district in New York could not require the daily reading of a state-written nondenominational prayer, even though students who did not want to say the prayer could leave the room.[53] The next year, the Court held that a Pennsylvania law requiring the reading aloud of ten Bible selections each school day and a Maryland law requiring the recitation of a Bible chapter or the Lord's Prayer during school were both unconstitutional.[54] Although opinion surveys consistently show strong public support for allowing prayer in the classroom, the Court continues to resist. In recent years, it has tossed out an Alabama law requiring a moment of meditation and a Rhode Island practice in which ministers offered prayers at school graduations.[55]

A recent case involving the establishment clause shows how complex the civil liberties cases the Supreme Court confronts can be. During the 1993 Christmas season, members of the Ku Klux Klan asked to place a cross in a public plaza located near the Ohio statehouse, a place often used for speeches and demonstrations. A state agency denied the Klan a permit to raise a cross, because it feared doing so would represent government endorsement of a particular religion. In a 7 to 2 decision in *Capitol Square v. Pinette* (1995), the Supreme Court held that religious speech is fully protected under the First Amendment, and that as long as other groups were allowed to use the plaza, the Klan had to have equal access.[56] The Court majority, however, splintered on one point. Four of the justices did not think that the question of state endorsement of religion applied to this case, while the three

In 1995, the Supreme Court ruled 7 to 2 that the Ku Klux Klan had a right to erect a cross in a public park near the state capitol in Columbus, Ohio. The Klan and its opponents wrestled over erecting the cross in 1993.

others thought it did apply but that no reasonable person would think that the state of Ohio was affirming the Klan's message. Among the groups that praised the Court's decision protecting the Klan's rights was Lubavitch, an organization of Orthodox Jews that has long campaigned for the right to erect Hanukkah menorahs on public grounds.[57]

The Supreme Court has set forth a number of arguments for determining where to draw the line between church and state, but for many years the most influential opinion came from a 1971 case, *Lemon v. Kurtzman.* In that decision, the Court overturned a Rhode Island law allowing the state to supplement the salaries of teachers at private elementary schools by up to 15 percent. The Court established a three-part test for judging the constitutionality of such measures: "First, the statute must have a secular legislative purpose; second, its principal or primary effect must be one that neither advances nor inhibits religion . . . [and] finally, the statute must not foster 'an excessive government entanglement with religion.' "[58] The Court believed that allowing the state and any particular religion to become "entangled" might eventually endanger an individual's right to freely exercise his or her religious beliefs. But for the last few years, the more conservative justices on the Court have tried to overturn the test devised in *Lemon,* thinking it is too unfriendly toward religious activities. Although the Court has yet to devise a replacement rule, it has recently decided two important state and religion cases—*Rosenberger* and *Capitol Square*—without any serious reference to *Lemon,* suggesting that the old rule is no longer in use. As our nation's populace changes, we may need the flexibility to fine tune and modify the rules that prevent the establishment of a state religion.

The Free Exercise Clause

Debate over the free exercise clause largely revolves around the distinction between beliefs and action. The Supreme Court's initial decision on the free exercise clause came in an 1878 case involving a polygamist from the Utah territory.[59] Although polygamy violated federal law, the defendant, a Mormon, argued that it was an important part of his religion, and he was therefore exercising his First Amendment rights. In upholding his conviction, the Court drew a sharp distinction between belief, which the government could not impede, and action based on those beliefs, which the government had a clear right to outlaw.

In 1993, the Supreme Court overturned a Hialeah, Florida, ordinance banning animal sacrifices. The Court held that members of the Santeria faith have the right to perform animal sacrifices because such rituals are central to the exercise of their religious faith.

Since the 1940s, the Supreme Court has generally moved away from the distinction it drew in 1878 between belief and action, holding that some actions are protected by the free exercise clause.[60] In 1943, the Court ruled that Jehovah's Witnesses could not be compelled to salute the flag, thereby reversing the position it had taken in a similar case only three years earlier.[61] In 1972, the Court allowed Amish children in Wisconsin to ignore a state law requiring public school attendance until age sixteen.[62] The Court reasoned that the right of the Amish to practice their religious beliefs, which call for minimizing contact with people from other faiths, outweighed the state's interest in requiring children to receive an education. And in 1993, the Court found that the city of Hialeah, Florida, had violated the First Amendment when it passed a series of ordinances designed to prevent practitioners of the Santeria faith from conducting animal sacrifices.[63]

The Supreme Court does not, however, always rule in favor of those exercising their religious beliefs. In a 1990 decision, the Court upheld the denial of unemployment benefits to two men fired by a private drug rehabilitation organization for using peyote, a hallucinogenic drug, during an American Indian religious ritual.[64] In that ruling, the Court abandoned its previous principle that the government had to demonstrate a compelling state interest to restrict religious practices and held that the state could restrict activities as long as the restrictions were not directed at religious groups alone. Therefore, the state of Oregon could outlaw the use of peyote, even for religious purposes. (A number of other states did exempt religious use of the drug.)

Congress and the president, however, joined together in 1993 to force the Supreme Court to tip the balance back toward individual religious liberties, returning to the stricter compelling state interest standard it had used before 1990 to judge whether a law restricting religious practices passed constitutional scrutiny. The Religious Freedom Restoration Act also held that even when the government could meet the compelling interest standard, it must institute laws that would restrict religious practices the least.[65] As this law demonstrates, the courts are not the only vehicle for determining civil liberties; the elected branches of government also play a role.

The First Amendment is a cornerstone of American politics and American society. Yet a constant tension exists between the rights of the individual and the interests of society. Because the balance between these two competing rights shifts with changes in political events and social mores, our understanding of the liberties embedded in the First Amendment has evolved over the past two centuries. No doubt the balance will continue to change over the next two as well.

THE SECOND AMENDMENT: THE RIGHT TO BEAR ARMS?

The Second Amendment states: "A well regulated Militia, being necessary to the security of a free state, the right of the people to keep and bear Arms, shall not be infringed." A poll taken in 1995 found that 75 percent of all American voters believe these words guarantee them the right to own a gun.[66] President Bill Clinton, a Yale-trained lawyer and a former professor of constitutional law at the University of Arkansas, said after the bombing of a federal building in Oklahoma City in 1995 that Americans have the freedom to bear arms as well as the freedom to speak and the freedom to assemble.[67] The National Rifle Association (NRA), the country's most prominent opponent of gun-control laws, argues vociferously that Americans have a constitutional right to keep and bear arms.

Although many Americans believe that the Constitution gives them the right to own guns, the Supreme Court has never recognized such a constitutional right. Indeed, no federal court has ever declared a law regulating the private ownership of firearms unconstitutional on Second Amendment grounds.[68] In 1991, retired Chief Justice Warren E. Burger publicly criticized the NRA for perpetuating the myth that Americans have a constitutional right to keep and bear arms. According to Burger, the Second Amendment "has been the subject of one of the greatest pieces of fraud, I repeat the word 'fraud,' on the American public."[69] Instead of granting individuals the right to keep and bear arms, the Court has long held that the Second Amendment only guarantees states the right to maintain militias—or citizen armies—without excessive interference from the federal government.

To understand why the Supreme Court has consistently ruled that the Second Amendment does not grant individuals the right to keep and bear arms, we first need to discuss the role of state militias. Only then can we discuss the Court's rulings and legislative efforts to regulate firearms.

State Militias

British rule left many American colonists deeply distrustful of a standing or professional army. King George III used professional troops to compel the American colonists to obey laws they opposed and to prevent the colonists from having their own weapons. The first shots of the Revolutionary War were fired in 1775 when British troops went to Lexington to seize weapons that the citizens of Massachusetts had stockpiled at a local armory. In light of this history, it is hardly surprising that the colonists came to see militias composed of all able-bodied adult white males as the great bulwark against government oppression.[70]

The reliance that the colonists placed on militias can be clearly seen in the constitutions the newly independent states wrote in the 1770s and 1780s. Virginia's famed Declaration of Rights, which was adopted in June 1776, said that "a well-regulated militia, composed of the body of the people, trained to arms, is the proper, natural, and safe defence of a free State."[71] Pennsylvania's constitution, adopted two months later, declared that "the people have a right to bear arms for the defence of themselves and the state."[72] Indeed, the distrust of a national army ran so deep in Revolutionary America that the Articles of Confederation did not provide for the creation of one. Individual states instead preferred to rely on their own militias.

Fears of a national army and faith in the state militias diminished somewhat in the 1780s as the militias fared poorly in responding to Shays's Rebellion and other disturbances.[73] When the delegates met in Philadelphia in 1787 to write the Constitution, they explicitly gave Congress the authority to create a national army and navy, to set national standards for organizing and arming state militias, and to order the state militias into service on behalf of the country to enforce federal laws, to suppress domestic insurrections, and to repel foreign invasions. Many Antifederalists opposed these provisions of the Constitution, in part because they feared having a national army and in part because they feared that Congress might use its authority to set national standards to bar the states from having militias. To allay these fears and to secure ratification, the Federalists agreed to amend the Constitution to prevent the federal government from interfering with state militias. That agreement produced the Second Amendment.[74]

In the early years of the United States, state militias provided the vast bulk of the country's land forces; when George Washington first took office, the federal army consisted of fewer than 840 soldiers.[75] The performance of the militias was mixed—on several occasions they nearly fought federal troops—and their reputation suffered a "crippling blow as the result of their terrible performance in the War of 1812."[76] They eventually went into decline, and "by the 1840s the militia system envisioned in the early days of the republic was a dead letter."[77] State militias based on the entire adult male population gave way to so-called organized militias composed of elite groups of volunteers. In 1903, Congress passed a law that transformed the organized militias into what we now know as the National Guard. Although the federal government pays and equips the various state National Guards, they are trained by their respective states and under the control of their respective governors until the federal government calls them into service.

Supreme Court Rulings

Unlike the case with the First Amendment, the Supreme Court has held to a consistent interpretation of the Second Amendment. For more than a century, the Court has argued that the Second Amendment was intended to prevent federal interference with state militias rather than to guarantee the right of individuals to own guns.

The first major Second Amendment case was *United States v. Cruikshank,* decided in 1876. In that case, the Supreme Court ruled that gun ownership "is not a right guaranteed by the Constitution. Neither is it in any manner dependent upon that instrument for its existence. The Second Amendment declares that it shall not be infringed; but this, as has been seen, means no more than that it shall not be infringed by Congress."[78] In subsequent cases, "the Court has consistently held to the *Cruikshank* doctrine that the Second Amendment does not apply to the states" (see table 4.1).[79] This means the states are free to restrict or regulate gun ownership.

Ten years after *Cruikshank,* the Supreme Court ruled unanimously in *Presser v. Illinois* that states can ban "private armies" and otherwise regulate militias. The Court again held that the Second Amendment grants states, and not individuals, the right to form well-regulated militias: "We think it clear that the sections under consideration, which only forbid bodies of men to associate together as military organizations, or to drill or parade with arms in cities and towns unless authorized by law, do not infringe

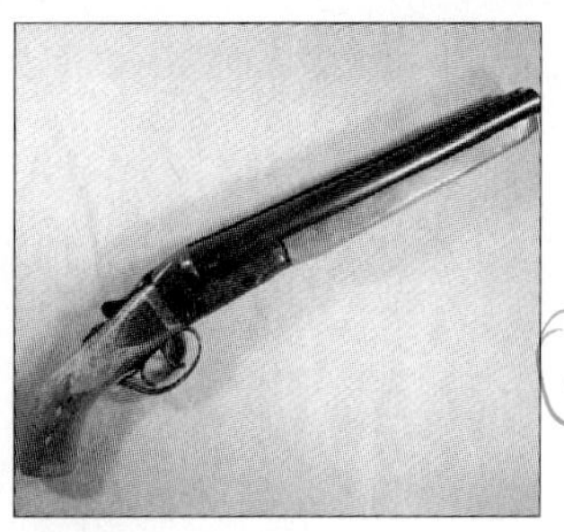

Jack Miller was charged with violating the National Firearms Act of 1934 when he carried a sawed-off shotgun across state lines. The Supreme Court rejected his claim that the National Firearms Act violated the Second Amendment.

the right of the people to keep and bear arms."[80] With this ruling, the Court rejected the claim that individuals can create their own militias. In 1894 and again in 1897, the Court repeated its view that the Second Amendment does not guarantee individuals the right to own guns.[81]

Whereas all the nineteenth-century cases dealt with the validity of *state* laws, the Supreme Court first considered the constitutionality of *federal* laws regulating firearms in the 1939 case of *United States v. Miller*. Jack Miller had been charged with violating the National Firearms Act of 1934 when he carried a sawed-off shotgun across state lines. Miller contended that the Firearms Act violated the Second Amendment. The Court disagreed, arguing that the "obvious purpose" of the Second Amendment was "to assure the continuation and render possible the effectiveness of" state militia forces. As a result, "in the absence of any evidence tending to show that possession or use of a 'shotgun having a barrel of less than eighteen inches in length' at this time has some reasonable relationship to the preservation or efficiency of a well regulated militia, we cannot say that the Second Amendment guarantees the right to keep and bear such an instrument."[82]

The Supreme Court revisited the question of the constitutionality of federal gun control laws in 1980. In its decision, the Court said: "These legislative restrictions are neither based on constitutionally suspect criteria, nor do they trench upon any constitutionally protected liberties."[83] Three years later, the Court let stand without comment or dissent a lower court ruling that the town of Morton Grove, Illinois, had the authority to ban handguns within the city limits. The lower court flatly rejected the argument that Americans have a constitutional right to own guns: "We conclude that the right to keep and bear handguns is not guaranteed by the Second Amendment."[84]

Despite the consistency of the Supreme Court's rulings, a few legal scholars argue that some if not all gun control laws should be ruled unconstitutional.[85] Scholars who criticize the Court's interpretation of the Second Amendment do so on a variety of grounds, but three criticisms stand out. First, critics argue that the Court has misinterpreted the founders' intent. In this view, the Court has simply ignored a constitutional right, in much the same way as it for many years refused to recognize that state-mandated segregation violated the equal protection provision of the Fourteenth Amendment (see chapter 5). Second, critics argue that the wording of the *Miller* case indicates that the Court would recognize the right to own guns if it can be shown the right bears a "reasonable relationship" to national defense. Third, critics argue that, contrary to conventional wisdom, the Court's position on the Second Amendment is not entirely settled. Because the Court has heard only a handful of gun control cases—in part because until recently, government regulation of firearms was minimal—different cases based on different facts might lead the Court to recognize at least a limited right for individuals to keep and bear arms.

Most legal scholars dismiss the criticisms of the Supreme Court's interpretation of the Second Amendment. First, they argue that the history and text of the amendment make it clear that the founders were seeking to prevent the federal government from controlling state militias rather than seeking to guarantee individuals the right to bear arms. (The dispute over what the founders intended by the Second Amendment illustrates the difficulty with using original intent to interpret the Constitution.) Second, they argue that the attempt to interpret *Miller* as justifying a right to gun ownership "is foolish on its face, both because sawed-off shotguns can and do have some military value, and because such a line of reasoning would justify private ownership of militarily useful weapons from bazookas and howitzers to tactical nuclear weapons."[86] Third, they argue that the critics have declined to test their arguments about the Second Amendment in court, preferring instead to challenge gun control laws on other grounds, because they know the case law is settled. As the attorney for one gun control advocacy group puts it:

"The NRA knows that every time the arguments about the history and meaning of the Second Amendment are put before a court of law, its version of an absolute, inalienable 'right' is shown to be nothing but an illusion."[87]

Gun Control Laws

Although the Supreme Court has interpreted the Second Amendment as allowing federal, state, and local government to regulate the sale, possession, and use of firearms, federal gun control laws impose only modest restrictions on gun ownership. The federal government did not pass its first gun control law until 1919.[88] Over the next seventy years, Congress enacted a variety of laws that placed relatively minor restrictions on gun ownership.

In recent years, efforts to enact more stringent federal gun control laws have picked up steam. In 1993, Congress passed the Brady Bill, named after James Brady, the press secretary who was gravely wounded in 1981 when John Hinckley tried to assassinate President Ronald Reagan. The Brady Bill requires a five-day waiting period for the purchase of a gun so that authorities can conduct a background check to see if the purchaser is a convicted felon or has a history of mental illness. In 1994, Congress passed a law banning various types of assault weapons. Despite these laws, however, the federal government places relatively few limits on gun ownership, especially when compared to the very stringent laws found in other advanced industrialized democracies. The lack of restrictive federal gun control laws stems from the political clout of groups such as the NRA rather than from any significant constitutional barrier to gun control laws; this is a good example of a situation in which political power determines the effective rules of the political system.

Partially in response to local and state politics, the restrictiveness of state and local gun control laws varies widely. Most state constitutions have provisions relating to the right to keep and bear arms, but the texts of those provisions differ, as do the interpretations state courts give to them. In general, highly urbanized states such as New York and Massachusetts tend to have the most restrictive gun laws, whereas highly rural states such as New Mexico and Idaho tend to have the least restrictive gun laws. Moreover, most states have also enacted so-called preemption legislation, which bars county and local government from imposing gun laws stricter than those the state has passed.[89]

In addition to regulating individual gun ownership, states may, in keeping with the Supreme Court's decision in *Presser v. Illinois,* regulate the activities of militias. As figure 4.3 shows, forty-two states ban or regulate private militias and paramilitary groups. These anti-militia laws became the subject of debate in 1995 when the Oklahoma City bombing focused public attention on the widespread growth of paramilitary groups in the United States. Critics of the militia movement argue that groups such as the Michigan Militia and the U.S. Militia Association have flourished because states have refused to enforce anti-militia laws. Many law enforcement officials and legal scholars argue, however, that these groups do not meet the legal definition of a militia. To quote one legal scholar: "What is called the Michigan Militia is a private organization. They could call themselves the Michigan Nuts. They are not a militia in any legal sense. There is no law against grown men dressing up in camouflage uniforms and playing soldier with legally acquired weapons."[90]

The prominence of private militias has brought renewed attention to the meaning of the Second Amendment. But unlike the case with the First Amendment, and, as we will see shortly, with the amendments in the Bill of Rights that deal with the rights of criminal suspects, the Supreme Court has consistently interpreted the Second Amendment in the same way. Contrary to widespread public belief that the Constitution guarantees Americans the right to own guns, the Court has long held that no such

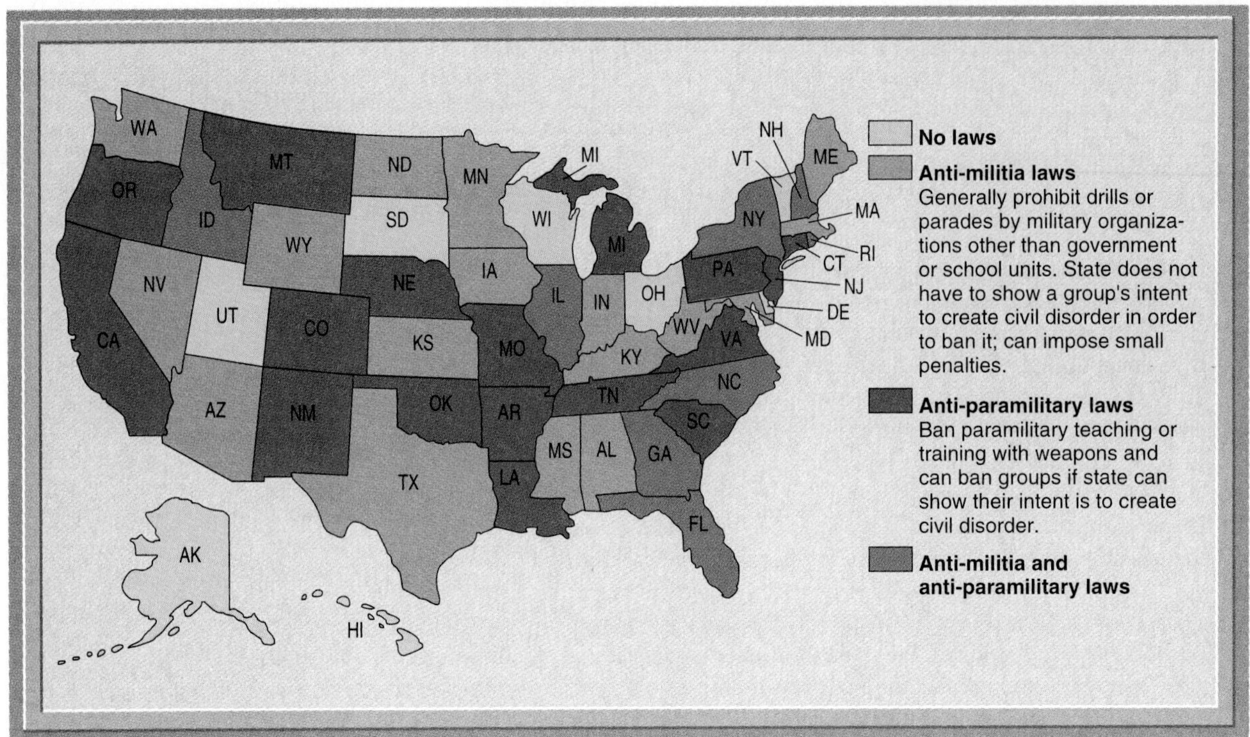

FIGURE 4.3
Regulating Paramilitary Groups
Many states have laws banning or restricting the activities of paramilitary groups.
Sources: Data from "Regulating Paramilitary Groups," *New York Times*, 10 May 1995, and from Klanwatch Project.

fundamental right exists. Instead, for more than one hundred years, the Court has concluded that the Second Amendment only guarantees the states the right to maintain well-regulated militias without excessive interference from the federal government. Proponents of the view that the right to bear arms is a fundamental civil liberty that the Constitution guarantees pledge to press their case, but the Supreme Court shows few signs of being prepared to change its interpretation.

Government and the Rights of Criminal Suspects

Whereas the First Amendment protects the rights of people to speak and write freely, to assemble peaceably, and to practice their religious beliefs, and the Second Amendment protects the right of states to maintain well-regulated militias, several provisions in the Bill of Rights protect the rights of people suspected of committing crimes. The Fourth, Fifth, Sixth, and Eighth Amendments set forth the rules governing the relationship between the federal government and criminal suspects. Proponents of the Bill of Rights insisted on these provisions to limit the federal government's ability to abuse its powers. As a result, the Bill of Rights contains many rules that limit what the government can do to fight crime. As with the First Amendment, however, and unlike the Second Amendment, the limits imposed on government behavior have changed over time. Moreover, the conflict between the rights of the individual and the interests of society that is so prominent in debates over the First Amendment also figures prominently in the area of criminal procedure. As the conflict rages on, the rules keep changing.

The Fourth Amendment: Search and Seizure

The Fourth Amendment was written to prevent the police from searching homes and seizing property without just cause. In most circumstances, police officers must obtain a search warrant before they can search someone's home for evidence of a crime, and judges are to grant a warrant only when the police can show probable cause exists to believe they might find incriminating evidence. In *Wolf v. Colorado* (1949), the Supreme Court extended the Fourth Amendment's requirement for a search warrant to the states.[91] But the *Wolf* decision had no power because it did not forbid states from using information obtained from illegal searches in court. The *Mapp* decision in 1961 changed that.[92]

In establishing rules to govern the conduct of searches, the Supreme Court has sought to balance the protection the Fourth Amendment offers the individual against the realities of police work. The Court has recognized that in many situations, it is unrealistic to expect the police to obtain a search warrant before they look for incriminating evidence. As a result, the Court has created numerous exceptions to the requirement that the police obtain a warrant before conducting a search.

One such exception applies to the ability of police officers to stop motorists. Since 1925, the Supreme Court has allowed police officers to stop and search a car based on probable cause, that is, when they have good reason to think they will find evidence of a crime. But does the police officers' right to stop and search a car extend to searching the package on the back seat or the luggage in the trunk? The Court has changed its view of the constitutionality of such searches over the years, with the most recent ruling giving the police considerable latitude to search a car and its contents.[93] The Court also has given the police the right to search mobile homes, airplanes, and other motor vehicles in most instances.

Police officers also do not need a search warrant to act on evidence in plain view. What constitutes plain view? The Supreme Court confronted this question in a 1968 case in which it held that officers who are legally in a position to see items in plain view may seize those items and use them as evidence.[94] The Court later established three standards for plain view search and seizure: the police must be in position lawfully, the evidence in plain view must be found inadvertently, and it should be immediately obvious to the police that the items in question are illicit.[95]

The Supreme Court has found that aerial surveillance does not violate Fourth Amendment protections. In *California v. Ciraolo* (1986), the police, acting on a tip, used a helicopter to fly over a suspect's backyard to see a marijuana crop they could not see from the ground. They used their visual inspection to get a search warrant, and they arrested Ciraolo. The Court upheld Ciraolo's conviction, noting the police were free to use public airspace to gain incriminating information.[96]

In addition to balancing the protection of the Fourth Amendment with the realities of police work, the Supreme Court has had to reconcile it with the advent of new technology. Take, for instance, the question of whether the police need a search warrant to tap someone's phone. When the Court first addressed the issue in 1928, it held that no search warrant was necessary because electronic eavesdropping fell outside the scope of the unreasonable search and seizure clause.[97] Over time, however, the Court changed its position; in 1967, it held that people "had a reasonable expectation of privacy," which therefore required the police to obtain a search warrant before listening in on a conversation.[98] In 1968, Congress passed a law requiring the Attorney General to obtain court approval for wiretapping.[99] In recent years, the courts have required search warrants for eavesdropping on cellular phone conversations.[100] The expectation of privacy has become an important standard in determining unreasonable search and seizure (and, as we will see, in other areas of the law as well), but this expectation is subject to limits. For example, the Court has held that individuals cannot expect to maintain the privacy of garbage left at the curb.[101]

What happens when the police gather evidence illegally? The answer lies in the **exclusionary rule,** which bars government officials from using evidence obtained in

"YOU MEAN THESE APPLY TO THE RIFFRAFF TOO?"

During the 1960s, the Supreme Court, under the leadership of Chief Justice Earl Warren, extended coverage of the Bill of Rights to many state-level criminal procedures. These protections of people facing criminal prosecution were unpopular then, and they continue to be controversial today.

From *The Herblock Gallery*, Simon & Schuster, 1968. Reprinted by permission.

Exclusionary rule
The doctrine, stemming from the Fourth Amendment, that the government cannot use illegally obtained evidence in court.

In recent years, Congress has debated legislation to expand police powers.

violation of the Fourth Amendment to gain a criminal conviction. The Supreme Court created the exclusionary rule at the federal level in 1914, but did not apply it to the states until 1961.[102] In recent years, the Court has whittled away at the absolute nature of the exclusionary rule, in some cases allowing tainted evidence to enter court if the police acted in good faith in obtaining it.[103] In 1995, the Supreme Court ruled that Phoenix, Arizona police could use evidence of criminal conduct they found in a search triggered by a computer's erroneous report that a valid arrest warrant was in place.[104]

The exclusionary rule gives the police an incentive to follow proper legal procedure when they conduct a search; if they do not, they risk losing a conviction. But the exclusionary rule has always been politically unpopular. Many Americans believe it enables criminals to go free on a "technicality." The best evidence we have on the frequency of such technicalities is a federal government report that found that only around 1 percent of all federal cases involve questions about improper collection of evidence.[105] (Other studies report similar numbers, ranging from 0.6 percent to 2.4 percent of all cases.)[106] Still, in recent years, both Democrats and Republicans have introduced bills in Congress that would limit the exclusionary rule. For example, in 1995, Sen. Orrin Hatch (R-Utah), the chair of the Senate Judiciary Committee, introduced a bill that would abolish the exclusionary rule. To deter police misconduct, Hatch's bill would instead allow victims of illegal searches to sue police and collect judgments for both actual and punitive damages.[107] (Punitive damages are monies assessed to punish a wrongdoer and deter future transgressions.) In this, as in many other cases, the political process may determine an individual's civil liberties.

The Fifth Amendment: Criminal Procedure for a Person Accused

The Fifth Amendment lays out several liberties designed to protect a person accused of committing a crime. Among the most prominent is that no person "shall be compelled in any criminal case to be a witness against himself." Although individuals can refuse to testify against themselves by invoking the Fifth Amendment, they can voluntarily confess, and prosecutors can use "nontestimonial" evidence such as fingerprints and DNA samples. In addition, if a person is granted immunity from prosecution—that is, the government promises to waive charges for the specific crime at issue—he or she can be compelled to testify.

Since individuals have an absolute right to refuse to incriminate themselves, debate has focused on the circumstances under which confessions may be considered voluntary. The Supreme Court first held in 1936 that law enforcement officials cannot use physical torture to force a confession.[108] By 1959, the Court was examining the "totality of the situation" to see if the police had coerced a confession by "third degree" tactics such as long interrogations by teams of interviewers that wear down a suspect's will to resist.[109]

In 1966, the Supreme Court issued a landmark decision in *Miranda v. Arizona* that established procedural rules to protect people subjected to police interrogations.[110] As anyone who watches television knows, the police must inform suspects of their **Miranda rights:** the right to remain silent during questioning, the right to know that any statement may be used as evidence against them, and the right to speak to an attorney before questioning. The police not only must inform a suspect of these rights, but they must also establish that he or she understands them.

Miranda rights
The rights against self-incrimination that the Fifth Amendment guarantees. Miranda rights include the right to remain silent during questioning, the right to know that any statements suspects make may be used as evidence against them, and the right to speak to an attorney before questioning.

Since 1966, the Supreme Court has identified situations in which the violation of a suspect's Miranda rights does not automatically invalidate an arrest. If a suspect provides evidence without being informed of his or her Miranda rights, the evidence may still be used if it inevitably would have been uncovered.[111] In a similar vein, the Court has held that a suspect may be jailed despite a coerced confession if other evidence at the trial would sustain a guilty verdict.[112] The Court has also created a public-safety exemption that allows the police to gain information and act on it if public safety is threatened.[113]

What difference does the requirement to issue a Miranda warning make to law enforcement? One estimate is that the obligation to read Miranda rights to suspects has caused confession rates to drop by around 17 percent.[114] That suggests that perhaps as many as 4 percent of all criminal cases are not successfully prosecuted because of Miranda requirements. Like the exclusionary rule, the Miranda requirement has been the subject of political debate. Some legislators want to limit it, or abolish it altogether.[115]

In addition to establishing a right against self-incrimination, the Fifth Amendment also provides protection against double jeopardy—trying a person acquitted of a crime on the same charge a second time. The protection against double jeopardy was adopted to prevent the government from harassing innocent people by repeatedly trying them for the same offense.

Some situations might seem to suggest a person has been placed in double jeopardy, but the Supreme Court does not agree that these situations constitute double jeopardy. For instance, individuals who commit an act that breaks both state and federal laws can be tried by both jurisdictions. Take, for example, the trials of the four Los Angeles police officers accused of beating motorist Rodney King in the early 1990s. The officers were acquitted in state court of criminal charges that they had used excessive force in arresting King. They were then tried (and two of the officers were convicted) in federal court for violating King's civil rights. The officers were tried twice for the same act, but under different laws in different jurisdictions.

The Sixth Amendment: Procedures for People Charged with a Crime

The Sixth Amendment extends several protections to people charged with committing crimes, including the right to an attorney, the right to a jury trial, and the right to confront witnesses. The Supreme Court recognized a right to legal counsel for people charged with capital crimes for the first time in 1932. In that ruling, the Court directed state governments to provide an attorney for defendants who could not afford one if the defendant might face the death penalty.[116] Not until 1963, however, in *Gideon v. Wainwright,* did the Court require the states to provide legal counsel in all felony cases. The *Gideon* decision marked an important change in policy because most criminal prosecutions take place in state courts.[117] In 1972, the Court extended the guarantee of legal counsel to most misdemeanor cases involving possible jail time.[118] As a

Clarence Gideon's pencil-written petition to the Supreme Court led to the Gideon v. Wainwright *decision, which guaranteed a lawyer to anyone accused of a felony.*

In The Supreme Court of The United States
washington D.C.
clarence Earl Gideon
Petitioner — Petition for awrit
vs. — of Certiorari Directed
H.G. Cochran, Jr., as — To The Supreme Court
Director, Divisions — State of Florida.
of corrections State — No. 890 Misc.
of Florida — OCT. TERM 1961
U. S. Supreme Court

To: The Honorable Earl Warren, Chief
Justice of the United States
Comes now the petitioner, Clarence
Earl Gideon, a citizen of The United states
of America, in proper person, and appearing
as his own counsel. Who petitions this
Honorable Court for a Writ of Certiorari
directed to The Supreme Court of The State
of Florida, To review the order and Judge-
ment of the court below denying The
petitioner a writ of Habeus Corpus.

result of these rulings, people charged with committing a crime are now guaranteed access to legal counsel at most, but not all, pre-trial, trial, and post-trial stages, including one appeal after a felony conviction.

The Supreme Court did not apply the Sixth Amendment's guarantee of a jury trial to state courts until 1968, and even then it required jury trials only in "serious" cases.[119] State trials do not have to follow the procedures used in federal trials in other regards as well. Juries in criminal cases in state courts do not have to have twelve members, as they do in federal courts, although the Court has declared five-member juries are too small.[120] In a similar vein, state courts do not need a unanimous jury vote to convict a person of a crime, although federal courts require unanimity.[121]

The Supreme Court has applied the Sixth Amendment right to confront one's accusers to state courts since 1965.[122] In recent years, the most explosive question involving the right to confront witnesses is whether a person accused of child molestation has the right to confront the child making the accusation. In 1988, the Court held that a screen that had been placed between a defendant and the teenage girls who accused him of molesting them violated his right to confront his accusers. The Court held open the possibility, however, that some protection might be afforded children who needed it. Indeed, in 1990, the Court upheld the conviction of a man in a Maryland case where a six-year-old child testified by closed-circuit television.[123] Again, while the Court upholds the rights of the individual (even one charged with a crime), those rights are not absolute and unlimited. They must always be weighed against the rights of the larger community.

The Eighth Amendment: Cruel and Unusual Punishment

While the Fourth Amendment deals with gathering evidence, the Fifth with persons accused of a crime, and the Sixth with formally charging a person with a crime, the Eighth Amendment addresses what comes after a conviction—it prohibits "cruel and unusual punishment." The Supreme Court has never found capital punishment—the death penalty—cruel and unusual. In 1972, the Court did find that death sentences were being imposed in an arbitrary, and therefore unconstitutional, manner.[124] Four years later, the Court upheld a death penalty law that had been rewritten in response to its earlier objections.[125] Since the late 1970s, the number of executions has escalated, and the public has maintained its substantial support for the death penalty. Indeed, the number of states with a death penalty has increased, and the federal government has increased the number of federal crimes punishable by death. Recent capital punishment cases have challenged *how* the death penalty is applied. The Court has held that someone as young as sixteen years old may be put to death, but not someone fifteen years old, and that the mentally retarded may be executed, but not people who are legally insane.[126]

In writing the Bill of Rights, the founders took several steps to protect the rights of criminal suspects and to prevent the federal government from abusing its police powers. Over the past two centuries, the Supreme Court's interpretation of the rights conveyed by the Fourth, Fifth, Sixth, and Eighth Amendments has changed. As we saw with the First Amendment, the Court has struggled to find the appropriate balance between the rights of the individual and the rights of society. In the past, changes in the political and social climate of the country have influenced the balance between these competing rights. No doubt the same will hold true in the future, and the rules governing the rights of criminal suspects will continue to change.

Privacy as a Constitutional Right

Americans take their right to privacy as a given. But is there a *constitutional* right to privacy? The Constitution does not mention privacy, although hints of such a right appear in the Bill of Rights. Because most Americans cherish their right to privacy while the Constitution says nothing about the scope of that right, privacy issues have fueled some of the country's most bitter political and legal battles.

The Supreme Court's most complete discussion of the right of privacy came in *Griswold v. Connecticut* (1965).[127] At that time, Connecticut had a law forbidding the use of birth control, although the ban was not regularly enforced. When an activist challenged the law, the Supreme Court declared it unconstitutional. The justices supporting the Court's majority position found a right to privacy in several places in the Constitution: the First Amendment's right to association, the Third Amendment's prohibition against quartering soldiers, the Fourth Amendment's ban on unreasonable search and seizure, the Fifth Amendment's self-incrimination clause, and the Ninth Amendment's declaration that the Constitution did not explicitly enumerate all individual rights. (As box 4.2 discusses, the use of the Ninth Amendment was somewhat unusual and controversial in this particular context.) The Court then determined that the zone of privacy a married couple enjoys makes a law prohibiting the use of contraceptives unconstitutional. Several years later, the Court extended the zone of privacy to cover the use of birth control by unmarried couples.[128]

The *Griswold* decision laid the foundation for the Supreme Court's most controversial decision in recent decades: ***Roe v. Wade*** (1973).[129] In *Roe*, the Court held that a woman's right to privacy allows her to obtain an abortion during the first trimester of pregnancy. The Court further held that states can impose reasonable regulations on abortions during the second trimester and can prohibit abortions under most circumstances in the third trimester.

Roe v. Wade
A 1973 Supreme Court decision that a woman's right to privacy prevents states from barring her from having an abortion during the first trimester of pregnancy. States can impose reasonable regulations on abortions during the second trimester and can prohibit abortions under most circumstances in the third trimester.

The political furor *Roe* created cannot be exaggerated. Pro-life organizations have tried to convince the Supreme Court to overturn the decision, and they have lobbied state legislatures to impose stringent restrictions on abortions. Pro-choice groups, on the other hand, have fought to preserve (and expand) the abortion rights *Roe* established. For its part, the Court has allowed states to impose some restrictions, such as barring government funds from being used to pay for abortions and requiring women under the age of eighteen to notify their parents before having an abortion.[130] The Court also appears to have abandoned the trimester system set forth in *Roe*.[131] But thus far, the Court has refused to overturn *Roe* and thereby leave it up to the states to decide whether abortion should be legal.

Although the Supreme Court has established that the right to privacy applies to birth control and abortions, it has not extended privacy rights to all areas of personal activity. For example, in 1986 the Court ruled that a Georgia law against sodomy was

Point of Order

BOX 4.2

The Ninth Amendment: What Does it Mean?

Amendment IX.

The enumeration in the Constitution, of certain rights, shall not be construed to deny or disparage others retained by the people.

The Ninth Amendment.

The first eight amendments to the Constitution enumerate specific rights granted to individuals to protect them from the federal government. The Ninth Amendment breaks from that pattern. It states, "The enumeration in the Constitution, of certain rights, shall not be construed to deny or disparage others retained by the people." In other words, the Ninth Amendment states that the people have rights the Constitution does not list, but it also says nothing about what those rights are. Thus, rather than granting more or fewer specific rights, the Ninth Amendment is ambiguous. What does it mean, and how have the courts used it to define our civil liberties?

It is easier to answer the second part of the question than the first. The Supreme Court seldom refers to the Ninth Amendment in legal argument. One case in which it did was *Griswold v. Connecticut,* a case involving the constitutionality of a Connecticut law banning the use of birth control. In finding Connecticut's law unconstitutional—and thereby expanding each American's right to privacy—the Court relied heavily on the Ninth Amendment. But some legal scholars sharply criticized the Court's decision, so much so that in recent years the Court has tended to make decisions on privacy issues based on other provisions of the Constitution.

The reason for the Court's reluctance to invoke the Ninth Amendment takes us back to our first question—what does the amendment mean? The answer is that no one knows for sure. Indeed, legal scholars disagree vehemently over how the Ninth Amendment affects our civil liberties. A major reason this disagreement exists is that we know relatively little about the history of the amendment, why it was written the way it was, and what the people who supported it thought it would do.

In the absence of a shared understanding of the history of the Ninth Amendment, legal scholars have had considerable freedom to speculate about the amendment's meaning and purpose. Some prominent legal scholars take an expansive view of the Ninth Amendment, arguing that it gives federal judges the authority to establish rights not specifically mentioned in the Constitution or its amendments. This is essentially the approach that Justice Douglas took in writing the Supreme Court's opinion in the *Griswold* case. As you might imagine, this expansive interpretation of the Ninth Amendment places tremendous power in the hands of the Supreme Court.

Other prominent legal scholars reject an expansive reading of the Ninth Amendment. They argue that such an interpretation would allow judges to open up a "Pandora's Box" of new constitutional rights. In rejecting an expansive interpretation, critics point out that the Ninth Amendment explicitly refers to other rights "retained by the people." They argue that this phrase indicates that the founders intended for the amendment to refer to well-known rights that the American people already had. If one accepts this interpretation, then the meaning of the Ninth Amendment depends on our understanding of what rights people had at the time the amendment was written. And to determine what those known rights were, we need to look at both state constitutions and at common law of that time. (Common law is the collection of rules and principles long used in custom and the judicial recognition of those customs.) Under this restricted interpretation, the founders intended the Ninth Amendment merely to reassure Americans that the enumeration of rights contained in the first eight amendments did not threaten their existing rights.

The ongoing debate over the meaning of the Ninth Amendment reflects the importance of the rules in American politics. One interpretation gives judges broad powers that can change how government and citizens may interact, while the other limits the powers judges may exercise. This all underscores the enduring power of rules.

Sources: Robert Bork, *The Tempting of America: The Political Seduction of the Law* (New York: Touchstone, 1990), pp. 183–85; James A. Curry, Richard B. Riley, and Richard M. Battistoni, *Constitutional Government: The American Experience* (St. Paul, Minn.: West, 1989), p. 410; H. L. Pohlman, *Constitutional Debate in Action: Civil Rights and Liberties* (New York: HarperCollins, 1995), pp. 131–37.

Does the Bill of Rights imply a "right to privacy"? The U.S. Supreme Court said it did in Griswold v. Connecticut; *this later became the basis for* Roe v. Wade, *which made abortion legal.*

constitutional, thereby rebuffing the defendant's argument that his sexual practices were covered by a right to privacy.[132] The Court has also indicated that the right to privacy does not necessarily mean a right to die, finding that the state may have a right to regulate the circumstances under which decisions about life support or euthanasia are made.[133]

Our concepts of the civil liberties guaranteed by the Bill of Rights are very different from what the founders envisioned in the late eighteenth century. At times, the Supreme Court and the elected branches of government have expanded civil liberties; at other times, they have narrowed them. In most cases, however, the Court, Congress, and other governmental institutions have recognized that individual freedoms must be balanced against the rights of society.

Summary

The Constitution sets forth the fundamental rules governing the relationship between the government and its citizens. These rules attempt to guarantee certain civil liberties, most of which Americans cherish as fundamental rights and freedoms. But although we think of these liberties as absolute and fixed concepts, they are neither. Part of government's task is to balance competing rights; in doing so, it must continually redefine the rules that govern our civil liberties.

Our civil liberties are rooted in the Bill of Rights. The Bill of Rights guarantees all Americans an extensive set of civil liberties, including freedom of speech, the right to assemble peaceably, and protection against unreasonable search and seizure (though not the right to own guns). Yet none of our civil liberties is absolute. The Supreme Court and Congress have long recognized that the rights of the individual must be weighed against the rights of society. One of the Court's tasks is to decide how to balance competing rights—where to draw the line when individual rights conflict with the common good.

If the civil liberties the Constitution provides are not absolute, neither are they fixed. As the membership of the Supreme Court and the values of society both change, so does the meaning of the Constitution. For many years, for example, the Court declined to apply the Bill of Rights to state government. In 1897, however, the Court changed its mind; over the past hundred years, the justices have gradually used the due process clause of the Fourteenth Amendment to extend the civil liberties guaranteed in the Bill of Rights to limit state and local laws.

The civil liberties we enjoy are quite different from what the founders envisioned because of the flexibility of the Constitution and the dynamics of a growing, changing society. At times our civil liberties have expanded, and at other times, they have narrowed. Throughout our history as a nation, however, we have striven to find a fair balance between the rights of the individual and the rights of society, and we will undoubtedly continue to do so.

Key Terms

Bad tendency doctrine
Civil liberties
Clear and present danger standard
Establishment clause
Exclusionary rule
Free exercise clause
Incitement standard
Libel law
Miranda rights
Obscenity law
Original intent
Pentagon Papers
Prior restraint
Roe v. Wade

Readings for Further Study

Abraham, Henry J., and Barbara A. Perry. *Freedom and the Court: Civil Rights and Liberties in the United States,* 6th ed. New York: Oxford University Press, 1994. A leading text explains the evolution of civil liberties.

Alderman, Ellen, and Caroline Kennedy. *In Our Defense: The Bill of Rights in Action.* New York: Morrow, 1991. An accessible set of stories about important cases that test our understanding of our civil liberties.

Alderman, Ellen, and Caroline Kennedy. *The Right to Privacy.* New York: Knopf, 1995. An engaging discussion of the evolution of the right to privacy in U.S. law.

Friendly, Fred W., and Martha J. H. Elliott. *The Constitution—That Delicate Balance.* New York: Random House, 1984. Another very accessible analysis of many of the important cases in the development of American constitutional law.

Levy, Leonard W. *Original Intent and the Framers' Constitution.* New York: Macmillan, 1988. Levy examines the historical evidence on original intent and analyzes court decisions on each major right the Bill of Rights grants.

Lewis, Anthony. *Gideon's Trumpet.* New York: Vintage, 1964. The story of Clarence Earl Gideon's successful Supreme Court appeal, which overturned his conviction for burglary on the grounds that he had no legal counsel at his trial.

Strossen, Nadine. *Defending Pornography: Free Speech, Sex, and the Fight for Women's Rights.* New York: Scribner, 1995. The president of the American Civil Liberties Union argues that censorship, not pornography, poses the greatest danger to women's rights.

Walker, Stephen. *In Defense of American Liberties: A History of the ACLU.* New York: Oxford University Press, 1990. A rich history of the American Civil Liberties Union and its decades-long battle to expand American civil liberties.

Chapter 5

Civil Rights

Civil Liberties and Civil Rights

Discrimination Against African Americans

From Slavery to Emancipation

Jim Crow

The First Civil Rights Organizations

The Brown Decision

The Civil Rights Movement

Congress Responds

The Continuing Fight Against Discrimination

Discrimination Against Asian Americans, Hispanic Americans, American Indians, and Others

Asian Americans

Hispanic Americans

American Indians

Other Minorities

Discrimination Against Women

Campaigning for the Right to Vote

The Fight for Equal Rights on Capitol Hill

The Fight for Equal Rights in the Courts

The Continuing Struggle Against Sex Discrimination

Extending Civil Rights

People with Disabilities

People with Age Claims

Gays and Lesbians

The Burden of Proof

Affirmative Action: Equal Opportunity or Equal Outcomes?

Summary

Key Terms

Readings for Further Study

In the summer of 1995, the University of California Board of Regents met to consider a proposal to end thirty years of racial and gender-based preferences in admissions, hiring, and contracting. Over time, these preferences had substantially increased the number of women and minorities attending and working at the system's nine campuses. But these preferences were now under fire in the country's most ethnically diverse state. While African Americans and Hispanic Americans had benefitted from the preferences, Asian Americans—a significant minority in California, as we saw in chapter 3—thought such policies limited their opportunities for higher education. A petition drive was under way to put a proposition on the state ballot to end all racial and gender-based preferences at the state and local levels. Surveys showed the measure enjoyed broad support. And Gov. Pete Wilson, a member of the Board of Regents, was making opposition to racial and gender-based preferences a major plank in his planned campaign for the Republican Party's presidential nomination.

The proposal before the Board came from Regent Ward Connerly, an African-American businessman from Sacramento. Connerly argued, "It is impossible for me to conclude that a preference for some based on race is not a disadvantage, is not discrimination against others."[1] Connerly's position was backed by state Assemblyman Nao Takasugi, who as a young man was interned in a detention camp with other Japanese Americans during World War II. Takasugi stated, "I have lived a life of hardship and challenges. It was also a life of goals achieved through hard work and merit . . . not based on the color of my skin but based on my own achievement. I wouldn't have it any other way."[2] Among those speaking against the proposal was Dr. Haile Debas, dean of the prestigious medical school at the University of California, San Francisco, and an immigrant from Ethiopia, who countered, "My success represents a personal triumph. But I publicly acknowledge that without the environment created by affirmative action, the doors would have been closed to me."[3] After listening to supporters and opponents for more than six hours, and having their meeting interrupted first by a bomb threat and later by a noisy demonstration, the regents voted in favor of ending racial and gender-based preferences in admissions, hiring, and contracting.[4]

The University of California Regents found themselves debating racial and gender-based preferences during the summer of 1995 because discrimination has a long and tragic history in American society. Despite a promise to "establish justice" and "secure the blessings of liberty," the original text of the Constitution made discrimination legally permissible. Although the word *slavery* was not used, Article I, Section 9 and Article IV, Section 2 essentially condoned the bondage of African Americans. Moreover, Article I, Section 2 stipulated that when counting the population to apportion seats in the House of Representatives, slaves should be considered equal to three-fifths of a free person; American Indians (called Indians in the Constitution) were not to be counted at all unless they paid taxes (that is, lived off their tribal reservations). None of the articles guaranteed equal rights for women, and the Supreme Court would later rule that the Constitution did not require that women be allowed to vote.[5]

Ever since the signing of the Constitution, some people have fought to see the blessings of liberty extended to all Americans, regardless of race, gender, or ethnicity. In many battles they have succeeded, and government has changed the rules that govern our civil rights. American citizens can no longer buy and sell slaves. Women, African Americans, American Indians, and members of other groups can vote. The battle over civil rights has at times exposed the ugly side of American society, but it also has demonstrated the capacity of the courts and other governmental institutions to translate the promises of the Constitution into reality, at least in some areas. Today, many Americans find themselves debating, as the University of California regents did, the question of what steps the government should take to aid the victims of discrimination.

In July 1995, the University of California Board of Regents voted to end the University's affirmative action program. The decision sparked demonstrations and even a bomb threat.

In this chapter, we examine the evolution of civil rights in the United States and the role politics plays in defining them. We explore how African Americans pioneered the civil rights movement and how other groups—including Asian Americans, Hispanic Americans, American Indians, women, people with disabilities, people with age claims, and gays and lesbians—have fought to ensure that they, too, enjoy the freedoms the Constitution promises. We conclude the chapter with a look at affirmative action, demonstrating the conflicts that may arise when two sets of rights collide. When this happens, our interpretations of civil rights change as government seeks to manage the conflict; often, as we shall see, political considerations determine the final balance. Groups on both sides battle hard to establish rules that favor their side. They know the rules matter—because the rules determine the rights real people exercise every day in the United States.

Civil Liberties and Civil Rights

The distinction between civil liberties and civil rights is difficult to draw. Both involve the federal government's relationship with individuals. As we discussed in chapter 4, the term *civil liberties* usually applies to the freedoms the Bill of Rights guarantees (although some are in the body of the Constitution). These liberties include freedom of speech, freedom of religion, and the right to assemble peaceably. In a very general sense, the civil liberties listed in the Bill of Rights restrain government—they prohibit government from taking negative actions that tread on individual rights.

The term **civil rights** usually refers to the notion of equality of rights for all people regardless of race, sex, ethnicity, religion, sexual orientation, and so on. Civil rights are rooted in the courts' interpretation of the Fourteenth Amendment and in laws that Congress and the state legislatures pass. Broadly speaking, civil rights require government to take positive actions to protect individual rights—for example, to desegregate public schools.

Civil rights
The equality of rights for all people regardless of race, sex, ethnicity, religion, and sexual orientation. Civil rights are rooted in the courts' interpretation of the Fourteenth Amendment and in laws that Congress and the state legislatures pass.

In practice, civil liberties and civil rights are closely linked. But sometimes the two can conflict. For example, laws designed to protect minorities from so-called hate speech can infringe on the rights of others to exercise their freedom of speech. (As we saw in chapter 4, the First Amendment applies even to speech that many Americans find reprehensible.) How can we balance the rights of some individuals to be protected from discrimination with the rights of other individuals to speak their minds as they see fit? Finding such a balance is not always an easy task. As we will see, the pursuit of civil rights—government's attempt to ensure equality of rights—can sometimes conflict with civil liberties.

Until the end of the Civil War, African Americans were bought and sold as slaves. The experience with slavery and racism has shaped the relationship between African Americans and the legal system.

Discrimination Against African Americans

Although many groups have participated in the struggle to ensure equal rights for all Americans, the battle for civil rights is most closely identified with African Americans, and their victories have been extended to benefit other groups. The leading role African Americans have played in the push for civil rights reflects their unique experience in America. The United States did not ban slavery until the end of the Civil War, and many African Americans were denied full political rights until well into this century. The experience with slavery and racism has shaped the relationship between African Americans as a group and the legal system.

To examine the problem of discrimination against African Americans, we must review the African-American journey from slavery to emancipation, and then explore the steps that many states took to deny African Americans the rights they won at the end of the Civil War. We will then discuss the appearance of the first civil rights organizations, their success in challenging discriminatory laws, and the birth of the civil rights movement. We will conclude the section by examining the steps Congress has taken to protect and promote the civil rights of African Americans and by discussing the continuing controversy over what steps the government may properly take to help the victims of discrimination. Though African Americans have made great strides in changing the rules to expand their civil rights, these rule changes have yet to bring them social and economic equality.

From Slavery to Emancipation

African Americans first arrived in what would become the United States in 1619. Many came initially as indentured servants who agreed to work for an employer for a fixed number of years in order to pay for their passage to America. By the latter half of the seventeenth century, however, slavery had taken hold in the thirteen colonies, especially in the South. As we discussed in chapter 2, the status of African Americans was a major issue at the Constitutional Convention in 1787. Delegates from southern states strongly defended slavery, whereas delegates from northern states were inclined to limit and eventually terminate the practice. Because southern delegates made it clear that they would desert the Convention rather than accept a constitution that abolished slavery, northern delegates dropped their efforts to insert a provision in the Constitution that would have banned slavery. In this case, as would be true many times in later years, political pressures molded the rules that denied African Americans their civil rights.

In addition to allowing the practice of slavery to continue, the founders inserted language into the Constitution that barred Congress from stopping the slave trade before 1808. As soon as the ban lapsed, Congress made the importation of slaves illegal. The buying and selling of slaves already in the country continued unabated, however, until the Civil War. Although slavery became an increasingly divisive and unpopular policy, the Supreme Court continued to find it constitutional, most notably (as we saw in chapter 2) in the *Dred Scott* decision of 1857.[6] In that case, the Court held that African Americans were not citizens of the United States, and therefore, they were not entitled to the liberties granted in the Constitution.

During the Civil War, President Lincoln issued the Emancipation Proclamation, which freed only those slaves living in the Confederacy. Slavery was finally made illegal everywhere in the country with the ratification of the Thirteenth Amendment in 1865. (Mississippi did not ratify the amendment until 1995, making it the last state to do so.) But while the Thirteenth Amendment made slavery unconstitutional, it did not guarantee that African Americans would be able to exercise the political rights available to other Americans. Many southern states quickly passed laws, called *Black Codes,* that barred African Americans from (among other things) buying and selling property, signing business contracts, and serving on juries. By severely limiting the legal rights of African Americans, the southern states were effectively forcing them back into slavery.

Congress responded to the Black Codes by passing a series of civil rights laws between 1866 and 1875. Congress also proposed the Fourteenth Amendment, which the states ratified in 1868. That amendment granted citizenship to "All persons born or naturalized in the United States," thereby nullifying the *Dred Scott* decision. The amendment also stipulated, among other things, that no state shall "deprive any person of life, liberty, or property, without due process of law," and it promised that all people would receive equal protection under the law. As we discussed in chapter 4, since the turn of the century, the Supreme Court has used the language of the Fourteenth Amendment to extend the Bill of Rights to cover the actions of state governments. The Court has also used it to advance the civil rights of African Americans and other groups. But in the second half of the nineteenth century, the Court would not take to heart the Fourteenth Amendment's injunction to provide all Americans with "equal protection of the laws." In effect, the Court ignored the spirit of this rule.

In addition to the Thirteenth and Fourteenth Amendments, Congress proposed the Fifteenth Amendment as another way to protect the civil rights of African Americans. Ratified by the states in 1870, the Fifteenth Amendment gave African-American men the right to vote for the first time. For a brief time, many African-American men enjoyed a measure of political equality with white men. Between 1869 and 1877, two African Americans from the South were elected to the Senate, and fourteen were elected to the House. (Until the early twentieth century, the vast majority of African Americans lived in the South.) A major reason the Fifteenth Amendment succeeded initially was that the federal troops still occupied the southern states, and while their record was by no means perfect, they did much to protect African Americans from intimidation and retaliation by white Southerners. (Federal troops occupied the South from 1865 to 1877, a period of time known as *Reconstruction.*)

Although Congress acted in the years immediately following the Civil War to guarantee (at least in writing) the *political* rights of African Americans, it did little to protect or improve their *economic* condition. Despite a promise Union Gen. William Tecumseh Sherman made to African Americans in the last months of the Civil War, Congress refused to pass legislation to confiscate southern plantations and give each former slave "forty acres and a mule."[7] Without land of their own to farm or an education to fall back on—slaveowners generally prevented their slaves from learning to read and write—and faced with the hostility of most white Southerners, African Americans had few opportunities to escape poverty. As a result, at least in terms of economic conditions, their lives as free citizens in many respects resembled the lives they had led as slaves.

With the passage of the Thirteenth, Fourteenth, and Fifteenth Amendments, African Americans initially enjoyed a measure of political equality with whites. Between 1869 and 1877, two African Americans were elected to the Senate and fourteen were elected to the House.

Source: National Portrait Gallery, Smithsonian Institution.

Jim Crow

The political victories that African Americans had won in the heady days immediately following the Civil War began to dissipate during the mid-1870s. In 1876, the outcome of the presidential election between Republican Rutherford B. Hayes and Democrat Samuel J. Tilden was disputed. (Tilden had won a majority of the popular vote, but the question of who had won a majority of the electoral votes was open to debate.) In the end, southern Democrats agreed to support Hayes for president in return for a Republican promise to withdraw federal troops from southern states and to drop the federal government's efforts to protect African Americans living in the South. With the end of Reconstruction came the end of congressional efforts to bar discrimination against African Americans for nearly half a century—a sad instance when political deal making resulted in new rules that restricted the civil rights of African Americans.

Just as African Americans found themselves abandoned by the political branches of the federal government, they found the federal courts equally unwilling to give life to the spirit of the Civil War amendments and legislation. In 1873, the Supreme Court handed down a ruling that interpreted the Fourteenth Amendment in a very narrow fashion, so narrow, in fact, that it virtually nullified the amendment as a source of legal protection for African Americans.[8] In its decision, the Court noted that the Fourteenth Amendment distinguished between national citizenship and state citizenship. The Court used this distinction to argue that, with the exception of a few broad rights such as the right to travel and the right to enter into contracts, the amendment was not intended to guarantee individual rights against state government actions. In essence, then, the Court held that state governments were not obliged to honor the rights (such as those set forth in the Bill of Rights) conferred upon Americans as a result of their national citizenship.

Three years later, the Supreme Court handed down two rulings, both on the same day, that curtailed the political rights of African Americans even further. In one case, the Court ruled that federal laws that punished individuals who violated the rights of African Americans were unconstitutional.[9] This ruling gutted Congress's ability to extend equal rights to African Americans. In the other case, the Court ruled that the Fifteenth Amendment did not guarantee all men over age twenty-one the right to vote.

The Ku Klux Klan peaked at a membership of about 5 million in the 1920s.

Instead, the Court argued, the amendment simply listed reasons that could not be used to deny citizens the right to vote.[10] The Court's decision gave the states permission to enact laws, such as literacy tests and poll taxes, that effectively denied African Americans the right to vote. The net result was to rob the Fifteenth Amendment of much of its meaning. It would be nearly a century before African Americans in the South (and in some parts of the North) would regain the right to vote. (Indeed, no African American from the South would serve in Congress from 1901 until 1973.)[11]

With the federal government no longer willing to protect the rights of African Americans, legal discrimination became a constant part of African-American life despite the promises contained in the Thirteenth, Fourteenth, and Fifteenth Amendments. Many southern states adopted **Jim Crow laws** that suppressed the rights of African Americans. (The term *Jim Crow* came from an early eighteenth-century Kentucky plantation song. By the mid-nineteenth century, the term was synonymous with the legal suppression of African-American rights.)[12] The result was **de jure segregation,** with African Americans required by law to live and work separately from white Americans. Many state governments actually maintained segregation in the workplace by making it illegal to hire African Americans for many jobs. Other laws barred African Americans from using the same public accommodations as whites. Throughout the South, hospitals, public parks, cemeteries, prisons, and even drinking fountains and rest rooms were all segregated by race. In the North, meanwhile, Jim Crow laws were far less common, but social practices effectively discriminated against African Americans and thereby limited their opportunities for education and employment.

Jim Crow laws
Laws that discriminated against African Americans, usually by enforcing segregation.

De jure segregation
Government-imposed laws that required African Americans to live and work separately from white Americans.

African Americans periodically challenged the constitutionality of Jim Crow laws in court, but they repeatedly came away disappointed. The most important such case was *Plessy v. Ferguson* (1896), in which the Supreme Court upheld segregated public facilities. This ruling established the **separate-but-equal standard** (see box 5.1), which declared that segregated facilities were acceptable as long as they were "equal."[13] Most prominent among the public facilities where the Court sanctioned segregation was the public school system. School segregation was so common, the Court noted in *Plessy,* that Congress had created and supported segregated schools in the District of Columbia. Only Justice John Harlan, a former slaveowner himself, disagreed with the ruling of the majority. In a dissent that would remain famous long after his death, Harlan wrote: "Our Constitution is color blind, and neither knows nor tolerates classes among citizens. In respect of civil rights, all citizens are equal before the law."

Separate-but-equal standard
The now-rejected Supreme Court doctrine that separation of the races was acceptable as long as each race was treated equally.

State-sanctioned discrimination made it easy for private groups, most notably the Ku Klux Klan (KKK), to terrorize African Americans. The Klan was originally formed in 1865 in Tennessee by a small group of ex-Confederate soldiers who wanted to resist the Union occupation. Its practice of terrorizing African Americans prompted Congress to pass a law in 1872 (which the Supreme Court declared unconstitutional in

The People Behind the Rules

BOX 5.1

Who Were Plessy and Brown?

In the 1890s, Homer Adolph Plessy challenged the Louisiana law requiring "equal but separate accommodations for the white and colored races." He lost.

Few names loom larger in the history of American civil rights than Plessy and Brown, the names in two of the most important Supreme Court decisions. Yet most people know little about these two individuals. Who were they, and how did they become such important actors on the stage of American history?

Homer Adolf Plessy

Homer Adolph Plessy was an African-American civil rights activist from New Orleans who chose to challenge one of Louisiana's Jim Crow laws, state statutes that legalized segregated public facilities. In 1890, the Louisiana state legislature had followed the lead of several other southern states and passed a law requiring that "all railway companies carrying passengers in their coaches in this State, shall provide equal but separate accommodations for the white, and colored, races." Until a few years earlier, most southern railroads had allowed African Americans to mix with whites in second-class, though not in first-class. Although the railroads in Louisiana were not actively enforcing the law, Plessy's fellow activists arranged for him to be arrested in the whites-only passenger car of the East Louisiana Railway. The first judge he faced was John H. Ferguson of the Criminal District Court of New Orleans. Ferguson ruled that the law did not violate the Fourteenth Amendment, as Plessy had argued; the Supreme Court ultimately upheld his decision in the infamous case that preserved both their names, *Plessy v. Ferguson*. From this case stemmed the separate-but-equal standard that legitimized discrimination for the next half century.

Oliver Brown

The case that led the Supreme Court to repeal the separate-but-equal standard was *Brown v. the Board of Education*. Oliver Brown was a railroad worker in Topeka, Kansas. In September 1950, he attempted to enroll his daughter Linda in the third grade at the Sumner School, which was located four blocks from the Browns' home. The Sumner School was for white children only, however, and the Brown family was African American. Because Topeka, like many other American cities, had a segregated school system, Linda had been forced to attend the Monroe School, which was located about a mile from her home. After officials at the Sumner School refused to accept Linda as a student, Oliver Brown sued the local school board at the urging of the local chapter of the NAACP. Brown's legal challenge wound its way through the legal system, eventually winding up in the Supreme Court. Chief Justice Earl Warren, writing on behalf of a unanimous Court, held that segregated school systems denied African-American children equal protection under the law.

Both *Plessy v. Ferguson* and *Brown v. the Board of Education* pitted individual rights against the rights of society. Although the outcome of each case was very different, Plessy and Brown share one distinction: few Americans have had a greater impact on the rules that govern our civil rights than Homer Plessy and Oliver Brown.

Source: See Richard Kluger, *Simple Justice* (New York: Vintage Books, 1975).

1883) making it a crime for any individual to deprive another of his or her rights. The original Klan collapsed shortly after it was founded, but it was revived in 1915. Its membership grew rapidly, peaking at 5 million in 1924. The power of the Klan in the southern states led to its label as "the invisible empire of the South."[14]

The Klan frequently used violence to intimidate African Americans as well as any whites who opposed segregation. To serve as a warning of impending violence, Klan members initiated the practice of cross burning. Beatings were the most common form of violence, but at times violence escalated to murder. Klan members (and nonmembers as well) often practiced **lynching,** that is, the unlawful killing, usually by hanging, of a person by a mob. Lynchings were exceptionally brutal and sadistic events, perhaps none more so than one that took place in Livermore, Kentucky, in 1911:

Lynching
The unlawful killing, usually by hanging, of a person by a mob.

> A Negro charged with murdering a white man was seized and hauled to a local theater, where an audience was invited to witness his hanging. Receipts were to go to the murdered white man's family. To add interest to the benefit performance, seatholders in the orchestra were invited to empty their revolvers into the swaying black body while those in the gallery were restricted to a single shot.[15]

Lynchings were especially common in the 1890s, with an average of one African American lynched every two-and-a-half days.[16] In all, more than three thousand African Americans were lynched in the South and elsewhere in the United States between 1880 and 1960.[17]

Despite the barbarity of the attacks on African Americans, the federal government repeatedly refused to step in to protect them. Successive presidents insisted that state and local governments must control mob violence, and Congress refused to pass legislation that would have made lynching a federal crime. State and local officials, however, usually failed to prosecute whites who lynched or otherwise terrorized African Americans, either because they approved of the attacks—many government officials belonged to the Klan or sympathized with it—or because they feared that doing so would cost them their jobs.

The First Civil Rights Organizations

In response to the spread of Jim Crow laws, a number of organizations formed to fight for the rights of African Americans. The most important was the National Association for the Advancement of Colored People (NAACP), founded in 1909 by black sociologist W. E. B. Dubois and others. The goal of the NAACP, whose founding members included African Americans and whites, was to end racial discrimination and legal segregation. The organization began a slow but steady battle to rewrite the rules and policies discriminating against African Americans.

The NAACP used many different strategies to advance the cause of African Americans, but it achieved the most success by filing lawsuits. In seeking vindication in the courts, the NAACP's legal team faced daunting odds. In many parts of the country, the deck was clearly stacked against African Americans. Take, for example, the prosecution of black sharecroppers in Arkansas in 1919. Their attempts to unionize had brought a violent response from landowners and local authorities, culminating in a pitched battle between the two sides. One account shows that

> Nearly one hundred blacks were indicted by an all-white grand jury on various charges; twelve were charged with murder. (A lone white man arrested was considered to be a union sympathizer.) Though the trials were brisk—none lasted more than forty-five minutes—they positively meandered compared to the five minutes (on average) required of the juries to return the guilty verdicts. In five days, twelve men were sentenced to die in the electric chair and eighty others were sentenced to prison terms of from one to twenty years.[18]

NAACP lawyers appealed the death sentences, and the Supreme Court later overturned each sentence because the sharecroppers had been denied due process, or the right to be tried according to fundamental, established legal principles.[19] Here, the existing rules of government were newly applied to protect the rights of African Americans.

Despite facing a very hostile legal environment, the NAACP won some important victories. In 1915, the Supreme Court accepted its argument that election laws containing *grandfather clauses* were unconstitutional.[20] (When southern states adopted literacy tests to deny African Americans the right to vote, they protected the voting rights of illiterate whites by stipulating that anyone who failed a literacy test could still vote if their grandfathers had had the right to vote before 1867—that is, before African Americans could legally vote in the South.) In 1917, the NAACP persuaded the Court that laws barring African Americans from buying homes in white neighborhoods were unconstitutional.[21] In 1938, the NAACP convinced the Court that the state of Missouri's refusal either to admit African Americans to the University of Missouri law school or to establish a separate African-American law school violated the Constitution. (Missouri's policy had been to pay for its African-American citizens to attend law school in other states.) The decision meant that, at a minimum, states were obligated to establish law schools for African Americans "substantially equal to those which the State there offered for persons of the white race."[22]

In 1944, the NAACP Legal Defense and Education Fund—created out of the NAACP in 1939 so that the NAACP itself could concentrate on lobbying the political branches of government—won a major victory in the fight to secure voting rights for African Americans. That year, the Supreme Court ruled that the southern practice of white-only primaries was unconstitutional.[23] At the time, Republican candidates seldom won elections in the South, so the real political battles generally took place in the Democratic primaries. Because they were barred from voting in the primaries, African Americans were denied the right to help pick candidates, and thereby effectively denied the right to help choose elected officials. The states had argued that the political parties administered the white primary, and that the parties were private organizations and thus entitled to discriminate if they wished. The Court disagreed.

In addition to its victories in the courts, the NAACP and other civil rights organizations won some victories by working through the other branches of government. For example, despite the heroic contributions of African-American soldiers throughout American history, the armed forces remained segregated at the end of World War II. One of President Truman's top advisors later recalled that by the late 1940s,

> the Army and the Air Force had only one black Colonel each, and no one of higher rank. The Navy had a grand total of four black officers, the Marine Corps only one. . . . I thought the Navy at times resembled a Southern plantation that had somehow escaped the Civil War. Blacks swabbed the decks, shined the shoes, did the cooking, washed the dishes, and served the food. Virtually no other jobs were open to them. The Army . . . had established a quota for black Americans in the Army of 10 percent—a policy Army leaders actually thought of as progressive. They trained with white troops but lived in segregated barracks, shopped at segregated stores, rode on segregated trains, and served in segregated units.[24]

Civil rights organizations campaigned to end such discrimination, taking their case to the White House and Congress, and President Harry Truman responded. In 1948, he issued landmark executive orders ending segregation in the armed services and in all other parts of the federal government.[25]

Finally, civil rights activists pushed on social and economic fronts as well. During World War II, for example, African-American leaders increased pressure on major league baseball to break the color barrier and sign African-American ballplayers.[26] In October 1945, the Brooklyn Dodgers took the lead by signing Jackie Robinson, a UCLA alumnus and World War II army officer playing in the Negro baseball leagues. When Robinson broke into the majors in 1947, African Americans around the country greeted his arrival as a major step forward.[27] Few teams, however, rushed to sign other African-American ballplayers, and only a handful joined Robinson in the majors over the next few years. Those that followed in Robinson's footsteps found playing in minor league cities, especially in the South, a humiliating experience. Curt Flood, an outstanding player with the St. Louis Cardinals, said of his days in the minor leagues that

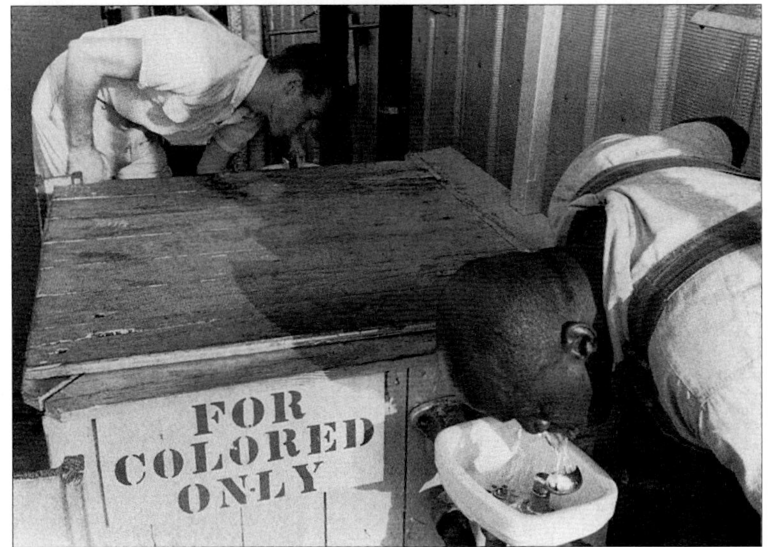

Before the passage of civil rights legislation in the 1960s, laws in many states banned African Americans and other minorities from using facilities reserved for whites.

> of the many indignities to which I was subject, few angered me more than the routine in [the] bus. When we were in transit and the team made a dinner stop, I wasn't permitted in the dining room. I had to go to the back door of the restaurant, like a beggar. . . . If I had to relieve myself, the bus would stop along the highway and I would hide from traffic as best I could.[28]

Because legal and social discrimination remained, African Americans continued to suffer a multitude of indignities in everyday life to remind them of their second-class status in the United States.

The Brown Decision

Even though by the late 1940s the NAACP had won important legal victories and President Truman had ended segregation in the armed forces, segregation remained firmly embedded in American life. That would finally begin to change in the 1950s, as the Supreme Court handed down a series of rulings that recognized the promise of equal protection the Fourteenth Amendment made to all Americans. In other words, the Court began enforcing the rules and policies already in place for white Americans.

The main legal battleground was the issue of segregated schooling. In two important rulings handed down in 1950, the Supreme Court effectively ended racial segregation in law schools and graduate schools. In the first case, the Court found that the state of Texas had established an African-American law school clearly inferior to the white law school at the University of Texas "in terms of number of faculty, variety of courses and opportunities for specialization, size of the student body, scope of the library, [and] availability of law review and similar activities."[29] In the second case, the Court ruled against the state of Oklahoma's decision to allow an African-American student to attend graduate school at the University of Oklahoma only if he sat in separate sections of the classroom, library, and cafeteria facilities. In the Court's view, these restrictions impermissibly impaired the student's "ability to study, to engage in discussions and exchange views with other students, and, in general, to learn his profession."[30]

The two decisions the Supreme Court handed down in 1950 failed to overturn the separate-but-equal standard set forth in *Plessy*. Instead, they set the standard for judging whether a state or local government had provided "substantially equal" facilities so high that it was nearly impossible to meet. It would not be until 1954, and the landmark case of ***Brown v. Board of Education,*** that the Court would finally overturn *Plessy*.[31] (The lead lawyer for the NAACP Legal Defense and Education Fund in the case was Thurgood Marshall, who thirteen years later would become the first African American appointed to the Supreme Court.)

Brown v. Board of Education The landmark 1954 Supreme Court decision holding that separate was not equal and public schools must be desegregated.

Thurgood Marshall *first established himself as a national figure through his work as the director of the NAACP Counsel of Legal Defense and Education Fund. In that capacity, he led the legal team that argued the landmark* Brown v. Board of Education *case before the Supreme Court. He was later named a Supreme Court justice.*

The *Brown* case addressed the fundamental question of whether segregated schools are constitutional (see box 5.1). A unanimous Supreme Court ruled they are not. In the words of Chief Justice Earl Warren:

> We conclude that in the field of public education the doctrine of "separate but equal" has no place. Separate educational facilities are inherently unequal. Therefore, we hold that the plaintiffs and others similarly situated . . . are, by reason of the segregation complained of, deprived of the equal protection of the laws guaranteed by the Fourteenth Amendment.[32]

The Court held that separate educational facilities are inherently unequal because they irreparably damage the self-esteem of African-American children—"To separate [African-American children] from others of similar age and qualifications solely because of their race generates a feeling of inferiority . . . that may affect their hearts and minds in a way unlikely ever to be undone."[33] Thus, fifty-eight years later, the Court redressed the historic wrong it had done to African Americans in *Plessy.*

The Supreme Court's ruling in *Brown v. Board of Education* was courageous in many respects. Many people, both inside and outside of government, wanted the Court to find school segregation constitutional. Chief Justice Warren found himself overtly pressured to rule against the NAACP's position. President Dwight Eisenhower, who had nominated Warren to the Court only a year earlier, invited the Chief Justice to dinner at the White House. He used the dinner to defend segregationists: "These are not bad people. All they are concerned about is to see that their sweet little girls are not required to sit in schools alongside some big overgrown Negroes."[34] Despite the pressure from Eisenhower, Warren actively worked to convince justices who were initially inclined to find segregation constitutional to vote with the majority, thereby allowing the Court to speak in a unified voice on a highly controversial issue.

Brown v. Board of Education II The 1955 Supreme Court decision that stated that the nation's entrenched system of segregated schools should desegregate with "all deliberate speed."

Massive resistance The policy many southern states followed in the wake of the first *Brown* decision of fiercely resisting desegregation.

Although the Supreme Court ruled against school segregation in *Brown v. Board of Education,* the case left open the question of *how* to dismantle the nation's entrenched system of segregated schools. In 1955, in a case known as ***Brown v. Board of Education II,*** the Court settled that question by stating that schools were to desegregate with "all deliberate speed."[35] The Court also assigned the lower federal courts the task of supervising school desegregation.

Although some states began the desegregation process the *Brown* decision mandated, many did not. State and local governments throughout the South initially engaged in **massive resistance,** the policy of fiercely resisting desegregation.[36] Confrontations between the federal courts and state and local officials erupted. In 1957, the governor of Arkansas ordered the state's National Guard to prevent nine African-American students from enrolling at an all-white high school in Little Rock. When the governor's actions led to mob violence, President Eisenhower, who had long been reluctant to have the federal government enforce desegregation orders the federal courts had issued, finally sent

When segregationists refused to allow African-American students to enter formerly all-white schools, federal troops sometimes had to come in to restore order and enforce desegregation laws.

U.S. troops to Little Rock to restore order and to allow the nine students to enroll.[37] Elsewhere, states passed laws "requiring state schools to be closed if blacks and whites were placed in the same facilities."[38] The state of Virginia closed down the public schools in Norfolk for the entire 1958–59 school year rather than integrate them. Some states set up programs that paid the tuition of white students who attended private schools, which at that time had a legal right to discriminate against African Americans. (The Supreme Court eventually ruled that private school segregation was unconstitutional as well.)[39] As a result of these and other tactics, in 1964, ten years after the Supreme Court handed down its decision in *Brown,* "97.75 percent of the South's black schoolchildren still attended all-black schools."[40] And in 1969, the Court was still pushing schools to obey its desegregation orders from a decade and a half earlier.[41]

Resistance to desegregation was equally fierce on college campuses. In 1962, the governor of Mississippi personally tried to prevent James Meredith from registering as the first African-American student at the University of Mississippi in Oxford. When President Kennedy announced in a televised address that Meredith must be allowed to register, segregationists in Oxford began to riot and two people were killed. Peace was restored and Meredith was allowed to register only after Kennedy ordered nearly 20,000 troops to the town.[42] The refusal to desegregate an all-white college until the federal government threatened to use force was repeated the following year in Alabama. Gov. George Wallace, who at his inauguration months earlier had vowed "segregation now, segregation tomorrow, segregation forever," blocked the door to the registration building at the University of Alabama to keep the first two African Americans from registering.[43] Wallace quickly backed down, however, when Kennedy issued the order to send troops to the campus.

As the federal courts sought to desegregate public schools in the first decade after the *Brown* decision, the Supreme Court extended the principle that separate is inherently unequal by striking down laws that mandated segregation in public places such as parks, swimming pools, and courtrooms. Yet because of public resistance to the Court's rulings, especially intense in the South but by no means unique to that region, the day-to-day lives of African Americans changed remarkably little. African Americans who insisted on their rights often faced beatings and even murder at the hands of ardent segregationists, and law enforcement officials often turned a blind eye to such crimes. The Court's promises would become reality only as a result of the rise of the civil rights movement.

The Civil Rights Movement

Civil rights movement
The mobilization of people to push for racial equality.

Following the initial *Brown* decision, African Americans, as well as many white Americans, joined civil rights protests that generated significant public pressure to put an end to segregation. The **civil rights movement** organized protests that would eventually reshape public opinion and lead Congress to take action to protect the rights of African Americans.

The civil rights movement was born in 1955 in Montgomery, Alabama with a simple act of defiance. Rosa Parks, a forty-three-year-old seamstress and active member of the NAACP, boarded a city bus and sat in a front seat reserved for whites. When the bus driver ordered her to move to the back of the bus, as the law required her to do, Parks refused. She was arrested and fined $10 for violating the city ordinance. Parks's arrest prompted Montgomery's African-American community to boycott the city's buses. The boycott lasted for a year, ending only when the Supreme Court affirmed a lower court ruling that laws requiring segregation on city buses are unconstitutional.[44]

Civil disobedience
The nonviolent refusal to obey what one perceives to be unjust laws.

The Montgomery bus boycott thrust its leader, the Rev. Dr. Martin Luther King, Jr., into the national spotlight. King and the organization he led, the Southern Christian Leadership Conference (SCLC), pioneered the idea of **civil disobedience**—the nonviolent refusal to obey what one perceives to be unjust laws—as a means to force an end to racial discrimination. In his famed "Letter from Birmingham Jail"—he was arrested in Birmingham, Alabama in April 1963 for parading without a permit—King explained that civil disobedience "seeks to create such a crisis and foster such a tension that a community which has constantly refused to negotiate is forced to confront the issue [of segregation]. It seeks so to dramatize the issue that it can no longer be ignored."[45] Thus, King and the SCLC hoped that civil disobedience would make the plight of the African-American community a national (and even worldwide) concern and force changes in U.S. law.

One type of civil disobedience was the sit-in. In 1960, four first-year African-American students at North Carolina Agricultural and Technical College in Greensboro sat down to eat at a white-only lunch counter at a local Woolworth's store. The African-American waitress refused to serve them, saying that "Fellows like you make our race look bad."[46] The four students sat at the lunch counter all afternoon, then returned the next day to continue their sit-in protest. Despite threats of violence, other students quickly joined the sit-in—by the sixth day of the protest, some four hundred students showed up at Woolworth's. Others in the South and later elsewhere quickly emulated the Greensboro sit-in to protest segregation.[47]

The Greensboro sit-in inspired the "freedom rides" of the summer of 1961. Organized by the leaders of the Congress of Racial Equality (commonly referred to by its acronym, CORE, and at the time a more militant civil rights organization than the NAACP), the freedom rides were intended to pressure government to desegregate public facilities such as bus stations. In May, two buses containing African-American and white volunteers left Washington, D.C., to travel around the South, challenging local and state Jim Crow laws. Concentrating their initial efforts on Alabama, the "freedom riders," as they came to be called, met strong resistance; a mob in Birmingham beat them (the local police chief said that police could not protect them because it was Mother's Day and most police officers were off-duty visiting their mothers), and white supremacists in Anniston burned one of their buses. President Kennedy and his brother, Attorney General Robert Kennedy, responded to the violence by sending six hundred federal marshals to protect the riders. Later that summer, the Interstate Commerce Commission ordered the desegregation of all terminals used in interstate transportation.[48]

Another tactic the civil rights movement used to promote the cause of African-American rights was the protest march. Sometimes the marches turned violent as police officers and segregationists attacked the protesters. In a 1963 march organized by Rev. King, more than one thousand African-American students marched to protest the segregation of public facilities in Birmingham, Alabama. Rather than ignore or

Marches and mass protests across the nation helped persuade Congress to pass the Civil Rights Act of 1964.

arrest the demonstrators, Birmingham authorities doused them with water from high-pressure fire hoses and then unleashed police dogs on them. The following year in Selma, Alabama, King organized another march to demand that restrictions on African-American voting rights be lifted. The march broke up when Alabama state troopers clubbed some marchers and segregationists beat and shot others.

In addition to practicing civil disobedience, the civil rights movement also worked within the law to promote the rights of African Americans. Many civil rights organizations launched efforts in the South to register African Americans to vote, calculating that if more African Americans voted, they could elect officials opposed to discriminatory laws. As with civil disobedience, however, their attempts to register African Americans to vote often made civil rights workers the targets of segregationist violence. For example, African-American and white college students mounted a voter registration drive in Mississippi in the summer of 1964. By the end of the summer, eighty had been beaten, thirty-five shot, and at least six killed, including three who were apparently murdered with the help of a local sheriff and his deputy.[49]

As you can see, the people who took part in the civil rights protests of the early 1960s often did so at great personal risk. Yet the courage these protesters demonstrated helped to change public opinion—and ultimately the rules and policies that perpetuated legalized discrimination—throughout the United States. Many white Americans who initially believed that the protesters were asking for too much too soon found the violent attacks on demonstrators repulsive and concluded that segregation had to end.

Congress Responds

The *Brown* decision and the rise of the civil rights movement placed early pressure on Congress and President Eisenhower to enact stronger civil rights legislation. In 1957, Congress responded by passing the Civil Rights Act. From the viewpoint of substance, the bill accomplished little. Its major provision created a Civil Rights Commission, a nonpartisan and temporary body charged with investigating and documenting civil rights violations. From a symbolic viewpoint, however, the bill was tremendously important. It marked the first time in the twentieth century that a coalition of northern Democrats and Republicans had been able to overcome the adamant opposition of southern Democrats to civil rights legislation. Three years later, Congress passed another civil rights bill. Among other things, the Civil Rights Act of 1960 established criminal penalties for people who used the threat of force to obstruct federal court orders on civil rights matters. The rules were changing as the federal government responded to the steady pressure of the civil rights movement.

FIGURE 5.1
African Americans Elected to Office, 1970–1993

Since the passage of the Voting Rights Act of 1965, the number of African Americans elected to political office at the federal, state, and local levels has increased substantially.

Source: Data from Harold W. Stanley and Richard G. Niemi, *Vital Statistics on American Politics,* 5th ed. (Washington, D.C.: CQ Press, 1995), p. 369.

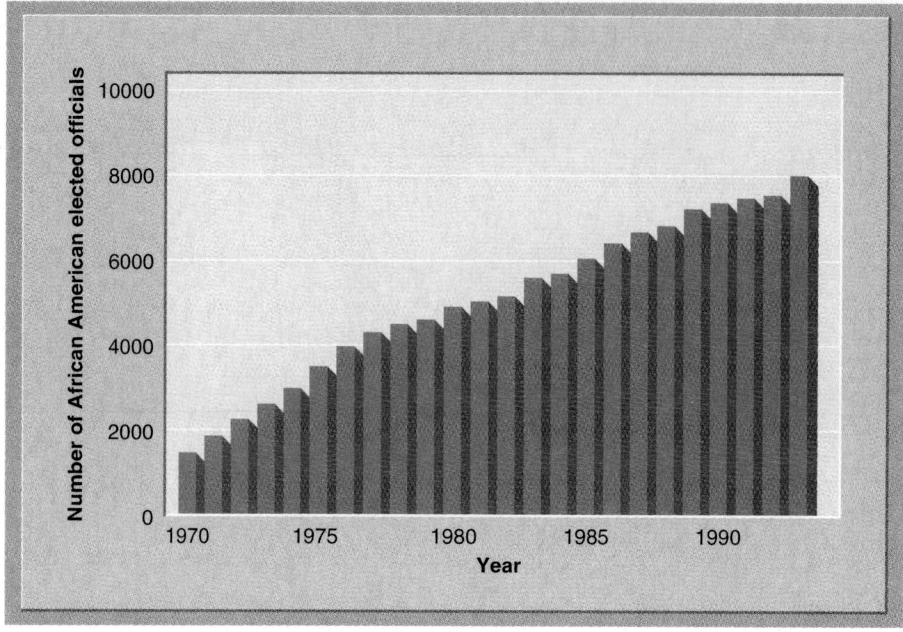

The Civil Rights Acts of 1957 and 1960 fell far short of guaranteeing African Americans their constitutional rights. But support among the American public for stronger civil rights legislation grew, especially in the wake of the television and newspaper photos of police dogs and fire hoses unleashed on demonstrators in Birmingham. Many members of Congress agreed it was time to take stronger action, including some not known for liberal view on matters of race; for example, as civil rights protests spread, the generally conservative Senate Minority Leader Everett Dirksen (R-Ill.) remarked that equality before the law was "an idea whose time had come."[50] The push for stronger civil rights legislation also gained momentum following the assassination of President Kennedy in November 1963. Not only did many in Congress regret not acting on a civil rights bill the slain president had introduced in Congress, but his successor, Lyndon Johnson, made civil rights his top legislative priority.

Civil Rights Act of 1964
An act of Congress that outlaws racial segregation in public accommodations and employment and prevents tax dollars from going to organizations that discriminate on the basis of race, color, or national origin.

With strong backing from President Johnson, himself a southerner, Congress passed the **Civil Rights Act of 1964.** The landmark bill outlawed segregation in public accommodations such as theaters, restaurants, and motels, and it barred tax dollars from going to organizations that discriminated on the basis of race, color, or national origin. The act also made job discrimination illegal, and it created the Equal Employment Opportunity Commission to enforce fair employment policies. The Civil Rights Act of 1964 is by far the strongest piece of civil rights legislation ever passed. It gave African Americans and others who had been denied full rights greater opportunities to participate in the mainstream of American social and economic life.

Voting Rights Act of 1965
An act of Congress that bars states from creating voting and registration practices that discriminate against African Americans and other minorities.

Equal rights for all Americans was enhanced the following year with the passage of the **Voting Rights Act of 1965.** Although the Fifteenth Amendment was adopted to guarantee African Americans the right to vote, as we have seen and as chapter 7 discusses further, many southern states adopted registration laws that made it difficult, if not impossible, for most African Americans to vote. The Voting Rights Act outlawed most registration and voting practices that discriminated against African Americans and other minorities. Perhaps even more important, it gave the Justice Department authority to review registration and voting laws in states in which less than 50 percent of the population was registered. Over the following two decades, the Voting Rights Act led to a dramatic increase in the number of African Americans registered to vote. As the number of African-American voters increased, so did the number of African Americans elected to political office, especially at the local level.[51] As figure 5.1 shows, changes in registration and voting laws have had a real and profound effect on the political power of African Americans.

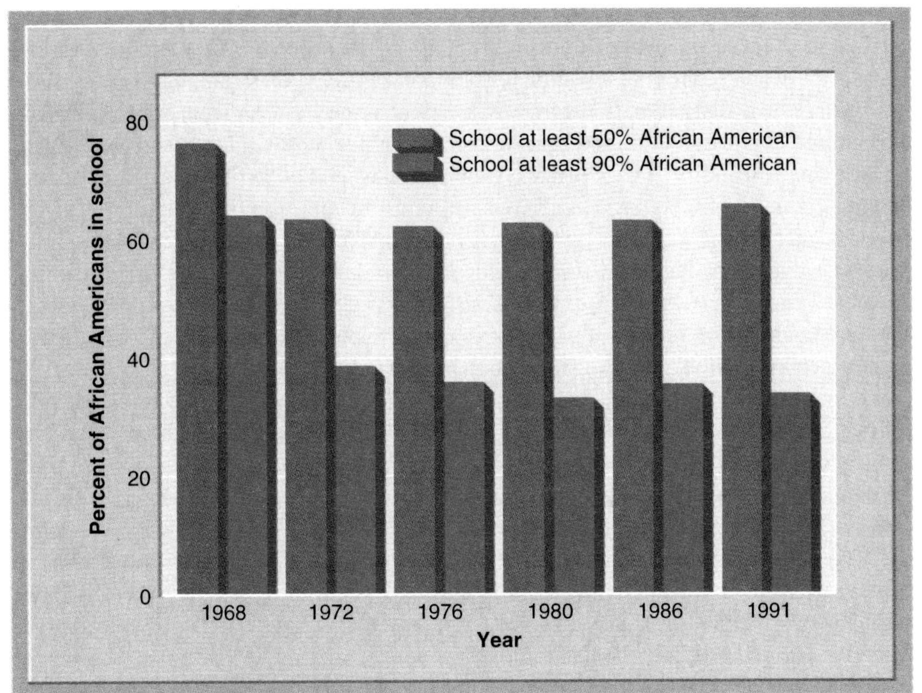

FIGURE 5.2
School Integration in the United States

U.S. schools are now more integrated than they used to be, but many children still attend schools in which minority groups overwhelmingly dominate the enrollment.

Source: Data from Harold W. Stanley and Richard G. Niemi, *Vital Statistics on American Politics*, 5th ed. (Washington, D.C.: CQ Press, 1995), pp. 365–66.

Congress has passed other civil rights legislation since the mid-1960s, but none has matched the importance of the Civil Rights Act of 1964 and the Voting Rights Act of 1965. In 1968, Congress banned racial discrimination in housing, and in 1974 it outlawed discrimination in the extension of credit. The most recent civil rights bill, the Civil Rights Act of 1991, essentially clarified disputed provisions of earlier legislation and expanded several interpretations of earlier laws that the Supreme Court had narrowed. Of course, passing a law does not in itself root out discrimination. As much attention is now devoted to enforcing existing laws as to writing new ones.

The Continuing Fight Against Discrimination

Have African Americans won their fight for equal rights under the law? As with many questions, the answer depends on one's vantage point and one's expectations.

In some respects, the change in race relations in the United States over the past forty years is nothing short of remarkable. In 1954, the year the Supreme Court handed down its decision in *Brown,* African Americans in many parts of the country were barred from attending school with whites, forced to ride in segregated buses, and effectively denied the right to vote. Moreover, African Americans were virtually absent from national political life. Forty years later, racial discrimination is no longer legal; African Americans serve prominently in Congress, the executive branch, and the Supreme Court; and one African American (the Rev. Jesse Jackson) finished second in the race for the presidential nomination of the Democratic Party while another (Gen. Colin Powell) was a favorite for the presidential nomination of the Republican Party before deciding not to run.

Yet if the United States has moved dramatically away from the segregated society it once was, it has by no means become a society in which, to borrow the famous words of the Rev. Martin Luther King's "I Have a Dream" speech, people are judged not "by the color of their skin, but by the content of their character."[52] Despite the fact that government-mandated segregation is illegal, **de facto segregation**—that is, segregation that results from the acts of individuals rather than the government—persists. For example, as figure 5.2 shows, while the percentage of African-American children attending integrated schools has increased over time, many still attend schools where the majority of students are minorities. Moreover, various measures of education, income, and health reveal that African Americans

De facto segregation
Segregation that results from the actions of individuals rather than the government.

continue to lag behind white Americans. Indeed, as their differing reactions to the verdict in the O. J. Simpson murder trial in 1995 show, African Americans and white Americans seem at times almost to inhabit two very different Americas.

Thus, racial discrimination remains a potent issue in American politics, raising thorny political, legal, and moral questions. As the dispute over admissions qualifications for the University of California system suggests, and as we will discuss at greater length later in this chapter, much debate surrounds the question of what steps the government may properly take to fight discrimination. This debate has been just as difficult for judges as it has been for elected officials. For example, ever since handing down its *Brown* decision, the Supreme Court has struggled with the question of how to achieve desegregated schools. For many years, the Court supported forced busing as a way to achieve school desegregation, but in recent years, it has moved to limit the practice.[53] The Court's change in direction in part reflects the public's backlash against busing and other remedial programs that are viewed as special treatment for African Americans, but it also reflects the tremendous difficulty the justices have in balancing the rights of African Americans (and other ethnic and racial minorities as well) against the rights of the white majority.

The complexity of many civil rights issues and the lack of easy answers helps to explain why the civil rights movement is not the force it once was in American politics. Most civil rights organizations have watched their memberships decline sharply since the early 1970s. The NAACP almost went bankrupt in 1995 amidst an internal squabble over charges that its leaders had engaged in financial mismanagement. Meanwhile, Reverend King's old organization, the SCLC, exists in name only.[54]

As traditional civil rights organizations seek to rejuvenate themselves, they are finding their claim to leadership challenged by other voices in the African-American community. In some respects, this is nothing new. The African-American community, like other communities in American society, has always harbored a wide range of views. Even at the height of the civil rights movement, Martin Luther King and other civil rights leaders were challenged on the one hand by conservative African Americans who argued that they were asking for too much too fast, and on the other hand by militant African Americans who argued that they were too eager to accept the rules of white society. Among the most important militants was Malcolm X, a leading member of the Nation of Islam (or Black Muslim faith), who called for creating a separate African-American nation built apart from white society and paid for by white reparations for slavery.[55] Shortly before he was assassinated in 1965, Malcolm X left the Nation of Islam and modified his views on black separatism, admitting the possibility of interracial brotherhood.

Many of these same divisions remain in the African-American community. Conservative African-American intellectuals argue that many of the problems currently facing African Americans are rooted in the African-American community itself and that most government programs designed to help African Americans perpetuate the problems rather than solve them.[56] While recognizing that racism exists in the United States, conservative African Americans contend that African Americans must rely more on themselves and on the opportunities available to them. As the writer Shelby Steele puts it, "There is today, despite America's residual racism, an enormous range of opportunity open to blacks in this society. The nexus of this new [African-American] identity must be a meeting of black individual initiative and American possibility."[57]

For their part, militants continue to advocate radical steps such as the creation of an independent African-American nation separate from white America. The most prominent advocate of black separatism for many years has been Louis Farrakhan, the head of the Nation of Islam, though in recent years he has taken some steps toward the political mainstream. Farrakhan is an enormously controversial figure; his supporters hail him as an unbending defender of African-American interests, and his critics denounce him as a racist and an anti-Semite. African Americans themselves are deeply divided over Farrakhan; a poll conducted in 1995 found that 41 percent of African Americans viewed him unfavorably, while 41 percent viewed him favorably.[58] Moreover, few

In 1995, Louis Farrakhan and the Nation of Islam brought hundreds of thousands of African-American men to the Million Man March in Washington, D.C.

African Americans believe that Farrakhan's views reflect what they think—the same 1995 poll found that only 14 percent of African Americans think he reflects the mainstream of African-American thought. Nonetheless, Farrakhan successfully organized the Million Man March, which brought hundreds of thousands of African-American men to Washington, D.C., in October 1995 to participate in the largest civil rights demonstration in U.S. history.[59]

It remains to be seen whether traditional civil rights organizations will succeed in rejuvenating themselves to tackle the civil rights issues of the twenty-first century or whether they will cede their leadership of the African-American community to other groups. However, no one can deny the successes that civil rights organizations achieved during the twentieth century in securing rule changes that protect the civil rights of African Americans. Moreover, these changes benefitted many other minority groups in the United States in the years to follow.

Discrimination Against Asian Americans, Hispanic Americans, American Indians, and Others

Although African Americans were the only group of Americans forced into slavery, Asian Americans, Hispanic Americans, and American Indians have also endured virulent racism, legal under our political rules for many years, that has denied them their political rights. The advances of the African-American civil rights movement have benefitted each of these groups, but their own unique histories give them somewhat different problems to solve. Each of their victories, whether in the courts or other political arenas, has improved not only their own prospects for gaining civil rights, but also the prospects of other groups.

Asian Americans

Like African Americans, Asian Americans have long endured official discrimination.[60] A particular source of discrimination for many years was immigration policy, which, like the rules governing the rights of African Americans, has changed as American society has changed. For much of the nineteenth century, the United States had no immigration laws; indeed, the young nation openly welcomed immigrants. In the 1860s, many Chinese began to come to the United States to work on building railroads in the West. In the 1870s, railroad construction slowed, and as the competition for jobs increased, anti-Chinese sentiment and violence grew. In 1882, Congress passed the Exclusion Act, which barred all immigrants from China for ten years. Rather than diminish anti-Chinese violence, however, the law seemed only to fuel it. In 1892, Congress passed legislation that prohibited Chinese immigration indefinitely.[61]

U.S. immigration policy also discriminated against immigrants from Japan. In 1890, the government of Japan allowed its citizens to emigrate for the first time, and by 1900, 24,000 Japanese immigrants had arrived in California.[62] Although Japanese immigrants constituted less than 2 percent of the state's population, anti-Japanese racism quickly surfaced, and the California state legislature began to consider proposals to restrict their rights. To head off legislation that he feared would damage America's standing in Asia, President Theodore Roosevelt negotiated a "Gentleman's Agreement" with Japan in 1907. Under the terms of the agreement, Tokyo "voluntarily" agreed to restrict Japanese emigration to the United States.[63]

In 1921 and 1924, Congress formally changed the rules and revamped the country's immigration laws, this time by imposing a "national origins quota system" that limited the number of immigrants allowed into the United States from outside the Western Hemisphere. The quotas were tied to the percentage of each ethnic group already living in the United States, but people from Asia (and Africa) were barred from immigrating. In 1952, Congress relaxed the ban on immigration from some Asian countries, but it retained the national origins quota system. Despite the change, Asian immigrants continued to be penalized because Asian Americans constituted such a small share of the American population; hence, the number of Asians admitted into the United States was correspondingly small. Congress abolished the national origins quota system in 1968 and replaced it with a first-come, first-served system that gives preference to foreign relatives of American citizens and to people with special skills.

Once in the United States, immigrants from Asia often found themselves subjected to official discrimination. In 1913, the California state legislature passed a law that effectively barred Japanese immigrants—as well as immigrants from other Asian countries—from owning agricultural land in the state.[64] Racism was the motivating factor behind the law—state legislators railed against the prospect of interracial marriage, and the governor openly worried that the Japanese were "driving the root of their civilization deep in California soil."[65] The state legislature had targeted land ownership because Japanese immigrants to California had been extraordinarily successful as farmers—by 1910, they accounted for 20 percent of the state's agricultural output.[66] Over the next ten years, more than half a dozen states would follow California's lead and pass laws barring Asian immigrants from owning land.[67]

Asian immigrants were vulnerable to discriminatory laws because U.S. laws had long designated them, unlike immigrants from Europe, as "aliens ineligible to citizenship." (Children born in the United States of Asian immigrant parents were, however, considered American citizens.) In 1914, Takao Ozawa, a Japanese immigrant who had come to the United States as a student to learn about democracy, was turned down when he applied for citizenship. Ozawa, who had studied law at the University of California, prepared his own case, challenging the constitutionality of laws denying Asian immigrants the right to be naturalized—that is, to become American citizens. Ozawa's case wound its way through the legal system for eight years before finally reaching the Supreme Court. In a landmark decision, the Court held that immigrants from Asia could not become American citizens because the Constitution limited naturalization to "free white persons and to aliens of African nativity and persons of African descent."[68] Immigrants from Asia would remain ineligible for American citizenship until 1952, when Congress finally passed legislation removing all racial discrimination from the country's immigration laws.

Even when people of Asian ancestry held American citizenship because they had been born in the United States, they could not count on equal protection under the law. During World War II, President Franklin Roosevelt ordered the relocation of all people of Japanese ancestry living on the West Coast—most of whom were American citizens

In the 1944 Korematsu v. United States *decision, the Supreme Court upheld the government's right to imprison U.S. citizens in internment camps, such as this one at Manzanar, California, solely because of their Japanese ancestry. In 1988, Congress formally apologized for these actions.*

because Japanese immigration had long since ended—to detention camps. The government did not force Americans of German and Italian heritage to relocate.[69] The Supreme Court upheld the legality of the relocation order as well as several other directives that restricted the rights of people of Japanese ancestry. In its rulings, the Court gave much greater weight to the government's claims that Japanese Americans posed a potential risk to national security than to the internees' argument that the orders violated their civil rights.[70] Not until 1988 did Congress pass a law that formally apologized for the internment and provided financial compensation to the survivors.[71]

Although the legal system discriminated against Asian Americans until well into the twentieth century, they did on occasion win legal vindication. In one landmark civil rights case in 1886, for example, the Supreme Court overturned a San Francisco ordinance intended to prevent Chinese from operating laundries.[72] As rules protecting the rights of minority groups accumulated with the key civil rights decisions of the 1950s and the congressional legislation of the 1960s, Asian Americans gained a fuller measure of protection for their civil rights.

Like many other non-English speaking minorities, Asian Americans have often faced discrimination because of their language. In the early 1970s, Chinese parents in San Francisco sued the local school district because it had failed to establish a program to help students who were not native English speakers to overcome the language barrier. The case eventually reached the Supreme Court, which agreed with the parents, concluding that the Civil Rights Act of 1964 required school districts to provide special assistance to Chinese-speaking students.[73] The basic principle behind the Court's ruling—that public schools should teach students in a language they can understand—has been extended to other non-English speaking minority groups, including Hispanic Americans, Filipino Americans, and Vietnamese Americans. The result has been the rapid growth of bilingual education throughout the United States—a good example of how a change in rules can influence policy outcomes that affect everyday lives.

In recent years, Asian Americans have worried that because they have been so successful economically—as chapter 3 discusses, Asian-American households are on average the wealthiest in the United States—they are now subject to discrimination of a different sort. In 1994, for example, Chinese Americans in San Francisco filed suit against the city school district to overturn a court-ordered desegregation plan. That plan, which went into effect in 1983, defines nine racial groups among San Francisco's students and mandates that no group may compose more than 45 percent of the student body in any school. To maintain that balance, administrators have had to shuffle students among schools. In one instance, the school district set different standards for members of various ethnic groups seeking admission to the city's premier high school. Thus, Chinese-American applicants must score higher than whites, other Asian Americans, and students from the other six ethnic groups on the school's admissions test. The lawsuit the Chinese Americans filed challenges the legality of the school district's policy. (Discrimination cases often take years to decide, and the San Francisco case has not been resolved.)[74]

Hispanic Americans

Like African Americans, many Hispanic Americans have been the victims of rules and policies that perpetuate discrimination. In states with large Hispanic populations such as California and Texas, many Hispanic children were forced for many years to attend segregated schools. Like African Americans, Hispanic Americans had to turn to the courts to force desegregation.[75]

Many Hispanic Americans have also been discriminated against because they speak Spanish rather than English. This was long a particular problem at the ballot box, as many states had laws requiring voters to pass an English literacy test. In 1966, the Supreme Court upheld the constitutionality of a provision of the Voting Rights Act of 1965 that outlawed such tests.[76] And as we just saw, as the result of a case involving Chinese Americans, school districts are now required to provide bilingual education programs to Hispanic-American children.

Immigration issues affect many Hispanic Americans, especially those living in the Southwest. Hispanic Americans have applauded some court rulings on immigration matters. In 1971, for example, the Supreme Court ruled that legal residents—people living legally in the United States who are not citizens—are entitled to welfare benefits (a right legislation passed in 1996 significantly reduces), and eleven years later it ruled that the children of illegal residents have the right to attend public schools.[77] Hispanic Americans have criticized other court rulings, however. Most notably, the Court has ruled that the U.S. Immigration and Naturalization Service has broad powers to arrest and search illegal aliens.[78] Many Hispanic Americans worry that such power will be abused, and as a result, that the rights of Hispanic citizens will be violated.

The Hispanic community's concerns about immigration issues intensified in 1986 after Congress passed the Immigration Reform and Control Act, which among other things imposed substantial fines on employers who hire illegal residents. Many Hispanic Americans fear that employers will make it a rule not to hire any Hispanic, even if he or she is an American citizen or a legal resident, to avoid inadvertently violating the 1986 law. A 1996 law reinforced these concerns by making it harder to sue employers for discrimination in hiring.

American Indians

American Indians have had a unique relationship with the federal government and have lived under a unique set of laws and rules. The Constitution did not grant them citizenship. Instead, for more than one hundred years after the writing of the Constitution, the prevailing belief was that American Indian tribes constituted their own political communities separate from the United States. As a result, the federal government pushed American Indians onto reservations, the dimensions of which continually shrank as the United States enveloped and devoured their land.

The passage of the Civil War amendments did not change the relationship between American Indians and the federal government. In 1884, the Supreme Court ruled that American Indians were not citizens of the United States, hence neither the Fourteenth nor Fifteenth Amendments applied to them.[79] In 1924, Congress passed the Indian Citizenship Act, which finally gave American Indians the right to vote. Despite passage of the citizenship act, however, some state laws effectively prevented American Indians from voting. For example, Arizona and New Mexico denied them the right to vote until 1948, and Utah did so until 1956.[80]

Beginning in the 1960s, American Indians emulated the civil rights movement, staging protests, seizing federal lands, and suing the United States for violating treaties.

The success African Americans had in ending years of rules that allowed legalized discrimination also affected American Indians. In 1968, Congress passed the Indian Civil Rights Act, which finally extended most of the rights contained in the Bill of Rights to American Indians living on reservations. The 1960s also saw American Indians begin to emulate the tactics of the civil rights movement. They occupied government buildings, held sit-ins, and staged demonstrations to bring attention to discrimination against American Indians. In 1969, for example, several American Indian groups seized Alcatraz Island, an island in San Francisco Bay that was home to an abandoned federal prison. The groups argued that according to the terms of a treaty the U.S. government had signed with the Sioux Nation in 1868, American Indians were entitled to all unused federal lands. Although the occupation lasted for nineteenth months, it failed to produce significant changes in federal policy toward American Indians.

Sometimes protests by American Indians led to violence, as happened in 1973 when members of the American Indian Movement (AIM) seized hostages in the town of Wounded Knee, South Dakota, the site at which the U.S. Cavalry had massacred more than two hundred Sioux prisoners in 1890. The occupation lasted more than two months and left two members of AIM dead and one federal marshal seriously wounded. When the federal government agreed to review the implementation of treaties it had signed with American Indian tribes, the occupation ended.

In addition to engaging in civil disobedience, American Indians, like African Americans and other groups, have also turned to the courts for redress. A major objective of their litigation has been to force the federal government to abide by the terms of the many treaties it has signed with American Indian tribes. In a series of cases, American Indians have won the return of parts of their ancestral lands in the western United States. In other cases, the government has had to compensate them financially for their lost lands. In 1980, for example, the Supreme Court upheld the decision of a lower court to award the Sioux Nation $17.1 million plus interest as compensation for the government's seizure of the Black Hills of South Dakota a century earlier.[81] American Indians have also won court cases that have forced the federal government as well as state governments to abide by treaty obligations that give them special hunting and fishing rights.

The idea that the United States and the American Indian community form separate nations persists. Many American Indians continue to live on reservations where tribal courts rather than state courts enforce tribal law. In 1987, the Supreme Court cited the special status of American Indians under U.S. law in upholding the right of a California tribe to run a high-stakes bingo parlor without state regulation.[82] Congress responded to the Court's decision by passing the Indian Gaming Regulatory Act, which stipulates that if a state allows some form of gambling, American Indian tribes must be allowed to run their own gambling operations on tribal lands.[83] (The tribes must negotiate the precise details of the gambling operations with the government of the state the tribal lands are located in.) Many tribes have taken advantage of the Indian Gaming Regulatory Act to open casinos, thereby generating considerable revenue for tribal coffers. Despite this new influx of money, American Indians as a group remain among the poorest in the United States. Their unique political status and the unique rules that govern them have not benefitted them socially or economically.

Other Minorities

Traditionally, the courts held that civil rights laws did not apply to members of white ethnic groups, such as Arab Americans, Irish Americans, and Polish Americans. In 1987, however, the Supreme Court expanded the scope of minority groups that are protected by civil rights laws. In a case involving an Arab American who was denied tenure at a private college in Pennsylvania, a unanimous Supreme Court ruled that the Civil Rights Act of 1866 protects members of all minority groups against a wide range of discriminatory acts.[84] As a result of the Court's ruling, members of any ethnic group can now sue if they believe they have been discriminated against in violation of the law on the basis of their race or ethnicity. If they can establish that the law has been broken, the courts can award them monetary damages.

Discrimination Against Women

Although women constitute slightly more than half the population in the United States, the rules set forth in the Constitution originally did not guarantee them political rights. For more than one hundred years, women were denied the right to vote and were discriminated against in many other ways as well. For example, in 1873, the Supreme Court upheld a decision by the Illinois state supreme court to reject a woman's application for a license to practice law simply because of her sex.[85] A few decades later, the Court held that Oregon could set the maximum number of hours a woman could work (noting "that a woman's physical structure and the performance of maternal functions place her at a disadvantage") and that New York could bar women from working as waitresses at night (though the state allowed them to work as entertainers).[86]

The Supreme Court's rulings in these and other cases were based on a belief widely shared in American society in the nineteenth and for much of the twentieth century: women are a weaker sex that men need to protect. The Court made its views on the proper place of women explicit when it upheld the Illinois law denying women the right to practice law:

> Man is, or should be, woman's protector and defender. The natural and proper timidity and delicacy which belongs to the female sex evidently unfits it for many of the occupations of civil life. The constitution of the family organization, which is founded in the divine ordinance, as well as in the nature of things, indicates the domestic as that which properly belongs to the domain and functions of womanhood. The harmony . . . of interests and views which belong, or should belong, to the family institution is repugnant to the idea of a woman adopting a distinct and independent career from that of her husband. . . .
>
> . . . The paramount destiny and mission of woman are to fulfill the noble and benign offices of wife and mother. This is the law of the Creator.[87]

In keeping with this line of thinking, laws were designed both to protect women from activities believed harmful to them and to keep them from breaking out of the roles society deemed proper for them.

For more than one hundred years, women's rights activists have challenged the idea that women need the protection of men and have fought to repeal laws that endorse sex discrimination. The focus of their efforts, though, has changed over time. Throughout the nineteenth century and during the first two decades of the twentieth century, the women's movement focused on securing the right to vote. Since the rebirth of the women's movement in the 1960s, women's rights activists have focused on eliminating discriminatory laws and practices. The women's movement has had many successes, first on Capitol Hill and then in the courts. As a result of these victories, women now play a more prominent role in American economic and political life.

Campaigning for the Right to Vote

The **women's movement**—the effort to guarantee equal rights for women—first surfaced on a national scale in 1848 when Elizabeth Cady Stanton and Lucretia Mott organized the first women's rights convention in Seneca Falls, New York. The convention delegates endorsed a manifesto, written by Stanton, that catalogued a long list of "injuries and usurpations" men had inflicted on women. Borrowing heavily from the language of the Declaration of Independence, this Declaration of Sentiments proclaimed:

Women's movement
The mobilization of people to push for equality between the sexes.

> We hold these truths to be self-evident: that all men and women are created equal; that they are endowed by their Creator with certain inalienable rights, that among these are life, liberty, and the pursuit of happiness; that to secure these rights governments are instituted, deriving their just powers from the consent of the governed. Whenever any form of government becomes destructive of these ends, it is the right of those who suffer from it to refuse allegiance to it, and to insist upon the institution of a new government, laying its foundation on such principles, and organizing its powers in such form as to them shall seem most likely to effect their safety and happiness. . . .
>
> Now, in view of this entire disenfranchisement of one-half of the people of this country, their social and religious degradation,—in view of the unjust laws . . . and because women do feel themselves aggrieved, oppressed, and fraudulently deprived of their most sacred rights, we insist that they have immediate admission to all the rights and privileges which belong to them as citizens of the United States.[88]

The women's movement met with at best mixed success in the first two decades after the Seneca Falls convention. For example, the state of New York passed several laws allowing women to own property and to enter into contracts, as well as to guarantee them shares of their husbands' estates. By the beginning of the Civil War, however, most of these laws had been modified or repealed under pressure from men who opposed expanding the rights of women.[89] Likewise, in 1861, Kansas became the first state to give women the right to vote in elections involving local schools, but it would be many years before more than a handful of states would follow Kansas's lead.[90]

Elizabeth Cady Stanton was a pioneer in the women's rights movement. She helped organize the Seneca Falls Convention, the first women's rights conference, in 1848.

Following the Civil War, women's groups allied themselves with the movement to give African Americans the right to vote, hoping that women would attain the same right as well. This hope came to naught, however. The Fourteenth Amendment introduced the word *male* into the Constitution for the first time, and it explicitly spoke of the right to vote as a right belonging to men. Meanwhile, the Fifteenth Amendment guaranteed the right to vote regardless of "race, color, or previous condition of servitude," but it made no mention of sex.

Disappointed with the results of their alliance with the movement to recognize the rights of African Americans, women's rights activists formed their own organizations to push for the extension of **suffrage,** or the right to vote, to women (see box 5.2). The first success came in 1869, when the Wyoming Territory gave women full suffrage. The Utah Territory followed suit the next year. Victories were in short supply over the next four decades, however, and by the end of 1910, only five states (Colorado, Idaho, Utah, Washington, and Wyoming) had given women the right to vote. The movement for women's suffrage gained steam over the next half dozen years—as women's rights activists repeatedly picketed the White House and Congress—and by 1918, fifteen states had given women the right to vote. Finally, in 1919, Congress passed a constitutional amendment

Suffrage
The right to vote.

The People Behind the Rules

BOX 5.2

The Women's Movement Then and Now

Although the U.S. Constitution is frequently hailed for guaranteeing individual rights, as originally written, it denied equal rights to women. As the work of the woman suffrage movement and the National Organization for Women both illustrate, for more than one hundred years women's rights activists have fought to ensure that our fundamental rules of government extend equal rights to women as well as to men.

The National Woman Suffrage Association

The Woman Suffrage Movement

The Constitution as it was written in 1789 did not grant women the right to vote. In 1869, two organizations formed to lobby for a change in the rules: the extension of suffrage (the right to vote) to women. These two organizations were the National Woman Suffrage Association (NWSA) and the American Woman Suffrage Association (AWSA).

The two groups had different philosophies. NWSA was the more militant; it sought to win passage of a federal amendment giving women the right to vote and to advance women's rights more generally. In contrast, AWSA worked solely on suffrage issues, and it concentrated its efforts on the state level. AWSA won its first major victory in 1890 when Wyoming's admission to the Union made it the first state to give women the right to vote.

In 1890, NWSA and AWSA finally joined ranks, creating the National American Woman Suffrage Association (NAWSA). The new organization lobbied both federal and state governments. By 1912, NAWSA had over 75,000 members, and it had persuaded nine states to give women the right to vote. NAWSA gained more momentum when the Woman's Christian Temperance Union, a conservative group with great influence in the South, began to advocate woman suffrage.

The turning point for the cause of woman suffrage came with the American entry into World War I. When President Woodrow Wilson said the United States would make the "world safe for democracy," NAWSA demanded that he begin at home by giving women the right to vote. Under growing public pressure to live up to his rhetoric, Wilson abandoned his opposition to woman suffrage. In the meantime, NAWSA's persistent efforts to influence congressional elections had paid off by producing a pro-suffragist Congress.

NAWSA finally achieved its goal in 1920 after Congress passed and the states ratified the Nineteenth Amendment. With its primary objective accomplished, NAWSA formally disbanded. Much of its membership was absorbed into a new organization dedicated to educating women about their new political responsibilities, the League of Women Voters.

Continued

giving women the right to vote, and in 1920, the states ratified the Nineteenth Amendment. The constitutional rules on suffrage were finally extended to the female half of the U.S. population. As both women and African Americans discovered, though, securing the right to vote was merely a first step in the fight for civil rights.

The Fight for Equal Rights on Capitol Hill

The passage of the Nineteenth Amendment gave women the right to vote, but it did not eliminate laws and social practices that discriminated against them. Yet for several decades the women's movement lay dormant, partly because some groups were satisfied with having won the right to vote and partly because other groups argued over the movement's proper objectives and tactics.

The women's movement reemerged in the 1960s. Betty Friedan's immensely influential book, *The Feminine Mystique,* prompted many women to begin to question how society allocated roles according to sex. The actions of the civil rights movement

THE PEOPLE BEHIND THE RULES

BOX 5.2 CONTINUED

National Organization for Women

National Organization for Women

Despite the successes of NAWSA, when the National Organization for Women (NOW) was founded in 1966, American women were in many ways second-class citizens. Airlines could fire stewardesses simply for gaining weight or marrying, newspapers had separate listings for male and female jobs, and almost no women held political office. The founding members of NOW resolved at their first meeting to take all necessary "action to bring women into full participation of American society *now*."

Over the next quarter century, NOW fulfilled its vow to push women's issues to the forefront of the political debate and to rewrite the rules of the political game in ways that broadened the freedom of women. NOW no longer dominates the women's movement as it once did. Its very success inspired the formation of many other women's groups, including groups such as Concerned Women for America that oppose NOW on almost every issue. But NOW's 250,000 members still make it the largest feminist organization in the United States.

NOW has fought legislative battles on a wide range of issues, including abortion rights, paid maternity leave, and more vigorous enforcement of civil rights. But NOW is most closely associated with efforts to make the Equal Rights Amendment (ERA) a part of the Constitution. Congress passed the ERA in 1972. When it appeared in 1978 that the required three-fourths of the states would not ratify the ERA within the seven-year time limit set by law, NOW persuaded Congress to extend the ratification period for another three years. Despite the extension, the proposed constitutional amendment expired on June 30, 1982 without being ratified.

Conservative critics regularly denounce NOW as a militant fringe group. While attacks from the right are to be expected, NOW also draws criticism from other groups in the women's movement. They complain that NOW is too enamored with its rhetoric and too busy fighting old battles to recognize that new problems face women in the 1990s. Even Betty Friedan, the first president of NOW, argues that the organization has "too narrow a focus."

Patricia Ireland, current president of NOW, remains unbowed in the face of the critics. "We lead public opinion, we do not follow it. That's who we are. Sure, it has its down side. Taking a leadership position makes people uncomfortable. But my ultimate value isn't comfort. My ultimate value is progress for women."

Sources: Jane Gross, "Does She Speak for Today's Women?" *New York Times Magazine*, 1 March 1992; L. Sandy Maisel, ed., *Political Parties and Elections in the United States: An Encyclopedia* (New York: Garland Publishing, 1991); and Edward L. Schapsmeier and Frederick H. Schapsmeier, *Political Parties and Civic Action Groups* (Westport, Conn.: Greenwood Press, 1981).

also provided a powerful example to emulate. In 1966, a group of professional women founded the National Organization for Women (NOW) with Friedan as their first president. NOW dedicated itself to winning equal rights for women (see box 5.2).

Unlike the civil rights movement, the women's movement won its first major victories on Capitol Hill rather than in court. For decades, women had worked alongside men in many occupations, often performing the same work for less pay. With the **Equal Pay Act of 1963,** Congress recognized the equal-pay-for-equal-work movement by banning wage discrimination based on sex, as well as race, religion, and national origin. The initial impact of the Equal Pay Act was limited, however, because it required equal pay only for substantially equivalent jobs rather than those merely comparable. As a result, employers had considerable freedom to classify positions in ways that kept women in lower-paying jobs. Moreover, state laws and employer practices that barred women from holding jobs that might expose them to physical danger or to toxic substances remained legal.

Equal Pay Act of 1963
An act of Congress that banned wage discrimination based on sex, race, religion, and national origin.

A more important victory in the cause of equal rights for women came with the passage of the Civil Rights Act of 1964. Although the primary purpose of the act was to guarantee the civil rights of African Americans, it included a section prohibiting job discrimination on the basis of sex. Ironically, the provision was the result not of pressure from women's groups, but rather of a failed attempt to derail the overall bill. Rep. Howard Smith (D-Va.), an opponent of equal rights for African Americans, sponsored the provision prohibiting job discrimination on the basis of sex, believing that the prospect of extending civil rights protection to women would make the entire civil rights bill unacceptable to his colleagues. Much to Smith's surprise, and to the surprise of many of his colleagues, the House passed his amendment and it became law.

Congress passed several other pieces of legislation in the 1970s that the women's movement favored. Title IX of the 1972 Higher Education Act bars colleges and universities that receive federal funds from discriminating on the basis of sex. Title IX has been a prominent issue on the nation's sports pages in recent years because it has been used to gain equal standing for women's collegiate athletic programs. The Equal Opportunity Credit Act of 1974 prohibits financial companies from discriminating on the basis of sex or marital status when lending money or issuing credit cards. This act removed most of the legal barriers that had traditionally made it very difficult for women to borrow money in their own name. Finally, in 1978 Congress enacted legislation that prohibits job discrimination against pregnant women.

The women's movement had renewed legislative success following Bill Clinton's election in 1992, which restored control of both the White House and Capitol Hill to the Democrats for the first time in a dozen years. In 1993, Congress passed the Family and Medical Leave Act. This law requires employers to give eligible employees up to twelve weeks of unpaid leave each year if the employee or the employee's spouse has a baby, or if the employee or a family member becomes seriously ill.[91] In 1994, Congress passed the Violence Against Women Act. This law contains a variety of provisions designed to punish domestic violence and other attacks against women, to help women who have been victims of violence, and to prevent violence in the future. The most controversial provision of the law holds that anyone who commits a violent crime motivated by gender bias is guilty of a federal civil rights violation and that the victim of such an attack can sue his or her attacker for damages.[92] Critics of the provision—which applies to both sexes but was primarily intended to protect female crime victims—argued that it would overwhelm the federal courts with domestic abuse cases better handled by state courts. During its first two years in operation, however, relatively few cases were filed under the Violence Against Women Act.[93]

Although the women's movement has enjoyed great success on Capitol Hill, it has fallen short of its goals in the state legislatures. In 1972, Congress passed the Equal Rights Amendment (ERA), which simply stated: "Equality of rights under the law shall not be denied or abridged by the United States or by any state on account of sex." Within a few years, thirty-five states had ratified the amendment (see figure 5.3). Despite the considerable political efforts of NOW and other groups in the women's movement, the ERA failed to win the approval of the three additional states needed for the amendment to enter into force. The ERA died largely because conservative women's groups mobilized to defeat it.

Although the effort to pass a national equal rights amendment failed, sixteen states include an equal rights provision in their state constitution. In recent years, however, supporters of the ERA have failed to make additional headway on the state level. In 1992, for example, voters in Iowa rejected a proposal to add an equal rights amendment to their state constitution. Despite the failure of the ERA, its opponents and supporters agree that many, though not all, of its intended benefits already have been achieved through legislation and judicial decisions that have rewritten the rules to prohibit many types of sex discrimination.

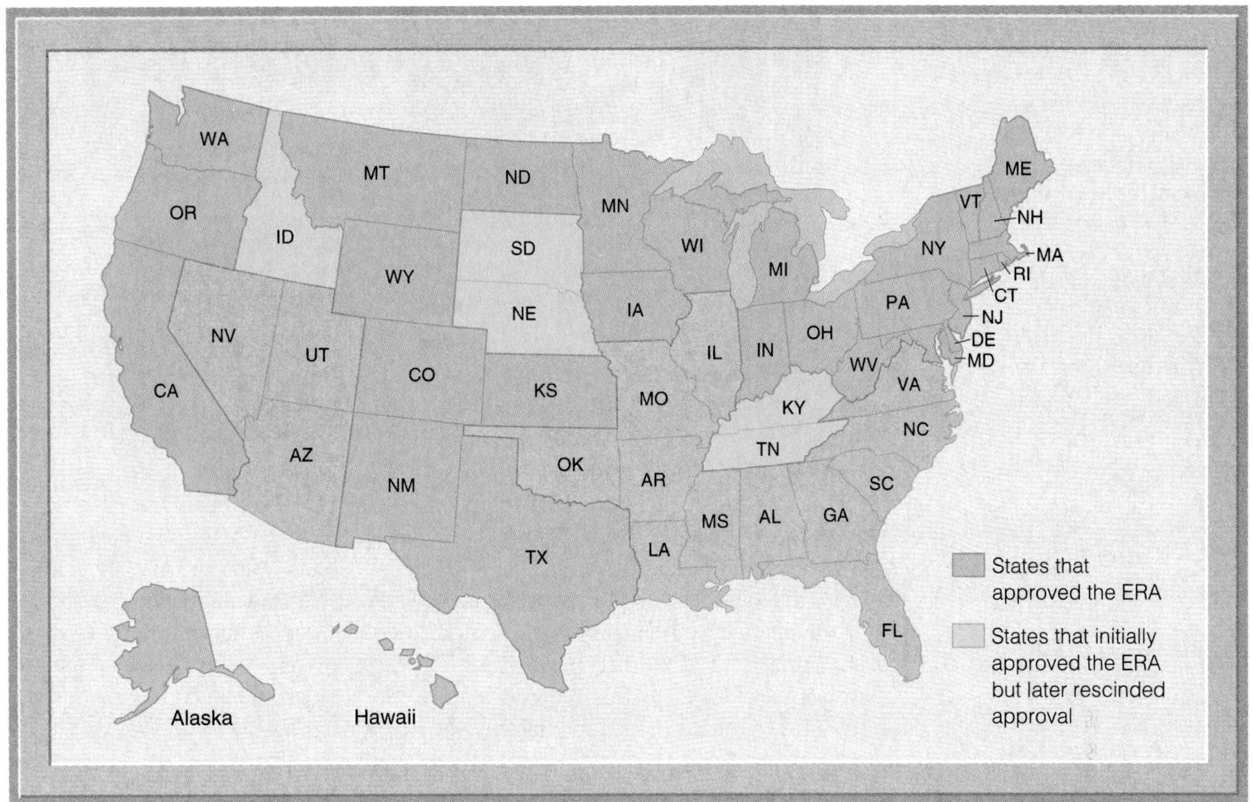

FIGURE 5.3
State Action on the Equal Rights Amendment

The Equal Rights Amendment passed Congress by a wide margin in 1972 and was submitted to the states. Although many states ratified the amendment within a year, the amendment never gained the required approval of thirty-eight states (three-quarters of the states), even after Congress extended the deadline for approval thirty-nine months.

Source: Data from Harold W. Stanley and Richard G. Niemi, *Vital Statistics on American Politics,* 4th ed. (Washington, D.C.: CQ Press, 1994), pp. 18–19.

The Fight for Equal Rights in the Courts

The courts were relatively slow to join the fight against sex discrimination. It was not until 1971 that the Supreme Court first struck down a law on the grounds that it discriminated against women.[94] The case in question involved an Idaho law that mandated that a man should always be chosen before an equally qualified woman to be the executor of a will. The law's intent was to limit the need to hold hearings on who should be the executor. In invalidating Idaho's law, the Court ruled that giving a "mandatory preference to either sex over members of the other, merely to accomplish the elimination of hearings on the merits, is to make the very kind of arbitrary legislative choice forbidden by the equal protection clause of the Fourteenth Amendment."[95]

The Supreme Court followed its 1971 ruling with a string of decisions that outlawed different classes of sex discrimination. Many of these rulings affect the treatment of women in the workplace. For example, newspapers cannot designate jobs listed in help-wanted ads as *male* and *female*.[96] Companies cannot refuse to hire mothers because they fear these women will need to take time off to take care of their children; nor can they force pregnant women to take maternity leave, or punish women who do take maternity leave.[97] Companies cannot force women to pay more into their pension plans each month while they are working or pay them less out of their pension plans each month after they retire simply because they are likely to live longer than male employees.[98] And companies cannot bar women of child-bearing age from working in jobs that might render them infertile or harm their fetus should they become pregnant.[99] In this latter case, the Court demonstrated unequivocally that it had shed the once dominant notion that the law has a special obligation to protect women from dangers to their well being. Other Supreme Court rulings affect how government treats women. For example, in 1996 the Court ruled that states cannot maintain all-male colleges.[100]

In applying the principle of equality between the sexes, the Supreme Court has thrown out several laws that discriminate against men. In a 1976 case, the Court held that an Oklahoma law that required women to be at least eighteen to buy beer but required men to be at least twenty-one was unconstitutional.[101] In 1979, the Court struck down an

Women have made significant progress in gaining access to higher education, including Ivy League colleges, U.S. military academies, and prestigious law and medical schools. In 1995, Rebecca Marier became the first woman to graduate first in the class from the U.S. Military Academy of West Point.

Alabama law that barred men from suing for alimony in a divorce, and in 1982, it struck down a Mississippi law that barred men from attending a state nursing school.[102]

Although the Supreme Court has struck down many laws that discriminate on the basis of sex, it has held that discrimination is legal in some areas. For example, the Court has upheld the law that requires men but not women to register for the military draft.[103] Laws for statutory rape that apply to men need not apply to women.[104] The government can give property tax exemptions to widows that it does not give to widowers, and it can treat men and women differently when allocating Social Security benefits.[105] And government agencies and private employers may take sex into account in certain hiring and promotion decisions.[106] The general trend, however, has been to remove sex-based distinctions from the law.

The Continuing Struggle Against Sex Discrimination

We noted earlier in the chapter that the civil rights movement has achieved substantial but by no means complete success in ensuring that African Americans enjoy an equal place in American society. The same may be said about the women's movement. Today, as a result of changes in the rules of American politics, American women enjoy more equality than ever before, but in many areas their opportunities continue to lag behind those of men.

On the positive side, women have broken into fields that for many years were denied to them. This has been especially true in the political arena. Women now play a prominent role as lobbyists (see chapter 10), members of Congress (see chapter 11), Supreme Court justices (see chapter 14), and as governors and state legislators (see chapter 15). Women also hold important positions in the federal bureaucracy, both as political appointees and as members of the civil service. For example, women now constitute 35 percent of the 25,000 lawyers that work for the executive branch.[107]

Women have also made impressive gains in gaining access to education. All-male colleges have all but disappeared, and women now attend prestigious undergraduate schools such as the Ivy League colleges and the U.S. military academies. Women have made similar gains in graduate education. For example, as late as 1970, women constituted only 3 percent of law school students; in 1996, the figure stood at nearly 50 percent.[108] As a result of greater access to education, women have made rapid inroads into high-paying and traditionally male-dominated professions such as law and medicine. For example, the percentage of female lawyers has grown steadily since the mid-1970s, now standing at 23 percent.[109] Women now account for 20 percent of all physicians.[110]

Finally, women have made great strides as entrepreneurs. Since the mid-1970s, the number of female-owned businesses has tripled. Women now own more than six million businesses, or roughly one-third of all U.S. companies. Indeed, between 1988 and 1992—the latest date for which data exist—women formed their own companies at a faster rate than men did. Today, companies owned by women employ more workers than all the Fortune 500 companies combined.[111] The growing number of female-owned businesses has led to the formation of groups like the National Women Business Owners that are dedicated to translating women's increased economic power into increased political power.

On the negative side, however, women are still underrepresented in government and in corporate America as a percentage of their share of the American population. For example, while one in every two Americans is a woman, in 1997, only one in ten members of Congress was a woman. Similarly, women account for only two of the nine Supreme Court justices and just 12 percent of all federal court judges.[112] And, of course, no woman has yet been elected president or vice president. Things aren't much better at the upper echelons of America's colleges and universities. "Only 3 percent of medical school deans and 5 percent of department heads are [women]. At Harvard Medical School, the 1994 class was 52 percent female; yet only 7 percent of the tenured professors are women."[113] In America's law schools, women constitute only 8 percent of the deans and 16 percent of tenured professors.[114]

In the private sector, women who enter the labor force often find themselves shunted into low-paying jobs such as secretaries, maids, and child-care workers that have traditionally been held by women. When women take a professional job, they often encounter an invisible "glass ceiling" that limits their ability to rise to the top of the corporate ladder. For example, a federal commission reported in 1995 that even though women make up almost one-half of the American workforce, they hold just 5 percent of senior management jobs. (Women have had more success obtaining middle management jobs such as assistant vice president and office manager; women now hold roughly 45 percent of these slots.)[115] Moreover, as women climb through the corporate ranks, they frequently find they are rewarded less handsomely than men are. For example, national surveys show that women who work as lawyers for Fortune 500 companies earn "less than their male counterparts at every level of seniority, with pay gaps that range as high as 35 percent."[116]

In light of the hardships women continue to confront in the workplace, women's rights activists continue to push for new rules of government that will redress inequalities between the sexes. But what the precise problems are and what steps the government should take are matters of considerable controversy. For example, sexism is only one possible explanation for why women on average earn less than men in the workforce. Because many women suspend their schooling or careers to have and raise children, or choose not to enter the workforce at all, the percentage of women in senior management positions may never mirror the percentage of women in the population. Moreover, as we have seen in this chapter and in chapter 3, many of the differences between men and women in the workplace have narrowed over the years. This suggests that, with time, many of the inequalities in today's workplace will diminish further. For example, one reason we see so few women in senior management jobs today may be that for many years women could not rise to middle management jobs. Now that so many women hold middle management positions, the number of women in senior management positions is likely to increase in the future.[117]

The debate over what to do to promote equality between the sexes is further complicated by disagreements, even among women, over what constitutes impermissible sexual discrimination and what government should do about it. Much as we saw earlier in our discussion of the African-American community, women disagree among themselves over the nature of the problems they face and the proper solutions. Take for example the issue of pornography. Feminists such as law school professor Catharine MacKinnon argue that pornography exploits women and denies them the equal protection promised by the Fourteenth Amendment. As a result, they argue on civil rights grounds that the First Amendment should not be interpreted to protect "sexually explicit materials that subordinate women through pictures or words."[118] In contrast, other feminists, such as Nadine Strossen, the president of the American Civil Liberties Union, argue that censorship, not pornography, poses the greater danger to women's rights.[119] These feminists oppose any effort to narrow the protections the First Amendment provides.

At the same time, some women are highly critical of some of the goals the women's movement has sought to accomplish.[120] Groups such as Concerned Women for America and the Independent Women's Forum reject policies such as affirmative action and gender equity in education as unfair, misdirected, and counterproductive.[121] Moreover, these groups, which many women support, argue that if the cause of equal rights is pushed too far, women will suffer rather than benefit. For example, they argue that pure equality would deprive women of important protections in divorce proceedings and child custody cases. As a result of these divergent views on what is best for women, the question of how far the rules of government should go to promote women's rights will remain a hotly debated topic for years to come.

Extending Civil Rights

Since the 1970s, many groups have pressed federal and state governments to recognize their status as victims of discrimination and to recognize and protect their civil rights. Three groups in particular stand out: (1) people with disabilities; (2) people with age claims; and (3) gays and lesbians. The push to extend civil rights to new groups poses a particular problem for the Supreme Court, which must decide at what point a discriminatory law becomes unconstitutional. To help it decide, the Court has developed a set of rules for determining who bears the burden of showing that a discriminatory law fails to pass constitutional muster.

People with Disabilities

In recent years, people with physical or mental disabilities have appealed to Congress and the Supreme Court for recognition and guarantees of their civil rights. They have met with some success in advancing their cause, more through congressional action than court decisions. In 1968, Congress passed the Architectural Barriers Act, which required buildings built with federal funds to be accessible to persons with physical difficulties. In addition, several other pieces of legislation in the 1970s and 1980s attempted to make public transportation more accessible to people with physical disabilities.[122]

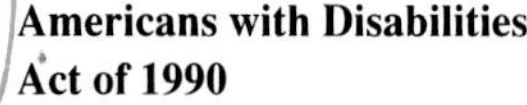

Americans with Disabilities Act of 1990
An act of Congress that seeks to minimize job discrimination, maximize access to government programs, and ensure access to public accommodations for people with disabilities.

The most significant legislation advancing the rights of people with disabilities is the **Americans with Disabilities Act of 1990** (ADA). The ADA is a comprehensive bill that seeks to minimize job discrimination, maximize access to government programs, and ensure access to public accommodations such as hotels, restaurants, and museums. This legislation is a good example of government taking a positive step to ensure equal rights. But unlike the Civil Rights Act of 1964, which stipulates that racial discrimination must be eliminated regardless of cost, the ADA allows cost to be considered in the search for a remedy when people with disabilities face discrimination. This compromise is meant to balance the right of persons with disabilities to gain access to a building or facility against the right of a business owner to avoid unreasonable costs. For example, under the ADA, "restaurants do not have to provide menus in Braille; waiters can read them to blind customers."[123]

Experience with the ADA shows that it has not led to the explosion of lawsuits that some opponents feared. By one count, the Justice Department and the Equal Employment Opportunity Commission together have handled fewer than twenty-five ADA suits a year, with only 650 cases brought nationwide.[124] Still, concerns about the scope of the legislation arise occasionally as new groups push for coverage under the ADA's provisions. For example, activists on behalf of Multiple Chemical Sensitivity sufferers—people who say that various scents, odors, and chemicals make them ill—have been pushing to have their ailments covered even though little scientific evidence supports the existence of their condition.[125] Should Multiple Chemical Sensitivity sufferers be successful, employers might be forced to (among

In recent years, people with disabilities have fought for recognition of their civil rights.

other things) ban people from wearing perfume in the workplace. But to this point, the rules governing the application of the ADA have not changed, and the ADA has not prompted much litigation. Presumably, the rules the ADA imposes have benefitted those with disabilities without unduly infringing on the rights of others.

People with Age Claims

Another class of people occasionally seeking civil rights guarantees is people of certain ages. Older Americans have been the most successful in this regard; they have gained substantial protection from discrimination, again more because of acts of Congress (responding, no doubt, to the political pressures older Americans can bring to bear in the voting booth) than from the courts. In 1967, Congress passed the Age Discrimination in Employment Act, which bars job discrimination based on age. The Age Discrimination Act of 1975 extended protection against age discrimination to any program receiving federal money. And Congress has also made mandatory retirement ages illegal in most circumstances, though the Supreme Court has upheld them in certain job categories where convincing cases can be made that older people as a class are less able to perform the required work.[126]

Younger people have had less success in overturning laws that discriminate against them. States have passed and the courts have upheld a wide variety of laws that discriminate against the young, including drinking laws, driving laws, parental consent requirements for contracts, marriage laws, and, in some states, abortion laws. The one major success younger Americans won came in 1971 when the states ratified the Twenty-sixth Amendment, which lowered the minimum voting age to eighteen.

Gays and Lesbians

In June 1969, homosexual patrons of the Stonewall bar in New York City finally tired of police harassment and fought back. What became known as the Stonewall riots resulted in the mobilization of a previously unorganized group and gave birth to the modern gay rights movement. In the almost thirty years since Stonewall, gay rights organizations have pressed to extend civil rights laws that protect other groups to cover gays and lesbians. While the movement has enjoyed some success at the state and local levels, it has won very few victories at the national level.

President Bill Clinton has shown some sympathy for gay rights, but Congress has been reluctant to follow his lead. During the 1992 presidential campaign, for example, Clinton pledged that if elected, he would overturn the Defense Department policy that banned gays and lesbians from serving openly in the military. Following the election, members of Congress, officials in the Defense Department, and leaders of conservative interest groups attacked Clinton's pledge. After a bitter political fight, Congress passed legislation that relaxed the military's policy of discriminating against gays and lesbians only slightly. Under the "Don't Ask, Don't Tell, Don't Pursue" policy, the military is barred from asking soldiers about their sexual orientation and from initiating inquiries into the subject, but gay and lesbian soldiers are allowed to remain in the armed forces only if they do not reveal their sexual orientation to other members of the military.[127] The constitutionality of the "Don't Ask, Don't Tell, Don't Pursue" policy has been challenged in court, but it will be several years before the issue is resolved.

In 1995, President Clinton became the first president to publicly endorse gay rights legislation when he endorsed a legislative proposal known as the Employment Non-Discrimination Act. In writing to Sen. Ted Kennedy (D-Mass.) in support of the bill, Clinton noted that "discrimination in employment on the basis of sexual orientation is currently legal in forty-one states. This is wrong."[128] In 1996, the Employment Non-Discrimination Act came within one vote of passing in the Senate, but the House declined to take up consideration of the bill.

While Congress and the president have argued over whether gays and lesbians merit civil rights protection, the Supreme Court has not recognized any special standing for gay rights. As we discussed in chapter 4, in a 1986 case involving the right to privacy, the Court upheld a Georgia law outlawing sodomy. (The man who had been arrested under the sodomy statute had not been prosecuted for the crime—no one had been for years—but he chose to pursue the case to have the law declared unconstitutional.) A majority of the justices concluded that the right to privacy does not extend to consensual homosexual sex because the Court recognizes fundamental rights only when they are based on values "deeply rooted in this Nation's history and tradition." The claim that the right to privacy extended to homosexual sex failed to meet this standard because "proscriptions against [sodomy] have ancient roots."[129] Many observers have taken the Court's decision in this civil liberties case to mean that the justices are unlikely to rule that gays and lesbians enjoy the civil rights protections that some other groups, such as African Americans and women, enjoy.

Outside of Washington, D.C., a handful of states have taken steps to limit discrimination against gays and lesbians. Cities and towns have been even more eager to act on behalf of gay rights. In passing such laws, local officials can point to public opinion polls that show that a majority of Americans favors legal safeguards against discrimination on the basis of sexual orientation.[130]

Despite the support expressed in public opinion polls, state and local government decisions to extend civil rights protections to gays and lesbians have frequently provoked backlashes. In 1993, residents of Cincinnati voted by an overwhelming margin to repeal the city's gay rights protections, and in 1994, residents of Austin, Texas, voted by an equally large margin to repeal a city ordinance granting health insurance to "domestic partners" of city employees—gay or heterosexual. After the city council in Portland, Oregon passed an ordinance in 1992 prohibiting discrimination against homosexuals, conservative opponents placed an initiative on the state-wide ballot that would have required Oregon schools to teach that homosexuality is "abnormal, wrong, unnatural, and perverse" and that would have required "that all governments discourage homosexuality."[131] On election day in 1992, Oregonians rejected the measure by a healthy margin. Two years later—after three more cities in Oregon adopted anti-discrimination ordinances and after conservatives moderated the language (but not the effect) of their ballot initiative—Oregonians again rejected the effort to limit gay rights, but this time by a much smaller margin.[132]

Gay rights has been a similarly controversial issue in Colorado. In 1992, the citizens of Colorado voted to amend the state's constitution to forbid state and local government from passing laws that would extend civil rights protections to gays and lesbians. The constitutional amendment invalidated ordinances in Denver and

In 1992 and 1994, Oregon voters rejected efforts to limit homosexuals' civil rights.

other Colorado communities banning discrimination against homosexuals. Gay and lesbian groups challenged the new amendment in the Colorado courts, arguing that it would effectively deny them equal participation in the political process. In 1994, the Colorado Supreme Court agreed, though it did not go so far as to rule that gays and lesbians are a legally protected minority. The state of Colorado appealed the case to the U.S. Supreme Court, which in 1996 found the amendment unconstitutional because it "classifies homosexuals not to further a proper legislative end but to make them unequal to everyone else."[133] The precise impact of the Court's decision is a matter of dispute, and it is unclear whether the decision marks a shift in the position the Court staked out in the 1986 sodomy case. (Indeed, the Court's majority opinion in the Colorado case made no reference to the sodomy case.) Gay and lesbian groups hailed the ruling in the Colorado case as a landmark legal victory that makes it likely that other laws discriminating against homosexuals will be found unconstitutional. Supporters of the Colorado amendment argued, however, that the Court had left open the possibility that laws discriminating against homosexuals will pass constitutional muster if they serve some legitimate government purpose.

A gay rights issue that has moved to the forefront of political debate in recent years is same-sex marriage. In 1993, the Supreme Court of Hawaii ruled that unless the state of Hawaii demonstrated that it had a compelling reason for denying homosexual couples the right to marry, the practice violated the state's constitution. The court gave the state until 1997 to make its case, but few legal experts expect it to prevail. If Hawaii does recognize a right for gays and lesbians to marry, the other forty-nine states may have to grant legal recognition to same-sex marriages performed in Hawaii—whether they want to or not—because the U.S. Constitution stipulates that "full faith and credit shall be given in each state to the public acts, records and judicial proceedings of every other state." To fend off the possibility of being forced to recognize same-sex marriages, Utah passed a law in 1995 that denies recognition to all out-of-state marriages that do not conform to Utah law. Within a year, more than a dozen other states enacted similar legislation, and Congress passed the Defense of Marriage Act, which bars federal recognition of same-sex marriages and permit states to disregard same-sex marriages performed in other states.[134] If Hawaii does legalize same-sex marriages, the federal courts may be called on to decide whether the "full faith and credit" clause of the U.S. Constitution requires other states and the federal government to grant legal recognition to these marriages.

The Burden of Proof

As you can see, since the 1970s, a number of different groups have asked the Supreme Court to recognize their status as victims of discrimination and to recognize and protect their civil rights. Because the Court has held that discrimination per se is not unconstitutional—recall, for example, that it has found some laws that discriminate on the basis of sex and age are constitutional—it has had to develop rules to determine which parties bear the burden of proof in determining when a discriminatory law is unconstitutional.

Rational scrutiny
A legal standard for judging whether a discriminatory law is unconstitutional. Rational scrutiny requires the government only to show that a law is reasonable and not arbitrary.

Strict scrutiny
A legal standard for judging whether a discriminatory law is unconstitutional. Strict scrutiny requires the government to show a compelling reason for a discriminatory law.

Intermediate scrutiny
A legal standard for judging whether a discriminatory law is unconstitutional. Intermediate scrutiny lies somewhere between the rational and strict scrutiny standards. It requires the government to show that a discriminatory law serves important governmental interests and is substantially related to the achievement of those objectives, or a group to show that the law does not meet these two standards.

As the law now stands, the Supreme Court employs a three-tiered standard for evaluating the constitutionality of a discriminatory law. Under the standard of **rational scrutiny,** the government needs only to show that a law is reasonable and not arbitrary. Here, the burden of proof rests with the individual or group challenging the government to prove that a law is unreasonable or arbitrary. Under the standard of **strict scrutiny,** the government must show a compelling reason for a discriminatory law. Here the burden of proof rests with the government, and it usually finds it difficult to meet this burden of proof. The standard of **intermediate scrutiny** lies somewhere between the rational and strict scrutiny standards.[135] Under the intermediate scrutiny standard, a discriminatory law must "serve important governmental interests and must be substantially related to the achievement of those objectives."[136] Here, the government and the group challenging the law share the burden of proof. (In a 1996 case, the Court raised questions about the continued validity of the three-tiered standard for judging the constitutionality of a discriminatory law when it introduced the idea of "skeptical scrutiny." As box 5.3 discusses, it remains to be seen whether skeptical scrutiny represents an entirely new standard or simply restates the intermediate scrutiny standard more forcefully.)

Rational, intermediate, and strict scrutiny apply different standards to different groups of people, as box 5.3 discusses in greater detail. Even with these standards, however, civil rights law remains one of the most complex aspects of American law, and it may become more complex in the future. For example, researchers have found persuasive evidence that businesses routinely discriminate against people on the basis of height, weight, and looks in making hiring decisions. As a result, people who are short, overweight, or unattractive earn less than other Americans.[137] People who believe they have been discriminated against on the basis of their height, weight, or looks are now testing their legal claims to protection against discrimination in the courts.

Affirmative Action: Equal Opportunity or Equal Outcomes?

Civil rights laws are intended to guarantee equal rights for all Americans. But what exactly does it mean to say that the government should ensure equal rights? You will recall from the first section of this chapter that civil rights legislation generally requires government to take positive steps to ensure equality. But what specific steps should government take? And how far should it go? These questions are at the crux of many disputes over civil rights.

Ensuring equality of rights is a demanding task. One way to understand the problem of how to ensure equal rights is to think of rights as items on a scale. On one side of the scale are the rights of an individual or group, on the other, the rights of the rest of society. Exactly how to achieve a balance is often a matter of considerable debate. For example, most Americans believe the government should protect against discrimination in the workplace. But what steps should the government take to achieve this goal? The question of whether equal rights means *equality of opportunity* or *equality of outcome* has been at the heart of civil rights debates since the mid-1960s.

Affirmative action
Programs designed to take positive actions to increase the number of women and minorities in jobs and educational programs.

The issue that most clearly exemplifies the conflict between equality of opportunity and equality of outcome is **affirmative action.** Affirmative action programs, such as those the University of California Board of Regents debated in the story that opened this chapter, require government to take positive actions to increase the number of underrepresented groups in certain positions, usually in the workplace. Using the scale

POINT OF ORDER

BOX 5.3

Standards of Judicial Scrutiny: Who Is Protected Under Civil Rights Laws?

The Supreme Court has the power to strike a balance between individual and societal rights.

Civil rights are not absolute. In its attempt to balance society's rights and the individual's rights, government constructs rules or standards that sometimes place limits on individual rights. One example of such a set of rules is the Supreme Court's three-tiered standard for proving a law does not discriminate improperly against a certain person or group: rational scrutiny, strict scrutiny, and intermediate scrutiny. The political climate of the times influences the way the Court applies this three-tiered standard.

Since the early years of the twentieth century, the Supreme Court has held that any method of classification that groups people by some characteristic must be rational (that is, reasonable and not arbitrary) and must be directly related to some legitimate state goal. This is a relatively easy standard for the government to meet, and the Court almost never overturns a law it subjects to so-called rational scrutiny. (One recent exception is the 1996 case *Romer v. Evans,* which involved an amendment to the Colorado Constitution barring state and local government from giving civil rights protections to homosexuals. The Court held the amendment was unconstitutional because it did not "bear a rational relationship to a legitimate government purpose.")

Later, the Court developed a much tougher rule—the strict scrutiny standard. This standard says that in certain cases, government must work much harder to prove that a law that differentiates between groups is constitutional. For example, the Court has ruled that differentiating on the basis of race or national origin is a suspect classification scheme. In such cases, the Court will automatically assume that any law that classifies people according to race or ethnicity is unconstitutional unless the government can prove otherwise. The Court almost always overturns laws that differentiate between people on the basis of race or nationality. (Two exceptions to this rule were *Korematsu v. United States* and *Hirabayashi v. United States.* These cases upheld President Franklin Roosevelt's decision to order the internment of more than 75,000 Japanese Americans in detention camps during World War II.)

In 1976, the Supreme Court created a third standard, known as intermediate scrutiny, for determining whether a law improperly distinguishes between different groups in society. Current Supreme Court Justice Ruth Bader Ginsburg filed a brief at that time as an attorney, asking the Court to apply the strict scrutiny standard to any law that discriminates between men and women—in effect, to make gender a suspect classification. The Court declined the request, but it did agree that gender-based laws should meet a standard somewhere between the easy-to-meet standard of rational scrutiny and the difficult-to-meet standard of strict scrutiny. Hence, it created the intermediate scrutiny standard. The Court subsequently subjected laws that distinguish between children born in and out of wedlock to intermediate scrutiny. Laws subjected to intermediate scrutiny have a fair chance of being upheld.

In a 1996 case involving the Virginia Military Institute (VMI), a state-supported, all-male military college, the Supreme Court threw the three-tiered standard of rational, intermediate, and strict scrutiny into some doubt. In ruling that VMI's ban on women was unconstitutional, the Court, in an opinion written by Justice Ginsburg, applied a "skeptical scrutiny" standard, which holds that a state must demonstrate an "exceedingly persuasive justification" for any official action that treats men and women differently. It remains to be seen, however, whether the skeptical scrutiny standard marks an entirely new standard or simply restates the idea of intermediate scrutiny in more forceful terms. As Chief Justice William Rehnquist noted in his concurring opinion, the Court's new verbal formulation has injected an "element of uncertainty" in the legal analysis of sex discrimination.

Since the 1970s, the Supreme Court has been asked to rule that other classification schemes require strict or intermediate scrutiny. So far, the Court has refused to do so. Among those groups that have argued for protected status but that have never been granted strict or intermediate scrutiny are age groups, people with disabilities, and gays and lesbians. These groups seek the protection of such rules because the rules matter. The rules on rational, intermediate, and strict scrutiny radically affect the civil rights of real people in everyday life.

Dueling views on affirmative action: Some people view affirmative action as a means to correct discrimination against women and minorities.

H. Clay Bennett/Reprinted with special permission of North America Syndicate.

analogy, imagine that on one side of the balance we have disadvantaged minority groups, on the other, the advantaged majority. Most people agree the balance has long been weighted on the side of the majority and that it needs to be tipped toward the minority side. But the question is, how far? What is the proper balance? Is it enough to make rules that *try* to ensure equal opportunity? Or do we need to establish rules that *guarantee* equal outcomes?

Which positive actions are both permissible and desirable lies at the heart of the affirmative action dispute. At a minimum, positive action means taking steps to notify people that an equal opportunity exists. Many large U.S. corporations, for instance, put the phrase "equal opportunity employer" on their stationery. At the other end of the spectrum, affirmative action takes the form of quotas or set-asides—rules that guarantee a number of positions for members of certain groups.

The affirmative action movement began under President Johnson in the mid-1960s, as the federal government directed organizations that received public money to take affirmative steps to increase the participation of underrepresented groups. This led to a series of programs designed to bring more minorities and women into the nation's educational system as well as its workplace. In the years since then, affirmative action programs frequently have triggered heated political and legal debate.

The debate over affirmative action centers on whether the law should treat everyone equally regardless of personal characteristics other than ability, or whether it should compensate groups that have faced discrimination in the past by giving them special advantages. Proponents of affirmative action contend that only positive actions can redress the effects of decades of discrimination. Opponents argue, however, that affirmative action creates a system of **reverse discrimination** in which whites, and especially white men, are denied equal protection under the law. This demonstrates the complex problems that can arise when competing sets of rights collide. Minorities should have a right to an equal chance at education and employment, but the white majority should also have this right. How can government create rules that balance these two sets of rights—that ensure the underrepresented group an equal chance without violating the rights of the rest of society?

Reverse discrimination Laws and policies that discriminate against whites, especially white males.

The Supreme Court has had numerous opportunities to judge the constitutionality of affirmative action. The Court's first major ruling came in the case of Allan Bakke, a white male who was denied admission to the medical school at the University of California–Davis even though his grades and test scores were higher than those of several minority students admitted under a special program. Indeed, the school had set aside sixteen of the one hundred admissions slots for minority students. The Court ruled

Others see affirmative action as another form of discrimination.

that the school could consider minority status a factor when making its admissions decisions, but that it could not impose a quota system. With the Court's ruling that quotas were unconstitutional, Bakke was admitted to medical school.[138] The change in the rules made a difference in who was admitted, in which way the balance tipped.

Subsequent Supreme Court decisions have left the constitutionality of affirmative action programs somewhat unclear. The Court has upheld voluntary affirmative action programs, and it has allowed quotas in instances in which past discrimination was proved.[139] The Court has also allowed affirmative action programs for women when a "manifest imbalance" exists in a specific work force.[140] The Court has ruled, however, that some set-aside programs, such as Richmond, Virginia's requirement that 30 percent of all city contracts must go to minority contractors, are unconstitutional because no past discrimination was demonstrated.[141] And in 1995, the Court, in a majority opinion written by Justice Sandra Day O'Connor, suggested that federal affirmative action programs must meet a strict scrutiny test.[142] This decision forced the Clinton administration to review government programs to see what, if any, changes should be made in order for them to survive legal challenge.[143] In initiating the review, President Clinton promised that his goal was to "mend, not end" the government's affirmative action programs.[144]

What sorts of affirmative action policies does the federal government pursue? A list compiled in 1995 identified more than one hundred programs with some affirmative action component.[145] They ranged from "programs as precise as setting aside a fixed percentage of crime assistance grants for minority or female-owned institutions, and as general as urging recipients of federal agriculture or housing assistance to use minority-owned banks."[146] The Clinton administration reduced the number of federal affirmative action programs in 1996 when it imposed a three-year moratorium on all government set-aside programs. Although the administration left open the possibility that it might revive set-asides at the end of the three years, it set such stringent conditions for reviving the programs that revival is unlikely. As one administration official put it, "as a practical matter, set-asides are gone."[147]

What difference have the government's affirmative action programs made? The answer is not clear, in large part because it is difficult to collect and judge evidence on the question. Minority-owned firms are disproportionately few in number and in size, and a significant number of them depend heavily on government set-asides to direct business their way.[148] Many minority business owners fear that if the government's affirmative action rules change, they will lose their businesses, in part because discriminatory practices will reemerge, but also because their firms are too small or not well enough connected to land government contracts.[149] But many of these federal government programs, though they once enjoyed bipartisan support, are now under attack as the owners of non-minority firms raise reverse discrimination claims.[150]

In the end, the government is searching for policies that correct for past discrimination without producing reverse discrimination. Developing such policies, which would achieve a balance between both sets of rights, is crucial as increasing numbers of individuals and groups seek rules that give them equality of status and rights under the law. One possible solution is "place, not race," a notion the Clinton administration has discussed. Such a policy might steer government contracts to companies located in economically distressed areas rather than to businesses whose owners represent certain races.[151] The Regents of the University of California developed a variant of that approach as a substitute for race-based affirmative action programs. Their policy would base admissions on factors such as "unusual persistence and determination" in overcoming disadvantaged social and educational circumstances in addition to grades and standardized test scores.[152] Pressure on governments to change affirmative action programs is likely to continue. In 1996, for example, California voters passed Proposition 209, which would end all the state's affirmative action programs.

Is the Constitution flexible enough to allow the federal government to create rules that correct for the lingering effects of past discrimination without triggering claims of reverse discrimination? History suggests it is. Exactly what rules will the Court and Congress establish to attain this balance? Realistically, political pressures will probably determine which rules are created and how they work.

Summary

The Constitution sets forth the fundamental rules governing the relationship between the government and its citizens. These rules attempt to guarantee certain civil rights. But although we think of these rights as fixed concepts, they are not. Part of government's task is to balance competing rights; in doing so, it must continually redefine the rules that govern our civil rights. And these rights matter greatly to real people in everyday life.

The flexibility of the Constitution is evident in the struggle of the civil rights movement. Throughout the nineteenth century and much of the twentieth century, the Supreme Court refused to recognize that all Americans were entitled to equal protection under the law regardless of race, creed, color, or gender. African Americans found themselves disenfranchised first by rulings that sanctioned slavery and, then, after slavery was abolished, by rulings that insisted that separate treatment was equal treatment. American Indians were denied citizenship rights, and Hispanic Americans and Asian Americans frequently confronted laws that limited their right to work and educate their children. Even women, who constituted half the American population, found that they were not full citizens in the eyes of the law.

Over the past four decades, the civil rights movement has breathed life into the promise of the Fourteenth Amendment that no person shall be denied equal protection under the law. Working through both the legal and political systems, African-American civil rights leaders succeeded in forcing both the Supreme Court and Congress to take steps to end legalized discrimination. The success of African Americans at forcing changes in rules and policies in turn inspired other minorities, as well as women, to demand that the government protect their rights as well. And in recent years, other groups, most notably people with disabilities, have been motivated by the civil rights movement to demand that they, too, be allowed to enjoy the full fruits of American citizenship. Gays and lesbians, however, have generally been unable to gain specific coverage under civil rights laws.

The very success of the civil rights movement has created new tensions and conflicts in American politics as protecting the rights of one group may infringe on the rights of another. These tensions and conflicts are most obvious in affirmative action programs. Proponents argue that we need affirmative action to reverse the effects of decades of discrimination, while opponents contend it curtails the rights of the majority. The Supreme Court has sought to chart a middle course between both camps, looking on the one hand to promote the interests of groups that have suffered discrimination while on the other hand attempting to avoid charges that it is promoting reverse discrimination. Undoubtedly, the Court will eventually define new rules in response to these new tensions in our increasingly diverse society. Just what those rules will be, however, is hard to predict. They will most likely be ushered in on the prevailing political winds as new members join the Court and new issues take center stage in American politics.

Key Terms

Affirmative action
Americans with Disabilities Act of 1990
Brown v. Board of Education
Brown v. Board of Education II
Civil disobedience
Civil rights
Civil Rights Act of 1964
Civil rights movement
De facto segregation
De jure segregation
Equal Pay Act of 1963
Intermediate scrutiny
Jim Crow laws
Lynching
Massive resistance
Rational scrutiny
Reverse discrimination
Separate-but-equal standard
Strict scrutiny
Suffrage
Voting Rights Act of 1965
Women's movement

Readings for Further Study

Andrews, Pat, ed. *Voices of Diversity: Perspectives on American Political Ideals and Institutions.* Guilford, Conn.: Dushkin, 1995. An excellent collection of primary sources on the struggle for civil rights.

Branch, Taylor. *Parting the Waters: America in the King Years, 1954–1963.* New York: Simon & Schuster, 1988. An award-winning account of the civil rights movement in the decade leading up to the passage of the 1964 Civil Rights Act.

Carter, Stephen L. *Reflections of an Affirmative Action Baby.* New York: Basic Books, 1991. A law school professor uses an autobiographical perspective to weigh the costs and benefits of affirmative action programs.

Irons, Peter. *The Courage of Their Convictions: Sixteen Americans Who Fought Their Way to the Supreme Court.* New York: Free Press, 1988. Compelling stories of sixteen people whose lawsuits challenged, and in many cases changed, our conception of civil rights.

Kluger, Richard. *Simple Justice.* New York: Vintage Books, 1975. A now-classic examination of the African-American struggle for civil rights, with particular attention paid to the history of *Brown v. the Board of Education.*

Lazarus, Edward. *Black Hills/White Justice: The Sioux Nation versus the United States, 1775 to the Present.* New York: HarperCollins, 1991. A lawyer tells the story of the longest running legal fight in U.S. history: the Sioux Nation's one-hundred-year effort to secure restitution for the federal government's seizure of the Black Hills of South Dakota.

Mansbridge, Jane. *Why We Lost the ERA.* Chicago: University of Chicago Press, 1986. A leading political scientist examines the political battle fought over the Equal Rights Amendment.

Sniderman, Paul M., and Thomas Piazza. *The Scar of Race.* Cambridge: Harvard University Press, 1993. A first-rate work of social science showing the complexity of racial attitudes current in American politics.

Part Two

Individuals and Groups in American Politics

6
Public Opinion

7
Voting and Participation

8
The News Media

9
Political Parties

10
Interest Groups

CHAPTER

6

PUBLIC OPINION

The People's Limited Knowledge of Politics
- *The Distribution of Knowledge*
- *Sources of Knowledge*
- *People with Knowledge: Issue Publics*

The Nature and Acquisition of Opinions and Values
- *Family and Friends*
- *School*
- *The Media*
- *Lifetime Learning*

Ideologies
- *Liberalism*
- *Conservatism*
- *Changes Over Time*
- *Sources of Ideologies*
- *The Process of Molding Ideologies*

Public Opinion on the Issues
- *Ideological Thinking by the Public*
- *Abstract Symbols Versus Concrete Policies*
- *Public Opinion on Clusters of Related Issues*
- *Changes in Opinion Over Time*
- *Causes of Change*

Summary

Key Terms

Readings for Further Study

During the fall of 1994, America's newspapers were filled with stories about the Contract With America, the ten-point platform that Republican candidates for the House of Representatives were campaigning on.[1] House Republican leaders had drafted the Contract, in the words of Rep. Henry Hyde (R-Ill.), to fight "the perception that is fostered by Democrats . . . [that we] are naysayers, aginers, obstructionists, and experts in gridlock. We think it is important to emphasize the things we stand for."[2] To draw public attention to the Contract, almost every Republican candidate for a House seat signed it in an elaborate public ceremony on the steps of the U.S. Capitol. House Republican leaders then arranged to have *TV Guide*—the magazine with the largest readership in America—publish the Contract.[3] Newt Gingrich, the leader of the House Republicans, spent the fall of 1994 criss-crossing America to talk about the Contract.

The House Republicans' effort to publicize the Contract With America sounds like an ideal example of political candidates telling the public where they stand on the issues of the day. Yet many Americans appear to have missed the message. Immediately after the November election, a public opinion poll found that 72 percent of the public had never heard of the Contract With America, let alone knew what was in it. Newt Gingrich, the architect of the Republican victory and the man who would soon be elected speaker of the House of Representatives, hardly fared much better. Sixty-five percent of those polled said they did not know enough about Gingrich to have an opinion about him.[4]

Despite knowing little about the contents of the Contract With America or the specific policy changes Newt Gingrich and his colleagues were proposing, many Americans said they supported Republican efforts to chart a new course for the country. For example, one poll taken shortly after the election found that 52 percent of those asked approved of "the Republican congressional leaders' policies and plans for the future," while only 28 percent disapproved.[5] Moreover, members of Congress and the administration took these opinions seriously. After all, this was the voice of the people.

The fundamental principle of democracy is that the people rule. The people decide who will hold office, and through these officeholders, the people decide public policy. To understand our elected officials and the policies they establish, we must begin by examining public opinion—what the people think about politics and political issues. Those opinions are the basic input to the system of political rules that produces public policy.

Although public opinion should guide public policy, converting opinion into policy is not an easy task. The problems extend beyond merely sorting out the conflicting opinions different members of the public express as to the best policies. As the example of the Contract With America attests, the public lacks knowledge about many issues government officials must confront. In addition, most people do not think ideologically—that is, their opinions are not guided by a consistent underlying philosophy. The result is that public opinion on some issues is contradictory. For example, most Americans want a balanced federal budget, but they balk when they are asked to pay for it with either increased taxes or cuts in government services.

In this chapter, we will examine the public's limited knowledge about politics. We will discuss how people acquire their opinions and how a relatively small number of people fit their opinions together into ideologies, or coherent philosophies about politics. Finally, we will examine the public's mix of opinions on a variety of issues—especially economic and social issues—to show where they are liberal, moderate, and conservative. By exploring all these elements of public opinion—knowledge, ideologies, and opinions—we will see how daunting a task it is for government officials to base public policies on public opinion.

The People's Limited Knowledge of Politics

The public's limited knowledge about the Contract With America is typical of its lack of knowledge about many aspects of politics. As table 6.1 shows, only a few basic facts about politics are known to virtually all Americans. Huge numbers of people do not know what an economic recession is or what the terms *liberal* and *conservative*

Republican candidates for the House of Representatives in 1994 went to great lengths to publicize their Contract With America, including staging an elaborate signing ceremony on the steps of the U.S. Capitol. Nonetheless, polls taken after Election Day found that nearly three out of every four Americans had not heard of the Contract.

TABLE 6.1 The Public's Knowledge About Politics and Issues

Most Americans do not know much about politics or political issues.

Year	Item of Knowledge	Percent Who Know
1987[d]	The right to trial by jury	83%
1989[a]	The name of their state's governor	73
1996[g]	Which political party is the majority in the U.S. House of Representatives	70
1995[f]	Lance Ito was the judge in the O. J. Simpson murder trial	64
1989[a]	What a recession is	57
1996[g]	Newt Gingrich is Speaker of the U.S. House of Representatives	50
1980[e]	Definitions of *liberal* and *conservative*	42
1996[g]	What the federal minimum wage was	42
1991[b]	What majority is needed to override a presidential veto	37
1989[a]	What percentage of Americans live below poverty line	18
1991[c]	Canada was America's largest foreign trading partner	8
1991[b]	William Rehnquist was Chief Justice of the United States	5

Sources: (a) 1989 National Survey of Political Knowledge, quoted from Michael X. Delli Carpini and Scott Keeter, "Measuring Political Knowledge," paper delivered at the Midwest Political Science Association Meeting, Chicago, Illinois, April 1992; (b) 1990–91 National Election Study surveys, quoted from Michael X. Delli Carpini and Scott Keeter, "Measuring Political Knowledge," paper delivered at the Midwest Political Science Association Meeting, Chicago, Illinois, April 1992; (c) *Gallup Poll Report,* No. 307, April 1991, p. 30; (d) NORC General Social Survey, quoted by Robert S. Erikson, *American Public Opinion,* 4th ed. (New York: Macmillan, 1991), p. 46; (e) Norman R. Luttbeg and Michael M. Gant, "The Failure of Liberal-Conservative Ideology as a Cognitive Structure," *Public Opinion Quarterly* 49 (Spring 1985): 85; (f) Princeton Survey Associates, *News Interest Index Poll,* The Roper Center, 9–12 February 1995; and (g) The Pew Research Center for the People and the Press, "TV News Viewership Declines," 13 May 1996, p. 76.

mean.[6] Knowledge about policy debates is even more limited. For example, in 1995, Congress debated how much to cut spending on foreign aid. While seven out of ten Americans believed the United States spent "too much" on foreign aid, and two out of three said they wanted to cut foreign aid programs, the public had a greatly exaggerated sense of how much the United States actually spends on foreign aid. On average, those polled estimated that 18 percent of the federal budget went to foreign aid programs—eighteen times more than the actual amount of 1 percent.[7]

The willingness of people to express opinions about a wide range of issues, even when their knowledge of those issues is sketchy, extends even to nonexistent events. For instance, in 1995, the *Washington Post* set out to determine how closely Americans

Point of Order

BOX 6.1

Public Opinion Polling Methods

Today most polls are conducted over the telephone.

Scholars learn a great deal of what they know about public opinion from public opinion surveys, or polls. The basic principles of surveys are quite simple. If the sample—the group of people who are asked questions—is representative of the entire population, if the sample is large enough, and if the questions are properly worded and ordered, then the answers are very likely to reflect the opinions of the entire population.

The best, most representative type of sample is what statisticians call a *simple random sample*. To draw such a sample, one would need a complete list of people in the population (for example, the United States). People would be randomly selected from the list, perhaps by writing everyone's name on separate pieces of paper and thoroughly mixing the pieces of paper in a huge bowl. If the bowl were mixed well enough that everyone had an equal chance of selection, we would have the perfect random sample.

No such complete list exists, but pollsters have developed methods to get around this. Using census data and sophisticated sampling techniques, pollsters draw random samples of regions and then neighborhoods within the regions. An exact list of households (if the survey is conducted in person by interviewers in the respondents' homes) or telephone numbers (if the survey is conducted by telephone) is needed only at the end of the sampling process. Just as in a simple random sample, everyone has an equal chance of being selected for the survey. The result is a sample representative of the entire population. (Actually, the survey "population" for many polls includes only "non-institutional adult residents." That is, they include all adults who live in the United States and who do not reside in "institutions" such as prisons, military housing, old age homes, or college fraternities, sororities, and dormitories. Survey organizations exclude institutional populations to save money.)

To provide an accurate description of the population, a sample must also be large enough. It often surprises people that the size of the population does not matter, only the size of the sample. A survey of 1,000 respondents will

Continued

follow the news. To do so, they asked people whether they thought that the 1975 Public Affairs Act should be repealed. Twenty-four percent said yes, while 19 percent responded it should not. The poll contained only one small hitch: the 1975 Public Affairs Act doesn't exist. Thus, 43 percent of those polled expressed an opinion about an imaginary law. As one of the people who oversaw the poll concluded, "the simple fact is that on a lot of big policy issues, there really isn't any informed public opinion."[8]

The explanation for the public's lack of knowledge about politics is not that people are fools. Rather, for most people, politics is unimportant. When national surveys ask people to identify their hopes and fears, few identify political problems. (To

POINT OF ORDER

BOX 6.1 CONTINUED

work just as well to estimate public opinion in the United States (population 250 million) as in Normal, Illinois (population 40,000). To see why this is so, try flipping a coin a number of times. After the first 10 tosses, the percentage of heads may not be close to 50 percent. But after 100 tosses, the percentage of heads will be much closer to 50 percent, and after 1,000 tosses, the percentage will be very close. In fact, the chances are 95 percent that the number will fall between 46.9 percent and 53.1 percent. The 3.1 percent variation from 50 is called the sampling error.

Just as the sampling error decreases as you toss the coin an increasing number of times, the sampling error gets smaller as the sample size grows in a survey. In other words, the bigger the sample, the more accurate the result—no matter what the total population size. The sampling error on a sample of 500 is 4.4 percent. With 1,000 respondents, it falls to 3.1 percent. With a sample of 1,500, it falls to 2.5 percent. Typical commercial polls use samples of about 1,000 people.

The final considerations in polling are question wording and question ordering. Slight changes in how questions are asked can change how people respond. For instance, a survey of two randomly selected samples found that 19 percent of those in the first sample favored "forbidding" public speeches against democracy, whereas 42 percent of those in the second sample favored "not allowing" such speeches. The polls produced very different answers to what were essentially identical questions because the questions differed in tone; *forbidding* sounds much harsher than *not allowing*, even if the two phrases are synonymous. In a similar vein, mentioning a famous person when asking about a specific policy proposal can skew poll results. Questions about "cutting government spending" and "Newt Gingrich's plans for cutting government spending" will elicit different answers because the second version of the question taps into what people think about Newt Gingrich personally as well as what they think about the issue of government spending. Because of the potential problem with question wording, pollsters try to write questions that use neutral wording and that focus on one policy or idea at a time.

Question order can also influence how people answer survey questions. One lengthy poll asked respondents whether they favored increasing defense spending, cutting it, or keeping it at existing levels. Later in the survey, the pollsters repeated the question, this time immediately after asking whether people favored increasing, cutting, or maintaining spending on education. The second version of the question implied a tradeoff between spending on education and spending on defense. As a result, the second version found support for cutting defense spending was ten percentage points higher than the first did, even though both questions were asked of the *same people in the same poll.*

Because of sampling error and the effects of question wording and question ordering, we must think of surveys as providing only rough indications of what the public thinks. Moreover, when evaluating polls, keep in mind that not all pollsters play by the rules of their profession. Interest groups can use poll results to influence government decisions, so some pollsters have an incentive to bias their results. For example, after drafting the Contract With America, the Republican National Committee (RNC) commissioned polls designed not to determine what Americans thought about the specifics of their legislative proposals, but rather to discover which descriptions of the proposals had the most popular appeal. For example, the RNC discovered that people responded very favorably to the term *citizen legislature,* so it named the term-limits plank in the Contract "The Citizen Legislature Act." Republicans subsequently trumpeted the RNC's polls as demonstrating that the Contract was popular with voters, even though these polls indicated that alternate descriptions of the very same policy proposals elicited lower levels of popular support.

Sources: Floyd J. Fowler, Jr., *Survey Research Methods* (Newbury Park, Calif.: Sage Publications, 1993); James G. Gimpel, *Fulfilling the Contract: The First 100 Days* (Boston: Allyn and Bacon, 1996), p. 6; John Mueller, *Policy and Opinion in the Gulf War* (Chicago: University of Chicago Press, 1994), p. 2; Eric R. A. N. Smith and Peverill Squire, "The Effects of Prestige Names in Question Wording," *Public Opinion Quarterly* 54 (Spring 1990): 97–116.

understand just how polling organizations survey public opinion, see box 6.1.) Far more common are answers about people's health, jobs, families, and events or conditions that affect their daily lives more directly than politics.[9] Most Americans find it hard to see connections between their lives and the decisions made in Washington or their state capital. Moreover, politics ranks far behind movies, books, sports, and other leisure activities as a source of entertainment. Few people have any real incentive to follow or learn about politics.

Surveys about public interest in politics reveal the low level of importance most people assign to politics. For instance, when a national survey asked people in 1996

Americans display much less interest in politics and political events than in other events.

whether they were following news about the presidential election campaign "very closely, fairly closely, not too closely, or not at all closely," only 22 percent said they were following the campaign very closely; the rest expressed less interest.[10] This lack of interest affects our democracy because the few who are interested and knowledgeable can exert disproportionate influence on decision makers.

The Distribution of Knowledge

Knowledge about politics is not uniformly distributed across the public. Some people know more and some know less. Who these people are matters because knowledge is a political resource that gives power to individuals and groups.

In general, people are likely to learn more about politics if they have the *opportunity* to learn, the *capacity* to learn, and an *interest* in learning.[11] One or more of these three elements shows up in many demographic, social, and psychological characteristics related to political knowledge. The most prominent demographic traits associated with knowledge are high education, income, and occupation. Social characteristics such as being active in political or even nonpolitical organizations also produce more political knowledge. And psychological characteristics, especially interest in politics and feelings of political efficacy—the sense that one can have an impact on political decisions—lead to greater political knowledge as well.

Demographic Characteristics

The single most important trait related to knowledge about politics is demographic—education.[12] Simply put, well-educated Americans are far more likely to be knowledgeable about politics than poorly educated Americans. Education combines all three elements of learning: schools offer the opportunity to learn, and those who progress to higher levels of education must have both the capacity for and an interest in learning. Courses in high school and college on civics, government, and history play an important role in teaching students about politics, but education's effect is not limited to what students learn in classrooms. College life surrounds students with opportunities to learn about politics. Rallies, protests, and debates are common campus events that draw in even those students who are not studying politics. By the time they leave college, most students follow politics in daily newspapers. This habit creates a continuing source of information that lasts a lifetime.[13]

At the other end of the education spectrum lies the political wasteland of illiteracy. According to a 1993 study, 23 percent of adult Americans are either completely illiterate or can perform only basic tasks such as signing their names.[14] Because so much political information and debate is carried in newspapers and magazines written at a higher level (for example, *Time* and *Newsweek* magazines are written at a high school senior reading level), people who are illiterate or who can read only at a low level miss a great deal.[15] The U.S. National Center for Education Statistics estimated that in 1985 only 21 percent of the nation's twenty-one- to twenty-five-year-olds could read well enough to synthesize the main argument from a lengthy newspaper editorial.[16] The other 79 percent were at a serious disadvantage.

Occupation and income, which along with education constitute a person's **socioeconomic status,** also have substantial effects on political knowledge. People with white-collar jobs usually work in offices and deal with paperwork, which offers them more opportunities to learn than those in blue-collar jobs. People with higher incomes are also more likely to be the targets of political appeals than those with lower incomes.[17] Moreover, high-status jobs and incomes put people in contact with others who have more education and who are more likely to be interested in politics. Thus, those who have a good job or a high income also benefit from some of the indirect effects of education. These demographic characteristics are typical of people who know about political issues.[18]

Socioeconomic status
Social status as measured by one's education, income, and occupation.

Social Characteristics

People who are knowledgeable about politics also share certain social characteristics. In general, any activity that brings people into contact with others and provides opportunities to talk about politics increases learning. Consequently, people who join and become active in organizations, even if they are not political organizations, are likely to learn more about politics. Union members and participants in religious, civic, and other types of organizations, for instance, tend to become more knowledgeable.

Psychological Characteristics

The main psychological characteristics associated with people who know more about politics are interest in politics, a sense of political efficacy, and a tendency toward activism. Survey researchers measure interest with questions about whether respondents are interested in the current campaigns, whether they care who wins, and whether they follow politics. In every case, those who are more interested know more about politics.[19]

The second psychological trait associated with people who know more about politics, a sense of political efficacy, is a source both of interest and of knowledge. Efficacy is the belief that one can have some effect or influence on politics. Many people without a sense of political efficacy believe there is no point in bothering to learn about politics because they cannot influence any political decisions. Therefore, those who do not feel efficacious tend to know less than those who do. Polls measure sense of efficacy with questions such as whether respondents think that public officials care what they think.[20]

Finally, those who participate actively in politics know more than those who do not. Any kind of activity, from attending campaign rallies to working for candidates, gives people opportunities to learn. Whether people become active because of their interest in politics or because of apolitical reasons such as doing a favor for an activist friend, the result is a learning experience. At least in theory, people in a democracy should be knowledgeable about government and issues in order to govern themselves wisely. Because activists have a disproportionate influence over policy decisions and rules, it is fortunate that they also have a lot of knowledge about politics. In other words, those who exercise more influence in politics also know more about politics.

Sources of Knowledge

Aside from schools—which provide background information on government and politics—the principal sources of political information are the news media, which provide information on current issues and political events. Since 1960, almost 90 percent of all Americans claim to have followed campaigns on television. A somewhat smaller percentage of people claim to have followed campaigns in newspapers, declining from about 80 percent in the early 1960s to 66 percent in the mid-1990s.[21] Studies of how Americans spend their time have found that the proportion of adult Americans who say that they "read a newspaper yesterday" declined from 71 percent in 1965 to 50 percent in 1996.[22] In addition, surveys show that people believe television news has improved and newspapers have gotten worse.[23] Thus, more and more people have come to think of television as their primary source of news.

The decline in newspaper reading and the growing dependence on television has disturbing implications because television offers much less information. As anyone who has compared the newspaper and television coverage of the same event can tell, newspaper coverage is far more thorough. Television news usually consists of a series of short reports on unrelated subjects—usually chosen for their action, drama, and splashy pictures. As we shall see in chapter 8, many observers argue that television's need for exciting pictures leads television journalists to ignore important political issues and to concentrate on trivial aspects of politics such as campaign rallies, crowds, and the candidates' witty or embarrassing statements.[24] Defenders of television news counter that television can interest viewers in issues that otherwise would attract little attention—such as the struggle against apartheid in South Africa.[25] Moreover, although television news may be less informative than newspapers, regular followers of television news do learn from it.[26] Still, the decline in the reliance on newspapers as an information source seems to be reducing the public's overall level of knowledge about politics.

People with Knowledge: Issue Publics

The public's lack of knowledge about the Contract With America, despite the tremendous publicity it received, can now be understood in context. Many people—even those who watch television regularly—know almost nothing about politics and policy issues; but others know a great deal. People who follow a particular issue closely, are well informed about it, and have strong opinions on the issue are called **attentive publics** or **issue publics.**[27]

Attentive publics or **issue publics**
People who follow a particular issue closely, are well informed about it, and have strong opinions on it.

Some people belong to many issue publics. They closely follow a wide range of issues. Other people pay attention to only one or two issues. Farmers, for instance, may follow farm policy; auto workers may know a good deal about tariffs on Japanese cars; students at public universities may follow policies that set tuition increases. And some people take a special interest in campaign promises such as the Contract With America.

Issue publics are especially important to elected officials because these people know and care a great deal about a narrow range of policy issues and, as we will see in chapter 7, are often willing to vote or spend their time and money to support their opinions in campaigns. Thus, pleasing issue publics is especially important to politicians seeking reelection.[28]

Issue publics, then, are small groups of Americans who tend to know more about politics and exert more influence over particular issues. Not surprisingly, members of issue publics have the characteristics associated with greater political knowledge. They generally are highly educated, have high incomes and good jobs, are active in political or other organizations, and are interested in and feel efficacious about politics. The first three of these characteristics, which make up socioeconomic status, are critical. People with higher socioeconomic status are far more politically knowledgeable than people with lower socioeconomic status. As we shall see in the discussion of

People who follow a few select issues closely, as some students follow the issue of tuition hikes, are issue publics.

interest groups in chapter 10, this knowledge gives them a substantial advantage in political disputes. When a conflict over policy arises and the government must decide how to manage the conflict, the greater knowledge people of high socioeconomic status have gives them a better chance to get what they want from government.

The Nature and Acquisition of Opinions and Values

Democracy depends on more than people's knowledge of politics; it depends on their preferences about government policies. Those preferences, or **opinions** (which are sometimes also called **attitudes**), are based both on factual knowledge and on underlying **values,** or principles. For instance, the general value of tolerance leads many people to hold the opinion that Congress should pass laws protecting gays and lesbians against discrimination.[29]

Opinions or **attitudes**
Preferences on specific issues.

Values
Basic principles which lead people to form opinions on specific issues.

Public opinion may or may not be based on an informed appraisal of the issues. Yet as the polls on the Contract With America and the public's initial support for the Republican congressional leaders' policies show, people are willing to express opinions even if they are not knowledgeable about the issue in question. They develop their opinions from what they know about the issues, from their values, and from the advice they receive from other people.[30]

People do not acquire opinions in the same way they learn facts. The process by which one acquires values and develops opinions from society is called **socialization.** Throughout life, from early childhood to old age, people undergo socialization. They develop new opinions and change old ones. The most important sources of socialization are family, friends, school, and the media.[31]

Socialization
The process by which people acquire values and opinions from their societies.

Family and Friends

Parents have substantial influence over their children's values and attitudes when they are young. Long before formal schooling begins, parents start teaching their children facts about the world and values to guide them in it. Moral and religious values often receive special attention, but parents teach other political and social values as well—from racial prejudices to political preferences.[32]

Most socialization is informal. In fact, parents and children are often not even aware of it. Children pick up on and learn from the casual comments of parents in conversations with other adults, their reactions to television news broadcasts, and a host of other cues. The emotional bonds between parents and children become a powerful teaching tool. Given the informal nature of these messages, it should not be surprising to find that the children of more politically interested and involved parents both learn more and are more likely themselves to become interested and involved in politics. If parents talk more about politics, their children are likely both to learn what their parents think and to learn that politics is interesting and important.[33]

As children grow older, their peers begin to influence their attitudes and opinions as well. The approval of friends grows in importance, especially during adolescence. For some, the initial values acquired from parents are strengthened; for others, they are weakened. The party loyalty of a child from a conservative family growing up in a liberal neighborhood can be the hidden prize in a contest of loyalties.[34]

Children may learn value judgments before they have any clear idea of the situations in which they apply. By fifth or sixth grade, for example, most children understand the party labels *Democrat* and *Republican,* and they respond with their party's candidate when questioned about their voting preferences in presidential elections. Yet few fifth and sixth graders understand much about the presidency, Congress, or the political issues at stake in the elections.[35] Their choices stem more from their desire to be like their parents and friends than from any detailed consideration of political issues.

By the time children reach young adulthood, many shift away from their parents' views. A comprehensive study of high school seniors and their parents compared the party loyalties of the two groups and found a high but far from perfect level of parent-child agreement.[36] Almost 59 percent of the parent-student pairs agreed, while only 7 percent took opposing stands—one Democratic, the other Republican. Most disagreement consisted of a parent or child claiming to be an independent while the other identified with a party. In a follow-up study of the same people eight years later, the researchers found agreement had declined to only 48 percent, but still only 8 percent had aligned with opposing parties.[37]

When the researchers examined the extent of parent-child agreement on a range of political issues such as racial integration, school prayer, and free speech they found much lower levels of agreement. Moreover, their follow-up study showed that agreement declined further as the years passed. The implication is that it is far easier to teach basic values such as party identification than to pass on specific opinions about public policies. While values are usually acquired through socialization, opinions on specific policies form in response to other influences such as individual reasoning, guidance from friends, or information from trusted political leaders. Whatever one's views, they are rarely carbon copies of those of one's parents.[38]

School

Schools are another source of cues for acquiring values and opinions. Many of these cues are intentionally built into the system to teach patriotism, respect for the law, and acceptance of the basic democratic and capitalist values of our political system—the daily pledge of allegiance and required history and civics classes, for instance. Indeed, teaching obedience and respect for authority are major goals of elementary schools. Yet these blunt efforts to socialize students are not always effective.[39] For example, in the case of the high school seniors and their parents that we just discussed, the researchers looked at the differences between students who did and did not take high school civics classes. They found that the African-American students who took the class had greater knowledge and expressed greater support for democratic values than those who had not taken it, but they did not find differences among any other groups. For most students, the civics classes did not have the intended effect.

Teachers mold opinions as well as teach facts.

Other political cues in school are less obvious, but no less important. Students often acquire the values of their teachers and peers, as a classic study of the power of socialization at Bennington College in the 1930s shows.[40] The faculty at Bennington was predominantly liberal, whereas the students came mostly from well-to-do, conservative families. The political preferences of the first-year students matched those of their parents fairly closely—both groups were conservative. But the preferences of the juniors and seniors who had been under the influence of their more senior peers and the Bennington faculty changed substantially. Unlike their parents, the juniors and seniors were predominantly liberal. At this stage, the school seemed more influential than parents in the students' lives.

The Media

Along with family, friends, and school, the mass media also socialize people, often from a very early age. Many children begin watching television when they are only babies. During the winter months, elementary school children typically spend more hours watching television than attending school. By the time of high school graduation, the average graduate will have watched 15,000 hours of television and attended only 11,000 hours of class.[41] Heavy users of mass media tend both to know more about current events and to support basic American values such as freedom of speech and tolerance. They also tend to hold the moderate political beliefs that television typically portrays.[42]

The mass media are influential in many ways, not just through news shows. Movies and television in the 1950s promoted racial and ethnic stereotypes, reinforcing prejudices. By the 1980s, many stereotypes had changed or been abandoned. Television programs and films now commonly present bigots as fools to be pitied or scorned. Yet despite the television industry's decision to embrace the norm of tolerance, many stereotypes persist. Minorities and women still appear more commonly in weaker supporting roles rather than leading roles. For example, a 1995 study found that Latinos are "mired in the stereotypes of a previous generation" and "serve as window dressing on mainstream, primetime television."[43] Another recent study showed that more than 40 percent of all MTV videos

Videos that portray women primarily as sex objects can help create stereotypes.

(other than those containing only footage of rock concerts) portrayed women as "being less than a person, a two-dimensional image. This characterization includes 'the dumb blonde,' the sex object and the whimpering victim."[44]

People often acquire mistaken impressions from the entertainment media. As media critics often observe, far more murders are committed on television and in movies than in real life. These fictional murders have real effects on public opinion, however. Heavy television watchers exaggerate the crime rate in the country, fear crime more than those who watch television less, and respond with calls for more police, more prisons, and longer sentences for criminals.[45] Entertainment affects the public's perceptions of society, so it indirectly affects public policy through public opinion.

Lifetime Learning

Socialization does not end when a person leaves high school or college; it continues throughout one's life. New jobs, new friends, new neighborhoods, and new political issues can either change people's values and attitudes or solidify them.[46]

In a follow-up to the Bennington study, researchers tracked down the participants in the original study after more than twenty years.[47] They found a high level of stability in the former students' attitudes. In the 1960 election, thirty of the thirty-three most liberal students from the 1930s voted for the Democratic candidate, John Kennedy; twenty-two of the thirty-three most conservative students from the 1930s voted for the Republican, Richard Nixon. The most important factor in explaining the few who changed views during the intervening years seemed to be whether the former student had married a liberal or a conservative and the political views of her friends. Having a spouse and friends who supported one's views resulted in little change; being surrounded by those who disagreed caused a good deal of change. Thus, the four years at Bennington College had a powerful influence, but not one that could necessarily withstand later influences.

The Bennington students of the 1930s do not differ very much from today's students. All children learn their initial values and attitudes from their parents. Over time, these beliefs change as other influences enter their lives—friends, schools, and the mass media, among others. In the realm of politics, party identification is more stable than virtually any other attitude, but as the Bennington study shows, it, too, can change over the years. Socialization factors—family, friends, schools, and the media—play a large role in determining public opinion, and through public opinion, they influence public policy.

Ideologies

Most people have opinions about a wide range of issues. As we just discussed, people's opinions are based on their knowledge and their underlying values and are shaped by socialization. Opinions, however, do not exist in isolation. They are related to other opinions. When opinions and values fit together into a general philosophy about government, we call them an ideology.

Ideology
An elaborate set of interrelated beliefs with overarching, abstract principles that make people's political philosophies coherent.

The term **ideology** has been defined in many ways, but the core of most definitions—and the one used here—is that an ideology is an elaborate set of interrelated beliefs with overarching, abstract principles that provide people with coherent philosophies about politics.[48] This means that an ideology is both a list of opinions (for example, conservatives should oppose high tax rates on corporations and government regulation of businesses) and a principled explanation of why those opinions fit together (for example, the principle of minimal government interference in the marketplace implies that the government should let businesses keep as much of their profits as possible and should avoid regulating them).

The role of ideologies is more than just to fit opinions together in an intellectually pleasing fashion. Ideologies focus conflict in society. Ideologies tell us not only what to think, but also where we should agree and disagree with our opponents. The ideology of Marxism, for example, tells us that class distinctions are the most important divisions in society, and that divisions within classes—such as race or ethnicity—should be ignored.[49] By establishing this, Marxism guides its adherents in identifying conflicts and in choosing the correct side to take. Other ideologies, including those that dominate American politics, point toward other conflicts.

The two ideologies most widespread in America today—**liberalism** and **conservatism**—agree on the basic principles of democracy and capitalism. These principles are well known to most Americans. *Democracy* means people control their government through elections and assumes that all people should have the same legal and political rights. Some writers describe this principle as *equality*. *Capitalism* means private ownership of the means of production and the free pursuit of profit in the marketplace. Closely associated with the idea of capitalism is the principle of *freedom,* the absence of government interference in one's economic activity and one's personal liberty.[50] Democracy and capitalism, then, are roughly synonymous with equality and freedom.

Liberalism
The political philosophy that government should play an expansive role in society (except in the area of personal morality) with the goal of protecting its weaker citizens and ensuring political and social equality for all citizens.

Conservatism
The political philosophy that government should play a minimal role in society (except in the area of traditional moral values) with the goal of ensuring all its citizens economic freedom.

Although the ideologies of liberalism and conservatism agree on our basic democratic-capitalist system, they disagree on the balance between the two principles. Democracy and capitalism conflict with each other in many situations. Consider campaign contributions as an example. A wealthy person can afford to give far more money to candidates and thus, insofar as money buys influence, can exert more influence than a poor person. Should the wealthy person be allowed the *freedom* to give a huge amount, or should contributions be limited to preserve political *equality* between the rich and poor? As we shall see in the discussions that follow, conservatives place great value on freedom, whereas liberals value equality more.

Liberalism

Modern-day liberalism differs significantly from the classical liberalism described in chapter 2. Today, the central principle of liberalism is that the government should play an extensive role in society, protecting poorer and weaker citizens. In economic matters, liberals are willing to curtail economic freedom and restrain capitalism in order to increase political and economic equality. In short, liberals believe that government should take an active role in moving society toward *equality of outcomes,* as described in chapter 5. In social matters, however, liberals favor a much smaller role for government, believing that the government should not restrict individual freedoms, even when the majority wants to do so. In foreign affairs, liberals believe that U.S. foreign policy should play down the use of military force and should focus instead on humanitarian and economic aid (see box 6.2).

In terms of specific issues, liberalism implies that the government should take the following actions:

- Make the wealthy pay more in taxes, raise minimum wages, and pass other laws to redistribute wealth from those who have more to those who have less.
- Regulate businesses to protect unions, to ensure safe working conditions, to reduce pollution, and to protect consumers.
- Guarantee minimum levels of health care, income, and housing for the poor, elderly, and people with disabilities—using government programs such as Medicare, Medicaid, welfare, and the Food Stamp program.
- Prevent discrimination against racial, religious, or ethnic minorities, homosexuals, people with disabilities, and people with extreme or unpopular ideas.
- Assist underdeveloped foreign nations with economic and humanitarian aid.

Not all liberals, or people who are to the **left** of center, agree with all these positions. People naturally choose their own opinions. But when a person agrees with most or all of the ideas on this list, we would describe that person as a liberal.

Left
The liberal end of the political spectrum.

The People Behind the Rules

BOX 6.2

The Liberals: Sen. Edward M. Kennedy and the Rev. Jesse Jackson

One way to learn about liberalism is to look at the records of two prominent liberals—Sen. Edward M. Kennedy (D-Mass.) and the Rev. Jesse Jackson. Although both belong to the Democratic Party, they are to the left of most of their fellow Democrats.

Sen. Edward M. Kennedy (D-Mass.)

Edward M. Kennedy

Edward Kennedy, the youngest brother of President John F. Kennedy, was elected to the U.S. Senate in 1962 when he was only thirty years old. He spent his first few years in office learning the rules and norms of the Senate and playing a supporting role in legislative fights. By the late 1960s, following years of upheaval during the civil rights movement, the anti-Vietnam War movement, and the assassinations of civil rights leader Rev. Dr. Martin Luther King, Jr., and his own brother, Sen. Robert F. Kennedy (D-N.Y.), the youngest Kennedy emerged as a powerful liberal leader.

In the decades that followed, Kennedy led the fight for a wide range of legislation. He worked for immigration reform—seeking to relax the rules so that more people could become U.S. citizens. He fought for freedom of choice in abortion, sponsoring the 1993 bill that made blocking an abortion clinic a federal crime. He supported busing to achieve integration of public schools and a wide range of affirmative action programs to increase the numbers of women and minorities hired in desirable jobs. He opposed capital punishment. When he was chair of the Labor and Human Resources Committee in the Senate in the late 1980s and early 1990s, Kennedy successfully pushed bills increasing AIDS education and treatment by $1 billion; creating "Star Schools" to improve math, science, and foreign language education; banning the use of lie detectors in federal courts; extending civil rights, and strengthening fair housing laws, which prevent discrimination in housing. In foreign affairs, Kennedy opposed the 1991 Gulf War and has consistently called for deep cuts in Pentagon spending.

Rev. Jesse Jackson

Jesse Jackson

Jesse Jackson entered politics as the student body president of North Carolina Agricultural and Technical State University, where he led civil rights sit-ins, marches, and other demonstrations in the early 1960s. After graduation, he moved to Chicago, where he attended the Chicago Theological Seminary and was ordained as a Baptist minister in 1968. While in Chicago, Jackson met Martin Luther King and worked with him and the Southern Christian Leadership Conference (SCLC). In 1966, King appointed Jackson to head the Chicago chapter of Operation Breadbasket—a program through which Jackson worked to improve the economic position of African Americans and to eliminate housing segregation in Chicago.

In 1971, Jackson left SCLC and founded PUSH—People United to Serve Humanity. As the leader of PUSH, Jackson led a string of marches, protests, and boycotts to fight discrimination and to improve the social and economic status of African Americans. In 1984 and again in 1988, Jackson ran for the Democratic nomination for the presidency. During his campaigns, he called for cutting defense expenditures and spending the resulting savings on domestic programs such as education, health, housing, and jobs programs. He favored increasing the taxes on the wealthy and cutting taxes on the working class and poor. He vigorously opposed abortion in the 1970s, but by 1984 he had reversed himself—supporting free choice in abortion. In foreign affairs, he favored putting pressure on South Africa to end apartheid and pulling U.S. aid out of countries he considered right-wing dictatorships.

Sources: The Almanac of American Politics, 1994 (Washington, D.C.: National Journal, 1993), pp. 597–98; *Candidates '88* (Washington, D.C.: Congressional Quarterly Press, 1988); and Allen D. Hertzke, *Echoes of Discontent: Jesse Jackson, Pat Robertson, and the Resurgence of Populism* (Washington, D.C.: CQ Press, 1993), chap. 3.

Conservatism

The central principle of conservatism is that the government should play a minimal role in society, except to uphold traditional moral standards. In economic matters, conservatives oppose governmental limitations on businesses or individual behavior, preferring to let the free market determine economic outcomes. Although conservatives favor a welfare "social safety net," they favor lower benefits than liberals do, and they prefer that private charities assist the poor so that the government is involved as little as possible. More broadly, conservatives believe that government should be limited to ensuring *equality of opportunities* in economic matters, not equality of outcomes. In social matters, however, conservatives favor a more expansive role for government, believing that majorities ought to be able to limit personal behavior on moral grounds. In foreign affairs, conservatives believe that the United States should use military aid to promote its interests overseas; they place less priority on economic and humanitarian aid (see box 6.3).

In terms of specific policies, conservatism implies that the government should take the following actions:

- Make tax rates flatter so that everyone pays the same or nearly the same percentage, regardless of total income.
- Oppose efforts to increase the minimum wage, to raise tariffs on imported goods, and to place more regulations on how businesses operate.
- Limit social welfare benefits for the poor, elderly, and people with disabilities.
- Uphold "traditional" values by strengthening laws against pornography and oppose laws designed to protect the rights of homosexuals.
- Favor laws outlawing abortion.
- Pursue U.S. foreign policy interests with military aid.

Not all conservatives, or people who are to the **right** of center, agree with this list of positions. But when people agree with most of these ideas, we describe them as conservative.

Right
The conservative end of the political spectrum.

Looking at liberalism and conservatism together, we see both consensus and conflict. Both agree on the general principles of democracy and capitalism, although they disagree on the balance between those principles. The conflicts between the two ideologies center on economic, social, and foreign policies. On economic policies, conservatives favor the interests of the wealthy by emphasizing economic growth, whereas liberals favor the interests of the poor by supporting income redistribution. On social policies, conservatives favor traditional moral standards and want to allow the majority to impose standards on the minority, whereas liberals prefer to prevent the government from legislating moral or religious standards. In foreign affairs, conservatives focus on preparing for military threats, whereas liberals emphasize efforts to aid the poor of other nations.

Changes Over Time

Ideologies are not fixed sets of ideas; they change over time in response to changes in society. Industrialization, urbanization, technological development, immigration, population growth, and other economic and social trends have all caused shifts in ideologies over time. Some of these modifications have been huge, others small.

At the end of the 1700s, when the United States was founded, most of the people were independent farmers with little need for government services. *Classical liberals* saw government as a potential threat to the individual rights and liberties of these citizens and thus sought to keep government small.[51] Yet with industrialization in the late 1800s and the struggle of workers to form labor unions, liberals began to see the government's potential as a protector of the rights of weaker citizens, rather

The People Behind the Rules

BOX 6.3

The Conservatives: Sen. Phil Gramm and Patrick J. Buchanan

To learn about conservatism, consider the records of two prominent conservatives—Sen. Phil Gramm (R-Tex.) and Patrick J. Buchanan. Gramm and Buchanan stand at the opposite end of the political spectrum from Kennedy and Jackson. Both Gramm and Buchanan are to the right of most of their fellow Republicans.

Sen. Phil Gramm (R-Tex.)

Sen. Phil Gramm

Phil Gramm grew up in Columbus, Georgia and went to school at the University of Georgia, where he earned first his B.A. and then a Ph.D. in economics. When he finished his doctorate, he moved to Texas to teach at Texas A&M. He entered politics by speaking around the state, praising free markets and denouncing government interference in business. Following an unsuccessful bid for the Democratic nomination for the U.S. Senate, Gramm finally entered office by winning a seat in the House of Representatives as a Democrat in 1978.

In Congress, Gramm focused his attention on economic issues. He received a seat on the Budget Committee, but then turned on his Democratic colleagues when he co-sponsored President Reagan's 1981 budget cutting bill and pushed other conservative policies. Two years later, Tip O'Neill—the Democratic speaker of the House—punished Gramm by removing him from the Budget Committee. Gramm resigned from the House, switched to the Republican Party, and won his old seat back in a special election. In 1984, Gramm won a seat in the Senate when the incumbent senator retired.

Once in the Senate, Gramm moved quickly to the forefront in budget politics. He helped craft the Gramm-Rudman deficit reduction law, which required automatic budget cuts if the budget deficit was not cut to specific levels each year (see chapter 16). Since then, he has regularly played a leading role in budget negotiations—always working for spending cuts, smaller government, and a balanced budget.

In other areas, Gramm opposed President Clinton's health care reforms because they increased government interference in the health care industry, and he fought against President Clinton's anti-crime legislation because the bill included social spending to prevent crime, rather than just tougher penalties for criminals. He also opposed the Brady gun control bill, which requires a waiting period before the purchase of a handgun and a national criminal background check for would-be firearm purchasers. In foreign affairs, Gramm—a confirmed free trader—supported the North American Free Trade Agreement (NAFTA), and he normally votes to support the Pentagon.

Patrick J. Buchanan

Patrick J. Buchanan

Pat Buchanan got his start in journalism, as an editorial writer for the St. Louis *Globe-Democrat*. When Richard Nixon won the presidency in 1968, Buchanan joined him as a speech writer. After the Watergate scandal forced Nixon to resign in 1974, Buchanan worked briefly for President Gerald Ford. He later returned to the world of journalism and then moved back to the White House as Director of Communications when Ronald Reagan won the presidential election in 1980.

In his unsuccessful bid for the 1996 Republican presidential nomination, Buchanan attacked President Clinton for raising taxes and for embracing liberal congressional legislation. Buchanan repeatedly called for limiting immigration, both legal and illegal. Buchanan also joined in the attack on the federally funded National Endowment for the Arts (NEA) for giving grants to artists whose work some considered obscene or anti-religious. He also took a hard-line pro-life stand, opposing abortion even in cases of rape and incest. In foreign affairs, Buchanan led the unsuccessful fight against NAFTA and the General Agreement on Tariffs and Trade, which President Clinton signed and Congress eventually approved. Buchanan wants to push the United States toward a more isolationist stand—eliminating foreign aid, bringing troops home from around the world, and reducing involvement in international organizations such as the United Nations and the World Bank.

Sources: The Almanac of American Politics, 1996 (Washington, D.C.: National Journal, 1995), pp. 1259–63; Patrick J. Buchanan, *Right from the Beginning: An Autobiography* (Boston: Little-Brown, 1988); Tom Mathews with Howard Fineman and Eleanor Clift, "Why Is Buchanan So Angry?" *Newsweek*, 27 January 1992, pp. 22–24; Michael Riley, "What Does Pat Want?" *Time*, 16 March 1992, pp. 23–24.

Ronald Reagan once denounced Medicare as "socialism"; twenty years later, as president, he praised it.

than as a threat to them. By the 1900s, a new "reform liberalism" had begun to emerge with the belief that government intervention in the marketplace could do more good than harm.[52]

Less dramatic changes in ideologies occur over shorter spans of time as new issues arise and old issues evolve. When Medicare, the federal health care program for the elderly, was debated in Congress in 1964, conservatives denounced it as "socialized medicine." A spokesperson for the American Medical Association—a vehement opponent of Medicare—argued that Medicare would be a giant step down the path to socialism in the United States; he declared that "medical care for the aged is a foot in the door of a government takeover of all medicine."[53] Yet by the time that spokesperson, Ronald Reagan, was elected president sixteen years later, the one-time socialist threat had become a popular program that liberals and conservatives both supported. Indeed, Medicare became so popular that when Republican members of Congress tried to restructure the program in 1995—at least in part to contain its skyrocketing cost—polls showed that the American public was deeply critical of the proposed changes.[54] In this case, as in many others, new ideas became accepted and the nature of the political conflicts changed over time.

Sources of Ideologies

Ideologies have their roots in two types of soil: in abstract ideas about the roles of individuals and the government in society, and in real-life groups of people helped or harmed by the ideas. Ideologies do not exist in a vacuum. Rather, they serve as justifications for groups seeking power, money, and other benefits. As a group's circumstances change, the ideology most closely associated with the group may be altered to rationalize new claims on social benefits.

As an example of how ideologies bend to group interests, consider how some conservatives reacted to a proposal the Clinton administration made in 1993 to require ranchers to pay market prices when they leased land from the federal government for their livestock to graze on. The administration wanted to end the long-standing practice of letting ranchers lease federal lands at below-market prices. Although conservatives usually argue that the free market should be allowed to operate with as few hindrances as possible and that government should be run more like a business, conservative members of Congress from Western states fought the proposal—and eventually succeeded in killing it—because it would have raised the cost of doing business for ranchers in their states. The principle of free markets yielded to the practical influence of the ranchers' claims. Of course, liberals also sometimes bend their ideology to satisfy group interests. For example, most liberals prefer to spend less money on defense. Yet when cutting defense spending means cutting spending on weapons programs or military bases that employ large numbers of their constituents, liberal lawmakers often vote for more defense spending. So when we speak of liberalism and conservatism, we must explain not only the ideas that make up those ideologies, but also the social groups that will benefit or lose if those ideas prevail.

Ideologies form around economic, racial, ethnic, religious, and gender groups. Probably the most important sets of groups that ideologies form around are economic groups. Conservatism offers a rationalization for the wealthy and business interests to have the freedom to gain an even larger share of society's wealth; liberalism offers a rationalization for redistributing wealth so that the poor and working class get a larger share—moving them toward equality.

Racial, ethnic, and religious groups are also significant sources of ideological cleavages. Not only do members of these groups often share similar economic situations, but they also share similar cultural and religious values. Together with providing a sense of group identity, these values can lead a group to demand social benefits from the government. These can range from tangible economic benefits such as those benefits affirmative action programs for minorities provide to intangible benefits such as laws symbolizing the cultural superiority of a group (for example, English-only laws, which establish English as the only language in which official government business can be conducted).[55]

The temperance movement to ban alcoholic beverages in America is a good example of the politics of cultural superiority.[56] Although some Protestant churches had objected to drinking since before the American Revolution, the temperance movement gained its greatest strength in the early 1900s when huge numbers of Catholic immigrants arrived from countries such as Ireland, Italy, and Poland in which drinking was socially and religiously acceptable. As the growing immigrant Catholic population began to threaten the Yankee Protestants' political control in some areas, the Protestants responded with calls for laws banning the sale or consumption of alcoholic beverages—laws that would symbolize Protestant superiority. In 1919, the temperance forces won passage of the Eighteenth Amendment to the Constitution, which established Prohibition. Fourteen years later, the political tides had changed as more immigrants became naturalized citizens with voting rights, and the Twenty-first Amendment repealed Prohibition.

The fight over temperance is typical of many ideological conflicts between social groups. The conservatives—mostly Yankee Protestants—sought laws against drinking to uphold the traditional moral value of abstinence. The liberals—mostly ethnic European Catholics—sought to resist those laws. The battleground was government policy; the prize both sides sought was a rule.

Since the late 1960s, gender has become the basis for ideological divisions as well. As we saw in chapter 5, the women's movement has identified and challenged a range of government policies and social practices in which men and women have been treated differently—from discrimination in education, jobs, and government benefits to private clubs and sexist language.[57] The movement also has sought to establish the principle of reproductive rights (for example, the right to family planning and the right to choose abortion) and to establish government policies that aid women in other ways (for example, creating government-subsidized child care and parental leave for birth or adoption). As the women's movement expanded, it quickly became an established aspect of liberalism (although the label *feminist* seems to have fallen out of fashion).[58] For their part, conservatives began to defend the "traditional" roles of women in families.[59]

The Process of Molding Ideologies

So far we have been discussing changes in ideologies without explaining who causes the changes. Ideologies are not modified by some vague process, of course, but by people. The politicians, journalists, political writers, and academics who debate political issues in speeches, newspaper columns, political magazines, and books are modifying ideologies with their arguments. No one person can declare the true liberal or conservative position on an issue, but as influential liberal or conservative leaders debate issues, a rough consensus emerges. When liberal leaders such as Sen. Edward Kennedy (D-Mass.) argue for legislation establishing a right to parental leave from one's job after the birth of a child, and conservative leaders such as then-Sen. Robert Dole (R-Kans.) oppose it, less prominent liberals and conservatives follow along. In this manner, ideologies evolve over time.

Only a small number of people participate in the process of molding ideologies. Most people—even most politicians, journalists, writers, and academics—are no more than consumers of the ideological packages the few create. The debates over what society should do about various problems and what "true" liberals or conservatives should think include few participants and many observers. The results of the debates—the packages of liberal and conservative positions—are passed down to the rest of the public through the news media, classrooms, and other forums. From these sources, depending on which leaders we trust, we learn whether we should favor or oppose new rules and policies.[60]

Public Opinion on the Issues

Describing public opinion is a difficult task because of the many confusing and seemingly contradictory views people hold. We can see this contradictory nature when we look at how people's opinions fail to fit into sets of liberal, moderate, or conservative ideologies, or when we compare Americans' opinions on abstract symbols with their opinions on concrete policies. In both cases, people seem to hold conflicting opinions, which shows that few Americans think ideologically. Although most Americans do not think ideologically, clear patterns do show up in their opinions. When we look at public opinion on clusters of related issues, we can see these patterns, which help us to understand public opinion and the demands people put on government.

Ideological Thinking by the Public

Although most politicians and political activists see politics in terms of ideological battles, only a relatively small portion of the mass public thinks in ideological terms—that is, thinks about politics in terms of overarching, abstract principles relating a broad set of beliefs about policies. Estimating how many people think ideologically is difficult, but clearly only a minority does. One study found that in 1980, only 42 percent of the population could even crudely define the terms *liberal* and *conservative*.[61] The proportion of the population that understands the terms apparently has not changed in decades.[62]

Studies of **attitude consistency** show similar results. Attitude consistency is the degree to which one's opinions on political issues are all roughly at the same point on the ideological spectrum. That is, if one holds all liberal opinions, all moderate opinions, or all conservative opinions, then one is consistent; but if one holds a mixture of liberal, moderate, and conservative positions at the same time, then one is inconsistent. Although holding an ideologically consistent set of opinions is not the same as ideological thinking, it is closely related.[63] Repeated studies show that most of the public hold some mix of liberal, moderate, and conservative opinions.[64] Our political leaders may think in ideological terms, but most of the people who vote for them do not.

Attitude consistency
The degree to which a person's political opinions all fall at about the same point on the liberal-conservative dimension.

The studies showing that few people think ideologically imply that the public only weakly understands the political debates that dominate the world of politicians and journalists. As we discussed earlier in this chapter, the public has a weak grasp of the many facts needed to understand debates about public policy. Here we see that the public also has a weak understanding of the philosophies that help us evaluate the meaning of those facts.

FIGURE 6.1

Percent of Americans Who Identify Themselves as Politically Moderate, Conservative, or Liberal

Most Americans label themselves as moderate, but more people identify themselves as conservatives than as liberals—suggesting a more conservative electorate.

Source: Data from surveys by National Opinion Research Center, General Social Survey, 1974–1994.

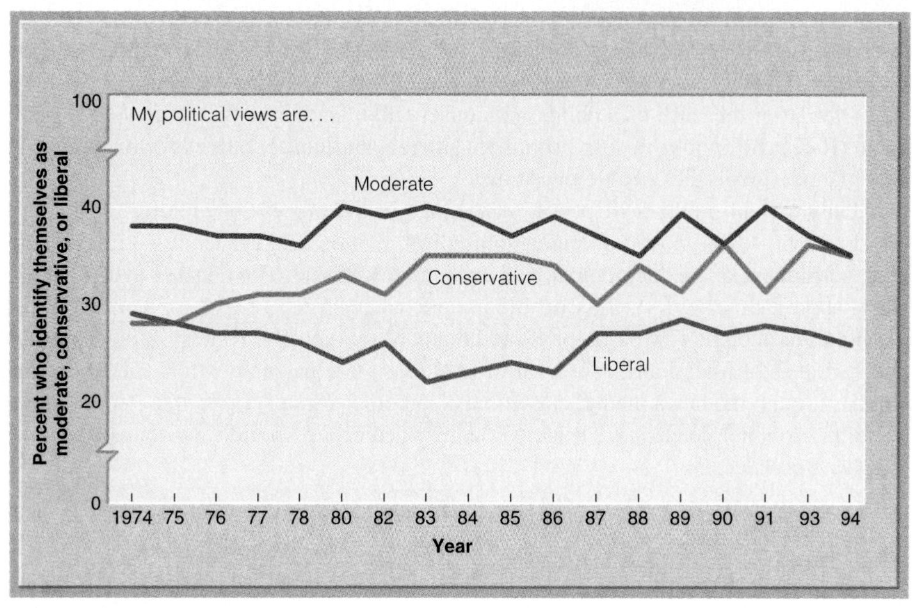

Abstract Symbols Versus Concrete Policies

The contradictory nature of the American public also becomes apparent when we consider the difference between people's support for conservative symbols and their support for liberal policies. In broad terms, the American public is best described as "both ideologically 'conservative' *and* programmatically 'liberal.' That is, Americans are opposed to 'big government' and respond favorably to the myths and symbols of competitive capitalism, in the abstract. When it comes to assessing specific government programs or the behavior of actual business enterprises, however, they support government spending in a variety of domestic areas and are profoundly suspicious of big business."[65]

The mix of liberal and conservative opinions is not some quirk of survey research methods. Rather, it stems from the public's lack of interest and political knowledge. Relatively few people know enough or spend enough time thinking about politics to recognize the connections between abstract statements with which they agree (for example, "free enterprise"—which implies less government intervention in the marketplace) and government programs that they like (for example, the minimum wage and government regulations to protect the environment—both of which imply more government intervention). Most people neither recognize nor resolve the contradictions among their opinions.

A good place to begin looking at symbols is by examining the ideological labels Americans use, as figure 6.1 shows. According to a survey conducted in 1994, more adult Americans claimed to be conservative (35 percent) than liberal (26 percent), with the rest describing themselves as moderate. As one might guess, the conservative lead grew during the Reagan years, but only slightly—gaining about 6 percentage points. Some voters shifted to the right, but no great surge of conservatism occurred.

Many abstract statements of conservative values attract majority support. For instance, a poll taken in 1995 asked people whether they agreed with the Republican proposal to "create an 'opportunity society' in which the federal government assures all Americans of an equal chance to prosper based on each individual's merits," but does not "guarantee minimum living standards or provide social benefits for its citizens." Of those polled, 41 percent said they "somewhat agreed," and an additional 22 percent said they "agreed strongly."[66] These figures would seem to indicate that the American public is predominantly conservative.

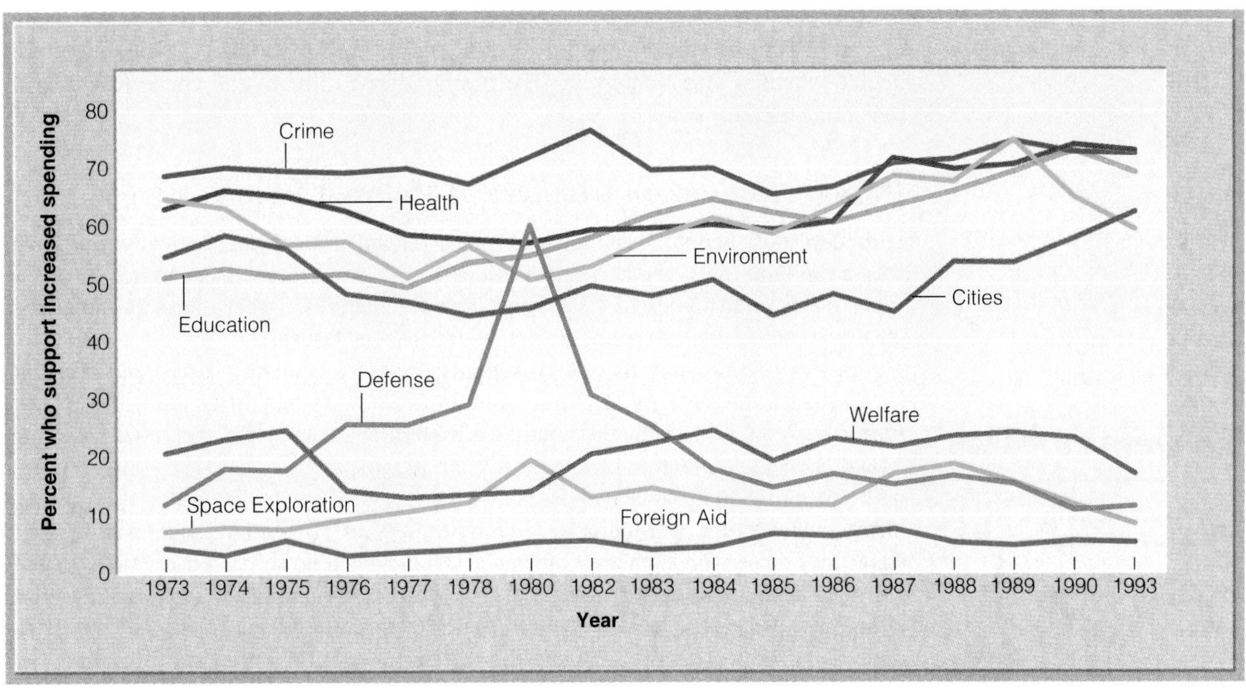

FIGURE 6.2
Percent of Americans Who Support Increased Spending

Most Americans want to increase spending in most policy areas—suggesting a more liberal electorate.

Source: Data from National Opinion Research Center General Social Surveys, 1973–1993.

Turning to concrete policy issues, however, we see signs of a more liberal electorate. For more than two decades, Americans have been polled about various aspects of government spending. They are presented with a list of problems and asked whether "we're spending too much money on it, too little money, or about the right amount." As we discussed earlier, conservatives generally prefer smaller government and less spending, whereas liberals tend to prefer larger government and more spending. This can be seen in campaign rhetoric when conservative candidates claim that liberals are "big spenders" who want to solve problems by "throwing money at them." Rhetoric aside, as figure 6.2 shows, in 1993, majorities of those polled supported increases in spending on the environment, health, education, the problems of the cities, and crime. Not many people supported increased defense spending, which should be a high priority according to conservative ideology. Indeed, increased defense spending has not been a high priority for most Americans, except for a brief period at the end of the 1970s and beginning of the 1980s.

Many observers regard the welfare system as a weak point of liberalism. Figure 6.2 confirms this claim; a majority of the public favors reducing spending on welfare. Yet when the same question was asked about spending for "assistance to the poor," the liberal, pro-spending majority reappeared.[67] Thus the public believes that the welfare system works poorly, but nevertheless is willing to help the poor. The only programs other than welfare that people wanted cut were defense, space exploration, and foreign aid. In sum, questions on specific government programs paint a more liberal picture of the American people than questions about ideological labels.[68]

Faced with the conflicting evidence presented here, one might ask, "How should we describe the public? Is it liberal or conservative?" This question can be answered two ways—"neither" and "both." First, most people are neither very liberal nor very conservative. They are moderate, or lean only slightly to the left or right. Second, most people have a mix of liberal, moderate, and conservative opinions. Some of those opinions conflict. For instance, some people want to increase spending on virtually every government program, cut taxes, and balance the budget—all at the same time (which is a serious problem for those who must work out

Guindon

A liberal throwing money at a problem.

Conservatives often accuse liberals of trying to solve social problems by spending money on them and thereby increasing the size of government.

the federal budget, as chapter 16 explains). Because they never address the problem of *how* to balance spending and taxes, they never have to sort out their opinions and decide which is most important. Their contradictory liberal and conservative opinions remain unresolved.

Economic issues
Issues relating to the distribution of income and wealth in society.

Social issues
Issues based on moral or value judgments.

Public Opinion on Clusters of Related Issues

Although most people's opinions are not arranged in neat, ideologically consistent sets, people do think about political issues and their opinions make sense. When we focus on different types of issues and look for patterns, rather than contradictions, clear patterns distinguish economic issues from social issues.

Public opinion analysts often distinguish between economic issues and social issues because the patterns of public opinion on these issues differ markedly.[69] **Economic issues** deal with the distribution of wealth in society—the tax system, welfare, Social Security, regulation of businesses and unions, and similar issues. **Social issues** relate to morals and value judgments—civil rights, women's equality, abortion and birth control, drugs, pornography, life-styles, sexual orientation, and related issues. Typically, those with higher incomes and educations tend to be conservative on economic issues (in part because this is to their economic benefit) and more liberal on social issues (because education fosters more tolerant attitudes). Those with lower incomes and educations tend to be the opposite—liberal on economic issues and conservative on social issues.

Americans frequently express one set of opinions when asked about abstract issues and a contradictory set of opinions when questioned about specific issues.

Economic Issues

The basic pattern among economic issues is that groups tend to favor policies that will benefit them economically. The wealthy tend to prefer tax cuts and flatter tax rates—so that taxes on the wealthy will drop—and reductions in government services—especially those, such as welfare, that go to the poor. In contrast, the poor tend to prefer tax increases and more progressive tax rates—so that the wealthy will pay more—and increases in government services—especially those that go to the poor. Economic self-interest also is apparent in the way many other groups view policies: farmers tend to support federal crop subsidies; renters tend to favor rent control; business owners tend to favor reduction in government regulations unless the regulations protect their businesses.

A typical example of these patterns can be seen in the debate over the minimum wage. In 1995, President Clinton proposed raising the minimum wage from $4.25 to $5.15 per hour. As table 6.2 shows, overwhelming majorities of all groups surveyed supported the increase, but the strongest support came from the lowest-income respondents (86 percent in favor) and the weakest from the highest-income respondents (62 percent in favor).

Aside from noting the economic self-interest table 6.2 reveals, we can make two other useful observations. First, we can see that the opinions of various groups are not monolithic, or uniform. Many of the wealthy supported the minimum wage increase, while some of the poor opposed it. Opinions are mixed within every income group. This is a typical finding. When we describe public opinion about any group, we should always be careful to avoid exaggerating tendencies. When we say that the poor tend to be liberal on economic issues, we usually mean that more of the poor support liberal proposals compared to the wealthy. But this can still mean that both groups support the proposals—as in the case of a minimum wage increase.

Second, we can observe other typical group differences in party, ideology, education, race, and gender. In addition to revealing income differences, table 6.2 shows that President Clinton's proposal garnered more support from Democrats, liberals, those without college educations, non-whites, and women than from Republicans, conservatives, those with postgraduate educations, whites, and men. These patterns are typical of public opinion on most economic issues. Age, however, did not form distinct patterns of support. The young are generally neither more liberal nor more conservative than the old on economic issues.

Men, whites, the well educated, the wealthy, and Republicans were more likely to take the conservative stand of opposing President Clinton's proposal to increase the minimum wage than were women, non-whites, the poorly educated, the poor, and Democrats.

TABLE 6.2 Support for President Clinton's Minimum Wage Increase

	Approve	Disapprove	No Opinion
Nationwide	77%	21%	2%
Sex			
Male	72	26	2
Female	83	16	1
Age			
18–29	81	18	1
30–49	75	23	2
50–64	77	23	*
65+	79	19	2
Race			
White	76	22	2
Non-white	88	12	0
Education			
College postgraduate	64	34	2
College graduate	69	28	3
Some college	73	25	2
No college	84	15	1
Income			
$75,000+	62	35	3
$50,000+	67	30	3
$30–49,999	74	24	2
$20–29,999	82	17	1
$0–19,999	86	13	1
Party Identification			
Republican	63	34	3
Independent	80	18	2
Democrats	89	11	*
Ideology			
Liberal	84	15	1
Moderate	83	16	1
Conservative	68	30	2

Question: "As you may know, President Clinton has proposed raising the minimum wage in this country over two years—from four dollars and 25 cents an hour to five dollars and 15 cents an hour. Do you favor or oppose this proposal?"

*Less than one percent

Source: The Gallup Poll Monthly, No. 353, February 1995, p. 15.

Social Issues

The most important pattern among social issues is that the well educated tend to be liberal and the poorly educated tend to be conservative. This stems from the fact that education leads people to become more tolerant, and tolerance lies at the root of many social issues—tolerance for people of different races or ethnicities, tolerance for people with different religions or sexual orientations, and tolerance for people who make moral judgments different from one's own. Consequently, the well educated tend to take liberal positions on social issues, whereas the poorly educated tend to take conservative positions. Those with good educations are more likely to favor government intervention to prevent discrimination against racial, religious, or ethnic minorities, homosexuals, the handicapped, and people with extreme or unpopular ideas. By the same token, the well educated are less likely than the poorly educated to support government action to uphold "traditional" values at the expense of individual freedom.[70]

A typical example of the relationship between education and opinion on social issues appears in the public's opinions about the legality of homosexual relations among consenting adults, as table 6.3 shows. In 1992, 69 percent of all college graduates thought that homosexual relations should be legalized, but only 38 percent of those

The young, the well educated, and the wealthy are more likely to take the liberal stand of favoring rights for homosexuals; elderly people, the poorly educated, and the poor are more likely to take the conservative stand of opposing homosexual rights.

TABLE 6.3 Attitudes Toward Homosexual Relations

	Legal	Not Legal	No Opinion
Nationwide	48%	44%	8%
Sex			
Men	51	44	5
Women	47	43	10
Age			
18–29	59	38	3
30–49	55	38	7
50–64	41	50	9
65+	30	58	12
Race			
White	49	44	7
Non-white	47	43	10
Education			
College graduate	69	25	6
Some college	57	38	5
No college	38	53	9
Income			
$50,000+	70	26	4
$30–49,999	49	43	8
$20–29,999	46	46	8
$0–19,999	43	51	6
Party Identification			
Republicans	41	54	5
Independents	55	34	11
Democrats	48	46	6
Ideology			
Liberals	65	29	6
Moderates	56	37	7
Conservative	33	60	7

Question: "Do you think homosexual relations between consenting adults should be legal or should not be legal?"
Source: The Gallup Poll Monthly, No. 321, June 1992, p. 6.

who had not attended college agreed. A similar pattern is evident among income groups—70 percent of those with the highest incomes believed homosexual relations should be legal, but only 43 percent of those with the lowest incomes thought so.

Table 6.3 also reveals a second important pattern related to social issues. The young tend to be more liberal than the old. (Remember, however, that this is generally not true concerning economic issues—for example, recall the minimum wage poll results shown in table 6.2). In the case of opinions about homosexual relations shown in table 6.3, people under age thirty are almost twice as likely as those over age sixty-five to oppose laws that prohibit homosexual activity.

The relationship between age and opinions on social issues has its roots in social change. At least since the 1950s, each generation has been more liberal and more tolerant than the previous generation. Many ideas about social issues that were unpopular fifty years ago—equality of the races, equality of the sexes, the acceptability of homosexual relationships—have now gained a far larger measure of acceptance. As society changes from generation to generation, the young have usually led the way. In terms of public opinion, this means that at any one time, the young are typically more liberal on social issues than are older people.[71]

One of the central areas of conflict in American society is another social issue—what role the government should play in guaranteeing civil rights for minorities and in working toward racial and ethnic equality. Should school children be bused to different schools to achieve racial balance? Should minorities receive special opportunities in school admissions or jobs to make up for past discrimination? Should the government

TABLE 6.4 Approval of Interracial Marriage

Men, the young, non-whites, the well educated, and the wealthy are more tolerant of interracial marriage than are women, the elderly, whites, the poorly educated, and the poor.

	Approve	Disapprove	No Opinion
Nationwide	48%	42%	10%
Sex			
Male	52	37	11
Female	44	46	10
Age			
18–29	64	28	8
30–49	56	34	10
50+	27	61	12
Race			
White	44	45	11
Non-white	70	19	11
Education			
College graduate	70	20	10
Some college	58	34	8
High school graduate	40	47	13
Less than high school graduate	26	66	8
Income			
$50,000+	61	34	5
$30–49,999	52	33	15
$20–29,999	49	44	7
$0–19,999	37	51	12
Party Identification			
Republican	46	44	10
Independent	53	36	11
Democrat	45	46	9

Question: "Do you approve or disapprove of marriage between blacks and whites?"

Source: George Gallup, Jr. and Frank Newport, "For First Time, More Americans Approve of Interracial Marriage than Disapprove," *The Gallup Poll Monthly*, No. 311, August 1991, p. 60.

make any effort to help lift more minorities into the middle class? As we discussed in chapter 5, civil-rights-related questions such as these have played a prominent role in American history.[72]

On virtually every civil rights issue, minorities favor far stronger government action than whites. When asked in 1995 whether they approved of affirmative action programs "designed to give preferential treatment to racial minorities in areas such as getting jobs and promotions, obtaining contracts, and being admitted to schools," 66 percent of non-whites approved, but only 36 percent of whites did.[73] Similarly, a poll conducted in 1991 asked people whether they approved or disapproved of "marriage between blacks and whites." Roughly 70 percent of non-whites but only 44 percent of whites said they approved (see table 6.4).

In addition to finding racial patterns on civil rights opinions, we also see the same sort of education and age patterns that appear in other social issues. In the case of interracial marriage, table 6.4 shows that 70 percent of college graduates approve, but only 26 percent of those who have not graduated from high school approve. Similarly, those under age thirty were more than twice as likely to approve of interracial marriage as those fifty and older.

Our final example of a social issue is abortion. Since the Supreme Court ruled in *Roe v. Wade* (1973) that states could not make abortion illegal, abortion has been among the most divisive social issues in the nation.[74] Liberal political leaders tend to be **pro-choice** (that is, favor a woman's right to choose abortion) and conservative leaders tend to be **pro-life** (that is, favor making abortion illegal), yet a substantial amount of disagreement exists both among liberal political leaders and among conservative political leaders, as well as in the population.[75] In other words, the liberal and conservative positions on abortion do not line up neatly with the liberal and conservative positions on other major issues.

Pro-choice
Favoring the policy of allowing women to choose whether to have abortions.

Pro-life
Favoring the policy of making abortion illegal.

Women, the young, the well educated, high income earners, Democrats, and liberals are somewhat more in favor of legal abortion than men, the elderly, the poorly educated, low income earners, Republicans, and conservatives.

Table 6.5 Attitudes Toward Abortion

	Always Legal	Legal Under Certain Circumstances	Always Illegal
Nationwide	33%	50%	15%
Sex			
Men	29	53	14
Women	36	47	15
Age			
18–29	34	44	19
30–49	39	46	12
50–64	26	57	15
65+	24	59	13
Race			
White	33	50	14
Non-white	30	49	18
Education			
College postgraduate	43	49	7
College graduate	41	48	9
Some college	37	47	14
No college	26	52	18
Income			
$75,000+	50	45	4
$50,000+	38	54	7
$30–49,999	37	47	11
$20–29,999	34	45	19
$0–19,999	25	52	20
Party Identification			
Republicans	25	57	16
Independents	37	44	15
Democrats	36	49	12
Ideology			
Liberal	43	43	12
Moderate	38	49	11
Conservative	22	54	21

Question: "Do you think abortions should be legal under any circumstances, legal only under certain circumstances, or illegal in all circumstances?"

Source: The Gallup Poll Monthly, No. 354, March 1995, p. 30.

Although abortion is not a typical social issue, as table 6.5 shows, the college educated are still much more likely to say that abortion should always be legal than are those who did not attend college. Largely because the well educated have high incomes, a strong relationship also exists between income and opinion on abortion. In addition, the percentage of young Americans who say they are pro-choice is about ten points higher than the percentage of pro-choice elderly, and Democrats and liberals are more likely to be pro-choice than are Republicans and conservatives.

As table 6.5 also shows, the percentage of women who believe that abortion should always be legal is seven points higher than the percentage of men who think so; however, men and women are equally likely to believe that abortion should always be illegal. In other words, we find women leaning slightly toward a pro-choice position. This has not always been the case; as recently as 1989, surveys routinely found no differences between men's and women's positions on abortion.[76] Although abortion is often described as a "women's issue," women and men have generally held similar views on the matter.

Taking a step back and looking broadly over the range of public opinion on issues, we see that when we analyze public opinion in terms of specific economic and social issues, it becomes easier to make sense of it. As we saw in the previous section, people have contradictory opinions about some issues, but as we see here, that does not mean their opinions are random or chaotic.

Attitudes on economic issues are heavily influenced by economic self-interest—wealthier people tend to favor policies that benefit the wealthy; poorer people usually favor policies that benefit the poor. Attitudes on social issues are heavily influenced by education—well-educated people generally prefer more tolerant social policies, whereas poorly educated people usually prefer less tolerant social policies. Other patterns emerge as well. The young tend to be more liberal on social issues than the elderly, and whites tend to be more conservative on civil rights issues than non-whites. Together these patterns help us to describe public opinion and to understand the conflicting demands that the public makes on government officials.

Changes in Opinion Over Time

For the most part, public opinion is fairly stable over time. Indeed, the key point to make about changes in public opinion is that there aren't many. The most thorough investigation of change in public opinion over time found a "remarkable degree of stability in Americans' collective policy preferences."[77] The study collected all the public opinion time series available from the major commercial and academic survey organizations from 1935 to 1990 and discovered that fewer than half of the opinions changed, and most of the changes were quite modest. Fewer than 7 percent of all public opinion items changed as much as 20 percentage points, and fewer than 2 percent changed as much as 30 percentage points (the size of the 1980 shift in opinion on defense spending in figure 6.2).

When changes in opinion do occur, they tend to be modest, such as the 7 percent point increase from the late 1970s to 1994 in people identifying themselves as conservative (see figure 6.1). Large movements, such as the 30 percent jump in the number of people who thought that the government was spending too little on defense in 1980, are uncommon.

When public opinion does shift dramatically, it usually does so in response to dramatic events that capture the public's attention. For example, worries about the 1979 Iranian seizure of the American embassy in Teheran and the Soviet invasion of Afghanistan less than a month later, coupled with Ronald Reagan's 1980 presidential campaign calls for a bigger military, caused the surge of people clamoring for more money to be spent on defense.[78] Within two years, however, the American hostage crisis in Iran was over, the Soviet invasion was largely forgotten, and the public's willingness to spend more on the military returned to its original level.

The public's response to the growing threat of the Gulf War following the August 1990 Iraqi invasion of Kuwait offers another example of a rapidly changing public mood. As late as the beginning of December, nearly three-fifths of the public said the United States should rely solely on economic sanctions to force Iraq out of Kuwait, no matter how long it took. By early January, as President Bush's January 15 deadline for Iraqi withdrawal approached, support for sanctions had fallen by 20 percentage points.[79] In mid-January, after President Bush ordered U.S. troops to liberate Kuwait, more than 80 percent of the people said they backed his decision.[80]

Happily, hostage crises and wars are not common events, and so public opinion remains fairly stable on the whole. When changes do occur, they typically happen slowly, over long periods of time. We can describe these trends by once more breaking issues down into social and economic issues.

Since World War II, most changes in attitudes on *social* issues have headed in a liberal direction.[81] The public has moved to the left on a wide range of social issues—civil rights for minorities, equality for women, abortion, divorce, civil liberties, and sexual customs. Most of these changes in opinion have led to more liberal public policies.

Consider, as an example of change, opinions on civil rights issues, which have shifted relatively quickly over the last forty years. As recently as the 1960s, equal rights for minorities were controversial, but as figure 6.3 shows, school integration is now almost universally accepted. Our society has also made progress toward more

FIGURE 6.3
Percent of White Respondents Who Supported School Integration, Intermarriage, and Open Housing

Support for racial equality has been steadily growing, but many Americans still do not support complete equality between the races.

Sources: Data from the National Opinion Research Center General Social Surveys. NORC data from 1956 to 1983 are from Howard Schuman, Charlotte Steeh, and Lawrence Bobo, *Racial Attitudes in America: Trends and Interpretations* (Cambridge, Mass.: Harvard University Press, 1985), pp. 74–75, 88–89.

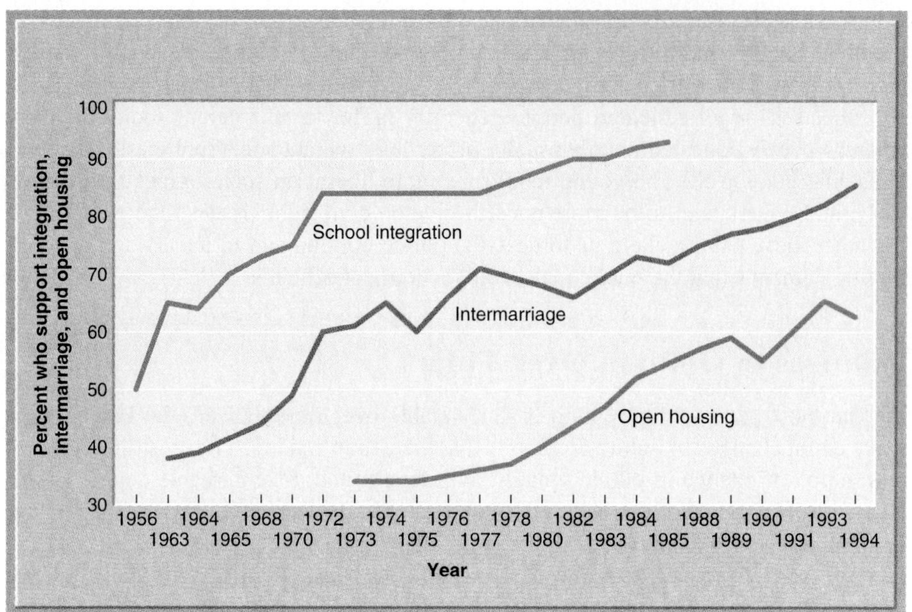

tolerant attitudes about open housing and interracial marriage; however, as figure 6.3 shows, substantial minorities of whites still support both forms of discrimination. (Note that figure 6.3 shows the results when people are asked whether they approve of a *law* against interracial marriages, not whether they personally approve of interracial marriages, which was the subject of table 6.4. Forty-five percent of whites disapprove, but only 16 percent would support a law banning interracial marriage.) In sum, support for racially intolerant laws has been steadily declining since the 1960s, but America is clearly a long way from being a nation without racial prejudice.[82]

On economic issues, changes in public opinion have been mixed. Support for Social Security has been high since the 1930s and remains steady.[83] Most other *entitlement programs*—federal programs such as Medicare and veterans benefits that provide direct benefits to individuals—have also remained highly popular. (See chapter 16 for a full discussion of entitlement programs.) From 1974 to 1980, a conservative trend caused support for big government, welfare, business regulation, environmental protection, and taxes to fall. Beginning in 1981, however, those trends reversed as public opinion on most economic issues began to move in a liberal direction.[84]

Crime is the one topic that has shown no liberal trend whatsoever. Public support has grown in the last thirty years for wider use of capital punishment, stiffer sentences, and increased spending to fight crime. In this area, public opinion has become more conservative.[85]

Causes of Change

Most movements in public opinion, like the changes in ideology discussed earlier in this chapter, can be traced to social or economic forces. The growth in support for women's equality, for instance, came about partly because of World War II. When America mobilized for war, many women entered the work force to replace men who had joined the military. Although some women left the work force when the war ended, many stayed. Moreover, many who worked during the war and then dropped out eventually returned to work. The growing number of working women became a major force underpinning the demands for equality.[86]

Social and economic forces alone may not be enough to produce changes in public attitudes. Often individuals or organizations play an important leadership role in bringing issues to the public's attention. For example, as we saw in chapter 5, the growth in racial tolerance in the United States over the past fifty years depended critically on the leaders of the civil rights movement. Until the 1950s, most Americans largely ignored civil rights. Many people did not approve of the system of racial segregation in the South, but they allowed it to continue. In a series of sit-ins, marches, and other protests, the Rev. Dr. Martin Luther King, Jr., and other civil rights leaders forced the problems of segregation and racism onto the front pages and television screens of America. When the public finally confronted the problem, both laws and attitudes began to change.[87]

With racial attitudes, as in most cases, change came slowly. The 1964 Civil Rights Act and the 1965 Voting Rights Act brought fairly quick changes to the laws governing racial relations, especially in the South. Yet racial prejudices diminished more slowly. As the survey data in figure 6.3 show, thirty years after the end of most forms of legalized segregation, 16 percent of the white population in America still thinks laws should prevent interracial marriage.

The framers of the Constitution worried about the whims of the majority—the possibility that public opinion could change rapidly.[88] That fear might have been justified two hundred years ago, but, as we have seen in this section, it is not justified now. Public opinion is quite stable. When sudden change occurs, it usually results from a dramatic event such as a war. Far more common is slow movement in public opinion, such as the changes in opinions about racial policies. When public opinion does shift, we can usually find the causes in social and economic changes in society and in the activities of political leaders.

SUMMARY

In a democracy, public opinion should guide the government's decisions. One might suppose that this means that the government should enact whatever policies the people want; that whenever a conflict arises, the government should do as the majority prefers. Yet our discussion of public opinion should make it clear that the matter is not so simple. The people's limited knowledge of politics, their inconsistent values and opinions, and their lack of a coherent ideology make it difficult for officeholders to gauge public opinion accurately.

Huge numbers of people do not know many basic facts about government and politics—from the campaign promises in the Contract With America to the name of the Chief Justice of the United States. Few people have any detailed understanding of the issues involved in congressional debates. Although almost everyone has some knowledge about some political issues, few have much detailed information. From the point of view of government officials, judging what the public would want if it knew the facts is extremely difficult.

To complicate matters, knowledge is not distributed equally in the population. The better educated, those with high incomes and high-status jobs, those who feel interested in and efficacious about politics, and those who are active in politics generally know a good deal more than the rest of the population and exert a disproportionate amount of influence.

People don't acquire opinions in the same way they learn facts about politics. People develop their values and opinions from those around them—from their families in early childhood, and from friends, teachers, and co-workers in later life. The mass media—including both news and entertainment media—also play an important role in molding people's beliefs.

To see how people's values and opinions fit together, it helps to consider the role of ideology. The prevailing ideologies in the United States are liberalism—which emphasizes the government's role in protecting its weaker citizens—and conservatism—which calls for government to play a minimal role in society, except to protect traditional moral standards. Ideologies are not fixed. Rather, they evolve over time in response to changing social, demographic, and technological changes in society. As new issues arise and old issues change, political leaders debate them, and in doing so, bring about slow shifts in what we think of as liberalism and conservatism.

An evaluation of the public's political knowledge shows that, unlike most political leaders, ordinary people usually do not think in ideological terms. Many people cannot even describe the dominant ideologies of liberalism and conservatism. Rather than holding consistent sets of liberal, moderate, or conservative views, many people hold a range of opinions from liberal to conservative. Moreover, some people call themselves conservatives but actually favor liberal policies; for example, they think the government should cut back on regulations and let business alone (a conservative stand) but that the government should also increase regulations to protect workers' health and to prevent businesses from damaging the environment (a liberal stand). In short, the public often sends out vague or contradictory messages to government officials.

To sort out these opinions, it helps to break them down into specific economic and social issues. When we do this, we see the role of self-interest: the wealthy tend to be conservative on economic issues, whereas the poor tend to be liberal. On social issues, the well educated (who also tend to be upper income) tend to be liberal, whereas the poorly educated tend to be conservative.

Looking at the history of public opinion in the last fifty years, we find that the public has become far more liberal on social issues, whereas trends on economic issues have been mixed. On some economic issues, people are more liberal; in other areas, they have become more conservative. Crime is the only area in which all of the trends indicate the public is becoming more conservative.

The problem for government officials, then, is how to take public opinion into account. Doing so is difficult because the public so often sends mixed messages. Because public opinion can be hard to decipher in the precise terms needed for legislation and government decision making, we should perhaps think of it as only a rough guide to government policy. This vagueness allows political parties and interest groups to speak on behalf of the people and act as intermediaries between the people and their government.

Key Terms

Attentive publics
Attitude consistency
Attitudes
Conservatism
Economic issues
Ideology
Issue publics
Left
Liberalism
Opinions
Pro-choice
Pro-life
Right
Social issues
Socialization
Socioeconomic status
Values

Readings for Further Study

Abramson, Paul R. *Political Attitudes in America: Formation and Change.* San Francisco: W. H. Freeman, 1983. A study of change in basic attitudes over the last three decades—including examinations of party identification, political trust, and feelings of political efficacy. Abramson skillfully analyzes these attitudes to help explain the decline in voter turnout since 1960.

Carpini, D., Michael X., and S. Keeter. *What Americans Know About Politics and Why It Matters.* New Haven: Yale University Press, 1996. An important and comprehensive analysis of what Americans know about politics, and a compelling argument that political knowledge is a powerful resource that helps knowledgeable Americans prevail in political conflicts.

Dolbeare, Kenneth M., and Linda J. Medcalf. *American Ideologies Today.* New York: Random House, 1988. A description and analysis of modern American values and political ideologies. Dolbeare and Medcalf explain the history of our ideologies and discuss how we might expect them to change in the future.

Erikson, Robert S., Norman R. Luttbeg, and Kent L. Tedin. *American Public Opinion.* 4th ed. New York: Macmillan, 1991. An outstanding textbook on American public opinion, which examines all the issues discussed in this chapter, but in far greater detail.

Graber, Doris. *Mass Media and American Politics.* 5th ed. Washington, D.C.: CQ Press, 1996. An outstanding textbook examining the influence of the mass media on public opinion and elections in America.

Jennings, M. Kent, and Richard G. Niemi. *The Political Character of Adolescence: The Influence of Families and Schools.* Princeton, N.J.: Princeton University Press, 1974. A classic study of the transmission of values and opinions from parents to their high-school-age children. Jennings and Niemi based their study on a nationwide survey of high school seniors and their parents conducted in 1965 and a follow-up survey conducted in 1973.

Mayer, William G. *The Changing American Mind: How and Why American Public Opinion Changed Between 1960 and 1988.* Ann Arbor: University of Michigan Press, 1992. A comprehensive history of American public opinion since 1960. Mayer not only documents trends in opinion, he systematically examines explanations for those trends and shows why public opinion changed.

McClosky, Herbert, and John Zaller. *The American Ethos.* Cambridge: Harvard University Press, 1984. A fascinating study of the two major traditions of American belief—capitalism and democracy. McClosky and Zaller blend a historical analysis of American beliefs and American culture with an analysis of modern survey data on what Americans and their political leaders think.

Page, Benjamin, and Robert Y. Shapiro. *The Rational Public.* Chicago: University of Chicago Press, 1992. An examination of public opinion on virtually every aspect of domestic and foreign policy from the 1930s to 1990. Page and Shapiro show how public opinion guides public policy, and they argue that public opinion is collectively rational—that it makes sense viewed in its entirety.

CHAPTER

7

VOTING AND PARTICIPATION

Who Votes?

The Effect of Individual Voter Characteristics

The Effect of Registration Laws

The Effect of Campaign Contacts

The Puzzling Decline of Voter Turnout

Does Turnout Matter?

Political Activists

Who Becomes an Activist?

Types of Activists

How Voters Make Choices

Party Identification

Candidate Characteristics

Issues

Changes Over Time

Voting and Social Groups

Summary

Key Terms

Readings for Further Study

The 1996 elections could have been a historic turning point for America. This can be said of only a handful of elections in our past. If Bob Dole had taken the White House, then together with Republican majorities in the House and Senate, he would have had the opportunity to steer public policy in a new and more conservative direction.

Although the outcome of the 1996 election could have fundamentally changed the direction of our nation's government, the campaign itself seemed almost ordinary, as if people did not recognize what was at stake. From its beginning in the harsh winters of Iowa and New Hampshire to its frenzied conclusion in November, an army of candidates and campaign workers struggled all across the country. Around one billion dollars were spent. Yet politics remained of little interest to many Americans. In the midst of a national debate about the country's future, people complained about too much negative advertising and too many television campaign commercials. On Election Day, only about half of all eligible voters bothered to vote.

The central activity that characterizes democracy is voting. When we think of democracy, we think of elections. Yet most people do not participate in most elections. Some sit out elections and watch the results come in on television; some cannot even muster the interest to find out who won. At the same time, others become intensely involved—stuffing envelopes, walking through neighborhoods to talk with potential voters, organizing rallies, and performing the dozens of other tasks that make up campaigning. Who chooses to participate and who chooses to sit at home greatly influence which candidates win and what policies become law. As we shall see, both the characteristics of individual citizens and the rules of the political system determine who participates.

When people do go to the polls, their choices depend on many things. Some committed activists never know a moment's doubt about how they will vote. Other, less interested citizens decide, sometimes at the last moment, on the basis of a few stray facts they have learned in the last weeks of the campaign.

In this chapter, we will examine voter participation, political activism, and voting choice. We will begin by looking at who votes and why, and then we will examine other forms of political participation, exploring why certain individuals choose to become activists. Finally, we will discuss why people choose to vote for particular candidates. Perhaps not surprisingly, we will see that people's voting decisions are based not only on the issues, but also on party identification, the characteristics of the candidates, and the past performance of the incumbent president. Finally, we will look at the tendencies of various social groups to vote Democratic or Republican. Who votes and why, and how they vote, are crucial questions in a democracy—because those who join the conflict are usually the ultimate winners.

Who Votes?

More people vote than engage in any other kind of political activity. Even so, only about half of all Americans who were eligible to vote voted in the 1996 presidential election, and far fewer people voted in primaries and other elections. The opportunity to vote may characterize a democracy, but not all citizens take advantage of this opportunity.

Voter turnout
The percentage of people who actually vote.

Voter turnout, or the percentage of people who actually vote, depends on many factors. Here, we will examine three of the most crucial: individual voter characteristics, registration laws, and campaign contacts.

The Effect of Individual Voter Characteristics

People who vote, like those who are knowledgeable about politics, tend to have certain socioeconomic, demographic, and psychological characteristics. We will discuss each of these types of characteristics in turn.

Only about half of eligible citizens voted in the 1996 presidential election; the rest found excuses for staying home.

Socioeconomic Characteristics

In the United States, the most important variable explaining whether one votes is a socioeconomic characteristic: *education.* As table 7.1 shows, those with college educations report voting at almost twice the rate of high school dropouts. The reason is that

> The personal qualities that raise the probability of voting are the skills that make learning about politics easier and more gratifying and reduce the difficulties of voting. Education increases one's capacity for understanding complex and intangible subjects such as politics, as well as encouraging the ethic of civic responsibility. Moreover, schools provide experience with a variety of bureaucratic problems, such as coping with requirements, filling out forms, and meeting deadlines.[1]

Family income and *occupational status*—which along with education make up socioeconomic status—also strongly influence voter turnout. As table 7.1 shows, turnout rises sharply from low to middle income levels, and those with white-collar jobs vote at far higher rates than laborers. Although income and occupational status to some extent reflect the effect of education, both contribute independently to turnout. Having more money to spend on political interests and holding a high-status job draws people into social circles in which more people are interested in politics. Moreover, having the skills needed to participate (which are associated with white-collar jobs) makes participation easier.

Demographic Characteristics

Besides being affected by socioeconomic characteristics, voter turnout is also affected by demographic characteristics such as race, ethnicity, age, and gender. *Race* and *ethnicity* seem to make a substantial difference in turnout rates. In 1992, non-Hispanic whites reported voting at the highest rate, 78 percent, while African Americans, Hispanic Americans, and Asian Americans voted at lower rates. However, if we take socioeconomic status into account by comparing non-Hispanic whites, African Americans, Hispanic Americans, and Asian Americans with similar levels of education and income (for example, low-education whites versus low-education African Americans, or high-education whites versus high-education African Americans), race and ethnicity make only small differences in turnout rates.[2] The lower average educations and incomes of these racial and ethnic groups, which we discussed in chapter 3, reduce the likelihood that members of these groups will vote, and, hence, limit their political power at election time.

Turnout also depends on one's *age.* As people grow older, they gain knowledge and other resources that make participation easier. They learn more about the parties and candidates, and they become more attached to them over time. People also gain the social contacts that make participation easier as they age. Community ties such as homeownership, marriage, and children develop, and with those ties greater interest in politics and higher voter turnout develop as well. By the time people are in their eighties, some begin to lose the ability to participate. But poor health and other problems cause only a slight drop in turnout among the elderly. They remain far more likely to vote than those under thirty.[3]

The people most likely to vote are the well educated, the wealthy, those with high-status occupations, whites, the elderly, strong party identifiers, those with a high sense of political efficacy and high interest in campaigns, those who read about campaigns in newspapers, and those who live outside of the South and Border states.

TABLE 7.1 Percentage of Self-Reported Turnout in the 1992 Election

Education	*Turnout*	*Gender*	*Turnout*
0–8 years	56	Men	77
9–11 years	47	Women	76
High school graduate	73		
Some college	85	***Strength of Party Identification***	
College graduate	91	Strong identifiers	88
Higher degree	95	Weak identifiers	76
		Leaning independents	74
Income		Pure independents	61
$0–9,999	55		
10–19,999	68	***Efficacy***	
20–29,999	72	Low	65
30–39,999	82	Medium	79
40–49,999	88	High	85
50–74,999	88		
75,000+	89	***Interest in Campaign***	
		Very much	91
Occupation		Somewhat	75
Professional	90	Not much	44
Managers/technical	88		
Sales/clerical	82	***Read Newspapers About Campaign***	
Service	73	Read	89
Skilled labor	68	Did not read	68
Unskilled labor	61		
		Region	
Race/Ethnicity		New England/Mid-Atlantic	80
White	78	North Central	82
African American	71	South	68
Hispanic American	61	Border	66
Asian/Indian	58	West	82
Age			
18–25	56		
26–35	74		
36–45	80		
46–55	83		
56–65	85		
66+	81		

Note: Turnout is self-reported. People often claim to have voted when, in fact, they have not; therefore, these turnout percentages are inflated.

Source: Data from the 1992 American National Election Survey.

Franchise
The right to vote.

A final demographic characteristic worth mentioning is *gender*—not because men or women vote at very different rates in the 1990s, but because they used to do so in the past. When women first won the **franchise,** or right to vote, in 1920, the voting rate among women was substantially lower than among men.[4] Many women in 1920 had been socialized to believe that politics was men's business and that they should stay out of it. As recently as the 1950s, women were still about 10 percent less likely to vote than men.[5] But beginning in the late 1960s, the women's movement changed the role of women in politics. The movement sought to change both the way society treated women and the way in which women were socialized to think of themselves. The result was that women, especially younger women—who were socialized after the women's movement began—started to vote at the same rate as men. In fact, since 1984, white women have often voted at a slightly higher rate than white men in presidential elections.[6]

Psychological Characteristics

In addition to socioeconomic and demographic characteristics, psychological characteristics such as party identification, sense of political efficacy, group consciousness,

From the suffrage movement to the feminist movement, the voting rate among women increased. It is now often slightly higher than the voting rate among men.

and interest in politics all contribute to voter turnout. *Strength of party identification* significantly influences turnout. People who identify strongly with one of the political parties are more likely to show up at the polls on Election Day than weak identifiers or independents because strong identifiers generally both know and care more about politics. (We will explain party identification in more detail later in this chapter).

A strong *sense of political efficacy*—the feeling that one can have an effect on politics and political decision makers—also motivates people to vote.[7] As we explained in chapter 6, people who believe they cannot affect government have less incentive to learn about politics and are, therefore, less knowledgeable than those who feel they can. Lacking a strong sense of efficacy, by the same token, makes one less likely to vote. Those who feel ineffective view voting and other types of political participation as wasted efforts.

Another psychological characteristic that explains participation is **group consciousness.** Several studies have found that African Americans and women who identify strongly with their race or gender and whose racial and gender identities are very important to them are more likely to participate.[8]

Group consciousness Identification with one's social group (for instance, black consciousness).

Finally, people who are *interested in politics* and who follow politics in newspapers and magazines are also more likely to vote than those who are not interested and who do not follow politics in the print media. This generalization does not hold true for those who follow politics on television, apparently because so many people watch television casually, with little real interest, and because television news does not convey much solid information about politics. Those who read about politics learn a good deal; those who only watch television do not.[9] The difference shows up in voting turnout.

Another attitude that deserves mention is *trust in government,* even though it seems to have little or no influence on turnout. A fairly popular notion is that people don't vote because they don't trust government leaders, they are cynical about politics and politicians, and they feel alienated. Indeed, survey measures of trust in government indicated a decline during the 1960s and 1970s—paralleling the decline in voter turnout. For instance, the following question has been asked regularly in national surveys since the 1950s: "How much of the time do you think you can trust the government in Washington to do what is right—just about always, most of the time, or only some of the time?" In 1964, 76 percent of the respondents said "just about always" or "most of the time." By 1980, only 25 percent gave such trusting responses. Although the public gained confidence in government during the 1980s, raising the confidence level to 35 percent, that gain did not last. By 1994, the level of trust had fallen to 23 percent—well below the levels of the 1950s and 1960s.[10] When political scientists examined the data carefully, however, they discovered that trust in government has little or no impact on turnout.[11] People don't refrain from

Feeling a strong sense of group pride makes people more likely to vote.

voting just because they do not like or trust politicians. If they believe their votes can affect politicians and policies, they vote despite their low opinions of officeholders and candidates.

All these characteristics paint a picture of the American most likely to vote: well educated with a high-status job and a high income; white and over thirty years old; a strong party identifier with a strong sense of political efficacy, a sense of group consciousness, and a high interest in politics. People with these traits are the most likely to vote, but—as we saw in chapter 3—they are hardly typical American citizens. Our system of rules gives every citizen the right to vote, but many people decline to exercise that right. When they decline, they allow those who do vote to determine who will be elected to public office.

The Effect of Registration Laws

The characteristics of individual voters are not the only influences on decisions about whether or not to vote. Registration and voting laws also affect turnout by changing the costs of voting from state to state. The more difficult and time consuming it is to vote, the less likely people are to do so. Moreover, by manipulating voting laws, legislators can influence how many people—and, more important, which people—vote. Ultimately, these rules can greatly affect which policies the government adopts and who wins political conflicts.

Registration laws dramatically demonstrate the important effects rules have on outcomes. These effects can be seen most clearly when one compares turnout in the United States with turnout in other industrial democracies. As figure 7.1 shows, of twenty-four industrial democracies, only Switzerland has a lower turnout rate than the United States; most of the other countries have turnout rates more than 30 percentage points higher. Two rules account for these differences. First, almost all other industrial democracies have automatic voter registration. That is, the government automatically registers voters; individual citizens are not responsible for initiating the registration process. In fact, "the United States is the only country where the entire burden of registration falls on the individual rather than the government."[12] A second rule that affects voter turnout is that many industrial democracies have some system of compulsory voting; they penalize their citizens for failure to vote (although in some cases, the penalties are never enforced). Together, these two rules raise turnout in most of these countries to levels far higher than in the United States.

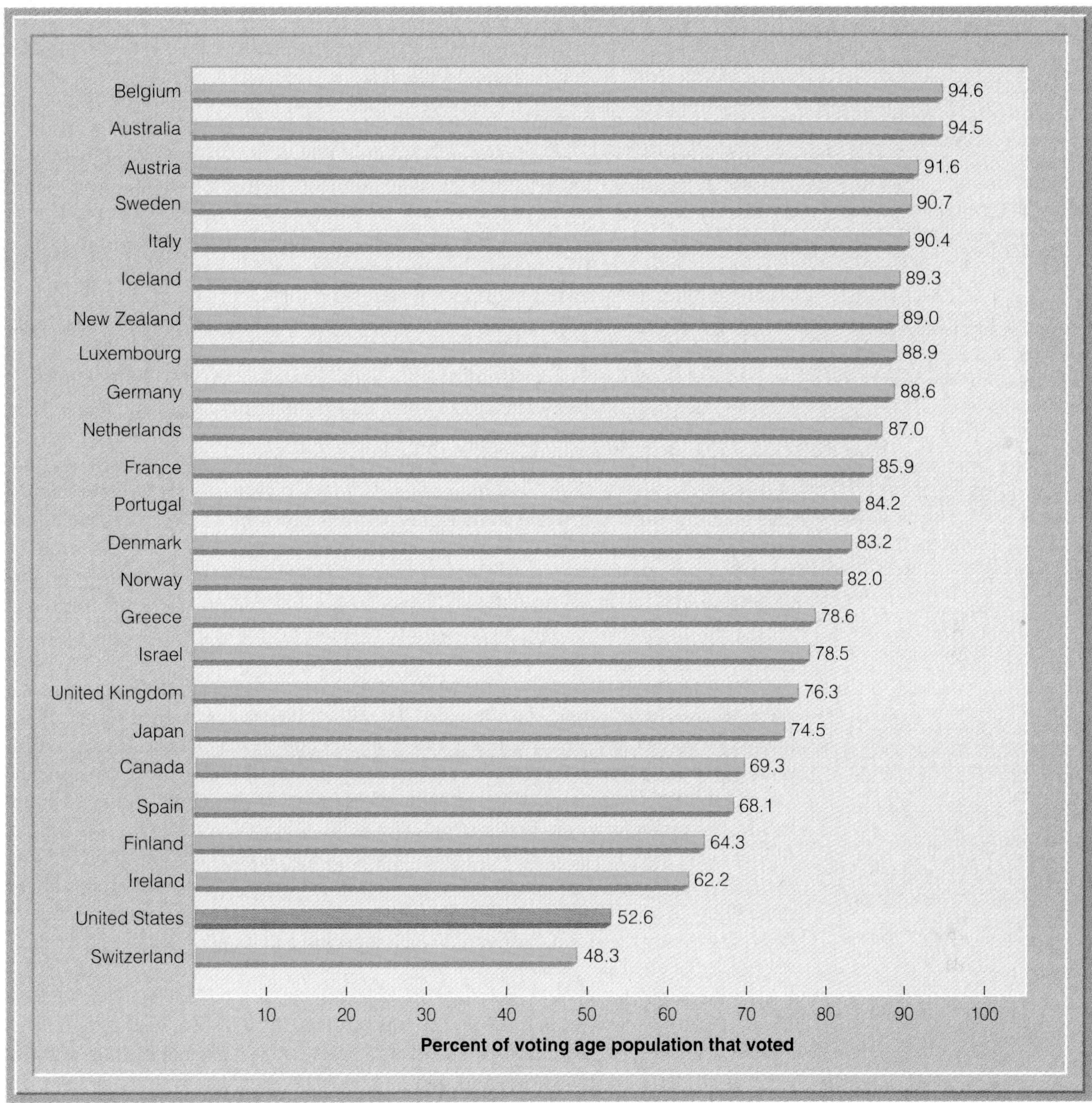

FIGURE 7.1
Ranking of Countries by Turnout

The United States has one of the lowest turnout rates of any industrial democracy.

Source: Data from David Glass, Peverill Squire, and Raymond Wolfinger, "Voter Turnout, An International Comparison," *Public Opinion,* December/January 1984, p. 50.

Automatic registration and compulsory voting also affect *who* votes. For example, the pattern of higher turnout among those of high socioeconomic status does not appear in countries with automatic registration and compulsory voting.[13] People with low incomes and poor educations vote at rates very similar to those with high incomes and good educations. The class bias in turnout vanishes. In short, the rules exert a powerful influence on who votes.

Looking now at turnout within the United States, we can see that registering to vote seems to be the major obstacle for most Americans. In states with lenient registration laws, voting participation is high; in states with tougher laws, participation is lower. The most important aspect of the law is the **closing date,** or the last day before the election when one can register to vote in the upcoming election.[14] States with Election Day registration have substantially higher turnout than those that close off registration thirty days before the election. Other laws that contribute to higher turnout rates

Closing date
The last day before the election when one can register to vote—usually described in number of days before Election Day.

in some states include those requiring voter registration offices to be open at least forty hours each week, and on weekends or evenings, and those allowing absentee registration (for example, registration by postcard).

In general, southern states have the toughest voter registration laws in the nation. Their restrictive voting policies are a legacy of the post-Civil War drive to disenfranchise African Americans and to reduce the political clout of poor whites.[15] Before the Twenty-fourth Amendment to the Constitution abolished **poll taxes** (which required citizens to pay a tax if they chose to vote) in 1964 and the Voting Rights Act of 1965 eliminated **literacy tests** and other barriers thrown up to prevent voting (see box 7.1), turnout in some southern states lagged below 10 percent. Although turnout increased enormously following the successes of the civil rights movement of the mid-1960s, turnout in the South remains below the national average, as table 7.1 shows.

Poll tax
Before 1964, the tax that people paid in some states if they chose to vote.

Literacy test
A test of ability to read and write, used in the South to prevent people from voting.

With the passage of the National Voter Registration Act in 1993, Congress took another large step toward easing voter registration laws. Known commonly as the Motor Voter Act, the law requires all states to offer people the opportunity to register by mail or when they go to motor vehicle bureaus, welfare agencies, disability offices, or military recruitment centers.[16] As with most reforms of voting and election rules, partisan controversy surrounded almost every aspect of the motor voter bill. Republicans in the Senate resisted the provisions of the bill requiring states to provide voter registration forms at agencies that assist people with disabilities or that deal with welfare clients; Democrats fought back, hoping to increase the turnout of groups they expected would vote for them. In the end, the Democrats won.[17]

What has been the effect of the Motor Voter Act? It has clearly led to a dramatic surge in voter registration. An estimated 11 million new voters signed up under the law in 1995. Georgia alone added more than 500,000 new voters, a 19 percentage point increase. Moreover, contrary to expectations, the Republican Party—not the Democratic Party—appears to be the bigger beneficiary of easing registration requirements. For example, in the first sixteen months the Motor Voter Act was in effect in Florida, new Republican registrants outnumbered new Democratic registrants four to three. The major reason Republicans have come out ahead is that poor people, who are more likely to vote Democratic than Republican, have not taken advantage of the new law. New voters registering at motor vehicle bureaus outnumber people registering at welfare offices by four to one.[18]

At the polls, the Motor Voter Act has apparently made a much smaller difference. Despite early predictions that the law would substantially increase voting, turnout in 1996 was about five percentage points lower than in 1992. Although making registration easier may have caused some people to vote who otherwise would not have, the drop in voter interest in the campaign between 1992 and 1996 washed away any potential turnout gains.[19] Nonetheless, both parties regard the struggle over the law as worthwhile because they believe that such laws make a difference in who votes and who prevails in our political conflicts—if not this time, then perhaps next time.

The Effect of Campaign Contacts

A staple of American campaigns since the early days of the Republic has been the drive to persuade citizens to vote (see box 7.2). For some people, simply being asked to vote—even if the person asking is a stranger—is enough to bring them out to the polls on Election Day. The result is that every election brings with it voter registration and get-out-the-vote drives.

Efforts to mobilize voters come from many directions. Most large campaigns use registration and get-out-the-vote drives as one part of their overall strategy, taking advantage of the fact that it is usually easier and more efficient to gain votes by increasing the turnout among a candidate's supporters than by converting a candidate's

Point of Order

BOX 7.1

The Voting Rights Act of 1965

Today, virtually all Americans take the right to register and vote for granted. Yet as recently as the early 1960s, that right was not extended to huge numbers of Americans in the South. The rules governing registration and voting can have a huge impact on voter turnout. Seldom has that been more clearly demonstrated than in the case of the Voting Rights Act of 1965.

Because of restrictive voter registration laws in southern states, a legacy of the Civil War, registration and voter turnout in the South have always been lower than in other parts of the country. All southern states discriminated against African Americans, and some sought to lessen the electoral impact of poor whites as well. In 1960—after civil rights workers spent almost a decade in massive efforts to register African Americans—the average percentage of southern whites registered to vote was 61.1 percent, while the average percentage of African Americans was only 29.1 percent. The state with the widest racial gap was Mississippi, where 63.9 percent of all voting age whites were registered, but only 5.2 percent of African Americans were registered.

The Voting Rights Act of 1965 radically changed the rules by directly involving the federal government in local voter registration and by establishing an extensive set of regulations. The act swept away a wide range of requirements and tests that some states used to prevent African Americans from voting—including tests of literacy, educational attainment, knowledge, and good moral character. In one of the most important sections of the act, Congress allowed the federal courts to appoint federal observers and examiners empowered to register voters. In effect, the federal government took on the oversight of registration and voting in southern elections and in other scattered areas across the nation that had shown patterns of racial or ethnic discrimination.

Perhaps the section of the Voting Rights Act that best reflects the problem Congress faced is the "preclearance" section. Congress feared that if one method of discrimination were made illegal, southern states would immediately replace it with another. To prevent this, Congress required states and counties with records of blatant discrimination to submit proposed changes in registration and voting laws to the U.S. Attorney General or to the Federal District Court for the District of Columbia, which must give permission or "clearance" *before* the changes could take effect. To gain clearance, the jurisdiction proposing the change would have to prove that there was no discriminatory intent behind the change and that there would be no discriminatory impact.

As recently as the early 1960s, voter registration laws restricted the rights of some Americans to vote. The Voting Rights Act of 1965 swept away many of these discriminatory rules.

The Voting Rights Act had an immediate effect. By 1968, registration and turnout in the South jumped sharply, and it continued to rise in the following years (at a time when turnout outside of the South was falling). By the 1990s, the racial gap in registration still existed, but the gap was far smaller than it had been before passage of the Voting Rights Act. In 1994, for instance, 64 percent of whites and 58 percent of African Americans were registered.

The struggle minorities must face for voting rights is by no means over. Although most barriers to registration and voting have been torn down, some remain. More important, more subtle methods exist to limit the political influence of minorities in elections. Thus, every election year, the battle over minority political power continues in courtrooms across the nation. These disputes flare up because, as the effects of the Voting Rights Act of 1965 show, the rules do matter.

Sources: "Assessing the Effects of the U.S. Voting Rights Act," *Publius* 16 (Fall 1986); Paul Allen Beck and Frank J. Sorauf, *Party Politics in America*, 7th ed. (New York: HarperCollins, 1992), p. 211; Chandler Davidson, ed., *Minority Vote Dilution* (Washington, D.C.: Howard University Press, 1984); Steven F. Lawson, *In Pursuit of Power: Southern Blacks and Electoral Politics, 1965–1982* (New York: Columbia University Press, 1982); Harold W. Stanley and Richard G. Niemi, *Vital Statistics on American Politics*, 5th ed. (Washington, D.C.: CQ Press, 1995), p.79; *Statistical Abstract of the United States, 1980*, 101st ed. (Washington, D.C.: U.S. Bureau of the Census, 1980), p. 514; and *Statistical Abstract of the United States, 1990*, 110th ed. (Washington, D.C.: U.S. Bureau of the Census, 1990), p. 264.

THE PEOPLE BEHIND THE RULES

BOX 7.2

The Politics of Voter Turnout: William Marcy "Boss" Tweed and Willie Velasquez

The means by which parties, campaign organizations, and other groups register voters and get them out to the polls have changed enormously since the last century. In the mid-1800s, few laws regulated the behavior of parties and campaigns, and those that did often went unenforced. Most parts of the country did not even require voters to register until the late 1800s. Now all states but North Dakota require voter registration, and carefully regulate registration and turnout efforts.

William Marcy "Boss" Tweed—a nineteenth-century party boss in New York City—organized massive voting fraud drives to maintain his political power.

William Marcy "Boss" Tweed

New York City's Tammany Hall, led by William Marcy "Boss" Tweed after the Civil War, was notorious among big city party machines. New York had a voter registration law, but Tweed had little trouble getting around it. A U.S. House of Representatives report on the 1868 election described Tweed's practice of organized "repeating," or sending people to vote more than once:

> On the 30th and 31st of October, when only two days intervened until the day of the election, gangs or bodies of men hired for the purpose, assembled at these [Tammany Hall] headquarters where they were furnished with names and numbers [of voters], and under a leader or captain, they went out in ones and twos and threes and tens and dozens, in nearly every part of the city, registering many times each, and when the day of election came these repeaters, supplied abundantly with intoxicating drinks, and changing coats, hats, or caps, as occasion required to avoid recognition or detection, commenced the work of "voting early and often," and this was carried on by these vagabonds until, wearied and drunken, night closed on the stupendous fraud which their depravity had perpetrated.

The practice of repeating helped Boss Tweed and his cronies to dominate politics in New York City during the 1860s and 1870s.

Willie Velasquez—a Latino political leader in the 1970s and 1980s—organized more than 1,000 registration and get-out-the-vote drives to empower Latinos like these. The woman's shirt says, "Your vote is your voice."

Willie Velasquez

By 1992, the Tammany Halls and repeat voters of America had all but disappeared. Today's voter registration and turnout organizations are often more like the Southwest Voter Registration Education Project (SVREP). Founded by Willie Velasquez in 1974, the SVREP registered people by sending thousands of volunteers door to door armed with clipboards and voter registration forms. First in Texas and then all across the Southwest, Velasquez organized Hispanic Americans and persuaded them that the path to political power was through registration and voting. SVREP's slogan said it all: "Su voto es su voz"—Your vote is your voice.

Over the years, Velasquez led more than a thousand registration drives and filed dozens of lawsuits under the Voting Rights Act to defend the interests of Hispanic Americans. Unlike Tweed, whose goal was personal wealth and political power, Velasquez sought to increase the power of the people. He believed that voting power could accomplish that:

> If your streets and drainage are bad, register and vote. If you don't like the way the schools are educating your kids, register and vote. If City Hall doesn't pay attention to you, register and vote.

Willie Velasquez died in 1988 at the age of forty-four. In the words of Michael Dukakis, then Governor of Massachusetts and the 1988 Democratic presidential candidate, Willie Velasquez "changed the world."

Sources: Richard Avena, "One Last Vote for Willie Velasquez," *Los Angeles Times,* 18 June 1988; David Lauter, "Dukakis Eulogizes Latino Political Leader," *Los Angeles Times,* 19 June 1988; U.S. House of Representatives, Report No. 41, 1868, p. 40, quoted in M. R. Werner, *Tammany Hall* (New York: Greenwood Press, 1928) (reprinted 1968), p. 138.

INSTRUCTIONS TO PRECINCT WORKERS

Precinct work is the single most important aspect of a political campaign. Its purpose is to inform the voters about the candidates and the issues in the upcoming election and to record favorable voters so that they can be reminded to vote on Election Day–April 15.

Go to all voters on your precinct list except Republicans or American Independents. Introduce yourself and ask for the voter by name. Indicate that you are campaigning for the BCA candidates. Talk to the voter. If the voter is favorable, mark a (+) next to his/her name; if the voter is unfavorable, mark a (-) next to her/his name; if the voter is undecided, mark a (0). Check to see if all the other voters in the household feel the same way.

If the voters support our candidates, ask them if they will help with the campaign, put up a poster, etc. If voters will help or if they want more literature please write down their names and addresses with the appropriate comments on the "Comment Sheet."

If the voter is not home mark a (NH) next to her/his name and leave some literature on the door knob or under the door. DO NOT LEAVE LITERATURE IN THE MAILBOX–IT IS ILLEGAL! At a later date go back to the voters who were not home or were undecided.

If the voter has moved mark an (M) next to his/her name. Try to get the voter's new address and telephone number (by asking the present occupants, etc.) so we can tell the voter where her/his polling place is on election day. Write the voter's new address and telephone, if known, on the precinct list. Return the "comment" sheets to the office on a weekly basis, so we can take care of them.

If you have any questions, need help finishing your precinct or need more literature, bumper strips, buttons, etc., contact the campaign office.

FIGURE 7.2
Instructions to Precinct Workers

A typical set of instructions for precinct canvassers seeking to get out the vote on Election Day.

opponents.[20] Campaigns, therefore, often put huge amounts of money into their registration and get-out-the-vote drives, targeting people they think are likely to support their candidate. Figure 7.2 reproduces a typical set of instructions that a political party—in this case the Democratic Party—gives to workers who are charged with trying to get out the vote.

Nonpartisan interest groups also work to increase turnout for their own purposes. Unions, civil rights groups, churches, and others seek to increase voting among their members to increase their influence with politicians or to try to get the politicians they favor elected.

Efforts to mobilize voters come in many forms. Some efforts rely on expensive mass mail campaigns and telephone banks. Other efforts rely on volunteer labor provided by people such as college students, who walk door to door in their communities encouraging their party's or group's supporters to vote. Although these activities may seem small in scale, they actually make a substantial difference in voter turnout and sometimes determine who wins the elections.

One electoral innovation that may relieve political parties and interest groups of much of the burden of turning out voters on Election Day is to allow people to mail in their ballots. Over the years, some local governments have experimented with mail-in voting. In 1996, Oregon filled a vacant U.S. Senate seat by holding the nation's first mail-in congressional election. Ballots were mailed to all the state's voters, and they had three weeks to mail the ballots back or drop them off at specified locations. When the ballots were finally counted, voter turnout exceeded 65 percent of registered voters, a record for a special election in Oregon. Moreover, the mail-in vote cost the state

In 1996, Oregon became the first state to conduct a congressional election entirely through the mail.

of Oregon about $1 million less than a traditional election in which voters go to the polls.[21] The success of Oregon's mail-in Senate election has led to calls for greater use of mail-in voting, but critics oppose any move away from the tradition of filling out a ballot in secret in a polling booth. They argue that mail-in voting will lead to a rise in voting fraud as people forge ballots and try to coerce their family and friends into voting for particular candidates.[22]

Overall, social scientists know a great deal about voter turnout in any given year. The 1996 turnout patterns look very similar to those seen in previous elections. Although people from all parts of society vote, those who have better educations, better jobs, and higher incomes, who are white and middle-aged or older, who strongly identify with a political party and feel a strong sense of political efficacy, who identify with a group, and who are interested in and read about politics in newspapers are more likely to vote than those who do not have these characteristics. People who live in states with lenient registration requirements are more likely to vote than those who live in states with tough requirements. Finally, people contacted through political campaigns or voter registration and get-out-the-vote drives are more likely to vote than those not contacted.

All of these patterns of voter characteristics, registration laws, and campaign contacts hold true in every year for which data are available. Yet these findings do not explain changes in turnout over time. Explaining why turnout has decreased over the years is difficult.

The Puzzling Decline of Voter Turnout

In a democracy, it would be ideal if every eligible citizen voted. But since 1896, turnout has been declining. The drop in voting participation has not been steady, but over the course of the century, turnout has declined from nearly 85 percent to around 55 percent (see figure 7.3).

The decline in voter turnout used to puzzle political scientists because they expected the rising level of education since the turn of the century and the easing of voter registration laws since the 1960s to lead to an increase in voter participation, contrary to what actually happened.[23] Several explanations for the decline have been proposed, some of which are controversial.

Analyses of the decline focus on two periods—the years immediately after 1896 and the post-1960 decline. Two competing explanations for the drop in voting participation after 1896 have been proposed. One side claims that economic tensions between

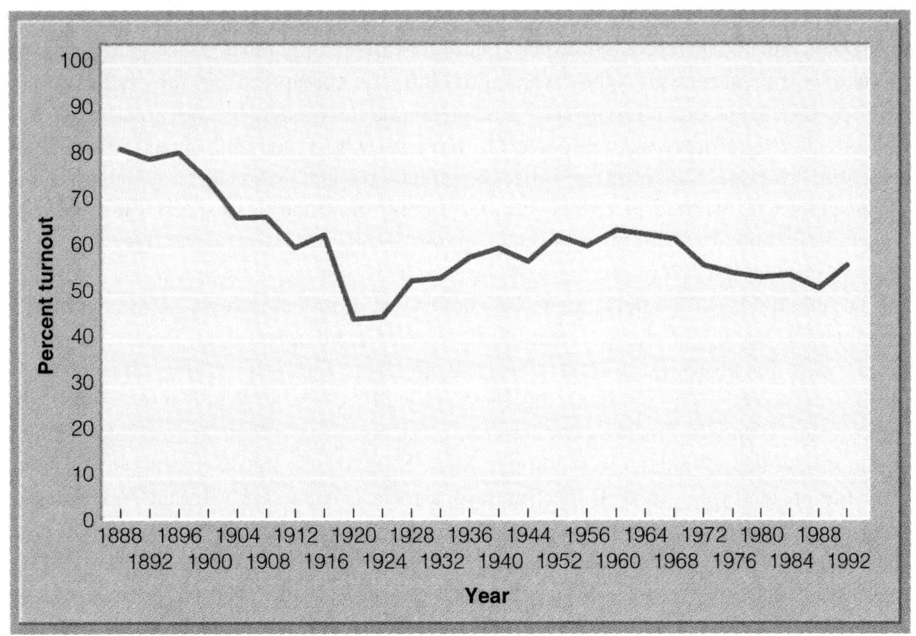

FIGURE 7.3
Voter Turnout, 1888 to 1992

Turnout declined sharply from 1896 to 1920, increased until 1960, and then began another uneven decline. In 1992, 55 percent of the eligible electorate voted. In 1996, however, turnout dropped again, to about 50 percent.

Source: Data for 1888–1988 from Paul R. Abramson, John H. Aldrich, and David W. Rohde, *Change and Continuity in the 1988 Elections,* rev. ed. (Washington, D.C.: CQ Press, 1991), pp. 89, 91. Data for 1992 from Paul R. Abramsom, John H. Aldrich, and David W. Rohde, *Change and Continuity in the 1992 Elections.* (Washington, D.C.: CQ Press, 1994), pp. 102–103.

industrialists and workers rose during the late 1800s and came to a head during the depression of 1893 to 1896. Even though the Democrats turned their backs on their own party's president, Grover Cleveland, and gave the nomination to the populist William Jennings Bryan, the Democrats were crushed at the polls. Republican William McKinley won the presidency by putting together a business-worker coalition that survived and prospered for the next thirty years. The success of this coalition forced the Democratic Party to favor business interests as well in their pursuit of office, and resulted in both parties putting forth "corporate-conservative" platforms that offered little to the working class. Lacking any real choices between the parties, so the argument goes, many people dropped out of politics and stopped voting.[24]

The other argument about the decline of voter turnout after 1896 claims that turnout declined not because the parties shifted toward business interests but because of changes in voting laws.[25] Scholars who accept this argument point to three key changes: the introduction of the **Australian ballot** (ca. 1889–1896), the passage of laws requiring people to register to vote (ca. 1890–1920), and the passage of the Nineteenth Amendment to the Constitution (1920). With the introduction of the Australian ballot, state governments took over the task of printing ballots from political parties. This allowed people to cast secret votes for the first time. The passage of registration laws meant that voters could no longer simply show up at the polls on Election Day. Instead, to be eligible to vote, they first had to register with the local government—usually well in advance. The Nineteenth Amendment gave women the right to vote.

Australian ballot
A government-printed ballot (as opposed to one distributed by political parties) that allows people to vote in secret.

Many scholars believe that these three changes in voting laws led to lower turnout rates. The Australian ballot lowered voter turnout because corrupt party bosses could no longer force people to go to the polls and vote for them. The bosses could still force people to go to the polls, but because of the secret ballots, the bosses could no longer ensure that voters would vote for them. The result was that, instead of using threats to win elections, the party bosses had to use persuasion. Forcing unwilling voters to turn out on Election Day was no longer effective (see chapter 9). Voter registration laws reduced turnout because they made it difficult for people to vote more than once on Election Day. And the Nineteenth Amendment lowered overall turnout because it extended the franchise to women, who as a group did not vote as often as men did. As we mentioned earlier, before the 1920s, most women had been socialized to believe that politics was men's business; consequently, even when they had the right to vote, many women chose not to do so. This meant that while the number of eligible voters roughly doubled, the percentage of eligible people who actually voted decreased.

Like most rule changes, the reforms of the registration and voting laws between the 1880s and 1920 were anything but neutral. Some people pushed for the reforms for good government reasons—they wanted to eliminate corruption and they believed that women should be treated equally.[26] But other people wanted the reforms because of the effects the reforms were expected to have on who voted and on who would win elections. Among the reforms' most prominent backers were upper class, Yankee Protestants who wanted to reduce turnout among the poor—especially those of Irish and Italian ethnicity, who were building majorities in many Northeastern cities. In addition to reducing corruption, the new voter registration requirements made it difficult for large numbers of the poor, many of whom were illiterate, to register, thus giving an advantage to the upper classes.[27] Similarly, women from upper class, Protestant households were far more likely than women from poor, European ethnic households to think that politics was women's business as well as men's. When women won the right to vote, upper class women voted at a far higher rate than lower class women, again giving the advantage to the upper class.[28] Finally, as we discussed earlier, voter registration was welcomed in the South as a means to prevent African Americans—and in some states, poor whites—from voting.[29] In short, registration and voting rules were regarded as powerful weapons in political conflicts across the nation.

The debate about the reduction in turnout after 1960 differs from the debate about the earlier drop because survey researchers left a record covering the later period.[30] Analyses of survey data have identified several population trends that account for part of the drop in turnout after 1960—decreases in the average age of the population, in the electorate's strength of party identification, in the electorate's sense of political efficacy, and in the number of people who regularly read newspapers. In other words, after 1960, a larger and larger portion of the electorate consisted of people less likely to vote.[31]

In addition to changes in the population, a change in the rules caused turnout to drop. The Twenty-sixth Amendment to the Constitution, ratified in 1971, gave the right to vote to eighteen-, nineteen-, and twenty-year-olds. This rule change, like the one in 1920, added a very low turnout group to the electorate and therefore lowered the overall turnout rate, beginning with the 1972 presidential election.

Still, these changes, even taken together, do not fully explain the decline in voting participation. The last piece of the puzzle, which scholars only recently identified, is the decline in parties' and campaigns' efforts to contact people and persuade them to vote. Because parties have turned away from grassroots organization and toward television and direct mail campaigning, voter turnout has fallen.[32]

Does Turnout Matter?

Does higher or lower turnout in an election affect who wins? Many politicians and journalists believe that elections with high turnout favor Democratic candidates, whereas elections with low turnout favor Republicans. The reasoning is that people of high socioeconomic status, who tend to vote Republican, generally turn out to vote, but people of low socioeconomic status turn out only for some elections. It would follow that as turnout increases, the additional voters would more likely be Democrats. When the question was finally studied, however, that argument turned out to be flawed.

A classic study of voter turnout conducted in the 1970s found that if all states relaxed their voter registration laws to match those in the most lenient states in 1972 (the year of the data used in the study), turnout would increase about 9 percent.[33] Although the turnout among low-socioeconomic voters would go up more than the turnout for those with high status, all socioeconomic groups would show overall increases in turnout. In addition, people with low incomes, low educations, and low-status jobs are not, as some assume (and as we shall see later in this chapter), all Democratic voters. Many would vote for Republicans, just as many high-socioeconomic voters would vote for Democrats. When all the numbers were added up, the study estimated that the result of the hypothetical 9 percent increase in turnout would actually yield a Republican advantage of less than one-half of 1 percent—a difference so small the authors could not be sure it was real. Most other studies that followed came to the same conclusion. A modest increase in turnout of 10 or 15 percent would be unlikely to make any difference in who wins.[34] Some scholars, however, have found evidence suggesting that the Democrats would benefit from higher turnout.[35]

Although most studies suggest that a 10 to 15 percent increase in voter turnout probably would not affect many election outcomes, scholars are unsure about what would happen if the United States ever experienced a huge increase in voter turnout. What if turnout were 80 or 90 percent—as it is in many European nations—instead of 50 or 55 percent, as it is in presidential elections in the United States?[36] We know that the Voting Rights Act of 1965, which raised turnout enormously in the South, had a substantial impact on who won office and what policies they favored.[37] So we cannot be sure that other dramatic changes would not ensue if a surge in turnout occurred in the United States.

Although general swings in the turnout rate do not seem to give either party an advantage, both major parties spend a great deal of time and money registering voters and getting them to the polls on Election Day. These efforts work not because higher or lower turnout will benefit one of the parties, but because the parties target particular groups they know will vote for them in overwhelming numbers. Republicans register voters only in Republican-leaning communities, while Democrats focus their efforts only in areas where they expect people to vote for their candidates. When the parties run their get-out-the-vote drives, they call only on voters already registered with their parties. Thus, each party targets its own supporters.

We have now learned that individual voter characteristics, registration laws and rules, and campaign contacts all have a pronounced effect on who chooses to vote. But voting is not the only way to participate; people can participate actively in the American political system in many other ways.

Political Activists

Even though voting is the most common way to try to influence who wins elections or what policies the government will adopt, it is not the only way to exert influence. Other forms of political activism are more influential than voting because political activists can often swing many votes beyond their own. Still, despite the potential to have a tremendous impact on who gets elected and what they do once in office, few people participate beyond voting.

Who Becomes an Activist?

Most Americans do not qualify as political activists, people whose involvement in politics goes beyond the mere act of voting. As figure 7.4 shows, only very small numbers of people report having worked in campaigns, joined political clubs, attended rallies, or donated money. This is true even though casually attending a political rally or even making a minor gesture such as placing a bumper sticker on one's car makes one an activist by these standards. Clearly, the number of hard-core political activists in the United States is very small.

In general, the causes of activism are similar to the causes of voting—they center around socioeconomic, demographic, and psychological characteristics. The most important differences between activists and nonactivists stem from socioeconomic status. People with higher incomes, better jobs, and more schooling are more likely to become activists than those who fall lower on these measures of socioeconomic status. In other words, activists overrepresent the upper class and underrepresent the lower class.

FIGURE 7.4
Participation in Politics

Voting is the most common form of participation. Many people also talk about politics, trying to persuade others how to vote. Very few participate in any other specific way.

Source: Data from the 1992 American National Election Study.

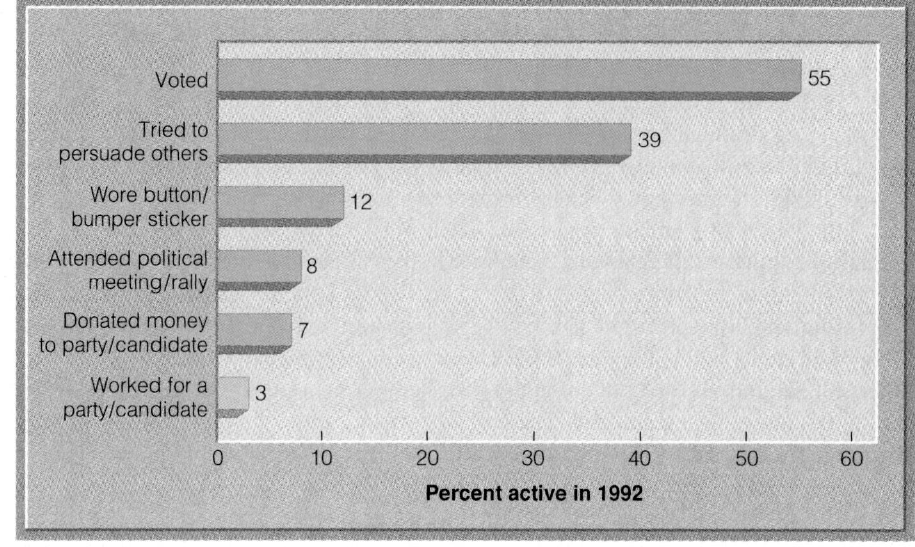

Other factors besides socioeconomic status affect activism. Whites are more likely to participate than non-whites; the middle-aged and elderly are more likely to participate than the young; and those who feel stronger party identification, who feel more efficacious and more interested in politics, and who read more about politics in newspapers are more likely to become active. Finally, those people who are contacted by other activists and asked to join active political efforts often do—again, simply because they were asked.[38]

Types of Activists

Beyond the general causes of activism, some evidence suggests that different people specialize in different types of activity. A classic study of political participation published in 1972 found that 11 percent of Americans were "complete activists," who participated in every way possible; a large number, 22 percent, were complete "inactives," who did not participate at all, even by voting.[39] The study classified everyone between these two extremes as falling into one of five groups: 21 percent were "voting specialists," who did nothing but vote; 15 percent were "campaigners," who focused their attention on campaigns; 20 percent were "communalists," who avoided the conflict of campaigns and focused instead on community problem solving through civic or charitable groups; 4 percent were "parochial participants," who became involved only by contacting public officials about problems—often personal ones; and 7 percent were unclassifiable. The general picture of participation the 1972 study presents is broader and more varied than one might suspect by focusing narrowly on participation in elections.

The 1972 study was later criticized for ignoring another form of participation—political protest.[40] In the late 1960s, when the authors of the study were gathering their data, political protests were widespread, but often regarded as unconventional. Within a decade, however, protests of various sorts—such as marches, pickets, and strikes—became more common and more widely accepted. By the 1990s, for instance, marches and sit-ins had become regular tactics that both pro-choice and pro-life forces used in the debate over abortion. The best estimate of the extent of protest behavior comes from a major nationwide study of civic participation conducted in 1990, which found that 6 percent of the public had participated in some kind of protest, demonstration, or march within the previous two years.[41]

More recently, some scholars have questioned the claim that people take part in different modes of participation. For instance, one study examined political activism from

Protests—once considered unconventional—are now a standard form of political participation.

1952 to 1988 and found no evidence that people specialized in different types of activities. This study found only three broad differences among people—some were nonvoters, some were only voters, and some were active in various ways beyond voting.[42]

Although relatively few people participate in politics in any way other than voting, activists are very influential. They staff the campaigns, register the voters, and perform all the other tasks that produce our elected officials. Moreover, because they participate in the demonstrations and write the letters that public officials read when they try to decipher public opinion, they affect many decisions. In short, activists may be few in number, but they are not small in influence in our political system.

How Voters Make Choices

Who turns out to vote obviously helps determine who wins. But once people are in the voting booths, how do they make up their minds? What influences their choices? Newspaper and television election coverage offers many answers—the candidates' television ads, their campaign strategies, their personalities, their spouses' personalities, their behavior during the Vietnam War, their stands on the issues, their experiences, their physical appearances, and a dozen other factors.

To some extent, all of these answers are right. But to arrive at a useful explanation or theory of voting behavior, we must reduce this long list to a few major causes. The list most political scientists use consists of party identification, candidate characteristics, and issues. The most important of these three factors, and one the news media do not often discuss, is party identification.

Party Identification

People identify with political parties in the same way they identify with religions or ethnicities. **Party identification** is more than an emotional or psychological attachment; it is a way in which people think of themselves and an influence on how they behave.

Party identification
The psychological feeling of belonging to a particular political party, which influences voting behavior.

As we discussed in chapter 6, children begin to learn about politics from their parents early in life. Children begin identifying with political parties when they are as young as eight to ten years old.[43] In fact, children often identify with political parties before they understand what parties or elections are. Their parents socialize them to accept the political labels. At least in the early years, party preference is not a reasoned choice. Although many children break away from their parents in later years, the early learning has a powerful influence.

TABLE 7.2 Percentage of Voters Who Identify with a Party, 1952–1994

The distribution of party identification has remained fairly stable over time, with Democratic identifiers outnumbering Republican identifiers.

	Strong Democrats	Weak Democrats	Independent Democrats	Pure Independents	Independent Republicans	Weak Republicans	Strong Republicans	Apolitical
1952	22%	25%	10%	6%	7%	14%	14%	3%
1956	21	23	6	9	8	14	15	4
1960	20	25	6	10	7	14	16	3
1964	27	25	9	8	6	14	11	1
1968	20	25	10	11	9	15	10	1
1972	15	26	11	13	11	13	10	1
1976	15	25	12	15	10	14	9	1
1980	18	23	11	13	10	14	9	2
1984	17	20	11	11	12	15	12	2
1988	18	18	12	11	13	14	14	2
1992	18	17	14	12	12	15	11	1
1994	15	18	13	10	12	15	16	1

From Bruce E. Keith, et al., *The Myth of the Independent Voter*, page 14. Copyright © 1992 The Regents of the University of California, Berkeley, CA. Data for 1992 and 1994 were compiled by the authors; data are from the 1952–1994 SRC/CPS American National Election Studies.

To understand the role party identification plays in our lives, we must start by examining the way it is measured. Political scientists measure party identification with the following questions:

> "Generally speaking, do you usually think of yourself as a Republican, a Democrat, an Independent, or what?"

If the respondent answers "Democrat" or "Republican," the next question is:

> "Would you call yourself a strong Democrat [Republican] or a not-so-strong Democrat [Republican]?"

If the respondent answers "Independent," he or she is asked:

> "Do you think of yourself as closer to the Republican Party or the Democratic Party?"

From these questions, we can construct a scale ranging from "Strong Republican" to "Strong Democrat" and a residual category of people who identify with minor parties or who have no interest in politics or parties whatsoever.

As table 7.2 shows, in 1994, 46 percent of all Americans identified themselves as some kind of Democrat, while 43 percent identified themselves as Republicans. Although the Democrats have an advantage, we shall see in the following discussion that this advantage does not always guarantee victory at the polls.

The most obvious effect of party identification is on voting choice. People who think of themselves as Democrats generally vote for Democratic candidates, while those who think of themselves as Republicans generally choose Republican candidates. Table 7.3 shows the impressive loyalty rates of strong identifiers—in 1992, 93 percent of the strong Democrats voted for Bill Clinton, while 2 percent of the strong Republicans voted for him. Typically, Republicans are slightly more loyal to their candidates than Democrats are to theirs. The higher loyalty rate of Republican identifiers over the years is a major advantage for Republican candidates because it helps to offset the greater number of Democratic identifiers.

Table 7.3 reveals another curious fact: people who say they are independent, but who lean toward one of the major parties, behave just like partisan voters. In fact, in eight of our eleven presidential elections from 1952 to 1992, independent Democrats were more likely to vote for the Democratic candidate than those who said they were weak Democrats. Independent Republicans were more loyal than weak Republicans about half the time. So although people may call themselves independents, if they say

TABLE 7.3 Party Identification and Vote for Democratic Presidential Candidates, 1952–1992

People who identify with parties usually vote for their party's presidential candidate, but Republicans are generally more loyal to their nominee than Democrats are.

	Percentage Who Voted for the Democratic Presidential Candidate											Voted for
	1952	**1956**	**1960**	**1964**	**1968**	**1972**	**1976**	**1980**	**1984**	**1988**	**1992**	**Perot 1992**
Strong Democrats	82%	85%	90%	94%	80%	66%	88%	83%	87%	93%	93%	4%
Weak Democrats	61	62	71	81	54	44	72	53	63	67	69	18
Independent Democrats	59	65	86	89	50	58	70	41	76	88	71	23
Pure Independents	17	15	49	75	22	25	41	21	22	32	41	37
Independent Republicans	7	7	13	25	4	12	14	11	5	14	11	27
Weak Republicans	5	7	11	40	9	9	21	5	6	16	15	25
Strong Republicans	2	1	2	9	3	2	3	4	2	2	2	11

From Bruce E. Keith, et al., *The Myth of the Independent Voter*, page 68. Copyright © 1992 The Regents of the University of California, Berkeley, CA. Data for 1992 were compiled by the authors; data are from the 1952–1992 SRC/CPS American National Election Studies.

they lean toward one of the parties, they are, for practical purposes, partisan voters. As one voter admitted in 1996, "I have never aligned with a party, but I have generally voted Republican all my life."[44]

As one might suspect, table 7.3 also shows that people who consider themselves pure independents are often the strongest supporters of independent or third party presidential candidates. In 1992, Ross Perot drew more support from people who thought of themselves as pure independents than from any other group. He received his weakest support from strong Democrats and strong Republicans—people already satisfied with their parties.

A less obvious, but no less important, aspect of party identification is its role as a *perceptual screen* that helps people interpret the world of politics.[45] Much of what we learn about politics from the mass media is ambiguous. Was the candidate's speech good? Will the president's economic proposal help reduce unemployment? How should the United States respond to the breakup of the Soviet Union or the conflict in Bosnia? Answering these questions is often difficult because people lack the necessary knowledge and because of the many value judgments required. Party identification provides guidance in these matters by identifying which political leaders to trust and which to doubt. The result is that people who identify with different parties "see" things differently.[46]

To see how party identification functions as a perceptual screen, consider people's assessments of who told the truth when Paula Jones accused President Clinton of sexually harassing her when she was an Arkansas state employee and he was the governor.[47] As figure 7.5 shows, people's opinions tended to match their party identifications. Although Republicans and Democrats heard similar news accounts of the Jones-Clinton dispute, 75 percent of the Democrats believed Clinton, while only 36 percent of Republicans did.[48]

The fact that people view evidence through partisan eyes and find their own party's leaders more believable than the other party's leaders influences more than candidate evaluations. Party identification also influences what positions people favor on the issues.[49] As we discussed in chapter 6, people generally don't know much about politics—especially about complicated policy matters. When people have to decide

FIGURE 7.5
Partisan Perceptions of the Truth

Bill Clinton and Paula Jones: Which one you believe may depend on your party identification.

Source: Data from *The Year in Figures* (Washington, D.C.: Times Mirror Center for the People and the Press, 1995), p. 8.

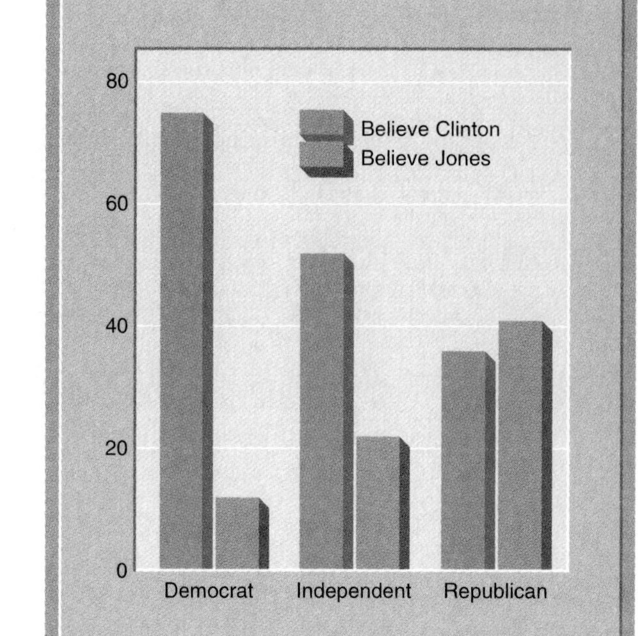

where they stand on complex questions such as economic trade policy or whether to support the Democratic or Republican proposals to reform Medicare, they have little choice but to look to someone for guidance. Consequently, although people do not blindly follow their party's leaders, they do look to them for advice on political issues.

Party identification's influence on voter evaluations of the candidates and voter policy preferences is important because those factors also affect voting choices. Thus, party identification has both a direct effect on voting and a number of indirect effects—swaying what we think of the candidates' stands on the issues, for instance, which in turn influences how we vote. For these reasons, party identification is the most important cause of voting choices. We must note, however, that even though most voters see the candidate through partisan eyes, party identification only *influences* how people evaluate the candidates; it does not strictly *predict* the voter's perceptions.

Candidate Characteristics

Candidate characteristics
The candidate's character, personality, experiences, past record, and physical appearance.

The candidates' personalities, experiences, past records, and even their physical appearances make up another set of voting influences called **candidate characteristics.** Relying on some candidate characteristics in deciding how to vote makes perfect sense. Whether the candidate has experience in elective office, how well he or she handled previous jobs, and whether the candidate seems intelligent, honest, and trustworthy are important considerations. A voter might reasonably choose an experienced candidate he or she disagrees with on some issues over a less experienced candidate with whom he or she agrees on all the issues. In the 1996 election, for instance, surveys revealed that 20 percent of the voters thought that sharing "my view of government" was the most important candidate quality, but another 20 percent thought that being "honest and trustworthy" was the top priority, and 16 percent thought that having a "vision for the future" was most important.[50]

Some voters are influenced by other candidate characteristics because of irrational prejudices. As a result, they may not vote for a candidate who is African American, Hispanic American, female, or of a different religion.[51] A poll conducted in 1994 asked, "If your party nominated a black for President, would you vote for him if he were qualified for the job?" Nine percent of the respondents said "No."[52] Similarly, some people refuse to vote for women. The same 1994 poll found that 21 percent of

Many actors, athletes, and public figures become successful politicians, some of whom include Rep. Sonny Bono (former pop singer); Rep. Steve Largent (former professional football player); and Sen. John Glenn (former astronaut).

the respondents agreed with the statement, "Most men are better suited emotionally for politics than are most women." In addition, when asked, "If your party nominated a woman for President, would you vote for her if she were qualified for the job?" 8 percent said "No."[53] In a tight election, that 8 percent can spell the difference between victory and defeat. As we see from these surveys, racial, religious, and gender prejudices no longer dominate American elections, but they still play a large enough role to affect the outcomes of some elections.[54]

More subtle prejudices also affect voter choice. Many political observers believe that being overweight or short puts a candidate at a disadvantage. Other characteristics or experiences can give candidates advantages—heroism of some kind has launched the careers of many politicians. Although it is hard to figure out why being an actor, athlete, or astronaut can be considered a qualification for office, Congress boasts quite a few. In 1997, Congress had a former actor (Sen. Fred Thompson, R-Tenn.), a former astronaut (Sen. John Glenn, D-Ohio), a former major league baseball pitcher (Rep. Jim Bunning, R-Ky.), a former professional football player (Rep. Steve Largent, R-Okla.), and one half of the former pop duo Sonny and Cher (Sonny Bono, R-Calif.).[55] Clearly, then, candidate characteristics influence voting behavior.

Issues

Issues lie at the heart of democratic elections. Through elections, we control what policies our government will follow in the coming years. Yet as we saw in chapter 6, few people know much about the details of public policy. This lack of knowledge does not eliminate the role of issues in elections, but it does affect the types of issues politicians and journalists emphasize during campaigns and the roles these issues play.

Issues influence voting decisions in two ways, retrospectively and prospectively. In **retrospective issue voting,** the voter decides how to vote on the basis of *past* policy outcomes. That is, the voter considers recent history and decides whether the incumbent has performed well enough to be retained in office. In this case, a

Retrospective issue voting Deciding how to vote on the basis of past policy outcomes.

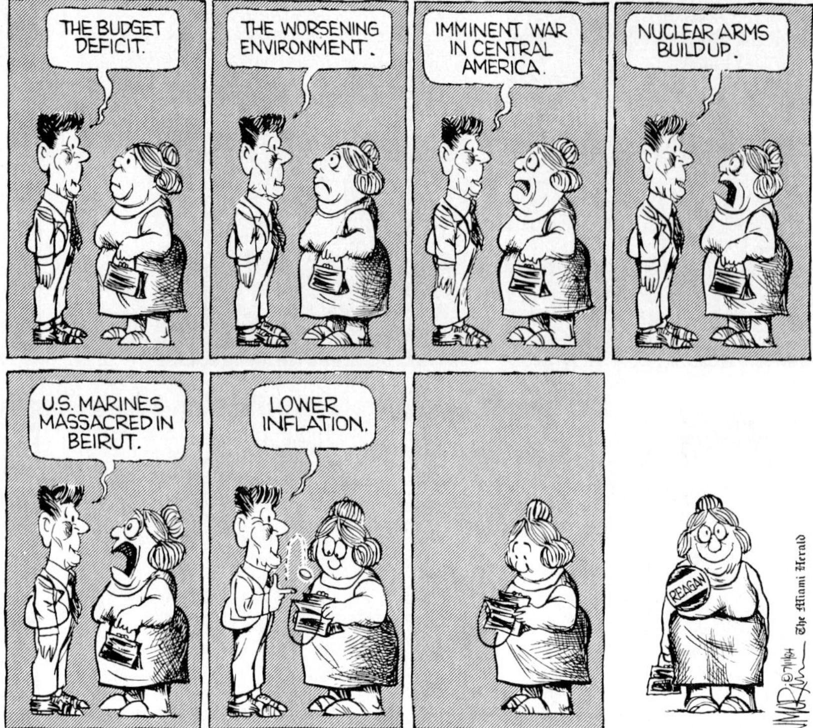

Voting studies show that economic retrospective voting is a powerful force—as this cartoonist explaining Ronald Reagan's appeal in 1984 well understood.

voter might ask, has the unemployment rate been too high in the last couple of years?[56] His or her vote would depend on the answer. In **prospective issue voting,** the voter decides how to vote on the basis of what policies the candidates promise to pursue when elected. That is, the voter chooses between alternative sets of *future* government policies. In this case, a voter might ask, should we allow women to have the option of abortion, or should we make abortion illegal?[57] Again, this voter might decide how to vote based on the expectation that the candidate will carry out policies the voter prefers.

Prospective issue voting
Deciding how to vote on the basis of a candidate's likely future policies.

Retrospective Issue Voting

An important aspect of retrospective voting is that it does not require voters to understand the specific details of public policy. They may need to know only a few generalities about how well the economy has been doing recently to form judgments about how well the president has been handling his job. From these judgments about past performance, people can develop expectations about how well the economy and the president will perform in the future.

When retrospectively evaluating an incumbent president's performance in office, most voters focus on the economy and consider the president's past performance as a good predictor of future performance. If the economy has been doing well, voters tend to reward the incumbent with reelection; if the economy has been weak, voters tend to throw out the incumbent and vote in the opposition party's candidate. In other words, voters act as the "rational god of vengeance and of reward."[58] Because of this behavior, political scientists can predict presidential elections fairly accurately on the basis of economic indicators such as change in gross domestic product, the unemployment rate, and the inflation rate.[59]

The conventional wisdom regarding retrospective voting is that people "vote their pocketbooks" by rewarding or punishing incumbents for the voters' *personal* economic situations. Yet when researchers began investigating the question, they found that most people seem to be **sociotropic voters.** That is, they seem to be influenced far

Sociotropic voters
People who vote on the basis of their community's economic interests, rather than their personal economic interests.

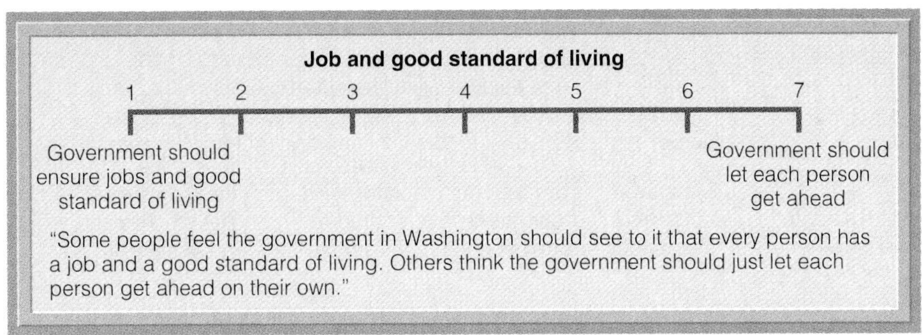

FIGURE 7.6
A Seven-Point Issue Scale

Issue scales, such as this jobs/standard of living scale, help us to understand the influence issues have on voting decisions.

Source: From *Codebook,* American National Election Study, 1992.

more by their community's or the nation's economic condition than by their own economic situations. The evidence for this pattern of behavior is that public opinion survey questions about personal economic situations poorly predict how people will vote, but questions about the respondent's perceptions of the nation's economic situation predict voting choices fairly well.[60] In other words, when people lose their jobs or suffer financial hardships, they do not necessarily blame the incumbent administration in the White House. However, when the unemployment rate goes up and people in their communities begin to lose their jobs, many voters do blame the incumbent administration.

The 1996 presidential election was a typical race. President Clinton received nearly two-thirds of the votes from voters who believed that the national economy was doing well. Senator Dole received slightly more than half of the votes of those who thought that the nation was performing poorly. He suffered, however, from the fact that a clear majority of the people thought the economy was in good or excellent shape.[61] Retrospective voting combined with a good economy thus played a strong role in Dole's defeat.

Prospective Issue Voting

It might seem reasonable that prospective issue voting—voting on the basis of policies a candidate promises to pursue in the future—should be a dominant factor in voting decisions. Yet one of the earliest and most disturbing findings about voting behavior was that prospective issues do not actually have much influence on voting decisions. That is, whether voters agree or disagree with candidates on public policies issues seems to make only a small difference in how they vote.

In a major study conducted in the 1950s, several researchers proposed that three conditions must be met for issues to influence choices.[62] In order for an issue to play any role in a voter's decision, the voter must (1) be aware of the issue and have an opinion on it; (2) have some idea about what the government is currently doing on that issue; and (3) see a difference between the policies the two candidates propose in response to the issue. Although these conditions may seem easy to satisfy, we should remember that, as we saw in chapter 6, few people in the American public are well informed about politics and public policy. This lack of knowledge helps explain why the researchers found that only one-quarter to one-third of the electorate met the three conditions necessary to characterize voters as engaging in prospective issue voting.

More recent studies paint a somewhat better—but still not glowing—picture of the electorate.[63] To help judge the presence of prospective issue voting, researchers use a series of issue questions in which survey respondents are presented with a scale (see figure 7.6). The respondents are asked to define which point on the scale best reflects their views and which points best reflect the views of the two presidential candidates. The researchers then suggest the following criteria for issue voting. An issue can influence someone's vote if (1) the voter can place him or herself on

In most presidential elections, more than half of the public fails to meet the four necessary conditions for issue voting.

TABLE 7.4 Four Criteria for Issue Voting, 1992

	Percentage of Sample Who:			
	I	II	III	IV
Issue Scale	**Placed Self on Scale**	**Placed Both Candidates On Scale**[a]	**Saw Difference Between Clinton and Bush**	**Saw Clinton as More "Liberal" Than Bush**
Government spending/ services	82	68	63	50
Defense spending	87	69	68	52
Jobs and standard of living	87	76	68	53

[a]If respondent could not place self on scale, respondent was not questioned further on that issue.

From Paul R. Abramson, et al., *Change and Continuity in the 1992 Elections*. Copyright © 1990 CQ Press, Washington, D.C. Reprinted by permission.

the scale; (2) the voter can place both candidates on the scale; (3) the voter sees a difference between the candidates; and (4) the voter correctly places the Democratic candidate to the left of the Republican candidate. Although these criteria differ from those used in the study conducted in the 1950s, they spring from the same basic ideas. For an issue to matter at the polls, the voter must care about it enough to offer an opinion and must correctly distinguish differences between the two candidates on the issue.

Table 7.4 presents the data researchers compiled using this method for the 1992 election. For the first issue, government spending and services, 82 percent of the voters in the national sample had opinions about whether government services should be increased or cut, and 68 percent thought they understood the positions of the presidential candidates—Bill Clinton and George Bush—on the issue. Sixty-three percent thought Clinton and Bush disagreed, and 50 percent correctly realized that Clinton favored spending more on government services than Bush. Therefore, if this issue had any effect on people's voting decisions, it could only be among these 50 percent of the voters.

The question of government spending is typical of many political issues. We may think that everyone knows and cares about major political issues, but, in fact, many people either don't know or don't care.

Easy issues
Simple issues that allow voters to make quick, emotional decisions without much information.

Hard issues
Complicated issues that require voters to have information about the policy and to spend time considering their choices.

Although most prospective issues do not seem to have much effect on voting decisions, some do. To examine which issues are more or less likely to influence voting outcomes, it helps to divide issues into two categories: easy and hard.[64] Simple or **easy issues**—those that allow voters to give quick, emotional responses to symbols—usually dominate election debates. For example, issues such as crime or abortion don't require much thought for many people—virtually everyone supports fighting crime and many voters have well-established pro-choice or pro-life stands on abortion. Candidates can therefore package these issues in thirty-second television spots or sound bites in speeches for the nightly news. **Hard issues**—those that are complicated and require some knowledge of the subject and some thought before coming to a conclusion—do not play much part in voters' decisions. Issues such as how to provide health care to all Americans, how to reduce the budget deficit, or how best to support the emerging democracies of eastern Europe cannot readily be reduced to campaign slogans or sound bites for television. They rely too much on the voters' knowledge of the issues and willingness to consider the problem carefully. The few who do follow these issues, of course, have a disproportionately large influence on the decisions officeholders make.

Abortion is a prospective *issue (what should future government policy be) and an* easy *issue (basic value judgments drive attitudes).*

Changes Over Time

Party identification, candidate characteristics, and issues all influence voters' choices in elections, but the relative importance of each factor changes from one election to the next. Calls to party unity have dominated some past presidential elections; issueless appeals to vote for the more "trustworthy" or "experienced" candidate have dominated others; while strident debates about public policy have characterized still other campaigns.

Several factors may change the nature of voter decisions over time. Dramatic events or conditions, such as wars or deep recessions, can focus the nation's attention on particular issues, reducing the impact of party identification or candidate characteristics. In more normal times, however, the candidates and the journalists who cover them decide the nature of the campaigns. When campaigns stress issues and ideological conflicts, the voters mirror the candidates by giving issues more weight in their voting choices. Alternatively, when campaigns focus on character or scandal, the voters pay less attention to issues.[65]

The ability of voters to pass the issue voting criteria, described in table 7.4, reflects the strategic choices candidates and journalists make about what to emphasize in campaigns. For instance, in the 1984 presidential election—one characterized by an intense ideological campaign between the conservative Ronald Reagan and the liberal Walter Mondale—more people passed the issue voting tests than in any other year since the data became available in 1972. By contrast, in the 1976 presidential election—an election characterized by President Ford's stress on experience and Jimmy Carter's stress on trust and the Watergate scandal—fewer people knew enough about the issues to meet the issue voting criteria than in any other recent election.

The people may want the candidates to talk about the issues, but the decision is up to the candidates and the journalists who cover them. If the candidates avoid the issues or the journalists choose not to discuss them, the people can do little to change things. They must then revert to making decisions based on other factors—party identification and the characteristics of the candidates.

In the 1976 presidential election, in the aftermath of the Watergate scandal, voters paid more attention to character than issues. Some of the high-ranking officials convicted in the Watergate trial included (from top left, clockwise): John Mitchell, attorney general; H. R. Haldeman, White House chief of staff; Charles Colson, presidential special counsel; and John Ehrlichman, chief domestic affairs advisor.

Voting and Social Groups

A final way to look at voting is to examine which candidates and parties different social groups favor. These voting patterns largely reflect the groups that make up the Democratic and Republican parties (see chapter 9). That is, in terms of our previous discussion, people's party identifications vary from one social group to another.

To illustrate the social composition of the Democratic and Republican parties, table 7.5 presents a portrait of the electorate in the 1996 presidential election. The outlines of the party coalitions are clear here (we will discuss Perot's supporters at the end of this section). What is clear is that all groups split their votes between Democrats and Republicans. Stereotypes such as "all the rich vote Republican" or "all the poor are Democrats" are wild exaggerations.

Beginning at the top of the table, we see that Democrats win a majority of the votes of the poor, whereas Republicans win a majority of the votes of the wealthy. Bill Clinton beat Bob Dole 59 percent to 28 percent among those with incomes under $15,000; by contrast, Dole beat Clinton 54 percent to 38 percent among those with incomes over $100,000.

The pattern of voting by education is similar to that of voting by income. As education level rises, Republican Party support increases as well—except among those with the highest levels of education. Democratic candidates generally do better among voters with postgraduate educations than they do among college graduates. Bill Clinton was no exception.

TABLE 7.5 Voting by Social Groups in the 1996 Presidential Election

Groups favoring the Democratic Party include the poor, the poorly educated, people in union households, African Americans and Hispanic Americans, Catholics, Jews, women, and liberals. Groups favoring the Republican Party include the wealthy, college graduates, whites, Asian Americans, white Protestants, men, and conservatives.

		Percentage Voting for		
Percentage of Total	Group	Clinton	Dole	Perot
Family Income				
11	$0–14,999	59	28	11
23	$15,000–29,999	53	36	9
27	$30,000–49,999	48	40	10
39	over $50,000	44	48	7
9	over $100,000	38	54	6
Education				
6	Not a high school graduate	59	28	11
24	High school graduate	51	35	13
27	Some college	48	40	10
26	College graduate	44	46	8
17	Postgraduate education	52	40	5
Union Household				
23	Union household	59	30	9
Race/Ethnicity				
83	White	43	46	9
10	African American	84	12	4
5	Hispanic American	72	21	6
1	Asian American	43	48	8
Religion				
46	White Protestant	36	53	10
29	Catholic	53	37	9
3	Jewish	78	16	3
Gender				
48	Men	43	44	10
52	Women	54	38	7
Ideology				
20	Liberals	78	11	7
47	Moderates	57	33	9
33	Conservatives	20	71	8
Total Vote		**49**	**41**	**8**

Note: Each row totals to 100 percent.

 New York Times, November 10, 1996. Data from 16,627 exit polls conducted by Voter News Service.

Union members and their families are also more likely to vote for Democratic candidates than are non-union families. To some extent, this reflects the Democratic Party's long association with unions.

Along racial and ethnic lines, whites and Asian Americans tend to support Republicans, whereas African Americans and Hispanic Americans tend to support Democrats. By religion, white Protestants tend to vote Republican, whereas Catholics lean toward the Democratic Party and Jewish voters are strongly Democratic.

Women tend to vote more Democratic than men. In the 1996 election, women were 9 percent more likely to vote for Clinton than were men. When we look at the difference in support for Dole, however, we see only a 6 percent difference. This difference in voting between men and women is often described as the **gender gap.** The gender gap was larger in 1996 than in any previous presidential election, but it has never been very large—averaging 7 or 8 percent in most surveys.[66] Although the gender gap is a small percentage, its political impact is huge; had only men been allowed to vote, Bob Dole would have won the 1996 election.

Gender gap
The difference between men's and women's voting rates for either a Democratic or Republican candidate.

Finally, those who identify themselves as liberals are far more likely to vote for Democratic candidates than are those who identify themselves as conservatives. Conversely, of course, conservatives are more likely than liberals to vote Republican.

Ross Perot's presidential vote differs from either the Democratic and Republican coalitions in that he drew votes fairly evenly from all groups. If anything, Perot received slightly more votes from the poor and from those who had not graduated from college than from the wealthy and college graduates, but the differences were quite small. In this way, Perot looks somewhat like a Democrat. However, Perot drew relatively few votes from African Americans or Hispanic Americans, which makes him look somewhat like a Republican. Yet all of these differences are quite small. In sum, Perot appealed to a broad cross-section of Americans. We cannot say of Perot, as we can of Democratic and Republican candidates, that particular types of voters were especially likely to support or oppose him.

Although voting patterns change somewhat from one election to the next, the results in table 7.5 are typical of most post-1930s presidential elections (of course, with the exception of Perot supporters). People who are upper income, well-educated, nonunion, white, Protestants, and who think of themselves as conservatives tend to support Republican candidates. Lower income, poorly educated, union members, who are African American or Hispanic American, who are Catholic or Jewish, and who think of themselves as liberals tend to support Democratic candidates. Since the late 1970s, women have also been slightly more likely than men to support Democratic candidates. These groups make up the party coalitions of the 1990s.

SUMMARY

Although the rules of the political system in the United States allow virtually everyone eighteen and older the opportunity to vote and participate, they do not guarantee that these people will choose to do so. There is no guarantee that "the will of the people" will be reflected in the election winners or the policies they set for our nation. Who votes or becomes politically active and how those people make their choices has a great impact on which candidates win and which policies become law.

Slightly more than half of eligible voters turn out in presidential elections; even fewer vote in other elections. People with high incomes, good educations, and high-status jobs—that is, people of high socioeconomic status—are more likely to vote than those with low incomes, poor educations, and low-status jobs. Whites are likely to vote at higher rates than are African Americans, Hispanic Americans, or Asian Americans, but these differences are caused by socioeconomic status. Middle-aged and elderly Americans are more likely to vote than the young. Finally, strong party identification, strong feelings of political efficacy, group consciousness and interest in politics, and reading about politics make people more likely to participate.

Although voting is a personal act, the decision about whether to vote and whom to vote for depends on more than the personal characteristics of the voters; it also depends on the rules of the political system. Voting and registration laws can substantially change the turnout rate. States with laws that make it more difficult or time consuming to register and vote have lower turnout rates than states with more lenient laws.

Aside from personal characteristics and rules, the behavior of campaigns and party organizations also influences turnout. Contacts from campaigns or voter registration and get-out-the-vote drives help bring people to the polls. As we shall see in chapter 9, the rules governing the behavior of political parties also affect these campaign efforts.

Voter turnout has declined since the turn of the century. The debate about the drop in turnout early in the century centers on whether changes in the parties' positions on the issues or changes in the rules governing registration and voting caused the decline. The post-1960 decline seems to be attributable to voters' personal characteristics, voting rules, and party strategy. Personal characteristics of voters have contributed to the decline because the average age of the population has fallen, and people identify less with political parties, feel less efficacious about politics, and are less likely to read newspapers than they were before 1960. Changes in rules have also contributed to the post-1960 decline—more young voters became eligible to vote with the passage of the Twenty-sixth Amendment to the Constitution, which added a relatively low turnout group to the electorate. Finally, parties and campaigns have put less effort into contacting and mobilizing voters over the past few decades.

The causes of activism are similar to the causes of voter participation, except that the level of political activism is far lower than the level of voting. Some evidence suggests that different types of people tend to specialize in different political activities. One study found seven different types of activists, from complete activists to nonparticipants; another study found only three types: nonvoters, voters, and activists.

Three broad sets of forces influence people's voting decisions—party identification, candidate characteristics, and issues. Of these, party identification is the most influential and issues the least. When looking at the role of issues in elections, one must distinguish between retrospective voting and prospective voting. People who vote retrospectively look back at the recent records of incumbent politicians and evaluate them, while those who vote prospectively look forward and vote on the basis of candidate promises and what they want the government to do in the future. When people do vote prospectively, they tend to do so on the basis of easy issues, which allow voters to give quick, emotional responses. Hard issues, which require some knowledge of the subject and careful thought, generally do not have much effect in elections.

Voting choice depends not only on the individual's preferences, but also on the strategic choices the candidates and journalists make about whether to emphasize party labels, particular candidate characteristics, or particular issues. Therefore, even if individuals' preferences were fixed, the ways in which candidates present different aspects of their personalities and different issues can alter the choices voters face and therefore change the outcomes.

In short, who wins elections depends on many factors—on who votes; on whether the rules in a given state encourage or discourage voting; on whether campaigns, parties, or other groups make an effort to contact voters; on people's preferences about party labels, candidate characteristics, and issues; and on the strategies and behavior of the candidates and journalists who cover them. An election outcome depends on much more than the personal preferences of the citizens. The people, the politicians, the journalists, and the rules under which they compete all play roles in determining who prevails in any given election.

Key Terms

Australian ballot
Candidate characteristics
Closing date
Easy issues
Franchise
Gender gap
Group consciousness
Hard issues
Literacy test
Party identification
Poll tax
Prospective issue voting
Retrospective issue voting
Sociotropic voters
Voter turnout

Readings for Further Study

Abramson, Paul R., John H. Aldrich, and David W. Rohde. *Change and Continuity in the 1992 Elections.* Washington, D.C.: CQ Press, 1994. A sophisticated but easily readable analysis of who turns out to vote and how they make up their minds. This study examines the central questions of voting analysis from the most important theoretical perspectives.

Keith, Bruce E., David B. Magleby, Candice J. Nelson, Elizabeth Orr, Mark C. Westyle, and Raymond E. Wolfinger. *The Myth of the Independent Voter.* Berkeley: University of California Press, 1992. A penetrating study of the behavior of people who call themselves political independents. Keith and his colleagues argue that the rise of independents was mythical and that most people still behave as if they are partisans.

Piven, Frances Fox, and Richard A. Cloward. *Why Americans Don't Vote.* New York: Pantheon, 1988. An investigation of why the turnout rate has dropped so sharply since the last century. Piven and Cloward argue persuasively that manipulation of registration laws is to blame.

Rosenstone, Steven J., and John Mark Hansen. *Mobilization, Participation, and Democracy in America.* New York: Macmillan, 1993. A pathbreaking study of why people vote and participate in other ways in our political system. The study reveals the key role parties and campaigns play when they choose whether to mobilize voters and activists.

Salmore, Stephen A., and Barbara G. Salmore. *Candidates, Parties, and Campaigns: Electoral Politics in America,* 2d ed. Washington, D.C.: CQ Press, 1989. A description and analysis of political campaigns. Salmore and Salmore discuss the changing role of parties and the changing style of campaigns in recent decades, as well as describing how campaigns are waged today.

Tate, Katherine. *From Protest to Politics: The New Black Voters in American Elections,* enlarged edition. Cambridge: Harvard University Press, 1994. An in-depth examination of black political behavior in the 1984, 1988, and 1992 elections, with special attention to the impact the Rev. Jesse Jackson's campaigns had on the Democratic presidential nominations.

Westlye, Mark C. *Senate Elections and Campaign Intensity.* Baltimore: Johns Hopkins University Press, 1991. A comprehensive and systematic study of modern Senate elections. Westlye draws on a wealth of survey and election data to show why we choose our senators.

Wolfinger, Raymond E., and Steven J. Rosenstone. *Who Votes?* New Haven: Yale University Press, 1980. In this classic study of who turns out to vote, Wolfinger and Rosenstone use census data to examine the demographic and social characteristics of voters.

CHAPTER

8

THE NEWS MEDIA

Do the News Media Matter?

The News Media and Public Opinion

The News Media and the Political Agenda

The News Media and Government

The Changing Face of the News Media

Changes in Journalistic Conventions

Changes in Readership and Viewership

Changes in Media Ownership

Freedom of the Press

Limits to Press Freedom

The Electronic Media

Reporting the News

What Is News?

Telling the Story

Evaluating the News Media

Ideological Bias

Cynicism

News as Entertainment

On the Campaign Trail

Reporting Leaks

The News Media and Democracy

Summary

Key Terms

Readings for Further Study

In November 1993, Bill Clinton sat down to an interview with two reporters from *Rolling Stone*. Like most presidential interviews, the questions covered a wide range of topics, from gun control to foreign policy to violence on television. As the interview came to a close, one of the reporters mentioned a conversation he had had that morning with a voter Clinton had met during the campaign. The voter had said he was disappointed in how little the administration had achieved during its first ten months in office, and he wanted the reporter to ask Clinton "what he's willing to stand up for and die on." A visibly angry Clinton responded to the question by denouncing the news media. "That is the press's fault, too, damn it. I have fought more damn battles here for more things than any president has in twenty years . . . and not gotten one damn bit of credit from the knee-jerk liberal press."[1]

Bill Clinton was not the first president to accuse the press of being unfair and inaccurate. Thomas Jefferson suggested that newspaper editors should divide their papers "into four chapters, heading the 1st, Truths. 2d, Probabilities. 3d, Possibilities. 4th, Lies."[2] Harry Truman pitied "the great body of my fellow citizens, who, reading newspapers, live and die in the belief that they have known something of what has been passing in the world in their time."[3] George Bush complained during the 1992 campaign that journalists ignored his accomplishments and exaggerated his failures: "When the Berlin Wall fell, I half expected to see a headline: WALL FALLS, THREE BORDER GUARDS LOSE JOBS. And underneath, it probably says, CLINTON BLAMES BUSH."[4]

Although not new, complaints about the news media are nonetheless troubling. By all accounts, the success of American democracy rests on the existence of a free press. After all, the media are responsible for finding out what government is doing and reporting that information to the public; without a free press, the people could not govern themselves, for they would have no way to monitor the actions of government and to decide whether they like what it is doing. As James Madison put it: "A popular Government without popular information, or the means of acquiring it, is but a Prologue to a Farce or a Tragedy; or, perhaps both."[5] Yet our very dependence on newspapers, radio, and television for information gives the media the potential to influence public opinion and government behavior.

The existence of a free press, then, creates a tension: democracy demands a free and vigorous news media, yet such a news media may abuse its power. How can the rules of our political system support freedom of the press while restraining the media's potential to shape the course of political debate? The answer is that the same structural rules that ensure freedom of the news media to report on issues also ensure that the news media do not possess unbridled power. Just as the First Amendment declares that Congress shall make no law abridging the freedom of the press, it also guarantees every American citizen the right to speak freely. As a result of this guarantee, the United States enjoys an enormous array of different media voices, ranging from liberal magazines such as *The Nation* to conservative television shows such as the *McLaughlin Group*. The great diversity in media voices makes it less likely that any one media outlet will determine what Americans think.

In this chapter, we explore the news media's role in American politics. We will begin by asking whether the media influence political debate in the United States. We will see that the answer is complex; what the news media report often reflects what the American people are thinking and what government is doing, rather than the reverse. In the second section of the chapter, we will review the changing nature of the news business. We will see that the rules of American politics give the news media great freedom to define their role in the political arena, and that, as a result, their role has changed greatly over the past two centuries. In the third section, we will analyze the rules that both guarantee and limit the freedoms the media have to report the news. In the fourth section, we will look at the media's tremendous power to define what is news, and we will explore how the media follow self-imposed rules to keep this power in check. Finally, we will evaluate several complaints that the news media have abused their power and harmed the democratic process in the United States.

President Bill Clinton sometimes expresses his frustration with the media. Because we depend on the media for information, they have the potential to influence our opinions as well as the behavior of the government.

Do the News Media Matter?

The authors of the Constitution believed that democracy could not flourish without a free press. In their view, the press—the term *news media* was invented in the twentieth century to include radio and television—is essential to enable the people to watch over government. Thomas Jefferson, who, as we have seen, could be quite critical of the press, went so far as to write: "Were it left to me to decide whether we should have a government without newspapers, or newspapers without a government, I should not hesitate a moment to prefer the latter."[6]

But to what extent do the media actually matter in American politics? Are they neutral channels of information, or do they shape the course of political debate in the United States? As we saw in chapter 6, the media are but one factor influencing people's deep-seated beliefs about politics. Moreover, in most instances, the media appear to have only a small impact on fundamental beliefs such as a person's political affiliation and faith in government.[7] People's deep-seated beliefs about politics seem to be more heavily influenced by their families, friends, and schooling.

If the news media lack the power to dictate the fundamental beliefs of the American public, they nonetheless have a significant, though complex, influence on the course of American politics. To see why, we need to examine how the news media affect public opinion on specific issues, shape the political agenda, and influence what government does.

The News Media and Public Opinion

Most Americans believe the news media exert considerable influence over public opinion in the United States.[8] That belief seems perfectly reasonable. After all, most of our knowledge about what government does, both at home and abroad, comes from reading the newspaper, watching television, or listening to the radio.

Yet, in practice, it is difficult to determine the impact of the news media on public opinion. One difficulty comes in trying to disentangle the effect of media coverage from the effect of the event itself. For example, did the sharp rise in President George Bush's public approval rating in the wake of the 1991 Gulf War stem from how the news media covered the war or from the simple fact that U.S. military forces won a decisive victory? Another difficulty stems from the enormous array of media voices in

Americans obtain their news and information from a wide variety of media sources, including traditional outlets such as the evening newscasts on network television and nontraditional outlets such as Rush Limbaugh's radio talk shows.

the United States. Are public attitudes toward Republican plans to cut taxes shaped more by an editorial in the *Wall Street Journal,* a story on ABC's *World News Tonight,* or a satirical skit on NBC's *Saturday Night Live?*

A third difficulty in assessing the impact of the news media is the fact that people choose which media voices, if any, they will listen to. Because people are free to listen to *Rush Limbaugh* or to change the station, the news media may not influence opinion even when they advocate a specific point of view.

In grappling with these problems, researchers have found that news coverage has at most a modest effect on public opinion on specific issues. One study looked at polls of public opinion on eighty different issues. In analyzing the results of the surveys, the study found that news commentators had a bigger impact on changes in public opinion than other sources of information such as the president and members of the opposition party. Yet in most instances, the change in public opinion attributable to the news media was small.[9]

Selective perception
A phenomenon in which people perceive the same event differently because they have different beliefs and personal experiences.

A major reason for the news media's limited influence on public opinion is **selective perception:** people often see the same events differently because they have different beliefs and personal experiences. For instance, public opinion polls conducted during O. J. Simpson's murder trial showed that whites and African Americans disagreed sharply over whether he was guilty.[10] Given the importance of selective perception, it is not surprising that researchers have found that the news media are most likely to influence opinion when a person knows little about an issue or has no strong beliefs concerning it.

The News Media and the Political Agenda

Political agenda
The list of issues that people think are important and that government officials are actively debating.

Even though stories that appear in the news media have at most a moderate effect on what Americans think, they have considerable influence over what Americans think about. Researchers have found that the news media play a major role in shaping the **political agenda,** the list of issues that people think are important and that government officials are actively debating. For example, if the news media run a series of stories on the problems that people with disabilities face in their everyday lives, more people will think about the obstacles society creates, worry about how to remove those obstacles, and communicate their concerns to public officials. In many ways, it makes sense that the news media choose the stories that affect which issues become important to people and government. After all, we depend on the news media to tell us what is happening in the world around us.

Television has the greatest impact on which issues the public thinks about because it is so widely watched. Using a series of carefully designed experiments that manipulated how much coverage was allotted to particular issues, researchers found that the more people were exposed to television news coverage on a given issue, the more likely they were to believe the issue was an important national problem. This finding suggests that "By attending to some problems and ignoring others, television news shapes the American public's political priorities."[11] Moreover, "the more removed the viewer is from the world of public affairs, the stronger the agenda-setting power of television news."[12]

Although newspaper, radio, and television coverage affects the political agenda, the agenda-setting power of the news media should not be exaggerated. The studies on agenda setting show only that people's opinions about the importance of an issue vary with the amount of news coverage; these studies do not show that the media consciously manipulate the political agenda. Why the news media cover some stories and not others is an important question we will examine later in the chapter. Here, it is sufficient to point out that, in many instances, the media follow rather than lead the public when it comes to choosing news stories. In 1995, for example, the O.J. Simpson murder trial was a hot topic in the nation's newspapers and on radio and television news shows. The media's interest in the trial was not the result of a conspiracy on the part of journalists; instead, it reflected the public's voracious appetite for stories about the Simpson case.

The News Media and Government

If the news media do influence public opinion and the political agenda, do they also influence what government does and does not do? The answer, once again, is complex. On the one hand, the news media's coverage of an issue can put tremendous pressure on government officials to act. Immediately following the Gulf War, for example, Americans began to see pictures of how Iraqi troops were punishing Kurds living in northern Iraq for having supported U.S. efforts to oust Saddam Hussein. After initially refusing to protect the Kurds, President Bush reversed course and provided American protection.[13] News coverage can have a similar effect on Congress.[14] As Rep. Howard Berman (D-Calif.) notes, Congress is "a very big institution and it's very hard to get everybody's attention on something which isn't on the front pages every day."[15]

Yet the relationship between the news media and government is not a one-way street. Because news coverage has the potential to influence both public opinion and the political agenda, officials at all levels of government actively try to influence news coverage. Presidents have the greatest power to influence which stories the media cover because they are the single most important political figure in the United States.[16] Simply by giving a speech, a president can pluck an issue from obscurity and put it in the national spotlight. Indeed, the ability of the president to influence the political agenda is a major source of presidential power, as we shall see in chapter 12.

Presidents, members of Congress, and other government officials also devote considerable effort to **spin control**—the practice of trying to persuade journalists to cover news stories in ways that put policies one likes in the most favorable light. (People outside of government who want to influence public policy, such as leaders of interest groups and political parties, also engage in spin control.) Because government officials work so hard to influence news coverage, the news media's influence is often less powerful than the public supposes. Rather than setting a lead for government to follow, in many instances, the news media are actually following the lead government sets.

Spin control
The practice of trying to persuade journalists to cover news stories in ways that put policies one likes in the most favorable light.

As you can see, the role of the news media in American politics is complex. Americans clearly depend on newspapers, radio, and television to keep them informed about what government is doing and not doing. And which stories the news media choose to cover, as well as how they cover the news, can significantly affect both public opinion and government behavior, and therefore public policy. Yet the relationship between the news media and the American people and government is a two-way street. In many instances, the news media's reports reflect what the American people are already thinking and what the government is already doing, rather than the reverse.

THE CHANGING FACE OF THE NEWS MEDIA

Although the authors of the Constitution believed that a free press is essential to the success of democracy, the nature of the news business has changed dramatically over the past two centuries. The most obvious change has been in technology. In April 1775, for example, local militia in Massachusetts clashed with British soldiers at Lexington and Concord, but people in Savannah, Georgia, did not read of the first battles of the American Revolution for another five weeks.[17] In contrast, in January 1991, U.S. warplanes attacked Iraq. Halfway around the world, the American public watched the start of the Gulf War on television as it happened.

Although technological developments have produced the most obvious changes in the media over the past two hundred years, the news media have changed in other ways as well. In this section, we discuss three such changes: (1) changes in the conventions of journalism; (2) changes in the sources from which the public obtains its news; and (3) changes in the pattern of media ownership. All these changes illustrate the immense freedom the media have to define their role in the American political system.

Changes in Journalistic Conventions

The newspapers Thomas Jefferson criticized differ greatly from the ones we read today. Then, newspapers were a *partisan press;* that is, they had formal ties to political parties or other political interests. A typical paper sold for six cents, at a time when the average worker earned less than a dollar a day. The high cost of a paper confined circulation to the wealthy. Even then, sales did not cover costs, so most newspapers required subsidies to continue operating. The subsidies typically came from business and political groups. In return for providing a subsidy, these groups expected that news reports and editorials would be slanted to promote their interests. The link between party and press accounts for the sometimes vicious edge found in the partisan press. The targets of a newspaper's ire might find themselves denounced as "serpents," "guileful betrayers," "an abandoned liar," or "an ill-looking devil."[18]

The 1830s ushered in the era of the *penny press.* With each paper selling for only one cent, the penny press revolutionized journalism. First and most important, the penny press relied on mass circulation to succeed, thereby expanding the number of Americans who read. Second, the penny press emphasized human interest stories rather than business and political news in its bid to attract readers. Third, the penny press covered its costs by relying on advertising and sales rather than on subsidies from business and political groups. Thus, the penny press had no formal party ties. It was not, however, nonpartisan. Penny papers frequently favored one party or another, but unlike the partisan press, the penny press did not see exerting political influence as its primary purpose.[19]

Yellow journalism
A form of journalism, popular at the end of the nineteenth century, that emphasized sensational and sometimes lurid news coverage.

The 1890s saw the rise of **yellow journalism.** Taking its name from *The Yellow Kid,* a comic strip popular at the time, the yellow press emphasized sensational and even lurid news coverage. Its leading practitioners were Joseph Pulitzer (for whom the Pulitzer Prize is named) and William Randolph Hearst (see box 8.1). The yellow press often crossed the line that separates reporting the news from making the news. When Cubans rebelled against Spanish rule in 1895, for example, the yellow press ran a stream of stories urging American intervention. When the United States finally declared war against Spain in 1898, one of the papers Hearst owned, the *New York Journal,* gleefully asked on its front page, "How do you like the *Journal's* war?"[20]

0,000 REWARD.—WHO DESTROYED THE MAINE?—$50,000 REWARD.

NEW YORK JOURNAL
AND ADVERTISER.

NEW YORK, THURSDAY, FEBRUARY 17, 1898.—16 PAGES. PRICE ONE CENT

TRUCTION OF THE WAR SHIP MAINE WAS THE WORK OF AN ENEMY.

$50,000!
0,000 REWARD!
r the Detection of the Perpetrator of the Maine Outrage!

Assistant Secretary Roosevelt Convinced the Explosion of the War Ship Was Not an Accident.

The Journal Offers $50,000 Reward for the Conviction of the Criminals Who Sent 258 American Sailors to Their Death. Naval Officers Unanimous That the Ship Was Destroyed on Purpose.

$50,000!
$50,000 REWARD!
For the Detection of the Perpetrator of the Maine Outrage!

NAVAL OFFICERS THINK THE MAINE WAS DESTROYED BY A SPANISH MINE.

Mine or a Sunken Torpedo Believed to Have Been the Weapon Used Against the American Man-of-War—Officers and Men Tell Thrilling Stories of Being Blown Into the Air Amid a Mass of Shattered Steel and Exploding Shells—Survivors Brought to Key West Scout the Idea of Accident—Spanish Officials Protest Too Much—Our Cabinet Orders a Searching Inquiry—Journal Sends Divers to Havana to Report Upon the Condition of the Wreck. Was the Vessel Anchored Over a Mine?

Assistant Secretary of the Navy Theodore Roosevelt says he is convinced that the destruction of the Maine in Havana Harbor was not an accident.

The Journal offers a reward of $50,000 for exclusive evidence that will convict the person, persons or Government criminally responsible for the de- of the American battleship and the death of 258 of its crew.

The suspicion that the Maine was deliberately blown up grows stronger every hour. Not a single fact to the contrary has been produced.

Captain Sigsbee, of the Maine, and Consul-General Lee both urge that public opinion be suspended until they have completed their investigation. taking the course of tactful men who are convinced that there has been treachery.

Spanish Government officials are pressing forward all sorts of explanations of how it could have been an accident. The facts show that there was a before the ship exploded, and that, had her magazine exploded, she would have sunk immediately.

Every naval expert in Washington says that if the Maine's magazine had exploded the whole vessel would have been blown to atoms.

Newspapers that practiced yellow journalism used the sinking of the U.S.S. Maine *to whip up public support for what became the Spanish-American War. Although many newspapers accused Spain of sinking the ship, the cause of the explosion aboard the* Maine *remains a mystery.*

Besides yellow journalism, the turn of the century saw the rise of a type of investigative reporting called **muckraking.** The name originated with President Theodore Roosevelt, who criticized some journalists for raking muck (or manure) in what he considered their excessive zeal to expose the unsavory aspects of government and business. Muckrakers, however, took the name as a badge of honor. They saw themselves as crusading against injustice, raking away the muck to expose wrongdoing. Ida M. Tarbell revealed the unfair business practices that John D. Rockefeller used to build the Standard Oil Company, and Lincoln Steffens uncovered political corruption in several major cities. Muckrakers published mostly in magazines such as *Collier's, Cosmopolitan, Ladies Home Journal,* and the *Saturday Evening Post.*

Muckraking
An early form of investigative journalism popular at the beginning of the twentieth century.

Neither the muckrakers nor the yellow press believed their job was to be objective. But after World War I, objectivity emerged as the touchstone of American journalism. In 1923, the American Society of Newspaper Editors drew up a code of ethics, called the Canons of Journalism, that outlined the principles of an **objective press.** At its core, objectivity holds that journalists should "Tell the News Straight!"; opinion should appear only on the editorial page and not in news reports.

Objective press
A form of journalism that developed in the 1920s and which continues to predominate today. It emphasizes that journalists should strive to keep their opinions out of their coverage of the news.

Although the idea of objectivity sounds lofty in principle, the development of an objective press came about largely for economic reasons. To appeal to the mass audiences needed to attract the advertising dollars so vital to profits, newspapers (and subsequently radio and television) had to present the news so that it appealed to people with divergent views on the issues of the day. That could be done only by removing as much overt bias as possible from news coverage. As we shall see later in this chapter, the news media often fall short of pure objectivity. Nonetheless, for journalists today, objectivity remains the standard.

The People Behind the Rules

BOX 8.1

William Randolph Hearst and Ted Turner

The media may exert power over public opinion, but who controls the media? Two of the most powerful and colorful figures in news media history are William Randolph Hearst and Ted Turner.

William Randolph Hearst

William Randolph Hearst

William Randolph Hearst was born in 1863 to a California family that had made its fortune in mining and ranching. He entered the newspaper business at the age of twenty-two when he returned home to San Francisco to work on the family newspaper, the *Examiner*, after being expelled from Harvard for decorating chamber pots with the likenesses of faculty members. In 1887, Hearst was given control of the paper, and the twenty-four-year-old quickly showed he had a knack for the newspaper business. He encouraged his reporters to sensationalize their stories, and the *Examiner's* circulation (and profits) soared.

In 1895, Hearst used the profits from the *Examiner* as well as funds from his family's fortune to buy a New York paper called the *Morning Journal*. As with the *Examiner*, Hearst directed the *Journal's* reporters to emphasize stories about sex and crime. Once again, the *Journal's* circulation quickly skyrocketed, and many other newspapers began to imitate its yellow journalism.

The *Journal* also used its pages to champion what it saw as the people's interests. Many of the paper's crusades targeted issues of local concern, such as municipal corruption. Others focused on national concerns. For example, the *Journal* worked hard to whip up public sentiment for a war with Spain over Cuba, and it was widely rumored (though never proved) that Hearst cabled the *Journal's* correspondent in Havana: "You furnish the pictures, and I'll furnish the war." The *Journal* also pushed what many at the time considered to be a radical political agenda: a graduated income tax, direct election of senators, and destruction of business trusts. The often venomous tone the *Journal* used to attack its opponents further cemented Hearst's reputation as a rabble-rouser.

With the fame he earned as the *Journal's* publisher, Hearst turned his sights to political office. In 1902, he was elected to the House of Representatives from New York City and served two terms. In 1904, he failed in his attempt to win the Democratic presidential nomination, and the next year, ballot fraud cost him the New York mayoral race. In 1906, he ran for governor of New York but was defeated in a bitter race by Charles Evans Hughes (who would later become Chief Justice of the United States). Hearst subsequently ran independent campaigns for the White House and the mayor's office, but his efforts excited few voters.

Despite Hearst's failures as a politician, his newspaper empire grew steadily. At its peak in 1935, Hearst papers appeared in nineteen cities and accounted for nearly 14 percent of all newspapers sold on weekdays and 25 percent of those sold on Sunday. The newspaper chain Hearst left behind at his death in 1951 remains one of the largest in the country.

Continued

Changes in Readership and Viewership

The second half of the twentieth century has seen an information explosion in the United States. In 1995, the United States counted more than 1,500 television stations, 10,000 radio stations, and 1,700 daily newspapers, not to mention a dizzying array of journals and magazines.[21] Americans do not want for news and information, although, as we saw in chapter 6, Americans are not necessarily better informed than they used to be.

The explosion of media outlets, however, obscures four important changes within the news business: (1) the declining number of daily newspapers; (2) the rise of cable television; (3) the rise of political talk shows on radio and television; and (4) the rapid growth of the Internet.

The People Behind the Rules

BOX 8.1 CONTINUED

Ted Turner

Ted Turner

Ted Turner claims to have watched *Citizen Kane,* the fictionalized portrayal of the life of William Randolph Hearst, more than one hundred times. Turner's fascination with the newspaper publisher is not surprising; his life parallels Hearst's in many ways.

Turner was born in 1938 to a wealthy Georgia family. He attended Brown University, but was expelled during his senior year for entertaining women in his dorm room. After a stint in the Coast Guard, he returned to Georgia in 1960 to work for the family billboard company. When his father committed suicide, Turner took over the firm and reversed its flagging fortunes. He then branched out into television by buying Channel 17, a small UHF station in Atlanta. Turner's recipe of old movies, network reruns, and Atlanta Braves games proved immensely profitable, especially after Channel 17—now known as WTBS—began to appear on cable systems across the country. In 1978, armed with the profits generated by his so-called superstation, Turner announced a new venture: a twenty-four-hour all-news cable channel.

The announcement drew guffaws from veterans in the news media. Not only was Turner proposing something revolutionary, but he was a neophyte when it came to journalism. The only newscast on Channel 17 was a spoof of the news that aired at three o'clock in the morning. The show featured a German shepherd, attired in a shirt and tie, as a co-anchor, and a correspondent who wore a paper bag over his head. Given Turner's cavalier attitude toward the news, many of his employees openly worried that the news channel would drown the otherwise profitable Channel 17 in a sea of red ink.

But Turner proved to be a visionary. Cable News Network (CNN) went on the air June 1, 1980, followed by a second all-news channel, Headline News, in 1981. By 1985, the two channels were generating more than $20 million a year in profits, and in 1995, Time-Warner bought CNN and Turner's other television properties for $7.5 billion. Many Americans now make CNN their primary news source. Indeed, CNN has had such an impact that it is now required viewing for government officials. At the start of the Gulf War, for example, officials in the Bush administration admitted they were getting much of their information from watching CNN.

One area in which Turner's life has not (thus far) paralleled Hearst's is politics. Rather than seeking political office, Turner has focused his efforts on promoting world peace and protecting the environment. He staged the Goodwill Games in Moscow in 1986 and in Seattle in 1990. He created the Better World Society, which, until its demise in 1991, sought to use documentaries to educate Americans about pollution, hunger, and the arms race. And he started the Turner Tomorrow Awards, which seek to inspire people to write about how to solve global problems by awarding a $500,000 prize. One of Turner's remaining ambitions reportedly is to win the Nobel Peace Prize.

Sources: Edwin Emery, *The Press and America: An Interpretative History of the Mass Media,* 3d ed. (Englewood Cliffs, N.J.: Prentice-Hall, 1972); Priscilla Painton, "The Taming of Ted Turner," *Time,* 6 January 1992, pp. 34–39; Hank Whittemore, *CNN: The Inside Story* (Boston: Little, Brown, 1990).

The Decline of Newspapers

The number of daily newspapers has declined over the past half century. In 1995, nearly 175 fewer newspapers were operating than was true five decades earlier.[22] In 1950, most major cities had several daily papers; today, 98 percent have only one.[23] Many newspapers died because more and more people stopped reading them. At the end of World War II, newspaper market penetration was 135 percent, meaning that more newspapers were sold in the United States than there were households. By 1994, newspaper market penetration had fallen to 62 percent.[24] And while total newspaper circulation rose by 6 million between 1950 and 1994, the population of the United States increased by more than 100 million over the same period.[25] Newspaper reading has fallen more sharply in the United States than in other advanced industrialized

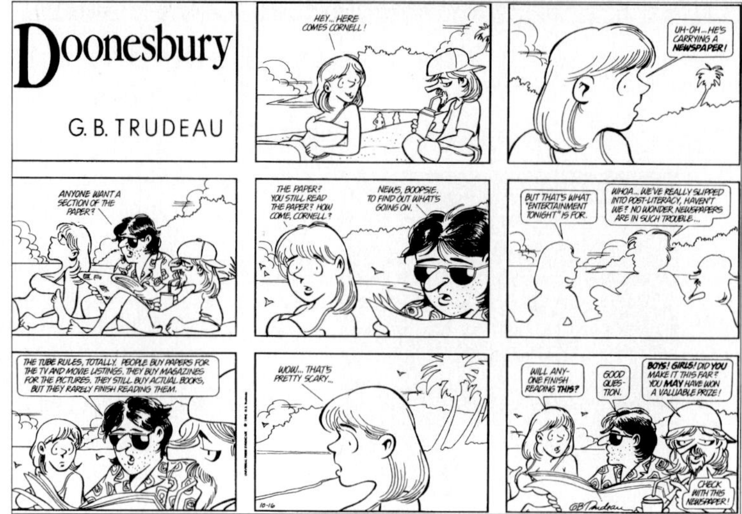

Daily newspaper reading has dropped sharply in the United States, especially among young adults.

democracies; whereas 78 percent of Germans surveyed in 1993 reported reading a newspaper the day before, only 49 percent of Americans did.[26] Much of the newspaper industry's problem in the United States traces to young adults. In the 1960s, 60 percent of Americans between the ages of eighteen and twenty-nine read a newspaper regularly. In 1995, only 21 percent did.[27]

The public's declining interest in newspapers largely results from the rise of television. While few Americans owned televisions in 1950, 98 percent of all American households own one today.[28] And as table 8.1 shows, most Americans say they obtain most of their news from television rather than from newspapers or radio. The tremendous importance of television as a news source raises serious questions about the quality of the information people have about the world around them. As we discussed in chapter 6, newspapers generally cover news events much more thoroughly than television does.

The Rise of Cable Television

Broadcast television
Television stations that make their programming available over the airwaves without charge. Most local cable companies include broadcast television channels as part of their basic package of services.

Despite the increased popularity of television, so-called **broadcast television,** stations that transmit their programming over the airwaves without charge, faces problems of its own. One problem is tight budgets. The three leading broadcast television networks—ABC, CBS, and NBC—were sold in the mid-1980s to major corporations that placed a greater emphasis on financial success. The increased emphasis on profits forced news shows to cut their budgets substantially.[29] Foreign news coverage took an especially hard hit as the networks closed many of their overseas news bureaus. At NBC, for example, "the Paris bureau is now just an answering machine."[30] At the same time, people are less likely to watch the evening news. During the 1980s, the network newscasts saw their share of the television audience shrink 20 percent.[31] The decline in audience share makes network newscasts less attractive to advertisers, and in turn, makes it harder for the newscasts to turn a profit.

Cable television
Television programming not originally transmitted over the air, as with broadcast television, but rather carried via coaxial or fiber optic cable into the homes of people who pay a monthly fee.

The problems network news departments face stem from increased competition from **cable television,** programming not originally transmitted over the airwaves, as with broadcast television, but carried via cable into the homes of people who pay a monthly fee. With the advent of cable television, Americans now have many more choices of what to watch than they did even a decade ago. But cable television offers more than old movies and sitcom reruns—it also offers an array of new sources of news and information. Cable's most visible contributor to news is the Cable News Network. Originally derided as "Chicken Noodle News," Ted Turner's

TABLE 8.1 Sources from Which Americans Get Their News (in percent)

Unlike Americans of thirty-five years ago, most Americans now say they get most of their news from television rather than from newspapers.

Poll Year	Television	Newspapers	Radio	Magazines	People
1959	51%	57%	34%	8%	4%
1961	52	57	34	9	5
1963	55	53	29	6	4
1964	58	56	26	8	5
1967	64	55	28	7	4
1968	59	49	25	7	5
1971	60	48	23	5	4
1972	64	50	21	6	4
1974	65	47	21	4	4
1976	64	49	19	7	5
1978	67	49	20	5	5
1980	64	44	18	5	4
1982	65	44	18	6	4
1984	64	40	14	4	4
1986	66	36	14	4	4
1988	65	42	14	4	5
1990	69	43	15	3	7
1992	69	43	16	4	6
1994	72	38	18	8	n.a.

Note: Each poll asked: "First, I'd like to ask you where you usually get most of your news about what's going on in the world today—from the newspapers or radio or television or magazines or talking to people or where?" The percentages sum to more than one hundred for each year because survey respondents were allowed to give multiple answers.

Sources: Data from Burns W. Roper, *Trends in Attitudes Toward Television and Other Media* (New York: Roper Organization, 1983), p. 5; Harold W. Stanley and Richard G. Niemi, *Vital Statistics on American Politics*, 5th ed. (Washington, D.C.: CQ Press, 1996), p. 89.

brainchild (see box 8.1) now reaches more than 50 million homes in the United States.[32] Besides CNN, cable television provides CNN Headline News, C-Span I and C-Span II (which cover the U.S. House and Senate), CNBC, and local access channels. For the minority of Americans who follow the news closely, television offers a smorgasbord of choices.

Yet the increase in the percentage of people who get their news almost exclusively from television may simply mean, as chapters 6 and 7 pointed out, that the American public is less well informed. Even though information bombards modern citizens, most Americans do not pay close attention to political issues. And those who obtain their political knowledge from television learn from short stories with quick, splashy visual images—not from in-depth analysis.

The Rise of Talk Radio

Although most Americans report getting their news from television, political talk shows on radio have emerged in recent years as an important force in American politics. Many observers argue that Bill Clinton's skillful use of **talk radio** helped him to capture the White House in the 1992 election. Likewise, many observers believe that a steady drumbeat of criticism of the Democratic Congress on talk-radio shows helped propel the historic Republican takeover of the House and Senate in the 1994 elections.

Talk radio
Political talk shows on radio. Since the early 1990s, talk radio has emerged as an important force in American politics.

Originally derided as "Chicken Noodle News," CNN has become a major source of news and information for millions of Americans.

The popularity of talk radio is clear from the dramatic rise in the number of radio stations featuring political talk shows—from fewer than 250 such stations in the mid-1980s to more than 1,000 in 1995.[33] Rush Limbaugh, by far the most popular talk-show host, broadcasts five times a week on more than 650 radio stations across the country and draws an estimated audience of 20 million.[34] Public opinion surveys estimate that roughly half of all Americans listen to talk radio at least once a week, and as many as 25 percent listen three or more times a week.[35]

Fans of talk radio argue that it serves an important function in our democracy by enabling Americans to hold in-depth discussions of pressing political issues. Critics complain that talk radio is more likely to distort than to clarify issues because talk-show hosts need controversy to attract an audience. Critics also complain that radio talk shows favor conservative causes. Roughly 70 percent of radio talk-show hosts with an identifiable ideology are conservative, and by a more than two-to-one margin, listeners say that talk shows are more critical of Democrats than Republicans.[36]

Analysts disagree over whether the audience for talk radio is more conservative than the country as a whole, but they agree that it is not representative of the country in many important ways. Members of the talk-radio audience are more likely to be registered to vote (90 percent as compared to only 60 percent of the adult public as a whole); more likely to be male (60 percent compared to 50 percent); more likely to be college educated (39 percent compared to 16 percent); and more likely to be wealthy (30 percent earn more than $60,000 per year as compared to only 20 percent of the general public).[37] To the extent that talk radio influences elections and government policy, then, it reflects the concerns of an atypical group of Americans.

The Rapid Growth of the Internet

A relatively new technology that may dramatically change the way Americans learn about political issues and communicate their political views is the Internet, a worldwide network of computer networks also referred to as the "information superhighway" and "cyberspace." Surveys indicate that somewhere between 10 and 15 million Americans had access to the Internet in 1995.[38] Most experts believe the number of Internet users will increase many times over in the next several decades.

With the Internet only in its infancy, the news media are just starting to exploit its potential.[39] The *New York Times,* the *Wall Street Journal,* and more than one thousand other newspapers now post some or all of their news articles on the World Wide

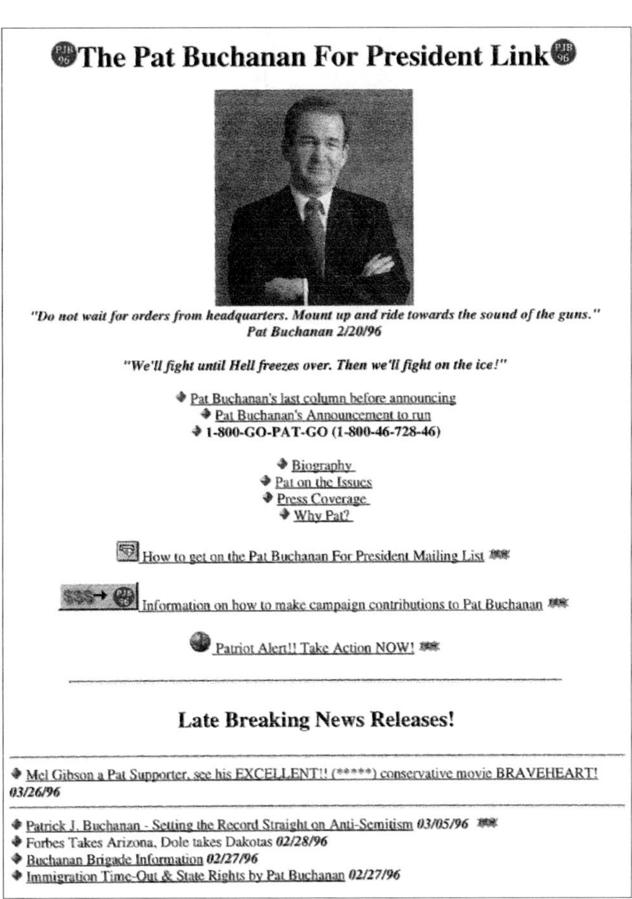

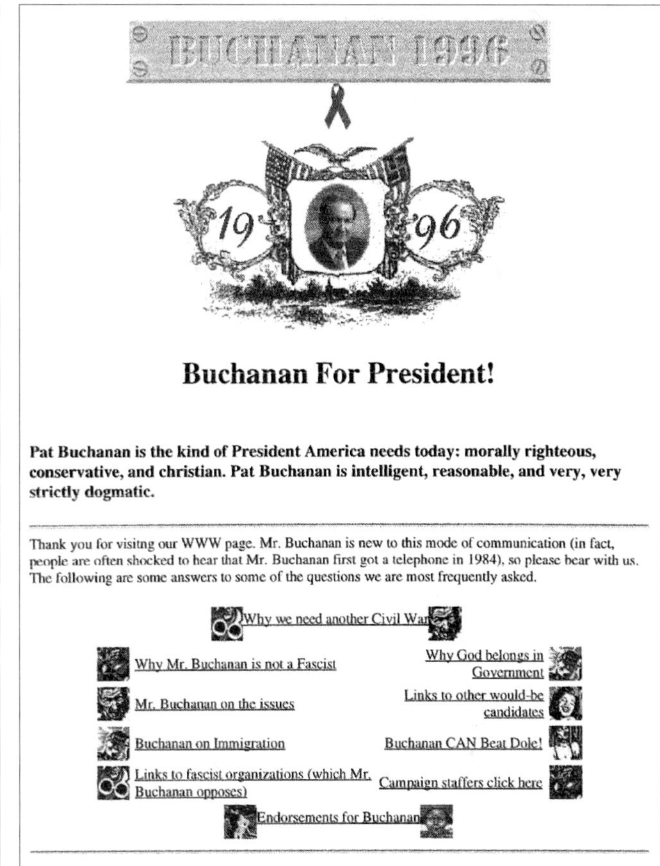

In 1996, presidential candidates rushed to set up "home pages" on the World Wide Web, but their critics soon followed suit with imitation home pages that satirized the candidates' views. (Note the swastika on the flag on the imitation home page on the right.) Some observers worry that many Americans will not be able to separate fact from fiction on the Internet.

Web—a portion of the Internet that enables users to transmit graphs, videos, and sound as well as text. In the future, subscribers will be able to use the Internet to obtain personalized copies of newspapers and television news shows that feature only articles on subjects that interest them.

Government agencies, elected officials, candidates for public office, and political interest groups are also learning how to use the Internet as a tool of education and persuasion. One of the first things Republicans did after taking control of the House of Representatives in 1995 was to make it possible for Americans to get copies of pending legislation through the Internet.[40] Likewise, all the major candidates in the 1996 presidential campaign set up *home pages*—electronic addresses on the World Wide Web—where Americans could obtain information about the candidates' stands on various issues, read biographies of their lives, and even sign up to work for a campaign.[41]

The exact impact of the Internet on American politics stirs much debate. Optimists contend that the Internet will improve the quality of political debate by making it easier for Americans to learn about issues that matter to them and to communicate their views to public officials. Pessimists worry, however, that many Americans, and particularly poor Americans, will not have access to the Internet and those that do will be buried under a mound of information they are not prepared to evaluate.

Changes in Media Ownership

The changes in what Americans read and watch have been accompanied by changes in the patterns of media ownership. Today, the news media are big business. The nine most influential national news organizations—ABC, CBS, NBC, the *New York Times*, the *Washington Post*, the *Wall Street Journal*, the *Los Angeles Times*, *Newsweek*, and *Time*—are all owned by corporations that rank among the five hundred largest in the United

When Walt Disney Company bought Capital Cities/ABC, critics complained that this and other media mergers would diminish editorial diversity and further blur the line separating entertainment from news.

Jimmy Margulies/Reprinted with special permission of North America Syndicate.

States. Even more striking than the size of many media companies is the trend toward greater concentration in ownership. In 1981, just forty-six corporations controlled a majority of the business in newspapers, radio, television, magazines, books, and movies. Nine years later, the number had shrunk to twenty.[42] And in 1995 alone, Walt Disney Company bought Capital Cities/ABC (the parent company of ABC), Westinghouse bought CBS, and Time-Warner bought Turner Broadcasting (the parent company of CNN).

The trend toward increased concentration of ownership is most evident with newspapers. Between 1960 and 1985, newspaper chains, that is, companies that own more than two daily newspapers in different cities, increased their share of total daily newspaper circulation from 46 to 77 percent.[43] In 1995, for instance, the Gannett Company owned *USA Today* as well as ninety-two other dailies, and Knight-Ridder owned twenty-seven daily newspapers, including the Detroit *Free Press,* the Miami *Herald,* and the Philadelphia *Inquirer*.[44]

Ownership of radio and television stations is less concentrated than newspaper ownership. The reason is that for many years, government policy deliberately sought to prevent concentrated "ownership" of the airwaves. Because the laws of physics limit the number of broadcast channels, and because of the belief that the public is best served by having a variety of broadcast voices, the federal government has since the 1940s limited ownership of television and radio stations. For many years, broadcast companies were subject to a 7–7–7 rule on cross-ownership—a single company could own at most seven AM, seven FM, and seven television stations. In the early 1980s, the rule was changed to 12–12–12, with no more than two of each in the nation's largest media markets. And in 1992, the limit on radio stations was raised to twenty AM and twenty FM outlets. The rules on media ownership were loosened on the grounds that the success of cable television and the development of other technologies for delivering television to America's homes had reduced the possibility that a few broadcasters could dominate the nation's airwaves.

In 1996, the push to deregulate the telecommunications industry culminated in the passage of the Telecommunications Competition and Deregulation Act.[45] The new law eliminated many of the restrictions on media ownership. Most important, it freed companies to own as many local television stations as they want as long as the combined audiences of their stations do not exceed 35 percent of the American public. The bill also eliminated the national limit on the ownership of radio stations and loosened the rules restricting ownership of multiple stations in the same city. Most experts expect that the decision to relax the restrictions on media ownership will lead to further concentration in the industry as companies take advantage of the new rules.[46]

Even with the remaining limits on ownership, a single broadcast company can influence what many Americans see and hear. In 1996, for instance, Westinghouse owned fifteen television stations that reached 33 percent of the American public, and ABC owned eight stations that reached 25 percent of the public.[47] And these figures understate the reach of the networks. Through the affiliated stations that make up each broadcast network, ABC, CBS, and NBC reach virtually the entire country with their news and entertainment programming. CNN reaches more than half of all American households.[48] This demonstrates the tremendous potential of a single company to influence the political views of huge numbers of people.

Although most radio and television stations are owned by companies seeking to make a profit, noncommercial or public broadcasting also exists. Established in 1967, the Public Broadcasting System consisted in 1996 of 345 television stations, plus 548 radio stations linked together as National Public Radio.[49] In place of advertising revenue, public broadcasting depends on government funding, foundation and corporation grants, and viewer and listener donations. The Corporation for Public Broadcasting, an independent federal agency, oversees public broadcasting. To insulate programming decisions from political pressure, the corporation handles only administrative issues. But its ability to withhold funding from programs it dislikes gives the corporation some say in programming decisions.[50] This is a good example of how the rules that empower the news media may also restrict their power.

Is the increased concentration of media ownership a matter of concern? Some observers argue that it is. They fear that as more and more media outlets are owned by a handful of large corporations, the diversity of news coverage and editorial opinion will diminish. The result will be a homogenized news media that restricts rather than promotes robust debate on the issues the country faces. The ultimate fear is that the number of independent media companies will shrink so far that the checks on media power will erode, and the few large companies that remain in business will have extraordinary influence over what Americans think.

Whether the increased concentration of media ownership has in fact homogenized news coverage and diminished editorial diversity is unclear. Efforts to study the question have produced mixed results.[51] Yet despite the increased concentration of media ownership, three key factors tend to promote news and editorial diversity in the United States. First, as we have just seen, the federal government regulates ownership of the electronic media with an eye toward preserving a diverse array of broadcast voices. Second, the expansion of cable television and the Internet increasingly exposes Americans to new sources of information. Third, media companies are in business to make money, and they do so by meeting the needs of their audience. If a substantial number of Americans should become dissatisfied with existing news coverage, some company is likely to try to provide coverage more to their liking.

Freedom of the Press

Thomas Jefferson wrote that "Our liberty depends on freedom of the press, and that cannot be limited without being lost."[52] The American press today enjoys the freedom that Jefferson believed was so vital to liberty. Unlike journalists in many African and Asian countries, journalists in the United States do not need a government license to work. Unlike journalists in China and North Korea, they do not need to clear their stories with a government censor. And unlike journalists in Great Britain, they seldom need worry that government officials may limit their right to report on a story. For journalists in the United States, freedom from government censorship and harassment rests in the blanket declaration of the First Amendment: "Congress shall make no law . . . abridging the freedom . . . of the press." This rule underpins our cherished notions of the news media's right to report and the people's right to know.

At first glance, the rule set forth in the First Amendment might seem to give the news media unbridled power. After all, it suggests that the media are not only free to decide which issues are important, but free to report on them in any way they please.

Yet very real constraints limit the power of the media. As we saw in chapter 4, the courts have long recognized limits to "freedom of the press." Newspapers, radio, and television must all observe libel and obscenity laws. Journalists also must overcome a variety of obstacles to gather the news. And, because the number of broadcast channels is limited, radio and television must follow regulations that do not apply to the print press.

Limits to Press Freedom

Several legal checks restrict the freedom of the media to report the news, including libel laws, obscenity laws, and prior restraint. The most common legal check by far is libel law. As chapter 4 discussed, the media cannot legally write or broadcast a story that unjustly injures a person's reputation. The media are also barred from publishing or showing obscene materials, though as a practical matter, obscenity laws seldom affect news coverage. A third possible legal check on the news media is prior restraint. As we saw in our discussion of the Pentagon Papers and *Business Week* cases in chapter 4, however, the circumstances under which the courts will bar the media in advance from reporting a story are extremely limited.

Besides these legal checks, the media find that several other factors constrain their ability to report the news, including government secrecy, government pressure, and limited access to news stories. After World War II, the federal government created a system for classifying government documents—some twenty million documents are now marked secret each year. Less than half a million of these involve national security matters. Most involve politically or personally sensitive material such as policy proposals and background checks on government personnel.[53] Because much of the classification system was created through executive orders issued by presidents rather than by laws passed by Congress, the media violate no laws when they obtain and publish government secrets. The one exception involves publishing classified information about intelligence operations, which is forbidden by law.

Freedom of Information Act
An act of Congress passed in 1966 that created a system through which anyone can petition the government to declassify secret documents.

Concerns about excessive secrecy led Congress to pass the **Freedom of Information Act** in 1966. The act created a system through which anyone can petition the government to declassify documents. In practice, the act has displeased many. On the one hand, some in government argue that it leads to the publication of information that should remain secret. Many journalists, on the other hand, argue that the government declassifies information grudgingly, continuing to impede their ability to gather the news.

In addition to confronting government secrecy, the news media also find that government pressure to some degree constrains their ability to report the news. In some circumstances, the government may threaten to prosecute reporters for violating espionage laws, as the Reagan administration did on several occasions.[54] More commonly, government officials pressure the media by ostracizing journalists they dislike. Journalists depend heavily on access to officials for their stories, so when they lose access, they lose stories. A spokesperson for Ronald Reagan punished journalists he disliked by seeing that no one in the White House press office took their calls.[55] After a CNN reporter asked President George Bush about published allegations that he had a long-running affair with his appointments secretary, a Bush spokesperson vowed that the reporter "would never work around the White House again."[56] Of course, officials do not actually have to deny access to put pressure on journalists. The mere possibility that an important government official may respond to a critical story by refusing to return phone calls may be sufficient to temper the zeal of some reporters.

Another way government officials try to pressure the news media is by accusing reporters of bias. Officials hope that journalists will respond to such charges by leaning over backwards to be fair. Thus, complaining about the media is, as one adviser to President Bush put it, rather like a coach "playing the referees" in the hope of winning by intimidation.[57]

During the Gulf War, the Defense Department imposed a pool reporting system that required journalists in the war zone to travel in small groups accompanied by a military escort. Many journalists complained that pool reporting made it more difficult for them to cover the news.

Along with facing government secrecy and pressure, the media sometimes meet constraints when the government denies them access to news stories. This happens most often with regard to U.S. military operations. Because many military officials believe that news coverage undermined public support for the Vietnam War, they have been determined to prevent journalists covering a future war from having the same freedom to report that journalists enjoyed in Vietnam (as well as in World War II and Korea). When the United States invaded Grenada in 1983, the Defense Department declined to include journalists with the invasion force. The military even prevented journalists from reaching Grenada on their own, going as far as to send a fighter plane on a mock bombing run of a boat journalists chartered.[58]

Not surprisingly, journalists cried censorship. The Defense Department responded to the complaints by creating a system of **pool reporting,** a procedure under which military officers escort small groups of selected reporters through the war zone. The pool system figured prominently during the Gulf War as Saudi society and geography made it easy to limit media access to the front. Many journalists criticized the pool system, though, arguing that it prevented them from covering the news. Some journalists, so-called unilaterals, refused to participate in the pool system and operated on their own.[59] After the war ended, seventeen major news organizations issued a report that denounced the military's restrictions on reporting as "real censorship" that confirmed "the worst fears of reporters in a democracy."[60] None of the complaints, however, prompted the Defense Department to abandon the pool system.[61]

Pool reporting
A system the Defense Department instituted in the 1980s for reporting from a combat zone during wartime. With pool reporting, military officials escort small groups of reporters when they interview American troops.

The restrictions on news reporting—libel laws, obscenity laws, prior restraint, government secrecy and pressure, and limited access to stories—might seem to put a considerable damper on the ability of the media to report the news. Yet in practice, only a tiny minority of news stories run afoul of any of these restrictions. Instead, as the First Amendment promises, journalists in the United States have a great deal of freedom to pursue and report on the vast majority of news stories.

The Electronic Media

The electronic media, that is, television and radio, must deal with numerous regulations that do not apply to the print press. Two factors explain the rationale for additional constraints on the electronic media. One is the so-called scarcity argument. The number of broadcast channels is limited, which in turn limits competition among electronic media. In contrast, anyone offended by newspaper coverage can in theory start a new newspaper. The other argument is that the airwaves belong to the public and not to any individual or corporation; hence, more government control is warranted.

Federal Communications Commission (FCC)
An independent federal agency that regulates interstate and international communication by radio, television, telephone, telegraph, cable, and satellite.

The agency that oversees the electronic media is the **Federal Communications Commission (FCC),** an independent federal regulatory agency headed by a seven-member commission. The president appoints the members of the panel. The FCC's job is to regulate the electronic media in "the public interest, convenience, or necessity." Since its creation in 1934, the FCC's jurisdiction has grown to include AM and FM radio, broadcast television, cable television, commercial satellites, CBs, and cellular telephones.

The FCC has four main tasks. One is to administer the rules on cross-ownership. Another is to set technical standards for the communications industry. In 1993, for example, the FCC chose the technical standard for high-definition television, a new technology used to make televisions that produce much crisper and clearer images. By setting such technical standards, the FCC ensures that telephones and televisions bought in one region will work throughout the country.

The third task the FCC performs is to license television and radio stations to use the public airwaves. (Individual cities and towns control the charters for cable television.) Radio and television stations must renew their licenses every five to seven years. The FCC denies renewal applications only when stations violate its regulations—which, it turns out, seldom occurs.[62] Since radio and television stations can be worth tens and even hundreds of millions of dollars, station owners have a strong incentive to heed the wishes of the FCC.

The fourth task of the FCC is to set and administer broadcast standards. The standards define things such as how frequently stations must identify themselves and what words and images they can use on air (decency standards). For instance, in 1995, the FCC fined the company that produces Howard Stern's radio show $1.7 million for the "shock jock's" indecent comments on air.[63] A more important broadcast regulation for politics is the **equal-time provision,** which requires radio and television stations to provide all candidates for the same public office with access to the airwaves under the same conditions. Thus, a station cannot give free air time, say, to one candidate for Congress and deny it to another.[64] The equal-time provision does not, however, apply to news coverage. Congress passed the law requiring the FCC to monitor compliance with the equal-time provision because it wanted to ensure a level playing field for political debate in the United States.

Equal-time provision
A federal law that stipulates that if a radio or television station gives or sells air time to a candidate for political office, it must provide all candidates for public office with access to the airwaves under the same conditions.

Fairness doctrine
A regulation the FCC adopted in 1949 and repealed in 1987. It required broadcasters to provide "reasonable opportunities for the expression of opposing views on controversial issues of public importance."

Another broadcast standard that regulated how the electronic media handled political issues for almost forty years was the **fairness doctrine,** which required stations to provide "reasonable opportunities for the expression of opposing views on controversial issues of public importance." Like the equal-time provision, the fairness doctrine did not apply to news coverage, but unlike the equal-time provision, it was an FCC-created rule rather than a law Congress passed. The FCC created the fairness doctrine in 1949 to prevent stations from using their public affairs programming to advance a particular party or candidate.

Critics of the fairness doctrine complained that it was never applied to unpopular points of view, that many stations shied away from political issues entirely to avoid violating the doctrine, and that it violated the First Amendment. On the last point, the Supreme Court disagreed. Although the Court has struck down laws requiring newspapers to provide equal space for opposing points of view, it ruled that the shortage of broadcast channels justified the fairness doctrine.[65] As a practical matter, however, the issue is moot. In 1987, the FCC repealed the fairness doctrine on the grounds that the growth of cable television made it unnecessary. Efforts by members of Congress to enact the fairness doctrine into law failed to make much headway.

Although radio and television are subject to greater federal regulation than newspapers, they still enjoy tremendous freedom to choose what they will broadcast. Unlike governments in many other democracies, the federal government cannot dictate the content of radio and television programs. Indeed, while the FCC can require the electronic media to follow certain broadcast standards, the legislation that created the agency specifically forbids it from censoring individual programs or otherwise interfering with the right to free speech. Of course, as critics of the fairness doctrine suggest, federal regulations may indirectly influence programming content. But even here, the effect of government regulations on programming content is unintended and, in all likelihood, quite minor.

Reporting the News

How do the media decide what is news? And once they decide which stories to cover, how do they determine how to tell a story? The answers to these two questions are critical precisely because we depend on newspapers, radio, and television to tell us what is happening in the world. As we discussed earlier, whether the media decide to cover an issue or ignore it plays an enormous role in shaping the political agenda. Moreover, the way the media cover a story has an enormous potential to influence the public's views on an issue.

What Is News?

What constitutes "news" is a subjective matter. Every day, thousands of events happen that could be news—the president begins a ten-day trip to Asia, Congress debates a crime bill, the mayor announces the city budget. But the news media cannot cover every possible story. Each newspaper, magazine, and newscast has a limited *news hole,* the amount of space left for news stories after it takes all advertisements, commercials, and features into account. Network television news has an exceptionally tight news hole, only twenty-two minutes. (Commercials take up the other eight.) Because space is limited, journalists must choose which stories they will cover and which they will not.

How do journalists select the news? Three specific selection criteria stand out: conflict, proximity, and timeliness.[66]

Conflict

Journalists gravitate toward conflict. Wars, fires, heated debates, scandals—these stories dominate the news. The reason for the bias toward conflict is simple: journalists see their job as ferreting out bad news. As Sam Donaldson, the long-time ABC correspondent puts it, the reporter's job is "to find out who did botch what, where, when, why, and how, and what's on the front burner for possible botching tomorrow."[67] Defining news as conflict means that the media tend to cover the failures of government rather than its successes, which helps to explain why President Clinton complained to *Rolling Stone* that the press was treating his administration unfairly. The news media's emphasis on failure can breed an adversarial relationship between journalists and politicians.

Proximity

The news media select stories that are likely to affect the lives of their audience. As one scholar describes it, "Newspaper and wire service reporters quite early in their professional lives absorb the rough rule of thumb that, in terms of reader interest, '10,000 deaths in Nepal equals 100 deaths in Wales equals 10 deaths in West Virginia equals one death next door.' "[68] Thus, a newspaper in a farm state such as Kansas is far more likely to cover the new government policy on farm subsidies than its counterpart in a big city such as New York. In turn, what Kansans identify as pressing public policy issues may differ sharply from what New Yorkers do. The divergence of interest and proximity will be an increasingly important factor in shaping news coverage as the population in the United States becomes more diverse and technological advances make it possible to increase the number of media outlets.

News reporting often becomes pack journalism as large numbers of journalists cover the same story.

Timeliness

The media prefer to cover the new and the unusual. As an old saying in journalism puts it, "It's only news when man bites dog." The corollary to this is that routine events lose their attractiveness as news. In late 1984, for example, famine in Ethiopia became a major story. By early 1985, however, the story had disappeared from the news, even though famine continued to plague Ethiopia and other countries in Africa. The story faded because the media came to see it as old hat. As an executive for NBC News remarked: "What I'm about to say sounds very cruel, but when you hear that we have another famine story from Ethiopia there is a tendency to assume that it's just more of a story that seems to be eternal."[69]

Other Influences on News Selection

Pack journalism
The tendency of journalists to cover stories because other journalists are covering them and to ignore stories that other journalists aren't covering.

In addition to conflict, proximity, and timeliness, two other factors also influence the selection of specific news stories. First, journalists select news stories with an eye to what their colleagues are reporting—that is, **pack journalism** often governs news reporting.[70] "Reporters feel pressure not necessarily to get the exclusive or the scoop but to get the story everyone else is covering. In their cost-benefit calculations, they worry more about the embarrassment of having missed a story than the satisfaction of having beaten everyone else to the punch."[71] The key agenda setters are the *New York Times* and the *Washington Post.* Robert Parry, a veteran reporter for both the Associated Press and *Newsweek,* says that if the *Times* and *Post* decide something is "not news, it's very hard to convince your editors at AP and even at *Newsweek* that it *is* news. Because they don't see it in the morning papers that they read. So they think, is this a guy who is off on his own tangent, following something that really isn't a story, that's going to get us in trouble?"[72] Although pack journalism is commonplace, it has a distinct weakness: because reporters travel in groups and watch the same events, they are far more susceptible to manipulation at the hands of government officials than if they worked on their own.

Second, television adds another factor in deciding what's news, namely, the availability of exciting, splashy video. Because viewers want to see more than Peter Jennings reading out loud, whether a story gets on the air may depend less on its intrinsic newsworthiness than on whether it comes with dramatic video images. A CBS executive explained the problem by comparing television's zeal for covering natural disasters such as erupting volcanoes with its aversion to covering complicated issues such as the debt problems affecting the world's poorer countries. "The volcano wasn't there yesterday and is there today—that's television news. But with a low-level simmering

TABLE 8.2 Story Topics Selected for Network Evening Newscasts, 1973–1981 (in percent)

By far the most popular story topics on the network evening newscasts are stories on domestic politics, domestic economics, and international politics.

Topic	ABC	CBS	NBC
Domestic politics	30.7%	34.6%	33.0%
Domestic economics	20.4	19.0	17.5
International politics	18.3	17.2	18.3
Sports and human interest	6.1	5.2	6.6
Science, technology, art	4.8	5.3	5.2
Social policies	3.5	3.9	4.3
International economics	2.8	1.6	2.3
Miscellaneous	13.4	13.1	13.0

Note: Figures may not add to 100 percent due to rounding.

Source: Adapted from Daniel Riffe, Brenda Ellis, Momo K. Rogers, Roger L. Van Ommeren, and Kieran A. Woodman, "Gatekeeping and the Network News Mix," *Journalism Quarterly* 63 (Summer 1986): 315–21.

sort of issue like the debt, it just doesn't work. People the next morning say, 'Gee, did you see the footage of that volcano last night on the news?' But nobody gets up in the morning and says, 'Gee, did you hear about that debt in Brazil?' "[73]

Absent from the list of criteria the media use to select news stories is the importance of a story. Many journalists argue, however, that their focus on conflict, proximity, and timeliness generally produces the most important stories of the day. But as the waning coverage of the Ethiopian famine attests, some stories of great significance may fail to meet the media's definition of news.

Despite the fact that news is the product of subjective choice, journalists agree to a great extent on what constitutes the news of the day. This is seen most clearly on the evening news on ABC, CBS, and NBC. Studies find that on a typical night, roughly half the stories on each newscast are the same.[74] The networks agree even more on the most important story of the day. One study found that 91 percent of the time, two of the three networks lead their evening newscast with the same story, and 43 percent of the time, all three lead with the same story.[75]

What stories do the media cover? The answer obviously varies among media outlets. Table 8.2 shows the story choices of the evening network newscasts over an eight-year period. By far the most popular topics are stories on domestic politics, the domestic economy, and international politics. In contrast, the network newscasts devote relatively little time to sports, science, and international economics. Table 8.2 also reconfirms the point that journalists agree to a surprising extent on what constitutes news. All three network newscasts present roughly the same mix of stories. They agree to an amazing degree on which issues matter to the American public.

Telling the Story

The power of the news media rests in two areas: defining the issues by deciding what qualifies as news and then deciding how to report on those issues. We have just discussed the rules that journalists use to decide what constitutes news. Once they determine an event is news, what rules do journalists follow in telling the story to their audience?

It is tempting to answer that journalists tell their stories by holding a mirror up to reality. But while journalists can strive to be impartial, they cannot be mirrors. Telling a story requires answers to dozens of questions. Should the story on the local school board meeting lead off with the discussion of teacher salaries or the debate on overcrowded classrooms? Should the story run on page one or page ten? Does the story merit a photo? If so, should the shot be of a single member of the school board or all of them? Because people can disagree over the "right" answers to these questions, purely objective news coverage is unattainable.

Journalists rely heavily on government sources for news.

TABLE 8.3 The Affiliation of Sources the News Media Uses (in percent)

Source Affiliation	Local Newspaper	Local Television	National Newspaper	Network Television
U.S. government	15.9%	7.7%	32.3%	32.5%
State government	14.9	14.8	5.4	2.6
Local government	17.2	26.8	5.9	2.1
Foreign government	0.4	0.0	11.1	11.4
Affiliated U.S. citizen	36.0	28.2	25.1	32.9
Unaffiliated U.S. citizen	6.0	14.1	4.3	8.1
Foreign citizen	0.4	0.0	4.2	1.7
Other	9.3	8.5	11.8	8.5
Number of sources	804	142	2,363	234

Note: The local newspapers analyzed were the *Charlotte Observer*, the *Asheville Citizen*, the *Fayetteville Observer*, and the *Raleigh News and Observer*. The national newspapers analyzed were the *New York Times* and the *Washington Post*. The local television stations were three stations in Indianapolis, Indiana, and two stations in Terre Haute, Indiana.

Sources: Data from Dan Berkowitz, "TV News Sources and News Channels: A Study in Agenda Building," *Journalism Quarterly* 64 (Summer-Autumn 1987): 511; Jane Delano Brown, Carl R. Bybee, Stanley T. Weardon, and Dulcie Murdock, "Invisible Power: Newspaper News Sources and the Limits of Diversity," *Journalism Quarterly* 64 (Spring 1987): 49.

How do journalists square the impossibility of pure objectivity with the desire to tell the news impartially? They do so by following rules designed to minimize subjective reporting. While government enacts rules such as libel law to ensure fair reporting, journalists set their own rules for reporting objectively. Four basic rules stand out:[76]

Rule 1: Keep personal preferences out of the story. From their first day in journalism school, reporters learn that reporting and advocacy do not mix. Journalists are not supposed to inject their personal feelings into a story.

Rule 2: Avoid using obviously value-laden words. The words used to describe a person or an event have tremendous power to color how readers and viewers see the world. People who would vote for a "conservative" candidate might oppose a "reactionary" one. Troops that "slaughter" their foes are viewed differently than troops that "kill" their foes. To avoid slanting a story, reporters shy away from words such as *reactionary* and *slaughter* that convey clear value judgments.

Rule 3: Get both sides of the story. Journalists assume that news stories have two sides (no more and no less). So when they cover a story, they seek the views of each side. Thus, when the Supreme Court rules on an abortion case, reporters interview leaders of both the pro-choice and pro-life movements for their reactions. Journalists are not, however, supposed to decide which side is right. That decision belongs to the audience.

Rule 4: Rely on "responsible" sources for information. Journalists define responsible sources as people who occupy positions of authority. As table 8.3 shows, positions of authority mean first and foremost government officials. Both local and national media rely heavily on government sources for news. When reporters seek sources outside of government, they speak mainly to people who work for organizations ("affiliated U.S. citizen") rather than to average people ("unaffiliated U.S. citizen"). Thus a story on the health of the auto industry is more likely to feature interviews with General Motors executives than with unemployed auto workers.

Journalists themselves admit they sometimes fail to follow the four basic rules of objective journalism. This happens most often when a consensus exists in society on an issue.[77] For instance, journalistic detachment frequently disappears when journalists

When the news media showed several American students kissing the ground after returning to the United States from Grenada in October 1983, many people concluded that the Reagan administration was justified in deciding to invade the small Caribbean nation. In fact, many students believed the invasion had put their lives in unnecessary danger.

cover U.S. military actions abroad.[78] During the Gulf War, CBS anchor Dan Rather ended one news bulletin by saluting American troops in Saudi Arabia.[79] Likewise, reporters frequently use value-laden words when describing criminals and communists. Most Americans consider these individuals societal outcasts; hence, they do not receive evenhanded treatment.

Yet even scrupulous attention to the rules does not guarantee objective or even fair reporting. Journalists can suppress their personal opinions but still (inadvertently or willfully) slant the story by whom they quote and what they show. The United States, for example, invaded Grenada in 1983, ostensibly to rescue American students endangered by a coup on the island. The students themselves disagreed over whether they had been in jeopardy. Still, film of the students returning to the United States focused on the few who kissed the ground upon arriving. Although the photos were accurate, they distorted reality by implying that most or all of the students supported the invasion.[80]

By the same token, avoiding value-laden terms does not end the problem of word usage. Many words carry more subtle value judgments. As press critic A. J. Liebling notes, when the media cover labor disputes and strikes, they describe management as making "offers" while labor unions make "demands."[81] Bombs are often planted by IRA "gunmen" but Palestinian "terrorists." The difference in wording may well reflect the fact that many more Americans are of Irish descent than Palestinian descent.

The injunction to get both sides of the story also creates problems. With some stories, attempts to balance one view against another distorts the issue. As famed CBS newsman Edward R. Murrow once complained, strict adherence to the command to present both sides of the story would require journalists to balance the views of Jesus Christ with those of Judas Iscariot.[82]

The reliance on responsible sources creates still other problems. One is that journalists often have no story if responsible sources will not talk about an issue. When public criticism of President Reagan's policy toward El Salvador rose in 1981, Reagan "administration officials simply stopped talking about Central America to reporters and . . . news coverage, especially on television, immediately dried up."[83] The other problem is that responsible sources inevitably bias news coverage toward the views of political and economic elites. As one researcher argues, the beliefs and desires of the poor and the powerless generally don't interest the media "until their activities produce social or moral disorder news."[84]

Thus, while journalists may try to be fair and objective, they are forced to make many subjective decisions when they report the news. Deciding what is a news story and exactly how to tell it gives the media, whether they seek it or not, great potential influence over public opinion and public policy. It is precisely the potential power of the news media to set the political agenda for government and to influence the terms of debate that has prompted many to complain about how journalists carry out their jobs.

Many conservatives in the United States believe that the news media have a liberal bias.

Evaluating the News Media

We noted at the start of this chapter that the success of American democracy rests on the existence of a free press. Without it, the American people would be unable to monitor much of what the government does and to decide whether they like the policies their elected officials are pursuing. Yet dependence on the news media for information about government creates a potential problem: the press may abuse its power by distorting the information it provides. If the news media fail to report accurately, or if they ignore some stories in favor of others, the results could compromise the democratic process in the United States.

How well, then, do the media perform their job of reporting the news? The answers to that question vary. Virtually everyone at one time or another takes offense at how the media cover the news. Indeed, much criticism of the news media comes from journalists. Far more than any other profession, journalists publicly discuss their job performance. Magazines such as *American Journalism Review* and *Columbia Journalism Review* debate whether journalists have performed their jobs well. Many newspapers devote space on their editorial pages each week to an ombudsperson, a person whose job is to evaluate the work of the paper. The news media are especially susceptible to criticism because, as we have seen, reporting a story requires journalists to make so many subjective choices.

In this section, we review five common complaints about the news media: (1) they are ideologically biased; (2) they are excessively cynical; (3) they increasingly treat news as entertainment; (4) they do a poor job of covering elections; and (5) they complicate the task of governing by reporting stories based on leaks of confidential government information. Each of these complaints raises questions about whether the news media are harming the democratic process in the United States.

Ideological Bias

Many Americans believe the news media are ideologically biased. Although some complain that the media favor conservative causes, most complaints accuse journalists of a liberal bias. Republicans have been especially persistent in lambasting reporters for "liberal-left" journalism, but as we saw at the start of the chapter, even some Democrats have accused the media of tilting toward the left.

At first glance, the claim that the media promote liberal causes and undermine conservative ones might seem odd. After all, three times in the 1980s, the American public voted overwhelmingly for conservative candidates for president; conservative

TABLE 8.4 Positions of the General Public, College-Educated Professionals, and Journalists on Selected Issues (in percent)

Journalists are far more likely than the average American to consider themselves liberal, and while they share many of the public's views on economic issues, they are more liberal on social issues.

Position	Public	College-Educated Professionals	Journalists
Consider self			
Liberal	23%	38%	55%
Conservative	19	30	17
Economic Issues			
Sympathize with			
Business	33	52	27
Labor	32	27	31
Government regulation of business			
Favor	22	26	49
Oppose	50	57	41
Government aid to those unable to support themselves			
Favor	83	81	95
Oppose	11	12	3
Government should reduce income inequality			
Favor	55	56	50
Oppose	23	24	39
Social Issues			
Allow women to have abortions			
Favor	49	68	82
Oppose	44	28	14
Prayer in public schools			
Favor	74	58	25
Oppose	19	36	67
Affirmative action			
Favor	56	67	81
Oppose	21	20	14
Death penalty			
For	75	67	47
Against	17	26	47

Note: The poll was conducted in 1985. It surveyed 2,993 members of the general public plus 2,703 news and editorial staff members on 621 papers. The top editor at 587 of the newspapers was also interviewed. All respondents were asked the same questions. The figures exclude "neutral" and "don't know" responses.

Source: Data from William Schneider and I. A. Lewis, "Views on the News," *Public Opinion* 8 (August/September 1985): 7.

hosts, as we have seen, dominate talk radio; and, as his attack on the press suggests, Bill Clinton received considerable negative news coverage both as a candidate and as president.[85] Moreover, by historical standards, modern journalism is the epitome of impartiality. No major newspaper would stamp the word *fraud* on the forehead of each picture of Bill Clinton as one New York paper did to Rutherford B. Hayes. Nor would the media today run an editorial declaring that "if bad institutions and bad men can be got rid of only by killing, then the killing must be done" as a Hearst paper did when William McKinley was president.[86] (McKinley was assassinated five months after the editorial, though the two events were not connected.)

Despite anecdotal evidence to the contrary, claims that the media favor liberal causes persist. To assess such claims, many scholars have turned to survey research.[87] As table 8.4 shows, journalists are far more likely to consider themselves liberal than does the public, though roughly equal percentages of both groups see themselves as conservative. And while journalists share many of the public's views on economic issues, they are far more liberal on social issues. Journalists are also more liberal than other college-educated professionals they might be expected to resemble. (Nearly 90 percent of journalists are college educated, compared to only 16 percent of the public.)[88] Finally, Washington-based journalists are more liberal than their colleagues elsewhere in the country.[89]

Do these surveys mean that the media favor liberal views in their reporting? No. Surveys tell us nothing about what journalists write. And the gap between what journalists think and what they write may be large. After all, the journalistic conventions we discussed in the last section are designed specifically to minimize the impact of a journalist's beliefs, whether liberal or conservative, on how the news is reported.

The emphasis placed on survey data also mistakenly assumes that the news reflects the work of lone journalists. But most reporting is a team effort. Group journalism is most pronounced in television. A report on the nightly news involves the work of many people besides the correspondent: research assistants, the sound and camera crews, the field producer, the managing editor, and the anchor. Newspaper reporters likewise must deal with bureau chiefs, copy editors, and managing editors. This teamwork helps temper individual opinions that might otherwise be more noticeable.

Journalists also must report to an array of corporate executives—many of whom are conservative. Corporate executives generally hire reporters who avoid advocacy in their reporting.[90] Indeed, the ability of corporate executives to hire and fire reporters raises the possibility that media coverage will have a conservative rather than a liberal bent as journalists curry favor with the people who set their salaries. And while the op-ed pages of the nation's newspapers feature a mix of liberal and conservative columnists, newspaper editorials show a conservative bent. For example, a study of some 1,500 newspapers in presidential election years 1976, 1980, and 1984 found that newspapers endorsed Republican candidates for president 80 percent of the time.[91] As you can see, then, journalistic conventions, team reporting, and corporate ownership all help limit bias in the news media.

Because survey research cannot evaluate the possibility of media bias, some scholars sift through actual news stories looking for signs of bias. Several studies of the 1992 presidential campaign, for example, found that President Bush received more negative news coverage than either Bill Clinton or Ross Perot. But such studies should be treated with great caution. Not only are definitions of "positive" and "negative" coverage inherently subjective, but such studies implicitly assume that each candidate should receive the same treatment. Such an assumption is unreasonable. Some candidates receive more negative news coverage because they run poor campaigns or fail to address the problems the public cares about. In the case of the 1992 campaign, for example, many observers argued that President Bush "acquired his negative coverage the hard way: he earned it."[92]

As the studies of the 1992 campaign suggest, charges that the news media favor liberal causes are impossible to disprove. Examples of unfair reporting will always be available because the very nature of reporting requires journalists to make dozens of decisions that reasonable people may disagree with. Indeed, as NBC News anchor Tom Brokaw points out, the subjectivity inherent in reporting the news means that "Bias, like beauty, is most often in the eye of the beholder."[93]

Cynicism

Talk of the possible ideological bias of the news media obscures a more pervasive bias in news coverage: the tendency to focus on the failures of government and to ignore its successes. As we saw earlier in the chapter, most journalists believe their job is to ferret out bad news. Indeed, journalists turn the old adage "no news is good news" on its head; in most news rooms, "good news is no news."[94]

Journalists defend their preoccupation with failures and misdeeds by arguing that the media's role is to act as a watchdog that monitors the actions of government. As one journalist puts it: "Our function in a democracy is to hold up to the public things that they have the ability to change, through their votes or pressures on public officials. We don't need to tell people that their roads are okay, because they don't need to do anything about that."[95] To carry out this watchdog role, journalists must inevitably be skeptical of what government does.

To many observers, however, the news media have gone beyond acting as a watchdog and have become an attack dog that assumes the worst about government officials and institutions. Speaker of the House Newt Gingrich complained in 1995 that the news media are "pathologically negative and cynical."[96] Some scholars agree. One recent study argued that "the press is contemptuous of politicians, whether liberal or conservative" and another concluded that the greatest impact of the news media lies in their "encouragement of cynicism."[97] Implicit in these criticisms is the fear that cynical news coverage will erode the public's faith in the country's democratic institutions.

Have the news media crossed the line that separates healthy skepticism from debilitating cynicism? As with charges of ideological bias, this is a difficult question to answer. One reason is that cynicism often lies in the eyes of the beholder. For example, Republicans might view a story questioning Newt Gingrich's fundraising practices as excessively cynical while Democrats see the same story as a solid piece of reporting. At the same time, journalists often have good reason to be cynical. Politicians have been known to change positions on an issue to curry favor with voters, and government agencies have been guilty of incompetence and duplicity.

The difficulty in agreeing on what constitutes excessive cynicism may help to explain why opinion polls show mixed results on the topic. A poll conducted in 1995 found that 54 percent of the journalists surveyed agreed that "the press is too cynical." However, two-thirds of these journalists disagreed with the statements that "the press is too adversarial" and "the press is too focused on reporting the misdeeds and personal failings of public figures." To further complicate matters, the poll found that a majority of Americans thinks that journalists are no more cynical than they are.[98]

If the degree of cynicism in news coverage is open to debate, virtually everyone agrees that the news media are more adversarial today toward government officials and institutions than they were several decades ago. When Franklin Roosevelt was president, for example, journalists generally respected his wish not to be photographed using crutches or a wheelchair. As a result, many Americans had no idea of the extent of Roosevelt's physical disabilities. Most observers attribute the rise of adversarial news coverage to the Watergate scandal of the early 1970s. As Ben Bradlee, who as editor of the *Washington Post* helped to break the Watergate story, puts it: "Journalism was forever changed by the assumption—by most journalists—after Watergate that government officials generally and instinctively lied when confronted by embarrassing events."[99]

Some media critics would like to see the news media return to a more deferential approach to news gathering. It is by no means clear, however, that the country would be better off with the type of reporting that prevailed before Watergate. Deferential news reporting carries its own risks. For example, one of the reasons McCarthyism became such a powerful and destructive force in American politics in the early 1950s was that few journalists dared to challenge Sen. Joseph McCarthy's (R-Wis.) false claims that many federal government officials were communists or communist sympathizers.

News as Entertainment

The media frenzy over the murder trial of O. J. Simpson illustrates a third complaint with news coverage: the tendency to treat news as entertainment. This tendency stems from the fact that the news media in the United States are privately owned. They make money by running advertisements, and the amount they can charge for advertising depends on the size of the audience they attract. But as the rise of cable television heated up the competition, newspapers, radio, and broadcast television saw their audiences diminish and their profits fall. Many media outlets have responded to the profit squeeze by favoring stories that emphasize the emotional, the novel, and the sensational.

Although the advent of cable television has made it easier for Americans to follow the news on television, they are much more likely to watch sports and entertainment channels such as ESPN than news channels such as CNN and C-SPAN.

TABLE 8.5 Size of the Audience for Cable News Channels Compared with Cable Entertainment Channels

Channel	Average Daily Number of Homes Watching
ESPN	525,000
CNN	**338,000**
Arts & Entertainment Network	335,000
Discovery Channel	313,000
Country Music Network	99,000
Cartoon Network	75,000
Comedy Central	66,000
C-SPAN	**less than 1,000**

Source: Data from Mark Robichaux, "Slicing It Thin," *Wall Street Journal*, 9 September 1994.

Of course, sensational news coverage hardly began with the Simpson trial (see box 8.2). But in recent years, more and more news stories have tended toward the interesting rather than the important. Bill Moyers, a prize-winning television commentator, complains: "Our center of gravity shifted from the standards and practices of the news business to show business. Pretty soon . . . tax policy had to compete with stories about three-legged sheep, and the three-legged sheep won."[100]

The trend away from "hard" news is perhaps most visible in local television news, where the operating maxim often is "If it bleeds, it leads."[101] But network television also shows a greater appetite for "soft" news. The nightly newscasts regularly devote their final few minutes to human interest stories, and the number of stories on show business nearly doubled from 1988 to 1990.[102] Many newspapers, in the meantime, are trying to attract new readers by increasing their sports coverage, adding life-style sections, and making news stories shorter.[103] Many newspapers are also following *USA Today's* lead in trying to attract readers through color graphics and photos—in short, by making themselves look more like their true competitor, television.

Media executives defend the move away from hard news on the grounds that they are giving the public what it wants. If the public demanded more in-depth coverage of banking regulations or of the positions of presidential candidates, they argue, they would gladly provide it.[104] This argument has considerable merit. As table 8.5 shows, fewer Americans watch CNN than ESPN on an average day, and the audience for C-SPAN lags behind that of Country Music Television, the Cartoon Network, and Comedy Central. But media executives may underestimate the American appetite for news. On the first night of the Gulf War, CNN saw its audience grow thirteen-fold.[105]

Whether the decline of hard news is due to a pandering news media or an apathetic public, the trend is troubling. By emphasizing the interesting over the important, the media can distort the public's perception of the problems facing the country. In turn, one must wonder how well a democracy can function if its citizens are ill-informed.

On the Campaign Trail

Horse-race journalism
News coverage of elections that focuses on which candidate is leading in the polls rather than on the substantive issues in the campaign.

To judge by the post-mortems of recent presidential campaigns, the news media do a poor job of covering elections. Critics single out three mistakes in particular. The first is that the media devote too much time to **horse-race journalism,** stories that focus on who's ahead in the race rather than on the issues in the campaign. One study of the 1992 election found that 29 percent of the campaign-related stories that ABC, CBS, and NBC aired on their evening news shows during the primary and general election campaigns dealt with which candidate was leading, whereas 38 percent dealt with the stands that each candidate took on the issues and 33 percent examined the character of the candidates.[106] Critics complain that by portraying elections as contests between individuals rather than as clashes of ideas—in essence, treating elections as sporting

Point of Order

BOX 8.2

The Changing Rules of News Coverage

ANSWERED PRAYERS

Brooklyn girl found safe in woods

DAILY NEWS

HEY, PAULA

Her X-rated suit seeks 700G from Clinton

PAULA JONES GOES PUBLIC IN LURID DETAIL SEE PAGES 4 & 5

KNICKS BOUNCE NETS

SEE SPORTS

Tabloid journalism focuses on the sensational, as when Paula Jones accused President Bill Clinton of having sexually harassed her when he was governor of Arkansas.

The media have come under fire over the past decade for sensationalizing the news. Critics have cried that the popularity of shows such as *A Current Affair* and *Hard Copy* has prompted the network television news shows to emphasize stories about sex, crime, and scandal. Critics also have denounced the media's growing interest in what politicians do in their bedrooms. Whereas journalists in the 1960s closed their eyes to John F. Kennedy's philandering, the alleged marital infidelities of Gary Hart, George Bush, and Bill Clinton have been the subject of intense media scrutiny.

For all the handwringing over tabloid television and voyeuristic journalism, sensationalist news coverage is nothing new in American society; rather it has waxed and waned in accordance with America's changing social mores. The first newspaper published in the United States, *Publick Occurrences, Both Foreign and Domestic*, reported in its first issue in 1690 that a local man had hanged himself and that the king of France was sleeping with his daughter-in-law. Given that *Publick Occurrences* was published in the Puritan-dominated Massachusetts Bay Colony, it is perhaps not surprising that the paper was barred from publishing a second edition.

Sex and scandal featured prominently in the 1828 race for the presidency. Newspapers that favored the candidacy of Andrew Jackson printed stories alleging that President John Quincy Adams had procured a young woman for the Russian czar while he was U.S. ambassador to Russia and that he had engaged in premarital sex. Newspapers that supported Adams's reelection returned fire with stories such as: "General Jackson's mother was a COMMON PROSTITUTE, brought to the country by the British soldiers. She afterward married a MULATTO MAN, with whom she had several children, of which number General JACKSON IS ONE!" Many newspapers also accused Jackson of living with his wife while she was still married to her first husband.

Sensationalist news coverage flourished during the heyday of yellow journalism. Many newspapers regularly gave prominent coverage to the lurid and the sensational. Stories with headlines such as "Real American Monsters and Dragons," "The Mysterious Murder of Bessie Little," and "Startling Confession of a Wholesale Murderer Who Begs to Be Hanged" were typical of the fare that William Randolph Hearst offered his readers. And newspaper editors knew at the turn of the century what Madison Avenue would discover decades later: sex sells. In describing the illustrations that would accompany a story about Halley's comet, a staff member for Joseph Pulitzer's paper the *Sunday World* suggested that "if you can work a pretty girl into the decoration, so much the better."

Because the American news media are privately owned and therefore need to turn a profit, they inevitably will emphasize the novel over the important whenever there is a public demand for it. When social mores become more lax, as they have in the United States over the past two decades, the news media will relax their rules on what constitutes an acceptable news story. Conversely, should social mores in the United States become more conservative, the media no doubt will push the rules of news coverage back in the direction of hard news.

Sources: Edwin Emery, *The Press and America: An Interpretative History of the Mass Media*, 3d ed. (Englewood Cliffs, N.J.: Prentice-Hall, 1972), pp. 355, 359; Todd Gitlin, "Media Lemmings Run Amok!" *Washington Journalism Review*, April 1992, p. 32; Mitchell Stephens, *A History of News: From the Drum to the Satellite* (New York: Penguin Books, 1988), pp. 187–88.

events—horse-race journalism does little to inform voters about whether any candidate is proposing viable solutions to the problems they consider important.

A second common criticism of campaign coverage is that journalists allow the candidates to manipulate them. Candidates often stage **photo opportunities** (or "photo ops" for short), carefully planned events designed to attract flattering news coverage.

Photo opportunities
Events that political candidates and government officials stage to allow newspaper photographers and television news crews to take flattering photos.

Although journalists frequently debate the ethics of reporting stories that delve into the private lives of government officials, the need to attract an audience often leads them to put aside their ethical qualms.

Presidents, like other politicians, often stage photo opportunities designed to attract flattering news coverage.

For example, a candidate may give a speech in front of the Statue of Liberty in the hope that when voters sees pictures or videos of the event, they will think of the candidate as a patriot. Although these events may contain little hard news, journalists nonetheless cover them, turning many news reports into what amounts to unpaid political advertising. At the same time, the fear of being charged with bias leads many journalists to strive to give both political parties equal treatment, even when equal treatment is not justified. During the 1988 presidential campaign, for example, George Bush's aides attacked the character of the Democratic nominee, Michael Dukakis. For several weeks, Dukakis and his advisers refused to accuse Bush's aides of negative campaigning because they knew that the journalistic commitment to balance "could be exploited to make it seem that each [candidate] bore responsibility" for negative campaigning.[107]

A third common criticism of election coverage is that the news media seldom let the candidates speak at length about their views. As figure 8.1 shows, the average length of a **sound bite** on the network evening news shrank more than 75 percent between 1968 and 1988. Sound bites shrank for several reasons. Video replaced film, which made it easier to cut up speeches in time for the evening news. Correspondents seeking to avoid manipulation by the candidates increasingly substituted their own analysis for canned speeches. And the conviction among television executives that the public has a dwindling attention span spawned a general trend within television news toward shorter, faster-moving stories.[108] Critics worry that shrinking sound bites deny voters the opportunity to hear the candidates explain their policy proposals and instead encourage politicians to speak in slogans.

Sound bite
A short excerpt from a person's speech or conversation that appears on radio or television news.

Many newspapers and television news shows have responded to these three criticisms by increasing the space they allot to stories on the issues, limiting their coverage

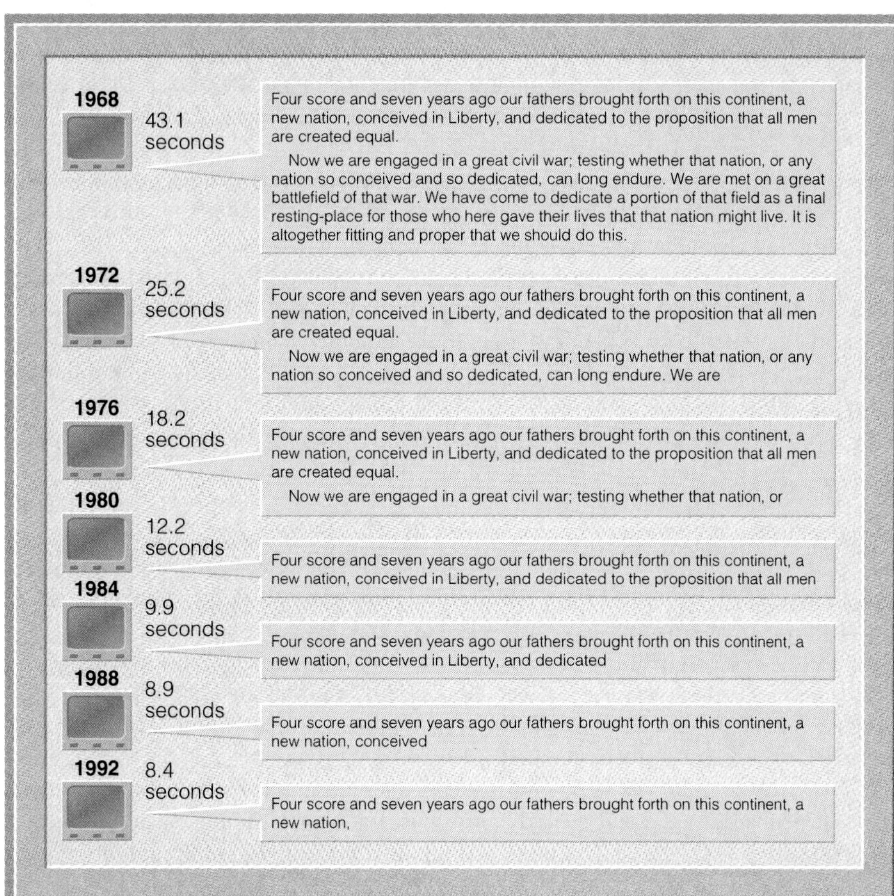

FIGURE 8.1
The Shrinking Sound Bite

The average length of campaign sound bites on the television network evening news shrank more than 75 percent between 1968 and 1988. This means Americans seldom hear presidential candidates speak at length about their views.

Source: Data for 1968–1988 from Daniel Hallin, "Sound Bite News: Television Coverage of Elections, 1968–1988." Woodrow Wilson Center for Scholars, 1991. Data for 1992 provided by the authors.

of photo opportunities, and running extended excerpts of each candidate's basic campaign speech. Whether these and other reportorial changes have improved the coverage of campaigns, however, is debatable. The public gave news coverage of the 1992 presidential campaign only slightly higher marks than coverage of the 1988 campaign, even though many news organizations made a concerted effort in 1992 to focus their coverage on issues rather than personalities.[109]

As newspapers and television news shows struggle to respond to complaints about how they cover elections, these media may be becoming less relevant to the election process.[110] In traditional campaigns, candidates rely heavily on attracting news coverage in their efforts to reach the voters. In 1992, however, candidates anxious to avoid inquisitive journalists turned to radio and television talk shows as a way to bypass the press and speak directly to voters. Candidates continued to make use of talk-show campaigning in 1996, and as we saw earlier in this chapter, they also sought to get their messages out to the voters through the Internet.

Does talk-show campaigning serve the public interest? Many Americans, angry at what they see as the arrogance of the news media, applaud the willingness of candidates to go over the heads of the press corps and talk directly to voters. And many Americans argue that by appearing in non-conventional forums, candidates reach voters who feel alienated from politics. Some journalists concur. Tim Russert, moderator of NBC's *Meet the Press,* observed in 1992 that talk shows "generated an enormous amount of interest by people who normally weren't turned on by the political process."[111]

But most journalists denounce talk-show campaigning as a new form of political manipulation. They argue that most Americans who attend or call in to talk show programs lack the training and aggressiveness needed to push candidates to explain their positions, a fact that candidates exploit to their advantage. Journalists also complain that the hosts of talk shows and network morning shows treat candidates with kid gloves, as when Harry Smith of CBS's *Morning Show* "responded to news that Bush's economic plan was twenty-nine pages long—compared to twenty-two pages for Clinton's—with the observation: 'That is certainly a more substantial plan, I guess, if it's got more pages in it.' "[112]

Whether one believes that talk-show campaigning shows democracy at its best or worst, future candidates will continue to use non-traditional formats for two reasons. First, candidates want media coverage to show them in the best possible light, and journalists are trained to ask the sorts of questions candidates hate to answer. Second, because more and more Americans don't watch the evening news shows, candidates find them less useful for reaching voters. So candidates have turned their sights to radio and television talk shows, the place where much of the audience, and much of the voting public, has gone.[113]

Reporting Leaks

Leaks
Confidential government information surreptitiously given to journalists.

In September 1991, Clarence Thomas seemed headed for quick confirmation as an associate justice of the Supreme Court. Then National Public Radio and *New York Newsday* reported that former co-worker Anita Hill had accused him of sexual harassment. The story, which was based on a **leak**—that is, confidential government information given surreptitiously to the journalists—led to unprecedented public hearings on Thomas's moral fitness to serve on the Court.[114] The incident also brought to the fore yet again complaints that the news media's willingness to report stories based on leaks threatens the democratic process in the United States.

Those who complain about the news media's reliance on leaks sometimes contend that leaks jeopardize national security. But very few stories based on leaks involve true national security issues. The vast majority instead deal with more mundane matters of governing, such as who the president will nominate for a vacant seat on the Supreme Court or whether federal agencies agree on the merits of the president's health care proposal. Many government officials find such leaks maddening because an ill-timed leak can make it much harder for them to accomplish their policy goals and can put their agencies or themselves in an unflattering light. For example, a president would find it much harder to convince Congress to pass a health care reform bill if it became public knowledge that White House economic advisers had concluded the reform proposal was too expensive.

Although complaints about leaks are commonplace, they should be taken with a grain of salt. After all, the reason the news media can write so many stories based on leaks is that many government officials are willing to leak confidential information. A survey conducted in 1983 found that 42 percent of government officials admitted leaking information to the media.[115] Indeed, many of the most vociferous complaints about leaks come from officials who are leakers themselves.[116] The willingness to leak stories extends to the highest levels of government. For instance, Donald Regan, secretary of the treasury and chief of staff during the Reagan administration, writes that he and other White House aides sought to influence news coverage of the administration by instituting "a policy of leaking information to journalists on a systematic basis. In effect, White House aides were assigned to tell reporters the innermost secrets of the Administration."[117]

As Regan's comments suggest, officials leak stories to the news media because leaks can advance their personal and policy goals. Officials recognize that news coverage can move an issue onto the political agenda or help mobilize public opposition to new policy proposals. Among the officials who admitted leaking stories in the 1983 survey, for example, 73 percent said they leaked information to draw attention to an issue or policy, 32 percent to send a message to someone else in the government, and 19 percent to derail a policy they opposed or damage a colleague they disliked.[118] In the case of the Reagan White House, officials calculated that leaking stories would enable them to influence both *what* the news media covered and *how* they covered it.

As leaking has become common practice in American politics, some journalists worry that leaks do more to damage the news media than government.[119] Leaks transform the media from observers into participants as officials try to use journalists as conduits for shaping policy. Worse yet, the need to cultivate a source may encourage journalists to treat leakers favorably and perhaps even to drop a potential story for fear of antagonizing a prized source of inside information. For example, some observers believe that a Lebanese newspaper rather than the American media uncovered how the Reagan administration secretly traded arms for hostages in the mid-1980s because American journalists depended too much on White House officials for their stories. As one journalist put it: "The media committed one of its biggest sins, basically sleeping with our sources, and as a consequence we blew the biggest story of the Reagan Administration."[120]

Yet despite the disadvantages, leaks are also one of the most powerful tools journalists have for getting at the heart of a story and keeping the American public informed. The Watergate scandal of the early 1970s, which forced Richard Nixon to resign the presidency, is a prime example. Investigative reporters Bob Woodward and Carl Bernstein were able to break the Watergate story only because a source, known only as Deep Throat, leaked vital information about the Nixon administration's illegal activities.[121] By reporting leaks, then, the news media can promote democracy by providing a powerful check on government power.

The News Media and Democracy

What are we to conclude about how well the media perform their job of reporting the news? Although criticisms of the news media are frequently exaggerated, even journalists agree they are far from perfect in doing their jobs. Bias can infect their stories; they may at times be too cynical; hard news increasingly must compete with soft news for print space and air time; coverage of election campaigns often emphasizes the contest at the expense of content; and government officials may selectively leak information to manipulate news coverage. Yet the freedom all Americans have to criticize what they see as poor reporting encourages the news media to improve their performance and helps check the abuse of media power. Thus, despite their occasional errors and excesses, the news media remain a vital component of the American democratic process.

Summary

Freedom of the press is essential to the health of a democracy. Without a lively news media, we would not be able to monitor the actions of government. Yet our very dependence on newspapers, radio, and television for information gives the news media great power to influence public opinion and government behavior. Although the media in no way dictate what we think, they do influence politics in the United States. The media have some effect on the way we view political issues, and they have a substantial impact on the political agenda. Nonetheless, the power of the media should not be exaggerated. What the news media report often reflects what Americans are thinking and what government is doing, rather than the reverse.

Although the authors of the Constitution believed that a free press is essential to the success of democracy, the nature of the news business has changed dramatically over the past two centuries. Partisan journalism has given way to objective reporting, television has surpassed newspapers as the preeminent source of news, and news has become big business. All of these changes illustrate the immense freedom the media have to define their role in the American political system.

To encourage vigorous reporting, American law extends great freedom to journalists. Unlike many other countries, the United States does not censor the media or require journalists to apply for licenses. The one exception to limited regulation is the electronic media. Because of the small number of broadcast channels, the government limits ownership of radio and television stations and sets some rules for public affairs programming. But in the main, these regulations have relatively little effect on the content that the electronic news media broadcast.

The choices journalists make determine which events become news. Reporters generally define news as events that are conflictual, relevant, and timely. When they report the news, journalists try to tell the story straight, though pure objectivity is impossible.

Because reporting requires journalists to make subjective choices, criticism of the news media is inevitable. Many people claim that the media favor liberal causes, but convincing evidence of a persistent liberal bias in the media is hard to come by. A more pervasive bias in news coverage is the tendency of the news media to focus on the failures of government rather than its successes. Many critics complain that the news media have become so focused on misdeeds that news coverage has become cynical.

Another criticism of the news media is their growing tendency to treat news as entertainment. As greater competition has squeezed media profits in recent years, newspapers, radio, and television have increasingly come to favor soft news over hard news.

The news media also have been criticized for doing a poor job of covering elections. Critics complain that journalists engage in horse-race journalism, allow campaign staffs to manipulate them, and chop candidates' speeches into shorter and shorter sound bites. The news media have tried to improve their coverage of elections, but the public says it sees little improvement. Moreover, the traditional news media are finding themselves pushed to the margins of the political debate as candidates make increased use of talk shows and other non-traditional venues to reach voters.

Finally, the news media have been criticized for reporting stories based on leaks of confidential government information. On closer inspection, however, the issue is more complicated than the criticisms suggest. Government officials frequently leak information to draw attention to an issue, to send a message to others in government, to derail a policy they oppose, or to damage a colleague they dislike. Although journalists worry that government officials selectively leak information to influence news coverage, they also know that leaks are one of the most powerful tools they have for getting at the heart of a story and keeping the American public informed.

Key Terms

Broadcast television
Cable television
Equal-time provision
Fairness doctrine
Federal Communications Commission (FCC)
Freedom of Information Act
Horse-race journalism
Leaks
Muckraking
Objective press
Pack journalism
Photo opportunities
Political agenda
Pool reporting
Selective perception
Sound bite
Spin control
Talk radio
Yellow journalism

Readings for Further Study

Ansolabehere, Stephen, Roy Behr, and Shanto Iyengar. *The Media Game: American Politics in the Television Age*. New York: Macmillan, 1993. Three scholars examine the impact of television on American politics.

Auletta, Ken. *Three Blind Mice: How the TV Networks Lost Their Way*. New York: Random House, 1991. A newspaper columnist shows how the advent of cable television and other technological advances led to major upheavals at the three broadcast networks.

Bennett, W. Lance, and David L. Paletz, eds. *Taken by Storm: The Media, Public Opinion, and U.S. Foreign Policy in the Gulf War*. Chicago: University of Chicago Press, 1994. A collection of essays examining the role the news media played in covering the Gulf War.

Bradlee, Ben. *A Good Life: Newspapering and Other Adventures*. New York: Simon & Schuster, 1995. A longtime editor of the *Washington Post* recounts his life in the newspaper business, including his role in breaking the story of the Watergate scandal.

Carter, T. Barton, Marc A. Franklin, and Jay B. Wright. *The First Amendment and the Fourth Estate: The Law of the Mass Media*, 5th ed. Mineola, N.Y.: Foundation Press, 1991. A comprehensive overview of the legal regulations affecting the news media.

Entman, Robert. *Democracy without Citizens: Media and the Decay of American Politics*. New York: Oxford University Press, 1989. A political scientist argues that the news media in the United States have encouraged the decay of democratic citizenship and virtually compelled politicians to practice demagoguery.

Fallows, James. *Breaking the News: How the Media Undermine American Democracy*. New York: Pantheon Books, 1996. A veteran Washington journalist argues that television distorts our understanding of what is news, turns reporters into celebrities, and undermines democratic values.

Graber, Doris A. *Mass Media and American Politics*, 5th ed. Washington, D.C.: CQ Press, 1996. Graber examines how the mass media affect the way political campaigns are run and how the voters view candidates and campaign issues.

Chapter

9

Political Parties

What Is a Political Party?
Party Functions

Characteristics of U.S. Political Parties
The Spatial Theory of Elections
The U.S. Two-Party System Versus Multiparty Systems
The Spatial Model Applied to Real Politics

The History of U.S. Parties and Elections
The First Party System (1796–1824)
The Second Party System (1828–1856)
The Third Party System (1860–1892)
The Fourth Party System (1896–1928)
The Fifth Party System (1932–?)
Critical Elections and Party Realignment Theory
From Realignment to Dealignment?
The Uncertain Future

Modern Party Organization
Local Organizations
State Organizations
National Organizations
Relationships Among Party Organizations

Summary

Key Terms

Readings for Further Study

On the evening of November 5, 1996, President Bill Clinton, Republican presidential candidate Robert Dole, independent presidential candidate Ross Perot, and hundreds of other candidates for the Senate, the House, and state and local office anxiously listened to election returns. The television networks announced the outcome for President Clinton early in the evening. Many other candidates, however, did not learn the results of their efforts until late that night, and, in some cases, days or even weeks later.

Despite President Clinton's early victory, his interest in the election results continued throughout the night. He cared about the results of more than just his own race because every time a Democratic candidate won a race for a seat in the House or Senate, a governorship, or any one of many other offices, it strengthened his hand for governing the nation. Bill Clinton wasn't running alone; he was running as part of a Democratic team.

Who were all those candidates and how did they come to run together under the same party label? In what sense were they a team? And why do two teams, the Democrats and Republicans, dominate American politics?

Parties were not written into the Constitution. Indeed, they were never even considered when the founders debated the Constitution. Instead, politicians created parties to help them achieve their goals—winning elections and making public policy. For these reasons, the nature of parties changes over time and differs from one part of the country to another. Parties change because the people who make them up and who seek office respond to public preferences and to the rules and laws that govern competition for elected office—both of which vary over time and from place to place. To serve as a means for the people to control government decisions, the parties must respond to public opinion. Yet to serve as vehicles for politicians to win elections, they must respond to the rules of the system as well.

In this chapter, we will examine what political parties are and what functions they perform for the political system—from contesting elections to organizing the government and providing a means for people to hold their elected officials accountable. We will discuss why our nation has two centrist parties rather than a multiparty system. We will sketch out America's electoral history so that we can examine how parties have behaved over the last two hundred years, and we will describe the current state of party organizations—including the roles they play in elections today.

What Is a Political Party?

People have many images of political parties: the hoopla of presidential nominating conventions, smoke-filled backrooms full of politicians, and local party workers canvassing their neighbors for votes. All of these images reflect different aspects of the truth.

Political party
A coalition of people seeking to control the government by contesting elections and winning office.

Political cleavages
Divisions in society around which parties organize.

The core of a political party's purpose, and the basis on which most scholars define parties, is their role as *electoral organizations.* A **political party** is a coalition of people seeking to control the government by contesting elections and winning office. A party differs from a single candidate's campaign because a party runs an entire slate of candidates for a wide range of offices rather than just one campaign for one office. A party also differs from an interest group because a party seeks to win offices rather than to influence those in office to win benefits from the government.

Party coalitions form around the basic **political cleavages,** or divisions, in society. For instance, on economic issues, today's Democratic politicians are mostly liberal—they represent the working class, the poor, and most minority groups in political conflicts. Today's Republican politicians are generally economic conservatives—they represent the wealthy and business interests. Thus, the two major parties offer opposing views on economic issues.

Of course, not all Democrats are liberal on economic issues, nor are all Republicans conservative. The overlap stems largely from the fact that economic differences are not the only important political cleavage in American society. A second basic cleavage divides people on social issues. As we saw in chapter 6, Democrats tend to be

President Clinton and Vice-President Gore celebrate their 1996 re-election victory on Election Night in Little Rock, Arkansas.

liberal and Republicans tend to be conservative, but people's positions on social and economic issues do not always fall neatly along party lines; to some extent, these cleavages are cross-cutting. This means that within each party, we find some politicians who are liberal on economic issues and conservative on social issues, and vice versa. Because the cleavages do not form one perfect dividing line, most Democratic politicians are liberal and most Republican politicians are conservative, but both parties contain a mixture. So, although the parties offer voters a choice, the choice may not always be clear.[1]

To contest elections, the Democrats and the Republicans have developed a network of party organizations, from their national committees in Washington, D.C., to state committees and down to county committees. In some towns and cities, parties are even organized at the neighborhood level. In addition, both parties have formed a number of affiliated organizations for special purposes such as raising money for congressional candidates and training campaign managers. These organizations work to recruit and nominate the candidates who run under the party's banner, to help the candidates win office once they are nominated, and to manage the party's affairs between elections.

Party Functions

A useful way to think about political parties and to see how they provide a means for the people to control their government is to consider the functions parties may perform in our political system. We say *may* perform because parties do not always perform these functions, and when they do, they may not perform them fully. At different times and different places in the country, parties have taken on different roles and behaved differently. The degree to which parties perform various functions depends on what party leaders and activists think will help them win elections and control the government. As we shall discuss later in this chapter, party leaders look at the rules governing campaigns and elections as well as other factors such as current campaign technology, public preferences on the issues, and voter loyalties when they decide how best to organize their parties.[2] In other words, parties are changeable. They adapt to circumstances. So when we generalize about what functions parties perform, we must qualify our statements by noting that parties do not *always* do these things.

Broadly speaking, the parties link the people and the government by providing *organization* and *information*. The organization is easy to see—party headquarters, committees, campaigns, nominations, and so forth provide it. The information is less obvious, but no less vital. Parties provide information because the parties organize around basic political cleavages. The party labels, therefore, inform voters and other candidates roughly where candidates stand on the issues. When a voter knows little about the candidates up

The Mule is the symbol of the Democratic Party. The Elephant is the symbol of the Republican Party—often called the "Grand Old Party" or "GOP" for short.

Courtesy of the Republican National Committee, Washington, D.C.

Both Democratic and Republican leaders recruited Dwight Eisenhower, the enormously popular general who commanded the Allied forces in Europe during World War II, to run for the presidency in 1952. But such efforts at recruitment are rare; most candidates are self-starters.

for election (which is unfortunately all too common, as we saw in chapter 6), party labels provide essential cues about which side the candidates are likely to take on issues. If a voter knows only the candidates' names and party labels, for instance, the voter can make a fair guess that the Democrat will favor more spending on jobs programs or education and the Republican will favor less. Similarly, party labels provide information to activists and other politicians about whether given politicians are likely allies.

A look at seven specific functions that the parties usually perform shows how they help the political system work by organizing and providing information.

First, parties *recruit candidates* to run for office. In some cases, party leaders seek out potential candidates, urge them to run, and offer them support. Both the Democrats and the Republicans recruited Dwight Eisenhower, the enormously popular general who commanded the Allied forces during World War II, to run for president in 1952.[3] Far more commonly, *self-starting candidates* seek out party leaders (among others) and ask for their support. In either case, the party leaders help bring together candidates and campaign donors, activists to work in the campaigns, and the people with the technical skills needed in campaigns—campaign managers, fundraisers, pollsters, public relations specialists, and others.

Second, parties *nominate candidates.* Through party primaries, caucuses, conventions, or other means, parties bestow the right to run using the party labels. In doing so, they reduce the field of candidates to only a few—and usually to only two serious competitors, the Democratic and Republican nominees. In eliminating most of the candidates, nominations simplify the choices for voters and give them a more manageable task—learning about only two candidates instead of a pack of them.

Direct primary
An election in which voters and not party leaders directly choose a party's nominees for political office.

The most common method of nominating candidates today is the **direct primary**—an election in which voters and not party leaders directly choose a party's nominees for office. There are three different types of primaries, which vary according to who is allowed to vote. *Closed primaries,* used in about forty states, require voters to indicate their party affiliations before Election Day, when they register to vote. *Open primaries* allow voters to choose which party primary they will vote in on Election Day, when they arrive at the polls. *Blanket primaries* permit voters to cast their ballots for candidates from any party, casting one vote for each office. In all types of primaries, the winner of the primary becomes the party's nominee and goes on to run in the general election against the nominees of other parties.

Caucus/convention system
A nomination method in which registered party members attend a party caucus, or meeting, to choose a nominee. In large districts, local caucuses send delegates to represent them at a convention.

An alternative nomination method is the **caucus/convention system**—in which registered party members attend a party caucus, or meeting, to choose a nominee. If the election were for a large district such as a state, the party would hold a number of local caucuses. Each caucus would then choose representatives, or delegates, to express their views and vote on their behalf at a statewide convention. In either case, people who consider themselves members of the party and who care enough to show up at the caucuses (which are far more time consuming than merely voting) make the nominations. Although the caucus/convention system gives state parties greater control over the nomination process, state parties can, as box 9.1 shows, exert control over the nomination process even in states with direct primaries by controlling who gets on the ballot.

Third, parties *mobilize voters.* Through party identification, parties develop emotional bonds with voters and use these bonds to encourage voting (see chapter 7). In a more practical vein, parties organize voter registration and get-out-the-vote drives all across the country. They are by no means the only groups to do this. Candidate campaign organizations and interest groups also run registration and get-out-the-vote drives. But parties often lead these activities.

Fourth, parties *contest elections.* They play a role in providing the candidates, the money, the managers, and the army of campaign workers that make up the campaigns. For most party activists, this is a party's core purpose—the campaigns.

Fifth, parties *form governments.* Once elected, officials organize governments along party lines. Presidents and governors normally choose from their own party ranks for appointments (see chapters 12 and 15). Members of Congress and state legislatures choose their leaders and fill their committees on the basis of party lines (see chapter 11). Forming governments along party lines makes sense because each party consists of politicians representing voters who generally take the same side on the basic cleavages dividing society—the cleavages around which the parties formed.

Sixth, parties *coordinate policy across independent units of government.* Few problems can be dealt with effectively by a single branch of government; rather, most require the cooperation of the president, Congress, and state and local governments. Party loyalties often provide the basis for building the coalitions needed to develop public policies, to enact them with legislation or executive action, and to implement them. The cleavages underlying the party coalitions bolster that loyalty.

Seventh, parties *provide accountability.* The party labels offer easy cues for voting decisions because they identify which side politicians are likely to take on particular issues. Moreover, voters who like recent government policies or performance can express their approval by voting for members of the party that controls the White House or the statehouse. Those who dislike recent policies or performance can vote to "throw the rascals out." The party labels make it easy for voters to identify whom to reward or punish.

Politicians, of course, did not set up political parties for the purpose of providing accountability. The politicians who invented parties thought that parties would help them win elections and control government. Accountability turned out to be a by-product—but a crucial one for our system of government.

As you can see, the seven functions that political parties serve extend well beyond just winning elections. Although the primary role of political parties is to act as electoral organizations, they also play a role in government—organizing it and forming the coalitions around which policy disputes are fought. In addition, they play a role in the electorate—organizing voters into large, informal coalitions of party identifiers and offering comprehensible choices to the voters.

By performing these functions, political parties form a critical link between the people and their government. They provide the organization and information that make understanding government, following politics, and choosing among competing candidates manageable tasks. Without parties, the chaotic free-for-all of elections would be difficult or impossible for ordinary citizens to understand. Indeed, some observers have suggested that mass democracy cannot function at all without political parties to organize it.[4]

Characteristics of U.S. Political Parties

Two of the fundamental characteristics of our political system are that we have a **two-party system** and that the dominant parties are **centrist,** or close to the political center. Since the development of political parties shortly after the founding of the nation, two major political parties have normally dominated U.S. politics. During a brief period from 1816 to 1824, only one party was strong enough to contest the presidency seriously, and serious minor party challenges and independent presidential candidacies have cropped up from time to time (for example, George Wallace's American Independent party in 1968 and Ross Perot's independent campaigns for the presidency in 1992 and 1996), but for the most part, only two parties have had a serious chance to win the presidency or any substantial number of seats in Congress. Since the formation of the Republican Party in 1854, those two parties have been the Democrats (who were organized in the early 1800s) and the Republicans.

Two-party system
A political system in which two major parties dominate.

Centrist parties
Parties close to the political center.

Our two major parties have always tended to take stands close to the political center; that is, we have centrist parties. Democrats and Republicans certainly disagree about a wide range of issues, but their disagreements are narrower than disagreements among parties in many other democratic nations.[5] For instance, several western European nations have communist and socialist parties, which favor far larger government roles in regulating business and economic relations in society. In the United States, by contrast, even the most liberal Democrats favor capitalism and would reject the more extreme, heavy-handed government interference in the marketplace that occurs in

Point of Order

BOX 9.1

The Politics of Getting on the Ballot: Sen. Robert Dole and the New York Republican Presidential Primary

Presidential hopeful Robert Dole and New York Senator Alfonse D'Amato during the 1996 primary season.

Before 1888, Americans who wanted to vote had to complete two tasks. First, they had to obtain a ballot from a precinct captain or other party worker. That ballot already listed the names of the party's candidates. Second, they had to cast the ballot in full public view, thereby showing everyone whether they had voted for the Democratic or Republican Party.

The introduction of the Australian ballot ended the practice of public voting. People now use government-printed ballots and make their choices in the privacy of voting booths. This reform has been widely hailed as a step forward for good government. Yet it also gave government control over the list of candidates on the ballot, and that is a form of political power. The travails of the candidates who dared to challenge Sen. Robert Dole (R-Kans.) in New York's Republican presidential primary in 1996 demonstrate the power inherent in controlling who ends up on the ballot.

To win a share of New York's delegates to the Republican National Convention, candidates first had to earn a spot on the state's primary ballot. New York's state law stipulated that to be listed on the primary ballot, a candidate had to do three things. First, the candidate had to pick a slate of three delegates and three alternates in each of the state's thirty-one congressional districts. Second, the candidate had to collect valid signatures (and other identifying information) from 1,250 registered Republicans in each congressional district between Thanksgiving Day 1995 and January 4, 1996. Third, the candidate had to submit the petitions to the appropriate election boards.

These three steps may sound easy and reasonable, but the details of the requirements show how difficult it is to

Continued

some other countries.[6] On the other end of the political spectrum, some western European countries have fascist or monarchist parties, which favor limiting who can participate in elections (usually on racial or ethnic grounds). In the United States, even the most conservative Republicans favor democracy and reject any proposal restricting the right to vote. So by standards of democracies around the world, the differences between the dominant American parties are relatively small; they tend to take stands not too far from one another.

The Spatial Theory of Elections

The *spatial theory of elections* helps us to understand why the United States has two centrist parties.[7] The spatial model was developed to explain how politicians and voters would behave if they were acting rationally to achieve their goals. It shows how different sets of rules create different incentives and so cause politicians and voters to behave differently. Under American election rules, politicians are more likely to achieve their goals if they join one of two centrist parties; under other types of election rules used in other nations, many parties can thrive. Different rules produce different outcomes.

To focus on the effects of rules, the spatial model simplifies the real world and attempts to identify the essential characteristics of our political system that influence

POINT OF ORDER

BOX 9.1 CONTINUED

get on the presidential primary ballot in New York. No signature is valid if it differs in any respect from the way in which the person signed his or her name at the time he or she registered to vote. None of the signatures are valid if someone who does not live in the congressional district gathers them, and none are valid if someone who was paid on the basis of the number of signatures gathered collected them. In the City of New York, the petitions must also be color-coded. In 1996, the approved color for Republican petitions was cherry red (not, mind you, fire engine red). Signatures on incorrectly colored paper are invalid. In addition to obtaining names, addresses, and signatures on the petitions, the campaigns must also identify every person's voting precinct and (in New York City) his or her State Assembly district. Any missing or incorrect information invalidates the petition. The petitions must be submitted to the correct election boards. Of course, any petitions accidentally submitted to the wrong election boards are invalidated. Finally, in 1996, lawyers from the New York State Republican Party scrutinized every petition (for every candidate other than Senator Dole), seeking to find errors that they could use to have the petitions invalidated.

For Dole, the process of getting on the primary ballot in New York was much less complicated. Dole was the choice of the state party and its two most prominent leaders—U.S. Sen. Alfonse D'Amato and Gov. George Pataki. As a result, the state party's army of 33,000 local party workers circulated the petitions and gathered the signatures Dole needed to be on the ballot. And Dole's petitions received only the lightest scrutiny from the party's lawyers.

Whether Senator Dole believed the process was unfair is unclear. Perhaps he believed that there was a certain justice to it. After all, he was frozen out of New York's primary in 1988 when the state's Republican leaders decided to support Vice President George Bush in his quest for the presidency.

In the end, though, Dole did not get the uncontested presidential primary that Senator D'Amato and Governor Pataki had worked so hard to produce. Just a week before New York voters went to the polls, a federal appeals court ruled that the state Republican Party's ballot access rules were unconstitutional because they imposed an "undue burden" on presidential candidates who are not the party's favorite. The result of the ruling was the first Republican presidential primary in the history of New York to be contested statewide. Despite the last-minute change in the rules, Senator Dole still triumphed in New York. When all the primary ballots were counted, he took all of New York's delegates to the Republican National Convention.

Sources: Michael S. Lewis-Beck and Peverill Squire, "The Politics of Institutional Choice: Presidential Ballot Access for Third Parties in the United States," *British Journal of Political Science* 25 (July 1995): 419–27; James M. Perry, "New York's Complicated Election Laws May Help State GOP Block Dole Rivals," *Wall Street Journal*, 27 July 1995; "Restrictive Republicans," *Wall Street Journal*, 10 April 1995; and Don Van Natta, Jr., "Ruling Puts Forbes on Primary Ballot Across New York," *New York Times*, 29 February 1996.

politicians and voters. As a description, therefore, the model does poorly; it doesn't take into account many of the complexities of particular elections. As a tool to help us understand how our system works, however, the model is useful.

The spatial theory assumes first that all political issues can be represented by a single left-right scale, and that all parties, politicians, and voters can be placed on this scale. The scale shown in figure 9.1, for instance, ranges from zero—an extreme liberal—to 100—an extreme conservative. On this scale, a liberal such as Sen. Ted Kennedy (D-Mass.) might be placed at 10, while a conservative such as Sen. Phil Gramm (R-Tex.) might be placed at 95. (Senators Kennedy and Gramm are profiled in boxes 6.2 and 6.3.) The more moderate 1996 Democratic and Republican presidential candidates, President Clinton and Senator Dole, would be somewhat closer to the center. The second assumption of the spatial model is that the voters know exactly where they and the candidates stand on the issue scale. That is, the model simplifies the real world by assuming that voters have "perfect information" about what politicians would do if they were elected. Third, the theory assumes that all people vote, choosing the candidate whose views are closest to theirs.

Median voter hypothesis
The theory that the best possible position for a politician who cares only about winning elections is the center—that is, in the position of the median voter.

From these assumptions, the spatial model suggests a conclusion known as the **median voter hypothesis**—namely, that the best possible position for a politician who cares only about winning elections is the center. The "center" is the position of the

Critics of the parties sometimes claim that the Democrats and Republicans are so similar they are indistinguishable.

Drawing by Handelsman; © The New Yorker Magazine, Inc. Reprinted by permission.

"I beg your pardon," said Alice, "but which of you is the Democrat?"

median voter, that is, the individual voter who has exactly half of all other voters to his or her left, and the remaining half of all voters to his or her right. On the scale in figure 9.1, the center is the midpoint of the scale, 50.

The logic behind the median voter hypothesis can be seen in figure 9.1. Consider first what would happen if the two parties chose Kennedy and Gramm as candidates. Because every voter votes for the candidate closest to him or her on the scale, the voters to the left of Kennedy would vote for Kennedy, and those to the right of Gramm would vote for Gramm. The midpoint between Kennedy (at 10 on the scale) and Gramm (at 95) is 52.5, so everyone to the left of 52.5 would vote for Kennedy, and everyone to the right of 52.5 would vote for Gramm. So Kennedy, with the 50 percent of the voters to the left of 50 on the scale, plus the additional voters between 50 and 52.5, would have a majority and win the election.

Now suppose that the Republicans nominated Bob Dole instead of Phil Gramm. The midpoint between Dole (at 80 on the scale) and Kennedy is to the left of center—at 45, which would yield a Republican victory. Because Dole is closer to the center, he would gain the half of the votes to the right of center and some to the left of center, because he would still be the closer candidate for voters from 45 to 50 on the scale. Those on the extreme right might prefer Gramm to Dole, but offered the choice between Dole and Kennedy, they would vote for Dole.

The major point the spatial model and the median voter hypothesis make is that, given American election rules, the candidate closer to the center should win the election. Therefore, if the parties care only about winning elections (as they do in the simplified world of the spatial model), they should nominate candidates as close to the center, or median voter, as possible. This, according to the median voter hypothesis, is why the Democrats and Republicans are centrist political parties.

To see why we have only two major political parties, consider the public's reaction to a minor party challenge. Figure 9.2 shows a hypothetical challenge from a right-wing party. If people vote for the candidate who is closest to them on the political spectrum, the challenge will draw off a substantial number of conservative votes that would otherwise go to the Republican, and thus make it extremely difficult for the Republican nominee to beat even a liberal Democrat. Therefore, minor party challenges from the left or right are not only unlikely to win, but they are also likely to harm the party closest to them on the political spectrum and help the party that is farther away (and with which they have the sharpest policy differences). In this way, minor parties in the United States are usually self-defeating.

The 1990 race for the U.S. House seat from California's first congressional district provides a concrete example of how minor party challenges can be self-defeating.

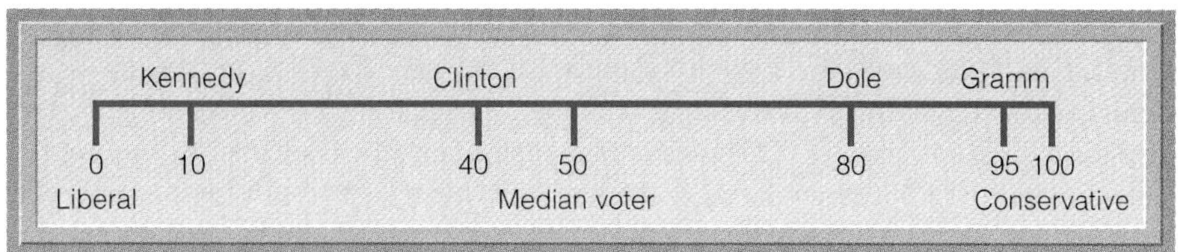

FIGURE 9.1
The Spatial Model of Elections

The *median voter hypothesis* predicts that candidates will move toward the median, or political center, because that position gives them the greatest chance of winning.

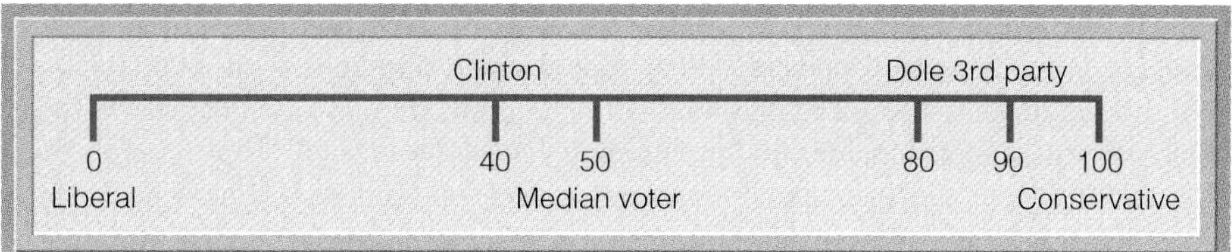

FIGURE 9.2
A Third Party Challenge

The spatial model of elections predicts that third party challenges will probably lose, and will hurt the major-party candidate who is closest to the third party.

The incumbent representative was Doug Bosco, a liberal Democrat who had won each of his previous three House campaigns with at least 62 percent of the vote. Members of the leftist Peace and Freedom Party, however, believed that Bosco was not sufficiently committed to liberal causes, and they ran a candidate against him in 1990. When the polls closed on Election Day, the Peace and Freedom Party's candidate, Darlene Comingore, had won 15 percent of the vote, with most of this support coming from people who otherwise would have voted for Bosco. Because the Democratic vote was split, Republican candidate Frank Riggs was able to beat Bosco by a 43 percent to 42 percent margin. Thus, by challenging Bosco, members of the Peace and Freedom Party helped elect someone with whom they disagreed even more sharply.[8] Looking at an example such as this, it is small wonder that serious minor party challenges from the left or right are rare.

The question of minor party challenges raises the question of how well the spatial model explains Ross Perot's independent campaigns for the presidency in 1992 and 1996. On most issues, Perot was in the political center, between Bill Clinton and his Republican rivals.[9] In each case, the model predicts that Perot should win votes from the center, although whether he would hurt Clinton or his opponents more should depend on exactly where he stands in relation to them on the issues. As we saw in chapter 7, Perot did receive the largest share of his votes from the center—moderates gave him more votes than either liberals or conservatives—but his support was drawn from a far broader range on the political spectrum than the model would have predicted. That is, both liberals and conservatives also gave Perot votes. In this respect, the spatial model predicted poorly. Most observers explain Perot's broad support by noting that he was, in large part, a protest candidate. Many people voted for him because they did not like either Clinton, Bush, or Dole.[10] So in the case of Perot, the spatial model provides insights, but not a complete explanation.

The U.S. Two-Party System Versus Multiparty Systems

Although the United States has two dominant, centrist parties, many other democracies around the world have more than two, some of which are not centrist. The difference is largely the result of the institutions, laws, and rules that govern different nations.

The United States has a **single-member, plurality electoral system.** In such a system, Congress and state legislatures are divided into districts; the House of Representatives, for instance, has 435 districts. Each district elects a single member as its representative, and the winner in each district is the candidate who receives a plurality of the vote—that is, more votes than any other candidate.

Single-member, plurality electoral system
A system in which each district elects a single member as its representative; the winner in each district is the candidate who receives a plurality of the vote.

Proportional representation system
A system in which legislators are elected at large and each party wins legislative seats in proportion to the number of votes it receives.

Many democratic nations, unlike the United States, have a **proportional representation** (PR) **system.** In such systems, each party puts forward a list of its nominees for the nation or for a large area such as a state or province, and citizens vote for the list as a whole. This means that each legislator is elected by and represents the entire nation or state rather than an individual district. In PR systems, the party wins seats in the legislature in proportion to the number of votes it receives. For instance, if a party receives 20 percent of the vote, it wins 20 percent of the seats in the legislature.[11]

The spatial model yields different predictions for single-member, plurality systems and proportional representation systems. In the United States and other single-member, plurality systems—as we explained in the previous section—a minor party challenge virtually always ends in defeat. Consequently, nations with these rules almost always develop two-party systems. This generalization is often called **Duverger's Law,** after the person who first observed it.[12]

Duverger's Law
The generalization that if a nation has a single-member, plurality electoral system, it will develop a two-party system.

In a PR system, however, minor parties can prosper. Consider the hypothetical example in figure 9.2. In a PR system, both the Republicans and the new right-wing party would win seats in the legislature. So proportional representation election rules often produce multi-party systems.

Comparing the single-member, plurality and proportional representation systems helps us to see how rules and institutional structures create incentives for politicians and citizens to behave in different ways to obtain their goals. Under American rules, politicians who want to become president join one of the major parties; in proportional representation systems, politicians seeking to lead their nations often have a wider choice of parties to join and may even do better by forming their own political parties.

The Spatial Model Applied to Real Politics

The spatial model is an abstract description of our political system. Because the model simplifies reality so much, one may wonder how it works in the real world. To address this question, we will discuss two examples—the politics of civil rights during the 1950s and 1960s, and the responses of the Democratic and Republican parties to their presidential election defeats in 1988 and 1992. As we shall show, the spatial model offers useful insights into real politics.

The Politics of Civil Rights

Party platform
An official statement of beliefs, values, and policy positions that a national party convention issues.

We have been speaking of parties taking and changing positions almost as if parties were individuals who could announce what they believe. Parties do take official positions in documents such as the Contract With America and in the **party platforms,** or statements of beliefs, that presidential nominating conventions issue every four years, but there is more to party positions than that.[13] Most people see the positions of presidents, presidential candidates, and party leaders as representing the positions of the party as well. To see how party positions change in the real world, consider how the Democratic and Republican parties changed their views during the 1950s and 1960s on the issue of civil rights.[14]

In the 1950s, both the Democratic and Republican parties took moderate, centrist stands on issues related to civil rights for African Americans. Of the two parties, the Republicans were slightly more supportive of civil rights, as they had been since they were founded in the 1850s as the anti-slavery party. The Democrats, by contrast, sought to avoid taking any firm stands on civil rights—a pro-civil rights stand would offend southern whites, who delivered the South to the Democrats in every presidential election; an anti-civil rights stand would offend northerners, who favored at least some progress toward integration.[15]

The parties' positions could be seen in their 1956 platforms. On the subject of the Supreme Court's decision in the historic *Brown v. Board of Education* case, which declared government laws mandating segregation in public schools to be unconstitutional (see chapter 5), the 1956 Democratic platform said almost nothing. It observed only that "recent decisions of the Supreme Court of the United States relating to segregation in publicly supported schools and elsewhere have brought consequences of vast importance to our Nation as a whole and especially to communities directly affected."[16] The Republican platform supported the Court's decision, saying, "The Republican Party accepts the decision of the U.S. Supreme Court that racial discrimination in publicly supported schools must be progressively eliminated."[17]

In the 1960 election, pushed by an escalating series of boycotts, sit-ins, marches, and mass demonstrations in favor of civil rights, both parties moved toward greater support for equality for African Americans. The Democratic candidate, Sen. John F. Kennedy, was regarded as slightly more supportive of civil rights because of a symbolic telephone call he made to Coretta Scott King while her husband, civil rights leader the Rev. Dr. Martin Luther King, Jr., was being held prisoner in an Atlanta jail.[18] Solid differences between the two parties' platforms, though, were hard to find.

By 1963, President Kennedy had still not taken action, so civil rights leaders turned up the pressure with more and larger marches and demonstrations.[19] Many of these protests resulted in violent police retaliation, especially in Birmingham, Alabama—where police attacked peaceful marchers with fire hoses, police dogs, and clubs. By June, President Kennedy decided that he had no choice but to act. In a nationwide address, he called for an end to segregation and for serious legislation against it, and shortly after, sent a tough civil rights bill to Congress.[20] Four months later, with the bill still struggling in Congress, President Kennedy was assassinated. His successor, Vice President Lyndon Johnson, although a southerner and a former opponent of civil rights, threw his full weight behind the bill and refused to compromise. The 1964 Civil Rights Act, which passed the following June, was even more comprehensive than the bill Kennedy originally had proposed.[21]

The electoral impact of the Democratic Party's turn in favor of civil rights was shattering. The solid South had voted Democratic for nearly one hundred years. That ended in the 1964 presidential election when the Republican candidate, Sen. Barry Goldwater of Arizona—an opponent of the Civil Rights Act—won five states in the deep South. African Americans, for their part, swung toward the Democrats, giving Lyndon Johnson more than 90 percent of their vote.[22]

By the 1968 election, the positions of the Democratic and Republican parties had clearly changed. The Democratic presidential candidate, Vice President Hubert Humphrey, was a long-time leader in the civil rights struggle and had been the Senate floor manager for the 1964 Civil Rights Act.[23] The Republican presidential candidate was Richard Nixon. Although Nixon had been a moderate on civil rights in 1960, he turned to a "southern strategy" of wooing the white South in 1968 by moving toward a "go slow" position on desegregation and by choosing the anti-busing governor of Maryland, Spiro Agnew, as his vice presidential running mate. The campaigns reinforced the differences. The Democrats and Republicans had split—one party pushing for faster movement on civil rights, the other party urging slower action.[24]

Since the 1968 election, white southern voters have moved even more toward the Republican Party.[25] When the Democrats and Republicans agreed on civil rights and chose to leave the South alone, the South stayed with the Democrats. But once the parties differed and offered a clear choice, many southern whites chose to switch parties and vote Republican.[26]

After they pushed civil rights legislation in the 1960s, the Democrats saw the once solid southern support for Democratic candidates crumble.

From *Herblock At Large*, Pantheon Books, 1987. Reprinted by permission.

This example of the politics of civil rights shows how the spatial model works in the real world. Parties do not usually take clear, unambiguous positions on issues. Rather, the views of presidential candidates and other party leaders, together with the statements in their parties' platforms, make up party positions. Because party leaders disagree among themselves and sometimes disagree with their party's platform, there are few precise party positions. Similarly, the voters have no "perfect information" about party positions. Yet out of the sound and fury of day-to-day politics, positions can be seen and voters do respond to them. Thus, we see that the abstractions of the spatial model correspond to the real behavior of politicians and voters.

The Politics of Presidential Election Defeat

The implications of the rules are not lost on politicians. Although few politicians may know the spatial theory of elections, most recognize the incentives built into the system. For example, in 1988, after the Democratic Party suffered its third consecutive defeat in the race for the presidency, party leaders and political pundits filled newspaper opinion columns and political magazines with articles debating what should be done to improve the party's chances before the next election.[27] Many writers argued that Democrats should move to the center, following the advice of the moderate Democratic Leadership Council, which was set up in 1985 to pull the Democratic Party back toward the center.[28] Others resisted the call for moderation, arguing that the Democratic Party must lead the voters to the left, rather than following them to the center.[29]

When Republicans lost control of the White House in 1992, they found themselves in the midst of a similar debate, though on the other end of the political spectrum. Moderates and conservatives debated whether the Republican Party should move toward the center or take a more conservative stand and try to persuade voters to agree with them. Sens. Warren Rudman (R-N.H.), Nancy Kassebaum (R-Kans.), Arlen Specter (R-Pa.), and other moderates formed the Moderate Majority Coalition in an effort to pull the Republican Party back toward the center. Meanwhile, Rep. Newt Gingrich (R-Ga.) and other conservative leaders resisted all efforts to push the Republican Party in a more moderate direction.[30]

In both of our examples—in the historic shift of the Democratic and Republican parties on civil rights stretching out over a decade, and in the months of soul searching after a presidential election defeat—we see the spatial model at work. The details may be messy, but one central point stands out: rules guide the behavior of politicians and voters. Since the rules of our single-member, plurality electoral system favor centrist parties, the parties debate their direction and periodically pull back toward center.

Before concluding our discussion of spatial models, we must comment on their limitations. Social scientists develop models to be useful simplifications of reality to help us understand it, not to be accurate descriptions of reality. Spatial models in particular are intended to help us understand the influence of election laws and the candidates' stands on the issues. To focus on the effects of laws and policy stands, the model simplifies reality by assuming that nothing else matters to voters. The model ignores candidates' personalities and experiences, along with the government's performance in managing the economy, scandals, wars, and a host of other variables. Yet as we saw in chapter 7, these variables do affect voters' choices. In short, the model is a poor description of many aspects of reality, and as a consequence, it does not always explain or predict correctly. Despite some lapses, however, the model helps us to understand the influence rules have on the behavior of politicians and voters.

The History of U.S. Parties and Elections

The electoral history of the United States is a story of continuity and change. Some things have remained the same over time—the basic rules that produced our two-party system, for instance. Other things have changed—from the people and their occupations to the basic political cleavages that divide our society. In looking at the history of parties and elections in the United States, we need to sort out patterns over time so that we can describe it with enough economy to gain useful insights.

The history of elections in the United States consists of periods in which each election looks largely like the others, separated by elections of heightened conflict in which the basic party coalitions abruptly shift. Because of these patterns, historians often divide the history of elections in the United States into five periods, or *party systems.*

The First Party System (1796–1824)

The Constitution does not mention political parties. In fact, the founders did not foresee the development of political parties. They recognized the idea of social groups with common interests, or *factions,* as they called them at the time, but they failed to see the rise of parties.[31] Instead, shortly after the first Congress was elected, its members invented political parties because the parties helped them achieve their goals under the newly written rules of the Constitution.

The first political parties formed around a conflict arising from the framing of the Constitution—how powerful should the federal government be? The Federalist Party, led by John Adams and Alexander Hamilton, sought a strong federal government that would benefit the predominantly northern capitalist interests. The Democrat-Republican Party, led by Thomas Jefferson and James Madison, sought a weak federal government so that the agrarian interests to the south and west could prosper more. The first party coalitions thus formed around regional, or *sectional,* economic interests.

Although we refer to the Federalists and the Democrat-Republicans as political parties, they were not parties in the modern sense. They began as congressional factions in Washington. As parties, they had little existence outside the capital in their early years. Not everyone was allowed to vote in the early Republic, and without universal white male suffrage, politicians had little need to build party organizations across the nation.[32]

The Federalist Party did not last long. Following John Adams's defeat in his reelection campaign in 1800, the Federalists became the minority party. Their opposition to the War of 1812 and support for unpopular policies forced the Federalists into virtual collapse. After 1816, they left the field to the Democrat-Republicans, failing even to nominate a presidential candidate. This led to a brief period of one-party dominance by the Democrat-Republicans known (somewhat inaccurately) as the Era of Good Feelings.

The Second Party System (1828–1856)

In 1828, Andrew Jackson captured the presidency by transforming the Democrat-Republican Party into the first mass political party.[33] (The party quickly came to be known as the Democratic Party, the name it still holds.) Jackson, along with his ally (and successor as president) Martin Van Buren, took advantage of the recently passed state laws expanding the right to vote and worked to develop a truly national party. They established and subsidized a chain of newspapers to push their party. They toured the nation helping to set up state and local party organizations to support Jackson's campaign and get out the vote on Election Day.[34] Their strategy of using party organization to draw people into voting and participation brought about a fundamental change in our system of democracy. The rules had changed.[35] No longer were politics and elections left to small handfuls of elites. Participation in politics surged as Jackson's party used the new convention system to select its nominees, and to adopt its platform.[36]

Jackson's success with the Democratic Party spurred the rise of the Whig Party. Like Jackson and the Democrats, the Whigs adapted to the laws extending the right to vote by building a coalition of northern industrialists and wealthy southern planters who opposed Jackson's western emphasis and his policies supporting the "common man." Although the Whigs won some presidential elections, their most prominent leaders—Daniel Webster and Henry Clay—never made it to the White House.

The Third Party System (1860–1892)

Throughout the early and middle 1800s, the morality of slavery became an increasingly contentious issue. Although both parties were divided over slavery, the Whig coalition of northerners—who mostly favored abolition—and southerners—who wanted to keep slavery—was especially divided. In 1854, the Republican Party formed to offer the voters a clear anti-slavery choice, and the Whigs collapsed shortly afterwards, not even nominating a presidential candidate in 1856.[37] In 1860, the Republican nominee, Abraham Lincoln, captured the White House, crystallizing political cleavages around the slavery issue and setting the nation on the path to the Civil War. The political system had successfully offered the voters a clear choice, but the losers were not willing to live with electoral defeat.

The Union victory in 1865 and the following twelve years of Reconstruction—the period during which the Union Army occupied the South—left white southerners united behind the Democratic Party. Outside the South, the sectional economic cleavages of the Jackson era remained, but the North shifted toward the Republicans. From the end of Reconstruction in 1877 until 1892, the Democrats and Republicans fought a series of close, competitive elections in which neither party managed to dominate.

The Fourth Party System (1896–1928)

William Jennings Bryan of Nebraska ran for the presidency as the Democratic Party nominee in 1896, 1900, and 1908. He lost all three times, enabling Republicans to solidify their control of the White House and ushering in the fourth party system.

In 1893, with Democrat Grover Cleveland in the White House, a massive economic depression hit the nation. The stock market collapsed, banks failed, and unemployment soared. In 1896, while the country was still reeling from economic problems, the Democrats nominated William Jennings Bryan, who ran on a populist platform attacking big business and calling for the free coinage of silver. The economic effect of using silver, in addition to gold, as the basis for the money supply would be to expand the money supply and fuel inflation. This would benefit farmers and other debtors at the expense of the northeastern bankers and industrialists, the principal moneylenders of the day. The Republicans countered by nominating William McKinley, who blamed the Democrats for the country's economic problems and defended business, the gold standard, and eastern interests against the "radical" westerners. Given the stark choice between opposing economic policies, the voters chose McKinley by a landslide.[38]

Following their crushing defeat, the Democrats were in disarray. They nominated Bryan twice more—in 1900 and 1908—but they slowly moved away from Bryan's populism toward what they thought was the political center, closer to the pro-business Republicans. The Republicans also moved toward the Democrats, led by President Theodore Roosevelt and other members of their progressive faction.[39] Nevertheless, for the next thirty-two years, Republican control of the White House was broken only by the two terms of Woodrow Wilson. Wilson first won the presidency in 1912 in a three-way race against the Republican incumbent—President William Howard Taft—and the former Republican president, Theodore Roosevelt.[40]

Throughout most of this period, Republicans held both houses of Congress and, with the exception of losing to Wilson, won the White House by lopsided margins. The closely fought elections of the post-Civil War years gave way to a solid Republican majority.

The Fifth Party System (1932–?)

As with the fourth party system, an economic collapse ushered in the fifth party system. The stock market crash of 1929 and the Great Depression that followed wreaked havoc, driving the unemployment rate up to 25 percent.[41] President Hoover's laissez-faire policies of limited government intervention in the economy did little to give people confidence in the Republican Party's ability to manage the nation's affairs. In the 1930 midterm elections, the Democrats picked up forty-nine seats in the House and eight in the Senate. Two years later, as the Depression raged on, the Democratic candidate, Franklin Delano Roosevelt, won the White House.

Once in office, Roosevelt immediately launched a pathbreaking series of reforms to turn the economy around—relief and jobs programs for the unemployed, aid for the elderly, agricultural price supports for farmers, banking regulation, and other efforts.[42] As chapters 2 and 17 discuss, these New Deal programs fundamentally altered relations between the federal government and state governments and established a new standard for federal government intervention in the economy. The political center had shifted to the left.[43]

In the elections that followed, further reforms cemented the new Democratic Party majority, labeled the **New Deal coalition.** Unlike previous party coalitions, which had been based on economic divisions between sections of the country, the New Deal coalition was an economic coalition that cut across regional lines. The poor, the working class, and union members in every part of the nation turned toward the Democrats, whereas the upper middle class and the wealthy moved toward the Republican Party. Only the South withstood the forces of realignment, remaining solidly Democratic during the Roosevelt years. Despite the economic appeal of the Republican Party to wealthier southerners, few shifted their allegiance away from the Democrats.[44]

New Deal coalition
The Democratic Party coalition that formed in 1932. It got its name from President Franklin Delano Roosevelt's New Deal policies.

Bolstered by the greater numbers of the working class, the Democrats began to dominate elections, as the Republicans had in previous years. Their domination lasted until the 1960s, when their grasp began to weaken. The changes to come, however, were unlike those leading up to the 1930s. Before we turn to the fall of the New Deal coalition, then, let us discuss the earlier shifts in party coalitions in more detail.

Critical Elections and Party Realignment Theory

The party systems we just described were separated by **critical elections** in which normal politics was disrupted and the basic party coalitions changed. The parties fought these elections—in 1828, 1860, 1896, and 1932—with unusual intensity. The parties became more ideologically polarized, voter turnout increased, and large blocks of voters switched parties.[45] The result in each case was that the balance between the two parties shifted or—in the case of 1860—an entirely new party arose. Scholars describe these shifts as **party realignments,** in which the basic cleavages dividing the parties change.[46]

Critical elections
Elections that disrupt party coalitions and create new ones in a party realignment.

Party realignment
A long-term shift in the electoral balance between the major parties.

There are two important theories about what causes the parties to realign. One theory argues that social, economic, and demographic forces build tensions within the political system and that the parties fail to respond to these tensions.[47] The period of rapid industrialization in America after the Civil War, for instance, also saw the number of farmers decline and urban areas undergo rapid growth. The two major parties ignored the new problems of urban areas and continued to woo the diminishing number of farmers. The recession of 1893 triggered a sudden shift in party coalitions as the parties suddenly began addressing the unfulfilled needs of the new urban, industrial sector in America.

The other major theory of party realignment contends that a major new issue arises that cuts across existing party lines.[48] If party leaders handle the issue well, the parties can adapt. But if party leaders straddle the issue and allow public passions to become inflamed, the issue may force a realignment. According to this theory, the rising tide of anti-slavery sentiment was just such an issue in the 1840s and 1850s. The Whig Party

Critical elections occur when large numbers of voters switch parties.

Drawing by Dana Fradon; © 1987 The New Yorker Magazine, Inc. Reprinted by permission.

"My God! I went to sleep a Democrat and I've awakened a Republican."

attempted to avoid confronting it, hoping to preserve its coalition of northerners and southerners. By the mid-1850s, however, this response became unacceptable to many northerners, who turned to a newly organized party—the anti-slavery Republicans.

Both theories of party realignment focus on the role parties play as linkages between the people and the government. The parties offer voters choices on the direction of public policy. Yet as years pass, social and economic changes occur and new issues arise. If the parties fail to adapt to the changes and to offer new choices on what the voters think are the most important issues, a realignment occurs. Thus, realignments are part of the process by which parties adjust to the changing demands people put on the government.[49]

From Realignment to Dealignment?

Once scholars recognized that party realignments followed a historical pattern, they began to look for evidence of a new, post-1932 realignment. Since previous realignments had occurred roughly once every generation, or about every thirty to forty years, scholars began to look for evidence that a sixth party system had begun to emerge in the 1960s. What they found, however, was quite different. Although the party coalitions did begin to change in the 1960s, the changes did not fit the pattern of a traditional realignment. Instead, a new pattern appeared.

To understand what scholars found when they began looking for evidence of a sixth party system, recall that the fifth party system began in 1932 with the New Deal realignment. For the next thirty years, a Democratic majority dominated American politics. Most voters identified themselves as Democrats, and Democrats controlled Congress for all but a few years. The only Republican to win the White House was Dwight Eisenhower.

In the 1960s, as theories about realignment theory would predict, the Democrats began to lose their dominant position in American politics. Many voters blamed them for failing to solve the nation's problems. As a result, the Democratic Party saw its commanding lead in party identification begin to slip. Yet unlike the realignments of the past, people did not switch their allegiances to the other party. In fact, the number of Republican identifiers began to slip as well, although not as sharply. Instead, people increasingly began to identify themselves as independents, as figure 9.3 shows. At the same time, they increasingly practiced ticket splitting, or voting for the presidential candidate of one party and the congressional or senatorial candidates of the other party (as figure 9.3 also shows). Party loyalties seemed to be weakening as people found it easier to vote for candidates of both parties in the same election.

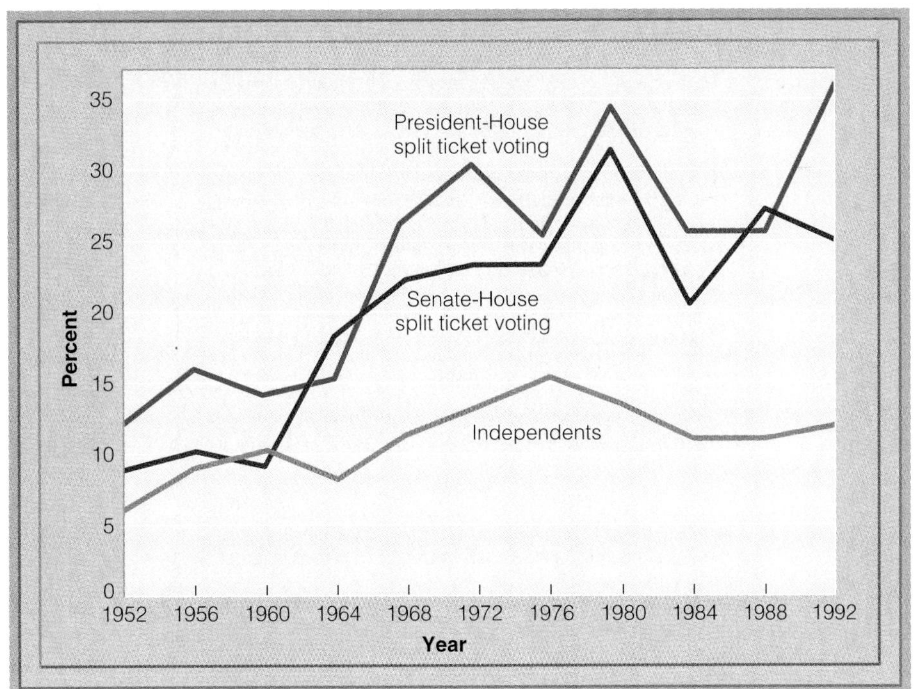

FIGURE 9.3
Signs of Party Dealignment

The increases in split-ticket voting and the number of people identifying themselves as independents indicate that party labels may matter less to people than they did in the past.

Source: Data are from SRC/CPS American National Election Studies.

Some observers see the rise in the number of people identifying themselves as independents and the rise in split-ticket voting as signs that, rather than realigning, voters have been *dealigning,* or distancing themselves from the two major parties. Put another way, these observers argue that since the late 1960s, the United States has been experiencing a period of **party dealignment** in which voters have become less partisan than they were in the past.[50] Many Americans are no longer loyal to either the Democratic or Republican parties.

Party dealignment
A trend in which voter loyalties to the two major parties weaken.

The evidence for dealignment, however, is ambiguous and subject to different interpretations. For example, while the number of people identifying themselves as independents rose in the 1960s and early 1970s, most of the new independents were actually independent in name only. Many people told survey interviewers they were independents but "leaned" toward one of the two major parties. As we saw in chapter 7, these so-called independents still voted as if they identified with one of the two major parties.[51]

In the same vein, dealignment is only one possible explanation for the rise in split-ticket voting. Some scholars argue that party loyalties have not weakened since the 1960s; rather, incumbents have become harder to beat. These scholars argue that presidential and congressional candidates make different appeals based on different sorts of issues. Because voters respond on the basis of different considerations when they vote for different offices, they end up splitting their ballots.[52] Again, the evidence for dealignment is ambiguous. Perhaps the electorate is dealigning, but perhaps other reasons explain ticket splitting.

To further complicate the debate over party dealignment, some evidence suggests that a party realignment is in fact occurring. Voters in the South and Rocky Mountain West are moving toward the Republican Party, whereas voters in the Northeast and Midwest are moving toward the Democratic Party.[53] Whether we are witnessing party dealignment or party realignment, it is clear that the New Deal party system that began in 1932 has changed enormously—so much so that many scholars argue that the New Deal party system is dead and that a new system has begun to form.[54]

The Uncertain Future

Since Ronald Reagan won the presidency in 1980, there have been signs that the trend toward dealignment, if there was such a trend, has stopped. The growth in the number

FIGURE 9.4
The Party Organization Hierarchy

Both the Democrats and the Republicans have hierarchically organized parties, but the organizations at the top do not have much control over the organizations below them.

of independents stalled, and the number of Republican identifiers increased during the 1980s. From 1981 through 1986, the Republicans held a majority in the Senate, for the first time since the 1950s. It seemed that a Republican realignment was finally happening. Yet by the end of the 1980s, that trend had weakened. The Democrats recaptured the Senate in 1986 and the White House in the 1992 election. In addition, the growth of Republican Party identifiers leveled off by the mid-1980s. Then, in 1994, the Republicans captured majorities in both the House and the Senate for the first time in forty years.[55] Following the election, polls showed a surge of voters identifying themselves with the Republican Party. Yet that surge was short-lived. As Republican plans to cut spending on popular programs began to attract attention, the Democrats began to revive. The 1996 elections changed little, leaving Bill Clinton in the White House and the Republicans in control of Congress. What will happen next is anyone's guess.

MODERN PARTY ORGANIZATION

Because parties exist primarily to contest elections, their formal organizations parallel the different levels of government (see figure 9.4). At the top of the organizations are the national party conventions, made up of the delegates who nominate the party's presidential ticket and write the party's platform and rules. Beneath the conventions are the national party committees, which manage the national party affairs between conventions. Also at this level are the Senate and House campaign committees, the congressional fundraising organizations that are independent of the national committees. The next rung down the ladder consists of the state party conventions and state party central committees. Below the state committees, in turn, are county central committees and in some areas legislative district committees, ward organizations, and precinct captains.

Although each party's formal organizational chart looks like a formal hierarchy, power and authority are not vested at the top, as they are in most organizations. Each party organization can make decisions independently on most questions and usually does not have to obey the decisions of the organization above it in the hierarchy. Perhaps the best way to understand party organizations is to think of them as being similar to the government under the Articles of Confederation (see chapter 2). The party organizations are loose confederations that agree to cooperate to achieve a common goal, yet cooperation is largely voluntary.

In many respects, the party organizations with the most independent power are those at the city and county levels. We shall, therefore, begin our examination of party organization at the bottom of the hierarchy.

Local Organizations

In the nineteenth century, the most important form of local party organization was the **party machine.** A machine is an organization built on the use of selective, material incentives for participation. Selective benefits are those that the party machine can give to its supporters and deny to others (for example, a contract for city services), as opposed to collective benefits, which everyone gets; material benefits have real monetary value (for example, a job) as opposed to nonmaterial benefits (see chapter 10). Of course, machines also use collective benefits that go to party supporters and opponents alike, such as public works like roads or airports, and nonmaterial benefits, such as statements of religious belief, to fortify their position, but these are not the keys to their success. Machines maintain power by doling out jobs, contracts, regulatory decisions, and other selective, material benefits in exchange for donations, campaign work, and support at the polls.

Party machine
A party organization built on the use of selective, material incentives for participation.

Party machines do not simply trade jobs for votes, nor do they buy votes with bribes. There are not enough jobs or money to do so. Instead, machines use selective, material benefits to raise an army of campaign workers who go door-to-door talking with voters and trying to persuade them to vote for the machine candidates.[56] Machines also use the campaign money they raise in all the other usual campaign methods. In the nineteenth century, this often meant giving precinct captains "walking-around money" so that they could buy small gifts for voters as tokens of friendship. Since the spread of radio and television, however, more and more machine money has gone into mass media campaigns.[57] Like other forms of party organization, party machines adapt to the rules of the system and the changes in campaign technology.

The best-known party machine since the 1950s was run by Chicago Mayor Richard J. Daley (see box 9.2). At its height of power from 1955 until Daley's death in 1976, the Cook County Democratic Committee controlled thousands of public and private sector jobs.[58] These **patronage jobs** were handed out to loyal party workers. The workers provided the machine with a loyal force of precinct captains, who would get to know every voter in their precincts and try to persuade them to vote for the machine's candidates. This one-two punch—a loyal force of precinct captains and a steady supply of small gifts and favors—made the Daley machine unbeatable.

Patronage job
A job given as a reward for loyal party service.

Although some weakened machines still survive in large northeastern and midwestern cities, most machines collapsed as the result of a series of Progressive Era reforms that swept the country from 1890 to 1920. In areas where support for progressives was strong, such as California, these reforms completely destroyed party machines and even weakened other types of parties. In other areas, such as Chicago, only some watered-down reforms passed, and machine politics survived.

Reforms That Affected Local Party Machines

The first blow to the party machines came just before the dawn of the Progressive Era—the introduction of the Australian idea of a publicly printed, secret ballot, known as the Australian ballot. Used first in Massachusetts in 1888, the reform quickly spread across the nation.[59] As we discussed in chapter 7, when people voted under the old system, they got their ballots from the local party and put them into

The People Behind the Rules

BOX 9.2

The Mayor and the Reformer: Richard J. Daley and Michael Shakman

When Chicago Mayor Richard J. Daley died, many journalists said the Chicago Democratic machine died with him. The machine died (or at least survives only on life support), but Daley's death was not the cause. If anyone killed the machine, it was a political reformer who helped change the rules—Michael Shakman.

Mayor Richard J. Daley

Richard J. Daley

Richard J. Daley was born May 15, 1902 in the Bridgeport section of Chicago, the neighborhood in which he was to live his entire life. He graduated from a Catholic high school, worked briefly in the stockyards, and then at age twenty-one took a position as a precinct captain for Democratic ward boss Joe McDonough. Along with that position in the party machine came a patronage job as clerk for the City Council. Daley rose both in the machine and in government jobs until 1955, when he was elected Mayor of Chicago—a job he would hold until his death in 1976.

As Mayor and Chair of the Cook County Democratic Committee, Daley presided over a local party machine that completely dominated Chicago politics. Not only did the machine hold all of the local elective offices, it controlled 35,000 government patronage jobs plus an additional 10,000 jobs in the private sector. Daley used the people in those jobs and the time and money they donated to the party to maintain his control. Although both Democratic and Republican reformers periodically challenged him in elections, none ever came close to winning.

Daley did not win merely because of his campaign workers and cash. He also won because he delivered good government—by Chicago standards. Chicago was, as its motto proclaimed, the city that worked. Under Daley's rule, government was efficient, in part because Daley could quickly resolve disputes between contending bureaucrats. Gridlock was never a problem. Moreover, Daley helped deliver federal subsidies for an enormous array of government development projects—including new expressways, a vastly expanded airport, and a revitalized downtown ("the Loop"). The rewards of having Daley as mayor were highly visible.

Michael Shakman

In 1969, Michael Shakman was a young attorney and University of Chicago graduate with an abiding interest in politics. When the state of Illinois decided it was time to revise its outdated constitution, Shakman sought election as one of Chicago's delegates to the state's constitutional convention. When the election was held, however, he lost to a candidate supported by Mayor Daley's political machine. Rather than accept defeat, Shakman decided to challenge the Daley machine in court.

The premise of Shakman's legal challenge was simple, and, to many observers, naive: political patronage is

Continued

ballot boxes in full view of the party's election watchers; consequently, the party could reward those who supported it and punish those who did not. The use of the Australian ballot, which allowed voters to enter a voting booth and vote in private, ended that system of reward and punishment and forced parties to persuade voters rather than threaten them.[60]

The next critical reform was the direct primary, which a few states adopted in the 1890s and which was extended to presidential nominations between 1904 and 1912. Under the old system, party committees—often dominated by bosses—selected nominees. In the primary system, voters in party primary elections choose the candidates they want to represent their party as nominees in the general election. When the party bosses lost the power to nominate candidates, they lost much of their ability to influence the behavior of elected officials as well. In some cases, voters chose anti-machine nominees; in other cases, the machine's own nominees

The People Behind the Rules

BOX 9.2 CONTINUED

Michael Shakman

illegal. Shakman pointed out that the precinct captains who had worked the neighborhoods on Election Day encouraging local residents to vote for his opponent were all city workers paid with city tax dollars to campaign. This gave machine candidates a nearly unbeatable edge over their opponents, who could not force city workers to help with their campaigns. In short, political patronage as it was practiced in Chicago virtually guaranteed that machine candidates would win political office.

Shakman eventually won two legal battles that devastated the patronage system the Chicago machine was built on. In *Shakman v. the Democratic Organization of Cook County* (1972), a federal district court initially ruled that *hiring* city or county employees based on tests of political loyalty was acceptable only if the employees had policy-making positions or some confidential political role. Working for the party could not be a requirement for holding jobs such as garbage collector, building inspector, street cleaner, or clerk. In 1976, the district court extended its previous ruling to prevent *firing* government employees in Cook County for failure to perform political favors for a party or candidate.

A federal appeals court partially overturned the Shakman decisions, but not before the newly elected, reform-minded Mayor Harold Washington accepted a consent decree in 1983 that made the Shakman decisions binding on the City of Chicago.

The Shakman decisions had a stunning effect on the Chicago machine. When Mayor Daley died in 1976, his machine controlled an estimated 35,000 government patronage jobs. When Harold Washington won the election for mayor in 1983, he had only 800 patronage jobs at his disposal to distribute to party loyalists.

A much weakened patronage system survives in Chicago, where Daley's son now serves as mayor. Few city jobs may be handed out as patronage, but some other government jobs in Cook County can be handed out in return for political favors. In addition, the machine still controls or influences many private sector jobs. (A 1996 Supreme Court decision weakened the ability of a party to use public contracts for patronage purposes.) Yet without the huge supply of city jobs, the machine began to break up. Only a shadow of its past strength remains.

Sources: Anne Freedman, "Doing Battle with the Patronage Army: Politics, Courts, and Personnel Administration in Chicago," *Public Administration Review* 48 (September/October 1988): 847–59; Alton Miller, *Harold Washington: The Mayor, The Man* (Chicago: Bonus Books, 1989), pp. 99–100; *O'Hare Truck Service, Inc., et al., v. City of Northlake et al.*, 95-191, (1996); Milton Rakove, *Don't Make No Waves . . . Don't Back No Losers* (Bloomington: Indiana University Press, 1975); Mike Royko, *Boss: Richard J. Daley of Chicago* (New York: Signet, 1971).

turned away from their patrons. In both cases, political power shifted from local party organizations to elected officials. The bosses lost power and the candidates became the dominant players.[61]

Along with the Australian ballot and the direct primary, a third critical reform was the spread of the merit civil service system, under which government employees were hired on the basis of merit alone. Under the old patronage, or *spoils* system, city and county employees were hired for political reasons and could be fired by party bosses if they became disloyal. The bosses justified the practice, in the candid words of William Marcy, a prominent nineteenth-century American politician, because "To the victor belong the spoils."[62] In the merit system, by contrast, employees are hired on the basis of merit—often determined by competitive examinations—and are protected from being fired for political reasons (see chapter 13). Without control over the supply of jobs to use as selective, material benefits, many party machines collapsed.

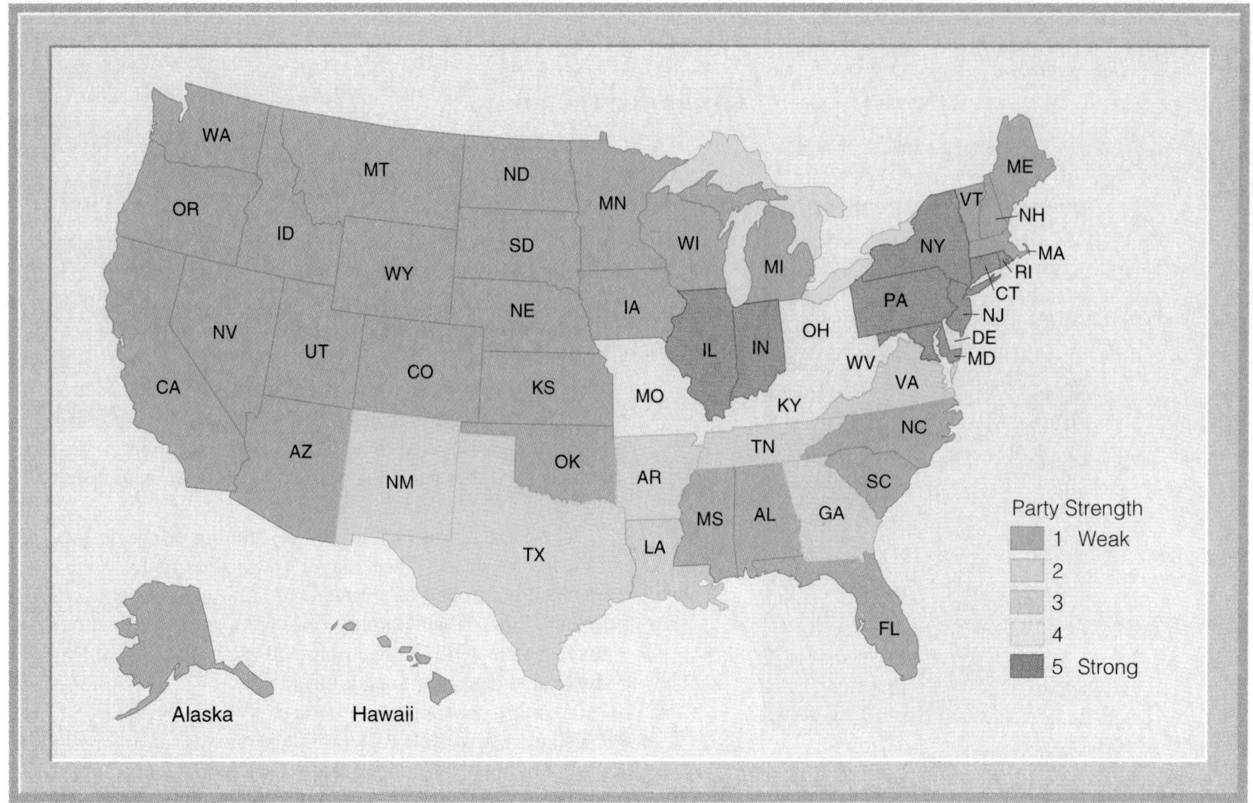

FIGURE 9.5
Party Strength in America

Over time, the strongest political parties have been in the northeast and midwest; the weakest parties have been in the west and the plains states.

Source: David R. Mayhew, *Placing Parties in American Politics,* 1986 Princeton University Press, Princeton, NJ.

The merit system was not a new idea. The federal government began hiring on merit as a result of the Pendleton Act of 1883, which Congress passed after a rejected job seeker expressed his disappointment by assassinating President Garfield. But from the 1890s through 1920, many states expanded civil service protection of employees so that they could not be fired for political reasons. Whenever jobs were converted from patronage to merit, the party machines lost power.

The progressive reforms did not pass everywhere. Some states, such as California, swept away party machines and made it as difficult as possible for the surviving party organizations to have any influence.[63] Other states, such as Illinois, passed only a few of the reforms, so that machines survived.[64] The remaining machines are in what the map in figure 9.5 describes as strong party states; they are mostly in the north central states and in the east.

Other Consequences of Local Reforms

The changes in rules that caused local party machines to collapse in many areas often went much further. Some progressive reformers sought not only to prevent corruption, but to destroy parties, which they considered inherently corrupt.[65] Additional reforms—formalizing party structure, requiring party leaders to be elected in primaries, inhibiting cooperation among campaigns and among different party organizations—enormously weakened parties. The result was that in progressive states, parties became weak and ineffective. Not only could parties not dominate politics, they were less influential than many interest groups.

The weakening of party organizations had two major consequences: it encouraged the rise of private clubs of partisans and promoted a shift to candidate-centered campaigns. The private clubs of partisans began to organize to perform the tasks officially regulated parties were not allowed to do—for instance, endorse candidates in the primaries. The club movement spread rapidly in the 1950s so that in some progressive states, such as California, a network of clubs developed to parallel the official party organizations.[66] In California, for instance, the California Democratic Council developed as a coalition of local clubs. These local clubs have regular meetings and engage in many of the activities of old-fashioned parties (except nominating candidates), but they can do so with almost no government regulation or interference.

The second consequence of weakening parties was the rise of **candidate-centered campaigns.** Instead of relying on the local party organizations to run a slate of candidates (which happened in traditional strong parties), individual candidates set up their own campaign organizations, raised their own money, and campaigned independently of other candidates in their party.[67]

Candidate-centered campaigns Campaigns in which candidates set up campaign organizations, raise money, and campaign independently of other candidates in their party.

Two other causes, in addition to the decline of party organizations brought about by the progressive reforms, contributed to the rise of candidate-centered campaigns—the spread of television and the passage of the campaign finance laws of the 1970s. The spread of radio in the 1930s and, far more important, television in the 1960s (described in chapter 8), had a major impact on campaigns and parties. Candidates who had relied on party organizations to contact voters no longer had to do so. Television offered a way to speak directly to voters without enlisting an army of campaign workers to walk door-to-door. Increasingly throughout the 1960s, candidates began to put more time, effort, and money into developing mass media campaigns.[68] Traditional party organizations simply became less relevant.

The new rules for campaign finance also influenced what candidates did when seeking office. Before the passage of the 1971 Federal Election Campaign Act (FECA) and its 1974 amendments, candidates could raise as much money as they wanted by soliciting donations of any size. But the new FECA laws restricted the size of donations for campaigns to federal offices (see chapter 12). The most important limitations were that individuals could contribute no more than $1,000 to each candidate per election and that political action committees, or PACs, could contribute no more than $5,000. Following the federal government's lead, a number of states passed similar laws limiting donations in state elections.[69] The consequence was that, instead of relying on a relatively small number of wealthy patrons, candidates now had to engage in mass fundraising.[70] Aided by computers and the new technology of mass mailing, candidates set up their own fundraising operations and thus became even more independent of political parties. In short, new rules and new technology combined to enable candidates to run independent campaigns.

With the club movement and the rise of candidate-centered campaigns, political parties in most areas of the country have been reduced to weak organizations that only assist the candidates with their campaigns. Candidates now commonly draw on the party organizations, on loose networks of local political activists, and on interest groups to staff and fund their campaigns. Because party organizations lack the strength to determine who wins the nomination and the election, they play only a supportive role to the candidates.

Although party organizations no longer dominate campaigns, they still matter. A 1979–80 survey of the 7,300 county-level party organizations in the United States showed a high level of activity. Most of them engaged in a wide range of activities—organizing fundraising and campaign events such as rallies, raising money for their own operations, and donating money to the campaign organizations of their parties' candidates, distributing campaign literature, operating phone banks, organizing door-to-door canvassing, and conducting other campaign efforts.[71]

Almost all local party organization activity focuses narrowly on campaigns and occurs during the campaign season. The campaigns are the exciting part of politics for party activists. When the campaigns start, the activists arrive; when the campaigns end, they turn to other pursuits.[72] As a result, during the off-season, parties are barely noticeable. The 1979–80 survey of county-level party organizations found that fewer than 15 percent had year-round offices or even telephone listings. Even fewer, less than 10 percent, had so much as a single, part-time paid staffer. Between campaigns, others carry on the business of politics.

Modern mass fundraising techniques, pioneered by people such as conservative Richard Viguere (shown here with a printer capable of printing 20,000 letters an hour), helped pave the way for candidate-centered campaigns.

The history of local parties over the course of the twentieth century, then, is one of declining influence. But it is also one of adapting to new rules and new technology. From the Progressive Era reforms to the FECA laws, the rules governing parties and campaigns have changed enormously. Similarly, the advent of radio, television, and the computer, which made modern mass fundraising possible, have also had a huge impact. Yet the parties have responded to these changes so that they can continue pursuing their goals—winning elections and controlling government.

State Organizations

State party organizations, like their local counterparts, usually lack political power. Every state has a Democratic and Republican state party organization, usually consisting of a state party chair, a party central committee, and a staff. Members of the central committee may be chosen in several ways. Most commonly they are elected in primaries or sent as representatives of lower-level party organizations.

Although state party organizations sit above local organizations in the party hierarchy, they generally have little control over them. Many state organizations, in fact, have little control over anything.

State parties lack power for the same reasons that local organizations often lack power—state party leaders do not control or even have much influence over nominations and elections. In almost all states, voters choose their party's nominees in primary elections. The state party leaders cannot give the nominations to whomever they want. Moreover, the candidates for the nominations build their own campaign organizations and raise money independently of the state parties. The state parties can donate money or other resources, but for many years, few had enough money to make much of a difference. A survey of state party leaders in the late 1970s showed that the average state party budget was only $341,000 and that state parties averaged only 7.7 staff members during election years.[73] This may now be changing. In the 1991–92 election cycle, state parties raised an average of $1.9 million. They also had larger and more professionalized staffs.[74] Still, in an age of multimillion dollar campaigns for statewide office, even these seemingly impressive resources may not do much to win influence with candidates.

Because they do not have legal control over nominations or the resources to have real power, state party organizations generally content themselves with providing services to candidates. They raise and distribute small amounts of money; they run voter registration and get-out-the-vote drives; they do public opinion polling and offer a variety of other useful services.

In a few cases where state party organizations play a role beyond being a service bureau, they do so because others provide the political muscle. In some states, for instance, when a party controls the governorship, the governor appoints the state party chair, who acts as a political agent of the governor. A typical job for such a chair is to handle the governor's patronage appointments.[75] The state party committees and the state chair rarely have much independent political power.

National Organizations

At the top of each party's hierarchy are the national party conventions and the national party committees—the Democratic National Committee and the Republican National Committee. In addition, each party's members in the House and Senate have campaign committees to raise funds for themselves. In short, it's somewhat crowded at the top.

Each major party has a national convention every four years to nominate its presidential and vice presidential candidates, to write its party platform, and to make changes in the party rules (the presidential selection process leading up to these conventions is discussed in chapter 12). Between the national conventions, the national committees and party chairs conduct party business. When they were originally created in the 1850s, the national committees' only role was to organize the presidential conventions and to help coordinate the presidential campaign in the fall. Aside from helping with presidential campaigns, the national organizations did almost nothing. Over time, the committees gained other responsibilities and became involved in state and local races, but they remain focused on national politics.

The Democratic and Republican National Committee chairpersons in 1996: Sen. Christopher Dodd (D-Conn.) (top) and Haley Barbour (bottom).

The national party committees, like state party committees, do not have much power (although, as we shall see, their power has recently been growing). They neither control the presidential nomination nor have much influence on that or any other election. Thus, like the state party organizations, the national party organizations have few resources and are limited in what they can do.

During the 1950s and 1960s, the national committees barely had enough money to provide more than token services.[76] At the end of the 1970s, however, the Democratic and Republican national committees and the four congressional campaign committees began to rebuild.[77] Paradoxically, the parties' resurgence stems largely from the same factors that forced individual candidates to become less dependent on local political parties—the FECA limits on campaign donations and the advent of computer-based mass-mail technology. The development of computerized mailing lists and mass-mailing techniques allowed parties to get into the fundraising business in the same way candidates did.[78] To be sure, the national parties were not alone in their efforts to raise funds, but they succeeded in raising far more money than ever before.

The parties used the money to build professional staffs offering a wide range of services—registration and get-out-the-vote drives, polling, issue research, candidate schools, campaign management schools, and of course, cash donations to candidates.[79] Their new-found resources and success allowed them to branch out and exert more influence in elections around the country. They have even entered state politics, attempting to build up state and local party organizations with the ultimate goal of electing more of their candidates to national office. As for the four congressional fundraising committees, they have parlayed their money and contacts into what may be described as a "national-party-as-intermediary" role—recruiting candidates for Congress and bringing together donors and candidates with good prospects for victory.[80] Thus they, too, have gained in stature since the 1970s. In general, all of the national party organizations have gained influence over the last two decades.

Relationships Among Party Organizations

Looking over the full range of party organizations, from local to national, we see a set of independent organizations and groups of candidates cooperating with each other to achieve a set of common goals. The cooperation in almost all cases is voluntary. Although we may loosely speak of the national parties as being above the state and local parties in the party hierarchy, the national party organizations have little real control over local party organizations. Their cooperation stems from the belief that if they work together, they will more likely achieve the party's goals of winning elections and controlling government.

What parties do has changed over time and differs even now from one part of the country to another. Parties have responded not only to voters' preferences, but to changes in rules and in campaign technology as well. In short, party history is the history of flexible organizations adapting to their times.

Summary

Politicians organized political parties to achieve practical political goals. They set up parties primarily to help them win elections and, to a lesser extent, to help them govern and pursue policy goals once elected. Despite the immediate practical nature of these goals, parties serve other specific purposes. They recruit and nominate candidates; they mobilize voters; they contest elections; they form governments and coordinate policy across independent units of government. By performing these tasks, parties help hold elected officials accountable for their actions. They perform a vital function for democracy.

The United States has a two-party system in which the election rules and laws encourage both parties to take stands near the political center. As the spatial theory of elections shows, in a single-member, plurality electoral system such as ours, politicians are more likely to win elections if they form two large, centrist parties. In a proportional representation system—more common in other democracies—there is much less incentive for large, centrist parties to form.

The history of American elections can best be described as consisting of five electoral periods—1796–1824, 1828–1856, 1860–1892, 1896–1928, and 1932 to the present. The periods were separated by elections of sharp conflict in which the coalitions making up the two parties realigned and in which new issues arose. The most recent realignment occurred in 1932, when the Republican dominance from the turn of the century on crumbled, a Democratic majority emerged, and the parties began to differ primarily along economic lines. Since the 1960s, however, this New Deal coalition has frayed, and some observers suggest that we are now in a period of party dealignment or are undergoing a new realignment.

Parties operate at the local, state, and national level. To be useful to politicians, parties had to adapt to local conditions over the years—especially to laws regulating party organization. When mass political parties first organized, no laws limited their behavior. Relying on patronage and other selective, material benefits, party machines grew to dominate politics in most parts of the nation. Then, in a series of reforms enacted during the Progressive Era, state legislatures instituted the use of the Australian ballot, established direct primaries, limited patronage, and otherwise restricted the power of machines. Parties changed their behavior, losing power but continuing to do whatever they could to help party members win office. With the passage of laws in the 1970s limiting the size of campaign donations and the development of mass-mail technology, parties again adapted—this time shaping a role for themselves in coordinating fundraising and other supportive activities among party donors, activists, and candidates across the country.

Although parties have changed enormously over the years, they still seek to win elections and thus still serve as links helping voters hold politicians accountable. To do so, they have adapted to two dynamics in the political system: changing voter preferences and changes in rules and campaign technologies.

Key Terms

Candidate-centered campaigns
Caucus/convention system
Centrist parties
Critical elections
Direct primary
Duverger's Law
Median voter hypothesis
New Deal coalition
Party dealignment
Party machine
Party platform
Party realignment
Patronage job
Political cleavages
Political party
Proportional representation system
Single-member, plurality electoral system
Two-party system

Readings for Further Study

Aldrich, John H. *Why Parties? The Origin and Transformation of Party Politics in America.* Chicago: University of Chicago Press, 1995. An examination of the histories of U.S. political parties from the 1790s to the Civil War and of modern parties after World War II. Aldrich shows why parties perform three essential tasks in our democracy—limiting the number of candidates for office, mobilizing voters, and maintaining the majorities necessary to attain policy goals once in office.

Beck, Paul A., and Frank J. Sorauf. *Party Politics in America,* 7th ed. Boston: Little, Brown, 1992. An outstanding textbook on American political parties, covering virtually every aspect of their history, their organization, and their relationship with the people and the government.

Canon, David T. *Actors, Athletes, and Astronauts: Political Amateurs in the United States Congress.* Chicago: University of Chicago Press, 1990. A definitive study of amateur politicians—people with no previous political experience—in elections and Congress. Canon examines why amateurs run for office, why they win, and how they behave once elected.

Downs, Anthony. *An Economic Theory of Democracy.* New York: Harper & Row, 1957. The classic analysis of parties and elections that introduced the spatial model of elections. With minimal use of formal mathematics, Downs offers an abstract way of understanding how election rules affect government decisions and public policy.

Ehrenhalt, Alan. *The United States of Ambition.* New York: Random House, 1991. An analysis of the rise of independent, ambitious, reelection-oriented politicians over the last thirty years. Using a series of case studies from across the nation, Ehrenhalt shows how the emergence of these new political entrepreneurs has reshaped the character of U.S. politics.

Hofstadter, Richard. *The Age of Reform: From Bryan to FDR.* New York: Vintage Books, 1955. A classic study of political reform from 1890 to 1940. Hofstadter examines and explains the sweep of reform from the Progressive Era through Franklin Roosevelt's New Deal.

Rakove, Milton. *Don't Make No Waves . . . Don't Back No Losers.* Bloomington: Indiana University Press, 1975. An insider's look at the Cook County Democratic machine of Chicago Mayor Richard Daley. Rakove, a political scientist and party worker in Chicago, both describes the machine and explains how it survived and prospered well into the 1970s.

Schlesinger, Joseph A. *Political Parties and the Winning of Office.* Ann Arbor: University of Michigan Press, 1991. A broad, theoretical look at how the rules governing our electoral system influence the behavior of politicians and political activists.

Sundquist, James L. *Dynamics of the Party System,* rev. ed. Washington, D.C.: Brookings Institution, 1983. A study of party history and the politics of realignment. Sundquist blends an electoral history of the United States with a groundbreaking theoretical analysis of why party coalitions rise and fall.

CHAPTER

10

INTEREST GROUPS

Defining Interest Groups
Interest Groups Versus Political Parties
The Roles of Interest Groups
The Growth of Interest Groups
The Diversity of Organized Interests
Economic Interest Groups
Citizen Groups
Government Interest Groups
Coalitions and Divisions
Interest Group Formation and Maintenance
Obstacles to Interest Group Formation
Overcoming Obstacles to Interest Group Formation
Interest Group Maintenance
Interest Group Bias
Interest Group Strategies
Creating Political Action Committees
Lobbying the Government
Mobilizing Public Opinion
Litigating
Interest Group Influence
External Factors
Internal Factors
The Balance Sheet on Interest Groups
A Love/Hate Relationship
Calls for Reform
The Contributions of Interest Groups
Summary
Key Terms
Readings for Further Study

In 1993, the Clinton administration proposed rewriting the nation's law regulating mining on federal lands. The existing law, which was passed in 1872 when Ulysses S. Grant was president and attracting settlers to the West was more important than protecting the federal treasury or the environment, allowed miners to buy public land for as little as $2.50 an acre, imposed no royalty fees (or taxes) on the gold, silver, or other minerals they extracted, and did not require them to restore the land they mined. Environmental groups applauded the administration's proposal to impose a royalty fee as well as environmental clean-up requirements, but mining companies denounced it. They argued vehemently that the proposal would drive up the cost of mining, force them to fire thousands of workers, and doom hundreds of mining communities in the West. Under pressure from mining companies and their employees, members of Congress from mining states battled the administration's plan. After nearly two years of legislative wrangling, they eventually defeated it.[1] The administration had no choice but to abide by a law that it estimated cost the taxpayers $100 million annually in lost royalties. Thus, in September 1995, the Interior Department sold 110 acres of federal land in Idaho to a Dutch mining company. The sale price for the land, which was believed to sit atop more than $1 billion in minerals, was $275.[2]

The defeat of the effort to rewrite the nation's mining law vividly illustrates the potential influence interest groups can have on public policy. Indeed, interest groups are so much a part of American politics that the United States has been called "the interest group society."[3] Yet for more than two hundred years, people have worried that interest groups distort public policy to serve narrow, selfish ends. In "Federalist No. 10," James Madison warned that, left unchecked, "factions"—the term *interest groups* appeared in a later era—would harm the public good.[4] Madison's fear echoes today in the many complaints that government is beholden to special interests.

Interest groups, like the other groups we are examining in this part of the book, both shape and are shaped by the rules of our political system. In earlier chapters, we showed how the structural rules of American government favor the individual; they allow any person or group to challenge the political system. The large number of interest groups in the United States is the result of these rules. And, just as important, interest groups have a strong hand in shaping what the government does; after all, they exist primarily to ensure that government policy favors their causes.

Do interest groups help or harm democracy in the United States? Do they enable the public to obtain what it wants from government, or do they block the wishes of the American people? Is the mining companies' success in their battle against the Clinton administration's proposal to rewrite the nation's mining law typical of interest group politics, or unusual? These are the questions we will explore in this chapter. We begin by discussing the role interest groups play in American politics. We go on to chart the growth of interest group activity since the end of World War II, to survey the increasingly diverse array of interest groups, and to analyze how interest groups form. We also review the strategies interest groups use to influence public policy and explain why some groups succeed and others fail. We conclude the chapter by assessing the vices and virtues of interest group politics and evaluating the effect interest groups have on American democracy.

Defining Interest Groups

Interest group
An organized group of people who share some goals and try to influence public policy.

"An **interest group** is an organized body of individuals who share some goals and who try to influence public policy."[5] The key phrase here is "to influence public policy." There are thousands of different organizations in the United States. Most pursue some private or social purpose, as is the case with the college or university you attend. These organizations become interest groups only when they deliberately try to affect local, state, and federal government policies. Thus, when colleges and universities seek to influence public policy, say, by urging Congress to spend more money on basic scientific research, they become interest groups.[6]

In 1993, the Clinton administration proposed requiring mining companies to pay a royalty fee (or tax) on minerals they mined on federal lands. Mining companies and their employees opposed the proposal, and they persuaded Congress to kill it.

To further understand the concept of interest groups, it is important to answer two questions: First, what distinguishes an interest group from a political party? Second, what roles do interest groups play in American politics?

Interest Groups Versus Political Parties

Since political parties and interest groups are both organized to influence public policy, you might wonder how the two differ. The answer lies in the difference between *aggregating* and *articulating* interests. As we saw in chapter 9, political parties nominate candidates who run under the party banner in elections for government office. To win these elections, political parties typically try to combine, or aggregate, numerous different interests and viewpoints into a single policy platform they hope will appeal to a broad range of voters. In contrast, most interest groups focus their attention on articulating a specific interest or viewpoint, such as gun control, lower taxes, or health care reform. As a result, most interest groups worry less about a politician's ideology or party affiliation than about whether he or she favors policies the group supports.[7]

Although political parties and interest groups are distinct entities, their fates are closely linked. Many interest groups are deeply involved in electoral politics, and some ally themselves with a political party. Labor unions, for example, traditionally support Democratic candidates, whereas the Christian Coalition helps the Republican Party recruit candidates for office. More generally, interest groups can address issues that political parties do not or cannot. Some issues simply are too narrow to be a high priority for either of the major political parties. Other issues are the subject of major disagreement within a party, which effectively prevents the party from advancing the interest in question. In either of these instances, an interest group can offer a useful alternative to a political party as a means of influencing public policy.

The Roles of Interest Groups

In seeking to influence public policy, interest groups try to protect existing rules or to establish new ones that benefit their particular interests. They exert their influence by performing five main functions: they represent the interests of their members to the government, enable people to participate in politics, educate government officials and the public about issues, build support for new policies, and monitor how the government administers programs.

Representation

Interest groups work first and foremost to see that public policy reflects the interests of their members. The Human Rights Campaign Fund works to advance the cause of gay and lesbian rights, the National Association of the Deaf Legal Defense Fund fights on behalf of the hearing impaired, and the Tobacco Institute promotes the interests of cigarette companies. Because the federal government has the power to set (or revise) the rules governing nearly every aspect of American society, almost every major interest group maintains an active presence in Washington, D.C. But interest groups also press their cause in state capitols and at city hall as well, as we will discuss at greater length in chapter 15.

Political Participation

Interest groups also enable people to participate in politics. Most people lack the time, training, or desire to run for and hold public office, or, as we saw in chapter 7, to participate in politics in other ways. For many Americans, then, interest groups offer a more convenient and less time-consuming way to shape public policy. Moreover, by uniting people who share a common cause, interest groups take advantage of the fact that there is strength in numbers.

Education

Interest groups devote considerable effort to education. They clearly want to educate government officials. But interest groups also work to explain government policy to their members and the broader public. When the Supreme Court handed down its decision in the 1992 abortion-rights case *Planned Parenthood of Southeastern Pennsylvania v. Casey,* for example, pro-choice and pro-life groups sent spokespersons to news shows across the country, took out newspaper advertisements, and launched direct-mail campaigns to explain their views of the ruling. The groups hoped their efforts would shape public opinion and thereby influence public policy.

Agenda Building

By educating their members, government officials, and the general public, interest groups help to push new issues onto the political agenda, the list of issues government officials are actively debating. A major topic of debate in the early 1990s, for example, was whether the federal government should require companies to give unpaid leave to the parents of newborn babies. A bill to mandate parental leave moved to the top of Congress's agenda and passed in 1993 only because labor unions and women's groups had fought for nearly a decade to build public support for the idea.

Program Monitoring

Because it matters not only which laws are passed but also how those laws are implemented, many interest groups monitor how the government administers programs. Sometimes the law even requires federal agencies to work with interest groups. To ensure that the administration takes American economic interests into account during international trade talks, for example, Congress requires U.S. negotiators to consult with labor, industry, farm, and consumer groups. If interest groups believe an agency is violating the intent of a law, they may alert sympathetic members of Congress, mobilize their membership, or even sue the government.

As you can see, interest groups play several important roles in American politics. By representing their members, participating in the political system, educating the general public, promoting their own agenda, and monitoring government programs, interest groups help shape the rules that define policy outcomes. Although interest groups matter, this does not mean they always help produce good public policy. Some citizens may not see their interests represented; groups may mislead the public about what the government is doing; and well-organized groups may distort public policy to benefit their own interests. At the end of the chapter, we return to the question of the pros and cons of interest group politics.

Interest groups have long been a feature of American politics. In 1773, the Sons of Liberty protested the tax policies of the British crown by throwing the Boston Tea Party.

The Growth of Interest Groups

With so many radio talk shows attacking "special interests," you might think that interest groups are a new phenomenon in American politics. They aren't. In 1773, a group of Bostonians banded together as the Sons of Liberty and protested the tax policies of the British crown by throwing the Boston Tea Party. Some sixty years later, the French writer Alexis de Tocqueville wrote that interest groups, or what he called associations, were an integral part of American politics. "Americans of all ages, all stations in life, and all types of disposition, are forever forming associations."[8]

Almost all the associations Tocqueville witnessed in his travels around the United States were groups with a limited geographical reach. One of the first interest groups organized on a national level was the American Anti-Slavery Society, founded in 1833. The number of national interest groups grew after the Civil War. The American Woman Suffrage Association and the National Woman Suffrage Association were both founded in 1869 to see that women won the right to vote (see chapter 5). The Grange was formed in the 1860s to promote the interests of farmers whose ability to get crops and livestock to market was threatened by the monopolistic practices of the railroads. The Woman's Christian Temperance Union was founded in 1874 to persuade Congress and state legislatures to prohibit the manufacture and sale of liquor.

Interest groups, then, are well ingrained in American politics. What is new about them in the 1990s is their sheer number. By one count, roughly six hundred interest groups were based in Washington in 1942; in 1995, there were more than seven thousand.[9] Even this number is a rough guess. No one knows the exact number of interest groups because they come in so many different shapes and sizes.

What accounts for the rapid growth in interest groups? The answer lies in a complex mix of factors. Americans have become increasingly better educated, and as a result, are more apt to recognize the benefits of joining an interest group. The civil rights and anti-war protests of the 1960s demonstrated the power of interest group politics and provided examples for new groups to emulate. Improvements in computer and communications technology have made it far easier for groups to target supporters with mailings and phone calls soliciting contributions. And the emergence of issues that cut across party lines, such as consumer rights and the environment, has encouraged people to look to interest groups for action.

The legacy of the 1960s, improvements in technology, and the rise of new issues have all led people to place more demands on the government. And as Congress and the White House have acted to meet these demands, government itself has stimulated the growth of interest groups. When the government intervenes in (or withdraws from) the economy and society, it affects the interests of many people. If people feel harmed by government action, they are likely to band together. Thus, when defense spending dropped sharply after the Vietnam War, numerous interest groups sprang up to argue for greater defense spending. In turn, when the Reagan administration initiated a massive military buildup in the early 1980s, the number of peace and arms control groups jumped sharply. At the same time, the government may directly create interest groups. Many of the Great Society programs of the 1960s required the federal government to create and work with local groups. If the number of interest groups in the United States today is any indication, we are indeed an interest group society.

The Diversity of Organized Interests

The astounding number of interest groups in the United States is matched by their incredible diversity. As we discussed in chapter 3, American society has become increasingly diverse, and this diversity has spawned a huge number of groups that flood government with conflicting demands and expectations. No simple typology fully captures the wide array of interest groups in the United States. Yet most interest groups fall into one of three categories: economic interest groups, citizen groups, and government interest groups.

Economic Interest Groups

The vast majority of interest groups work to advance the economic interests of their members. There are four main types of economic interest groups: business groups, labor unions, agricultural organizations, and professional associations.

Business Groups

Business groups are the most common interest group. How common depends on how one counts. If we count only formally organized interest groups, then business accounts for 25 percent of the interest groups in Washington.[10] If, however, we also count lobbyists and law firms hired to represent business interests, business interests constitute up to 70 percent of all the interest groups that knock at Washington's doors.[11]

Businesses promote their interests using three distinct types of organization. The organization with the broadest membership is the peak business association. Peak associations attempt, when possible, to speak for the business community as a whole. The most important peak business associations in the United States are the U.S. Chamber of Commerce, the National Association of Manufacturers (NAM), and the Business Roundtable. The Chamber represents an amalgam of local chambers of commerce and other groups, NAM represents more than ten thousand manufacturing firms, and the Business Roundtable represents the country's two hundred largest corporations.

Many businesses also try to advance their economic interests through trade associations. These organizations represent companies in the same line of business. Ford, GM, and Chrysler, for example, all belong to the Motor Vehicle Manufacturers Association, while Exxon, Gulf, and Sunoco all belong to the American Petroleum Institute. As a rule, trade associations focus on issues that affect their particular industry.

Finally, many businesses try to influence public policy directly. Most large firms have offices in Washington that handle relations with the federal government. Firms without an office in the nation's capital often hire a Washington law firm or lobbyist to represent their interests.

Organized Labor

The most important voice in organized labor is the AFL-CIO, which is essentially a union of unions. Its member unions include the Teamsters (1.3 million members in 1994), the American Federation of State, County, and Municipal Employees (1.2 million), the United Food and Commercial Workers International Union (1 million), and the United Auto Workers (771,000). But not all unions belong to the AFL-CIO. The powerful National Education Association, for example, which represents 2 million school teachers, remains independent.

Unions try to influence government policy on a wide range of issues. Besides issues of obvious interest to workers such as the minimum wage and safety regulations, many unions address broader political issues such as civil rights or health care. Yet the ability of unions to influence government policy has waned in recent years. As we discussed in chapter 3, union membership dropped sharply in the 1980s, in part because highly unionized manufacturing industries such as autos and steel laid off many workers to cut costs and in part because government policy favored management at the expense of unions. Union influence was further undermined when union officials failed to persuade their members to vote for the candidates the unions endorsed. In 1996, for example, 39 percent of labor households voted for Bob Dole or Ross Perot, even though most unions endorsed Bill Clinton.[12]

Agricultural Groups

General farm interest groups are one kind of agricultural interest group.[13] The biggest and most influential general farm interest group is the American Farm Bureau Federation. It represents the interests of large farms, and it tends to favor the Republican Party and conservative causes.[14] Less consequential for policy making are the American Agricultural Movement, the National Farmers Organization, and the National Farmers Union. These groups represent the interests of small farmers, and they tend to ally with the Democratic Party and liberal causes.

In recent years, general farm interest groups have seen their influence eroded by groups organized around specific commodities. Almost every crop and livestock has a corresponding interest group. Corn farmers join the National Corn Growers Association, rice farmers join the American Rice Growers Cooperative Association, and hog farmers join the National Swine Growers Association. Farm-oriented businesses such as pesticide manufacturers and farm-implement dealers also have their own organizations.

Professional Associations

Professional associations resemble labor unions. The main difference is that professional associations involve higher-status occupations that generally require extended formal training and even government licensing. The two best-known professional associations are the American Bar Association (ABA), the largest organization of lawyers, and the American Medical Association (AMA). While the ABA and the AMA garner the most headlines, almost every profession has its own association. Optometrists join the American Optometric Association, real estate agents the National Association of Realtors, and pharmacists the National Association of Retail Druggists. But not all professionals join the association that claims to represent them. For example, only 44 percent of doctors in the United States actually belong to the AMA.[15]

Besides groups organized along professional lines, some professional associations are organized to advance the interests of women and minorities in their membership. Examples include the American Association of University Women, the National Association of Black Accountants, and the National Association of Women Lawyers.

Citizen Groups

The civil rights and anti-war movements of the 1960s spurred the rise of **citizen groups.** Unlike economic interest groups, citizen groups mobilize to promote their visions of the public good rather than their own economic interests.[16] Because citizen

Citizen groups
Interest groups, also known as public interest groups, dedicated to promoting a vision of good public policy rather than the economic interests of their members.

The National Association for the Advancement of Colored People (NAACP) is the nation's largest and most prominent civil rights interest group.

groups seek to advance what they perceive to be the public good, they are often called public interest groups. This latter label is problematic; conservatives seldom hail the American Civil Liberties Union for advancing the public interest; nor do many liberals praise the work of the National Rifle Association. Moreover, people's visions of the public good often coincide with their economic interests. For example, students tend to think that low-cost, high-quality public education is in the public interest.

Citizen groups exist for almost every issue. Some groups favor broad political agendas. Americans for Democratic Action and People for the American Way support a wide array of liberal policy positions; the American Conservative Union and the Eagle Forum push a variety of conservative policies. Other citizen groups are known as *single-issue groups* because they target specific issues, such as civil rights (National Association for the Advancement of Colored People, or NAACP), the environment (Greenpeace), good government (Common Cause), and women's issues (National Organization for Women), to name just a few. As table 10.1 suggests, many distinct single-issue groups may exist on a given issue, with each taking a different emphasis and approach.

Although most citizen groups are secular in orientation, some interest groups are associated with the many religions people practice in the United States. Religious groups active in politics include the National Council of Churches, the U.S. Catholic Conference, and the American Jewish Congress.

Government Interest Groups

The federal government funds and regulates many of the programs state and local governments run. Given the preeminence of the federal government, state and local governments have their own interest groups. Most states and many large cities have a liaison office in Washington, and many also hire Washington law firms to represent them. State and local governments also have their own associations. Issues that affect the interests of state and local governments are likely to attract the attention of groups such as the National Governor's Association, the National Association of Counties, and the National League of Cities.

Foreign governments provide another set of government interest groups. Most embassies devote much energy to representing their country's interests to Congress and the executive branch. Foreign governments also hire lobbyists and public relations

TABLE 10.1 Interest Groups in the Environmental Movement

Any political issue is likely to give rise to many distinct interest groups, each with a different emphasis and approach.

Radical groups generally take a confrontational position in dealing with the business community and have strong visions of what the future of the environment should look like. Some examples include the following:

Citizens Clearinghouse for Hazardous Waste. Founded in 1981; based in Arlington, Va.; 20,000 individual members and 8,000 citizens groups; annual budget, $650,000.

Clean Water Action Project. Founded in 1971; based in Washington; 600,000 members; budget, $9 million.

Environmental Action Inc. Founded in 1970; based in Washington; 20,000 members; budget, $1.2 million.

Friends of the Earth Inc. Founded in 1969, merged with Oceanic Society and Environmental Policy Institute in 1990; based in Washington; 50,000 members; budget, $3.2 million.

Greenpeace USA. Founded in 1971; based in Washington; 1.8 million members; budget, $50.1 million.

National Toxics Campaign. Founded in 1984; based in Boston; 100,000 members; budget, $1 million.

U.S. Public Interest Research Group. Founded in 1983; based in Washington; one million members; budget, $285,000.

Mainstream groups are pragmatic reformers who are willing to work with both the business community and government to improve the environment. Some examples include the following:

Environmental Defense Fund. Founded in 1967; based in New York City; 150,000 members; budget, $15 million.

Izaak Walton League of America. Founded in 1922; based in Arlington, Va.; 50,000-plus members; budget, $1.6 million.

National Audubon Society. Founded in 1905; based in New York City; 550,000 members; budget, $40 million.

National Parks and Conservation Association. Founded in 1919; based in Washington; 190,000 members; budget, $4 million.

National Wildlife Federation. Founded in 1936; based in Washington; 5.8 million members; budget, $79 million.

Natural Resources Defense Council Inc. Founded in 1970; based in New York City; 160,000 members; budget, $13.5 million.

Sierra Club. Founded in 1892; based in San Francisco; 545,000 members; budget, $28 million.

Wilderness Society. Founded in 1935; based in Washington; 372,000 members; budget, $14 million.

Accommodating groups generally avoid confrontation with the business community and favor private action over government action. Some examples include the following:

Nature Conservancy. Founded in 1951; based in Arlington, Va.; 550,000 members; budget, $109 million.

Resources for the Future Inc. Founded in 1952; based in Washington; not a membership organization; budget, $7.1 million.

World Wildlife Fund and Conservation Foundation. Founded in 1961 and 1948, respectively; affiliated in 1985 and currently merging; based in Washington; one million members; budget, $50 million.

firms to advance their interests.[17] For example, after Iraq invaded Kuwait in 1990, the Kuwaiti government secretly bankrolled the creation of Citizens for a Free Kuwait, a group that paid one of America's largest public relations firms to help persuade Congress and the American people that the United States should use force to liberate Kuwait.[18]

Coalitions and Divisions

To influence public policy, interest groups seek to join forces with other groups that share their position on an issue. The coalitions that arise around such mutual interests often bear out the saying that politics makes strange bedfellows. Take the case of the 1993 battle over the North American Free Trade Agreement (NAFTA), an accord to lower trade barriers among Canada, Mexico, and the United States. The anti-NAFTA coalition consisted of several unlikely allies: small business owners, labor unions, environmentalists, consumer groups, and mining companies. Indeed, many of the groups in the anti-NAFTA coalition were more accustomed to opposing each other than to working together.[19]

While some issues produce coalitions composed of interest groups that do not normally work together, other issues may divide groups that usually are allies. For instance, the Sierra Club, Friends of the Earth, and Greenpeace U.S.A. opposed NAFTA, whereas the National Audubon Society, the National Wildlife Federation, the Environmental Defense Fund, and the World Wildlife Fund supported it.[20] Likewise, the AMA and most other medical organizations staunchly oppose proposals to limit the fees physicians and hospitals can charge their patients. Two of the largest associations of medical specialists, however, the 77,000-member American College of Physicians (which represents doctors of internal medicine) and the 74,000-member American Academy of Family Physicians (which represents family practitioners) both support limits on doctor and hospital fees.[21] Interest groups with similar orientations sometimes divide on public policy issues because they see their interests and the likely impact of government policy differently.

If like-minded interest groups are not always united on the issues, neither are the members of an individual interest group. Many groups suffer from cross-cutting cleavages (differences that cut across group lines) as individual members embrace different interests. For example, the gay rights group Act Up often finds itself "divided between radicals and moderates, young and old—between those who are H.I.V. positive and those who are not."[22] As a rule, the larger the organization and the more diverse its membership, the more prone it is to cross-cutting cleavages. Some of the members of an economic interest group may also be members of a citizen or government interest group, or even another economic interest group, with competing goals. The number and diversity of interest groups in the United States today reflect, as chapter 3 pointed out, an almost limitless potential for cross-cutting cleavages to arise as different groups—and even different individuals within groups—vie to sway policy rules and outcomes in their favor.

Interest Group Formation and Maintenance

The tremendous number and diversity of interest groups in the United States reflect the enormous influence government has on our lives. Many organizations formed for purposes unrelated to politics become involved in interest group politics because government policy directly affects their interests. People form businesses, for example, to make products and money, yet the profound influence the government has on the economy leads businesses almost inevitably into interest group politics. Likewise, colleges and universities are founded as educational institutions and not as interest groups. Yet because government decisions on matters such as student loans and scientific research affect higher education, many colleges and universities have joined the fray of interest group politics.

Although many interest groups are organizations that formed for reasons unrelated to politics, other interest groups form for the specific purpose of influencing government policy. The process of forming a new interest group can be quite difficult; in many instances, interest groups often fail to materialize. In particular, the interests of minorities, women, and the poor are less well represented in the United States than the interests of the wealthy and powerful. The discrepancies in interest group formation raise two critical questions: When do interest groups form? And, who in American society gets their interests represented?

Obstacles to Interest Group Formation

In 1991, the city of Syracuse, New York, faced a problem: too many stray cats and dogs. To solve the problem, the Syracuse City Planning Commission proposed barring city residents from owning more than three cats or dogs. But the commission seriously misjudged public sentiment. Cat lovers in Syracuse organized the Save Abandoned Cats and Kittens Society to fight any limit on pet ownership. After a flood of mail, phone calls, and adverse publicity, the commission dropped the proposed ordinance.[23]

The Save Abandoned Cats and Kittens Society of Syracuse illustrates one way interest groups form—as a spontaneous response to changes that threaten the interests of some people. When people respond to proposed changes by spontaneously forming an interest group, political scientists explain the group's formation in terms of *disturbance theory.*[24] In the case of the Save Abandoned Cats and Kittens Society, the disturbance that propelled the creation of a new interest group came from a proposed government regulation. But the disturbance can come from almost any source, including changes in social norms or even the actions of an existing interest group. For example, Tipper Gore, wife of then-Senator and later Vice President Al Gore, along with several friends, formed the Parents Music Resource Center in the late 1980s to combat what they saw as the increased vulgarity of popular music. Frontier of Freedom, a group dedicated to limiting government regulation of private property, formed in 1995 to counter the work of environmental groups such as the Environmental Defense Fund and the Sierra Club.[25]

Although a threat to the status quo may trigger the creation of interest groups, in many instances it does not. In Syracuse, for example, dog owners did not band together to organize the Save Abandoned Dogs and Puppies Society even though the city also proposed limiting dog ownership. Likewise, relatively few college students banded together in the 1980s to fight the decisions the Reagan and Bush administrations made to tighten restrictions on college loan programs.

What we need to explain, then, is not only why interest groups form, but also why they sometimes do *not.* To explain the failure to organize, political scientists often point to the **collective goods dilemma.**[26] When an interest group shapes public policy, it usually produces a collective good—a benefit available to members and nonmembers alike. Thus, if the Center for Auto Safety convinces government officials to require automakers to build safer cars, it cannot dictate that only its members get to drive the safer cars. Yet if an interest group cannot deny benefits to nonmembers, rational people have an incentive to be **free riders;** that is, to gain the benefits of the group's work without bearing any of the costs (for example, dues, meetings, and marches). Here's where the collective goods dilemma comes in: if everyone chooses to be a free rider, then the interest group will not form and no one will get any benefits. To return to the example of auto safety, if everyone acts rationally and refrains from paying dues and organizing meetings, groups such as the Center for Auto Safety will not form, and the benefits that come from their activity will be lost.

Collective goods dilemma
A dilemma created when people can obtain the benefits of interest group activity without paying any of the costs associated with it. In this situation, the interest group may not form because everyone has an incentive to let someone else pay the costs of group formation.

Free riders
People or groups who benefit from the efforts of others without bearing any of the costs.

Overcoming Obstacles to Interest Group Formation

Given the abundance of interest groups in the United States, we know that some groups do solve the collective goods dilemma. How do they do it? Most political scientists answer the question by highlighting the importance of political entrepreneurs—leaders who by dint of personal conviction or ambition will bear the cost of organizing others.[27] The driving force behind the Save Abandoned Cats and Kittens Society, for example, was Gretchen Brooks, known as the Cat Mother of Syracuse because she lived with more than twenty cats.[28] On the national level, the most prominent interest group entrepreneur is Ross Perot, who used his personal wealth to establish United We Stand America, an organization dedicated to (among other things) eliminating the federal budget deficit. Another well-known interest group entrepreneur is Ralph Nader, whom many view as the founder of the consumer movement.

In trying to organize an interest group, entrepreneurs may turn to patrons for help. One study found that 34 percent of economic interest groups and 89 percent of citizen interest groups received money from a patron to start operations.[29] Who are these patrons? They may be wealthy private citizens, corporations, nonprofit foundations, or existing interest groups. The government itself may even act as a patron. For example, "The National Rifle Association was launched in close consultation with the Department of the Army in the nineteenth century to encourage familiarity with firearms among citizens who might be called to fight in future wars, and the American Legion was begun during World War I with government support to encourage patriotism and popular support for the war effort."[30] More recently, federal grants were crucial to the creation of the American Public Transit Association and the American Council on Education, among other interest groups.[31]

Gretchen Brooks founded the Save Abandoned Cats and Kittens Society, which pressured the Syracuse City Planning Commission into dropping its proposal to bar city residents from owning more than three cats or dogs.

Material benefits
The actual goods and services that come from belonging to an interest group.

Solidary benefits
The emotional and psychological enjoyment that comes from belonging to an interest group whose members share common interests and goals.

Expressive benefits
The feelings of satisfaction people derive from working for an interest group cause they believe is just and right. Also known as purposive benefits.

Selective benefits
Any benefit given to a member of a group but denied to nonmembers.

If an interest group is blessed with wealthy patrons or a small budget it may be able to survive without recruiting members.[32] But most interest groups eventually try to recruit members. In general, people receive three types of benefits—material, solidary, and expressive—from joining an interest group.[33] **Material benefits** are actual goods and services that come from belonging to a group. Many states, for example, have so-called closed-shop rules, which means that people must belong to a union to get and keep certain jobs. Perhaps more commonly, interest groups try to entice members by offering material benefits not directly connected to the policy work of the group. The National Rifle Association's (NRA) $35 annual membership fee entitles one to a magazine subscription, a shooter's cap, and decals, and it also makes one eligible to apply for a low-interest credit card and inexpensive insurance policies.

People also join interest groups because membership provides them with **solidary benefits,** the enjoyment that comes from being associated with a group of similarly minded people. Solidary benefits are strongest in organizations built around a shared experience, such as nationality, religion, or race.

Besides material and solidary benefits, people derive **expressive benefits** from group membership. Also known as purposive benefits, expressive benefits are the feelings of satisfaction people derive from working for a cause they believe is just and right. Many people join groups such as the Eagle Forum, Greenpeace, or Common Cause because they support the group's goals.

All three types of interest group benefits—material, solidary, and expressive—are what political scientists call **selective benefits.** That is, they are benefits received by people who join the group and denied to people who do not join. As we discussed earlier, rational people may choose to be free riders if they can share in the collective good an interest group provides without having to join the group and pay some of the costs. But selective benefits go only to group members. Some people who would choose to be free riders without the selective benefits will join the group so they can get these selective benefits as well as share in the collective benefit.[34] For example, people who want to see the environment protected might not join the Sierra Club without some additional enticement, such as *Sierra Magazine* and the low-cost vacation tours of wilderness areas the Sierra Club offers to its members.

Of course, the precise mix of material, solidary, and expressive benefits that leads people to join interest groups varies from person to person. You might join the NRA primarily to receive the magazine and only secondarily because you endorse the NRA's opposition to gun control. Your next-door neighbor's reasons might be the reverse. The mix of material, solidary, and expressive benefits that interest group membership provides also varies from group to group. For example, an organization such as Veterans of Foreign Wars probably provides greater solidary benefits than a group such as the American Association of Retired Persons.

Interest Group Maintenance

Once interest groups become established, they must worry about retaining members.[35] Maintaining membership can often be difficult. Members may lose interest in the group. As we noted earlier, organized labor saw its membership decline in the 1980s. Citizen groups face an even more difficult task in retaining members since they must appeal to ideology rather than to more immediate concerns such as jobs. For instance, since the heyday of the civil rights movement ended in the mid-1970s, most civil rights groups have struggled to retain members. The NAACP has seen its membership fall by 40 percent, and the Southern Christian Leadership Conference—the Rev. Dr. Martin Luther King's old organization—exists in name only.[36]

Interest groups seek to retain members by continuing to provide material, solidary, and expressive benefits. Yet groups may tinker with the mix of benefits over time to attract and retain members. A group may add new material incentives to make membership more appealing, or it may seize on current events to reemphasize the expressive benefits that come with membership. The NRA, for instance, seized on the 1992 Los Angeles riots to dramatize its argument that gun control punishes only law-abiding citizens. In addition to changing the mix of membership benefits, groups may increase or decrease their reliance on patrons. As member contributions dropped with the warming of U.S.-Soviet relations in the late 1980s, for example, the Union of Concerned Scientists, a major arms control group, asked wealthy donors and private foundations to make up the shortfall.[37]

In extreme cases, changing events may force an interest group to redefine its mission in order to retain and attract members. With the passing of the Cold War, for example, the Project on Military Procurement became the Project on Government Procurement. Physicians for Social Responsibility, meanwhile, shifted its attention from the medical consequences of nuclear war to the medical consequences of environmental destruction, and several other groups shifted their attention from nuclear arms control issues to setting limits on the sale of conventional weapons to foreign countries.[38]

Interest Group Bias

Despite their great number, interest groups do not represent the interests of all people equally. Studies show time and again that the affluent and better educated are far more likely to belong to interest groups than the poor and less educated.[39] Most political scientists attribute the discrepancy to differing expectations about the benefits of organizing: the wealthy and the educated have more faith that the political system will respond to their demands. This is not to say that the poor cannot organize. The late Cesar Chavez successfully organized farm workers despite their low wages and, in most cases, limited formal education. The success of the United Farm Workers notwithstanding, interest groups are least likely to represent the interests of people on the margins of society.

Although the rules of American politics allow virtually anyone to form an interest group, it is difficult to form and maintain an effective group. In practice, interest

Interest groups often use current events to dramatize their cause and recruit new members.

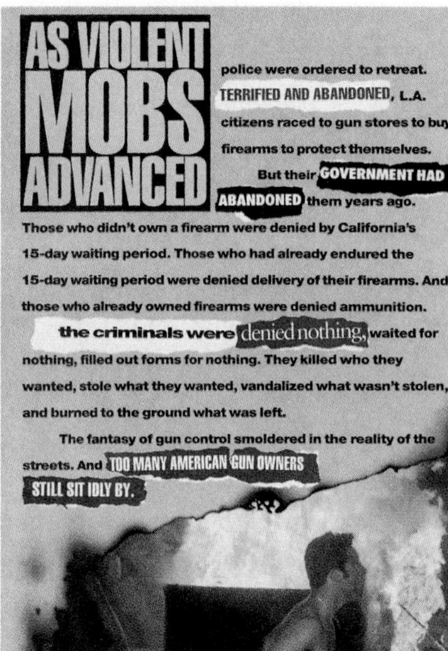

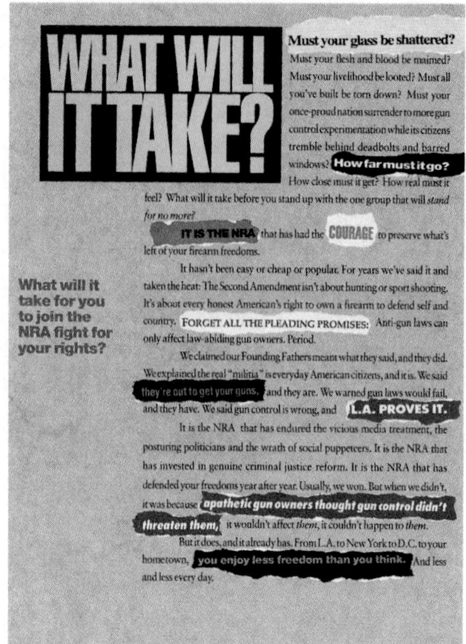

groups that have the backing of educated and well-to-do Americans are the most likely to survive. The bias of interest groups toward the affluent raises troubling questions about the nature of American democracy. Rich and poor Americans do not compete on a level playing field when it comes to interest group politics. How this disparity translates in terms of actual influence over government policy needs to be understood. First, however, we need to examine the strategies that interest groups use in their efforts to influence public policy.

Interest Group Strategies

We said at the start of the chapter that interest groups seek to influence public policy. But just how do they do so? The strategies that interest groups pursue fall into four distinct categories: creating a political action committee, lobbying government officials, mobilizing public opinion, and litigating.

Creating Political Action Committees

Political action committees (PACs)
Organizations that solicit contributions from members of interest groups and channel those contributions to election campaigns.

In the early 1970s, Congress passed several laws designed to clean up the financing of federal election campaigns—in essence, to prevent an elite few from "buying" the loyalty of elected federal officials. A cornerstone of the new legislation was a provision allowing interest groups to set up **political action committees (PACs),** organizations that solicit campaign contributions from group members and channel those funds to an election campaign. (The law had previously limited the use of PACs mostly to labor unions.) PACs now constitute the primary avenue by which interest groups contribute money to federal election campaigns.

Federal campaign finance law prohibits PACs from giving more than $5,000 per election to any candidate seeking a federal office. Under the law, primary, general, runoff, and special elections are all considered separate elections. The rules governing PACs do not, however, apply to campaigns for state and local office. (The laws regulating campaign finance vary widely from state to state; many states allow interest groups to give directly to political campaigns without creating a PAC or making the detailed spending disclosures required by federal law. As a result, our knowledge about how much money interest groups contribute to state and local elections is limited.)[40]

The number of PACs exploded in the 1970s before topping out in the 1980s at around 4,200. As you can see in figure 10.1, the most common type of PAC is a

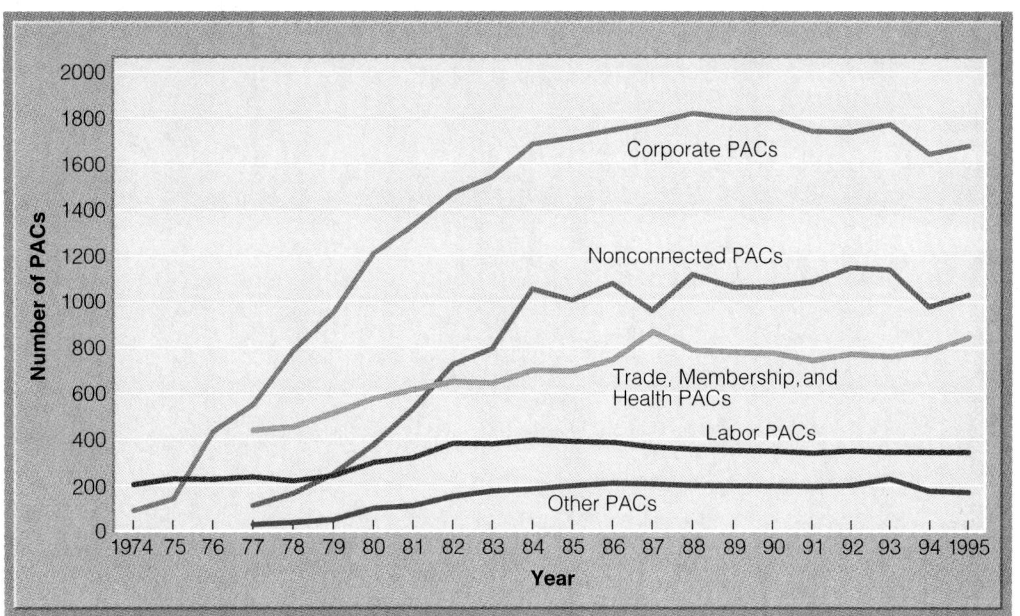

FIGURE 10.1 Growth in Political Action Committees (PACs), 1974–1995

The number of political action committees exploded in the 1970s before leveling off in the 1980s and 1990s.

Source: Data from Harold W. Stanley and Richard G. Niemi, *Vital Statistics on American Politics,* 5th ed. (Washington, D.C.: CQ Press, 1995), p. 161.

corporate PAC. The second most common is the nonconnected PAC, which is independent, at least in legal terms, from established interest groups. One nonconnected PAC is EMILY's List—the acronym stands for "early money is like yeast"—which gives money to Democratic women candidates who support abortion rights. Like EMILY's List, most (but not all) nonconnected PACs try to promote particular ideological positions rather than economic interests. Table 10.2 lists some PACs and their parent interest groups.

Over time, PAC spending has increased. During the 1993–94 electoral cycle, for example, PACs spent $387 million, more than double the amount they spent a dozen years earlier.[41] As figure 10.2 shows, corporate PACs give the most money, followed in order by PACs representing trade, membership, and health associations; labor PACs; and nonconnected PACs. While the total amount of PAC money is considerable, most individual PACs spend relatively little. During the 1993–94 election cycle, 75 percent of all PACs spent less than $50,000.[42] Some PACs, however, spend far more. EMILY's List spent $7.5 million during the 1993–94 election cycle, the NRA's Political Victory Fund spent $5.9 million, and the National Education Association's PAC spent $4.4 million.[43]

Who gets PAC money? A major portion of PAC money, perhaps as much as 50 percent for the average PAC, goes simply to pay the administrative expenses incurred in running the PAC and raising funds.[44] The vast bulk of contributions to political campaigns goes to candidates for Congress. During the 1991–92 election cycle, for example, 48 percent of PAC money, or roughly $188 million, went to congressional candidates. In contrast, presidential candidates received only $810,000.[45] The reason PACs favor candidates for Congress over candidates for the presidency is simple: the law enabling presidential candidates to receive public financing for their campaigns severely limits their ability to accept PAC contributions.

In addition to paying administrative expenses and contributing directly to political campaigns, PACs spend a small portion of their money on so-called independent expenditures. With an independent expenditure, a PAC promotes or attacks a candidate for office without formally coordinating its efforts with any political party or candidate. In 1994, for example, Americans for Limited Terms spent more than $300,000 on advertisements attacking Speaker of the House Thomas S. Foley (D-Wash.) because he opposed efforts to limit service in Congress.[46] A fifteen-term incumbent, Foley became the first sitting Speaker since 1862 to lose his bid for reelection. Despite Foley's defeat, it is important not to exaggerate the effect of independent expenditures. During the 1993–94 election cycle, less than $5 million in PAC money went to independent expenditures.[47]

FIGURE 10.2
Spending by Political Action Committees, (PACs), 1993–1994

Corporate political action committees spend the most money, followed in order by political action committees representing trade, membership, and health associations; labor unions; and nonconnected groups.

Source: Data from Harold W. Stanley and Richard G. Niemi, *Vital Statistics on American Politics,* 5th ed. (Washington, D.C.: CQ Press, 1995), p. 164.

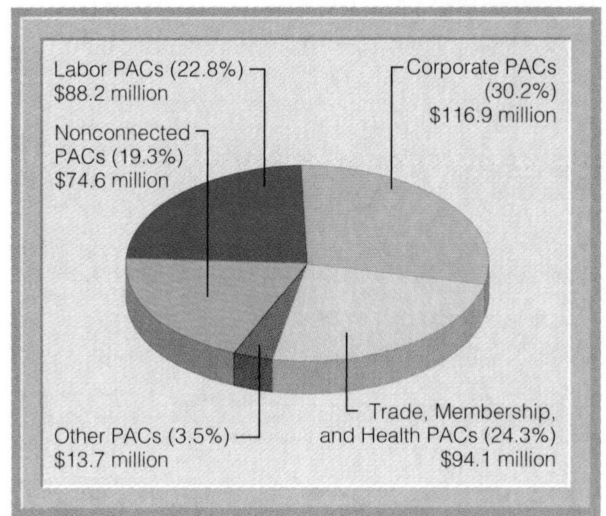

Many different interest groups have formed political action committees.

TABLE 10.2 Select Political Action Committees

PAC Name	Associated Corporation or Interest Group
AQUA PAC	Water Quality Association
BANKPAC	American Bankers Association
BEEF-PAC	Texas Cattle Feeders Association
BREADPAC	American Bakers Association
BUSPAC	American Bus Association
CABLE PAC	National Cable Television Association
COLT	American Horse Council, Inc.
COMPUTERPAC	Computer Dealers and Lessors Association
COTTON PAC	California Cotton Growers Association
EGGPAC	United Egg Association
FANNIE PAC	Federal National Mortgage Association
FLIGHT PAC	Association of Flight Attendants
FOOD PAC	Food Marketing Institute
IRISH PAC	Irish National Political Caucus
NUTPAC	Peanut Butter and Nut Processors Association
PORKPAC	National Pork Producers Council
POWER PAC	Florida Power Corporation
RAMS	American Sheep Association, Inc.
SANE PAC	Committee for a Sane Nuclear Policy
SIX-PAC	National Beer Wholesalers Association
TUNAPAC	United States Tuna Industry
WAFFLEPAC	Waffle House Inc.
WHATAPAC	Whataburger Inc. of Texas

Source: "Pacronyms," Federal Election Commission, August 1994.

As you can see, the vast bulk of PAC money actually spent on political campaigns is spent on elections to Congress. When it comes to contributing to congressional campaigns, spending patterns vary among PACs. Corporate and trade association PACs largely ignore party labels; they care more about backing someone who will win the election and support their views than they do about helping the Democratic or Republican parties. Labor PACs and ideological PACs, however, pay attention to party labels. It is easy to see why. Many of the issues important to labor PACs and ideological PACs divide Democrats from Republicans. It would hardly make sense, for example, for a labor PAC to contribute to the reelection campaigns of Republicans who favor

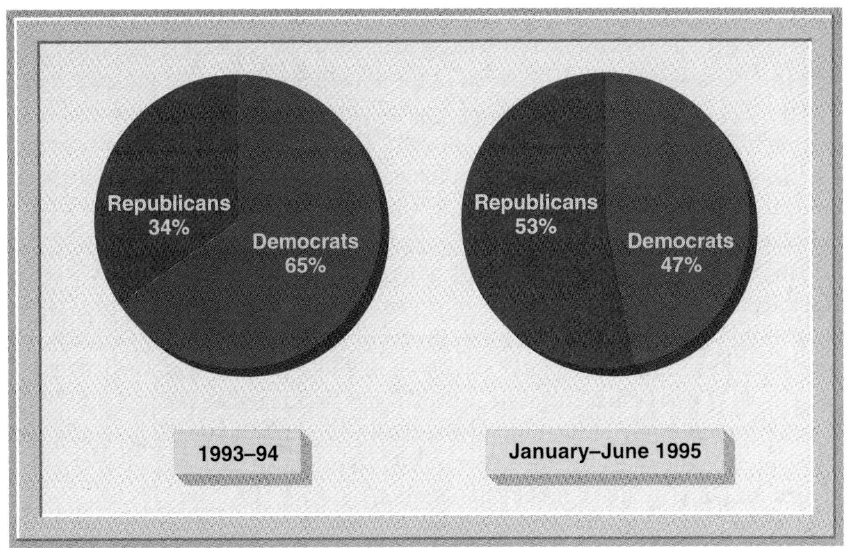

Figure 10.3
Changes in Political Action Committee (PAC) Contributions to Congress

When control of Congress shifted from the Democratic Party to the Republican Party following the 1994 congressional elections, the allocation of PAC spending between the two political parties changed as well. Each chart records the top 40 PACs' donations to members of Congress during the time period stated.

Source: Data from "The New Beneficiaries of the Top 400," *Washington Post National Weekly Edition*, 4–10 December 1995, p. 8.

laws making it harder to unionize. Nor would it make sense for a group such as the National Conservative Political Action Committee to help reelect a liberal senator such as Edward Kennedy.

Though some PACs ignore party labels, all PACs pay close attention to whether a candidate is likely to win. Because of the high reelection rates in Congress, PACs favor incumbents. During the 1993–94 electoral cycle, for instance, when political analysts talked frequently about the anti-incumbent mood of the American public, PACs gave eight times more money to incumbent representatives and five times more to incumbent senators than they did to challengers.[48] And party leaders and committee chairs—-especially those chairing the energy and tax committees—receive far more PAC contributions than average members of Congress.[49]

Of course, because PACs favor incumbent legislators, the party that benefits most from PAC contributions changes when partisan control of Congress changes. This is precisely what happened following the 1994 elections, when Republicans regained control of both houses of Congress for the first time in forty years. As figure 10.3 shows, during the 1993–94 election cycle, while Democrats were still the majority on Capitol Hill, they received nearly two-thirds of all PAC contributions to congressional candidates. In the first six months of 1995, though, the donation pattern changed; Republican candidates received a majority of PAC contributions. Again, the change occurred not because PACs suddenly decided they liked the policies of the Republican Party more than those of the Democratic Party—although many of them may well have—but because, beginning in January 1995, more incumbents and all committee chairs were now Republicans. And when Republican electoral prospects began to sag in early 1996, the flow of PAC money again began to favor the Democrats.[50]

What do PACs get for their campaign contributions? Much of the popular debate over campaign financing suggests that PACs are in the business of buying votes. Yet the testimony of PAC officials and political candidates, as well as a good deal of research by political scientists, indicates that the impact of PAC money is greatly exaggerated.[51] As one PAC official puts it:

> You certainly aren't going to be able to buy anybody for $500 or $1,000 or $10,000. It's a joke. Occasionally something will happen where everybody in one industry will be for one specific solution to a problem, and they may then pour money to one guy. And he suddenly looks out and says, "I haven't got $7,000 from this group, I've got $70,000." That might get his attention: "I've got to support what they want." But that's a rarity.[52]

The reality of how difficult it is for PACs to buy votes is illustrated by the fate of the Cable Television Reregulation Act of 1992, a bill the cable industry vehemently opposed. During the 1991–92 election cycle, ten senators received at least $13,000 each in campaign contributions from PACs associated with the cable industry. Despite the generosity of the cable PACs, seven of the ten senators voted for the cable bill.[53]

Why does PAC money do a poor job of buying votes? There are several reasons. One is the $5,000 limit on contributions. The immense cost of political campaigns, which can exceed 5 million dollars in a Senate race and 1 million dollars in a House race, means that individual PACs provide a tiny percentage of a candidate's funding. Hence, candidates frequently can afford to ignore a contributor's wishes. Another reason that PAC money does a poor job of buying votes is that contributions from competing PACs frequently cancel each other out. In the case of the Cable Television Reregulation Act, for example, many members of Congress received campaign contributions from PACs on both sides of the issue. A third reason PAC money does a poor job of buying votes is that most elected officials find it politically risky to abandon their policy preferences for the sake of a campaign contribution. Officials who change their position on an issue after receiving a PAC contribution make themselves an obvious target for political attack in the next election.

If PAC money generally does not buy votes, why do PACs continue to contribute to political campaigns? The answer is simple: to ensure access to elected officials.[54] Access clearly matters when you want to influence public policy; after all, it is hard to persuade elected officials to adopt policies you favor if you cannot get your foot inside the door. PACs that fail to make campaign contributions worry they will find themselves on the outside looking in when matters of public policy relevant to their interests are being discussed. As one PAC official explains it: "You know, some congressman has got X number of ergs of energy, and here's a person or a company who wants to come see him and give him a thousand dollars, and here's another one who wants to just stop by and say hello. And he has only time to see one. Which one? So the PAC's an attention getter."[55]

The links between campaign contributions and access to elected officials became quite evident during and after the 1994 elections. In October 1994, when polls showed Republicans might regain control of Congress for the first time in forty years, Newt Gingrich (R-Ga.) warned potential campaign contributors: "For anybody who's not on board now it's going to be the two coldest years in Washington."[56] After the Republicans won their stunning victory, they continued to press PACs for campaign contributions. For instance, Rep. Tom Delay (R-Tex.), the number three person in the House Republican leadership, sent letters to every PAC that had contributed to the campaign of Rep. Mike Kreidler (D-Wash.), who had lost his seat to Republican Randy Tate. The letters said: "While I was surprised to see you oppose Randy Tate, you now have the opportunity to work toward a positive future relationship."[57] Of course, Republican legislators are not alone in pressing PACs for campaign contributions. As one professional campaign fundraiser notes, "Some members will get on the phone and be threatening: 'If you don't come [to my fundraiser], I'll never vote for you again.' I'd like to think that doesn't happen, but I know it does, on both sides of the aisle."[58]

The fact that PAC contributions buy more access than votes suggests that the popular concern about PACs corrupting American politics is overstated. Instead of politicians being beholden to PACs, to some extent, PACs are beholden to politicians. If a group fails to contribute to campaigns, it risks losing access to elected officials. Thus, for interest groups, PAC contributions are to some degree an insurance policy (or, less charitably, protection money).

Lobbying the Government

Lobbying
Trying to influence governmental decisions, especially the voting decisions legislators make on proposed legislation.

With PACs, interest groups try to influence public policy by influencing who wins elected office. But interest groups do not stop there; they also try to influence what elected officials do once in office. Interest groups do this through **lobbying,** that is, attempting to influence governmental decisions, especially the voting decisions legislators make on proposed legislation. The phrase *to lobby* originated in seventeenth-century

Because so many lobbyists wait outside the offices of the Senate Finance Committee before a major vote in the hope of speaking with a senator, the corridor has earned the nickname Gucci Gulch, in honor of the expensive Italian shoes many lobbyists wear.

England, where people wishing to influence the government buttonholed members of Parliament in a large lobby off the floor of the House of Commons to plead their case. Not surprisingly, people who make their living trying to influence public policy are known as **lobbyists.**

Lobbyists
People who make their living trying to influence public policy.

Who are lobbyists? Some are staff members of the interest group they represent, others are "hired guns" who work for a law firm or a public relations firm the interest group retains (see box 10.1). Although lobbying is traditionally a male-dominated profession, more and more women are becoming lobbyists. In 1995, the chief lobbyists at more than forty firms—including Coca Cola, Ford, General Electric, and Hershey Foods—were women, and women headed up a number of prominent lobbying firms.[59] Most lobbyists are well paid—one study from the early 1980s found that lobbyists in Washington, D.C., earned more than $90,000 per year on average (though lobbyists for citizen groups earned far less).[60] The allure of high pay explains why so many legislators and their aides become lobbyists after they leave Congress. For example, of the 121 lawmakers who left Capitol Hill after the 1992 elections, forty-eight became lobbyists within the next year, as did at least fifty of their top aides.[61] Yet whether lobbyists come from Capitol Hill or elsewhere, all successful lobbyists share one trait: knowledge of how government works.

When lobbyists personally contact government officials to plead their case, they are engaging in **direct lobbying.** Interest groups devote much of their time to direct lobbying of members of Congress. The key to successful lobbying on Capitol Hill is information.[62] A journalist who spent a year observing the Senate writes, "more than 99 percent of lobbying effort is spent not on parties, weekend hosting, and passing plain white envelopes, but trying to persuade minds through facts and reason."[63] A successful lobbyist makes the same point even more bluntly: "Information is the currency of Capitol Hill, not dollars. And not friends."[64]

Direct lobbying
Trying to influence public policy through direct contact with government officials.

Information is the currency lobbyists use because members of Congress are forced to make decisions on far more issues than any person—even one with aides—can master. Members and their staff are so busy they may even rely on lobbyists to help them do their jobs. To quote one congressional staffer:

> My boss demands a speech and a statement for the *Congressional Record* for every bill we introduce or co-sponsor—and we have a lot of bills. I just can't do it all myself. The better lobbyists, when they have a proposal they are pushing, bring it to me along with a couple of speeches, a *Record* insert, and a fact sheet.[65]

The People Behind the Rules

BOX 10.1

Tommy Boggs and Marian Wright Edelman

Professional lobbyists work the halls of the Capitol to promote the interests of the groups they represent. Two of the most successful lobbyists in recent years are Tommy Boggs and Marian Wright Edelman.

Thomas Hale Boggs, Jr.

Thomas Hale Boggs, Jr.

Corporations and business groups that want a lobbyist who knows the corridors of power in Washington turn to Tommy Boggs. Known around the nation's capital as a top gun among lobbyists, Boggs's roster of clients reads like a who's who of the corporate and professional world: the Association of Trial Lawyers of America, Chrysler, Marathon Oil, the National Cable Television Association, New York Life, and Westinghouse, among others.

Politics comes naturally to Tommy Boggs. His father, Hale Boggs, served as majority leader in the House of Representatives. His mother, Lindy Boggs, became a member of Congress on her husband's death and served for twenty years. And one of Tommy's sisters, Cokie Roberts, is a correspondent for both National Public Radio and ABC News.

Early on, it looked as if Tommy Boggs would follow in his father's footsteps. After graduating from Georgetown University in 1961, he worked for the Joint Economic Committee of Congress and earned a law degree at Georgetown. In 1970, Boggs launched his own bid for Congress, running for a House seat from Maryland. He did not, however, enjoy his parents' electoral touch. He lost decisively to a two-term incumbent.

Despite never winning elected office, Boggs remains a power in Washington politics. As one of Washington's "superlobbyists," he has been in the thick of numerous legislative battles. Yet the corporations and groups that hire Boggs are by no means guaranteed victory. Like all Washington lobbyists, he has both wins and losses to his credit. As one Washington observer puts it: "What you buy with Tommy Boggs is access. Very few people are gonna say they won't see him. You buy acumen. This is somebody who understands how the process works."

Continued

Because members need information, lobbyists might be tempted to play fast and loose with the truth. Yet while lobbyists often minimize facts that hurt their case and may well exaggerate their political strength, they generally avoid misleading members of Congress.[66] The reason is that the long-term costs of lying far outweigh the short-term benefits. Lobbyists can do their jobs only as long as members trust their word. That trust will evaporate if members discover a lobbyist has lied to them.

Lobbyists devote much of their time to working with members of Congress who support their cause as well as with those who are undecided. Not surprisingly, lobbyists generally avoid wasting their time trying to lobby members who take the opposite side of the issue. In working with their legislative allies, lobbyists often become deeply involved in activities such as planning hearings, drafting legislation, and plotting strategy.[67] In 1995, for instance, House Republican leaders seeking to enact the Contract With America into law coordinated their efforts with lobbyists from groups such as the U.S. Chamber of Commerce, the National Federation of Independent Business, the Christian Coalition, and the Coalition for America's future.[68]

The People Behind the Rules

BOX 10.1 CONTINUED

Marian Wright Edelman

Marian Wright Edelman

An estimated 13 million American children live in poverty. More than 2 million children are abused or neglected each year, and more than 100,000 are homeless. The United States ranks twenty-fourth in the world in preventing infant mortality and twenty-ninth in preventing low-birth-weight babies. A leading voice in the fight to change these statistics is Marian Wright Edelman.

Born in Bennettsville, South Carolina, in 1939, Edelman graduated from Spellman College and then Yale Law School. In 1963, she joined the NAACP Legal Defense and Education Fund and moved to Mississippi to work in the civil rights movement. She became the first African-American woman admitted to the practice of law in Mississippi. Her work increasingly came to focus on fighting the extreme poverty of the Mississippi Delta. In 1968, she moved to Washington to better fight the war on hunger.

In 1973, Edelman used several foundation grants to establish the Children's Defense Fund. The fund soon established itself as the strongest and most persistent advocacy group on issues affecting poor, minority, and disabled children. In 1996, the fund organized the Stand for Children rally, which brought groups from across the country to Washington, D.C., to demand that every child in America receive adequate health care and a high-quality education.

Edelman is known as a tenacious lobbyist on behalf of children; some observers even say that on children's issues, she is the "101st Senator." But her tenacity irritates some members of Congress, including those who work with her. She has been criticized as "unrealistic" and "arrogant." Perhaps not surprisingly for a person who has seen poverty firsthand, Edelman dismisses the criticisms: "If political credibility rests on being a doormat or not feeling strongly about what you do, then I think we're in the wrong business."

Sources: Carol Lawson, "A Sense of Place Called Family," *New York Times,* 8 October 1992; W. John Moore, "The Gravy Train," *National Journal,* 10 October 1992, pp. 2294–98; Matthew S. Scott, "The Great Defender," *Black Enterprise,* May 1992, pp. 67–69; Hedrick Smith, *The Power Game: How Washington Works* (New York: Random House, 1988), p. 234; Joseph P. Shapiro, "The Unraveling Kids' Crusade," *U.S. News & World Report,* 26 March 1990, pp. 22–24; *Washington Representatives,* 15th ed. (Washington, D.C.: Columbia Books, 1991), p. 49; *Who's Who Among Black Americans* (Detroit: Gale Research, 1992), p. 417; and *Who's Who in America, 1990–1991* (Wilmette, Ill.: Marquis Who's Who, 1990), p. 304.

Although lobbying is commonly associated with Congress, interest groups also lobby the executive branch. Lobbyists would prefer to speak directly to the president and cabinet officials. For most lobbyists, however, such meetings are difficult to arrange; presidents and cabinet officials are far less accessible than members of Congress. The bulk of executive branch lobbying focuses instead on senior aides in the White House and at the various federal agencies. Every president since Gerald Ford has maintained an Office of Public Liaison to keep open lines of communication with major interest groups, particularly those that support the president.[69]

As with Congress, the main tool interest groups use to lobby the executive branch is information. To gain an advantage in dealing with federal agencies, interest groups frequently hire former executive branch officials as lobbyists. Groups hope to benefit from the knowledge former officials have about how an agency works as well as from their friendships with agency employees. Much debate surrounds the propriety of hiring former executive branch officials as lobbyists. Critics worry that officials may favor certain interest groups in order to get a well-paid job as a lobbyist and, once they become lobbyists, exploit their insider knowledge to benefit their employer. To limit influence peddling of this sort, federal law prohibits executive branch officials and members of Congress from lobbying on matters they worked on while in government for one year after leaving office. Bill Clinton went even further upon becoming president; he ordered that the top eleven hundred employees in the executive branch be barred from lobbying their old offices for five years after leaving government service.[70]

Mobilizing Public Opinion

Efforts to lobby the government are sometimes called *inside strategies* because they rely on gaining access to government officials. But interest groups can also try to influence public policy through so-called *outside strategies,* efforts designed to put pressure on government officials by mobilizing public opinion on the group's behalf.[71] The outside strategies that interest groups use to mobilize public opinion include education campaigns, grass-roots lobbying, and civil disobedience. All three outside strategies rely on one simple idea: government officials listen to what voters have to say.

Education Campaigns

One way interest groups try to mobilize public opinion is by educating the public about issues. Groups often find that one of the biggest obstacles to achieving their policy goals is the public's general ignorance of the issues. In turn, groups calculate that if they can raise public awareness about an issue, voters might demand government action. Thus, the Children's Defense Fund has sought to build political support for increased spending on social programs by educating Americans about the extent and consequences of childhood poverty in the United States.

Advocacy advertising Newspaper, television, and radio advertisements that promote an interest group's political views.

One popular educational technique is the media campaign, which encompasses a broad array of activities. At one end of the spectrum lie efforts to shape how the news media cover stories. Interest groups frequently send news organizations suggestions on stories to cover as well as information on stories they are covering. At the other end of the spectrum lies **advocacy advertising,** or the practice of buying newspaper, television, and radio advertisements that directly promote a group's views. In 1994, for example, the insurance industry financed a television advertising campaign in which a couple named Harry and Louise worried that President Clinton's plan to reform health care would make it harder for them to obtain the medical care they wanted. Many observers credited the Harry and Louise campaign with turning public and congressional opinion against the president's plan. As a rule, the great expense of advocacy advertising limits its use on a sustained basis to interest groups with deep financial pockets—which usually means big corporations.

Interest groups also try to educate the public by publishing research studies. Groups hope that people will read the studies themselves, or more likely, read or hear about the studies in the news media. In 1993, for example, the Sierra Club and U.S. Public Research Interest Group released a study showing that the mining industry had contributed $2 million to members of Congress between 1987 and 1992.[72] The two groups undertook the study because they wanted to show that mining companies were, in their view, using campaign contributions to buy support in Congress. The groups hoped the results of the study would discredit the mining industry in the eyes of the public and thereby increase pressure on Congress to rewrite the 1872 mining law.

A third way interest groups try to educate voters is by rating members of Congress in terms of how often each votes "correctly" on issues a group deems important. Most groups score members on a scale of 0 to 100, with 0 denoting a legislator staunchly opposed to the cause of the interest group and 100 denoting a legislator staunchly in favor. As you might imagine, liberal groups give Democrats high scores and Republicans low

Interest groups often engage in advocacy advertising to educate the public and their members about their cause.

scores, whereas conservative groups do just the opposite. Figure 10.4 shows the divergent scores awarded to two representatives, one liberal and the other conservative, by ten major interest groups.

Grass-Roots Lobbying

With **grass-roots lobbying,** interest groups go beyond education and actively try to mobilize their memberships and the broader public into action to influence policy. A common type of grass-roots lobbying is the petition drive, a technique that supporters of Ross Perot used to put the Texas billionaire's name on the 1992 presidential ballot. Another common type of grass-roots lobbying is the letter-writing and phone campaign. This rather old lobbying technique has enjoyed a renaissance in recent years with the growth of radio and television talk shows; many groups have found that talk shows are an effective way to mobilize voters to action. Interest groups calculate, with good reason, that members of Congress and executive branch officials will pay more attention to the letters and phone calls of a thousand voters than they will to the efforts of a dozen lobbyists.

Grass-roots lobbying
Trying to influence public policy indirectly by mobilizing an interest group's membership and the broader public to contact elected officials.

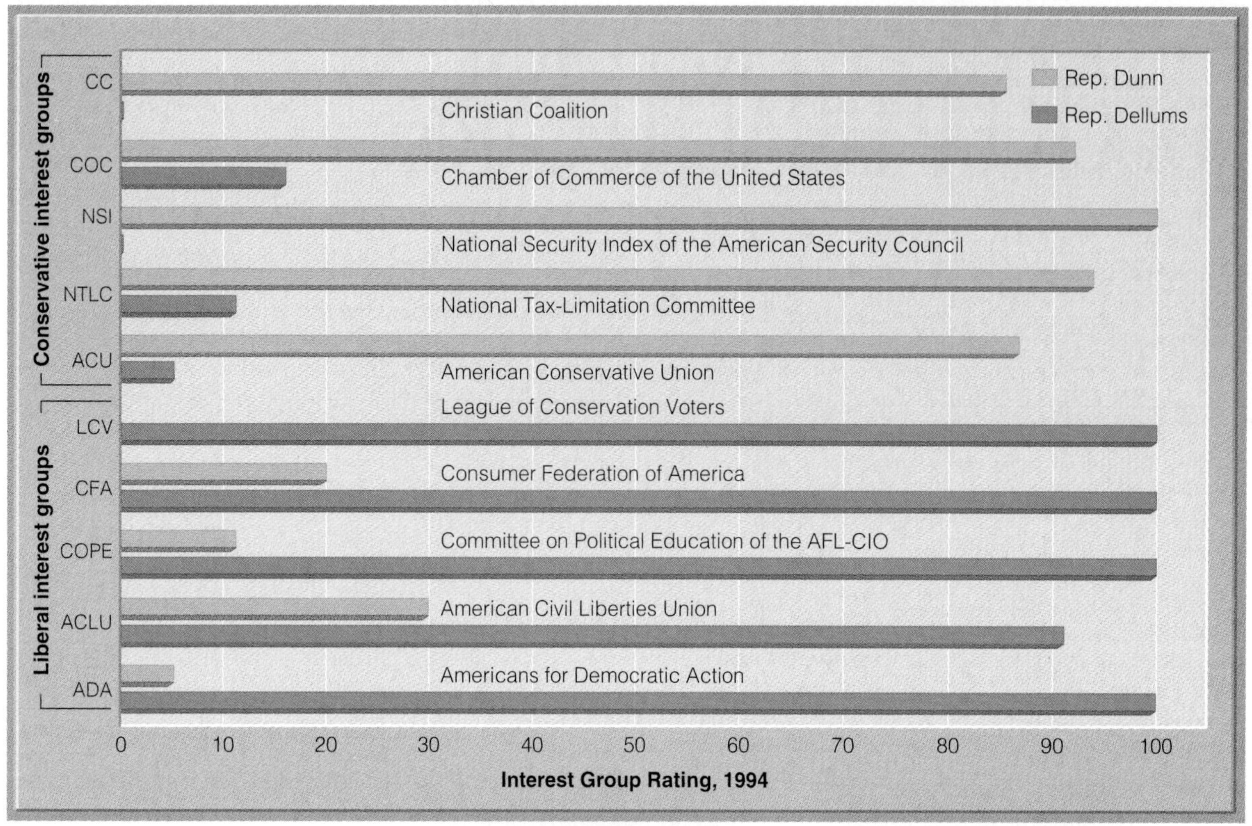

FIGURE 10.4
Interest Group Ratings of Two Members of the House of Representatives

Members of Congress who score high marks in ratings compiled by liberal interest groups usually score low marks in ratings compiled by conservative interest groups, and vice versa.

Source: Michael Barone and Grant Ujifusa, *The Almanac of American Politics, 1996* (Washington, D.C.: National Journal, 1995), pp. 119, 1423.

Rep. Ronald V. Dellums (D-Calif.)

Rep. Jennifer B. Dunn (R-Wash.)

Grass-roots lobbying may also involve protest marches and demonstrations as groups try to show Congress and the White House that their cause enjoys broad public support. Some protests come with a dash of political theater as groups try to maximize media coverage and thereby increase pressure on government officials. Peace groups often sponsor "die-ins" to illustrate the dangers of war, farmers occasionally drive their tractors to Washington in "tractorcades" to highlight their anger at agricultural policy, and pro-life advocates sometimes erect miniature cemeteries to dramatize their view that abortion is murder. Groups resort to political theater because they know, as we saw in chapter 8, that dramatic visual images attract the attention of the news media, especially television news.

A final type of grass-roots lobbying revolves around get-out-the-vote activities, a campaign strategy we discussed in chapter 7. A number of groups work on registering people to vote. One of the best known is the Rev. Jesse Jackson's Rainbow Coalition, which seeks to register minority voters. But organized labor runs the most extensive get-out-the-vote campaigns. Not only do labor unions run voter registration campaigns, but they also devote considerable time and effort to convincing union members and supporters to support the candidates the union endorses. When Election Day rolls around, many unions open phone banks so they can call labor supporters and encourage them to vote. In some instances, unions even arrange to drive voters to the polls.

Because grass-roots lobbying can be so effective in shaping government policy, wealthy interest groups (which usually means business groups) increasingly have sought to create synthetic grass-roots movements.[73] Such **astroturf lobbying** encourages individuals to contact their elected officials by making it very easy to do. Thus, groups send out preaddressed post cards with messages to members of Congress already printed on them, telephone potential supporters and connect them automatically to congressional offices, and advertise 800 numbers people can call if they want a letter to go to Congress in their name. For instance, the Coalition to End Abusive Securities Suits—a group with more than 1,450 members, including firms such as Intel and RJR Nabisco—advertised an 800 number people could call to demand that Congress make it harder for investors to sue companies for fraud when their stock prices fell. If you call the number,

Astroturf lobbying
Efforts, usually led by interest groups with deep financial pockets, to create synthetic grass-roots movements by aggressively encouraging voters to contact their elected officials about specific issues.

> in less than a minute . . . you have sent letters to your representative and senators. . . . It is not necessary to understand the issue or to know what the letter will say. You do not have to know who your legislators are, and you probably have not guessed that you are calling at the behest of some of the nation's richest companies.[74]

Astroturf lobbying obviously carries great potential for abuse. Just how great became clear in 1995 when the Competitive Long Distance Coalition, a group seeking to block passage of a telecommunications bill, hired a firm to generate letters from consumers. It turned out, however, that "as many as half of the telegrams that deluged House members were sent without the signatories' approval."[75]

Civil Disobedience

In some circumstances, interest groups break the law in order to pressure legislators into changing it. The Rev. Dr. Martin Luther King, Jr., forcefully advocated the practice of civil disobedience during the civil rights protests of the 1960s. More recently, the pro-life group Operation Rescue has seized on civil disobedience as a favored tactic. The group has tried to block the entrances to abortion clinics in several cities, despite court orders to the contrary. Another practitioner of civil disobedience is the environmental group Earth First!, which has illegally blocked logging of the forests by driving spikes into trees and by destroying the equipment of lumber companies.

Groups that practice civil disobedience hope that breaking the law will draw attention to what they see as unjust government policy. The success of the tactic depends first on having members who will risk going to jail and paying heavy fines. In most organizations, the number of such dedicated members is small. The success of civil disobedience also depends on the public's perception that the harm the group

Some interest groups practice civil disobedience in the hope that, by breaking the law, they will draw attention to what they see as unjust government policy.

causes by breaking the law is not excessive. In 1990, Earth First! was forced to disavow the practice of tree spiking after several lumber workers were maimed when their power saws struck spikes imbedded in trees.[76] Finally, civil disobedience works only if groups can sustain their protests over time. If not, the public quickly forgets the sacrifice of the protesters.

Litigating

Interest groups often influence public policy by going to court.[77] Sometimes groups seek test cases so they can challenge the constitutionality of existing laws. As chapter 5 noted, the NAACP has long pushed the cause of civil rights by finding people who have been discriminated against and then helping them challenge that discriminatory behavior in court. Other lawsuits seek to compel the government to enforce existing laws. In recent years, for example, environmental groups have initiated litigation to see that corporations scrupulously obey laws such as the Clean Air Act and the Endangered Species Act.

Besides seeking test cases and initiating their own litigation, interest groups can join lawsuits others file. Individuals or groups who wish to air their views in a lawsuit may petition the court for the right to file an ***amicus curiae*** (friend of the court) **brief** that argues why the court should rule in favor of one of the parties to the case. *Amicus curiae* briefs are most commonly filed in lawsuits that involve matters of great public interest such as civil rights and liberties. Table 10.3 lists some of the more than seventy interest groups that filed *amicus curiae* briefs with the Supreme Court in the 1989 case *Webster v. Reproductive Health Services.* The case involved a Missouri law that restricted access to abortion.

***Amicus curiae* brief**
Literally, friend of the court. A brief filed with the court by a person or group who is not directly involved in the legal action but who has views on the matter.

In sum, interest groups can pursue a variety of strategies in their efforts to ensure that the government considers their interests. Indeed, most interest groups use a combination of tactics—forming PACs, lobbying the government, mobilizing public opinion, and even going to court—to try to influence public policy. As we shall see, though, some groups are more successful in their efforts than others.

Interest Group Influence

What makes one interest group more influential than another? The answer to this question is a mix of external and internal factors.

TABLE 10.3 A Sampling of Interest Groups Filing *Amicus Curiae* Briefs in *Webster v. Reproductive Health Services*

Interest groups often file amicus curiae *briefs that argue why the court should rule in favor of one of the parties to a lawsuit.*

For Restrictions on Abortion Rights
Alabama Lawyers for Unborn Children
American Academy of Medical Ethics
American Collegians for Life
American Family Association
American Life League
Birthright, Inc.
Catholic Health Association of the United States
Center for Judicial Studies
Christian Advocates Serving Evangelism
Doctors for Life
Feminists for Life of America
Holy Orthodox Church
International Right to Life Federation
Knights of Columbus
National Right to Life Committee
New England Christian Action Council
Right to Life Advocates
Southern Center for Law and Ethics
Southwest Life and Law Center
United States Catholic Conference

Against Restrictions on Abortion Rights
American Civil Liberties Union
American Jewish Congress
American Library Association
American Medical Association
American Nurses Association
American Psychological Association
American Public Health Association
Americans for Democratic Action
Americans United for Separation of Church and State
Association of Reproductive Health Care Professionals
Bioethicists for Privacy
Canadian Abortion Rights Action League
Catholics for a Free Choice
National Association of Public Hospitals
National Coalition Against Domestic Violence
National Council of Negro Women
National Organization for Women
National Association of Women Lawyers

Source: Webster v. Reproductive Health Services (1989), 106 L Ed 2d 410, pp. 745–49.

External Factors

The ability of any interest group to influence public policy depends in part on external factors that lie beyond its immediate control. Who sits in the Oval Office, which party controls Congress, who chairs the relevant congressional committee, which way public opinion is moving, and even how world events are breaking all help determine whether a group gets its way. For example, business groups had more success pushing for less government regulation in 1996 when Republicans controlled Congress than in 1994 when Democrats did. Likewise, peace groups lobbying for cuts in defense spending found it easier to gain a hearing after the collapse of the Soviet Union.

The ability of an interest group to influence public policy also depends on whether other interest groups oppose its views. As we noted earlier, the formation of one interest group can prompt another group to form in opposition. The result is that interest groups on opposite sides of a policy debate expend considerable energies countering—and often negating—each other's efforts. But as we also noted, there is no guarantee that opposing interest groups will form. When opposition fails to materialize, an interest group is better able to push its cause. Edward J. Derwinski, Secretary of Veterans Affairs during the Bush administration, explained the tremendous success veterans groups have had in protecting veterans programs from budget cuts: "There is no anti-veterans group. It's just a one way street. Now we're not talking about a hell of a big army, but it's unopposed."[78] When an interest group is unopposed, members of Congress and executive branch officials face less pressure to resist the group's demands. Moreover, if no opposition exists to rebut the group's claims, government officials may come to see the policies the group advocates as good public policy.

Internal Factors

If the ability of an interest group to influence public policy depends partly on factors beyond its immediate control, the internal characteristics of a group also affect its ability to influence policy. Political scientists have identified four internal factors that affect interest group success: the size and commitment of a group's membership, the political skills of its leaders, its financial resources, and its objectives. Groups need not score high along all four of these dimensions to be successful. But few groups are likely to be influential without at least some strength in these areas.

Membership

All else being equal, government officials are most likely to listen to interest groups that represent large numbers of voters. But size tells only part of the story. College-age Americans, for example, wield little clout in Washington despite their rather sizable numbers. The reason can be gleaned from the comment then-Sen. Wyche Fowler (D-Ga.) made in 1992 dismissing a request by student lobbyists for a meeting: "Students don't vote. Do you expect me to come in here and kiss your ass?"[79] The commitment of a group's members matters as much as sheer numbers. For instance, mining companies succeeded in defeating the effort to rewrite the nation's mining law not because they represented a major chunk of the American public, but (in part) because they were cohesive and highly motivated.

Maintaining such cohesion and motivation can be difficult for some interest groups, especially those such as peak business associations and trade associations that are composed of many different groups or companies, each of which may have divergent interests. For example, the Edison Electric Institute—the trade association for the electric power industry—has been ineffective in shaping government policy on deregulation because of disagreements among its members. The disputes became so sharp that in 1996 several splinter groups formed, each promoting different policy alternatives and thereby weakening the ability of the Edison Electric Institute to speak for the power industry.[80]

Leadership

A skillful leadership greatly enhances the work of any interest group. The most effective interest group leaders combine two special skills. First, they understand the nuances of decision making in Washington and know how to represent the group's interest to government officials, the media, and the public. An interest group can waste its political capital if its leaders misjudge the mood on Capitol Hill, alienate the news media, or fail to mobilize public opinion on its behalf. Second, effective interest group leaders know how to manage their organizations. Decisions about how to recruit new members, how to deal with disputes within the group, and which issues to emphasize all affect the stability, and ultimately the success, of an interest group.

Financial Resources

As it does with many things in life, money matters in interest group politics. A large financial war chest enables a group to contribute to political campaigns, to host lavish parties for government officials, to hire the best lobbyists, to run nationwide media campaigns, and to buy the most advanced equipment for direct-mail operations. For example, deep financial pockets enabled the Coalition to End Abusive Securities Suits to engage in astroturf lobbying on behalf of its plan to make it harder for investors to sue companies for fraud.

Money does not, however, guarantee influence. During the 1992 debate over the bill to reregulate cable television, cable PACs outspent the bill's supporters nearly four to one.[81] The cable television industry also saturated the airwaves with advertisements denouncing reregulation. Despite the expensive attack campaign, Congress voted overwhelmingly for the bill.

By the same token, lack of money need not condemn an interest group to irrelevance. Many consumer and environmental groups, for example, cannot compete dollar-for-dollar with business and trade groups. These citizen groups compensate for their financial disadvantage by honing their skills at generating so-called free media. They become adept at using research studies, publicity stunts, and protest marches to attract media coverage of their causes.

Objectives

What an interest group hopes to do also affects its ability to influence public policy. As a general rule, interest groups find it easier to block changes in policy than to lobby for new policies. The defeat of the Clinton administration's proposed rewrite of the nation's mining law is a case in point. The reason interest groups find it easier to block changes in policy can be found back in chapter 2: the rules of the American political system favor the status quo. To block new legislation, an interest group often needs only to persuade a few key members of Congress or officials in the executive branch. Yet if a group wants to change a law, it faces the more arduous task of convincing a majority of both houses of Congress as well as the president.

Interest groups also find it easier to get what they want on issues that have a narrow rather than a broad impact on society. The reason is that the greater the number of people affected by the policy change an interest group wants enacted, the more likely that other groups will mobilize to fight the change. For example, in the early 1990s, Delta College in Michigan persuaded Congress to appropriate $8 million to build a planetarium on its campus.[82] Although you might wonder why the federal government would build a science facility for a two-year college that does not offer a major in the sciences, the fact that the planetarium affected relatively few people outside the Delta College community made it unlikely the appropriation would attract attention, let alone opposition. In contrast, pro-choice groups have failed to persuade Congress to pass legislation that would guarantee a woman's right to an abortion. Right-to-life groups vehemently oppose abortion, and they have lobbied furiously to make an abortion harder, if not impossible, to get.

In sum, external factors and internal group characteristics such as membership, leadership, financial resources, and objectives all help determine whether an interest group will succeed in its quest to shape a particular rule or policy outcome. We mentioned before that these factors often combine to favor more affluent and educated groups. Let's look now at the effect this may have on our democracy.

The Balance Sheet on Interest Groups

Where does the balance sheet on interest groups stand? Do they advance democratic dialogue? Or do they benefit political elites at the expense of the average citizen? To answer these questions, we need to review the love/hate relationship Americans have with interest groups, discuss the many calls for reforming interest group politics, and review the contributions interests groups make to American democracy.

A Love/Hate Relationship

We noted at the start of the chapter that the existence of interest groups has always raised troubling questions for American democracy. It seems that everyone denounces

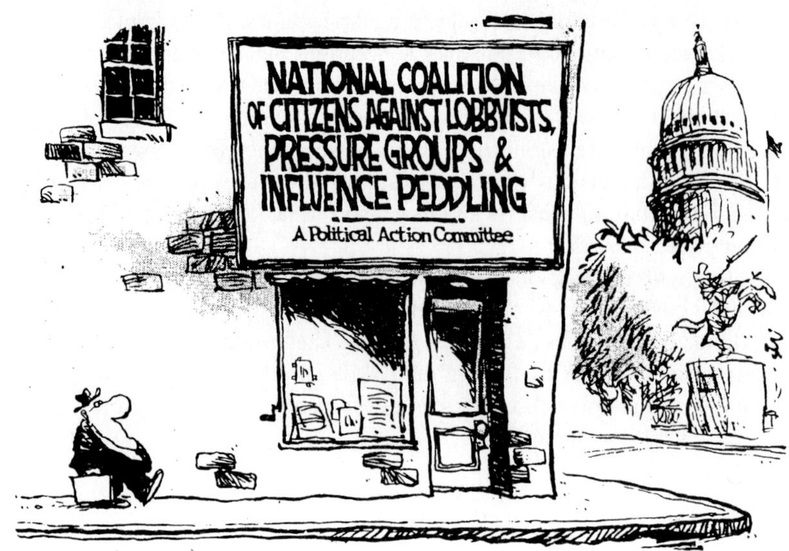

Americans say they dislike interest group politics, but joining interest groups seems to be in our blood. Whenever Americans join together to influence government—say, to reduce the power of special interests—we are engaging in interest group politics.

Jim Borgman/Reprinted with special permission of King Features Syndicate.

the harmful influence of special interests. For example, a poll conducted in 1994 found that 79 percent of those surveyed believed that lobbyists wield too much influence over government policy.[83]

Yet as Tocqueville and many others have pointed out, joining interest groups seems to be in our blood. By one count, seven out of ten Americans belong to at least one organization that lobbies the government.[84] Of course, most Americans do not recognize the extent of their own involvement in interest group politics: "The typical person giving to the American Cancer Society doesn't think he's giving to a lobbying group. But that's lobbying too."[85] Indeed, if you buy the *Consumer Reports* magazine published by Consumer's Union (which lobbies on banking, insurance, and product safety laws), join the Boy Scouts or Girl Scouts (which lobby to protect tax deductions for charitable contributions), or contribute to the American Foundation of the Blind (which lobbies on behalf of people with disabilities), you become involved in interest group politics.

Moreover, while most Americans dislike interest groups in the abstract, they give specific interest groups high marks, as figure 10.5 shows. America's love/hate relationship with interest groups explains why President Harry Truman answered a question about whether he would use lobbyists to push his legislative program through Congress by saying: "We probably wouldn't call those people lobbyists. We would call them citizens appearing in the public interest."[86]

The disagreement over the virtues of various interest groups suggests that attempts to distinguish "good" interest groups from "bad" interest groups won't work. As figure 10.5 shows, even groups that a majority of Americans views favorably are still disliked by many others. Indeed, the great diversity of Americans in terms of such matters as race, class, age, gender, region, and occupation means that we will never have a consensus on which groups promote the public good.

What, then, can we conclude about interest group politics? The one thing on which almost all observers agree is that the interest group "chorus sings with a strong upper-class accent"; the wealthy and the powerful are better represented than the poor and the powerless.[87] This is not to say that corporations or trade associations always get their way. They don't. But in politics, the saying that "the squeaky wheel gets the grease" holds true more often than not. No matter how meritorious their claims or how just their cause, people who are not organized are at a disadvantage when it comes to ensuring that their views are heard.

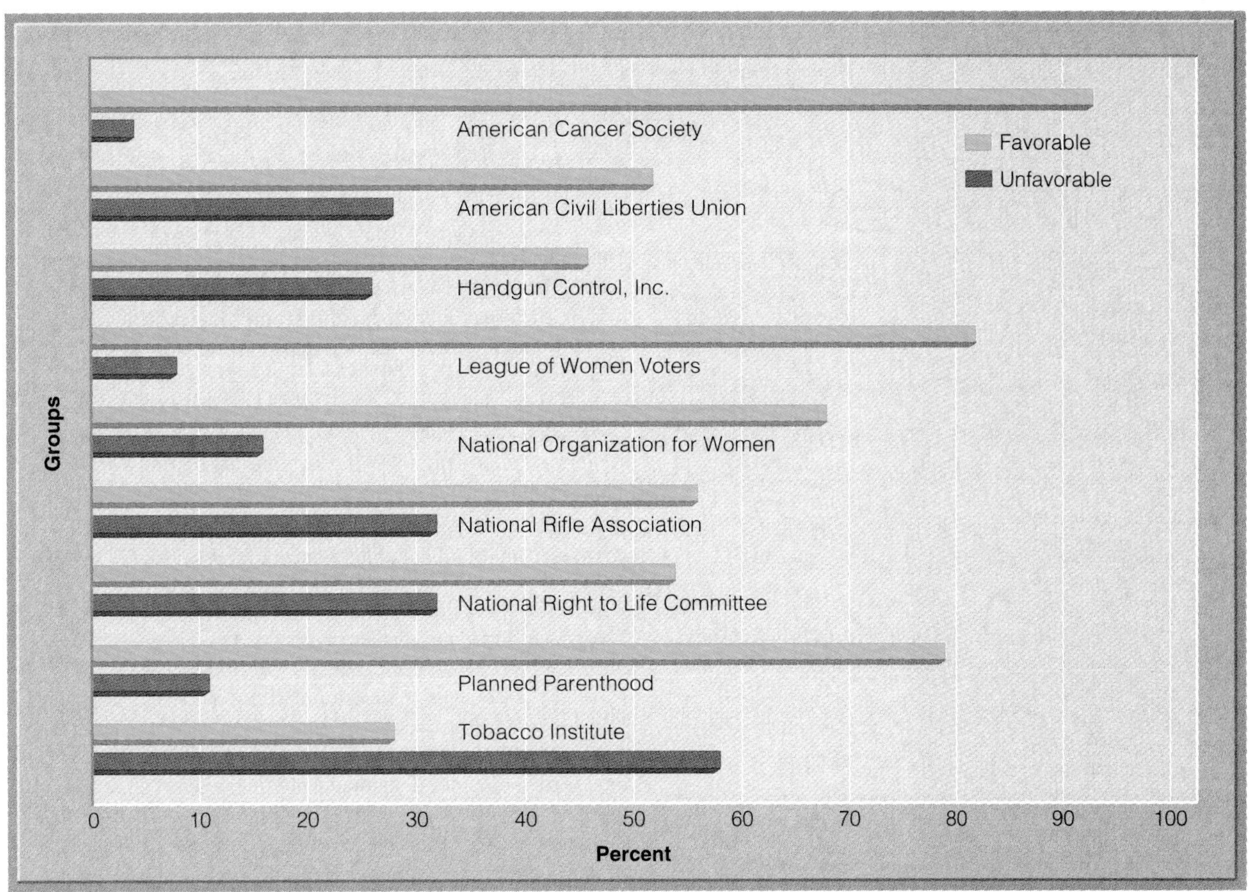

FIGURE 10.5
Public Attitudes Toward Specific Interest Groups

Americans hold favorable opinions of some interest groups but not others.

Source: Gallup Report, May 1989, pp. 25–27.

Calls for Reform

Complaints that interest group politics favors the wealthy and the powerful—and particularly the interests of the business community—have prompted numerous calls for reform. Reformers understand a point we have made time and again in this book: changing the rules of the political process can change the outcomes of that process.

Some changes have been made over the years to the rules governing interest groups. For instance, in the 1970s, Congress initiated public financing of presidential campaigns. And in 1995, Congress enacted several different reforms that affect its own relations with interest groups. The Senate adopted rules that forbid senators from accepting any gift worth more than $50 from a lobbyist.[88] The House went even further; it adopted rules barring representatives from accepting gifts from anyone other than family members or friends.[89] Congress also passed a law that imposes tougher disclosure requirements on groups that lobby the federal government, as box 10.2 discusses at greater length.[90]

While Congress has limited gift giving and toughened disclosure requirements for lobbyists, it has made little progress in passing other reform legislation. This is especially true in the case of campaign finance laws, which have attracted considerable criticism over the past decade. Democrats and Republicans agree that the current rules need to be changed, but they disagree over how to change them. Not surprisingly, Democrats favor changes they expect will help Democratic candidates, whereas Republicans favor changes they expect will help Republican candidates. As a result, reform legislation remains stalled on Capitol Hill.[91]

POINT OF ORDER

BOX 10.2

Limiting the Influence of Interest Groups: The Lobbying Disclosure Act of 1995

The Lobbying Disclosure Act of 1995 requires lobbyists to disclose more about their efforts to influence government policy.

Americans have long been suspicious of their elected officials. They believe that too often laws are made "behind closed doors" with the public interest "sold out" in deals cut with "special interests." Books with titles such as *The Best Congress Money Can Buy* and *The Government Racket,* as well as television news exposés of well-heeled interest groups paying for members of Congress to attend "conferences" at plush resorts, testify to and feed those suspicions.

Reformers have sought to reduce the influence of special interests by changing the rules of political decision making. In the last thirty years alone, several such rules changes have been enacted. For example, the use of direct primaries has expanded to promote broader public participation in the presidential nomination process (see chapters 9 and 12). Likewise, Congress has opened up the deliberations of its committees to greater public scrutiny, and it has passed laws requiring candidates for federal office to disclose the identity of contributors to their election campaigns (see chapter 12). In each of these instances, reformers were seeking to reduce the influence of special interests by exposing various aspects of the governing process to public view.

None of these changes, though, cut to the heart of the public's fears about interest group lobbying—who influences government officials? Congress took a potentially major step toward giving the public a better view of the lobbying process when it passed the Lobbying Disclosure Act of 1995. This law tries to accomplish many of the goals first set out, but not achieved, by the 1946 Federal Regulation of Lobbying Act. The new law does so by (1) broadening the scope of the 1946 law's definition of a lobbyist, and (2) strengthening the disclosure requirements on lobbyists.

The original 1946 law limited the definition of lobbying to the interaction between an individual or group and a member of Congress. The 1995 law expands the scope of lobbying activity by designating congressional staff members and most policy-making officials in the executive branch as potential subjects of lobbying. In addition, under the terms of the 1946 law, only individuals who spent a majority of their time lobbying members of Congress had to register with the government as lobbyists, and representatives of foreign interests were exempted from complying with the law. Under the new Lobbying Disclosure Act, however, any individuals or groups spending 20 percent or more of their time lobbying anyone defined as a policy maker in the legislative or executive branches must register with the House and Senate as a lobbyist. All agents of foreign interests must also register. As a result, although only about 6,000 lobbyists were registered with the federal government before the 1995 law went into effect, some observers estimate that under the terms of the new law, three to ten times more people will have to register.

The 1995 law also imposes important disclosure requirements on registered lobbyists. Individuals who receive more than $5,000 for their lobbying efforts in a six-month period, as well as organizations that spend more than $20,000 on lobbying in a six-month period, are required to file reports with Congress. These semiannual reports must identify the lobbyist's clients, the issues lobbied, specific bills lobbied, and the executive agencies and houses of Congress lobbied; the reports must also estimate how much each lobbying campaign cost. The reports do not have to identify the specific individuals that lobbyists contacted. A failure to abide by the new requirements is subject to fines of up to $50,000.

The registration and reporting requirements in the Lobbying Disclosure Act contain two important exemptions. First, individuals and groups are not required to report their efforts at grass-roots lobbying. Second, tax-exempt organizations—for example, the Red Cross, the Boy Scouts of America, and church organizations—are not required to participate in the disclosure process.

While the ultimate impact of the Lobbying Disclosure Act remains to be seen, supporters of the new law are optimistic. They clearly believe, as we have shown many times, that rules matter, and that changing the rules changes the dynamics of the political process. Rep. Barney Frank (D-Mass.), for example, explained that the law would achieve its goal of limiting special interest influence by ensuring that the "people will know a lot more about who does what in lobbying." Rep. John Bryant (D-Tex.) spoke directly to the public's suspicions about "closed door" politics when he observed that "the principal importance of this bill goes to the concern of the American public that unseen forces are controlling the outcome of a Congress that is daily wined and dined by interest groups."

Sources: Adam Clymer, "Congress Passes Bill to Disclose Lobbyists' Roles," *New York Times,* 30 November 1995; "Outlook," *U.S. News & World Report,* 8 January 1996, p. 17; Jonathan D. Salant, "Lobbying: Bill Would Open Windows on Lobbying Efforts," *Congressional Quarterly Weekly Report,* 2 December 1995, pp. 3631–33.

In addition to circumventing political gridlock, efforts to curb the perceived excesses of interest group politics must overcome constitutional obstacles. The founders clearly designed the American political system to give people great freedom to press their cause on the government. Thus, efforts to reform interest group politics risk violating the basic rules of American politics—most notably, the right, enshrined in the First Amendment, of individuals and groups to petition the government. The Supreme Court effectively gutted the first effort to regulate lobbyists, the Federal Regulation of Lobbying Act of 1946, on these grounds.[92] Proposals to ban PACs run a similar risk of violating the First Amendment. Can government outlaw a political activity simply because some people believe "it has succeeded in a way most political activity aims to succeed—because it has achieved some influence over public decisions?"[93]

Even if reformers succeed in passing new laws that limit PACs and pass constitutional muster, reform legislation may still not produce the benefits they expect. On many occasions, reform legislation has produced unintended (and undesirable) consequences as laws designed to fix one problem have created others. Once again, campaign finance laws provide a useful case in point. PACs were created to clean up campaign financing, but many reformers now attack them as a form of legalized corruption. Indeed, some experts worry that any effort to ban PACs will make things worse rather than better. As a leading scholar on campaign finance writes, "whatever the alternative to a PAC . . . the connection or interest that brings contributors together will be far less visible and the aggregate sums they contribute far harder to compute than they are with PACs."[94]

The Contributions of Interest Groups

Although interest groups may at times stir cynicism about politics, it is worth remembering that they also play a positive role in American politics. As we mentioned at the outset of the chapter, interest groups help represent the views and interests of the American people to the government, and they enable people to participate in politics. Interest groups also educate Americans about the issues facing our society, push new issues onto the political agenda, and help people monitor the actions of government.

The positive contributions of interest group politics are evident in two of the most important political changes in the United States in the twentieth century: universal suffrage and the cause of civil rights. Eighty years ago, women could not vote in federal and most state elections. Fifty years ago, Jim Crow laws effectively disenfranchised most African Americans. These injustices have now been remedied, largely because of the efforts of dedicated interest groups such as the National American Woman Suffrage Association and the National Association for the Advancement of Colored People.

Thus, despite frequent complaints that special interests are too powerful in American politics, limiting the freedom of interest groups to petition the government probably would do the democratic process in the United States more harm than good. Interest groups give ordinary citizens access to government and allow them to communicate their values and expectations. The Constitution—the set of rules for our political system—makes it clear this is an essential and cherished right.

Summary

Interest groups are organizations dedicated to influencing public policy. Although interest group politics is as old as the American republic, in recent years, the number of interest groups has exploded. Most interest groups work to advance the economic interests of their members. But other groups try to promote their visions of good public policy, and still others represent the interests of state, local, and foreign governments.

Interest groups frequently form when change threatens the interests of a group of people. But just as often, people fail to organize because of the collective goods dilemma—the incentive people have to leave it up to someone else to organize the group. In practice, the collective goods dilemma is usually solved by political entrepreneurs who, because of personal conviction or ambition, bear the cost of organizing other people. To recruit followers, political entrepreneurs try to provide a mix of material, solidary, and expressive benefits to members.

To influence public policy, interest groups contribute to political campaigns, lobby members of Congress and the executive branch, mobilize public opinion, and litigate. The ability of any interest group to influence public policy depends in part on external factors beyond its immediate control. But the success of a group also depends on internal factors, including the size and commitment of its membership, the political skills of its leaders, its financial resources, and its policy objectives.

The prevalence of interest groups in the United States has fueled claims that special interests have taken the government away from the people. But distinguishing good interest groups from bad ones is impossible. Americans don't agree on which interests should be promoted and which shunned. And while it is clear that the interests of the rich and the powerful are more faithfully represented, interest groups have historically been an important vehicle for remedying the injustices done to the poor and oppressed.

Key Terms

Advocacy advertising
Amicus curiae brief
Astroturf lobbying
Citizen groups
Collective goods dilemma
Direct lobbying
Expressive benefits
Free riders
Grass-roots lobbying
Interest group
Lobbying
Lobbyists
Material benefits
Political action committees (PACs)
Selective benefits
Solidary benefits

Readings for Further Study

Birnbaum, Jeffrey H., and Alan S. Murray. *Showdown at Gucci Gulch: Lawmakers, Lobbyists, and the Unlikely Triumph of Tax Reform.* New York: Random House, 1987. Two journalists report on how lobbyists influenced the writing and passage of the Tax Reform Act of 1986.

Bronner, Ethan. *Battle for Justice: How the Bork Nomination Shook America.* New York: Norton, 1989. A journalist tells how civil rights groups succeeded in defeating Ronald Reagan's nomination of Judge Robert Bork as an associate justice of the Supreme Court.

Cigler, Allan J., and Burdett A. Loomis, eds. *Interest Group Politics,* 4th ed. Washington, D.C.: CQ Press, 1994. A collection of essays that examines a wide variety of issues in interest group politics.

Olson, Mancur, Jr. *The Logic of Collective Action: Public Goods and the Theory of Groups.* Cambridge: Harvard University Press, 1965. An economist examines the incentives for and obstacles to interest group formation.

Schlozman, Kay Lehman, and John T. Tierney. *Organized Interests and American Democracy.* New York: Harper & Row, 1986. Two political scientists survey the techniques interest groups use to influence government decision making.

Sorauf, Frank J. *Inside Campaign Finance: Myths and Realities.* New Haven: Yale University Press, 1992. A political scientist explores the world of campaign finance and dispels some myths about political action committees.

Stern, Philip M. *Still the Best Congress Money Can Buy.* Washington, D.C.: Regnery Gateway, 1992. A former newspaper reporter and Democratic Party official argues that political action committees threaten representative democracy in the United States.

Wright, John R. *Interest Groups and Congress: Lobbying Contributions, and Influence.* Boston: Allyn & Bacon, 1996. A political scientist presents an engaging and authoritative review of how interest groups affect opinion and public policy in Congress.

Part Three

The Institutions of American Politics

11
Congress

12
The Presidency

13
The Federal Bureaucracy

14
The Courts

Chapter 11

Congress

The Structure of Congress
- *Bicameralism*
- *The House of Representatives*
- *The Senate*

The Evolution of Congress
- *Changing Attitudes Toward Service in Congress*
- *Change in the House*
- *Change in the Senate*

Getting There and Staying There—Congressional Elections
- *Incumbents and Reelection*
- *The Election Setting*
- *The Incumbents' Advantages*
- *The Challengers' Disadvantages*
- *Voters and Election Outcomes*

Serving in Congress
- *Who Serves?*
- *Congress as a Job*
- *Congress and Ethics*

Congress as an Organization
- *Political Parties in Congress*
- *Party Leadership in Congress*
- *Committees*
- *Staff*

The Business of Congress
- *The Legislative Process*
- *Decision Making*
- *Policy Oversight*

Congress and the Idea of Representation

Summary

Key Terms

Readings for Further Study

In February 1995, President Bill Clinton called for increasing the minimum wage from to $4.25 to $5.15 an hour. He defended the proposal on the grounds that "the only way to grow the middle class and shrink the underclass is to make work pay."[1] The president's proposal enjoyed unusually broad support, with close to 80 percent of the public backing it.[2] But the Republican majority in Congress was decidedly less enthusiastic about the proposed increase, fearing it would hurt small businesses and reduce job opportunities. House Majority Leader Richard Armey (R-Tex.), who had previously called for repealing the minimum wage, said he would fight the president's request "with every fiber in my body."[3] Without the support and interest of members of the majority party in Congress, Clinton's proposal to increase the minimum wage faced little prospect of passing. But in 1996, a rising public sense of economic insecurity forced the President's minimum wage proposal to the forefront of the congressional agenda. Ultimately, moderate Republicans feared that voting against a hike in the minimum wage would cost them at the polls, and they joined Democrats to pass the bill.

As President Clinton discovered firsthand, Congress stands at the heart of the American political system. The founders established it in the first article of the Constitution, making it, at least in their minds, the first among equal branches of government. They drew up rules that made the House of Representatives the closest link between the government and the people, and they mandated that all tax bills originate in it. The Senate was designed to be more insulated from public pressure, but it, too, exercises power over the actions of the president, the bureaucracy, and the courts. Congress clearly is positioned to influence policy making. More important, Congress is intended to be the public voice in our republican form of government—a government in which the public governs through its elected representatives.

Today's Congress is the product of both the original rules the founders set down in the Constitution and decisions made over the past two hundred years. In this chapter, we begin by examining the basic structure of Congress set forth in the Constitution. We then look at how the rules and norms of Congress have evolved since the House and Senate first met in 1789. Next, we turn to congressional elections—how members get to Congress and how they stay there. We explore service in Congress, focusing on who serves, Congress as a job, and Congress as an organization. We conclude by reviewing the lawmaking process and discussing the issue of legislative representation. The founders created rules designed to make Congress representative of the public. What exactly does this mean? Are the rules successful? And is the Congress of the 1990s the representative body the founders envisioned?

The Structure of Congress

We have argued throughout this book that rules influence politics. Nowhere is this lesson more obvious than in Congress. The Constitution established the fundamental structure of Congress, and, in doing so, largely determined the specific character of both the House and the Senate.

Bicameralism

When the delegates to the Constitutional Convention began to debate what the new national legislature would look like, they could have considered a wide range of possible structures. But most of the delegates agreed from the start that Congress would be a two-chamber or **bicameral legislature** that would operate independently of the other two branches of government. In choosing a bicameral structure for Congress, the delegates were adopting what was then (and still is) the most common structure for a legislature; the English Parliament and all but three of the colonial legislatures were bicameral.[4]

Bicameral legislature
A legislature with two houses—such as the House and the Senate.

One difference that distinguishes Congress from most other bicameral legislatures in the world is that both chambers wield substantial power. Although the House and Senate each have a few distinct responsibilities, for the most part, they share

Members of the House have unassigned seating. With 435 members, the House floor can become quite crowded and noisy. Usually, personal staff members are not allowed on the floor.

Senators have assigned desks. Their staff members can come to the floor.

lawmaking power. This shared power poses both advantages and disadvantages. On the one hand, it increases the number of voices that are heard when policy proposals are being considered. On the other hand, bicameralism with two powerful houses makes lawmaking more difficult. No bill can be sent to the president to sign into law unless both the House and the Senate have passed it. This rule makes the American legislative process conservative—not in terms of the partisan or ideological substance of the legislation passed, but in terms of making it difficult to change existing laws. In creating a bicameral legislature with two powerful houses, the founders purposely dispersed power to prevent one body of government from dominating all others. While the bicameral structure of Congress does preclude a concentration of power in one house, it also contributes to the "gridlock," or inability to move forward quickly and decisively, that often seems to characterize today's federal legislative process.

The House of Representatives

Although the founders made the House and the Senate equals in lawmaking, they structured the two chambers to have different virtues. The founders wanted the House to be sensitive to public opinion, and the rules governing election to the House reflect this goal. The Constitution requires all representatives to stand for election every two years, which creates the opportunity for a rapid change or **turnover** in House membership if the public so desires. The Constitution also requires that all vacancies that arise during a two-year term must be filled through elections. Unlike the Senate, where vacancies are usually filled initially by appointment, the House can claim that every one of its members was elected by the voters.

Turnover
Change in membership of Congress between elections.

The Constitution further ensures that the House will reflect public sentiment by requiring that the number of representatives in each state be proportional to the population. This means that states with larger populations have more representatives than states with smaller populations, although every state is guaranteed at least one representative.

The Constitution stipulated that the ratio of representatives to the population would be one for every 30,000 people, and it established the initial size of the House of Representatives at sixty-five members. To accommodate a growing population, the Constitution further stipulated that the number of seats a state was entitled to would change every ten years on the basis of the results of the national census. As the country added states and the population continued to increase, Congress responded by creating new House seats. After the first census in 1790, for example, the House expanded to 106 members. By 1860, the House had 243 members.

The rules Congress used to apportion seats changed over time.[5] By 1830, Congress had junked the prescribed constitutional ratio of constituents per representative, allowing bigger districts. (If the one to 30,000 ratio were still in effect, the House now would have more than 8,500 members.) In 1911, Congress decided to cap the number of House seats at 435, a number it reached in 1913 after New Mexico and Arizona entered the Union. The cap meant that in the future, those 435 seats would have to be redistributed or reapportioned among the states as the population grew or new states joined the Union. Congress bickered for nineteen years over a formula for **reapportionment** before finally adopting a new process in 1929, which it revised again in 1950. Since then, population changes have forced significant redistributions in seats among the states. For example, in 1910, California and Iowa each had eleven seats in the House. In 1997, however, California had fifty-two seats to Iowa's five.

Reapportionment
The redistribution of seats in the House of Representatives among the states, which occurs every ten years following the census, so that the size of each state's delegation is proportional to its share of the total population.

The Constitution specifies several other rules for the House, though none of them affects the character of the institution. All representatives must be at least twenty-five years of age and must have been U.S. citizens for at least seven years. (Thus, the 1997 House included among its members Jay Kim, R-Calif., who grew up in Korea, Tom Lantos, D-Calif., an immigrant from Hungary, and Ileana Ros-Lehtinen, R-Fla., a native of Cuba.) The only residency requirement is that representatives must be inhabitants of the state they are elected from; it is only by tradition that we expect them to live in the district they represent. And not surprisingly, given the role that taxes played in triggering the American Revolutionary War, the Constitution states that all tax bills must originate in the House.

The Senate

In contrast to the rules that establish the structure of the House, the rules creating the Senate were designed to establish a more mature body—members must be at least thirty years old and must have been citizens for at least nine years. As chapter 2 discussed, the Connecticut Compromise gave each state two senators. The founders also took two steps to insulate senators from the shifting tides of public opinion. First, they gave senators six-year terms, with only one-third of the Senate up for reelection in any election year. As a result, rapid turnover is far less likely in the Senate than in the House. Second, the founders stipulated that state legislatures rather than voters elect senators. Eventually, this method of electing senators became more and more unpopular. The adoption of the Seventeenth Amendment in 1913 finally mandated the direct, public election of senators. (By then, a majority of states had instituted binding advisory elections that directed the state legislature whom to elect to the Senate.)[6] Unlike vacancies in the House, vacancies in the Senate can be filled by appointment rather than by election (with the governor of the affected state making the choice). These structural rules attempt to achieve a balance by making the Senate more distanced from public opinion, while maintaining the House's sensitivity to it.

The Evolution of Congress

Although the Constitution specifies the basic structure of Congress, it says little about what rules should govern the day-to-day operation of the House and Senate. Article I stipulates that "The House of Representatives shall choose their Speaker and other Officers," that "the Vice President of the United States shall be President of the Senate," and that "the Senate shall choose the other Officers, and also a President pro tempore." Beyond these general guidelines, however, the Constitution says that "each House may determine the Rules of its Proceedings." Because members of Congress are free to adopt the sorts of rules and structures they want, norms and procedures in Congress have changed enormously over the past two hundred years as the interests of members themselves have changed. Moreover, because of the differences in size between the House and Senate, the two chambers have developed very different sets of rules governing their proceedings.

Changing Attitudes Toward Service in Congress

For close to a half-century, service in the House was deemed to be more prestigious than that in the Senate.[7] Overall, however, service in Congress was not thought to be of great importance for much of the nineteenth century. The real action was at the state level. Only slightly more than half of the original members of the House in 1789 returned to office in 1791, and similar turnover rates continued until well after the Civil War.[8] The situation in the Senate was worse. The Senate's first members "fled the Capitol . . . almost as fast as humanly possible."[9] Only two of the original twenty-six senators held their seats for more than six years—most left long before.

Several reasons explain the substantial turnover in congressional membership in the first half of the nineteenth century. Because many of the issues Congress was deciding were less important than those decided elsewhere, members who left voluntarily often did so to take another political office, usually at the state level.[10] For instance, during the first half of the nineteenth century, several speakers of the House gave up their posts to take what are by today's standards far less influential government jobs: receiver-general of the Pennsylvania Land Office, Virginia state treasurer, and lieutenant governor of Kentucky, to name a few examples.[11]

Another reason members left was the practice of rotation, an early version of term limits. In many House districts, particularly in the North, representatives served just one or, more commonly, two terms, and then retired so someone else could serve. Abraham Lincoln, for example, represented Illinois in the House for only one term because his district used the rotation rule.[12]

High congressional turnover also resulted from the lack of incentives for long service. Because congressional pay was low, members put their financial futures at risk by serving in Congress.[13] Moreover, life in Washington was not attractive, even to those who might have found congressional service satisfying. The then-new city was built on a drained swamp, and it lacked most of the amenities common to older cities. For several decades, members of Congress left their families home and lived in boarding houses or hotels during their stays in Washington. Before the advent of railroads, travel to and from the capitol was difficult for most members. Finally, the summer weather was miserable—Congress did not meet year-round until well into the twentieth century, after the Capitol was air conditioned.[14]

High turnover had important consequences for both the House and Senate. Length of service in Congress meant almost nothing. For example, Henry Clay first came to Congress in 1812 and was immediately elected speaker of the House (see box 11.1). He subsequently left Congress and then returned, again claiming the post of speaker. Such a career pattern is unheard of in the modern Congress. More typical is the career path of the current speaker of the House, Newt Gingrich (R-Ga.), which was marked by almost two decades of continuous service and relatively slow movement up the leadership ladder.[15]

High turnover also affected how members of Congress conducted themselves. Because they intended to serve only a short time, members had little to fear if their behavior offended their colleagues, and the decorum of Congress suffered for it. Conduct on the floor of the House, for example, included bringing hunting dogs to lie alongside one member's desk; verbal debates degenerating into threats of bodily harm; fisticuffs; beatings with canes; and even one fight in which a gun was fired.[16]

Members of Congress began to view their service as a career sometime during the second half of the nineteenth century. Many reasons can be offered to explain the shift. The most important is that changes in the economic and social fabric of the country, especially those produced by industrialization, urbanization, and immigration, created new political interests that only the federal government could satisfy. This, in turn, pushed Congress toward the center of decision making, and it made being a member of Congress more interesting and important than it had been.

The People Behind the Rules

BOX 11.1

The Political Careers of Henry Clay and Newt Gingrich

One of the biggest changes in Congress over the last two centuries has been the path members take to attain positions of power. Two speakers of the House demonstrate the dramatic changes: Henry Clay, who served as speaker in three different short stints during the early 1800s, and Newt Gingrich, who became speaker in 1995 after sixteen years of relatively slow movement up the rungs of power in the House.

Henry Clay

Newt Gingrich

Henry Clay

Henry Clay is one of the most important figures in American history. Known as the Great Compromiser, Clay dedicated much of his political career in the years preceding the Civil War to preventing the impending split between North and South. To this end, he was in large part responsible for the Missouri Compromise of 1820 and the Compromise of 1850.

Clay's service to the country was extensive and varied. To our modern eyes, the leaps his career took—from U.S. senator to speaker of the Kentucky House of Representatives to U.S. senator again to speaker of the U.S. House of Representatives to secretary of state—are incredible. No modern politician could expect to hopscotch among such a variety of powerful posts. In 1806, Clay was appointed to fill the last two years of an unexpired Senate term despite the fact that he was only twenty-nine, one year shy of meeting the constitutional requirement that senators be at least thirty years of age. (Clay was seated because none of his fellow senators challenged his right to the seat.) The next year, he returned home to Kentucky, where he served for two years as speaker in the Kentucky House of Representatives. He returned to Washington in 1809 when he was appointed to fill the last two years of another unexpired Senate term. In 1811, Clay was elected to the House, and almost immediately became speaker. He resigned the speakership in 1814 to become a member of the U.S. delegation that was negotiating a treaty to end the War of 1812 with Great Britain.

Clay returned to the House after completing the Treaty of Ghent, and he was again elected speaker. He left the House again in 1821, returned two years later, and served once more as speaker. After running unsuccessfully for president, Clay left the House in 1825, never to return. He served as Secretary of State under President John Quincy Adams. Later, Clay had two more tours of duty in the Senate, and he ran unsuccessfully for president two more times. He said of his failed bids for the White House, "I would rather be right than be President."

Newt Gingrich

In 1978, Newt Gingrich, a thirty-five-year-old history professor at West Georgia College, was elected to the House. Gingrich gained his seat on his third attempt; in 1974 and 1976, he had come close to knocking off a long-time incumbent. When the incumbent decided against running again in 1978, Gingrich won the race for the open seat.

As a first-term member of the House, Gingrich was assigned to relatively minor committees. His real interest, however, was in working toward making Republicans the majority party in the House. He quickly became a leader among younger, more conservative Republican members, and a thorn in the side of the Democrats. Gingrich, for example, leveled the ethics charges that eventually led Jim Wright to resign as the speaker of the House.

In 1989, Gingrich won a tough race against a more moderate Republican from Illinois to become the minority whip. Despite representing his party's more conservative wing, by the time Minority Leader Robert Michel decided to retire following the 1994 election, Gingrich was his unchallenged successor. Thus, when the Republicans took control of the House following the 1994 elections, Gingrich became the first Republican speaker in forty years. But it took Gingrich sixteen years of service to work his way up to the position of speaker—a position Clay reached almost immediately upon his election to the House at the age of thirty-four.

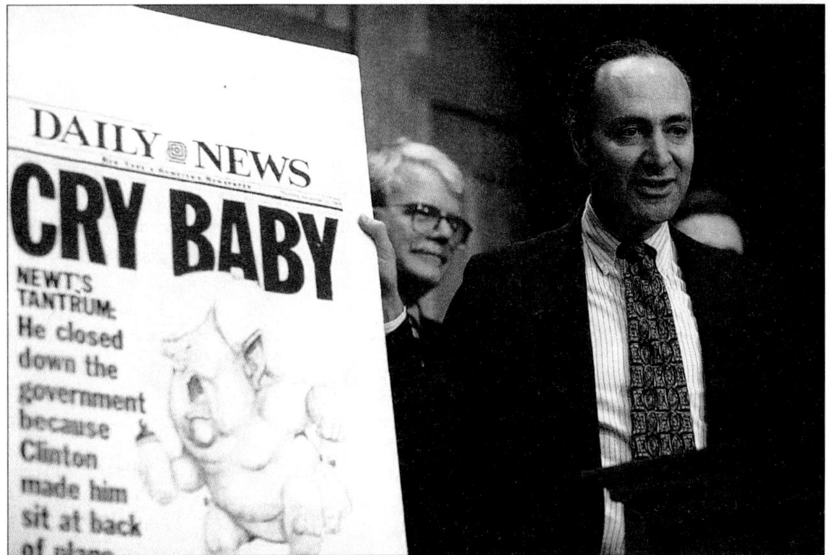

Norms of civility have held in Congress since the late 1800s, but they are sometimes violated. In 1995, Rep. Charles Schumer (D-N.Y.) was not allowed to call Speaker Gingrich a "crybaby" after Gingrich complained that President Bill Clinton had snubbed him aboard Air Force One, the presidential jet.

Change in the House

The House has undergone many changes since it first met in 1789. We can break these changes down into four distinct periods: the nineteenth century, the early twentieth century, the 1970s and 1980s, and the 1990s.

The Nineteenth Century

The shift toward viewing membership in Congress as a career affected both the House and the Senate, though it affected the House in particular. The most visible change involved member decorum. In the latter half of the nineteenth century, civility replaced outrageous behavior as strict rules and norms were developed to govern how members conducted themselves on the floor of the House and in committee meetings. For example, even in the midst of the most heated debate, members are now barred from denigrating their opponents. Although such rules often lead to excessive (and stilted) civility, they serve a practical purpose: they limit rancorous exchanges and thereby make every member's service more tolerable.

The shift toward viewing congressional service as a career also has changed the balance of power within the House. Until the beginning of the twentieth century, the speaker dominated the work of the House. The bulk of the speaker's power stemmed from the committee system. By 1820, the House had created a system of permanent, or standing, committees to help manage its workload. Each **standing committee** was given jurisdiction over a specific policy area, and it had an almost unlimited right to determine whether a bill within its jurisdiction would be put to a vote by the whole House. For example, in 1802, the House established the Ways and Means Committee to oversee the government's tax system. Any bill changing the tax structure had to pass through Ways and Means, giving that committee virtual control over tax policy.

Standing committee
A permanent committee in Congress with jurisdiction over a specific policy area. Such a committee has tremendous say over the details of legislation within its jurisdiction.

Members served on a committee at the discretion of the speaker. The speaker also had the power to assign bills to committee and to determine the rules under which the full membership of the House would debate and vote on bills. Members gained influence through their relationship with the speaker; length of service in the House did not matter. Members who were in the speaker's good graces received positions of power, whereas those who were not found themselves serving on minor committees.

The Early Twentieth Century

The speaker's domination of the House continued as long as members had no desire to make congressional service a career. As members began to serve longer, however, they chafed at the speaker's immense power. In 1910, rank-and-file members revolted

The seniority system is sometimes designated the "senility system," but it does guarantee that committee chairs are members with extensive service.

From *The Herblock Book,* Beacon Press, 1952. Reprinted by permission.

Seniority rule
The congressional norm of making the member of the majority party with the longest continuous service on a committee the chair of that committee.

and enacted new rules that stripped the office of the speakership of much of its authority. They gave the power to make committee assignments to special groups in each party. Under the **seniority rule,** which is actually an informal norm rather than a written rule, the member of the majority party with the longest continuous service on a committee became the chair of the committee. Although the importance of seniority had been increasing since after the Civil War, it did not become absolute until around 1916.[17] Members accepted the seniority rule because it meant they would acquire positions of power such as the chair of a committee if they served long enough.

From the revolt of 1910 until the early 1970s, power in the House was concentrated in the hands of committee chairs and other senior members. On most issues, members deferred to the committees. Members were expected to focus on the issues before their committees and to avoid meddling in the affairs of other committees. Junior members were expected to serve an apprenticeship while they learned the substance of the issues before their committees. Only as they gained seniority did they earn the opportunity to shape legislation.

Change in the 1970s and 1980s

Dissatisfaction with the power of committee chairs grew in the 1950s and 1960s. Democrats from northern and western states bridled at the disproportionate number of committee chairs southern Democrats held. The southerners held so many committee chairs because they had been elected at young ages, had never faced serious challenges in their one-party states, and, as a result, had gained substantial seniority.[18] The immense power of the southern committee chairs would not have been a major problem if these members shared the views of other Democrats. But they were much more conservative, and they used their committee positions to stifle the policy preferences of more liberal Democrats, especially in the area of civil rights.

Subcommittees
The smaller units of a standing committee that oversee one part of the committee's jurisdiction.

In the early 1970s, northern Democrats gained the upper hand within their party because of their own increased seniority and because many elderly southerners retired. The northern Democrats used their power to make significant changes in the rules of the House. Most important, they took power away from committee chairs and gave it to the chairs of the **subcommittees,** the smaller units of a standing committee that oversee one part of the committee's jurisdiction. Now more than eighty-four subcommittee chairs—many of them junior members—enjoy considerable influence. As former representative Morris Udall joked, "We've got so many committees and subcommittees now that if you can't remember somebody's name, you just say 'Hi, Mr. Chairman.'"[19]

The reform movement of the 1970s also targeted the seniority system. Over the years, many committee chairs had used their powers to impose their preferences on other committee members. To curtail such abuses, the Democratic **caucus,** which consists of all the Democratic members in the House, agreed in 1974 to elect committee chairs by secret ballot. (Since the Democrats were the majority party in the House, they had the responsibility for establishing the rules for selecting chairs.) In the first vote under the new rules, Democrats unseated three southern committee chairs who were legendary for their autocratic ways. But the vote did not mark a rejection of the seniority system itself. The caucus replaced two of the chairs with the next most senior member; the other new chair was fourth in seniority. After 1975, the caucus replaced very few chairs. The chairs knew, however, that they could be removed if they did not maintain the support of the caucus. And members realized that seniority did not guarantee that they would get to chair a committee.

Caucus
A closed meeting of members of a political party to discuss matters of public policy and political strategy, and in some cases, to select candidates for office.

The reform movement of the 1970s decentralized power in the House. Committee chairs accustomed to wielding extensive power found themselves having to share authority with subcommittee chairs. At the same time, committees no longer could write legislation and expect the full House to approve it without change. Individual members began to take advantage of the rules of the House to try to change or amend legislation once it came to the floor for a vote. From the mid-1970s to the mid-1980s, the number of amendments offered on the floor, and the number accepted, increased dramatically.[20] Thus, junior members had improved their prospects for influencing legislation, even in areas outside their committee jurisdictions.

The trend toward decentralization had important consequences for the House as an organization. Members found it more difficult to develop and agree on major legislation. Recognizing this problem, in the mid-1970s they adopted several changes designed to recentralize some powers in the hands of the party leadership. The speaker regained some, but by no means all, of the powers lost decades earlier. Under the new rules, the speaker had more say in committee assignments and more authority regarding the flow of legislation between committees and the floor.[21]

The nation's difficult budget situation in the 1980s accelerated the recentralization of power in the hands of the majority party leadership, and it increased the importance of the committees that oversaw taxes and spending. As the federal government's budget deficits grew, money for new programs became very tight, and the most important political battles were fought over legislation that determined how government money would be spent. Power over those bills was concentrated in the hands of relatively few people—party leaders such as the speaker and the members of the committees with the most input on budget bills. To some extent, members serving on other committees were left out of the process in which many important policy decisions were made.[22]

Under the Democrats, the trend toward recentralization was tempered by the legacy of the reforms of the 1970s. Strains of decentralization and recentralization coexisted somewhat uncomfortably together. Power continued to be diffused among many members, with subcommittees remaining important actors in the process and individual members continuing to amend legislation on the floor.[23] Senior members still exercised the most influence in the House, but junior members were deeply involved in lawmaking.[24] At the same time, the majority party leadership was stronger than at any time since the early part of the century. Budget constraints gave majority party leaders the opportunity to shape policy with input from relatively few members. But the reforms made the leadership dependent on the members for power; that is, the leaders were allowed to make decisions only as long as the membership was willing to accept the final package. Members were often willing to reject deals the leadership brought to the floor.[25] Moreover, members had more opportunities to remove leaders. Thus, the rules created a situation in which leaders had more power to shape policies than they had before, but rank-and-file members ultimately retained the ability to reject or constrain the decisions the leaders made.

Change in the 1990s

In 1995, the Republicans took control of the House for the first time in forty years, and with their new majority status came the responsibility of deciding what powers a Republican speaker would have. They ultimately decided to make relatively few changes to the formal powers of the speaker. One formal change they did make was to limit the speaker to four consecutive terms in office, a change that in the long run tends to reduce the power of the speaker.

Despite these term limits and the lack of formal rules changes, Speaker Newt Gingrich quickly assumed powers unrivaled by any speaker since the turn of the century. For example, Gingrich made committee assignments, and he violated the unwritten seniority rule in naming the chairs of several committees and subcommittees. He forced all returning Republicans on the important Appropriations Committee to sign letters of loyalty to the party's programs. He also centralized important decision-making powers in his hands. On one occasion, he forced a committee chair to reverse a hard-won position on a major telecommunications bill before the full House voted on it. On another occasion, he moved negotiations on the controversial 1995 farm bill from the Agriculture Committee to his office. The House plan to reform Medicare was developed by an ad hoc task force working for the speaker, not by the committees that oversee the issue.[26]

As power flowed to the speaker's office, it ebbed away from committee and subcommittee chairs. For the most part, committee and subcommittee chairs accepted their diminished status. Rep. Henry Hyde (R-Ill.), the chair of the Judiciary Committee who, as we saw in chapter 1, had to push his party's term-limits measure through his committee even though he strongly opposed it, observed, "There has not been time to implement items of my personal agenda. But they are small potatoes. I'm fully in accord with the priorities of this leadership."[27]

Speaker Gingrich succeeded in taking power away from committee and subcommittee chairs in the absence of any major change in the formal powers of the speaker's office because he had the loyal support of most House Republicans, and especially of first-term Republicans. As one former House member noted, "There is personal loyalty to him [Gingrich] that is without precedent in recent history."[28] But because Gingrich's expanded authority rested on personal loyalty rather than on the formal powers of the speaker's office, his powers faded some in 1996, as negative public reaction to him led his fellow Republicans to become more independent.

Change in the Senate

The Senate has undergone less visible change than the House. Although it has grown in size from twenty-six to one hundred members, the Senate continues to operate under rules that reflect its original small size. Senators have considerable freedom to debate policy proposals and to block legislation they dislike, and many senators have exploited these freedoms to see that their policy views are taken into account. As a result, individual senators have much greater influence over legislation than their counterparts in the House do.

Despite the tremendous continuity in its procedures, the Senate has seen some change over the past several decades. In the 1940s and 1950s, the Senate was often characterized as an elite men's club where a handful of senior members dominated decision making.[29] Junior members endured lengthy apprenticeships before earning the opportunity to participate, and they were expected to concentrate on a handful of policy areas.[30] During a committee meeting in the early 1960s, for example, one junior senator interrupted the discussion among the committee's senior members to ask the chair "if he would mind talking louder so we could hear what decisions were being made."[31]

In the 1970s, the Senate adopted several new rules that encouraged decentralization. Informal changes played an even bigger role, though, as new, more individualist senators refused to enter into apprenticeships while more senior members managed the business of the Senate. As a result, power in the Senate is now dispersed into the hands of many members. Even first-term senators can play key roles in policy

Even as a first-year member of the Senate in 1995, Rick Santorum (R-Pa.) was able to play a visible role in the budget battle. A few decades ago, first-term members were not expected to be important players in Senate decisions.

making.[32] For example, Sen. Rick Santorum (R-Pa.), who was only thirty-six years old when he was elected to the Senate in 1994, immediately involved himself in high-profile debates with senior members of both parties on the balanced budget amendment.[33] Such boldness would never have been expected or tolerated from a junior senator thirty years earlier.

Nonetheless, the formal rules in the Senate do not change as often or as much as they do in the House. The reason is that each chamber has different rules governing how much support is needed to change any rule. In the House, a simple majority is all that is needed to change a rule, which means that the majority party can dictate the rules as long as its members agree on them. In the Senate, however, two-thirds of the senators must approve any rule changes.[34] Thus, unless the majority party in the Senate holds sixty-seven seats, or can gain the consent of the minority party, the rules will not change.

Getting There and Staying There—Congressional Elections

The framers of the Constitution understood that how elected officials gain office influences their behavior once there. For example, the framers chose direct election and two-year terms to make representatives responsive to public opinion. In contrast, they chose six-year terms and election by state legislatures to insulate senators from the heat of public demands. Today, of course, members of both the House and the Senate are directly elected. But the difference in term lengths and, for most senators, differences in the number of people they represent influence the way representatives and senators win election and how they behave once in office.

Incumbents and Reelection

One overriding fact affects congressional elections: incumbents who choose to run for reelection almost always win. Moreover, they usually win by large margins. As figure 11.1 shows, the electoral success of incumbents is particularly striking for members of the House. Since 1952, representatives who run for reelection have won more than 90 percent of the time, while senators have won roughly 80 percent of the time. Even in 1994, a year when the media reported that an anti-incumbent mood was sweeping the

FIGURE 11.1
Percent of Incumbents Reelected, 1952–1996

Representatives have a higher reelection rate than senators, but both usually win.

Source: Data for 1952–1994 from Norman J. Ornstein, Thomas E. Mann, and Michael J. Malbin, *Vital Statistics on Congress 1995–1996* (Washington, D.C.: Congressional Quarterly, 1996), pp. 60–61; data for 1996, Helen Dewar, "Senate Takes More Conservative Bent," *Washington Post,* 7 November 1996, and John E. Yang, "Slimmer Majority for House GOP," *Washington Post,* 7 November 1996.

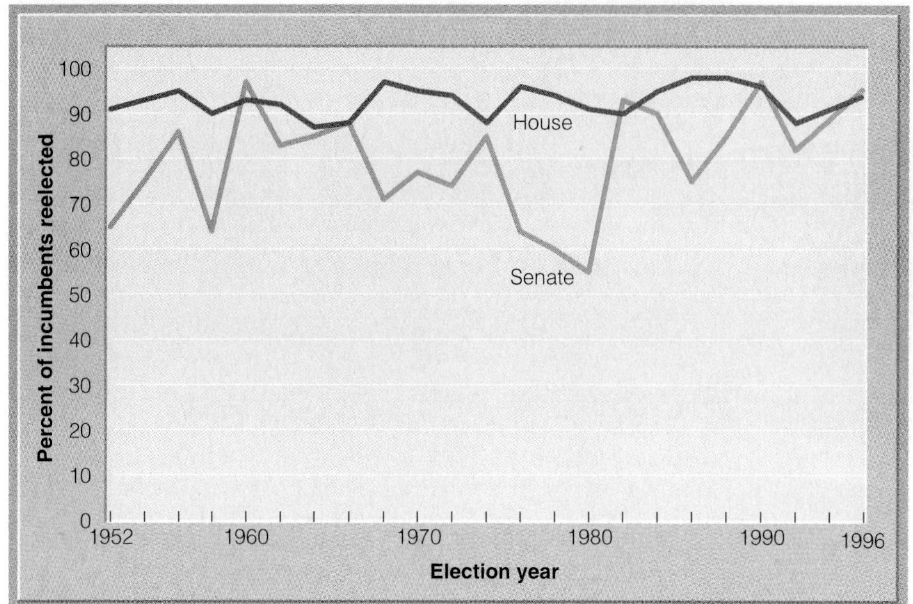

country, more than 90 percent of the representatives who ran for reelection won, as did 92 percent of the senators. (As a rule, incumbents fare well at the ballot box in most democracies. A recent study of national legislatures in eight other industrialized democracies found that incumbent reelection rates averaged 75 percent, ranging from a low of 61 percent in Canada and France to a high of 89 percent in New Zealand.)[35]

Although the reelection rate for congressional incumbents is very high, Congress still sees substantial turnover in its membership (though far less than the founders envisioned). In 1997, for example, 76 percent of the members of Congress had been in office for less than twelve years. How can substantial turnover coexist with high reelection rates? The answer is that each year, many incumbents decide against running for reelection. Some retire because of age or a desire to pursue other activities, some seek election to a higher office, and some decide they cannot win reelection.

Why do incumbents who run for reelection fare so well? And why do representatives fare better than senators? To answer these two questions, we will examine the setting in which elections take place, the advantages incumbents have, and the disadvantages that challengers face. We will also consider why incumbents lose.

The Election Setting

One way to answer both questions—why incumbents fare so well when they run for reelection and why representatives running for reelection fare better than senators—is to look at the setting in which elections take place. Especially important is the way in which congressional districts are drawn and the greater homogeneity of congressional districts when compared to states.

Redistricting and Gerrymandering

One possible explanation for why so many incumbents win reelection is that the maps of congressional districts are drawn to favor incumbents. Of course, such an explanation says nothing about why so many senators win reelection; after all, they represent states whose boundaries do not change. But it might explain the electoral success of incumbents in the House. In theory at least, district boundaries could be drawn in ways that promote the electoral prospects of incumbent representatives.

Single-member districts
A legislative district in which only one legislator is elected.

The Constitution does not stipulate how states should draw their House districts. All members now are elected from so-called **single-member districts,** which means that the voters living in a defined geographic area known as a district elect just one representative.

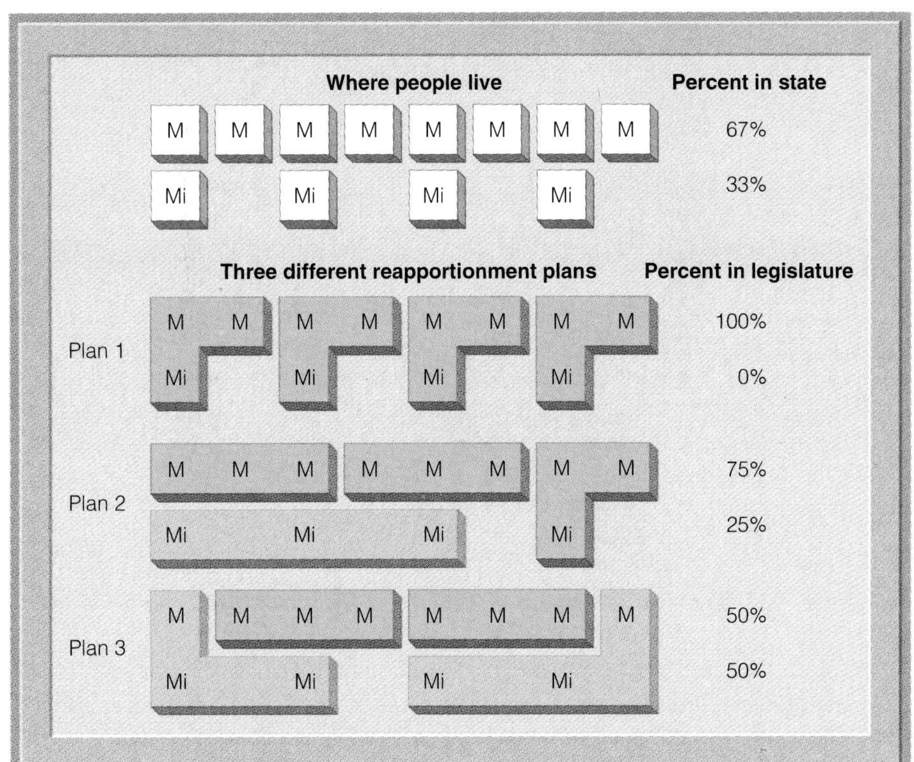

FIGURE 11.2
Hypothetical Redistricting
Even with the same distribution of majority and minority party members, different districting plans can produce very different results.

In the past, however, some members were elected from at-large districts, where everyone in the state voted for the representative. In 1842, Congress passed legislation requiring single-member districts, and in 1872, it also passed legislation requiring districts to be of roughly equal population. But these rules were not enforced on the states.[36] (Indeed, Congress outlawed multimember districts again in 1967.)

Until the early 1960s, state legislatures, which oversee redistricting, were not compelled to redraw district lines to take shifting populations into account. The result was that, in many states, voters were distributed unevenly across the districts, with some districts containing up to four times as many people as other districts. Typically, rural and Republican interests were overrepresented in such plans and urban and Democratic interests underrepresented.

In the early 1960s, the Supreme Court ruled that House districts must have roughly equal numbers of people, and it ordered states to redistrict on the basis of one person, one vote.[37] But the Court did not define the fairest way to draw congressional districts; indeed, the Court could not specify objective guidelines for redistricting. Figure 11.2 shows why. Imagine that a state has eight members of the majority political party (*M*) for every four members of the minority political party (*Mi*). How would you divide the state into four congressional districts? In the first plan, the district lines are drawn so that the *M*s have a majority in each of the four districts. In the second plan, the *Mi*s are heavily concentrated in one district, giving them the opportunity to control that single district. In the third plan, *Mi*s control half of the districts, giving them a chance to elect two of the four representatives, despite making up just a third of the population.

Figure 11.2 illustrates two important points. First, the way district boundaries are drawn matters. Substitute ethnic, racial, or socioeconomic groups for our imaginary political parties *M* and *Mi* and you can see how redistricting can determine the composition of the House of Representatives. Second, district lines are not neutral. No matter who draws them or what their intentions are, any set of lines will help one group and hurt another. There is no ideal set of districts in figure 11.2, no boundaries that guarantee perfect representation.

FIGURE 11.3
The Original Gerrymander—Massachusetts, 1812

The practice of drawing district lines for partisan political advantage has a long history in American politics.

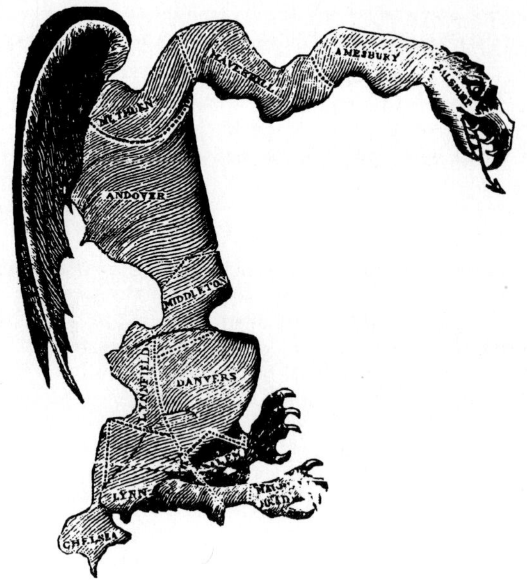

Gerrymandering
Drawing congressional district boundaries to favor one party over the other.

The fact that district lines are not neutral raises the possibility of **gerrymandering**—drawing district boundaries to favor one political party over another. (Gerrymandering gets its name from a redistricting plan drawn up by the political associates of Elbridge Gerry, a governor of Massachusetts in the early 1800s. Opponents of the plan drew a head and wings on the outline of one district—see figure 11.3—and said that it looked like a salamander. One wit among them observed that it looked more like a gerrymander.) The Supreme Court ruled in 1986 that gerrymandering violates the Constitution, though the Court did not say how to determine a gerrymander.[38] As with obscenity, the Court knows a gerrymander when it sees one, but it cannot specify exactly what it is. So parties retain the ability to draw district lines to their advantage.

Does the drawing of district lines explain the reelection success of incumbents? While it is clear that incumbents may gain some advantages from redistricting, their reelection success is not a result of the way their districts are drawn.[39] Incumbents in districts in which lines are redrawn fare no better or worse than their colleagues in unchanged districts.[40] Also, over the ten years that district boundaries are in effect, parties that gerrymander sometimes gain more seats than they deserve based on their percentage of the vote, but in other cases, they do worse.[41]

Although redistricting does not explain high reelection rates among incumbents, considerable concern remains that district boundaries may be drawn in ways that minimize the chances that minorities will be elected to Congress. Based on Congress's 1982 amendments to the Voting Rights Act of 1965, the Supreme Court has thrown out such redistricting plans. As a result, many state legislatures have sought to maximize the chance of minority representation in the House by concentrating particular minority groups in single districts.[42] In 1997, for example, the first district in Illinois, on Chicago's south side, was 70 percent African American. Nearby districts included the second district, which was 68 percent African American; the third district, which was 89 percent white; and the fourth district, which was 64 percent Hispanic American. One effect of concentrating minorities in a district is that, as we will see, the number of minorities elected to Congress has increased appreciably. But, in an ironic twist, because most African Americans and, to a lesser extent, Hispanic Americans support the Democratic Party, concentrating them in a few districts has resulted in fewer Democrats and more Republicans being elected to the House.[43]

How far can states go to create districts that make the election of minorities likely? The answer is that race cannot be a predominant factor in the drawing of district lines. In a 1993 case involving a congressional district in North Carolina (see figure 11.4), the Supreme Court ruled that the use of extreme measures to ensure the election of minorities

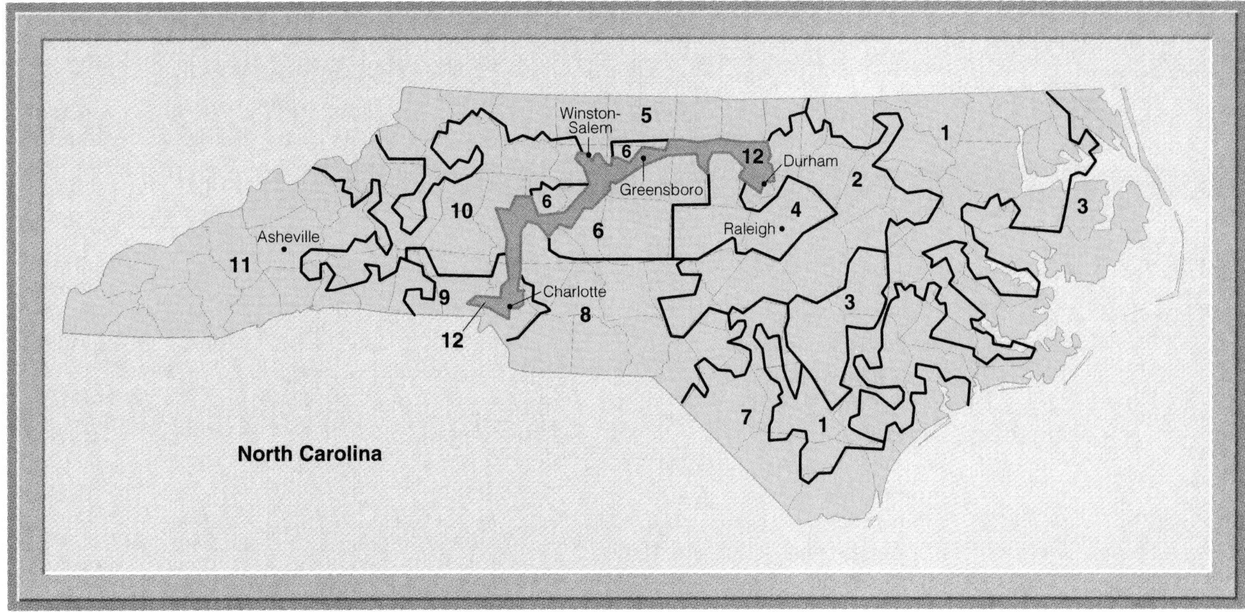

FIGURE 11.4
Racial Gerrymandering

The 12th district in North Carolina faced court challenges in 1993 and 1996. The district, which took its odd shape because state legislators wanted to draw an African-American majority district, was the subject of the Supreme Court's decision in *Shaw v. Reno* (1993). The district was tossed out by the Court in *Shaw v. Hunt* (1996).

From *Congressional Quarterly Weekly Report,* Supplement to No. 44, page 92, November 7, 1992. Congressional Quarterly, Inc., Washington, D.C. Reprinted by permission.

amounts to racial gerrymandering and may violate the rights of white voters to equal protection under the law.[44] Although the Court's ruling in that case only established that white voters had the right to sue North Carolina, the tenor of the decision indicated that the redistricting plan would not pass constitutional muster. In a 1995 case involving a district in Georgia, the other shoe dropped. The Court ruled that use of race as a "predominant factor" in drawing district lines would be presumed unconstitutional.[45] In 1996, the Court tossed out several districts in Texas as well as the disputed North Carolina district. In these cases, the Court held open the possibility that states might be allowed to create districts in which members of minority groups were the majority, but it ruled that race cannot be the predominant factor in drawing district lines and that districts must be geographically compact and not bizarrely shaped.[46]

Districts Versus States

Redistricting may not explain why so many representatives win reelection, but the number of congressional districts does help explain why House incumbents fare better than Senate incumbents. Races for the House usually involve smaller and more homogeneous groups of voters than Senate elections. (The exceptions to this generalization are the seven states that have a single representative—Alaska, Delaware, Montana, North Dakota, South Dakota, Vermont, and Wyoming.) Put simply, as the number of voters increases, so does their economic, ideological, and social diversity. The increased diversity makes it harder for Senate candidates to maintain a winning coalition of voters.

Table 11.1 uses the population characteristics from four California congressional districts to illustrate the tremendous diversity of many states. Notice how much the districts vary in terms of the percentage of households with children, median house values, and ethnic and racial makeup, even though the number of people living in each district is almost the same. The districts also have very different economies. The first district encompasses the redwood forests and northern coast of California. Its economy depends heavily on fishing, logging, and tourism. The twentieth district lies in the Central Valley, an area in which large farms grow cotton, melons, walnuts, and a host of other crops. The twenty-fourth and thirty-third districts are both in Los Angeles, but they represent very different communities. The twenty-fourth encompasses some very wealthy areas, including Malibu, and it is home to the entertainment and aerospace industries. In contrast, the thirty-third district includes many of the poorest neighborhoods in Los Angeles.

Senators usually face more diverse constituencies than representatives do.

TABLE 11.1 Comparisons of State and Selected District Demographics: California, 1990

	State of California	1st District	20th District	24th District	33d District
Population	30,857,000	572,870	573,555	572,287	570,893
Percent rural	7	13	9	3	0
Median household income	$35,798	$30,943	$21,140	$48,433	$20,708
Percent households married couple with children	26	27	35	25	34
Median house value	$195,500	$136,200	$63,400	$304,300	$154,400
Percent Hispanic American	26	11	55	13	83
Percent African American	7	4	6	2	4
Percent Asian American	10	4	6	6	4

Source: Data from Michael Barone and Grant Ujifusa, *The Almanac of American Politics 1996* (Washington, D.C.: National Journal, 1995), pp. 96, 145, 155, 179.

If people often do not have much in common with people living in other districts in the state, they usually have much in common with others living in the same district. They often hold similar kinds of jobs, cherish the same cultural heritage, and share the same political values. The relative homogeneity of congressional districts—and some districts are far more homogeneous than others—makes it easier for representatives to identify the interests of the district and to characterize their work in Washington in ways that appeal to voters. In turn, knowing what appeals to constituents helps members get reelected.

Now imagine the problem that confronts California's two senators. Not only must they develop a platform that appeals to the very different voters living in the four districts shown in table 11.1, but to the voters living in the state's other forty-eight districts as well! Crafting and communicating a political message that appeals to loggers in northern California, to farmers in the Central Valley, to movie stars in Beverly Hills, and to the poor of inner-city Los Angeles is difficult. California's senators run the risk that taking a stance on almost any issue will alienate some voters. In sum, larger and more diverse constituencies account, in part, for the lower reelection rate of senators.

The Incumbents' Advantages

Home style
The way in which members of Congress present themselves to their constituents in the district.

A second set of explanations for the high incumbent reelection rate argues that simply being in office gives incumbents many opportunities to make themselves better known to and better liked by their constituents. The way members of Congress present themselves to the voters in their district or state is known as their **home style.**[47] Members adopt home styles that suit their personalities and the districts they represent. Although a representative from Manhattan may adopt a style different from that of his or her colleague from Salt Lake City, the two share the same goal: to present themselves as accessible and trustworthy. Members go to great lengths to convince voters that they share the same values and that they are making the same decisions the voters would if they sat in Congress.

Members of Congress have many tools with which to shape their home style. They can trumpet their legislative successes, use the resources of their office to reach out to voters, and raise funds to run political advertisements that burnish their image. If members develop an effective home style, they will enter every election with advantages that any challenger finds difficult to match.

The Advantages of Responsibility

The responsibility of being an elected official carries with it several advantages. First of all, members of Congress have many opportunities to steer federal money into their districts and states. When members secure government funds to build a new bridge, to finance a research project at the local university, or to build a tank at a nearby defense plant, they can claim credit for improving the lives of their constituents.[48] For example, when Iowa City, Iowa received federal money to buy five new buses, Sen. Tom Harkin (D-Iowa) announced the grant, and his picture accompanied the story in the local paper.[49] As the federal budget tightens, members of Congress have even started to take credit for cutting funding. A press release for Rep. Henry Bonilla (R-Tex.), for example, trumpeted "Bonilla Eliminates Funding for Enforcement of Cardboard Baler Regulation," an action he thought would be popular with his supporters.[50]

A second advantage that members of Congress gain from occupying a position of responsibility is that voters want to know their views on the major issues of the day. This allows members to stake out policy positions that please their constituents.[51] In some instances, members disregard their own personal views and adopt the most politically advantageous position. In other instances, though, members take positions by framing their personal views to appeal to the maximum number of voters. For example, one representative wrote to his constituents to tell them: "I have worked hard on issues such as tax fairness, cutting federal red tape, creating jobs, making college education more affordable, improving our roads and airports, sensibly managing our resources, and at the same time eliminating government waste."[52] It is hard to imagine anyone taking the opposing side on any of these issues. Voting also gives members of Congress an opportunity to put themselves on record in support of politically popular positions.

In addition to claiming credit and taking positions, members of Congress take advantage of their position of responsibility by calling attention to their activities—in effect, advertising themselves.[53] Much of what happens in Congress is newsworthy, especially for local media. As a result, most members of Congress have press secretaries, and almost every congressional office issues press releases heralding the member's efforts to represent the voters back home.[54] The House, Senate, and both national party headquarters also have satellite facilities to tape the comments of members of Congress and send them to television stations back home.[55] Local media are eager to relay congressional press and video releases—sometimes edited, sometimes not—to the voters because their audiences want to know what is happening and because many of them need news items to fill their papers or airtime.

Resources of the Office

Along with the advantage that comes from being able to claim responsibility for government benefits, incumbents gain an advantage from the resources of their office. One such resource is the clout needed to help constituents deal with the federal bureaucracy. Servicing the needs of constituents is part of the representational duties of a member of Congress. But **constituent service** also makes good electoral sense. Most people speak fondly of members who persuade the Social Security Administration to reissue a lost check or who cut through the red tape blocking a cousin's effort to immigrate to the United States. During Sen. Edward Kennedy's (D-Mass.) successful 1994 reelection effort, for example, one lifelong Republican confessed, "My mother would die if she were alive to see [me vote for Kennedy, but] I don't care. He did me a very big favor. I had trouble getting my Medicare check and he took care of it for me."[56] Because constituent service can generate considerable goodwill at a relatively low cost, members have made sure that their office budgets are large enough to allow them to hire staffs to help constituents solve problems they may have with the federal government.

Constituent service
Favors members of Congress do for constituents—usually in the form of help in dealing with the federal bureaucracy.

A second resource that comes with a seat in Congress is the **franking privilege,** the right to send official mail for free. With the franking privilege, members of Congress can bypass the local media and reach voters directly. Although members almost always respond to letters from their constituents, the most prominent use of the franking privilege is the constituent newsletter (see figure 11.5). Newsletters are mass mailings that

Franking privilege
The right of a member of Congress to send official mail without paying postage.

FIGURE 11.5
Constituent Newsletters

Portions of newletters from then-Rep. Dave Nagle (top) and then-Sen. Pete Wilson (bottom). Representatives and senators are eager to perform constituent services. Their newsletters drum up business, telling people what services members of Congress can perform and how to contact them.

Courtesy of Dave Nagle, Waterloo, Iowa.

PAGE 4 CONGRESSMAN DAVE NAGLE

CONSTITUENT SERVICE GUIDE

Information for Help With Federal Programs

When you have a specific need or problem with the Federal government, sometimes it can be difficult to find the right office or person who can help you.

Listed here are some of the programs, services, and federal agencies that my office can help you with.

- Social Security
- Federal Student Loans
- Farm Services
- Federal Employment
- Government Contracts
- Medicare and Medicaid
- Small Business Administration
- Civil Services
- Housing
- Consumer Programs
- Disability Eligibility
- Retirement Eligibility
- Food and Nutrition Programs
- Immigration and Naturalization Service

In your inquiry, please include your full name and address, telephone number, and Social Security number.

Special Requests

ACADEMY APPOINTMENTS—Each year, Congressman Nagle nominates a number of qualified students to appointment at the four National Service Academies.

Please contact Toni Harn in the Waterloo office if you wish to apply for one of these academies.

WASHINGTON TOURS—Our office can arrange tours of various federal office buildings including the White House, the FBI Building, and the Supreme Court. These tours come in a very limited number and are offered on a first-come, first-served basis. So please, if your family or group is coming to Washington, let us know as early as possible.

PUBLIC APPEARANCES—I really enjoy speaking to community, civic, and school groups throughout our District. It helps keep you up to date and is a great opportunity for me to stay in touch with you.

If you would like me to address your group, please contact my Waterloo office and we'll do everything possible to work it out.

INTERNSHIPS—Internships are available in the District and Washington offices for college or high school students who would like to volunteer their time in the summer to learn about and participate in the workings of a Congressional office. Interns work with the staff performing routine office functions as well as other special projects. For more information please contact one of the offices.

U.S. FLAGS—Several sizes of American flags are available for purchase from my Washington office only. If you would like your flag flown over the Capitol Building on a specific date, please let us know. These orders take six weeks to fill.

Wilson Offices Here To Help

SAN FRANCISCO
450 Golden Gate Avenue
San Francisco, California 94102

LOS ANGELES
11000 Wilshire Boulevard
Suite 11221
Los Angeles, California 90024

SAN DIEGO
880 Front Street
Room 6-S-9
San Diego, California 92188

FRESNO
1130 O Street
Room 4015
Fresno, California 93721

WASHINGTON
Hart Senate Office Building
Suite 720
Washington, D.C. 20510

Caseworkers Can Help You To Cut Through Federal Red Tape

When artificial heart recipient William Schroeder took the opportunity of a get-well phone call from President Reagan to request that the President cut through the red tape Schroeder was encountering at the Social Security office, it was an example of the frustration Americans often feel when dealing with the federal bureaucracy.

Elected officials like myself can help you in such cases. I have a staff of trained individuals -- known as caseworkers -- who know how to negotiate the complicated twists and turns of federal regulations. Although my caseworkers are headquartered in my San Francisco office, all of my offices do casework.

Here's an example of how a case proceeds. You may recall reading about the six-month old French donkey that two San Diego veterinarians brought into the country in December only to be told by the U.S. Department of Agriculture that they could not prove that the animal was free of disease.

The vets argued the tests U.S.D.A. had used on the donkey were designed for horses and therefore worthless on donkeys. But in a classic Catch-22, U.S.D.A. ordered the donkey destroyed.

It took many of my staff members working on the case to save the donkey's life. But Sonnette -- French for "Little Bell" -- is safe now. Eventually she'll be bred as part of an effort to repopulate her nearly-extinct species.

My caseworkers aren't miracle workers -- they can only help solve problems with the federal government. But if you have such a problem, and you don't know where to turn, they may be able to help.

Pete Wilson
U.S.S.

UNITED STATES SENATE
WASHINGTON, D.C. 20510

PUBLIC DOCUMENT

OFFICIAL BUSINESS

BLK. RT.

Return Postage Guaranteed
ATTENTION POSTMASTER — OCR — PLEASE DO NOT MARK ON OR ABOVE THE LABEL.

8044

U.S. VOTER
MAIN STREET
ANYTOWN USA 12345-6789

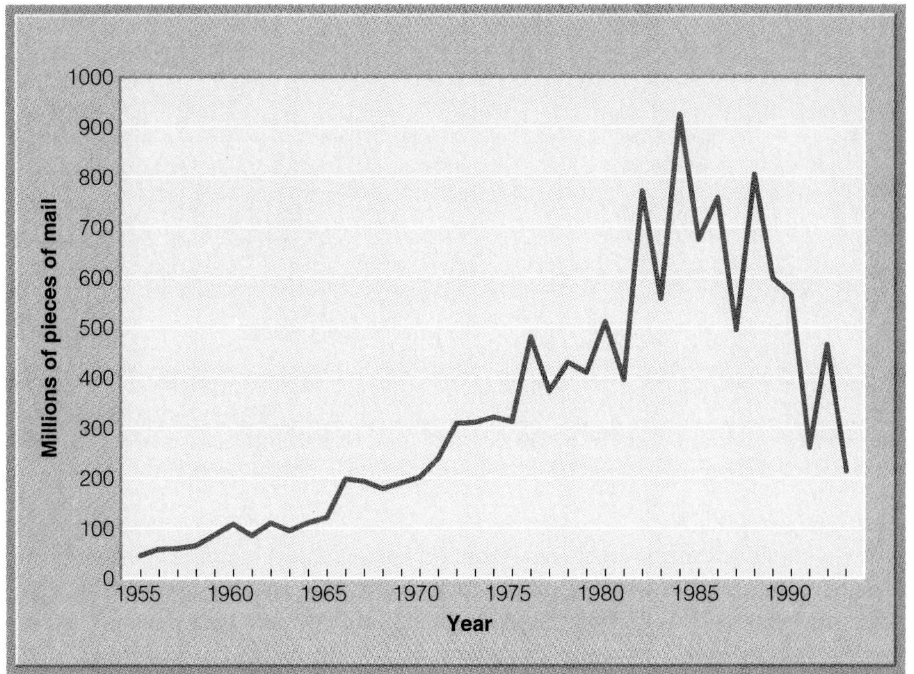

FIGURE 11.6
Use of Franking Privileges, 1955–1993

The use of franked mail increases in election years, but recent rule changes have decreased its usage.

Source: Data from Norman J. Ornstein, Thomas E. Mann, and Michael J. Malbin, *Vital Statistics on Congress 1995–1996* (Washington, D.C.: Congressional Quarterly, 1996), p. 344.

members use to tell their constituents what they are doing in Washington and to alert voters to the array of constituent services they provide. Predictably, newsletters portray the members who send them in a favorable light.[57]

Members have long believed that the frank is an important political resource. Former Speaker of the House Sam Rayburn (D-Tex.) reportedly told incoming members, "There are three rules for getting reelected: one is to use the frank, two is to use the frank, and three is to use the frank."[58] As figure 11.6 shows, members have heeded Rayburn's advice; the amount of money spent on franked mail and the number of pieces of franked mail have climbed over time. As you might expect, more franked mail is sent in election years than non-election years. In recent years, Congress has imposed some limits on the use of mass mailings, and the amount of mail sent has declined.

In addition to having the staff needed to provide constituent services and the right to send official mail for free, members of Congress have ample travel budgets for visiting their district or state. And most members return home frequently, where they are in great demand as speakers. Take, for example, the activities of Rep. Eliot Engel (D-N.Y.). Most weekends he attends as many as twenty events, working from 9:00 A.M. to 10:00 P.M. He holds "lobby days" when he sets up shop in the high-rise apartment buildings where his constituents live, meeting and greeting them as they come and go. According to one observer, "If there's a senior citizens' center he hasn't visited, it's in another state."[59]

Direct meetings with voters give members of Congress the opportunity to hear the concerns of their constituents firsthand. Such meetings between members and voters are what we expect in a democracy. But the meetings also give members valuable opportunities to make the case that they are doing a good job back in Washington. These meetings are made all the more valuable because most of them occur in nonpartisan forums such as senior centers. In these forums, members can emphasize their personal qualities. Thus, providing constituent services, sending franked mail, and taking opportunities to appear in the district give incumbents real advantages on Election Day.

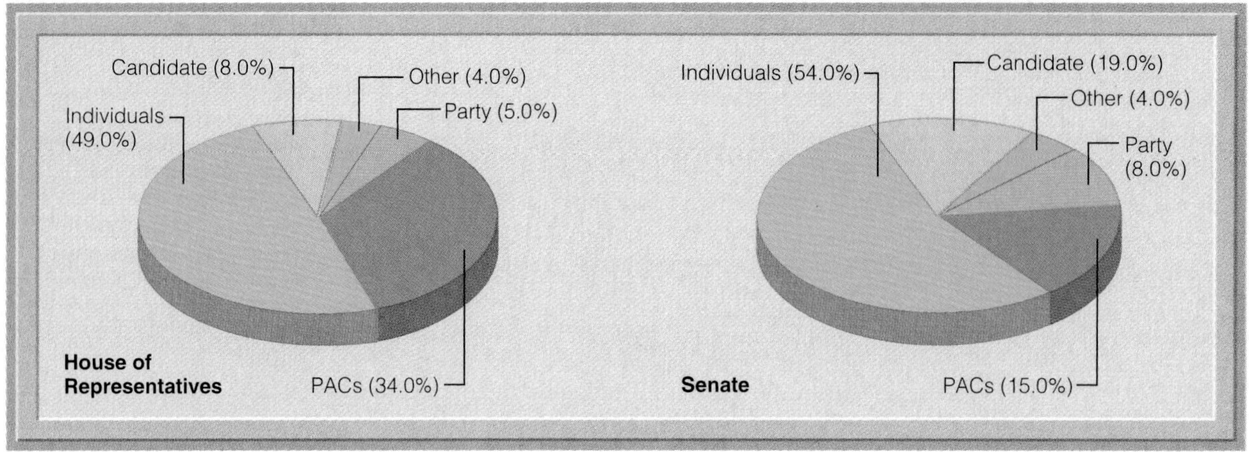

FIGURE 11.7
Sources of Funds for Congressional Candidates, 1994

Most campaign money comes from individuals, not PACs or parties. Senators rely less on PACs and more on individuals for campaign funds than representatives do.

Source: Data from Norman J. Ornstein, Thomas E. Mann, and Michael J. Malbin, *Vital Statistics on Congress 1995–1996* (Washington, D.C.: Congressional Quarterly, 1996), p. 103.

Campaign Money

Along with the advantages that come from occupying a position of responsibility and from having access to federal resources, incumbents have an advantage over their opponents when it comes to raising campaign funds. Money matters in elections because it pays for campaign workers, pollsters, offices, and advertising, among other things. And incumbents raise and spend large sums of money. In 1994, for example, House incumbents spent an average of $559,929 per race. Senators usually spend even more because they generally represent more voters; the twenty-six incumbents who ran in 1994 spent an average of more than $4.6 million, with Sen. Dianne Feinstein (D-Calif.) leading the way at more than $14 million.[60]

Since the passage of the Federal Election Campaign Act in 1971, individuals, political action committees (PACs), and political parties have been limited in the amount of money they can contribute to a candidate for Congress. Individuals may contribute only $1,000 per election—a primary election counts as one election, the general election another—and PACs, as chapter 10 discussed, may contribute no more than $5,000 per election. Political parties operate under even more complex rules, but are limited to $5,000 contributions for House candidates and $17,500 for Senate candidates per election. (A 1996 Supreme Court decision allows parties to spend unlimited sums independently of the candidates' campaigns.)[61]

Candidates may spend as much of their own money as they wish on their campaigns, and every election sees a few candidates who finance their campaigns out of their own bank accounts (often without success). For the vast majority of candidates, though, the limits on fundraising matter. As figure 11.7 shows, congressional candidates receive contributions from several sources, but the single largest source of campaign contributions is individual contributors. Because most individuals contribute much less than the $1,000 maximum, incumbents looking to raise several hundred thousand dollars for a House race or several million dollars for a Senate race must tap a large number of sources.

Incumbency makes the task of raising campaign funds much easier than it otherwise would be. A series of successful runs for office enables incumbents to build a large network of contributors. More important, the very fact that incumbents hold office makes them attractive to many contributors, especially PACs. This is not surprising. As we saw in chapter 10, interest groups want the opportunity to influence people in power, and they believe that campaign contributions buy them access. Given the reelection success that members of Congress enjoy, it makes sense for PACs to contribute to incumbents. Thus in the 1994 elections, House and Senate incumbents received more than $126 million in contributions from PACs, while their challengers took in just less than $20 million.[62] Indeed, PACs gave more money to open-seat candidates than they did to challengers, even though there were many more challengers.

Although House and Senate incumbents almost always raise the money they need to finance their campaigns, the limits on the size of individual campaign contributions mean that they must devote considerable time and energy to raising money for reelection.

Although Americans generally hold Congress in low regard, they like their own representatives and senators. Thus, most incumbents are reelected, even when voters claim they want to "throw the bums out."

Steve McBride, Independence (Kan.), Daily Reporter. Reprinted by permission.

Sen. Nancy Kassebaum (R-Kans.), who retired from the Senate in 1996 in part because she tired of the rigors of raising campaign funds, complained:

> Here we are forced to raise money all the time. I don't worry about money influencing our votes. I don't think that happens. But I worry about the energy it takes. We're out there raising money all the time. We don't sit down and talk to each other very much anymore. We don't have time. I just don't know how people find time to think or reflect.[63]

To fully understand Senator Kassebaum's fears, consider Senator Feinstein's 1994 reelection campaign. To prepare for her reelection effort, Senator Feinstein had to raise an average of $22,000 *a day* in 1993 and 1994. That required her to spend an enormous amount of time on the phone, asking potential contributors for money—time that could have been spent carrying out her legislative duties.[64]

The Ultimate Advantage of Office: Name Recognition

The advantages of responsibility, the resources of the office, and access to campaign contributions all combine to make members of Congress well known and better liked by their constituents. While only around 40 percent of voters can *recall* the name of their representative, and 60 percent can name a senator, name *recognition* is much higher; it stands at more than 90 percent for representatives and close to 95 percent for senators.[65] Name recognition matters because voters who enter the polling booth are more likely to vote for a name they recognize on the ballot. And while being known does not guarantee being liked, both public opinion surveys and election results suggest that voters like their legislators.

The popularity of individual members of Congress might seem remarkable given that public opinion polls show that the public holds Congress as a whole in low regard.[66] The explanation for this apparent contradiction is that voters distinguish between their legislator and the larger institution. Thus, while voters may disparage Congress, they do not see the people they elect as part of the problem. The problem lies instead with the people everyone else elects. The willingness of many people to hold individual legislators in high regard while disparaging legislators as a group is not unusual; most people draw the same distinction between individual bureaucrats they work with and the federal bureaucracy, and between their own doctors and the medical profession.[67] As astute politicians, many members try to take advantage of the distinction people draw between individuals and institutions by attacking Congress in their run for office.

The Challengers' Disadvantages

We know that congressional incumbents bring enormous advantages into a campaign, but what about their opponents? If a challenger can counter the incumbent's advantages, then a competitive race should ensue. If, however, a challenger enters the campaign at a disadvantage, the incumbent is likely to win. As we have mentioned, in most elections, the incumbents win and win big. Why are challengers unable to counter the advantages the incumbent enjoys?

The answer is that the candidates most likely to unseat an incumbent often decide it is too risky to run. To see why, it is important to recognize that some people make stronger candidates than others. The strongest candidates for Congress usually are people who already have been elected to political office.[68] By winning an election to, say, the city council or state legislature, potential challengers learn how to run a political campaign, establish some name recognition, develop lists of campaign contributors, and, perhaps, can exploit the resources of their office to their advantage. Of course, some people without electoral office experience make good candidates because of their celebrity or personal appeal.[69] But most strong challengers come from the ranks of the politically experienced.

If holding political office makes someone a stronger candidate for Congress, it also raises the costs of a failed campaign. In most situations, challengers must give up their current office (by not seeking reelection) to run for Congress. Many potential candidates decide that the risk of losing their current position is too great given the usually dismal prospects for winning a congressional campaign.[70] As a result, few House incumbents face strong challengers. Indeed, in the average election year, the prospects of unseating a House incumbent are so dim that in roughly one out of every seven districts no one bothers to run.[71] Senators usually face more competitive opposition, but many of them also face weak challengers.[72]

Does it matter if a better challenger runs? In a word, yes. Challengers who appear to have a good shot at winning a race find it easier to raise campaign contributions. For example, most PACs contribute only to the campaigns of challengers who have a credible shot at winning. But the standard that PACs use to determine credibility is money raised! As one challenger observed after he lost a bid for a House seat: "The PACs, seeing no 'viability' (their word for a snowball's chance in hell) in my election, weren't about to invest in my race. I faced the American campaign Catch 22: I couldn't raise money until I showed momentum, I couldn't show momentum until I raised money."[73]

Again, an inability to raise funds diminishes the chances of victory. Studies show that the more money challengers spend, the better they do.[74] Money does not guarantee victory, of course, but without an ample campaign treasury, challengers find it hard to reach voters. Most House races are uncompetitive precisely because the challenger lacks the money needed to counter the incumbent's advantages. On average, challengers in Senate races have an easier time raising money, and, as a result, they tend to have closer contests.

Voters and Election Outcomes

If challengers face an uphill battle in trying to win a seat in Congress, why do incumbents ever lose? One set of answers points to how incumbents behave. Some members of Congress succumb to "Potomac Fever" and lose touch with the interests of their constituents.[75] Senators are somewhat more vulnerable to the charge they are out of step with the people back home because they are more likely to face well-funded challengers who can buy the political advertising needed to make the charge stick. Some incumbents also put their seats in Congress in jeopardy through personal impropriety. For example, many of the House incumbents who lost in the 1992 elections had been tarred by the so-called Rubbergate scandal in which some members repeatedly overdrew their checking accounts at the now-defunct House bank.[76] And several senators who went down to defeat in recent years were linked to unethical behavior.

Midterm elections
The congressional elections that take place midway through a president's four-year term.

The second set of explanations for why some incumbents lose despite their tremendous advantages looks beyond individual behavior and points instead to national political forces. Some incumbents who belong to the president's political party almost always lose their congressional seats in the **midterm elections,** the elections held at the midpoint of the president's four-year term. These losses partly reflect the fact that voting in midterm elections constitutes a referendum on the president's performance rather than the member's.[77] For example, the Republicans' stunning success in the 1994 midterm elections was attributed in part to public dissatisfaction with President Clinton.

On rare occasions, parties may be able to overcome the voters' usual focus on local problems and candidates by seeking to nationalize the election, as the Republicans attempted to do with their Contract With America in 1994. But incumbent defeats in midterm elections also reflect strategic behavior on the part of challengers. Stronger challengers from the party not holding the White House enter midterm elections because they think it improves their odds for election, particularly when the president is riding low in the public opinion polls.[78]

If incumbents belonging to the president's political party face tougher going during midterm elections, incumbents benefit during presidential elections if their political party has a strong presidential candidate. Indeed, candidates who win big in the presidential race may significantly increase the vote for the party's congressional candidates. In recent presidential elections, however, the strength of this *presidential coattail effect* has diminished. This is not necessarily because the impact of the presidential vote has lessened, but rather because incumbents now win by such large margins. Incumbents who regularly win with 65 percent of the vote have little to fear from an opposition party's presidential coattail effect of four or five points.[79]

The president's shrinking political coattails have been accompanied by the rise of **divided government,** when one party controls the White House and the other is the majority in at least one house of Congress. Although divided government has occurred throughout American history, it has become, as chapter 9 points out, much more common in the last few decades. Bill Clinton's victory in 1992 marked the first time in twelve years that the voters put both the White House and Congress in the hands of one political party. But two years later, divided government returned as voters gave control of Congress to the Republicans. One possible explanation for divided government is that voters consciously put the presidency and Congress in different hands to encourage the two parties to compromise on policy differences.[80] While such calculated behavior runs contrary to what we know about American voters, some survey evidence indicates that voters like divided control of government.[81]

Divided government
When the president is of one party and the other party has a majority in at least one house of Congress.

Another explanation for the rise of divided government is that voters hold contrasting ideas about what they want from the two offices. On the one hand, voters want a president who will hold the line on taxes and cut government spending, yet, on the other hand, they expect their member of Congress to bring government resources home.[82] This line of reasoning would predict Republican control of the White House and Democratic dominance in Congress—especially in the House—the trend experienced from the late 1960s until the mid-1990s. (The 1994 and 1996 elections raise doubts about this explanation.)

To sum up, the election setting, incumbents' advantages, challengers' disadvantages, and voter behavior all tend to favor incumbents' reelection, especially in House races. Nonetheless, because so many incumbents decide against running for reelection, Congress still sees substantial turnover in its membership (though far less than the founders envisioned).

Serving in Congress

As we have just seen, seats in Congress are the targets of intense competition. Incumbents fight to stay in office, and challengers search for ways to unseat them. But when the dust from the electoral competition finally settles, what kinds of people end up serving in Congress? And what is the job of being a member of Congress like?

Who Serves?

What sort of people succeed in getting elected to Congress? Does Congress represent a cross-section of the American public? If not, what are the consequences for representative government?

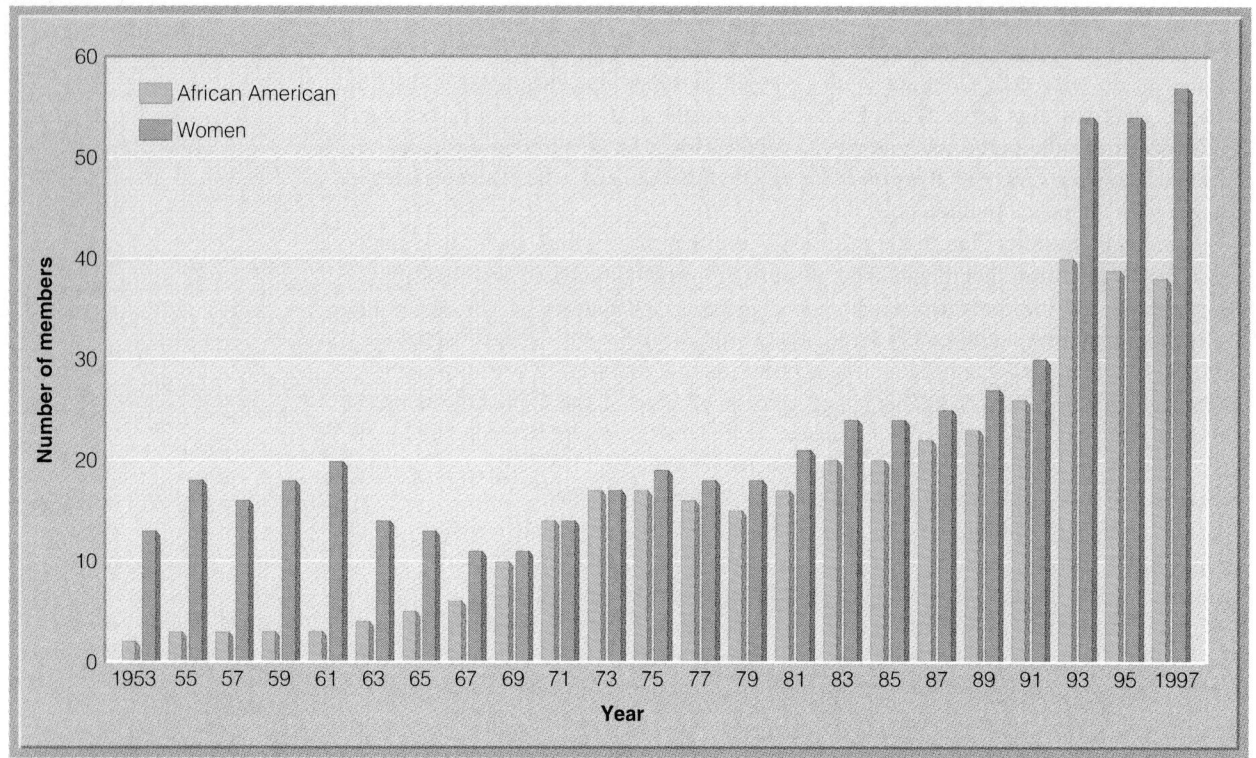

FIGURE 11.8
Women and African Americans in Congress, 1953–1997

The number of women and African Americans in Congress has grown rapidly in the last few years, but they are still underrepresented compared to their numbers in the American public.

Source: Data from Norman J. Ornstein, Thomas E. Mann, and Michael J. Malbin, *Vital Statistics on Congress 1995–1996* (Washington, D.C.: Congressional Quarterly, 1996), pp. 38–39; *USA Today*, "105th Congress: A Closer Look," 7 November 1996.

When the first Congress convened in 1789, all of its members were white males. In the 1990s, white males continue to predominate. Although Congress now counts among its members women, African Americans, Asian Americans, Hispanic Americans, and Native Americans, the number of women and minorities has grown slowly, as figure 11.8 shows. For female members, the biggest change relates to the way they have acquired their seats in Congress. Until the last several decades, most women serving in Congress took their seats by replacing their dead husbands. Now, as box 11.2 discusses, most are elected on their own.[83] As more women occupy elected offices at the state and local level, more women are in a position to run for Congress, and as more women run, more are elected.[84] As for African Americans, their relatively small gains in Congress have come in large part because of the Supreme Court's rulings on the laws governing redistricting.[85] With few exceptions, African Americans, Hispanic Americans, and Asian Americans are elected from districts with significant numbers of minority voters.[86]

Because white males predominate, neither the House nor the Senate is descriptively representative in the sense that the percentage of female and minority members reflects their percentage in the general population. Yet the lack of *descriptive representation* in Congress may not have significant consequences for *policy* or *political representation*.[87] A Congress that is descriptively representative might very well vote the same way on the same issues as it does now. For example, table 11.2 compares the voting records of Sen. Barbara Boxer (D-Calif.) and Sen. Kay Bailey Hutchison (R-Tex.). The two differ in a predictable way on a number of important social, economic, and defense issues; Boxer votes like other Democrats, whereas Hutchison usually sides with her Republican colleagues. In 1995, for example, Boxer voted with a majority of Democrats against the Balanced Budget Amendment, while Hutchison, like most Republicans, supported the measure. The fact that both are women does not mean that they vote alike. (Some evidence suggests, however, that the priorities of women legislators differ from those of men. Several studies of members of Congress have found that regardless of their political affiliation,

Table 11.2 Comparisons of the 1993–1995 Voting Records of Sen. Barbara Boxer (D-Calif.) and Sen. Kay Bailey Hutchison (R-Tex.)

Vote	Boxer	Hutchison
Clinton deficit plan (D 50–6; R 0–44)[a]	For	Against
North American Free Trade Agreement (D 27–28; R 34–10)	Against	For
Handgun purchase waiting period (Brady Bill) (D 47–8; R 16–28)	For	For
Cut Trident Missile funds (D 34–22; R 6–38)	For	Against
Product liability reform (D 15–30; R 46–7)	Against	For
ADA rating 1994[b]	95	10
ACU rating 1994[c]	0	96

Source: Selected key votes from Michael Barone and Grant Ujifusa, *The Almanac of American Politics 1996* (Washington, D.C.: National Journal, 1995), pp. 94, 1267.

[a]The parentheses contain the vote within each party, with the yes vote listed first.

[b]Americans for Democratic Action, a liberal group, which gives higher ratings to members of Congress who vote for liberal legislation.

[c]American Conservative Union, a conservative group, which gives higher ratings to members of Congress who vote for conservative legislation.

Democrats tend to vote like other Democrats, and Republicans tend to vote like other Republicans.

women legislators tend to place greater importance on health, welfare, and education issues and less importance on business issues than men do.)[88]

Regardless of their race, gender, or ethnicity, members of Congress tend to vote in ways consistent with the desires of their constituents, particularly on highly salient issues. Thus, while it is true that almost every African-American member of the House is a liberal, it is not race that dictates their behavior. Most of them represent very liberal districts. When their constituents are more conservative, they tend to be more conservative as well. In 1995, for example, Rep. Ron Dellums (D-Calif.) narrowly failed in his bid to convince Congress to stop production of the B-2 bomber. Dellums lost in large part because seventeen of his colleagues in the Congressional Black Caucus voted to continue the program, which had support in their districts.[89]

Other demographic characteristics also poorly predict the views of members of Congress. For example, two Senate Democrats, Herb Kohl of Wisconsin and Frank Lautenberg of New Jersey, are both self-made millionaires and former corporate executives. In Congress, they have liberal voting records. In contrast, the most conservative Republican members of Congress in 1997 included Speaker Newt Gingrich, House Majority Leader Dick Armey, and Sen. Phil Gramm (R-Tex.). All were college professors before they entered politics. Like occupation, personal wealth, or other cross-cutting cleavages, religion cuts many ways. About 29 percent of all members of Congress are Catholic, roughly the same percentage as in the general population. But Catholics in Congress are found on either side of any controversial issue, including abortion. Descriptive representation, then, is not identical to policy or political representation. Although white males dominate Congress, they and their female and minority colleagues seem to vote according to their constituents' views much of the time.

Congress as a Job

Many people have sought a seat in Congress. They campaign at great cost in terms of time, energy, and money, and, in the end, only a small handful succeed. For those who do, what are the advantages and disadvantages to the job?

The People Behind the Rules

BOX 11.2

Changing Paths to the Senate: The Careers of Margaret Chase Smith and Olympia Snowe

In 1994, Olympia Snowe became the second woman elected to the U.S. Senate from the state of Maine. A comparison of Snowe's path to the Senate with that of Maine's first female senator, Margaret Chase Smith, illustrates important changes in the routes available to women seeking high political office in the United States.

Margaret Chase Smith

Margaret Chase Smith

Margaret Chase Smith was born in 1897 to a family of modest means in Skowhegan, Maine. She never attended college, and after graduating from high school she worked as a telephone operator, a circulation manager for a weekly newspaper, a grade school teacher, and an executive at a woolen mill. In 1932, she married Clyde Smith, a newspaper owner and an activist in the Republican Party. In 1937, Mr. Smith was elected to the U.S. House of Representatives. When he became gravely ill in 1940, he asked his constituents to continue his policies by electing his wife to succeed him, something they did in the special election following his death. Thus, Margaret Chase Smith became one of only nine women serving in the House at that time.

In 1948, Smith ran for the Senate, easily defeating three male rivals in the Republican primary and another man in the general election. When she was sworn into office, she was the only woman serving in the Senate, a distinction she held for many years. Her service was marked by a strong independent streak. In the early 1950s, she joined with a small group of other Republican senators to criticize their colleague, Sen. Joseph McCarthy (R-Wis.), who had made sensationalistic charges of communist influence in the U.S. government. Smith challenged McCarthy's claims, saying "I don't want to see the Republican Party ride to political victory on the four horsemen of calumny—fear, ignorance, bigotry, and smear."

In 1952 and again in 1968, Smith was mentioned as a possible vice presidential candidate. She ran for the presidency in 1964, and she received several votes at that year's Republican National Convention. She finally lost her Senate seat in 1974. Smith ran that last campaign as she had her other races, hiring no campaign staff, putting out no advertising, and appearing in the state only for weekend receptions. Although questions were raised during the 1974 campaign about Smith's advanced age, she lived in good health until her death in 1995.

Continued

Serving in Congress is a full-time job with significant attractions. It is prestigious, and members enjoy immense personal satisfaction from being considered important. Congress offers other rewards as well. The Constitution requires that members be paid for their service. Congressional pay has always been a politically sensitive issue. Originally, members were paid $6 a day. In 1816, members raised their pay to $1,500 a session to cover what they claimed was the growing cost of serving in Congress. A public furor ensued, and in 1817 members voted to rescind the raise. Thus, early on, the trend on congressional salaries was set: members vote to raise their pay only when they are willing to withstand the inevitable public anger.[90]

In 1997, members of Congress earned $133,644. In the early 1990s, public outrage over what many saw as a conflict of interest forced Congress to outlaw *honoraria*—

The People Behind the Rules

BOX 11.2 CONTINUED

Olympia Snowe

Olympia Snowe

Olympia Snowe was born in 1947 in Augusta, Maine, and she was orphaned as a child. She graduated from the University of Maine in 1969 and soon took a job as a legislative staffer for Rep. William Cohen (R-Maine). Snowe first won elected office in 1973 when, like Smith before her, she was elected to take the seat of her deceased husband—in this case, a state representative who died in an auto accident. After four years in Maine's lower house, Snowe was elected to the state senate. After two years in that post, she was elected to the U.S. House of Representatives, taking the seat of her former boss, William Cohen, who was elected to the Senate. During her eight terms in the House, Snowe established herself as leading Republican moderate. She voted with the more conservative element of the Republican Party on many economic issues, but she took more liberal positions on issues such as abortion and the environment.

In 1989, Snowe married John McKernan, the governor of Maine and once one of her colleagues in the House of Representatives. In 1990, McKernan's unpopularity with the people of Maine almost cost Snowe her seat in the House. She won reelection again in 1992, and then raised and spent more than $2 million to beat a strong opponent for Maine's open Senate seat in 1994. When she was sworn in as senator in 1995, she became one of eight women serving in the Senate.

As a senator, Snowe has followed the same moderate course she charted as a representative. She joined with other Republican moderates to temper the policies favored by their conservative colleagues on social issues, but at the same time agreed with conservatives on the need to balance the federal budget and to shrink the size of the federal government.

The careers of Senators Smith and Snowe resemble one another in some respects. Both sought elective office after their husbands died, and both were moderate Republicans who often found themselves taking positions outside their party's mainstream. In other ways, however, their careers are quite different. The social prejudices of Smith's era strongly discouraged women from standing for election, and it is unlikely that she would have won a seat in Congress if her husband had not died in office. In contrast, Snowe, like many other women of her generation, worked her way up through the political ranks. And while the number of women serving in Congress with Senator Snowe does not reflect their share of the population, many more populate Capitol Hill today than in the days of Senator Smith. Indeed, in 1996, Maine voters elected Republican Susan Collins to their other Senate seat.

Sources: Michael Barone, Grant Ujifusa, and Douglas Matthews, *The Almanac of American Politics 1976* (New York: Dutton, 1975), p. 344; Michael Barone and Grant Ujifusa, *The Almanac of American Politics 1982* (Washington, D.C.: Barone and Company, 1981), pp. 452–57; Michael Barone and Grant Ujifusa, *The Almanac of American Politics 1996* (Washington, D.C.: National Journal, 1995), pp. 592–95; David S. Cloud, "GOP Moderates Refusing to Get in Line," *Congressional Quarterly Weekly Report,* 30 September 1995, pp. 2963–65; Richard Severo, "Margaret Chase Smith Is Dead at 97; Maine Republican Made History Twice," *New York Times,* 30 May 1995; Patricia Ward, *Politics of Conscience: A Biography of Margaret Chase Smith* (Westport, Conn.: Praeger, 1995).

money members earned for giving speeches, usually to interest groups—as part of a political deal to raise member pay to its current level. But members continue to enjoy other benefits besides their substantial salary. The pension plan is very generous—former Speaker Thomas Foley (D-Wash.), for example, receives a pension estimated at $124,000 a year.[91] Members can buy life insurance at a very low cost, and they pay nothing for health care. They can use a wide array of facilities in and around the Capitol, including restaurants, gyms, barber shops, and a stationery store, all for less than the general public would pay for the same services.[92]

Although the rewards of congressional service sound appealing, the job has its disadvantages. The average member of Congress devotes an enormous amount of time to the job; one estimate has representatives working more than twelve hours a day.[93] As figure 11.9 shows, members spend time attending committee and subcommittee meetings, participating in floor debates, working with staff, meeting with constituents and lobbyists, raising campaign funds, traveling to and from the district, and engaging in a host of other activities.

The time members of Congress devote to their job forces most of them to sacrifice other interests. The strain on their personal lives is apparent. One representative gave the following reason for his decision to leave Congress in 1996: "I missed [my daughter] Jordan's first steps. I heard her first word over the phone."[94] In a similar but harsher vein, a representative retiring in 1994 commented, "It is a good job for someone with no family life, no life of their own, no desire to do anything but get up, go to work, and live and die by your own press releases, and there are *plenty* of people here that fill that bill. So it is a great job for deviant human beings."[95] Indeed, the job can become so consuming that routine activities of life are ignored. Veteran Rep. James Leach (R-Iowa), for example, had to have his wife show him how to use a bank's automatic teller machine just days before he assumed the chair of the House Banking and Financial Services Committee.[96] Pressures from younger members forced Speaker Gingrich to create a bipartisan House Family Quality of Life Advisory Committee in 1995 to try to make service more "family friendly." Still, one member noted that year that the House adjourned after 9:00 P.M. more than half the time, lamenting that "the only time we see our families is when we take a picture of them out of our wallets."[97]

There are other costs as well. Although members of Congress are well paid relative to the general population, they make far less than most people who hold positions of similar importance. (Or even some people holding positions of less importance. For example, every bench warmer in the National Basketball Association makes more than a member of Congress does.) Most members would make more money if they went to work in the private sector. Moreover, members suffer because they have to pay to live both in Washington and back home. Many try to cut expenses by sharing apartments in Washington with other members of Congress or by living with family or friends when they return home. Sen. Thad Cochran (R-Miss.), for example, owns a home in Washington so his family can be with him, and he stays with his parents when he returns to the state.[98]

The tremendous demands of congressional service prompt some members to leave Congress. Yet, for most, the reasons to stay outweigh the reasons to leave. As one representative reflected, "The demands of a congressional career can tend to crowd out other facets of a person's life . . . [but] I'm not complaining. I recognized the trade-offs, and I accepted them willingly. I would do so again."[99]

Congress and Ethics

Americans have always held the ethics of their elected representatives in low regard. In 1897, Mark Twain wrote, "It could probably be shown by facts and figures that there is no distinctly native American criminal class except Congress."[100] In recent years, talk of corruption on Capitol Hill has reached a fevered pitch. But have members of Congress become more corrupt?

The best evidence suggests the answer is no. Cases of individual corruption—for example, taking a bribe in exchange for a vote—are far fewer now than in the past. (Indeed, Congress used to be so lax about such concerns that bribing a member was not declared illegal until 1853.)[101] Starting in the 1970s, Congress imposed strict legal and ethical regulations on itself, regulations that constitute perhaps the most stringent rules governing any legislative body in the world.[102] In 1995, for example, the House of Representatives adopted strict rules barring members from accepting free meals, gifts, or trips from anyone but family and close friends. (Earlier in the year, the Senate adopted less severe gift rules.)[103]

In recent years, the rules have become so demanding that more and more previously routine activities have come under public and press scrutiny. For example, when the *Charlotte Observer* asked if it was proper for Sen. Lauch Faircloth (R-N.C.), a millionaire hog farmer, to sponsor bills designed to help the hog industry, the senator submitted his actions to the Senate Ethics Committee for review. The committee held that Senator

Rep. James Leach in the District—Tuesday, May 31, 1994

8:00 A.M. – 10:30 A.M.
United Airlines
United Airlines Flight #603
Leaves Washington National at 8:00 A.M.
Arrives Chicago O'Hare at 9:00 A.M.
United Airlines Flight #5285
Leaves Chicago O'Hare at 9:40 A.M.
Arrives Cedar Rapids at 10:30 A.M.

12:00 P.M.
Cedar Rapids East Rotary Club

2:00 P.M. – 4:00 P.M.
Tour of Mercy Hospital
Cedar Rapids

4:15 P.M. – 4:45 P.M.
Meeting w/ Lou Blair
Cedar Rapids
Mr. Blair is a retired administrator of St. Luke's Hospital in Cedar Rapids. He would like to talk to JL about healthcare reform and modified single payer proposal he supports

5:00 P.M.
Live interview—KCRG-TV Live at 5
Cedar Rapids

5:30 P.M. – 6:45 P.M.
Dinner w/ members of Iowa Medical Society
Cedar Rapids

7:00 P.M.
Meeting w/ Campaign Finance Reform Supporters
Mercy Medical Center, Cedar Rapids

Rep. James Leach in Washington, D.C.—Wednesday, June 22, 1994

8:00 A.M. – 9:00 A.M.
Name: *Breakfast for Congressman Ed Royce*
Location: Capitol Hill Club

8:00 A.M. – 9:00 A.M.
Name: *Society of Statesmen/Chowder and Marching Society/Wednesday Group Breakfast Meeting*
Location: H-130 Capitol
Note: w/ Dr. Gail Wilensky, Senior Fellow at Project Hope

10:00 A.M. – 5:00 P.M.
Name: *House of Representatives in Session*

10:00 A.M. – 10:10 A.M.
Name: *Conference Call with Parliamentarians for Global Action*
Location: Representative Leach's office

11:15 A.M. – 11:30 A.M.
Name: *8 Students from West High School in Iowa City*
Location: Representative Leach's office

11:30 A.M. – 11:45 A.M.
Name: *National Association of Mutual Insurance Companies*
Location: Representative Leach's office
Note: Marilyn Schwickerath of Cerro Gordo Mutual, Bernie Lindsey of American Mutual, Cliff Strovers of Poweshiek Mutual, Daryl Lang of Brown Township Mutual, Marilyn Simon of Bohemian Farmers Mutual, Larry Jansen and Brent Larsen of Grinnell Mutual

12:00 P.M. – 1:30 P.M.
Name: *Congressional Roundtable Luncheon*
Location: EF-100 Capitol
Note: James Moody, Chief of the FBI's Organized Crime Unit, and Nancy Lubin, Professor at Georgetown University

12:30 P.M. – 1:30 P.M.
Name: *Congressional Arts Caucus Luncheon*
Location: HC-5
Note: w/ Jane Alexander, chair, National Endowment for the Arts, and Sheldon Hackney, chair, National Endowment for the Humanities

1:45 P.M. – 2:00 P.M.
Name: *Wayne Alcott and Larry Toll of US West*
Location: Representative Leach's office
Note: To discuss current telecommunications legislation w/ Don Brown of Communications Workers of America

2:00 P.M. – 2:30 P.M.
Name: *Dr. Jane Hamilton-Merritt*
Location: Representative Leach's office
Note: To discuss chemical and biological warfare

2:45 P.M. – 3:00 P.M.
Name: *Congressional Youth Leadership Council*
Location: Representative Leach's office
Note: 5 students from the 1st District to discuss legislative process

4:00 P.M. – 4:30 P.M.
Name: *Jack Rehm, CEO, Meredith Publishing*
Location: Representative Leach's office

5:00 P.M.
Name: *House Wednesday Group hosted by Congressman Bill Clinger*
Location: H-122 Capitol

5:30 P.M. – 7:30 P.M.
Name: *Reception for Congressman Gary A. Franks*
Location: Capitol Hill Club

6:00 P.M. – 8:00 P.M.
Name: *Congressional Members Working Group on Latin America*
Location: HC-4 Capitol

FIGURE 11.9
A Daily Schedule for a Member of Congress

Members of Congress have full schedules, both in their districts and in Washington, D.C.

Courtesy of Representative James Leach, Davenport, Iowa.

The House of Representatives often schedules sessions that last well into the night. This can cause problems for members such as Rep. Tim Roemer (D-Ind.) who must juggle his work and caring for his son, Matthew.

Faircloth's activities were acceptable because they would benefit all hog producers (including a number of Faircloth's constituents) and not just himself.[104] Similar concerns have cropped up about the actions of other members of Congress, suggesting that members will continue to be held more accountable for their behavior in office.[105]

Congress as an Organization

Congress consists of 535 individuals. Each of its members assumes office as an equal. As we discussed earlier, the Constitution imposes almost no organization or structure on either house. What we could have, then, is an organization of 535 individually elected members, each pursuing his or her own policy agenda, with no mechanism in place to impose order and manage the conflicts that inevitably arise. Yet Congress has rules and structures that enable (or force) it to make decisions. How has order been imposed where chaos might reign?

The answer is political parties. Their very existence makes it possible to create the system of party leaders, committees, and staff that form the organizational heart of the modern Congress.

Political Parties in Congress

As we discussed in chapter 9, the framers of the Constitution had no use for political parties. Yet, voting blocs emerged very quickly in Congress.[106] The reason for their formation is simple: organization begat organization. When members of Congress who favored the policies of George Washington's administration began working together, opponents countered with their own organization. As these organizations evolved into political parties, they simplified and structured decision making in Congress. In particular, they enabled members to unite in the pursuit of common goals.

Political parties have become so ingrained in congressional politics over the past two hundred years that it is hard to envision how Congress could operate without them. But do not misconstrue the role of political parties in Congress. Only rarely do they control congressional decision making or develop and impose policy agendas on their members. When members of Congress find that their political interests or policy preferences diverge from those of their party, they usually go their own way. Thus, in Congress we can talk about *conditional party government,* wherein the majority party acts cohesively and under the leadership's direction only when substantial policy agreement exists among its members on important issues.[107]

Members of Congress can ignore the wishes of their political party because they know they do not owe their election to the party. As we discussed in chapter 9, political parties in the United States are weak and decentralized organizations that work only when their members share common interests. Only in a few states do political parties control who is nominated as their candidate. In most states, individuals launch their candidacy, raise money, campaign, and win the nomination without the help or advice of what passes for the party organization. In short, parties lack clout because they cannot take away the jobs of maverick members.

What role, then, do political parties play in Congress? Parties matter because they provide the basic stuff of organization, the glue that binds some members together and allows the imposition of leadership and structure. Every leadership position in both the House and Senate is filled through the parties. Members get their committee assignments through their party. Even the few members elected as something other than a Democrat or a Republican are assigned committee seats by one of the parties.

Party Leadership in Congress

Most organizations can function effectively only with leadership. Congress is no exception; both House and Senate have developed leadership structures to help them conduct business. Because the majority and minority parties in the House organize their leadership differently, and because of differences between the House and Senate, we discuss majority and minority party leadership in each chamber separately.

Majority Leadership in the House

Despite the lack of constitutional guidance, both the House and the Senate have adopted similar leadership structures. The House's speaker is the only major difference between the two bodies. Although the full House membership formally elects the speaker, in reality, the members of the majority party decide before each two-year session of Congress which of their members will be given the job. On an organizational vote such as this, members cast their ballots along straight party lines, which means that the candidate of the majority party wins. During this century, speakers have always been senior members, but not the *most* senior members, and they tend to come from the moderate ranks of their party. Speakers generally hold office until they retire or their party loses the majority. The only recent exception was Jim Wright (D-Tex.), who resigned the speakership in 1989 after he was accused of unethical behavior.[108]

The rules of the House give the speaker substantial formal authority. As we discussed earlier, these powers have changed over time; recent speakers have had more authority than speakers in the mid-twentieth century had, but less than speakers in the nineteenth century had. The speaker's power comes from being the chief parliamentary officer of the House, which enables the speaker to exercise great control over the referral of legislation to committee, the scheduling of legislative debate, and the recognition of members during floor debate. Because of these duties, the speaker rarely takes part in debates and usually votes only in the event of a tie.

The speaker is also the leader of the majority party in the House, and this role gives the speaker other powers. Under the Republicans, for example, the speaker chairs the party's Steering Committee, the group that assigns Republican members to committees and names the chairs of committees and subcommittees. The speaker casts five of the thirty votes on the Steering Committee.[109] As a result, the speaker has considerable say over committee assignments, decisions that strongly influence the course of each member's career.

In addition to the formal powers of the office, the speaker has informal powers. Foremost among these is the ability to bestow (or withhold) favors. For example, speakers are responsible for making a small number of patronage appointments in the House, and they can help members raise campaign funds. Speakers can use these and other favors to win support from members of their own party or even, on occasion, members of the opposition.

A second informal power of the speaker is information. Speakers (and all other congressional leaders) sit at the center of the information flow in Congress. This information

The Speaker of the House often helps his party members by attending fundraisers for them in their districts. Here, Speaker Gingrich helps Jim Nussle (R-Iowa) raise campaign funds in his district. The Speaker may decline to help members who do not reciprocate with their votes in the House.

varies greatly, from the scheduling of floor debates to the policy preferences of individual members. In a very real sense, speakers (and their staff) collect intelligence; they know more about what is going on in the institution than anyone else does, and they use that information to their advantage.

The speaker is joined in the formal leadership structure by the majority leader and majority whip. Both positions are elected by the majority caucus. The majority leader assists the speaker on scheduling matters and helps to develop the leadership's position on major issues. The majority leader also speaks for the party on the floor of the House. The whip sits at the center of a two-way information flow. (The term *whip* comes from the English term *whipper-in,* the person in a hunt who keeps the hounds together in pursuit of the fox.) The whip is the leadership's chief vote counter, the person who monitors the mood of members before a vote to see which way it is apt to go. In turn, the whip keeps members abreast of the legislative schedule and informs them about the party leadership's preferences. The whip works with a large group of assistant whips, usually organized along regional lines.

Although the speaker, majority leader, and majority whip wield tremendous influence, they lack the power needed to ram their own policy agendas through the House. As a result, most majority party leaders work to facilitate the development and passage of legislation that a majority of their party supports. The party leaders accomplish this by making such legislation a priority, marshaling support for it, and bringing it to the floor for a vote under favorable conditions. Ambivalence or outright opposition on the part of the leadership does not automatically kill a bill, but it does diminish the chances for its passage.[110] In working to pass legislation favored by their party, majority party leaders know that if their party unites, the bill will pass.

In practice, however, majority party leaders lack the tools needed to compel party discipline; in other words, they cannot always depend on every member of the party to follow their lead. As one representative described the difficulties that majority party leaders face in trying to lead: "It's like herding cats and everybody has their own idea about how to save Western civilization."[111]

The case of Rep. Mark Neumann (R-Wis.) illustrates the limited powers of the party leadership.[112] Neumann first came to Congress in 1995 as a strong supporter of Newt Gingrich. The new speaker rewarded Neumann by giving him a seat on the powerful Appropriations Committee as well as on its prestigious National Security Subcommittee, plum assignments for a first-term member. For the most part,

Neumann proved to be a strong supporter of the Republican leadership. On some issues, however, he criticized the leadership for compromising on the principles set forth in the Contract With America. When the leadership watered down several provisions in the defense appropriations bill, Neumann helped defeat the bill on the floor of the House.

Neumann's opposition to the defense appropriations bill infuriated the chair of the Appropriations Committee. With the consent of Speaker Gingrich, he punished Neumann by taking away his seat on the National Security Subcommittee and reassigning him to a less prestigious appropriations subcommittee. Neumann's fellow first-term members, however, quickly rallied to his support. Meeting with Speaker Gingrich, one first-term member asserted: "This was an attempt to deal with Mr. Neumann that was also an attempt to send a message to the freshmen. We weren't sent here to kow-tow to anybody. We were sent here to vote our conscience."[113] Within hours, Neumann's situation improved. He was not restored to his seat on the National Security Subcommittee—the leadership could not back down from that decision. Instead, he was given a prized slot on the Budget Committee in addition to his already influential appropriations post. The lesson of the Neumann incident is clear: even the most powerful leadership that the House has seen in decades is limited in the punishment it can inflict on even the most junior members of its party.

Minority Leadership in the House

The minority leader and minority whip lead the minority party. The minority leader faces problems different from those of the majority party leader. The minority party cannot prevail in House voting unless it is unified *and* can attract enough support from members of the majority party to become the functional majority, as has happened with the appearance of the **Conservative Coalition,** an alliance of Republicans and southern Democrats that has formed from time to time over the last half century.[114] Operating from this position of weakness puts minority leaders in a bind. They can choose one of three strategies: to cooperate with, compete with, or obstruct majority party proposals.[115]

Conservative Coalition
The Conservative Coalition appears when a majority of southern Democrats votes with a majority of Republicans against a majority of northern Democrats.

If the minority party cooperates with the majority, it gains some input into policy, but at the cost of being identified with the policies of the majority party. The minority party is unlikely to get credit if the policies succeed, and it cannot attack the majority party if the policies fail. Because the minority party hopes someday to become the majority party, cooperating with the majority party may produce short-term advantages but long-term disadvantages.

Electoral incentives, then, discourage cooperation with the majority party and, with it, the minority party's chance to influence policy. In choosing not to cooperate with the majority party, the minority party may decide to develop a competing policy program of its own. Although such a program will lack the votes needed to pass in the House, the minority party calculates that voters at the next election will find its program preferable to the one the majority party is offering. The minority party also might forego developing its own policies and decide instead to focus on blocking legislation that the majority party favors. Such an obstructionist strategy has the advantage of preventing the majority party's preferences from becoming policy, but at a cost of preventing the minority party from developing an alternative program to take to the voters.

Minority party leaders in the House—which from 1955 until 1995 meant Republicans—have pursued a mix of cooperative, competitive, and obstructionist strategies over the last four decades. And chronic tension existed among House Republicans over which strategy was most effective. In 1989, for example, House Republicans elected Newt Gingrich as the new whip largely because he favored a militant opposition to the Democrats quite unlike the cooperative approach associated with minority leader Robert Michel.[116] When the Democrats became the minority party in 1995, they, too, had to grapple with these problems. In some instances they cooperated with the majority; in others, they offered competing proposals or simply worked to obstruct the majority's will.[117] They quickly learned the opportunities and limitations of being in the minority. As one of their members, Rep. Charles Schumer (D-N.Y.), observed, "The luxury of being in the minority is the freedom to change and think of new ways of doing things. You cannot do it the old [majority party] way and always worry about getting 218 votes. The fact is, like it or not, we don't have 218 votes."[118]

Leadership in the Senate

Under the Constitution, the vice president of the United States serves as the president, or presiding officer, of the Senate. The vice president usually appears in the Senate only on ceremonial occasions or when needed to break a tie on an important bill. The Constitution created the position of president pro tempore to preside over the Senate in the vice president's absence. The most senior majority party member is named the president pro tempore, but the post is largely honorific. Presiding over the Senate is a tedious chore, usually assigned to junior members of the majority party as a sort of hazing.

For more than a century, the Senate did without official party leaders. The Democrats named their first official party leader in 1920, and the Republicans followed suit in 1925.[119] The position assumed the importance we now attach to it during the 1950s, when Sens. Lyndon B. Johnson (D-Tex.) and Robert A. Taft (R-Ohio) were party leaders.[120] Both men used their stints as majority leader to increase the power and status of the position. Now the majority leader is almost always considered the most important person in the Senate. Like the other leaders in the House and Senate, the majority leader gets far more national media attention than most members and becomes not only a spokesperson for the party, but a recognized national political figure.[121]

The nature of the Senate does not, however, allow its leaders to exercise the same level of power their counterparts in the House enjoy. The Senate's rules make it hard for leaders in the Senate to get anyone to follow them. For example, the majority leader is in charge of the schedule, but even this power is at the mercy of virtually every member of the Senate. The objection of even the most junior minority party senator is often sufficient to disrupt the majority leader's plans. Thus, as one congressional observer notes, "The Senate has become a band of 100 individual operators. . . . There's very little a leader can do to impose his will on the members any more."[122] As a result, the power of Senate leaders rests largely on their own personal qualities and ambitions. Lyndon Johnson, for example, epitomized the energetic leader. His power over the Senate stemmed from his unchallenged knowledge of the needs and wants of his fellow senators as well as his forceful and occasionally overbearing personal style. His successor as majority leader, Sen. Mike Mansfield (D-Mont.), offered a stark contrast. Mansfield was a quiet person, much less driven by the need to pursue his own policy agenda. Yet, most observers considered Mansfield an effective leader as well. Effective leaders, in both the House and Senate, play the important role of managing conflict, keeping some semblance of order, and keeping the difficult business of lawmaking running smoothly.

Committees

To observe that committees are where Congress does its work is trite but true. Committees were created as a labor-saving device, allowing each chamber to handle its workload by assigning a few members to concentrate on particular areas, leaving others to deal with different problems. Virtually all legislation is reviewed by a committee before it is considered for debate and a vote on the floor of either house. Most bills are introduced and then sent immediately to a committee, and most never make it out of committee—which, in effect, kills them. The ability of committees to determine which bills go to the floor gives them considerable power.

Certainly, the place committees occupy in the legislative process makes them powerful. That is, being a "gatekeeper" on legislation that is introduced gives them an

Committees do much of the work of Congress. Their gatekeeping role—deciding which bills may go to the floor—makes them powerful actors in the legislative process.

extraordinary opportunity to decide whether the legislation will be pursued. Committee power is also enhanced by the fact that the committee members who review a particular piece of legislation dominate a **conference committee** on it.[123] (A conference committee is an *ad hoc* committee of House and Senate members formed to resolve the differences in a bill that passes each body with different provisions.) But committee power rests on another source, as well: information. Members can acquire expertise on the issues that come before their committees. Knowledge about a particular subject gives committee members an advantage over their noncommittee colleagues who do not understand the ins and outs of the issue. Thus, noncommittee members may defer to their committee colleagues with the expertise.[124]

Conference committee
An *ad hoc* committee of House and Senate members formed to resolve the differences in a bill that passes each body with different provisions.

The House and the Senate have essentially the same workload, yet the House has 435 members to handle it while the Senate has only a hundred members. The House divides its work among nineteen standing committees, while the Senate has seventeen standing committees. Standing committees continue from session to session and are charged with examining and reporting legislation to the full House or Senate. Both the House and the Senate also have special and **select committees,** almost all of which are created for only specific lengths of time and which lack authority to report legislation. Several joint House-Senate committees oversee administrative matters and conduct research.

Select committees
Congressional committees that typically are created for only specific lengths of time and that lack authority to report legislation.

House committees have more members than Senate committees, but the average representative serves on far fewer committees than the typical senator: 1.8 in the House to 3.1 in the Senate. The number of subcommittee assignments reflects the same difference: representatives serve on an average of 2.9 subcommittees, senators on 6.2 subcommittees.[125]

Because representatives serve on fewer committees, they focus their attention on a smaller number of issues than senators do. Representatives generally concentrate on the areas under their committees' jurisdictions, and over time, most become experts on their subjects. Senators tend to be spread very thin by the many demands on their time. Their far-flung committee assignments enable them to have a say on a wide range of issues, but out of necessity, they tend to be generalists rather than specialists.

The 1996 committee assignments of Sen. Arlen Specter (R-Pa.) and Rep. Curt Weldon (R-Pa.) illustrate the difference between the Senate generalist and the House specialist. Senator Specter served on the Appropriations Committee, the

Judiciary Committee, the Veteran's Affairs Committee, and the select Intelligence Committee, which he chaired. He sat on eight subcommittees, two of which he chaired. These positions gave Specter a platform from which to address a wide array of issues. Over the course of his career, he has been active on a wide range of issues including crime, education, health care, low-income energy assistance, and foreign policy. In contrast, Representative Weldon served on the National Security Committee, where he chaired the Military Research and Development Subcommittee, and on the Science Committee. Like Specter, Weldon is an active legislator, but most of his efforts are confined to legislation involving military readiness and civilian disaster management.

Committee assignments matter more to representatives than to senators. Representatives find their influence is generally confined to those areas their committee assignments cover. As a result, which committees they sit on greatly affects the legislative activities they pursue. Not surprisingly, representatives seek slots on committees that help them reach their political goals, regardless of whether those goals are to protect the interests of their constituents, promote particular policies, or become influential in the House.[126] Thus, the roster of the Agriculture Committee is heavily weighted with members from farming districts, and the Resources Committee, which oversees the use of federally owned lands, is dominated by representatives from western states, where most federal land is located. Because committees such as Agriculture and Resources tend to attract members who represent particular economic interests, the decisions those committees reach may be biased in favor of those interests.[127] But committees with broader jurisdictions tend not to become captured by specific interests.

The party groups that make committee assignments in the House—which both Democrats and Republicans call the Steering Committee—take member preferences into consideration. (The ratio of majority to minority party members on almost every committee reflects the ratio in the full House or Senate.) They also weigh party interests by balancing state, regional, and ideological concerns. Members assigned to the most powerful committees in the House—Appropriations, Commerce, Rules, and Ways and Means—are limited to that single post.[128] Other members usually serve on one major and one minor committee.

Representatives usually keep their initial committee assignments because their influence increases as they accumulate seniority on a committee. The only members who change assignments are those willing to sacrifice their seniority on a less important committee to gain a position on one of the most powerful committees. Because seniority usually determines who becomes chair, members may wait many years before they can assume the top committee post. But in 1995, at the behest of Speaker Gingrich, Republicans ignored seniority in selecting the chairs of three powerful committees: Appropriations, Commerce, and Judiciary. Gingrich picked Rep. Robert Livingston (R-La.), the fifth Republican in rank on the committee, to head Appropriations. (The first Republican in committee seniority was Joseph McDade, R-Pa., who was under indictment on corruption charges.) On the Commerce and Judiciary committees, Gingrich passed over Rep. Carlos Moorhead (R-Calif.), who was first in line for both chairs; he named Thomas Bliley (R-Va.) and Henry Hyde (R-Ill.) instead. These decisions do not, however, signal the end of seniority. The men who jumped the line were hardly junior members: Hyde was first elected in 1974, Livingston in 1977, and Bliley in 1980. The chairs of the other committees all went to the Republican with the most seniority. Indeed, the average Republican committee chair in 1996 was only slightly younger and less senior than the Democratic chairs had been two years before.

In the Senate, every senator is assigned to one of the four top committees—Appropriations, Armed Services, Finance (the counterpart to Ways and Means), and Foreign Relations—before any senator gets a second such position. Almost every majority party senator chairs either a committee or a subcommittee. Senators are much more likely than representatives to change committee assignments because many senators like to move to committees overseeing issues they find of current interest.

Staff

Congress employs a large number of people to assist members in their work. Each representative receives a set sum of money with which to hire personal staff, while senators receive an amount based on the number of people they represent. Both representatives and senators hire people to track legislation and research issues, and almost all have press secretaries. Many personal staff are assigned to handle constituent problems. More than 45 percent of the personal staff of House members and more than 35 percent of Senate staff members work in district or state offices rather than in Washington, D.C.[129]

In addition to the staff that work directly for members of Congress, some people work for committees. In most cases, the committee staff are experts on some aspect of the committee's business. Members also rely on three congressional support agencies for information. The Congressional Research Service performs extensive research on subjects members request. The General Accounting Office and the Congressional Budget Office provide members and committees with the expertise necessary to keep track of the extensive activities of the federal government.

The number of personal, committee, and support staff in Congress has grown tremendously since the early 1970s, so much so that some observers now complain that the staff constitute a fourth branch of government. In 1995, however, Republicans fulfilled one of their pledges in the Contract With America by reducing the number of congressional staff members. In addition, the Republicans abolished the Office of Technology Assessment, a congressional support agency that reported to Congress on scientific matters. The Republicans also eliminated funds for legislative service organizations such as the Congressional Black Caucus, the Congressional Hispanic Caucus, and the Congressional Human Rights Caucus, which provide staff to enable members to work together on issues of common interest. (Some of these organizations have carried on, using members' personal staff).[130]

The growth of congressional staff has come largely in response to the growing size of the federal government and the desire of members of Congress to counter the executive branch's vast advantage in information and expertise. And while some personal staff work primarily to promote their member's electoral prospects, most congressional staff work to provide members with information they can use to increase their influence in the policy-making process. Staff thereby extend the members' reach, allowing them to be active on more issues than they could be otherwise. For example, then-Sen. Robert Dole (R-Kans.) remained a major player in the debate over health care reform in 1994 even though at the time he had his hands full carrying out his duties as the Senate minority leader; his top aide, Sheila Burke, acted on his behalf at numerous meetings and negotiations.[131] Indeed, on many issues, staff members can play a critical and influential role in the legislative process.[132]

The Business of Congress

Congress is the country's supreme lawmaking body. But what is the legislative process, the set of rules that turns a policy proposal into a law? How do members of Congress decide whether to support the legislation they are asked to vote on? And what steps do members of Congress take to ensure that the laws they pass work as intended? In this section, we consider each of these questions in turn.

In his role as Senate Majority Leader, Robert Dole relied heavily on his top aide, Sheila Burke, to help him run the Senate.

The Legislative Process

The legislative process formally begins when a member of Congress introduces a bill.[133] Only members can introduce a bill. Anyone else who wants Congress to consider a piece of legislation—even the president—must have a representative or senator do it for them. A bill may be introduced either in one chamber alone or in both chambers simultaneously, and it is generally considered first in committee and then on the floor. The same version of the bill must pass both the House and the Senate before it can go to the president for his signature. As figure 11.10 shows, the process a bill follows is essentially the same in both houses, with the important exception of an additional hurdle, the Rules Committee, in the House.

Policy Initiation

Ideas for bills come from many sources, including the White House, executive agencies, interest groups, industry, and even professors. Members of Congress and their aides sometimes develop policy proposals on their own, but more often than not, members borrow ideas others have generated. In short, members usually act as policy entrepreneurs rather than policy innovators.

As soon as members begin the process of translating an idea into a bill, they begin to look for support. Before submitting a bill, the sponsor usually circulates a "dear colleague" letter informing other members about the bill and why it is needed. The sponsor hopes to convince other members to become co-sponsors, thereby increasing the chances the bill will become law. By the time most bills are introduced into Congress, they have a number of members listed as co-sponsors.

The Committee Process

Once a bill is introduced—dropped into a wooden hopper in the front of the House or handed to a clerk in the Senate—it is assigned a number, preceded by "H.R." for House bills and "S." for Senate bills. From time to time, members reserve numbers for special purposes. For example, one former representative, H. R. Gross, always introduced a bill, H.R. 144 (144 of something is a gross).[134] Once introduced, a bill is referred to a committee. In the House, the speaker decides where a bill will go, and in the Senate, the presiding officer does, but both are constrained by the defined jurisdictions of the various

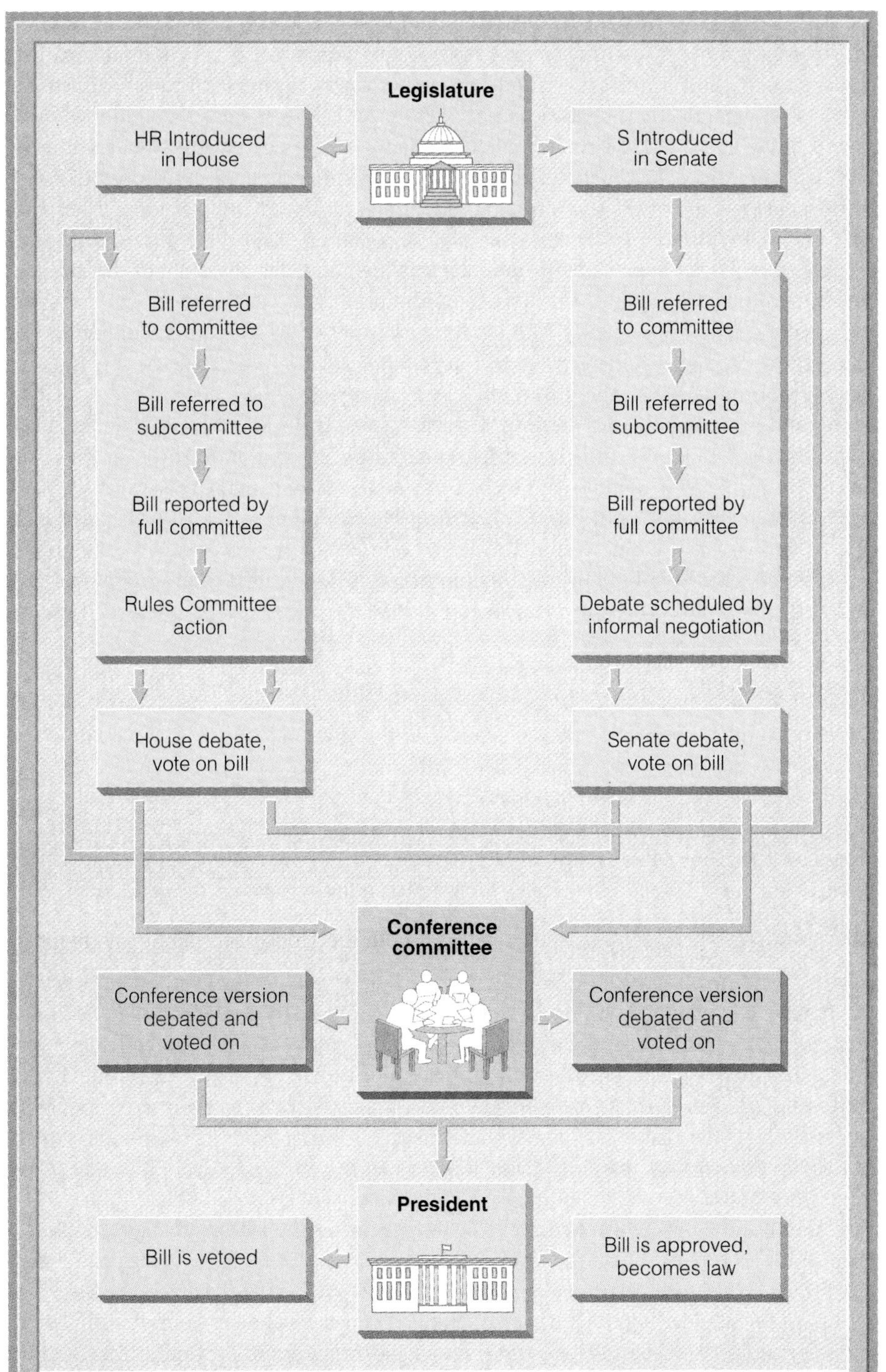

FIGURE 11.10
How a Bill Becomes a Law

A bill must overcome many obstacles before it is signed into law. Most bills never make it out of committee.

Source: William F. Hildenbrand and Robert B. Dove, "Enactment of a Law: Procedural Steps in the Legislative Process" (Washington, D.C.: Government Printing Office, 1982), p. 233.

committees and other precedents. Which committee gets a bill can matter, as some committees may be more receptive than others. In 1995, for example, House Republican leaders rewrote legislation involving parts of the Coastal Zone Management and the Marine Protection, Research, and Sanctuaries acts so as to reroute them around the House Resources Subcommittee on Fisheries, Wildlife, and Oceans, the body that would normally tackle such issues. The reason for this extraordinary action? House leaders thought the chair of that subcommittee, Rep. James Saxton (R-N.J.), was too sympathetic to environmental groups.[135]

Under most circumstances, the committee that gets the bill refers it to one of its subcommittees. Most bills never pass beyond this point. For a subcommittee to take any action on a bill, some subcommittee member must express interest in it. Even that may not be enough if the chair does not want to pursue it. If the subcommittee wants to proceed with the bill, hearings are held so that witnesses can testify about its merits. Most subcommittee hearings are low-profile events that generate little participation from committee members and attract no attention from the media. Although hearings can serve many different purposes, the most important is to provide a forum in which affected groups can express their opinions and members can learn about the substantive and political impact of the proposed legislation.

A markup session usually follows the hearings. At this meeting, subcommittee members decide what changes the bill needs to secure a majority vote to send it to the full committee. Members may make no changes or they may rewrite the bill. Participation matters at the markup; members who participate can influence a bill significantly.[136] Once a bill passes the subcommittee, the entire process can play out again in the full committee, with more hearings and markup sessions. While committees can and do kill bills by refusing to send them to the floor, subcommittee decisions carry great weight in many committees.[137] For many years, it was very difficult for members to force a committee to send a bill to the floor. In 1993, however, the House voted to make the so-called discharge process less difficult to invoke.[138]

The House Floor

Once a committee passes a bill and sends it to the floor, usually with a recommendation to pass, the House and Senate follow different procedures. In the House, bills are put on one of five legislative calendars, which make up an archaic and complex system that bears no relationship to the calendar used in everyday life. Most bills of any significance do not have to wait for the workings of the legislative calendars to bring them to the floor. Instead, the Rules Committee issues a special rule that takes them off the calendar and sends them to the floor.

The Rules Committee exists only in the House. (The Senate Rules and Administration Committee serves a different purpose.) The House Rules Committee regulates the flow of legislation to the floor and sets the conditions under which the full House will consider a bill. Unlike the membership of most other committees, the Rules Committee membership is stacked heavily in the majority party's favor. As we mentioned earlier, the speaker selects the members of the majority party who serve on the Rules Committee, which makes the committee sensitive to the wishes of the majority party leadership. As a result, majority party leaders can use the Rules Committee to determine when and under what conditions the full House will consider a bill.

Before the House considers a bill, it first votes on the rule the Rules Committee proposes. The rule itself can be very simple or, as figure 11.11 shows, extremely complex. It almost always limits the amount of time a bill can be debated. The rule may also limit the number and type of amendments members can offer. Some bills come to the floor under a closed rule, meaning no amendments may be offered, while others come to the floor under a restricted rule, which means members can offer only certain amendments. The Rules Committee can also write an open rule, which permits members to offer any amendment.

Sometimes the Rules Committee crafts rules designed to provide members of the majority party with political cover on tough votes. The King-of-the-Hill rule, for example, states that the last amendment passed in a given sequence is the one that takes effect. The majority party finds the King-of-the-Hill rule helpful when the minority party is proposing amendments that members find politically difficult to oppose. Under the rule, the House votes on the opposition's amendments first, which allows members of the majority party to go on record in favor of them. The amendment the majority party leadership prefers comes up for a vote last, and supersedes and replaces

H. Res. 416

Resolved, That at any time after the adoption of this resolution the Speaker may, pursuant to clause 1(b) of rule XXIII, declare the House resolved into the Committee of the Whole House on the state of the Union for consideration of the bill (H.R. 4296) to make unlawful the transfer or possession of assault weapons. The first reading of the bill shall be dispensed with. All points of order against consideration of the bill are waived. General debate shall be confined to the bill and shall not exceed two hours equally divided and controlled by the chairman and ranking minority member of the Committee on the Judiciary. After general debate the bill shall be considered for amendment under the five-minute rule. The amendment in the nature of a substitute recommended by the Committee on the Judiciary now printed in the bill shall be considered as read. All points of order against the committee amendment in the nature of a substitute are waived. No amendment to the committee amendment in the nature of a substitute and no other amendment to the bill shall be in order. At the conclusion of consideration of the bill for amendment the Committee shall rise and report the bill to the House with such amendment as may have been adopted. The previous question shall be considered as ordered on the bill and any amendment thereto to final passage without intervening motion except one motion to recommit with or without instructions.

FIGURE 11.11
Example of a House Rule

Rules govern how a bill will be considered on the floor, determining how long debate will last and how many and what type of amendments will be offered.

Source: Congressional Record, 5 May 1994, p. H3064.

the earlier amendments as long as it wins a majority of votes. In 1995, the new Republican majority created a Queen-of-the-Hill rule, which stipulates that the amendment garnering the most votes wins.[139]

As the King-of-the-Hill and Queen-of-the-Hill rules suggest, the vote on a rule often determines what kind of bill will emerge from the floor debate. Once a rule is adopted, the House dissolves itself into the Committee of the Whole, a parliamentary device that makes it easier to consider amendments. (The Committee of the Whole is made up of every member of the House.) Once amendments are disposed of, the Committee of the Whole dissolves and members vote on the bill. The House may follow many different voting procedures. Some procedures, such as voice votes, allow members to vote without making their position on the issue public. Since its inception in 1973, however, electronic voting has become the most common voting procedure. Members put something akin to a personal credit card into one of forty voting stations distributed around the House floor, and their vote registers on several scoreboards. Electronic voting has resulted in far more recorded votes; thus, it has increased member accountability to interest groups and the public.

The Senate Floor

Bills are brought to the Senate floor at the discretion of the majority leader, who works most of the time with the consent of the full Senate. When a bill makes it to the floor, debate is unlimited. A member can talk for as long as he or she desires or is physically able. The tactic of preventing a vote on a bill by talking it to death is known as a **filibuster.** A filibuster can be stopped only when at least sixty senators vote to invoke **cloture,** a procedure that limits the length of a debate. (Sen. Strom Thurmond of South Carolina holds the record for a one-person filibuster. In 1957, he spoke for more than twenty-four hours straight in a failed effort to block a vote on a civil rights bill.) Only about half of all filibusters actually block a bill or convince sponsors to revise their proposal, but that figure is sufficient to encourage members to undertake them.[140]

Filibuster
The tactic of stalling a bill in the Senate by talking endlessly about the bill in order to win changes in it or kill it.

Cloture
The procedure to stop a filibuster, which requires a supermajority of sixty votes.

The right to filibuster, or talk for as long as one wishes, gives senators a great deal of power. Here, Sen. Strom Thurmond (D-S.C.—he later switched to the Republican Party) leaves the Senate floor following his record twenty-four-hour filibuster against a civil rights bill in 1957.

Many bills, particularly the most important pieces of legislation, come to the Senate floor covered by a *unanimous consent agreement.* The majority leader negotiates these agreements, which can go into effect only if no senator objects. Unanimous consent agreements can be used, among other things, to limit debate and the number and sort of amendments senators can offer. Thus, unanimous consent agreements allow the Senate to streamline its deliberative procedures. Still, as box 11.3 shows, individual senators can impede the Senate's consideration of bills in ways their House counterparts cannot.[141]

The voting procedures in the Senate also differ from those used in the House. Most votes in the Senate are roll-call votes in which a clerk reads the names of each member and the senators respond by stating their position. Not surprisingly, the Senate is almost always in session for many more days than the more regimented House.

The Conference Committee

When the House and Senate pass different versions of the same bill, a conference committee usually meets to resolve the differences. The power to appoint the conference committee formally rests with the speaker of the House and the presiding officer of the Senate. In practice, however, the conferees are almost always chosen by the chairs and ranking members of the committees that sent the bill to the floor. (A ranking member is the minority party member with the most seniority on the committee. He or she acts as the minority party leader on the committee.)

Conference committees range in size from very small to very large; one conference in 1981 had more than 250 members. The conference committee is free to revise the bill, almost to the point of completely rewriting it, as happened with the landmark Tax Reform Act of 1986.[142] Once a conference committee reaches agreement, both chambers must approve it without any changes for the agreement to be sent to the president. If members do try to change the bill the conference committee reported, they risk forcing the appointment of a new conference committee or killing the bill entirely.

Decision Making

The number of subcommittee, committee, and floor votes cast each session reaches well into the thousands. How do members decide how to vote?

Point of Order

BOX 11.3

The Byrd Rule and Senate Voting on the Budget

The Byrd Rule played a role in the 1995 budget battle.

Reprinted by permission: Tribune Media Services.

Because rules structure how legislatures make decisions, rules can determine which side wins and which side loses in a conflict. One example of the power rules have to determine winners and losers is the operation of the Byrd Rule in the Senate during the epic budget fight in 1995.

In 1985, then-Senate Majority Leader Robert Byrd (D-W.V.) pushed through a new rule that governed how the Senate handled budget bills. In most circumstances, the Senate operates with unlimited debate, and only a unanimous consent agreement or a cloture vote can curtail it. One exception is consideration of budget bills (formally known as reconciliation measures), on which a twenty-hour limit on debate is imposed. The limit exists so that budget bills cannot be held hostage to a filibuster. But because filibusters are not allowed, senators have an incentive to attach extraneous (or non-germane) amendments to budget bills, knowing that their colleagues can do relatively little to stop them. The Byrd Rule, as it came to be known, was instituted to make it more difficult for individual senators to attach extraneous provisions to budget bills.

The exact details of the Byrd Rule are fairly complex; the Senate has developed more than a dozen different criteria for determining when a provision of a budget bill is extraneous. The general thrust of these criteria is that the provisions of a budget bill are germane only if they are aimed at reducing the federal government's budget deficit. Provisions that increase the budget deficit and provisions that do not have a substantial impact on government revenues and spending are deemed extraneous. Thus, if a provision were added to a budget bill to expand the scope of the student loan program, the provision would be extraneous because it would increase government spending and, hence, the deficit. In a similar vein, a provision in a budget bill that made abortion illegal would also be extraneous, this time because deficit reduction is not the primary purpose of the provision.

If a provision of a budget bill is extraneous under the Byrd Rule, any senator may raise a point of order against it on the floor. Under the rules of the Senate, the offending provision is thereby struck from the bill. The point of order can be waived, and the provision reinstated in the bill, only if *three-fifths* of the senators agree to do so. Because the Byrd Rule can be waived only with the support of sixty senators, it is difficult to add extraneous provisions to budget bills.

Of what relevance is the Byrd Rule? As the 1995 budget battle unfolded, House Republicans sought to include many of their significant policy proposals in one massive budget bill. They calculated that President Clinton would have a harder time vetoing Republican policy proposals if those proposals were attached to a bill appropriating the money needed to run the federal government. But what the House Republicans forgot was that Senate Democrats could defeat their strategy by invoking the Byrd Rule once the bill came to the Senate. In November 1995, for example, Rep. John Doolittle (R-Calif.) commented, "We're just now becoming aware there is a major problem" because of the Byrd Rule.

And it was a major problem for the Republicans, who only had fifty-three votes in the Senate, or seven votes fewer than they needed to waive a point of order. Senate Democrats invoked the Byrd Rule and stripped one extraneous provision after another from the budget bill. Gone were provisions that would have transferred federal land to California for use as a low-level radioactive waste dump, imposed a five-year limit on welfare, increased the eligibility age for Medicare recipients from 65 to 67 years of age, and sold a government oil reserve, among a host of other things.

The damage was not confined to the votes in the Senate. In the conference committee called to reconcile the Senate and House versions of the budget bill, other provisions were deleted because Republican leaders realized that Senate Democrats could use the Byrd Rule to challenge them when the bill returned to the Senate floor for a final vote. Of course, Republicans had the option of resurrecting the deleted provisions by introducing them as individual bills. But they lost the tactical advantage they hoped to gain by attaching them to budget measures.

The Byrd Rule was imposed to prevent senators from adding extraneous measures to budget bills and thereby abusing the budget process. When the Republicans were in the minority, they used it to their advantage. In 1995, with the tables turned, Democrats exploited the rule to their benefit.

Sources: Christopher Georges, "Byrd Procedural Rule Is Threatening to Derail Substantial Portions of the Republican Agenda," *Wall Street Journal*, 8 November 1995; Christopher Georges and Greg Hitt, "GOP Conferees Reach Accord on Medicare Bill," *Wall Street Journal*, 9 November 1995; George Hager, "Reconciliation Now a Major Tool," *Congressional Quarterly Weekly Report*, 28 October 1995, p. 3286; Walter J. Oleszek, *Congressional Procedures and the Policy Process*, 4th ed. (Washington, D.C.: CQ Press, 1996), pp. 74–75; Alissa J. Rubin, "Senate's Last-Minute Changes Kept Floor Activity Lively," *Congressional Quarterly Weekly Report*, 4 November 1995, p. 3360; Charles Tiefer, *Congressional Practice and Procedure* (Westport, Conn.: Greenwood Press, 1989), pp. 89–91.

Sen. Barbara Boxer (D-Calif.) gets more than ten thousand letters a day—not counting the five thousand or so mass mailings lobbying groups send daily to every member of Congress. Members of Congress value the mail they receive because it gives them some idea of their constituents' thoughts about issues. But sometimes constituents are vague about what they want their members of Congress to do.

Voting Cues

In many instances, the question of how to vote is easy for members of Congress to answer. They know how to vote on issues on which they are experts, say, because their committee held hearings on the bill or because they have a personal interest in the legislation. Members also know how to vote on the few issues on which their constituents have intense and uniform preferences. Given the political power of the senior citizen lobby, for example, most members do not have to read the details of a bill to know they will vote against any effort to cut Social Security benefits. And often Congress votes on symbolic resolutions or on politically attractive issues that almost everyone can support. In 1995, for example, the Senate voted 97 to 0 to "to require a minimum mandatory sentence of thirty years in prison for acts of terrorism against shipments of high-level radioactive waste."

Yet on many votes, members know little about the issue at stake, their constituents lack well-formed opinions, and the legislation is substantive rather than symbolic. What do members do then? In these circumstances, members look elsewhere for guidance, or cues, on how to vote. Voting cues come from a wide variety of sources besides personal ideology and constituent opinion: party leaders, members of the committee that reported the bill, members from the same state, and friends. Members use the views of others to help them make up their own minds because they cannot possibly master all the issues they are asked to vote on. Put simply, voting cues are decision-making shortcuts that members hope will enable them to avoid making bad policy and bad political decisions.

One common voting cue is party, as undecided members look to see how others in their political party intend to vote. Party members tend to vote alike not because their leaders can discipline them but because they tend to represent similar sorts of people with similar preferences. Some issues can become highly partisan, with a majority of congressional Democrats taking one side of an issue and a majority of congressional Republicans taking the other side. On important votes, party leaders communicate their preferences clearly: whips and their assistants may stand at the chamber doors signaling thumbs up or thumbs down. But members have great flexibility in deciding how to vote, and they rarely vote with their party on every issue.

Even members of Congress who do not support military spending in general are likely to fight to protect their districts from the economic damage the closing of a local military base causes.

Brian Duffy, *The Des Moines Register*. Reprinted by permission.

Many bills do not excite partisan passions. Most look something like a 1991 bill to "bypass laws that require that meat products for use in schools be inspected at the point of processing by federal officials."[143] Sponsored by a Kansas representative on behalf of Pizza Hut, Inc., the bill sought to allow commercial pizza companies to sell pizzas in school cafeterias. Few members were experts on the specific issues the bill raised (market access, food safety, and childhood nutrition); few constituents cared, or even knew, about the bill; and neither political party had a position on pizza in schools. Most members had to look to other voting cues, such as their assessment of the sponsor of the legislation and the views of their colleagues, in deciding how to vote. As Representative Hyde has observed, voting is usually "an exercise in mutual trust. I've been here twenty-one years, and you can't tell me that when they wave those continuing resolutions around at 2 A.M. that are 1,200 pages long, that they have been read by anybody. You have to do it that way. Otherwise, we'd have to stop what we were doing for two weeks just to read."[144]

Personal Versus Constituent Preferences

Members of Congress are sent to Washington to represent the interests of their constituents, but they also have their own personal policy preferences. Sometimes the two conflict. Take the example of Sen. Alan Cranston (D-Calif.). In the mid-1970s, he was a staunch supporter of the B-1 bomber, despite his position as a leading proponent of efforts to cut defense spending. Cranston's contradictory behavior shocked no one because California businesses were scheduled to receive nearly a third of the money spent on the B-1.

While a member's personal preferences sometimes conflict with those of his or her constituents, they more often coincide. The reason lies in the nature of the recruitment process for Congress. The need to reside in a district for much of one's life to build a coalition of supporters, and to win an election makes it likely that members will share the policy views of many of their constituents. To return to the example of Senator Cranston, in the mid-1980s, he voted against funding the Strategic Defense Initiative (SDI), or Star Wars, even though it would have pumped far more money into California's economy than the B-1 program did. Cranston was able to vote according to his policy preferences because "the anti-SDI lobby in California was large, well organized, and drew much of its support from individuals in [his] electoral coalition. The anti-B-1 movement was never strong in California."[145] In other words, Cranston's own preferences and those of many of his constituents meshed.

As Senator Cranston's behavior illustrates, members of Congress constantly calculate possible trade-offs between their personal agendas and their understanding of what their constituents want.[146] Sometimes constituent apathy, division, or agreement leaves members free to vote as they see fit. At other times, members swallow their preferences to avoid alienating their constituents. How much electoral risk a member will tolerate in pursuit of his or her policy preferences varies with the individual.

Policy Oversight

Policy oversight
Efforts by Congress to see that the legislation it passes is implemented, that the expected results have come about, and whether new laws are needed.

The business of Congress does not end with voting on bills. Congress is also responsible for **policy oversight,** seeing that the legislation it passes is implemented, that the expected results come about, and whether new laws are needed. Policy oversight is important because the complexity of many issues and the limited time members can devote to any single issue generally force Congress to pass legislation that is short on details. As a result, the bureaucracy has discretion to use its expertise to fill in the necessary details. And as we will discuss at greater length in chapter 13, bureaucrats can use their discretion in ways contrary to what members of Congress had in mind when they passed the legislation.

As important as policy oversight is, it is a daunting endeavor. The federal bureaucracy is enormous; it spends more than $1.5 trillion dollars each year, employs millions of people, and administers thousands of programs. Members of Congress could not monitor a tenth of what the federal government does even if they and their staffs ignored all their other responsibilities. Moreover, the complexity of many issues makes it difficult for members to assess the effectiveness of government programs. For example, after the Gulf War, military experts disagreed over whether American weapons had performed as successfully on the battlefield as the Department of Defense claimed. Few members have the expertise needed to evaluate such disputes.

Police-patrol oversight
Congressional oversight hearings designed to take a wide-ranging look for possible problems.

Given the abundance of programs to oversee, how do members of Congress decide which ones to examine? In general, they take two different approaches to the task of policy oversight: the police-patrol approach and the fire-alarm approach. **Police-patrol oversight** takes place when members hold hearings and request information on the off chance they might uncover something wrong.[147] For example, when the various committees in Congress conduct their annual budget reviews, they usually ask how government monies have been spent and request evidence that programs have accomplished their goals.

Because executive agencies heed the wishes of Congress most of the time, police-patrol oversight may not uncover instances in which an executive branch agency has defied the will of Congress. But the real merit of police-patrol oversight lies in its deterrent value; agencies that fear a congressional inquiry will abide by the wishes of Congress. Indeed, members of Congress often use police-patrol oversight to send signals to executive agencies about how they expect agencies to behave.[148] For instance, when the Social Security Administration (SSA) proposed requiring people to take a treadmill stress test to document any disability claims, the chair of the Senate Special Committee on Aging responded that it was "amazing that SSA continues to push this mistaken policy . . . Congress may be forced to pass a law preventing SSA from relying so heavily on treadmill tests. We hope SSA will reconsider and avoid a run-in with Congress."[149]

Police-patrol oversight has one distinct disadvantage from the viewpoint of a member of Congress: systematically examining the executive branch may provide no chance to curry favor with the voters. If a police patrol fails to uncover any abuses, members have nothing to show their constituents for their efforts. If it does uncover a problem, the abuse may not harm or interest constituents; hence, no opportunity exists for members to garner credit.

Fire-alarm oversight
Congressional oversight hearings designed to investigate a problem after it has become highly visible.

To compensate for the disadvantages of police-patrol oversight, members of Congress also engage in **fire-alarm oversight,** investigating problems after they become highly visible. In fire-alarm oversight, members rely on constituents, the media, or some other aggrieved party to sound the alarm about a problem. For example, when the Equal Employment Opportunity Commission (EEOC) proposed guidelines in 1994 to stem religious harassment in the workplace, a diverse coalition of groups, including

Sometimes police patrols miss a problem, and not enough fire alarms ring to draw attention to a major problem, as happened with the savings and loan disaster.

Reprinted by permission: Tribune Media Services.

the American Civil Liberties Union and the Christian Coalition, argued that they violated the First Amendment. Congress immediately intervened and voted to urge the EEOC to rework the proposal. In response to the overwhelming signal Congress sent, the EEOC withdrew the proposal in short order.[150] The advantage of fire-alarm oversight in the eyes of members is that it enables them to focus on issues that matter to voters, thereby increasing their chances of winning points with the voters. As you might imagine, the disadvantage to fire-alarm oversight is that members might hear the alarm only after great damage has occurred.

Congress and the Idea of Representation

By proposing and refining legislation, making decisions to support or oppose a bill, and overseeing the effects of past legislation, Congress fulfills its duty to make laws and rules to govern the nation. But in the process of governing, Congress has another obligation—to represent the will of the people. But what exactly does representation entail? This seemingly simple question has long divided political philosophers. The *delegate theory of representation* holds that members should vote according to the preferences of their constituents. In contrast, the *trustee theory of representation* contends that voters have entrusted members with the responsibility of deciding what constitutes good public policy. Both theories raise thorny questions. If members act as delegates, which constituents should they look to when deciding how to vote? The majority on each issue? Members of their political party? People who donated to their campaign? Conversely, if members disregard constituent opinion, as the trustee theory says they may, does Congress cease to be a representative body?

Whichever theory of representation you find more appealing, in practice, members of Congress are both free to vote as they please and constrained by constituent opinion. The voters back home know little about the day-to-day activities of Congress, which gives members a tremendous amount of freedom in deciding how to act. Members even have considerable freedom to ignore the wishes of the interest groups that donate to their campaigns. Although interest groups carefully follow congressional business, they can ill afford to destroy their long-term relationship with a member because he or she votes against them on a specific issue.

Yet for all the freedom that members of Congress have in planning their legislative activities, they know that ultimately their position in Congress depends on maintaining constituent support. According to the rules, representatives must stand for election every two years, and senators every six years. Members who stray too far from the wishes of their constituents will quickly become former members of Congress.

Representation, then, hinges on elections. Citizens have a powerful weapon: they can replace a member of Congress with someone who better reflects their preferences. Of course, voters may find it hard to gather the information they need to evaluate how

Voting in Congress can be complex, and sometimes members can be on both sides on an issue.

Reprinted by permission: Tribune Media Services.

the current member measures up. Not only does it take time and effort to learn what members have done during their term in office, but members frequently use parliamentary procedures such as the King-of-the-Hill rule to take both sides of controversial issues. Nonetheless, as long as members must worry about what voters think, representation is maintained. The rules largely work, and the representative body the founders envisioned—although the details have changed—still exists.

Summary

The framers of the Constitution established Congress as a bicameral legislature that operates independently of the executive and judicial branches of government. Although the House and Senate are equals in lawmaking, the framers structured them to have different virtues. To ensure the House would be sensitive to public opinion, the framers stipulated that representatives would stand for election every two years, thereby creating the opportunity for rapid turnover in House membership. In contrast, the framers gave senators six-year terms to give them some distance from the whims of the voters. Having two powerful houses makes it difficult to make things happen. Simply stated, "a bicameral body of 535 [is not] designed to be fast on its 1,070 feet."[151]

Although the Constitution specifies the basic structure of Congress, the House and Senate have the authority to decide what rules will govern their day-to-day operations. As a result, congressional norms and procedures have changed as the interests of members themselves have changed. The House has seen the most change, with authority at first concentrated in the office of the speaker, then dispersed to the committees, and eventually to the subcommittees. Generally, the Senate continues to operate under many of its original rules. Despite the tremendous continuity in its procedures, the Senate has decentralized its authority to some degree since the early 1970s.

The change in congressional rules and norms has been accompanied by a change in congressional elections: unlike incumbents in past elections, incumbents who now run for reelection almost always win. Some explanations for the success incumbents enjoy point to the setting in which congressional elections occur. Although the relative homogeneity of most congressional districts helps explain why House incumbents usually fare better than Senate incumbents, the way district lines are drawn does not appear to explain the success of House incumbents. Better explanations for their electoral success point to the advantages members of Congress enjoy because they are officeholders and the disadvantages challengers face in mounting a campaign.

Members of Congress come from all parts of American society, but white males continue to predominate. The absence of descriptive representation in Congress may not have significant repercussions for political representation. Gender, race, ethnicity, and other demographic attributes do not appear to determine how members of Congress vote. Instead, members' votes tend to reflect the views of their constituents.

Serving in Congress is a full-time job with significant attractions. It is prestigious, it pays more than $130,000 per year, and it comes with many perks. But congressional service has its price. Members devote many hours to the job, and most members are forced to sacrifice other interests. Yet the number of members who run for reelection suggests that most members find the costs of the job tolerable.

Members of Congress assume their offices as equals, and chaos is one possible result when 535 equals each pursue their own interests. Yet Congress has managed to avoid chaos because of the existence of political parties. Although parties do not control congressional decision making, they do provide the basic stuff of organization, the glue that binds members together and allows for the imposition of leadership. Without political parties, the House and Senate would have a more difficult time maintaining the system of leaders, committees, and staff that form the organizational heart of Congress.

The organizational structure of Congress is designed to enable the institution to fulfill its role as the nation's supreme lawmaking body. To turn a policy proposal into a law, members must navigate a bill through subcommittee, committee, floor, and, finally, conference committee deliberations. When deciding how to vote, members consider their own views, constituent opinion, and a host of other voting cues. The job of a member of Congress does not end with the passage of legislation. Members are also responsible for overseeing the executive branch to ensure that laws are implemented and that the expected results are achieved.

Does Congress represent the American public? In practice, members of Congress are both free to vote as they please and constrained by constituent opinion. The voters back home generally know little about the day-to-day activities of Congress, and interest groups often cannot afford to punish members who vote contrary to their wishes. Yet for all the freedom members have, they know that ultimately their seat in Congress depends on maintaining the support of constituents. Thus, as long as members face the prospect of competitive elections, representation is maintained, and the voters have the last word.

Key Terms

Bicameral legislature
Caucus
Cloture
Conference committee
Conservative Coalition
Constituent service
Divided government
Filibuster
Fire-alarm oversight
Franking privilege
Gerrymandering
Home style
Midterm elections
Police-patrol oversight
Policy oversight
Reapportionment
Select committees
Seniority rule
Single-member districts
Standing committee
Subcommittees
Turnover

Readings for Further Study

Dodd, Lawrence C., and Bruce I. Oppenheimer, eds. *Congress Reconsidered,* 6th ed. Washington, D.C.: CQ Press, 1997. A collection of articles by political scientists describing and analyzing the modern Congress.

Fenno, Richard F., Jr. *When Incumbency Fails: The Senate Career of Mark Andrews.* Washington, D.C.: CQ Press, 1992. A noted scholar of Congress shows the relationship between activity in Washington and reelection considerations back home.

Fowler, Linda L. *Candidates, Congress, and the American Democracy.* Ann Arbor: University of Michigan Press, 1993. A leading scholar's first-rate review of congressional elections.

Mayhew, David R. *Congress: The Electoral Connection.* New Haven: Yale University Press, 1974. A pathbreaking analysis of Congress that begins by asking the reader to imagine what Congress would be like if members cared only about reelection.

McGrath, Dennis J., and Dane Smith. *Professor Wellstone Goes to Washington.* Minneapolis: University of Minnesota Press, 1995. An interesting campaign diary by two reporters who followed Paul Wellstone's atypical Senate campaign.

Ornstein, Norman J., Thomas E. Mann, and Michael J. Malbin. *Vital Statistics on Congress 1995–1996.* Washington, D.C.: CQ Press, 1996. A compendium of important statistics on virtually every aspect of Congress.

Rohde, David W. *Parties and Leaders in the Postreform House.* Chicago: University of Chicago Press, 1991. An excellent study of the effects of the 1970s reforms on the House of Representatives.

Waldman, Steven. *The Bill: How the Adventures of Clinton's National Service Bill Reveal What Is Corrupt, Comic, Cynical—and Noble—About Washington.* New York: Viking, 1995. A journalistic account of the twists and turns leading to the adoption of legislation creating AmeriCorps and changing the student loan system.

Young, James Sterling. *The Washington Community 1800–1828.* New York: Harcourt, Brace & World, 1966. A fascinating account of service in Congress and life in Washington during the first decades of the nineteenth century.

CHAPTER

12

THE PRESIDENCY

The Development of the Presidency

The Presidency on Paper: Constitutional Rules

The Presidency in Practice: Applying the Rules

The Advent of the "Modern" Presidency

Selecting a President

The Nomination Process

The General Election

The Electoral College

Consequences for Governing

The Presidency as an Institution

The Powers of the Presidency

The Organizational Structure of the Presidency

The Workings of the Presidency

Assessing the Presidency as an Institution

The Presidency in American Politics

The Political Context: Permanent Crisis

Presidential Strategies

Presidential Relationships

Summary

Key Terms

Readings for Further Study

On a crisp December evening in 1995, President Bill Clinton pressed the button on a switch, first used by Calvin Coolidge, to light the national Christmas tree. With the lights ablaze, Clinton reminded those who had gathered for the ceremony that the Christmas season is a time that "we give gifts and we count our blessings." He went on to speak of his hopes for peace around the world—in Northern Ireland, in the Middle East, and in Bosnia. He told his audience that the United States had a responsibility to be a peacemaker in the world, even though that role "imposes extra burdens" on Americans. To that end, he asked for special prayers for U.S. troops beginning peacekeeping operations in Bosnia and concluding them in Haiti.

The president's performance during the tree-lighting ceremony illustrates the dual roles we expect presidents to play. On the one hand, by lighting the tree and symbolically ushering in the nation's celebration of Christmas, Clinton was fulfilling his ceremonial and nonpolitical duty as the representative of the American people. But at the same time, Clinton was making political points, asking the public to understand and support a controversial decision he had made a month earlier to send U.S. troops to Bosnia. This merging of political and nonpolitical roles is commonplace for presidents, because we expect them to be both a unifying symbol of our nation and a politically adept policymaker and leader.

Presidents perform their duties according to their personal styles and preferences. Ronald Reagan, for example, displayed the suave aplomb of an actor who had spent a lifetime in the public eye, whereas Jimmy Carter behaved in a simple, almost painfully earnest fashion. But regardless of the differences in the way they perform the tasks of the presidency, every president must respond to the same basic expectations for the office. The presidency is a stable office, structured by rules set forth in the Constitution and shaped by statutory laws and informal expectations that have accumulated over two hundred years. The rules create order, structure, and continuity as new presidents perform the duties of the office.

In this chapter, we examine how the rules of American politics shape the presidency and how presidents shape the rules. We will see the dynamic interplay of the presidency on paper, as the rules set forth in the Constitution define the office, and the presidency in practice, as presidents interpret and reshape the rules to achieve their objectives. We begin by tracing the development of the presidency from its colonial roots to the appearance of the modern presidency in the 1930s. We go on to describe the political and institutional underpinnings of the office of the presidency by first reviewing the presidential selection process and then by examining the workings of the presidency as an institution. We will see how changes in political and institutional rules have molded the presidency into a highly individual and influential office. Finally, we will look at the modern presidency and its interactions with the rest of the political system. We will see that although the presidency has gained power over two centuries of American history, that power remains limited.

The Development of the Presidency

The presidency has evolved in response to many influences, including both the structural rules outlined in the Constitution and the way presidents have interpreted those rules over the past two hundred years. These two influences have combined to mold the modern presidency.

The Presidency on Paper: Constitutional Rules

The constitutional rules that govern the presidency give the president power, but they also constrain that power. From the writing of the Constitution up to the present day, Americans have expressed an ambivalence about the presidency. On the one hand, we

The colonists saw King George III of England as a tyrant, and that shaped their views of executive power. Many mistrusted executives. As a consequence, the Articles of Confederation did not create an independent executive office.

recognize the need for a strong leader with the authority to make swift executive decisions. But on the other hand, we are cautious about vesting too much power in any one individual or branch of government.

As we saw in chapter 2, a deep distrust of executive power shaped the writing of the Articles of Confederation. The oppressive rule of King George III and his colonial governors convinced the authors of the Articles of Confederation to create a national government that had a legislature but no independent executive. By doing without an executive leader, the authors of the Articles of Confederation hoped to prevent the emergence of an American tyrant.

By the mid-1780s, however, the national government's fragmented approach to foreign affairs and other matters convinced many Americans that the decision to do without an executive was a mistake. They believed that the national government needed an independent executive who could implement a cohesive national policy. Thus, when the Constitutional Convention met in 1787 to write the Constitution, one of the foremost topics of discussion was the creation of a new national executive.

Although most of the delegates accepted the need for an executive in principle, their initial proposals envisioned a presidency with modest powers (see box 12.1). In the end, delegates who favored a stronger presidency largely succeeded in pressing their point. The final provisions written into the Constitution created an office of the presidency with three primary characteristics: (1) institutional and political independence from the other two branches of government; (2) shared powers with other institutions; and (3) vaguely defined powers.

Institutional and Political Independence

The Constitution gives the office of the presidency a strong institutional and political foundation. In keeping with the doctrine of the separation of powers, the founders established the presidency as a separate and independent branch of government. As we shall see, the Constitution gives the presidency certain powers that its constitutional coequals, Congress and the Supreme Court, cannot challenge. In a practical sense, then, neither Congress nor the Supreme Court directly controls or supervises the president.

POINT OF ORDER

BOX 12.1

Alternative Arrangements for the Presidency Considered at the Constitutional Convention

Can you imagine a national government in which the presidency consists of a three-member team appointed by Congress for a single seven-year term? Strange as such an arrangement sounds, it is one of the possibilities that might have emerged from the Constitutional Convention in 1787. The founders wanted executive leadership, but they were unsure how to design an office that provided energy and direction without the potential for tyranny. As a result, they considered a variety of arrangements for the presidency.

To understand the complexity and consequences of the choices the founders faced, consider some of the questions they had to grapple with:

The Constitutional Convention at work.

Should a Single Person or a Group of People Occupy the Presidency?

The Virginia Plan said nothing about the composition of the presidency, while the New Jersey Plan proposed creating a plural executive. The delegates to the Constitutional Convention eventually concluded that a plural executive would sap the executive of energy and accountability without making tyranny any less likely. As a result, they chose to assign the presidency to a single person rather than to an executive team.

Who Chooses the President?

Some delegates to the Constitutional Convention suggested that Congress should elect the president; others said the president should be elected by the people. Both proposals, and especially the suggestion for direct popular elections, stirred strong opposition. Critics of the plan allowing Congress to choose the president argued that it would deny the presidency the political independence it needed to succeed. Critics of the plan allowing the people to elect the president warned about the prospect of mob rule. Divided over how to elect the president, the delegates set up a committee to study the matter. The committee returned with a compromise proposal in which neither Congress nor the people chose the president. Their solution was the electoral college. If the committee had not devised the electoral college proposal, it is likely that the fears most delegates had about mob rule would have led the Convention to give Congress the authority to elect the president. Such an outcome, no doubt, would have seriously weakened the presidency.

One Long Term or Many Short Terms?

Closely tied to the issue of who should choose the president were the questions of how long presidents should be allowed to serve in office and whether they should be eligible for reelection. The founders wanted presidents to be able to stand for reelection because they judged that the prospect of facing reelection would encourage presidents to discharge their duties faithfully. But if Congress selected the president, allowing presidents to stand for reelection would be counterproductive; Congress simply would have too much influence over an incumbent president. As long as Congress was the leading choice to elect presidents, the delegates favored giving the president a long term of office with no possibility for reelection. Once the Convention adopted the proposal for the electoral college, however, the delegates moved quickly to give presidents a four-year term of office and to allow them to run for reelection.

Over the course of our nation's history, sixteen incumbents have been reelected. The prospect of single terms for George Washington, Thomas Jefferson, Andrew Jackson, Woodrow Wilson, Franklin Roosevelt, and Ronald Reagan underlines the significance of the choices the founders made at the Constitutional Convention. A single-term presidency would have produced much different dynamics in the relations presidents have with the rest of government and with the American people. Once again, we see that the choices the founders made about the structural rules of American politics carried consequences—in short, the rules mattered.

Source: Sidney M. Milkis and Michael Nelson, *The American Presidency: Origins and Development, 1776–1993,* 2d ed. (Washington, D.C.: CQ Press, 1994), chap. 2.

The Constitution also gives the presidency an important degree of political independence from the other two branches of government. Congress plays no significant role in the presidential selection process, except for the unlikely instance in which no presidential candidate wins a majority of the votes in the electoral college. Of course, the Constitution does stipulate that Congress can remove a president from office if the House of Representatives impeaches (that is, formally accuses) the president and the Senate then convicts him or her of "Treason, Bribery, or other High Crimes and Misdemeanors" by a two-thirds vote. But because Congress cannot select the next president, **impeachment** makes a poor weapon for trying to influence the White House; after all, the new president may be even less to Congress's liking. Moreover, by tradition, Congress uses the impeachment process only in extraordinary situations. Because Congress cannot select presidents and because political norms limit its ability to remove presidents from office, presidents enjoy considerable freedom from Congress.

Impeachment
Formally charging a government official with having committed "Treason, Bribery, or other High Crimes and Misdemeanors." Officials convicted of such charges are removed from office.

Another source of political independence for the presidency comes from its four-year term of office and the provision that presidents can stand for reelection. As originally written, the Constitution placed no limit on the number of terms a president could serve. The combination of a long term in office and unlimited opportunities for reelection made it harder for Congress to defeat presidential initiatives simply by stalling until the president's term in office ended. As chapter 1 discussed, following Franklin Roosevelt's record four terms as president, Congress passed and the states ratified the Twenty-second Amendment, which states that "no person shall be elected to the office of the President more than twice." Even with this term limit, presidents still have up to eight years to press for adoption of their legislative and administrative goals. And because the Constitution gives presidents political, as well as institutional, independence, the presidency is an office with which the other two branches have to contend.

Shared Powers

Although the doctrine of separation of powers influenced how the delegates to the Constitution wrote the structural rules governing the office of the presidency, the doctrine of checks and balances did as well. Once again, the founders' fear of executive tyranny led them to check the president's ability to act by dispersing powers between the presidency and the other two branches of government, allowing the other branches to review or even reverse some of the president's actions. As we saw in both chapters 2 and 11, for example, presidents can sign treaties and nominate people to federal judgeships and senior posts in the executive branch, but no treaty becomes operative and no appointment becomes permanent until the Senate agrees. Likewise, as we saw in chapter 4 and will see again in chapter 14, the federal courts can declare a president's actions unconstitutional. In short, the Constitution constrains as well as empowers the president.

Vague Definition of Authority

Although the founders feared executive tyranny and sought to prevent its emergence by creating a political system based on checks and balances, they defined the scope of the president's powers only vaguely.[1] As chapter 2 discussed, the delegates to the Constitutional Convention disagreed on the proper scope of presidential authority. Some wanted to bestow substantial powers on the president, whereas others feared that creating a powerful presidency would promote tyranny. In the end, the delegates agreed to finesse their differences by making the precise boundaries of presidential power ambiguous. Yet, as we shall see shortly, this very ambiguity created opportunities for presidents to reinterpret and expand the powers of their office in ways that most of the delegates to the Constitutional Convention never intended.

To be sure, Article II of the Constitution does list several specific or **enumerated powers** of the presidency. A moment ago, we mentioned the president's treaty and appointment powers, and as we saw in chapter 11, Article I specifically empowers the president to veto congressional legislation, either directly or by refusing to sign a bill passed during the last ten days of a session of Congress. (This second type of veto is

Enumerated powers
Powers explicitly identified in the text of the Constitution.

Pocket veto
The power of the president to veto a bill passed during the last ten days of a session of Congress simply by failing to sign it.

called a **pocket veto.**) The Constitution also stipulates that presidents are vested with "the executive Power"; that they may direct the head of an executive department to provide them with advice; that they have the power to pardon people suspected or convicted of federal crimes; that they may recommend legislation to Congress; that they may call Congress into special session if "extraordinary Occasions" warrant it; that they may order the adjournment of Congress if members cannot agree among themselves on when to adjourn; that they have the authority to receive ambassadors; and that they have the power to "take Care that the Laws be faithfully executed."

Although this list of enumerated powers may seem lengthy, it is relatively short compared to the list of powers the Constitution specifically assigns to Congress in Article I. Instead of being based solely on enumerated powers, much of the authority of the presidency stems from its **implied powers,** that is, powers the presidency is assumed to have because they are necessary for executing the enumerated powers of the office. Many of the implied powers of the presidency come from the Constitution's statement that "the executive Power shall be vested in a President of the United States of America." Other implied powers of the presidency stem from the fact that the Constitution names the president as the commander in chief of the armed forces of the United States. The founders used the title "commander in chief" simply to designate a post at the top of the military chain of command rather than to denote an independent source of political power.[2] For most of U.S. history, however, and especially since World War II, presidents have argued that the commander-in-chief clause gives them wide powers in foreign policy. Because so much of presidential authority is implied rather than enumerated, presidents have been able to expand the powers of their office over the past two hundred years.

Implied powers
Governmental powers not enumerated in the Constitution; authority the government is assumed to have in order to carry out its enumerated powers.

Although the delegates to the Constitutional Convention created rules that make the presidency a powerful and independent branch of government, they also hedged the president's power with checks the other two branches hold. Perhaps most important, they only vaguely defined the powers of the presidency. These three characteristics of the structural rules governing the presidency have two important consequences for American politics. First, they set the stage for continual though usually healthy conflict among the three coequal branches of government. Second, they make the acts of individual presidents especially important. Since the president has considerable power and independence, and because the Constitution does not specifically spell out all the powers of the presidency, the structural rules of American politics allow presidents to define the implied powers of the presidency through their actions while in office.

The Presidency in Practice: Applying the Rules

In addition to being shaped by the rules set forth in the Constitution, the office of the presidency has been shaped by the decisions and behavior of the forty-one men who have been president.[3] Over the course of the past two hundred years, various presidents have established new rules by asserting the existence of implied duties and powers, and these precedents have been incorporated into our view of the presidency. In essence, past presidents have shaped and reinterpreted the rules that govern the office of the presidency today, just as today's presidents are shaping the rules of the presidency for the future.

As the first president, George Washington established many important precedents.[4] With the help of Secretary of the Treasury Alexander Hamilton, he led Congress by proposing and lobbying for the passage of a legislative program. He fended off congressional intrusions into the presidency by establishing the principle of confidentiality between a president and his advisers, by limiting the Senate's role in appointing executive officers to providing consent rather than advice, and by denying Congress a role in establishing formal diplomatic relations with foreign countries. He established the presidency as the leader of the executive branch by closely supervising the executive departments. Finally, Washington enhanced the legitimacy of the presidency by stepping down after two terms. By relinquishing his position, he helped allay fears of executive tyranny and created an informal limit on how many terms future presidents might serve. After all, who deserved to serve longer than Washington?

Many people viewed Andrew Jackson's vigorous leadership as president with alarm. Here we see Jackson portrayed as a monarch trampling on the Constitution and the laws of Congress. Yet his active leadership served as a model for presidents of the twentieth century.

Thomas Jefferson created a role for the president as a party leader.[5] As we saw in chapter 9, political parties had emerged in the nation's early years to coordinate the actions of like-minded politicians. As president, Jefferson used his claim to be party leader to push his fellow party members in Congress to support his policy initiatives. It subsequently became the norm for presidents to assume the role of party leader and to demand that their fellow party members in Congress be loyal to the administration's policy initiatives.

Andrew Jackson was the first president to lead a mass-based political party, and he persuaded the public to accept the president as the voice of the people.[6] During the first four decades under the Constitution, people saw Congress as speaking for them while they saw presidents as necessary but threatening; presidents provided much needed leadership, but many feared they might become tyrants. Jackson's election in 1828 was the first time that virtually all white males over the age of twenty-one were eligible to vote. (In earlier elections, most states had limited voter eligibility by requiring voters to own property.) Jackson used the expanded electorate to buttress his claim that the presidency's national constituency made it the true voice of the people. In contrast, he characterized Congress as a collection of localized special interests that did not act in the best interest of the nation. Jackson's view of the president's role in American politics provides a key justification for the leadership role that most twentieth-century presidents have assumed.

Abraham Lincoln's handling of the Civil War marked a high point in the exercise of presidential power during the nineteenth century. Lincoln took several steps that he knew exceeded his authority, as when he ordered the secretary of the navy at the start of the war in April 1861 to take funds from the U.S. Treasury to buy military goods. Because Congress had not authorized the purchase—it was not in session and therefore unable to give the required approval—Lincoln's order usurped Congress's power of the purse. Although the Supreme Court declared after the Civil War ended that some of Lincoln's wartime decisions were unconstitutional, Lincoln showed that, under the right circumstances, presidents can take virtually any action they deem necessary, without regard to legal or constitutional boundaries.[7]

Presidential power, however, ebbs and flows. For nearly forty years after Lincoln was assassinated, the United States was led by a succession of weak presidents who

Franklin Roosevelt moved quickly and decisively in his efforts to lead the nation out of the Great Depression. His many speeches to Congress and the American people, combined with his extensive legislative agenda, stamped the presidency as the preeminent source of leadership. He established the era of the "modern" presidency. His successors have all felt compelled to follow in his footsteps as a leader.

were dominated by Congress. Theodore Roosevelt and Woodrow Wilson revived the activist role of the presidency in the first two decades of the twentieth century. Roosevelt's expansive view of the president's powers enabled him to take the initiative on a wide range of foreign and domestic issues. Wilson reclaimed the president's roles as party leader and voice of the nation, and he used both roles to persuade Congress to pass a large legislative agenda.[8] When the United States entered World War I, Congress gave him wide-ranging powers over the economy.[9]

The Advent of the "Modern" Presidency

The role and structure of the presidency changed dramatically during Franklin Delano Roosevelt's (FDR) presidency. The changes were so great that most scholars credit Roosevelt with ushering in the era of the "modern" presidency.[10] Since FDR, presidents have been expected to be active, preeminent national leaders representing the interests of the nation as a whole and providing leadership in a variety of roles.

The Impact of FDR

Why was FDR's presidency so pivotal? Before he took office, presidents were not expected to lead the nation, to actively promote and implement new policy. They might try to lead if they had the personality to do so and the political climate was favorable, but they were not expected to be active, preeminent national leaders. When FDR was sworn into office in 1933, however, the country was in the depths of the Great Depression. Public faith in government was ebbing, and people were willing to accept strong, even authoritarian leadership. Roosevelt responded with a take-charge style and an extensive legislative agenda that restored the public's trust in the federal government. In the early days of his presidency, he delivered many major speeches, held press conferences twice a week, and persuaded Congress to pass more than a dozen major laws.[11] From 1941 to 1945, he led America in fighting World War II.

By the time of FDR's death in April 1945, he had established the presidency as the preeminent source of national leadership. Members of Congress, officials in the federal bureaucracy, and the American public began to expect strong policy leadership from the president. As a result, all of FDR's successors from Truman through Clinton have either felt compelled to follow the example he set of active, national leadership or have known they would be measured against it.

Institutionalized Leadership: The Presidency's Many Roles

The expectations institutionalized during FDR's presidency, the duties the Constitution defines, and the precedents presidential practices have established have combined to create leadership roles that we expect presidents to play in their relations with other political actors.[12] While presidents play many such roles, six stand out.

First, the president is the nation's *chief of state*. This role consists of the ceremonial and largely nonpolitical duties that presidents perform on behalf of the nation as a whole, such as lighting the national Christmas tree, throwing out the first ball at the start of the baseball season, or awarding medals to citizens for their achievements.

Second, the president is the nation's *chief legislator*. In this role, presidents offer guidance and set priorities for Congress by proposing and pursuing a legislative agenda and by using the veto power to block bills they oppose. Presidents who fail to offer Congress a substantial agenda open themselves to criticism from their own party, from members of Congress, and from the news media.

Third, the president is the nation's *chief executive*. Presidents appoint (subject to Senate confirmation) the leaders of federal agencies and attempt to direct their actions through executive orders. As chapter 13 shows, Congress and the presidency share responsibility for overseeing the work of the bureaucracy, but most people hold presidents responsible for the federal bureaucracy, expecting them to correct ineffective or abusive agency actions.

Fourth, the president is the nation's *opinion leader*. The public expects the president to identify and propose solutions to the problems the country faces. Theodore Roosevelt spoke of this role when he described the presidency as a bully pulpit from which presidents could shape the public's priorities, offer proposals to address those priorities, and mobilize the public on their behalf.

Fifth, the president is the nation's *chief diplomat*, representing the United States to the rest of the world. The founders' belief in the need for a leader to fulfill this role helped motivate them to create the presidency as an independent office. Presidents negotiate treaties, send and receive ambassadors, and are expected to speak out on the nation's behalf when foreign policy crises arise.

Finally, the president is the nation's *commander in chief*. This role is written into the Constitution itself. Over the years, presidents have used their position as commander in chief to justify actions they have taken, often without congressional approval, to protect the nation's security from foreign military threats.

The historical development of the presidency demonstrates how the institution (as defined in the rules of the Constitution and laws passed by Congress) and individual presidents (as each reshapes the rules and expectations of the office) interact to create our expectations for the modern presidency. Had the rules defining the office been different—had the Constitution more sharply limited presidential power, for example, or had FDR been a more passive president—then our expectations of presidential roles and the behavior of individual presidents might be quite different as well.

Selecting a President

The process by which Americans select a president has changed dramatically over the course of our nation's history. Just as constitutional rules and precedents have helped push the president to a position of preeminence as a national leader, the changing rules for selecting a president have placed increasing importance on individual candidates and their skills as political leaders.

The process of selecting a president takes place in three stages. First, candidates secure their party's nomination; next, they run in the general election; and finally, the results of the general election are used to allocate votes in the electoral college, which determines which candidate wins. The rules governing each of the three stages have long been points of contention and, in the case of the nomination and general election stages, have undergone major changes. These changes, in turn, have significantly influenced both the election process itself and how presidents have behaved once in office.

The Nomination Process

The task of selecting presidential nominees for the nation's first two elections in 1789 and 1792 was simple: everyone expected George Washington to be president. When Washington declined to run for a third term in 1796, a very informal process produced John Adams, Washington's vice president, and Thomas Jefferson, Washington's first secretary of state, as the two leading nominees. Since 1800, however, the business of nominating candidates has fallen to political parties. And over the course of our nation's history, political parties have used three different sets of nomination rules and procedures to choose their candidates: (1) congressional caucuses; (2) party conventions; and (3) direct primary elections.

Congressional Caucuses

Caucus
A closed meeting of members of a political party to discuss matters of public policy and political strategy, and in some cases, to select candidates for office.

Congress controlled the presidential nominating process from 1800 through 1824. The two major parties of the time, the Democrat-Republicans and the Federalists, each organized a **caucus,** or an informal meeting, in which their members in Congress selected a nominee. This procedure was later dubbed "King Caucus" by critics because it undermined the constitutional principle that the executive branch should be independent of the legislative branch. Since King Caucus meant that members of Congress decided who would be nominated as president, it also meant they could deny a president the chance to run for reelection. The threat of being denied renomination weakened the presidency and made Congress more dominant during the first two decades of the nineteenth century.[13]

Party Conventions

In 1824, the congressional caucus system broke down when candidates who lacked the votes needed to win in the Democrat-Republican Party caucus decided to attack the process as undemocratic. A national system to replace King Caucus did not emerge for another eight years. In the interim, nominations were determined on an *ad hoc* basis at the state and local levels. In 1824 and 1828, for example, Andrew Jackson was nominated for president by the legislature in his home state of Tennessee. But by 1832, when Jackson was running for reelection, the two major groups contending for the presidency settled on a new nomination process—namely, party conventions—although each did so for a different reason.

The anti-Jackson group, the Whigs, understood that their prospects for beating "King Andrew," as they derisively called him, were slim. Everyone who opposed Jackson had to rally behind one candidate. To achieve that unity, they decided to hold a national convention, or party meeting, an innovation the small Anti-Masonic party had first used in 1830.[14] They met in Baltimore in December 1831 and named Henry Clay as their candidate.

President Jackson's advisers also decided to hold a national convention in 1832, but for a different reason. As box 12.2 discusses in greater detail, Jackson's main adviser, Martin Van Buren, and others wanted to dump Vice President John C. Calhoun from the ticket because of fundamental disagreements on major issues. They thought a national convention would be the best way to remove Calhoun, because Jackson's people would control the convention and could produce whatever outcome they wanted. Jackson's Democrat-Republican Party met in Baltimore five months after the Whigs. Delegates were allowed to vote only on the vice presidential nomination, and they cast their ballots for Martin Van Buren.[15] Thus, the rules governing the nomination process changed in the early part of the nineteenth century because political elites wanted to change them, not because the American public demanded it.

As the convention system took hold, each state party organization developed a process for choosing delegates to its party's national convention. State party delegates were chosen in a series of party conventions, with each convention choosing delegates to attend the convention at the next level. Local, county, and then state-level conventions took place, with state convention delegates choosing delegates to the national party convention. The national delegates from all the states then met together at a national convention to choose the party's presidential nominee (see figure 12.1).

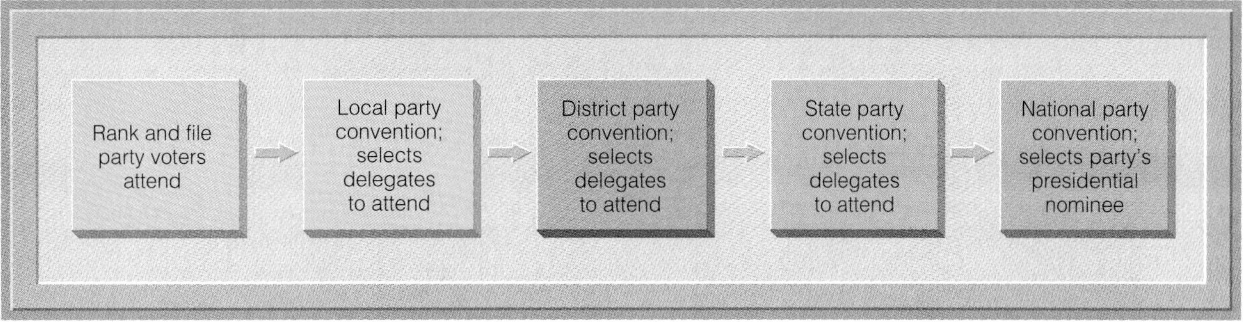

FIGURE 12.1
The Party Convention Presidential Nominations System
The many stages of the party convention nominating system enabled party organizations to select delegates to state and national nominating conventions. This gave the parties, rather than the voters, the power to nominate candidates. As a result, prospective candidates had to be responsive to the party organization's wishes and demands.

Because state party leaders typically dominated the local, county, and state conventions, they wielded enormous power under the state convention system. State party leaders would pick loyal delegates who could be counted on to follow their lead. At the national convention, the candidates would acquire delegates by courting state party leaders, extracting their support in exchange for promising to reward the states with favors and benefits. The bargaining was usually protracted, and quite often the convention would vote several times before one candidate acquired the votes needed to win the nomination. (Indeed, in 1924, it took the Democratic Party 103 ballots to select its presidential nominee.)[16] But in the end, the eventual nominee had the endorsement of many state party organizations. In return, state party leaders had considerable influence over whom their party nominated for president.

Direct Primary Elections

The next major change in the rules shifted control of the presidential selection process from state party conventions to direct primary elections in which voters themselves determined which delegates would attend the national party convention. This shift placed increased emphasis on the candidates and their ability to win the support of the public and decreased emphasis on the parties.

Early in the twentieth century, the **Progressive movement** sought to reform the presidential selection process and reduce the influence of state party leaders by persuading states to change their rules for selecting candidates. Progressives urged the states to use primary elections to choose delegates to the national conventions, thereby giving the public a more direct say in choosing party nominees. But, as figure 12.2 shows, after an initial surge in adoptions, most states reverted to the use of conventions. From 1924 to 1968, primaries were used to select fewer than 40 percent of all party delegates. Moreover, many of these primaries were only advisory, which meant that the outcome of the primary election did not determine the distribution of delegates. (For example, a candidate might win 60 percent of the votes in a state's Democratic primary, but receive only 35 percent of that state's delegates because the delegates were selected through a different process.)

Progressive movement
An early twentieth-century political movement that sought to advance the public interest by reducing the power of political parties in the selection of candidates and the administration of government.

Consequently, through the 1968 election, serious presidential candidates did not rely on primaries as the fundamental way to win delegates. Nonetheless, two factors made primaries attractive to some candidates. First, primaries offered lesser-known candidates who lacked party leaders' support a way to draw public attention and win delegates. Second, primaries gave candidates a way to show party leaders they had popular support and were thus worthy of the party's support. For example, John Kennedy used the 1960 West Virginia primary to prove to Democratic Party leaders that conservative Protestants would support a Roman Catholic, thereby making himself a more viable candidate.[17]

Although states determine their own delegate selection rules, the national parties can set guidelines for the states to follow. For example, after the tumultuous 1968 presidential election, the national Democratic Party adopted a series of rule changes that gave the states a strong incentive to adopt primaries. In 1968, Democrats were deeply divided over the Vietnam war. The Johnson administration was committed to continuing the

The People Behind the Rules

BOX 12.2

Martin Van Buren: Living and Dying by the Two-Thirds Rule

Martin Van Buren

Martin Van Buren is an obscure name to most Americans. At best, he is remembered as the answer to a trivia question: Who was the last sitting vice president to be elected president before George Bush in 1988? But Van Buren played an important role in the development of the American political system—he is credited with developing a political theory justifying political parties in general and the two-party system in particular. His experience with the *two-thirds rule* highlights how rules affect who gets to serve in office.

Van Buren was born in 1782, making him the first person born an American to serve as president. He worked his way through the political ranks in his native New York, serving as state senator, attorney general, U.S. senator, and governor. Along the way his political skills earned him the nickname "the little magician." (Van Buren was only five feet, six inches tall.)

In 1828, Van Buren was a leading Northern supporter of Andrew Jackson's campaign for the presidency. After winning the presidency, Jackson rewarded Van Buren by naming him secretary of state. He quickly became one of the president's closest advisers, but he was forced to resign his position before the end of Jackson's first term because of what became known as the Petticoat Wars. The controversy erupted when Secretary of War John Eaton married a woman with an allegedly promiscuous past. Despite pressure from President Jackson—a widower whose own late wife had been the subject of scandalous rumors—the wives of other cabinet officials refused to socialize with Mrs. Eaton. Van Buren was the only cabinet member to support the Eatons, a position that increased the bad blood between him and Vice President John Calhoun. Van Buren feared the controversy was hurting the president, and he and Eaton eventually resigned their posts. President Jackson subsequently nominated Van Buren to be ambassador to England. The Senate refused to confirm Van Buren's nomination, however, when Vice President Calhoun broke a tie vote by casting his ballot against him. Despite these setbacks, Van Buren continued to have the president's ear, and when Jackson ran for reelection in 1832, he was able to exact revenge against Calhoun.

Van Buren and others had little trouble convincing President Jackson, who had had an earlier falling out with his vice president, to drop Calhoun from the ticket. Doing so was easier said than done, however, because Calhoun enjoyed considerable support in the Democrat-Republican Party. Van Buren and another Jackson advisor found the

Continued

war, whereas most liberals wanted to end U.S. involvement. Sen. Eugene McCarthy (D-Minn.) opposed the war and challenged Johnson for the nomination in the New Hampshire primary, which then, as now, is the nation's first primary. (The Iowa caucuses, which since 1972 have been held before New Hampshire's primary, hold the distinction of being the nation's first significant nomination event. In caucuses, party members meet face-to-face to discuss their candidate preferences; as a result, these meetings require more time and effort than voting in a primary.) When Johnson failed to beat McCarthy by a large margin, he withdrew from the presidential race.

With Johnson out of the race, the Democratic Party organization rallied behind Vice President Hubert Humphrey, who promised to continue Johnson's war policies. In response, Democrats who opposed the war began to contest the Democratic state primaries. Sen. Robert Kennedy (D-N.Y.) emerged from the primaries as the leading challenger to Humphrey, but he was assassinated following his win in the California primary. When the Democrats convened in Chicago for their national convention, Humphrey, who had run a traditional campaign emphasizing state conventions, was

The People Behind the Rules

BOX 12.2 CONTINUED

solution to their problem in what was then a new phenomenon in American politics, the national party convention. They arranged for the Democrat-Republican Party to hold its first national convention. At the convention, Van Buren pushed for the adoption of a two-thirds rule, which required that all nominees had to win the backing of two-thirds of the convention delegates. The convention then renominated Jackson by acclamation. But the real question was, who would be the vice presidential nominee? As Van Buren had calculated, Calhoun failed to muster the necessary two-thirds vote. With Calhoun's nomination defeated, Van Buren himself won the vice presidential nomination. The Jackson-Van Buren ticket won easily in the general election.

When Jackson announced he would not seek a third term as president in 1836, Van Buren was in line to be the Democrat-Republican Party's presidential nominee. Jackson strongly endorsed him, and no one else became a candidate for the party's nomination. Once again, a national party convention determined the party's nominees. At the convention there was considerable debate over the wisdom of using the two-thirds rule. After prodding from Van Buren and after the Virginia delegation switched its vote, the convention decided to retain the two-thirds rule. Van Buren was easily nominated, and he won the general election.

Although Van Buren proved to be an unpopular president—he became known as Martin Van Ruin when the Panic of 1837 plunged the country into a severe economic recession—he was renominated in 1840 without opposition. (The 1840 convention also formally changed the party's name from Democrat-Republican to Democratic.) Van Buren was not, however, reelected. Despite the loss, he continued to be a major figure in the Democratic Party, and he entered the 1844 election as the leading candidate for the Democratic nomination. At the national convention, Van Buren won a majority of the votes, but he failed to muster the required two-thirds. Ultimately, the delegates turned to James Polk, the speaker of the House (and to this day, the only man to move from that position to the White House). How did Van Buren respond to his loss? The man who had instituted and strongly supported the two-thirds rule now denounced it as undemocratic. (In a final irony, Van Buren, the man who developed a political theory justifying the two-party system in the United States, finished his political career in 1848 as the presidential candidate of a third party, the Free Soil Party.)

The two-thirds rule made and broke Martin Van Buren's presidential aspirations. Before the Democratic Party abolished the two-thirds rule in 1936, one other prominent Democrat won the support of a majority of his party delegates only to lose the party's nomination because he failed to reach the magic two-thirds mark. (The unfortunate candidate was Speaker of the House Champ Clark of Missouri, who in 1912 lost the nomination to Gov. Woodrow Wilson of New Jersey.) Over the years, the two-thirds rule was justified as a device to ensure that the Democratic Party's presidential nominees enjoyed broad, national support. But as with all rules, it helped some candidates and hurt others. Martin Van Buren happened to feel the effects of the two-thirds rule from both sides.

Sources: Paul T. David, Ralph M. Goldman, and Richard C. Bain, *The Politics of National Party Conventions* (Washington, D.C.: Brookings Institution, 1960), pp. 17–20; Richard Hofstadter, *The Idea of a Party System* (Berkeley: University of California Press, 1969), pp. 226–54; John L. Moore, *Speaking of Washington* (Washington, D.C.: Congressional Quarterly, 1993), pp. 240–41; Robert B. Morris, ed., *Encyclopedia of American History* (New York: Harper & Brothers, 1953), pp. 169–74; and Austin Ranney, *Curing the Mischiefs of Faction* (Berkeley: University of California Press, 1975), pp. 71–72.

the leading candidate. Though he had entered *no* primary elections, Humphrey still had won more than half of the primary delegates because most of them were not bound to any candidate.[18] Following heated debate over the merits of the nominating process inside the convention hall, and despite protests on the streets outside, the Democrats nominated Humphrey as their presidential candidate.

Many Democrats believed that Humphrey's nomination lacked legitimacy because he had not faced the voters in the primaries and because the delegates to the Democratic National Convention in Chicago did not reflect the diversity of the party's membership. These dissatisfactions, coupled with Humphrey's loss to Richard Nixon, led the national Democratic Party to adopt two major sets of rule changes in its nominating process. The first set sought to increase the participation of women, minorities, young adults, and other groups that had been underrepresented at the national conventions. The second set of proposed rule changes sought to ensure that delegates to the party's national convention were allocated in proportion to the support each candidate had among the party's rank and file. Many state party organizations decided that primary

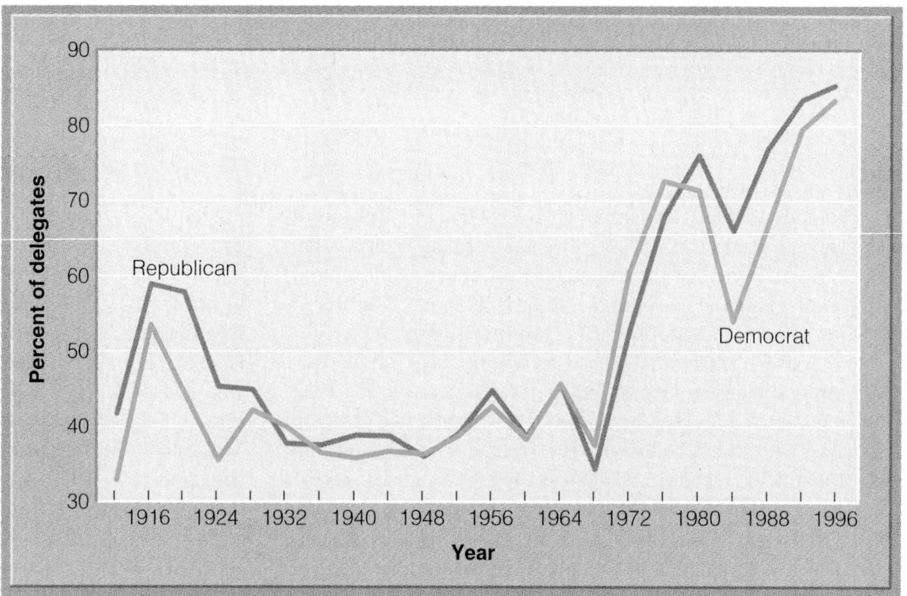

FIGURE 12.2
Percent of Delegates Chosen by Primary, 1912–1996

The convention system dominated the selection of delegates to national nominating conventions until the 1970s. Since then, the overwhelming majority of delegates have been selected through state primaries. This trend has weakened state party organizations by giving the power to nominate presidential candidates to those who vote in the primaries.

Source: Data from Stephen J. Wayne, *The Road to the White House 1996* (New York: St. Martin's, 1996), p. 11.

elections were the easiest way to satisfy both sets of rules and so avoid having their delegates challenged at the national convention.[19] As state legislatures adopted presidential primaries because of the changes in Democratic Party rules, the Republican Party was swept along, and a number of changes were forced on it as well.[20] Consequently, primaries have become the main method both parties use to choose delegates.

Primaries have changed the nature of the presidential nomination process in four ways: they have elevated the importance of early nominating events, encouraged candidates to start their campaigns months and even years ahead of the election, prompted the states to hold their primary races earlier, and, most important, weakened the influence of state party organizations. Primaries elevate the importance of the early contests because candidates who do well early find it easier to raise campaign funds and receive media coverage. Conversely, candidates who do poorly early on, or who sit out the early contests altogether, usually find themselves unable to raise campaign funds or attract media attention.[21] This creates a self-reinforcing cycle that dooms candidates who perform poorly in the early contests to eventual defeat. Only candidates with extraordinarily deep resources can hope to withstand missteps early in the campaign. For example, in 1996, then-Sen. Robert Dole (R-Kans.) did worse than expected in winning the caucuses in Iowa and lost the New Hampshire primary. But he had already raised a large campaign war chest, and he possessed the built-in visibility that comes with being Senate Majority Leader. As a result, he weathered the early setbacks and went on to win the Republican nomination. The experience of one of Dole's challengers, Lamar Alexander, is more typical of candidates who do poorly in the early races. Failing to finish better than third in either Iowa or New Hampshire, Alexander withdrew from the race just two weeks after the New Hampshire primary.

The need to do well in early primaries has encouraged candidates to start their campaigns earlier than they did in the past. Until the 1970s, presidential candidates seldom announced their candidacies more than a few months before the first primary. In 1968, for example, no Republican candidate announced his candidacy more than a year before the general election. But because a poor showing in an early primary can now force a candidate out of the race, most candidates today formally enter the race more than a year before the first primary, after informally testing the political waters even earlier. For example, in contrast to the race in 1968, during the 1996 campaign, nine Republicans announced their plans to run for president more than sixteen months before the general election.[22] Some candidates begin to campaign informally even earlier. For example, within six months after the 1992 election, Sen. Robert Dole

Protests by dissidents within the Democratic Party against Hubert Humphrey's nomination in 1968 culminated in rioting outside the party's national nominating convention. The party responded by adopting reforms that led many states to adopt primaries in order to choose delegates to the national convention.

and Sen. Phil Gramm (R-Tex.) had visited Iowa and New Hampshire to talk to the voters and to meet with state party leaders.[23] Dole went so far as to schedule a brief vacation in New Hampshire in August 1993; the "vacation" consisted of "four days of nonstop [political] events."[24] Dole, Gramm, and other prospective candidates test the political waters in this fashion because they want to get their campaigns up and running and to gain name recognition among the voters.

In addition to elevating the importance of early primary elections and encouraging candidates to start their campaigns months or even years before the first primary election in New Hampshire, the increased importance of primary elections has prompted many states to hold their primaries earlier in the election year. This process, known as **frontloading,** is illustrated in figure 12.3. In 1968, New Hampshire was the only state to hold its primary on or before March 16. In contrast, in 1996, thirty-one states held their presidential primaries on or before March 16. The desire to hold the first primary or caucus has created conflicts. States move up the dates of their contests so their voters play a more prominent role in determining whom each party selects as its nominee. In most years, states that hold late presidential primaries discover that their elections are essentially irrelevant because a candidate has already won a majority of the delegates to the national convention by the time their vote is held. The Democratic Party has rules to prevent states from leapfrogging Iowa and New Hampshire as the first nominating events, and both states have passed laws requiring that their nominating event be the first of its type. But in 1996, that did not stop Louisiana Republicans from moving their party's caucuses ahead of Iowa to make Louisiana the first caucus state, or keep Arizona and Delaware from trying (unsuccessfully) to hold their primaries before New Hampshire.

Frontloading
The decision states make to move their primaries and caucuses to earlier dates to increase their impact on the nomination process.

The final and most significant consequence of the increased importance of primaries is the weakening of state party organizations. Under the convention system, state party organizations chose delegates to the national party convention. In the primary system, however, voters in the primaries do the choosing. By shifting control of the nomination process from state party officials to voters, the primary system undermined the party-oriented character of nomination and general election campaigns, thereby freeing presidential candidates from party influence.[25]

As we have discussed, the rules governing the presidential nomination process have changed greatly over the past two centuries. The power to decide who will be a party's next presidential nominee has shifted from congressional caucuses to state party conventions to primary elections. In turn, control over the nominating process has shifted from Congress to the state party organizations and, finally, to the voting

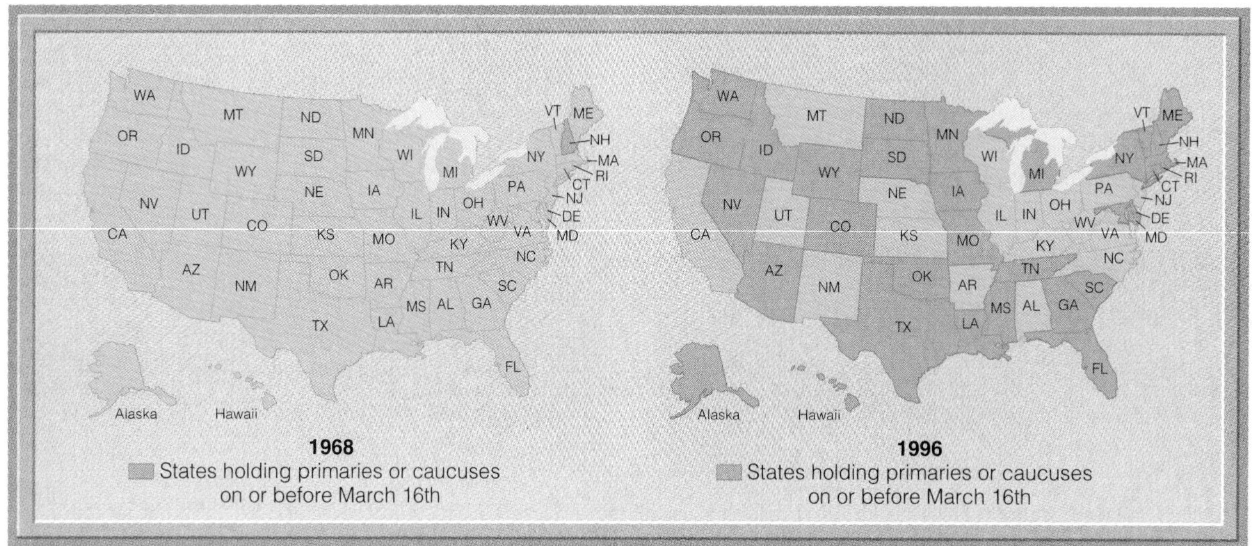

FIGURE 12.3
Frontloading the Presidential Nomination Process

Most states now hold their primaries by mid-March. This development, called frontloading, means candidates must start campaigning very early to stand a chance of winning their party's nomination.

Source: Michael L. Goldstein, *Guide to the 1996 Presidential Election*, (Washington, D.C.: Congressional Quarterly, 1995), pp. 29–31.

public. These rule changes also have shifted the burden of securing a nomination from party leaders to the candidates. Although party leaders acting together once had the power to decide who would be the next nominee, individual candidates are now in a better position to secure their own nominations, with or without the support of party leaders.

The General Election

After the Democratic and Republican parties each have selected a nominee, the next stage in the presidential selection process is the general election. During this stage, the nominees from each party, plus any independent or third party candidates, take the contest before the entire American public. Just as rule changes in the nomination process have weakened the role political parties play and given individual candidates more influence, changes in the conduct of the general election have strengthened the candidate's role and weakened the role of party leaders.[26] Two of these changes are the emergence of radio and television and new campaign finance laws.

The Emergence of Radio and Television

Radio and television have radically altered the way presidential campaigns are run. They have had two important effects on the election process. First, they allow each candidate to address voters directly in their homes, increasing the visibility of the candidate and decreasing the candidate's reliance on the party organization to get the message to the voters. Second, the broadcast media have made elections more expensive as campaigns now must craft effective commercials. Presidential candidates today spend more than one-half of their campaign funds on activities related to television.[27] Since parties have neither the expertise nor the financial resources candidates need to make use of the media, candidates must build their own resources. This again increases the candidate's role in the election process.

Campaign Finance Laws

As figure 12.4 shows, the costs of campaigning for president have skyrocketed over the last forty years. The growing importance of money in presidential campaigns has led to four significant changes in the rules regulating how candidates finance their campaigns: (1) the Federal Election Campaign Act (FECA) of 1971; (2) the 1974 amendments to FECA; (3) the Supreme Court's 1976 decision in *Buckley v. Valeo;* and (4) the 1979 amendments to FECA.

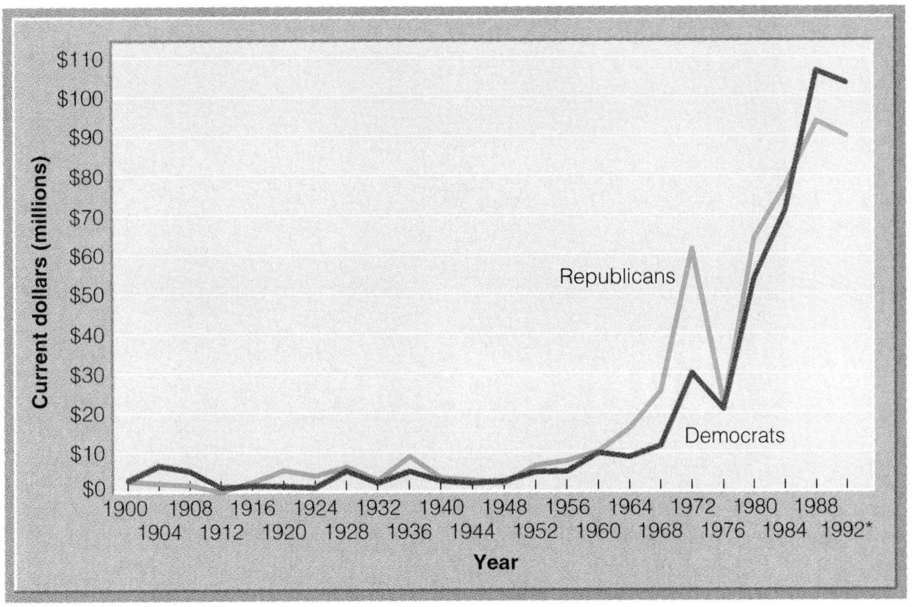

*In addition, Ross Perot spent $64.7 million of his own money to finance his campaign.

FIGURE 12.4
General Election Campaign Costs, 1900–1992

The expense of presidential campaigns grew dramatically once candidates began to rely heavily on television advertising to carry their message to the voters. Campaign financing reforms adopted in the 1970s have done little to limit the growth of overall spending.

Sources: Data for 1900–1976: Herbert E. Alexander, *Financing Politics* (Washington, D.C.: Congressional Quarterly, 1984), p. 7; for 1980: Herbert E. Alexander, *Financing the 1980 Election* (Lexington, Mass.: Lexington Books, 1983), p. 299; for 1984: Herbert E. Alexander and Brian A. Haggerty, *Financing the 1984 Election* (Lexington, Mass.: Lexington Books, 1987), p. 331; for 1988: Herbert E. Alexander and Monica Bauer, *Financing the 1988 Election* (Boulder, Colo.: Westview Press, 1991), p. 41; for 1992: Herbert E. Alexander and Anthony Corrado, *Financing the 1992 Election* (Armonk, NY: M. E. Sharpe, 1995), p. 115.

The Federal Election Campaign Act of 1971 The first serious attempt at campaign finance reform occurred in 1971, with the passage of the Federal Election Campaign Act (FECA). (Chapter 11 discusses how FECA applies to congressional campaigns.) FECA allowed presidential candidates to contribute no more than $50,000 to their own campaigns. It also placed limits on how much they could spend on media advertising, and it required candidates to disclose the names of anyone who contributed more than $100 to their campaigns. However, the original version of FECA did not limit the size of individual contributions or the total amount candidates could spend on their campaigns.

The 1972 presidential election campaign convinced many people that the original version of FECA did not go far enough in reforming campaign finance and that it was necessary to limit both the size of campaign contributions and the total amount of campaign spending. During the 1972 campaign, Democratic candidate George McGovern raised $30 million in campaign funds, more than any other previous candidate for president. Nonetheless, his campaign treasury was dwarfed by the $61.4 million incumbent President Richard Nixon raised. The controversy surrounding Nixon's fundraising techniques was heightened by the Watergate scandal, which began when police in Washington, D.C., caught low-level employees from Nixon's campaign trying to plant listening devices in the offices of the Democratic National Committee at the Watergate building. Further investigation uncovered that Nixon's reelection campaign had secretly received large campaign contributions from wealthy contributors. The Watergate scandal persuaded Congress to amend FECA in 1974.

The 1974 Amendments to FECA The 1974 amendments to FECA sought to reduce the impact of campaign contributions in three ways.[28] First, the amendments created a system for public financing of presidential campaigns. (This innovation had its roots in a 1971 law that permitted people to direct one dollar of their income taxes to the Presidential Election Campaign Fund.) Under this system, candidates receive public funds at two stages: (1) during the nominating campaign, when candidates who meet certain eligibility requirements receive government contributions that match the first $250 of each private contribution; and (2) during the general election, when candidates whose parties meet a different set of eligibility requirements—which traditionally means the nominees of the Democratic and Republican parties but in 1996 included Ross Perot's Reform Party candidacy—can finance their campaigns entirely with federal funds.

Presidential candidates, such as Bill Clinton in 1996, now rely heavily on TV advertising to carry their messages to the voters. They commonly spend more than one-half of their revenues on TV-related expenses.

Second, the 1974 amendments limited the size of the contributions that candidates can accept, as well as the amount that candidates can contribute to their own campaigns. Individual contributors can give no more than $1,000 per candidate per contest up to a maximum of $25,000 per year, and PACs can contribute up to only $5,000 per candidate per election. The 1974 changes retained the requirement that candidates could contribute no more than $50,000 of their own money to their campaign.

Third, the 1974 amendments limited the amount of money candidates can spend during both the nomination process and the general election. These limits are increased before each election to reflect the effects of inflation and growth in the number of eligible voters. In 1996, candidate spending was limited to $31 million for the nomination stage and $62.2 million for the general election. The Federal Election Commission was created to administer these rules.[29]

***Buckley v. Valeo* (1976)** The third important change in campaign finance laws occurred in 1976, when the Supreme Court handed down its decision in the case of *Buckley v. Valeo.* The *Buckley* case undermined the impact of the FECA reforms by invalidating two of their key provisions. First, the Court distinguished between contributions to a candidate's campaign and **independent expenditures** made on behalf of a candidate. The Court ruled that the government can limit contributions but that it cannot regulate independent expenditures—that is, money that groups or individuals spend on behalf of a candidate without formal contact with that candidate. In the eyes of the Court, limits on independent expenditures infringe impermissibly on the right of free speech.

Independent expenditures Funds raised and spent without contact with the supported candidate.

Since the Supreme Court handed down its decision in *Buckley v. Valeo,* independent expenditures have become a significant part of the campaign process. Between 1980 and 1992, groups spent $49.8 million on independent expenditures, with more than $40 million of that amount going to support Republican candidates. However, independent expenditures have become less important over time, declining from a high of $17.4 million in 1984 to a low of $4.4 million in 1992.[30]

Many independent expenditure campaigns have proven quite effective. During the 1988 presidential campaign, for example, supporters of George Bush ran an independent television ad campaign asserting that Bush's opponent, Michael Dukakis, was soft on crime. The ad told how Willie Horton, an African American convicted of murder, had raped a Maryland woman while on release from a Massachusetts prison as part of a prison furlough program that operated during Dukakis's governorship. The Willie Horton ad misleadingly raised the volatile issues of race and crime, implying that Dukakis was responsible for Horton's release and that Horton's actions were typical of participants in the furlough program.[31] The false implication damaged Dukakis's electoral chances, but he could not meaningfully confront his accusers because they were not formally linked to Bush's campaign.

The Willie Horton ad, run in 1988 against Democratic nominee Michael Dukakis, is the most notorious example of independent expenditures in a presidential election. The ad attacked Dukakis as "soft on crime." It was produced and run not by the Bush campaign, but by an independent conservative group.

The second key FECA provision that *Buckley v. Valeo* invalidated was the limit on the amount of money candidates can contribute to their own campaigns. The Supreme Court ruled that any law that limits self-contributions in all circumstances amounts to an unconstitutional restriction on a candidate's right to free speech. The Court did rule, however, that the federal government can limit how much money candidates contribute to their own campaigns if the candidate agrees to accept public funding. In this situation, the Court argued, limits on self-contributions are constitutional because public funding is designed to ensure that candidates can speak out.

As a result of *Buckley v. Valeo,* candidates who choose not to accept public funding do not have to abide by FECA's limits on total spending. They can contribute as much of their personal wealth to their campaigns as they want. As a practical matter, however, most presidential candidates take public funding and abide by the limits on self-contributions. The only two significant presidential candidates to decline public funding were billionaire Ross Perot in 1992 and multimillionaire Steve Forbes in 1996, both of whom decided to fund their campaigns largely out of their own pockets. (In his 1996 campaign, however, Perot accepted public funds.)

The 1979 FECA Amendments The final important change in campaign finance laws occurred when Congress adopted the 1979 amendments to FECA. Like the *Buckley* decision, these amendments undermined the limits the 1974 amendments placed on campaign spending. The 1979 amendments were intended to expand the role political parties play in elections by allowing them to collect and spend unlimited sums of **soft money,** expenditures designed to increase voter participation by strengthening party organizations, registering voters, and getting out the vote on Election Day. In 1980 and 1984, Republicans made much better use of this tool, raising more than $15 million in each election, whereas Democrats raised only $10 million total in the two elections together. Since then, however, Democrats have gained the upper hand. In 1988, Democrats outspent Republicans $23 million to $22 million, and in 1992, the Democrats' advantage jumped substantially; they outspent Republicans $22.1 million to $15.6 million. In 1996, soft money expenditures exploded, to more than $100 million for each party.[32]

Soft money
Expenditures political parties make during an election for any activity that serves the purpose of increasing voter turnout.

Candidate-Centered Campaigns

As a result of the changes in both the nominating and general election stages, individual candidates increasingly control their own campaigns, so that we now have candidate-centered campaigns.[33] Each candidate constructs his or her own organization of personal loyalists and hired experts whose main duty is to win the election. This loyalty often weakens cooperation with the party. For example, in 1972, Richard Nixon created his own campaign organization, the Committee to Re-Elect the President (CREEP); the Republican Party had no role in organizing, financing, or conducting his campaign. Likewise, in 1976, Jimmy Carter campaigned for president by running against the Washington establishment, implicitly criticizing members of his own party.

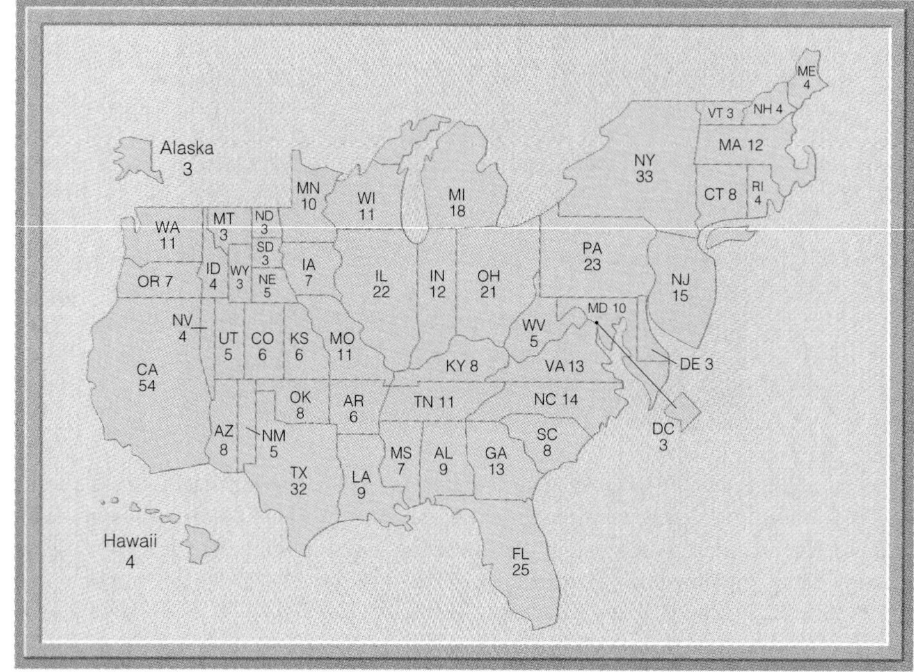

FIGURE 12.5
Electoral Votes per State for the 1996 Election

This map of the United States demonstrates the relative importance of large-population states such as California and New York in the electoral college.

But some candidates do work with their parties. Ronald Reagan in 1984 and George Bush in 1988 attended to the wishes of the Republican Party and, as a result, received their party's help in raising funds and organizing grass-roots activities.[34] Thus, candidates work with their party if they wish to, but not because they have to. In essence, the candidates themselves decide the extent to which they will coordinate their campaign activities with those of their party.

The Electoral College

Electoral college
The body of electors, whose composition is determined by the results of the general election, that chooses the president and vice president. To win in the electoral college, candidates must secure a majority of the electoral vote.

The general election stage ends when the public casts its votes on Election Day. But the popular vote is not the final step in selecting a president. Instead, following the nomination and general election stages, the contest moves to the **electoral college.** In this final stage of the selection process, the results of the popular vote are used to choose electors who will vote in the electoral college. The votes of these electors actually determine who will be president. The rules governing the electoral college significantly affect the way the candidates conduct their campaigns, the winner's margin of victory, and even who wins.[35]

The Constitution sets forth most of the rules governing the electoral college. Each state casts electoral votes equal to the number of its senators and representatives. Thus, California, which has two senators and fifty-two representatives, casts fifty-four electoral votes, whereas Montana, which has two senators and one representative, casts three. Although the District of Columbia has no senators or representatives, since the ratification of the Twenty-third Amendment in 1961, it has been entitled to cast three electoral votes. In all, the electoral college has a total of 538 electoral votes. Figure 12.5 shows the relative weight each state has in the electoral college.

Unit rule
A winner-take-all system which requires that the candidate with the most popular votes receive all of that state's electoral votes.

The Constitution permits each state to decide how to allocate its electors among the competing candidates. Every state but Maine and Nebraska uses the **unit rule,** which means that the candidate with the most popular votes in a state—that is, a plurality—receives *all* of that state's electoral college votes. To win in the electoral college, the Constitution requires that a candidate receive a majority of the electoral votes to win, currently 270 votes out of 538. In the absence of a majority, the newly elected House of Representatives elects the president from the top three finishers, with each state delegation casting one vote, and the newly elected Senate elects the vice president from the top two finishers, with each senator casting one vote.

The states' use of the unit rule and the constitutional requirement that presidents must win a majority of the votes in the electoral college provide excellent examples of how rules affect outcomes. The unit rule has two important consequences for presidential elections. First, it makes it far more important for candidates to win the most populous states rather than the least populous states. To see why, consider the following comparison. The candidate who wins the general election in California receives every one of California's fifty-four electoral votes, even if he wins the general election by only one vote. In contrast, if his opponent wins the general election in Montana, she receives only three electoral votes, even if everyone in Montana voted for her. As you can see, the use of the unit rule gives presidential candidates good reason to focus their efforts on states with large populations where they have a chance to win. Conversely, candidates tend to overlook the least populous states because winning them, even by landslide margins, adds little to their electoral vote total.

Grover Cleveland (top) won the popular vote in 1888, but still lost the race for the presidency to Benjamin Harrison (bottom). This undemocratic outcome resulted from the states' widespread use of the unit rule when casting their votes in the electoral college.

The second consequence of the unit rule stems from the first: the winner-take-all requirement can lead to an electoral college vote that looks very different from the popular vote. In most cases, the person who wins the popular vote wins by an even larger margin in the electoral college. In 1980, for example, Ronald Reagan beat Jimmy Carter by roughly 10 percentage points in the popular vote—a comfortable win, but not a landslide. Yet, when the votes in the electoral college were counted, Reagan had swamped Carter, winning 91 percent of the electoral votes. At the extreme, a candidate could sweep the electoral college vote despite winning the general election by only fifty-one votes, provided, of course, that the candidate wins by a one-vote margin in every state and the District of Columbia.

The tendency of the electoral college vote to distort the outcome of the popular vote might appear to be only a curiosity. After all, whether you win by one vote or by a million, a win is a win. Yet the distortion the electoral college creates is more than a curiosity because the possibility exists that a candidate could win a majority of the popular vote and still lose the electoral college vote. To see how, imagine an election in which a candidate loses the general election in California by one vote but wins the general election in Montana by 10,000 votes. Our candidate leads her opponent by 9,999 popular votes, but she trails by a margin of 54 to 3 in the electoral college! If this pattern of narrow losses in the more populous states and landslide victories in the less populous states were repeated throughout the country, the winner of the popular vote would lose the electoral college. And this is not just a theoretical possibility. Twice in American history, the winner of the popular vote lost the electoral college vote and the presidency: Samuel Tilden lost to Rutherford B. Hayes in this way in 1876, and Grover Cleveland repeated the trick in his loss to Benjamin Harrison in 1888.[36] The unit rule can have a very undemocratic effect on the outcome of presidential elections.

Like the unit rule, the rule requiring candidates to win a majority of the electoral college vote also can have an undemocratic effect. If no candidate wins a majority, the decision of who should be president is taken out of the hands of the public and put in the hands of the House of Representatives. As long as only two candidates have a chance of winning electoral votes, the only way the election can end up in the House is if there is a tie in the electoral college—and that has never happened. If only two candidates receive votes, one is virtually certain to receive a majority. But occasionally, a third party candidate may be able to win electoral votes in a few states. This can prevent either of the two major candidates from securing a majority, as happened to Andrew Jackson in 1824. Jackson won a plurality of the popular and electoral votes, but with three other candidates in the race, he failed to win a majority in the electoral college. The election went to the House of Representatives, which chose John Quincy Adams, who had finished second in both the popular and electoral college vote. The country has narrowly avoided a similar outcome several times more recently. For example, in 1960, a shift of less than 5,000 votes in both Illinois and Missouri would have deprived both Kennedy and Nixon of electoral college majorities (fifteen electoral votes were cast for Sen. Harry Byrd of Virginia that year), and a shift of less than 7,000 votes in both Delaware and Ohio in 1976 would have tied Carter and Ford in electoral votes, again throwing the election to the House of Representatives.[37]

The possibility that the winner of the popular vote could still lose the race for the presidency has triggered calls to adopt some form of direct popular election. But changing the rules governing presidential elections would dramatically alter the dynamics of presidential politics and could lead to a cure worse than the disease. To understand why, remember that moving to a direct popular election would eliminate the use of the unit rule. In turn, eliminating the unit rule would encourage candidates with limited regional or national appeals to run for president because they no longer would have to worry about winning a plurality of the popular vote in a large number of states. With more candidates in the race, the popular vote would likely be spread across a larger number of candidates, which would make it far less likely that the winning candidate would receive a majority or even a large plurality of the popular vote. Indeed, direct popular elections would even make it possible to elect a president the vast majority of the American public opposed. Because direct presidential elections contain the potential for such undesirable consequences, they are not likely to be adopted.

Consequences for Governing

The many changes in the nomination, general election, and electoral college stages of the presidential selection process have encouraged modern presidents to move away from their parties and to create more personalized presidencies. Other developments in American politics have also weakened parties. As chapter 7 showed, voters have become more willing to split their tickets between the two major parties, and, as chapter 11 discussed, members of Congress also run candidate-centered campaigns in which they downplay their party affiliation.

With weakened political parties, modern presidents cannot rely on their parties to create a single governing coalition that will support them across the broad spectrum of problems facing the nation. Instead, modern presidents must create new coalitions to support each issue on their agenda. This shift in the nature of the president's leadership role has had major implications for the way presidents structure and run their presidencies.

The Presidency as an Institution

Tremendous changes have affected the presidency as an institution. As we just discussed, the rules that bring the candidate to the fore during the election process also bring the president to prominence in the governing process. As the presidency has increased and political parties decreased in strength and significance, modern presidents have relied less on their parties and more on their staffs to accomplish their goals in office. This change has had several consequences for the power of the president, the organizational structure of the presidency, and the way in which presidents work to secure their personal and policy goals.

The Powers of the Presidency

We noted earlier that the Constitution for the most part defines the powers of the presidency only in vague terms. In practice, this vagueness has permitted a dynamic and flexible interpretation of presidential powers, and, in general, presidential powers have expanded as the president has become an increasingly visible, influential, and active national leader. We can trace the growth in presidential power by examining first the sources and then three models of presidential power.

Bill Clinton vetoed the Republicans' Medicare reform bill in 1995 with a pen Lyndon Johnson used to sign Medicare into law.

Sources of Presidential Power

The power of the presidency is grounded in one or more of three sources: the Constitution, statutory laws passed by Congress, and precedents set by earlier presidents. As we mentioned earlier, the specific constitutional powers assigned to the president include the veto power, the treaty power, and the appointment power. These powers give the president considerable say in the policies of the federal government. Take, for example, the veto power. Between 1789 and 1994, Congress overrode only 99 of 1,446 regular vetoes, a success rate of roughly 7 percent. Presidents also used the pocket veto to block passage of an additional 1,069 bills.[38] Thus, in 1995, President Clinton was able to block congressional Republicans from enacting their plans to cut taxes and restructure Medicare because they could not garner enough votes to override his vetoes. Because presidents can almost always make their vetoes stick, the *threat* of a presidential veto often is sufficient to convince Congress to make its legislation reflect the preferences of the White House.

A second source of presidential power is statutory law—that is, legislation passed by Congress. When passing legislation, Congress frequently includes provisions that give presidents some discretion in deciding how to implement the law. For instance, during Harry Truman's presidency, more than 1,100 different laws gave him some degree of discretionary authority.[39] Congress delegates such discretion because it often lacks the time and expertise needed to write all the details of legislation and because experience has shown that giving the executive branch some flexibility to carry out the spirit of a law often serves the public interest best.

One example of how statutory law can enhance presidential power is the president's *reprogramming authority*, or the power to redirect government spending. The Constitution gives the power of the purse to Congress, but most appropriations bills give the president limited authority to reprogram funds as circumstances warrant. Congress gives the president this power because it cannot anticipate all the events that may influence how money should be spent over the course of a year. Most reprogramming decisions are routine, and they enable the federal government to spend more wisely. At times, however, presidents use their reprogramming power to pursue their own policy objectives. For example, when Richard Nixon sent troops into Cambodia in 1970, he initially funded the operation by reprogramming foreign aid appropriations intended for other countries.[40] In 1991, George Bush accelerated $9.7 billion in government spending to try to stimulate the economy as part of his reelection campaign.[41] In these ways, presidents can shape congressional priorities to better match their personal preferences.

Statutory law may also enable presidents to take more complete advantage of their constitutional powers. For instance, the Constitution allows presidents to "recommend to [Congress's] consideration such measures as he shall judge necessary and expedient." For more than a century, however, the president lacked the institutional apparatus needed to use that authority fully, particularly when it came to federal spending. Federal agencies simply made their legislative and budgetary requests directly to Congress, without presidential involvement. In 1921, however, Congress passed the Budget and Accounting Act, which gave presidents the authority and the staff needed to review, revise, and assemble the budget requests of federal agencies into a comprehensive budget and to review and revise each agency's legislative proposals before they were submitted to Congress. This process is now referred to as the power of **central legislative clearance.** Presidents use this power to shape Congress's legislative agenda by presenting it with a comprehensive package of bills and budget proposals each year. In 1996, Congress passed a law giving the president a version of the line-item veto. Technically called enhanced recission, it enables the president to selectively withhold funds from government agencies. Chapter 16 discusses the implications of this new power in greater detail.

Central legislative clearance
The power the Budget and Accounting Act of 1921 granted to the president to create a package of legislative proposals and budgets for congressional consideration.

In addition to the Constitution and statutory law, presidential power is grounded in custom and precedent. When Congress, the courts, and the public accept as legitimate presidential actions previously thought to lie beyond the proper scope of presidential authority, the power of the presidency is enhanced. As William Howard Taft, the only man to serve both as president and Chief Justice of the United States, once put it: "So strong is the influence of custom that it seems almost to amend the Constitution."[42] In general, precedents redefine the scope of the implied powers of the presidency, that is, the powers the presidency is assumed to have but that are not specifically mentioned in the Constitution.

The evolution of the president's dismissal power, or the ability to fire or retain federal appointees, illustrates how precedent can serve as a source of power.[43] The Constitution says nothing about the president's power to dismiss executive appointees, and throughout the nineteenth century, presidents and Congress argued over whether the Senate's consent was needed to fire an executive officer, as it is to appoint one. Indeed, when President Andrew Johnson was impeached in 1868, one of the articles of impeachment charged him with dismissing his secretary of war without Senate approval. (The Senate fell one vote short of convicting Johnson, who remains the only U.S. president ever to be impeached.) Not until the early twentieth century, however, did presidential arguments that the power to dismiss was separate from the power to appoint gain general acceptance.[44]

Models of Presidential Power

Examining the sources of presidential power is one way to see the gradual changes in rules that have expanded the powers of the presidency. Another is to look at what presidents have understood their powers to be. Past presidents have adhered to three competing conceptions of presidential power: the Restricted, Prerogative, and Stewardship models.

The most limited conception of presidential power is identified with President William Howard Taft and is known as the *Restricted Model.* Taft claimed that presidents are permitted to exercise only those powers explicitly granted to them by the Constitution or statutory law, or that could be clearly implied from those sources. According to the Restricted Model, presidents can propose and veto legislation because the Constitution explicitly authorizes the president to do both. The president should not, however, lobby Congress on legislation because the Constitution makes no provision for it. Presidents who adhere to the Restricted Model of presidential power tend to be passive and reactive.

The most expansive conception of presidential power is identified with Abraham Lincoln and is known as the *Prerogative Model.* Lincoln held that when the existence or integrity of the nation is at stake, presidents may take any action, without regard to constitutionality or legality, to protect it. Adhering to that precept, he violated the Constitution to achieve the higher goal of maintaining the Union. Some presidents since Lincoln have made recourse to prerogative powers on occasion, especially in foreign policy, but no subsequent president has used it as a general model for his presidency.[45]

Between these two extremes lies the *Stewardship Model,* which is associated with President Theodore Roosevelt. The Stewardship Model turns Taft's Restricted Model on its head. Roosevelt claimed that because presidents alone represent the entire nation, they have a duty to act as stewards of the national interest. In that role, they can take any action not explicitly prohibited by law or the Constitution. Presidents following the Stewardship Model actively seek power and use it to lead the country.

While most nineteenth-century presidents adhered to the Restricted Model, modern presidents have all conceived of their power in terms of the Stewardship Model. This influences the way they interpret and reshape the rules of the presidency, because they believe they have the power to take any action not expressly prohibited by the Constitution or statutory law. In turn, conceiving of presidential power in terms of the Stewardship Model helps presidents who can no longer rely extensively on their political parties to help them accomplish their goals. A more expansive view of the inherent power of the presidency gives them the influence and flexibility they need to create new coalitions of supporters for their programs.

The Organizational Structure of the Presidency

The organizational structure of the presidency has changed dramatically over the past two centuries. From 1789 to today, the office has grown in size, complexity, and power as the presidency has become a more active and powerful position.

Historical Development

Historically, the presidency was a small and personal office. Presidents relied on family and friends to serve as staff; those who agreed to help did so without pay or were paid by the president himself. For example, George Washington hired his nephew to be his personal secretary, and Andrew Jackson created a "kitchen cabinet" of close political friends who advised him on policy and politics. Congress appropriated funds to hire some presidential aides in 1857 and gradually appropriated more money for White House staff over the next sixty years. Still, presidential staffs remained small and informal until 1939.[46]

As the presidency grew in prominence and power, the presidential staff grew in number and complexity as well. Once again, Franklin Roosevelt's presidency marks the turning point in defining the modern presidency. As FDR enacted his New Deal programs, the executive branch became more active, and the federal bureaucracy grew. The president's administrative duties expanded as well. To handle his growing administrative burden and to help coordinate the various agencies and staff that reported to him, FDR in 1939 used authority Congress had given him to create the Executive Office of the President (EOP). The EOP is an "umbrella" organization that includes several influential agencies that perform key functions for the president.

The EOP grew steadily in size from FDR's presidency through the 1960s. Staff support expanded as presidents were expected to provide leadership in more policy areas. At its peak during the Nixon administration, the EOP employed nearly six thousand people spread across twenty agencies.[47] In the aftermath of the Vietnam War and the Watergate scandal, however, congressional criticism and public mistrust of a too-powerful presidency led Presidents Ford and Carter to reduce the size of the EOP to roughly its present size—twelve staff agencies, which together employ about two thousand workers. Figure 12.6 provides a brief description of these agencies and the functions that each performs.

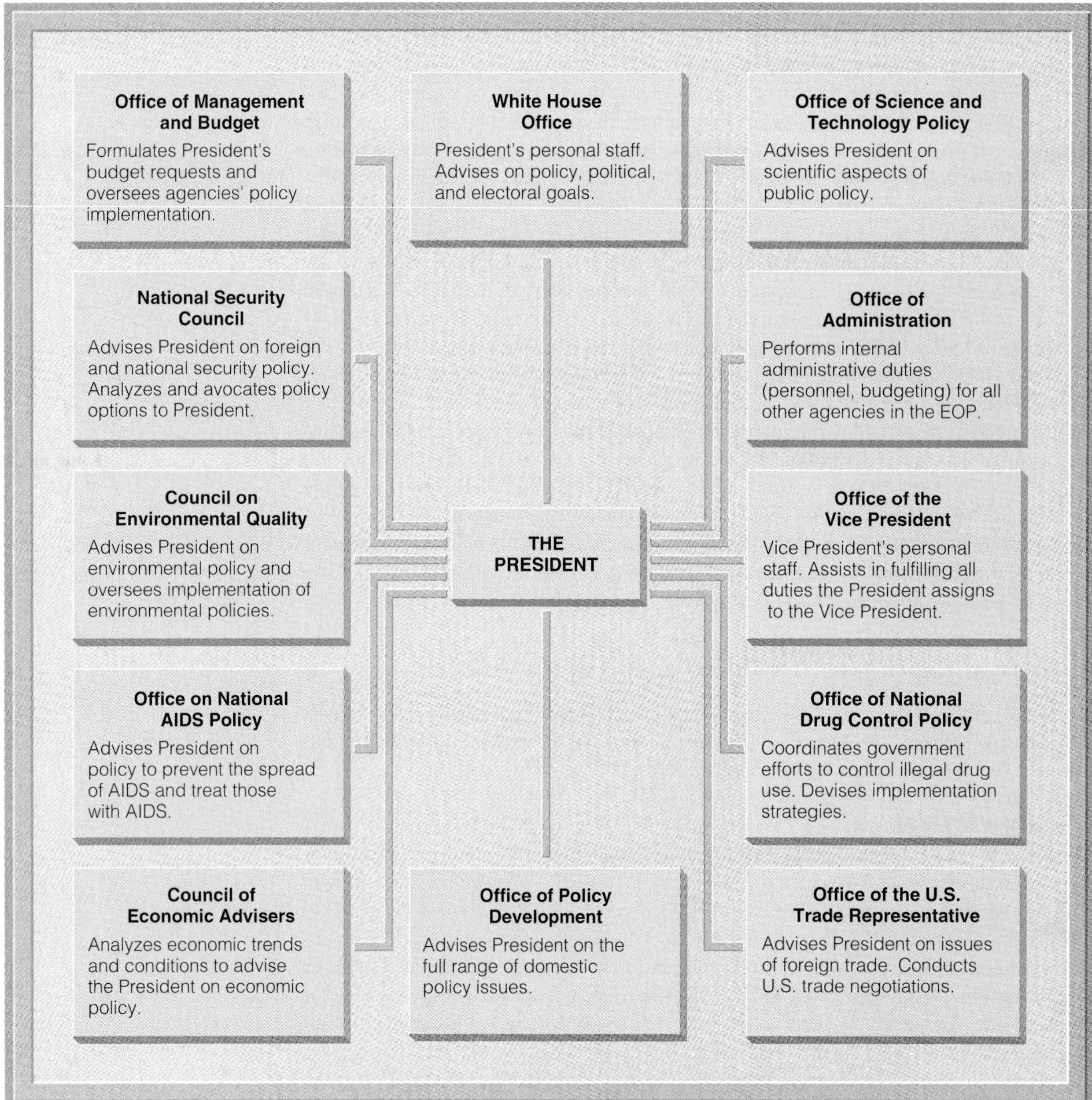

FIGURE 12.6
Agencies in the Executive Office of the President, 1996

The Executive Office of the President houses a wide variety of agencies that provide advice and assistance to presidents on virtually every policy and political problem they confront.

Source: Adapted from *Carroll's Federal Directory: Executive, Legislative, Judicial,* January/February 1996 (Washington, D.C.: Carroll Publishing, 1995), pp. 125–33.

Key Agencies of the Contemporary EOP

While each of the twelve agencies in the EOP is important to the workings of the presidency, four merit special attention: the White House Office, the Office of Management and Budget, the National Security Council, and the Office of the Vice President.

In many respects, the most important agency in the EOP is the White House Office. It employs roughly five hundred people whose primary task is to meet the immediate personal and policy needs of the president. Figure 12.7 identifies the key units in the White House Office during the Clinton presidency. The people who work for the White House Office include the president's primary advisers on policy and political matters, administrators who manage the internal operation of the White House and supervise the workings of the rest of the bureaucracy, and aides who conduct relations with important actors such as Congress, the mass media, and special interest groups. As you might imagine, presidents try to staff the White House Office with loyal aides who will carry out their wishes.

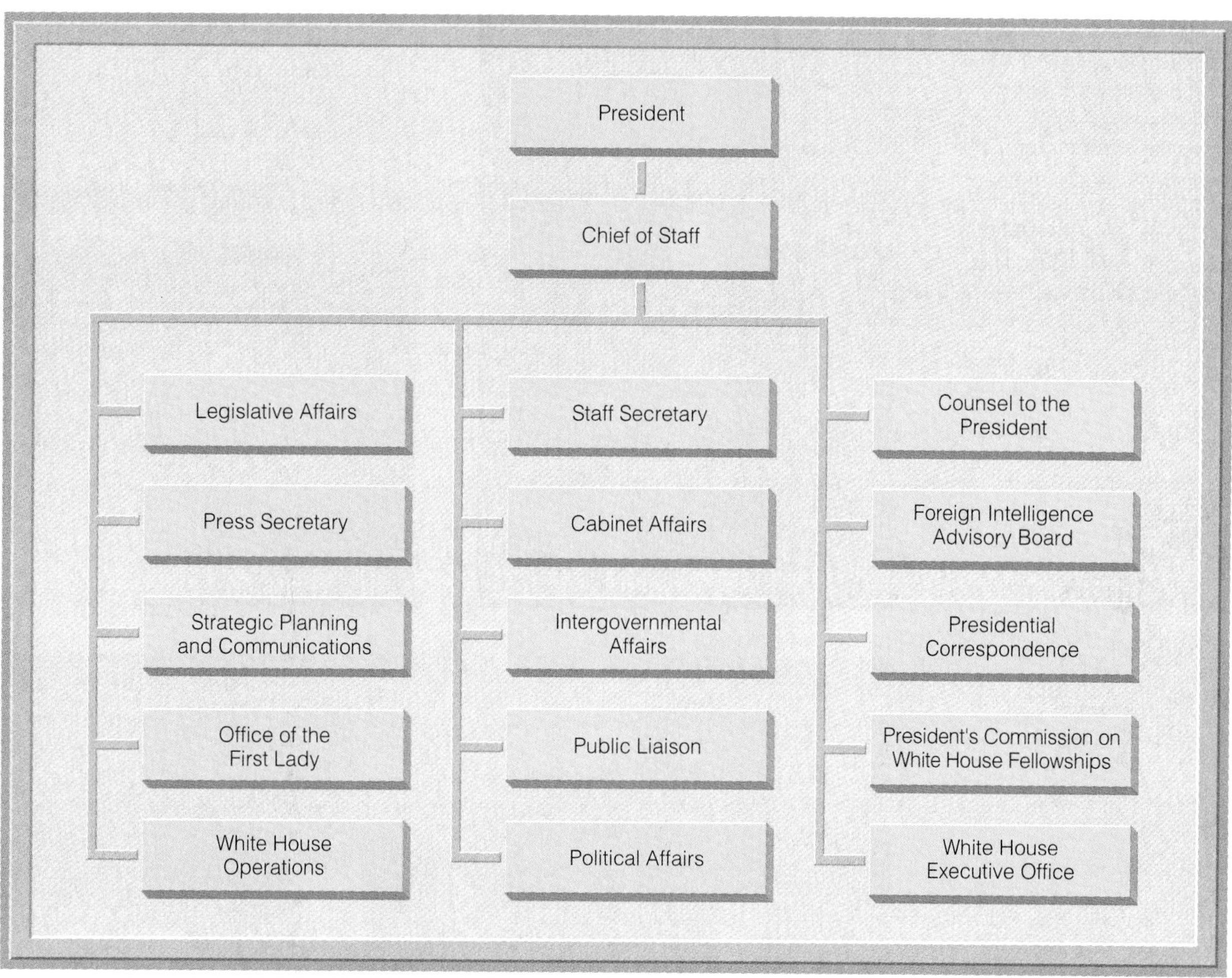

FIGURE 12.7
Structure of the White House Office, 1996

The White House staff has grown dramatically from the days of Andrew Jackson's "kitchen cabinet." Today's White House Office is a large and complex organization. Staffed with people who are deeply committed to the president, it serves as the cornerstone of political and policy assistance to modern presidents.

Source: Adapted from *Carroll's Federal Directory: Executive, Legislative, Judicial,* January/February 1996 (Washington, D.C.: Carroll Publishing, 1995), pp. 125–33.

The White House Office also includes the Office of the First Lady. Traditionally, the president's wife served as the nation's hostess, welcoming guests to the White House. She stayed away from politically controversial issues. Many first ladies in the modern era have pursued government policies that particularly interested them and enjoyed broad public support: Lady Bird Johnson advocated beautifying America's highways, Nancy Reagan urged Americans to "Just Say No" to drugs, and Barbara Bush helped promote literacy. On occasion, first ladies have played more prominent political roles. Eleanor Roosevelt, for example, was a leading figure in publicizing the civil rights movement during the 1930s.[48] Jimmy Carter openly acknowledged that his wife, Rosalynn, was one of his most important advisers, and she was the first presidential spouse to regularly attend cabinet meetings.[49] Hillary Rodham Clinton undertook a political role unprecedented in its prominence when President Clinton put her in charge of drafting a proposal to overhaul the nation's health care system. When Congress refused to pass legislation enacting the reforms she had helped to craft, Mrs. Clinton retreated from the political spotlight and assumed the more traditional roles of the first lady. (White House aides called this resumption of a more traditional role "the *Redbook* strategy" because they were trying to appeal to *Redbook* magazine's audience, the average American woman.)[50] Nonetheless, Mrs. Clinton clearly extended the boundaries of the role of the first lady. It remains to be seen whether her successors (be they first ladies or first gentlemen) will follow in her footsteps.

The Office of Management and Budget (OMB) helps the president draft the annual federal budget request and oversee the work of the federal bureaucracy. OMB was created by the Budget and Accounting Act of 1921 as the Bureau of the Budget

Hillary Rodham Clinton vastly expanded the possible roles of the First Lady. She lobbies members of Congress. She represents the nation at international conferences. In addition, she performs her traditional duties of serving as the nation's official host for important state events.

(BOB), and it became part of the EOP in 1939. In 1970, President Nixon expanded the size and functions and changed the name of the agency. OMB's career civil servants review the budgetary and legislative requests each federal agency makes to Congress to ensure that they conform to the president's priorities. OMB also helps presidents direct the bureaucracy by making sure that laws and presidential directives are implemented according to the president's wishes.

The National Security Council (NSC), created in 1947, consists of the secretaries of state and defense, the vice president, and the president. The NSC provides a forum for discussing foreign policy options. It is supported by a staff of policy experts appointed by the president. Since the Kennedy presidency, the NSC staff has been an important source of foreign policy advice and advocacy.

The Office of the Vice President serves the needs of the vice president. The importance of the vice presidency has changed over the past two hundred years. John Adams, our first vice president, called the vice presidency "the most insignificant office that ever the invention of man contrived or his imagination conceived."[51] Most nineteenth-century vice presidents were undistinguished politicians whose sole role was to attract votes during the general election. Vice presidents gained a measure of prominence in the early twentieth century as they began to participate in cabinet meetings, serve as emissaries to foreign governments, and act as liaisons with Congress. Nonetheless, as late as the 1930s, Franklin Roosevelt's first vice president, John Nance Garner, observed that the vice presidency "isn't worth a pitcher of warm spit."[52]

The Office of the Vice President has gained in stature in recent years as presidents have entrusted their vice presidents with more important duties. Nelson Rockefeller (under Gerald Ford), Walter Mondale (under Jimmy Carter), George Bush (under Ronald Reagan), and Dan Quayle (under Bush) all served as advisers to the president on a range of policy and political questions.

Al Gore built upon the recent tradition of an active vice presidency by playing important roles for President Clinton in both domestic and foreign policy. As we shall see in the next chapter, Gore led a task force charged with finding ways to restructure and revitalize the federal bureaucracy. He also acted as a key liaison to the environmental community. In foreign affairs, Gore played a leading role in strengthening relations with Russia and South Africa.[53] The staff in the Office of the Vice President advises the vice president and works to see that he or she is able to carry out whatever tasks the president assigns.

In sum, the organizational structure of the presidency was relatively small and stable for more than one hundred and fifty years. Over the past fifty years, however, it has grown in both size and complexity. As the presidency has evolved from a small, personal office into a conglomerate of support agencies under the umbrella of the EOP, presidents have found themselves able to rely on a larger number of people and agencies to accomplish their goals. In turn, this expansion has changed the way presidents work.

The role of the vice president has come a long way since the days of Franklin Roosevelt's first vice president, John Nance Garner. Today, Vice President Al Gore fulfills many important tasks, such as representing the United States overseas.

The Workings of the Presidency

A third way the presidency as an institution has changed during the past half-century, along with the changes in the powers of the presidency and the organizational structure of the presidency, is the way in which the office works. The workings of the presidency are influenced by both internal and external factors. These factors, like the structural rules set forth in the Constitution, combine both to empower and constrain the president.

Internal factors that affect the workings of the presidency include the functions the agencies of the EOP perform for the president, the president's style of managing those agencies, and the president's conception of the role staff should play. Internal factors tend to give presidents the ability to run their presidencies as they wish. External factors include the expectations that others have for the president and what they believe he or she should accomplish. External factors tend to constrain the president.

Internal Factors—Functions of EOP Agencies

The agencies that make up the EOP advise presidents on public policy, help presidents conduct relations with others in and out of government, and assist presidents as they look ahead to reelection.

As figure 12.6 shows, each agency in the EOP has a specific role to play in advising and supporting the president on public policy. For example, the National Security Council recommends foreign policy options, the Council of Economic Advisers helps formulate economic policy, and the Office of Policy Development advises presidents on a wide range of domestic policies.

Some agencies in the EOP also act as liaisons to Congress and interest groups, helping presidents build political support for their policy initiatives. This is especially true of various units of the White House Office. For example, every president since Dwight Eisenhower has used the Office of Legislative Affairs to develop support on Capitol Hill for his legislative agenda. Likewise, every president since Gerald Ford has used the Office of Public Liaison to improve his relations with interest groups.

And the Office of Strategic Planning and Communications helps presidents present a dignified, professional image and present persuasive messages to the public through the national press corps.

In addition to advising the president on public policy and acting as liaisons with groups in and out of government, agencies in the EOP also act to advance the president's prospects for reelection. Again, this is especially true of the White House Office, which over the past thirty years has developed into a shadow campaign organization. The reason is that once presidents enter office, they usually transfer their key campaign aides into important positions in the White House. These aides advise the president both on policy and electoral matters. When the time for reelection nears, these aides often move out of the White House staff and back into the president's reelection campaign staff.

One example of the dual policy and electoral roles played by units in the White House Office is illustrated by the Office of Public Liaison. Not only does it work to enlist the support of interest groups for the president's legislative agenda, it also tries to keep the president's fences mended as the White House looks to the next election. White House opinion pollsters also play dual policy and electoral roles. They measure the public's reactions to the president's proposals to determine how best to mobilize support for the administration's legislative agenda. But they also routinely survey the public to determine which issues will have the most appeal in the next election and to determine the president's political standing with the voters.[54] Bill Clinton has relied more heavily than any of his predecessors on public opinion analysts, commissioning three to four polls each month to assist him in achieving both his policy and political goals.[55]

Thus, the functions the agencies of the EOP perform have evolved over time. In particular, the liaison and reelection functions of EOP agencies have both become more prominent as political parties have weakened. The White House and other EOP agencies have stepped in to fill the role parties once played in helping presidents both lead the government and win reelection.

Internal Factors—Presidential Management Styles

Modern presidents have developed different management styles, which range from an informal "spokes of the wheel" style to a highly structured "pyramid" style. No president employs a pure version of either style. Rather, each president draws on features of both, but tends to place relatively greater emphasis on one or the other.[56]

As figure 12.8 shows, in a wheel style of management, the White House has few layers of hierarchy, and the president is accessible to many different assistants. Presidents who use the wheel style of management prefer to take a hands-on approach to the presidency. They are less likely to appoint a strong chief of staff to oversee the White House's administration, preferring to assume that task themselves. They frequently change staff assignments, and they may fail to clearly divide responsibility among their aides. Franklin Roosevelt, John Kennedy, Jimmy Carter, and Bill Clinton (see box 12.3) all tended toward the wheel style of management, though each also adjusted his style over the course of his administration and from issue to issue.

In contrast to the wheel style, the pyramid style of management creates a fairly formal and hierarchical command structure within the office of the presidency. As figure 12.8 shows, a White House organized according to the pyramidal style has several layers of authority and more formal and rigid staff assignments, with clear lines of authority and duties. One staff member is typically designated as chief of staff and given authority to oversee other White House aides. Presidents who resort to the pyramid style of management generally limit their contact to a small number of senior staff. Dwight Eisenhower, Richard Nixon, Ronald Reagan (see box 12.3), and George Bush all tended toward the pyramid style of management to varying degrees.

Each management style has advantages and disadvantages. Proponents of the wheel approach claim that it enables presidents to receive more complete and accurate information about what their administrations are doing. By communicating with many different aides, including those who hold only midlevel appointments, presidents are more likely to

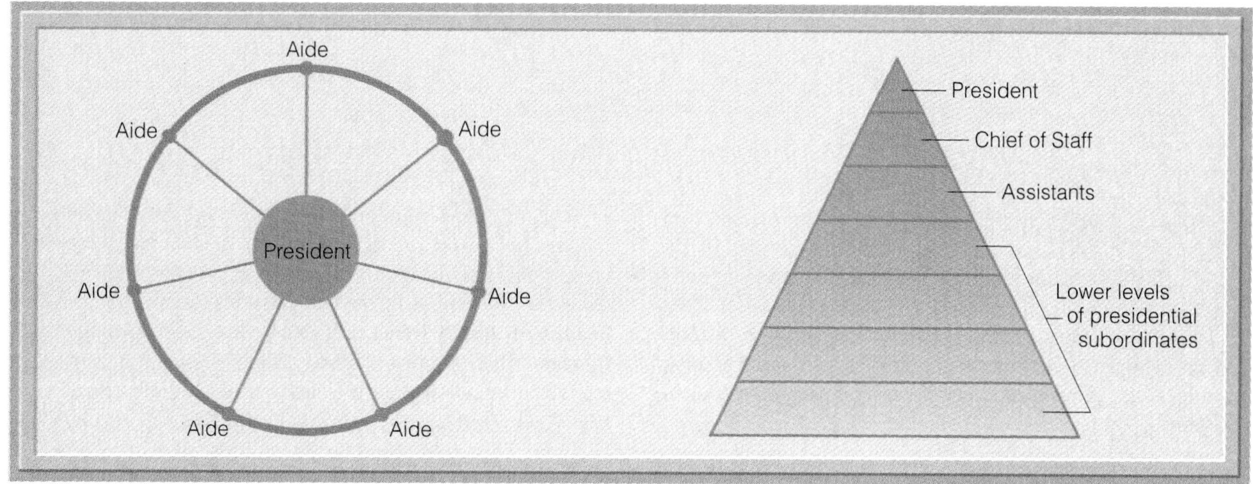

FIGURE 12.8
The Spokes of the Wheel and Pyramid Styles of Presidential Management

Although no president employs a pure version of either management style, most lean toward one or the other on the basis of their experiences, party membership, and length of time in office. For example, while George Bush used a fairly structured pyramid approach to management, Bill Clinton embraced the more free-flowing spokes of the wheel style.

know what is happening both inside and outside of government. Yet the wheel style places enormous demands on a president's time, since no one else in the White House is empowered to make key decisions. And the more time presidents spend on internal White House matters, the less time they have to make important political and policy decisions. Thus, the wheel style forces presidents to pay a high price for being well informed.

The advantages and disadvantages of the pyramid approach tend to be exactly the opposite. The strength of the pyramid style is that it places relatively few administrative demands on the president. Those duties are assigned to the chief of staff. Moreover, the clear chain of command limits disputes over who has authority to make decisions. The pyramid style's weakness is that it can leave presidents insulated from political reality because they depend on a small number of aides for information. No one wants to be the bearer of bad tidings, especially if it puts oneself or one's boss in a bad light, so as the number of people with access to the president declines, and the number of layers through which information must pass increases, it becomes more likely that bad news will never make it to the president's desk. As a result, presidents who rely on the pyramid style of management may develop a distorted understanding of what Americans and their elected representatives in Congress are thinking.[57]

Why do presidents develop a preferred management style? Each president's management style depends on his prior political experiences, his political party affiliation, the size and complexity of the EOP during his administration, and how long the president has served in office.

Prior political experience leads presidents to favor one style over the other. Most Republican presidents have had executive backgrounds in large organizations: Eisenhower in the U.S. Army, Nixon as vice president, Reagan as governor of California, and Bush in a variety of executive branch offices, including the vice presidency. As a result, Republicans tend to be more comfortable with the pyramid style. Only Gerald Ford, as a long-time member of the House, had a predominantly legislative background, and he was the most wheel-oriented Republican president. In contrast, most Democrats have had political careers that predispose them toward the wheel style. Truman, Kennedy, and Johnson spent most of their careers in the Senate, which has a decidedly non-pyramidal structure. Although Carter and Clinton served as governors, both served in smaller states and did not need large staffs.

Party is important because presidents tend to model themselves on predecessors from their party. Modern Democratic presidents have tended to emulate FDR's wheel style. In contrast, Republicans have tended to model their presidencies on Eisenhower's formal, pyramidal approach.

The size and complexity of the presidency has led presidents elected since the 1960s to rely more on the pyramid style than earlier presidents did. As the presidency has grown in size, the wheel style's high administrative costs have made it less attractive.

THE PEOPLE BEHIND THE RULES

BOX 12.3

Contrasting Management Styles: Reagan and Clinton

All presidents today must not only lead the nation, they also must oversee and coordinate the activities of the roughly five hundred members of the White House staff. Yet different presidents bring different management styles to the Oval Office. To see just how different presidential management styles can be, compare how Ronald Reagan and Bill Clinton approached the task of running the White House.

Ronald Reagan and Bill Clinton had decidedly different presidential management styles.

Reprinted by permission: Tribune Media Services.

Ronald Reagan

Ronald Reagan directed his administration by voicing general goals and letting his subordinates work out the details. During his first term, he employed a well-organized staff structure based on a "Troika" of key aides: Michael Deaver, James Baker, and Edwin Meese. These three assistants then managed the workings of the rest of the White House. In Reagan's second term, his style of management became even more formal and pyramidal, as he appointed Donald Regan chief of staff to replace the Troika. Regan ran the White House in a highly structured fashion, staffing the office with carefully chosen subordinates rather than peers who could challenge his authority. President Reagan left day-to-day operational decisions to Regan.

Reagan's supporters praised his ability to delegate authority; his detractors denigrated his detachment. Both were right. Praise for his hands-off style produced, for example, an article in the business magazine *Fortune* headlined "What Managers Can Learn from Manager Reagan." But hosannas turned to ridicule when it became known in late 1986 that members of his National Security Council staff had secretly (and illegally) traded weapons with Iran to secure the release of Americans held hostage in Lebanon and then (again, illegally) used some of the profits to aid the Contra rebels in Nicaragua. Reagan defended himself against resounding public and congressional criticism of the Iran-Contra Affair by claiming he was unaware of what his most senior aides were doing.

Bill Clinton

Bill Clinton takes a very hands-on, wheel style approach to managing his presidency. He provides ambiguous job descriptions to his top aides, and he often keeps in touch with lower-level White House aides by dropping in on them in their offices to discuss policy. Clinton's hands-on approach is reflected in how his first chief of staff, Mack McLarty, operated. Rather than relying on the pyramidal structure Donald Regan favored, McLarty employed an "inclusive, nonhierarchical" approach. He did not require that the flow of information to the president go exclusively through his office, and he permitted as many as eight advisers direct access to Clinton (compared to three or four during Reagan's terms). Clinton's second chief of staff, Leon Panetta, imposed more structure on the Clinton White House.

Clinton's management style has met with a fair degree of success. His administration convinced Congress to approve both a major deficit reduction bill and the North American Free Trade Agreement. But Clinton's management style has also drawn sharp criticism. Critics complain that too many aides have a say in policy making and that the lines of decision-making authority are too blurred; as a result, they claim the Clinton White House takes too long to develop domestic policy initiatives and was too slow to respond to events overseas.

Sources: Stephen Hess, *Organizing the Presidency,* 2d ed. (Washington, D.C.: Brookings Institution, 1988), chap. 9, and Burt Solomon, "A Modish Management Style Means. . . . Slip-sliding Around the West Wing," *National Journal,* 30 October 1993, pp. 2606–7.

President Clinton relies heavily on personal assistants and staff members who are committed to ensuring the success of his presidency.

Finally, presidents tend to shift their management styles toward the pyramid approach as their administrations progress. Early on, presidents promise open administrations, assuring the cabinet, Congress, and the public access to the president, which fits the wheel model. Moreover, the first tasks facing a president concern policy formulation: what to do and how to do it? These factors lead presidents to seek input and to tolerate debate and dissent, attitudes that lend themselves to the wheel style. However, as they move further into their terms, presidents find their task shifts to implementing policies. This is easier to accomplish with the pyramid style's formal chain of command.

Internal Factors—The Role of Staff

Closely related to a president's management style is his or her concept of the role the presidential staff should play. This is another area in which the presidency has gained influence over the past half-century, as presidents have rewritten the informal rules that govern their use of staff. In general, presidents have abandoned the idea of hiring objective, neutral staff in favor of hiring staff members who are politically loyal.

When the EOP was first created, most of the agencies were staffed according to the principle of **neutral competence,** which holds that staff members should be permanent career civil servants whose task is to provide competent and objective advice to every president rather than to advocate each president's policy preferences.[58] The exception to this rule was staff that presidents appointed to work in the White House Office. These temporary employees were expected to serve the political interests of the president who appointed them. According to the principle of neutral competence, then, most presidential staff members were committed to the presidency as an institution, but not necessarily to the policy goals of a particular president. Obviously, the norm of neutral competence limited what the president's staff was willing to do for him.

Neutral competence
The belief that staff members (usually career civil servants) should be able to work competently for any president, regardless of partisan affiliation or policy preferences and without advocating the policies of individual presidents.

Most presidents grow dissatisfied with staff members who fail to respond to their immediate political needs. As a result, they have tried to weaken the norm of neutral competence and to politicize most agencies in the EOP. For example, during the 1960s, Lyndon Johnson pressured the Bureau of the Budget (now known as OMB) to abandon its neutral perspective and advocate his policies, while Richard Nixon and Jimmy Carter imposed new layers of political appointees on OMB to gain greater control of its operation.[59] David Stockman, Ronald Reagan's first director of OMB, ordered the agency to alter its projections of government spending and revenue to support Reagan's claim that he could raise defense spending, cut domestic spending, lower taxes, and still balance the budget.[60]

Presidents also have politicized the workings of the key presidential agency on foreign policy, the staff of the National Security Council (NSC). John Kennedy ended the practice of filling positions on the NSC staff with career officers from the departments of defense and state, and instead appointed outside experts who shared his views on foreign policy. Richard Nixon gave Henry Kissinger, his national security adviser and the head of the NSC staff, enormous powers to conduct foreign policy, relegating the State Department to a peripheral caretaker role. Members of the NSC staff assumed a key role in implementing foreign policy on behalf of Ronald Reagan in the mid-1980s. Members of Reagan's NSC staff secretly (and in violation of U.S. law) sold weapons to Iran in a bid to secure the release of several Americans held hostage in Lebanon. Some of the proceeds from these secret sales were then routed to the Contra rebels in Nicaragua, an act that violated legislation restricting U.S. aid to the Contras. The resulting scandal, known as the Iran-Contra Affair, rocked the Reagan administration and damaged Ronald Reagan's reputation.

The politicization of the institution of the presidency is one of the most important trends of the modern era.[61] As the OMB and Iran-Contra examples show, presidents who have loyal staffs dedicated to serving their personal aims are far better positioned to pursue their goals than presidents whose staffs adhere to the norm of neutral competence. In short, by politicizing the EOP, recent presidents have increased their personal power.

But as the founders feared, and episodes such as Iran-Contra confirm, too much personal power encourages presidents to abuse their authority. Remember that our constitutional rules give Congress and the courts the ability to check presidential power. Less formal rules also constrain the presidency and keep it in check. These rules spring from the expectations of people and forces external to the presidency.

External Influences—The Expectations of Others

We have reviewed the effects of internal factors, such as styles of presidential management and conceptions of staff roles, on the power and workings of the presidency. The last factor that influences the power and workings of the presidency is the expectations of outside political actors. When these expectations are so ingrained that new presidents and presidential staffs instinctively meet them, we can say that these expectations have been *institutionalized*—they have become a part of the institution and are unlikely to change even when new presidents take office or when they hire new staffs. Institutionalized expectations, then, are essentially informal rules.

The importance of institutionalized expectations is seen in the widely accepted belief that presidents should propose legislation for Congress to consider and thereby set the nation's political agenda. As we discussed earlier, this expectation dates back to the aggressive legislative agenda Franklin Roosevelt put forward to combat the Great Depression. Since FDR, presidents with limited legislative agendas have paid a heavy price in the form of criticism from Congress, the news media, and the public. For example, Dwight Eisenhower took office in 1953 without a specific legislative agenda in mind. When it became clear he had few legislative proposals to submit to Congress, even his fellow Republicans joined in the chorus of criticism. Within a year, Eisenhower had generated an agenda of proposals for Congress to consider.[62] Likewise, George Bush was criticized during his bid for reelection for having offered Congress and the American public little in the way of a domestic legislative agenda.

A second example of how external expectations become institutionalized, and thereby constrain presidential behavior, can be found in the president's annual State of the Union message. The Constitution requires the president "from time to time to give to the Congress Information of the State of the Union," but it does not stipulate how the president is to deliver the message. Every president from Thomas Jefferson through William Howard Taft presented the State of the Union message to Congress in the form of a letter. Woodrow Wilson, however, revived the practice of George Washington and John Adams and delivered the State of the Union address in a speech before a joint session of Congress. The practice of delivering the State of the Union address in a speech to Congress is now so ingrained that it is unthinkable that a president would return to the practice of delivering it in a letter.[63] Indeed, Congress, the media, interest groups, and the public now expect the president to use the State of the Union speech to spell out a vision for the country's future.

As the examples of presidential proposals to Congress and speeches on the State of the Union show, institutionalized expectations constrain the discretion of the presidency. The expectations of Congress, the news media, and the public all impose political accountability on the White House and direct the president's efforts toward some activities and away from others. Without institutionalized expectations and the criticisms that arise when they are violated, fewer checks would limit the power of the presidency and presidents would have greater opportunity, as the founders feared, to abuse their power.

As you can see, then, the workings of the presidency have become increasingly complex as the presidency has grown in size, structure, and power. Within this more complex environment, presidents still try to use the factors they can control—such as defining the functions of an agency, establishing a management style, and influencing the role that staff members play—to enhance their power. At the same time, factors outside the presidents' control—such as the expectations and unwritten rules created by others in the American political system—curb their power and help prevent presidents and their staffs from abusing it. Over time, there is a constant push and pull as presidents push for power, and other political actors rein presidential power back in.

Assessing the Presidency as an Institution

Just as changes in the rules governing the presidential selection process have increased the power and personal nature of the presidency, changes in the institution of the presidency have also tended to make the modern presidency a more individualized and influential office.

For the most part, the changes that have taken place in the presidency as an institution have increased the power of the president. By adopting the Stewardship Model of presidential authority and boldly acting in ways not expressly prohibited by the Constitution or statutory law, modern presidents have increased their power. The organizational structure of the presidency has become much larger and more complex, and as a result, presidents have had more staff to help them pursue their goals. Finally, the workings of the presidency reflect a more powerful and personalized modern institution. Because modern presidents have loyal staffs to help them win support and advance their more aggressive personal and policy goals, they are more likely to achieve these goals.

Still, despite the empowerment of the modern presidency, several forces constrain presidential power, including constitutional rules, statutory laws, the courts, and informal rules embodied in the expectations of the public and other political actors. Although modern presidents reach—and sometimes overreach—for power, and the flexible rules of the American political system allow them to do so, the rules also work to rectify past abuses of presidential power and to prevent future abuses.

The office of the presidency, then, is a dynamic, continually changing institution, marked by a tension between empowerment and constraint. Although the office of the presidency has gained influence over the past two hundred years and especially over the past sixty, the balance of power is by no means set in stone. Each new president has the opportunity to test the limits of presidential authority, just as other political actors are free to challenge the president's authority. Because presidents do not operate in a vacuum but must instead deal with other government officials, interest groups, and the broader public, we need to look at the place the presidency occupies within the American political system.

The Presidency in American Politics

Thus far in our discussion of the presidency, we have focused on the office of the presidency itself. Now that we have seen how the presidency has evolved, how the rules of the presidential selection process have changed, and how rules and circumstances have

An important feature of the modern presidency is the insistent demand that the president take the lead in developing solutions to the nation's problems. However, it is equally true that those demanding leadership do not necessarily feel obliged to follow the president's suggestions. This can cause serious conflict within the government.

Mike Keefe, *The Denver Post.* Reprinted by permission.

changed the institution of the presidency, let's draw back and examine the presidency against the broader background of the rest of the American political system. We can see how the modern presidency fits into the larger political system by focusing on the political context within which presidents operate, the strategies they use to achieve their goals, and their relations with other political actors.

The Political Context: Permanent Crisis

Modern presidents operate within a political context that has been called a "permanent crisis."[64] As the presidency has gained power and prominence over the past sixty years, the American public has come to look to the president to address pressing national problems, and it expects the president to produce quick, effective, and even painless solutions. At the same time, presidents face constraints that make it difficult to find and implement solutions. Not only may Congress and the American public balk at following the president's lead, but time and institutional constraints frequently hamper presidential efforts to address national problems.

Conflicting Expectations of Leadership: Initiative and Responsiveness

One of the most important developments of the modern era has been the emergence of the presidency as the primary focus of American society's expectations for leadership. Whenever a problem claims the country's attention, we expect the president to find a solution. Congress, the federal bureaucracy, interest groups, and the public all look to the president to set the course for the nation.

But while Americans look to the White House for leadership, we are by no means obligated to follow the president's lead. Indeed, one of the most serious obstacles presidents face is that people urge them to lead but often refuse to follow. While we want presidents to produce bold and timely initiatives, we also expect them to protect our interests when devising solutions to the nation's problems. For example, when Bill Clinton took office, a majority of the public believed that the nation's health care system was in crisis—costs were skyrocketing, and millions of Americans had no health insurance. Many on Capitol Hill and elsewhere urged the president to find a solution. The president made health care reform the centerpiece of his legislative agenda, and he placed the first lady, Hillary Rodham Clinton, in charge of developing a reform proposal. Once the president made his proposal public, however, dozens of groups attacked it and members of Congress offered competing plans. Despite the administration's intensive efforts, Congress refused to pass its health care proposal.[65] As Clinton's experience shows, presidents at times find it very difficult to meet the conflicting expectations others place on them.

Presidents try to "hit the ground running"—that is, to quickly enact their agenda with Congress—because midterm elections usually produce a new, less supportive Congress. The Republicans' 1994 victory forced Clinton to respond to their agenda instead of pushing for adoption of his own initiatives.

Reprinted by permission: Tribune Media Services.

Time Constraints

Not only must presidents address a host of important issues, but they must also do so within a relatively brief period of time. Presidents cannot afford the luxury of making long-term plans. Rather, they must move quickly to generate concrete results that meet the expectations of Congress, the bureaucracy, interest groups, and, most important, the American voters. This combination of insistent demands and limited time creates the sense of permanent crisis in the White House.

Modern presidents want to hit the ground running when they first enter office.[66] They usually (but not always) enjoy a "honeymoon" period for the first several months of their term as Congress, the press, and the public defer somewhat to their leadership. Yet after the first **One Hundred Days**—a benchmark chosen largely because at that point in Franklin Roosevelt's first term Congress had passed a substantial portion of his New Deal legislation—presidents typically find Congress, journalists, and the public judging their presidency. As presidents enter their second year in office, they face even greater pressure to enact their legislative program. The reason is that the president's party usually loses seats in Congress in the **midterm elections**—that is, the congressional elections held at the midpoint of a four-year presidential term—and, as a result, Congress generally becomes even less willing to follow the president's lead. For example, in 1994, the Democrats lost control of both the House and Senate, and the Republicans who took control of Capitol Hill were hostile to most of President Clinton's legislative agenda. By the fourth year, both the president and Congress are looking to the next election, further diminishing their incentive to cooperate. Should a president be reelected, his fifth and sixth years may provide a modest echo of the opportunities of the first two, but the last two years are spent as a "lame duck," defending achievements from the attacks of Congress. In short, even when presidents succeed in serving for eight years, the political winds are often unfavorable much of the time.[67]

One Hundred Days
A benchmark period for assessing a new president's performance, based on the first three months of Franklin Roosevelt's presidency, when he gained passage of more than a dozen major bills as part of his New Deal agenda.

Midterm elections
The congressional elections that take place midway through a president's four-year term.

Institutional Constraints

Presidents contending with the public's demands for action and the limits time imposes must also contend with the institutional constraints the Constitution imposes. Although we have emphasized throughout this chapter the gradually growing scope of presidential authority, we must always view this power against the larger backdrop of our constitutional rules. Only in certain limited circumstances can presidents act independently to accomplish their aims. Our system of shared powers means that presidents must gain the cooperation of others—Congress, the bureaucracy, and interest groups—if they are to succeed in translating their vision of good public policy into reality.

Cooperation is often not forthcoming because presidents frequently have goals and perspectives different from those of members of Congress, bureaucrats, and interest groups. Presidents possess a uniquely national orientation. Their national electoral constituency

Presidents possess many resources they can use to bargain for the support of members of Congress. This Doonesbury cartoon pokes fun at President Clinton for the perception that widespread "wheeling and dealing" took place to win congressional support for the North American Free Trade Agreement (NAFTA) in 1993.

Doonesbury BY GARRY TRUDEAU

forces them to address problems from a national perspective. In contrast, each member of Congress sees problems in terms of their impact on his or her local constituency; agencies see issues through the prism of their particular mission; and interest groups advocate their specific needs and wishes without regard to national agendas. Only presidents must contend with the wide range of issues seeking space in the set of national priorities. To meet the demands placed on them as a national leader confronted by these many constraints, modern presidents have developed strategies for advancing their political agendas.

Presidential Strategies

Scholars have identified two strategies that presidents use in their efforts to provide national leadership: bargaining and going public.

The Bargaining Strategy

Bargaining strategy
Direct negotiations the White House conducts with other political actors, such as members of Congress and leaders of interest groups, that attempt to reach mutually beneficial agreements.

Presidents try to influence other political actors by bargaining for their support. To make this **bargaining strategy** effective, presidents must be good negotiators skilled at interpersonal relations and able to construct supportive coalitions with leaders in Congress, the federal bureaucracy, and interest groups. A president who can persuade political actors with conflicting aims and desires to support his or her programs is more likely to succeed than one who cannot. Often, part of the persuasive process means promising groups some benefit or favor in return for their support, or threatening to use presidential powers (such as the veto power) if they try to pass legislation the administration opposes.[68]

Presidents are more likely to succeed in their bargaining strategy when they possess a reputation for being an effective leader. Presidents acquire such a reputation when their past behavior instills confidence among their supporters and fear among their opponents. Congress, the bureaucracy, interest groups, and the public are much more likely to follow the lead of a president with a string of policy successes than the lead of a president with a string of policy failures. Put another way, success tends to breed success for the White House. Presidents are also helped in their bargaining when they are personally popular with the public, because popular support enhances the legitimacy of their claim to national leadership.[69] Presidents can use high public approval ratings to argue that they have the public's confidence and support, and, thus, that Congress should follow their lead.

The Going Public Strategy

As we saw in previous chapters, by the 1970s, congressional authority had become fragmented among dozens of subcommittees and the number of interest groups had

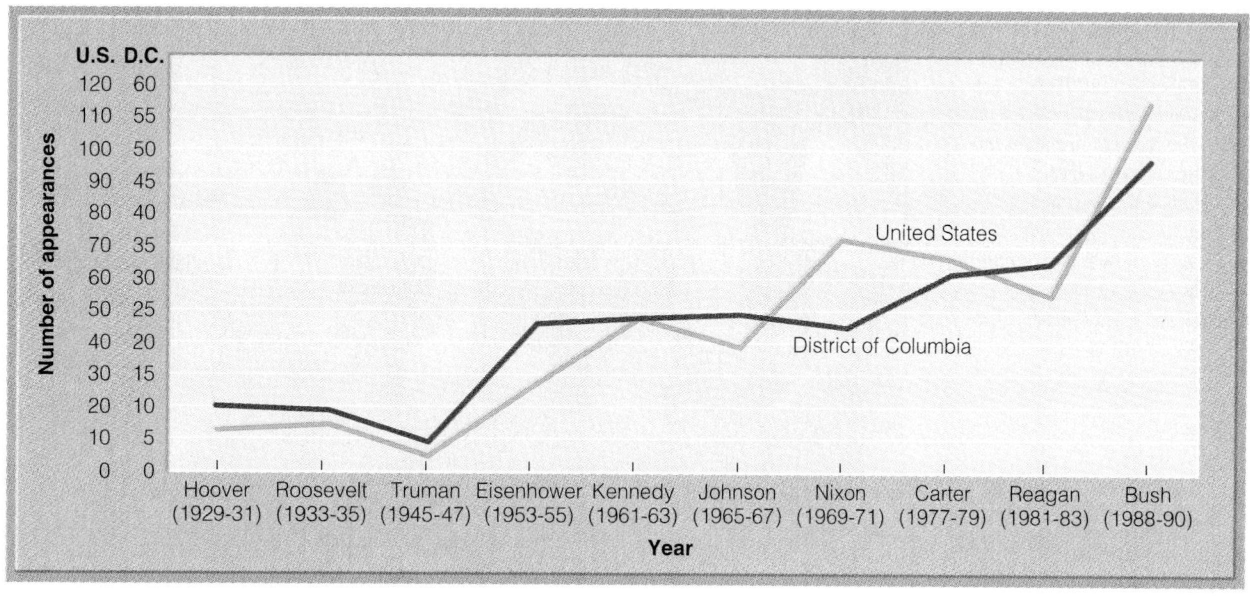

FIGURE 12.9
Presidential Public Appearances, 1929–1990 (yearly averages for first three years of first term)

Presidents have increasingly turned to the public to support their agendas. As a result, the number of presidential public appearances has grown through the era of the modern presidency.

Samuel Kernell, *Going Public: New Strategies of Presidential Leadership*, 2d ed. Copyright © 1993 CQ Press, Washington, D.C. Reprinted by permission.

exploded. Because these changes made it harder to build coalitions to support legislation, presidents have begun to try to win support for their policies by using a **going public strategy,** that is, by appealing directly to the American people.[70] Of special importance to the going public strategy is mass communications technology. To build support for their policies, presidents frequently give televised addresses to the nation, hold news conferences, or grant interviews to journalists. Presidents also pursue the going public strategy by traveling around the country giving speeches to major organizations and by meeting with representatives of groups the policies in question are likely to affect. Figure 12.9 describes the trend toward an increased number of presidential public appearances. By going public, presidents hope to mobilize public support, which, in turn, will put pressure on Congress to pass their proposals.

Going public strategy
Direct presidential appeals to the public for support. Presidents use public support to pressure other political actors to accept their policies.

Of course, presidents may combine the bargaining and going public strategies, appealing to the public for support while bargaining with key leaders in Congress and among interest groups. Ronald Reagan, for example, relied heavily on public support to build momentum for his program of tax and budget cuts in 1981, but he also bargained with members of Congress to build majorities in both houses.[71] Bill Clinton also combined the bargaining and going public strategies in his successful 1993 effort to persuade Congress to pass the North American Free Trade Agreement. While Vice President Al Gore went on the *Larry King Show* to debate the merits of the agreement with Ross Perot, Clinton and his aides cut deals with members of Congress who claimed to be undecided over whether to support the accord.

Presidential Relationships

Presidents work with many groups both in and out of government to achieve their goals. Modern presidents must maintain particularly good relationships with other political actors; they cannot rely as heavily on party loyalty to gain support for their programs as their predecessors did. To achieve their goals and retain their stature as national leaders, presidents must maintain good relations with Congress, the American public, and the bureaucracy.

Presidents must communicate and negotiate with the leaders of Congress to fulfill their role in the legislative process, even when the leaders are from the opposition party. Here, President Clinton and Vice President Gore meet with Speaker Gingrich and Senate Majority Leader Dole to discuss the 1996 budget.

Presidents and Congress

As we discussed earlier, modern presidents are expected to play the role of chief legislator by presenting a package of legislative proposals to Congress. This power to propose legislation is one of the presidency's most important powers because it helps presidents to set Congress's legislative agenda. Presidents use both bargaining and going public strategies to form coalitions and win congressional support. Whether Congress enacts a president's proposals, however, depends heavily on the relationship between the president and Congress.

The most important influence on a president's relationship with Congress is whether the president's party is the majority party in Congress. This is important for two reasons. First, as we saw in chapter 11, members of Congress are more likely to vote with members of their own party and against members of the opposition party. Even though presidents cannot count on total party loyalty, when the president's party is the majority party, the president's legislative agenda is more likely to win congressional support.[72] Second, when the president's party is the majority party in Congress, it controls the legislative process. As we also saw in chapter 11, control of the legislative process gives the majority party a decided advantage in passing the legislation it favors. In contrast, when **divided government** exists—that is, when the opposition party controls at least one house of Congress—presidential proposals are much less likely to make their way through Congress. In addition, presidents faced with divided government must spend more of their time opposing the agenda of the opposition party, usually a difficult and time-consuming task.[73]

Divided government
When the president is of one party and the other party has a majority in at least one house of Congress.

The contrast between Clinton's first two years in office, during which he faced a Democratic majority in Congress, and his second two years, when he confronted a Republican majority, illustrates why presidents prefer to avoid divided government. Although Clinton lost his bid to revamp the nation's health care system, he still recommended and Congress enacted a wide range of bills during his first two years in office. By early 1995, however, he was nearly a forgotten man as Speaker of the House Gingrich and the new Republican majority in Congress took center stage. Even though Clinton subsequently assumed greater prominence by vetoing Republican legislation and thereby forced congressional Republicans to negotiate with him, he clearly lost the aura of leadership and initiative that marked his first two years.

Although members of Congress frequently criticize and oppose presidential proposals, most presidents still secure passage of a substantial portion of their agenda.[74] We cannot assess with certainty how much influence presidents exert on the legislative process on Capitol Hill, but no one doubts that every president will continue to act as a key agenda setter and chief lobbyist for bills sent to Congress.

Presidents and the Public

Because the public eye has focused increasingly on the president as national leader over the past sixty years, presidents must develop good relations with the public. Advances in modern mass communications have enabled today's presidents to appeal directly to the public, and presidents regularly use their ready access to the news media to try to shape the public's interpretation of important events.[75] Presidents also have created elaborate structures within the office of the presidency to help them deal with the public. All presidents now employ public opinion polling experts to recognize and interpret the public's views, and they also employ speech writers and media consultants to help them cultivate the proper image with the public.[76]

Despite concerted efforts to maintain popularity with the American public, figure 12.10 shows that most presidents experience declining popularity over the course of their four-year terms, although their popularity does tend to rebound somewhat in the fourth year as the next election approaches. Two factors help contribute to this pattern of decline. First, presidents begin their terms with an exaggerated sense of public support. The public, including many who voted for the other candidate, rallies around a new president, giving the president the benefit of the doubt and hoping for the best. This behavior contributes to the honeymoon effect described earlier, and quickly disappears once the president begins to act on the promises made during the campaign. A second reason for decline is an "expectations gap" that develops as the president's term proceeds.[77] During the campaign, candidates overpromise to attract votes. Once in office, the winners decide that they either should not or cannot deliver on their promises, and so they fail to meet the expectations of those who supported them. President Clinton, for instance, promised during the 1992 campaign to end a blockade that prevented Haitian refugees from entering the United States. Once in office, he decided he had been in error and continued the blockade.[78] Clinton was also unable to end the ban on gays in the military or reform health care as he had promised to do during the 1992 campaign.[79]

Presidents care so much about their public image because, as we have seen, greater popularity often means greater influence on Capitol Hill. To be sure, popularity does not guarantee that presidents will get their way in Congress.[80] For example, even though George Bush's public approval rating at the close of the Gulf War stood briefly at 89 percent, the highest approval rating recorded since modern polling began, Congress still rejected his personal appeal on behalf of a high-priority housing bill.[81] Although public popularity does not always translate into political power, presidents who have little public support lose much of their ability to lead Congress, the federal bureaucracy, and the American people.

Presidents and the Federal Bureaucracy

Presidents must not only cultivate good relations with Congress and the public, they must also persuade the federal bureaucracy to support and implement their programs. Although we often think of the president as the "head" or director of the federal bureaucracy, in reality, the president cannot command the obedience of agencies in the executive branch. As we shall discuss at greater length in the next chapter, presidents must share their authority over the federal bureaucracy with Congress and the courts. As a result, presidents must bargain with and persuade agencies to do their bidding, all the while competing with the conflicting demands Congress, the courts, and interest groups place on the bureaucracy.

Presidents use a number of resources to influence the behavior of the federal bureaucracy.[82] First, presidents are responsible for appointing the heads of federal agencies, and they usually try to appoint people who share their political preferences. Second, presidents influence agencies through their budget-making power. Because presidents can recommend that Congress cut or increase spending for an agency, every agency has an incentive to heed the wishes of the White House. Third, presidents have some authority to reorganize the structures and duties of federal agencies. Finally, presidents can issue an **executive order** that directs a federal agency to take some specific action. Although Congress has the power to block each of these four moves, presidents usually can force a federal agency to obey their wishes *if* they are willing to devote time and effort to the issue.

Executive order
A presidential directive to an agency of the federal government that tells the agency to take some specified action.

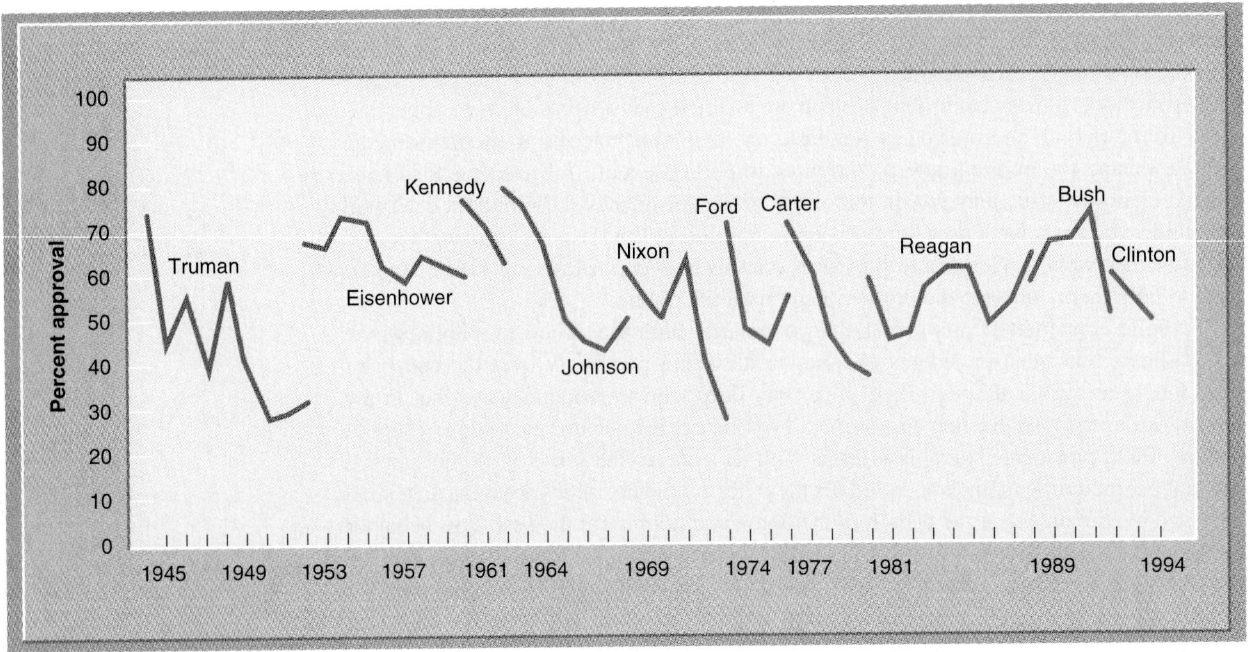

FIGURE 12.10
Public Annual Average Approval Rating of the President, 1945–1994

Most presidents experience declining levels of public approval over the course of their term due to artificially high initial levels of support and high public expectations that most presidents fail to fulfill. This gives presidents an incentive to accomplish their goals early in their terms.

Source: Lyn Ragsdale, *Vital Statistics on the Presidency: Washington to Clinton*, Copyright © 1996. Congressional Quarterly, Inc., Washington, D.C.

In practice, however, presidents usually find that the overwhelming nature of their workload prevents them from concentrating their attention on a single federal agency for any sustained period of time. And as presidential interest in an agency wanes, that agency's responsiveness to presidential wishes erodes.[83] Moreover, when confronted with criticism that it has failed to comply with the preferences of the White House, a federal agency typically can blame its failure on its need to respond to political pressure from other political actors such as Congress and interest group clienteles. In short, presidents must compete for control of the federal bureaucracy.

As we have seen, then, modern presidents frequently cannot exercise their powers independently of the rest of government; all their actions take place in a political system characterized by shared powers and conflicting priorities. The expectations we place on modern presidents—to take bold initiatives, but respond to our desires; to act quickly and decisively; and to work within the rules and boundaries laid down in the Constitution—create a permanent atmosphere of crisis. Presidents respond by adopting strategies that help them manage political conflict and meet the expectations of national leadership; they bargain with other actors in the political system, and they appeal to the public to mobilize support for their programs. To make these strategies effective, presidents must maintain positive relationships with Congress, the federal bureaucracy, and the public.

Thus, while changing rules and norms have empowered the presidency and brought the president prominence as a national leader, they have also limited the way presidents perform their roles. The ambivalence of the founders is still present today; the presidency is shaped by rules that infuse it with power, yet constrain its ability to act.

SUMMARY

The United States has a president because early Americans discovered through their experience with the Articles of Confederation that the federal government could not function well without one. Yet in recognizing the need for a president, the founders worried about vesting too much power in any one individual or branch of government. As a result, the structural rules set forth in the Constitution try to balance the need for executive leadership with protections against tyranny. Thus, while the Constitution gives the president specific or enumerated powers to act, the founders also checked the ability of presidents to act by sharing many of these powers with the other two branches of government.

Yet the president's role in American politics has been defined not only by the structural rules of the office, but also by the actions of the forty-one men who have served in the White House. In keeping with the expectations of the founders, most eighteenth- and nineteenth-century presidents were fairly passive executives, reacting to Congress rather than leading it. All that changed when Franklin Roosevelt assumed office in 1933. FDR established the modern presidency with his forceful national leadership during the Great Depression and World War II. All of FDR's successors have felt compelled to fill the role of national leader.

Just as the president's role in American politics has changed over the past two hundred years, so has the presidential selection process. Initially, the parties in Congress controlled the nomination stage, but by the 1830s, state parties had gained the upper hand and selected candidates at their national conventions. In the 1970s, the increased use of primaries diminished the parties' role, giving greater control to the candidates themselves and the people who voted in the primary elections. The general election process has also changed significantly. The rise of television has given candidates even more control over their campaigns, and campaign finance laws have failed to limit the growth in campaign spending. The one aspect of the presidential selection process that has not changed is the electoral college. As has been the case for two centuries, the unit rule and majority rule determine how the outcome of the popular vote will translate into votes in the electoral college, and, as a result, which candidate wins the presidency.

The institution of the presidency has also changed in three important ways since George Washington was president. First, the powers of the presidency have grown. Because the Constitution defines the powers of the presidency in relatively vague terms, presidents have been able to interpret the rules in ways that expand their authority. Second, as the federal government has grown larger and more complex, and the expectations for presidential leadership have grown as well, the institution of the presidency has evolved from a small, informal organization into the Executive Office of the President (EOP), a larger, more formal organization employing some two thousand people. Third, the way presidents work in office has changed. The growing size and complexity of the presidency has forced presidents into a more hierarchical, pyramidal style of management, and whereas presidents once expected staff members in the EOP to provide neutral competence, they now expect those staff members to work on behalf of their programs. Although these developments have tended to enhance presidential power, a rising tide of expectations about what presidents are supposed to accomplish has tended to constrain presidential power.

In discharging their responsibilities and attempting to fulfill the expectations of Congress and the public, presidents operate within a political context that has been described as permanent crisis. Because the presidency has gained power and prominence since the days of Franklin Roosevelt, the American public now looks to the White House for answers to pressing national problems. But the increase in presidential power and the public's high expectations for the president have not changed one fundamental structural reality about American politics: presidents still share many of the powers of government with Congress, the bureaucracy, and the courts. Presidents can bargain with members of Congress and appeal directly to the public to support their programs, but they cannot compel obedience from Capitol Hill or even federal agencies. In the end, presidents often must rely on their powers of persuasion to accomplish their policy goals.

Key Terms

Bargaining strategy
Caucus
Central legislative clearance
Divided government
Electoral college
Enumerated powers
Executive order
Frontloading
Going public strategy
Impeachment
Implied powers
Independent expenditures
Midterm elections
Neutral competence
One Hundred Days
Pocket veto
Progressive movement
Soft money
Unit rule

Readings for Further Study

Jamieson, Kathleen Hall. *Packaging the Presidency: A History and Criticism of Presidential Campaign Advertising,* 2d ed. New York: Oxford University Press, 1992. An informed and informative blow-by-blow account of advertising developments and their effects in every presidential election from 1952 through 1988.

Jones, Charles O. *The Presidency in a Separated System.* Washington, D.C.: Brookings Institution, 1994. An award-winning discussion of the limited potential for presidential leadership. Jones contrasts the common perception of a powerful office with the realities that hem in the presidency on all sides.

Kernell, Samuel. *Going Public: New Strategies of Presidential Leadership,* 3d ed. Washington, D.C.: CQ Press, 1997. The most authoritative revision of the Neustadt model of presidential influence. Kernell argues that presidents increasingly rely on public support rather than personal bargaining to achieve their goals in government.

Milkis, Sidney M., and Michael Nelson. *The American Presidency: Origins and Development, 1776–1993,* 2d ed. Washington, D.C.: CQ Press, 1994. A concise yet remarkably complete review of the historical development of the presidency from Washington through Bush.

Nathan, Richard P. *The Administrative Presidency.* New York: Macmillan, 1986. Originally published as a case study of the Nixon presidency, the current version demonstrates more generally how presidents can use the administrative powers of their office to achieve policy goals even when Congress rejects their legislative initiatives.

Neustadt, Richard. *Presidential Power and the Modern Presidents.* New York: Free Press, 1990. The definitive starting point for any discussion of the modern presidency. A must read for any serious student of the institution.

Polsby, Nelson W., and Aaron Wildavsky. *Presidential Elections,* 9th ed. Chatham, N.J.: Chatham House, 1996. The authoritative treatment of presidential elections in the modern era. It encompasses virtually every facet of elections and how they have evolved over the past forty years.

Chapter

13

The Federal Bureaucracy

What Is Bureaucracy?

The Structure and Tasks of the Federal Bureaucracy

Types of Federal Agencies

The Tasks of the Federal Bureaucracy

Development of the Federal Bureaucracy

Constitutional Foundations

The Growth of the Federal Bureaucracy

The Expanding Functions of the Federal Bureaucracy

Changes in the Federal Bureaucracy's Personnel System

The Politics of the Federal Bureaucracy

The Political Character of the Federal Bureaucracy

The Goals of the Federal Bureaucracy

The Political Resources of the Federal Bureaucracy

Political Constraints on the Federal Bureaucracy

Iron Triangles and the Federal Bureaucracy

The Evolving Role of the Bureaucracy

Reinventing the Federal Bureaucracy

Summary

Key Terms

Readings for Further Study

Since the 1960s, the Food and Drug Administration (FDA) has required pharmaceutical companies to demonstrate both the safety and effectiveness of any new drug before doctors can prescribe it to the general public. The FDA had traditionally been encouraged to "go slow"; we would rather have the FDA take a long time making sure drugs are safe and effective than to have unsafe or ineffective drugs make it through the system undetected.[1] As a result, by the 1980s, drug testing had become an expensive process that usually took several years to complete. But then an odd thing happened: the length of time the FDA took to test drugs began to plummet. In 1987, the average new drug took almost three years to test. By 1992, that average had fallen by almost one-half, to nineteen months. And for drugs tested in a special drug approval program created in 1993, the rate was down to 13.5 months.[2]

What caused the FDA to change its behavior so dramatically? The answer lies not in the discovery of new technologies or in a natural drive within the FDA for greater efficiency. Rather, the FDA changed its behavior because it found itself facing political pressure to balance its concern for safety with the awareness that each day spent testing a new drug deprives patients of its potentially beneficial, even life-saving effects. In the mid-1980s, interest groups representing people with Acquired Immune Deficiency Syndrome (AIDS) attacked the FDA for taking too long to approve new medicines. These activists were joined by Ronald Reagan and members of Congress, who had pledged to reduce government regulation of American industry, and by the pharmaceutical industry, which wanted to speed the testing process so it could get new drugs to market faster and start generating revenues.[3] Although the FDA (and much of the medical community) initially resisted political pressure to speed up the drug approval process, in the end, the agency gave patients with life-threatening diseases greater access to experimental drugs and dramatically shortened the time required to test new drugs.

Bureaucracy
In general usage, the set of government agencies that carries out government policies. The bureaucracy is characterized by formalized structures, specialized duties, a hierarchical system of authority, routine record-keeping, and a permanent staff.

In our study of political institutions, we have repeatedly made the point that institutions both shape and are shaped by the rules of American politics. As the FDA policy on experimental drugs demonstrates, the **bureaucracy** is no exception. The experience of the FDA highlights three important lessons about the place of the federal bureaucracy in American politics. The first is that the bureaucracy helps shape the nation's policy rules. Federal agencies administer government policy, and the decisions they make greatly affect our lives. Indeed, most of the direct contact Americans have with the federal government is with the bureaucracy rather than Congress or the president. When Americans mail their income tax returns to the Internal Revenue Service, receive a check from the Social Security Administration, or visit a national park maintained by the National Park Service, they are dealing with federal agencies, and they are affected by the policy rules those agencies create.

If the experience of the FDA reminds us that the federal bureaucracy helps determine the rules that affect our everyday lives, it also teaches us a second lesson about the bureaucracy: the rules of American politics affect the bureaucracy. In our system, the president, Congress, the courts, interest groups, and the public all possess some degree of political power. Because the rules empower citizens to protest, interest groups to lobby, and the president and Congress to exert pressure on the bureaucracy, the FDA responded to the combined efforts of AIDS activists, President Reagan, members of Congress, and the pharmaceutical industry. The bureaucracy's powers are limited by the constitutional rules that disperse power among other groups.

But by no means is the bureaucracy simply a mindless tool in the hands of Congress, the president, or the courts. These other political actors may sketch out the broad outlines of government policy, but the bureaucracy fills in the details. And because it has the discretion to make and implement rules—to decide who wins or loses in conflicts over government policies and services—the bureaucracy possesses political power. This leads us to the third lesson the FDA example has to offer: the bureaucracy is a political institution. Political pressures—such as the organization of AIDS activists, the election of a president who pledges to cut bureaucratic red tape, and an industry with a vested interest in reforming an agency—affect the bureaucracy, and the bureaucracy's actions affect the political environment. To understand the federal bureaucracy, then, it is crucial to understand its political nature.

We begin our study of the role of the federal bureaucracy in American politics by defining the characteristics that distinguish a bureaucracy from other forms of political organization. We go on to examine the structure and tasks of the federal bureaucracy, showing how the agencies in the federal bureaucracy make and implement rules. We then discuss the evolution of the bureaucracy—how changes in society and in the rules of government have shaped the size, functions, and hiring practices of the federal bureaucracy over the course of American history. Finally, we discuss the political character of the federal bureaucracy, focusing on its goals, its political resources, and the constraints others place on its power. We analyze some of the typical patterns of cooperation that develop among federal agencies, the congressional committees they report to, and the interest groups they affect.

We conclude the chapter by asking a question—can we "reinvent" the federal bureaucracy to meet the demands of the twenty-first century? An increasingly diverse society presents government with an increasingly diverse—and often conflicting—list of demands. Whether the bureaucracy can successfully manage and respond to the growing expectations of the American public depends on the rules government sets for the bureaucracy and the bureaucracy's ability to shape effective new rules for the future.

In the past decade, the time the FDA takes to test and approve new drugs has dropped dramatically in response to pressures from a diverse range of actors, including presidents Reagan and Bush, Congress, the pharmaceutical industry, and AIDS activists. The FDA's sensitivity to these pressures demonstrates the political character of the bureaucracy.

What Is Bureaucracy?

Americans often have unkind things to say about government bureaucracy. They tend to see it as "overstaffed, inflexible, unresponsive, and power-hungry, all at once," and they see its employees, known as **bureaucrats,** as "lazy, snarling, or both."[4] Jokes about bureaucratic ineptitude are a staple on late-night television talk shows, as comedians such as Jay Leno and David Letterman draw huge laughs lampooning bureaucrats for such misadventures as taking fourteen pages to lay out the recipe for making fruit cake.[5] And Americans regularly complain that the federal bureaucracy wastes their tax dollars and drowns the country in a sea of bureaucratic red tape.[6]

Bureaucrats
A term used generally to identify anyone who works within a large, formal organization. More specifically, it refers to career civil service employees of the government.

Yet for all the jokes and complaints about bureaucratic ineptitude, bureaucracy is an inescapable part of modern government. The United States is simply too large and the issues too complex for Congress and the president to run the country themselves. They must create other agencies to administer the policy decisions they reach—to carry out the rules.

But what precisely distinguishes a bureaucracy from other forms of political organization? The great German sociologist, Max Weber (1864–1920), defined the ideal, or model, bureaucracy as an organization that possesses five distinctive characteristics:[7]

1. *Specialization*—The organization has a well-defined division of labor. Jobs are divided up and assigned to subsidiary groups within the organization that have expertise in that particular task.

2. *Hierarchy*—The organization has a clear chain of command in which workers are arranged in order of rank or authority.

3. *Formality*—The organization has a formal set of rules and procedures to ensure that it performs its duties in a consistent manner.

4. *Record-keeping*—The organization retains written records of its decisions and actions.

5. *Professionalization*—The organization is staffed with full-time career workers who are paid a regular salary and hired and promoted on the basis of their competence.

Americans often complain that the federal bureaucracy is overstaffed and unresponsive, but bureaucrats perform important tasks for the American people.

AUTH © The *Philadelphia Inquirer*. Reprinted with permission of UNIVERSAL PRESS SYNDICATE. All rights reserved.

The many agencies that make up the federal bureaucracy generally exhibit most of the characteristics Weber identified as typical of the ideal bureaucracy. Virtually all federal agencies are permanent organizations in which workers are assigned to different levels in the organizational hierarchy on the basis of the authority they wield. Almost all federal agencies follow well-developed rules and procedures in performing their specialized tasks, and they are required by law to keep detailed records of their actions. Finally, most federal employees today are permanent, career-oriented people who are, in principle, hired, compensated, and promoted on the basis of merit.

The Structure and Tasks of the Federal Bureaucracy

Although the agencies that make up the federal bureaucracy generally share the five characteristic features that Weber identified with bureaucracy, they vary widely in terms of their organizational forms and duties. Some federal agencies are huge and actually are composed of hundreds of subsidiary agencies, bureaus, and offices; others are so small they have very few subunits. While some federal agencies are responsible for national security matters, others deal with health, economic, or safety issues. Despite these differences, all federal agencies perform three general tasks: they administer the rules of public policy, develop new rules as the need arises, and determine when their rules have been broken or their procedures ignored.

Types of Federal Agencies

The agencies that make up the federal bureaucracy vary widely in organizational structure, size, and responsibility. Figure 13.1 gives examples of the four main kinds of organizations within the federal bureaucracy: executive departments, independent regulatory commissions, government corporations, and independent agencies.

Executive Departments

Executive departments are the primary form of organization in the federal bureaucracy; in 1997, the United States had fourteen executive departments in all. Executive departments were the first bureaucratic organizations Congress created, and they continue to carry out most of the federal government's responsibilities. Executive departments are hierarchically organized, and they are headed by a single individual, usually known as the secretary. Thus, the person in charge of the Defense Department is known as the

EXECUTIVE DEPARTMENTS

State, Treasury, Defense, Justice, Interior, Agriculture, Commerce, Labor, Health and Human Services, Housing and Urban Development, Transportation, Energy, Education, Veterans Affairs

INDEPENDENT AGENCIES*

Environmental Protection Agency, Federal Emergency Management Agency, General Services Administration, National Aeronautics & Space Administration, Office of Personnel Management, Peace Corps, Small Business Administration, U.S. Information Agency, U.S. Arms Control and Disarmament Agency, Merit Systems Protection Board

INDEPENDENT REGULATORY COMMISSIONS*

Federal Communications Commission, Federal Maritime Commission, Federal Reserve Board, Federal Trade Commission, National Labor Relations Board, Securities and Exchange Commission, Consumer Product Safety Commission, Commodity Futures Trading Commission, Nuclear Regulatory Commission, Federal Election Commission, Equal Employment Opportunity Commission, Occupational Health and Safety Review Commission

GOVERNMENT CORPORATIONS*

Federal Deposit Insurance Corporation, Export-Import Bank of the United States, Tennessee Valley Authority, Federal Financing Bank, Inter-American Foundation

* Principal examples of agencies within this category

FIGURE 13.1
Organization of the National Bureaucracy

This description of the principal agencies of the federal bureaucracy illustrates the wide range of activities the federal government is involved in.

Source: Adapted and updated from Harold Seidman and Robert Gilmour, *Politics, Position and Power*, 4th ed. (New York: Oxford University Press, 1986), pp. 254–57; The United States Government Manual, 1994/95 (Washington, D.C.: Office of the Federal Register, 1994), pp. vi–vii.

secretary of defense, and the person in charge of the State Department is known as the secretary of state. The secretaries of defense and state, like the secretaries of all other executive departments, are appointed by the president with the **advice and consent** of the Senate, which means that a majority of the Senate must approve, or confirm, the president's choice. The president also has the power to fire the secretary of an executive department, and as we saw in chapter 12, the Senate has no say over whether to remove the secretary of an executive department from his or her post.

Advice and consent
Refers to the provision in Article II of the Constitution that requires the president to gain the Senate's approval of appointees to a variety of government positions.

The secretaries of the fourteen executive departments in the federal bureaucracy, along with other key government officials, make up the **cabinet,** a group that, in theory, advises the president on all aspects of public policy. In practice, however, most presidents make little use of the cabinet as a source of advice, preferring instead to rely on the White House staff. Although the cabinet tends to have little impact on presidential decision making, the fact that an executive department has cabinet-level status is important. Being a member of the cabinet gives secretaries greater stature in Washington politics, stature they can use as a political resource to advance the interests of their departments.[8]

Cabinet
An informal designation that refers to the collective body of individuals appointed by the president to head the executive departments. The cabinet can, but rarely does, function as an advisory body to the president.

As a result of their great size, executive departments consist of dozens and even hundreds of subsidiary agencies, bureaus, and offices, each of which handles some small part of the department's responsibilities. To give you a sense of what these subsidiary agencies do and how they fit into the overall organization of a department, figure 13.2 presents the organizational chart for the Department of the Treasury. As you can see from the figure, which is actually a simplified view of how the department is organized, the secretary of the treasury oversees a wide array of different agencies, bureaus, and offices, including the U.S. Mint, the Bureau of Alcohol, Tobacco, and Firearms, the Secret Service, the Office of the Comptroller of the Currency, and the Internal Revenue Service. In turn, the responsibilities of the many subsidiary agencies in the Department of the Treasury span the policy spectrum, ranging from domestic

The president's cabinet consists of the secretaries of the government's fourteen executive departments and other designated officials. While the cabinet seldom serves as an important source of advice, its individual members are often close confidants of the president. The prestige of cabinet rank also assists cabinet members in their political conflicts.

matters such as tax policy and corporate finance to foreign policy matters such as international monetary policy and trade and investment policy.

Independent Regulatory Commissions

Independent regulatory commissions constitute the second major type of organization within the federal bureaucracy. Whereas some executive departments date back to 1789, the first independent regulatory commission, the Interstate Commerce Commission (ICC), was not established until 1887. (Chapter 17 discusses the history of the ICC, which was abolished in 1996.) All independent regulatory commissions are charged with performing the same basic function: promoting the public interest by writing and enforcing rules that regulate the operations of some sector of private industry. For example, the Consumer Products Safety Commission works to ensure that companies produce goods that are not likely to harm consumers, and the Nuclear Regulatory Commission regulates the nation's nuclear power plants.

Independent regulatory commissions differ dramatically from executive departments in terms of size, leadership structure, and political independence from the president. To begin with, independent regulatory commissions are much smaller than most executive departments; whereas the Defense Department had more than 850,000 employees in 1995, the Federal Communications Commission had only 2,100.[9] Independent regulatory commissions also differ from executive departments in that they are headed by a commission, usually consisting of three to eleven people, rather than by a single secretary. The chair of a commission is the first among equals, lacking the authority the secretaries of executive departments enjoy. Finally, as the name implies, independent regulatory commissions enjoy greater political independence from the president than executive departments do. The reason has to do with the nature of each commissioner's appointment. Like the secretaries of the executive departments, commissioners are appointed by the president and confirmed by the Senate. Instead of serving at the pleasure of the president, though, commissioners serve fixed terms that are staggered over time. As a result, when new presidents take office, they confront independent regulatory commissions headed by people previous presidents appointed, and they can appoint new commissioners only when vacancies open up.

Government Corporations

In addition to executive departments and independent regulatory commissions, a third type of bureaucratic organization is the *government corporation*. Government corporations are, in essence, government-owned companies that sell services or products to the public to generate their own revenues. For example, the Postal Service pays for its

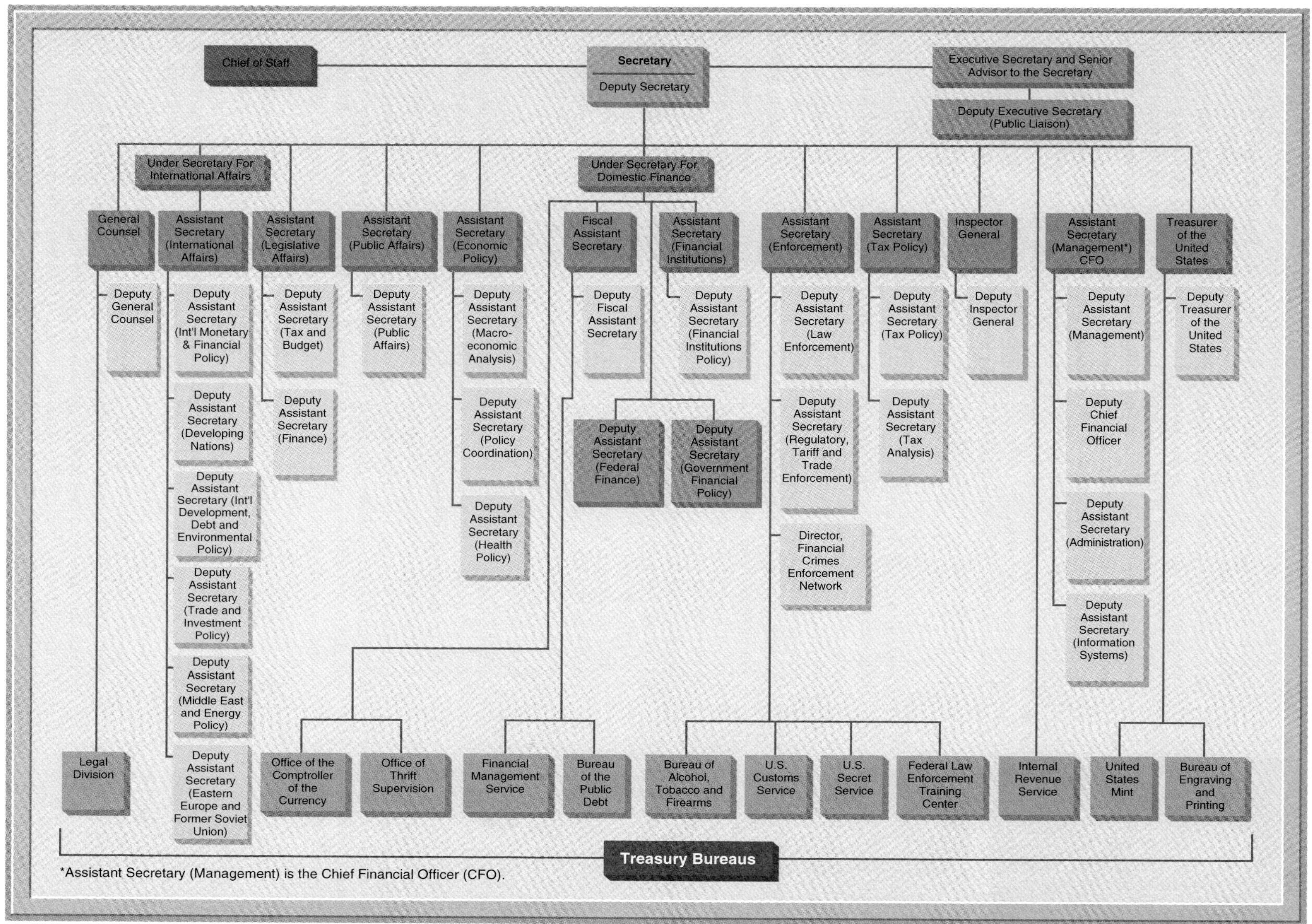

FIGURE 13.2

The Department of the Treasury: An Organizational Chart

This simplified depiction of the primary components of the Treasury Department illustrates the breadth of duties as well as the internal complexity that characterizes most departments.

Source: United States Government Manual, 1994/1995 (Washington, D.C.: U.S. Government Printing Office, 1994), p. 492.

Recently the Postal Service began to promote stamp collecting as a hobby because stamps purchased and placed in a collection book make much more money for the Postal Service than stamps placed on an envelope and mailed.

operations by selling stamps and charging for other postal services. Therefore, it has worked hard to produce stamps, such as those of Elvis Presley and Marilyn Monroe, that customers will retain rather than use, since the Postal Service pockets more money from the sale of stamps that are never used for postage.[10] The Tennessee Valley Authority pays for its operations by charging its customers for the electricity generated by the dams and nuclear power plants it operates. And the Federal Deposit Insurance Corporation (FDIC) charges banks a fee in return for insuring customer deposits against a possible banking collapse. Some government corporations are headed by single individuals, while others have plural leadership.

In principle, government corporations are self-supporting agencies; they sell their services at prices that enable them to break even each year. When a government corporation fails to generate enough revenue to cover its expenses, however, the federal government will supplement the corporation's income. Thus, when the Federal Savings and Loan Insurance Corporation (FSLIC) exhausted its financial reserves after many of the savings-and-loan companies it insured went bankrupt in the 1980s, Congress bailed it out by giving it more money and merging it with the larger and more financially stable FDIC.

Independent Agencies

The category of *independent agencies* encompasses all other types of federal agencies. Independent agencies are not part of any executive department, and their leaders usually lack the cabinet-level status of department secretaries. Some independent agencies, such as the National Aeronautics and Space Administration (NASA), are headed by individuals, whereas others, such as the Merit System Protection Board, are headed by a commission. Some, such as the Small Business Administration, provide a service; others, such as the Environmental Protection Agency, perform a regulatory function. With the exception of the Central Intelligence Agency, independent agencies do not enjoy the same sort of political prestige as executive departments. The relative lack of political prestige has important implications for the well-being of independent agencies. As we shall see later in this chapter, the more power an agency possesses, the better it can fulfill its mission and ensure its own survival. Cabinet-rank status contributes to the deference that others accord an agency, and so to its ability to achieve its own goals.

The Tasks of the Federal Bureaucracy

Despite major differences in organization, structure, and political accountability, all agencies in the federal bureaucracy perform three key tasks: rule administration, rule making, and rule adjudication.

Rule administration
The core function of the bureaucracy—to carry out the decisions of Congress, the president, or the courts.

Rule administration involves carrying out, or administering, the public policy decisions Congress, the president, or the courts make. For example, the Environmental Protection Agency (EPA) administers laws Congress passes to clean up the nation's air and water. Likewise, when the president declares a state eligible for disaster relief in the wake of a flood, earthquake, or hurricane, the Federal Emergency Management Agency (FEMA) administers federal relief programs. As you can see, rule administration is the most basic function of any agency; after all, Congress and the president create bureaucratic agencies because they themselves lack the time and resources needed to implement the public policy decisions they make.

Rule making
Formulating the rules for carrying out the programs a bureaucratic agency administers.

To administer public policy, agencies often must engage in two other kinds of activities: rule making and rule adjudication. In **rule making,** a federal agency drafts regulations—that is, rules—that govern the operation of government programs. The federal bureaucracy writes new regulations and revises old ones because Congress frequently passes laws long on broad guidelines but short on details. As we saw in chapter 11, Congress in many instances gives federal agencies the authority to flesh out the details of legislation because the issues are too complex and members too pressed for time to provide the specifics themselves. Of course, the discretion agencies have to translate the spirit of a congressional mandate into detailed rules gives bureaucrats tremendous influence over the substance of public policy. As we will see later in the chapter, this freedom of maneuver on occasion enables bureaucrats to frustrate the will of Congress.

Every type of government agency administers rules. Examples include (clockwise from top left) the Agriculture Department working with farmers, the Environmental Protection Agency cleaning toxic waste sites, the Federal Emergency Management Agency assisting victims of natural disasters, and the Tennessee Valley Authority generating hydroelectric power to sell to public utilities.

How extensive is rule making among federal agencies? We can glean some idea from figure 13.3, which shows the number of pages published each year in a government document known as the *Federal Register*. By law, a federal agency's rule cannot go into effect until thirty days after its publication in the *Federal Register,* so the annual length of the *Register* provides a crude measure of the amount of rule making that takes place. As you can see, bureaucratic rule making rose sharply from the 1940s, when Franklin Roosevelt was president, through the late 1970s, when Jimmy Carter was president. The amount of rule making dropped after Ronald Reagan's election in 1980, as administration officials sought to make good on his pledge to halt, if not reverse, government regulation of the economy. In 1990, with George Bush in the White House, the amount of rule making began to rise sharply once again, and it continued to rise during Bill Clinton's administration.

In addition to making rules, many federal agencies are responsible for determining whether the rules they administer and formulate have been broken, a process known as **rule adjudication.** Whereas federal agencies operate as Congress does when they make rules, they operate as the courts do when they adjudicate rules. More than twenty-five federal agencies employ a combined total of nearly 1,300 administrative law judges.[11] These judges, who exercise great independence because they cannot be fired except for gross misconduct, review evidence and determine whether the defendants violated any relevant rules or laws. For example, the National Labor Relations Board employs administrative law judges to hear complaints that unions or businesses have violated provisions of the National Labor Relations Act.[12] Rule adjudication has grown in importance over the past fifty years because more federal agencies have gained the responsibility of regulating economic activity in the private sector.

Rule adjudication
Determining whether an agency's rules have been violated.

The federal bureaucracy is a huge conglomerate of diverse, specialized agencies charged with carrying out government policies. All of these agencies administer,

FIGURE 13.3
Measuring Agency Activity, 1940–1994

The 1970s saw a dramatic rise in the amount of rule making government agencies engaged in as the federal government's role in providing all kinds of services grew. Rule making declined markedly in the first half of the 1980s in response to Ronald Reagan's efforts to reduce government activity. It has, however, resumed its upward climb.

Source: Compiled from successive volumes of the *Federal Register* (Washington, D.C.: U.S. Government Printing Office).

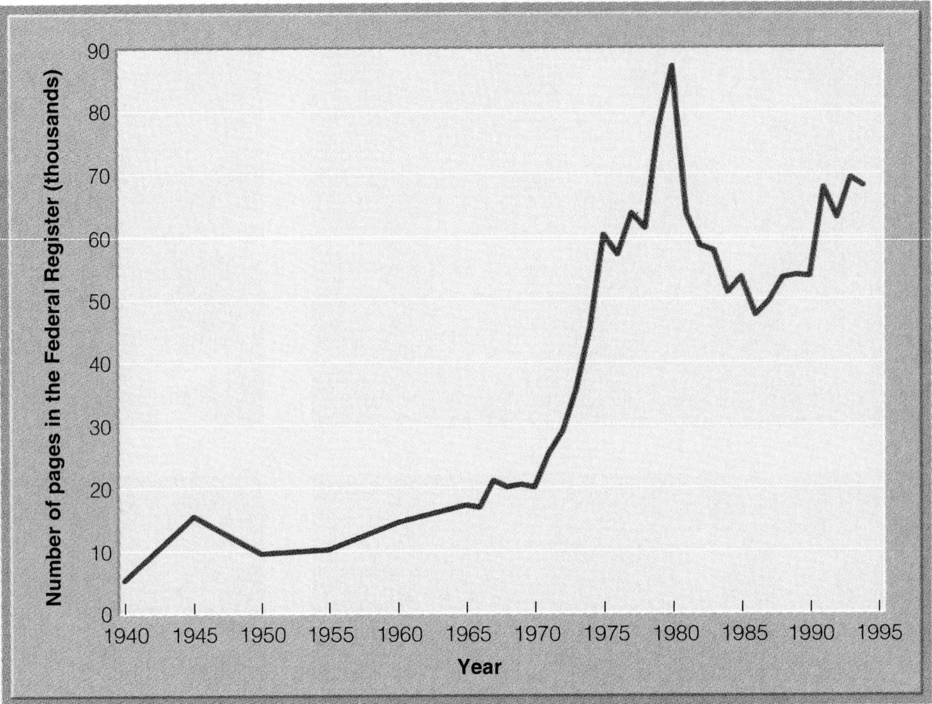

make, and enforce rules. But how did the bureaucracy become the large, complex institution it is today? This is the question we will answer next, as we trace the development of the bureaucracy.

DEVELOPMENT OF THE FEDERAL BUREAUCRACY

On a visit to almost any American city, you can find visible evidence of the reach of the federal bureaucracy: post offices, military recruiting stations, Social Security offices, agricultural extension offices, and offices for a mind-numbing array of other federal bureaus and agencies. To staff the far-flung federal bureaucracy, the federal government employed slightly less than 3 million civilian employees in 1995.[13] Yet the federal government was not always such a massive presence in American life. When Thomas Jefferson sat in the White House, the federal government employed roughly 2,700 civilians.[14]

The tremendous growth in the size of the federal bureaucracy raises several important questions: What is the constitutional status of the bureaucracy? How rapidly did it grow, and is it still growing today? And how have the functions of the bureaucracy and the rules used to hired bureaucrats changed over the past two centuries?

Constitutional Foundations

Chapters 11 and 12 noted that the Constitution specifies the basic structure of both Congress and the presidency. This is not true for the federal bureaucracy. Rather than stipulating the creation of specific federal agencies, the Constitution gave both Congress and the president authority to devise and operate a bureaucracy that would meet the changing needs of a growing country. Congress has the power to create new agencies—which, by implication, means it can abolish or reorganize existing ones—and it decides how much money each agency can spend in a given year. The president has the power to appoint (subject to Senate confirmation) the heads of federal agencies. The Constitution also directs the president to "take care that the laws be faithfully executed," a provision that authorizes the president to order the federal bureaucracy to carry out government policy.

As you can see, the federal bureaucracy is something of a constitutional hybrid. It bridges the gap between the legislative and executive branches of government—it is

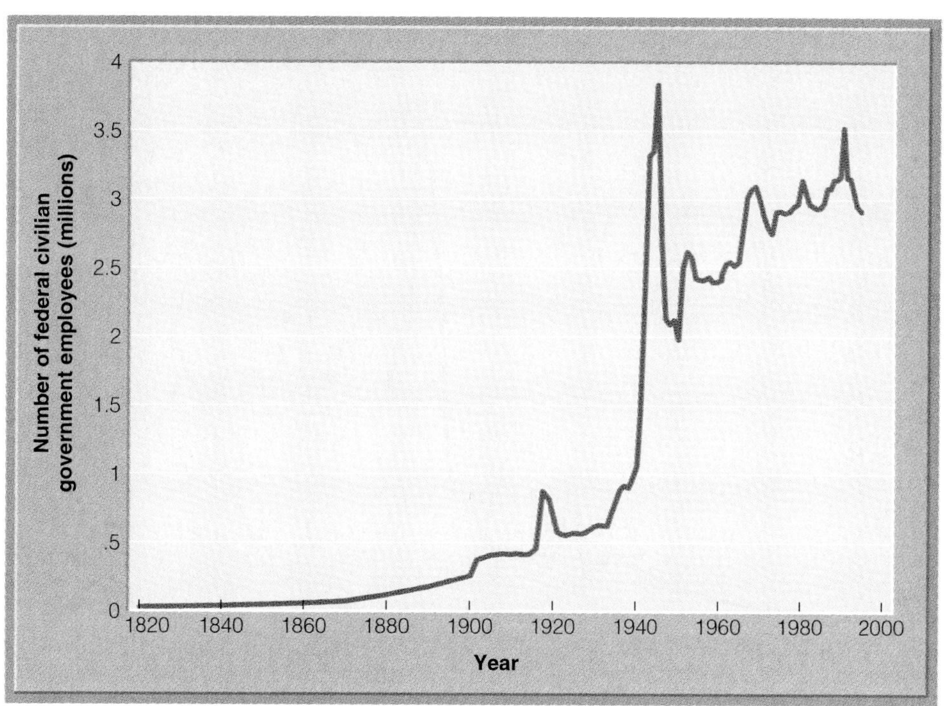

FIGURE 13.4
Total Number of Federal Civilian Government Employees, 1816–1995

Our perception of the federal government's size is affected by what aspect of the government we look at. This figure shows that total federal employment has grown fairly steadily since the 1930s, apart from the abrupt increase that accompanied World War II.

Source: Data from Harold W. Stanley and Richard G. Niemi, *Vital Statistics on American Politics*, 5th ed. (Washington, D.C.: CQ Press, 1995), p. 250.

created by Congress, under the direction of the president, and accountable to both. Of course, agencies vary in the degree to which they respond to the wishes of Congress or the president. Secretaries of the executive departments tend to be more responsive to the White House because they serve at the pleasure of the president. In contrast, the commissioners of independent regulatory commissions serve fixed terms that place them beyond the president's direct control.

The Growth of the Federal Bureaucracy

Because the Constitution does not specify the structure of the federal bureaucracy, one of the major tasks the first Congress had to accomplish when it met in 1789 was to create agencies for the new government. In doing so, the first Congress created a simple bureaucratic structure consisting of three executive departments: the Department of State, the Department of War, and the Department of the Treasury. The first Congress also created the positions of attorney general and postmaster general. The attorney general is the federal government's chief legal official and a member of the president's cabinet. (The attorney general was put in charge of the Justice Department when that agency was created in 1870.) The postmaster general was placed in charge of the Department of the Post Office, which had been created under the Articles of Confederation. The postmaster general was added to the cabinet when Andrew Jackson became president and was dropped from the cabinet when the post was abolished in 1971 as part of a reorganization of the Postal Service.

By the standards of the 1990s, the early federal bureaucracy was extremely small. In 1816, the federal government employed fewer than 5,000 civilian workers. As figure 13.4 shows, that number grew slowly throughout the nineteenth century and the first three decades of the twentieth century. Then the total number of federal civilian employees skyrocketed, increasing more than four-fold between 1931 and 1951. The number of federal employees grew so rapidly in the 1930s and 1940s because of the Great Depression and World War II. These events provided the impetus to rewrite many of the rules of American government. For example, to help restart the stalled American economy, President Franklin Roosevelt and Congress enacted a series of programs known as the New Deal that greatly expanded the federal government's role

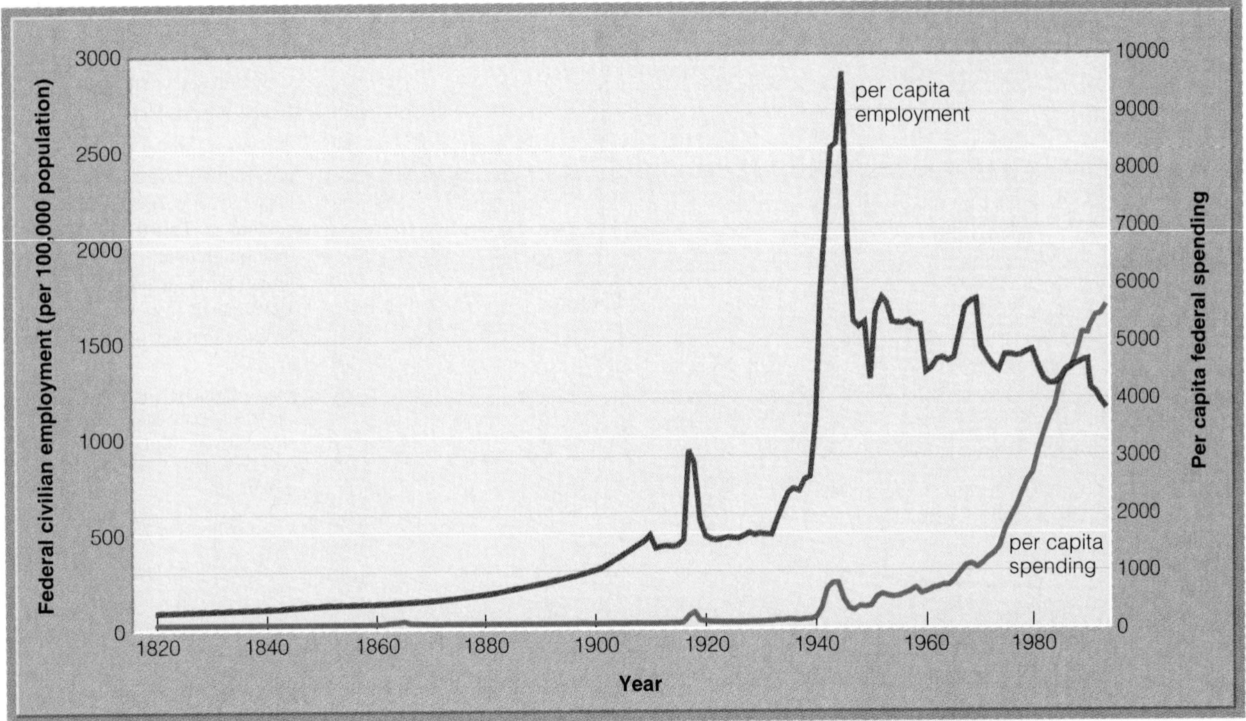

FIGURE 13.5
Growth of the Federal Government, 1816–1994

In contrast to figure 13.4, figure 13.5 shows that per capita federal employment has actually declined since the 1950s. The figure also shows that the federal government spends more money every year, but it does so while employing proportionately fewer people.

Sources: Data from *Historical Statistics of the United States: Colonial Times to 1970* (Washington, D.C.: U.S. Bureau of the Census, 1975), pp. 14, 1114–15, and Harold W. Stanley and Richard G. Niemi, *Vital Statistics on American Politics,* 5th ed. (Washington, D.C.: CQ Press, 1995), pp. 250, 387–88.

in American society. And once Japan attacked Pearl Harbor in December 1941, the federal government needed to hire many more people to run the war effort; indeed, the federal work force expanded to 3.8 million workers in 1945 before falling back to 1.9 million in 1950. In the nearly five decades since then, the number of federal civilian employees has grown much more slowly and has actually declined in recent years.

Figure 13.4 shows the *absolute* number of federal civilian employees. But what does change in the size of the federal work force look like when we take into account the growing size of the American population? After all, one reason a bureaucracy might hire more workers is to meet the needs of a growing population. To answer the question, figure 13.5 shows the number of federal civilian employees per every hundred thousand Americans for the years 1820 to 1993. As you can see, figure 13.5 tells much the same story as figure 13.4 for the years 1820 through 1951: the size of the federal work force grew in both absolute and relative terms, with peak employment reached during World War II. The big difference between figures 13.4 and 13.5 lies in the decades since 1951. Although the absolute number of federal civilian workers increased 18 percent between 1951 and 1995, the number of federal civilian workers per hundred thousand Americans actually *fell* by more than 25 percent. In sum, in 1995, the federal bureaucracy was serving the needs of the American public with relatively fewer workers than it was four decades earlier.

Although the number of federal civilian employees has declined in recent years once change in the size of the population is taken into account, figure 13.5 also shows that per capita spending by federal agencies increased dramatically in the second half of the twentieth century. To understand why federal agency spending rose so sharply, we need to look at how Congress and the president changed the rules to expand the number of functions the federal bureaucracy is called upon to perform.

The Expanding Functions of the Federal Bureaucracy

The history of the federal government is a history of expanding duties and responsibilities. As Americans have come to demand more services from the federal government, federal agencies have assumed more functions. These functions fall into four categories: national maintenance, clientele service, private sector regulation, and income redistribution. In many instances, a single agency performs more than one of these functions. In a similar vein, in many cases more than one federal agency may carry out the same function.

National Maintenance

Early in American history, the functions of the federal government were limited largely to carrying out a small number of tasks essential to maintaining the country: collecting tax revenue (the job of the Treasury Department), defending the country against external threats (the War Department), conducting relations with other countries (the State Department), enforcing federal laws (the attorney general), and promoting internal communications (the Post Office).

As long as the federal government limited itself to these core duties, growth in the size of the federal bureaucracy was driven largely by growth in the size of the country itself. For example, the Post Office accounted for most of the early growth in the number of federal employees as it added more workers to deliver the mail to a growing population.[15] The acquisition of new territories also drove bureaucratic growth; Congress created the Interior Department in 1849 to manage the western territories.

Clientele Services

Midway through the nineteenth century, organized interest groups began demanding that the federal government go beyond its traditional national maintenance functions to serve the particular needs of their members. Washington responded to the demands by creating new agencies designed to provide these groups, or clients, with services. In the 1850s, for example, farming interests began lobbying for greater federal involvement in agricultural policy, and Congress responded in 1862 by creating the Department of Agriculture. During the 1880s, labor organizations followed the example the farm groups set and demanded the creation of a department designed to serve their interests. Congress responded in 1884 by creating the Bureau of Labor. Pressures from business interests led Congress (over the objections of labor groups) to create a combined Department of Commerce and Labor in 1903. Finally, at the insistence of the American Federation of Labor, Congress established separate Departments of Commerce and Labor in 1913.

Part of the growth in both federal employment and spending since the 1930s can be traced to the expansion of the clientele services the federal government provides to American citizens. The New Deal launched the country on an era of government activism intended to stimulate the economy and provide for the public's general welfare. In 1953, Congress created the Department of Health, Education, and Welfare (renamed the Department of Health and Human Services in 1979) to administer the nation's health, education, and income assistance programs. In the 1960s, the federal bureaucracy expanded again in response to the passage of the Great Society programs, President Lyndon Johnson's effort to reduce economic and racial inequality in the United States. Many new agencies were created or expanded into executive departments. Thus, in 1965, the Housing and Home Finance Agency was elevated in status and renamed the Department of Housing and Urban Development. A year later, Congress merged programs and activities from eight separate departments into the Department of Transportation. Over the next three decades, three more executive departments were created: the Department of Energy in 1977, the Department of Education in 1979, and the Department of Veterans Affairs in 1989.

The creation of new federal agencies designed to serve the needs of specific segments of American society accounts for much of the growth in the total number of federal civilian employees between 1951 and 1995. The growth in the number of federal agencies also accounts for the even more spectacular growth in federal spending. As we discuss at greater length in chapters 15 and 16, most federal spending takes the form of grants to state and local governments and direct payments to individuals. By increasing its grants to state and local governments and its direct payments to individuals, the federal government expanded the services it could provide without having to hire more employees.

Regulatory agencies were created to protect the public from unfair and unsafe business activities and products. In many cases, regulatory agencies must compel businesses to comply with their regulations. However, agencies and businesses often cooperate. For example, since 1993, the major automakers and the federal government have been working together to produce a new line of cars that is more fuel efficient and less polluting.

Regulation of the Private Sector

In addition to maintaining the basic needs of the country and serving the needs of specific segments of American society, the federal bureaucracy has grown because it has acquired the responsibility of regulating the American economy. The federal government first moved into the regulatory arena in 1887 when it created the Interstate Commerce Commission (ICC) to end the predatory business practices of the railroad industry. (The ICC's jurisdiction eventually expanded to include trucking, bus lines, water carriers, oil pipelines, and express delivery agencies before it was abolished in 1996.) In 1913, Congress created the Federal Reserve Board to regulate the activities of commercial banks, and in 1914, it created the Federal Trade Commission to regulate the trade practices of businesses. The regulatory responsibilities of the federal government expanded yet again during the administration of Franklin Roosevelt. In 1934, Congress created the Federal Communications Commission (see chapter 8) to regulate the emerging field of electronic communications and the Securities and Exchange Commission to regulate the operation of the stock market.

As chapter 17 discusses at greater length, the regulatory agencies created before 1960 were responsible largely for regulating economic matters, such as the price of goods and services, the amount of competition in the marketplace, and the kinds of information sellers must disclose to buyers. During the 1960s, however, Congress expanded the focus of government regulation to include social regulation, rules that emphasize "the conditions under which goods and services are produced, and the physical characteristics of products that are manufactured."[16] Toward that broader end, Congress created agencies to protect the environment, employees in the workplace, and consumers. The Environmental Protection Agency (EPA) and the Occupational Safety and Health Administration (OSHA) were created in 1970, and the Consumer Products Safety Commission in 1972. These agencies have broad mandates that extend beyond the traditional practice of regulating particular industries. The EPA, for example, can regulate pollution from all sources, including industrial plants, automobiles, landfill sites, animal feed lots, and all places where pollution appears (soil, air, and water.) The wide-ranging nature of the mandate Congress gave the EPA means the agency has extensive influence across a wide segment of American society. The broadening scope of the government's regulatory duties helps account for figure 13.3's pattern of growth in the volume of regulations the government issued in the 1970s.

Income Redistribution

The fourth function of the federal bureaucracy, and the one most recent in origin, involves the redistribution of income. Redistribution refers to government efforts to shift resources, either directly or indirectly, between classes of people in society, from richer to poorer or vice versa. In the wake of the Great Depression, the federal government increasingly assumed a role in maintaining the economic and social welfare of the American people. As a result, income redistribution became an important part of government policy and yet another factor contributing to the expansion of the federal bureaucracy.

Chapters 16 and 17 discuss in considerable detail the ways in which the federal government redistributes income among American citizens. Here it is sufficient to make two points. First, most of the redistributive efforts of federal agencies involve direct payments to individuals. For example, the Social Security system, established in 1935, makes cash payments to elderly Americans as well as to dependent children of deceased workers and to Americans with disabilities. Likewise, Aid to Families with Dependent Children (AFDC), established as part of the same legislation that created Social Security, provides cash benefits to needy families. As the number of people eligible for programs such as Social Security and AFDC has increased, the budgets of the federal agencies that make the transfer payments have grown as well.

The second point about the federal government's attempts to redistribute income is that while some programs transfer money from the rich to the poor, as AFDC does, some transfer money to the wealthy. For example, many federal programs make direct payments to wealthy individuals and firms. Much of the money the Department of Agriculture pays to keep farmers in business goes to wealthy corporate farmers. Likewise, the Social Security Administration mails the largest social security checks to elderly Americans who had the highest incomes during their working years, regardless of whether they are currently rich or poor. Thus, income redistribution is not a one-way street. Both the wealthy and the poor can benefit from government policies if the government deems their well-being a proper goal of government policy. It all depends on the rules.

Changes in the Federal Bureaucracy's Personnel System

The past two centuries have seen dramatic changes in the size of the federal bureaucracy and in the sorts of functions it is expected to undertake. The past two centuries also have seen dramatic changes in the bureaucracy's personnel system, the rules that govern the hiring and firing of federal employees. The question of who works for the federal bureaucracy is important because bureaucrats are responsible for implementing public policy, and so they greatly shape the actions of the federal government. In the United States, the rules used to hire and fire federal employees have changed in response to changes in the nation's political climate. In turn, these changes have affected the way in which the federal bureaucracy performs its work.

Government by Gentlemen

From the time the nation was founded until 1829, the federal bureaucracy consisted of political appointees recruited primarily from the elite classes in American society, and service in the bureaucracy was viewed as a high calling. The pool of eligible appointees was limited for the most part to white males who had demonstrated their loyalty to the party in power, who possessed high social standing and an advanced education, and who had relatives who were government officials. Both the Federalist and the Democrat-Republican parties followed this pattern, sometimes called "government by gentlemen" because the "business of governing was prestigious, and it was anointed with high moral imperatives of integrity and honor."[17]

The Spoils System

The era of "government by gentlemen" gave way in 1829 to the **spoils system,** the practice of hiring and firing federal workers on the basis of party loyalty and support in election campaigns. The spoils system was implemented by Andrew Jackson, the first president to be elected with election rules that allowed nearly all adult white males to vote, and it got its name when Sen. William Marcy defended Jackson's practice of appointing his political supporters to government jobs by arguing that "to the victor belong the spoils of the enemy."[18] Jackson wanted to make the federal bureaucracy more

Spoils system
The method used to hire and fire government employees during most of the 1800s. Government employees of the new president's choosing would replace those a previous president had appointed. Government jobs were the "spoils" (or rewards) of the electoral "wars." This system was also known as patronage.

A disgruntled job seeker's assassination of President James Garfield helped push Congress to reform the federal employment system. In place of the existing patronage system, Congress adopted the civil service system, which requires that people be hired on the basis of their ability to do their work rather than their political connections.

responsive to presidential leadership, and he believed that most government jobs required little more than common sense. As a result, he made party loyalty the primary consideration in hiring people to work for the federal government.

Under the spoils system, the spoils—that is, government jobs—went to the victor in an election. The result of this winner-take-all approach was that a great deal of turnover occurred in government jobs each time a new administration came to the White House. Members of the defeated political party would lose their government jobs, and members of the victorious political party would replace them. The ability of presidents to reward their followers with government jobs is known as **patronage.** Presidents often found patronage very helpful for building political support for their proposals. For example, Abraham Lincoln used his patronage powers to secure political support for his policies on the Civil War.[19]

Patronage
The practice of rewarding partisan supporters with government jobs. Also known as the spoils system.

The spoils system held sway from Jackson's presidency until the 1880s. Although nineteenth-century presidents found patronage useful for winning political support and ensuring that bureaucrats responded to their wishes, the spoils system bred cynicism among the American public about the integrity of federal employees. Many federal employees began to see their jobs not only as rewards but as a means of self-enrichment. Political corruption grew rampant. By the 1870s, a growing public awareness of government corruption, along with a mistrust of how ethnic groups such as Irish Americans had used patronage to gain political power in large cities, led to increased calls for a new personnel system based on merit rather than political ties. The push for reform gained momentum in 1881 when a disgruntled job seeker assassinated President James Garfield. Two years later, Congress passed the Pendleton Act of 1883, which held that people should be hired on the basis of their qualifications rather than their political connections.

The Civil Service System

The Pendleton Act established the third type of personnel system for the federal bureaucracy and the one that remains in effect today: **civil service.** In a civil service system, the rules for hiring workers stress the competence of the job applicant rather than his or her political affiliation. In other words, civil service puts a premium on *what* you know, rather than *who* you know. At first, the federal civil service system encompassed only 10 percent of the federal work force, and people who held these jobs became known as civil servants. Over the years, however, the number of federal jobs subject to the rules of civil service was gradually enlarged. By 1994, more than 80 percent of all civilian bureaucratic employees fell under some part of the civil service system, with 55.2 percent participating in what is known as the General Schedule Classification System, and another 27.2 percent working under the Postal Service System.[20] The president, however, retains the power to appoint people to jobs in the highest levels of the federal bureaucracy, subject to Senate confirmation in most instances.

Civil service
The method by which most government employees have been hired, promoted, and fired since the 1880s. Personnel decisions are based on merit, or the competence of the individual to do the job, rather than the individual's political loyalties.

In addition to expanding to encompass most federal jobs, the civil service system has changed in other ways as well. One major change has been the effort to recruit more women and minorities. Historically, both groups were grossly underrepresented in the federal bureaucracy. In the early 1970s, Congress took steps to remedy the problem by requiring the federal government to follow affirmative action guidelines in making hiring decisions (see box 13.1). As a result of this change in hiring rules, the proportion of government jobs going to women and minorities grew significantly in the 1970s and 1980s. By 1993, women made up about 50 percent of the federal work force and minorities 28 percent—both roughly comparable to their proportions of the general population.[21] Women and minorities continue, however, to be underrepresented at the highest levels of the civil service.[22] Thus, while some progress has been made, the objectives of the affirmative action policy have yet to be fully achieved.

The Civil Service Reform Act of 1978 further revised the operations of the civil service system. Among the many changes that the law mandated, two are especially important. First, the act reorganized the agencies that oversee the civil service system. Before the passage of the Civil Service Reform Act, the Civil Service Commission had the dual tasks of advising presidents on personnel policy and protecting civil servants from the political interference of elected officials. In practice, these two responsibilities often came into conflict because many presidents wanted to influence the behavior of career bureaucrats. Jimmy Carter proposed to remedy the conflict-of-interest problem by abolishing the Civil Service Commission and dividing its duties between two new agencies. Congress then enacted Carter's proposal, which created the Office of Personnel Management to advise the president on personnel matters and the Merit System Protection Board to administer the civil service system.

The Civil Service Reform Act also created the Senior Executive Service (SES), which consists of civil servants who have reached the highest ranks of their careers. The purpose of the SES is to enable the most senior career civil servants to move into high-level policy-making positions in the federal government that are traditionally reserved for political appointees. Individuals who join the SES retain the basic protections of the civil service system, but the president can shift them from one job to another on the basis of his or her personal policy preferences. For example, a Democratic president can replace a conservative member of the SES who holds a senior post in the Defense Department with a liberal member of the SES. The conservative member of SES must then receive a commensurate job elsewhere in the federal bureaucracy. Thus, the SES helps civil servants by giving them opportunities to undertake more challenging work, and it helps presidents by enabling them to fill important government jobs with people who share their policy preferences.

Thus far, we have painted the bureaucracy as a huge institution that is accountable to both Congress and the president and that provides an expanding set of government services to the American public. We have seen how the bureaucracy shapes rules and how rules and other changes affect the bureaucracy. Now let's look at how the bureaucracy performs its tasks, focusing particularly on the third lesson about the bureaucracy we are discussing in this chapter: the fact that the bureaucracy is a political institution.

The Politics of the Federal Bureaucracy

Americans historically have believed that the federal bureaucracy is and should be nonpolitical.[23] Yet as we noted at the beginning of the chapter, federal agencies are fundamentally political organizations. They do not simply implement the decisions of Congress and the president; they also make rules and policies. And just as the laws Congress passes and the president signs benefit some Americans and hurt others, so do the rules and policies the federal bureaucracy develops. Thus, to understand the role federal agencies play in American politics, it is important to understand the inherently political nature of their jobs, the goals they try to accomplish, the source of their political power, and the constraints that limit their power.

POINT OF ORDER

BOX 13.1

Who Gets the Job? The Effects of Veteran's Preference and Affirmative Action Rules on Government Hiring

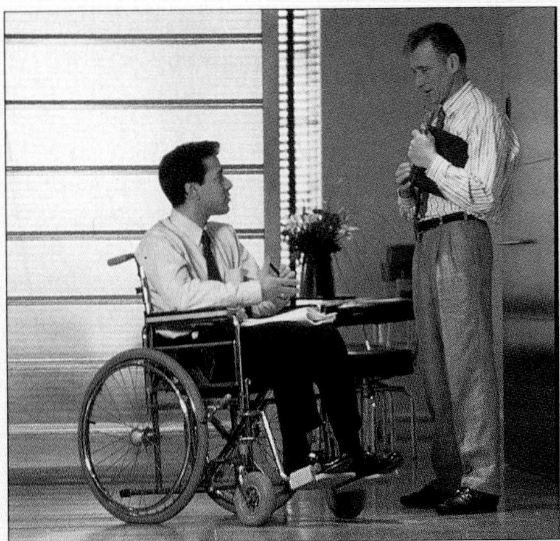

Congress has modified the federal government's merit-based personnel system to help achieve important social goals. Military veterans receive special consideration in hiring decisions, and affirmative action laws have helped increase the proportions of women and minorities the government employs.

The criteria used to hire career federal civil servants provide a clear example of how government rules distribute benefits. With the passage of the Pendleton Act in 1883, the government made merit (the ability to do the job) the primary standard for making hiring decisions. Under this system, job applicants are tested and scored on a 100-point scale that measures their ability to perform different types of jobs. If merit were the only consideration the federal government used in hiring new workers, then it would hire the people with the highest scores. Over the years, however, Congress has modified the merit system to provide special benefits to specific groups of Americans.

One group that benefits from the modified merit system is military veterans. The federal civil service systems adds a bonus of between five and fifteen points to the test scores of all applicants who have served on active military

Continued

The Political Character of the Federal Bureaucracy

An enduring feature of the American public's attitude toward government bureaucracy is the belief that bureaucracies are, and should be, politically neutral organizations that carry out the administrative tasks elected officials assigned to them. In this view, Congress and the president should *formulate* policy and the bureaucracy should *implement* it. From this perspective, then, bureaucratic administration is simply a mechanistic process for implementing the wishes of elected officials efficiently and effectively.[24]

The American expectation that government bureaucracy should be politically neutral has greatly affected the development of the federal bureaucracy. For example, the push in the 1870s and 1880s to create a civil service system sprang from the desire to hire workers who could perform skilled tasks and who would be protected from the political pressures their presidentially appointed superiors imposed. The move to create independent regulatory commissions stemmed from the similar belief that bureaucracies should be politically neutral organizations. Proponents believed that providing members of a commission with fixed and staggered terms in office would minimize the possibilities for political interference and thereby enable the commissioners to act in the best interests of the American public.

POINT OF ORDER

BOX 13.1 CONTINUED

duty. The number of bonus points increases if the veteran has war-related disabilities or served in the Vietnam War. Spouses, widows, widowers, and mothers of military veterans also may have bonus points added to their test scores under certain circumstances. Other sections of the American public that benefit from the modifications to the merit system are women and minorities. The federal government is an affirmative action employer. This means that when a federal agency is filling a position, and all candidates have roughly equal merit, women and minority candidates receive strong consideration or even preference based on their gender or ethnic background. The rules direct the federal agency to try to hire women and minority candidates. To meet the federal government's affirmative action employment targets, federal agencies must set numerical goals for the employment of women and minorities, and they must establish timetables for achieving those goals.

Veteran's preferences and affirmative action have affected the composition of the federal work force. Not counting postal workers, one-third of all federal employees are military veterans. In contrast, veterans make up only 10.6 percent of the civilian labor force in the United States. Women make up about 50 percent and minorities 28 percent of federal employees, roughly equal to their numbers in the population. In contrast, in 1970, before the hiring preferences were established, women made up only 33 percent of the federal work force and minorities only 20 percent.

Veteran's preferences and affirmative action are controversial policies because they make exceptions to the conventional notion of merit. Proponents argue that these policies advance goals that are important to the country. They argue that the veteran's preference rewards people who have served the country and thereby encourages other Americans to serve in the military. Along the same line, affirmative action tries to correct past discrimination and ensure that the people who work in the federal bureaucracy mirror the American public.

Opponents challenge veteran's preferences and affirmative action on the grounds that the two policies run contrary to the idea of merit hiring. Critics recognize the value of the veteran's preference in helping veterans find jobs when they first leave the military, but oppose allowing veterans who have already obtained gainful employment to use it. Many attempts have been made to limit the use of the veteran's preference, but politically powerful veterans' organizations have lobbied hard to protect a rule that benefits so many of their members. As for affirmative action, it is criticized for rewarding people who themselves have not experienced discrimination. As we saw in chapter 5, some opponents even label the policy as reverse discrimination because it consciously denies equal treatment to white males. The controversy over affirmative action has generated many attempts in both Congress and the courts to expand, as well as limit, its scope.

Veteran's preferences and affirmative action show that even the seemingly technical rules governing who the federal government hires have a tremendous effect on which groups of Americans benefit from government policy. As a result, many groups try to change the rules of government in ways that will benefit their members.

Sources: James W. Fesler and Donald F. Kettl, *The Politics of the Administrative Process* (Chatham, N.J.: Chatham House, 1991), pp. 115–18; George J. Gordon, *Public Administration in America,* 4th ed. (New York: St. Martin's, 1992), p. 291; *Statistical Abstract of the United States* (Washington, D.C.: U.S. Bureau of the Census, various years).

Although the notion of bureaucratic neutrality is appealing, close examination of the administrative tasks of federal agencies shows that bureaucracies are inherently political institutions. To begin with, implementing the decisions of Congress, the president, and the courts requires that federal agencies do much more than mechanically put the wishes of others into effect. Because Congress, the president, or the courts lack the time needed to specify all the details of public policy, as well as the clairvoyance needed to anticipate all possible future developments, bureaucracies by necessity must try to translate broad principles and goals into concrete programs. The power to give meaning to what may be no more than a general principle gives bureaucrats a range of discretion as they decide how to fulfill their duties. As we shall see, agencies use their power to administer policy and shape policy rules to pursue their own interests and their own visions of good public policy as well as to respond to the demands of other political actors.

The work of the federal bureaucracy is also political because Congress and the president seldom speak with a single, coherent voice. Both want to direct the actions of the bureaucracy, but neither can unilaterally command its obedience. Instead, they must compete for its allegiance. Federal agencies can turn this competition to their

The People Behind the Rules

BOX 13.2

Managing Public Lands: James Watt and Bruce Babbitt

Bureaucracies are political institutions, and changes in the political climate affect federal agencies. A change in the leadership of a federal agency can profoundly affect how the agency operates, as a comparison of the Department of the Interior under Secretaries James Watt (1981–1983) and Bruce Babbitt (1993–present) shows. The Interior Department, created in 1849 to manage federally owned land, must weigh and manage conflicting demands. Environmental groups want to preserve public land and ensure the health of the ecosystem. Ranching, mining, logging, and oil businesses want to develop the land's economic potential. Although both Watt and Babbitt grew up in the West—Watt in Wyoming and Babbitt in Arizona—the Interior Department weighed these competing demands quite differently during Watt's and Babbitt's terms in office.

James Watt

James Watt

Before becoming secretary of the interior, James Watt had a long history of working on behalf of interests that wanted to develop the economic potential of the nation's natural resources. During the 1960s, Watt advocated economic development of federally owned land as a staff member in the U.S. Senate and as a lobbyist for the U.S. Chamber of Commerce. He then served as deputy assistant secretary of the Interior and as head of the Bureau of Outdoor Recreation during the Nixon Administration. President Gerald Ford appointed Watt to the Federal Power Commission in 1975. In the late 1970s, he served as president of the Mountain States Legal Foundation, an organization that lobbied the federal government to make public land more accessible to private industry.

Ronald Reagan appointed Watt as secretary of the interior in 1981, and Watt quickly moved to enact many of the pro-business policies he favored. Early on, he directed the department to cut off all communication with environmental interest groups and with congressional staffers who favored protecting the environment. In 1982, he ordered the largest sale in U.S. history of leases for coal exploration and development on public land. The decision drew sharp criticism when it turned out that the Interior Department had sold the leases at less than one-half of their estimated market value. Watt attracted even more criticism when he doubled the acreage open to petroleum companies for offshore oil exploration, including many areas critics argued were environmentally fragile. And he largely halted the expansion of the country's national parks and wildlife refuges.

Because of these policy decisions, Watt's three-year term as secretary was marked by controversy. Environmental groups denounced his policies for exploiting the nation's natural bounty for immediate economic gain, and they worked with their allies in Congress to block many of his proposals. Yet Watt's career as secretary

Continued

advantage since they can play Congress and the president against each other. For example, if the Defense Department favors the president's proposal to spend more than Congress wants on defenses against nuclear missiles, it can produce studies showing the wisdom of the president's idea. In contrast, if the Defense Department opposes the president's decision to remove U.S. troops from South Korea, it can give Congress studies showing that the president's proposal will increase the chances of war in Asia. In short, the fact that federal agencies serve two masters gives them some freedom to shape public policy to advance their own interests and their own vision of good public policy.

In sum, the work of the federal bureaucracy is inherently political. The changes in how the Interior Department manages public lands under leaders with divergent policy goals attests to this (see box 13.2). Federal agencies do not mechanically implement

The People Behind the Rules

BOX 13.2 CONTINUED

came to an abrupt halt not because of his policy decisions but because he made a remark widely viewed as grossly inappropriate for a senior government official. In 1983, he described a commission he had to create to investigate his coal leasing policies as consisting of "every kind of mixture you can have—I have a Black. I have a woman, two Jews, and a Cripple." The public outcry over the comment forced Watt to resign. Although he did not accomplish all of his pro-business goals, Watt's term as secretary of the interior provides a good example of how the policy preferences of the head of a federal agency can greatly shape its operations.

Bruce Babbitt

Bruce Babbitt

Bruce Babbitt made a name for himself as a strong advocate for the environment during his thirty years of public service before his appointment as secretary of the interior. He served as attorney general and then as governor of Arizona. In 1988, he ran for the Democratic presidential nomination. Although he failed in his bid to be president of the United States, he subsequently became president of the League of Conservation Voters, a leading environmental group. In 1993, Bill Clinton named Babbitt secretary of the interior.

Although strongly identified with the environmental movement, Babbitt, unlike Watt, kept the channels of communication open to both environmentalists and private industry. Under Babbitt, the Interior Department placed more emphasis on protecting public lands than on developing them. After three years in office, Babbitt had forged a number of compromises that, while not satisfying his environmental supporters or silencing his business community critics, were viewed as progress after twelve years of Republican control of the department. After several false starts, he revised regulations for cattle grazing on federal lands, developed a plan to require the sugar industry to begin paying for cleanup of the damage it inflicted on the Everglades, and devised a solution (since superseded by the courts and Congress) to the dispute between logging interests and environmentalists over the logging of public lands that provide a habitat for the endangered spotted owl. Thus, Babbitt showed during his tenure as secretary of the interior that whoever heads the department sets the tone for its operations.

Sources: Paul J. Culhane, "Sagebrush Rebels in Office: Jim Watt's Land and Water Politics," in *Environmental Policy in the 1980s: Reagan's New Agenda,* ed. Norman J. Vig and Michael E. Kraft (Washington, D.C.: CQ Press, 1984); Margaret Kriz, "Cabinet Scorecard: Interior Secretary Babbitt," *National Journal,* 6 November 1993, pp. 2640–41; Margaret Kriz, "Quick Draw," *National Journal,* 13 November 1993, pp. 2711–16; Timothy Noah, "Babbitt, Once the Darling of Environmentalists, Discovers Some Decisions Are Costing Him Allies," *Wall Street Journal,* 3 May 1994.

orders they receive from elected officials or the courts. Rather, because the process of implementing policy almost by necessity gives them discretion, and because they are responsible to both Congress and the president, federal agencies have some freedom to shape their own rules and pursue their own political goals.

The Goals of the Federal Bureaucracy

Government agencies have two types of goals: *mission goals* and *survival goals.* Mission goals are the policy objectives that justify the creation and existence of an agency. The Department of Transportation, for example, was created to promote the development of the nation's transportation systems. Most employees in an agency see its mission goals as a matter of good public policy. Thus, employees for the Department of

In 1995, congressional Republicans sought to abolish the Commerce Department. In a clear demonstration of the power survival goals can have, Commerce Department officials worked hard to defeat the Republican proposal.

Transportation generally believe that the federal government should do its best to build and maintain interstate highways, improve the nation's airports, and encourage mass transit use.

Survival goals refer to the desire bureaucrats have to see the agency they work for grow and prosper. Civil servants typically are career-oriented individuals whose personal advancement hinges on the success of their agency, which is usually defined in terms of whether the agency's budget, work force, jurisdiction, and power are growing. No matter what an agency's original mission goals, it invariably seeks to survive and prosper once it exists. Indeed, "executive agencies often come to regard preserving their own organizational well-being as the most important of all public goods."[25] Thus, agency officials may work to keep their agency alive even when others believe its mission goals have become obsolete. For example, in 1995, congressional Republicans proposed abolishing the Commerce Department, which is home to agencies such as the Census Bureau, the National Weather Service, and the Patent and Trademark Office. Republicans argued that most of the department's functions were either unnecessary, duplicated by other agencies, or best performed by the private sector or other federal agencies. They also estimated that abolishing Commerce would save the federal government $8 billion over five years.[26] Rather than meekly accepting the Republican proposal, Commerce Department officials argued that the agency performed vital services, and they eventually succeeded in keeping it in business. (For their part, congressional Republicans succeeded in sharply cutting the Commerce Department's budget.)

The desire that agencies have to grow and prosper almost inevitably brings them into conflict with other political actors, be they Congress, the president, other federal agencies, state and local governments, or interest groups. The reason is that when one agency grows in power, other agencies and interests almost invariably lose power. In the early 1980s, for example, defense spending rose rapidly as the Reagan administration launched a major buildup of U.S. military forces. Concerned that defense spending was taking too much away from spending on social programs, liberal members of Congress and their interest group allies fought to cut funding for the Defense Department and to increase funding for domestic agencies. Thus, when an agency grows in size and power, it almost always makes some enemies. To protect themselves against potential enemies, agencies try to develop their own independent bases of power.

The Political Resources of the Federal Bureaucracy

Power is "the lifeblood" of government agencies.[27] Agencies want political power because their view of good public policy may differ substantially from the views other government agencies, elected officials, and the public hold. They also want power to ensure their own survival. Agencies that have their own power bases can protect themselves from opponents and perhaps even expand their influence over public policy. They develop these power bases by exercising discretion in their policy areas, establishing strong client support, and developing policy expertise.

Administrative Discretion

Agencies establish their political power in part through their rule-making responsibilities. As we saw earlier in the chapter, agencies exercise discretion in deciding how to administer policy. They can use that discretion to implement policies to reflect their view of good public policy and to benefit their self-interest. For example, the fact that the Environmental Protection Agency is responsible for generating many of the rules needed to carry out the nation's clean air laws gives it considerable power to influence the health of the American economy as well as the health of individual Americans. Similarly, the fact that the Justice Department is responsible for deciding when evidence is sufficient to prosecute someone for breaking a federal law gives the department tremendous power on matters involving the federal criminal justice system.

In addition to the power that comes from discretion in implementing public policy, the two main sources of power for a government agency are the support of its clientele and its specialized knowledge, or expertise.[28] Because agencies differ in terms of clients and expertise, they also differ in terms of the amount of political power they wield.

Clientele Support

We mentioned earlier that whenever a government agency provides a service or regulates behavior, it seeks to help a targeted segment of society. Those intended beneficiaries compose the agency's **clientele.** In most instances, an agency's clientele consists of organized interest groups, though congressional committees or subcommittees may be part of an agency's clientele as well.

Clientele
The recipients of the services a government agency's programs provide.

The power an agency exercises depends heavily on the power of its clientele. An agency supported by large, well-organized, and well-funded interest groups is likely to fare much better in achieving its goals than an agency that lacks such support. As we discussed in chapter 10, interest groups can help an agency by pressuring Congress and the president to give it bigger budgets, greater powers, or new duties. Because interest groups make campaign contributions and mobilize voters, both members of Congress and the president have an incentive to listen to interest group pleas on behalf of a federal agency.

The Defense Department and the State Department illustrate the two extremes when it comes to clientele support. A wide array of groups benefits from the operations of the Defense Department, including the companies that manufacture weapons and other products for the armed services, the people who work for defense contractors, the cities and towns located near military bases, and the more than 1.5 million people who serve on active duty. Because these clients represent a sizable segment of the American public, the Defense Department exercises tremendous political power. (Were it not for the power of its clients, the Defense Department's budget no doubt would have decreased far more sharply and rapidly following the end of the Cold War than it has.) In contrast, the State Department is a classic case of an agency without a politically significant clientele. Very few groups benefit directly from the work of the State Department, so few groups advocate its interests before Congress or the president. Not surprisingly, federal spending on foreign aid—which the State Department and its subordinate agencies oversee—fell by 17 percent between 1990 and 1996, even before taking into account the effect of inflation.[29]

Agencies do not have to stand idly by waiting for their clientele groups to act on their behalf. In many instances, agencies try to improve their political positions by helping to organize their clients into politically significant groups. For example, the Labor Department advocated the expansion of labor unions, at least in part because workers are much more powerful when they are formally organized into unions than

Government agencies differ dramatically in the political clout their clienteles exercise. The State Department has traditionally been at a disadvantage because it lacks a strong clientele. In contrast, the Defense Department benefits from the support of the many groups that have a stake in its mission.

when they act as individuals. Similarly, federal agencies often give grants to state or local governments, and they encourage the recipients to organize into groups. These groups can then urge Congress and the president to give the granting agency more funds and greater say in the distribution of grants.[30] Thus, agencies benefit from serving powerful clienteles, and they have an incentive to try to strengthen their clienteles.

If a clientele is especially powerful, an agency may come to depend so heavily on it that it loses much of its autonomy and becomes a "captive agency."[31] Sometimes the clientele that captures an agency is the intended beneficiary of the agency's activities. For example, the Department of Agriculture is very sensitive to the wishes of agricultural interest groups because they form the core of the department's power base. In other situations, an agency may be captured by other groups, as is often the case with independent regulatory commissions. The reason independent regulatory commissions are created is to regulate business practices within some industry and thereby produce benefits for the general public. Yet the public is an unorganized and unmotivated client, so it exerts relatively little influence on behalf of a commission. In contrast, an industry is often well organized and strongly motivated to oppose any actions that might hurt its profitability. As a result of this imbalance, independent regulatory commissions frequently are captured by the industries they regulate. This leads to regulations that often serve the interests of the industry rather than those of the broader public.

Agency Expertise

Expertise
Specialized knowledge acquired through work experience or training and education.

In addition to gaining political power from administrative discretion and the support of clientele groups, agencies gain power from the **expertise** their employees develop. As civil servants undergo special training and education, and as they acquire hands-on experience from years on the job, they may develop specialized knowledge that very few people outside the agency can match. An agency can then use its employees' expertise to argue that it "knows best" and that members of Congress and the president should adopt the policies it prefers. Since most members of Congress and most occupants of the Oval Office are likely to lack the same level of expertise, they may be inclined to accept the agency's recommendations. As a result, agencies can use their expertise to see that the government follows their policy preferences.

The political value of expertise depends on two critical factors: the extent to which an agency's employees are the only ones who possess expertise on the issue in question, and the size of the knowledge gap between the experts and non-experts. The experience of the Social Security Administration (SSA) illustrates the value of holding a monopoly, or exclusive possession, on expertise. In the 1930s and 1940s, the SSA persuaded Congress to adopt the policies it preferred because Congress lacked the economic expertise needed to challenge the analyses the SSA produced. By the 1960s, however, congressional committees had developed their own staffs of economic experts, which enabled Congress to make independent judgments about the merits of the SSA's recommendations.[32]

The effect a large knowledge gap has on the political power of an agency is clear in the very different experiences of the National Aeronautics and Space Administration (NASA) and the State Department. When NASA advised Congress during the 1960s on the best way to implement President Kennedy's goal of reaching the moon, most members did not have access to independent scientific advice and were inclined to accept the advice of NASA's scientists. NASA gained considerable prestige and power as a result. In contrast, White House officials and many members of Congress believe they know as much about diplomacy and foreign policy as the foreign service officers in the State Department. As a result, they do not hesitate to challenge or dispute the advice the department offers or to second-guess its actions. Unable to convince other government officials that it possesses a special expertise, the State Department finds itself seriously constrained in deciding how to conduct diplomatic relations.

Admiral Frank Kelso, Chief of Naval Operations, testifying before Congress in 1993 on the effect allowing gays and lesbians to serve openly in the military would have on the morale of the armed forces. Agencies such as the Defense Department rely on their expertise to help persuade Congress to accept their recommendations.

Differences in Agency Power

Agencies differ widely in their ability to achieve their mission and survival goals.[33] Agencies with politically strong clienteles and formidable levels of expertise have much greater say over the course of public policy than agencies with weak clienteles or expertise perceived to be common knowledge. Thus, while some agencies are recognized as powerful players in the federal government and have more influence in creating rules, others must act much more deferentially.

Political Constraints on the Federal Bureaucracy

Although government agencies seek political power to ensure their survival and to promote their policy preferences, they are by no means all-powerful. Because the rules of American politics disperse and balance power, no individual or institution possesses unrestrained power over the system. The bureaucracy, like other institutions, exercises power, but always within constraints. Congress, the president, interest groups, other federal agencies, and the courts all may challenge an agency's decisions. Such challenges make an agency accountable for its actions and encourage it to do more than simply respond to its own preferences, its self-interest, or the interests of its clientele.

Congress

The Constitution gives Congress important powers over the bureaucracy, including the authority to create (and therefore abolish or modify) agencies, to determine their structure and responsibilities, and to appropriate funds for their use. These are truly "life and death" powers from the agencies' viewpoint, and as a result, Congress wields enormous influence over the workings of the federal bureaucracy.

Congress exercises its bureaucratic powers primarily through its committees and subcommittees. Each committee oversees the operation of agencies that fall within its jurisdiction and makes recommendations regarding the operation and funding of those agencies to the parent body—the House or the Senate. Committees oversee agencies by a variety of means. The most common methods include direct communications between committee staff and the agency, hearings held to oversee or reauthorize agency programs, and evaluations of agency programs performed by congressional support agencies such as the General Accounting Office and the Congressional Research Service.[34]

Congress's decision to assign oversight responsibilities to its committees has significantly affected its relations with the bureaucracy. Committees tend to be controlled by members whose constituents are also the clienteles of the agencies the committees are charged with overseeing.[35] For example, legislators from farm states are more likely to serve on the agriculture committees, and legislators with military bases in

During the 1992 presidential campaign, Bill Clinton promised to end the Defense Department's ban on allowing gays and lesbians to serve openly in the military. Once in office, Clinton discovered that despite his position as commander in chief, the military resisted his plan.

their districts are more likely to serve on the armed services committees. These committee members have a greater incentive to cooperate with the agency they oversee than members whose constituents have little or no stake in the operations of the agency. As a result, the committees charged with overseeing a federal agency often are more inclined to help that agency than the House or Senate as a whole is.

The President

Presidents often find themselves in conflict with the federal bureaucracy over the resources the agencies should receive and the manner in which agencies should administer policy. Because the nation cannot afford to give each federal agency all the money it wants, presidents must set spending and policy priorities, a process that makes some agencies winners and others losers. Agencies that win are those whose budgets increase and whose policy proposals move to the top of the president's political agenda. The agencies that lose are those forced to make do with smaller budgets and whose policy proposals are ignored or opposed by the White House.

Of course, when presidents seek to set spending and policy priorities for the federal bureaucracy, they must compete with the more specialized policy aspirations of agencies and their clienteles. And often presidents get bloodied in the resulting political battle. Take, for example, Bill Clinton's promise during the 1992 presidential election campaign to end the ban on allowing gays and lesbians to serve openly in the armed forces. After he was inaugurated in January 1993, Clinton found his proposal denounced by members of the military, their allies on Capitol Hill, and conservative interest groups. Thus, despite his position as commander in chief, Clinton eventually was forced to accept a substitute policy on gays and lesbians that effectively gutted his campaign promise.

Although the battle over gays and lesbians in the military reminds us that presidents do not always get their way in battles with the federal bureaucracy, they do win more often than not. The reason is that the rules of American politics give presidents several powers they can use to enforce their spending and policy priorities. First, the Constitution charges the president with seeing that the laws are faithfully executed. This power permits presidents to oversee the work of federal agencies. Second, presidents appoint (subject to Senate confirmation) the leadership of most agencies. Presidents who use the appointment power effectively can influence how agencies implement policy.[36] For example, after more than a decade of relaxed enforcement of various regulatory policies under agencies headed by Republican appointees, President Clinton appointed individuals with a more activist orientation to agencies such as the Occupational Safety and Health Administration, the Food and Drug Administration, and the Consumer Product Safety Commission. These agencies, in turn, have been much more aggressive and vigilant as they enforce regulations affecting the industries within their jurisdictions.[37]

In addition to using their oversight and appointment powers, presidents can constrain the power of the federal bureaucracy by exercising their right to propose budgets and legislation to Congress. Although Congress is ultimately responsible for appropriating all government expenditures, presidential budget proposals are usually the starting point for most debates on federal spending and public policy because presidents have the power to both propose budgets to Congress and to veto appropriations bills with which they disagree. The burden then rests with an agency and its allies on Capitol Hill to build a majority coalition that will change the president's budget, a task that often proves difficult. Thus, when Ronald Reagan proposed lower budgets for the Environmental Protection Agency in the early years of his administration, Congress largely followed his lead. As a result, the agency was forced to reduce its research and enforcement activities, an outcome that pleased a president who thought that environmental regulations were unduly hampering the growth of the American economy.[38]

The fourth way presidents can influence the behavior of the federal bureaucracy is by reorganizing the structures of individual agencies. Reorganization can strengthen or weaken an agency. In 1970, for example, Richard Nixon sought to demonstrate his personal commitment to the environment and to strengthen the government's ability to protect the environment by consolidating the government's many environmental programs under the leadership of the newly formed Environmental Protection Agency.[39] In contrast, in 1971, Nixon sought to undermine the government's core welfare program, AFDC. Political support for AFDC was weak, but the program was administered by the Department of Health, Education, and Welfare (HEW) along with several other assistance programs that enjoyed strong political support. Nixon moved the more politically popular assistance programs into another part of HEW and then imposed spending cuts and other changes on AFDC that he hoped would reduce the welfare rolls.[40]

Finally, presidents can use the Office of Management and Budget (OMB) to curb the power of the federal bureaucracy. As we discussed earlier in the chapter, agencies issue rules as part of their task in administering government policies. Since the 1970s, these rules have had to be cleared by OMB before they can be issued. If the president objects to a proposed rule, OMB can block its implementation or force the agency to rewrite it to the president's liking.[41] The sharp decline in the rule-making activities of the federal bureaucracy in the 1980s, as depicted in figure 13.3, owed largely to President Ronald Reagan's adroit use of the OMB clearance process to block the imposition of new rules he disliked.

Interest Groups

One of the most potent checks on the power of the federal bureaucracy comes from the opposition of interest groups whose interests have been harmed by the actions of an agency. Very few agencies pursue policies that harm no one. For example, in 1995, the Food and Drug Administration proposed rules to limit the sale of cigarettes to minors. Even though most people agree that minors should be discouraged from smoking, the FDA's proposal triggered a torrent of protests from tobacco companies, advertising agencies, magazine publishers, sponsors of sporting events, and even some charitable groups that receive contributions from tobacco companies.[42] In general, the more important an issue is to the groups that oppose it, and the more powerful those opponents are, the less likely an agency is to get its own way.

Groups that believe they have been or are about to be harmed by a federal agency may look to the president for help.[43] In the early 1970s, many companies found that the cost of adhering to new Environmental Protection Agency regulations was squeezing their profit margins. The companies responded by urging President Nixon to intervene on their behalf and convince the agency to relax its regulations. The Bush administration actually formalized the process of responding to complaints from the business community about burdensome government regulation when it created the White House Council on Competitiveness. Under the leadership of Vice President Dan Quayle, the Council advocated business interests, forcing federal agencies to revise regulations that it believed damaged American economic competitiveness.[44]

The surveillance flights that produced evidence of Soviet missiles in Cuba in 1962 were delayed several days as the CIA and the Air Force squabbled over which organization should make the flights.

Groups that oppose an agency's actions may also turn to Congress for help. For example, in 1995, the Occupational Safety and Health Administration (OSHA) proposed regulations to protect workers from "repetitive strain injuries." Such injuries occur to employees in occupations such as meat packing and computer programming because these employees have jobs that require them to make the same movements over and over all day long. Business groups, including the National Association of Manufacturers and the National Federation of Independent Business, denied that employees suffered repetitive strain injuries on the job. These groups appealed to the Republican majorities in Congress for relief from the regulations. In the face of this pressure, OSHA withdrew the proposed regulations.[45]

Other Agencies

In addition to the constraints Congress, the president, and interest groups impose, the aspirations of agencies with overlapping or competing jurisdictions also constrain the power of an agency to act as it sees fit. While agencies occasionally cooperate with one another, they much more commonly view one another as potential competitors for clients and resources. As a result, agencies engage in "bureaucratic imperialism" as they try to establish themselves as the lead organization in a contested policy area.[46]

A good example of how federal agencies fight one another can be found in the events leading up to the Cuban Missile Crisis of 1962. The crisis arose when the United States discovered that the Soviet Union was installing nuclear missiles in Cuba, a discovery that brought the two superpowers to the brink of war. (War was averted when Soviet leaders eventually agreed to remove the missiles from Cuba.) The discovery of the missiles was delayed for ten crucial days while the State Department, the CIA, and the Air Force squabbled over a proposal to send a U-2 spy plane to take aerial photographs of what they believed were missile launch sites. The State Department opposed the plan, arguing that the United States would find itself in a diplomatic crisis if the Cuban military shot down the plane. The CIA and the Air Force both supported the proposed flight, but they disagreed over who should run the operation. The CIA wanted its pilots to fly the mission because the flight involved covert intelligence gathering, while the Air Force insisted that, given the high risk that the plane might be shot down, a uniformed military officer should make the flight. After ten days of haggling, an Air Force officer, flying a CIA-owned U-2 plane, made the flight that took the pictures that provided definitive evidence that the Soviets were preparing to install nuclear missiles in Cuba.[47]

Bureaucratic arguments are by no means limited to agencies in the foreign policy bureaucracy. Domestic agencies engage in jurisdictional disputes as well. The ongoing competition between the Federal Aviation Administration (FAA) and the National Traffic Safety Board (NTSB) over regulating the airline industry illustrates this type of dispute. The FAA is charged with both promoting air travel and regulating the airline

Agencies are often caught up in heated political disputes. The struggle over logging in Oregon pitted the environmental movement against the logging industry. Regardless of its decision, the Interior Department was certain to disappoint one side.
William Costello © 1993. Reprinted by permission.

industry. As a result, critics have accused it of regulating in the interests of the airline industry rather than the public.[48] In contrast, the NTSB is responsible for investigating accidents involving transportation vehicles and making recommendations for improving travel safety. These overlapping jurisdictions have led to frequent conflicts between the two agencies. In just the last five years, for example, the NTSB has criticized the FAA for failing to train flight personnel properly, to require the use of child safety seats, and to ground certain types of aircraft. The NTSB aired these criticisms as part of its effort to prod the FAA to be more vigilant in protecting the safety of the flying public.[49]

The Courts

A final check on the power of the federal bureaucracy comes from the federal courts. They are often the last refuge for groups that oppose an agency's decisions. The courts can overturn the decisions of federal agencies because the rules of American politics authorize federal judges to review the legality of decisions the government makes.

As we shall see in the next chapter, the federal judiciary is much less sensitive to political pressure than the other two branches of government are. Because federal judges generally do not need to satisfy politically influential interests, they are free to base their decisions on their interpretations of the law rather than on the wishes of the majority or the pleadings of a powerful interest group. The politically insulated nature of legal deliberations makes the courts an attractive access point for groups that have failed to persuade Congress and the president to overturn an agency's decisions. In court, what matters more than political power is whether a group can mount a compelling legal argument that an agency has exceeded its authority or otherwise violated the law.

Instances in which the federal courts limit or overturn the actions of federal agencies abound. A classic example came during the 1980s when environmental groups failed to persuade the Interior Department to stop companies from clear-cutting old forests on federal property in Oregon. Interior Department officials instead favored the interests of the logging industry, which wanted to cut the very old trees because the timber from these old-growth forests commanded higher prices in the market. Unable to persuade the Interior Department to change its policy, environmental groups turned to the federal courts. They asked the courts to bar further logging in the old-growth forests on the grounds that clear-cutting endangered the habitat of the spotted owl, which was protected under the provisions of the Endangered Species Act. Successive federal courts agreed, and they issued injunctions barring further logging. Although President Clinton and Congress subsequently became involved in trying to resolve the issue, the courts remain a potent tool for environmentalists as they struggle to protect these forests.[50]

As you can see, the agencies that make up the federal bureaucracy are political institutions. Their ability to exercise discretion and the often contradictory instructions coming from Congress and the White House enable them to inject their preferences into public policy. To promote their mission and survival goals, agencies seek to gain power by expanding their clientele and by taking advantage of their specialized expertise. Of course, not all federal agencies are equally successful in acquiring political power, and none is free to act entirely as it sees fit. Congress, the president, interest groups, other federal agencies, and the courts all can challenge an agency's decisions. Indeed, because federal agencies constantly interact with these other political actors, particularly congressional committees and interest groups, a predictable pattern of interaction known as the "iron triangle" often results.

Iron Triangles and the Federal Bureaucracy

Iron triangles
The alliance of a government agency, congressional committee or subcommittee, and political interest group for the purpose of directing government policy within the agency's jurisdiction to the mutual benefit of the three partners.

Many observers of the federal bureaucracy have noticed that federal agencies, congressional committees, and interest groups sometimes form a three-way alliance of mutual cooperation. The alliances among these three groups have earned a variety of names, including policy subgovernments, policy whirlpools, cozy triangles, and **iron triangles.** Despite the different names, all of the terms highlight the same common theme: federal agencies, congressional committees, and interest groups working on the same issues often join to shape public policies within their realm of influence to their mutual advantage.[51]

Iron triangles operate most effectively when they form around narrowly defined policy issues. Thus, they typically involve specialized subunits of an agency rather than entire departments, the members of a subcommittee rather than the parent committee, and narrowly focused interest groups rather than the interest group community as a whole. Literally dozens of iron triangles can operate within the federal government at any one time, with each exercising significant influence over its own narrow slice of public policy.

Participants in Iron Triangles

Figure 13.6 illustrates the pattern of mutual interests that holds together the participants in an iron triangle. Consider first the political interest group. It participates in an iron triangle to get Congress to pass laws that favor its interests and to get the bureaucracy to carry out those laws in a favorable manner. To advance its goals, an interest group can offer valuable services to both members of Congress and the agency. For example, it can help members of Congress by contributing to their election campaigns, endorsing their bids for reelection, researching policy issues, and formulating draft legislation. Members find that all of these services help them win reelection and make public policy. As for helping federal agencies, interest groups often lobby Congress on behalf of an agency's budget requests and legislative proposals.

Members of congressional committees participate in the iron triangle to advance their chances for reelection and to gain potential allies for their legislative proposals. To that end, they have something to offer both interest groups and federal agencies. Members can provide the legislative votes needed to enact into law the proposals an interest group favors. Members provide much the same kind of benefit to federal agencies. Members with seats on an appropriate congressional committee can work to protect the agency from criticism as well as push to expand the agency's duties and budget.

Federal agencies have a stake in maintaining the iron triangle because they must solicit support for their budgetary and legislative requests. As we saw earlier, interest groups that are the clients of an agency constitute an important source of political power in Washington, and the support of the appropriate congressional committees goes a long way toward convincing the full House and Senate to approve an agency's requests. In exchange for the assistance that interest groups and congressional committees offer, the agency can implement the law in a way that aids the interest group, and it can help members perform constituency service and other activities.[52]

Limitations on Iron Triangles

Iron triangles are a common feature of government because they meet the needs of their participants so effectively. Yet iron triangles are not the sort of rigid and impenetrable structures that their name suggests. The formation of iron triangles is not inevitable, and their power is not beyond challenge.

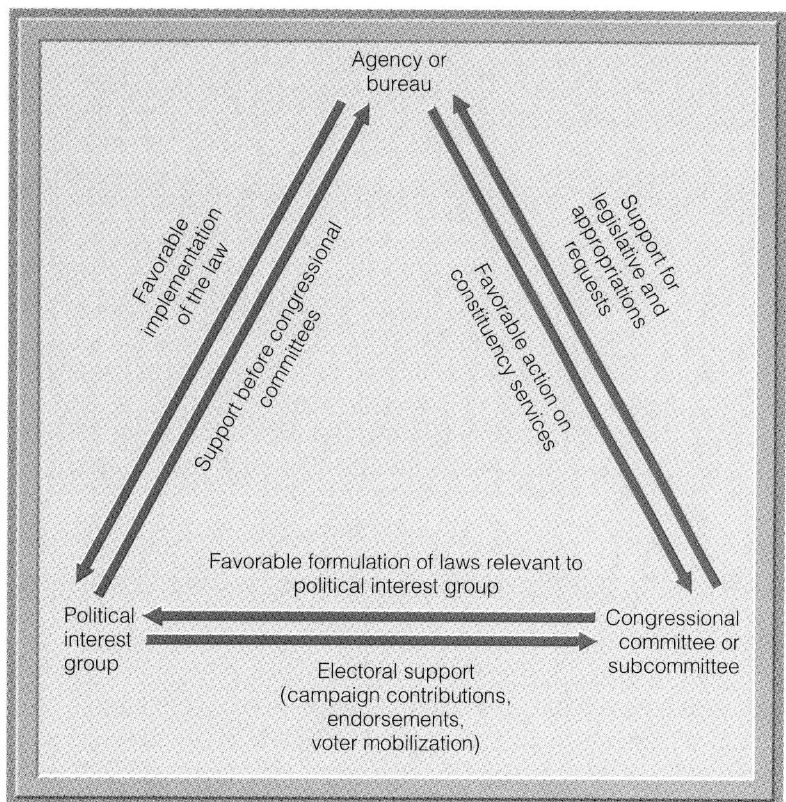

FIGURE 13.6
The Workings of an Iron Triangle

The durability of an iron triangle depends on the extent to which each participant is able to benefit from and help the other two.

Iron triangles are most likely to form when a federal agency and the congressional committees that oversee it face a cohesive and powerful set of interest groups. If the affected interest groups are either poorly organized or bitterly divided, however, an iron triangle is unlikely to develop. For example, no iron triangle could hope to form on a divisive issue such as abortion.

When iron triangles do exist, they are likely to be thwarted when their issue becomes the center of public attention. At such times, the president or Congress may be able to muster support from national majorities for policies that the iron triangle opposes. A classic example of outsiders overriding an iron triangle's policy preferences involved tobacco. When public, congressional, and presidential concerns over the health effects of smoking gained prominence during the 1960s, the iron triangle in tobacco found itself under attack. Although it initially succeeded in fending off attempts to regulate both cigarette smoking and cigarette advertising, opponents eventually won out.[53] Of course, when the spotlight of public attention shifts to other issues, the participants in the iron triangle can reassert their control over policy.

Political Implications of Iron Triangles

Does it matter that iron triangles sometimes exist? In a word, yes. Iron triangles make it difficult for the federal government to formulate comprehensive policies, and they subordinate the interests of the nation as a whole to the interests of small subgroups in American society.

Iron triangles obstruct the ability of the president and Congress to formulate comprehensive public policy because their very nature inclines them to look at issues from a parochial, or narrow, view rather than from a national perspective. Consider, for example, Ronald Reagan's attempt in 1985 to eliminate the Small Business Administration (SBA). Despite repeated efforts to close down SBA as part of his broader effort to reduce government spending, Reagan failed. Widespread support for the agency from small business interest groups, opposition from the congressional committees that

Under the sustained pressure of public scrutiny, the tobacco iron triangle gradually lost control over the government's policies toward smoking. Ultimately, the government imposed warning labels and advertising restrictions, and it has imposed significant restrictions on smoking in public areas.

oversee SBA, and a discreet campaign by Reagan's own SBA director to keep the agency alive meant that, in the end, the SBA remained "alive and well."[54] Because participants in iron triangles tend to put self-interest ahead of the national interest—or, more charitably, take their self-interest to *be* the national interest—they complicate presidential and congressional efforts to pass comprehensive legislation.

In addition to making it difficult to pass comprehensive legislation, iron triangles shape public policy rules to benefit their members at the expense of the general public. The reason stems from the way in which participants in an iron triangle evaluate the benefits and costs of a legislative proposal. They are very sensitive to how much they stand to benefit from a program they support, and they will identify every possible benefit and use the information to justify the program. In contrast, participants in an iron triangle have every reason to ignore the costs of a program because the American taxpayer usually bears those costs. To take one example, farmers, members of the agriculture committees in Congress, and the Department of Agriculture pay close attention to what they stand to gain from the government's policy of crop subsidies. They worry less about how much those subsidies will add to the federal budget because the cost of the subsidies is spread across the entire American public.

The ability of iron triangles to obstruct national legislation and bias public policy in favor of narrow interests appears to be highly undemocratic. Iron triangles have also been criticized for promoting inappropriate and even irresponsible policies.[55] Yet iron triangles flow directly from the decision the founders made at the Constitutional Convention to decentralize political authority in the United States. As we discussed in chapter 2, the founders believed that the best way to protect the rights of the minority from a tyranny of the majority was to structure the rules of politics so that small groups would have opportunities to block or promote legislation they had strong preferences on. Iron triangles provide minorities with just such an opportunity. Of course, as we have seen, the majority also has the opportunity to override the decisions iron triangles make, but only if the majority becomes concerned with the issue.

The Evolving Role of the Bureaucracy

As we look to the future, it is important to realize that iron triangles are becoming less of a force in American politics. In the wake of a number of changes in American society and politics, fewer iron triangles exist, and those that do are less important in making public policy.[56]

Beginning in the 1970s, the political forces that promoted the rise of iron triangles began to give way. The most important change was a development we discussed in chapter 10, namely, the tremendous rise in the number of organized interest groups. As interest groups multiplied in the 1970s and 1980s, so did the competition for the attention of congressional committees and federal agencies. Since iron triangles operate most effectively when a federal agency and the congressional committees that oversee it face a cohesive interest group community, the appearance of new interest groups with competing policy agendas caused many iron triangles to collapse. The result was to make policy making, and the federal agencies themselves, more responsive to broader segments of the American public.

Iron triangles have often been replaced by less structured policy making arrangements that are more open to participation. These structures have been called **issue networks** or "hollow core" policy making processes.[57] These arrangements permit the involvement of a wider range of participants, both in and out of government, who may take opposing positions on the issues involved. The results are more conflictual interactions and less predictable policy decisions.[58]

Issue networks
A loose collection of groups or people in and out of government who interact on a policy issue on the basis of their interest and knowledge rather than just on the basis of economic interests.

Reinventing the Federal Bureaucracy

Although the decreased prominence of iron triangles has made the federal bureaucracy more responsive to the demands of the American people, the change has not altered the public's view of the bureaucracy. Complaints about government red tape and bureaucratic ineptitude remain a staple of American politics. A 1996 poll found that 61 percent of American adults say the federal government is almost always wasteful and inefficient, while only 35 percent say the federal government often does a better job than people give it credit for.[59] Politicians are quick to respond to the public's dissatisfaction with how government operates. Ronald Reagan, George Bush, and Bill Clinton all won election to the White House in part by campaigning *against* the federal bureaucracy, with Clinton going so far as pledging to "reinvent government." But can a president—or anyone else—make the federal bureaucracy more efficient and effective?

In September 1993, Clinton attempted to make good on his pledge to reinvent government by releasing a report prepared by the National Performance Review, a task force chaired by Vice President Al Gore. Entitled *From Red Tape to Results: Creating a Government that Works Better and Costs Less,* the report contained more than eight hundred recommendations for streamlining what the vice president called "old-fashioned, outdated government."[60] The recommendations affected almost every federal agency. They proposed merging the Drug Enforcement Agency and the Bureau of Alcohol, Tobacco, and Firearms into the Federal Bureau of Investigation; reducing the number of field offices the Army Corps of Engineers, the Department of Agriculture, and the Department of Housing and Urban Affairs maintain; and allowing Americans to pay their federal income taxes by credit card.[61] The administration claimed that enacting all of the recommendations would save the federal government $108 billion over five years and eliminate more than a quarter million federal jobs by 1998 (though some budgetary experts called these figures overly optimistic).[62]

Not surprisingly, the findings of the National Performance Review (NPR) drew bipartisan applause. At the same time, however, many people expressed skepticism that the attempt to rewrite the rules of the federal bureaucracy would succeed. Presidents as far back as Theodore Roosevelt have commissioned task forces to find ways to improve how the federal bureaucracy operates, often with little to show for the effort in the end. For instance, only nine years before the Clinton administration conducted its National Performance Review, the Reagan administration formed the Grace Commission to review the performance of the federal bureaucracy. Like the National Performance Review, the Grace Commission received considerable applause for its proposals to streamline the federal government. Despite the fanfare, though, relatively few of the Grace Commission's recommendations were enacted into law.[63]

Many recommendations to rewrite the rules of the federal government are proposed and then abandoned because "the political gain is less than the political cost."[64] Although President Clinton had the authority to enact as many as 70 percent of the recommendations

Like many of his predecessors, President Bill Clinton wants to streamline the federal bureaucracy. Here he joins Vice President Al Gore to publicize the potential benefits of enacting the recommendations of the National Performance Review.

the NPR made with the stroke of his pen, the proposals with the biggest cost savings required congressional approval. And defenders of the agencies and programs targeted for major changes could be expected to lobby their allies in Congress to block the proposed changes. As a result, most presidents abandon their reform efforts because they eventually decide that fighting Congress and the bureaucracy tooth and nail over restructuring agencies most Americans have never heard of will bring them little political benefit.

Although it is tempting to conclude that agency officials oppose reform proposals simply to ensure the agency's survival, opposition to reform proposals may also be based on the merits of the status quo. As we mentioned in chapter 10 when discussing campaign finance reform, attempts to rewrite the rules of politics may solve one problem but create others. The move by Congress and the Reagan administration in the early 1980s to relax government regulation of the savings-and-loan industry illustrates how reform can produce unintended and undesirable consequences. Proponents of deregulation argued that reducing government intervention would enable individual savings and loans (S&Ls) to become more profitable. This, in turn, would enable them to lend more money to people who wanted to buy homes. Deregulation did not work as planned, however. Freed from the most intrusive government regulations, many savings and loans spent lavishly and invested in risky real estate ventures. By the end of the 1980s, many S&Ls had gone bankrupt. Because the Federal Savings and Loan Insurance Corporation insured most of the failed S&Ls, the federal government had to spend billions of dollars to bail out the industry.

In light of these obstacles to bureaucratic reform, what has been the record of the NPR proposals? After three years, the results were mixed. On the one hand were some clear successes.[65] The Agriculture Department, for example, announced it would shut down 1,274 field offices (one-third of the total) over five years, which would eliminate 11,000 employees at a projected savings of $3.6 billion.[66] More generally, the NPR surprised most experts by achieving almost all of the $12.6 billion in savings projected for its first year.[67] On the other hand, some agencies successfully fought off reform proposals.[68] For example, senior officials in the Justice Department and the Treasury Department let it be known on Capitol Hill that they opposed the proposal to merge the Drug Enforcement Agency and the Bureau of Alcohol, Tobacco, and Firearms with the Federal Bureau of Investigation.[69] This opposition persuaded the White House to drop the merger proposal.

In sum, rewriting the rules of the federal bureaucracy so that it operates more efficiently and more effectively is difficult to do. Part of the reason lies in the survival goals of agencies, and part lies in the conflicting demands the American public places on the bureaucracy. As we discussed earlier in the chapter, it is almost a law of politics that organizations, like human beings, have a drive to survive. Regardless of whether federal agencies and programs have outlived their usefulness, they muster all their political power to avoid being downsized or abolished. Bureaucratic resistance to reform proposals is likely to be especially fierce because bureaucrats who have spent their entire working lives with an agency are likely to believe deeply in the agency's mission. Indeed, we would be deeply suspicious of a naval officer who thought the United States could do without aircraft carriers and submarines, and we would look askance at a member of the National Park Service who advocated the sale of America's national parks.

And while bureaucratic self-interest accounts for some of the inefficiency and ineffectiveness of the federal bureaucracy, the often incompatible expectations of the American public do as well.[70] We expect the federal bureaucracy to treat all Americans equally regardless of their wealth or political stature, but we also expect it to be flexible enough to respond to the needs of people whose problems do not fit neatly into standard categories. We expect the federal bureaucracy to act quickly in response to problems, but we also expect it to avoid acting hastily and wasting taxpayer dollars. We expect the federal bureaucracy to give American companies the room they need to grow and create jobs, but we also expect it to prevent companies from selling unsafe products, polluting the environment, and defrauding investors. We expect the federal bureaucracy to end poverty, hunger, and illiteracy, but we also expect it to spend less of our tax money. Given such a tall order, it is perhaps not surprising that the federal bureaucracy often disappoints the people it serves.[71]

SUMMARY

The rules set forth in the Constitution define the organizational and political context in which the federal bureaucracy must operate. Most important, the Constitution assigns the power to oversee federal agencies to both Congress and the president. Whereas the rules authorize Congress to create and fund agencies, they authorize presidents to appoint senior agency officials (subject to Senate confirmation) and to see that agencies faithfully enact laws. Paradoxically, serving two political masters means that the federal bureaucracy is not entirely under the total control of either. The constitutional rules that divide control of the bureaucracy between Congress and the presidency give federal agencies some freedom to follow their own public policy preferences.

The federal bureaucracy has developed over time in response to political pressures and rule changes. As the public made more demands on the federal government, Congress created new agencies and added more employees and additional duties to existing agencies. At the same time, the rules governing who works in the federal bureaucracy and under what conditions also have changed in response to changing political pressures. For much of the nineteenth century, political loyalty was the primary criterion for hiring federal workers, but the American public increasingly came to view this practice as corrupt and inappropriate. Beginning in the 1880s, the federal bureaucracy moved away from the spoils system and toward a new set of rules—a civil service system in which merit rather than political or party loyalty is the primary standard for hiring new workers.

Although many Americans believe that federal agencies should be apolitical organizations that simply administer the decisions of Congress and the president, the administrative tasks of the federal bureaucracy are inherently political. Congress and the president lack the time needed to specify all the details of public policy, and they often give contradictory directions. As a result, federal agencies have some freedom to decide how to fulfill their responsibilities. To that end, each agency's performance is colored by its defined mission and by its desire to survive and grow as an organization.

To carry out their mission and survival goals, agencies seek to acquire power. The two most important sources of agency power are the support of well-organized clientele groups and the agency's own expertise. Agencies that serve politically powerful clients and that have highly valued expertise are well positioned to achieve their goals. This is not to say, of course, that these agencies can act as they see fit. All federal agencies operate within constraints that Congress, the president, interest groups, competing agencies, and the courts impose. The rules of American politics disperse power, which gives the bureaucracy some influence but also imposes constraints.

To enhance their influence in policy making, many federal agencies take part in a coalition known as an iron triangle, a three-way alliance of mutual cooperation that involves an agency, the congressional committees that oversee it, and interest groups affected by the agency's decisions. The participants work together to enact policies that benefit the interest group, help members of the committees get reelected, and enable the agency to grow and prosper. Iron triangles are most likely to succeed when their activities generate little public attention and the affected interest groups are unified in their views. In the 1970s and 1980s, however, the political environment became increasingly hostile to iron triangles. As the number of interest groups multiplied, many agencies found themselves involved in issue networks, facing a host of new interest groups with competing policy agendas. The appearance of interest group competition made policy making, and the federal agencies themselves, more responsive to a broader segment of the American public.

Despite the increased responsiveness of the federal bureaucracy, Americans continue to complain about the inefficiency and ineffectiveness of the federal government. Presidents dating back to Theodore Roosevelt have commissioned task forces to find ways to improve the management of the federal government, but most proposals to rewrite the rules of the federal bureaucracy have fallen by the wayside. The failure of most reform efforts stems from two factors: bureaucratic self-interest and the conflicting demands of the American people. Bureaucracies seldom volunteer to cut their budgets or scale back their activities; instead, their goals are to survive and to prosper. At the same time, Americans place a diverse set of demands on the federal government, with the result that the federal bureaucracy faces a series of complex and often contradictory goals that impede its efficiency and effectiveness. The rules of American politics that allow a diversity of voices to define the goals of government also make it difficult for government to respond with a unified, cohesive set of public policy rules.

Key Terms

Advice and consent	Clientele	Rule adjudication
Bureaucracy	Expertise	Rule administration
Bureaucrats	Iron triangles	Rule making
Cabinet	Issue networks	Spoils system
Civil service	Patronage	

Readings for Further Study

Fesler, James W., and Donald F. Kettl. *The Politics of the Administrative Process.* Chatham, N.J.: Chatham House, 1991. A thorough, up-to-date review and analysis of the tasks, processes, characteristics, and problems of the bureaucracy.

Goodsell, Charles T. *The Case for Bureaucracy: A Public Administration Polemic,* 3d ed. Chatham, N.J.: Chatham House, 1993. A useful corrective for stereotypical criticisms of the bureaucracy. Demonstrates that bureaucratic behavior is generally acceptable and responsible.

Kettl, Donald F., and John J. DiIulio, Jr., eds. *Inside the Reinvention Machine: Appraising Governmental Reform.* Washington, D.C.: Brookings Institution, 1995. A thorough review of the accomplishments and shortcomings of the National Performance Review's attempt to "reinvent" government.

Meier, Kenneth J. *Politics and the Bureaucracy: Policymaking in the Fourth Branch of Government,* 3d ed. Belmont, Calif.: Brooks/Cole, 1993. A concise yet thorough discussion of bureaucratic politics. Especially valuable for its treatment of recent developments in the bureaucracy's relationship with Congress, the presidency, the courts, and interest groups. Concludes with discussions of possible reforms.

Quarles, John. *Cleaning Up America: An Insider's View of the Environmental Protection Agency.* Boston: Houghton Mifflin, 1976. An engaging account of the origins and early years of the EPA. Illustrates the many political pressures agencies confront in fulfilling their administrative duties.

Rourke, Francis E. *Bureaucracy, Politics and Public Policy,* 3d ed. Boston: Little, Brown, 1984. An excellent introduction to the broad topic of politics in the bureaucracy. Discusses both the goals and resources of the bureaucracy, as well as the constraints it operates within.

Rubin, Irene S. *Shrinking the Federal Government: The Effects of Cutbacks on Five Federal Agencies.* New York: Longman, 1985. Uses comparative case studies to assess the effects of budget cutbacks on government agencies. In an era of limited budgets, this book provides relevant and important analyses of how agencies cope with fiscal constraints.

Seidman, Harold, and Robert Gilmour. *Politics, Position, and Power: From the Positive to the Regulatory State,* 4th ed. New York: Oxford University Press, 1986. A classic, comprehensive discussion of the functions and politics of the bureaucracy. A challenging book with commensurate rewards.

Wilson, James Q. *Bureaucracy: What Government Agencies Do and Why They Do It.* New York: Basic Books, 1989. Wilson analyzes why some government agencies work well and others do not.

CHAPTER

14

THE COURTS

The Federal Courts

- *The Constitution and the Federal Courts*
- *Congress and the Federal Courts*
- *The Federal Court System*

The Federal Courts as Policy Makers

- *Judicial Review, Judicial Activism, and Policy Making*
- *Limitations on the Courts*

The Supreme Court as a Political Institution

- *The Characteristics of the Court*
- *The Politics of Nomination and Confirmation*
- *Presidential Legacies on the Supreme Court*

Decision Making at the Supreme Court

- *Hearing a Case*
- *Individual Decision Making*
- *Supreme Court Opinions*
- *Voting Patterns*
- *Who Wins Before the Supreme Court?*

The Lower Federal Courts

- *District Courts*
- *Courts of Appeal*
- *Nomination and Confirmation*

State Courts

- *Organization*
- *Judicial Selection*
- *Length of Service*
- *State Laws*

Summary

Key Terms

Readings for Further Study

In 1995, a unanimous Supreme Court held in *Rubin v. Coors Brewing Co.* that a federal law preventing brewers from listing a beer's alcohol content on the label violated the brewers' right to free speech.[1] The law, which the Coors Brewing Company had contested, had been written just after the end of Prohibition, and it reflected the federal government's desire to prevent brewers from luring customers with higher alcohol content.[2] While the Court recognized that the government had a legitimate interest in trying to promote public safety through the labeling restriction, it noted that the government undercut its own efforts in three ways: by allowing states to determine whether alcohol content could be mentioned in advertising (which can happen in thirty-two states), by allowing brewers to label higher-alcohol beers "malt liquor" and lower-alcohol beers "nonalcoholic," and by allowing alcohol content to appear on labels for other products, such as wine and hard liquor. Thus, the Court considered the current regulation irrational and threw it out. Now brewers may tell prospective customers the alcohol content of their beer on its label.

The Supreme Court's ruling in *Coors* highlights an important lesson about democracy in the United States: every day, judges make decisions, large and small, that affect the way Americans live. Yet while Americans have the right to choose who represents them in Congress and who will serve in the White House, they have no direct say in who sits on the Supreme Court or any other federal court, and in a number of states they have only limited say over who serves on state courts. How does a judiciary that often lies beyond the direct control of the public fit into the concept of a democracy?

The answer lies in the nature and purpose of the court system in the United States. All democracies need a formal system that allows individuals, groups, and government agencies to challenge people they believe have violated the rules and infringed on their rights. Without such a system, political might will triumph over individual rights, and societal conflict will likely escalate into violence. Thus, although the courts have few democratic qualities, they are an integral part of our democracy because they can protect the rights of individuals and restrain the government from overstepping or abusing its power.

In this chapter, we will examine the role the courts play in our democracy. We begin by looking at what the Constitution says—and does not say—about the federal courts, and we examine the way Congress has structured the federal judiciary. We then discuss how the federal courts have become important policy makers by exercising their power to decide the legality of government actions, how justices are picked for the Supreme Court, and how they decide cases once they reach the bench. We also analyze the work of the lower federal courts. We conclude the chapter by examining the state courts, which handle the vast majority of legal cases in the United States. Although state courts mirror some of the basic attributes of the federal judiciary, they also differ in important ways from the federal courts.

The Federal Courts

The federal court system is a joint creation of the Constitution and Congress. The Constitution established the federal judiciary as one of the three branches of government, but it says remarkably little about what the federal court system should look like. Instead, the founders delegated to Congress the task of designing a court system that would fit the needs of the new country. Over the next two hundred years, Congress fulfilled its constitutional duty by passing legislation that created (and abolished) federal courts as the needs of an ever-changing country demanded.

The Constitution and the Federal Courts

The delegates to the Constitutional Convention firmly believed that the success of American democracy depended on the creation of a court system independent of the executive and legislative branches of government. To this end, Article III of the Constitution created the federal judiciary as a separate branch of government.

In 1995, the Supreme Court ruled that the federal government could not bar brewers from listing the alcohol content of their beer. The ruling illustrates how the courts make decisions, large and small, that affect the way Americans live.

Although the founders believed deeply in the idea of an independent judiciary, they spent relatively little time discussing it, and they provided little guidance on how to organize the federal courts. Article III says "the judicial power of the United States shall be vested in one supreme Court," and it lists the subjects on which the federal courts can rule (although Congress is authorized to make exceptions to the list). Article II gives the president the right to appoint federal judges with the advice and consent of the Senate, and it gives Congress the right to remove judges and other government officials through the impeachment process. Overall, however, the Constitution is silent on the question of how to organize the federal courts. Indeed, while the Constitution specifically creates the Supreme Court, it says nothing about how many justices should serve on it.

Instead of providing a blueprint for the federal court system, the Constitution charged Congress with designing one. The founders delegated the task to Congress because they disagreed over how many federal courts the country needed. Some argued that all court cases should originate in state courts, thereby negating the need for any federal courts other than the Supreme Court.[3] Rather than allowing the Constitutional Convention to flounder over a dispute on how to organize the judiciary, the founders authorized Congress to decide the matter.

Congress and the Federal Courts

Over the past two hundred years, Congress has passed many laws affecting the organization of the federal judiciary. The first was the Judiciary Act of 1789. One key provision of the act stipulated that the Supreme Court would consist of a Chief Justice and five associate justices. The act also settled the question of how many federal courts there should be by creating a federal court system consisting of the Supreme Court, circuit courts, and district courts.

Although the Judiciary Act of 1789 set important precedents, it has been modified many times. For example, the Supreme Court initially was created with six seats.

Congress changed the number of Supreme Court justices more than half-a-dozen times during the nineteenth century, so that the Court had as few as five members at one point and as many as ten members at another. The current number of nine justices was set in 1869. Since then, there have been several attempts to make the Court larger. The most famous was the so-called court-packing scheme of 1937 in which President Franklin Roosevelt asked Congress to pass a law requiring the appointment of one additional justice for each sitting justice over the age of seventy. This would have immediately increased the size of the Court to fifteen members. Roosevelt hoped that a larger Court stacked with his appointees would be more sympathetic to his New Deal programs, but ultimately his plan failed to secure congressional support, and the number of justices remained at nine.[4]

Likewise, over time Congress has changed elements of the court system. In the Court of Appeals Act of 1891, Congress created powerful courts of appeals; the original circuit courts withered and were finally abolished in 1911. Since 1911, the Supreme Court, appeals courts, and district courts have remained the three basic levels in the federal judiciary.[5] And as the American population has grown, Congress has responded by adding to the number of appeals and district courts.

Constitutional courts
The three-tiered system of federal district courts, courts of appeal (originally circuit courts), and the Supreme Court. Article III of the Constitution provides for the creation of these courts.

Legislative courts
Various administrative courts and tribunals that Congress establishes, as Article I of the Constitution provides.

Legal scholars refer to the Supreme Court, appeals courts, and district courts as **constitutional courts** because Article III of the Constitution provides for their creation and because that Article's safeguards against removal from the bench and salary cuts apply to the judges appointed to them. In addition to its responsibility for organizing the constitutional courts, Congress can also establish **legislative courts,** so-called because their legal basis stems not from Article III, but from a clause in Article I allowing Congress "to constitute tribunals." Legislative courts are usually designed to deal with specific issues or to administer specific congressional statutes. In 1988, for example, Congress established the Court of Veterans Appeals to review the decisions the Department of Veterans Affairs makes. Legislative courts enjoy less independence than constitutional courts. Judges on the Court of Veterans Appeals, for example, serve for fifteen-year terms, whereas constitutional judges serve for life.[6] Other legislative courts include the U.S. Court of Military Appeals, the Court of International Trade, and the U.S. Tax Court. Although legislative courts can be important in specific circumstances, the constitutional courts handle most federal litigation, and they are the focus of our attention in this chapter.

The Federal Court System

Figure 14.1 shows the three tiers in the current configuration of the federal court system. The Supreme Court sits atop the federal judiciary. Almost all of the cases it takes are on appeal from other courts. The decisions the Supreme Court makes are final unless Congress and the president go to extraordinary lengths—such as passing new laws or proposing constitutional amendments—to overturn them, or the Court chooses to reverse itself. Although the Court can decide very broad issues, such as the constitutionality of laws, many of its holdings (or rulings) are decided on very narrow grounds. Thus, only a few of its decisions each year gain much public attention; many are of interest to relatively few people.

Beneath the Supreme Court are the thirteen courts of appeals. As figure 14.2 shows, twelve of the courts of appeals have a geographical jurisdiction. Congress created the Thirteenth Court of Appeals in 1982. Called the Court of Appeals for the Federal Circuit, it fields cases dealing with specialized subjects such as patents, copyrights, and trademarks. The courts of appeals form the middle tier of the federal judiciary, and they hear appeals of decisions that the district courts and some federal administrative agencies make.

The lowest tier in the federal court system comprises the ninety-four district courts (eighty-nine districts in fifty states, plus one each in the District of Columbia, Puerto Rico, Guam, Virgin Islands, and Northern Marianas Islands.) The district courts are almost always the courts of original jurisdiction, meaning they are the first court to hear a

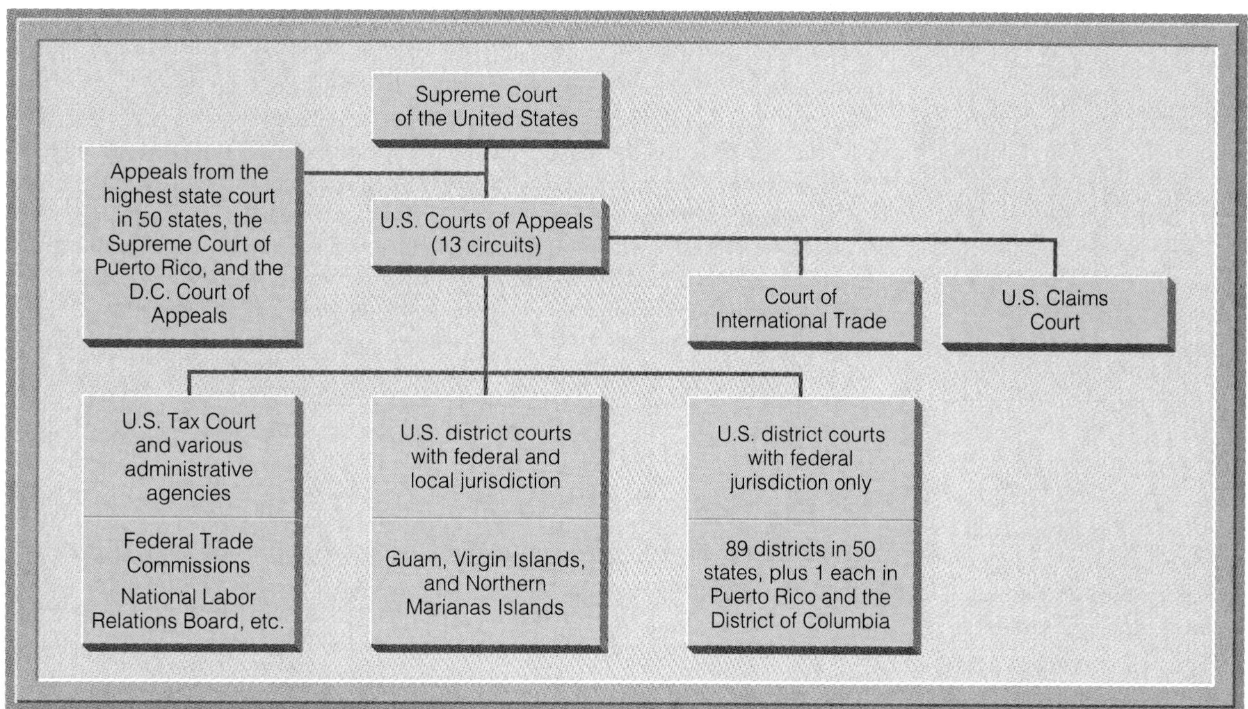

Figure 14.1
The U.S. Federal Court System

The federal court system has three tiers: district courts, courts of appeals, and the Supreme Court.

From Administrative Office of the United States Courts as appeared in Harold W. Stanley and Richard G. Niemi, *Vital Statistics on American Politics,* 3d ed. Copyright © 1992 CQ Press, Washington, DC. Reprinted by permission.

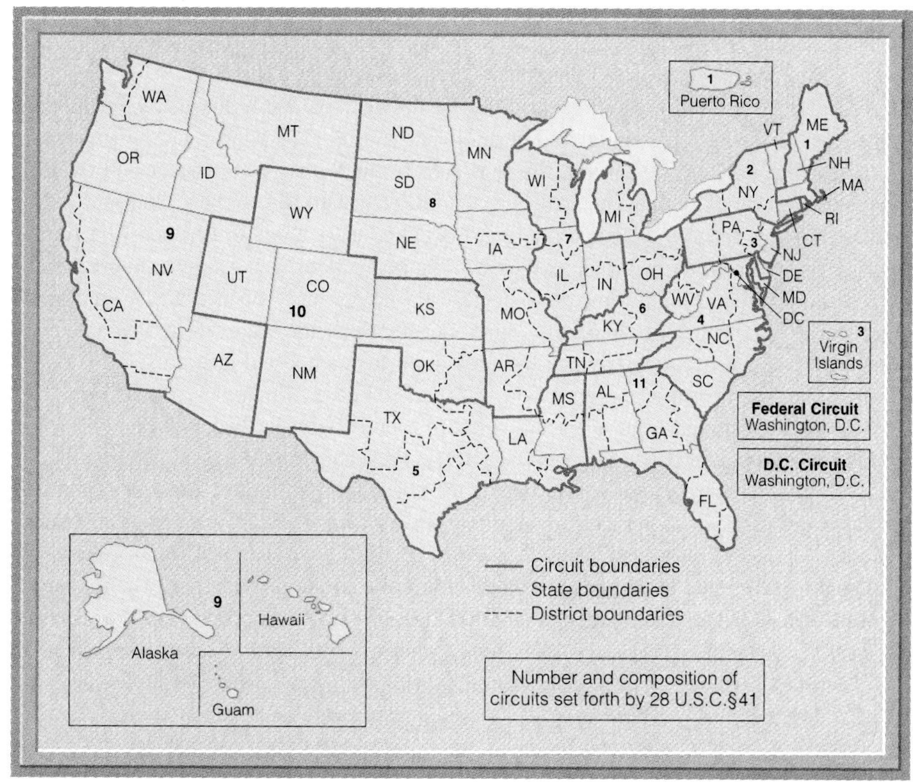

Figure 14.2
The Thirteen Federal Judicial Circuits and Ninety-Four U.S. District Courts

The courts of appeals and the district courts are organized geographically.

From Administrative Office of the United States Courts as appeared in Harold W. Stanley and Richard G. Niemi, *Vital Statistics on American Politics,* 3d ed. Copyright © 1992 CQ Press, Washington, DC. Reprinted by permission.

case. In a district court, a single judge presides over a trial to determine guilt or innocence in federal (but not state) criminal cases or to assess responsibilities or fault in federal civil cases. District courts handle more than 280,000 cases each year.[7]

Most of the cases that reach the Supreme Court were heard first in one of the ninety-four federal district courts and then in one of the thirteen appeals courts. The vast majority of legal cases, however, never make it to a federal appeals court, let alone the Supreme Court. Only about 10 percent of cases in district court are appealed to courts of appeals. In turn, only a small percentage of the cases the courts of appeals decide are appealed to and taken up by the Supreme Court. Legal cases also can make it onto the docket of the Supreme Court through other routes. For example, the decisions of each state's highest court can be appealed directly to the Supreme Court when a substantial federal question is involved, as can other cases that Congress may specify. Nonetheless, the most common route is federal district court to federal appeals court to Supreme Court.

The Federal Courts as Policy Makers

The founders envisioned the federal courts as independent bodies, applying the laws and policies established by the legislative and executive branches of government. Yet the federal courts almost immediately became policy makers when the Supreme Court established the power of judicial review. This power gives the federal courts great influence over the way our democracy operates and over our everyday lives.

Judicial Review, Judicial Activism, and Policy Making

By sketching the federal court system in broad outlines only, the Constitution left unclear what powers the federal judiciary would exercise. As a result, the federal courts spent the first two decades after the Constitutional Convention defining their role in the American political system. In these years, the federal courts established two key rules of the American political system: the rulings of the federal judiciary are superior to those of state courts, and the federal judiciary has the authority to overturn the decisions of both the executive and legislative branches of government.

Article VI of the Constitution stipulates that the U.S. Constitution is to be held superior to state constitutions and laws. The Judiciary Act of 1789 confirmed the supremacy of the federal judiciary by giving the Supreme Court the right to review and overturn state court decisions on laws or treaties that conflicted with federal law. And in the 1796 case of *Ware v. Hylton,* the Supreme Court declared a state law to be unconstitutional.[8] Thus, almost immediately, the federal courts asserted superiority over state courts.

Although the Constitution does declare the supremacy of the U.S. Constitution over state laws, it does not explicitly empower the Supreme Court to review and overturn the decisions of Congress and the president. Instead, Chief Justice John Marshall claimed that right for the Supreme Court in the 1803 case ***Marbury v. Madison.***

Marbury v. Madison
The Supreme Court decision in 1803 that established the principle of judicial review.

The case stemmed from a dispute between members of the Federalist Party and the Democrat-Republican Party. On March 2, 1801, President John Adams, a Federalist, appointed William Marbury to be a justice of the peace in Washington, D.C. The next day, Adams's last in office, the proper appointment papers were filled out and signed, but acting Secretary of State John Marshall (who had just recently been named Chief Justice of the Supreme Court) failed to deliver the papers before the stroke of midnight, when Adams's term of office expired. Subsequently, Adams's Democrat-Republican successor, Thomas Jefferson, ordered his secretary of state, James Madison, not to give Marbury the papers.

Marbury filed suit with the Supreme Court, asking it to issue a *writ of mandamus* ("we command" in Latin) to Madison; that is, he wanted a Court order forcing Madison to give him his appointment papers. Marbury could request a writ of mandamus because a section of the Judiciary Act of 1789 provided for it. The Court did not make a decision on the case until February 1803, in its first meeting since December 1801. The Court's opinion, written by Chief Justice Marshall, was a legal and political masterpiece. In it, Marshall, an ardent Federalist, scolded President Jefferson for not giving Marbury his

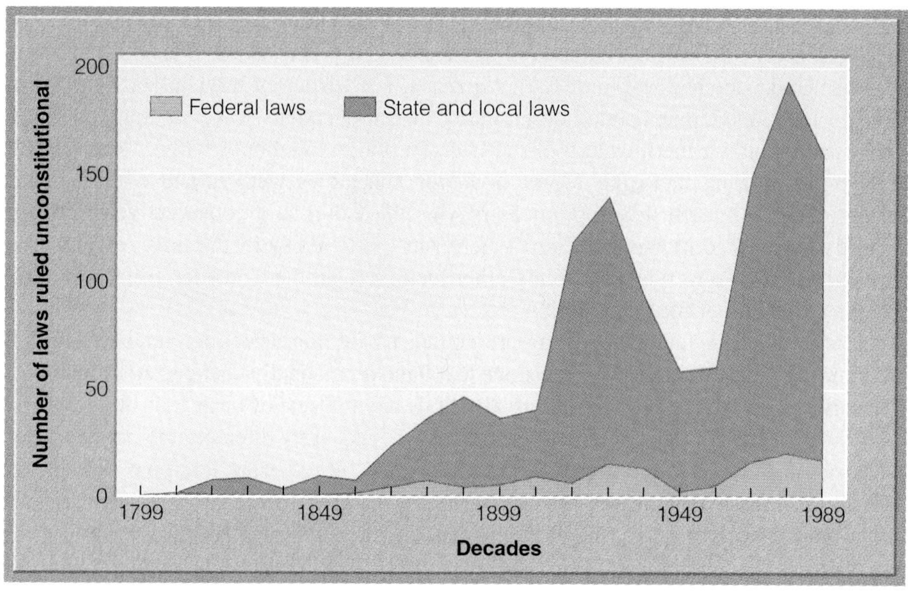

FIGURE 14.3
Laws Declared Unconstitutional, 1799–1989

The number of state and federal laws the Supreme Court has declared unconstitutional each decade has increased over time.

Source: Data from Harold W. Stanley and Richard G. Niemi, *Vital Statistics on American Politics*, 4th ed. (Washington, D.C.: CQ Press, 1994), p. 308.

rightful position. But Marshall went on to say that the Court did not have the power to force the president to deliver the appointment papers because the Court found the section of the Judiciary Act giving them that power to be an unconstitutional extension of the Court's jurisdiction. Thus, the Court claimed the right to declare a law unconstitutional by nullifying a law Congress had passed to increase the Court's power.[9]

The Supreme Court's ruling in *Marbury v. Madison* established the doctrine of **judicial review.** This doctrine, a bedrock principle of American jurisprudence, allows the Supreme Court, none of whose members must stand for election, to declare the acts of the president and Congress unconstitutional, and thus null and void. Federal district courts and courts of appeals also may rule that legislation is unconstitutional, and their rulings are binding unless a higher court reverses them.

Judicial review
The doctrine allowing the Supreme Court to review and overturn decisions made by Congress and the president.

President Thomas Jefferson and members of Congress recognized at the time that Chief Justice Marshall was claiming a new power for the Supreme Court. Yet neither Jefferson nor Congress moved to kill the doctrine of judicial review. The White House and Capitol Hill agreed to accept the new doctrine partly because both Jefferson and a majority in Congress agreed with the substantive decision that the Court had reached in *Marbury,* if not with the reasoning it used. A second reason that the White House and Capitol Hill accepted judicial review was the persuasiveness of Marshall's skillfully written opinion. Although the Constitution did not explicitly grant the power of judicial review, Marshall argued convincingly that it did so implicitly.[10]

A third reason Congress and the president accepted the doctrine of judicial review was that the Supreme Court used its new-found power sparingly. Indeed, the Court did not declare another act of Congress unconstitutional for more than fifty years. (The second instance came in *Dred Scott v. Sandford,* the tragic 1857 case that helped set the stage for the Civil War.) As figure 14.3 shows, in recent years, the Supreme Court has become more willing to overturn federal, state, and local laws, though judicial review is still a rather rare event. Even so, judicial review remains a powerful weapon. The threat that the Supreme Court may overturn a law often influences how Congress, state legislatures, and city councils draft legislation.

The power the federal courts have to decide which laws are and are not constitutional raises concerns. Many observers worry that judicial review has evolved into **judicial activism** as federal judges overturn laws to impose their policy preferences on the public rather than to uphold the Constitution. A problem arises, however, when it comes to distinguishing between judicial review, which is acceptable, and judicial activism, which, to many people, is not. In most instances, the distinction lies in the eye of the beholder.

Judicial activism
The vigorous use of judicial review to overturn laws and make public policy from the federal bench.

To see how difficult it is to distinguish between judicial review and judicial activism, consider the criticisms leveled against the Supreme Court over the past four decades. Under the leadership of Earl Warren, Chief Justice of the United States from 1953 to 1969, the Court handed down many liberal decisions. Liberals applauded the Court for upholding the meaning of the Constitution, while conservatives accused the justices of ignoring it. In the 1980s, however, the tables were turned when Ronald Reagan and George Bush's appointees pushed the Court in a conservative direction. Liberals began to criticize the Court's activism, particularly in the areas of personal and civil rights. Conservatives, on the other hand, lauded the Court for adhering to the essential meaning of the Constitution.

Concerns about judicial activism are neither trivial nor academic. Since the 1950s, the Supreme Court has rendered decisions that have dramatically changed American life. It has overturned state laws prohibiting abortions and the sale of birth control devices. It has fundamentally restructured the criminal justice system by directing the police to follow strict procedures when investigating crimes and by requiring that poor defendants receive a lawyer. On all sorts of issues, from legislative redistricting to environmental issues to free speech to prayer in the public schools, the Court has changed the way government operates and the way Americans live. Clearly, judicial review might give judges bent on judicial activism powers inconsistent with common notions of democracy because judges are free to impose their views on the public through the legal system.

Limitations on the Courts

Despite the doctrine of judicial review and the potential for judicial activism, the federal judiciary does not exercise unlimited power. Four factors curb the power of the courts: the reactive nature of the courts, their inability to enforce their rulings, the ability of the president and Congress to draft new laws, and public opinion.

American courts are by their very nature reactive. In our legal system, courts can rule only on cases brought before them; they cannot seek out cases to decide or issue rulings on hypothetical cases. (They can, however, shift the focus of a case from the issues the litigants want to discuss to matters the justices find more compelling. For example, the famed case of *Mapp v. Ohio* (1961) initially involved obscenity issues. Yet, because the police had seized the obscene materials without a search warrant, the Court used the case to rule that evidence obtained from an illegal police search must be excluded from a trial.[11] There is evidence that the Court answers questions not raised by the parties with some frequency.)[12] For example, if Supreme Court justices want to change previous abortion decisions, they must wait until a relevant case is appealed to them; they cannot go out and drum up business. In contrast, the president and Congress are both free to initiate policy. Additionally, decisions the courts reach tend to be on small, specific points, producing policy changes that are narrowly focused rather than expansive.[13] The courts tend to take small steps, not large ones, in changing policy.

The second limitation on the power of the courts is that they depend on other government agencies to enforce their decisions. As we saw in chapter 5, many southern states initially refused to obey the Supreme Court's ruling in *Brown v. the Board of Education* that they desegregate their schools. The refusal to obey court decisions also arises on far less prominent matters. For example, in 1989, the Supreme Court ruled that states cannot exempt religious periodicals or books from sales taxes.[14] In Rhode Island, however, shopkeepers continued to exempt bibles and other "canonized scriptures" from the sales tax, as a 1982 state law required them to do. Even after the state division of taxes notified all Rhode Island book stores in 1992 that the exemption was now illegal, many stores continued to exempt religious books. Even more striking is that Rhode Island's legislative leaders failed to support the repeal of the unconstitutional religious exemption from the state statutes when some legislators introduced legislation that would have done just that.[15]

In addition to being limited by the reactive nature of the legal system and a lack of enforcement power, the power of the courts is limited by the ability of Congress and the president to write new laws. Sometimes Congress responds to Supreme Court decisions by proposing amendments to the Constitution. When the Supreme Court overturned a federal law lowering the voting age to eighteen in 1970, Congress and the states nullified the Court's decision by adopting the Twenty-sixth Amendment a year later.[16] The Eleventh, Fourteenth, and Sixteenth Amendments also were adopted to overcome Supreme Court decisions.[17] Similarly, after the Court handed down a 1990 decision that made it easier for states to restrict religious practices, Congress and the president responded in 1993 with the Religious Freedom Restoration Act. As we noted in chapter 4, this act returned the standard the courts were to use to the stricter interpretation used before the 1990 decision.[18]

Not all attempts to overturn the Supreme Court's decisions, however, succeed.[19] Members of Congress have submitted hundreds of proposed constitutional amendments to overturn the ban against official school prayer. None has passed. And when the Court ruled in 1989 that the First Amendment protected an individual's right to burn the American flag, outraged members of Congress immediately tried (and failed) to amend the Constitution to outlaw flag burning as a form of political protest. In other cases in which the courts find a law is flawed, Congress may simply rework the offending provision. As we will discuss at greater length in chapter 16, the Supreme Court in 1985 overturned Gramm-Rudman, a bill designed to cut the federal budget deficit, because it contained a provision that violated the separation of powers. Congress responded by rewriting the offending provision to comply with the Court's objections.[20]

The final limitation on the power of the courts is public opinion. The founders designed the courts to be isolated from public and political sentiments. But as Justice Felix Frankfurter observed, "The Court's authority—possessed of neither the purse nor the sword—ultimately rests on sustained public confidence."[21] Although the public hardly follows the courts in any detail—on average, only 30 percent of Americans say they follow important Supreme Court cases closely—public opinion of the Court does change in response to its decisions.[22] For example, when the Warren Court handed down a series of unpopular decisions protecting the rights of people accused of crimes, public confidence in the courts dropped.[23]

The risk the Supreme Court faces is that a series of unpopular rulings will anger the public and move Congress to pass laws that restrict the independence of the judiciary. And the justices recognize the risk they run. During their deliberations on the abortion-rights case *Planned Parenthood of Southeastern Pennsylvania v. Casey* (1992), the justices were acutely aware of the need to maintain the legitimacy of the Court in the public eye (see box 14.2 later in the chapter). Yet throughout its history, the Court rarely has been out of step with the mainstream of public opinion for an extended period of time, although it is quicker to respond on some issues, such as criminal procedure, than it is on others, such as civil rights.[24] Indeed, as figure 14.4 shows, with the exception of a liberal period under Chief Justice Earl Warren, the Court has tended toward moderate decisions. The reason for this congruence is not that justices respond to current political passions, though they sometimes may, but rather that, as we will see, the political process by which judges are appointed to the bench keeps the courts in touch with public sentiment.

The Supreme Court as a Political Institution

Supreme Court justices wield considerable power. Acting collectively, they have the power to set the course the law will follow, even to the extent of overruling the preferences of the president and Congress. But like all federal judges, the justices attain their seats on the Supreme Court through a highly politicized process. How does politics affect the selection of justices? Does a politicized process ensure a more democratic system, or undercut it? Obviously, who serves—and how they get to the bench—matters.

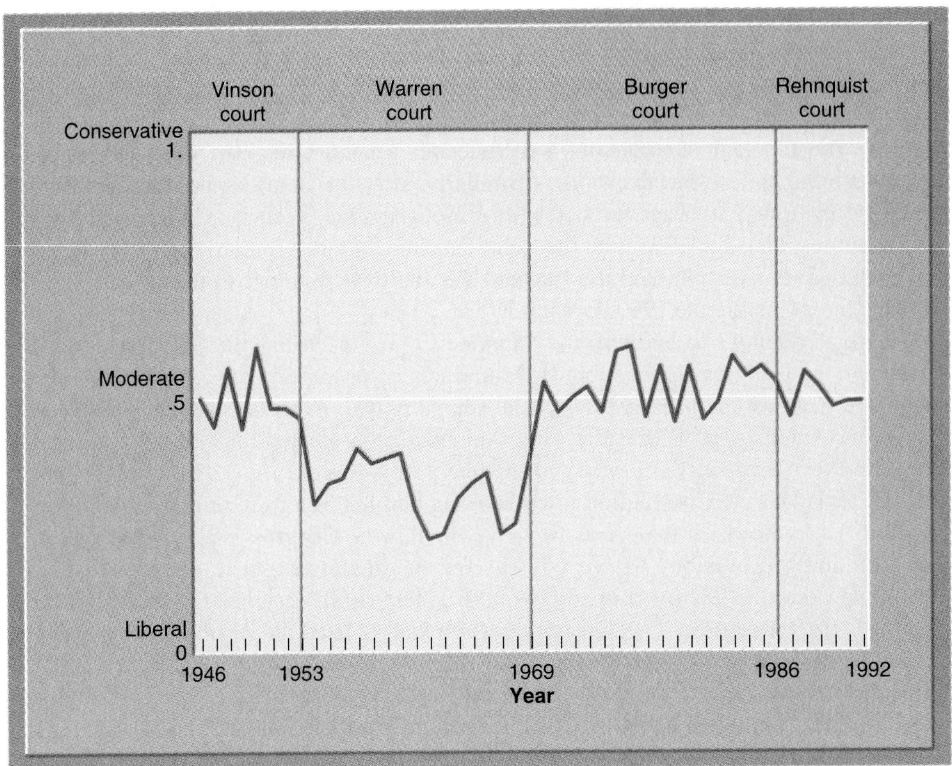

Figure 14.4
The Supreme Court's Ideological Direction, 1946–1992

With the exception of the Warren Court, the modern Supreme Court generally makes moderate decisions.

Source: Calculated from *The United States Supreme Court Judicial Database* by Professor Timothy Hagle, University of Iowa.

The Characteristics of the Court

To understand how the Supreme Court operates, it is necessary first to explain the basic characteristics of the Court: who serves, the typical career path of a justice, the special powers of the chief justice, the average length of service on the Court, and the rewards of service.

Who Serves?

Since the Court's inception, slightly more than one hundred people have served as justices. As is the case with presidents and members of Congress, almost all of the justices have been white Protestants, and all but two have been men. Several Catholics have served, though little attention was paid to their religion. Controversy did surround the nomination of the first Jewish justice, Louis Brandeis, in 1916. (Indeed, one of the other justices refused to talk to Brandeis for the first three years he served on the Court and even refused to sit next to him when the Court had its picture taken.) The first African-American justice, Thurgood Marshall, was not appointed until 1967. Upon his retirement in 1991, he was succeeded by another African American, Clarence Thomas. The first woman justice, Sandra Day O'Connor, was named only in 1981. In 1993, Ruth Bader Ginsburg joined her. No other minorities or women have served on the Supreme Court.

How They Arrive at the Court

Although each Supreme Court justice has followed a different career path, they all share one common trait: they all have been lawyers. (The Constitution does not require justices to be lawyers, nor does it establish a minimum age as it does for Congress and the presidency.) Most justices have served previously as judges at either the state or federal level. Even William Howard Taft, the president who later became chief justice, served as a state and federal judge early in his career. If anything, previous judicial experience has become even more important in recent decades. Every appointee since William Rehnquist and Lewis Powell in 1971 has had judicial experience. But some

The first woman appointed to the Supreme Court, Justice Sandra Day O'Connor (third from left) meets with the Court's second female member, Ruth Bader Ginsburg, in 1993.

notable members of the Court have not served on the bench before joining the Supreme Court. For example, Earl Warren was the governor of California and had been the 1948 Republican nominee for vice president when President Eisenhower appointed him chief justice in 1953. The comparison of the resumes of William Rehnquist and Sandra Day O'Connor in box 14.1 shows the different paths they took to the Court.

The Chief Justice

The chief justice is considered first among equals on the Supreme Court, but the job's importance and standing has evolved over time. The Constitution mentions the position only in passing; Article I, Section 3 requires that the chief justice preside over any impeachment trial of a president. As mentioned earlier in this chapter, the Judiciary Act of 1789 specified a chief justice, along with five associate justices. Since the mid-1860s, the official title of the post of chief justice has been "Chief Justice of the United States," further distinguishing it from the positions of the associate justices, who are justices "of the Supreme Court."[25] Like the other justices, the chief justice is nominated by the president and confirmed by the Senate. Even sitting members of the Court must be reconfirmed if they are elevated to chief justice. The chief justice typically is the most publicly prominent member of the Court. The chief justice, for instance, usually administers the oath of office to the president and speaks for the federal courts to Congress and the public. The chief justice plays this latter role because he—so far every chief justice has been a man—is responsible for carrying out numerous administrative tasks, such as chairing the organizations that oversee the management of the federal courts.

Chief justices can influence the direction of the Supreme Court in several ways. The chief justice presides at the public hearing in which the lawyers in a case present their oral arguments, chairs the conference where the justices decide each case, determines who will write the opinion of the Court when he is part of the majority, and initiates the discuss list.[26] This last power is important. The discuss list contains those cases appealed to the Court that the chief justice believes are important enough to warrant further discussion. Only about 20 to 30 percent of all cases appealed to the Supreme Court make it onto the discuss list. The other justices may add to the discuss

THE PEOPLE BEHIND THE RULES

BOX 14.1

The Career Paths of William Rehnquist and Sandra Day O'Connor

In 1952, two promising students graduated from Stanford University's prestigious law school: William Rehnquist and Sandra Day O'Connor. Both had attended Stanford as undergraduates. Both had distinguished law school records—O'Connor was an editor of the Law Review and earned other academic honors, and Rehnquist graduated first in their class. Both would eventually gain the highest prestige in their profession by becoming Supreme Court justices. But in reaching the Supreme Court, the two justices followed very different career paths.

Rehnquist's credentials landed him the most prestigious position a law school graduate can covet: a clerkship with a Supreme Court justice. After he completed his clerkship, Rehnquist practiced law in Phoenix, Arizona, and became involved in Republican politics. One of the people he worked with in Arizona, Richard Kleindienst, later became a deputy attorney general in the Nixon administration. Kleindienst appointed Rehnquist as the head of the Justice Department's Office of Legal Counsel. In that position, Rehnquist dealt with constitutional law matters, and he did his job with such skill that President Nixon appointed him to the Supreme Court in 1971. President Reagan nominated Rehnquist to be chief justice in 1986.

Sandra Day O'Connor followed a different road to the Supreme Court. Despite her remarkable record in law school, O'Connor had a difficult time finding a job after graduation. Many firms, including one in Los Angeles whose partners included William French Smith—who as Reagan's attorney general would bring O'Connor to the president's attention—offered her a job only as a legal secretary. Finally, she worked as a deputy county attorney while her husband finished law school. She followed her husband to Germany while he was in the military, working there as a civilian attorney for the Army. After her husband's tour of duty was finished, they returned to Phoenix.

The Stanford Law School Class of 1952 included two future Supreme Court justices, William Rehnquist (back row, furthest left) and Sandra Day O'Connor (first row, second from left).

O'Connor spent eight years raising her three sons and engaging only part-time in various legal activities. In 1965, she returned to work full-time outside the home, taking a position as an assistant attorney general for Arizona. O'Connor was appointed to fill a vacancy in the state senate in 1969, and she was elected to that seat in her own right the next year. In 1972, she was elected majority leader, the first woman in the country to hold that position. O'Connor was elected to the bench in Maricopa County in 1974 and was appointed to the Arizona Court of Appeals by Democratic governor Bruce Babbitt in 1979. Two years later, President Reagan upheld a campaign pledge to name a woman to the Supreme Court by nominating O'Connor to fill the first vacancy of his term.

Source: Elder Witt, ed., *The Supreme Court and Its Work* (Washington, D.C.: Congressional Quarterly, 1981), pp. 185–87.

list the chief justice starts, but they may not subtract from it. Thus, the chief justice always has the opportunity to convince his colleagues to hear a case he thinks warrants attention.[27] Because of the leadership role chief justices play, Supreme Court eras are usually associated with a particular chief justice, such as the Warren Court (1953–1969) or the Burger Court (1969–1986).

Length of Service

Justices can serve for life—and most serve until they die or retire from public life. But service on the Supreme Court has not always been attractive. One of George Washington's original appointees declined the offer, preferring instead to take a state office. Another served just two years and never attended any sessions before he resigned to become the chief justice of the South Carolina State Supreme Court. Among Washington's original appointees, most served only a few years and only one served as long as ten.

A seat on the Supreme Court became more appealing, and members began to serve longer, once the Court established itself as an important part of the American political system. William O. Douglas had the longest career of any Supreme Court justice, serving from 1939 to 1975, a period that spanned seven presidencies. Lengthy service on the Court is now the norm—the last ten justices to die or retire from office served an average of twenty-five years each. Such long tenures explain why presidents regard a Supreme Court nomination as one of the most important decisions they will make—the justices they appoint are likely to be on the bench long after the president has left the White House.

William O. Douglas served on the Supreme Court from 1939 to 1975—longer than anyone in history. Lifetime appointments to the federal bench cause the courts to respond slowly to public opinion.

Rewards of Service

The attraction of a seat on the Supreme Court today is easy to see. Becoming a justice represents the pinnacle of a legal career, even though the $164,100 salary in 1995 was much lower than any of the justices could expect to make in private practice. (The chief justice earned slightly more, $171,500.) Each justice is allowed to select his or her own law clerks—the best and brightest law school graduates—a practice that allows even elderly justices to shoulder the heavy workload. During the first half of the nineteenth century, many members served until they died, but the creation of a pension system in 1869 has since induced most members to retire from the bench. Usually advancing age and failing health trigger their decision, but some members have tried to time their departures to improve the prospects that they will be replaced by someone with a similar approach to the law.[28]

The Politics of Nomination and Confirmation

The Constitution states that the president nominates federal court judges subject to Senate approval. Because both presidents and senators want the Supreme Court to champion their view of the law, the nomination and confirmation of a Supreme Court justice is an inherently political process. At times the process may appear unseemly, but the mix of presidential nomination and Senate confirmation means that elected officials determine who serves on the Supreme Court, and, in turn, ensures that the Court remains in touch with the electorate.

Every president has many opportunities to appoint judges to district and appeals courts, but whether a vacancy opens up on the Supreme Court during a presidential term depends on a number of variables, including the age and tenure of the Court's members.[29] William Howard Taft, for example, appointed six justices during his one term as president, whereas Jimmy Carter did not have the opportunity to nominate a single justice during his four years in office.

Because appointments to the Supreme Court offer presidents the chance to affect judicial decisions far into the future, they want to choose competent, capable people who think as they do *and* who can win Senate confirmation. Presidents occasionally nominate a justice who belongs to the other political party—as Richard Nixon did when he picked Lewis Powell, a Democrat—but usually they stay within their own partisan camp. Perhaps surprisingly, given the partisan overtones of almost every nomination, most nominees are confirmed with little controversy. But twelve appointments have been formally rejected by a Senate vote, and another seventeen were withdrawn before the Senate could consider them.[30]

Nominations become contentious for several reasons.[31] When a president appears politically weak, the Senate is less likely to approve his nominees. For example, after Lyndon Johnson announced he would not seek reelection in 1968, he tried to fill a Supreme Court vacancy. Although Democrats controlled the Senate, Republicans were able to block confirmation of his nominee, arguing that the next president should make the selection. A president's nominees may also run into trouble when his party is the minority party in the Senate. Richard Nixon, for example, saw the Democratic-controlled Senate reject his nominations of Clement Haynsworth and G. Harrold Carswell in 1969 and 1970, and a Democratic-controlled Senate rejected Ronald Reagan's nomination of Robert Bork in 1987.

Supreme Court confirmations have become contentious since the Senate rejected Robert Bork's nomination.

Bruce Beattie/Copley News Service. Reprinted by permission.

Supreme Court nominations also can become controversial if the nominee is perceived to lack the necessary credentials for the post or has exhibited behavior some people regard as improper. For example, Harrold Carswell's credentials for a seat on the Supreme Court were so weak that one Republican senator was forced to defend him by arguing that, "There are a lot of mediocre judges and people and lawyers and they are entitled to a little representation [on the Court], aren't they?"[32] Douglas Ginsburg, whom Ronald Reagan nominated to the Supreme Court in 1987, was forced to withdraw from consideration because he admitted using marijuana while he was a law professor. And although many Democrats disliked Clarence Thomas's legal and political views, his nomination was not seriously threatened until a former subordinate, Anita Hill, accused him of sexual harassment.

Besides becoming controversial because the president is politically weak or because of shortcomings in the credentials or character of the nominee, a Supreme Court nomination may become contentious if a nominee's legal and political views clash with those of powerful members of the Senate. In the past few decades, only the nomination of Robert Bork was contested wholly on the nominee's views, though ideological differences are usually what drives senators to try to defeat a nomination. (Senators prefer to attack a nominee's credentials or character rather than his or her political views because it protects them from charges that they are making the Supreme Court a partisan political issue.) Bork's legal views came under attack because he had taken controversial positions on a wide range of social and legal issues in his distinguished career as a Yale law professor and as a court of appeals judge. Worried that his confirmation would give conservative justices a majority on the Court, liberal senators used Bork's writings to argue that his beliefs were out of step with those of a majority of Americans.

Although Bork's nomination was defeated, and Reagan's second choice, Ginsburg, withdrew, President Reagan succeeded in appointing a conservative when the Senate confirmed his third choice, Anthony Kennedy. Similarly, even after the Senate rejected Nixon's nominees, Haynsworth and Carswell, it confirmed his third choice, Harry Blackmun. The lesson is simple: although it may take some perseverance, presidents can almost always appoint a Supreme Court justice who they believe shares their legal views. But in recent years the nomination contest has become more contentious, with presidents subjected to more pressures as they decide on a nominee, and all steps of the process taking longer as supporters and opponents gather information and map political strategies.[33]

Presidential Legacies on the Supreme Court

Do justices vote the way the president who selected them wants? Not necessarily. Among the justices serving on the Court in 1996, Ronald Reagan's three appointees (Sandra Day O'Connor, Antonin Scalia, and Anthony Kennedy) and Richard Nixon's last remaining choice (William Rehnquist) were clearly conservative, as we would expect. Similarly, President Bush's selections reflected his more muddled ideological disposition: one was a moderate (David Souter) and the other a hard-line conservative (Clarence Thomas). President Clinton's choices also seemed consistent with his preferences: a moderate (Stephen Breyer) and a liberal (Ruth Bader Ginsburg). But among the generally liberal members of the Court was John Paul Stevens, who was named to the bench by Gerald Ford, a Republican. Overall, presidents are usually happy with their selections, but the voting behavior of some justices clearly comes as a surprise.

Although observers frequently generalize about a justice's conservative or liberal leanings, on particular issues, a justice may take positions that contradict his or her usual behavior. Justice O'Connor, for example, is generally conservative, but on cases involving sex discrimination in the workplace, she sometimes sides with the Supreme Court's liberals—perhaps because of her own experience with sex discrimination (see box 14.1). Justices Kennedy and Scalia surprised their conservative supporters when they agreed with the Court's majority that flag burning is a constitutionally protected form of speech.

A justice's legal views also may change over the course of his or her career.[34] Former Justice Blackmun, for example, was thought to be so conservative when he first joined the Supreme Court that he and the conservative Chief Justice Warren Burger—a lifelong friend from Minneapolis and another Nixon appointee—were referred to as the "Minnesota Twins."[35] But over time, their voting records diverged widely, with Blackmun championing many liberal positions. In sum, a judge's ideology can be complex and variable, making it tricky to reduce it to a simple label such as liberal or conservative. Thus, even when presidents get the people they want on the bench, there is no guarantee the results will be what they wanted.[36]

Many liberals were troubled by the knowledge that President Reagan's judicial appointments would still be on the bench long after Reagan left the White House. Most still serve today.

From *Herblock At Large*, Pantheon Books, 1987. Reprinted by permission.

Decision Making at the Supreme Court

When justices take their seat on the Supreme Court, they are assuming one of the most powerful posts in American politics. The immense responsibility that the justices bear for deciding the course of American law raises four key questions: What procedures does the Court follow when deciding whether to hear a case? How do individual justices decide which way to rule on a case? How does the Court communicate its opinion in a case to the public? And do some groups in American society enjoy an advantage over others when it comes to arguing their positions before the Supreme Court?

Hearing a Case

The Supreme Court meets annually in one regular session, starting on the first Monday in October. The term lasts until the Court has finished the business before it or has decided to lay over to the next session any undecided cases. In most years, that means the Court is in session until June or July. The Court meets in a special session when it must decide a case that cannot wait for the regular term.

Cases may reach the Supreme Court by several routes. In a few rare situations, most notably in disputes between states or between a state and the federal government, the Supreme Court has original jurisdiction, meaning it is the first court to hear the case. Another unusual route to the Supreme Court is certification, when an appeals court requests a review to settle a question of law. But the majority of cases presented to the Supreme Court are appeals of court of appeals decisions, and most of the rest come directly from state supreme courts when an important federal issue is at stake. Technically, most appeals ask for a **writ of certiorari,** an order the Supreme Court issues requiring a lower court to send the records of a case to it for review.

Writ of certiorari
A Supreme Court order for a lower court to send it the records of a case—the first step in reviewing a lower court case.

FIGURE 14.5
Cases Filed in the U.S. Supreme Court, 1938–1993

More and more cases are being appealed to the Supreme Court.

From Harold W. Stanley and Richard G. Niemi, *Vital Statistics on American Politics,* 5th ed. Copyright © 1995 CQ Press, Washington, DC. Reprinted by permission.

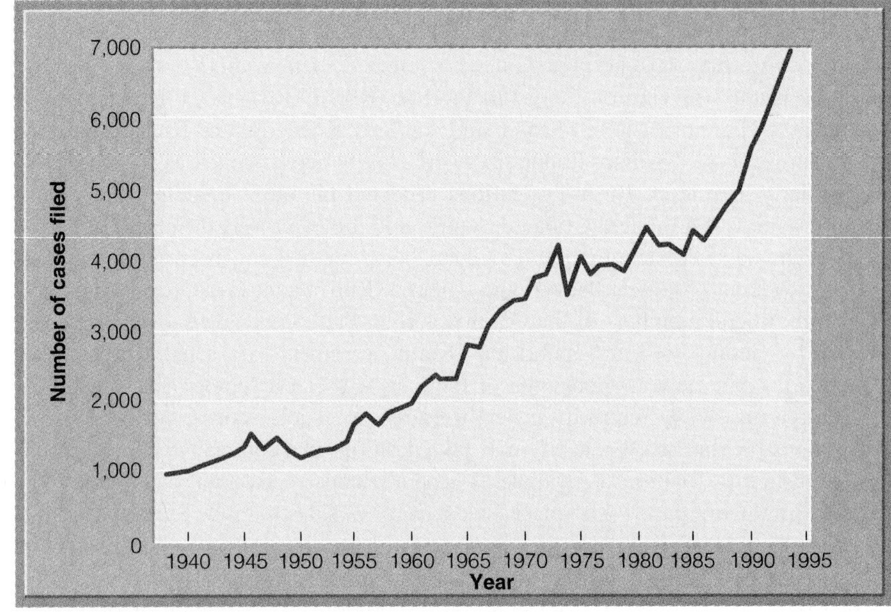

Since 1988, when Congress changed some of the rules governing how cases reach the Supreme Court, the justices have had almost complete control over which cases they will hear. The Court is asked to hear far more cases each year than it has the capacity to handle, and, as figure 14.5 shows, the number of cases appealed to the Supreme Court has escalated over the last fifty years. Despite the growing number of appeals, the number of cases the Court decides to hear has declined. Over the past two decades, the Court has heard an average of slightly more than 150 cases each year, but in recent years it has heard far fewer cases.[37] With a few exceptions, the Court can pick and choose the cases it wishes to hear.

All of the cases appealed to the Supreme Court are first reviewed to determine if they raise legal issues the Court needs to address. Most of the cases the Court is asked to hear fail to make it past an initial screening the justices' law clerks perform. The 20 to 30 percent of the cases deemed important enough for consideration by the chief justice or any one of the associate justices are placed on the discuss list.[38] The discuss list is brought before a conference that only the nine justices attend. The decision on which cases to accept is based on the **Rule of Four:** if at least four justices want to hear a case, it goes on the schedule. The Rule of Four is used to manage the demands on the Court's time by focusing the attention of the justices on the most important cases.[39]

Rule of Four
The Supreme Court rule that at least four justices must decide that a case merits a review before it goes on the Court's schedule.

Which cases are heard?[40] Procedural considerations eliminate some from consideration. These considerations include whether there is an issue to be adjudicated (a case may be moot by the time it reaches the Supreme Court) and whether the person or group bringing the suit has a legal right, or standing, to do so. Other variables also matter in deciding whether the Court will hear a case. The Court is most likely to hear cases in which the federal government is appealing, lower courts have issued conflicting decisions, or one or more uninvolved but interested parties, called ***amicus curiae,*** ask for a review.[41] The term *amicus curiae* literally means "friend of the court," and the rules of the Supreme Court allow for almost unlimited *amicus curiae* participation.[42] As we discussed in chapter 10, more than seventy different groups, including church organizations, medical associations, and others, filed *amicus curiae* briefs with the Court in the 1989 abortion-rights case of *Webster v. Reproductive Health Services.*[43] In a 1994 Court case involving a suit over whether 2 Live Crew's version of Roy Orbison's classic song "Pretty Woman" was a parody protected by the First Amendment or a copyright infringement, amicus briefs in favor of the rap group's position were filed by, among others, the American Civil Liberties Union,

Amicus curiae
Literally, friend of the court. A person or group that files a legal brief in a case they are not directly involved in.

NBC, political humorist Mark Russell, and *Mad Magazine*. Taking the side of the music company holding the rights to "Pretty Woman" were Michael Jackson, Dolly Parton, and the estates of Leonard Bernstein, Ira Gershwin, and Cole Porter. (The Court ultimately sided with 2 Live Crew.[44]) The presence or absence of amicus briefs may give the Court an important signal as to whether a case warrants its attention.[45] If the Court refuses to take up a case, the last decision reached on the case becomes final.

Once the Supreme Court accepts a case, it is usually scheduled for an oral argument, typically at least three months later. (The Court disposes of some cases by issuing per curium—unsigned—opinions and memorandums.) A few weeks before the hearing, the lawyers for each side submit their written arguments, or briefs. The oral argument allows the lawyers for each side to present their case before the Court. Although oral argument on a single case often continued for days in the nineteenth century, today, each side is limited to only thirty minutes. During a lawyer's presentation, the justices often interrupt to ask questions. Indeed, on one recent occasion a lawyer's argument on behalf of a convict on death row had barely begun when the justices raised questions that instigated a discussion among themselves. When the red light on the lawyer's lectern flashed, signaling the end of the allotted thirty minutes, Chief Justice Rehnquist said, "Thank you Ms. Foster . . . I think you did very well in the four minutes the court allowed you."[46] These short hearings may have much less effect than the written briefs do on a justice's final decision, but some justices find the oral arguments useful in highlighting the important issues the briefs raise.[47]

Individual Decision Making

How do individual justices make decisions? Decisions usually rest on a combination of precedent and the justice's personal judicial beliefs.[48] In some sense, each case argued before the Court has distinctive elements; otherwise there would be no reason for the members of the Court to want to decide it. But almost every case is similar to some other case or cases the Court has decided before. For example, the Court has taken up numerous cases involving free speech. Each case raises certain core issues. Yet each case also presents a new twist on the issue, which gives the Court another opportunity to fine-tune the law on First Amendment rights.

The question that confronts each justice on each case is how bound is he or she to the line of argument previous Supreme Court decisions laid out on this issue? What is the role of ***stare decisis,*** or precedent—the idea that current decisions should be based on past judgments? The answer to this question is somewhat elusive. On occasion, members of the Court will agree on the relevant precedent and employ it without controversy. In a few situations, the Court will choose to reverse itself and overturn a precedent. For example, in 1955, the Court held that a 1934 law making it a crime to lie to an agency or department of the federal government applied to Congress. From then on, the law was used to prosecute people for lying to Congress. But in 1995, the Court changed its mind, ruling that the law only applied to statements made to the executive branch.[49] As the dialogue in box 14.2 demonstrates, however, explicitly overturning a precedent has a potential political cost to the Court. Justices worry that if they overturn too many decisions, the public will conclude that the Court swims with the political tide rather than adheres to legal principles.

Stare decisis
The doctrine that previous Supreme Court decisions should be allowed to stand.

More typical is a case in which precedents are less obvious or lead in different directions. A liberal justice and a conservative justice may agree on the basic facts of a case but rely on different precedents or legal reasoning to reach conflicting decisions. Because the relevance of past cases is often open to dispute, each justice is invariably influenced by his or her past experiences, judicial philosophy, and political beliefs when making legal decisions.[50] It would be hard to imagine, for example, that Thurgood Marshall's experiences as an African American living in a segregated society did not influence the decisions he later reached as a Supreme Court justice.

Point of Order

BOX 14.2

Precedent, Public Opinion, and the Supreme Court's Legitimacy

It is sometimes difficult for Supreme Court justices to determine how much weight to give to precedent and when to overturn a previous Supreme Court decision. For example, in 1992, the Supreme Court issued a much anticipated decision on the constitutionality of a Pennsylvania law that imposed strict regulations on abortion. Abortion-rights supporters argued that the law clearly sought to make it more difficult for women to obtain an abortion, while abortion-rights opponents argued that the law was needed to protect the well-being of women having abortions. In any event, the act did not outlaw abortions. Abortion-rights supporters hoped the Supreme Court would strike down Pennsylvania's law as unconstitutional, while abortion-rights opponents hoped the Court would use the case to overturn the 1973 decision in *Roe v. Wade,* which established a constitutional right to abortion, and declared abortion unconstitutional.

The decision the Supreme Court handed down in *Planned Parenthood of Southeastern Pennsylvania v. Casey* left both sides disappointed. The majority opinion was a rare collaborative effort written by Justices O'Connor, Kennedy, and Souter. Chief Justice Rehnquist authored one of the dissents. Among the issues they debated was *stare decisis*—the role precedent, or previous decisions, should play in reaching the current decision. The justices also touched on the question of the Court's legitimacy and public opinion. The following excerpts illustrate the role precedent played in the arguments of the justices.

Justice Sandra Day O'Connor

Justice Anthony Kennedy

Justices O'Connor, Kennedy and Souter

> The root of American Governmental power is revealed most clearly in the instance of the power conferred by the Constitution upon the Judiciary of the United States and specifically on this Court. As Americans of each succeeding generation are rightly told, the Court cannot buy support for its decisions by spending money and, except to a minor degree, it cannot independently coerce obedience to its decrees. The Court's power lies, rather, in its legitimacy, a product of substance and perception that shows itself in the people's acceptance of the Judiciary as fit to determine what the Nation's law means and to declare what it demands. . . .
>
> The Court must take care to speak and act in ways that allow people to accept its decisions on the terms the Court claims for them, as grounded truly in principle, not as compromises with social and political pressures having, as such, no bearing on the principled choices that the Court is obliged to make. Thus, the Court's legitimacy depends on making legally principled decisions under circumstances in which their principled character is sufficiently plausible to be accepted by the Nation.
>
> The need for principled action to be perceived as such is implicated to some degree whenever this, or any other appellate court, overrules a prior case. This is not to say, of course, that this Court cannot give a perfectly

Continued

Point of Order

BOX 14.2 CONTINUED

Justice David Souter

Chief Justice William Rehnquist

satisfactory explanation in most cases. People understand that some of the Constitution's language is hard to fathom and that the Court's Justices are sometimes able to perceive significant facts or to understand principles of law that eluded their predecessors and that justify departures from existing decisions. However upsetting it may be to those most directly affected when one judicially derived rule replaces another, the country can accept some correction of error without necessarily questioning the legitimacy of the Court.

There is . . . a point beyond which frequent overruling would overtax the country's belief in the Court's good faith. Despite the variety of reasons that may inform and justify a decision to overrule, we cannot forget that such a decision is usually perceived (and perceived correctly) as, at the least, a statement that a prior decision was wrong. There is a limit to the amount of error that can plausibly be imputed to prior courts. If that limit should be exceeded, disturbance of prior rulings would be taken as evidence that justifiable reexamination of principle had given way to drives for particular results in the short term. The legitimacy of the Court would fade with the frequency of its vacillation. . . .

The Court's duty in the present case is clear. In 1973, it confronted the already-divisive issue of governmental power to limit personal choice to undergo abortion. . . . Whether or not a new social consensus is developing on that issue, its divisiveness is no less today than in 1973, and pressure to overrule the decision, like the pressure to retain it, has grown only more intense. A decision to overrule *Roe's* essential holding under the existing circumstances would address error, if error there was, at the cost of both the profound and unnecessary damage to the Court's legitimacy, and to the Nation's commitment to the rule of law.

Chief Justice Rehnquist

We believe that *Roe* was wrongly decided, and that it can and should be overruled consistently with our traditional approach to stare decisis in constitutional cases. . . . The joint opinion of Justices O'Connor, Kennedy, and Souter cannot bring itself to say that *Roe* was correct as an original matter, but the authors are of the view that "the immediate question is not the soundness of *Roe's* resolution of the issue, but the precedential force that must be accorded to its ruling. . . ." Our constitutional watch does not cease merely because we have spoken before on an issue; when it becomes clear that a prior constitutional interpretation is unsound we are obliged to reexamine the question. . . .

The Judicial Branch derives its legitimacy, not from following public opinion, but from deciding by its best lights whether legislative enactments of the popular branches of Government comport with the Constitution. . . .

Source: Planned Parenthood of Southeastern Pennsylvania v. Casey, 112 S. Ct. 2791 (1992).

Californians took notice of their former governor's role in Reynolds v. Sims.

© San Francisco Chronicle. Reprinted by permission.

"Earl! You of all people!"

The Supreme Court's decision in *Reynolds v. Sims* (1964) shows not only how justices can bring their view of the world to bear on a decision, but also how serving on the bench can change that view. The Court decided in *Reynolds* that state legislatures must apportion their legislative districts strictly on the basis of population. Before the *Reynolds* decision, a number of states, including California, had one house in which seats were apportioned as they are in the U.S. Senate, with no assurance that equal numbers of people lived in each district. This way of allocating legislative seats effectively gave certain groups in the state more political clout. In *Reynolds,* the Court held that seats in both houses of a state legislature must be apportioned as they are in the U.S. House of Representatives, with each state divided into districts of equal population so that every citizen of the state is equally represented.

The author of the *Reynolds* decision was Chief Justice Earl Warren. When he was governor of California, Warren had led a successful fight to defeat a state ballot proposition that would have apportioned the state senate on the basis of population. As Chief Justice, he assigned himself the *Reynolds* decision, in part to atone for his past partisan sins:

> My own state was one of the most malapportioned in the nation. . . . The last attempt [to change the apportionment system] was made in 1948 when I was governor. I joined . . . in opposing it. It was frankly a matter of political expediency.
>
> I thought little more about this until *Baker v. Carr* came to the Supreme Court. . . . I concluded that it was a matter for the courts to decide when I . . . remembered my California experience. I then decided that rather than merely join the opinion of one of the other Justices, after having taken the political stand I had in California, I should now squarely face up to the question from a judicial viewpoint. Accordingly, I assigned the state malapportionment cases to myself, knowing that this would create much comment in California.[51]

Supreme Court Opinions

A few days after the Supreme Court hears a case, the nine justices meet alone—with no clerks, stenographers, or other staff present—to discuss the case, along with others they have recently heard. The conference begins as the chief justice offers his analysis of the case and says how he will vote to decide it. The discussion then proceeds in order from the most senior member of the Court (based on length of Court service) to the most junior.[52] In most cases, after the most junior member of the Court has spoken, the chief justice announces a tally of the vote. If the Chief Justice is in the majority, he assigns himself or one of the justices who voted with him to draft the Court's **majority opinion,** the written document that announces to the public the Court's decision on a case and the reasoning the Court used to arrive at that decision. If the chief justice sides with the minority, the most senior justice in the majority determines who will write the opinion.

Majority opinion
The document announcing and usually explaining the Supreme Court's decision in a case.

Majority Opinions

The selection of a justice to write the majority opinion is an important decision. Different justices are likely to write different opinions. Chief justices often assign themselves important cases. But even if they assign a major case to another justice, that choice may determine what sort of decision is written. The last several chief justices have waited until roughly two weeks after a conference before making assignments on cases in which they were in the majority. Such a delay allows the chief justice to accumulate assignments, then distribute them to make the workload more or less even among his colleagues, yet also maintain his flexibility in assigning important decisions.[53]

Once a justice drafts a majority opinion, it is circulated among the other eight justices. Each justice is free to offer suggestions and criticisms. Indeed, the vote taken in the conference is not binding. On occasion, justices change their position on a case after the conference because they find the draft opinion persuasive or because they disagree with it. In a 1989 civil rights case, for example, Justice Kennedy initially sided with the Supreme Court's liberals, but later changed his mind and agreed with the conservatives, swinging the Court's majority with him. Indeed, Kennedy often waits to see how the argument in a decision develops before he commits to it, a practice that has led some law clerks to call him "Flipper" behind his back.[54] But all the Court's members realize that a decision becomes final only when five or more members of the Court agree to sign the majority opinion.

The importance of the majority opinion extends beyond simply announcing which side won. By presenting the reasoning behind the decision it reached, the Court majority sends a signal to lower courts, lawyers, potential litigants, and others about how they are likely to treat similar cases in the future. The opinion, then, is important for what it says and for what it does not say. In a sense, it is the best road map available for figuring out how the law is evolving.

Concurring and Dissenting Opinions

Occasionally a justice will agree with the decision in a case but not with the reasoning used to reach it. In this situation, a justice may write a **concurring opinion,** which lays out how he or she would have preferred the Supreme Court to have arrived at its decision. Justices who disagree with the decision may write a **dissenting opinion,** which explains why they disagreed with the Court's ruling. Dissents are usually more than just sour grapes. They can lay the groundwork for future decisions. During the first decades of the twentieth century, for example, Justice Oliver Wendell Holmes wrote a series of dissents that favored laws giving the federal government more control over commerce. In 1938, the Court finally adopted Holmes's reasoning.[55] Indeed, dissents have become so important over the last few decades, that since the 1970s, the senior justice on the losing side assigns responsibility for writing one, just as the senior justice in the majority assigns the Court's opinion.[56]

Concurring opinion
A statement from one or more Supreme Court justices agreeing with a decision in a case, but giving an alternative explanation for it.

Dissenting opinion
A statement from one or more Supreme Court justices explaining why they disagree with a decision in a case.

Concurring and dissenting opinions perform a valuable function because they state the terms of disagreement clearly and explicitly. But they have become commonplace only since the 1940s. They became more common in large part because Chief Justice Harlan Stone (1941–1946) encouraged his colleagues to engage in open and vigorous argument and because several justices who joined the Supreme Court in the 1940s were less committed to the established norms of doing business.[57] On occasion, the tendency to air differences has led the Court to issue decisions in which a majority agrees on the outcome but not on the reasoning behind it. In such situations, a final ruling giving guidance on the law in that issue is deferred to another time when the members of the Court can come to agreement.

Voting Patterns

In recent years, a substantial percentage of cases each session has been decided by unanimous votes: 43 percent in the 1994–95 Supreme Court term, and 38 percent in

In recent years, a single vote has decided a number of important Supreme Court cases. That raises the possibility that any change in Court membership could produce very different decisions.

the 1993–94 term. But the decisions in many other cases hinge on a single vote. During the 1994–95 term, 20 percent of cases came down to a 5 to 4 decision, with Justices Kennedy or O'Connor usually being considered the key vote—and often writing the Court majority's opinion. Thus, with a significant number of close cases, Justices Kennedy and O'Connor have become the critical swing votes, able to decide the direction of the majority decision. Other justices are somewhat more predictable. Conservative Justices Scalia and Thomas agreed with each other 83 percent of the time in 1994–95, while Clinton's more liberal appointees, Breyer and Ginsburg, ended up on the same side in 79 percent of the cases. In contrast, Justices Stevens and Thomas disagreed on 89 percent of the cases. Indeed, Stevens often found himself standing alone, writing the only dissent to majority opinions close to 10 percent of the time.[58]

Who Wins Before the Supreme Court?

Who wins before the Supreme Court? It is reasonable to expect that litigants who appear before the Supreme Court on a regular basis have an advantage over those who do not. After all, groups that regularly argue cases before the Court are likely to have resources and expertise that others lack.

The federal government is the most frequent litigant before the Supreme Court. The federal government is represented in Supreme Court cases by the solicitor general, who is appointed by the president. The solicitor general decides which cases the government should ask the Court to review and, with the assistance of staff members, prepares the government's position on the cases the Court accepts. Not surprisingly, the federal government won more than 67 percent of the cases it was involved in between 1953 and 1988.[59] Regardless of whether the opposing litigant is a state government, a corporation, a labor union, or an individual, the Supreme Court usually rules in favor of the federal government. Several arcane legal rules that incline the Court to favor the positions the federal government takes aid the federal government's enviable winning percentage. In addition, the solicitor general usually brings only strong cases before the court; likely losers are not pursued.

In ruling so often in favor of the federal government, the justices are not merely repaying favors to their employer. Supreme Court justices, like all federal judges, enjoy considerable independence. The Constitution makes it difficult for Congress or the president to remove a justice, and it bars Congress and the president from punishing justices by cutting their pay. Thus, when a special prosecutor probing the Watergate scandal asked the Supreme Court to order President Nixon to hand over tapes of conversations recorded in the Oval Office, the justices—three of whom Nixon had nominated—voted unanimously to grant the request. (Justice Rehnquist, the fourth Nixon appointee on the Court at that time, did not participate in the decision because he had been a member of the Justice Department during the Nixon administration.) The Court's decision led to Nixon's resignation.

Aside from the federal government, no other litigants appear to have an advantage when arguing before the Supreme Court. Perhaps surprisingly, corporations and other litigants that can afford high-powered and expensive legal counsel do not fare appreciably better than poor Americans. The ability to pay for legal counsel is not a determining factor in part because "even poor defendants with interesting cases can attract skilled and experienced counsel and the financial support of powerful interest groups."[60] Moreover, when deciding a case, the justices look past the resources of particular litigants to the merits of their cases. Although the resource differences between rich and poor matter at lower levels of the court system where access to legal expertise is much more uneven, they do not have much impact at the very top.[61]

The Lower Federal Courts

As we noted earlier, Congress, using the power the Constitution gives it, created two lower federal courts: district courts and the courts of appeals. Like Supreme Court justices, judges in the lower federal courts are appointed in a political process. As we shall see, this process may actually help make the lower federal court system more democratic, because elected officials who represent the areas where the judges will serve strongly influence the selection of federal judges.

District Courts

The district courts, which hold trials and establish the facts of a case, are the starting and ending point of most federal cases. Most federal cases are civil rather than criminal cases: of all federal cases in 1994, 238,590, or 84 percent, were civil cases. More than half of all district court cases involve statutory actions, petitions from prisoners, civil rights violations, tax suits, and bankruptcies. Most of the rest involve enforcement of contracts and various liability claims. Relatively few federal cases involve crimes; most criminal cases involve state laws and state courts.[62]

District court judges exercise less discretion than appellate judges or Supreme Court justices. Much of their job is to apply the law as Congress and the Supreme Court have defined it. But district judges still have some opportunities to exercise discretion as they apply the law, particularly in new areas where the law is not well developed.[63]

Courts of Appeal

Courts of appeal decide cases appealed to them from the district courts. Unlike district courts, they do not determine the facts of a case. Instead, they focus on legal issues that a case tried in district or state court might raise, such as whether a trial was conducted fairly or whether a judge applied the law correctly. Usually a panel of three appeals court judges hears an appeal and renders a judgment. As a rule, judges on the appeals courts have more flexibility than district court judges to interpret and extend the law.

Nomination and Confirmation

Like Supreme Court justices, district and appeals court judges are nominated by the president and confirmed by the Senate. However, members of the Senate have much greater say in the selection of nominees for the lower federal courts than they do for the Supreme Court. In most circumstances, the president selects nominees for district and appeals courts by following the tradition known as **senatorial courtesy:** the president asks a senior senator in his party from the state or region where the vacancy occurs to supply a list of possible nominees. If there is no senator of his party from the state or region, the president will ask a member of his party from the House or a state party leader to supply the list. If the president declines to nominate any of the suggested choices, another list will be prepared. Although presidents have more freedom to nominate whomever they want for appeals courts than for district courts, they generally refrain from nominating a candidate who lacks the support of party members from the affected state or region.[64]

Senatorial courtesy
The practice a president follows in choosing a nominee for a district or appeals court judgeship. The president selects a nominee from a list supplied by the senior senator of the president's party from the state or region where the vacancy occurs.

Partisan politics clearly influences the naming of federal judges. Take, for example, a vacancy that arose on the Eighth U.S. Circuit Court of Appeals in 1991. The Eighth Circuit includes seven midwestern states. President Bush's rumored choice for the post was a district court judge from Arkansas. After Sen. Charles Grassley (R-Iowa) complained, Bush appointed a district court judge from Iowa. According to Grassley, "We just implored them to look at it from a political standpoint, that Iowa

Presidents usually appoint people from their own party to the federal bench.

TABLE 14.1 Characteristics of Federal Court Appointees (in percent)

	Ford	Carter	Reagan	Bush	Clinton (through 1994)
District Courts					
Partisanship					
Democrat	21	93	5	5	89
Republican	79	4	93	89	3
Independent	0	3	2	6	8
Race, Ethnicity					
White	89	79	92	89	65
African American	6	14	2	7	25
Hispanic American	2	7	5	4	8
Asian American	4	1	1	0	1
Sex					
Female	2	14	8	20	32
Number of Appointees	52	202	290	148	107
Courts of Appeals					
Partisanship					
Democrat	8	82	0	5	89
Republican	92	7	97	89	6
Independent	0	11	1	5	6
Race, Ethnicity					
White	100	79	97	89	72
African American	0	16	1	5	17
Hispanic American	0	2	1	5	11
Asian American	0	4	0	0	0
Sex					
Female	0	20	5	19	28
Number of Appointees	12	56	78	37	18

Source: Sheldon Goldman, "Bush's Judicial Legacy: The Final Imprint," *Judicature* 76 (April/May 1993): 287, 293; Sheldon Goldman, "Judicial Selection Under Clinton: A Midterm Examination," *Judicature* 78 (May-June 1995): 281, 287.

having a Republican senator, Arkansas not having Republican senators, they were going to be relying on Chuck Grassley to a greater extent for help. They weren't going to get it out of Democratic senators from Arkansas."[65]

Although the president and members of Congress reap clear political benefits from choosing judges on political grounds, it is less obvious how the selection process benefits the judicial system. Yet injecting politics into the selection process actually helps make the judicial system more democratic. Allowing elected officials from the state or region to influence who is named to the bench makes federal judges more politically representative of the areas they serve in than they otherwise might be. Over time, presidents can shift the partisan character of the bench. President Reagan, for example, selected seventy-eight court of appeals judges and 290 district court judges during his eight years in office, filling close to 50 percent of all federal judgeships.[66] These appointments gave the lower courts a discernible conservative bent.[67]

As table 14.1 shows, presidents appoint judges from their own party. But while federal judges may be politically representative, they are not demographically representative. Presidents tend to select white, middle-aged males. The federal bench started to become noticeably more diverse under Democratic President Jimmy Carter. Republican Presidents Reagan and Bush appointed fewer African Americans—which is not surprising given that more African Americans identify with the Democratic Party than the Republican Party—but they did appoint a growing number of Hispanic Americans to the bench.[68] The number of women appointed as federal judges also has grown over time. The highest proportions of women and minorities appointed to the federal bench, however, occurred during the Clinton administration.

State Courts

Whether it is through a speeding ticket, a dispute over the terms of a contract, or an accusation of criminal wrongdoing, the interaction most Americans have with our country's legal system is with state, not federal, courts. In contrast to the 280,000 cases that federal district courts handle each year, state trial courts handle almost 100 million.[69] For this reason, most of what we think, hear, and read about in regard to the American legal system has to do with state laws, not federal laws. And, as we will see, not only do state courts operate differently from the federal courts, states also vary dramatically in the way they organize their court systems, in the methods they use to select judges, in their limits on the length of judicial service, and in the laws they have on the books.

Organization

State courts exhibit a wide variety of forms, structures, and names. Every state has a highest court, or court of last resort, although Texas and Oklahoma have two such courts, one for civil cases and the other for criminal cases. Most states refer to their highest court as the supreme court, and its role is usually similar to its federal namesake. (New York and Maryland call their highest courts the court of appeals, however, and to make matters more confusing, New York calls its lower courts supreme courts.)

One of the important roles state supreme courts play is to interpret state constitutions. In many cases, state constitutions provide civil rights protections that go beyond those afforded to citizens by the U.S. Constitution.[70] For example, in 1988, the U.S. Supreme Court held that federal law officials did not need a warrant to search a person's garbage.[71] But state courts in New Jersey and Washington subsequently held that their state constitutions required state law officials to obtain a warrant before rifling through a suspect's garbage.[72] Indeed, some state supreme courts have established a right to privacy based on their state constitution, thereby guaranteeing abortion rights.[73] Some state supreme courts become legal pathbreakers, establishing precedents that other states and the federal courts cite in later disputes.[74]

The other tiers of most state judicial systems differ somewhat from the federal system. Intermediate appeals courts, similar in purpose to the federal appeals courts, are found in thirty-seven states. Most states have trial courts of general jurisdiction where most cases are handled. Again, the names vary—California and several other states call theirs superior court, while elsewhere they are called circuit court, district court, or court of common pleas. Some states have several different types of major trial courts. In addition to the major trial courts, all states but Illinois and Iowa have trial courts of limited jurisdiction, including family court, juvenile court, and even justices of the peace.

Judicial Selection

The method by which judges gain the bench varies from state to state and by level within some states. But most states do not follow the federal model of judicial selection. In Rhode Island, for example, the state legislature selects justices for the state supreme court, and the governor appoints and the state senate confirms most other state court judges. Voters in Wisconsin elect all state judges in nonpartisan elections, whereas voters in Mississippi elect all state judges in partisan elections.

Missouri and a number of other states use a mix of appointment and election to select judges. In Missouri, for example, a seven-member nonpartisan commission initially screens potential appellate court justices. The commission then submits the names of three candidates for a judgeship to the governor. The candidate the governor selects is appointed to the bench but must face the voters in the first general election after serving for a year. The nonpartisan ballot on which the judge's name appears allows voters to either confirm (retain) or reject the judge. If the judge is retained, he or she must again get voter approval to stay on the bench at the end of each twelve-year term.[75]

Missouri Plan/Merit System The system some states use to select judges, appointing them but requiring them to stand for periodic reelection.

Many judicial reformers favor variants of this procedure, which is usually called the **Missouri Plan** (because it was first introduced in that state) or the **Merit System,** because it supposedly reduces the role of partisan politics in the selection of judges. Judges covered by retention elections strongly favor them, in large part because it removes them from partisan politics.[76] Incumbent judges, however, do even better in retention elections than incumbent legislators in seeking reelection; less than 1 percent of judges are not retained.[77] There is no evidence, however, that any particular system produces better judges or influences the sorts of decisions the courts render.[78]

Do different selection processes produce different sorts of people on the bench? One study of African Americans serving as state court judges suggests that the relationship between the judicial selection system and minority representation is not clear. More African-American judges are found in states using partisan and nonpartisan judicial elections than in states using some other system—which is not surprising since most states with significant African-American populations use elections. But even in these states, most African-American judges initially gain the bench by appointment. Because most states with elective systems allow the governor to fill a vacancy between elections, most African-American judges are appointed to the bench by the governor.[79] But, minority judges facing retention election fare almost as well as their white colleagues, winning at a 96 percent rate.[80]

Length of Service

States differ from the federal government not only in how they select judges, but also in deciding how long judges may serve on the bench. Whereas federal judges are appointed for life, most state judges serve for specific terms. In addition, while federal judges can be removed only through impeachment and conviction, many states have a variety of other mechanisms for removing judges from the bench, including reelection defeat, recall, and action by a judicial disciplinary commission.

The federal system of appointing judges for life protects their independence from politics. States that use elections sacrifice judicial independence in favor of encouraging political responsiveness and judicial accountability. In many states, however, judges seeking reelection must "raise huge sums of money, often from special interest groups that have a tangible stake in the outcome of cases before the courts."[81] Not surprisingly, most incumbent judges, like their legislative counterparts, win reelection. But in theory, at least, voters can remove state judges whose behavior or rulings displease them.

State Laws

The laws that judges are asked to uphold vary, sometimes dramatically, across the fifty states. For example, in thirty-eight states, a judge may impose the death penalty on a person convicted of first-degree murder; in the other twelve states, the maximum punishment is life in prison. As figure 14.6 shows, in 1996, twenty-eight states allowed a person to carry a concealed weapon. The same variations occur across the country; acts that are illegal in some states (gambling or prostitution) are legal in others, and the penalties attached to a crime also vary from state to state. Although the federal Constitution and the U.S. Supreme Court's interpretation of it impose some uniformity on our legal system, significant differences across the states are still evident.

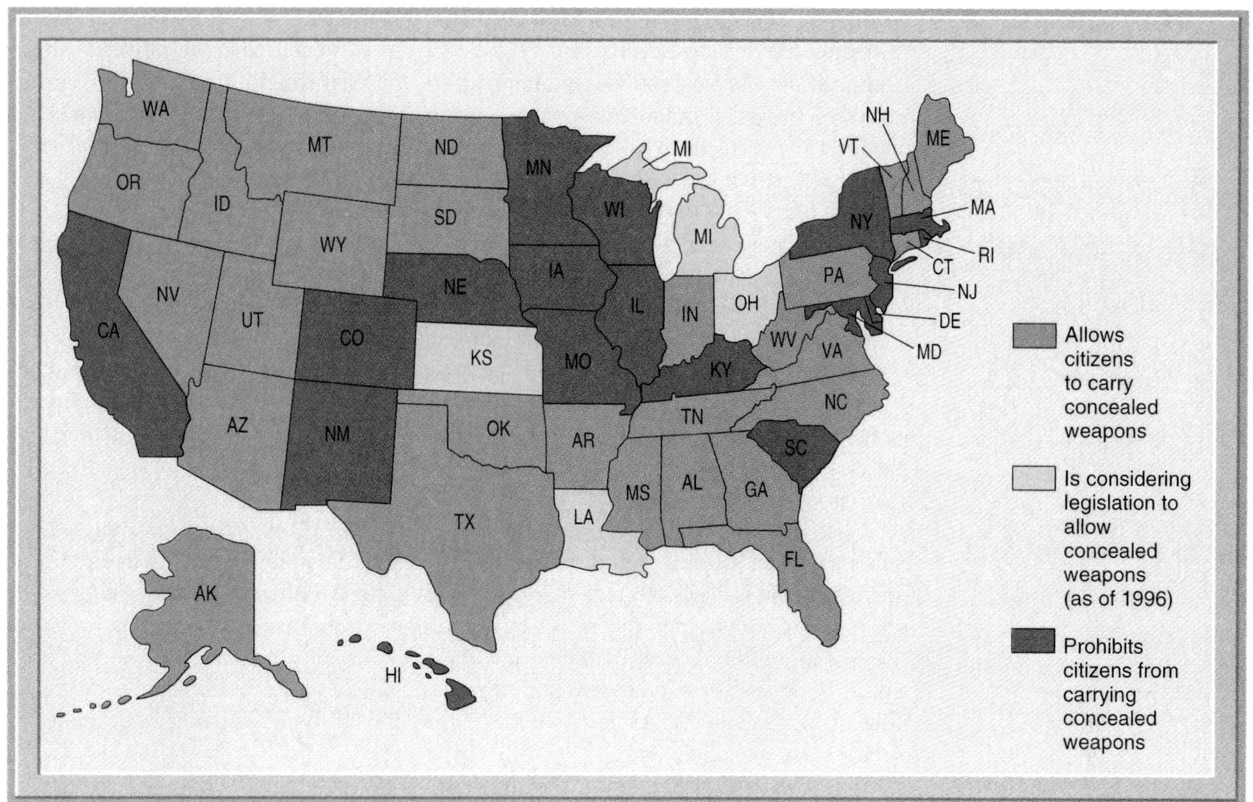

FIGURE 14.6
States Allowing Concealed Weapons, 1996

A citizen's legal right to carry a concealed weapon varies by state.

Source: "Handguns State by State," *USA Weekend*, 29–31 December 1995.

SUMMARY

Although the founders were almost unanimous in their support for creating an independent federal judiciary, they left it to Congress to specify the details of the federal court system. Over the years, Congress has passed many laws regarding the structure and organization of the federal judiciary. The main thrust of these laws has been to create a three-tiered system of constitutional courts: district courts, courts of appeals, and the Supreme Court. Congress has also established legislative courts to deal with specific issues or to administer specific congressional statutes.

The founders thought the federal courts would simply apply the laws and policies Congress and the president establish. Almost immediately, however, the federal courts became policy makers themselves. Early on, the Supreme Court asserted the doctrine of judicial review, the right of federal courts to declare both federal and state laws unconstitutional and therefore null and void. Although judicial review now constitutes a bedrock principle of the American legal system, some critics complain that federal judges use judicial review as an excuse for imposing their policy preferences on the public rather than for upholding the Constitution. Complaints about judicial activism notwithstanding, the power of the federal judiciary is limited by the reactive nature of the courts, their inability to enforce their rulings, the ability of the president and Congress to draft new laws, and the force of public opinion.

The Supreme Court is the nation's highest court. More than one hundred justices have served on the Court. All have been lawyers, only two have been female, and only two have been African American. The chief justice is considered first among equals on the Supreme Court, and all nine justices are nominated by the president and confirmed by the Senate. Because the justices serve for life and have the power to shape American law for generations, the nomination and confirmation of a justice is an inherently political process. Senators are most likely to contest a nomination when a president is politically weak, when a nominee's credentials are questionable, or when his or her legal views clash with those of powerful senators.

The Supreme Court hears only a small portion of the cases appealed to it. If the Court decides to hear a case, it schedules an oral argument. To reach their decisions, the justices rely both on legal precedent and on their own experiences, judicial philosophies, and political beliefs. The justices render their decision in the form of a majority opinion that outlines the reasoning they used to reach their decision. Justices who agree with the conclusion the majority reached but not with the reasoning behind it may write concurring opinions. Justices who disagree with the majority opinion in its entirety may write dissenting opinions. The federal government wins a majority of the cases it argues before the Supreme Court; no other group in society enjoys the same success rate.

District courts and courts of appeals constitute the lower federal courts. Like Supreme Court justices, judges in the lower federal courts are appointed in a political process. In their case, elected officials representing the areas where the judges will serve strongly influence the selection of an appointee. The district courts form the lowest rung in the federal judiciary; they hold trials and establish the facts of a case. Courts of appeal focus on legal issues that a case tried in a district or state court might raise. Appeals court judges generally have more flexibility than district court judges to interpret and extend the law.

In addition to the federal judiciary, each state maintains its own separate court system. Most state courts operate differently from the federal courts, and states vary dramatically in the way they organize their court systems, in the methods they use to select judges, in their limits on the length of judicial service, and in the laws they have on the books.

As we have seen in this chapter, both federal and state courts lack many of the qualities we normally associate with democratic politics. Yet, at many levels, the court system appears responsive to political shifts in the public. The main reason for this responsiveness is that either voters (in many states) or their elected representatives (at the federal level) control the process by which judges gain the bench.

KEY TERMS

Amicus curiae
Concurring opinion
Constitutional courts
Dissenting opinion
Judicial activism
Judicial review
Legislative courts
Majority opinion
Marbury v. Madison
Missouri Plan/Merit System
Rule of Four
Senatorial courtesy
Stare decisis
Writ of certiorari

Readings for Further Study

Bork, Robert H. *The Tempting of America: The Political Seduction of the Law.* New York: Free Press, 1990. An analysis of contemporary legal theory by the prominent conservative jurist whose nomination to the U.S. Supreme Court was rejected by the Senate.

Carp, Robert A., and Ronald Stidham. *The Federal Courts,* 2d ed. Washington, D.C.: CQ Press, 1991. A leading textbook on the organization and politics of the lower federal courts.

O'Brien, David. *Storm Center: The Supreme Court in American Politics,* 4th ed. New York: Norton, 1996. A useful historical analysis of the Supreme Court.

Segal, Jeffrey A., and Harold J. Spaeth. *The Supreme Court and the Attitudinal Model.* New York: Cambridge University Press, 1993. Two leading judicial scholars examine the relationship between the attitudes of justices and their decision-making behavior.

Silverstein, Mark. *Judicious Choices: The New Politics of Supreme Court Confirmations.* New York: Norton, 1994. An interesting and current examination of how the nomination process works.

Simon, James F. *The Center Holds: The Power Struggle Inside the Rehnquist Court.* New York: Simon & Schuster, 1995. A journalist who became a law school professor explores the struggle between conservative and liberal justices for control of the Rehnquist Court.

Stumpf, Harry P., and John H. Culver. *The Politics of State Courts.* New York: Longman, 1992. A very good textbook examining the structure and politics of state courts.

Walker, Thomas G., and Lee Epstein. *The Supreme Court of the United States.* Washington, D.C.: CQ Press, 1993. A first-rate introduction to the Supreme Court as a political institution by two of the best political scientists who study the courts.

Part Four

The Policy Process in American Politics

15
The Federal System and State Government

16
The Federal Budget

17
Domestic Policy

18
Foreign Policy

CHAPTER

15

THE FEDERAL SYSTEM AND STATE GOVERNMENT

Relations Between Federal, State, and Local Government
- *Federal Aid to State and Local Governments*
- *Other Forms of Federal Influence*
- *The Changing Nature of Federalism*

State Government and Politics
- *State Constitutions*
- *Governors*
- *State Legislatures*
- *Interest Groups in State Politics*
- *The Public and Direct Democracy*
- *Summing Up*

State Budgets
- *Raising Revenues*
- *Budgeting*
- *Spending*

Local Government
- *Forms of Local Government*
- *Local Government Structures*
- *Local Government and Representation*
- *The Costs of Local Government*
- *Privatization of Government Services*

Who Delivers? Public Opinion and Level of Government

Summary

Key Terms

Readings for Further Study

When the 104th Congress convened in January 1995, the leaders of the new Republican majority pledged to shift many powers from the federal government back to the states. In keeping with this pledge, Congress subsequently passed the National Highway System bill, which freed the states to set their own speed limits on the nation's highways and to decide whether to require motorcyclists to wear helmets. But while Congress returned control of many transportation and safety matters to the states, on some matters, it retained power in federal hands. For example, Congress voted to keep national seat belt requirements on the books. It even imposed a new demand on the states, requiring them to adopt "zero tolerance" laws that would make it illegal for underage drinkers to drive, even if they are not legally drunk, or risk losing some federal highway funds.[1]

The highway safety debate illuminates two key points about American politics. The first is that the rules that govern the relationship between the federal government and state governments matter, because they determine how much influence the federal government has over the policies set within the states. The second is that the rules within each state matter, because they determine the policies that affect people's everyday lives. Because the federal government helps to finance many state and local programs, it has potentially tremendous influence over the policy choices state and local governments make. But most of the laws Americans live under are made at the state and local levels, not at the federal level. Although the federal government can pressure cities and states to conform to its wishes, in many instances, state and local governments have the freedom to make their own policy choices. Thus, a combination of federal and state rules determine the policies that serve, protect, and limit Americans in their everyday lives.

In this chapter, we examine both aspects of state politics—how state and local governments fit into the federal system and how governments within the states operate. We begin by looking at the changing relationship between the federal government and state and local government, discussing how federal aid has become a major source of revenue for state and local governments and has increased the influence of the federal government over state and local policies. We go on to explore how state governments operate, focusing especially on state budgeting, government institutions, interest groups, and the public's role in state politics. Finally, we look at local government. We conclude the chapter by discussing how citizens assess the relative performance of federal, state, and local government.

As the public's expectations of government evolve, the rules governing the relationship between the federal government and state governments change, and the rules within each state change in response. As with other aspects of American politics, the rules matter, because the rules determine who wins and loses in the competition for government programs and services.

When Congress allowed states to set their own speed limits in 1995, several states immediately upped their limits. Wyoming Gov. Jim Geringer helped post the new, higher limit in his state.

Relations Between Federal, State, and Local Government

We have said that the federal government helps pay the cost of many city and state programs. But how much aid does Washington provide? What rules structure the allocation of aid, and how do those rules affect the policy choices made in state capitals and mayors' offices around the country? What other tools does Washington use to influence cities and states? Answers to these questions will help us understand how state and local governments fit into the national political system.

Federal Aid to State and Local Governments

Federal aid to state and local governments dates back to our nation's origins. During the 1800s, the most important form of federal aid consisted of grants of land to the states to support the creation of colleges and universities; direct cash payments to cities and states were rare. All of that changed, however, in the 1930s, with the shift

During this century, the federal government has become an important source of revenue for state and local governments.

TABLE 15.1 Patterns of Federal Aid to State and Local Governments

Year	Total Federal Grants-in-Aid (in millions)	Federal Grants as a Percentage of State and Local Government Expenditures
1902	7	<1.0%
1913	12	<1.0
1922	108	2.1
1932	232	3.0
1940	945	10.2
1950	2,486	10.9
1960	6,974	13.4
1970	24,100	19.0
1980	91,500	25.8
1990	135,400	19.4
1995	235,500 (est.)	n.a.

Sources: Advisory Commission on Intergovernmental Relations, *Significant Features of Fiscal Federalism, Volume 2: Revenues and Expenditures* (Washington, D.C.: U.S. Government Printing Office, 1992), p. 60; *Historical Statistics of the United States: Colonial Times to 1970, Part 2* (Washington, D.C.: U.S. Bureau of the Census, 1975), pp. 1125–28.

from dual to fiscal federalism. Federal aid is now a major source of revenue for cities and states, which gives the federal government considerable influence over the policy choices that state and local governments make.

Dual Federalism

For the first 140 years of U.S. history, the federal government provided minuscule amounts of aid to state and local governments. As table 15.1 shows, as late as World War I, federal grants constituted less than 1 percent of all state and local revenues. Federal aid was low because the idea of **dual federalism,** which held that the federal government and state governments should work in parallel without much interaction, governed the relations between Washington and the states. Because the doctrine of dual federalism meant no federal aid, state and local governments covered the cost of almost all of their programs through their own taxes. In turn, Washington had relatively little input into the decisions cities and states made.

Dual federalism
An interpretation of federalism that held that the national government was supreme within those areas specifically assigned to it in the Constitution, and the states were supreme in all other areas of public policy.

Fiscal Federalism

The tradition of dual federalism collapsed in the 1930s with the advent of President Franklin Roosevelt's New Deal programs. As we discussed in chapter 2, the New Deal ushered in the era of **fiscal federalism,** which holds that the federal government has a role to play in providing financial assistance to state and local governments. Until the mid-1960s, fiscal federalism had a strong element of cooperation between the levels of government, as they often worked together to solve problems such as unemployment. But in more recent years, fiscal federalism has taken on a less cooperative and more conflictual tone.

Fiscal federalism
The principle that the federal government should play a major role in financing some state and local government activities.

As table 15.1 shows, the amount of federal aid to state and local governments has soared since the 1930s. By the time Dwight Eisenhower left the White House in 1961, the federal government provided $7 billion in aid to cities and states, or roughly 13 percent of all state and local expenditures. The trend toward increased federal aid to cities and states was boosted during the 1960s when President Lyndon Johnson and Congress sought to end poverty in the United States by enacting the Great Society programs—an ambitious and expensive set of programs designed to increase educational and job training opportunities for the poor while improving their general quality of life. By 1970, the federal government's share of state and local expenditures stood at 19 percent. Over the next decade, Congress further accelerated the trend toward increased federal aid by expanding the scope of assistance programs and relaxing the eligibility criteria so that most middle-class towns and cities could qualify. As a result, when Ronald Reagan took the oath of office in 1981, the federal government was providing more than $91 billion in aid, a thirteen-fold increase in a span of twenty years, and federal assistance accounted for over 25 percent of all state and local expenditures.

Rather than continue the trend of having Washington underwrite more and more of the cost of state and local government, President Reagan worked to eliminate federal aid programs. In doing so, he was motivated by his twin desires to reduce how much the federal government spent on domestic programs and to reduce the federal government's influence over state and local politics.[2] As a result, the rules changed, and the federal government's contribution to state and local revenues fell, reaching 19 percent in 1990. Despite the significant drop in the share of state and local spending supported by Washington, the total amount of federal aid has grown, and it remains one of the major sources of state and local revenues.

Forms of Financial Assistance

Federal assistance may be divided into three general types: categorical grants, block grants, and revenue sharing. Since the 1930s, the backbone of federal aid to state and local governments has been **categorical grants-in-aid**—programs that Congress creates and national agencies administer to fund narrow, specific categories of activities, such as building highways or paying welfare recipients. Categorical grants may be project- or formula-based, but either way, they give recipient governments little discretion in spending the money. *Project grants* are awarded on a competitive basis; a federal agency accepts applications from cities and states and then funds the projects it deems the most worthy. This procedure gives the granting agency great power to decide who gets a grant, leaving open the possibility of political favoritism. In contrast, *formula grants* automatically set the number of dollars a recipient government gets based on certain objective local conditions, such as the population and the unemployment rate. But formula grants are not immune to politics. Congressional battles over setting the formulas often include detailed discussions of which locales stand to win or lose, and many of the formulas are designed to ensure that money is spread across the country.[3] Although categorical grants are an attractive source of financing for state and local programs, they come with strings attached, particularly for the more numerous project grants. Recipients usually must follow very detailed rules, written in Washington, that govern how the money can be spent.

Categorical grants-in-aid
Grants of money from the federal government to pay for specific state and local government activities under strict federal guidelines.

The number of categorical grant programs rose ten-fold during the 1960s, and with this increase came numerous complaints that the grants were too difficult to administer and the rules too rigid to meet the needs of state and local governments.[4] In response to these criticisms, Congress in the early 1970s instituted a system of **block grants,** allocating federal funds for broad policy purposes rather than for specific purposes, as categorical grants do. Because block grants come with fewer federal rules attached, state and local governments may spend the money on a variety of activities within the designated policy area. A city that receives a law enforcement block grant, for example, can use the money to purchase police cars, hire new police officers, improve its communications network, or any of a variety of other actions. As with categorical grants, block grants may be made on the basis of individual projects or general formulas.

Block grants
Grants of money from the federal government that state and local governments may spend on any program serving the general purpose of the grant.

In 1972, Congress supplemented categorical and block grants by instituting **general revenue sharing,** a program that allocated federal funds to state and local governments on the basis of a formula that took into account a community's needs and its willingness to tax its own citizens. Recipients were allowed to use the money as they saw fit. Because no federal rules dictated how the money was spent, revenue sharing marked a significant retreat by the federal government from its habit of trying to shape state and local government policy choices. Although some supporters of revenue sharing hoped it eventually would replace all categorical and block grants, the program ended in 1986 as part of the Reagan administration's effort to restrain the growth in federal aid to cities and states.

General revenue sharing
A program giving federal money to state and local governments with no restrictions on how it will be spent.

The Persistence of Categorical Grants

In 1995, the federal government provided roughly $235.5 billion in financial assistance to the nation's cities and states.[5] Almost 90 percent of federal aid was allocated through categorical grants, with the bulk allocated through about two dozen formula-based programs.[6] Categorical grants have persisted as the dominant form of aid despite the complaints of state and local governments, efforts to replace them with revenue sharing, and Ronald Reagan's repeated attempts to cut domestic spending.

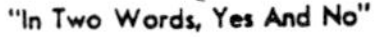

Federal grants and other monies given to the states usually come with strings attached.

From *The Herblock Book*, Beacon Press, 1952. Reprinted by permission.

Why have categorical grants persisted? Federal officials like them for two reasons. First, categorical grants provide the federal government with a way to hold recipient governments financially accountable for their actions. Because cities and states must follow the detailed rules that come with a categorical grant, the federal government can track how the money is spent, ensuring effective and efficient spending. In contrast, block grants and revenue sharing limit the federal government's ability to monitor how aid is spent, raising the possibility that the state or local government will not spend the money as federal officials wish. Federal government officials thus have a strong interest in retaining categorical grants.

Second, categorical grants are attractive because they enable members of Congress to claim credit for directing federal dollars into their home districts. As we pointed out in chapter 11, members find that claiming credit for federal programs that benefit their constituents can boost their prospects for reelection. Because categorical grants are tied to specific purposes, they provide members with opportunities to claim credit. With more general block grants and revenue sharing, however, members of Congress can claim no specific credit because state and local officials decide how to spend the money. As a result, until recently, there was little political support in Congress for expanding block grants or reviving revenue sharing.

When the Republicans took control of Congress in 1995 for the first time in forty years, they called for greatly expanding the use of block grants. They argued that state and local governments would be able to use federal aid more wisely and productively if they were freed from having to follow the detailed guidelines that come with categorical grants. In the end, however, President Clinton and his fellow Democrats on Capitol Hill largely blocked Republican efforts to expand the use of block grants, and categorical grants continue to be the primary type of federal aid. But for the first time in decades, the way the federal government funnels money to the states is being seriously challenged.

Consequences of Financial Assistance

The rules governing the distribution of the immense amount of federal aid to state and local governments have had several consequences: increased federal power over the states, increased lobbying of the federal government by states and localities, and an increased emphasis on the importance of the federal Census. First and foremost, increased federal aid gives the federal government tremendous leverage over the policy choices cities and states make. The federal government does not directly provide most domestic services; police and fire protection, education, sanitation, libraries, welfare, and most other public services are all programs that state and local governments pay for and administer. By providing or denying funds to cities and states, however, Washington can influence the kinds of services they provide.[7] Thus, the federal government can use its financial leverage to accomplish policy goals it could not otherwise achieve. For example, in 1984, Congress passed a law stating that states that did not raise their legal drinking age to twenty-one by 1986 would lose 5 percent of their national highway funds, with more severe cuts to follow in succeeding years. Despite grumbling from several states that the federal government was intruding into their affairs, they all knuckled under to the pressure and raised their legal drinking age.[8]

A second consequence of the tremendous amount of federal aid that goes to cities and states is that state and local governments now actively lobby the federal government. During the era of dual federalism, state and local governments could afford to ignore much of what happened in Washington, D.C. But once federal aid became a

Local governments provide and control most public services.

major source of revenue, state and local governments had a vested interest in seeing that aid programs minimized their administrative costs and maximized their administrative discretion. As chapter 10 noted, state and local governments have their own interest groups, and most states and many large cities maintain their own liaison offices in Washington. Lobbying by cities and states contributed to the creation of block grants and revenue-sharing programs, and it is a major reason why the federal government often uses formula-based categorical grants.

The success that state and local governments have had in promoting formula-based grants has led to the third consequence of federal aid: the increased importance of the federal Census. Cities and states like formula-based grants because every community that meets the eligibility criteria receives aid, which minimizes the chances that politically well-connected communities can manipulate the allocation process in their favor. But no formula can end all controversy. Because federal aid is largely allocated on the basis of population, whom the Bureau of the Census counts and doesn't count affects how aid is allocated. Following the 1990 Census, several cities and states argued that the Census had undercounted the number of people living in their communities, thereby costing them federal aid.[9]

The use of formula-based grants to allocate federal aid has increased the importance of the federal Census. After the 1990 Census, some cities and states complained that the Census had undercounted the number of people living in their communities, thereby costing them federal aid.

By permission of Mike Luckovich and Creators Syndicate.

Other Forms of Federal Influence

Along with financial aid, the federal government also influences state and local governments through two other means: mandates and the relationships that picket-fence federalism creates.

Mandates

The federal government can influence state and local governments by issuing **mandates**—laws Congress passes that require other levels of government to take specified actions.[10] Whereas financial aid constitutes a "carrot" the federal government can use to encourage cities and states to enact its policy priorities, mandates are the "stick." In some circumstances, Washington orders cities and states to abide by its regulations. For example, the federal government has ordered cities and states to avoid discriminating on the basis of race, gender, or religion, and it can require them to meet clean air standards.

Mandates
Laws Congress passes that require state and local governments to undertake specified actions.

As you might imagine, Washington's use of mandates irritates many state and local officials. Their irritation has mounted in recent years because the federal government has continued to issue mandates even though a persistent federal budget deficit has prevented it from providing cities and states with the money they need to comply. The amount of money involved is significant. In Ohio, for example, the state government estimated that unfunded mandates cost the state more than $1.74 billion from 1992 to 1995.[11]

Because cities and states are required to satisfy federal mandates whether Washington provides the money or not, they must make tough choices about whether to raise taxes or cut existing programs. For example, the Asbestos Hazard Emergency Response Act, which Congress passed in 1986, required schools to remove asbestos from their buildings, at an estimated cost of $3.1 billion over thirty years. Although the federal government mandated the asbestos removal, it did not provide any money to reimburse other levels of government to cover the cost.[12] Washington left it up to cities and states to decide how they would pay for the cleanup.

Although federal mandates have been imposing costs on the states for years, unfunded mandates only burst onto the national political scene as a major issue in 1993. By 1995, however, the states had brought so much pressure to bear on Congress that it passed the Unfunded Mandate Reform Act of 1995.[13] The law, one of the first major pieces of the new Republican majority's agenda to be signed into law, changed the rules to make it harder for Congress to require state and local governments to undertake new programs without providing the money to fund them. Congress did not make the law retroactive, however, so the states still have to bear the cost of earlier unfunded mandates.

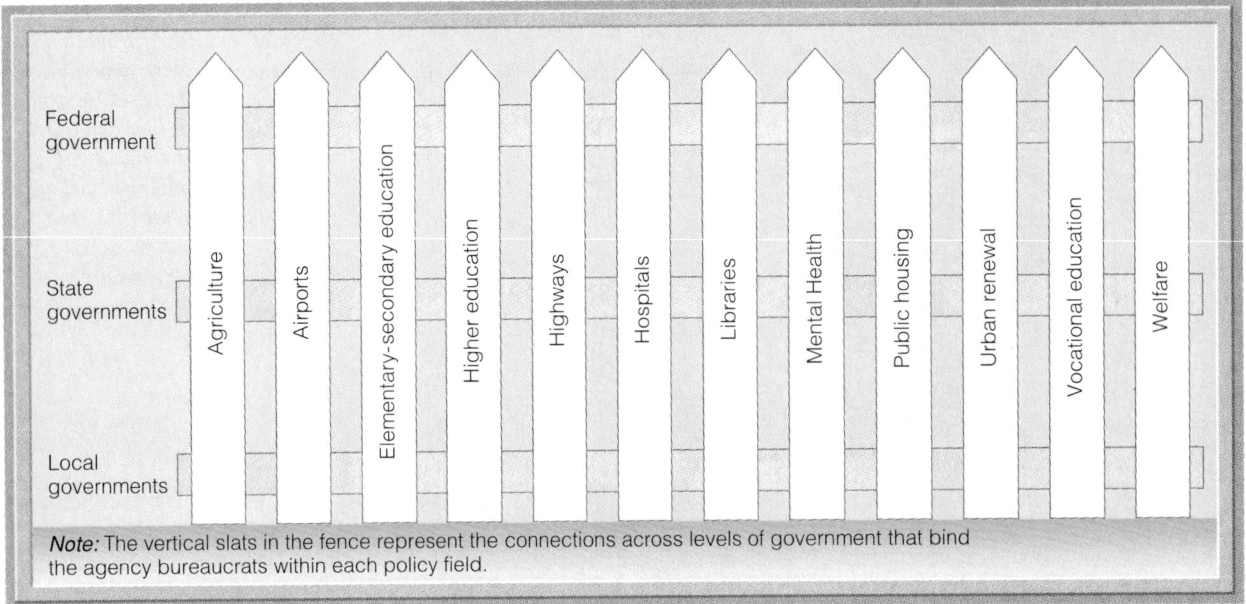

FIGURE 15.1
Picket-Fence Federalism

Strong working relationships often develop among federal, state, and local government officials working on the same issues.

Sources: George J. Gordon, *Public Administration in America*, 1986; and Deil S. Wright, *Understanding Intergovernmental Relations*, 1988.

Picket-fence federalism
The tendency of federal, state, and local agencies concerned with the same issues to coordinate their efforts with each other and to be insulated from other government agencies that deal with different issues.

Picket-Fence Federalism

Along with mandates, the federal government influences cities and states through the close working relationship that many federal, state, and local agencies have with one another. Figure 15.1 illustrates this phenomenon, which has been called **picket-fence federalism.**[14] Federal, state, and local agencies that work together on an issue often discover they have common interests. At the same time, agencies at all three levels become insulated from agencies that deal with other issues—for example, a state highway commission might work more closely with its federal counterpart than with the state agencies that deal with public housing or higher education. This tendency for agencies at all three levels of government to coordinate their efforts on a shared issue creates the separate "pickets" shown in figure 15.1. Since the federal agency on each picket channels federal funds to, and is usually larger and better staffed than, its state and local counterparts, it gains greater influence over the state and local agencies. In turn, the horizontal insulation of agencies from each other makes it more difficult for state and local officials to coordinate the work of the agencies they oversee. Some observers think that increased competition for scarce public funds within some issues areas—for example, between different groups pushing health programs for the elderly, young, people with AIDS, and many others—makes the picket-fence analogy less powerful today than it was a decade ago. But the relationships that exist among federal, state, and local agencies can still be very important.

The founders envisioned a small federal government with relatively limited powers. But, as we noted in chapter 2, the brevity and vagueness of the Constitution have allowed each generation to restructure the way the rules of American politics are played out. In the case of federalism, the federal government can exert power over state and local governments through aid programs, direct mandates, and the establishment of close working relationships with local and state agencies. Since the 1930s, the federal government has used its influence extensively. But more recent changes in policies and rules have again shifted some power back into the hands of state and local government.

The Changing Nature of Federalism

The rules that regulate the relationship between the federal government and state and local governments determine where political power lies in the United States. In the 1930s and again in the 1960s, Washington assumed a larger role in American political life as it increasingly came to underwrite the costs of state and local government. In

Starting with the Nixon administration, Republicans have worked to shift the balance of power toward the states. Although it was not part of the Contract With America, giving power to the states was an important part of the 1995 Republican agenda.

By Jack Ohman. Reprinted by permission: Tribune Media Services.

the 1980s, however, that trend came to a halt as the Reagan and Bush administrations succeeded in slowing the growth of federal aid and in shifting more of the cost of state and local government back onto the cities and states.

Although the retrenchment that took place in Washington in the 1980s created many headaches for state and local officials, especially when it came to finding new sources of revenue, it also increased their power. In seeking to curtail federal assistance to state and local governments, the Reagan and Bush administrations were motivated both by a desire to restrain federal spending and a desire to shift political power back to the cities and states. Moreover, the reluctance of both Ronald Reagan and George Bush to propose new domestic programs forced political activists to look at state governments in a new light. Proponents of many new programs found that they received a more cordial hearing in state capitals than in Washington. As a result, state and local governments have increased their say in policy decisions.[15] The changes in rules changed the centers of power and the targets of interest groups.

The dynamics of the federal system promise to change even more in future years. When Republicans took control of Congress in 1995, they vowed to take power away from the federal government and restore it to the states.[16] One obvious product of this movement was the bill forbidding unfunded mandates. But congressional Republicans were not content with simply limiting unfunded mandates. They also set to work on a variety of fronts to take power from Washington and to give it to the state capitals.

One example of the Republican effort to shift power to the states is the battle that took place in 1995 over Medicaid—the government program that provides health coverage for the poor and people with disabilities. The Republican-controlled Congress passed legislation that would have used block grants to turn much of the responsibility for structuring Medicaid coverage over to state governments. Still, the Republicans did not propose to terminate all the federal guidelines for Medicaid. For example, their legislation required the states to provide some health care coverage to pregnant women and children under the age of thirteen years. Likewise, it retained federal standards for nursing homes that care for Medicaid patients.[17] Although President Clinton vetoed the Medicaid reform legislation, Republicans continued to press the general policy of taking decision-making power away from the federal government and giving it to the states.

Like congressional Republicans, many state officials are eager to see the balance of power in the federal system shift in their favor.[18] Pressuring Congress to fund any future

In recent years, Republicans have advocated taking power from Washington and giving it to the states, but they have not resisted the urge to attach their own strings to programs.

mandates was just one step toward this goal. Some state legislatures are trying to compel other changes, although some of these changes are of questionable legality. For example, in 1995, the state legislature in Montana passed a bill requiring federal officers to get permission from local officials before making arrests or seizing property in the state. (Montana's governor vetoed the bill.) Next door in Idaho, the state legislature created a $1 million "constitutional defense fund" to finance lawsuits challenging what many legislators deemed unconstitutional mandates and regulations handed down by the federal government.[19] And in Montana, New Hampshire, and Virginia, state officials were so suspicious of the federal government that they declined to participate in Goals 2000, a federal program that gives money to states to help them meet eight education goals, including making American students tops in the world in science and mathematics.[20] (New Hampshire state officials eventually changed their minds, and the state joined the program.)[21]

The efforts of state legislatures to take power back from the federal government reminds us that the nature of federalism can change with time and events. Over the course of the twentieth century, the federal government has increased its financial aid to state and local governments and has thereby become more involved in state and local affairs. That involvement has in turn sparked political conflict over the proper nature of the relationship between the federal government and state and local governments. Many people today want to rewrite the rules governing that relationship and restructure the nature of relations between Washington and the states.

State Government and Politics

Throughout the first fourteen chapters of this book, we focused on how the federal government works rather than on how state governments work. The focus on the federal government is not as misplaced as it might seem, because in many ways, state governments are smaller versions of the federal government. Although the Constitution requires only that states adopt a republican form of government, all fifty states have the same three distinct branches of government with similar checks and balances among them. By the same token, however, state capitals are not carbon copies of Washington. Neither are all states alike. In this section, we turn our attention to the states, examining key aspects of state government and politics: state constitutions, governors, legislatures, interest groups, and direct democracy.

State Constitutions

Like the U.S. Constitution, state constitutions establish the basic rules of the political system in each state. The changeable nature of these rules is even more clear at the state level than at the federal level. The U.S. Constitution has been amended only twenty-seven times since it was written in 1789. Few state constitutions have enjoyed similar stability. Only Massachusetts's constitution, which was adopted in 1780, is older than the U.S. Constitution. Most states have had several constitutions; Louisiana leads the way with eleven. (Its current constitution was adopted in 1974.) States also have been quite willing to amend their constitutions. The Alabama constitution has been amended more than 535 times since it was adopted in 1901. Almost half of the states have amended their constitutions more than one hundred times.[22]

State constitutions have been far less stable than the U.S. Constitution for two reasons. First, state constitutions are much more detailed and specific than the federal constitution. Alabama's constitution, for example, runs some 174,000 words long, which makes it by far the nation's longest. To put that figure in perspective, the U.S. Constitution contains roughly 7,500 words. All this detail makes state constitutions less flexible and more often in need of change. The second reason state constitutions have changed so frequently is that, unlike the U.S. Constitution, most state constitutions make it easy for dissatisfied groups to pass constitutional amendments.

The history of state constitution making reveals an interesting pattern. Constitutions adopted around the time the U.S. Constitution was ratified tended to emulate it; they were relatively brief and written in broad, general language. During the nineteenth and early twentieth centuries, longer, more detailed state constitutions became the norm. "The Arkansas Constitution of 1874, for example, contained articles regulating 'Municipal and Private Corporations,' 'Horticulture, Mining and Manufacturing,' and 'Railroads, Canals and Turnpikes.' "[23] In the last half-century, however, states that have revised their constitutions have again written shorter and more flexible documents.[24]

Governors

Most Americans see their governor as an important political figure who has more effect on their daily lives than their elected officials in Washington do. Almost three-quarters of all Americans can recall the name of their governor, while only 40 to 50 percent can tell you the name of one of their U.S. senators.[25] Gubernatorial races bring more people to the polls than senatorial races, and voters care more about the outcomes of gubernatorial than senatorial races.[26] And, as the careers of Jimmy Carter, Ronald Reagan, and Bill Clinton attest, many governors become politicians of national stature.

Terms of Office

All but two states have shifted their governors to four-year terms of office. The move from one-, two-, and three-year terms to four-year terms was fueled by the desire to save the governor from perpetual campaigning. A longer term allows governors to learn their job and have a chance to pursue their policy agendas before they have to face the voters again.

Many states limit the number of terms their governors may serve. In Virginia, for example, the governor may serve only one four-year term. But limiting governors to one term of office brings with it one decided disadvantage—it tends to make it difficult for the governor to fulfill his or her campaign pledges. The reason is that a one-term governor is soon considered a **lame duck**—an officeholder whose political power is weakened

Lame duck
An officeholder whose political power is weakened because his or her term is coming to an end.

Christine Todd Whitman was elected governor of New Jersey in 1993. She immediately became a major figure in Republican Party politics.

because his or her term is coming to an end. Since state legislators and other government officials know that the governor cannot run for reelection, they have less incentive to cooperate with the governor's office. For this reason, a two-term limit is more common than a one-term limit. Indeed, thirty-five states emulate the Twenty-second Amendment of the U.S. Constitution and limit their governor to two four-year terms.

Some states do not place any limits on how many terms a governor may serve, though among those that do not, several have an informal norm that limits service to two terms. A few midwestern states have had governors serve for more than two terms. In 1994, for example, Terry Branstad was elected to his fourth four-year term in Iowa. Such lengthy service offers a governor the best chance to make a mark on the state.

Who Serves?

Almost all governors have been white males. A few minority members have held the office in states where their numbers are strong, notably Asian Americans in Hawaii and Hispanic Americans in New Mexico. Washington state voters elected Gary Locke, a Chinese American, governor in 1996. The only African American elected governor was Douglas Wilder of Virginia, who held office from 1990 to 1994. No Native Americans have served as governor, although in 1994, Idaho's Attorney General, Larry EchoHawk, a Pawnee, lost a close race for governor.

The first women to serve as governor followed their husbands' footsteps; indeed, some were just surrogates on the ballots. The first women were elected governor in 1924: Nellie Taylor Ross in Wyoming, who filled the term of her dead husband, and Miriam "Ma" Ferguson in Texas, who was on the ballot because her husband, a former governor, was ineligible to hold the office again. Ferguson was reelected in 1932. (Ma Ferguson's campaign slogan, "Two governors for the price of one," clearly signaled to voters what they would be getting if she were elected.) No woman was elected governor again until the 1960s, when Lurleen Wallace won in Alabama. But like Ma Ferguson, Wallace ran as a stand-in for her husband, George, whom the state constitution barred from running for reelection.[27]

In recent years, several women have been elected governor in their own right. The first woman elected governor whose husband had not been governor was Ella Grasso of Connecticut in 1974. Two years later, Dixie Lee Ray was elected governor in Washington. Since then, women have been elected governor in several states, including Kansas, Kentucky, Nebraska, New Hampshire, New Jersey, Oregon, Texas, and Vermont.

Most governors come from the ranks of either the Democratic or Republican parties. Unlike the case with the presidency, however, some independent or third party candidates have been elected governor. For example, in 1990, voters in both Alaska and Connecticut chose independents, and the voters of Maine did likewise in 1994 (see box 15.1). In some cases, these independent candidates are individuals previously elected to office as either a Democratic or a Republican who, for one reason or another, bolted their political party when they ran for governor. In other cases, the independent candidates have been wealthy individuals who had not held public office before becoming governor.

Formal and Informal Powers of the Office

Although the powers that governors exercise vary from state to state, almost every governor has formal powers a president would envy.[28] But this was not always the case. In the past, most governors operated under rules that limited their ability to lead their states.

Over the past several decades, however, governors in most states have gained new powers, making them powerful political leaders. The number of other statewide elected administrators has declined in recent years, but the states still vary considerably in the number of such posts. In North Dakota, for example, in addition to the governor, voters also elect the lieutenant governor, secretary of state, attorney general, treasurer, auditor, agricultural commissioner, commissioner of insurance, labor commissioner, tax commissioner, superintendent of public instruction, and three public service commissioners. In contrast, in Maine, New Hampshire, and New Jersey, the governor is the only elected administrative official. In those states, executive power is much less fragmented than it is in North Dakota, where the governor has to contend with a host of competing elected administrators. Governors are at an advantage when they can appoint people to head administrative agencies because it enables them to staff state government with loyal subordinates, people likely to follow the governor's lead.[29] There is, of course, no guarantee that independently elected officials will do so. In addition, appointments can give the governor considerable leverage when negotiating with legislators and others in the policy-making process because the governor can use appointments to reward political support.[30]

Many states have also changed their constitutions to give their governors greater say in the budget-making process, to allow them to fire selected state employees, and to enable them to initiate plans to reorganize the state bureaucracy. In addition, most states have given their governors more staff. In 1956, for example, governors' offices averaged eleven staff members; in 1990, the average was more than fifty.[31] The increase in staff has increased the governors' power by giving them greater access to information.

The most important formal power any executive has is the veto. Every state gives its governor the same veto power the president has: the ability to reject a bill in its entirety. (In 1996, North Carolina voters passed a constitutional amendment giving their governor the veto.)[32] But most states go even farther. Forty-three states permit a **line-item veto,** which authorizes the governor to delete some provisions from a bill while allowing the rest to become law. Governors in some states enjoy extraordinary line-item veto power. In Wisconsin, for example, the governor can veto words and even letters and digits in a bill. In the 1987–1989 budget bill, for example, Wisconsin Gov. Tommy Thompson altered a provision that mandated courts to hold a juvenile for "not more than forty-eight hours" for certain offenses; by excising certain words and letters, he turned "forty-eight hours" into "ten days." Although legislators challenged this clear example of a change in the intent of legislation, the courts upheld the governor's right to do so.[33] But Wisconsin voters finally reined in the governor's powers in 1990 by passing what was called the "Vanna White" amendment to the state constitution, a measure that prevents the governor from striking letters to make new words.[34]

Line-item veto
The ability of an executive to delete or veto some provisions of a bill, while allowing the rest of the bill to become law.

Eleven states give their governor the power to reduce spending provisions, and fifteen allow an **executive amendment,** a procedure by which the governor rejects a bill but returns it to the legislature with changes that would make it acceptable.[35] This is a powerful weapon. In Illinois, for example, the legislature eventually accepts most of the governor's suggested amendments on vetoed bills.[36]

Executive amendment
A procedure allowing governors to reject a bill by returning it to the legislature with changes that would make it acceptable; the legislature must agree to the changes for the bill to become law.

The People Behind the Rules

BOX 15.1

An Independent in the Governor's Mansion: Angus King of Maine

American history provides a long list of independent or third party candidates who have tried to win the White House. All of them failed. But the record on the state level is different; several independent candidates have been elected governor. The most recent was Angus King, who was elected governor of Maine in 1994. King's path to the governor's mansion reveals the possibilities and problems in taking the independent route.

King grew up in Virginia. After graduating from law school, he moved to Maine to work as a legal-aid lawyer for the poor. He then worked on the staff of U.S. Sen. William Hathaway (D-Maine) for several years before starting his own law practice. King later served as a corporate counsel, and in 1989, he formed Northeast Energy Management, Inc., an energy conservation company. In 1994, King sold his company for $20 million, giving him the financial resources he needed to make an independent bid for the governorship.

In deciding to run for governor, King had another advantage besides money. For eighteen years, he had hosted a public affairs program on Maine public television. This experience made him comfortable in front of television cameras and microphones, something many candidates who are not professional politicians lack. Moreover, the show gave King the policy background and name recognition among political insiders to make him a credible candidate for governor.

In the general election, King faced some formidable opponents: Democrat Joseph Brennan, a former two-term governor, and Republican Susan Collins, a former aide to the outgoing governor. In addition, the Green Party, a political group dedicated to environmental causes, fielded a candidate. In the end, King squeaked out a victory, getting 35 percent of the vote to 34 percent for Brennan, 23 percent for Collins, and 6 percent for the Green Party's candidate. King fared better with Republican voters than with Democrats, and in the state where Ross Perot got his highest vote percentage in 1992, King won the votes of many Perot supporters as well.

Campaigning as a political outsider is one thing; governing as one is something else. Once in office, King found himself the target of some stinging criticism for his political miscues. At the end of the 1995 legislative session, one political observer commented, "Those of you who voted for Angus King for governor because he said he wasn't a politician now have considerable evidence he was telling the truth. King has spent the entire legislative session displaying the political savvy of a muskmelon." Of course, being an independent places a governor at a disadvantage because there is no natural constituency to call on to support your proposals. Neither the Democrats nor the Republicans in the legislature have a vested interest in seeing a political independent succeed. For example, after Governor King gave his State of the State address in 1996, leaders of *both* parties criticized his proposals.

Gov. Angus King

Not all of the problems Angus King encountered as governor can be blamed on his independent status or lack of political experience. One other source of considerable difficulty has been that control of Maine's legislature is split between the Republicans and Democrats, with majority status changing regularly due to special elections and party switches. Despite his missteps, King has had enough success that some Democrats have speculated about the possibility of naming him as their party's candidate in 1998. But in the end, being an independent governor in a partisan world is not easy.

Sources: Michael Barone and Grant Ujifusa, *The Almanac of American Politics 1996* (Washington, D.C.: National Journal, 1995), p. 590; Paul Carrier, "Economy Is First, Says King," *Portland Press Herald,* 24 January 1996; Al Diamon, "Politics and Other Mistakes," *Casco Bay Weekly,* 6 June 1995; Al Diamon, "Politics and Other Mistakes," *Casco Bay Weekly,* 28 September 1995; Charles Mahtesian, "Angus King: Insider's Outsider," *Governing,* January 1995, p. 18; Bill Nemitz, "Okay, Kids, Time to Quit the Sandbox," *Portland Press Herald,* 17 January 1996.

In many states, governors use the veto power liberally, and the number of vetoed bills has increased in recent years.[37] In 1995, for example, Gov. Gary Johnson of New Mexico set what may be a national record by vetoing 48 percent of the 424 bills sent to his desk.[38] Similarly, in 1992 and 1993, Gov. Pete Wilson of California rejected 21 percent of the 2,681 bills sent to him, and the legislature failed to override a single one.[39] Indeed, few legislatures override vetoes.[40] The state legislature with the least success in overriding vetoes may well be New York's; it failed to override a single veto between 1873 and 1976.[41]

Governors can make their vetoes stick for three reasons. First, in thirty-eight states, an override requires a two-thirds majority; in another six states, a three-fifths majority is needed. Most governors can muster the relatively few votes they need to sustain their vetoes. Second, many state legislatures pass most of their bills in the last few days of the legislative session, enabling the governor to veto their work after they have adjourned and cannot respond. Third, some legislators introduce bad bills at the behest of important constituents and push them through the legislature expecting the governor to veto them. In these situations, the legislator can claim credit for passing the bill, while letting the governor take the blame for not allowing it to become law.[42]

Governors also have informal powers that increase their influence, particularly over the actions of the legislature. They receive much more media attention than any other politician in the state.[43] This publicity advantage allows them to set the policy agenda, and if they are skillful, to frame public debate on the issues.[44] For example, South Carolina's governorship is considered among the least powerful in the country. Yet, when Richard Riley occupied the post from 1979 to 1987, he used his domination of the media to push through a series of important educational reforms.[45] Similarly, then-Gov. Bill Clinton used the media to rally public support for his controversial education reform package in Arkansas in 1983.[46] Indeed, the ability to work well with the media and to use them to communicate policy decisions to the voters is a key characteristic of successful and popular governors.[47]

Gubernatorial Elections

Governors, like other incumbents in American elections, win much more often than they lose.[48] But governors are reelected at a lower rate than are senators, representatives, or state legislators, and on average, governors get a lower percentage of the vote than other elected officials do. Voters hold governors responsible for problems in ways they do not hold other politicians accountable. For example, issues closely identified with governors, such as education, health, crime, and the environment, usually are more salient to voters than national issues, such as defense and foreign policy, that often occupy members of Congress. Because governors also get much more news coverage than other elected officials, they are more vulnerable to blame when things do not go well. Thus, it is not surprising that governors have more difficulty getting reelected.[49]

State Legislatures

Over the last three decades, state legislatures have changed dramatically. Member salaries have increased markedly, sessions have grown longer, and facilities and staff have greatly improved.[50] Because state legislatures have become more professional, their members are serving longer, and they have, by and large, increased both their influence over policy and their independence from the governor. At the same time, the mix of people who serve in state legislatures has changed, as have the rules governing how long state legislators may serve in office.

Organizational Arrangements

The fifty state legislatures vary along every imaginable dimension. They range in size from the twenty-member Alaska state senate to the four-hundred-member New Hampshire House of Representatives. The forty state senators in California each represent roughly 744,000 people—making their districts larger than the districts of members of the U.S.

House of Representatives—while the average state representative in New Hampshire has fewer than 3,000 constituents. State legislatures also differ in how much they pay their members, how much staff they provide, and in the number of days they meet each year.

Every state but one has a bicameral legislature. Most states call their lower house the House of Representatives, although a few call it the Assembly or House of Delegates. Every state calls its upper house the Senate. Most states designate two-year terms of office for state representatives (or members of the assembly or delegates, as the case might be) and four-year terms for state senators. But a few states mandate two-year terms for members of both houses, and a couple of states, most recently, North Dakota in 1996, give all of their legislators four-year terms.

Nebraska provides the lone exception to the rule of bicameral state legislatures; it has a one-house state legislature known as the Unicameral. In addition to being the only one-house legislature in the United States, the Unicameral is also the only legislature in the nation whose members are elected in nonpartisan elections. Nebraska's citizens voted to switch from a partisan bicameral legislature to a nonpartisan unicameral legislature in 1934, during the Great Depression. Voters hoped the switch would reduce the cost of running the legislature and make the legislative process more efficient. It is not clear, however, that the Unicameral functions better than other state legislatures.[51] For example, the Unicameral costs more to run per citizen than the larger two-house state legislature next door in Iowa. Still, proponents of unicameral legislatures have promoted the idea in Iowa, California, South Dakota, and other states.[52]

Professionalization

Most state legislatures have experienced dramatic changes in the last several decades. Until the 1960s, most governors exercised far more political power than their state's legislature did. State legislators were poorly paid, rarely received staff or even offices, and were often limited by law in the number of days they could meet in session; most were populated with farmers, lawyers, or businesspeople serving in the legislature part-time, outside their regular profession. Thus, most legislators did not serve for long, and they never acquired the sorts of expertise about issues and government operations that they needed to be a strong political force. Legislators were only able to respond to the governor's initiatives.

During the 1960s, state legislatures undertook a series of reforms, collectively referred to as *professionalization,* that greatly strengthened their power. The reforms came about in large part because of the efforts of Jesse Unruh, who turned the California Assembly into the model of a professional legislature during his tenure as Speaker of the Assembly, and the Citizens Conference on State Legislatures, a reform group that proposed guidelines for establishing more professional state legislatures. Many legislatures increased member pay to make service more attractive and affordable. They also expanded and improved staff resources and facilities, enabling legislators to counter the governor's traditional advantages in expertise and staff. And many legislatures lifted laws limiting how often the legislature could meet so that legislators could meet year round.

Reformers, then, have consciously sought to make state legislatures more professional, that is, more like the U.S. Congress. How successful have their efforts been? The answer varies from state to state.[53] The state legislatures in California, Massachusetts, Michigan, and New York are the most professionalized. These four legislatures pay well, meet in unlimited sessions, and provide ample staff. A few legislatures, such as those in Pennsylvania and Ohio, are substantially professionalized. Most others, however, are not, with the legislatures in New Hampshire, North Dakota, South Dakota, Utah, and Wyoming being the least professionalized. New Hampshire, for example, pays its state legislators only $100 per year.

Does this mean that the less professional legislatures are less effective? Not necessarily; the benefits of professionalization are not clear-cut. Legislators in more professionalized legislatures serve longer and come to know more about how government works. They also have more staff. With more information at their fingertips, legislators in professionalized legislatures are better able to generate their own policy initiatives, which in turn makes them less inclined to accept the governor's preferences. The public, however, is not impressed by professionalized legislatures; they give them lower approval ratings than they give less professionalized legislatures.[54]

Overall, partisanship—whether the same party controls both the legislature and governorship—still dominates the relationship between governor and legislature, regardless of professionalization.[55] States in which the same party holds the governorship and controls the state legislature have much smoother executive-legislative relations than states in which political control is divided. The public, however, gives state government higher approval ratings to states with split party control.[56]

During his tenure as Speaker of the California Assembly during the 1960s, Jesse Unruh started the national movement to professionalize state legislatures.

Who Serves?

Historically, state legislators were overwhelmingly white males, many of whom were lawyers. Reformers argued in the 1960s that professionalization would redraw the face of each state legislature because it would make it easier for women and minorities to run for election. As the Citizens Conference on State Legislatures claimed: "Other things being equal, the diversity of legislatures will increase as it is economically possible for larger numbers of people to consider running for office."[57]

As reformers hoped, the number of women and minorities serving as state legislators has increased over the past few decades. In 1995, women held 20 percent of all state legislative seats, African Americans 8 percent, and Hispanic Americans 2 percent.[58] Very few Asian Americans and American Indians serve in state legislatures.[59] However, as you might expect, members of minority groups are more often elected in the states where they constitute larger proportions of the population. In California, for example, Hispanic Americans are an increasingly important political bloc. In 1997, Cruz Bustamante became the first Hispanic American selected Speaker of the California Assembly.

The number of women in state legislatures is much higher now than twenty years ago, but there were actually slightly fewer in office in 1995 than in 1993—probably because fewer women ran in 1995 than two years before.[60] (The last point is important because women are just as likely as men to win state legislative races.)[61] But contrary to reformers' hopes, women tend to be found in larger numbers in less professionalized legislatures such as those in Vermont and New Hampshire. In recent years, however, they also have found success in somewhat more professionalized state legislatures in conservative states such as Arizona and Colorado.[62] Moreover, women constitute almost the same percentage of all Republican state legislators (19 percent) as they do of all Democratic state legislators (22 percent).[63]

The influx of women and minorities into state legislatures has made the legislatures more attuned to issues that affect these groups, particularly where they form a substantial portion of the membership.[64] There is evidence, for example, that African-American women in state legislatures focus their policy agendas on education, health care, and economic development.[65] And unlike their counterparts several decades ago, women elected to state legislatures in recent years are just as politically experienced as men and are just as likely to see themselves as effective legislators.[66] Younger women with children, however, are still much less likely to serve in state legislatures than younger men who are fathers.[67]

The occupational backgrounds of state legislators have also changed. During the first half of the twentieth century, state legislatures were disproportionately populated by lawyers and farmers; each group represented more than 20 percent of the membership.[68] By 1995, the percentage of attorneys serving in state legislatures had dropped to 16 percent. The percentage of farmers holding legislative office has declined to 8 percent, largely because farmers are a decreasing percentage of the nation's population. Farmer-legislators are most common in Iowa and North Dakota.[69]

A wide variety of other occupations is now represented in state legislatures. Most prominent among these are educators, business owners, and business employees. The percentage of homemakers, students, and retirees combined stands at around 9 percent. These groups are concentrated in the highly unprofessionalized New Hampshire and Vermont legislatures.

As one might expect, given the successful attempts to professionalize state legislatures, the number of members who work as full-time legislators has grown sharply. Forty years ago, few legislators claimed to work full-time at the state house; now 14 percent do, and this figure probably is low.[70] In Michigan, for example, observers believe that two-thirds of the members are full-time legislators, but few of the members will publicly admit it because they fear that being labeled a professional politician will hurt their chances for reelection.[71] Those who admit to being full-time legislators are concentrated in the most professionalized legislatures, such as Massachusetts and New York.[72]

Elections, Turnover, and Term Limits

State legislators, like congressional incumbents, win reelection at high rates and by wide margins.[73] Legislators in more professionalized bodies seem to enjoy slightly more success than average, but reelection rates are high in almost every state.[74] Nonetheless, turnover rates in state legislatures are very high, especially when compared to Congress.[75] For example, in 1995, almost 25 percent of state legislators were in their first term.[76] Turnover is related to professionalization; the more professionalized the legislature, the lower the turnover rate.[77]

In California and a few other states, turnover is high even though the legislature is very professionalized. One reason for the high turnover rate in California is that state legislators have relatively more opportunities to run for a seat in the U.S. House of Representatives; recall that California has more seats in Congress than in its own state senate. As a result, ambitious politicians are willing to give up their seat in the statehouse for a chance to go to Capitol Hill.[78] But in 1990, voters in California gave their legislators another reason to leave quickly: they voted to make California one of the first states to limit how many terms a person may serve in the legislature.

As figure 15.2 shows, the push for term limits has caught on in other parts of the country. In 1990, voters in Oklahoma and Colorado joined with voters in California to impose term limits on their state legislators. Two years later, term-limit measures passed in all twelve states in which they appeared on the ballot, and Maine voters imposed limits on their legislators in 1993. Idaho, Massachusetts, and Nevada joined the list in 1994, as did Louisiana in 1995. (Nebraska voters passed term limits in 1992, but the Nebraska Supreme Court tossed out the measure in early 1994. The state's voters then passed new limits in November 1994 only to have the Court toss them out again.) In only one state, Utah in 1994, have legislators placed limits on themselves, but even there, they were pressured by the threat that Utah voters would use a ballot measure to impose term limits.[79] Many term-limit measures restrict a person from serving more than six years in office. Although critics have complained that term limits violate state constitutions, the limits have withstood challenge in the courts.[80]

The term-limit movement has been pushed by several national organizations, with one organization, U.S. Term Limits, supplying much of the money term-limit supporters use in each state. For example, in 1994, U.S. Term Limits gave $52,870 out of the $73,260 that Idahoans for Term Limits raised, $230,000 out of the $255,100 that Nebraskans for Term Limits gathered, and $76,000 of the $104,500 that term-limit supporters in Maine collected.[81] There is some evidence that voters have responded to term-limit campaigns in part because of their continuing dissatisfaction with and cynicism about the way government works.[82] But there also is a partisan edge to the debate; some sophisticated voters see term limits as a device to dislodge the majority party in their state from office. This usually, but not always, means Republicans are more likely to favor limits, while Democrats are less likely to support them.[83] Similarly, it is not surprising, given their long-time status as the minority party in many states, that Republican legislators are far more likely than Democrats to support term limits.[84]

As we discussed in chapter 1, proponents of term limits argue that dislodging long-time incumbents will make legislatures more responsive to the average voter. But barring senior legislators from continuing to serve also robs a legislature of continuity and expertise, although some evidence indicates that members of legislatures with

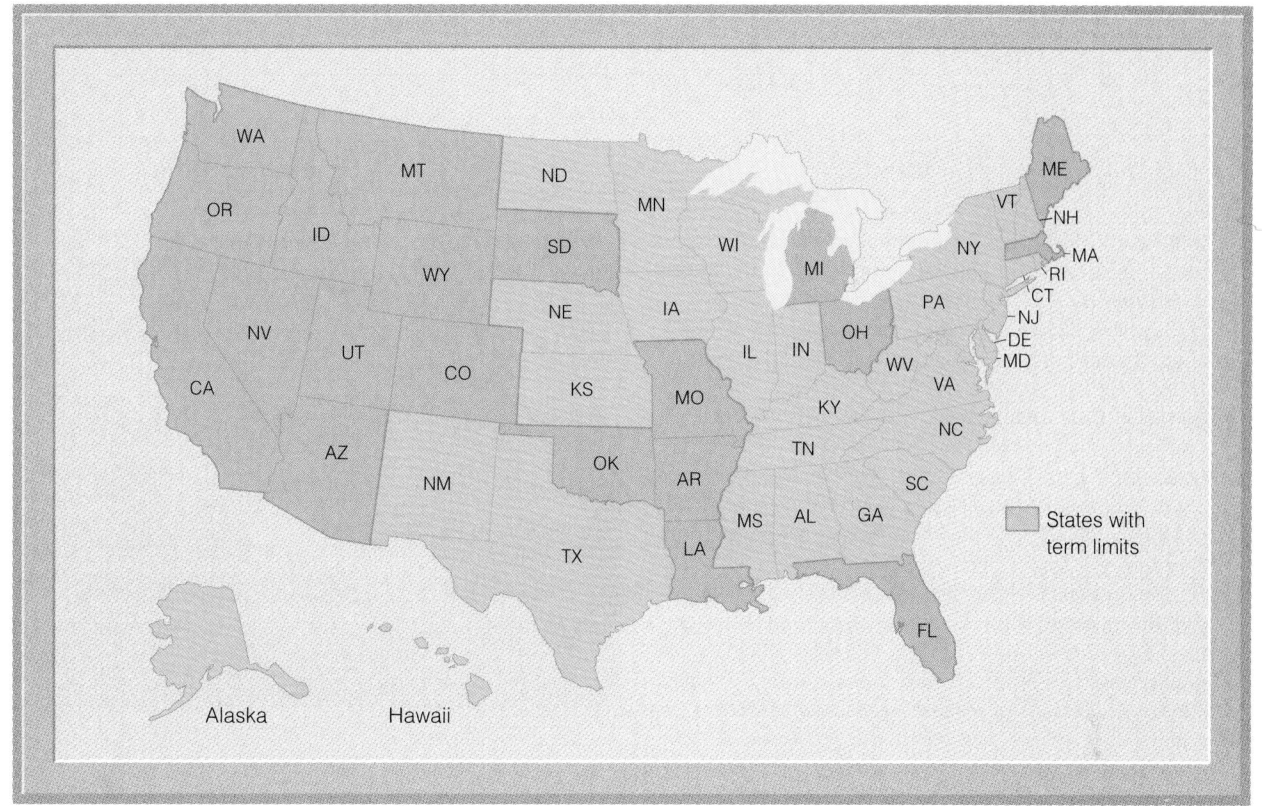

FIGURE 15.2
Term Limits and State Legislatures

Term limits for state legislators have been an important issue in the 1990s, and voters have put limits in place in nineteen states. Only the Utah state legislature has imposed term limits on itself.

Sources: National Conference of State Legislatures; U.S. Term Limits.

term limits double their efforts to master legislative rules and public issues.[85] Depending on the length of service allowed, term limits may have scant effect on many of the less professionalized state legislatures where few legislators serve longer than the limits in any event.[86] The full effects of term limits will not be apparent until the new rules have pushed experienced legislators out the door, an effect to be felt first in California and Maine in 1996 (see box 15.2).

Interest Groups in State Politics

At the beginning of the twentieth century, politics in many states was dominated by a few large interest groups. In California, for example, the Southern Pacific Railroad wielded enormous political power, and Anaconda Copper exercised near total control of politics in Montana. Although the ability of a few private interests to dominate state government largely disappeared by the 1950s, interest group activity at the state level continued to be restricted to a handful of groups, usually those with a substantial interest in the state's economy. Most national interest groups, and especially business interest groups, focused their attention on lobbying Congress and the executive branch because they made most of the important policy decisions.

The preoccupation interest groups had with Washington, D.C., changed in the 1980s. As the Reagan administration sought to curtail federal assistance and to shift decision-making authority back to cities and states, interest groups began to pay more attention to what was happening in Albany, Austin, Sacramento, Springfield, Tallahassee, and other state capitals.[87] Lobbying of state governments exploded. A 1990 survey counted more than 42,500 registered state lobbyists, an increase of 20 percent in only four years.[88] Another study showed that the number of interests registered to lobby state legislatures increased threefold between 1975 and 1990.[89] Indeed, because many interest groups now use the same techniques to lobby both federal and state governments, some observers argue that we are witnessing the "nationalization" of state politics.[90]

POINT OF ORDER

BOX 15.2

Changing The Rules: The Effects of Legislative Term Limits on the California Assembly

The California Assembly

In the early 1990s, term limits swept the nation. By 1996, twenty-one states had imposed term limits on their state legislators. But all these laws were passed before anyone had had any experience with the consequences of living under a term-limit law—the first legislators the laws affected were in California and Maine, and they were only prevented from running again starting in 1996. Thus, an examination of the California Assembly, the lower of the two houses in the California state legislature and a chamber whose members are now limited to six years in office, gives us a glimpse into the consequences of changing the rules and imposing term limits.

The California Assembly has traditionally been considered the model of a professional legislative body. Its members are well paid, work at the job full-time, and have impressive staff resources. Yet in 1990, California voters approved a term-limits law and voted to cut the budget for running the Assembly and state senate by 40 percent. The message the voters seemed to be sending was, "We think that doing away with professional politicians and big government will result in better public policy."

What has happened in the California Assembly since the voters approved term limits and cut its budget? One result is hardly surprising—members of the Assembly, who by and large are professional politicians, have looked for opportunities to move on to other, usually higher, offices. That is nothing new; members of the Assembly have always used it as a springboard. But with term limits in place, the search for opportunities to leave has been hastened, and this has taken a toll on the operations of the Assembly. For example, in 1995, the Republican leader in the Assembly resigned from his post, in large part because he was being forced out of office by term limits and he wanted to concentrate on campaigning for a seat in the state senate. Indeed, by 1995, many members appeared to be thinking less about their constituents and the pursuit of good public policy and more about currying favor with people and interests who could assist them in attaining higher office, or help them find work once their days in the legislature came to an end.

What about the people who have replaced members of the Assembly who left because of term limits? Contrary to the hopes of supporters, term limits do not appear to change the nature of the people elected to the Assembly or how they behave once in office. Analyses show that new members behave much like their more senior colleagues and

Continued

There are, of course, important differences in interest group activity across the fifty states. Interest groups are more powerful in some states than in others, and which groups are active varies from state to state.[91] It is no surprise, for example, that the United Auto Workers is more active in Michigan than in Hawaii, or that the Farm Bureau has a stronger presence in Iowa than in New Jersey. But we can make two important generalizations about interest groups and state politics; both relate to economics. First, the more diverse the state economy, the more diverse the types of interest groups active in the state. Second, the larger a state economy, the more interest groups in the state.[92]

Across the states, business groups tend to exercise more power than other groups.[93] But the single most influential interest group in state politics is the public school teachers lobby, which in most states means the local chapters of the National Education Association.[94] In Alabama, for example, teachers became politically active

Point of Order

BOX 15.2 CONTINUED

former members. They, too, are professional politicians, and they raise their campaign money in the same ways and from the same people and interests as their predecessors. Moreover, they are just as partisan in their voting behavior.

But newer members of the Assembly differ from the members they have replaced in one key respect—they have less knowledge about how to operate the institution. For instance, following the 1994 elections, the Assembly found itself embroiled in a bitter power struggle over who should be the next speaker. As the more senior members who understood the parliamentary rules shaped the terms of the debate, most first- and second-term members found themselves pushed to the sidelines.

Some senior members of the Assembly have worked to groom new leaders to take the places of those pushed out. During the 1993–94 session, for example, many first- and second-term members were handed important committee and leadership posts, a change from past practice when seniority played a bigger role in allocating top positions. But as 1996 approached, members began to understand that term limits placed them in a bind when making decisions about leadership positions. If they selected a third-term member for a top post, he or she would be gone once the session ended. If they chose a first- or second-term member, they were getting a leader with little experience. In addition, many members began to realize that their lack of legislative seasoning left the Assembly weak relative to the state senate (where members are limited to eight years), and, more important, to the governor. Observers who had expected experienced staff to compensate for inexperienced legislators were surprised to learn that turnover among staffers mirrored that of their employers, leaving few people around to provide institutional memory.

Finally, term limits has encouraged a decline in civility within the Assembly. Members realize that because of term limits, they will not work with each other for very long. This creates a scenario much like the nineteenth-century U.S. House of Representatives, where, as we saw in chapter 11, rapid turnover meant that proper decorum and civil behavior were the exception rather than the rule. During the Assembly's 1995 legislative session, for example, members made obscene gestures and said uncivil things to each other on the Assembly floor. Such behavior breeds hard feelings and makes it difficult for people to work together. But with term limits, members have little incentive to adopt rules and norms that promote decorum.

Overall, changing the rules by imposing term limits has changed the California Assembly. But most reforms have unintended consequences and leave unfulfilled promises. Term limits in the California Assembly is no exception.

Sources: Elizabeth A. Capell, "The Impact of Term Limits: Early Returns from California," *Extension of Remarks,* July 1994, pp. 6–7, 9, 15; Richard A. Clucas, "The First Post-Term Limits Election in California," *Extension of Remarks,* July 1994, 4–5, 15; Ken DeBow, "Decline of the California Legislature: Why New Faces Won't Help," presented at the 1996 annual meeting of the Western Political Science Association, San Francisco; Timothy A. Hodson, "Conventional Wisdom or Wishful Thinking: Staff Influence in Post Term Limit Legislatures, *Extension of Remarks,* July 1994, pp. 8–9; Timothy Hodson, Rich Jones, Karl Kurtz, and Gary Moncreif, "Leaders and Limits: Changing Patterns of State Legislative Leadership Under Term Limits," presented at the 1995 annual meeting of the Western Political Science Association, Portland, Ore.; Charles R. Kesler, "Reaping What Voters Sowed," *Los Angeles Times,* 15 September 1995; Peverill Squire, "Career Opportunities and Membership Stability in Legislatures," *Legislative Studies Quarterly* 13 (February 1988): 65–82; Peverill Squire, "The Theory of Legislative Institutionalization and the California Assembly," *Journal of Politics* 54 (November 1992): 1026–54; Bill Stall, "Brulte Resigns as GOP Leader in Assembly," *Los Angeles Times,* 19 August 1995.

in the 1970s, and by 1987, 41 percent of state legislators were teachers, former teachers, or people married to teachers.[95] In addition, the Alabama Education Association has been able to register more lobbyists than any other interest in the state.[96]

Teachers have enjoyed substantial political success because they enjoy several organizing advantages.[97] First, teachers live in every town (and legislative district); thus they can exert constituent pressure on all legislators. Second, as is true of most well-educated people, teachers are more disposed than the average American toward joining political groups. Third, state legislatures greatly influence education funding and directives. This means that teachers who work for public schools have a strong incentive to lobby state government. Indeed, in 1993 and 1994, New York State United Teachers, the state's main teachers union, spent far more money lobbying in Albany and gathering campaign contributions for state office than did any other group, including professional associations for doctors, trial lawyers, and bankers.[98]

As a general rule, the states have taken a more aggressive role than the federal government in regulating interest group lobbying. All fifty states require lobbyists to register and to disclose who employs them. Most states also require lobbyists to file reports listing their business expenditures.[99] The strongest regulations tend to be enacted in states with more professionalized legislatures and in states with a lower tolerance for political corruption.[100]

States have also actively regulated campaign finance. All fifty states impose regulations of some sort on political action committees. But again, the regulations vary. Some states provide public funds for candidates in some or all state elections. Some states bar corporations, labor unions, and public utilities from contributing to campaigns, while others impose no contribution limits.[101] Each state has its own web of regulations governing the interaction of interest groups and public officials. But regardless of the details of those regulations, interest groups are paying increased attention to state governments.

The Public and Direct Democracy

Under the U.S. Constitution, Americans can pass formal judgment on the work of the federal government only by voting in congressional and presidential elections. In contrast, state constitutions provide an array of mechanisms that enable voters to record their views on the work of the state government. In many states, the rules allow voters to revise the state's constitution, overturn bills the state legislature passes, enact their own bills, and even vote to remove elected officials from office. Each of these mechanisms is a form of **direct democracy.**

Direct democracy
Mechanisms such as the initiative, referendum, and recall—powers that enable voters to use the ballot box to set government policy.

Referendum
An election held allowing voters to accept or reject a proposed law or amendment passed by a legislative body.

Initiative
A proposed law or amendment placed on the ballot by citizens, usually through a petition.

Referenda and Initiatives

Two ways voters can directly control state policy are through referenda and initiatives. A **referendum** is a rules change, proposed by a legislature and put to a direct public vote, whereas an **initiative** is a voter-proposed change. Every state but Delaware requires that amendments to the state constitution be put to a vote in a statewide election known as a *constitutional referendum.*[102] Seventeen states also provide for a *constitutional initiative* in which citizens can put a proposed constitutional amendment on the ballot, usually after they have collected a set number of signatures on a petition. (The Massachusetts state constitution also provides for an indirect initiative, whereby the legislature may pass an acceptable version of the proposed amendment before it is put to the voters.) In every state except one, only a majority of voters must support a constitutional amendment for it to pass. The exception is New Hampshire, where a two-thirds majority is needed.

In half the states, voters can demand a *citizen* or *popular referendum* in which a measure the state legislature has passed is placed on the ballot and made subject to voter approval. Like the rules on constitutional initiatives, the rules governing a popular referendum usually require sponsors of the measure to collect a set number of signatures on a petition. Half of the states also allow the legislature itself to put measures it has passed before the voters for approval in a *legislative referendum.* Both popular and legislative referenda give voters the opportunity to override the decisions of their elected representatives.

In some states, citizens need not wait for the legislature to act. Voters in eighteen states may use a *direct initiative* to sidestep the state legislature and place a proposed piece of legislation directly before the voters. Direct initiatives enable citizens to tackle issues that state legislators may wish to avoid or are unable to settle. A recent example is term limits. With the exception of Utah, every state that now has a law limiting the number of terms legislators may serve enacted that law as the result of a direct initiative.

In recent years, the use of referenda and initiatives has increased. In 1996, for example, voters in California passed measures to eliminate state affirmative action programs and to legalize marijuana for medical purposes, voters in Alabama passed a "Sportsperson's Bill of Rights" guaranteeing a right to hunt and fish, and Oklahoma voters passed a crime victim's rights bill. Yet the increased use of referenda and initiatives reflects more than greater political interest or unhappiness among the general public. National political activists have seized on direct democracy as a way to translate their policy preferences into law in individual states. (Recall how much out-of-state money flowed into term-limit campaigns.) As a result, a national group that can afford to round up the signatures needed to hold an initiative in a particular state can set the policy agenda in that state. Indeed, more money was spent in California in 1990 on initiative campaigns than on lobbying the legislature.[103]

For voters, referenda and initiatives pose a problem. Because interest groups rather than political parties usually push these measures, voters cannot use party affiliation to decide how to vote. Of course, voters can do their own research on an issue, but that takes time, and many referenda and initiatives involve issues of great interest to activists and far less interest to everyone else. Moreover, as figure 15.3 illustrates, some referenda and initiatives are exceptionally detailed and complex, making it impossible for all but the most dedicated and well-informed voters to decipher them.

Because referenda and initiatives typically involve matters of little interest to the general public and because they can be so complex, most voters rely on advertising to gain information about what a referendum or initiative means. In short, they may use advertisements as a shortcut to becoming informed.[104] The information gleaned from political advertisements may be biased, however, especially if only one side can afford to make its case heard. Because reliable information can be scarce, surveys find that voters are much more likely to change their minds about a referendum or an initiative during the course of a campaign than they are to change their minds about a candidate.[105] While referenda and initiatives may in theory be direct democracy in action, they are a vehicle that well-financed interest groups can use to maneuver the public into voting for the groups' policy preferences.

Although a well-financed interest group can help improve the chances that a ballot measure will pass, money by no means guarantees victory. Consider, for example, the fate of two measures that appeared on California's ballot in 1994. The first proposed that California establish an ambitious system of state-financed health care. The proposal's opponents, led by insurance companies, spent some $7 million to defeat the plan, far more than the $2.3 million that its supporters spent. On Election Day, 73 percent of California's voters said no to the health care proposal. The second ballot measure proposed to ease restrictions on smoking in public places. Once again, spending was lopsided; proponents of the measure raised almost $14 million—some $12.5 million from the Philip Morris Company alone—while their opponents spent only $400,000.[106] Yet even though proponents spent heavily, more than 70 percent of California's voters said no to easing restrictions on public smoking.

Recall

In 1996, voters in Minnesota made it the seventeenth state to give citizens the right to vote to recall elected officials. Residents of Montana can go even further and recall appointed officials. Recall votes are not common, but even the threat of one may have a powerful effect on state officials. In 1987, for example, a group of Arizona citizens launched a petition to recall Republican Gov. Evan Mecham because of alleged unethical and perhaps even corrupt behavior. Within four months, they had collected more than enough signatures to force a recall election. The political pressure on the Arizona Republican Party became immense, and ultimately, the state legislature beat the voters to the punch: they impeached and convicted Mecham, thereby removing him from office.[107] Because the rules allowed voter recall, Mecham lost his job much more quickly than probably would have been the case if he had been governor of a state without a recall process.

In 1995, recall elections were used to remove two members of the California Assembly from office, not because of corruption or unethical behavior, but for political reasons. Both Assembly members were Republicans who had voted with Democrats in a series of votes on who would be the next speaker of the Assembly. The recall efforts were led by other Republicans who wanted to punish colleagues they considered turncoats. The two were the first state legislators to be recalled in California since 1914.

Proposition 186: Text of Proposed Law

This initiative measure is submitted to the people in accordance with the provisions of Article II, Section 8 of the Constitution.

This initiative measure expressly amends the Constitution by adding sections thereto, and repeals and adds sections to various codes; therefore, existing provisions proposed to be deleted are printed in ~~strikeout type~~ and new provisions proposed to be added are printed in *italic type* to indicate that they are new.

PROPOSED LAW

CALIFORNIA HEALTH SECURITY ACT

SECTION 1. This initiative establishes a California health security system that will protect California consumers, taxpayers, and employers from the skyrocketing cost of health care. Savings will be achieved by limiting health care costs, eliminating waste, and emphasizing disease prevention. Under the time-tested single-payer system established by this act and administered by an elected Health Commissioner, the practice of medicine will remain private. Under the health security system, all Californians will have free choice of health care provider, regardless of employment, and access to comprehensive health care, including long-term care. The health security system will provide these services for the same or less money in real dollars than is spent on health care in California today.

SECTION 2. Division 13 (commencing with Section 25000) is added to the Welfare and Institutions Code, to read:

DIVISION 13. CALIFORNIA HEALTH SECURITY ACT

CHAPTER 1. FINDINGS AND INTENT

25000. This act shall be known and may be cited as the California Health Security Act.

25001. Findings and declarations.

The people of the State of California find and declare as follows:

(a) Californians have a right not to be financially ruined when they or their loved ones become sick or ill.

(b) California employers have a right not to be driven into insolvency by the spiraling cost of employee medical benefits.

(c) Californians have a right to high-quality health care.

(d) Californians should be guaranteed the freedom to choose their own doctor or other health care provider.

(e) Californians should not be at risk of losing their health benefits if they change or lose their jobs.

(f) California taxpayers are bearing enormous financial costs because many Californians do not have a regular health care provider. This lack of primary care leads to expensive overuse of emergency facilities resulting in exorbitant financial costs that are ultimately borne by the taxpayers.

(g) Because health care costs are rising faster than wages and prices, the number of uninsured and under-insured Californians is growing at an alarming rate. Over five million Californians presently have no health insurance. Children, low-income working and unemployed individuals, and individuals with disabilities and chronic conditions, in particular, are having a harder and harder time getting all types of medical care.

(h) In spite of the fact that employers and individuals spend huge amounts of money purchasing health insurance from insurance companies, the insurance they purchase often does not provide adequate medical care or real protection from financial ruin, especially if a loved one develops a catastrophic illness or needs long-term care.

(i) Enormous savings will be achieved in California upon institution of a single payer for health care. Savings will be achieved by decreasing wasteful administrative overhead, bargaining for the best possible prescription drug prices, providing more cost-effective primary care, and by providing long-term care at home. The current health care system is so wasteful that the savings will be enough to fund universal coverage for all medical care services and extend benefits to include long-term care, mental health care, and some dental services, and increase the resources available to prevent disease, all for the same amount of money currently spent on health care in California.

(j) The quality of health care can be improved in California upon institution of a single-payer for health care. Quality can be improved by changing those features of the health care system that underserve consumers and which subject some to the risks of unnecessary medical treatments.

(k) Since people always need health care services, prices for those services often do not respond to normal supply-and-demand market forces. As a result, health care costs much more than it should to provide for the health care needs of Californians. Any health care delivery system relying on price competition is unlikely to keep costs in check or provide universal health services to the population. Price control is therefore necessary to achieve cost containment and to make quality health care accessible to all.

(l) Because the best way to control health care costs in the long run is to prevent disease, funding for public health measures, and for research directed at the causes and prevention of disease, should be directly related to the overall cost of illness to society.

(m) Health care consumers need to participate in developing and reviewing public policies affecting the quality, accessibility, and accountability of health care service providers. Health care consumers therefore have the right voluntarily to join and support a democratically-controlled Health Care Consumer Council that will represent their interests before administrative, judicial, and legislative bodies, and that will have an efficient and honest system for funding.

(n) Safeguarding the quality and accountability of the health care system requires that there be a Health Commissioner who is elected by a direct vote of the people of California.

25002. Purpose and Intent.

The people enact this act to accomplish the following purposes:

(a) To replace the current hodgepodge of government programs, private health insurance, and health care expenditures by individuals with a comprehensive and sensible health security system that will provide all medically appropriate care specific to individual needs, including preventive, mental health, and long-term care, as well as prescription drug coverage, and some dental care for all Californians.

(b) To control health care costs without compromising quality, primarily by eliminating wasteful overhead and excessive expenditures that do not contribute to the quality of health care.

(c) To finance the health security system in a manner that is fair, and spend no more money per individual in real dollars than is now being spent on health care in California.

(d) To provide incentives by which competition can improve quality and service in the health care system. When consumers have freedom of choice of health care providers, instead of a restricted choice of health plans based on what they can afford, providers have an incentive to provide the best quality care and service, in order to attract patients. When providers have freedom of mode of reimbursement, such as a choice of fee-for-service, capitation, or salary, under an overall budget, they can focus on taking the best possible care of their patients, without bureaucratic intrusion into the relationship between individual providers and their patients.

(e) To allocate health security system funds effectively in order to make the highest standards of care available for all Californians.

(f) To address the current and future health care needs of all Californians through emphasis on public health measures, changes in training and distribution of health care workers, and an intensive program of research into the causes of disease and the most effective means of preventing illness.

(g) To convert the current health care delivery system from one focused on emergency care to one focused on primary health care services and the promotion, restoration, and maintenance of health. These reforms will integrate all health care services and emphasize preventive services, early intervention, vigorous

FIGURE 15.3

Example of a Ballot Initiative

Ballot initiatives can be very complex, as suggested by this first of sixteen pages of text for the California Health Security Act put to California's voters in 1994. The proposition ultimately failed.

Source: California Ballot Pamphlet, General Elections, 8 November 1994.

California Republicans also went after a newly elected Democratic member of the Assembly who, they claimed, had double-crossed the voters of his district by voting for a Democratic candidate for speaker after allegedly saying he would not. That recall effort failed. But holding all three recall elections cost the state hundreds of thousands of tax dollars.[108]

Summing Up

State government institutions, interest groups, and the public are the forces that drive state politics. While state governments are similar to the federal government in many ways, they are very different in others. Governors exercise more power in their states than U.S. presidents do over the federal system; state legislatures exercise less power

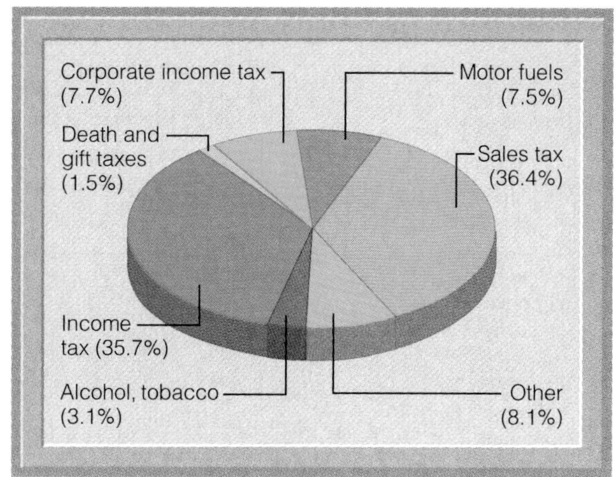

FIGURE 15.4
State Revenue Sources, 1993

States rely heavily on sales taxes and individual income taxes to generate most of their revenue.

Source: Data from *Statistical Abstract of the United States 1995*, 115th ed. (Washington, D.C.: U.S. Bureau of the Census, 1995), p. 312.

than the U.S. Congress. The public can vote directly on some state and local policies, but not on national issues. And interest groups are more regulated—and often more influential—at the state level.

As state and local governments have gained influence, however, the public has looked to them for an increasing number of programs and services. The increased demand has placed new pressures on state government. Like their federal counterparts, state political leaders are focusing on their budgets as they grapple with determining the programs and services they can afford to provide.

STATE BUDGETS

States raise and spend money in many ways. Some rely heavily on income taxes, whereas others do not. A few can rely on taxes on drilling and mining, but most cannot. Some states have high taxes and provide many public services; others tax less and do less. In this section, we examine how states raise and spend money and how the differences among states affect their policy choices.

Raising Revenues

States impose three basic types of taxes: taxes on property, sales, and income. During the first decades of the twentieth century, property taxes were the major source of state tax revenue. In response to fiscal pressures the Great Depression generated, states imposed sales taxes and transferred the right to tax property to local governments. In the 1940s, states added taxes on individual and corporate incomes. Although the relative mix of sales and income taxes has changed over the past several decades, states have not added any major new types of taxes during the past four decades. In recent years, however, they have turned increasingly to less traditional sources of revenue, including state lotteries and other forms of gambling.

Figure 15.4 shows the average breakdown for state tax collections in 1993. As you can see, states rely heavily on two sources of revenue: a general sales tax and individual income taxes. Taxes on motor fuels, corporations, and alcohol and tobacco products generate smaller sums. Property taxes, the staple at the beginning of the century, now contribute very little to state coffers.[109]

Figure 15.4 presents the national average. But many states differ markedly from the average in terms of their sources of revenue. Alaska, for example, relies heavily on taxes on the drilling and mining of its oil and mineral riches, so much so that Alaskans pay neither a personal income tax nor a general sales tax. The result, as table 15.2 shows, is that Alaskans bear the lowest overall tax burden in the United

The overall state tax burden varies greatly from state to state.

TABLE 15.2 Differences in State Taxes

Rank	State	Taxes on a Family of Four Earning $84,158 in Income in 1994
1.	New York	$10,529
2.	Maryland	$10,471
3.	Rhode Island	$10,294
4.	Maine	$10,132
5.	Connecticut	$9,996
6.	Wisconsin	$9,976
7.	Massachusetts	$9,513
8.	Ohio	$9,088
9.	New Jersey	$8,832
10.	Minnesota	$8,822
11.	Michigan	$8,793
12.	Oregon	$8,787
13.	Nebraska	$8,613
14.	Montana	$8,541
15.	California	$8,496
16.	Hawaii	$8,471
17.	Idaho	$8,448
18.	Georgia	$8,378
19.	North Carolina	$8,308
20.	Utah	$8,172
21.	West Virginia	$7,809
22.	New Mexico	$7,809
23.	Vermont	$7,788
24.	Arizona	$7,788
25.	Pennsylvania	$7,781
26.	Arkansas	$7,761
27.	Illinois	$7,755
28.	Iowa	$7,723
29.	South Carolina	$7,678
30.	Kentucky	$7,632
31.	Oklahoma	$7,622
32.	Colorado	$7,503
33.	Indiana	$7,416
34.	Virginia	$7,303
35.	Kansas	$7,159
36.	Delaware	$6,781
37.	Mississippi	$6,759
38.	Missouri	$6,698
39.	Louisiana	$6,625
40.	North Dakota	$6,552
41.	Alabama	$6,157
42.	New Hampshire	$5,506
43.	Washington	$5,463
44.	Texas	$5,290
45.	South Dakota	$5,151
46.	Tennessee	$5,073
47.	Florida	$4,686
48.	Nevada	$4,238
49.	Wyoming	$3,104
50.	Alaska	$2,291

Source: Kelly Smith, "Alaska Is Tax Heaven; New Yorkers Have Hell to Pay," *Money*, January 1995, pp. 92–93.

States; that is, the average Alaskan pays less in state taxes than other Americans. Indeed, all seven of the states that do not tax personal income are among the lowest tax states in the country.

States also vary in their reliance on a general sales tax. In addition to Alaska, the states of Delaware, Montana, New Hampshire, and Oregon have no general sales tax. The sales tax rate varies from state to state (and even within states, because many give their county and local governments the right to impose their own sales taxes). Most sales tax states exempt prescription drugs, and about half also exempt food. New Mexico, however, taxes both. Excluding food, prescription drugs, and other necessities of life makes the sales tax less regressive than it would otherwise be.[110] States without a sales tax must compensate for the lost revenue by relying more on other types of taxes. Oregon, for example, relies more on income taxes than any other state.[111]

Like sales tax rates, income tax rates vary from state to state. It is difficult to compare income tax rates across states because each state has different rules regarding the kinds of income and expenses that are exempt from taxes. For example, some states allow taxpayers to deduct the taxes they pay to the federal government from the income subject to state tax; others do not. Such deductions effectively lower the real tax rate. Attempts to compare tax rates are also difficult because most states have a progressive income tax in which the tax rate increases with income. Only a few states have a flat tax rate in which everyone's income is taxed at the same rate.

Although it is difficult to compare income tax rates across states, general trends in income tax rates are clear. Spurred by a nationwide tax revolt that began in the late 1970s and was epitomized by Ronald Reagan's election as president, many states tried in the 1980s to reduce their tax rates. But as states saw their expenditures begin to outstrip their revenues in the early 1990s, the trend reversed; more states began to contemplate increasing their tax rates, especially the rates the wealthy pay.[112] Indeed, budget shortfalls have caused several states without an income tax to consider imposing one. Connecticut, for example, imposed a state income tax for the first time in 1991 after a bitter political battle.[113]

During the 1980s, the budgetary problems facing many states prompted them to look elsewhere for money. One revenue source that grew in importance was so-called sin taxes, taxes on alcohol and tobacco. (Some people support sin taxes less for their revenue-generating potential than because they may force people to drink and smoke less, thereby reducing health care costs.) Again, the tax rates applied to alcohol and tobacco vary by state. The range on tobacco products is amazing: tobacco-producing states such as Kentucky and North Carolina levy a tax of only a few cents per pack of cigarettes, while the tax in Massachusetts and Minnesota is twenty-five times as much. One constraint states face in setting tax rates on alcohol and tobacco (and other taxes as well) is the rates in nearby states. If taxes soar too high, people living near the state border may buy their cigarettes and alcohol in a neighboring state, denying their home state the revenue it hoped to generate.

Because the public usually frowns on higher taxes, governors and legislators increasingly have looked to develop revenue sources that do not require taxes. One popular source of non-tax revenue is a state lottery. New Hampshire instituted the first modern state lottery in 1964. By 1996, thirty-six states, including all the major industrial states, had lotteries. In some states, lottery revenues are dedicated to specific expenditures. For example, lottery revenues in California go to education, and in Iowa, they are used to finance economic development. But in some states where lottery revenues have been earmarked for a special purpose, concerns have been raised that the money is used *in place of* regular tax funds in the budget, rather than adding to it, as voters thought would be the case.

Another source of state revenue that has gained in popularity is gambling, which generates money for the state from licenses and taxes on the profits. For many years, gambling was illegal in every state but Nevada (which legalized it in 1931), largely because powerful religious interests argued that it undermined public morality. In 1976, New Jersey legalized gambling in Atlantic City as part of an effort to revitalize the downtrodden seaside resort community. In 1989, Iowa responded to its budgetary woes by permitting gambling on riverboats plying the rivers along the state's borders. Riverboat gambling quickly became the rage as several other states along the Mississippi followed Iowa's lead. By 1994, ten states had legalized commercial casino gambling. But since then, other states have rebuffed well-financed efforts to do likewise.

Rainy day fund
Surplus revenue a state government holds in reserve for budget emergencies and shortfalls.

One possible explanation for why more states have not legalized gambling is that economic conditions improved across the country in the mid-1990s, which boosted government tax receipts and eased the pressure to find new sources of revenue.[114] Indeed, tax receipts went up so much that in 1996, most states had balanced budgets, and many were running surpluses. These surpluses were so large in a few states that observers worried that the states had too much money stashed away in **rainy day funds,** accounts to be used for emergencies or to protect the state when the economy turns sour.[115] Many governors have promised to use the budget surpluses to cut taxes, but state legislators are reticent to do so. They argue that their states should keep the money in reserve in case of future budget shortfalls, especially if the Republicans in Congress succeed in returning responsibility for many government programs to the states.[116]

Budgeting

Most states make their budgetary decisions much as the federal government does. The main similarity is that the governor, like the president, has the right to make the initial budget proposal. (In some states, the governor must share this power with others.)[117] Making the initial budget proposal is an important power because it enables the governor to set the parameters of the debate, in many cases reducing the legislature's role to making changes only at the margins.

State budgetary processes differ from the federal budget process, however, in two important respects. First, as we mentioned earlier, most governors have a line-item veto that allows them to cut spending they dislike. There is evidence, however, that governors are just as likely to use the line-item veto to shape spending to their partisan preferences as they are to use it to lower the overall budget.[118] In addition, state legislatures can structure line-item budgets in ways that make it difficult for governors to veto spending they oppose.[119] Thus, the power of the line-item veto as a tool to control spending may be overstated. Second, every state but one has a constitutional or statutory requirement that the state government balance its budget. Vermont is the one exception, but by tradition, it balances its budget.[120]

The balanced budget requirements so common in state government should not be taken literally. They do not prevent states from running a deficit, and they do not always bar states from accruing debt. In 1992, for example, state debts totaled almost $372 billion.[121] (Indeed, one reason state governments appear to have balanced budgets while the federal government does not is that states use different budget and accounting practices than the federal government does.) Deficits can occur because the budget is a forecast of how much money a state will have coming in and how much money it plans to spend. The forecast can be wrong for many reasons, particularly if the economy fails to perform as expected. Thirty-six states have laws that prohibit them from carrying deficits into the next fiscal year, so the government must take immediate steps to correct a budget shortfall once one becomes apparent. These corrective steps include giving the governor power to make budget cuts and using money set aside in rainy day funds to cover the deficit.[122]

Some states borrow to cover deficits, although sixteen states have strict constitutional controls on the borrowing process. Borrowing increases a state's long-term costs because it must repay not only the money it borrowed but also the interest on the loan. States that run chronic deficits become poor credit risks and have to pay higher interest rates on the bonds they issue to raise money. As states ran into budgetary problems in the early 1990s, all but a few saw their credit ratings drop.[123] States also issue bonds to cover expenditures to construct roads, schools, hospitals, sports facilities, college dormitories, and the like. States have a variety of different controls governing the issuance of such bonds, but state constitutional limits on debt do not appear to slow the growth of state debt.[124] Many bonds now issued do not guarantee repayment of the debt through taxes; instead, they pledge the revenues the facility being financed will generate.[125]

Spending

The spending priorities of states differ from those of the federal government. The federal government, for example, pays the full cost of defending the United States. States pay for the vast bulk of public spending on schools and prisons. As relations between Washington and the states have become increasingly complex over time, however, state spending priorities have changed.

As recently as the 1970s, education took far and away the biggest chunk of state funds, with roads and highways also claiming a respectable percentage of the budget. But by the early 1990s, the composition of state budgets had changed, largely in response to federal mandates and increased public demands for other services. Education remains the biggest single component in state budgets, but it has declined as a percentage of state spending. Roads and highways also get a smaller percentage of state funds. In turn, state spending on human services and health care has increased dramatically, as have the costs of running prisons and paying interest on state debts.[126] Indeed, in their fiscal year 1994 budgets, states for the first time spent more on Medicaid—the federal-state health program for low-income people—than on their colleges and universities.[127] And in 1995, California spent more on its Department of Corrections than it did on the University of California and California State University systems combined.[128]

Although every state faces much the same demand for spending, some difference in spending emphases are noticeable across the states. Many large, heavily urbanized states, for example, tend to spend more money per citizen on fighting crime than smaller, more rural states.[129] Similarly, New York and other large-population states spend far more money on welfare than smaller-population states such as Alaska and Nevada.[130] Expenditures for public education also vary, with East Coast and Western states tending to devote larger portions of their budgets to all levels of education than do other states, particularly those in the South.[131]

Because states vary in the priorities and rules they set for raising revenues, budgeting, and spending, the resident of one state may enjoy more or different services than a similar individual in another state. This is also true within a single state, as local governments write their own rules and policies.

Local Government

The U.S. Constitution says nothing about local government. Thus, unlike the federal government and state governments, cities and towns have no independent constitutional standing in the United States. Instead, the power to create local governments rests with state governments. Each state decides not only what types of local governments will exist within its borders, but also what their geographic boundaries will be and what powers they may exercise. One result is that local government comes in different forms and employs different structures. Despite this variety, local government in many respects constitutes the most representative level of government. And as the cost of running local government has risen in recent years, some local governments have responded by privatizing some of their public services.

Forms of Local Government

Local government comes in many forms. Most state constitutions provide for the creation of counties, which are charged with actually administering many state services much as states administer federally funded programs. In New England, towns perform the same functions as counties. Most Americans live in municipalities or cities. Unlike counties, cities are created by the specific action of the state. A city comes into legal existence only when the state incorporates it by granting it a charter that spells out its jurisdiction, powers, and duties.

In addition to counties, towns, and municipalities, states also create a wide variety of single-purpose governments. The most common are school districts and special fire or water districts. These districts deliver government services to an area that may cross city or county lines. For example, most metropolitan regions have a special district known as a public transit authority responsible for providing public transportation to the cities and towns in the region.[132]

The number of local governments in the United States has declined dramatically since World War II. The main reason for the decline has been the effort over the years by state and local governments to save money by consolidating school districts. In 1942, the states oversaw 155,067 different local governments, 70 percent of which were school districts. By 1992, however, the number of local governments had shrunk to 85,006, only 17 percent of which were school districts.[133]

Local Government Structures

Local governments are organized in a variety of ways.[134] Municipalities generally use one of three different governing structures: mayor-council, city commission, and council-manager. Each form of government has strengths and weaknesses. The most popular form of government, particularly in larger cities, is the *mayor-council form.* The mayor-council structure can have either a strong mayor or a weak mayor. A strong mayor system invests the mayor with the sort of executive leadership powers the president and governors enjoy. In a weak mayor system, the mayor is essentially the figurehead leader of a council, and the council performs all executive functions. Some people prefer the strong mayor system because it enhances the political accountability of the executive, a position echoing the arguments made about the presidency during the Constitutional Convention (see box 12.1).

The *city commission form* of government fuses legislative and executive functions in one elected group. Commissioners make policy as a group, but each commissioner also heads a major department of government. Under this system, one commissioner is named mayor to preside over commission meetings. One concern with the city commission system is that elected officials do not always have the managerial skills needed to successfully lead their departments.

The *council-manager form* of government is designed to place administrative power in the hands of a city manager. The city manager is a professional administrator the elected city council hires to implement the policies it sets. Under this system, it is not uncommon for the city manager to become a powerful force in setting city policy, contrary to the system's intention to separate administration from politics. But many observers credit this form of government with professionalizing city administration.

In most counties, an elected body, usually called a board of supervisors or commissioners, governs. This board often shares power in the county with other elected officials, such as a sheriff, county attorney, and county clerk. But most executive power is vested in the board. Some counties use a council-administrator system, an arrangement similar to the council-manager form of city government. Still others come under a county council-elected executive arrangement. Under this system, executive power rests with an elected executive, while legislative power rests with the board. As with the various forms of city governments, the different county arrangements allow counties to place different emphases on political accountability and administrative professionalization and skill.

Local Government and Representation

Although the Constitution does not mention local governments, they play an important role in the lives of Americans. Local governments provide most basic public services, so the decisions made at City Hall greatly affect the level of police protection, the quality of public schooling, the price of public transportation, and hundreds of other issues, large and small. At the same time, people tend to view their local government as the most representative level of government. Local government does reflect America's ethnic and racial diversity to a far greater extent than do the federal and state governments.

While few minority members have been elected governor or senator, many have served as mayor, councilperson, or school board member. In 1993, for example, almost 7,500 of the 8,000 African Americans holding elected office in the United States served at the local level.[135]

Many large cities have suffered budget problems in recent years. Washington, D.C.'s Tower 10 fire truck sat at a repair center in 1995 until the city paid its bill. When in service, the truck helps provide fire protection for the White House.

The Costs of Local Government

The role of local government has become increasingly important as federal aid to cities and towns has risen. For example, in 1932, federal aid to local government amounted to only $10 million. By 1981, that aid had grown to $21 billion, but by 1990, it had declined to $20 billion. In 1992, that $20 billion in federal aid represented less than 4 percent of the $572 billion local governments raised. State governments provided some 34 percent of the money local governments had; the rest they raised on their own.[136]

Local governments rely heavily on property taxes for their self-generated revenue; other taxes contribute relatively little to local government treasuries. In 1992, for example, property taxes accounted for close to 76 percent of all tax dollars local governments raised; income taxes and corporate income taxes contributed just 6 percent.[137] Heavy reliance on property taxes poses a number of problems for local governments. Property taxes are the main source of funding for primary public education, which leads to inequities in school finances between communities with high and low property values. For two decades, the federal and state courts have struggled to devise solutions to this problem.[138] In most situations, raising property taxes to generate more money is not an acceptable answer. It is very unpopular, particularly among older, retired people who tend to have difficulty keeping up with increasing tax rates.[139] Voter rebellions against rising property taxes have prompted most states to impose limits on the ability of local governments to raise property taxes.[140]

Privatization of Government Services

Over the last two decades, many state and local governments have sought to save their taxpayers money by turning government services over to private companies. The **privatization** movement began in earnest in the 1970s when Phoenix, Arizona hired private businesses to take over trash collection, a task its city workers had performed. Since then, many of the services local governments used to provide are now contracted out to private companies, as figure 15.5 shows.

Privatization
Turning government programs over to private companies to run, or selling government assets to the private sector.

Indianapolis has been particularly aggressive about privatizing services. In 1995, the city had fewer employees on its payroll than it had twenty years earlier, and under Mayor Stephen Goldsmith, it had cut its budget by more than $100 million since 1992.[141] But Indianapolis has not pursued a simple-minded strategy of privatization. Instead, the administration introduced competition to the bureaucracy, allowing city departments to bid for contracts against private concerns. In many instances, city workers won the contracts, and the city ended up with better service at lower cost.[142]

Privatization has also begun to move beyond the provision of services to the private ownership of items such as highways. Indeed, in 1995, a privately owned, fourteen-mile long highway between Washington, D.C. and Dulles International Airport in Virginia opened, and in California, four new privately constructed and owned lanes were added to a busy highway.[143] It may be that private money will provide other public facilities that government cannot or is not willing to afford, with those who use the facilities paying the cost.

Privatization is more likely to occur where local governments already operate under "good government" laws—particularly policies that promote merit systems rather than patronage in hiring government workers and that promote the use of purchasing standards.[144] The existence of good government laws usually signifies that a local community values efficiency and effectiveness over patronage. As a result, it normally has laws on the books that make it easier for government officials to contract services to the private sector.

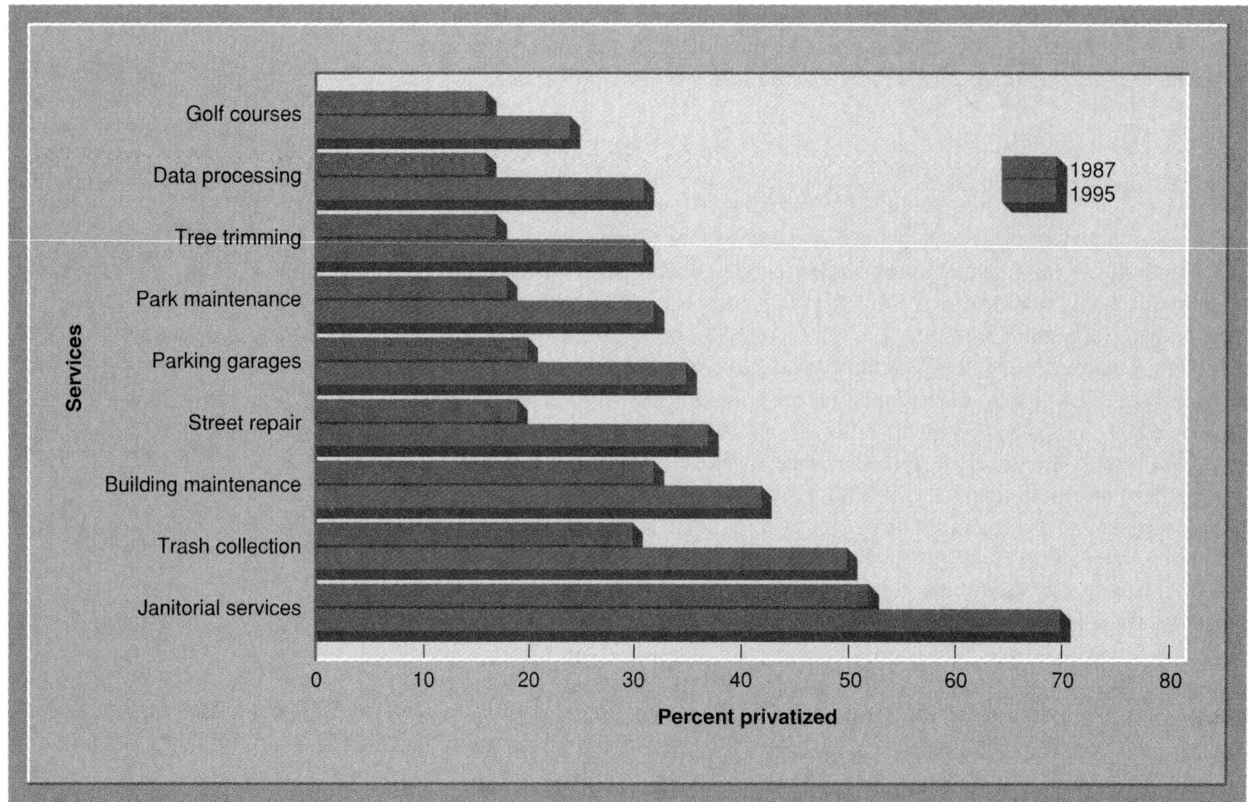

FIGURE 15.5
Privatization of Local Government

The percentage of local governments contracting out a variety of services has climbed steadily in recent years.

Sources: Data from David Wessel, "The American Way," *Wall Street Journal,* 2 October 1995, and Mercer Group, Inc.

But privatization is not a panacea for all government spending problems. In Iowa, for example, the state government hired a private company to clean highway rest stops, saving quite a bit of money compared to having state workers perform the task. But the private company had problems doing the job, and when the public began to complain about dirty bathrooms, the state government fired the company. In the end, other private companies won the job, but at a higher cost than when state government did the chore itself.

Overall, as local governments have acquired more revenue outside of state control, they have become more independent in making and implementing policy. Indeed, they are far ahead of the federal government in promoting privatization. As a result of their independence, local governments are and will continue to be important participants in American politics.

WHO DELIVERS? PUBLIC OPINION AND LEVEL OF GOVERNMENT

Three levels of government serve Americans: federal, state, and local. Which level of government do people think gives them the most for their tax dollars? The answer has changed over time. During the 1970s, more people had confidence in how the federal government spent their money than in how their local and state governments did. Since 1979, however, public confidence in the federal government has dropped.[145] Today, people are more likely to think that their local and state governments are giving them the most for their money.

Congressional Republicans played to these changed attitudes in 1995. As part of their Contract With America, they worked to shift responsibility for many government programs from Washington to the state capitals. By and large, Americans are sympathetic to that goal. In one survey that year, almost 70 percent of respondents said they trusted their state government to do a better job running programs and services than the federal government would. Almost every group of Americans, whether Democrat or Republican, liberal or conservative, shared this belief. (The only exception was African Americans; they split about evenly on the question.) Americans trusted state governments to do a better job fighting crime, running welfare programs, setting workplace safety rules, and operating the Medicare and Medicaid programs. People favored the federal government over state governments only in protecting civil rights.[146] Another national poll suggested that people also looked to the federal government rather than state governments to protect the environment.[147]

But it may be that people have the most faith in their local government. In response to a 1992 question asking their level of trust and confidence in the three levels of government, people ranked local government much higher than state government, which they in turn ranked above the federal government. Twenty years earlier, people expressed more overall trust and confidence in each level, but the order was reversed.[148] So it is not that people now think the world of their state and local governments; they just think much less of the national government than in the past.

SUMMARY

For much of American history, state and local governments had few dealings with the federal government. That changed in the 1930s when the New Deal prompted a sizable increase in federal assistance to cities and states. The Great Society programs of the 1960s carved out an even larger financial role for the federal government, allowing the federal government to exercise influence through aid programs, mandates, and picket-fence federalism. In the 1980s, however, Republican presidents Reagan and Bush sought to shift the cost of governing, as well as the authority to govern, back onto cities and states. As a result, state and local governments have regained influence over many programs. And when Republicans took control of Congress in 1995, they attempted to shift even more decision-making authority back to the states.

State governments in many ways resemble the federal government. They all have the same three distinct branches of government, and they all operate according to the same system of checks and balances. But states do differ from the federal government and from each other. Each state has its own constitution, which sets forth the rules that shape politics in that state. In every state, the governor is the single most powerful political figure, and voters hold their governors to a higher standard of accountability than they do other politicians. State legislatures vary enormously in size, organization, and influence.

Over the past two decades, interest groups have begun to pay more attention to state governments. Business groups constitute the most powerful category of interest groups. The single most powerful lobby, though, has been public school teachers. They have been successful because they live in every town and city, are eager to organize, and have strong incentives to lobby. States have been more aggressive than the federal government in regulating interest groups. All fifty states require lobbyists to disclose who they work for, and every state regulates political action committees.

One area interest groups have been active in is promoting ballot initiatives. Unlike the U.S. Constitution, many state constitutions promote direct democracy, mechanisms that allow voters to use the ballot booth to set the policy of state government. In many states, voters can revise the state constitution, overturn bills the state legislature passes, enact their own bills, and even vote to remove elected officials from office. Many interest groups have seized on these ballot initiatives as a way to translate their policy preferences into law.

States raise and spend money in many different ways. Sales taxes and income taxes are the two biggest sources of revenue in most states. As budgetary problems have increased over the past decade, states have relied more and more on sin taxes on alcohol and tobacco and on revenues generated by lotteries and gambling. States need to keep revenue in line with spending because virtually every state has a law that requires a balanced budget. State spending looks much different from federal spending. Most state revenues are spent on education and prisons, which make up only a small portion of the federal budget.

Local governments are the offspring of state governments. They come in many different forms, with the states determining which forms may be used. In recent decades, local governments have become more independent of their parent states, with the federal government sending some financial aid directly to them. This has increased their independence and power. Local governments have been in the forefront of the privatization movement.

Public assessments of the effectiveness of federal, state, and local government have changed over time. In the 1970s, Americans were more likely to credit the federal government than state or local government with spending their tax dollars wisely. In recent years, however, Americans have expressed more confidence in local government than in state or federal government.

Key Terms

Block grants
Categorical grants-in-aid
Direct democracy
Dual federalism
Executive amendment
Fiscal federalism
General revenue sharing
Initiative
Lame duck
Line-item veto
Mandates
Picket-fence federalism
Privatization
Rainy day fund
Referendum

Readings for Further Study

Altschuler, Bruce E. *Running in Place: A Campaign Journal.* Chicago: Nelson-Hall, 1996. A political scientist's interesting account of another political scientist's unsuccessful campaign for a seat in the New York Assembly.

Aron, Michael. *Governor's Race: A TV Reporter's Chronicle of the 1993 Florio/Whitman Campaign.* New Brunswick, N.J.: Rutgers University Press, 1994. A reporter's fascinating day-by-day chronicle of Christine Whitman's election as governor of New Jersey.

Beyle, Thad L., ed. *Governors and Hard Times.* Washington, D.C.: CQ Press, 1992. A collection of essays on ten of the new governors elected in 1989 and 1990 that analyzes the problems facing them and their states in the early 1990s.

Burns, Nancy. *The Formation of American Local Governments.* New York: Oxford University Press, 1994. A political scientist examines the reasons behind the dramatic increase in the number of special districts created in recent decades, and their relationship to federal, state, and existing local governments.

Gray, Virginia, and Herbert Jacob, eds. *Politics in the American States: A Comparative Analysis,* 6th ed. Washington, D.C.: CQ Press, 1996. A collection of articles by political scientists examining a number of areas of state politics and public policies in some depth.

Loftus, Tom. *The Art of Legislative Politics.* Washington, D.C.: CQ Press, 1994. An interesting account of state politics by the former speaker of the Wisconsin State Assembly.

Rosenthal, Alan. *Governors and Legislators: Contending Powers.* Washington, D.C.: CQ Press, 1990. A thorough examination of the relationship between governors and state legislatures.

Rosenthal, Alan. *The Third House: Lobbyists and Lobbying in the States.* Washington, D.C.: CQ Press, 1993. A study of how lobbyists operate in the states.

CHAPTER

16

THE FEDERAL BUDGET

Budgets, Deficit Spending, and the National Debt

The Growing Federal Budget

The Rise of Deficit Spending

The Exploding National Debt

The Consequences of an Exploding National Debt

Where Does Government Revenue Come From?

Government Revenue in Historical Perspective

Income and Payroll Taxes

Where Does Government Spending Go?

The Changing Nature of Government Spending

The Growth of Entitlement Programs

Limiting Entitlement Programs

What About Pork?

Why Do Budget Deficits Persist?

Congress and the President

The American Public

The Budgetary Process

The Budgetary Process from George Washington to Richard Nixon

Budgetary Reform in the 1970s

Budgetary Reform in the 1980s

Budgetary Reform in the 1990s

A Balanced Budget by 2002?

More Reforms?

Is the Budget Process Irrational?

Summary

Key Terms

Readings for Further Study

In mid-November 1995, Sudjai Pattuma, a St. Louis resident born in Thailand, learned that his brother in Italy had fallen gravely ill. He wanted to visit his brother, but he needed a passport to make the trip. So he flew to Chicago, the site of the only government office in the Midwest that will issue a passport in one day. Yet when Mr. Pattuma arrived at the Federal Building in downtown Chicago, he discovered that it, along with most of the rest of the federal government, was closed until further notice.[1] Mr. Pattuma was not the only person who found the federal government shut down on that frigid November morning. On a typical day, some 700,000 people visit the nation's national parks, 55,000 tourists visit monuments and museums in Washington, D.C., 28,000 retirees apply for Social Security benefits, and 700 young men and women join the armed services.[2] In mid-November 1995, they all found the federal government closed for business.

Why was the federal government shut down? The answer lies in the inability of Congress and the president to agree on a new budget for the federal government. By law, the president and Congress have until September 30 of each year to agree on a budget for the next fiscal year. (A fiscal year is a twelve-month accounting period, which for the federal government runs from October 1 to September 30). Quite often, Congress and the president fail to complete work on the budget by September 30, but they keep the government open by passing short-term spending bills that keep things running until they reach a final agreement. In 1995, however, President Clinton and the Republican majority in Congress were too far apart in their views to reach any long-term agreement. When a short-term spending bill expired in mid-November, the federal government lost its authority to spend money and it had to shut down all non-essential services. A week later, a new short-term spending bill was passed, but then the same pattern was repeated: the short-term spending bill expired, and parts of the federal government shut down until Congress and the president agreed on a new short-term spending plan. Congress and the president did not reach agreement on a final budget until April 1996, seven months into the fiscal year.

The shutdowns of the federal government in late 1995 and early 1996 illustrate a simple but harsh reality that all governments face: the programs people would like the government to fund far outstrip the government's resources. In this case, the Republicans in Congress and President Clinton had very different ideas about how much money the government should bring in through taxes, and how it should spend the money it raised. During the 1996 fiscal year, the U.S. government spent more than $1.6 trillion ($1,600,000,000,000), but it could not afford to fully fund everything the president and Congress wanted to do. Nor could it afford to meet all of the public's expectations for education, health care, law enforcement, and many other programs. The government's inability to fund every program means that it must decide which programs it will fund and which it will not. These decisions about spending priorities are set during the budgetary process. And because dollars are policy, budgetary decisions represent the most important decisions the president and Congress make each year.

In this chapter, we examine the federal budget. We begin by discussing the dramatic growth in government spending over the past two hundred years. We go on to review government revenue sources and to look at what the government spends its money on. We then explore why, in recent years, the federal government has failed to balance revenues and spending and has instead run massive budget deficits. We examine the rules of the budgetary process, focusing on efforts the president and Congress have made to bring government spending into line with government revenue, and we explain why these efforts have failed. Finally, we consider whether the process the federal government uses to set its budget makes sense.

Budgets, Deficit Spending, and the National Debt

For good or for ill, the budget of the federal government greatly affects the well-being of the American public. To put the current debate over government spending in

In 1995 and again in 1996, non-essential parts of the federal government shut down because Congress and the president could not agree on a budget.

context, this section reviews the growth of the federal budget over the past two hundred years, the rise of deficit spending since 1960, and the rapid increase in the national debt since 1980.

The Growing Federal Budget

The size and composition of the federal budget have changed dramatically since the days of George Washington. During Washington's presidency, the federal government spent roughly $3 to $5 million annually. Several times in the 1790s, government spending exceeded government revenues, creating the first **budget deficits.** (Deficits occur when the government spends more money than it brings in during a fiscal year.) To make up for the gap between spending and revenue, the government borrowed money (much as you might do to pay your tuition). The money that Washington's government borrowed, in turn, formed the first **national debt.** (The national debt is the total amount of money the government owes—that is, the accumulation of unpaid annual deficits.) Because the government did not immediately repay the money it borrowed, the national debt began to grow.

Budget deficit
The amount by which government spending exceeds government revenues in a single year.

National debt
The total amount of money the federal government owes to pay for accumulated deficits.

The budget deficits that occurred under George Washington and his immediate successors, however, tended to be small and infrequent. Throughout the nineteenth century, government revenues usually equaled expenditures, thereby creating a **balanced budget.** In some years, government revenues actually exceeded expenditures, creating a **budget surplus.** Balanced budgets were expected, in part because many politicians saw them as a way to limit the growth and power of the federal government.[3] Indeed, in the nineteenth century, the federal government generally ran budget deficits only when the country was at war and faced an urgent need to increase military spending.

Balanced budget
A federal budget in which spending and revenues are equal.

Budget surplus
The amount by which government revenues exceed government spending in a single year.

As presidents and Congresses struggled throughout the nineteenth century to keep government spending in line with government revenues, the size of the federal budget grew slowly. The federal budget did not exceed $1 billion in spending—or less than a fourth of what the government spent in 1995 on disaster relief alone—until the close of the Civil War in 1865. After the Civil War, government spending dropped sharply. The federal budget did not exceed $1 billion again until World War I.

The growth in federal spending picked up speed after World War I, and it accelerated further after World War II. The federal government's budget first broke the $100 billion mark in 1962, and it topped $1 trillion for the first time in 1987. The federal budget is expected to exceed $2 trillion by the end of the century.

What accounts for the rapid growth in federal spending over the past sixty years? The answer lies in the vast expansion of the federal government's role in American life. When the Great Depression prompted President Franklin Roosevelt to push through Congress the programs that made up the New Deal, the federal government assumed new responsibilities for stimulating the national economy and maintaining social welfare. After World War II, America's new-found role as a superpower led the federal government to increase dramatically the size and cost of the military. And in the 1960s, President Lyndon Johnson championed the establishment of the Great Society, a set of programs that greatly expanded the federal government's role in reducing economic and racial inequality. As the federal government's responsibilities expanded in all these areas, it spent rapidly increasing sums to meet its new obligations.

The Rise of Deficit Spending

The growth in government spending has accompanied a change in political attitudes toward deficit spending. The theories of British economist John Maynard Keynes, who argued that national governments should use deficit spending to stimulate the economy during a recession, influenced President Roosevelt and his advisers. The Roosevelt administration ran record budget deficits to end the Depression and to finance the cost of World War II. Despite Roosevelt's use of deficit spending, the expectation of a balanced federal budget remained strong. When the country returned to economic prosperity after the war, the federal government returned to the tradition of balancing its budget.

In the early 1960s, however, the inhibitions against deficit spending faded away. During the Johnson administration, the budget began to balloon as new social programs such as Medicare—created in 1965 to help the elderly and people with disabilities pay for immediate (as opposed to long-term) health care—were created and the cost of the Vietnam War began to escalate. The president and Congress did not want to cut spending, and when they finally raised taxes, the revenue was insufficient to balance the budget.[4] As figure 16.1 shows, since that time, budget deficits have become commonplace. Congress and the president continue to be unwilling or unable to raise enough revenue to pay for government spending or to cut spending to match revenues. With the exception of fiscal year 1969 (when a change in accounting rules produced a surplus that barely shows up on the graph), the budget has been in the red every year since 1961.

Budget deficits have become a potent political issue in American politics not only because they have become chronic, but also because they have grown tremendously in size. As figure 16.1 shows, the size of the budget deficit grew especially rapidly under Presidents Reagan and Bush. In 1992, the budget deficit reached a record, totaling almost $300 billion (even higher by some accounting rules). To put that figure in perspective, consider that the budget deficit in 1992 totaled more than $1,200 for every man, woman, and child in the United States; that firing every civilian and military employee of the federal government would have reduced the size of the budget deficit in 1992 by only 25 percent; and that the federal government would have run a budget deficit in 1992 even if it had reduced defense spending to zero.

The federal government ran up increasingly larger budget deficits in the three decades after 1969, despite the fact that its revenues were growing rapidly. The problem was that revenues did not keep pace with spending. In 1993, President Clinton and Congress agreed on a package of spending cuts and tax increases designed to reduce the size of the budget deficit. Even so, in 1994, the deficit was still $203 billion, dipping to $107 billion in 1996. Although both figures represent substantial progress, the deficit is still very large.

So far, we have looked at the federal government's budget deficit in terms of its raw or *absolute* size. Another—and in the view of many economists, better—way to evaluate the federal deficit is to examine its size *relative* to the country's gross domestic product, a measure of the country's total economic output and, hence, its ability to

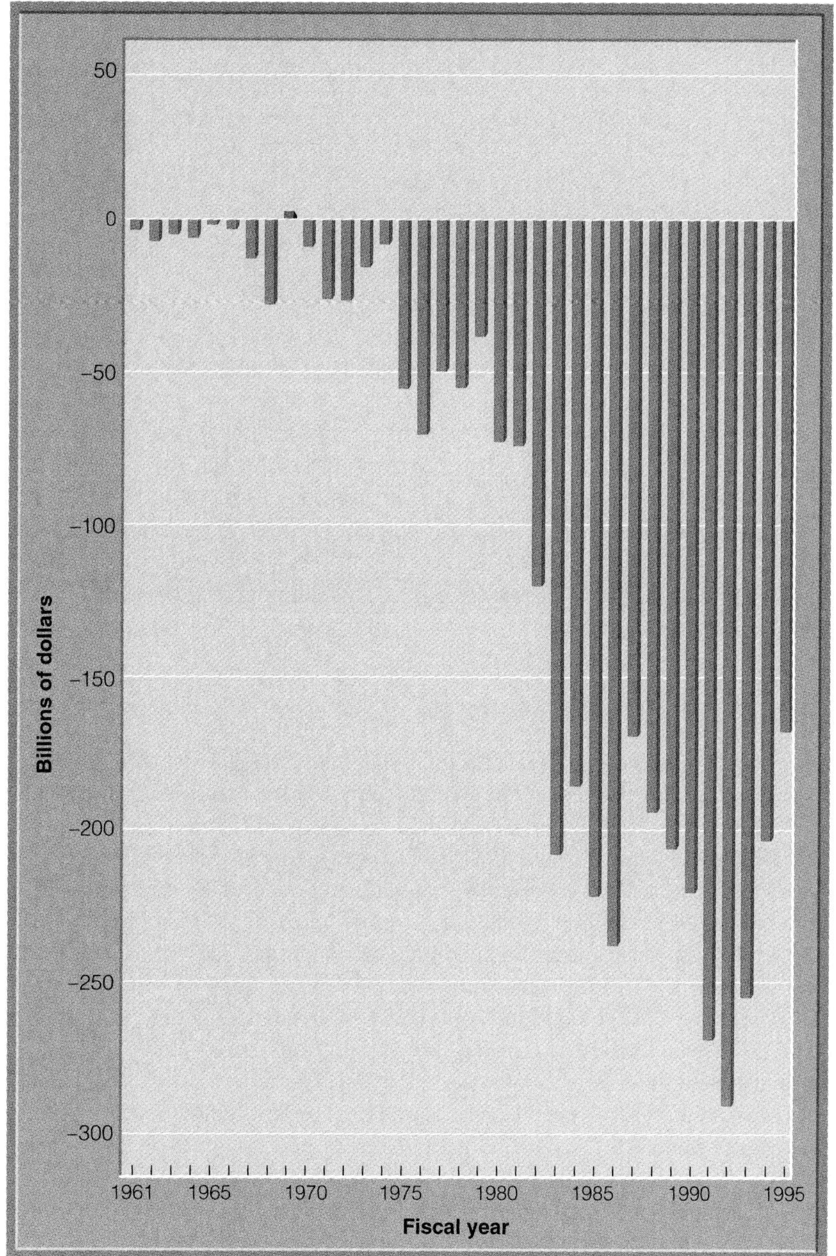

FIGURE 16.1
Budget Surplus and Deficit, 1961–1995

Budget deficits have been a chronic problem for more than thirty years, but particularly since 1980.

Sources: Data from *Statistical Abstract of the United States, 1992,* 112th ed. (Washington, D.C.: U.S. Bureau of the Census, 1992), p. 315; *Statistical Abstract of the United States, 1995,* 115th ed. (Washington, D.C.: U.S. Bureau of the Census, 1995), p. 333.

repay its obligations. If the federal budget deficit is growing more rapidly than the gross domestic product, then the deficit is becoming a bigger burden on the country. Conversely, if the deficit is growing less rapidly than is the gross domestic product, then the deficit is becoming less of a burden on the country. (An analogous situation would be if your indebtedness increased last year by, say, 5 percent because you spent more than you earned. That additional indebtedness might be a cause of concern if you failed to get a raise last year, but you might not think much about it if your income went up 50 percent. In the latter case, you would be better able to repay your debts.) Looking at the relative size of the federal deficit casts a more positive light on the efforts of the Clinton administration and Congress to curb deficit spending. Between 1992 and 1996, the federal deficit as a share of gross domestic product fell by more than half, as cuts in the absolute level of the federal deficit were coupled with moderate growth in the nation's economy.

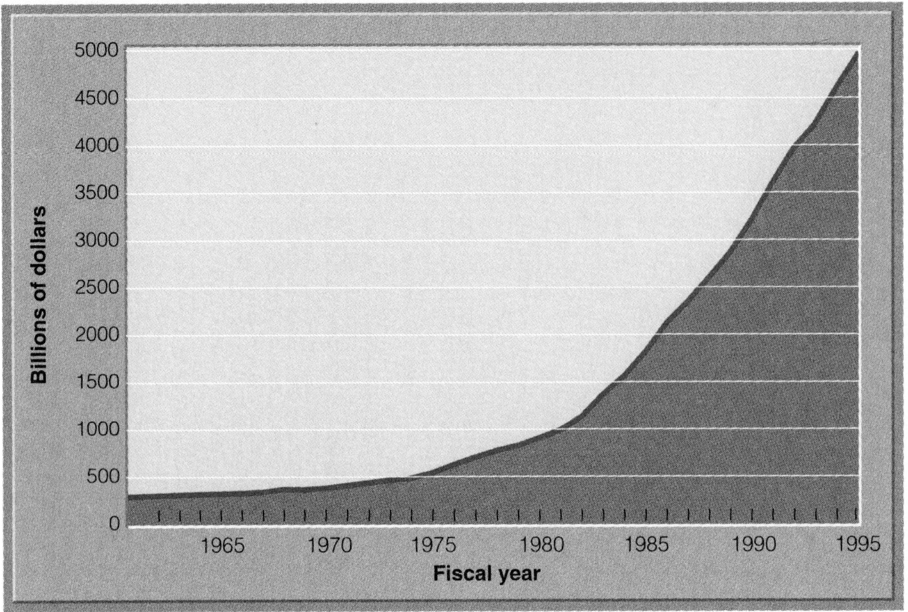

FIGURE 16.2
Growth in National Debt, 1961–1995

Because of chronic annual deficits, the total national debt has exploded over the last decade.

Source: Data from *Statistical Abstract of the United States, 1995,* 115th ed. (Washington, D.C.: U.S. Bureau of the Census, 1995), p. 333.

The Exploding National Debt

As figure 16.2 shows, the growth of deficit spending over the last three decades has led to an explosion in the size of the national debt. As we mentioned earlier, the federal government first went into debt during George Washington's presidency. Nonetheless, it took from 1789 to 1981, or 192 years, for the national debt to reach $1 trillion. Over the next twelve years, the national debt quadrupled, reaching $4 trillion in 1993. Bill Clinton supplied another way to look at the rapid increase in the size of the debt during the Reagan and Bush administrations in his address to a joint session of Congress early in 1993: "I well remember twelve years ago President Reagan stood at this podium and told you and the American people that if our debt were stacked in $1,000 bills, the stack would reach sixty-seven miles into space. Well, today that stack would reach 267 miles."[5]

We have said that the federal government finances its budget deficits by borrowing. But from whom does it borrow money? Or, to put the question another way, to whom does the government owe the debt? As of 1995, American investors, including individuals, mutual funds, pension funds, and banks, held about 66 percent of the debt. The federal government held close to 11 percent in various trust funds required to invest in government securities. State and local governments held another 6 percent. Thus, most of the debt we owe to ourselves. But foreigners hold 21 percent of the debt.[6] Because foreign investors profit when they lend money to the federal government—as do American investors—deficit spending entails a transfer of American wealth to foreign citizens and governments. In the overall budget picture, however, the sum of money paid in interest to foreign investors is small: in 1992, it represented $39 billion, or 2.8 percent of all the money the federal government spent.[7]

The United States is not the only industrialized country suffering from debt problems. Although the absolute size of the American national debt swamps that of any other country, when debts are calculated in relative terms as a percentage of a nation's gross domestic product—essentially, the size of its economy—the United States fares better than some countries and worse than others. For example, Italy and Belgium have debts that total more than 1.3 times the size of their entire annual gross domestic product, whereas the debt of the United States is roughly 69 percent of its gross domestic product. But Germany, one of America's main economic competitors, has a national debt equal to slightly less than 50 percent of its gross domestic product.[8]

Most Americans believe the federal government should balance its budget, but businesses and private households in the United States are further in debt than the federal government.

Dan Foote/Pen Tip International Features. Reprinted by permission.

The Consequences of an Exploding National Debt

Are a ballooning federal budget deficit and an escalating national debt matters for concern? To answer the question, it is important to recognize that debt itself is not inherently evil. Borrowing may make sense if the money is used to finance productive investment. For example, businesses borrow money to modernize their factories in the hope that modern plants will mean bigger profits, and many college students borrow money for college in the hope that a bachelor's degree will enable them to earn more in the future. (Indeed, businesses and private households in the United States are further in debt than the federal government.)[9] Thus, the country may benefit if the government borrows to build highways, train workers, develop new technologies, or otherwise improve the economy.

If debt is not inherently evil, neither is it always beneficial. Much of the discussion about the national debt focuses on two problems. The first is that a rapidly growing national debt can retard economic growth. Whenever the federal government borrows money, it competes against other borrowers for loans, thereby raising interest rates higher than they otherwise would be. Higher interest rates may discourage firms from borrowing money to invest in the new factories and technologies needed to spur economic growth. Thus, some economists argue that the federal government can best stimulate the economy by learning to live within its means.[10]

The other problem with increasing budget deficits, and the one that fuels much of the political debate, is the fear that the deficit spending goes less to finance productive investment and more to pay for current consumption. (An example of the difference between investment and consumption is the difference between using money to pay your tuition—investment, which is likely to help you earn money—and using money to pay for a spring break trip—consumption, which means the money you used is gone.) Borrowing to finance programs such as health care, veterans benefits, and military pensions, as opposed to investing in education or new technologies, will not make the country better prepared to pay tomorrow's bills. And, as we shall see later in the chapter, the cost of paying the interest on the borrowed money is taking up an increasing portion of the federal budget. If the national debt continues to balloon, the federal government will spend more and more money simply to pay interest on the debt. In fiscal year 1996, interest payments alone totaled more than the budgets of the Departments of Commerce, Education, Energy, Interior, Justice, Labor, State, Transportation, and Veterans Affairs, the budgets of the National Aeronautics and Space Administration (NASA) and the Environmental Protection Agency, and the operating expenses of the White House, Congress, and

FIGURE 16.3
Government Revenue Sources, 1900

In 1900, the federal government obtained most of its money from excise taxes and customs duties.

Source: Data from *Historical Statistics of the United States: Colonial Times to 1970* (Washington, D.C.: U.S. Bureau of the Census, 1975), p. 1106.

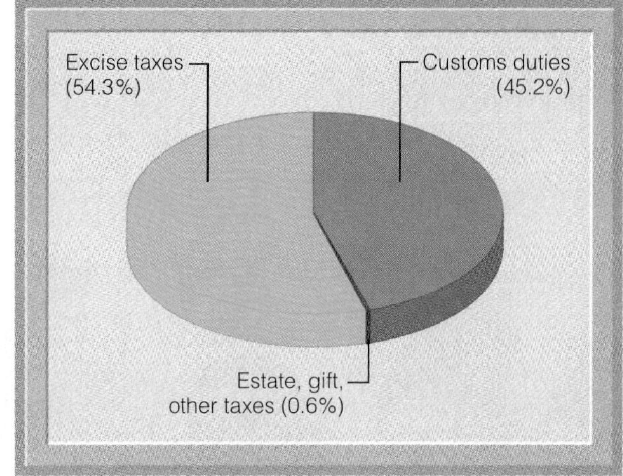

the judicial branch *combined*.[11] Obviously, interest payments are money lost for other uses; these funds cannot be used to improve schools, build a space station, find a cure for cancer, or clean up the environment.

WHERE DOES GOVERNMENT REVENUE COME FROM?

The rapid growth in the national debt has made reducing the federal budget deficit a hot political topic. In 1995 and 1996, the Republican majority in Congress made deficit reduction the centerpiece of its legislative agenda. Indeed, the political appeal of a balanced budget plan was so strong in 1995 that President Bill Clinton abandoned his original budget proposal—which projected deficit spending throughout the 1990s—and proposed his own plan for balancing the federal budget.

The federal government can reduce its budget deficit by increasing its revenues—which usually, but not always, means raising taxes—by cutting spending, or by some mix of the two. (Printing more money and reneging on the national debt are unacceptable alternatives for a number of reasons.) To put deficit reduction efforts in perspective, we now examine where government revenue comes from. In the next section, we will examine where government spending goes.

Government Revenue in Historical Perspective

The federal government's revenue sources have changed dramatically over the past two hundred years. Until the early 1900s, the government obtained much of its revenue from customs duties (also called tariffs), which are taxes on imported goods. As figure 16.3 shows, in 1900, nearly half of all government revenue came from customs duties. The other half came from excise taxes, mostly on alcohol and tobacco products. A small portion of government revenue came from estate and gift taxes and a few other sources.

The federal government gained a new source of revenue in 1913 with the adoption of the Sixteenth Amendment to the Constitution. The amendment allowed the federal government to impose an income tax on individuals and corporations. Although the government had enacted an income tax during the Civil War and again in 1894, the Supreme Court ruled in 1895 that the Constitution prohibited a federal income tax.[12] After ratification of the Sixteenth Amendment, Democrats and progressive Republicans quickly joined with newly elected President Woodrow Wilson in passing an income tax. (The Supreme Court ultimately upheld this tax.)[13]

Initially, the federal income tax affected very few people.[14] Indeed, many members of Congress voted to impose a federal income tax because they knew that it would not affect most of their constituents. As one member of Congress from Kansas

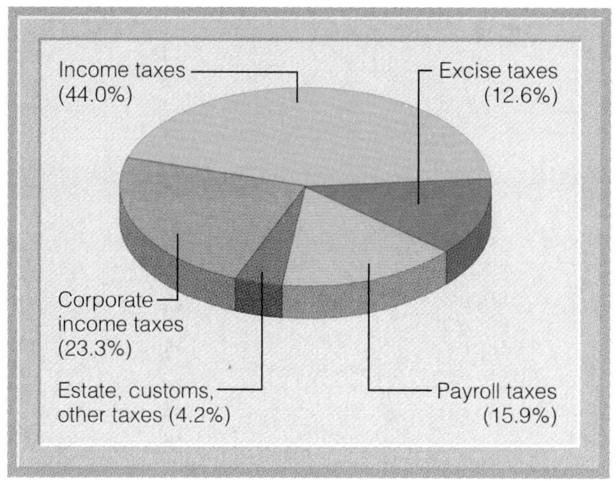

FIGURE 16.4
Government Revenue Sources, 1960

By 1960, the individual income tax was the largest source of revenue for the federal government.

Source: Data from *Statistical Abstract of the United States, 1980*, 100th ed. (Washington, D.C.: U.S. Bureau of the Census, 1980), p. 260.

observed bluntly at the time the tax was debated, "I stand here as a representative of the Republican Party of the central West to pledge to you my word that the great western states will be found voting . . . for an income tax. Why? Because they will not pay it!"[15] Indeed, in 1913, only 358,000 Americans, or about 0.8 percent of the population, filed income tax returns.[16] And until World War II, tax rates remained very low and the average American paid very little, if anything. But by the early 1940s, income taxes had become the major source of federal revenue.

The federal government gained another source of revenue with the passage of the **Social Security Act of 1935.** The act imposed a payroll tax (often labeled FICA on a pay stub) on all wage earners to pay for Social Security and associated programs. As with the first income taxes, Americans initially paid only a small payroll tax. Over time, however, payroll tax rates and the amount of government revenue they provide have risen sharply.

Social Security Act of 1935
The act of Congress that created the Social Security tax (Federal Insurance Contribution Act—FICA) and Social Security programs.

The addition of income and payroll taxes led to a tremendous change in the composition of federal revenues in the middle part of the century. As figure 16.4 shows, by 1960, almost half of all government revenue came from taxes on the incomes of individual Americans. Taxes on corporate incomes accounted for nearly one-quarter of all government revenue, and payroll taxes contributed another 16 percent. Meanwhile, customs duties, which were once the single largest source of government revenue, fell to less than 5 percent.

Since 1960, the federal government has refrained from adding new revenue sources, despite calls from some economists for a national sales tax or a value-added tax (a tax imposed on a product at each stage of production, as it increases in value). The federal government has, however, expanded the reach of existing taxes. Payroll taxes have increased to cover the costs of Medicare. The federal government also has extended excise taxes to include gasoline, tires, and a few other items in addition to alcohol and tobacco.

Although the federal government has not imposed any new types of taxes over the past three decades, the mix of revenue sources has changed. As figure 16.5 shows, in 1995, individual income taxes contributed roughly the same percentage of total revenue as they did in 1960. The share of government revenue coming from corporate income taxes dropped by more than half, however, and the share generated by excise taxes fell by nearly two-thirds. Meanwhile, the share of government revenue generated by payroll taxes more than doubled.

Income and Payroll Taxes

In 1997, the individual taxpayer provided, through income and payroll taxes, more than 80 percent of the federal government's revenue. Yet, some Americans earn a great deal of money each year, and some earn very little. How is the federal tax burden distributed across the American public? The answer depends on whether you are talking about individual income taxes or payroll taxes.

FIGURE 16.5
Government Revenue Sources, 1995

Although income taxes remain an important source of federal government revenue, payroll taxes are almost as important.

Source: Data from *Statistical Abstract of the United States, 1995*, 115th ed. (Washington, D.C.: U.S. Bureau of the Census, 1995), p. 334.

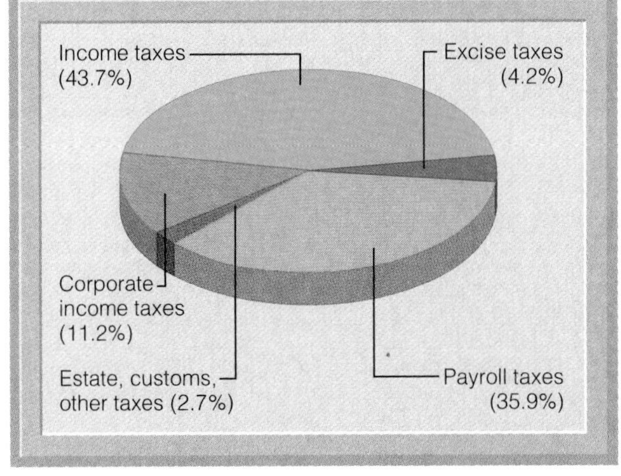

Progressive tax
A tax system in which those with high incomes pay a higher percentage of their income in taxes than those with low incomes.

The income tax has always been intended to be a **progressive tax**—the more money a person makes, the higher the tax rate he or she pays. The highest tax rate has varied over time, from a low of 7 percent in 1913 (applied to annual incomes of $500,000 and higher) to 91 percent during most of the 1950s and 1960s (on annual incomes of $200,000 and higher).[17] These percentages are somewhat misleading, however. The federal tax code has always provided tax breaks (or, less charitably, loopholes) that allow people to declare some income exempt from taxation, thereby lowering their tax burden.

In the 1960s, and especially in the 1980s, the federal government lowered income tax rates, especially the top rate, and eliminated many tax breaks. But as part of President Clinton's first budget package, Congress raised the top tax rate from 31 to 36 percent. Individuals with more than $250,000 in taxable income also had to pay a 10 percent surtax—making their effective tax rate 39.6 percent. But most Americans were taxed at 15 percent. Moreover, people with very low incomes were not required to pay any income tax. (Indeed, the Earned Income Tax Credit actually supplements the incomes of the working poor.) Despite the tremendous changes in tax rates, most Americans have not seen much change in their federal income tax burden since the 1950s, once inflation is taken into account. (Again, compare figures 16.4 and 16.5.)

The progressive character of the federal income tax is revealed when we examine who pays it. The top 1 percent of wage earners, who earn about 14 percent of the nation's income, pay almost 29 percent of the income taxes the federal government takes in. The top 50 percent of wage earners, who account for 85 percent of all income, produce 95 percent of the revenue the federal government gets from the income tax. The bottom 50 percent of wage earners, who account for 15 percent of all income, produce only 5 percent of the federal government's tax revenue.[18] Thus, the more you make, the more you pay as a percentage of your income.

The picture looks very different when it comes to payroll taxes. Unlike income taxes, payroll taxes are not progressive; the same percentage is removed from every employee's check, and all employees must pay the tax, no matter how little they earn. The payroll tax also applies to employers, who must pay the federal government an amount equal to every employee's contribution. Like income taxes, payroll taxes started at very low rates: in 1965, the rate was 3.625 percent and was applied only to the first $4,800 of income, making the highest payroll tax bill $174.[19] Over time, however, rates increased. In 1997, the payroll tax rate was 7.65 percent (split 6.20 percent for Social Security and 1.45 percent for Medicare). The Social Security portion of the tax applied to all wages up to a total of $65,400. As part of President Clinton's budget package, all wages were made subject to the Medicare portion of the payroll tax starting in 1994. Thus, a college professor earning $62,700 paid the same amount of

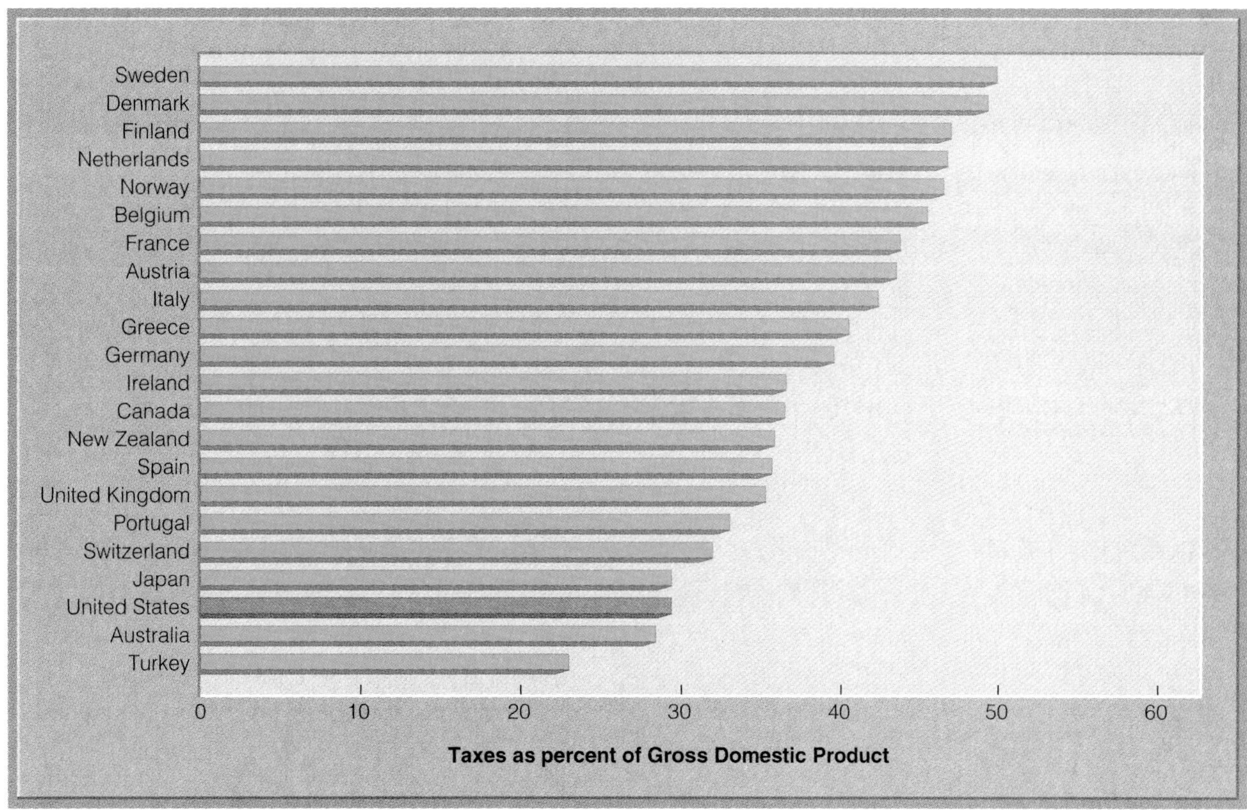

FIGURE 16.6
Comparing Tax Burdens: National, State, and Local Taxes, 1992

Overall, Americans pay less in taxes than citizens in most other industrialized countries.

Source: Data from *Statistical Abstract of the United States, 1995*, 115th ed. (Washington, D.C.: U.S. Bureau of the Census, 1995), p. 860.

money in Social Security tax in 1996 as multibillionaire Bill Gates. But Mr. Gates paid more for the Medicare portion of the payroll tax because all of his income from wages—though not income from other sources—was subject to it. Because people earning above the payroll tax limit for Social Security spend a smaller percentage of their income on payroll taxes than people earning below the limit, the payroll tax is considered a **regressive tax.**

Regressive tax
A tax system in which those with high incomes pay a lower percentage of their income in taxes than those with low incomes.

The federal government's reliance on individual Americans for most of its revenue has tremendous political ramifications. People know that the federal government takes a big bite out of their wages, and they dislike having that bite made larger. But while Americans know what their total income tax bill is each year—after all, they must file their income tax returns by every April 15—most fail to appreciate how much they pay in payroll taxes. It is easy to see why. Americans are not generally asked to file annual returns on their payroll taxes, and the employer's matching contribution is money the employee never sees. Thus, while most Americans are correct to think that they pay more taxes to the federal government than they did in the past, they probably do not have the story quite right. Income taxes are not the source of the increased pain, payroll taxes are. Indeed, by the early 1990s, many Americans paid more in payroll taxes than in income taxes.[20]

Americans might, however, take some small comfort in knowing that they actually shoulder a smaller tax burden than people in most other industrialized democracies. Figure 16.6 shows total government tax revenues as a percentage of each country's gross domestic product. (Comparing the total tax burden, including state and local taxes in the United States, is appropriate because, as we pointed out in chapter 2, countries are organized in different ways, with some unitary and others confederal.) Even with government's increasing revenue appetite over the last several decades, Americans pay less of their incomes in taxes than most citizens elsewhere, not more.

FIGURE 16.7
Percent of Federal Spending by Type, 1940–1995

Payments to individuals are a bigger part of federal government spending now than they were fifty years ago, whereas defense spending takes roughly the same share.

Sources: Data from *Statistical Abstract of the United States, 1992,* 112th ed. (Washington, D.C.: U.S. Bureau of the Census, 1992), p. 317; *Statistical Abstract of the United States, 1995,* 115th ed. (Washington, D.C.: U.S. Bureau of the Census, 1995), p. 333.

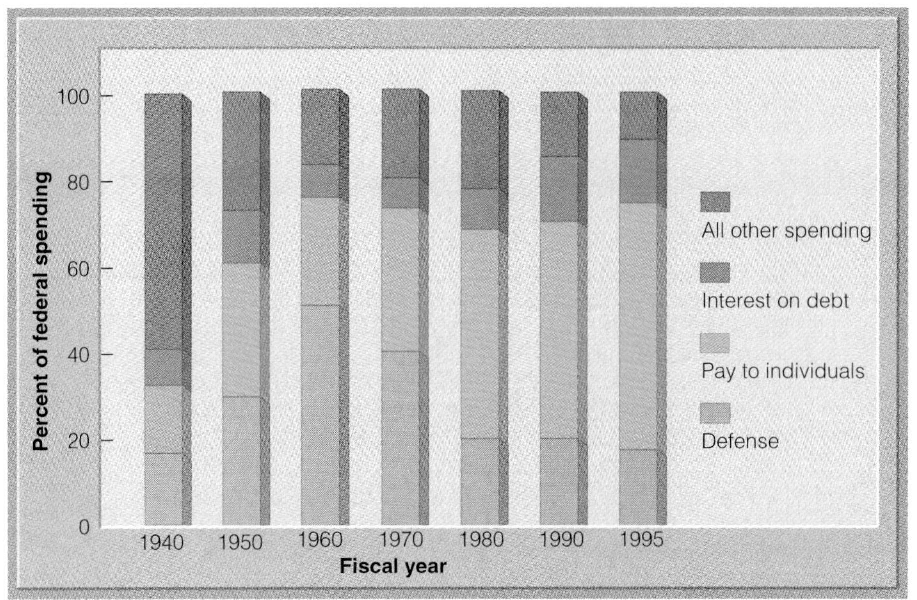

WHERE DOES GOVERNMENT SPENDING GO?

As we mentioned earlier, the level of federal spending has grown dramatically over the past half century. Whereas the federal government spent less than $10 billion in 1940, it spent more than $1.6 trillion dollars—that is, more than $1,600 billion, or more than 160 times as much—in 1996. The growth in federal spending has been accompanied by major changes in what the government spends money on. In the 1990s, an overwhelming percentage of the federal budget goes to direct payments to individuals, to payments on the national debt, and to the military. The tasks we normally associate with the federal government—drug enforcement, air traffic control, national parks, medical research, and so forth—consume only a small portion of the budget.

The Changing Nature of Government Spending

One area where the changes in federal spending show up is defense. As figure 16.7 shows, in 1940, the federal government spent less than 20 percent of its budget on defense. With the onset of the Cold War, however, spending priorities changed. Defense spending took a growing chunk of the federal budget in the 1950s and claimed roughly half of federal spending in 1960. In the more than three decades since then, however, the share of the budget devoted to defense has declined, so much so that in 1995, defense spending as a percentage of the budget was about the same as it was in 1940. Of course, since 1940, the absolute level of defense spending has grown enormously (as is true for every category of federal spending). But as figure 16.8 shows, even with increased spending on defense early in the Reagan administration, growth in defense spending has lagged behind increased spending for other components of the federal budget.

Between 1940 and 1980, interest payments on the national debt were remarkably stable as a percentage of the national budget, which suggests that the debt was not growing more rapidly than either the population or the national economy. In the 1980s, however, the percentage of the budget devoted to interest payments nearly doubled, rising to more than 15 percent in 1995. To put that growth in perspective, interest payments in 1990 were twenty-three times the size of the *entire national budget* in 1940.

Although the past five decades have seen changes in the share of the federal budget devoted to defense and interest payments, the most dramatic spending shifts have been in two other categories: direct payments to individuals and all other spending. In 1940, shortly after Franklin Roosevelt and Congress established Social Security and

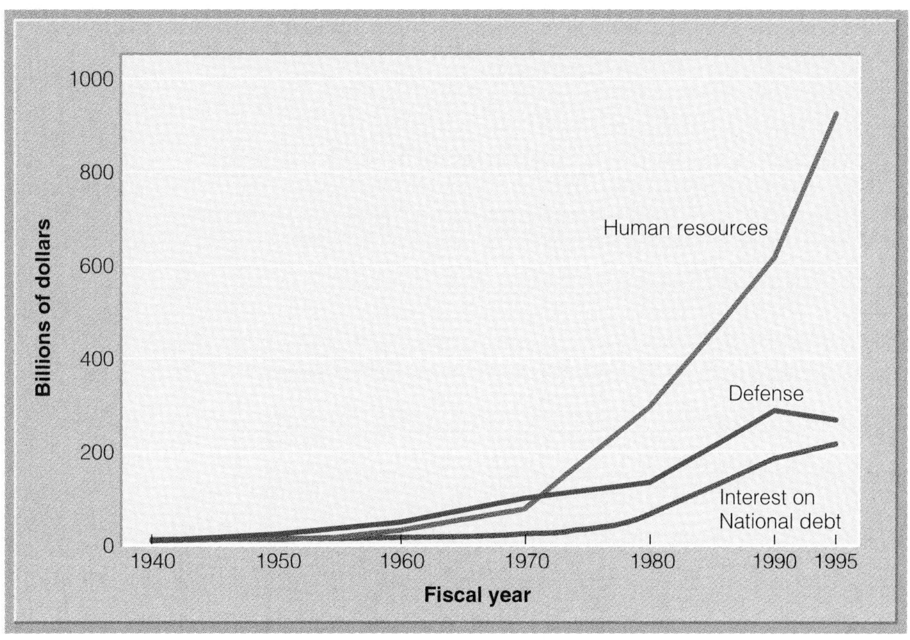

FIGURE 16.8
Changing Federal Spending, 1940–1995

Although all spending has increased over time, money going to human resources has increased much faster than that allotted to defense or to paying interest on the national debt.

Source: Data from *Statistical Abstract of the United States, 1995,* 115th ed. (Washington, D.C.: U.S. Bureau of the Census, 1995), p. 335.

several other social programs, payments to individuals consumed less than 20 percent of the budget. By 1980, that number had increased to nearly 50 percent. In contrast, in 1940, roughly 55 percent of all federal dollars went to the services we associate with government: building roads, running parks, fighting crime, and so forth. But by 1995, spending on all of those programs constituted less than 20 percent of federal spending.

The Growth of Entitlement Programs

Figure 16.8 shows that the most rapidly growing segment of the federal budget is spending on human resources, mostly in the form of direct payments to individuals. Most of these benefits are paid through **entitlement programs.** The name comes from the fact that people who meet the program's eligibility requirements are legally entitled to its benefits. For example, any person who earns less than 130 percent of the federal poverty rate and who has less than $2,000 in liquid assets such as a bank account is eligible to receive food stamps. Such a person will receive the food stamps even if the federal government has not budgeted enough money for the program.

Entitlement programs
Programs, created by legislation, that require the government to pay a benefit directly to any individual who meets the eligibility requirements the law establishes.

Social Security

The largest entitlement program by far is Social Security, which is actually two separate programs—the Old Age and Survivors Insurance program created in 1935 and the Disability Insurance program created in 1956. Social Security paid close to $340 billion in 1995 to some 41 million Americans. As we discussed earlier, a payroll tax finances Social Security.

The money each recipient receives from Social Security is determined by a formula that takes into account that person's lifetime earnings. Since 1972, federal law has required that Social Security benefits be tied (or indexed) to the rate of inflation as measured by the Consumer Price Index (see box 16.1). This means that when the cost of living rises, Social Security benefits rise, too. In 1997, for example, the annual **cost-of-living adjustment (COLA)** raised the monthly benefit 2.9 percent from the previous year, to an average of $745. For members of Congress, the law mandating COLAs was politically irresistible because it was popular with senior citizens who wanted their benefits protected from the ravages of inflation.[21] Social Security benefits also enjoy a partial exemption from income taxes, although President Clinton's first budget reduced the exemptions. In 1994, single individuals earning more than $34,000 annually and married couples earning more than $44,000 paid income taxes

Cost-of-living adjustment (COLA)
An increase in Social Security or other benefits designed to keep pace with inflation.

POINT OF ORDER

BOX 16.1

Measuring Inflation and Its Consequences for the Budget

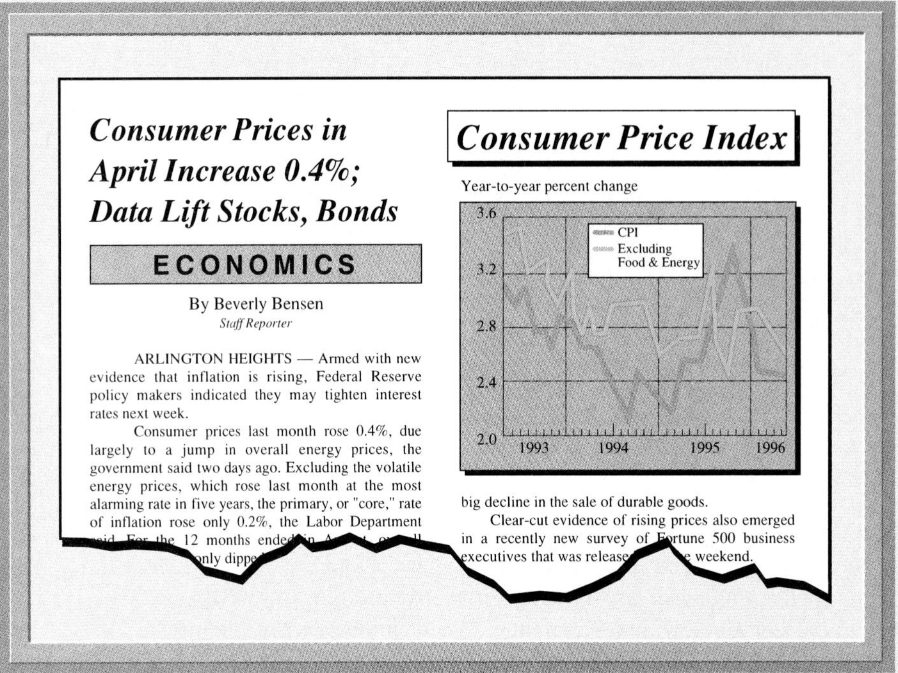

Consumer Prices in April Increase 0.4%; Data Lift Stocks, Bonds

ECONOMICS

By Beverly Bensen
Staff Reporter

ARLINGTON HEIGHTS — Armed with new evidence that inflation is rising, Federal Reserve policy makers indicated they may tighten interest rates next week.

Consumer prices last month rose 0.4%, due largely to a jump in overall energy prices, the government said two days ago. Excluding the volatile energy prices, which rose last month at the most alarming rate in five years, the primary, or "core," rate of inflation rose only 0.2%, the Labor Department

big decline in the sale of durable goods.

Clear-cut evidence of rising prices also emerged in a recently new survey of

The federal government uses the Consumer Price Index (CPI) to adjust federal benefits such as Social Security to reflect changes in the cost of living.

Each month, the Bureau of Labor Statistics publishes the Consumer Price Index (CPI)—a measure of inflation, or how much the cost of goods and services has increased. Few statistics are followed as closely as the CPI. For example, investors use the index to judge whether inflation is becoming a serious threat, and they adjust their behavior accordingly. But the CPI also has a tremendous impact on the federal budget. Many federal benefits (most notably Social Security) as well as income tax brackets are indexed (or tied) to changes in the cost of living. Thus, when the Bureau of Labor Statistics reports that the CPI has gone up over the past year, the federal government must pay beneficiaries of Social Security and other programs more benefits (which increases government spending), and it must move the upper limit of each tax bracket higher (which costs the government revenue). Because the CPI affects the federal budget in such a fundamental way, Congress and the president have begun to consider whether the rules used to determine the CPI should be rewritten.

The Bureau of Labor Statistics first published an inflation index in 1919. Over the years, the Bureau has tinkered with its method for determining the CPI, but in general, its basic approach has remained the same: it tries to measure how the price of a fixed "market basket" of goods and services an urban wage earner might purchase has changed over time. Currently, the CPI "is based on prices of food, clothing, shelter, fuels, transportation fares, charges for doctors' and dentists' services, drugs, etc., purchased for day-to-day living." The Bureau collects prices on a monthly and bimonthly basis from eighty-five areas around the country, covering 57,000 housing units and 19,000 establishments. The Bureau then takes the data it collects,

Continued

on 85 percent of their Social Security benefits. For these people, the other 15 percent of their Social Security income was exempt from taxes. But only 13 percent of Social Security recipients paid any income tax on their benefits in 1994.[22]

Despite the size and importance of Social Security, most Americans do not understand how it works. For example, only about 15 percent of the public knows that Social Security is the biggest single item in the federal budget.[23] And about half of

Point of Order

BOX 16.1 CONTINUED

weights the various prices to reflect their importance in a typical consumer's budget, and averages them across the regions sampled.

Economists and statisticians have argued for many years about whether the CPI measures the inflation rate accurately. The emerging consensus is that the CPI overstates the actual inflation rate, but the experts disagree over how much. For example, the Congressional Budget Office suggests the CPI exaggerates the actual inflation rate by 0.2 to 0.8 percent per year; Alan Greenspan, the chair of the Federal Reserve, argues that it exaggerates the actual inflation rate by 0.5 to 1.5 percent per year; and a blue-ribbon panel of economists that Congress commissioned to evaluate the CPI concluded that it exaggerates the actual inflation rate by 0.7 to 2 percent per year.

Experts agree on why the CPI overstates inflation. First, the current method for calculating the CPI fails to take into account substitution effects, which occur when a consumer buys a cheaper generic product rather than its more expensive name-brand competitor, or switches to chicken when steak gets too expensive. Second, in recent years, shopping patterns in the United States have changed. Many Americans have switched from shopping in department stores (which the Bureau of Labor Statistics uses in calculating the CPI) to shopping in lower-cost discount stores. Third, the current method for calculating the CPI fails to incorporate new products into the market basket in a timely fashion. Fourth, the current method for calculating the CPI fails to capture improvements in product quality, such as the increasing capabilities of personal computers.

Does it matter if the CPI overstates the actual inflation rate? In terms of the federal deficit, the answer is yes. To see why, consider what would happen if the annual CPI between 1996 and 2005 were 2 percent rather than 3 percent. Over the next ten years, that 1 percentage point reduction per year would save the federal government a total of $634 billion! Moreover, because the current method for calculating the CPI exaggerates the actual inflation rate, "the overindexing will itself become the fourth-largest spending program in the budget by 2005," overtaking all other expenditures except Social Security, health care, and national defense. In short, a new and more accurate measure of the actual inflation rate would save the federal government money *and* help balance the federal budget.

While experts agree that the rules used to calculate the CPI need to be changed, doing so is politically difficult. To see why, consider Social Security benefits. In 1995, the average married couple on Social Security received $14,160 in benefits. If the CPI were 3 percent per year for the next five years, their Social Security benefits—indexed to the CPI—would rise to $16,416. In contrast, if the CPI were to rise 2 percent per year over those same five years, the same married couple would end up receiving $15,635, or almost $800 less. As you can see, correcting the rules used to calculate the CPI so that it doesn't overstate the actual inflation rate means that people who receive government benefits will receive less than they would under the current method. And because many of these beneficiaries are the elderly—who, as we have noted before, are among the Americans most likely to vote—politicians approach the prospect of tinkering with the CPI with great trepidation.

In 1995, congressional Republicans embraced a proposal to revise the rules used to calculate the CPI as part of their plan to achieve a balanced federal budget. In doing so, however, they opted for a proposal to reduce the CPI by 0.2 percent, which is far smaller than the reduction most economists call for. President Clinton indicated that he was sympathetic to such a reduction, but he did not formally endorse it.

By 1996, neither Congress nor the president had agreed on legislation requiring the Bureau of Labor Statistics to change the rules it uses to calculate the CPI. Nonetheless, the Bureau did announce plans to make some changes in the way it calculates the CPI starting in 1997. These revisions are expected to cut the reported inflation rate by between 0.1 percent and 0.3 percent. Even that small reduction will save some $30 billion over seven years. But it is likely that Congress and the president will continue to examine how the federal government measures inflation. Determining how much the cost of living has really increased may be a key to balancing the budget in the future.

Sources: David Fischer, "Conquering Inflation," *U.S. News & World Report,* 20 November 1995, pp. 77–79; Robert D. Hershey, Jr., "Panel Sees a Corrected Price Index as Deficit-Cutter," *New York Times,* 15 September 1995; Robert J. Samuelson, "What's in a Number?" *Newsweek,* 23 October 1995, p. 52; *Statistical Abstract of the United States, 1995,* 115th ed. (Washington, D.C.: U.S. Bureau of the Census, 1995), pp. 489–90; Herbert Stein, "The Consumer Price Index: Servant or Master?" *Wall Street Journal,* 1 November 1995; David Wessel, "Why the CPI Fix Looks So Likely," *Wall Street Journal,* 11 December 1995.

Americans 55 years or older mistakenly think the money they pay (or paid) in Social Security taxes is set aside in a personal account for their retirement.[24] It is not. "Social Security, in fact, has always been an intergenerational chain letter. Throughout the program's history, today's workers have been paying the benefits for today's recipients, and the recipients have always received far more than they ever paid in."[25] (People under age 55 understand this fact much better.)[26]

The fact that Social Security is a pay-as-you-go system, in which current workers pay for the benefits paid to current retirees, is key to understanding both the popularity of Social Security and why many experts believe it must be fundamentally restructured. For the first several decades Social Security was in place, the number of workers far outnumbered the number of retirees. This simple demographic fact meant that for many years, the federal government could pay for Social Security by imposing only a small payroll tax on workers. And this meant, in turn, that Social Security benefits became quite generous relative to each beneficiary's contributions. (Ida May Fuller of Ludlow, Vermont, who received the first monthly Social Security check in 1940, paid only $22 in taxes and collected more than $20,000 in benefits.)[27] Until recently, retirees received all their Social Security contributions back *with interest* within about four years after retiring—and the average person lives more than fifteen years after retiring.[28] For example, in 1993, "a typical middle-income couple who retired in 1981 ha[d] already received back, with interest, not only the total value of their previous Social Security and Medicare taxes, but *also the total value of their lifetime federal income taxes.*"[29]

Any program that asks for little in contributions but provides a lot in benefits is destined to be politically popular. Yet the changing demographics of the United States make it impossible to sustain the generosity of Social Security. As we discussed in chapter 3, the American population is aging. Whereas in 1950, there were fifteen workers for every retiree, in 1990, there were only five, and experts predict that by 2030, there will be fewer than three.[30] To make up for this shortfall, the federal government has gradually been forced (as we mentioned earlier in this chapter) to require workers to pay more in payroll taxes and (to a lesser degree) to accept lower benefits. As a result, many retirees in the near future will take longer to recoup their contributions, and many may end up taking out less than they contributed.[31] One recent analysis, for example, shows that "a single worker born in 1930 with average earnings, can expect to get back about 90 percent of the total payroll tax paid, plus interest, while the same kind of worker born in 1950 will end up with just 55 percent."[32] And some experts fear that workers now entering the workforce will be forced to pay high payroll taxes over the course of their careers and will receive relatively few benefits when they retire in forty years.[33]

Whatever misconceptions Americans may have about how Social Security works, the program remains extraordinarily popular.[34] Its popularity explains why elected officials are loath to tamper with it, long referring to Social Security as the "third rail" of American politics: "Touch it and die."[35] Indeed, the political power of the senior citizen lobby helps explain why in 1990, more than 28 percent of the federal budget went to programs for the elderly, while just a bit more than 5 percent went to programs for children.[36] On a per capita basis, the elderly received $13,890 in benefits from the federal government, whereas children got just $1,271.[37] (The disparity obviously contributes to the findings, reported in chapter 3, that children are much more likely to live in poverty than the elderly.) But political support to reform Social Security is emerging. A poll conducted in 1996 found that less than 10 percent of people under age fifty expect benefits to be as generous for them as for the people currently receiving them. Indeed, most younger people think they will receive lower benefits, or no benefits at all.[38]

Other Entitlement Programs

Even though Social Security is the largest entitlement program, many other entitlement programs also serve the American public. For example, Medicare serves some 36 million people, at a cost of close to $160 billion in 1995. Medicaid, also created in 1965 to help provide medical care for low-income people, has some 33 million beneficiaries. In 1995, nearly 27 million people used food stamps.[39] Around 1.7 million military retirees and their surviving families and 1.6 million retired federal workers receive retirement benefits from the federal government.

Although Social Security affects far more Americans than most entitlement programs, the others are also extremely popular. Medicare enjoys strong support among

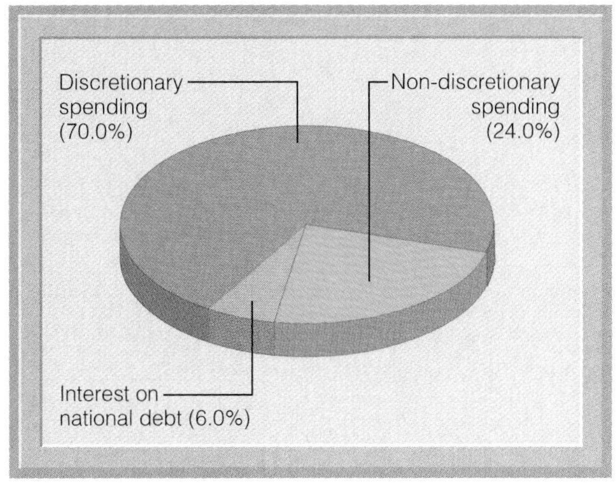

FIGURE 16.9
Discretionary Federal Spending, 1962

Discretionary spending made up more than two-thirds of the federal budget in 1962.

Source: Data from Harold W. Stanley and Richard G. Niemi, *Vital Statistics on American Politics*, 5th ed. (Washington, D.C.: CQ Press, 1995), p. 391.

the elderly. Military leaders insist that generous pensions are needed to convince people to make the military a career, and veterans say that their benefits are a just reward for their service to the country. Entitlement programs also draw political support from groups that benefit indirectly. For example, farmers and food companies support the Food Stamp program because it helps them sell more of their products. Every entitlement program has staunch supporters who resist cutting funding for their favorite program. This makes it difficult to limit entitlement programs and to restrain their growing appetite for federal funds.

Limiting Entitlement Programs

The growing federal budget deficit has prompted much talk in academic and financial circles about the need to cut the cost of entitlement programs. But administration officials and members of Congress usually prefer to steer clear of talk about cutting entitlements. The reason is simple: they do not want to take the political heat for trying to reduce benefits.

The difficulty that Congress and the president have in cutting an entitlement program is amplified by their inability to control entitlements through the budgetary process. As we said earlier, federal law stipulates that everyone who meets the eligibility requirements for an entitlement program must receive its benefits. Thus, if unemployment rises, the government must provide unemployment benefits to everyone who qualifies, even if that means spending on unemployment benefits will exceed what was budgeted.

The only way Congress and the president can reduce the cost of an entitlement program is to rewrite the law that established it. They can then tighten eligibility requirements, reduce the benefits provided, or enact some mix of both. But changing the rules governing entitlement programs risks starting a political donnybrook, as Republican members of Congress learned in 1995 when they proposed making significant changes to Medicare and Medicaid. Supporters of the two programs mobilized political support and largely rebuffed the proposed changes.

Because Congress and the president cannot use the budget process to limit entitlements, these programs are often referred to as **non-discretionary spending.** Interest on the national debt also represents non-discretionary spending since the government must make the interest payments. In contrast, expenditures on most other federal programs involve **discretionary spending** that can be controlled through the budgetary process. For example, the president and Congress can use the budgetary process to raise or lower spending on nuclear weapons, cancer research, and foreign aid.

Non-discretionary spending
Federal spending on programs such as Social Security that cannot be controlled through the regular budget process.

Discretionary spending
Federal spending on programs that can be controlled through the regular budget process.

The issue of discretionary spending is crucial because the share of the federal budget that can be controlled through the budgetary process has fallen sharply over the past three decades. As figure 16.9 shows, in 1962, non-discretionary spending on entitlements and interest payments on the debt consumed 30 percent of the budget, leaving

FIGURE 16.10
Discretionary Federal Spending, 1995

Discretionary spending decreased to only one-third of the federal budget in 1995.

Source: Data from Harold W. Stanley and Richard G. Niemi, *Vital Statistics on American Politics*, 5th ed. (Washington, D.C.: CQ Press, 1995), p. 391.

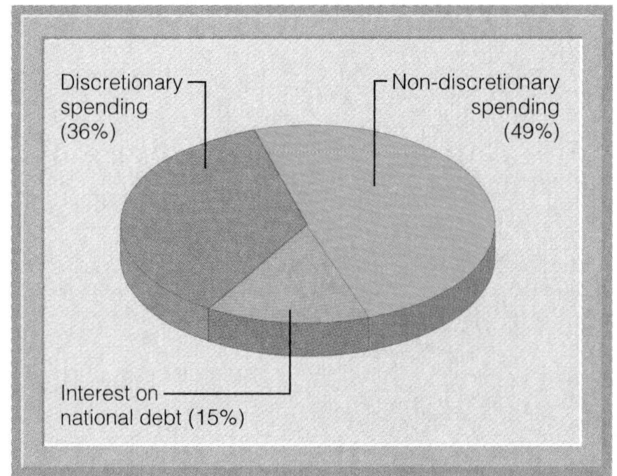

70 percent for discretionary spending. As figure 16.10 shows, however, in 1995, the figures were reversed. The rising share of the budget devoted to non-discretionary spending makes it far more difficult to reduce the budget deficit.

What About Pork?

Pork barrel
Legislation that appropriates government money for local projects of questionable value that may ingratiate a legislator with his or her constituents.

To this point we have said nothing about government spending on **pork barrel** projects—the portion of discretionary spending that funds programs, often of dubious value, designed to benefit individual congressional districts. (The term *pork barrel* refers to the nineteenth-century practice of packing salted pork in barrels; the term likens members of Congress to hungry diners reaching in for their share of the goodies.)[40] We have all heard tales of how members of Congress lavish money on pet projects: $43 million to establish Steamtown, a railroad theme park in Scranton, Pennsylvania; $6.4 million to build an "authentic" Bavarian resort in Kellogg, Idaho; $3 million to build private parking garages in Chicago; and $1 million to preserve a sewer in Trenton, New Jersey, as a historic monument, to name just a few well-known examples. While these and other federal projects might seem frivolous, members of Congress can take credit for directing these federal dollars to their states and districts. Even Sen. Phil Gramm (R-Tex.), a staunch proponent of cutting federal spending and balancing the federal budget, brags to his constituents that "I'm carrying so much pork, I'm beginning to get trichinosis."[41]

What portion of the budget goes to pork-barrel projects? It is difficult to know precisely since one person's pork is another's essential government service. Take, for example, the record of Sen. Robert Byrd (D-W.V.), one of the most powerful members of the Senate. Senator Byrd considers his congressional activities "West Virginia's billion-dollar industry." By some accounts, he has channeled $1.5 billion in federal money into his home state. At his behest, West Virginia has become home to a new FBI Identification Center, the Treasury Department's Bureau of Public Debt, an IRS processing center, and a host of other public facilities. Yet listen to his justification of these endeavors to the voters back home: "You, the federal taxpayers of this country, have invested $7 billion—that's billion with a B—for the mass transit system in Washington. Now that's pork. What I'm doing is spreading good seed that will bear fruit a hundredfold [in West Virginia]. Prosperity flows along concrete rivers."[42]

Corporate welfare
Government subsidies or tax breaks of questionable value to private corporations.

Even allowing for differences in definition, pork-barrel projects constitute a small part of federal spending. By most estimates, pork-barrel spending accounts for less than $10 billion, or 1 percent, of the federal budget.[43] A much bigger expense to the federal treasury are subsidies and tax breaks to corporations, or what critics have come to call **corporate welfare.** Each year, the federal government provides money to corporations or agrees to reduce their taxes, ostensibly for the purpose of helping them remain competitive in the

Most people consider Steamtown, a railroad theme park in Scranton, Pennsylvania, that was built with federal funds, an example of pork barrel politics.

marketplace but sometimes only because they are politically well-connected. For example, the federal government "builds roads in national forests to make it easier for private industry to bring out timber, gives low-interest loans through the Rural Electrification Administration that hold down the cost of running ski resorts in Aspen, Colorado, and casinos in Las Vegas, Nevada, and is providing $333 million to help American automobile manufacturers create a new generation of 'clean' cars to help keep them competitive."[44]

Just how much does corporate welfare—or what supporters prefer to call corporate support—cost the government each year? The exact number is hotly disputed. The Congressional Budget Office puts the number at $30 billion, Congress's Joint Committee on Taxation says it might be as high as $60 billion, and critics of corporate subsidies and tax breaks argue that the cost runs as high as $160 billion.[45] Despite the different estimates, most everyone agrees that corporate subsidies and tax breaks cost the federal government far more money than pork barrel projects such as Steamtown.

Whatever the exact cost of corporate subsidies and tax breaks, college students might fairly ask why the federal government is spending millions helping the wealthy to ski and gamble when it is not fully funding Pell Grants. Yet, as we just saw with pork barrel projects, what constitutes corporate welfare lies in the eye of the beholder. (This is why estimates of what the government spends on corporate welfare vary so widely.) The most strident critics of corporate welfare believe that any corporate subsidy or tax break is by definition wasteful, since they believe the marketplace and not the government should determine all business decisions. In contrast, proponents of corporate subsidies and tax breaks argue that they stimulate economic growth and provide jobs for thousands of Americans. For instance, the timber industry argues that without the roughly $6 million the federal government provides each year to build roads in national forests, it would be too expensive in many parts of the country to log. Thus, if timber subsidies were reduced, timber companies would have to lay off workers, and these workers would ultimately have to turn to the government for unemployment and other benefits. (Whether such claims are true tend to be a matter of debate.)

The debate over the need for corporate subsidies and tax breaks is likely to intensify in coming years for the simple reason that they represent a sizable government expense. Even so, corporate welfare is not likely to become a partisan issue—Democrats and Republicans take both sides of the debate. For instance, in 1995, Secretary of Labor Robert Reich campaigned publicly against programs he considered corporate welfare. But he received little support from other members of the Clinton administration, many of whom argued that the federal government should increase aid to major corporations to increase America's economic competitiveness. Likewise, while Republicans traditionally condemn government interference in the marketplace, they frequently work to keep corporate subsidies and tax breaks alive. For example, in 1995, House Republicans voted for a 29 percent increase in the budget for the Agriculture

Department's market-promotion program—which pays for American companies (and even some foreign ones) to advertise their goods and services overseas—even though they came to office pledging to reduce the size of government.[46]

Why Do Budget Deficits Persist?

Why has the federal government run larger and larger deficits over the past three decades? Presidents often blame Congress, and Congress in turn points 535 fingers at the president. Both share responsibility for the problem, but the American public is the main culprit. When Congress and the president set the budget, they are responding to the will of the public. And the public is of two minds, on the one hand calling for more government services, and on the other hand calling for lower taxes. These contradictory demands are a recipe for government red ink.

Congress and the President

Since 1921, presidents have been charged with introducing a single budget to Congress. In recent years, Congress has stayed within the overall spending total the president has established.[47] In the twenty-seven years between 1968 and 1994, for example, Congress appropriated less money than the president requested in twenty-two years and more money than the president requested in only five years.[48] Moreover, since 1981, no president has come close to submitting a balanced budget. (In late 1995, following the lead of the Republican majority in Congress, President Clinton produced a plan to balance the budget in seven years.)

The failure of Presidents Reagan, Bush, and Clinton to submit a balanced budget might make it seem that the president is to blame for America's chronic budget deficits. But that view oversimplifies the case. When presidents decide how much money to request, they often anticipate the preferences of Congress. For example, Ronald Reagan asked for more domestic spending than he would have preferred because he knew if he asked for less, Congress would have rejected his proposed budget and substitute a (higher) one of its own. And on occasion, Congress does ignore the president's preferences on how much the government should spend. Congress sometimes even underfunds programs that by law must be fully funded (by intentionally underestimating expected costs) and gives the money instead to other programs its members favor. Such tactics force the president to return to Capitol Hill to ask for a supplemental appropriation that will fund the required program in full.[49]

In the end, both the president and members of Congress bear responsibility for the persistence of budget deficits. While it is true that only Congress can appropriate federal monies, it is also true that a presidential veto usually can keep an appropriations bill from becoming law.

The American Public

Although the president and members of Congress are responsible for drawing up the federal budget, they do not operate in a vacuum. When they make budgetary decisions, they are usually doing what elected officials are supposed to do in a democracy—responding to the wishes of the public.

Public opinion surveys consistently show that 70 to 85 percent of the American public wants the federal budget balanced. When asked how the government should balance the budget, more than 80 percent of Americans opt for cutting spending, while fewer than 10 percent favor raising taxes. But when asked which government programs should be cut, most Americans fail to identify programs they would be willing to trim. After the 1994 election, for example, 64 percent of Americans thought federal spending on education should increase; only 6 percent thought it should decrease. Majorities also thought the federal government should spend more to fight crime, provide health care, take care of the homeless, and conduct AIDs research. Only defense spending aroused much support

Public opinion polls repeatedly show that the American public wants the federal government to balance its budget but opposes proposals to cut spending on most government programs or to raise taxes.

By permission of Mike Luckovich and Creators Syndicate.

for a spending cut, and only 23 percent took that position. Otherwise, people either wanted to spend more or to keep funding at current levels for government programs.[50] Another survey in 1995 found strong resistance to proposed cuts in spending on environmental programs, public housing, the National Service Corps, and summer jobs programs for young people.[51]

Part of the explanation for the public's seemingly contradictory opinions is that most people do not have a very good grasp of the federal budget. In a survey conducted in 1994, for example, 61 percent of people supported cutting entitlement programs to help eliminate the deficit. But in that same survey, 66 percent opposed cuts in "programs such as Social Security, Medicare, Medicaid and farm subsidies," which are, of course, the biggest entitlement programs.[52] Similarly, in a poll taken in 1995, some 70 percent thought the U.S. spends too much on foreign aid. Respondents were then asked what percentage of the budget they thought foreign aid constituted, and what the appropriate level of spending should be. The median response on the first question was 15 percent; the median answer on the second was 5 percent. In reality, of course, foreign aid constitutes about 1 percent of the federal budget.[53] (Some 27 percent of the public mistakenly thinks foreign aid is the largest component of the budget.)[54] Eliminating all foreign aid would make only a small dent in an annual budget deficit of more than $100 billion.

The public's lack of knowledge about the particulars of federal spending extends to the tax code as well. Although Americans generally oppose tax increases, they often fail to recognize how they benefit from exemptions in the tax code. Figure 16.11 shows the six tax breaks that cost the federal treasury the most in terms of lost revenue in 1996. The federal government lost the most money, some $67 billion, by not taxing employer-paid health benefits. The second most costly tax break is the exemption on pension contributions and their accrued interest; this cost the government $59 billion. No taxes are levied on the interest homeowners pay on their mortgages, which cost the federal treasury another $54 billion. If the federal government eliminated the three biggest tax breaks, the federal budget would be balanced and perhaps even run a small surplus. But the tax breaks listed in figure 16.11 and many smaller ones also enjoy great public support. Elected officials who try to repeal these tax breaks risk defeat in the next election.

The public's attitudes toward spending and taxes mean that individual members of Congress have no political incentive to balance the budget. Constituents want the budget balanced, but not if it means raising their taxes or cutting programs they like. As one anonymous member of Congress commented, "I think most of us are frustrated with the cynicism we find out there. . . . It's frustrating to . . . have to face

FIGURE 16.11
Top Tax Breaks, 1996

By giving tax breaks, the federal government gives up billions of dollars of revenue.

Source: Data from *Statistical Abstract of the United States, 1995,* 115th ed. (Washington, D.C.: U.S. Bureau of the Census, 1995), p. 339.

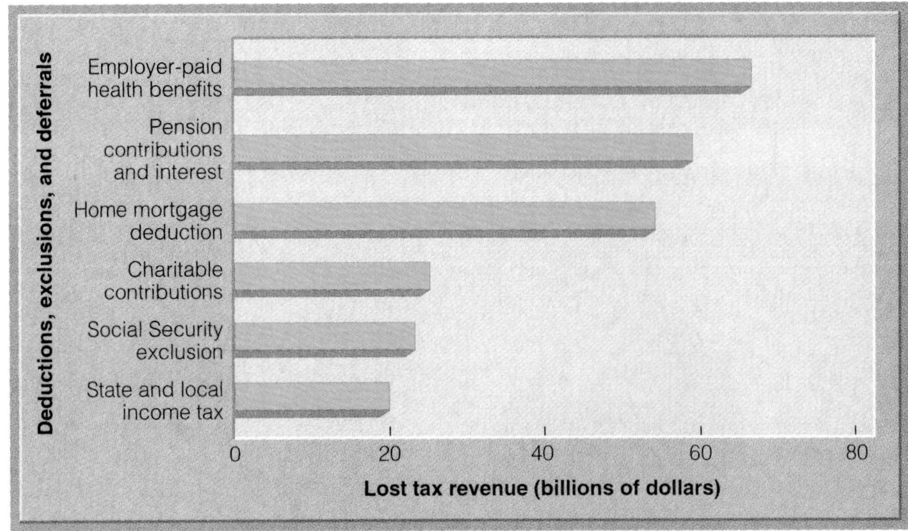

an angry mob of people who demand that the budget deficit and their taxes be reduced but who won't give up their favorite programs."[55] Members respond to the public's wishes by protecting the interests of their constituents. The battle cry on Capitol Hill is: "If spending is cut, it should be cut in someone else's district." In this sense, what one member blasts as pork another defends as good and necessary. Because no one agrees on whose programs should be cut, members find it easiest simply to provide the goods their constituents want and to let future generations decide how to pay for the national debt.

THE BUDGETARY PROCESS

The incentive the president and members of Congress have to provide voters with benefits and to protect them from taxes creates an inherent bias toward deficit spending. One way to control the government's appetite for spending is to design a budgetary process that imposes fiscal discipline on the president and members of Congress. As the budget deficit has grown over the past three decades, Congress has adopted several different procedural reforms that have sought to impose fiscal discipline on members. But as we will see, procedural reforms and rule changes cannot substitute for the will to control government spending, although the amount of time Congress and the president devote to the subject has grown enormously.

The Budgetary Process from George Washington to Richard Nixon

During the nineteenth century, the federal government followed a very simple budgetary process, in keeping with the low level of spending.[56] Individual agencies in the executive branch essentially submitted their budget requests directly to Congress, without soliciting the president's input. Congress at first appropriated funds in lump sums, giving agencies discretion in spending the money. But when members of Congress grew distrustful of the executive branch, they shifted more toward *line-item budgeting,* which specifies exact sums of money for specific purposes.

As the budget grew in response to the country's growth, members of Congress changed the budgetary process to cope with their increased workload. Until the mid-1860s, the House Ways and Means Committee and the Senate Finance Committee handled both tax and appropriations bills. But the growth of the budget forced both the House and the Senate to create appropriations committees. This gave power over government revenues to one group of legislators (Ways and Means in the House and Finance in the Senate) and control over spending to a different group (the appropriations committees in each chamber).

Although separating decisions about revenues from decisions about spending created the potential for budgetary confusion, the process worked relatively well throughout the rest of the nineteenth century. During World War I, however, the federal government ran very large deficits, raising the national debt from $1 billion to $25 billion in less than three years. One response to the government's sudden surge of red ink was the **Budget and Accounting Act of 1921.** This act authorized presidents to coordinate the spending proposals of government agencies with their own priorities and to submit a single budget to Congress. To assist the president in dealing with the budget, Congress created the Bureau of the Budget (BOB). The BOB initially was part of the Treasury Department, but it moved into the newly created Executive Office of the President in 1939. President Nixon reorganized and renamed the agency the **Office of Management and Budget (OMB)** in 1970. But Congress explicitly retained the right to review and change the president's budget.

Budget and Accounting Act of 1921
An act of Congress that created the Bureau of the Budget and allowed the president to review and coordinate the spending proposals of federal agencies and departments.

Office of Management and Budget (OMB)
The agency in charge of assisting the president in reviewing and coordinating budget requests to Congress from federal agencies and departments. Formerly the Bureau of the Budget.

The budget process remained essentially unchanged from 1921 until 1974. The president submitted a budget and Congress considered it—a process often described as "the president proposes and Congress disposes." Although no formal mechanism reconciled revenue and spending, the appropriations committees acted as the guardians of the federal treasury.[57] As one House Appropriations Committee chair observed, "You may think my business is to make appropriations, but it is not. It is to prevent their being made."[58] The norm in the House Appropriations Committee was to cut budget requests. This loosely coordinated budget process, based on mostly unwritten rules, tended to produce balanced budgets, in large part because the members of the House Appropriations Committee played the role of budgetary watchdogs.

The House Appropriations Committee's power to cut the budget, however, dissipated over time. This happened in part because of the rise in entitlement programs, which the House and Senate appropriations committees do not control. But, fundamentally, the House Appropriations Committee lost power because House members no longer wanted it to make difficult choices. As pressures for increased spending mounted, the House Appropriations Committee no longer had the power to guard the budget because it did not have the support it needed from the rest of the House to keep spending in line with revenues.[59]

Budgetary Reform in the 1970s

As we noted earlier, budget deficits began to become the norm rather than the exception for government spending in the mid-1960s. When the deficit suddenly escalated in the early 1970s, rising from $8.6 billion in 1970 to $26.4 billion in 1972, many observers blamed the budgetary process. They argued that the process was too fragmented to produce a coherent, balanced budget.[60] At the same time, many members of Congress worried that the enormous size of the budget gave the president too much power. They argued that the president had a terrific informational advantage because of OMB's expertise. Richard Nixon's behavior during his first years as president reinforced fears that the White House had too much power. The conservative Nixon impounded (refused to spend) funds a more liberal Congress appropriated; sometimes members of Congress learned about the impoundment of funds only by reading the newspaper.

Concerns over budget deficits and presidential impoundments combined to produce a significant reform of the budget process: the **Congressional Budget and Impoundment Control Act of 1974.** The Budget Act curtailed the president's ability to impound appropriated funds, and it created the **Congressional Budget Office (CBO)** to give Congress the same level of expertise that OMB gave the president. But the main purpose of the Budget Act was to impose collective responsibility on members of Congress themselves. Because the Ways and Means, Finance, and Appropriations

Congressional Budget and Impoundment Control Act of 1974
An act of Congress that created the new budget process and the Congressional Budget Office and that curtailed the president's power to impound funds.

Congressional Budget Office (CBO)
A nonpartisan congressional agency in charge of assisting Congress in reviewing and coordinating budget requests to Congress.

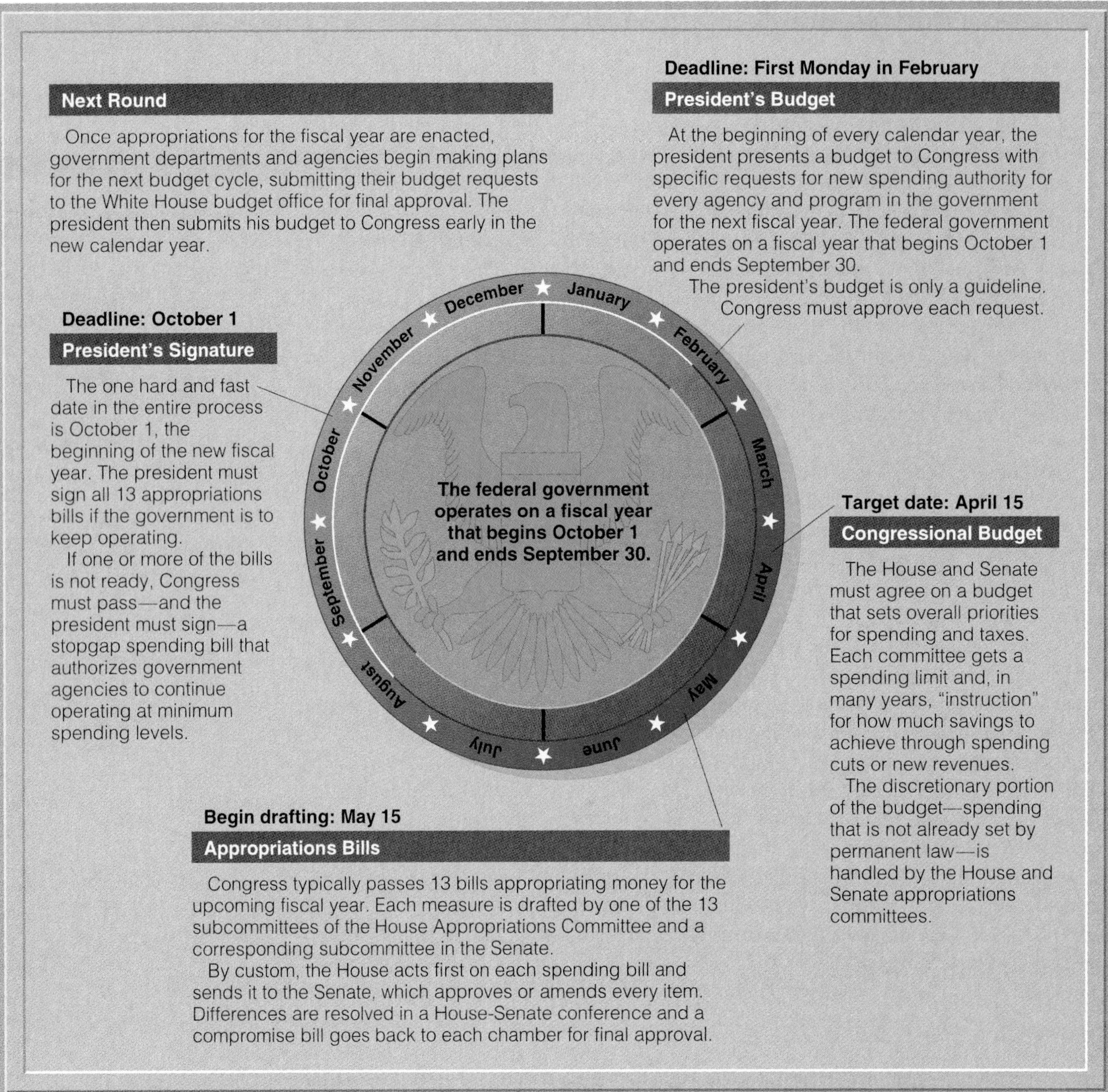

FIGURE 16.12
The Budget Cycle

The basic budget cycle the federal government currently uses begins when the president submits a budget to Congress and ends when all 13 appropriation bills are signed into law.

From "Where the Money Goes," *Congressional Quarterly* 51 (49), supp. 40, 11 December 1993, p. 9. Copyright © 1993 Congressional Quarterly, Washington, D.C. Reprinted by permission.

Continuing resolutions
Temporary laws Congress passes to keep the government running when Congress misses the deadline for passing the budget.

committees had failed to reconcile revenue and spending, the Budget Act also established budget committees in both the House and Senate. These new committees were responsible for shepherding two budget resolutions, one preliminary and the other final, through Congress each year. The purpose of the budget resolutions was to set a limit on total government spending and then to make sure that the sum of the various spending bills did not exceed that limit. Figure 16.12 outlines the timetable that the Budget Act created for the budgetary process.

A procedure that requires Congress to reconcile individual spending bills with an overall spending target sounds eminently sensible. In practice, however, the Budget Act of 1974 failed to work. Only four times since 1975 has Congress met the October 1 deadline the Budget Act established for assembling all pieces of the budget, and it has often had to resort to stop-gap measures called **continuing resolutions** to keep the government running.[61] In 1983, Congress gave up entirely on trying to pass a second budget resolution.

Even more significant is the failure of the budget resolutions to cap spending. During the early 1980s, individual appropriations bills were not trimmed to meet the

In 1985, this threesome loaned their names to a new anti-deficit law: from left, Senators Warren B. Rudman, Phil Gramm, and Ernest F. Hollings.

spending limits contained in the second resolution. Instead, Congress increased the spending limit to match whatever spending decisions it had adopted. Moreover, both spending resolutions were suspect because they usually contained favorable and unrealistic forecasts about the health of the economy.[62] Such "rosy scenarios" allowed members of Congress (and presidents as well) to inflate expected revenue and underestimate spending. The final failing of the reforms was the absence of any penalty if appropriations exceeded the spending limits adopted in the first resolution. With no mechanism for capturing excess spending, each succeeding deficit was tacked on to the national debt, with the results we have discussed.[63]

The failure of the Budget Act shows that changing the rules of the budgetary process will not work when no agreement exists in Washington on how to control government spending. Budget deficits grew despite the Budget Act not because of flaws in the legislation, but because Congress and the president disagreed over budgetary priorities. President Reagan, for instance, insisted on cutting domestic programs and opposed tax increases, while the Democratic majority on Capitol Hill favored protecting domestic programs and urged tax increases. When Reagan refused to raise taxes and Congress refused to cut domestic spending, budget deficits were inevitable, regardless of the provisions of the Budget Act.

Budgetary Reform in the 1980s

By the early 1980s, the rapidly escalating size of the federal deficit had exposed the failings of the Budget Act of 1974. Members concerned about the size of the deficit began to cast about for changes in the rules of the budgetary process that would impose fiscal discipline on Congress. What members settled on was legislation known as Gramm-Rudman-Hollings, in honor of its sponsors, Sens. Phil Gramm (R-Tex.), Warren Rudman (R-N.H.), and Ernest Hollings (D-S.C.).

Gramm-Rudman (as the reforms were commonly called) came in two versions. The first was rushed through a near-panicked Congress in the fall of 1985—it is one of the few bills to become law without having been reviewed by any congressional committee.[64] Many members of Congress voted for Gramm-Rudman because they wanted to do something to bring deficits under control, or, at least, because they wanted to show their constituents they were tackling the problem. But most members knew the bill contained a fatal constitutional flaw. Indeed, the bill contained a clause requiring the federal courts to hear the case on an accelerated basis. When the Supreme Court

Despite repeated efforts to bring the federal budget under control, budget deficits continue to exceed targeted levels.

TABLE 16.1 Federal Deficit Targets (in billions)

Fiscal Year	1987 GRH[a] Targets	1990 BEA[b] Targets	Actual Deficit
1988	144		155
1989	136		152
1990	100		195
1991	64	327	269
1992	28	317	290
1993	0	236	255
1994		102	203
1995		83	168
1996			107

[a]Gramm-Rudman-Hollings budget deficit targets.

[b]Budget Enforcement Act of 1990 budget deficit targets.

Sources: Statistical Abstract of the United States, 1995, 115th ed. (Washington, D.C.: U.S. Bureau of the Census, 1995), p. 333; James A. Thurber and Samantha L. Durst, "The 1990 Budget Enforcement Act: The Decline of Congressional Accountability," in *Congress Reconsidered,* 5th ed., ed. Lawrence C. Dodd and Bruce I. Oppenheimer (Washington, D.C.: CQ Press, 1993), p. 380; Jackie Calmes, "Budget Deficit Shrinks to Lowest Level in Two Decades, a Boon for Clinton," *Wall Street Journal,* 29 October 1996.

ruled in July 1986 that the first Gramm-Rudman law was unconstitutional, Congress was again spared from making difficult budgetary choices. (The bill gave the head of the General Accounting Office, a member of the legislative branch, power to impose across-the-board spending cuts on the federal government. The Supreme Court held that because such power properly rests with the executive branch, the bill violated the separation of powers.)[65] But continued concern over the deficit spurred Congress to pass another version of Gramm-Rudman in 1987, this one written to pass constitutional muster. (It allowed the head of the OMB, an executive agency, to impose the cuts.)

Like the Budget Act of 1974, both versions of Gramm-Rudman sought to impose collective responsibility on members of Congress. Both bills set annual deficit targets that over several years would produce a balanced budget. To ensure that the deficit reduction targets would be met, Gramm-Rudman stipulated that if Congress failed to produce a budget deficit less than or equal to the target for that year, then an automatic, "almost" across-the-board budget cut known as *sequestration* would be implemented. (The "almost" is important because some 70 percent of the budget, including programs such as Social Security, were exempt from the cuts.)[66] Supporters of Gramm-Rudman believed that members would put together budgets that met the deficit targets rather than risk maiming their favorite programs through the mandatory, across-the-board cuts sequestration required.

Table 16.1 shows the deficit targets for the second Gramm-Rudman bill along with actual budget deficits for each year. As you can see, the federal budget deficit grew rather than shrank while Gramm-Rudman was in effect. Why did Gramm-Rudman fail to reduce the deficit? The answer is the same reason the Budget Act of 1974 failed: Congress and the president could not agree on budgetary priorities. Like the 1974 reforms, Gramm-Rudman was susceptible to manipulation. Members overestimated revenue and underestimated spending, and they used accounting tricks to meet the target limits. (Congress once went so far as to shift the date for charging the budget for military pay from October 1 to September 30. This shifted the pay date from one fiscal year—the one they were setting the budget for—to the current fiscal year, in which there was no sanction for overspending.) And like the 1974 reforms, Gramm-Rudman only required Congress to produce a budget forecasted to meet the deficit targets. Once the members had voted to accept a particular forecast, they were no longer bound to meet it, and no penalties or spending cuts were imposed if the forecast proved faulty.

Budgetary Reform in the 1990s

Gramm-Rudman's failure to stem the growing tide of red ink in the federal budget prompted concerned members of Congress to search for another remedy. In 1990, President Bush and the Democratic leadership of Congress held extended negotiations over how to reduce the budget deficit. The negotiations became quite contentious, and at one point, the president allowed the government to run out of money, forcing many government operations to shut down for one weekend. Eventually, however, the president and Congress reached an agreement that was enacted into law as the Budget Enforcement Act of 1990 (BEA).[67]

An extremely complex law, the BEA changed the focus of budgeting by setting limits on expenditure growth and imposing sanctions for not meeting budgetary targets. In essence, the BEA divided the budget into three domains: defense, domestic policy, and international affairs. If spending exceeded the limit in any of the three domains, the excess had to come out of the next year's funds for that domain. Moreover, if members wanted to increase spending on a particular program, the BEA required them to find a way to pay for the new spending, either by raising taxes or by taking the money from another part of the same budget domain. (So-called *firewalls* barred members for three years from cutting funds in one budget domain to spend more in another.) Finally, the BEA required that any revenue beyond that projected had to be applied to bring down the deficit, and it required Congress to use better revenue and spending projections when setting the budget.

The BEA was projected to reduce budget deficits by some $490 billion over its five-year life span. But that meant only that the debt would be $490 billion less than it would have been without the BEA. Deficits (and an ever larger debt) would remain. As table 16.1 shows, the BEA set budget deficit targets that were much higher (and more realistic) than the Gramm-Rudman targets. Moreover, President Clinton's first budget raised taxes on the wealthy and cut some government spending. Even with the BEA's stringent provisions and Clinton's budgetary changes, the country still ran large deficits.

A Balanced Budget by 2002?

Perhaps the most prominent proposal on the legislative agenda that congressional Republicans put forth in 1995 and 1996 was legislation to balance the federal budget by 2002. With cohesive majorities in both Houses—powered in large part by a sizable group of first-year members devoted to balancing the budget—congressional Republicans were well-positioned to push through their proposals. And with the 1994 election results and the promises in the Contract With America, Republicans could (and did) claim to have a mandate from the American people to balance the budget.

But devising a detailed budget plan their own members could agree on proved a daunting task for Republican congressional leaders. For one thing, balancing the budget without raising income taxes or payroll taxes requires substantial cuts in federal spending. Early in the budget process, House Majority Leader Dick Armey (R-Tex.) predicted, "Once members of Congress know exactly, chapter and verse, the pain that the government must live with in order to get to a balanced budget, their knees will buckle."[68] And once congressional Republicans announced their complete budgetary package, one first-term member commented, "If we had come out with this [detailed plan] as our Contract [With America], they [the public] wouldn't have voted us in."[69]

Republican efforts to balance the budget were further hampered by another of their campaign promises: a pledge to cut taxes. Most economists believe that tax cuts will reduce the amount of revenue the government takes in—although a few argue that cutting taxes so stimulates the economy that more tax revenues are generated despite the lower rates. Because congressional Republicans were committed to cutting taxes, they had to find even more money to cut from the federal budget than they would have had to otherwise. But despite having to overcome many obstacles, including the very

The People Behind the Rules

BOX 16.2

Estimating the Numbers: June E. O Neill, Alice Rivlin, and the 1996 Budget Battle

During the great battle over the 1996 federal budget, the Republican majority in Congress kept pushing President Bill Clinton to propose a plan that would lead to a balanced budget in seven years. President Clinton claimed several times during the summer and fall of 1995 that he had done so, but the Republicans disputed his claim. They argued that the president's proposals would produce red ink for as far into the future as the eye could see. How could the president and congressional Republicans look at the same plans and arrive at such remarkably different forecasts of what they would do?

The answer lay in the numbers each side used to forecast how the economy would perform. The Republicans relied on pessimistic estimates the Congressional Budget Office (CBO) produced, while the president used more favorable appraisals his Office of Management and Budget (OMB) supplied. The CBO and OMB offered slightly different forecasts of the economic future, differences that translated into substantially different estimates of federal revenue and spending over the next seven years. In the end, President Clinton agreed to produce his budget plan using CBO numbers, but only after the CBO had consulted with the OMB experts and possibly revised its expectations upwards.

The politicians' maneuverings pushed the heads of the CBO and OMB to the forefront of the nation's most important policy debate in a generation. Who were these people whose economic projections would determine how the government would tackle the deficit?

June E. O'Neill

June E. O Neill

June E. O'Neill is a former economics professor at Bernard Baruch College in New York. She first gained experience in Washington working on the staff at CBO and then on the staff of the Council of Economic Advisers under Presidents Nixon and Ford. She was appointed director of the CBO in 1995 at the behest of Rep. John Kasich (R-Ohio), the new chair of the House Budget Committee and a leading Republican expert on the budget. Once in office, O'Neill took a step that reaffirmed her office's cherished reputation for independence—she announced that a Republican proposal

Continued

real concern that many voters might not like the cuts, the Republicans eventually produced a massive bill that proposed to balance the federal budget over seven years. The bill cut spending for many domestic programs, kept defense spending at about the same level, and still provided some $245 billion in tax cuts.

President Clinton vetoed the Republican budget plan. But, as box 16.2 discusses, after months of resisting the idea, he developed his own plan for balancing the federal budget over seven years. Clinton's proposal differed from the Republican proposal in key respects, and with Republicans controlling both houses of Congress, Clinton's plan had little chance of passing. As a result, the battle over the 1996 budget dragged on far into the fiscal year, with no agreement reached on the details of a seven-year plan. But as Congress passed individual appropriations bills and the president signed them, it imposed some substantial budget reductions. For example, federal spending on transportation in 1996 was set at $12.5 billion, an 8.9 percent reduction from the previous year. Thus, for the first time in recent history, many federal programs had to make do with less money than they did the year before.[70] And President Clinton's proposed budget

The People Behind the Rules

BOX 16.2 CONTINUED

to reform Medicare would save the federal government far less than the plan's supporters claimed. O'Neill's conclusion threw a monkey wrench into the Republican drive to produce a balanced budget, and it left Representative Kasich, who a few months before had said O'Neill was "highly qualified" for the top post at CBO, complaining that she and her staff had a "very stupid way of doing things." But O'Neill defended her office's work, noting, "everyone is annoyed with us at some time or another," and she helped ensure that members of both parties would accept OMB's word as authoritative.

Alice Rivlin

Alice Rivlin

In 1994, President Clinton selected Alice Rivlin to be the new Director of the OMB. Like O'Neill, Rivlin was an expert on the federal budget. She earned her doctorate in economics from Radcliffe in 1958, and for many years she was affiliated with the Brookings Institution, a Washington think tank. She served as the first director of the CBO, and she is credited with establishing its reputation for nonpartisan expertise. (One of the staffers who worked under her at the CBO was O'Neill.) The OMB that Rivlin took over in 1994 had long since shed its reputation for neutral competence in favor of advocating the president's programs. As one of the president's main advisers on budget matters, the OMB director now has a very high public profile. But because Rivlin had such a high political profile, she found it hard to convince Republicans that OMB's economic forecasts were accurate. (In 1996, President Clinton nominated and the Senate confirmed Rivlin as Vice-Chair of the Federal Reserve Board, a prestigious and important institution that chapter 17 discusses at greater length. Her successor at the OMB was investment banker Franklin D. Raines, the first African American to be OMB director.)

The budget is now the single most important policy decision facing the president and Congress, and the directors of CBO and OMB have become important and high-profile actors in the process. The economic forecasts they make determine how we judge competing budget plans.

Sources: George Hager, "Rivlin Brings Independent Streak to Director's Chair at OMB," *Congressional Quarterly Weekly Report,* 2 July 1994, p. 1770; Eric Pianin "We Have Seen the Enemy and . . . ," *Washington Post National Weekly Edition,* 11–17 September 1995, p. 32; Ronald G. Shafer, "Washington Wire," *Wall Street Journal,* 2 August 1996; David Wessel, "Art of Tweaking: White House's Altered Forecast on Economy Underlies Capitol Hill Budget Duel," *Wall Street Journal,* 3 November 1995.

for fiscal year 1997, which he unveiled in February 1996, forecasted a surplus by 2002 by proposing to spend less money than previously planned on Medicare, Medicaid, and welfare and by making significant cuts in discretionary programs. This plan was a dramatic shift from the budget he had proposed one year earlier, and it represented at least a moral victory for the Republican majority in Congress.[71]

The fight in 1995 and 1996 over balancing the budget in seven years not only forced significant cuts in some programs and reduced the rate of growth for many others, it changed the nature of the policy debate in Washington. Indeed, Republicans even took the risk of starting a discussion on entitlement reform, focusing on Medicare, Medicaid, and welfare, as we discuss further in chapter 17. (The presidential Bipartisan Commission on Entitlement and Tax Reform, chaired by Sen. Robert Kerrey (D-Neb.), tried to open the debate when it issued its report after the 1994 election, but its pleas about the exploding costs of the Social Security system mostly fell on deaf ears.)[72] But, although both President Clinton and the Republicans in Congress made difficult decisions by proposing substantial cuts in politically popular programs over seven years, neither plan would solve the nation's long-term budget problems. Unless entitlement reform far surpasses what the Republicans proposed in 1995 and 1996—when they offered changes to Medicare, Medicaid, and welfare, but not Social Security, the largest category in the budget—deficits will increase dramatically after 2002 as the baby boom generation retires and begins collecting benefits.[73]

More Reforms?

Many different budgetary reforms have been suggested over the past two hundred years. Two much-discussed rule changes are the proposal to give the president a line-item veto and the proposal to amend the Constitution to require Congress to balance the budget. Both these proposals seek to make it more likely that the federal government will balance its budget each year. Other budget reform proposals seek to change the way the federal government raises revenue. Most prominent among these is the flat tax, which would dramatically restructure the current system for taxing income.

The Line-Item Veto

Line-item veto
The ability of the executive to delete or veto some provisions of a bill, while allowing the rest of the bill to become law.

Every president since Jimmy Carter has asked for a **line-item veto.** (The notion goes back to the 1870s, when President Grant called for such a veto.)[74] The Constitution states that presidents can veto only entire bills. If a bill they favor comes with provisions they dislike, they must decide whether it is better to sign a bill with some flaws or no bill at all. With a line-item veto, presidents would have the authority to veto provisions they dislike while still accepting the bill. As Presidents Carter, Reagan, and Clinton—all former governors—noted, the line-item veto is common in state government; forty-three states give their governor a line-item veto.

Supporters argue that the line-item veto would enable the president to eliminate pork-barrel spending. Although this sounds sensible, the line-item veto comes with several flaws. To start with, as we have discussed, what constitutes pork lies in the eye of the beholder. Members of Congress (and their constituents) might disagree vehemently with the president about which programs are wasteful. Indeed, as we pointed out in chapter 15, the experience of state government suggests that governors use their line-item vetoes to shape spending to their policy preferences as much as to reduce spending.[75] Members also fear that a president might use the threat of a line-item veto to coerce them into supporting other policy proposals the White House favors. For example, a president might threaten to eliminate funds for highway construction in Texas as a way to pressure the Texas congressional delegation into supporting a White House proposal to reform the health care system.

Disagreement over what constitutes wasteful spending and fears of enhancing presidential power make it highly unlikely that Congress will pass a true line-item veto, since doing so would require it to propose a constitutional amendment. Because proponents of the line-item veto know they don't have the votes they need to propose an amendment, they have instead offered a variety of bills that seek to create the functional equivalent of a line-item veto through ordinary legislation. (Although these bills would not create a true line-item veto, they are routinely if somewhat inaccurately referred to as line-item veto bills, a practice we adopt here. The differences between a true line-item veto and its legislative substitutes are complex and need not detain us here.) In 1995, House and Senate Republicans passed very different (and incompatible) versions of the line-item veto.[76] A year later, however, at the behest of the Republican presidential nominee, then-Sen. Robert Dole (R-Kans.), House and Senate Republicans agreed on a line-item veto bill, which Congress passed and President Clinton signed into law.

The new line-item veto, technically known as enhanced rescission, went into effect on January 1, 1997. The law authorizes the president to veto spending on specific items mentioned in an appropriations bill or in the congressional report that accompanies each appropriations bill. The law also authorizes the president to veto any tax break that benefits fewer than one hundred taxpayers. But the president's line-item veto power applies only to dollar figures. The law does not allow a president to strike legislative prescriptions, language Congress inserts in appropriations bills directing the executive branch how to spend the appropriations. (Some states give their governors such authority.) Thus, if Congress directs the government to spend $10 million on AIDS research, the president cannot ignore the directive and spend the money on something else. The president's only options are to approve the line-item spending figure or veto it. When the president does veto a line item, Congress can pass a free-standing bill reinstating the spending. But the president can then exercise a constitutional veto, thereby requiring Congress to muster a two-thirds vote in both the House and Senate before the spending is reinstated.[77]

Supporters of the line-item veto argue that presidents will use it to strike wasteful government spending. Critics, however, argue that the law shifts too much power to the White House. Senator Byrd, a staunch supporter of congressional prerogatives, denounced the line-item veto as a plan that "James Madison and the framers would abhor."[78] In an unusual move, the Judicial Conference of the United States, the organization that represents federal judges, denounced the line-item veto as a threat to judicial independence because presidents could use it to punish judges or courts that make unpopular decisions. Moreover, the *threat* of a veto might influence how judges or courts decide cases.[79] While the Judicial Conference did not comment on the constitutionality of the law, many legal scholars say it violates Article 1, section 7 of the Constitution, which authorizes the president to veto whole bills but not parts of bills.

Even if the line-item veto passes constitutional muster, several factors are likely to limit its effectiveness in fighting deficit spending.[80] First, contrary to what many people believe, the appropriations bills that emerge from Congress do not list each individual expenditure. Much of the legally binding budget consists of general lump sums, while most allocations for specific projects are made in congressional reports, which are not legally binding. Even before the new line-item veto law, presidents were free to ignore these non-binding directions, but they and the agencies they oversee were usually loath to ignore them and make Congress angry.[81] Second, most of the federal budget is exempt from the line-item veto. Although the law gives the president authority to strike new benefits for entitlement programs such as Social Security and Medicare, it denies the president authority to strike existing benefits. Likewise, the line-item veto does not apply to interest on the national debt. Because entitlement spending and interest on the national debt constitute nearly two-thirds of federal spending, the line-item veto authority applies to only one-third of the budget. Third, because an ordinary statute rather than the Constitution authorizes the president to veto individual line items, Congress can suspend that authority whenever it wishes. For example, if Congress wants to spend more on defense and the president less, legislators can simply insert a provision in the defense appropriations bill stating that the line-item veto authority does not apply to the bill or to particular provisions within it.

The new line-item veto might even have the perverse effect of *promoting* deficit spending because it encourages members of Congress to be less responsible. With a line-item veto in place, members might choose to fund all the programs their constituents want and let the president take the political heat for vetoing popular projects. Indeed, on the same day the House of Representatives approved the line-item veto legislation, it voted to increase the amount of money the elderly can earn each year without having their Social Security benefits reduced. That single change would cost the federal government roughly $10 billion per year.[82]

The new line-item veto power may also change the dynamics of executive-legislative relations. As chapter 15 discusses, governors use the threat of a line-item veto less to cut spending and more to whip state legislators into line behind their spending priorities. As Rep. Nick Smith (R-Mich.) noted during debate over the line-item veto legislation, "I served under three governors while in the state legislature. Every one of these governors, liberal and conservative, used the leverage of the line-item veto to get the spending they wanted."[83] Much the same may happen in Washington. Yet fears that presidents will use the line-item veto to run roughshod over

Proposed constitutional amendments to require the federal government to balance its budget delay the requirement for balancing the budget for several years. As a result, legislators who support the amendment can reap an immediate political benefit, leaving others to make the tough choices needed to balance the budget in the future.

Reprinted by permission: Tribune Media Services.

Congress are overblown. Not only does Congress retain the authority to suspend the president's authority to veto line items, the legislation itself contains a sunset clause. Presidential authority to exercise a line-item veto will lapse in 2005 unless Congress votes to extend it. If presidents abuse the line-item veto, Congress undoubtedly will refuse to renew the power.

Balanced Budget Amendments

Various constitutional amendments have been offered to require Congress and the president to balance the budget. One almost passed in 1995, falling just one vote short in the Senate. (The final tally shows a two-vote deficit because Senator Dole changed his vote to no at the last minute, thereby protecting his parliamentary right as Senate majority leader to bring the amendment up again for another vote later in the session. Shortly before leaving the Senate in 1996 to concentrate on his presidential campaign, Dole forced another vote on the amendment, and it again failed.) A problem with all such measures is that they do not specify how to balance the budget. Moreover, a budget that runs deficits measured in the hundreds of billions of dollars cannot be cut quickly without wreaking havoc on the American economy and society. As a result, most balanced budget amendments delay the requirement for balancing the budget until some time in the future. Finally, it is unlikely that a balanced budget amendment would prevent budget deficits, or that it could even be enforced.[84] Many states that have constitutional provisions requiring a balanced budget still have managed to build their own debts.

Despite the practical problems with a balanced budget amendment, it has great popular appeal. After all, it sounds sensible to require the government to live within its means. But the rub comes in deciding *how* to balance the budget. Indeed, public support for a balanced budget amendment fades when people are confronted with its possible consequences. For example, one survey found that 68 percent of those polled supported the idea of a balanced budget amendment in the abstract. When they were then told that balancing the federal budget would require cuts in Medicare, Medicaid, and veterans benefits, support for the balanced budget amendment fell to 33 percent.[85]

The initial popularity of a balanced budget amendment with the average voter explains its continued popularity with many members of Congress. Politicians who support the balanced budget amendment can reap an immediate political benefit, leaving the hard choices needed to balance the budget to future years.

The Flat Tax

Americans don't like to pay taxes. In 1961, 46 percent of Americans thought their federal income taxes were too high, a figure that reached 66 percent in 1994.[86] When survey researchers asked people in 1995 what percentage of its income a family of four should have to pay in taxes, they found a remarkable consensus. Every group—rich and poor, white and African American, conservative and liberal—arrived at the same figure: 25 percent. In comparison, under the present tax code, the typical family of four pays 39 percent of its income in taxes.[87] So proposals to cut taxes have considerable popular appeal.

One plan to cut taxes would enact a **flat tax,** which would replace the current progressive tax system with one in which everyone would pay the same percentage on their taxable income. Flat tax plans have been around for many years; for example, Nobel Prize-winning economist Milton Friedman floated the idea in 1962.[88] In recent years, several members of Congress, including House Majority Leader Dick Armey, have introduced legislation to create a flat tax. But the idea of a flat tax did not inspire much public debate until 1996, when Malcolm S. "Steve" Forbes, Jr., made the idea the centerpiece of his unsuccessful bid to win the Republican nomination for president. (Surprisingly little notice is given to the fact that seven states have a flat tax on income; whether the flat tax promotes more rapid economic growth in those states is a matter of debate.)[89]

Flat tax
Any income tax system in which taxable income is taxed at the same percentage rate regardless of the taxpayer's income.

Although all flat tax plans propose to tax income at a single rate, they differ in setting what the tax rate will be, determining what kinds of income are exempt from taxes, and establishing which expenses are deductible when calculating taxable income. For example, the Forbes plan would have established a 17 percent rate on wages, but it would have made all income from dividends, interest, and capital gains exempt from taxes. (Capital gains are profits from the sale of assets such as stocks, bonds, and real estate.) The Forbes plan would also have made each person's first $13,000 in income, or $26,000 for a married couple, exempt from taxes, and give families a $5,000 deduction for each child. Thus, under the Forbes plan, a couple with two children would have paid no taxes on their first $36,000 in income. (Under the current income tax system, a typical family of four pays $3,000 in federal income taxes.)[90] In practice, then, the Forbes flat tax would effectively have created two rates, zero for people who earn less than the exempted amount, and 17 percent on income over the exempted amount for everyone else.[91]

The details of any flat tax proposal are critical because they determine how much money the federal government will raise in revenue. As the tax rate falls and as exemptions become more liberal, the federal government takes in less revenue. To avoid making the federal budget deficit larger, many people argue that any new tax system should be **revenue neutral;** that is, it should neither increase nor decrease government revenue from current levels. By this standard, the Forbes flat tax proposal fails to pass muster. According to most independent analyses, the Forbes plan would have lowered federal revenues by more than $100 billion, precisely because it would cut almost everyone's tax bill. The result would be a sharp jump in the size of the federal deficit, unless Congress and the president agreed to make offsetting cuts in federal spending. To make the Forbes flat tax plan revenue neutral, the tax rate would have to increase from an attractive 17 percent to more than 20 percent. Yet raising the tax rate that high would mean that the taxes of many middle-class Americans would go *up,* not down.[92]

Revenue neutral
A quality of any tax reform plan that will neither increase nor decrease government revenue.

Although the prospect of a smaller tax bill is one reason for the appeal of the flat tax, another is its simplicity. (The U.S. tax code has become incredibly complex over time. In 1913, the tax code filled a single four-hundred-page volume. Now it takes 40,500 pages in twenty-two volumes![93] And at 7 million words, the tax code is nearly ten times longer than the Bible.)[94] Because a flat tax would eliminate the vast majority of exemptions and deductions in the present tax code, supporters claim it will enable most taxpayers to file their income tax returns on a postcard. Not surprisingly, many people find the prospect of a greatly simplified tax appealing. Indeed, during his unsuccessful 1996 presidential campaign, Steve Forbes got his biggest applause when he promised that his flat tax proposal would kill the present tax code, "drive a stake through its heart," and bury it.[95] As a practical matter, however, the switch to a flat tax would not change the tax filing process for most people. Roughly 70 percent of Americans currently do not use the exemptions in the tax code; hence, they already file their taxes on a one- or two-page form.[96]

The appeal of the flat tax diminished somewhat during the battle over the 1996 Republican presidential nomination. To stop Steve Forbes's surge in the public opinion polls, his Republican opponents pointed out that the two greatest strengths of his flat tax proposal—lower tax bills and simplified tax returns—were also its two biggest weaknesses. Not only would a 17 percent flat tax in all likelihood increase the size of the federal deficit, but simplifying tax returns means forcing Americans to give up cherished tax breaks such as the home mortgage interest deduction. After the national media had discussed the idea of a flat tax for several months, polls found that a majority of Americans preferred a progressive tax rate over a flat tax system. Only the wealthiest Americans gave the flat tax much support, a finding in keeping with analyses that suggest they would benefit the most from such plans.[97]

Is the Budget Process Irrational?

A budget of more than $1.6 trillion is almost beyond comprehension. It is hard to fathom how to devise a rational way to budget such a large amount of money. Even if we could all agree on what constitutes worthwhile spending, just imagine how difficult it would be to ensure that the government spent every one of those $1.6 trillion wisely. The federal government has tried to allot small chunks of the budget using innovative techniques such as program-planning budgeting, management by objective, and zero-based budgeting, each of which requires agencies to justify funding for all of their programs. But each of these budgeting techniques failed, in large part because they overwhelmed the bureaucracy and Congress with work. No one had the time and expertise to conduct complete budgetary reviews on an annual basis.[98]

In general, although budgets almost always grow, they usually change only slightly from year to year. That is, the best predictor of how money will be spent in this year's budget is how it was spent in last year's budget. Although there may be a few significant shifts in spending, in a budget the size of the federal government's, adding a few billion for this program or taking a few billion from that program really makes changes only at the margins. Some people argue that such incremental budgeting is rational.[99] It simplifies budgeting decisions by focusing attention on a few programs, usually those that arouse some political controversy. But incremental budgeting also means that most spending continues on autopilot, with little or no evaluation of whether the money is being spent wisely.

In the end, budgeting is fundamentally a political, not a mechanical, process. Like all governments, the federal government makes budgetary decisions in response to political demands and to meet political realities. When deficits occur, as they have repeatedly over the past three decades, the reason is not irrational budgetary rules, but elected officials responding to constituent demands. Until Congress and the president reach a consensus on spending priorities and then summon the will to make politically difficult choices, budget deficits will persist.

Summary

Federal spending has grown enormously since George Washington was president. The federal government now spends more than $1.6 trillion every year. But the growth in spending has outpaced the growth of revenue. As a result, the federal government regularly runs budget deficits exceeding $100 billion. These massive deficits have led to a rapid increase in the size of the national debt. In 1997, the national debt was more than four times greater than it was only fifteen years earlier.

Reducing the size of the budget deficit will require the federal government to increase revenue, decrease spending, or both. The sources of government revenue have changed greatly over the past one hundred years. In 1900, the federal government got almost all of its revenue from customs duties on imported goods and excise taxes on tobacco and alcohol. In contrast, in 1995, more than 80 percent of government revenue came from the income and payroll taxes individual Americans paid.

Government spending patterns have also changed dramatically over the past one hundred years, and especially over the past sixty. In 1940, nearly two-thirds of government spending went to programs we normally associate with government, such as road construction, medical research, national parks, and so forth; only 20 percent went to entitlement programs that made direct payments to individuals. In 1995, the numbers were almost exactly the reverse. The expansion of entitlement programs such as Social Security, Medicare, unemployment insurance, and the Food Stamp program has greatly complicated the task of balancing the budget. Not only are most entitlement programs very popular, which discourages members of Congress from trying to cut benefits, but entitlements by their very nature cannot be controlled through the budgetary process. Reducing entitlement benefits requires Congress to rewrite the laws that created the programs in the first place.

Responsibility for the federal government's chronic budget deficit falls at the doorsteps of both Congress and the president. But responsibility also rests with the American public. When Congress and the president assemble budgets in which spending exceeds revenue, they are responding to the public's demand for more government services and lower taxes. Congress has passed several budgetary reforms designed to stem the flow of red ink, but none have succeeded. Budget deficits are the result of political decisions, not flawed budgetary processes. The federal government will not begin to balance its budget until Congress and the president win public support to make tough budgetary choices.

Key Terms

Balanced budget
Budget and Accounting Act of 1921
Budget deficit
Budget surplus
Congressional Budget and Impoundment Control Act of 1974
Congressional Budget Office (CBO)
Continuing resolutions
Corporate welfare
Cost-of-living adjustment (COLA)
Discretionary spending
Entitlement programs
Flat tax
Line-item veto
National debt
Non-discretionary spending
Office of Management and Budget (OMB)
Pork barrel
Progressive tax
Regressive tax
Revenue neutral
Social Security Act of 1935

Readings for Further Study

Gilmour, John B. *Reconcilable Differences.* Berkeley: University of California Press, 1990. An analysis of how Congress dealt with budget deficits from the 1960s through the 1980s that explains why the process changed and where it succeeded and failed.

Mackenzie, G. Calvin, and Saranna Thornton. *Bucking the Deficit: Economic Policymaking in America.* Boulder, Colo.: Westview, 1996. A political scientist and an economist provide an introductory yet comprehensive examination of the federal government and economic policymaking.

Penny, Timothy J., and Steven E. Schier. *Payment Due: A Nation in Debt, A Generation in Trouble.* Boulder, Colo.: Westview, 1996. A former member of Congress and a professor of political science examine the problems the federal debt will cause for upcoming generations.

Peterson, Peter G. *Facing Up: How to Rescue the Economy from Crushing Debt and Restore the American Dream.* New York: Simon & Schuster, 1993. A former secretary of commerce under President Nixon writes about the problems the national debt creates. He also offers a number of tough approaches to cutting the budget.

Savage, James D. *Balanced Budgets and American Politics.* Ithaca, N.Y.: Cornell University Press, 1988. An examination of balanced budgets and the changing arguments for and against them from colonial times to the Reagan years.

Stockman, David. *The Triumph of Politics: How the Reagan Revolution Failed.* New York: Harper & Row, 1986. An inside account of the budgetary politics of the early Reagan years written by President Reagan's former director of the Office of Management and Budget (OMB).

White, Joseph, and Aaron B. Wildavsky. *The Deficit and the Public Interest.* Berkeley: University of California Press, 1989. A detailed analysis of the politics of budget deficits that looks at the problem from a variety of perspectives.

Wildavsky, Aaron B. *The New Politics of the Budgetary Process,* 2d ed. New York: HarperCollins, 1992. A revised version of a classic book on the budgetary machinations of bureaucrats and members of Congress.

CHAPTER

17

DOMESTIC POLICY

Managing the Economy

From Government Restraint to Government Intervention

Managing the Economy by Taxing and Spending

Managing the Economy by Controlling the Money Supply

Can the Government Manage the Economy?

The Current Status of Economic Stewardship

Regulating Business

Basic Concepts and Categories

The Objectives of Economic Regulation

The Evolution of Economic Regulation

Social Regulation

Protecting Worker Safety and Health

Protecting the Environment

Promoting Social Welfare

Basic Concepts and Categories

The Evolution of Social Welfare Policy

The Current Status of Social Welfare Policy

The Future of Social Welfare Policy

Summary

Key Terms

Readings for Further Study

In the 1964 State of the Union address, President Lyndon Johnson declared "unconditional war on poverty in America." He pledged that the federal government would do what it could to create "better schools and better health and better homes and better training and better job opportunities."[1] Johnson's vision of a vigorous, "can do" federal government that would create the Great Society by promoting the public interest soon carried the day. Over the course of the 1960s, first under Johnson and then under his Republican successor, Richard Nixon, Congress passed legislation creating an array of programs that committed the federal government to fight poverty, provide medical care for the elderly and the poor, eliminate hazardous working conditions, prevent hazardous products from reaching the marketplace, protect the environment, and end discrimination in the workplace.

Three decades later, much of the enthusiasm for an activist federal role in domestic policy has vanished. Republicans are especially critical of the federal government's failings. They charge that President Johnson's War on Poverty has been "an unqualified failure" that has cost the country "trillions of dollars" and has had the "unintended consequence of snaring millions of Americans into the welfare trap."[2] Republicans claim that excessive intervention in the private sector has turned the federal government into "the problem rather than the solution" and that it is time to get "Washington off our backs."[3] Yet Republicans are not alone in their criticisms. Many of Lyndon Johnson's fellow Democrats are reluctant to defend his vision of a federal government with expansive domestic policy responsibilities. Indeed, in 1996, President Bill Clinton declared in his State of the Union speech that "the era of big government is over."[4]

The changing attitudes toward the War on Poverty and the Great Society programs illustrate how conflict continually arises and evolves over how active a role government should take in responding to domestic problems. Throughout the nineteenth century, the federal government played a very limited role in domestic policy. In the twentieth century, however, the federal government took on new responsibilities for managing the economy, regulating the practices of private businesses, and providing a social safety net for the American people. Thus, as the views of Congress and the president toward the proper role of the federal government change, the rules of domestic policy change to either limit or expand the federal government's ability to intervene directly in domestic concerns. These changes in the rules create different winners and losers in the conflict.

In this chapter, we examine the federal government's changing role in American life. We look at three broad tasks the federal government has assumed in domestic policy—managing the economy, regulating the practices of private business, and promoting social welfare. We begin by sketching out the growth of the government's tools for managing the economy, and then we assess the success of current efforts to guide the nation's economy toward a stable, prosperous future. In the second section, we first discuss the development and consequences of the federal government's efforts to regulate the competitive practices of business. We then review social regulation, analyzing in particular worker safety and health regulations and environmental regulations. In the third section, we discuss the historical development and current status of social welfare policy in the United States. We conclude our discussion of social welfare policy by reviewing the core issues in the debates over Social Security, welfare reform, and health care.

In all three of these areas—economic policy, regulatory policy, and social welfare policy—the rules change as the needs and views of the American public and their elected representatives change. And in domestic policy, as in all areas of government, changes in the rules of politics cause some groups to gain and others to lose. Which is preferable: a smaller, more limited federal government, or a larger one with more expansive responsibilities? The controversy rages on.

Managing the Economy

Most Americans now expect the federal government to manage the overall health of the national economy. They count on the government to promote the creation of new jobs,

In 1965, President Lyndon Johnson signed the legislation establishing Medicare, a key Great Society program, as former president Harry Truman, who had first proposed such a program in the late 1940s, looked on.

to keep inflation and interest rates low and stable, and to ensure that the economy grows at a steady rate. Yet while the idea that the federal government should manage the economy seems natural to us today, it is a relatively recent phenomenon. Indeed, at the beginning of the twentieth century, most people believed that the federal government should have no role in managing the economy. Thus, to understand the federal government's current role in managing the economy, we need to review how the government's role in economic management has changed over the course of the century as well as to discuss what tools the government has today to manage the nation's economy.

From Government Restraint to Government Intervention

At the opening of the twentieth century, the dominant economic wisdom was what we know today as *classical economics.* A fundamental principle of classical economics was that government should follow a **laissez faire** approach to the national economy. Taken from the French expression "let it be," laissez faire held that the government's only role in the economy was to ensure a stable supply of money; other than that, the government should leave the success or failure of private businesses up to the forces of the free market. This let-it-be approach to the economy applied even when economic growth faltered and unemployment rose. During economic hard times, classical economics held, the government should avoid intervening in the economy and simply allow the business cycle to run its course.

Laissez faire
An economic theory, dominant at the start of the twentieth century, that argued that the federal government's only role in the economy was to ensure a stable supply of money.

The last president associated with laissez faire economic policies was Herbert Hoover, who was elected in 1928. During Hoover's first year in office, the stock market crashed and the Great Depression began. Although he wanted the government to take a more activist role in leading the country out of its economic slump, Hoover lacked the popular and political support needed to institute major changes in how the government managed the economy. As a result, much of his administration's work was limited to assuring Americans that better days were just around the corner and urging them to help those in need. Hoover's let-it-be approach failed to solve the country's economic problems, and the economic picture worsened. Not surprisingly, Hoover lost the 1932 presidential race to his Democratic rival, Franklin Delano Roosevelt, and Hoover found himself labeled (somewhat misleadingly) by later generations of Americans as a president who believed strongly in a laissez faire approach to business and society.[5]

When Roosevelt began his first term as president in 1933, he faced a daunting challenge. The Great Depression had led to the collapse of thousands upon thousands of banks, farms, and businesses, and unemployment soared to 25 percent. Yet Roosevelt had something that Hoover had lacked, namely, the political support he needed to carve out a more activist role for the federal government. As a result, Roosevelt responded to the country's economic hardship by initiating a series of programs, known collectively as the New Deal, that sought to get the country back on its economic feet by expanding the federal government's power over the economy.[6] Ironically, many of these programs had their roots in proposals that the Hoover administration had originally developed.[7]

Roosevelt's New Deal programs slowly began to work. Unemployment edged down from 25 percent in 1933 to 14 percent in 1937. When the economy suddenly began to falter and unemployment shot up again in 1938, however, Roosevelt took a new approach to the country's economic problems.

The approach Roosevelt adopted in 1938 was based on the idea that government spending can be used to rejuvenate the economy—in short, if the government spends more money, and even if it goes into debt to do so, the extra money will help get private businesses going again and put people back to work. Accordingly, Roosevelt changed the rules. He persuaded Congress to put aside its traditional commitment to a balanced budget—even though he had endorsed the idea of balancing the budget during his first presidential campaign in 1932—and to launch an ambitious program of increased government spending. The federal government's deficit grew, but the hope was that the nation could spend its way out of the Depression. Although the United States never fully pulled out of the Depression until World War II—when deficit spending reached truly massive heights, as chapter 16 shows—Roosevelt established the federal government's role as manager of the economy and convinced American policy makers that they could use **fiscal policy**—that is, government taxing and spending decisions—as a management tool.[8]

Fiscal policy
Using the federal government's control over taxes and spending to influence the condition of the national economy.

Managing the Economy by Taxing and Spending

Franklin Roosevelt's decision to use fiscal policy to combat the Great Depression was inspired by the work of John Maynard Keynes, a British economist whose work revolutionized how governments attempt to manage their economies. In his seminal book, *The General Theory of Employment, Interest, and Money,* published in 1936, Keynes argued that capitalist economies do not always run at full throttle.[9] Instead, they experience periods of recession, or economic slowdown, and periods of growth. During recessions, both the supply of goods and services business produces and the demand for goods and services to purchase fall. Because businesses cannot sell their goods, they fire workers and produce fewer goods. Because fewer people have jobs, less money is available to buy goods. In the resulting cycle, unemployment rises and the country's **gross domestic product (GDP),** or overall economic output, falls.

Gross domestic product (GDP)
A measure of a country's total economic output in any given year.

Keynes believed that government can manage the economy and push it out of recession by employing certain policies—in effect, by changing the rules of fiscal policy according to the situation. To push a country out of recession, Keynes argued, a government should spend enough money to raise demand for goods and services, even if it must borrow money and run a budget deficit. This, in turn, would cause businesses to hire more people, which would give the new workers salaries to push demand up even further. In other words, Keynes said that deficit spending—spending more than the government is taking in—could pull nations out of recessions.

The other side of Keynes's theory was that the economy could run too fast. Businesses, seeking to expand production, could seek new workers by paying them more, thus bidding up the prices of workers and causing inflation. Similarly, consumers, seeking to purchase more goods than were available, could drive inflation by offering to pay more for goods. Eventually, prices might spiral so high that people could no longer afford basic goods; the economy might then nose-dive into a recession as people quit spending and businesses lose money and have to lay off workers. To prevent the economy from growing too rapidly and thereby creating unacceptable levels of inflation, Keynes argued that the government should cut its spending or raise taxes to soak up the excess demand and slow the economy down to a more stable level. That is, the government could use budget surpluses—taking in more tax revenues than it spends—to keep inflation in check.

Thus, in Keynes's view, the main tool for managing the national economy is simply the amount of the federal government's surplus or deficit spending: the decision to raise more in revenue than it spends (a surplus) or spend more money than it raises (a deficit). Keynes's theory, known as **Keynesian economics,** did not specify what governments should spend their money on or what taxes should be raised or cut; it only specified the overall amounts of deficit or surplus spending. Later work by Keynes and other economists refined and expanded upon his original idea by identifying factors that influence the health of the economy. Nonetheless, for Keynesians, the main tool for managing the national economy remains the size of the budget deficit or surplus.

Keynesian economics
An economic theory, based on the work of British economist John Maynard Keynes, that contends that the national government can manage the economy by running budget surpluses and budget deficits.

By the end of World War II, Keynes's activist approach to government management of the economy was firmly rooted in American politics. When Congress passed the Employment Act of 1946, it officially declared that the federal government was responsible for assuring full employment, stable prices, and a strong economy.

John Maynard Keynes revolutionized economics by arguing that governments can use fiscal policy to manage their national economies.

Although Keynesian economics gained wide acceptance among economists and politicians, it had a critical weakness. Slowing down an overheated economy by raising taxes and cutting services might work in economic theory, but in practice, persuading Congress to take such actions is often politically difficult. Some government programs such as welfare, food stamps, and unemployment insurance are automatic, *countercyclical programs.* This means that when the economy slows down and unemployment rises, government spending on these programs automatically increases; when the economy speeds up and unemployment falls, government spending on these programs falls. But most efforts to slow the economy by cutting government spending or raising taxes require Congress to pass laws, which members of Congress find politically difficult. Once a "temporary" jobs program or a "temporary" business tax cut to boost the economy has done its work, advocates for the program defend it in Congress and the temporary program often becomes permanent. Thus, Keynes's advice to increase spending when the economy falters generally leads to bigger government and greater deficit spending because the corresponding spending cuts and tax increases are usually not enacted when the economy improves.

Managing the Economy by Controlling the Money Supply

Although Keynesian economics and a belief in the merits of fiscal policy guided the federal government's efforts to manage the national economy in the 1950s, 1960s, and 1970s, some economists argued that Keynes had fundamentally misunderstood how the economy works and, as a result, that his policy advice was misguided. These economists offered a competing economic theory that contends that changes in a nation's money supply—that is, in the amount of money in circulation—are the primary if not the sole determinant of its economic health. Because these economists emphasize the importance of the money supply, they are known as monetarists and their views as **monetary theory.**

Monetary theory
An economic theory that contends that a nation's money supply, or the amount of money in circulation, is the primary if not sole determinant of the health of the national economy.

Unlike Keynesian economic theory, monetary theory was not suddenly presented to the world by a single, brilliant economist. Instead, the roots of monetary theory are found in the nineteenth-century debates over what the federal government should do regarding the money supply and setting up a central bank. During the nineteenth century, the United States was on a gold standard, which meant that people holding paper currency had the right to convert their currency into gold on demand. Because the supply of gold was limited, the 1800s saw heated debates over how much money should be minted and what the government should do to stabilize the value of money and prevent currency crises.[10] By the late 1800s, periodic currency crises were seriously disrupting the country's economic growth. This led to calls for Congress to create a powerful central bank that could stabilize the country's money supply.

The Board of Governors of the Federal Reserve System sets the nation's monetary policy.

Federal Reserve System An independent regulatory commission that Congress created in 1913 to oversee the nation's money supply.

In 1913, Congress finally responded by establishing the **Federal Reserve System,** often referred to by its nickname, the Fed.[11] By law, the Fed is an independent regulatory commission, which as we saw in chapter 13 means that it operates with relatively little direct interference from either the rest of the executive branch or from Congress. The reason Congress made the Fed independent of the rest of government is simple: the sponsors of the law creating the Federal Reserve System wanted to limit the ability of elected officials to manipulate the economy for political gain.

The structure of the Fed has changed little since it was established. The Fed has four parts: (1) the Board of Governors; (2) the Federal Open Market Committee; (3) the twelve regional Federal Reserve Banks; and (4) the commercial banks that are members of the Federal Reserve System, including all national banks and any state-chartered banks that choose to join. The president appoints the chair and vice-chair of the Fed (with the consent of the Senate); the commercial banks that are members of the system elect the directors of the Federal Reserve Banks. Thus, some Federal Reserve officials are appointed by the president with the Senate's approval, and some are elected by private businesses.

By the 1960s, leading monetary theorists such as Milton Friedman had developed sophisticated economic models showing how the Federal Reserve's management of the money supply influences the economy.[12] Friedman and his colleagues argued that to keep the national economy growing at a healthy pace, the government should expand the money supply at a steady rate that matches the growth rate of the economy. If the money supply expands too quickly, the excess money will drive down interest rates, which will make it cheaper for businesses and individuals to borrow money, which will encourage faster growth, which will fuel inflation. If the money supply expands too slowly, the lack of money will drive up interest rates, which will make it more expensive for companies and individuals to borrow money, which will slow down the economy and possibly even force it into a recession. Indeed, some monetary theorists argue that the Fed's refusal in the late 1920s to expand the money supply—a strategy that monetary theorists call a tight money policy—helped cause the Great Depression.[13]

The Federal Reserve System controls the money supply that lies at the core of monetary theory in three main ways: (1) by setting the discount rate; (2) by deciding how many treasury securities to buy or sell; and (3) by changing the required reserve ratio. The *discount rate* is the interest rate the Fed charges its member banks when it lends them money. If the Fed wishes to reduce the money supply and slow down the economy, it can raise the discount rate, making it more expensive to borrow money. Similarly, if it wishes to increase the money supply, it can lower the discount rate. The Fed's Board of Governors is responsible for deciding where to peg the rate.

The second primary method the Fed uses to affect the country's money supply is buying and selling *treasury securities*, or government IOUs. When the Fed wishes to change the amount of money in circulation, it does not simply turn on or off the presses that print money. Instead, the Fed buys or sells treasury securities. When the Fed sells treasury securities, it takes money out of circulation and leaves the purchaser with a bond—a piece of paper promising to repay the purchaser principal plus interest over a set period of time, which may range from as short as three months to as long as thirty years. When the Fed buys treasury securities, it redeems bonds, or pays back its IOUs, and thereby puts more money into circulation. Thus, decisions about the sale of treasury securities can also affect the money supply and indirectly influence whether the economy speeds up or slows down. Decisions about buying and selling treasury securities are up to the Federal Open Market Committee, made up of the Board of Governors plus the five elected representatives of the Federal Reserve Banks.

The third method the Fed uses to affect the country's money supply is changing the *required reserve ratio*. By law, banks must hold a specified percentage of their deposits as required reserves, that is, money they cannot lend. When the Fed raises the required reserve ratio, banks must keep more of their deposits on hand; as a result, they have less money to lend, which reduces the money supply. Conversely, when the Fed lowers the reserve requirement, banks have more money to lend, which increases the money supply. Because changing the required reserve ratio can produce dramatic changes in the money supply and the economy, the Fed seldom uses this method.

Guiding the economy by controlling the money supply is extraordinarily complicated. Economists may agree about the general causes of economic prosperity, but they disagree about technical questions such as when to change the discount rate and how many treasury securities to buy or sell in any given month. The controls over the money supply are, after all, fairly crude. Moreover, virtually all economists recognize that in order to work, monetary policy must be coordinated with fiscal policy.[14] The money supply decisions the Fed makes and the budget decisions Congress and the president make both influence the economy in ways that interact with each other. No group can operate without considering the actions of the others.

Some observers liken the problem of guiding the economy with fiscal and monetary policy to steering an ocean liner. When the captain turns the rudder sharply to the right, it takes the ship a long time to change course. If the captain waits too long before turning the rudder back, the ship may continue turning to the right far longer than the captain wished.

In 1997, the captain of our monetary policy was Alan Greenspan, the chair of the Federal Reserve System. Greenspan was credited with being one of the best chairs in the Fed's history. From the time President Reagan first appointed him in 1987, Greenspan moved the national economy toward recovery and economic expansion while avoiding missteps that would have triggered escalating inflation.[15] Because Greenspan proved so adept (though by no means perfect) at managing the nation's money supply, President Clinton reappointed him in 1996 to a third four-year term.

Can the Government Manage the Economy?

Keynesian and monetarist theories have come under fire in recent years from economists who argue that the ability of the federal government to use fiscal and monetary policy to manage the economy is actually very limited. In the early 1970s, Robert Lucas of the University of Chicago began to examine a question that Keynesian and monetarist theories left unaddressed—namely, how do firms and individuals react to changes in government policy? Using sophisticated mathematical models, Lucas posited what became known as the **Lucas critique,** the argument that if people act rationally, then their reactions to changes in government policy will often negate the

Lucas critique
An economic theory that contends that if people act rationally, then their reactions to changes in government policy will often negate the intent of those changes.

Robert Lucas won the Nobel Prize in economics in 1995 for his work on the Lucas critique, which argues that if people act rationally, their reactions to changes in fiscal and monetary policy will defeat the purpose of those changes.

intent of those changes. Moreover, the Lucas critique suggests that in some circumstances, firms and individuals will react to changes in fiscal and monetary policy in ways that will produce results opposite those that government officials intended.[16] (In 1995, Lucas won the Nobel Prize in economics for developing the Lucas critique.)

To understand the basic intuition behind the Lucas critique, consider what happens when the government decides to cut taxes. According to traditional Keynesian economics, this use of fiscal policy will stimulate the demand for goods and services, which in turn will encourage economic growth. The Lucas critique takes this line of thinking one step further, arguing that people know from past experience that government efforts to stimulate the economy will spur inflation and erode their earnings. Workers will therefore demand higher wages, and businesses will demand higher prices. The result will be higher inflation and continued unemployment, the exact opposite of what policy makers hoped to accomplish. Monetary policy can produce the same perverse outcome. When the Federal Reserve tries to slow economic growth to a more reasonable level by raising interest rates, it may well plunge the country into a recession as businesses and workers react to the higher rates by cutting back on their purchases of goods and services.

The Lucas critique suggests two simple, yet important, pieces of advice to government policy makers. First, the government cannot use fiscal and monetary policy to fine-tune the economy. Firms and individuals will react to government efforts to manipulate the economy in ways that will tend to cancel out what policy makers hope to achieve. Second, the government's only role in the economy should be to maintain a steady growth in the money supply. Because Lucas and his colleagues are so skeptical of the ability of the federal government to manage the economy, their arguments have come to be called the "new classical economics." Much like the classical economists of the nineteenth century, the new classical economists argue that the government should not intervene in the economy; it should follow laissez faire policies.[17]

In the mid-1980s, a group of economists who called themselves "new Keynesians" began to respond to the arguments of the new classical economists. They accepted much of the reasoning behind the Lucas critique, but they dissented on some key issues. In particular, they argued that the new classical economists were mistaken in their policy recommendations because their mathematical models assumed that wages and prices change quickly in response to changes in the economy. The new Keynesians argued that in the real world, wages can be "sticky"—in other words, they might not rise or fall quickly in response to changes in economic conditions.[18] Consequently, the new Keynesians argued that persistent unemployment could exist. Similarly, in some circumstances, prices might be sticky and not change rapidly in response to supply and demand. As a result, shortages and excess supplies of goods might develop. Because the new Keynesians believe that the actual economy does not work in precisely the fashion the mathematical models of the new classical economists predict, they argue that the government should intervene in the economy to deal with market failures such as high unemployment.[19]

In sum, economists continue to disagree over how the economy works and over what economic policies the government should follow. Whereas many economists believe that the government has a significant role to play in managing the economy, many others argue that its role is small at best. No resolution of their debates is in sight. But the rules or theories policy makers choose to put into play will affect the economy and create economic winners and losers.

The Current Status of Economic Stewardship

An old joke about economists suggests that if you bring twelve prominent economists together and ask their advice, you will get at least thirteen contradictory opinions. Yet the record suggests that although economists may disagree about minor matters, they have been right about the big ones. As figure 17.1 shows, fiscal and monetary policy controls have successfully stabilized the U.S. economy since World War II. Wide swings from boom to bust have largely disappeared.

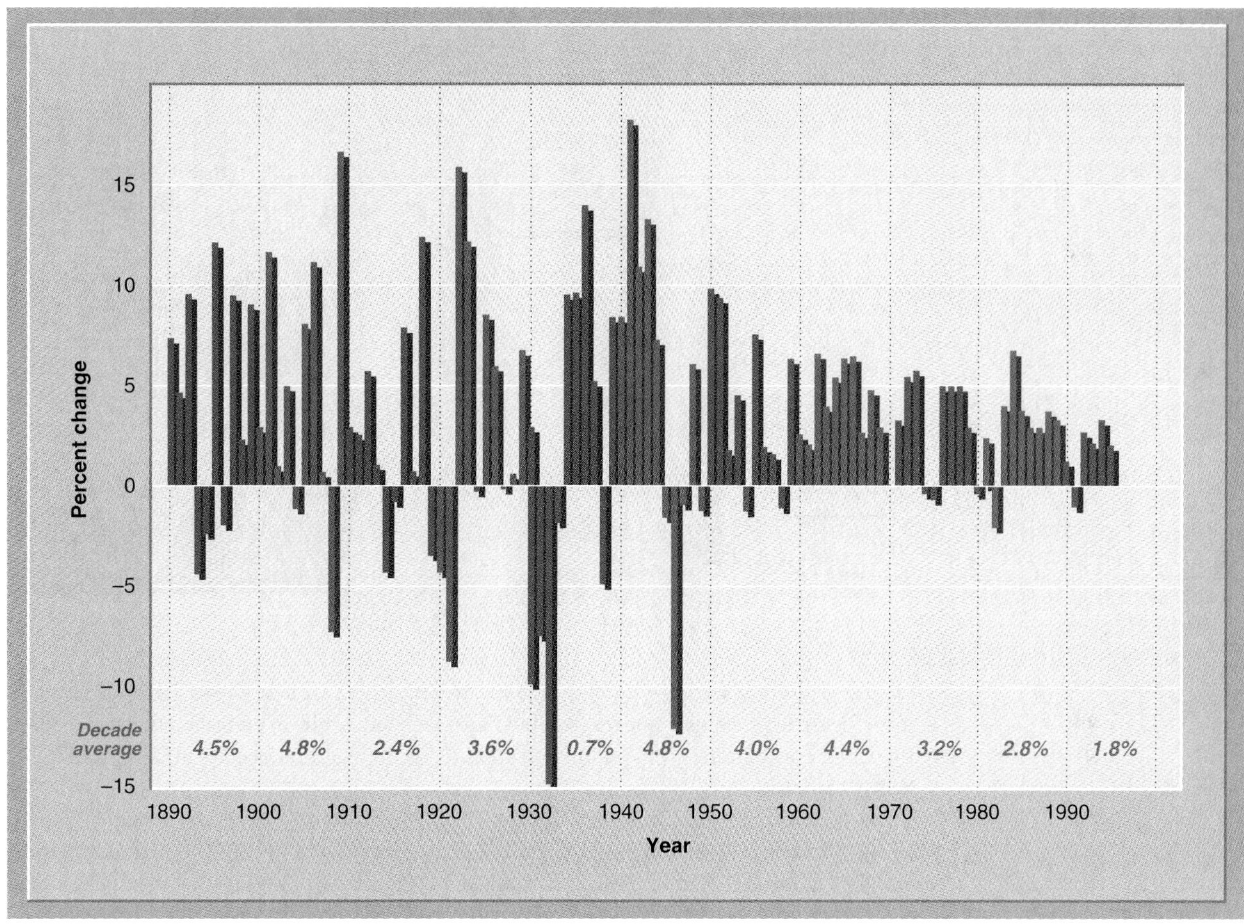

FIGURE 17.1
A Century of U.S. Economic Growth

The volatility of annual changes in gross domestic product, after inflation has been factored out, has diminished over the past half-century. Most economists attribute the disappearance of wide swings from boom to bust to the successful use of fiscal and monetary policy.

Sources: Data from "A Century of U.S. Economic Growth," *New York Times*, 17 March 1996; David Wyss, DRI/McGraw-Hill.

Despite the general success of our economic policy, many areas of conflict remain. Politicians, economists, and citizens continue to disagree about issues such as how America's wealth should be distributed and whether there are better ways to spur the economy.

The Distribution of Income and Wealth

Although discussions of the American economy frequently focus on topics such as unemployment, inflation, and economic growth, people care about more than just a few summary measures of the economy's success. They also care about how particular groups in American society are faring. One trend occurring over the last fifteen years is that the distribution of resources in American society has changed dramatically—the rich are increasingly laying claim to more of the country's economic pie, while the poor are laying claim to less. In 1980, the highest paid 20 percent of American families earned 41.5 percent of all income, while the lowest paid 20 percent received only 5.2 percent of all income. By 1995, the top 20 percent had increased its share to 48.7 percent of all income, while the share of the bottom 20 percent had dropped to 3.7 percent.[20] Nonetheless, the income gap between rich and poor in the United States remains much smaller than it was in the 1930s, and it is not radically larger than the gap in most other advanced industrialized democracies.[21]

America's wealth—which encompasses not only income but also assets such as real estate, stocks, bonds, and material goods—is even less equally distributed than its income. The richest 1 percent of all U.S. households—those with a net worth of at least $2.3 million each—own nearly 40 percent of the nation's wealth. The top 20 percent of U.S. households—those with a net worth of $180,000 or more—control more than 80 percent of the country's wealth. The concentration of wealth in the United States is greater than that in any European democracy. For example, the richest 1 percent of all

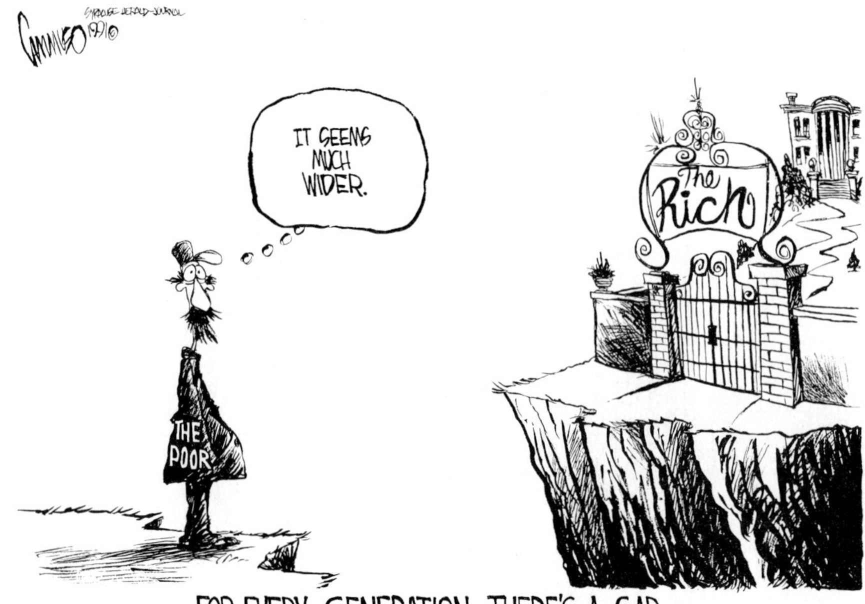

Studies indicate that in recent years, the gap between the rich and the poor in the United States has been growing.

Frank Cammusco/*Syracuse Herald-Journal*. Reprinted by permission.

British households holds 18 percent of the wealth in the United Kingdom, and the richest 1 percent of French households holds 26 percent of the wealth in France.[22] Moreover, the concentration of wealth in the hands of the rich has accelerated in the United States since the early 1980s.[23]

Much dispute surrounds the question of whether the substantial and growing disparities in income and wealth in the United States are good or bad. In general, conservative analysts minimize the importance of statistics on the distribution of income and wealth. Some argue that such figures are misleading because they often overlook how welfare programs improve the lot of the poor and because they say nothing about the turnover that occurs from year to year across different levels of income and wealth.[24] (For example, most young people look impoverished in statistics that measure income and wealth because they are just starting out on their careers. A few years down the road, they may be very wealthy.) Some conservative analysts argue that inequality is inherent in a free-market economy such as that of the United States; hence, there is no such thing as a fair distribution of income and wealth. As the Republican majority of the Joint Economic Committee of Congress put it in a report issued in 1995: "All societies have unequal wealth and income dispersion, and there is no positive basis for criticizing any degree of market-determined inequality."[25] Some conservative analysts go so far as to argue that high levels of inequality are good for the economy if the rich are encouraged to invest their savings in economically productive ventures. This would help promote economic growth, which in theory should benefit individuals at every income level. In short, in *relative* terms, the poor might end up with a smaller share of the pie, but in *absolute* terms they would end up with more pie than they might otherwise have received.

Not surprisingly, liberal analysts take a much more pessimistic view of the consequences of rising inequality.[26] They cite data showing that the poor are increasingly likely to stay poor, and as a result, they worry that the United States, which historically has prided itself on being an egalitarian society, is becoming a nation of haves and have-nots.[27] Liberal analysts fear that one consequence of dividing the country into haves and have-nots will be slower economic growth. The poor will increasingly lack the incomes they need to consume goods and services, which will deprive businesses of potential customers. At the same time, liberal analysts worry that rising inequality will tear at the nation's social fabric. The rich will be even better able to shift political and economic decisions in their favor, thereby producing further inequality. In turn, the poor might become increasingly envious of the rich, sowing the seeds of class conflict.

Ronald Reagan popularized the idea of supply-side economics, which his critics derided as "voodoo economics."

Copyright 1984 by Herblock in *The Washington Post*. Reprinted by permission.

Supply-Side Economics

To some extent, the increased inequality in the distribution of income and wealth in the United States in the 1980s was the consequence of **supply-side economics,** an economic theory developed by an influential group of conservative economists led by George Gilder and Arthur Laffer.[28] Proponents of supply-side economics believe that the government has become too large and that it is soaking up too much money from the private sector. They argue that if the government cuts taxes, reduces government spending, and eliminates many government regulations, resources will be freed up to fuel the economy to produce even more goods and services for everyone. In short, supply-siders argued that cutting taxes would increase the supply of goods and services to the benefit of all. (Because supply-side economics seeks to affect the economy by changing government spending and taxing decisions, it is a type of fiscal policy, though its underlying logic and policy recommendations differ sharply from those of Keynesian economics.)

Supply-side economics
An economic theory that argues that if the government cuts taxes, reduces spending, and eliminates regulations, resources will be freed up to fuel the economy to produce even more goods and services.

President Ronald Reagan championed the idea of supply-side economics. In the first years of his administration, Reagan persuaded Congress to enact large cuts in income taxes. At the same time, the Reagan administration pushed Congress to slow the growth of federal spending, if not actually cut it. Because the tax cuts primarily benefitted the rich—after all, they paid more income taxes to begin with—and because many of the spending cuts fell heavily on programs such as welfare and job training that go mostly to the poor and working class, one consequence was increased inequality in the distribution of income and wealth in the United States. As you might imagine, as it became clear that the distribution of income and wealth was becoming more unequal, supply-side economics became the subject of considerable controversy and was often derided by its critics as *Reaganomics* and *voodoo economics*.[29] (George Bush coined the term *voodoo economics* when he criticized Reagan's economic proposals during his unsuccessful bid to win the Republican presidential nomination in 1980.)

For their part, proponents of supply-side economics point out with pride that both inflation and unemployment fell sharply and the economy grew rapidly while President Reagan was in office. Whether supply-side economics was responsible for this good fortune is another matter. Monetarists argue that much of the credit for the healthy economy is owed to the Fed for administering a wise monetary policy. Keynesians frequently argue that in practice, supply-side economics looks a lot like Keynesian economics. The reason is that, while members of Congress were happy to cut taxes, they refused to accept the advice of supply-side economists and cut government spending on politically popular and very expensive programs such as Social Security and Medicare. As we saw in chapter 16, combining tax cuts with increased government spending produced massive budget deficits during the Reagan years. And as Keynesian economists had long argued, if government runs large budget deficits, it will stimulate economic growth.

Because of evidence of growing inequality in the distribution of income and wealth, and because of well-justified fears that Congress will not match politically popular tax cuts with politically unpopular spending cuts, proponents of supply-side economics have won few battles in Washington since the early 1980s.[30] Nonetheless, in 1996, Robert Dole centered his presidential campaign around a proposed 15 percent tax cut.

Industrial Policy

Industrial policy
The policy of seeking to strengthen selected industries by targeting them for governmental aid rather than letting the forces of the free market determine their fates.

Since the early 1980s, liberal economists have urged Congress and the president to develop an **industrial policy** to strengthen the American economy. These economists argue that the United States will prosper even more if the government helps specific industries rather than leaves their fate solely to the free market.[31] Government aid can come in a variety of forms, ranging from special tax incentives to government funds for research and development to exemptions from some types of government regulations. Whatever the form the aid takes, the basic idea behind industrial policy is for the government to select an industry it believes can become a world leader with the proper help and encouragement.

Many advanced industrialized nations have been quite successful with industrial policies. Japan, for example, has successfully bolstered its automobile and high technology industries into leading positions in the worldwide economy.[32] One of the few U.S. efforts in that direction so far has been Sematech, a government-industry research consortium that seeks to advance computer chip technology to boost U.S. industry.[33] On the whole, however, the United States has shied away from an organized industrial policy, partly because of deep-seated philosophical objections to government intervention in the marketplace and partly because of practical doubts about the ability of the government to pick industries likely to be "winners."

In steering our modern economy, the government uses both fiscal and monetary policy. Yet different people with different goals hold the controls. Congress and the president control the primary fiscal policy tool, the budget. They make decisions about the size of the surplus or deficit, as well as decisions about supply-side economics and industrial policy such as how big the government should be and whether it should favor particular industries. The independent Fed controls monetary policy. It makes decisions about the money supply by setting the discount rate and regulating the purchase and sale of treasury securities. Thus, while most Americans reward or blame the president for the performance of the economy (see chapter 7), the president must share management of the economy with many other people in government.

Regulating Business

Regulatory policy
Laws and government rules targeting private business for the purpose of (1) protecting consumers and other businesses from what the government deems unfair business practices; (2) protecting workers from unsafe or unhealthy working conditions; (3) protecting consumers from unsafe products; and (4) protecting a number of groups from discrimination.

As chapter 13 explains, regulation of the private sector is one of the four major functions of the federal bureaucracy. The government regulates private business in order to protect both consumers and other businesses from what the government decides are unfair business practices, to protect workers from unsafe or unhealthy working conditions, to protect consumers from unsafe products, and to protect a number of groups from discrimination. Although **regulatory policy** certainly affects the overall state of the economy, its primary aim is to manage these problems, not to affect the economy, as fiscal and monetary policies do.

Regulation first became an important federal activity a century ago, when Congress passed the Interstate Commerce Act of 1887. Since then, the federal government has become heavily involved in regulating the competitive practices of business. Beginning in the 1960s, it became involved in regulating the social effects of business activity as well.

The idea of regulation has always received a mixed response from the public. When public opinion surveys ask about government regulations on business in general, the public splits over whether they are desirable. When asked about specific regulations such as minimum wage laws, product safety laws, and environmental regulations, however, the public often favors regulations.[34] For example, as we noted in chapter 6 and again in chapter 11, nearly 80 percent of the public supported President Clinton's 1995 proposal to raise the minimum wage.[35] The tension between disliking regulation in the abstract and liking regulation in specific cases has fueled political conflict ever since the federal government began to regulate private business.[36] Those battles are still being fought in the 1990s. To understand them, we need to review some basic concepts and to discuss the federal government's role in economic and social regulation.

Basic Concepts and Categories

As chapter 13 discusses, the federal government carries out its regulatory duties through its executive departments (for example, the Department of Health and Human Services, which houses the Food and Drug Administration), its independent regulatory commissions (for example, the Nuclear Regulatory Commission), and its independent agencies (for example, the Environmental Protection Agency). These agencies regulate private sector activity in three ways: (1) through rule administration, which means the agencies implement the decisions of Congress, the president, or the courts; (2) through rule making, which means the agencies write their own regulations (because congressional, presidential, and judicial decisions are often long on broad guidelines but short on details); and (3) through rule adjudication, which means the agencies judge whether their regulations have been violated.

Regulatory efforts fall into two categories. First, **economic regulation** consists of rules affecting the competitive practices of businesses. Antitrust laws, which seek to prevent any single company or group of companies from suppressing competition, are an example of economic regulation. Second, **social regulation** consists of rules designed to protect Americans from dangers or unfair practices associated with how companies produce their products as well as from dangers associated with the products themselves. For example, regulations prevent the automobile industry from polluting the air, from practicing racial discrimination when they hire new employees, and from producing unsafe cars.

Economic regulation
Laws and governmental rules that affect the competitive practices of private business.

Social regulation
Laws and governmental rules designed to protect Americans from dangers or unfair practices associated with how private businesses produce their products or with the products themselves.

Economic and social regulation emerged at different times for different purposes, and they involve different patterns of governmental action. For these reasons, we will discuss each type of regulation separately.

The Objectives of Economic Regulation

Economic regulations enable the government to influence the competitive practices of industry. In doing so, the government can strive to accomplish one of two goals.[37] First, it may seek to encourage economic competition by preventing monopolies from forming and by deterring unfair forms of business competition. For example, in 1995, Microsoft, the largest computer software company in the world, sought to buy Intuit, the maker of Quicken, the world's most popular personal finance software. Microsoft hoped that by purchasing Intuit, it would take the lead in the rapidly growing (and immensely profitable) market for computerized home banking services. When it became

In 1995, Microsoft, the largest computer software company in the world, sought to buy Intuit, the maker of Quicken, the world's most popular personal finance software. The sale fell through when it became clear that federal regulators had concluded the deal would violate economic regulations.

clear that government regulators were unlikely to approve the deal—they feared that Microsoft's enormous size combined with Quicken's popularity would drive competitors out of the market—the deal for Intuit fell apart.

A second goal the government may strive to achieve is to use economic regulation to control the ability of firms to enter an industry or to control the prices they charge for their goods or services. The government typically steps in to control market entry or product pricing when competition in a given market is, for one reason or another, impractical or has undesirable side effects. For instance, Congress created the Interstate Commerce Commission (ICC) in 1887 because in many parts of the country, a single railroad company served the entire region. These companies faced no real competition—trucks and cargo planes had not been invented yet—so they could charge their customers exorbitant rates to ship goods. Because it did not make financial sense to create competition by constructing additional sets of rail lines, Congress instead directed the ICC to regulate how much railroads could charge their customers.[38] The same logic lies behind the regulation of other "natural" monopolies such as water, electricity, and other utilities.

Of course, politicians disagree about whether many conditions warrant regulation. Should Congress regulate cable television? Many people subscribe to cable services, but cable is hardly as economically essential as water, electricity, or transportation. When cable was first introduced, it was financially impractical for two or more cable companies to wire the same community, so cable companies had natural monopolies in their communities. As a result, Congress passed laws that regulated how much cable companies could charge their customers. Then the development of satellite dish technology presented an alternative to cable and weakened its monopoly. The anticipated development of cable services over ordinary telephone wires should further erode cable's domination of the market and open up even more competition. These trends prompted Congress in 1996 to do away with essentially all the rules that regulate cable company pricing. As many experts predicted, in the short run at least, the price of cable TV rose.[39] Increased rates may make the deregulation of cable TV a matter ripe for political conflict.

The Evolution of Economic Regulation

The federal government has been enacting economic regulations for more than one hundred years. During that time, regulatory policy has gone through three phases.[40] In the first phase, which lasted from the 1880s through the 1910s, the government first established a role for itself in regulating the economy. This began, as we have noted, when Congress established the ICC in 1887. Three other important laws passed during this first phase of government regulation of the economy were the Sherman Antitrust Act of 1890, the Clayton Antitrust Act of 1914, and the Federal Trade Commission Act of 1914. The Sherman Antitrust Act was designed to break up trusts, a form of business organization in which several large firms join together to dominate an industry and raise prices higher than they could charge in a competitive market. The Sherman Antitrust Act prohibited companies from fixing prices and creating monopolies. It did not, however, provide workable enforcement mechanisms. The Clayton Antitrust Act and the Federal Trade Commission Act were attempts to remedy the weaknesses of the Sherman Antitrust Act. As a result of the "trust-busting" efforts of the Federal Trade Commission (FTC) and the Antitrust Division of the Justice Department, trusts were eliminated by the 1930s.[41]

The second phase of economic regulatory activity began during Franklin Roosevelt's presidency. During this phase, Congress greatly expanded the federal government's role in regulating the economy. As part of the New Deal, Congress established a host of regulatory agencies, including the Federal Communications Commission in 1934 to regulate radio and television, the Securities and Exchange Commission in 1934 to oversee the stock market, and the Civil Aeronautics Board in 1938 to regulate the airline industry.[42]

By the early 1960s, the federal government had established four areas of economic regulatory policy: antitrust, financial institutions, transportation, and communications.[43] But the very size of the federal government's regulatory role prompted considerable criticism. The reason stemmed from the fact that Congress typically passed regulatory legislation that listed only broad goals such as promoting justice and protecting the public interest. Congress left it up to individual regulatory agencies to translate these broad goals into specific rules for specific industries. The ambiguity of congressional directives and the immense political pressure regulated industries placed on the regulatory agencies triggered charges that the purpose of government regulation had been subverted—instead of protecting the public, regulations were protecting industries.[44]

These charges gave rise to the third and most recent phase of economic regulation: deregulation. This phase began in the 1970s and continues today. By the 1970s, many consumer advocates had concluded that government regulation too often ended up hurting the public it was intended to protect. They argued that regulated industries were able to maintain inflated prices because the regulating agencies stifled price competition and blocked new firms from entering the market. For example, critics accused the Civil Aeronautics Board of preventing airlines from competing on ticket prices.[45] In response to these criticisms, the federal government, beginning with the Carter administration and continuing through the Clinton administration, deregulated (among others) the airline, trucking, savings and loan (S&L), and telecommunication industries. In the airline industry's case, Congress went so far as to abolish the Civil Aeronautics Board.[46] And as box 17.1 shows, the trend toward deregulation led to the demise of the ICC, the nation's oldest regulatory agency.

Proponents of deregulation argue that regulated industries are too often able to capture control of the bureaucrats who regulate them and manipulate regulations for their benefit rather than for the benefit of the public. Moreover, they contend, freeing markets from regulation stimulates competition and promotes both better products and lower prices.[47] In some cases, with airline deregulation perhaps the most notable example, deregulation has produced at least some of the benefits proponents claimed for it.[48] In other cases, however, deregulation has produced unintended consequences. For example, following the deregulation of the S&L industry, many S&Ls made risky loans and went bankrupt, leaving taxpayers responsible for their debts. The government has spent billions of dollars to cover the losses that bankrupt S&Ls incurred.[49]

Thus, the nation has learned that while deregulation has succeeded in some areas, it may not always be the best solution to problems of competitiveness within industries. Deregulation can lead to industry behavior that damages the public interest—making

Point of Order

BOX 17.1

The Demise of the Interstate Commerce Commission

The Interstate Commerce Commission closed its doors for good at the end of 1995.

Attitudes toward the federal government's proper role in domestic policy change over time. Public feelings about economic regulation are no exception. Indeed, as the establishment and recent demise of the Interstate Commerce Commission (ICC) illustrate, supporters and opponents of economic regulation can switch positions on the desirability of government regulation of the way American businesses operate.

The ICC was created in 1887 to protect the public from the monopolistic pricing practices of the railroad industry. In the 1930s, the agency's jurisdiction was extended to include the trucking industry. For many years, the ICC was viewed as a defender of the public interest. It regulated the pricing practices of railroads and trucking companies, preventing them from overcharging consumers for their services. In turn, railroad and trucking executives frequently complained that the ICC meddled in their affairs, raised their cost of doing business, and made their companies less profitable than they otherwise would have been.

While the ICC was created to protect the public, by the 1960s, consumer groups were accusing it of setting regulatory policies that benefitted the transportation industry rather than the public. In turn, railroad and trucking interests had become the ICC's staunchest defenders. While these industries continued to complain that the ICC's regulatory requirements were burdensome, they also recognized that the rules provided them with important benefits. For example, the ICC had regulations that restricted new firms from entering the trucking and railroad businesses. This effectively limited the number of competitors in both industries and allowed existing firms to charge higher prices. Likewise, the ICC's requirement that firms publicly announce any price changes in advance tended to result in higher consumer prices than would have occurred in an unregulated market.

Convinced that the ICC was hurting the public interest, consumer groups began to argue that the key to protecting consumers from artificially high prices lay not in regulating the railroad and trucking industries, but in deregulating them. Presidents Richard Nixon and Gerald Ford both tried but failed to persuade Congress to embrace deregulation. President Jimmy Carter then appointed deregulation advocates to the ICC, and these appointees took the first significant steps toward dismantling the agency's regulations. In a series of administrative and legislative actions that would extend over twenty years, the ICC was gradually stripped of its regulatory authority. Its budget and employment levels followed suit. By 1995, its jurisdiction had shrunk to those rare situations in which a single railroad or trucking firm actually monopolized a particular transportation route. Its staff, which had numbered 2,400 employees in the early 1960s, fell to 300.

Stripped of its mission and most of its political support, the ICC became a tempting target of those in Congress who wanted to cut federal spending and shrink the scope of government. While the dollar value of abolishing the ICC was minimal—it operated on a budget of only $40 million per year—the political value of eliminating a symbol of "big government" was significant. With virtually no dissent, and on a mere voice vote in the House, Congress agreed to close down the ICC. President Clinton's signature sealed the agency's fate. With little media attention and no fanfare, a "government closure team" took over the ICC's offices at the end of 1995, dumped years of agency reports and records into trash bins, and prepared the building for occupancy by another agency. Thus, even in the world of long-lived economic regulation, political conflicts are dynamic, and changes in the issues and positions of those involved have consequences for the rules of government.

Sources: Dan Carney, "ICC Bill Clears; Veto Possible," *Congressional Quarterly Weekly Report*, 23 December 1995, 3886; "President Signs Bill Terminating ICC," *Congressional Quarterly Weekly Report*, 6 January 1996, 58; David E. Sanger, "A U.S. Agency, Once Powerful, Is Dead at 108," *New York Times*, 1 January 1996; Richard W. Waterman, *Presidential Influence and the Administrative State* (Knoxville: University of Tennessee Press, 1989), chap. 4.

Table 17.1 Principal Agencies Engaged in Social Regulation

Agency	Year Established
Food and Drug Administration	1930
National Labor Relations Board	1935
Equal Employment Opportunity Commission	1964
Environmental Protection Agency	1970
Occupational Safety and Health Administration	1970
National Highway Traffic Safety Administration	1970
Consumer Product Safety Commission	1972
Nuclear Regulatory Commission	1975

The number of federal agencies responsible for social regulation grew sharply in the 1960s and 1970s as the American public demanded that the federal government do something about hazardous working conditions, unsafe consumer products, pollution, and discrimination in the workplace.

industry the winner and the public the loser in the conflict over regulatory policy. As a result, some moves have been made in the last decade to reregulate certain aspects of deregulated industries. Future developments in economic regulation will reflect an awareness of both the advantages and disadvantages of regulation and deregulation.

Social Regulation

Social regulation "affects the conditions under which goods and services are produced, and the physical characteristics of products that are manufactured."[50] In other words, the social regulation of business affects both working conditions and the safety and efficacy of the products themselves. As table 17.1 shows, social regulation dates back to the 1930s. The push for social regulation rose sharply in the 1960s and 1970s, however, as the public came to demand that the federal government do something about problems such as hazardous working conditions, unsafe consumer products, pollution, and discrimination in the workplace.[51]

Social regulation differs from economic regulation in two important ways. First, whereas economic regulations usually are industry-specific, social regulations tend to cut across industries. Government regulations on work and product safety, the environment, and equal opportunity are social regulations that apply to all industries. Second, social regulations are usually grounded in very specific, technical legislation rather than vague guidelines that require federal agencies to protect the public interest.

Social regulation runs the gamut from prohibiting employment discrimination to ensuring safety in the workplace to eliminating hazardous consumer products. The great diversity of social regulations makes it impossible to discuss each specific type. Instead, we will examine the evolution of and debates over two types of social regulation: policies protecting worker safety and health, and policies designed to protect the environment. (Chapter 5 discusses several of the laws Congress has passed to fight discrimination in the workplace.)

Protecting Worker Safety and Health

One of the best known and most controversial federal regulatory agencies is the Occupational Safety and Health Administration (OSHA). Congress established OSHA with the Occupational Safety and Health Act of 1970 and directed it to write and enforce rules to protect the health and safety of the American work force. Congress took this action because the high rate of worker injuries and deaths was a serious problem for the economy and because labor unions and middle-class environmental and consumer activists were pressing for action.[52] The legal foundations for the act came from the provisions of Article I of the Constitution—that Congress should provide for the general welfare and that Congress has the power to regulate interstate and foreign commerce.

Congress set up OSHA as an agency with broad powers to identify safety and health risks in working conditions and in products and to write and enforce regulations to reduce those hazards. OSHA has a staff of 2,400 inspectors who visit job sites, conduct safety tests of consumer products, and otherwise seek to ensure the health and safety of

The U.S. Occupational Safety and Health Administration (OSHA) came under attack in the mid-1990s as lawmakers wrangled over its role as a governmental regulator over private business.

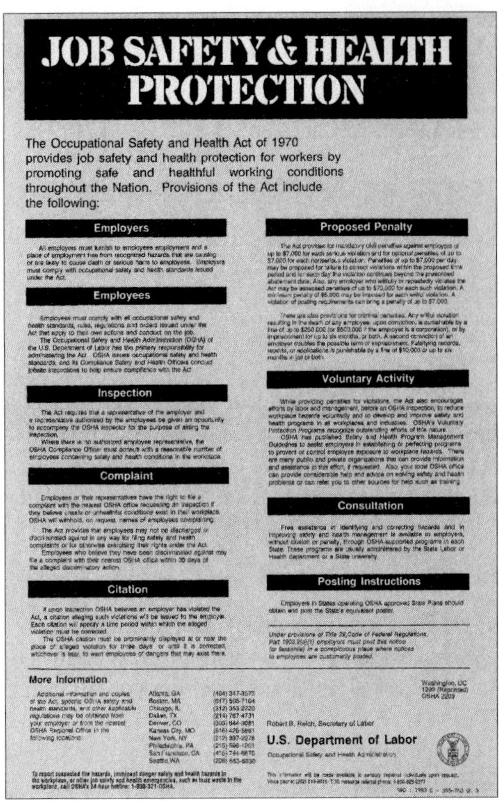

America's 93 million workers at their 6.2 million worksites, along with the safety of the products they make.[53] Since 1972, OSHA has established safety and health standards for asbestos, lead, vinyl chloride, pesticides, and a host of other hazards. OSHA enforces its regulations by issuing warnings to or in some cases fining businesses that fail to comply with its rules.

Criticism of OSHA began almost as soon as it hired its first regulator. Business leaders complained that OSHA wrote maddeningly complicated rules that interfered with businesses, failed to make workers safer, and cost too much.[54] They cited examples such as rules specifying exactly what size the letters in "Emergency Exit" signs had to be, claiming that OSHA had become an example of an overbearing government bureaucracy at its worst.[55]

Labor leaders and consumer advocates, in contrast, defended OSHA. They pointed to specific cases, such as the Love Canal toxic waste dump in upstate New York, in which government regulations would have saved money and prevented illnesses had they been in place. Had the owners of Love Canal invested $4 million initially, they would have saved $27 million in eventual cleanup costs.[56] Far greater savings would have been achieved if businesses had paid attention much earlier to the dangers of asbestos.[57] Defenders of OSHA also pointed to evidence that OSHA's regulations had reduced the rates of workplace injuries and illnesses.[58] While OSHA's supporters acknowledged that some of its regulations needed to be changed, they argued that, on the whole, the agency had succeeded in reducing health and safety risks to workers and consumers.

During the Reagan years, Congress cut OSHA's budget and staff, and the White House steered OSHA in a more business-friendly direction. OSHA complied, cutting many of its regulations, simplifying others, and reducing the penalties it charged for violations.[59] Business leaders cheered, while labor leaders and other critics of the Reagan administration charged that OSHA was allowing businesses to expose workers to unacceptable dangers.[60]

The Clinton administration initially sought to increase spending on OSHA, but in 1995, the agency came under attack once again. The new Republican majority on Capitol Hill moved to dismantle regulations that it claimed placed excessive burdens on private business.[61] The House, for example, passed a bill that (among other things) eliminated rules barring teenagers from using baler machines that crush cardboard cartons and from driving vehicles on the job, and it prohibited OSHA from doing anything to prevent repetitive-stress injuries in the workplace. This effort to scale back OSHA's regulations came to a halt, at least temporarily, when President Clinton and Congress reached an impasse in early 1996 over how to balance the federal budget (see chapter 16). Despite being unable to pass a law terminating the rules they found objectionable, Republicans did manage to cut OSHA funding by 15 percent.[62] This budget cut made it more difficult for OSHA to carry out its duties.

OSHA's supporters criticized the Republican efforts to limit the agency's work. They denounced one bill that sought to strip OSHA of much of its regulatory power as "the 'Death and Injury Enhancement Act' or DIE."[63] Officials in the Clinton administration were equally scathing in their criticism. Secretary of Labor Robert Reich accused Republicans of unleashing "carnage" in the workplace with the cuts they were making in OSHA's budget. Another administration official made the same point more gently: "Our resources to do surprise inspections of the workplace, one of the most important incentives for compliance with health and safety requirements, have been cut way back. It's like not having state troopers on the highway to enforce speed limits."[64]

As business and labor groups have fought over the proper role of OSHA, public opinion has continued to support both OSHA and the idea of having the government regulate safety and health conditions in the workplace. Indeed, public opinion surveys show that the public recognizes the economic costs of health and safety regulations and is willing to pay them.[65] Regardless of public opinion, the conflict over government regulation of private business will certainly not end. As the power wielded by business and labor changes over time, and as new health and safety issues arise with the development of new technology, OSHA's role will continue to evolve and the rules that govern it will continue to change.

Protecting the Environment

Since the 1960s, Congress has passed many laws designed to protect the environment. These laws have become a source of considerable political conflict because, like other types of social regulation, they create winners and losers. While environmental activists argue that the government needs to do more to protect the environment, private businesses complain that environmental regulations have become too costly and are costing the United States too many jobs. The conflict between those who want to do more to protect the country from pollution and those who want to do more to protect business from excessive regulation will shape the rules of environmental policy for years to come.

The Evolution of Environmental Policy

Before the mid-1960s, federal policy on the environment reflected a conservationist approach; the government's efforts were aimed largely at setting aside public lands for recreational use. The environmental movement had yet to ignite and Congress felt little pressure to take any action.[66] In 1962, however, urged on by Rachel Carson's disturbing book, *Silent Spring,* the public began to pay attention to the dangers of a polluted environment.[67] Congress responded by passing the Water Quality Act of 1965, the Clean Water Restoration Act of 1966, and the Air Quality Act of 1967. These laws gave the Department of Health, Education, and Welfare (later to become the Department of Health and Human Services) the power to establish clean water standards, provided federal funds for sewage treatment plants, and required the states to establish air quality standards (including automobile emission standards) with the advice and consent of the federal government.[68] Although these laws began moving the federal government into environmental regulation, none of them was stringent enough, according to environmentalist activists.[69]

The environmental movement received a second jarring boost in 1969 when an offshore oil drilling platform owned by Union Oil Company of California blew out, dumping 4.2 million barrels of oil into the Santa Barbara Channel along the California coast. The resulting publicity, including nightly television coverage of thousands of

Congress has given the Environmental Protection Agency (EPA) responsibility for overseeing a vast array of environmental regulations.

TABLE 17.2 The Responsibilities of the Environmental Protection Agency (EPA)

In the area of air quality, the EPA:

- Establishes national air quality standards.
- Sets limits on the level of air pollutants emitted from stationary sources such as power plants, municipal incinerators, factories, and chemical plants.
- Establishes emission standards for new motor vehicles.
- Sets allowable levels for toxins like lead, benzene, and toluene in gasoline.
- Establishes emissions standards for hazardous air pollutants such as beryllium, mercury, and asbestos.
- Supervises states in their development of clean air plans.

In the area of water quality and protection, the EPA:

- Issues permits for the discharge of any pollutant into navigable waters.
- Develops "effluent guidelines" to control discharge of specific water pollutants, including radiation.
- Develops criteria that enable states to set water quality standards.
- Administers grants program to states to subsidize the cost of building sewage treatment plants.
- Regulates disposal of waste material, including sludge and low-level radioactive discards, into the oceans.
- Cooperates with the Army Corps of Engineers to issue permits for dredging and filling of wetlands.
- Sets national drinking water standards to ensure that drinking water is safe.
- Regulates underground injection of wastes to protect purity of ground water.
- With the Coast Guard, coordinates cleanup of oil and chemical spills into U.S. waterways.

To control the disposal of hazardous waste, the EPA:

- Maintains inventory of existing hazardous waste dump sites.
- Tracks more than 500 hazardous compounds from point of origin to final disposal site.
- Sets standards for generators and transporters of hazardous wastes.
- Issues permits for treatment, storage, and disposal facilities for hazardous wastes.
- Assists states in developing hazardous waste control programs.
- Maintains a multibillion-dollar fund ("Superfund") from industry fees and general tax revenues to provide for emergency cleanup of hazardous dumps when no responsible party can immediately be found.
- Pursues identification of parties responsible for waste sites and eventual reimbursement of the federal government for Superfund money spent cleaning up these sites.

Source: Walter A. Rosenbaum, *Environmental Politics and Policy,* 3d ed. (Washington, D.C.: CQ Press, 1995), pp. 116–17.

dead fish and oil-coated birds, pushed both Congress and President Richard Nixon into aggressively seeking to regulate businesses and protect the environment.[70]

The passage of the National Environmental Policy Act (NEPA) in 1969 reflected the federal government's new approach to the environment. NEPA took several important steps. First, it set forth the basic goals and responsibilities of the federal government in protecting the environment. Second, it established the Council on Environmental Quality within the Executive Office of the President to advise presidents on the environment. Finally, NEPA created the **environmental impact statement** process, which requires federal agencies to analyze the environmental impact of any significant action they may take. Environmental groups have used the federal government's many environmental impact statements to influence, delay, and even block actions federal agencies proposed.[71]

Environmental impact statement
A document federal agencies must issue that analyzes the environmental impact of any significant actions they plan to take.

In 1970, President Nixon went further by consolidating the federal government's many environmental tasks into the Environmental Protection Agency (EPA), a new agency whose purpose was to protect the environment. Not to be outdone, Congress enacted new laws strengthening the Clean Air and Clean Water Acts, protecting wildlife, and extending environmental regulations into new areas. By the end of the 1970s, the EPA was left with a vast array of laws to administer, as table 17.2 shows.[72]

To regulate chemicals, including pesticides and radioactive waste, the EPA:

- Maintains inventory of chemical substances now in commercial use.
- Regulates existing chemicals considered serious hazards to people and the environment, including fluorocarbons, PCBs, and asbestos.
- Issues procedures for the proper safety testing of chemicals and orders them tested when necessary.
- Requires the registration of insecticides, herbicides, or fungicides intended for sale in the United States.
- Requires pesticide manufacturers to provide scientific evidence that their product will not injure humans, livestock, crops, or wildlife when used as directed.
- Classifies pesticides for either general public use or restricted use by certified applicators.
- Sets standards for certification of applicators of restricted-use pesticides. (Individual states may certify applicators through their own programs based on the federal standards.)
- Cancels or suspends the registration of a product on the basis of actual or potential unreasonable risk to animals, or the environment.
- Issues a "stop sale, use, and removal" order when a pesticide already in circulation is in violation of the law.
- Requires registration of pesticide-producing establishments.
- Issues regulations concerning the labeling, storage, and disposal of pesticide containers.
- Issues permits for pesticide research.
- Monitors pesticide levels in the environment.
- Monitors and regulates radiation in drinking water, oceans, rainfall, and air.
- Conducts research on toxic substances, pesticides, air and water quality, hazardous wastes, radiation, and the causes and effects of acid rain.
- Provides overall guidance to other federal agencies on radiation protection matters that affect public health.

In addition, the EPA:

- Sets noise levels acceptable for construction equipment, transportation equipment (except aircraft), all motors and engines, and electronic equipment.

Ronald Reagan, who was elected president in 1980, entered office with an entirely different view of environmental regulations—he saw them as undue burdens on business and major obstacles to economic growth. His appointees to agencies such as EPA and the Interior Department (see box 13.2) shared his opposition to the government's environmental policies. Although the Reagan administration sought to dismantle many environmental regulations, it met with only mixed success.[73] It succeeded in cutting the budgets for environmental programs—government spending in constant dollars (that is, adjusted for inflation) on natural resources and the environment fell dramatically between 1980 and 1981 and did not return to 1980 levels until 1993.[74] Yet by the end of Reagan's first term, Congress again began enacting legislation to protect the environment. Members of Congress were responding to opinion polls that showed public support for environmental protection rising throughout Reagan's presidency.[75]

George Bush ran for election in 1988 promising to be an "environmental president," and early in his term, he gained political credit for taking a more protective approach toward the environment than Reagan had. In 1990, for example, Bush reversed Reagan's policy of opposing legislation to strengthen the 1972 Clean Air Act, and together with Congress, he hammered out the 1990 Clean Air Act.[76] As Bush prepared to run for reelection, however, he deemphasized environmental issues and instead sought to attract political support from the business community by helping it obtain regulatory relief. As a result, during the second half of his presidency, Bush repeatedly blocked and watered down regulations designed to protect the environment.[77]

Bill Clinton came to office promising to renew public efforts at environmental protection, but his administration moved slowly on most matters. An Interior Department plan to conduct a biological survey of the nation was shelved after the department received complaints from landowners who feared the survey would lead to

At the center of a debate about environmental regulations: the spotted owl.

increased regulation of their lands. Clinton also abandoned an early proposal to protect public lands in western states by raising the fees the government charges for grazing.[78] Other legislative efforts—including bills designed to overhaul nineteenth-century laws regulating mining on federal lands (see chapter 10), to reform the superfund for cleaning up toxic waste dumps, and to reauthorize the Clean Water Act—foundered on Capitol Hill.[79]

Political Conflicts in Environmental Protection

One can easily see why environmental regulation generates political conflict. When the government imposes a regulation, it benefits one group, usually the public at large, and imposes costs on another group, perhaps a firm or an individual. For example, when the government mandates lower automobile emissions, the public gets cleaner air and it costs automobile companies more to make their cars and trucks. As one might expect, firms or individuals that bear the cost of regulations usually oppose them.

Four other factors shape the course of political debate over environmental regulations. First, environmental regulations (and other social regulations as well) tend to produce diffuse benefits spread across society while imposing focused costs that affect relatively few businesses or individuals. The benefits of environmental regulations are typically spread out across the United States, and many (if not most) Americans do not notice them. In contrast, the firm that must pay to clean up its toxic waste or the lumber company that cannot log timber for fear of harming the habitat of an endangered animal such as the spotted owl is acutely aware of the costs of regulation. Because benefits are diffuse while costs are concentrated, opponents of environmental regulation often have a greater incentive to fight against regulation than proponents have to fight for it.[80]

A second factor that affects the debate on environmental regulations is the fact that the benefits of some environmental regulations are hard to measure, but the costs are not.[81] For instance, it is difficult to measure the health benefits that come from having cleaner air or water. Medical researchers can see the benefits in terms of saved lives or reduced numbers of illnesses, but the general public cannot. Measuring the benefit to society of preserving an ancient forest or saving an endangered species is even more difficult. This "measurement" depends on the value one places on the forest or endangered species. In contrast, it is fairly easy to measure jobs and income lost because of environmental regulation. Because environmentalists sometimes find it impossible to produce definitive evidence that the benefits of regulation will exceed the costs, they frequently find themselves at a disadvantage in the political arena.

A third factor that affects the debate is that measuring the magnitude of environmental problems can be difficult. This is becoming increasingly so as the government addresses the more obvious forms of pollution and begins to address so-called second generation environmental issues such as global warming and ozone depletion. It is one thing to measure the presence and health effects of pollutants in the air; it is quite another to establish that industrial development is changing global weather patterns enough to produce a "greenhouse effect" that will wreak environmental havoc on the world.[82] As scientific certainty diminishes, critics of regulation gain an advantage.

Finally, protecting the environment becomes increasingly costly as the standards of environmental quality rise. As government seeks to reduce pollution even more, the costs associated with marginal improvements grow. This raises the stakes for the firms and individuals that must pay for these improvements, and it gives them incentives to resist regulation even more strenuously.

Future Directions for Environmental Policy

When President Clinton proposed to "reinvent government" (see chapter 13), he made environmental regulation a prime target. Traditional regulatory policy emphasizes a *command-and-control approach* to the environment in which agencies draft regulations dictating how to protect the environment (commands) and then create mechanisms for forcing targeted polluters to comply (controls). The regulations are detailed, specifying both the amount of pollution that any source may produce and how the pollution must be reduced. These regulations are also universalistic, leaving little room for adaptations to local situations. Because of its inflexibility, the command-and-control approach to regulation has drawn complaints from environmentalists as well as from the business community.

Two frequently mentioned alternatives to the command-and-control approach are *market incentives* and *pollution prevention*. With a market-incentives approach, the government would abandon its efforts to develop uniform, nationwide regulations that specify how to eliminate pollution. Instead, it would establish an overall level of pollution allowable for different geographic areas, and it would issue a permit to each potential polluter within a region specifying how much pollution it may produce. Polluters would then be allowed to trade permits. If one firm can reduce its pollutants cheaply, say, by closing down an unneeded plant, it could then sell its permit to a firm that can only reduce its pollutants at great expense. In theory, creating a market in which firms can trade pollution permits will produce a greater reduction in pollution at less cost than is true with the command-and-control approach.[83] Congress directed the federal government to create a market for air pollution permits as part of the 1990 Clear Air Act, but it is still too early to tell if the market-incentives approach will work as well in practice as it does in theory.

The second alternative to the command-and-control approach is pollution prevention. Unlike command-and-control methods, which emphasize government intervention to correct an existing problem, pollution prevention emphasizes avoiding pollution in the first place. The pollution-prevention approach has wide support from business and the public, and the Pollution Prevention Act of 1990 added it as one of EPA's policy options. The act requires EPA to give priority to programs designed to help industry produce less pollution and waste. Hundreds of firms are voluntarily revising their production activities to conform with the law.[84] As with the market-incentive approach, however, it is still too early to know if the pollution-prevention approach will live up to expectations.

While the jury is still out on the efficacy of the market-incentive and pollution-prevention approaches to environmental regulation, many of the Republicans who took control of Congress in 1995 wanted to scale back the environmental legislation passed over the preceding two decades. To this end, they proposed a revised version of the Clean Water Act that would have relaxed many of the law's regulatory requirements. The bill passed the House of Representatives but became bogged down in the Senate, where Democrats and moderate Republicans attacked it as the "dirty water act" and the "polluter's bill of rights."[85] The House also passed legislation containing a variety of provisions that would have prohibited the EPA from enforcing key aspects of the nation's laws regulating air and water pollution. At the insistence of the Senate, these provisions were later dropped from the legislation.[86] A third House bill sought to rewrite the Endangered Species Act of 1973 to eliminate many of its protections for biological species and ecosystems.[87] Even though these and several other efforts to scale back environmental regulations failed to become law, Republicans did substantially cut funding for environmental programs, thereby making it more difficult for the federal agencies responsible for the environment to carry out their duties.[88]

Whether Republicans will continue their efforts to scale back the reach of environmental regulation remains to be seen. Public opinion polls showed that their environmental proposals were unpopular with many Americans, and leading Republicans openly wondered if their policies on the environment were doing deep political damage to the party.[89] A poll that Republican members of Congress commissioned and a prominent Republican pollster conducted concluded in 1996 that "our party is out of sync with mainstream American opinion" and that "55 percent of Republicans do not trust their party when it comes to protecting the environment, while 72 percent of the Democrats do trust their party."[90] Although some Republicans argued that environmental activists had distorted the substance of their legislative initiatives, many others were clearly worried that the American public had come to believe their critics' claim that they were waging a "war on the environment."

The debate over environmental policy, like the debates over the wisdom of economic deregulation and the future of OSHA, reminds us that regulatory policy is a source of tremendous conflict in American politics. While government regulations may benefit consumers, workers, and the environment, they also impose costs on businesses and limit their freedom of action. Not surprisingly, businesses that are the targets of government regulation usually oppose new regulations and try to have existing ones repealed. As views on the desirability of government regulation change over time, the rules of regulatory policy change as well.

Promoting Social Welfare

Aid to Families with Dependent Children (AFDC)
A public assistance program that provides government aid to low-income families with children.

Although many Americans tend to think of welfare in terms of one particular welfare program, **Aid to Families with Dependent Children (AFDC),** many different government welfare policies and programs exist. To understand the broad range of social welfare policy in the United States, we need to discuss some basic concepts and categories, to trace the evolving role of the federal government in providing social welfare benefits, to review the current status of social welfare programs, and to identify the issues that will shape the future of social welfare policy. The rules we choose for social welfare policy may affect more Americans more dramatically and directly than any other type of domestic policy. They certainly create social "winners" and "losers"; who gains and who loses depends on the rules we adopt as the new century begins.

Basic Concepts and Categories

Social welfare policy
Government programs that provide goods and services to citizens to improve the quality of their lives.

Social welfare policy refers to government programs that provide goods and services to citizens to improve the quality of their lives. This broad definition includes many different types of programs. To show just how broad the notion of social welfare policy is, table 17.3 lists a variety of social welfare programs that the federal government or state governments have enacted at one time or another.

Since the idea of social welfare policy encompasses everything from Social Security to vocational rehabilitation, how should we organize this broad array of programs? Table 17.3 offers one way to classify social welfare programs, namely, to organize them according to their substantive purpose. Some programs seek to ensure that individuals have adequate incomes, others seek to provide them with nutritious diets, still others seek to protect their health, and so on.

Social insurance
Government programs, such as Social Security and Medicare, that require future beneficiaries to make contributions (otherwise known as taxes) and that distribute benefits without regard to the recipient's income.

Public assistance
Government programs, such as Medicaid and food stamps, that are funded out of general tax revenues and that are designed to provide benefits only to low-income people.

Means test
A requirement that people must fall below certain income and wealth requirements to qualify for government benefits.

A substantive approach, however, is not the only way to classify social welfare programs. A second approach differentiates policies that operate on the principle of **social insurance** from those based on **public assistance.** Social insurance programs (for example, Social Security and Medicare) require those who will receive benefits to make contributions (pay taxes), and they distribute benefits without regard to the recipient's level of income. For example, to receive Social Security benefits when you retire, you must pay Social Security taxes while you are employed. Once you retire, you receive benefits regardless of whether you are a millionaire or live in poverty. In contrast to social insurance programs, public assistance programs (for example, Medicaid and food stamps) are funded out of general tax revenues. Their benefits go only to recipients who qualify through a **means test,** which shows that they are poor enough to be eligible for the program.

Finally, social welfare programs can be classified according to the strategy they use to improve recipients' quality of life.[91] One strategy is *alleviative;* it encompasses programs that attempt to soften—or alleviate—the hardships of poverty. Most public assistance programs are alleviative. A second strategy is *preventative;* this strategy encompasses programs that require individuals to take action today (making contributions, for example, to a social insurance program) to prevent themselves from falling

The federal government and state governments administer a wide range of social welfare programs.

TABLE 17.3 Different Types of Social Welfare Policies

Income Maintenance Programs
Aid to Families with Dependent Children (AFDC)
Social Security
Supplemental Security Income (SSI)
Unemployment Compensation
Workers' Compensation
Nutrition Programs
Food Stamps
Meals on Wheels
School Breakfasts
School Lunch
Special Supplemental Nutrition Program for Women, Infants, and Children
Health Programs
Medicare
Medicaid
Public Health
Social Services Programs
Community Action
Community Mental Health
Job Training Partnership Act
Legal Services
Social Services for Children and Families
Social Services for the Elderly
Vocational Rehabilitation

Source: Adapted from Diana M. DiNitto and Thomas R. Dye, *Social Welfare Politics and Public Policy*, 2d ed. (Englewood Cliffs, N.J.: Prentice-Hall, 1987), p. 3.

into poverty later in life. A third strategy is *curative;* it encompasses programs such as Head Start and job training that seek to cure poverty by giving the poor the skills they need to lift themselves out of poverty.

The three different approaches to classifying social welfare programs are important because each highlights different ways the government can seek to maintain and improve the general welfare. In addition, the differences among social welfare programs help explain why each enjoys a different level of political support, and the different approaches fuel disagreements over how the federal government should structure its social welfare programs. For example, some Americans favor social insurance programs but want cuts in public assistance programs; others support alleviative programs but not curative programs. As we shall see, the political support behind each of these types of programs influences which rules are adopted and who gains or loses under those rules.

The Evolution of Social Welfare Policy

Social welfare policy in the United States has changed dramatically over the past century. In the nineteenth century, most people believed caring for the poor was the responsibility of the private sector or local government, not the federal government. The only federal social welfare program in the nineteenth century was one that offered pensions to soldiers who fought for the Union in the Civil War. The Great Depression of the 1930s led the federal government to carve out a prominent role in guaranteeing the welfare of American citizens. That role expanded yet again in the 1960s as Washington sought to eradicate poverty and provide health care to the elderly and the poor.

Head Start is an example of a curative social welfare program. It seeks to cure poverty by giving poor children the strong educational foundation they need to succeed.

Welfare as a Private Sector and Local Responsibility

For the first half of our nation's history, the norms (or informal rules) of American society worked to keep the federal government largely out of social welfare policy.[92] To begin with, the poor were often blamed for their own situation. Poverty was regarded as a product of a person's character: the able-bodied poor were lazy, shiftless, or spendthrifts, and therefore they did not deserve help. If people were in need, family members were expected to be the first source of assistance. Moreover, American society mostly viewed public assistance as a local rather than national responsibility. It was up to the community in which the poor lived to decide who was eligible for aid and to raise the resources needed to provide assistance—either through local churches and charities, or, in some cases, through local governments.[93] Finally, aid was meager; when it was provided, it was less than the amount a person could earn working at a low-wage job.

When federal and state governments finally did begin to become involved in social welfare policy, they did so by narrowly targeting groups of "deserving poor," rather than by offering general forms of assistance. The first federal social program, for example, gave benefits to veterans of the Civil War who fought on the Union side. From the 1880s through the 1910s, Congress passed a series of laws granting and then expanding pensions for disabled and elderly veterans. Congress justified the pensions on the grounds that these soldiers had fought for the Union and deserved to be compensated. After 1910, states began to develop their own social welfare policies. Forty state governments set up programs to give money to widowed mothers living in poverty so that they could care for their children without working. In sum, before the 1930s, state and federal programs targeted specific groups of "deserving" poor people, rather than providing general assistance to those in poverty.[94]

Social Security is the country's oldest and largest social welfare program. In 1995, Social Security paid out $336 million in benefits to more than 41 million Americans.

At the same time that the American government slowly edged into the business of providing social welfare benefits to a few, narrow groups, many European nations were establishing broad social welfare programs for all of their poor and elderly. Germany, for example, created a system of old-age pensions in 1889, and most of the rest of Europe had similar programs in place by 1914.[95] In contrast, the United States did not adopt its nationwide system of old-age pensions, what we call Social Security, until 1935. Thus, providing broad social welfare services became a governmental responsibility in the United States several decades after it did in Europe.

Nationalizing Social Welfare: The Social Security Act of 1935

Although most states had enacted limited social welfare programs by the mid-1930s, the inadequacy of these programs became clear during the Great Depression. As chapter 2 notes, the Great Depression deprived the states of the tax revenues they needed to fund public assistance. Moreover, with one out of every four American workers unemployed, the conventional stereotype of the poor as too lazy to work no longer held. Millions of people desperately sought work, but few jobs were available. People who had conscientiously saved for the proverbial rainy day found themselves with nothing to fall back on as banks across the country failed. Surely these people deserved help, yet they did not fit in the traditional category of the deserving poor. The federal government, under the leadership of President Franklin Roosevelt, stepped in to fill the gap.

The Social Security Act of 1935 laid the foundation of the federal government's role in social welfare policy. This legislation created two types of federal social welfare programs: (1) social insurance programs for the elderly and the unemployed; and (2) public assistance programs to help the elderly, the blind, and dependent children.

Social Insurance Programs The main social insurance program the Social Security Act created was the Old Age and Survivors program. (Recall that a social insurance program is a program that benefits all who contribute, regardless of income level.) In 1956, Congress added a new social insurance program, the Disability Insurance program. Taken together, these two programs constitute what we call Social Security—the oldest and largest social welfare program in the United States. The number of people receiving Social Security benefits has grown from 222,000 in 1940 to 42.2 million in 1994. Costs have also increased. In 1940, Social Security paid out just $32 million; in 1995, it paid out $336 billion.[96]

As chapter 16 discusses, Social Security is financed by a payroll tax (usually labeled FICA or OASDI on your pay stub)—in other words, it comes out of your pay before you receive your paycheck. Each recipient receives an amount based on that person's lifetime earnings. Since 1972, federal law has required that Social Security benefits be indexed to the rate of inflation; when the cost of living rises, so do Social Security benefits. The increase in payments is called a cost-of-living adjustment, or COLA.

In addition to creating the Old Age and Survivors Insurance program, the Social Security Act established a social insurance program that provides benefits to the unemployed. Employers pay special unemployment taxes on behalf of their employees. Should the employers lay those workers off, the workers are entitled to receive unemployment benefits. Unemployment insurance costs little compared to Social Security; in 1995, the total cost of the program was only $23.9 billion.[97]

Public Assistance Programs The second type of social welfare program the Social Security Act created is public assistance, which comes from general tax revenues and is granted only to those who qualify by income. The act established programs to assist the elderly (Old Age Assistance), the blind (Aid to the Blind), and children (AFDC). In 1950, Congress added a new public assistance program for people with disabilities (Aid to the Permanently and Totally Disabled). These public assistance programs are funded out of the federal government's general tax revenues.

For many years, the federal government left the job of administering (as opposed to financing) its public assistance programs to the states. Individual states set eligibility requirements and benefit levels as they saw fit. The states paid for the programs with grants they received from the federal government. Because states were free to run the programs as they saw fit, wide disparities developed among them in terms of benefits and eligibility requirements.[98] Some states offered meager benefits and severely restricted eligibility, while others were much more generous. In 1972, Congress standardized the benefits and eligibility requirements of the programs for the elderly, the blind, and people with disabilities by consolidating them into a single, federally administered program called Supplemental Security Income (SSI). The cost of SSI and its predecessor programs has grown substantially over the past half-century, rising from $495 million in 1940 to $24.6 billion in 1993.[99]

Unlike the programs for the elderly, the blind, and people with disabilities, AFDC, which aids poor families with children, continues to operate as a separate program with different levels of support from one state to another. Originally, AFDC provided benefits only for children, and it was called Aid to Dependent Children. In the 1960s, Congress made mothers eligible for benefits and changed the program's title to AFDC. By 1993, AFDC cost $22.7 billion.[100] Although AFDC has received a great deal of attention from liberal and conservative reformers who are dissatisfied with it, the program pays only modest benefits: in 1993, the average benefit per family of four was $377 per month, or $4,524 per year, well below the poverty threshold of $14,763 per year.[101] Moreover, if you take inflation into account, AFDC benefits actually fell by 43 percent between 1970 and 1993.[102]

The growth in the number of people receiving AFDC benefits in the 1970s spurred criticism of the program. Critics argued that AFDC made its recipients dependent on the government and thereby trapped them in poverty. Critics also accused AFDC of undermining the two-parent family and allowing absent parents to avoid taking responsibility for their children.[103] Finally, critics complained that AFDC was riddled with fraud and waste. During the 1970s and 1980s, the federal government improved the management of AFDC, restricted eligibility, and made greater efforts to force deadbeat parents to support their children. In addition, many states cut the amounts of money AFDC recipients received each month.[104] The cumulative effect of these changes was to remove many thousands of families from the program. Several studies suggest that, as a result, millions of children fell below the poverty line.[105]

The War on Poverty

The Social Security Act of 1935 introduced the first major wave of social welfare policies in the United States. The second major wave came about during the presidency of Lyndon Johnson as part of his Great Society program. The public's attention had been drawn to

The Food Stamp program provides beneficiaries—who must meet a means test—with stamps (or coupons) they can use to buy food.

the existence of widespread poverty by Michael Harrington's famous book, *The Other America.*[106] Johnson responded by using his surge of popularity following President Kennedy's assassination to persuade Congress to undertake the War on Poverty.[107]

One legislative landmark in the War on Poverty was the passage of the Economic Opportunity Act of 1964. The act created the Office of Economic Opportunity (OEO), which was charged with administering a host of different social services programs. Among OEO's programs were the Job Corps, which provided job training for poor youths; the Neighborhood Youth Corps, which offered poor youths an opportunity to gain work experience; and Head Start, which provided educational opportunities for disadvantaged preschool children. Unlike the Social Security Act, which created programs that sought to alleviate or prevent poverty, the Equal Opportunity Act created programs that sought to "cure" poverty by helping the poor pull themselves out of poverty.[108]

The other major landmark in the War on Poverty was the passage of the Food Stamp Act of 1964, which created the **Food Stamp program.** The Department of Agriculture administers this program, which provides benefits only to people who meet a means test. Participants receive stamps (or coupons) that they use to buy food. Originally, recipients purchased the stamps at a discounted price, but today they receive them free of charge. The Food Stamp program cost relatively little in its early years, but its cost eventually ballooned as the pool of recipients expanded and the purchase requirement was eliminated. The cost of the program also responds quickly to changes in the economy. When unemployment rises during recessions, huge numbers of people apply for food stamps to help them through hard times. During the 1991 recession, for example, the number of people receiving food stamps jumped by 3 million to a total of almost 24 million at a cost of approximately $18 billion.[109]

Food Stamp program
A public assistance program established in 1964 that provides stamps (or coupons) to low-income people to buy food.

Although the War on Poverty attracted considerable fanfare, its success in reducing poverty was limited. Many of the programs created under the Economic Opportunity Act lasted only a few years before they were eliminated, consolidated, or transferred to other departments and agencies. The OEO itself was abolished in 1975. A few of the more popular and successful programs, such as Head Start, remain in operation today.

Why were so many of the War on Poverty programs phased out? A major reason was their curative approach to poverty.[110] Because they worked to empower the poor, these programs often produced activist organizations that challenged established power centers in cities across the country. This strained relations between the War on Poverty agencies and more traditional social services providers.[111] At the same time, although the OEO may have helped to reduce poverty, it did not eliminate it, which made it hard to maintain congressional support for the programs. In contrast, the Food Stamp program survived because it took the more traditional alleviative approach to poverty and because it had strong political support. Members of Congress from farm states support the Food Stamp program because it helps the poor to purchase more food products, and members from poor regions support it because it feeds their constituents. In other words, both farm state residents and residents of poverty-stricken areas are winners under the rules that administer the Food Stamp program.

Health Care

At the same time that the Johnson administration was launching its War on Poverty, it was also creating a new role for the federal government in financing health care for American citizens. Until the 1960s, the federal government had been very hesitant to fund health services. Whereas public health insurance had become commonplace in Europe by the 1940s, Congress repeatedly rejected any form of national health assistance on the grounds that such programs would open the door to "socialized medicine."[112] Why do Americans mistrust the idea of a nationalized health care system, which is so common in other industrialized democracies? Two reasons may be our historic skepticism, dating back to the days of the American Revolution, of big government, and our tendency to look to the private sector to provide most goods and services.

Because the United States had a history of leaving most aspects of social welfare in private hands and because most Americans preferred to rely on private business rather than government to deliver goods and services, the federal government did not develop a publicly financed health care system. Instead, it used its tax policies to support the development of a private health insurance system. Employers could deduct payments to employee health insurance programs as a part of the cost of doing business, and thus they did not pay taxes on those expenditures. At the same time, employees could exclude the value of their health insurance benefits at work from their income, thus making those benefits more attractive than comparable increases in taxable income. As a result, the United States developed a very large private health insurance industry.

With the Democrats' landslide victory in the 1964 elections, supporters of national health care finally had an opportunity to enact a federally financed health care program. Congress responded by passing the Medicare Act of 1965.[113] Much as the Social Security Act did, the Medicare Act created both a social insurance program (Medicare) and a public assistance program (Medicaid). Both programs target certain groups of Americans; neither provides the sort of universal health care coverage most other advanced industrial democracies provide.

Medicare
A social insurance program that provides basic hospital insurance and supplementary insurance for doctors' bills and other health care expenses for people over the age of sixty-five.

Medicare is a social insurance program that provides basic hospital insurance and supplementary insurance for doctors' bills and other health care expenses for people over the age of sixty-five. Its benefits are not means-tested. Anyone receiving Social Security is also eligible for Medicare. Part A of Medicare is a compulsory program funded by payroll taxes. It pays for a share of the recipient's hospital costs. Part B of Medicare is a voluntary program. Participants may choose to buy insurance to pay their doctor bills. Participants pay about one-quarter of the cost of the Part B insurance; the federal government pays for the rest out of general tax revenues.[114]

Medicaid
A public assistance program that provides publicly subsidized health care to low-income Americans.

Medicaid is a public assistance program that provides publicly subsidized health care, that is, health care paid for by the government. Participation is means-tested, with benefits available only to people with low incomes. The program consists of federal grants to the states that are funded out of general tax revenues. States match the federal government's contribution, establish their own eligibility requirements and benefit levels, and administer the program. Anyone eligible for AFDC or SSI payments is eligible (meets the means or income test) for Medicaid. Most states model their programs on Medicare and make direct payments to doctors on behalf of the recipient.

Table 17.4 shows how the costs of Medicare and Medicaid have grown. As you can see, the cost of Medicare grew more than twentyfold between 1970 and 1993. As for Medicaid, its cost grew more than sixteenfold, between 1970 and 1993, making it the federal government's largest and fastest growing form of public assistance. The question of how to rein in the growing costs of Medicare and Medicaid is the subject of considerable debate.[115]

TABLE 17.4 Costs of Federal Medicare and Medicaid Programs (in millions of current dollars)

The costs of Medicare and Medicaid have risen sharply since 1970.

Year	Medicare	Medicaid
1970	$7,493	$6,310
1980	$36,802	$28,007
1990	$110,984	$79,685
1993	$150,370	$101,709

Source: Data from *Statistical Abstract of the United States, 1995*, 115th ed. (Washington, D.C.: U.S. Bureau of the Census, 1995), pp. 113, 116.

The Current Status of Social Welfare Policy

What is the current status of social welfare policy in the United States? There are at least four ways to answer this question: (1) by comparing social welfare policies in the United States with those in other advanced industrial democracies; (2) by analyzing how the share of the federal budget spent on social welfare programs has changed in recent years; (3) by examining what the federal government spends on different types of social welfare programs; and (4) by trying to measure the success of social welfare programs.

Social Welfare Policies in Other Advanced Industrial Democracies

By virtually any measure one chooses, the United States spends far less on social welfare and provides a lower level of services than either Europe or Japan.[116] For example, whereas the United States in 1994 allocated 29.1 percent of its public spending to social welfare programs, most industrialized democracies devoted more than 40 percent of their government budgets to social welfare programs.[117] Because European countries spend so much more on social welfare, their citizens receive greater government benefits. For example, unlike the United States, most European countries have national health care programs in which the national government rather than the individual citizen pays for medical services.[118] The United States provides fewer public social welfare benefits than other advanced industrial democracies largely because of the American tradition of relying on the private sector for assistance.

Social Welfare Versus Other Types of Government Spending

As we mentioned earlier, the definition of social welfare policy is imprecise, so some controversy inevitably surrounds how to measure spending on social welfare. A good (but by no means perfect) measure is the portion of the federal budget devoted to making payments to individuals. This number includes the social welfare payments to individuals we discussed in this chapter, other social welfare benefits such as veterans benefits, and federal government pensions. As we saw in chapter 16, payments to individuals consumed less than 20 percent of the federal budget in 1940. Yet by 1995, this figure stood at roughly 50 percent.[119] Thus, social welfare constitutes an increasingly important priority in the federal government's budget. From a politician's perspective, the huge number of people receiving some kind of direct benefits from the government makes cutting those benefits politically hazardous.[120] Thus, Congress is reluctant to cut benefits, even though they constitute a huge and growing portion of the federal budget.

Spending on Different Types of Social Welfare Programs

What relative emphasis does the federal government place on different categories of social welfare programs? The answer can be found in table 17.5, which compares how the federal government spent its social welfare dollars in 1970 and 1992.

As table 17.5 shows, the federal government places its greatest emphasis on the preventative and alleviative strategies we discussed earlier and the least emphasis on the curative strategy. The preventative strategy approach includes our two largest social insurance programs—Social Security and Medicare. In 1992, those programs accounted for two-thirds of the federal government's social welfare expenditures. Spending on

TABLE 17.5 Distribution of Social Welfare Expenditures Across Programs (as a percentage of all social welfare expenditures)

The federal government spends the biggest share of its social welfare expenditures on social insurance programs that take a preventative approach to the problem of social welfare. It spends the smallest share on programs such as job training and education that take a curative approach to social welfare.

Year	Social Insurance	Public Aid	Health/Medical	Veterans Programs	Education	Housing	Other
1970	58.4%	13.0%	6.5%	11.7%	7.8%	1.3%	2.6%
1992	66.1%	18.6%	4.3%	4.5%	2.7%	2.4%	1.5%

Source: Data from *Statistical Abstract of the United States, 1995,* 115th ed. (Washington, D.C.: U.S. Bureau of the Census, 1995), p. 375.

public aid, the primary example of the alleviative strategy, accounted for another 18 percent. That left little room for spending on service-oriented, curative strategy programs such as job training or education. Moreover, as a comparison of spending in 1970 and 1992 makes clear, the emphasis on the preventative and alleviative strategies has increased over the past two decades.

What accounts for these spending patterns? First, social insurance programs have their own earmarked source of revenue—namely, payroll taxes. Second, social insurance payments are popular with Americans of all ages.[121] These programs are not means-tested, so everyone who meets age and other eligibility criteria receives a payment regardless of income. Third, Social Security and Medicare largely benefit the elderly, who also happen to be a politically powerful interest group. People age sixty-five and over make up 13 percent of the population and, as chapter 6 discusses, they have an extremely high voter turnout rate. No politician wants to alienate such a powerful voting bloc. As a result, members of Congress find it politically difficult to enact legislation to restrict eligibility or lower benefits.

Measuring the Success of Social Welfare Programs

The success of the federal government's social welfare programs is a matter of sharp conflict. Conservatives claim that social welfare programs have failed; liberals claim that most of them work and that the rest need only moderate reform in order to work.[122] To a large extent, the question of success or failure turns on which measures one chooses to use.

Direct measures of the success of social welfare programs reveal a great deal of success in some areas and only mixed progress in others. Poverty has declined substantially in the United States, largely as the result of social welfare programs. It is, however, far from being eliminated.[123] As we saw in chapter 3, 22 percent of the population lived in poverty in 1960, but by 1970—after the expansion of Social Security and the introduction of food stamps, AFDC, Medicare, and Medicaid—only 13 percent lived below the poverty line.[124] After 1970, government social welfare programs ceased to expand and the proportion of our population living in poverty leveled off. It then began to edge up again in the 1980s.

The decline and eventual leveling off of the overall poverty rate in the United States obscures important differences among different groups of Americans. As we saw in chapter 3, the drop in poverty that the Great Society programs produced was especially rapid for the elderly. Before 1960, people over age sixty-five had a higher poverty rate than any other age group; by 1995, only 10.5 percent of those over sixty-five lived in poverty—below the national average of 13.8 percent.[125] One government study found that in 1984, the poverty rate would have been 55 percent among those over sixty-five if not for Social Security.[126] In contrast, the poverty rate among children has actually grown over the past two decades; in 1970, 14.9 percent of all children under the age of eighteen lived below the poverty line, whereas in 1995, the figure stood at 20.8 percent.[127]

The state of the nation's health has also improved as a result of social welfare programs. Measuring the health of a nation is difficult, but one widely used measure is the

Social welfare programs have had some successes. For example, following the creation in the 1960s of programs such as Medicaid and Food Stamps, the infant mortality rate in the United States dropped sharply.

infant mortality rate (that is, the percentage of children who die before their first birthdays). Following the introduction of Medicaid, which provides health care for the poor, and the AFDC and Food Stamp programs, which provide healthier diets, the infant mortality rate in the United States dropped quickly. In 1960, the rate stood at 26.0 per thousand live births, by 1975, it was only 16.1 per thousand, and by 1993, it was 8.3 per thousand.[128] Improved medicine certainly caused some of the decline in infant mortality, but the decline was sharpest among the poor—who directly benefit from social welfare programs. Consequently, experts agree that social welfare programs explain a large portion of the improvement in our nation's health.[129]

When one examines other possible effects of social welfare programs, the system seems less successful. The divorce rate, the percentage of children living in single-parent families, and the crime rate have all increased sharply since the 1960s. Some critics argue that the welfare system has caused these changes as unintended side-effects. Perhaps most disturbing of all, some conservative critics contend that the welfare system has produced an underclass of people who are permanently trapped in poverty because of the incentives the welfare system offers.[130] The extent to which the welfare system has caused these changes in our society is difficult to estimate, however, because divorce, single-parent households, and crime are increasing among both those who receive welfare and those who do not.[131]

The Future of Social Welfare Policy

Social welfare policy is an issue that unites as well as separates Democrats from Republicans. On the one hand, neither Democrats nor Republicans are eager to touch the country's largest social welfare program, Social Security, even though most impartial analyses show that the program is headed for bankruptcy unless Congress makes fundamental changes to it. On the other hand, Democrats and Republicans disagree sharply over what should be done in the important areas of welfare and health care. Whereas Democrats argue that the federal government should play a major role in lifting people out of poverty and ensuring that they have adequate medical care, Republicans argue for greater reliance on individual initiative and the workings of the marketplace.

Social Security

Social Security looms as a potential point of conflict between the generations in the years ahead. Two important questions lie at the core of the debate: (1) whom should the federal government spend its money on, and (2) is Social Security headed for insolvency?

As chapter 16 discusses, the federal government spends nearly eleven times more per capita on the elderly than on the young.[132] Three factors explain why this disparity in government spending exists. First, Social Security is a mandatory social insurance program for all workers, while programs for the young target only children in poor families. Second, because Social Security affects many more people, it enjoys greater political support and is less vulnerable to budget-cutting pressures. Third, the young, unlike the elderly, have no direct representation or access to power in government; hence, they aren't able to push for programs that affect their interests. One question facing the American public, therefore, is whether the federal government should continue to spend so heavily on Social Security for the elderly when far more children than senior citizens live in poverty. When the interests of the elderly and children conflict, how should the rules of social welfare be structured? Who should benefit? These are difficult questions that arouse considerable controversy.

The second issue surrounding Social Security concerns whether the program will remain solvent.[133] As chapter 16 notes, revenues from current payroll taxes pay for current Social Security benefits. The flaw with this pay-as-you-go system is that, over the years, the ratio of workers paying taxes to retirees drawing benefits has fallen. In 1950, for instance, as we have previously noted, there were fifteen workers for every retiree; in 1990, there were only five; and experts predict that by 2030, there will be fewer than three.[134] If this trend continues unchanged, some time in the next twenty years the annual cost of Social Security will exceed the revenue from payroll taxes; and once the surpluses that have built up over the years are exhausted, Social Security will become insolvent.

Proposals for keeping Social Security solvent include increasing payroll taxes, cutting benefits, tightening eligibility standards for recipients, and tapping general tax revenues. None of these options is attractive given the tremendous political support that exists in the United States for Social Security as well as the tremendous political opposition to increasing taxes. That is why during the acrimonious congressional debates in 1995 over how to shrink the size of the federal government, both Republicans and Democrats insisted that they would not touch Social Security. Nonetheless, if the ratio of workers to retirees continues to decline, Congress and the president will eventually be forced to confront the contentious question of how to keep Social Security solvent.[135]

Welfare Policy

Welfare policy in the United States, which usually means the AFDC and Food Stamp programs, reflects an uneasy balance between the public's desire to help people in need and its reluctance to give aid to the able-bodied or to those, such as impoverished drug addicts, who the public believe are responsible for their own poverty.[136] This tension has been reflected historically in the government's efforts to target the "deserving" poor—for example, Civil War veterans and widowed mothers—for assistance. The tension is evident today in public opinion polls about the poor and what the government should do to help them.

Although the public expresses dissatisfaction with our current welfare system, an overwhelming majority endorses the idea that the government should provide a social safety net of welfare programs for the poor (though this support has eroded somewhat in recent years).[137] We can see evidence of support in a public opinion survey conducted in 1993 that asked whether the government was "spending too much, too little, or about the right amount on assistance to the poor." Sixty-five percent responded too little, but only 12 percent said too much.[138] Questions about the sources of poverty, however, divide the public. For example, a poll taken in 1994 asked, "In your opinion, which is generally more often to blame if a person is poor—lack of effort on his own part, or circumstances beyond his control?" Forty-four percent said lack of effort; 34 percent said circumstances; and the rest said both or were undecided.[139] Finally, questions about specific welfare reforms enjoy different levels of support depending on whether the public sees the people in question as taking advantage of the system or trying to get back on their feet. A 1994 poll, for example, found that 61 percent of the public favors cutting all benefits to people who have not found jobs after two years; yet another poll shows that more than 90 percent of the public favors helping the poor get off welfare by paying for their child care.[140]

In 1995, Republicans took control of Congress for the first time in forty years. Led by Speaker of the House Newt Gingrich (R-Ga.), they sought to dismantle much of President Lyndon Johnson's Great Society.

Reprinted by permission: Tribune Media Services.

Whether to blame the poor or society for poverty remains at the core of our public debate over welfare reform.[141] Because many Americans believe welfare often goes to people who are to blame for their poverty and who do not actually need assistance, welfare reform became a hot topic of debate in the 1990s (see box 17.2).

Conservatives leveled many criticisms at the existing welfare program.[142] They argued that the program promoted dependence on government aid and created a class of people who had never worked and so lacked good work skills. They claimed that welfare contributed to the breakdown of the two-parent family by making it financially easier for unwed teenagers to have babies. In 1995, 32.4 percent of American families headed by a single woman lived in poverty, compared to only 10.8 percent for all families.[143]

Welfare's defenders saw the issue differently.[144] They denied that welfare encourages single-parent households and long-term dependency. They instead criticized welfare programs for providing inadequate education and job training, and they complained that programs that try to influence people's behavior (for example, by denying extra benefits to women who have additional children) put the poor at risk of homelessness, malnutrition, and other dangers.[145]

In 1996, President Clinton and the Republican Congress agreed on a welfare reform bill that addressed many of the conservatives' concerns.[146] Most important, the new law ended a 60-year guarantee of welfare to all eligible individuals by transforming the old entitlement program into a block grant to the states, and by giving the states the power to determine eligibility and benefit levels. The law also requires welfare recipients to find work within two years of receiving aid, bars recipients from getting benefits for more than five years, denies legal aliens access to most federal welfare benefits, and cuts the Food Stamp program. These changes should reduce the cost of welfare by $54 billion over the next six years.

Although the new welfare reform law began to fulfill President Clinton's 1992 campaign promise to "end welfare as we know it," but it may create new problems. Welfare experts warn that recipients may not receive adequate job training and that there may not be enough jobs for them. That could put hundreds of thousands of children and families on the streets.[147] If the experts' warnings prove true, then welfare reform will likely remain at the top of the nation's agenda.

Health Policy

The central issues in health care policy are cost and access. The government's health care costs have grown much faster than the cost of living. Spending on Medicaid leads the way, with an annual growth rate of 30 percent.[148] The cost of privately paid health care has skyrocketed as well. As a result, health care is consuming a large and growing

The People Behind the Rules

BOX 17.2

Who Receives Welfare? Image Versus Reality

The typical welfare recipient is a white, poorly educated, single mother who lives in dire poverty.

Welfare reform is a hot topic in American politics. Bill Clinton campaigned for the presidency in 1992 on a pledge to "end welfare as we know it." Polls show that roughly 70 percent of the American public believes that welfare programs do more harm than good. In 1996, President Clinton signed a Republican-inspired welfare reform bill into law. As government officials rewrite the rules governing the country's welfare programs, it is useful to ask: who typically receives welfare?

To judge by the complaints from conservatives that welfare encourages women to have children out of wedlock, and by the photos that accompany most stories in the media about welfare, the typical welfare recipient is a single African-American woman with several children who lives in the inner city. Moreover, in the popular imagination the typical recipient is a "welfare queen" who has been living a life of leisure at taxpayer expense for years. For example, polls show that roughly 50 percent of the American public believes that welfare recipients get more benefits than they need, and 80 percent believes that welfare recipients are so dependent on government benefits they will never get off welfare.

Is the popular image of the typical welfare recipient accurate? The answer is partly yes, but mostly no. As the popular imagination would suggest, the typical welfare recipient is a single, poorly educated mother under age thirty. Mothers in the age category of 15 to 44 who are receiving benefits from Aid to Families with Dependent Children (AFDC) are five years younger on average than mothers in the same age group who are not AFDC recipients (29.5 versus 34 years of age). They also have slightly more children (2.6 versus 2.1). Moreover, mothers receiving AFDC benefits are far more likely to have dropped out of high school than mothers who are not recipients. And AFDC recipients are far more likely to be female; AFDC provides benefits to roughly 4.3 million families headed by women and only 300,000 families headed by men.

Yet the common image of the typical welfare recipient is mistaken in four important ways:

Most welfare mothers are white. In 1995, roughly 55 percent of welfare recipients were white, 39 percent were African American, and 21 percent were Hispanic American. (These numbers add to more than 100 percent because Hispanic Americans can be of any race.) However, the percentage of white welfare recipients is smaller than the share of whites in the total population (75 percent). In contrast, the percentage of African-American and Hispanic-American recipients is greater than their respective shares of the total population (12 percent and 9 percent).

Few if any welfare recipients live like royalty. Roughly three-quarters of all welfare recipients live on a monthly family income of less than $1,000 per month, while 90 percent of nonrecipients live on more than $1,000 per month.

Welfare recipients live in suburbs and rural areas as well as cities. While the percentage of residents receiving welfare benefits is higher in inner cities, sizable numbers of welfare recipients live in the suburbs as well as in rural areas.

Most people do not stay on welfare permanently. How long people stay on welfare is difficult to measure and is a subject of great debate. One recent study found that more than 50 percent of welfare recipients left the welfare system within four years. Another study found that about 40 percent of women on welfare are short-term users, while 30 percent are periodic users. When compared to people who remain on welfare for more than five years, people who receive welfare for two years or less are likely to be minority members, to have dropped out of high school, and to have never married—those the popular wisdom suggests are most likely to make welfare a way of life.

Thus, the typical welfare recipient is different from what the public imagines. Yet as we have stressed throughout the book, concentrating solely on the average or typical person can be misleading. In particular, while most welfare recipients do not become permanently dependent on welfare, some do. One of the challenges that government officials face as they rewrite the rules governing welfare is how to redesign the system so that it discourages long-term dependency but still provides a safety net for those who need it.

Sources: Jeffrey L. Katz, "Sampling Welfare Users," *Congressional Quarterly Weekly Report,* 22 January 1994, p. 122; "Profile of Mothers Receiving Welfare Payments," *USA Today,* 3 March 1995; R. Kent Weaver, Robert Y. Shapiro, and Lawrence R. Jacobs, "The Polls—Trends," *Public Opinion Quarterly* 59 (Winter 1995): 606–27.

When Republicans sought to cut Medicare spending in 1995 and 1996, they met opposition from seniors as well as from the White House and congressional Democrats.

share of the economy. In 1950, the United States spent roughly 4 percent of its gross domestic product on health care. By 1970, that figure had risen to 7 percent, and by 1993 it had risen to 14 percent.[149] Some experts project that if no policy changes are made, by 2002, health care costs will consume one-fifth of the nation's GDP.[150]

The other major issue in health care policy is access to medical care. Even though the United States has the world's largest private health insurance industry as well as both Medicare and Medicaid, at any given time about 17 percent of Americans have no health insurance.[151] Most people who lack health insurance either are unemployed or work at low-paying jobs that do not provide medical benefits. Because doctor visits can be expensive, people without insurance tend to seek medical care only when their illnesses are more advanced and thus more expensive to treat. Other consumers of medical care finance part of the cost of treating the uninsured by paying higher bills and premiums as doctors and hospitals pass their expenses on to patients who have insurance. Finally, despite the fact that the United States pays more per capita for medical care than any other major industrial nation, many objective measures of our nation's health (for example, the infant mortality rate) indicate that the quality of our health care is among the lowest of the major industrial nations.[152]

In 1993, President Clinton attempted to deal with the problems of both cost and access by proposing to overhaul the health care system in the United States.[153] He sought to create a system of universal health insurance, or insurance covering all Americans, that would combine the current system of private insurers and employment-based coverage with government administration. Clinton's proposal attracted criticism from both Democrats, many of whom favored creating a government-run national health insurance program, and Republicans, most of whom preferred to rely on the private sector to solve the cost and access problems. Congress failed to act on Clinton's proposal before the 1994 elections, and the subsequent Republican victory dealt the final death blow to his plan.

When the Republicans took control of Congress in 1995, they sought to enact their own plans for dealing with escalating health care costs. As part of an ambitious effort to cut federal spending, the Republicans passed legislation that would have revamped both Medicare and Medicaid. The Republican plan would have reduced projected spending on Medicare, the federal government's health insurance for the elderly, by an estimated $270 billion over seven years. The savings would have come largely from paying doctors and hospitals less for their services, from encouraging elderly Americans to choose lower-cost forms of health insurance, and from requiring more affluent beneficiaries to pay more for their Medicare coverage. As for Medicaid, the Republican plan would have cut projected spending on the public assistance program for the poor by an estimated $163 billion over seven years. The Republicans' Medicaid reform plan also would have given state governments great freedom to decide who would be covered and what benefits they would get.[154] Not surprisingly, Democrats, led by President Clinton, denounced the Republican legislation as an effort to balance the budget on the backs of the poor and the elderly.[155] Both the Medicare and Medicaid legislation became caught up in an epic battle between the White House and Capitol Hill over the federal budget (see chapter 16). Ultimately, Republicans lacked the votes they needed to override the president's veto.

In health care, welfare, Social Security, and other aspects of social welfare policy, a tension exists that symbolizes the broader questions the United States faces in dealing with domestic policy: What responsibility does government have to address the problems of the people? What limitations should government face when intervening in these areas? Conflicts over domestic policy will continue as our society experiences changing pressures, and the rules of domestic policy will change as government responds.

Summary

In this chapter, we have considered three types of domestic policy: management of the economy, regulatory policy, and social welfare policy. In all three areas, the rules change as the needs and views of the American people and their elected representatives change. And in domestic policy, as in all areas of government, changes in the rules cause some groups to gain and others to lose. This creates an ongoing question for Americans: To what extent should the federal government intervene in the lives of people? How active a role should the government take in setting domestic policy?

Traditionally, the federal government adopted laissez faire domestic policy, allowing the economy, businesses, and individuals to manage without government interference. However, during the Great Depression of the 1930s, the federal government took on a new activist role. It now uses both fiscal tools (the budget) and monetary tools (the Fed's control over the money supply) to manage the economy. While these policies have generally been successful, many conflicts over economic policy remain. Today's economic theorists split in advocating either more or less government intervention in the economy.

The federal government currently engages in economic and social regulation. With economic regulation, the government seeks to promote economic competition when possible and to counter the harmful effects of monopoly when not. Social regulation became a significant government activity in the 1960s and 1970s. It seeks to protect Americans from dangers or unfair practices associated with how companies produce their products as well as from dangers associated with the products themselves.

The federal government's involvement in social welfare dates back to the New Deal. Today it includes both social insurance programs to protect the elderly and public assistance programs to help the poor. The bulk of social welfare is provided through social insurance programs. Debates over the future of social insurance programs will be shaped by the strong support they enjoy and by their growing cost. In contrast, the future of most public assistance programs is clouded by public skepticism over their effectiveness in alleviating poverty and helping the poor to become self-sufficient. Debate also centers around the most effective type of public assistance programs—alleviative, preventative, or curative—and whether the federal government or the states should administer such programs.

As the United States faces the rapid changes and challenges of the twenty-first century, it will need to adapt. In domestic policy, as in other areas of government, this means constantly reexamining and changing our rules and policies to reflect changes in society and in the world. And so the political conflict goes on—the groups compete—and the ever-changing rules of domestic policy create new winners and losers in American society. Just who those winners and losers will be over the next few decades remains to be seen.

Key Terms

Aid to Families with Dependent Children (AFDC)
Economic regulation
Environmental impact statement
Federal Reserve System
Fiscal policy
Food Stamp program
Gross domestic product (GDP)
Industrial policy
Keynesian economics
Laissez faire
Lucas critique
Means test
Medicaid
Medicare
Monetary theory
Public assistance
Regulatory policy
Social insurance
Social regulation
Social welfare policy
Supply-side economics

Readings for Further Study

Cook, Fay Lomax, and Edith J. Barrett. *Support for the American Welfare State: The Views of Congress and the Public.* New York: Columbia University Press, 1992. The authors argue that the "American welfare state is here to stay" because support for social welfare programs has deep roots with the American people and their elected representatives in Congress.

Gans, Herbert J. *The War Against the Poor: The Underclass and Anti-Poverty Policy.* New York: Basic Books, 1995. A leading sociologist argues that pejorative labels have been used to relegate the poor to the margins of society.

Greider, William. *Secrets of the Temple: How the Federal Reserve Runs the Country.* New York: Simon & Schuster, 1987. An absorbing account of how the Federal Reserve Bank manages the American economy.

Kettl, Donald F., and John J. Dilulio, Jr. *Cutting Government.* Washington, D.C.: Brookings Institution, 1995. Two leading scholars seek to answer the question: "If the federal government is to perform fewer tasks and to approach those that it does perform differently, who exactly will perform these tasks and how will they do it?"

Landy, Marc K., Marc J. Roberts, and Stephen R. Thomas. *The Environmental Protection Agency: From Nixon to Clinton,* expanded ed. New York: Oxford University Press, 1994. A well-written history of the Environmental Protection Agency.

Murray, Charles. *Losing Ground: American Social Policy, 1950–1980,* 10th anniversary ed. New York: Basic Books, 1995. A revised edition of a controversial book that argues that social welfare programs have had the unintended consequence of trapping the poor in poverty.

Norris, Donald F., and Lyke Thompson, eds. *The Politics of Welfare Reform.* Thousand Oaks, Calif.: Sage, 1995. An accessible collection of articles on the steps state governments have taken to overhaul their welfare programs.

Starr, Paul. *The Social Transformation of American Medicine.* New York: Basic Books, 1982. An award-winning book that shows why the United States developed a health care system that relies so heavily on private businesses rather than the government.

Chapter 18

Foreign Policy

A Brief History of U.S. Foreign Policy
- *The Era of Isolationism*
- *The Era of Globalism*
- *After the Cold War*

Foreign Policy Versus Domestic Policy
- *The Constitution and Foreign Policy*
- *The President's Inherent Advantages*
- *Precedent*
- *Supreme Court Rulings*
- *The Behavior of Congress*

Who Makes U.S. Foreign Policy?
- *The White House*
- *The Foreign Policy Bureaucracy*
- *Congress*
- *The Public*

Challenges to the United States in the Post–Cold War Era
- *Economic and Budgetary Constraints*
- *A Changing Foreign Policy Agenda*
- *Unilateralism Versus Multilateralism*

Summary

Key Terms

Readings for Further Study

In 1992, Croats, Muslims, and Serbs began to wage a war for control of Bosnia, a republic in the former Yugoslavia. The bitter fighting raged off and on for three years, and more than 250,000 men, women, and children were killed. Many observers feared that the fighting in Bosnia might spread to other parts of Europe, jeopardizing the political stability the United States had sought for nearly fifty years to preserve. In late 1995, at the behest of the United States, Croat, Muslim, and Serb officials finally agreed to sign a peace treaty. To give peace a chance to take root, Bill Clinton and America's European allies agreed to send more than 60,000 peacekeeping troops, including 20,000 Americans, to Bosnia. In defending the peacekeeping mission to the American people, President Clinton argued that American participation was necessary "to help stop the killings of innocent civilians, especially children, and at the same time to bring stability to central Europe, a region of the world that is vital to our national interests."[1]

The peacekeeping mission to Bosnia reminds us that the United States has interests that lie outside its borders. Because world events can have a dramatic effect on U.S. interests, the federal government must be able to chart a wise course in foreign policy. When asked about foreign policy, most people naturally think of national security issues such as the dispatch of U.S. troops to Bosnia. But U.S. involvement with the rest of the world extends far beyond military matters. Foreign policy encompasses all the decisions that govern America's relations with the rest of the world. Drug trafficking, global warming, human rights, immigration, nuclear proliferation, and trade are just a few of the issues on the foreign policy agenda. And, as we have seen throughout this book, changes in priorities and needs mean changes in rules, and new rules mean new outcomes. Foreign policy presents an especially challenging arena as the potential for conflict and the need to manage that conflict extend beyond the boundaries of the United States to nations around the globe.

We begin the chapter with a brief history of U.S. foreign policy, reviewing how the United States abandoned its traditional isolationism when it assumed the role of a global superpower after World War II. In the second section of the chapter, we analyze the differences between decision making on foreign policy and domestic policy, discussing how the inherent advantages of the presidency and changing interpretations of constitutional rules have increased the power of the executive branch at the expense of Congress when it comes to foreign policy. In the third section, we review the roles of the president, the foreign policy bureaucracy, Congress, and the public in making foreign policy. And finally, we explore the challenges the United States faces in the post–Cold War era.

A Brief History of U.S. Foreign Policy

Americans are accustomed to thinking of the United States as a global power. Yet for most of its history, the United States played a small role in world politics. Before World War II, both Democratic and Republican administrations generally avoided becoming entangled in the affairs of other countries, and especially the affairs of Europe. Pearl Harbor changed all that. The late 1990s may see yet another dramatic change in the direction of U.S. foreign policy. The collapse of the Soviet Union has triggered a debate over what role the United States should play in a post–Cold War world.

Because the choices and rules made in the past greatly influence the present, this section briefly surveys three periods in U.S. diplomatic history: the isolationist era (1789–1941); the era of globalism (1942–1989); and the post–Cold War era (1990 to the present).

Isolationism
A foreign policy built on the principle of avoiding formal military and political alliances with other countries.

The Era of Isolationism

For its first 150 years, the United States followed a policy of **isolationism,** avoiding what Thomas Jefferson called "entangling alliances" with other nations.[2] When war broke out

In 1995, Croats, Muslims, and Serbs signed a peace treaty for war-torn Bosnia. To help peace take root, President Clinton and European leaders sent in 60,000 peacekeeping troops.

in Europe in 1793, President George Washington had to decide whether the United States should side with France, as the French had sided with the American colonists fifteen years earlier. Unwilling to plunge a young and weak country into war, Washington announced the United States would pursue a policy of neutrality. Three years later, Washington laid down a general guideline for U.S. foreign policy in his Farewell Address: "The great rule of conduct for us in regard to foreign nations is, in extending our commercial relations to have with them as little *political* connection as possible."[3]

The young nation followed the advice of its first president to avoid formal political ties with other countries while pursuing business relationships abroad. The staying power of isolationism was the result of three factors. First, as a weak country with a small military, it made sense for the United States to keep out of foreign wars. Second, the geographic isolation of the United States from the great powers of Europe saved it from being drawn inadvertently into conflicts with larger and more powerful countries. Third, for much of the nineteenth century, most of America's energies were absorbed in settling the frontier—and conquering the American Indian population—and not in playing a major role on the world stage.

Although U.S. foreign policy can be characterized as isolationist for the century and a half preceding World War II, this does not mean that the United States ignored the rest of the world during that time. The main thrust of isolationism was to avoid political and military obligations to other countries. The United States eagerly sought, however, to develop its overseas trade. To that end, presidents negotiated an array of treaties with other countries on matters such as commercial relations and navigation of the seas. Most Americans believed that international trade would help develop the U.S. economy and promote international goodwill.

Along with avoiding political ties, isolationism primarily meant staying out of the affairs of Europe. Asia, and particularly Latin America, were another matter. Relatively early in U.S. history, presidents began to distinguish between the "Old World" of Europe and the "New World" of the Western Hemisphere. In a message to Congress in 1823, President James Monroe announced that the United States would not interfere in the affairs of Europe, but he warned Europeans that the Americas were "henceforth not to be considered as subjects for future colonization" and that the United States would "consider any attempt on their part to extend their system to any portion of this hemisphere as dangerous to our peace and safety."[4] With this speech, which laid the foundation for what became known as the **Monroe Doctrine,** the United States promised to stay out of European affairs and warned Europe to stay out of Latin America.[5]

Monroe Doctrine
A basic principle of U.S. foreign policy that dates back to a warning President James Monroe issued in 1823 that the United States would resist further European efforts to intervene in the affairs of the Western Hemisphere.

In his Farewell Address, George Washington urged his fellow Americans to pursue a policy of isolationism in foreign affairs, advice the United States followed for a century and a half.

When Monroe placed the Americas off limits to further European colonization, the United States lacked the military power to back up its threat. Nor was the United States heavily involved in Latin America for most of the nineteenth century; no president formally invoked the Monroe Doctrine until 1895.[6] But as the turn of the century approached, U.S. involvement in Latin America, and Asia as well, began to grow.[7] In the Spanish-American War of 1898, for instance, the United States acquired control of Puerto Rico and the Philippines from Spain, and it used the war as an opportunity and a justification to annex the formerly independent Hawaiian Islands. (The Philippines was given its independence in 1946.)

U.S. involvement abroad was especially prominent in Latin America at the turn of the century. Whereas the Monroe Doctrine originally sought to bar outside interference in the affairs of Latin America, by 1900, presidents had begun to use it to justify U.S. intervention in the region. In 1903, the U.S. Navy intervened to help Panama secede from Colombia, an event that enabled the United States to build the Panama Canal and to gain control over the canal zone. And between 1904 and 1934, the United States sent eight expeditionary forces to Latin America and conducted five extended military occupations, including one in Nicaragua that lasted nineteen years.

If the first decades of the twentieth century saw increased U.S. involvement in Asia and Latin America, they also witnessed the first major break with the tradition of staying aloof from European wars. When World War I began in Europe, President Woodrow Wilson urged Americans to be "neutral in thought as well as in action."[8] But Germany's decision to wage submarine warfare against U.S. shipping and its efforts to convince Mexico to attack the United States (and thereby reclaim New Mexico, Texas, and Arizona) combined to push the United States into the war.

With the end of World War I, the United States reverted to its tradition of isolationism. In 1919 and again in 1920, the Senate refused to approve the Treaty of Versailles, the treaty that President Wilson had helped negotiate to end World War I. The major point of controversy was the treaty's provisions creating a League of Nations. Critics complained that membership in the League violated the U.S. tradition of avoiding political alliances

In the wake of the Japanese attack on Pearl Harbor, the United States abandoned its isolationalist stance on foreign policy.

and that the League would draw the United States into conflicts in which it had no interests. Although supporters of the treaty formed a majority in the Senate, they lacked the two-thirds majority needed to prevail.[9]

With the rejection of the Treaty of Versailles, isolationist sentiment in the United States intensified. Throughout the 1920s and 1930s, isolationist forces in Congress, who counted their greatest strength among Republicans from the Midwest, fought efforts supporting a more internationalist foreign policy. Although many isolationists worried about the rise to power of Adolf Hitler in Germany and Benito Mussolini in Italy, they believed that U.S. interests would be best served by staying out of the affairs of Europe. For most Americans, that belief died on December 7, 1941, when Japanese planes bombed the U.S. fleet at Pearl Harbor.

The Era of Globalism

When the Japanese attacked Pearl Harbor, a shocked nation abandoned its traditional isolationism and embraced the war against the Axis Powers. As the war came to a close, however, many Allied leaders feared that the United States would disengage itself from world affairs as it had after World War I, leaving Europe and Asia to fend for themselves. These fears proved groundless, however. By 1950, the United States had abandoned its traditional isolationism for a foreign policy based on **globalism,** the idea that the United States should be prepared to use military force around the globe to defend its political and economic interests.

The turning point in U.S. policy came in 1947. Greek communists were waging a guerrilla war, and U.S. officials feared that a communist victory in Greece would destabilize Europe. After consulting with congressional leaders, President Truman proposed sending aid to Greece. In a speech to Congress defending the proposal, the president announced what became known as the **Truman Doctrine:** the United States must "support free peoples who are resisting attempted subjugation by armed minorities or by outside pressure."[10] For the first time, a president had defined U.S. interests in global terms.

The **Marshall Plan,** named after then-Secretary of State George C. Marshall, soon followed the Truman Doctrine.[11] Under this program, the United States provided massive amounts of aid to help rebuild war-torn Europe. Between 1948 and 1952, the United States spent nearly 1.5 percent of its gross national product each year, or the equivalent of $100 billion today, on aid to Europe. To put these figures in perspective, in 1993—as several nations struggled to emerge from communist rule and establish themselves politically and economically—the United States spent only 0.15 percent of its gross national product, or $9.7 billion, on official development assistance.[12]

Globalism
The idea that the United States should be prepared to use military force around the globe to defend its political and economic interests.

Truman Doctrine
A policy, announced by President Truman in 1947, that the United States would oppose communist attempts to overthrow or conquer non-communist countries.

Marshall Plan
A multibillion-dollar U.S. aid program in the late 1940s and early 1950s that helped Western European countries rebuild their economies in the wake of World War II.

Containment
A bedrock principle of U.S. foreign policy from the 1940s to the 1980s that emphasized the need to prevent communist countries, especially the Soviet Union, from expanding the territory they controlled.

Cold War
A phrase used to describe the high level of tension and distrust that characterized relations between the Soviet Union and the United States from the late 1940s until the early 1990s.

North Atlantic Treaty Organization (NATO)
A military alliance founded in 1949 for the purpose of defending Western Europe from attack. Members of NATO include the United States, Canada, and fourteen European countries.

Third World
A term loosely defined to mean the developing countries in Asia, Africa, and Latin America.

By defining U.S. interests in global terms, President Truman established what would become the overriding objective of U.S. foreign policy for the next forty years: the **containment** of communist expansion. U.S. officials especially feared Soviet expansionism. Although the United States and the Soviet Union had been allies during World War II, tensions between the two were so high by the late 1940s that people spoke of a **Cold War** (as distinct from a hot, or shooting, war). Fears of Soviet expansionism led the United States in 1949 to help create the **North Atlantic Treaty Organization (NATO),** a military alliance designed to protect Western Europe against a Soviet invasion (see figure 18.1). By making itself the guarantor of European security, the United States clearly cast off its traditional isolationism to assume a leading role in world politics.

The policy of containment was tested in June 1950 when communist North Korea invaded South Korea. Although the Truman administration had previously doubted the strategic importance of the Korean peninsula, the United States, acting with the approval of the United Nations, quickly came to South Korea's defense. After initially being almost driven off the Korean peninsula, U.S. and South Korean forces came close to defeating the North Korean army. They were forced to retreat once again, however, and the war turned into a stalemate when the People's Republic of China intervened on behalf of North Korea in November 1950. (Chinese communists had triumphed in China's civil war a year earlier.) By the time both sides signed an armistice in 1953, more than 54,000 Americans had died.

The failure to win in Korea did not undermine the U.S. commitment to containment. In Europe, the United States spent tremendous sums to deter a possible Soviet invasion. In the **Third World,** a term loosely defined to mean Asia, Africa, and Latin America, the United States continued to move aggressively against what it perceived as communist threats. It began to provide economic and military aid to anti-communist governments, and it encouraged them to form military alliances modeled after NATO. In some cases, the United States went so far as to help overthrow governments it perceived as too sympathetic to the Soviet Union.

In pursuing the policy of containment in the 1950s and early 1960s, presidents enjoyed considerable congressional and public support. When presidents did come under fire on foreign policy, they usually were criticized for being too passive rather than too aggressive in dealing with the communist threat. John F. Kennedy, for example, campaigned for the White House in 1960 criticizing the Eisenhower administration for allowing the Soviet Union to grab the lead in ballistic missile technology (a claim that turned out to be false). Kennedy later found himself criticized for being too soft in dealing with the Soviet Union.

The national consensus in favor of a policy of global containment crumbled in Vietnam.[13] Unlike the case with the war in Korea, the United States became involved in Vietnam slowly, over a period of years. The United States initially became involved in 1950 when the Truman administration responded to the communist victory in China by agreeing to pay part of the cost of French rule in Vietnam. (France, which had lost control of Vietnam to Japan during World War II, had subsequently tried to reestablish its colonial rule.) U.S. officials hoped that the French would block Chinese expansionism in the region. When Vietnamese communist troops forced France to withdraw from Vietnam in 1954, the country split in two and the United States threw its support behind the non-communist South. The first U.S. military advisers went to South Vietnam during the Eisenhower administration to try to stem a communist insurgency. U.S. combat troops did not arrive in South Vietnam in large numbers, however, until 1965. The number of U.S. soldiers in South Vietnam steadily increased over the next three years, peaking at 540,000 in 1968.

The communist insurgency continued despite the U.S. military buildup. As public criticism of the war began to surface in late 1967, the U.S. commander in Vietnam claimed the situation had reached the "point where the end begins to come into view."[14] Then, in January 1968, communist forces launched a surprise attack called the Tet Offensive. Although the attackers were eventually routed, television scenes of

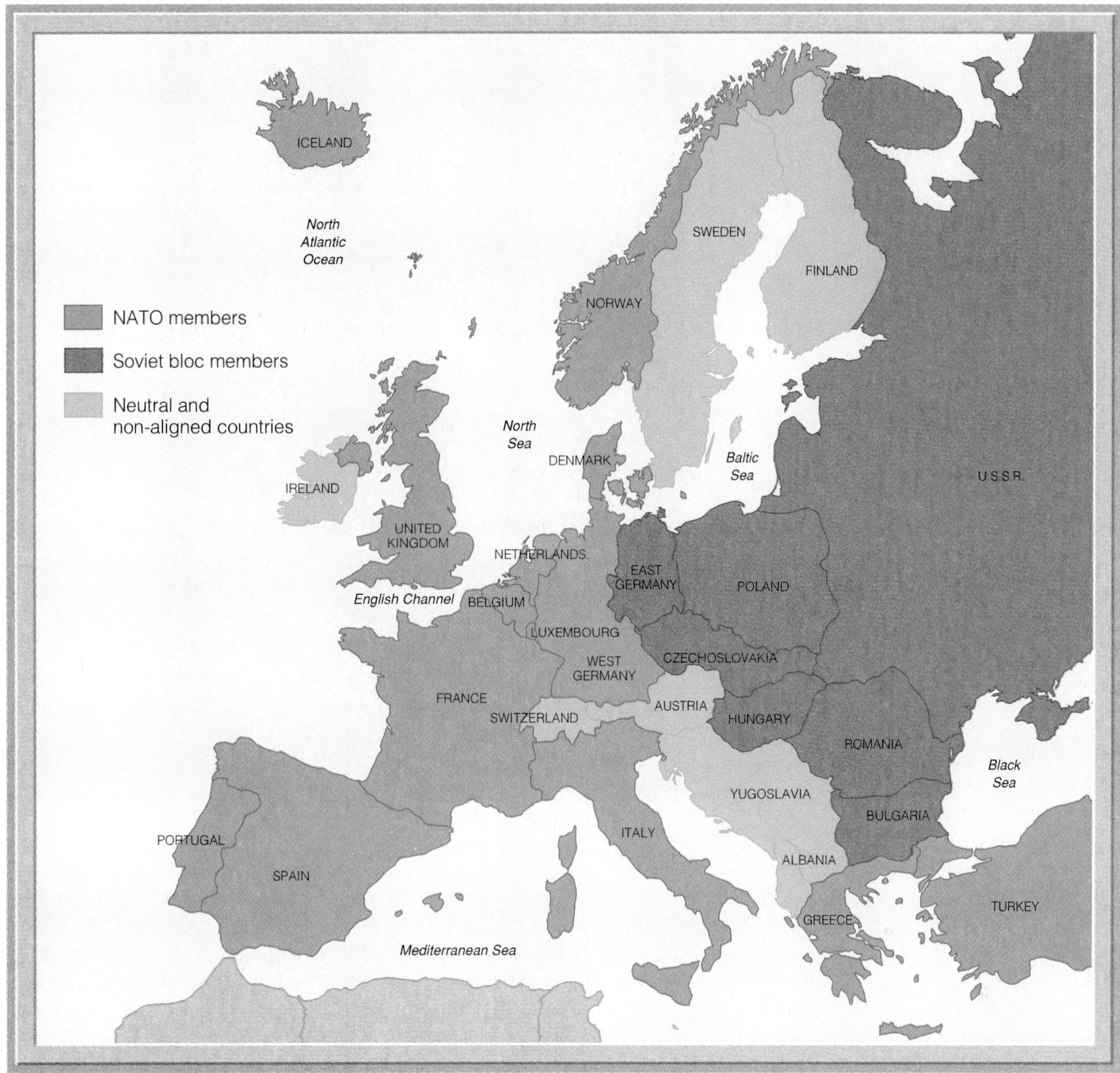

FIGURE 18.1
Cold War Military Alliances

During the Cold War, Europe was divided into three distinct political groups: the North Atlantic Treaty Organization, the Soviet bloc, and the neutral and non-aligned countries.

fighting on the streets of the South Vietnamese capital convinced many Americans that the war could not be won at an acceptable cost. In the ensuing public uproar, President Lyndon Johnson decided not to run for reelection. His successor, Richard Nixon, spent much of his first term seeking to extricate the United States from Vietnam. The signing of the Paris Peace Accord in 1973 marked the end of U.S. combat involvement in Vietnam. In all, more than 58,000 Americans died in the Vietnam War.

Vietnam drove a deep wedge into the U.S. national consensus on the merits of globalism. For so-called hawks, the Vietnam War was, in the words of Ronald Reagan, a "noble cause." In this view, the war would have been won if it had enjoyed greater public support. For so-called doves, Vietnam attested to the folly of viewing Third World struggles through the prism of the U.S.-Soviet rivalry. In this view, Vietnam was a war of national unification that had no significant impact on U.S. interests. Although Americans disagreed over the lessons of Vietnam, the war succeeded in curtailing direct U.S. military intervention in the Third World for a decade. Throughout the 1970s and into the 1980s, presidential efforts to intervene in places such as Angola, Lebanon, and Central America foundered over fears both in Congress and among the public of "another Vietnam."

The Vietnam War left more than 58,000 Americans dead, shattering the national consensus on globalism as the basis for U.S. foreign policy.

Detente
A policy the Nixon administration followed to develop more cordial relations with the Soviet Union.

While Vietnam diminished America's appetite for confronting communism outside of Europe, containment of the Soviet Union remained the focal point of U.S. foreign policy. The tone of U.S. policy toward the Soviet Union, however, varied greatly during the 1970s and 1980s. President Nixon initiated a policy of **detente,** or more cordial relations, with Moscow. Detente governed U.S. policy until 1979, when the Soviet invasion of Afghanistan plunged U.S.-Soviet relations into a deep chill. During the first Reagan administration (1981–1985), tensions between the United States and the Soviet Union reached levels not seen since the 1950s. Nonetheless, with the ascension of Mikhail Gorbachev to power in the Soviet Union in 1985, U.S.-Soviet relations gradually improved.

After the Cold War

The reforms Mikhail Gorbachev initiated in the Soviet Union unleashed a series of sweeping changes in Eastern Europe that eventually ended the Cold War and ushered in a new era in U.S. foreign policy. In October 1989, the Soviet army stood silent as the Berlin Wall fell. Within six months, the communist governments in the Soviet bloc were swept from power, and within a year, East and West Germany were reunited, removing one of the last tangible legacies of World War II. Then in August 1991, hardline communists failed in their bid to seize control of the Soviet Union. After the failed coup, the Soviet Union splintered into more than a dozen separate countries.

The decline and eventual collapse of the Soviet Union changed the face of the international system. As the lone remaining superpower, the United States suddenly found itself with new freedom of maneuver in world politics. In December 1989, U.S. troops invaded Panama and overthrew the government of Gen. Manuel Noriega, whom the United States accused of aiding the international cocaine trade. An even clearer example of the increased freedom of maneuver the United States enjoyed came in 1991 when President George Bush assembled and led a multinational coalition that liberated Kuwait from Iraqi occupation.[15] Although Panama and the Gulf War showed that the United States had thrown off some of its post-Vietnam reluctance to use force, they also revealed the limits of force as a foreign policy tool. The flow of drugs through Panama actually increased after Noriega's removal, and Saddam Hussein remained the leader of Iraq.

The decline and eventual collapse of the Soviet Union has prompted many calls for a new U.S. foreign policy. But people disagree over what that policy and the rules that accompany it should look like. The Clinton administration proposed to replace the policy of containment with one of **enlargement.**[16] Under the policy of enlargement, the United States seeks to promote the emergence of successful market democracies—that is, countries that, like the United States, combine a free market economic system with a democratic political system. The Clinton administration proposed to pursue the policy of enlargement through a variety of means: by promoting world trade, providing economic and technical aid to emerging democracies and market economies, and, as a last resort, using military force to resist anti-democratic forces. The policy of enlargement partially underlay President Clinton's decision in 1994 to threaten to invade Haiti if that country's military rulers did not return power to the democratically elected president they had overthrown. (When Haiti's military leaders did step down, a U.S. peacekeeping force went to Haiti to oversee its return to democratic rule.)

Enlargement
The policy President Bill Clinton proposed as a substitute for containment. It calls on the United States to promote the emergence of market democracies; that is, countries that combine a free market economic system with a democratic political system.

The policy of enlargement by no means garnered widespread approval in the United States. While President Clinton, and many Republican leaders as well, argued that the United States should continue to be engaged in the world and to continue to define its interests in global terms, others argued that the United States should disengage from world affairs and devote more attention to problems at home. This policy of **neo-isolationism** is popular with many Americans. For example, in one national public opinion poll conducted in 1995, twice as many people said they wanted the United States to be less active in world affairs (34 percent) as said they wanted the United States to be more active (17 percent).[17] Support for neo-isolationism is strongest among those with the least factual knowledge about government and politics. Another national poll conducted in 1995 found that 52 percent of less-informed voters believed it would be better if the United States stayed out of world affairs. In contrast, only 22 percent of the best informed voters said it would be better for the United States to stay out of world affairs.[18]

Neo-isolationism
The idea that the United States should reduce its role in world affairs and return to a foreign policy similar to the one it pursued before World War II.

As important as the debate over the future of U.S. foreign policy is, it is taking place amidst considerable public apathy about events beyond America's borders. During the 1992 and 1996 presidential campaigns, for example, voters expressed even less interest than usual in foreign policy. As a result, it remains to be seen what will replace containment as the cornerstone of U.S. foreign policy. The only certainty is that constructing new rules for foreign policy will be a complex process as the United States faces the conflicts and interests of dozens of nations in addition to its own domestic conflicts.

Foreign Policy Versus Domestic Policy

How does decision making on foreign policy differ from decision making on domestic policy? It is sometimes tempting to answer this question by invoking the concept of the **national interest,** the idea that a consensus exists about America's role in the world even though none exists about policies at home. While Americans agree that U.S. foreign policy should aim to promote peace and prosperity, the debates over issues such as Bosnia, aid to Russia, and trade with Mexico all show that Americans disagree, sometimes vehemently, over how best to achieve the nation's foreign policy goals. Indeed, how people define the national interest varies with their party affiliation, ideological beliefs, socioeconomic background, and ethnicity. To put it simply, Americans disagree just as sharply over rules and policies for our relations abroad as they do over rules and policies at home.

National interest
The idea that the United States has certain interests in international relations that most Americans agree on.

The precise limits on the president's foreign policy powers have long been debated. When Ronald Reagan and George Bush sat in the Oval Office, Republicans argued for a broad interpretation of presidential authority and Democrats for a narrow one. When Bill Clinton became president, the two parties switched positions.

Foreign policy, then, is subject to the same kinds of debate and division that characterize domestic policy. What distinguishes foreign policy from domestic policy is that presidents usually have more say over foreign policy. The president's greater success in shaping foreign policy is so marked that scholars sometimes speak of the United States as having **two presidencies,** a weak, embattled one at home and a strong, confident one abroad.[19] The strength of the president in foreign policy cannot be explained on the basis of a literal reading of the Constitution. Instead, the president's strength in foreign policy stems from four sources: the president's inherent advantages in foreign policy, precedents set by earlier presidents, the rulings of the Supreme Court, and the behavior of Congress.

Two presidencies
The argument that presidents have much greater influence over the content of foreign policy than the content of domestic policy.

The Constitution and Foreign Policy

Why do presidents have a greater say in making foreign policy than domestic policy? The Constitution itself does not provide an answer.[20] The framers of the Constitution, ever fearful of the potential for executive tyranny, gave the president relatively few specific (or enumerated) foreign policy powers. Article 2, Section 2 of the Constitution designates the president as "Commander in Chief of the Army and Navy of the United States" and specifies that, subject to the approval of the Senate, the president has the power "to make Treaties" and "appoint Ambassadors." Although today most people believe the position of commander in chief confers special powers on the president, the framers of the Constitution saw the position simply as an office and not as an independent source of decision-making authority.[21]

In contrast to the relatively limited authority it grants the president, the Constitution allocates considerable foreign policy powers to Congress. Article 1 assigns Congress the power "to provide for the common Defence," "to regulate Commerce with foreign Nations," "to define and punish Piracies and Felonies committed on the high Seas," "to declare war," "to raise and support Armies," "to provide and maintain a Navy," and "to make Rules for the Government and Regulation of the land and naval Forces." Article 2 specifies that the Senate must give its advice and consent to all treaties and ambassadorial appointments. And Congress's general power to approve government spending gives it potentially great influence over foreign policy.

The President's Inherent Advantages

If the rules set forth in the Constitution do not explain the president's tremendous influence over foreign policy, what does? One answer is the inherent advantages of the presidency, the informal powers that enable presidents to act swiftly and unilaterally in foreign affairs. Success in foreign policy, far more than in domestic policy, places a

Although the founders saw the position of commander in chief as an office rather than as a source of power, today the commander-in-chief clause in the Constitution is widely interpreted as conferring special powers on the president.

premium on speed, discretion, and flexibility. And as Alexander Hamilton put it in "Federalist No. 70," "decision, activity, secrecy, and dispatch will generally characterise the proceedings of one man, in a much more eminent degree, than the proceedings of any greater number."[22] The president's ability to initiate policy confers an additional advantage on the White House. In domestic affairs, presidential initiatives generally remain proposals *until* Congress assents. In foreign policy, however, presidential initiatives often become policy *unless* Congress acts to block them. Thus, if Congress ignores a president's proposal to raise taxes, the proposal dies. But if Congress fails to act on the president's decision to terminate a treaty or to send troops abroad, the president's proposal prevails. The inherent advantages of the presidency are the greatest in crisis situations. When Americans are taken hostage in a foreign land or an American ally comes under attack, the president may be forced to make quick decisions. Often these decisions leave members of Congress with little choice but to follow the lead of the White House. Of course, Congress has the authority to overturn many presidential decisions in foreign policy, including decisions to send U.S. troops into combat. But building a veto-proof majority in Congress is usually extremely difficult because of partisan, regional, and institutional divisions on Capitol Hill.

Precedent

The authority the president wields on foreign policy stems not only from the inherent advantages of the office but also from the way precedent, or past practice, has modified the rules set down in the Constitution. Presidents frequently cite precedents their predecessors have set to claim or justify new foreign policy powers, as the evolution of the war power attests (see box 18.1). Although the early presidents sometimes used force without congressional approval, none claimed an inherent right to order troops into combat. James Madison even vetoed a bill authorizing him to use the Navy to protect American merchant ships against pirates on the grounds that Congress could not delegate its war power. Madison's successors have not always shared his reluctance to take on that power. Presidents from Truman onward have argued that they have an inherent right as commander in chief to order troops into combat.[23] Thus, just as the Constitution has been interpreted and reinterpreted to meet the demands of an ever-changing domestic environment, presidents have used the flexibility of constitutional rules to their advantage in foreign policy.

Supreme Court Rulings

The Supreme Court has ratified the president's expanded authority in foreign affairs through its interpretation of the rules set forth in the Constitution.[24] Perhaps the most notable Court ruling is the 1936 case *U.S. v. Curtiss-Wright Export Corporation.* In this case, the Court held that, unlike presidential powers in domestic affairs, the president's

Point of Order

BOX 18.1

The War Power

Going to war is the most difficult decision a nation has to make.

The most weighty decision any country faces is the decision to go to war. The rules regarding the war power matter because wars bring about momentous changes in the lives of both individuals and nations. When a country goes to war, soldiers lose limbs and lives. Families lose loved ones. The economy reels or explodes in growth. The nation gains or loses credibility and respect on the world stage.

In the United States, the Constitution assigns the power to declare war to Congress. Congress has declared war four times: the War of 1812 (1812–1815), the Spanish-American War (1898), World War I (1917–1918), and World War II (1941–1945). In the case of the Mexican-American War (1846–1848), Congress did not formally declare war but rather passed a resolution recognizing that a state of war existed. The Civil War was undeclared because a declaration of war would have recognized the legitimacy of the Confederate government.

Although the Constitution assigns the war power to Congress, presidents have used their own authority to order U.S. troops into combat or into situations where hostilities are imminent since the early days of the Republic. The exact number of such instances is unclear. In 1971, Sen. Barry M. Goldwater (R-Ariz.) identified 192 instances in which the president used his own authority to send U.S. troops into combat. Twelve years later, Ronald Reagan cited 125 precedents for his decision to send U.S. troops to Lebanon.

Whatever the actual number of cases, until recently, presidents sent troops into actual or potential combat situations on their own authority only when the prospect for casualties was low. Most of the cases Senator Goldwater and President Reagan cited involved military action against brigands, pirates, and other stateless groups. When sustained combat was likely, presidents asked Congress for a formal declaration of war. Senator Goldwater implicitly acknowledged this distinction between levels of conflict when he noted that, of the 192 undeclared uses of force on his list, "nearly half involved actual fighting."

The willingness of presidents to order the use of force against sovereign states on their own authority grew after World War II. When North Korea invaded South Korea in June 1950, President Truman decided against asking Congress to declare war because he thought his critics might filibuster the resolution and dilute its symbolic effect. After it was reported in August 1964 that North Vietnamese boats had attacked U.S. ships in the Gulf of Tonkin, Congress passed a resolution approving President Johnson's decision to use force to prevent further aggression. Although Johnson used the Gulf of Tonkin Resolution to justify his decision several months later to send combat troops to Vietnam, few members of Congress thought at the time that they were voting for war.

Vietnam convinced many in Congress that a change in the rules was necessary—specifically, a change that would check the president's war powers. The result was the passage in 1973 of the War Powers Resolution. This rather complicated law specifies, among other things, that the president can send troops into combat for no more than sixty days (ninety days in some circumstances) unless Congress authorizes the deployment.

The War Powers Resolution has proven a failure. Every president but Jimmy Carter and Bill Clinton has denied its constitutionality, and administrations have exploited ambiguities in the law to prevent the sixty-day clock from starting. President Reagan did sign a 1983 bill that gave him authority to keep U.S. troops in Lebanon for eighteen months, but he repeated the claim that the War Powers Resolution is unconstitutional. The resolution did not figure in the invasions of Grenada and Panama or in the peacekeeping missions in Haiti and Bosnia.

When Iraq invaded Kuwait in August 1990, President Bush sent U.S. troops to Saudi Arabia. Yet, he, too, refused to invoke the War Powers Resolution. In November, he announced that the United States would liberate Kuwait by force if Iraq did not leave on its own, and he said that he did not need congressional approval to initiate hostilities. Public opinion, however, eventually forced the president to seek the approval of Congress. Although the resolution Congress voted on was technically not a declaration of war, most members regarded it as the functional equivalent of one. After more than twenty hours of debate, the resolution passed 250 to 183 in the House and 52 to 47 in the Senate. Four days later, the Gulf War began.

Sources: Ronald D. Elving, "America's Most Frequent Fight Has Been the Undeclared War," *Congressional Quarterly Weekly Report*, 5 January 1991, pp. 37–40; James M. Lindsay, *Congress and the Politics of U.S. Foreign Policy* (Baltimore: Johns Hopkins University Press, 1994) pp. 84–85, 147–53; Arthur M. Schlesinger, Jr., *The Imperial Presidency* (Boston: Houghton Mifflin, 1989).

foreign policy powers go beyond what the Constitution mentions. Although subsequent Supreme Court opinions disavowed the idea of extra-constitutional powers, presidents continue to cite *Curtiss-Wright* when claiming extensive foreign policy powers for themselves. Another Supreme Court case that expanded the president's powers in foreign policy was *United States v. Belmont.* In this 1937 ruling, the Court held that while treaties must be approved by two-thirds of the Senate, presidents can make equally binding international commitments by signing **executive agreements,** which do not necessarily require Senate approval. The Court's decision in *Belmont* restructured the constitutional rules and diminished the effectiveness of the Senate's treaty power (see box 18.2).

Executive agreements
International agreements that, unlike treaties, do not require the approval of two-thirds of the Senate to become binding on the United States.

The Supreme Court has also enhanced presidential power by declining to hear most lawsuits challenging the president's authority in foreign affairs. The federal judiciary routinely dismisses such cases on the grounds that the contested issues are not ripe for judicial decision or that they raise political and not legal questions. In the fall of 1990, for example, a federal district court refused to require President Bush to get congressional authorization before he ordered U.S. troops to liberate Kuwait—even though the Constitution gives only Congress the power to declare war. The judge in the case ruled that the request for such an order was "unripe."[25] The courts dismiss so many cases challenging presidential authority in foreign affairs because they believe that foreign policy raises issues that lie beyond their competence. The courts also fear that hearing such lawsuits will draw them into political conflict with the other two branches of government.[26]

The Behavior of Congress

Besides inherent advantages, precedent, and the rulings of the Supreme Court, the president's great strength in foreign policy stems from the behavior of members of Congress. Partisan and institutional divisions on Capitol Hill mean that without widespread agreement among members—something that is often missing on foreign policy—Congress will not act. Congressional influence is also complicated by a belief widely held on Capitol Hill (and among the public) that strong presidential leadership is essential for a successful foreign policy.[27] Thus, during the first days after the Iraqi invasion of Kuwait in 1990, the natural instinct of many members of Congress was to rally around President Bush's decision to send troops to the Persian Gulf.

In addition to divisions on Capitol Hill and beliefs about the necessity of strong presidential leadership, many members defer to the president on foreign policy because of electoral considerations. Members of Congress want to avoid stands on policy matters that leave them open to blame, and thus, to punishment at the polls. So when the public supports the president, legislators are likely to as well. For example, members of Congress usually feel comfortable challenging and criticizing suggestions that U.S. troops might be sent to another country. Once the president decides to send U.S. troops, however, many members fear they will be labeled unpatriotic if they attack the decision.

The influence of electoral considerations on the behavior of Congress helps explain the surge of congressional activism on foreign policy after Vietnam. The first two decades after World War II were marked by extensive (though by no means total) congressional deference to the president on foreign policy.[28] That deference was partly the result of agreement on the substance of policy. But it also stemmed from legislative fears that the public would see challenges to the president as unpatriotic. Once Vietnam shattered the nation's consensus on the merits of globalism, however, the public became much more tolerant of legislative challenges to presidential authority, and congressional activity increased. With the end of the Cold War, Congress has become even more involved in foreign policy.[29] The debate over the Gulf War gave some hint of renewed congressional activism. The Senate came within a handful of votes of denying President Bush authority to use force against Iraq.

Point of Order

BOX 18.2

Executive Agreements

The North American Free Trade Agreement (NAFTA) was handled as an executive agreement rather than as a treaty.

In 1967, President Johnson asked the Senate to approve a treaty the United States had signed with Thailand on the subject of double taxation. Although the president deferred to the Senate's treaty power on this rather minor (and obscure) issue, he felt no similar need to seek Senate approval when he subsequently decided to commit the United States to defend Thailand against communist aggression and send 40,000 troops to the Southeast Asian country. Johnson's ability to make a major international commitment to Thailand without securing the consent of the Senate illustrates one of the reasons presidents have gained considerable power over foreign policy in the past half-century: the rise of the executive agreement.

The United States has two tools for making binding commitments to other countries: treaties and executive agreements. Article 2 of the Constitution stipulates the rule governing treaties: they must win the approval of two-thirds of the Senate before they can take effect. If a treaty falls even one vote short of the magic two-thirds number, it is dead. Between 1789 and 1996, the Senate voted down seventeen treaties (out of the more than 1,400 signed), and it blocked another 118 by refusing to consider them.

An executive agreement carries the same force of law as a treaty, but the rules of American politics do not require that two-thirds of the Senate approve it. Indeed, most executive agreements require no congressional approval at all. For reasons having to do with statute, tradition, and political pragmatism, some executive agreements do require the approval of a majority of both the House and Senate. Under U.S. law, for instance, all trade agreements are handled as executive agreements and must be submitted to Congress for simple majority approval. Even when an executive agreement requires congressional approval, presidents prefer it to a treaty because they usually find it easier to round up majority support in both chambers than two-thirds support in the Senate.

Every president since George Washington has used executive agreements. As the following table shows, however, in recent decades, executive agreements have replaced treaties as the primary tool by which the United States makes commitments to other countries:

Years	Number of Treaties	Number of Executive Agreements	Executive Agreements as a Percentage of All International Agreements
1789–1839	60	27	31%
1840–1889	215	238	57
1890–1939	524	907	63
1940–1969	368	5,472	94
1970–1994	417	6,728	94

Not only did the use of executive agreements skyrocket after 1940, but presidents became more inclined to use them to make major commitments to other countries. The Yalta and Potsdam Agreements, which governed the division of Europe after the end of World War II, were both executive agreements, as were the Offensive Arms Pact of the Strategic Arms Limitation Talks (SALT I) and the Paris Peace Accord ending American involvement in Vietnam. Until Congress passed a law in 1972 requiring the White House to notify Capitol Hill of all executive agreements, presidents frequently kept the commitments they had made through executive agreements secret from members of Congress.

What distinguishes an executive agreement from a treaty? No one knows for sure. As the historian Arthur Schlesinger, Jr., writes,

> When Senator Gillette of Iowa asked the State Department in 1954 to make everything perfectly clear, the Department (or so Gillette informed the Senate) replied "that a treaty was something they had to send to the Senate to get approval by two-thirds vote. An executive agreement was something they did not have to send to the Senate." This reminded Gillette of the time when as a boy on the farm he asked the hired man how to tell the difference between male and female pigeons. The answer was: "You put corn in front of the pigeon. If he picks it up, it is a he; if she picks it up, it is a she."

Although no one knows what precisely distinguishes an executive agreement from a treaty, it is clear that presidents have increasingly used executive agreements to enhance their foreign policy powers at the expense of Congress.

Sources: Ellen C. Collier, "U.S. Senate Rejection of Treaties: A Brief Survey of Past Instances," Congressional Research Service, Report No. 87–305F, 30 March 1987, pp. 2–3; *Congressional Record,* 90th Cong., 1st sess., 1967, 113, pt. 15:20717; James M. McCormick, *American Foreign Policy and Process,* 2d ed. (Itasca, Ill.: F. E. Peacock, 1992), p. 276; Arthur M. Schlesinger, Jr., *The Imperial Presidency* (Boston: Houghton Mifflin, 1989), p. 104; Harold W. Stanley and Richard G. Niemi, *Vital Statistics on American Politics,* 5th ed. (Washington, D.C.: Congressional Quarterly, 1995), p. 260.

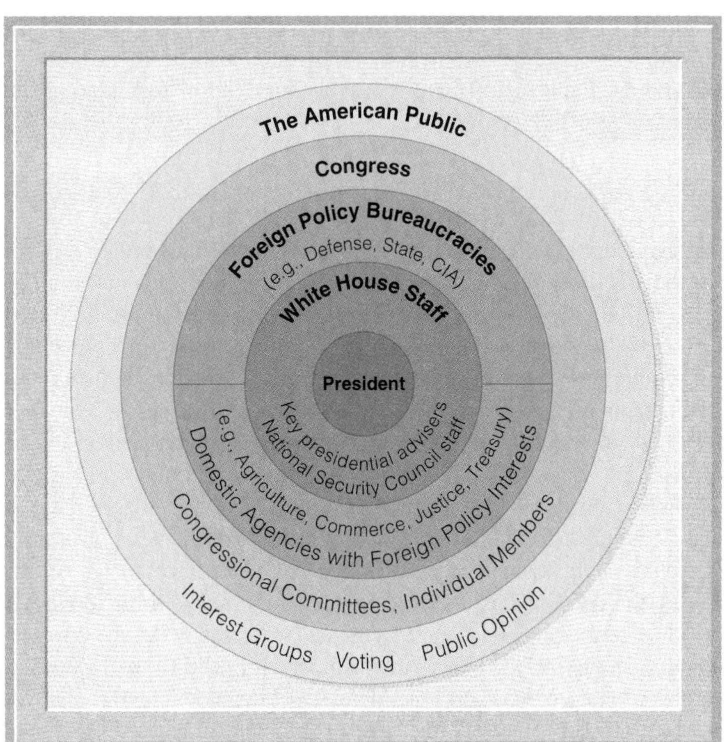

FIGURE 18.2
The Concentric Circles of Power in Foreign Policy Decision Making

Presidents and their advisers lie at the heart of foreign policy making in the United States, whereas the American public is furthest from the center of power.

Because of the inherent advantages of being a single person with executive authority, precedents previous occupants of the Oval Office have set, the rulings of the Supreme Court, the institutional disadvantages of Congress, and the reticence of its members to challenge foreign policy decisions in many instances, the president wields much more power over foreign than domestic policy. Nevertheless, the president does not dictate the content of U.S. foreign policy. As we shall see in the next section, other government officials and institutions also contribute to making foreign policy.

Who Makes U.S. Foreign Policy?

We have noted that both the president and Congress claim significant powers in U.S. foreign policy. But influence over the course of foreign policy decision making in the United States is not equally distributed between the two branches of government or across government institutions. Instead, it can be thought of as a series of concentric circles involving the White House, the foreign policy bureaucracy, Congress, and the public (see figure 18.2). At the heart of the decision-making process are the president and the White House staff. Next in importance are the agencies that make up the foreign policy bureaucracy. By virtue of their expertise and responsibilities, these agencies wield tremendous influence over both the formulation and implementation of foreign policy. Congress occupies the third circle. It influences foreign policy by passing legislation and shaping public opinion. Furthest from the center of power is the public. Because it does not play a role in the day-to-day affairs of governing, the public shapes policy largely by placing constraints on which policies the government can pursue.

Of course, figure 18.2 should not be taken literally. Presidential strength on foreign policy is not preordained. Through inattention or incompetence, presidents may see other actors eclipse their influence over specific foreign policies. For example, the Reagan administration was so out of touch with congressional and public sentiment in its efforts to support the Contra rebels in Nicaragua that by 1987, Congress was effectively setting U.S. policy in Central America.[30] Likewise, intense congressional criticism following the deaths of eighteen U.S. soldiers in Somalia in October

Presidents rely heavily on their national security advisers when they make foreign policy decisions.

1993 eventually forced the Clinton administration to withdraw all U.S. peacekeepers from the African country. Nonetheless, the general pattern of influence outlined in figure 18.2 holds. Each set of institutions plays a role in formulating the rules that guide foreign policy.

The White House

The president is the single most important actor in foreign policy. As we have discussed, presidents draw their powers from the Constitution, from the inherent advantages of the office, and from the fact that Congress and the public look first to the White House for leadership on foreign policy. And while no single individual can match the resources and expertise of the bureaucracy, presidents gain considerable influence from their power to appoint agency heads and to decide whose advice they will heed. Thus, during the Iran-Contra affair, when high-ranking officials in the Reagan administration secretly and illegally sold arms to Iran and funneled the profits to the U.S.-backed Contra rebels in Nicaragua, both Secretary of Defense Caspar Weinberger and Secretary of State George Shultz found themselves powerless to stop the plan because President Reagan chose to disregard their advice.[31]

One way the president is able to wield considerable power in foreign policy is through the National Security Council (NSC), a body created by the passage of the National Security Act of 1947.[32] By law, the members of the NSC are the president, the vice president, the secretary of state, and the secretary of defense. The law also designates the director of Central Intelligence and the chair of the Joint Chiefs of Staff as advisers to the NSC. (The Joint Chiefs of Staff is composed of the uniformed heads of the Army, Navy, Air Force, and Marines.) A staff of foreign policy analysts supports the work of the NSC. The head of this staff is commonly known as the national security adviser, though his or her formal title is assistant to the president for national security affairs.

The NSC staff was originally intended to be small and to act primarily to coordinate the activities of the foreign policy bureaucracy rather than to make policy. Over time, however, the NSC staff has grown to become a major player in policy formation. The national security adviser first came to play a substantial policy-making role during the Kennedy administration.[33] Then Henry Kissinger used the position to dominate foreign policy in the Nixon administration.[34] Though no subsequent national security adviser has wielded as much power as Kissinger, they have, to varying degrees, all been independent sources of policy ideas.

Presidents rely heavily on the national security adviser and the NSC staff for several reasons.[35] First, many of the people who work in the foreign policy bureaucracy are career bureaucrats who owe their loyalty to the agency they serve. In contrast, the NSC staff is composed entirely of presidential appointees, and not too surprisingly, they tend to be dedicated advocates for the president's wishes in foreign policy. Second, the president relies on the NSC staff because of its physical proximity. The national security adviser is based in the White House—rather than across town or across the Potomac River, as the secretaries of state and defense are—and thus can develop a close relationship with the president. Third, presidents find that the small size of the NSC staff makes it easier to control.

The Foreign Policy Bureaucracy

Although presidents are powerful on foreign policy, their influence has limits. U.S. foreign policy is also shaped by the agencies that make up the foreign policy bureaucracy: the State Department, the Defense Department, the intelligence community, and a number of other federal agencies. All of these agencies perform two roles: they offer expert advice to the president on foreign policy issues, and they implement the foreign policy decisions the president and Congress make.

As a repository of expertise, the foreign policy bureaucracy plays a major role in formulating policy proposals. This role enables agencies to influence policy by determining which proposals reach the president's desk and how those proposals are framed. The foreign policy bureaucracy also influences policy because it implements presidential directives.[36] Most presidents at one time or another have shared the frustration Franklin Roosevelt felt when dealing with the U.S. Navy: "To change anything in the Na-a-vy is like punching a featherbed. You punch it with your right and you punch it with your left until you are finally exhausted, and then you find the damn bed just as it was before you started punching."[37] The foreign policy bureaucracy often succeeds in derailing initiatives it dislikes because presidents lack the time they would need to monitor compliance with their directives.

In seeking to shape the content of U.S. foreign policy, the agencies that make up the foreign policy bureaucracy regularly compete with each other for power.[38] The State Department, the Defense Department, and the intelligence community jealously guard their turf and fight for presidential attention. Sometimes the competition for power even extends into an agency's suborganizations as they compete to see which will control the actions of the parent agency. These struggles among and within agencies influence the course of U.S. foreign policy.

The State Department

The State Department was originally founded to conduct and monitor all U.S. diplomatic relations with other countries. As the oldest cabinet-level bureaucracy, the State Department has grown as the U.S. role in world affairs has increased. Whereas the first secretary of state, Thomas Jefferson, oversaw the work of five employees and two embassies, in 1994, the secretary of state oversaw more than 25,000 employees working both in Washington and at some 270 embassies, missions, consulates, and other offices abroad (see box 18.3).[39] Approximately 10,000 messages, reports, and instructions flow in and out of the State Department each day, only a tiny fraction of which cross the desk of the secretary of state.[40] Still, with an annual budget of less than $4 billion, the State Department remains one of the smallest cabinet-level bureaucracies.

Even as the State Department grew in the decades following World War II, other agencies eclipsed its influence over policy.[41] The decline of the State Department was the result of several factors. First, the prominence of military issues during the Cold War naturally played to the strengths of other agencies, most notably the Defense Department. Second, the State Department's small size and lack of a vocal domestic constituency made it easier to push aside in the bureaucratic battles that attend policy making. Third, most presidents came to distrust the State Department as too cautious, too sensitive to the interests of other countries, and too quick to overlook the president's political interests at home.[42] As a result of all these factors, the State Department now plays a much less influential role in formulating foreign policy than it did in the past.

In part because of its weak political position, the State Department was the target of a major reorganization effort during the 104th Congress (1995–1997). Sen. Jesse Helms (R-N.C.), who became chair of the Senate Foreign Relations Committee following the Republican victory in the 1994 midterm elections, proposed a plan to require the State Department to absorb several smaller agencies that traditionally had operated independently of it, to eliminate some of its programs, and to reduce its staff. Many Democratic senators and some Republican senators opposed Helms's plan, arguing that it made too many changes to the State Department and that it would hobble the president's ability to conduct foreign policy. After much wrangling, Helms and his opponents agreed on a compromise bill that required the State Department to cut $1.7 billion from its budget over five years but gave departmental officials some discretion to decide how to achieve the savings.[43] President Clinton vetoed the bill, however, arguing that it "would seriously impede the president's authority to organize and administer foreign affairs agencies to best serve the nation's interests."[44] Despite the president's veto, the State Department continues to face budgetary pressures, and in the years to come it may have to reduce or abolish some of its functions.

The People Behind the Rules

BOX 18.3

The (Slowly) Changing Face of the Foreign Service

The 1947 Foreign Service Institute class of vice consuls.

Some Foreign Service officers in 1994.

The State Department bears primary responsibility for conducting U.S. foreign policy. At the heart of the State Department is the Foreign Service and its more than 4,900 Foreign Service officers. Chosen through rigorous competitive examinations that are separate from the Civil Service system we discussed in chapter 13, Foreign Service officers form an elite corps of professional diplomats who hold key positions within the State Department and who also represent the United States in its many embassies, missions, consulates, and other offices abroad. Yet as they work to represent U.S. interests overseas, Foreign Service officers themselves are not representative of the American people.

For much of the history of the Foreign Service, its officers were overwhelmingly white and almost exclusively male. Studies show that in the 1950s, Foreign Service officers were far more likely than other government employees or members of the American public to come from families whose fathers held prestigious occupations. The tremendous homogeneity of Foreign Service officers in terms of race, gender, and background helped promote the popular stereotype of Foreign Service officers as "upper-class men from the Northeast with degrees from Ivy League colleges."

In 1980, Congress passed legislation that among other things required the Foreign Service to be "representative of the American people." Despite the push for greater diversity, the demographic makeup of the Foreign Service has been slow to change. For example, in 1996, the percentage of female Foreign Service officers stood at 28.3 percent, up from 16.4 percent in 1980, but still well short of the percentage of women in American society. The results for members of minority groups were equally unimpressive. The percentage of African-American Foreign Service officers rose from 5.5 to only 5.6 percent between 1980 and 1996, the percentage of Hispanic Americans rose from 2.4 to 4.5 percent, the percentage of Asian Americans from 1 to 3.0 percent, and the percentage of American Indians from 0.2 to 0.4 percent.

Just as the demographic makeup of the Foreign Service has been slow to change, so has its male-oriented culture. In 1989, for example, a federal court ruled that the State Department had persistently discriminated against female Foreign Service officers. The court found that the department had hired more men than women for the Foreign Service and that it had given male Foreign Service officers higher performance ratings and more awards and honors.

Thus, the Foreign Service has taken some steps toward recruiting more women and minorities. But despite legislation to the contrary, it still falls well short of mirroring the diversity of American society. As one observer puts it, "If the Foreign Service is no longer a smug men's club, it is more like one than any other part of the U.S. government."

Sources: Charles W. Kegley, Jr., and Eugene R. Wittkopf, *American Foreign Policy: Pattern and Process,* 4th ed. (New York: St. Martin's Press, 1991), pp. 365–68; Barry Rubin, *Secrets of State: The State Department and the Struggle over U.S. Foreign Policy* (New York: Oxford University Press, 1985); United States Department of State, *Multi-Year Affirmative Action Plan, FY 1990–92,* 30 April 1991; United States Department of State, *Personnel Inventory Report,* 30 June 1996, p. 67; W. Lloyd Warner, Paul P. Van Riper, Norman H. Martin, and Orvis F. Collins, *The American Federal Executive* (New Haven: Yale University Press, 1963).

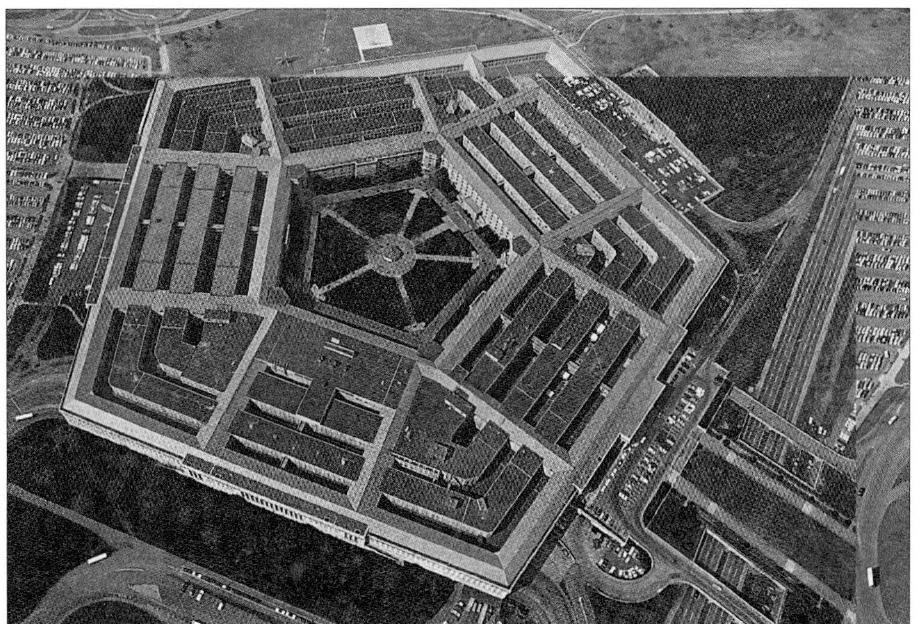

The Pentagon, headquarters of the Defense Department, is the world's largest office building, with three times the floor space of the Empire State Building in New York City. Located in Arlington, Virginia, the Pentagon houses more than 23,000 employees in offices that cover thirty-four acres.

The Defense Department

One agency that contributed to and benefitted from the State Department's declining influence is the Defense Department, otherwise known as the Pentagon after the shape of the building that houses it. The Defense Department, as its name implies, is responsible for defending the United States against foreign threats. The Defense Department is a relatively new agency, created when the National Security Act of 1947 merged the War Department and the Department of the Navy. The Defense Department is now the largest federal bureaucracy. In 1996, its budget was $265 billion, and it employed approximately 850,000 civilian workers, or roughly one-third of all federal civilian employees. These civilian workers were in addition to the 1.7 million Americans who served as members of the uniformed military.[45]

In many respects, the Defense Department is a collection of agencies rather than one cohesive bureaucracy.[46] The uniformed military consists of the four services—the Army, Navy, Air Force, and Marines—each of which has its own history, uniforms, and even battle songs. (The Coast Guard is part of the Transportation Department during peacetime and reports to the Navy during wartime.) The Defense Department also includes the Office of the Secretary of Defense (OSD), the civilian component of the Pentagon that supports and advises the secretary of defense. Inter- and intra-service rivalries, as well as tensions between the services and OSD, have long bedeviled decision making on defense policy. The ability of the secretary of defense to lead the various organizations that make up the Defense Department is limited. As former Secretary of Defense James Schlesinger writes, the responsibilities of the secretary of defense are "not matched by the powers of the office."[47]

The passing of the Cold War opened debate on how the Defense Department can best meet the challenges of the 1990s. Exactly how to restructure the Defense Department is a matter of great contention, though defense spending is not likely to increase significantly in the coming years and may even decrease.[48] As figure 18.3 shows, spending on national defense grew sharply in the 1980s, peaking at $295 billion in 1989. Between 1990 and 1995, however, defense spending fell by $35 billion, even before taking into account the effect of inflation. Once the effects of inflation are considered, defense spending actually fell 25 percent.[49] In addition to the decrease in defense

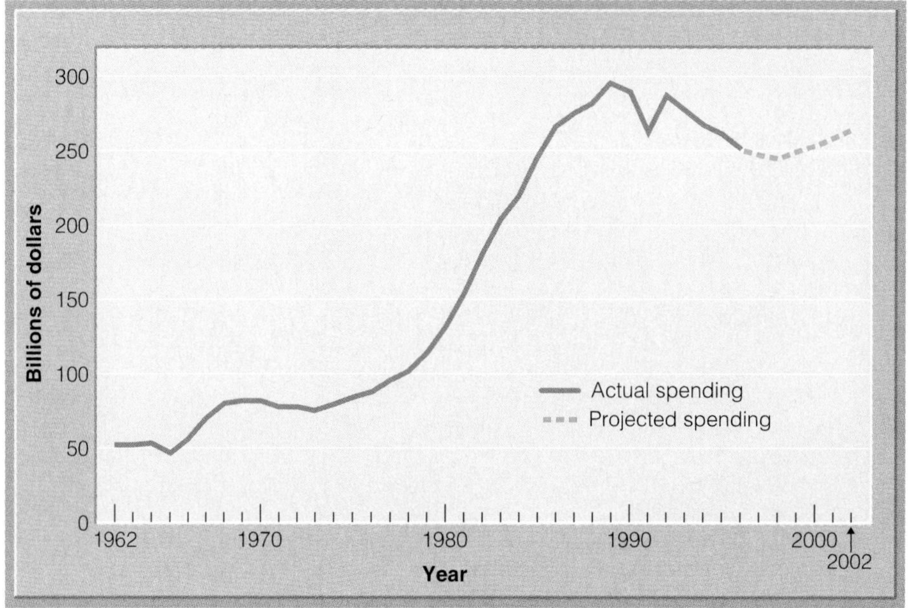

FIGURE 18.3
U.S. Defense Spending, 1962–2002 (in current dollars)

Annual spending on defense, which grew sharply in the 1980s as a result of the Reagan defense buildup, has declined since then.

Source: Data from *Budget of the United States Government, Fiscal Year 1997: Historical Tables* (Washington, D.C.: U.S. Government Printing Office, 1996), pp. 58–62.

spending, the number of Americans in uniform has fallen as well. Whereas there were 2.1 million Americans in uniform in 1990, the last year of the Cold War, in 1999, the Defense Department expects to have only 1.4 million people in uniform, a decline of roughly 26 percent.[50]

Whether defense spending has been cut too much or too little is a matter of great debate. Some people argue that defense spending has been cut too far too fast.[51] They argue that reductions in defense spending and personnel are likely to create a "hollow" military force that lacks the equipment and experienced personnel needed to respond effectively to threats to America's national security interests. The belief in the need to maintain or even increase defense spending was particularly strong among the Republicans who took control of Congress in 1995. They approved legislation that called for modest increases over the Bush and Clinton administrations' previous defense spending proposals.

Critics of defense spending argue that it remains too high.[52] They point out that in inflation-adjusted dollars, the Defense Department's budget for 1996 was more than 85 percent of the average amount the United States spent on defense between 1965 and 1990—a period when the United States fought a war in Vietnam and faced a formidable adversary in the Soviet Union.[53] Moreover, in 1996, the United States spent more than three times what any other country in the world spent on its military—Russia, the second biggest spender, had a defense budget of approximately $80 billion—and "more than all its prospective enemies and neutral nations combined."[54] Since the United States no longer faces the kind of military threats it faced during the Cold War, critics of current levels of defense spending argue that the Defense Department's budget should be cut even further.

The Intelligence Community

A third major foreign policy bureaucracy is the intelligence community, which is responsible for gathering information about activities that might affect U.S. interests around the world.[55] The best known intelligence organization is the Central Intelligence Agency (CIA), established by the same 1947 legislation that created the Defense Department and the NSC.[56] Another major intelligence organization is the National Security Agency, which bears primary responsibility for monitoring the communications of other countries.[57] The National Reconnaissance Office—an agency so secret that the government denied its very existence until 1992—oversees

The Central Intelligence Agency is the best known of the dozen agencies that make up the U.S. intelligence community.

space reconnaissance systems, better known as spy satellites.[58] Intelligence offices also exist within the Federal Bureau of Investigation and within the Departments of Defense, Energy, State, and Treasury. The director of the CIA heads up the intelligence community and serves as the primary adviser to the president and the NSC on intelligence matters.

The budget for the intelligence community is secret, but it was believed to be roughly $28 billion in 1996.[59] Although mention of the intelligence community usually conjures up visions of covert operations, the primary task of the intelligence agencies is to track and analyze economic, military, and political events around the world. However, the intelligence agencies are discouraged from formulating policy. Officials worry that if the intelligence agencies become identified with particular policies, they will be tempted to distort their advice to serve their policy interests.

Like the Defense Department, the intelligence agencies face an uncertain future in the post–Cold War era. The Clinton administration as well as some members of the intelligence community argue that the resources once used to monitor the Soviet Union should be redirected toward monitoring regional conflicts, nuclear proliferation, drug trafficking, environmental conflict, and economic espionage by foreign countries. Critics of this approach argue that the intelligence community should continue its traditional focus on military threats to American national security.[60]

Other Agencies

In addition to the State Department, Defense Department, and the intelligence community, many agencies normally thought of as domestic bureaucracies play a role in foreign policy. The Treasury Department, for instance, handles international monetary matters. The Departments of Agriculture and Commerce administer programs that affect America's agricultural and business interests abroad. The Justice

Department plays a leading role in combating drug-producing operations overseas through its Drug Enforcement Agency. Although it might seem at first glance that the involvement of these and other agencies in foreign policy making creates "too many cooks," their participation attests to the complexity and diversity of foreign policy issues.

Congress

As we saw earlier in the chapter, the Constitution assigns to Congress considerable powers in foreign policy.[61] Yet the extent of congressional influence over foreign policy has varied greatly over the years as perceptions of external threats to the country have changed. In the second half of the nineteenth century, for example, a time when the United States faced few threats from abroad, Congress so dominated foreign policy that these years have been called the era of "congressional government," "congressional supremacy," "government-by-Congress," and "senatorial domination."[62] In contrast, at the height of the Cold War in the 1950s and 1960s, Congress became so willing to defer to presidential leadership on foreign policy that one senator complained that members of Congress responded to even the most far-reaching presidential decisions by "stumbling over each other to see who can say 'yea' the quickest and the loudest."[63] And when many members of Congress became convinced following the Vietnam War that U.S. officials had exaggerated the threats facing the United States, Congress again became more active on foreign policy.

Increased congressional activism on foreign policy in the 1970s and 1980s prompted complaints that too many committees in Congress have a say in foreign policy.[64] As is true in the executive branch, the profusion of congressional committees with jurisdiction over some aspect of foreign policy owes more to the diversity and complexity of foreign policy issues than to organizational inefficiency on the part of Congress. Moreover, most of Congress's activity on foreign and defense policy occurs within the confines of eight committees: the House International Relations Committee and the Senate Foreign Relations Committee (which oversee foreign aid programs), the House National Security Committee and the Senate Armed Services Committee (which oversee defense programs), the House and Senate Intelligence Committees (which oversee intelligence programs), and the House and Senate Appropriations Committees (which appropriate the funds for all government spending).[65]

Congress influences foreign policy in three ways: by passing substantive legislation, by passing procedural legislation, and by shaping public opinion.[66] In passing substantive legislation, Congress specifies the substance or content of U.S. foreign policy. When Congress passes substantive legislation, it is usually invoking its appropriations power.[67] By law, the president cannot spend money Congress refuses to appropriate. For example, Congress stymied Ronald Reagan's plans to help the Contras overthrow the government of Nicaragua by limiting the amount and kind of aid the United States gave the rebels. Congress also can specify the substance of foreign policy by virtue of its constitutional power to regulate foreign trade. One notable instance in which Congress used its trade power was the 1986 bill that placed sanctions on South Africa in order to pressure Pretoria to end its policy of apartheid. In passing the legislation, Congress had to overcome several hurdles, including a presidential veto. The South Africa sanctions bill is the only time since 1973 that Congress has overridden a foreign policy veto.

Along with passing substantive legislation, Congress can influence foreign policy by passing procedural legislation, bills that change the procedures the executive branch uses to make decisions. Procedural legislation rests on the premise that changing the rules governing the decision-making process will change the policy that emerges from the executive branch. In trade policy, for example, legislation now requires the White House to consult with a wide range of consumer, industry, and labor groups whenever it is negotiating an international trade agreement. Sponsors of the law believe that including these groups in decision making makes it more likely that U.S. trade policy will reflect U.S. economic interests.[68]

In addition to passing substantive and procedural legislation, Congress can influence foreign policy by changing the climate of opinion in the country. When public opinion changes, policies frequently do as well. One example of a congressional effort to change public opinion and thereby U.S. policy came in 1990 and 1991 when many members of Congress believed the Bush administration was moving too slowly in response to the enormous changes sweeping the Soviet bloc. Legislators favoring a more conciliatory policy toward the Soviet Union introduced bills, gave speeches, appeared on TV talk shows, and wrote articles for the opinion pages of newspapers, all in a bid to put public pressure on the administration to act. All these efforts played a major role in forcing the Bush administration to recognize the end of the Cold War.[69] As this example suggests, members use a host of different techniques to influence public opinion. But these diverse activities share a common goal: to set the terms of debate on an issue in a way that increases support for some policy options and decreases support for others.

The Public

Individual Americans have the potential to affect the course of U.S. foreign policy. They can do so in two main ways: by becoming members of interest groups and by voting for presidential and congressional candidates who share their foreign policy preferences.

As chapter 10 notes, the number of interest groups in the United States has grown tremendously over the past several decades. Their growth in the area of foreign policy is no exception.[70] Many interest groups active on foreign policy are business and labor groups that wish to shape trade and foreign economic policy. Other groups are dedicated to representing ethnic interests, such as those of Jewish Americans, Greek Americans, or Arab Americans.[71] Still other interest groups active on foreign policy are citizen groups that champion issues such as defense spending, the environment, human rights, and immigration. As with any interest group, the ability of foreign policy interest groups to influence policy making depends on external events, the existence of opposing groups, and their own internal characteristics.

Although interest groups are an important means by which the American public can express its views on foreign policy, most Americans do not belong to an interest group expressly devoted to foreign policy. Instead, the primary way the American public influences foreign policy occurs in the polling booth. Most studies of voting suggest that foreign policy plays a small role in presidential and congressional elections.[72] Still, whether Americans voted for Bill Clinton, Bob Dole, or someone else determined who will pick the national security adviser and the cabinet secretaries, who in turn help determine U.S. foreign policy.

Although the public determines who will sit in positions of political power, it seldom determines the course of day-to-day policy decisions. Quite often, policy makers pursue policies that a substantial portion of the public opposes. In 1977, for instance, President Carter signed two treaties returning the Panama Canal to Panama, even though polls initially showed that more than 60 percent of the American public wanted the United States to retain control of the canal.[73] The Reagan administration provided aid to the Nicaraguan Contras despite the fact that a substantial majority of Americans opposed the policy.[74] President Bush began the Gulf War even though polls showed that Americans were almost evenly split over whether to use economic sanctions or military force to dislodge Iraq from Kuwait.[75] And President Bill Clinton sent U.S. troops to Haiti and Bosnia even though large majorities of Americans opposed both peacekeeping missions.[76]

As with domestic policy, interest groups often lobby and demonstrate in order to influence foreign policy.

One reason policy makers can disregard public opinion was discussed in chapter 6: the public lacks detailed knowledge about many policy areas, especially foreign policy.[77] Compared to the citizens of other countries, Americans know little about the world beyond their borders.[78] A second reason that public opinion does not guide U.S. foreign policy is apathy. Americans typically care far more deeply about domestic issues than foreign ones. For example, a national survey conducted in 1994 asked respondents to list the problems the country faced—77 percent of the total number of problems they listed were domestic or social in nature.[79] Likewise, when asked to name the single most important issue facing the country, Americans usually mention a domestic rather than foreign policy issue.[80]

Because most Americans are uninformed and apathetic about foreign policy, public opinion is easily swayed and may change dramatically in the span of a few days or weeks. For example, the Carter administration launched a major public relations effort to persuade the American public that the Panama Canal treaties would serve the interests of the United States. The campaign worked. By the time the Senate voted on the treaties, polls showed that a majority of the public had come to support them.[81] Likewise, the public virtually always rallies around the president during a crisis.[82] Polls taken the day the Gulf War started showed that despite earlier misgivings, roughly 80 percent of the public supported the decision to use force to liberate Kuwait.[83]

If, as we pointed out in chapter 6, public opinion does not guide government officials, it does place broad constraints on the policies officials can consider. Take the case of U.S. military interventions in the Third World. During the 1960s, presidents essentially had a free hand to send U.S. troops overseas—the Kennedy administration, for instance, sent more than ten thousand military advisers to South Vietnam without much thought about public reaction. After Vietnam, however, presidents had much less freedom to send troops overseas. The Reagan administration, for example, found itself embroiled in a bitter political debate when it proposed sending a few dozen military advisers to El Salvador. What changed in the two decades from Kennedy to Reagan was that the public was less willing to support foreign military operations.[84] In sum, public pressure affects Congress, the foreign policy bureaucracy, and the president as they make decisions on foreign policy.

Challenges to the United States in the Post–Cold War Era

The demise of the Soviet Union marked a watershed in U.S. foreign policy. For the first time in nearly fifty years, Americans began rethinking their relations with the rest of the world. As we discussed earlier, President Clinton and many Republican leaders argue that despite the end of the Cold War, the United States must remain engaged in world affairs. In contrast, many Democrats and Republicans argue that with the Cold War won, the United States should decrease its involvement in world affairs and turn its attention to pressing problems at home. This spirited debate is likely to continue throughout the 1990s.

As Americans debate the question of what role the United States should play in the world, they will confront three fundamental challenges: (1) economic and budgetary problems; (2) a changing foreign policy agenda; and (3) a growing need for multilateral rather than unilateral solutions to foreign policy problems.

Economic and Budgetary Constraints

The United States emerged from World War II as a military superpower and, even more clearly, an economic superpower. In the late 1940s, the United States accounted for 40 to 45 percent of the world's gross economic output.[85] U.S. firms led the way in technological innovation, and the United States ran consistent trade surpluses on the basis of its manufacturing prowess. The United States also invested heavily abroad, most notably through the Marshall Plan. The country's immense wealth enabled the U.S. government to pursue a global foreign policy.

In the 1990s, the United States remains an economic superpower. The U.S. economy is the largest in the world, and U.S. workers continue to be the most productive. But the U.S. share of the world's gross economic output has fallen by almost half, to roughly 20 to 25 percent.[86] Moreover, as table 18.1 shows, the United States lags behind its main economic competitors in many areas, and some observers worry about the long-term health of the U.S. economy. They argue that the United States has overcommitted itself in world affairs, especially when it comes to maintaining a military presence around the world. The result has been to divert resources from productive investments at home and to encourage a long-term decline in American economic power.[87] These theories of American decline have been hotly disputed, with critics arguing that the United States is in the midst of an economic renewal.[88] Whoever is right, the smaller U.S. share of world economic output and the economic problems facing the United States mean that the country can no longer dominate the international economy as it once did.

In addition to economic constraints, U.S. options in foreign policy face budgetary constraints.[89] As we discussed in chapter 16, since the early 1980s, the federal government has consistently run large budget deficits, and much of the political debate in the United States now revolves around which programs we should cut to bring the budget into balance. As a result of this budgetary pressure, new foreign policy programs that require substantial government spending are not likely to gain approval, and many old programs face reduction or elimination. As we saw when discussing the foreign policy bureaucracy, agencies such as the Defense Department saw their budgets fall in the first years following the end of the Cold War.

Although the United States is one of the wealthiest countries in the world as measured by gross national product per capita, it lags behind other major industrialized countries on other economic indicators.

TABLE 18.1 Comparisons of the U.S. Economy to the Economies of Other Major Industrialized Countries on Selected Indicators

A. Gross National Product Per Capita, 1993 (in U.S. dollars)		B. Growth in Gross National Product Per Capita, 1985–1993	
1. Japan	$34,160	1. Japan	3.2%
2. United States	**24,580**	2. Italy	1.8
3. France	21,530	3. Netherlands	1.7
4. Germany	21,020	4. United Kingdom	1.6
5. Netherlands	19,570	5. France	1.4
6. Canada	18,940	**6. United States**	**1.3**
7. Italy	16,800	7. Canada	0.7
8. United Kingdom	16,180	8. Germany	–0.3
C. Investment as a Percentage of Gross Domestic Product, 1993		**D. Average Trade Balance, 1984–1993 (in billions of U.S. dollars)**	
1. Japan	29.8%	1. Japan	$90.2
2. Germany	22.2	2. Germany	50.3
3. Netherlands	19.7	3. Canada	9.1
4. France	18.6	4. Netherlands	8.0
5. Canada	17.8	5. Italy	–0.4
6. Italy	17.1	6. France	–5.4
7. United States	**16.8**	7. United Kingdom	–21.8
8. United Kingdom	15.0	**8. United States**	**–119.3**
E. Annual Growth in Manufacturing Productivity, 1985–1993		**F. Ratio of Savings to Disposable Personal Income, 1993**	
1. Japan	4.0%	1. Italy	19.1%
1. United Kingdom	4.0	2. Japan	14.6
3. Italy	3.4	3. France	13.8
4. United States	**2.7**	4. Netherlands	12.3
5. France	2.6	4. Germany	12.3
6. Germany	1.7	6. United Kingdom	11.7
7. Netherlands	1.5	7. Canada	9.1
8. Canada	1.13	**8. United States**	**4.1**

Note: The figures for Germany exclude data for the former German Democratic Republic (East Germany).

Sources: International Financial Statistics 1994 (Washington, D.C.: International Monetary Fund, 1994), 128; *Statistical Abstract of the United States, 1995,* 115th ed. (Washington, D.C.: U.S. Bureau of the Census, 1995), pp. 855, 857, 866.

The impact of budgetary constraints on U.S. foreign policy is most obvious in foreign aid, where spending fell by 17 percent between 1990 and 1996 even before taking into account the effect of inflation.[90] The result, as table 18.2 shows, is that Japan, France, and Germany have surpassed the United States as the world's largest provider of foreign aid. Moreover, when the size of the American economy and population is taken into account, the United States ranks behind virtually every other industrialized country in providing foreign aid. Budgetary constraints explain why the Bush and Clinton administrations each proposed less than $1 billion in direct aid to the former Soviet Union—a pittance compared to the amount the Marshall Plan gave to Western Europe—despite widespread agreement on the need to aid Russia and its neighboring republics. Budgetary constraints are also likely to derail many of the proposals for combating global warming, drug trafficking, and nuclear proliferation.

The economic and budgetary problems facing the United States are making many Americans look more favorably on policies that limit U.S. involvement with other countries. Foreign aid provides perhaps the clearest example of this phenomenon. Public opinion polls repeatedly show that large majorities of the American public think the

TABLE 18.2 Amount of Official Development Assistance (ODA) Given by Industrialized Countries to Developing Countries, 1995.

The United States lags behind Japan, France, and Germany in terms of the total amount of foreign aid it provides. When the size of the U.S. economy and population is taken into account, the United States ranks behind virtually every other industrial democracy.

Total (in billions of U.S. dollars)			As a Percentage of GNP			Per Capita		
1.	Japan	$14.5	1.	Denmark	0.97%	1.	Denmark	$308
2.	France	8.4	2.	Sweden	0.89	2.	Norway	287
3.	Germany	7.5	3.	Norway	0.87	3.	Sweden	228
4.	**United States**	**7.3**	4.	The Netherlands	0.80	4.	The Netherlands	214
5.	The Netherlands	3.3	5.	France	0.55	5.	Switzerland	153
6.	United Kingdom	3.2	6.	Canada	0.39	6.	France	145
7.	Canada	2.1	7.	Belgium	0.38	7.	Japan	116
8.	Sweden	2.0	8.	Australia	0.34	8.	Belgium	102
9.	Denmark	1.6	8.	Switzerland	0.34	9.	Austria	94
10.	Italy	1.5	10.	Austria	0.32	10.	Germany	92
11.	Spain	1.3	10.	Finland	0.32	11.	Finland	77
12.	Norway	1.24	12.	Germany	0.31	12.	Canada	75
13.	Australia	1.14	13.	United Kingdom	0.29	13.	Australia	63
14.	Switzerland	1.08	14.	Japan	0.28	14.	United Kingdom	55
15.	Belgium	1.03	15.	Ireland	0.27	15.	Ireland	40
16.	Austria	0.75	15.	Portugal	0.27	16.	New Zealand	35
17.	Finland	0.39	17.	New Zealand	0.23	17.	Spain	33
18.	Portugal	0.27	18.	Spain	0.23	**18.**	**United States**	**28**
19.	Ireland	0.14	19.	Italy	0.14	19.	Italy	26
20.	New Zealand	0.12	**20.**	**United States**	**0.10**	20.	Portugal	25

Source: Organization of Economic Cooperation and Development, "Financial Flows to Developing Countries in 1995: Sharp Decline in Official Aid; Private Flows Rise," 11 June 1996, p. 12.

United States spends too much on foreign aid and that spending on foreign aid should be cut back sharply.[91] (Of course, as both chapter 6 and 16 note, most Americans have a grossly exaggerated idea of how much money the United States spends on foreign aid—it constitutes only 1 percent of the federal government's budget.)

Another example of how economic and budgetary problems are making many Americans look more favorably on policies that limit U.S. involvement with other countries is trade policy. For much of the Cold War era, the United States eagerly promoted **free trade,** an economic policy that holds that lowering trade barriers will benefit the economies of all the countries involved. In 1947, the United States helped create the **General Agreement on Tariffs and Trade (GATT),** the international organization for trade policy. (In January 1995, a new international agency, the World Trade Organization, replaced GATT.) GATT helped orchestrate a tremendous reduction in trade barriers, a development that in turn stimulated economic growth around the world. Yet when many Americans began to lose their jobs in the 1980s and early 1990s because of foreign competition, public enthusiasm for free trade waned. In 1993, opponents of free trade came close to defeating the North American Free Trade Agreement (NAFTA), an accord that sought to reduce trade barriers among Canada, Mexico, and the United States. NAFTA's critics argued that the agreement would cost the United States hundreds of thousands of jobs. If the American economy had been healthier, and high-paying jobs more plentiful, NAFTA most likely would have been a far less contentious issue.

Free trade
An economic policy that holds that lowering trade barriers will benefit the economies of all the countries involved.

General Agreement on Tariffs and Trade (GATT)
An international organization that existed between 1947 and 1995. GATT was used by its member countries to set many of the rules governing world trade. In 1995, it gave way to the World Trade Organization.

A Changing Foreign Policy Agenda

The second challenge facing the United States as it seeks to devise a new foreign policy for the post–Cold War era is the changing nature of the issues on the foreign policy agenda. As we have mentioned, the overriding objective of U.S. foreign policy

Foreign aid programs are unpopular with many Americans.

Gill Fox/*Bridgeport Post.* Reprinted by permission.

throughout the Cold War era was containing communist expansion. An inevitable result of the priority given to containment was that relations with the Soviet Union dominated the foreign policy debate in the United States. Other foreign policy issues were pushed to the sidelines as national security became identified with foreign policy.

With the Soviet Union no longer a threat to the United States, formerly lower-priority issues are now moving to the forefront of the foreign policy agenda. Trade policy is one such issue. Another is nuclear proliferation. Throughout the Cold War, U.S. officials focused on trying to prevent a nuclear war with the Soviet Union, an effort that led the two countries to sign several treaties designed to control the amount and kinds of nuclear weapons each had. Although U.S. officials did work to stop the spread of nuclear weapons to other countries, it was a lower-priority issue. Following the demise of the Soviet Union, however, the threat that nuclear weapons might spread across the world displaced the fear of superpower nuclear conflict as a major foreign policy issue. Countries such as Iran, Iraq, North Korea, and Pakistan all either have or are within range of building nuclear weapons.[92]

As some long-neglected foreign issues have gained prominence following the end of the Cold War, some entirely new foreign policy problems are appearing on the policy agenda. Because countries have become increasingly interconnected in the modern world, the United States faces a host of new and pressing foreign policy problems. Acid rain, biodiversity, drug trafficking, energy dependence, global warming, and natural resource depletion are all problems that were unknown to Presidents Truman, Eisenhower, and Kennedy. Yet each of these issues is likely to consume considerable time and effort on the part of U.S. officials in the twenty-first century.

Intermestic issues
Issues such as trade, the environment, and drug trafficking that affect both domestic and foreign interests.

The changing nature of the foreign policy agenda poses a challenge because it presents policy makers with unfamiliar problems. An even greater challenge lies in the fact that trade and many of the newly emergent problems are **intermestic issues** that straddle the line separating domestic policy from foreign policy.[93] In the case of trade, for instance, the president must negotiate with other heads of state as well as with domestic interest groups. For example, to convince Congress in 1993 to approve NAFTA, President Clinton had to make numerous concessions to groups that claimed the agreement would hurt them.[94] Likewise, efforts to save the world's rain forests and to ensure biological diversity will require presidents to pursue both international and domestic initiatives. When both domestic and international interests are involved, the number and complexity of conflicting interests increase tremendously. It is clearly much more difficult to create rules that effectively manage the conflicts among all these competing interests.

Presidents also find it much harder to lead on intermestic issues than on pure foreign policy issues because they cannot count on the automatic support of Congress or

The end of the Cold War has forced U.S. foreign policy officials to confront new and, in some ways, more complex problems.

Signe Wilkinson/Cartoonists & Writers Syndicate. Reprinted by permission.

the American people. Congress is likely to be active because intermestic issues involve decisions traditionally considered part of domestic policy. Legislators will not suddenly defer to the White House on trade or environmental policy simply because the president says they are key foreign policy problems. Moreover, intermestic issues directly affect the well-being of domestic groups; hence, a greater chance exists that any presidential or congressional initiative will face considerable constituent opposition and interest group activity. The changing foreign policy agenda is laced with intermestic issues that involve such potential problems.

Unilateralism Versus Multilateralism

The third challenge the United States must meet in rethinking its foreign policy is the increasing need to work with other countries to find multilateral solutions to common problems. A trademark characteristic of U.S. foreign policy is **unilateralism,** that is, the tendency to act in foreign affairs without consulting other countries. When isolationism reigned supreme in the United States, one of the major arguments against joining an alliance with other countries was that the United States needed to have a free hand to choose its destiny. Even when the United States assumed a global role after World War II, the bias toward unilateralism continued, as the country's great wealth enabled it to pursue policies without consulting other countries. In Korea, Vietnam, and elsewhere, the United States acted with relatively little help (and sometimes outright opposition) from its major allies.

Unilateralism
The tendency of the United States to act alone in foreign affairs without consulting other countries.

Economic and budgetary problems and the changing nature of the foreign policy agenda are making it harder for the United States to continue to resort to unilateral solutions to its foreign policy problems. Rising budgetary constraints in the late 1980s prompted the United States to ask other industrialized countries to finance a greater share of the costs of foreign policy. The Reagan and Bush administrations, for instance, encouraged Japan to offset the decline in U.S. aid by increasing its spending on foreign aid.[95] During the Gulf War, the Bush administration pressed both Europe and Japan to help underwrite the cost of liberating Kuwait.[96]

Even if the United States could afford to continue to act unilaterally, growing global interdependence will put pressure on U.S. officials to move away from unilateralism and toward **multilateralism,** that is, an approach in which three or more countries cooperate in seeking solutions to foreign policy problems. Fears of global warming illustrate the importance of multilateralism. The United States is the world's single largest producer of the heat-trapping gases responsible for global warming. Yet because so many countries produce these gases, changes in U.S. policy alone will not reverse the long-term potential for global warming.[97] In short, multilateral solutions are necessary to solve multilateral problems.

Multilateralism
An approach in which three or more countries cooperate for the purpose of solving some common problem.

Of course, the United States has considerable experience with multilateralism, as its membership in the United Nations and NATO both attest. But throughout the Cold

As U.S. negotiators discovered at the 1992 Earth Summit in Rio de Janiero, the solutions to many foreign policy problems now require the cooperation of many different countries.

War, the United States dominated most multilateral institutions and was able to force (or block) action regardless of the positions of other countries. And during the Gulf War, the United States contributed most of the troops, and U.S. officers rather than a multinational military command directed the fighting.

Yet, the ability of the United States to dominate multilateral institutions is fading. Europe and Japan argue that their economic wealth entitles them to a greater say in decision making in multilateral organizations. Moreover, because Europe and Japan no longer need the United States to protect them from the Soviet Union, they are less inclined to defer to U.S. leadership. A good example of the increased difficulty the United States faces in getting its way in international forums came during the 1992 Earth Summit in Rio de Janeiro. Europe and Japan rejected the positions the Bush administration took on global warming and biological diversity, and as a result, the United States found itself politically isolated at the summit.[98]

Because unilateralism is so ingrained in U.S. foreign policy, the merits of multilateralism are likely to be a constant source of political debate in the United States. The issue rose to the top of the political agenda in October 1993 when eighteen American soldiers were killed while participating in a United Nations peacekeeping mission in Somalia. Some critics mistakenly blamed the deaths on the failure of United Nations forces to send reinforcements quickly when the American soldiers became pinned down in a firefight. Congress subsequently debated a bill that would have barred the president from assigning U.S. combat troops to any United Nations mission under the command of a foreign officer without prior congressional approval.[99] Although the bill was defeated—as was a similar piece of legislation drafted two years later as part of the Contract With America—the debate underscored the concern many Americans have about letting other countries have a say in U.S. foreign policy.[100]

The merits of multilateralism became an issue again in late 1994 in the congressional debate over a new trade agreement the 124 members of GATT had negotiated. The most controversial aspect of the agreement was a provision that created the **World Trade Organization (WTO).**[101] Under the terms of the trade agreement, the WTO would operate as the successor organization to GATT and have enhanced powers to oversee and enforce compliance with multilateral trade agreements. Proponents of the WTO argued that these enhanced powers would benefit the United States because the international agency would be able to punish countries with trading practices that unfairly discriminated against U.S. exports.

World Trade Organization (WTO)
The international trade agency that began operation in 1995 as the successor to the General Agreement on Tariffs and Trade.

Opponents of the WTO argued that the international agency would undermine American **sovereignty,** that is, the right of Americans to determine what laws they wish to live under. Because the WTO would have the power to punish countries it deemed to have "unfair trading practices," critics argued that it could do the same to the United States. As a result, the United States might discover one day that the WTO

Sovereignty
The power of self-rule.

Some Americans argue that international organizations such as the World Trade Organization or the United Nations threaten U.S. sovereignty.

had found its environmental, consumer protection, and labor laws to violate international trade agreements. In making this argument, American critics of the WTO frequently pointed to what had happened under GATT after Congress passed a law in 1991 barring the import of tuna from several countries because their tuna fleets killed too many dolphins. The affected countries appealed the issue to GATT, which subsequently ruled that the ban violated international trade rules that prohibit countries from applying their domestic regulations to foreign countries. Not surprisingly, environmentalists denounced the ruling, arguing that it robbed them of a tool needed to protect wildlife.[102] Whereas GATT lacked the power to penalize the United States, the WTO would not.

In the end, Congress approved the trade agreement that created the WTO. (In contrast to the conditions surrounding the debate over NAFTA, economic conditions had improved by the time of the 1994 vote, and a much broader range of industries had an interest in seeing the trade agreement pass.) In doing so, however, Congress and the Clinton administration struck a deal that lets Congress revoke U.S. membership in the WTO if certain conditions occur. Under the terms of the deal, the Clinton administration agreed to create a panel composed of five federal judges to review the WTO's rulings. If the panel finds that the WTO has ruled against the United States unfairly three times in a five-year period, then Congress can pass legislation (subject to a presidential veto) directing the president to terminate U.S. membership in the WTO.[103] (The WTO decided its first case in 1996, ruling that a provision of the Clean Air Act that regulated the import of foreign gasoline violated international trade rules. While critics argued that this bore out their fears about the WTO, American trade officials admitted that the law in question, which was only a temporary measure, clearly discriminated against foreign refineries.)[104]

Economic and budgetary problems, changing needs and priorities, and an increasing need for multilateralism are three challenges the United States must confront as it seeks to chart a new course for foreign policy at the start of the twenty-first century. The days when the nation could make foreign policy decisions with a free hand—either because of its isolation from the rest of the world or its immense wealth and power—are over. As the United States struggles to remake its foreign policy, it faces a complex set of conflicting interests that span the globe. How the United States will decide to manage those conflicts, and how well it can manage them, remain to be seen.

SUMMARY

For the first 150 years of its history, the United States avoided foreign alliances. In the wake of World War II, however, the United States broke with its isolationist past and assumed the mantle of a global superpower. Containment of communism, and especially containment of the Soviet Union, became the cornerstone of U.S. foreign policy. The eventual demise of the Soviet Union marked the triumph of containment. Having won the Cold War, the United States now struggles to define the role it will play in the world in the 1990s.

Presidents influence foreign policy to an extent not true of any other policy domain. Their influence stems from four factors. First, presidents enjoy inherent advantages in foreign affairs. Congress cannot hope to match the speed and secrecy of presidential decision making. Second, presidents have used precedents to expand their authority in foreign affairs. Third, the Supreme Court often hands down rulings that grant the president great freedom in foreign policy, and it generally declines to hear cases that challenge presidential authority. Fourth, partisan and institutional divisions make it difficult for Congress to act in the absence of consensus, and members of Congress frequently defer to the president for electoral reasons and because they believe that success in foreign policy requires strong presidential leadership.

Although presidents have the greatest say in foreign policy, they must continually struggle to control the bureaucracy and to maintain the support of Congress and the public. The foreign policy bureaucracy exercises tremendous influence because it both formulates and implements policy. Congress makes its preferences felt through substantive and procedural legislation and by shaping public opinion. The public's great distance from the day-to-day affairs of government leaves it poorly positioned to affect most foreign policy decisions. But the public's willingness to support foreign policy initiatives places broad constraints on the actions the government can take.

As the United States heads toward the twenty-first century, it faces three major foreign policy challenges. First, the country's chronic budget deficit sharply limits the policy options the president and Congress can consider; programs that require major financial commitments are not likely to win approval. Second, the issues on the foreign policy agenda are changing. With the Cold War over, containment of communism has given way to issues such as trade, nuclear proliferation, and global warming. Not only are the newly emergent problems in some ways more complicated than containment, they are likely to prove even more divisive among the public. Third, the United States cannot afford, and many foreign policy problems cannot be solved by, the traditional U.S. reliance on unilateral action. Other countries are likely to contest U.S. leadership in world affairs, and some multilateral institutions will actually limit the freedom of maneuver the United States has historically enjoyed in foreign policy.

Key Terms

Cold War
Containment
Detente
Enlargement
Executive agreements
Free trade
General Agreement on Tariffs and Trade (GATT)
Globalism
Intermestic issues
Isolationism
Marshall Plan
Monroe Doctrine
Multilateralism
National interest
Neo-isolationism
North Atlantic Treaty Organization (NATO)
Sovereignty
Third World
Truman Doctrine
Two presidencies
Unilateralism
World Trade Organization (WTO)

Readings for Further Study

The Cambridge History of American Foreign Relations, vols. 1–4. New York: Cambridge University Press, 1993. Four of America's leading historians offer a lively overview of the history of U.S. foreign policy from the days of George Washington to the presidency of Bill Clinton.

Halperin, Morton H. *Bureaucratic Politics and Foreign Policy.* Washington, D.C.: Brookings Institution, 1974. The classic discussion of the organizational politics that drive decision making within the U.S. foreign policy bureaucracy.

Kennedy, Paul. *Preparing for the Twenty-First Century.* New York: Random House, 1993. A historian examines how transnational forces are likely to affect domestic and foreign policies in the next century.

Kissinger, Henry. *Diplomacy.* New York: Simon & Schuster, 1994. A former secretary of state and winner of the Nobel Peace Prize traces the evolution of diplomacy over the past three hundred years and explores the peculiar American approach to foreign relations.

Lindsay, James M. *Congress and the Politics of U.S. Foreign Policy.* Baltimore: Johns Hopkins University Press, 1994. A political scientist examines the tools Congress uses to influence foreign policy and shows how politics frequently drives members of Congress to discharge their constitutional duty to oversee the executive branch.

McNamara, Robert. *In Retrospect: The Tragedy and Lessons of Vietnam.* New York: Random House, 1995. The leading architect of America's entry into the Vietnam War reviews how the United States became involved in Vietnam and discusses the torment he felt as secretary of defense when the war began to go badly.

Nincic, Miroslav. *Democracy and Foreign Policy: The Fallacy of Political Realism.* New York: Columbia University Press, 1992. A political scientist considers and rebuts arguments that the U.S. political system makes it difficult to pursue a wise and effective foreign policy.

Schlesinger, Arthur M. *The Imperial Presidency.* Boston: Houghton Mifflin, 1973, 1989. A Pulitzer Prize-winning historian traces the growth of presidential power over two centuries and argues that presidents now exercise almost royal prerogatives in foreign policy.

Appendix

A

The Declaration of Independence

In Congress, 4 July 1776

The Unanimous Declaration of the Thirteen United States of America

When, in the course of human events, it becomes necessary for one people to dissolve the political bands which have connected them with another, and to assume, among the powers of the earth, the separate and equal station to which the laws of nature and of nature's God entitle them, a decent respect to the opinions of mankind requires that they should declare the causes which impel them to the separation.

We hold these truths to be self-evident: That all men are created equal; that they are endowed by their Creator with certain unalienable rights; that among these are life, liberty, and the pursuit of happiness; that, to secure these rights, governments are instituted among men, deriving their just powers from the consent of the governed; that whenever any form of government becomes destructive of these ends, it is the right of the people to alter or to abolish it, and to institute new government, laying its foundation on such principles, and organizing its powers in such form, as to them shall seem most likely to effect their safety and happiness. Prudence, indeed, will dictate that governments long established should not be changed for light and transient causes; and accordingly all experience hath shown that mankind are more disposed to suffer, while evils are sufferable, than to right themselves by abolishing the forms to which they are accustomed. But when a long train of abuses and usurpations, pursuing invariably the same object, evinces a design to reduce them under absolute despotism, it is their right, it is their duty, to throw off such government, and to provide new guards for their future security. Such has been the patient sufferance of these colonies; and such is now the necessity which constrains them to alter their former systems of government. The history of the present King of Great Britain is a history of repeated injuries and usurpations, all having in direct object the establishment of an absolute tyranny over these states. To prove this, let facts be submitted to a candid world.

He has refused to assent to laws, the most wholesome and necessary for the public good.

He has forbidden his governors to pass laws of immediate and pressing importance, unless suspended in their operation till his assent should be obtained; and, when so suspended, he has utterly neglected to attend to them.

He has refused to pass other laws for the accommodation of large districts of people, unless those people would relinquish the right of representation in the legislature, a right inestimable to them, and formidable to tyrants only.

He has called together legislative bodies at places unusual, uncomfortable, and distant from the depository of their public records, for the sole purpose of fatiguing them into compliance with his measures.

He has dissolved representative houses repeatedly, for opposing, with manly firmness, his invasions on the rights of the people.

He has refused for a long time, after such dissolutions, to cause others to be elected; whereby the legislative powers, incapable of annihilation, have returned to the people at large for their exercise; the state remaining, in the mean time, exposed to all dangers of invasions from without and convulsions within.

He has endeavored to prevent the population of these states; for that purpose obstructing the laws for naturalization of foreigners; refusing to pass others to encourage their migration hither, and raising the conditions of new appropriations of lands.

He has obstructed the administration of justice, by refusing his assent to laws for establishing judiciary powers.

He has made judges dependent on his will alone, for the tenure of their offices, and the amount and payment of their salaries.

He has erected a multitude of new offices, and sent hither swarms of officers to harass our people and eat out their substance.

He has kept among us, in times of peace, standing armies, without the consent of our legislatures.

He has affected to render the military independent of, and superior to, the civil power.

He has combined with others to subject us to a jurisdiction foreign to our constitution, and unacknowledged by our laws, giving his assent to their acts of pretended legislation:

For quartering large bodies of armed troops among us;

For protecting them, by a mock trial, from punishment for any murders which they should commit on the inhabitants of these states;

For cutting off our trade with all parts of the world;

For imposing taxes on us without our consent;

For depriving us, in many cases, of the benefits of trial by jury;

For transporting us beyond seas, to be tried for pretended offenses;

For abolishing the free system of English laws in a neighboring province, establishing therein an arbitrary government, and enlarging its boundaries, so as to render it at once an example and fit instrument for introducing the same absolute rule into these colonies;

For taking away our charters, abolishing our most valuable laws, and altering fundamentally the forms of our governments;

For suspending our own legislatures, and declaring themselves invested with power to legislate for us in all cases whatsoever.

He has abdicated government here, by declaring us out of his protection and waging war against us.

He has plundered our seas, ravaged our coasts, burned our towns, and destroyed the lives of our people.

He is at this time transporting large armies of foreign mercenaries to complete the works of death, desolation, and tyranny already begun with circumstances of cruelty and perfidy scarcely paralleled in the most barbarous ages, and totally unworthy the head of a civilized nation.

He has constrained our fellow-citizens, taken captive on the high seas, to bear arms against their country, to become the executioners of their friends and brethren, or to fall themselves by their hands.

He has excited domestic insurrections among us, and has endeavored to bring on the inhabitants of our frontiers the merciless Indian savages, whose known rule of warfare is an undistinguished destruction of all ages, sexes, and conditions.

In every stage of these oppressions we have petitioned for redress in the most humble terms; our repeated petitions have been answered only by repeated injury. A prince, whose character is thus marked by every act which may define a tyrant, is unfit to be the ruler of a free people.

Nor have we been wanting in our attentions to our British brethren. We have warned them, from time to time, of attempts by their legislature to extend an unwarrantable jurisdiction over us. We have reminded them of the circumstances of our emigration and settlement here. We have appealed to their native justice and magnanimity; and we have conjured them, by the ties of our common kindred, to disavow these usurpations, which would inevitably interrupt our connections and correspondence. They, too, have been deaf to the voice of justice and of consanguinity. We must, therefore, acquiesce in the necessity which denounces our separation, and hold them, as we hold the rest of mankind, enemies in war, in peace friends.

We, therefore, the representatives of the United States of America, in General Congress assembled, appealing to the Supreme Judge of the world for the rectitude of our intentions, do, in the name and by the authority of the good people of these colonies, solemnly publish and declare, that these United Colonies are, and of right ought to be, FREE AND INDEPENDENT STATES, that they are absolved from all allegiance to the British crown, and that all political connection between them, and the state of Great Britain is, and ought to be, totally dissolved; and that, as free and independent states, they have full power to levy war, conclude peace, contract alliances, establish commerce, and do all other acts and things which independent states may of right do. And for the support of this declaration, with a firm reliance on the protection of Divine Providence, we mutually pledge to each other our lives, our fortunes, and our sacred honor.

John Hancock [*President*]

NEW HAMPSHIRE
Josiah Bartlett
William Whipple
Matthew Thornton

MASSACHUSETTS BAY
Samuel Adams
John Adams
Robert Treat Paine
Elbridge Gerry

RHODE ISLAND
Stephen Hopkins
William Ellery

CONNECTICUT
Roger Sherman
Samuel Huntington
William Williams
Oliver Wolcott

NEW YORK
William Floyd
Philip Livingston
Francis Lewis
Lewis Morris

NEW JERSEY
Richard Stockton
John Witherspoon
Francis Hopkinson
John Hart
Abraham Clark

PENNSYLVANIA
Robert Morris
Benjamin Rush
Benjamin Franklin
John Morton
George Clymer
James Smith
George Taylor
James Wilson
George Ross

DELAWARE
Caesar Rodney
George Read
Thomas M'Kean

MARYLAND
Samuel Chase
William Paca
Thomas Stone
Charles Carroll, of Carrollton

VIRGINIA
George Wythe
Richard Henry Lee
Thomas Jefferson
Benjamin Harrison
Thomas Nelson, Jr.
Francis Lightfoot Lee
Carter Braxton

NORTH CAROLINA
William Hooper
Joseph Hewes
John Penn

SOUTH CAROLINA
Edward Rutledge
Thomas Heyward, Jr.
Thomas Lynch, Jr.
Arthur Middleton

GEORGIA
Button Gwinnett
Lyman Hall
George Walton

Resolved, That copies of the Declaration be sent to the several assemblies, conventions, and committees, or councils of safety, and to the several commanding officers of the continental troops; that it be proclaimed in each of the United States, at the head of the army.

Appendix B

The Articles of Confederation and Perpetual Union

1 March 1781. To all to whom these Presents shall come, we the under signed Delegates of the States affixed to our Names, send greeting.

Whereas the Delegates of the United States of America, in Congress assembled, did, on the 15th day of November, in the Year of Our Lord One thousand Seven Hundred and Seventy seven, and in the Second Year of the Independence of America, agree to certain articles of Confederation and perpetual Union between the States of Newhampshire, Massachusetts-bay, Rhodeisland and Providence Plantations, Connecticut, New York, New Jersey, Pennsylvania, Delaware, Maryland, Virginia, North-Carolina, South-Carolina, and Georgia in the words following, viz. "Articles of Confederation and perpetual Union between the states of Newhampshire, Massachusetts-bay, Rhodeisland and Providence Plantations, Connecticut, New-York, New-Jersey, Pennsylvania, Delaware, Maryland, Virginia, North-Carolina, South-Carolina and Georgia.

Article I. The Stile of this confederacy shall be "The United States of America."

Article II. Each state retains its sovereignty, freedom, and independence, and every Power, Jurisdiction and right, which is not by this confederation expressly delegated to the United States, in Congress assembled.

Article III. The said states hereby severally enter into a firm league of friendship with each other, for their common defence, the security of their Liberties, and their mutual and general welfare, binding themselves to assist each other, against all force offered to, or attacks made upon them, or any of them, on account of religion, sovereignty, trade, or any other pretence whatever.

Article IV. The better to secure and perpetuate mutual friendship and intercourse among the people of the different states in this union, the free inhabitants of each of these states, paupers, vagabonds and fugitives from justice excepted, shall be entitled to all privileges and immunities of free citizens in the several states; and the people of each state shall have free ingress and regress to and from any other state, and shall enjoy therein all the privileges of trade and commerce, subject to the same duties, impositions and restrictions as the inhabitants thereof respectively, provided that such restriction shall not extend so far as to prevent the removal of property imported into any state, to any other state, of which the Owner is an inhabitant; provided also that no imposition, duties or restriction shall be laid by any state, on the property of the united states, or either of them.

If any Person guilty of, or charged with treason, felony, or other high misdemeanor in any state, shall flee from Justice, and be found in any of the united states, he shall, upon demand of the Governor or executive power, of the state from which he fled, be delivered up and removed to the state having jurisdiction of his offence.

Full faith and credit shall be given in each of these states to the records, acts and judicial proceedings of the courts and magistrates of every other state.

Article V. For the more convenient management of the general interests of the united states, delegates shall be annually appointed in such manner as the legislature of each state shall direct, to meet in Congress on the first Monday in November, in every year, with a power reserved to each state, to recal its delegates, or any of them, at any time within the year, and to send others in their stead, for the remainder of the Year.

No state shall be represented in Congress by less than two, nor by more than seven Members; and no person shall be capable of being a delegate for more than three years in any term of six years; nor shall any person, being a delegate, be capable of holding any office under the united states, for which he, or another for his benefit receives any salary, fees or emolument of any kind.

Each state shall maintain its own delegates in a meeting of the states, and while they act as members of the committee of the states.

In determining questions in the united states in Congress assembled, each state shall have one vote.

Freedom of speech and debate in Congress shall not be impeached or questioned in any Court, or place out of Congress, and the members of congress shall be protected in their persons from arrests and imprisonments, during the time of their going to and from, and attendance on congress, except for treason, felony, or breach of the peace.

Article VI. No state, without the Consent of the united states in congress assembled, shall send any embassy to, or receive any embassy from, or enter into any conference, agreement, alliance or treaty with any King prince or state; nor shall any person holding any office of profit or trust under the united states, or any of them, accept of any present, emolument, office or title of any kind whatever from any king, prince or foreign state, nor shall the united states in congress assembled, or any of them, grant any title of nobility.

No two or more states shall enter into any treaty, confederation or alliance whatever between them, without the consent of the united states in congress assembled, specifying accurately the purposes for which the same is to be entered into, and how long it shall continue.

No state shall lay any imposts or duties, which may interfere with any stipulations in treaties, entered into by the united states in congress assembled, with any king, prince or state, in pursuance of any treaties already proposed by congress, to the courts of France and Spain.

No vessels of war shall be kept up in time of peace by any state, except such number only, as shall be deemed necessary by the united states in congress assembled, for the defence of such state, or its trade; nor shall any body of forces be kept up by any state, in time of peace, except such number only, as in the judgment of the united states, in congress assembled, shall be deemed requisite to garrison the forts necessary for the defence of such state; but every state shall always keep up a well regulated and disciplined militia, sufficiently armed and accoutred, and shall provide and constantly have ready for use, in public stores, a due number of field pieces and tents, and a proper quantity of arms, ammunition and camp equipage.

No state shall engage in any war without the consent of the united states in congress assembled, unless such state be actually invaded by enemies, or shall have received certain advice of a resolution being formed by some nation of Indians to invade such state, and the danger is so imminent as not to admit of a delay till the united states in congress assembled can be consulted: nor shall any state grant commissions to any ships or vessels of war, nor letters of marque or reprisal, except it be after a declaration of war by the united states in congress assembled, and then only against the kingdom or state and the subjects thereof, against which war has been so declared, and under such regulations as shall be established by the united states in congress assembled, unless such state be infested by pirates, in which case vessels of war may be fitted out for that occasion, and kept so long as the danger shall continue, or until the united states in congress assembled, shall determine otherwise.

Article VII. When land-forces are raised by any state for the common defence, all officers of or under the rank of colonel, shall be appointed by the legislature of each state respectively, by whom such forces shall be raised, or in such manner as such state shall direct, and all vacancies shall be filled up by the State which first made the appointment.

Article VIII. All charges of war, and all other expences that shall be incurred for the common defence or general welfare, and allowed by the united states in congress assembled, shall be defrayed out of a common treasury, which shall be supplied by the several states in proportion to the value of all land within each state, granted to or surveyed for an Person, as such land and the buildings and improvements thereon shall be estimated according to such mode as the united states in congress assembled, shall from time to time direct and appoint.

The taxes for paying that proportion shall be laid and levied by the authority and direction of the legislatures of the several states within the time agreed upon by the united states in congress assembled.

Article IX. The united states in congress assembled, shall have the sole and exclusive right and power of determining on peace and war, except in the cases mentioned in the sixth article—of sending and receiving ambassadors—entering into treaties and alliances, provided that no treaty of commerce shall be made whereby the legislative power of the respective states shall be restrained from imposing such imposts and duties on foreigners as their own people are subjected to, or from prohibiting the exportation or importation of any species of goods or commodities whatsoever—of establishing rules for deciding in all cases, what captures on land or water shall be legal, and in what manner prizes taken by land or naval forces in the service of the united states shall be divided or appropriated—or granting letters of marque and reprisal in times of peace—appointing courts for the trial of piracies and felonies committed on the high seas and establishing courts for receiving and determining finally appeals in all cases of captures, provided that no member of congress shall be appointed a judge of any of the said courts.

The united states in congress assembled shall also be the last resort on appeal in all disputes and differences now subsisting or that hereafter may arise between two or more states concerning boundary, jurisdiction or any other cause whatever; which authority shall always be exercised in the manner following. Whenever the legislative or executive authority or lawful agent of any state in controversy with another shall present a petition to congress stating the matter in question and praying for a hearing, notice thereof shall be given by order of congress to the legislative or executive authority of the other state in controversy, and a day assigned for the appearance of the parties by their lawful agents, who shall then be directed to appoint by joint consent, commissioners or judges to constitute a court for hearing and determining the matter in question: but if they cannot agree, congress shall name three persons out of each of the united states, and from the list of such persons each party shall alternately strike out one, the petitioners beginning, until the number shall be reduced to thirteen; and from that number not less than seven, nor more than nine names as congress shall direct, shall in the presence of congress be drawn out by lot, and the persons whose names shall be so drawn or any five of them, shall be commissioners or judges, to hear and finally determine the controversy, so always a major part of the judges who shall hear the cause shall agree in the determination: and if either party shall neglect to attend at the day appointed, without showing reasons, which congress shall judge sufficient, or being present shall refuse to strike, the congress shall proceed to nominate three persons out of each state, and the secretary of congress shall strike in behalf of such party absent or refusing; and the judgment and sentence of the court to be appointed, in the manner before prescribed, shall be final and conclusive; and if any of the parties shall refuse to submit to the authority of such court, or to appear or defend their claim or cause, the court shall nevertheless proceed to pronounce sentence, or judgment, which shall in like manner be final and decisive, the judgment or sentence and other proceedings being in either case transmitted to congress, and lodged among the acts of congress for the security of the parties concerned: provided that every commissioner, before he sits in judgment, shall take an oath to be administered by one of the judges of the supreme or superior court of the state, where the cause shall be tried, "well and truly to hear and determine the matter in question, according to the best of his judgment, without favour, affection or hope of reward:" provided also, that no state shall be deprived of territory for the benefit of the united states.

All controversies concerning the private right of soil claimed under different grants of two or more states, whose jurisdictions as they may respect such lands, and the states which passed such grants are adjusted, the said grants or either of them being at the same time claimed to have originated antecedent to such settlement of jurisdiction, shall on the petition of either party to the congress of the united states, be finally determined as near as may be in the same manner as is before prescribed for deciding disputes respecting territorial jurisdiction between different states.

The united states in congress assembled shall also have the sole and exclusive right and power of regulating the alloy and value of coin struck by their own authority, or by that of the respective states—fixing the standards of weights and measures throughout the united states—regulating the trade and managing all affairs with the Indians, not members of any of the states, provided that the legislative right of any state within its own limits be not infringed or violated—establishing or regulating post-offices from one state to another, throughout all the united states, and exacting such postage on the papers passing thro' the same as may be requisite to defray the expences of the said office—appointing all officers of the land forces, in the service of the united states, excepting regimental officers—appointing all the officers of the naval forces, and commissioning all officers whatever in the service of the united states—making rules for the government and regulation of the said land and naval forces, and directing their operations.

The united states in congress assembled shall have authority to appoint a committee, to sit in the recess of congress, to be denominated "A Committee of the States," and to consist of one delegate from each state; and to appoint such other committees and civil officers as may be necessary for managing the general affairs of the united states under their direction—to appoint one of their number to preside, provided that no person be allowed to serve in the office of president more than one year in any term of three years; to ascertain the necessary sums of money to be raised for the service of the united states, and to appropriate and apply the same for defraying the public expences—to borrow money, or emit bills on the credit of the united states, transmitting every half year to the respective states an account of the sums of money so borrowed or emitted—to build and equip a navy—to agree upon the number of land forces, and to make requisitions from each state for its quota, in proportion to the number of white inhabitants in such state; which requisition shall be binding, and thereupon the legislature of each state shall appoint the regimental officers, raise the men and cloath, arm and equip them in a soldier like manner, at the expence of the united states; and the officers and men so cloathed, armed and equipped shall march to the place appointed, and within the time agreed on by the united states in congress assembled: But if the united states in congress assembled shall, on consideration of circumstances judge proper that any state should not raise men, or should raise a smaller number than its quota, and that any other state should raise a greater number of men than the quota thereof, such extra number shall be raised, officered, cloathed, armed and equipped in the same manner as the quota of such state, unless the legislature of such state shall judge that such extra number cannot be safely spared out of the same, in which case they shall raise officer, cloath, arm and equip as many of such extra number as they judge can be safely spared. And the officers and men so cloathed, armed and equipped, shall march to the place appointed, and within the time agreed on by the united states in congress assembled.

The united states in congress assembled shall never engage in a war, not grant letters of marque and reprisal in time of peace, nor enter into any treaties or alliances, nor coin money, nor regulate the value thereof, nor ascertain the sums and expences necessary for the defence and welfare of the united states, or any of them, nor emit bills, nor borrow money on the credit of the united states, nor appropriate money, nor agree upon the number of vessels of war, to be built or purchased, or the number of land or sea forces to be raised, nor appoint a commander in chief of the army or navy, unless nine states assent to the same: nor shall a question on any other point, except for adjourning from day to day be determined, unless by the votes of a majority of the united states in congress assembled.

The congress of the united states shall have power to adjourn to any time within the year, and to any place within the united states, so that no period of adjournment be for a longer duration than the space of six Months, and shall publish the Journal of their proceedings monthly, except such parts thereof relating to treaties, alliances or military operations, as in their judgment require secrecy; and the yeas and nays of the delegates of each state on any question shall be entered on the Journal, when it is desired by any delegate; and the delegates of a state, or any of them, at his or their request shall be furnished with a transcript of the said Journal, except such parts as are above excepted, to lay before the legislatures of the several states.

Article X. The committee of the states, or any nine of them, shall be authorized to execute, in the recess of congress, such of the powers of congress as the united states in congress assembled, by the consent of nine states, shall from time to time think expedient to vest them with; provided that no power be delegated to the said committee, for the exercise of which, by the articles of confederation, the voice of nine states in the congress of the united states assembled is requisite.

Article XI. Canada acceding to this confederation, and joining in the measures of the united states, shall be admitted into, and entitled to all the advantages of this union: but no other colony shall be admitted into the same, unless such admission be agreed to by nine states.

Article XII. All bills of credit emitted, monies borrowed and debts contracted by, or under the authority of congress, before the assembling of the united states, in pursuance of the present confederation, shall be deemed and considered as a charge against the united states, for payment and satisfaction whereof the said united states, and the public faith are hereby solemnly pledged.

Article XIII. Every state shall abide by the determinations of the united states in congress assembled, on all questions which by this confederation are submitted to them. And the Articles of this confederation shall be inviolably observed by every state, and the union shall be perpetual; nor shall any alteration at any time hereafter be made in any of them; unless such alteration be agreed to in a congress of the united states, and be afterwards confirmed by the legislatures of every state.

And Whereas it hath pleased the Great Governor of the World to incline the hearts of the legislatures we respectively represent in congress, to approve of, and to authorize us to ratify the said articles of confederation and perpetual union. Know Ye that we the undersigned delegates, by virtue of the power and authority to us given for that purpose, do by these presents, in the name and in behalf of our respective constituents, fully and entirely ratify and confirm each and every of the said articles of confederation and perpetual union, and all and singular the matters and things therein contained: And we do further solemnly plight and engage the faith of our respective constituents, that they shall abide by the determinations of the united states in congress assembled, on all questions, which by the said confederation are submitted to them. And that the articles thereof shall be inviolably observed by the states we respectively represent, and that the union shall be perpetual. In Witness whereof we have here-unto set our hands in Congress. Done at Philadelphia in the state of Pennsylvania the ninth day of July, in the Year of our Lord one Thousand seven Hundred and Seventy-eight, and in the third year of the independence of America.

Josiah Bartlett, John Wentworth, Junr August 8th, 1778,	On the part and behalf of the State of New Hampshire.
John Hancock, Samuel Adams, Elbridge Gerry, Francis Dana, James Lovell, Samuel Holten,	On the part and behalf of the State of Massachusetts Bay.
William Ellery, Henry Marchant, John Collins,	On the part and behalf of the State of Rhode-Island and Providence Plantations.
Roger Sherman, Samuel Huntington, Oliver Wolcott, Titus Hosmer, Andrew Adams,	On the part and behalf of the State of Connecticut.
Jas Duane, Fra: Lewis, Wm Duer, Gouvr Morris,	On the part and behalf of the State of New York.
Jno Witherspoon, Nathl Scudder,	On the Part and in Behalf of the State of New Jersey, November 26th, 1778.
Robert Morris, Daniel Roberdeau, Jon. Bayard Smith, William Clingar, Joseph Reed, 22d July, 1778,	On the part and behalf of the State of Pennsylvania.
Thos McKean, Feby 22d, 1779, John Dickinson, May 5th, 1779, Nicholas Van Dyke,	On the part and behalf of the State of Delaware.
John Hanson, March 1, 1781, Daniel Carroll, DO	On the part and behalf of the State of Maryland.
Richard Henry Lee, John Banister, Thomas Adams, Jno Harvic, Francis Lightfoot Lee,	On the Part and Behalf of the State of Virginia.
John Penn, July 21st, 1778, Corns Harnett, Jno Williams,	On the part and behalf of the State of North Carolina.
Henry Laurens, William Henry Drayton, Jno Mathews, Richd Hutson, Thos Heyward, Junr.	On the part and behalf of the State of South Carolina.
Jno Walton, 24th July, 1778, Edwd Telfair, Edwd Langworthy,	On the part and behalf of the State of Georgia.[1]

Note: These Articles of Confederation are taken from *Journals of the Continental Congress,* Library of Congress edition, Vol. XIX (1912), 214.

The Articles of Confederation were agreed to by the Congress, 15 November 1777. They were, as appears from the list of signatures affixed to these Articles, signed at different times by the delegates of the different American states. On 1 March 1781, the delegates from Maryland, the last of the states to take action, "did, in behalf of the said state of Maryland, sign and ratify the said articles, by which act the Confederation of the United States of America was completed, each and every of the Thirteen United States, from New Hampshire to Georgia, both included, having adopted and confirmed, and by their delegates in Congress, ratified the same."

[1]The proceedings of this day with respect to the signing of the Articles of Confederation, the Articles themselves, and the signers are entered in the *Papers of the Continental Congress,* No. 9 (History of the Confederation), but not in the Journal itself. The Articles are printed here from the original roll in the Bureau of Rolls and Library, Department of State.

APPENDIX

C

FEDERALIST NO. 10

James Madison
22 November 1787

To the People of the State of New York.

Among the numerous advantages promised by a well constructed Union, none deserves to be more accurately developed than its tendency to break and control the violence of faction. The friend of popular governments, never finds himself so much alarmed for their character and fate, as when he contemplates their propensity to this dangerous vice. He will not fail therefore to set a due value on any plan which, without violating the principles to which he is attached, provides a proper cure for it. The instability, injustice and confusion introduced into the public councils, have in truth been the mortal diseases under which popular governments have every where perished; as they continue to be the favorite and fruitful topics from which the adversaries to liberty derive their most specious declamations. The valuable improvements made by the American Constitutions on the popular models, both ancient and modern, cannot certainly be too much admired; but it would be an unwarrantable partiality, to contend that they have as effectually obviated the danger on this side as was wished and expected. Complaints are every where heard from our most considerate and virtuous citizens, equally the friends of public and private faith, and of public and personal liberty; that our governments are too unstable; that the public good is disregarded in the conflicts of rival parties; and that measures are too often decided, not according to the rules of justice, and the rights of the minor party; but by the superior force of an interested and overbearing majority. However anxiously we may wish that these complaints had no foundation, the evidence of known facts will not permit us to deny that they are in some degree true. It will be found indeed, on a candid review of our situation, that some of the distresses under which we labor, have been erroneously charged on the operation of our governments; but it will be found, at the same time, that other causes will not alone account for many of our heaviest misfortunes; and particularly, for that prevailing and increasing distrust of public engagements, and alarm for private rights, which are echoed from one end of the continent to the other. These must be chiefly, if not wholly, effects of the unsteadiness and injustice, with which a factious spirit has tainted our public administrations.

By a faction I understand a number of citizens, whether amounting to a majority or minority of the whole, who are united and actuated by some common impulse of passion, or of interest, adverse to the rights of other citizens, or to the permanent and aggregate interests of the community.

There are two methods of curing the mischiefs of faction: the one, by removing its causes; the other, by controlling its effects.

There are again two methods of removing the causes of faction: the one by destroying the liberty which is essential to its existence; the other, by giving to every citizen the same opinions, the same passions, and the same interests.

It could never be more truly said than of the first remedy, that it is worse than the disease. Liberty is to faction, what air is to fire, an ailment without which it instantly expires. But it could not be a less folly to abolish liberty, which is essential to political life, because it nourishes faction, than it would be to wish the annihilation of air, which is essential to animal life, because it imparts to fire its destructive agency.

The second expedient is as impracticable, as the first would be unwise. As long as the reason of man continues fallible, and he is at liberty to exercise it, different opinions will be formed. As long as the connection subsists between his reason and his self-love, his opinions and his passions will have a reciprocal influence on each other; and the former will be objects to which the latter will attach themselves. The diversity in the faculties of men from which the rights of property originate, is not less an insuperable obstacle to a uniformity of interests. The protection of these faculties is the first object of Government. From the protection of different and unequal faculties of acquiring property, the possession of different degrees and kinds of property immediately results: and from the influence of these on the sentiments and views of the respective proprietors, ensues a division of the society into different interests and parties.

The latent causes of faction are thus sown in the nature of man; and we see them every where brought into different degrees of activity, according to the different circumstances of civil society. A zeal for different opinions concerning religion, concerning Government and many other points, as well of speculation as of practice; an attachment to different leaders ambitiously contending for pre-eminence and power; or to persons of other descriptions whose fortunes have been interesting to the human passions, have in turn divided mankind into parties, inflamed them with mutual animosity, and rendered them much more disposed to vex and oppress each other, than to cooperate for their common good. So strong is this propensity of mankind to fall into mutual animosities, that where no substantial occasion presents itself, the most frivolous and fanciful distinctions have been sufficient to kindle their unfriendly passions, and excite their most violent conflicts. But the most common and durable sources of factions, has been the various and unequal distribution of property. Those who hold, and those who are without property, have ever formed distinct interests in society. Those who are creditors, and those who are debtors, fall under a like discrimination. A landed interest, a manufacturing interest, a mercantile interest, a monied interest, with many lesser interests, grow up of necessity in civilized nations, and divide them into different classes, actuated by different sentiments and views. The regulation of these various and interfering interests forms the principal task of modern Legislation and involves the spirit of party and faction in the necessary and ordinary operations of Government.

No man is allowed to be a judge in his own cause; because his interest would certainly bias his judgment, and, not improbably, corrupt his integrity. With equal, nay with greater reason, a body of men, are unfit to be both judges and parties, at the same time; yet, what are many of the most important acts of legislation, but so many judicial determinations, not indeed concerning the rights of single persons, but concerning the rights of large bodies of citizens, and what are the different classes of legislators, but advocates and parties to the causes which they determine? Is a law proposed concerning private debts? It is a question to which the creditors are parties on one side, and the debtors on the other. Justice ought to hold the balance between them. Yet the parties are and must be themselves the judges; and the most numerous party, or, in other words, the most powerful faction must be expected to prevail. Shall domestic manufactures be encouraged, and in what degree, by restrictions on foreign manufactures? are questions which would be differently decided by the landed and the manufacturing classes; and probably by neither, with a sole regard to justice and the public good. The apportionment of taxes on the various descriptions of property, is an act which seems to require the most exact impartiality; yet, there is perhaps no legislative act in which greater opportunity and temptation are given to a predominant party, to trample on the rules of justice. Every shilling with which they over-burden the inferior number, is a shilling saved to their own pockets.

It is in vain to say, that enlightened statesmen will be able to adjust these clashing interests, and render them all subservient to the public good. Enlightened statesmen will not always be at the helm: Nor, in many cases, can such an adjustment be made at all, without taking into view indirect and remote considerations, which will rarely prevail over the immediate interest which one party may find in disregarding the rights of another, or the good of the whole.

The inference to which we are brought, is, that the *causes* of faction cannot be removed; and that relief is only to be sought in the means of controlling its *effects*.

If a faction consists of less than a majority, relief is supplied by the republican principle, which enables the majority to defeat its sinister views by regular vote: It may clog the administration, it may convulse the society; but it will be unable to execute and mask its violence under the forms of the Constitution. When a majority is included in a faction, the form of popular government on the other hand enables it to sacrifice to its ruling passion or interest, both the public good and the rights of other citizens. To secure the public good, and private rights, against the danger of such a faction, and at the same time to preserve the spirit and the form of popular government, is then the great object to which our enquiries are directed: Let me add that it is the great desideratum, by which alone this form of government can be rescued from the opprobrium under which it has so long labored, and be recommended to the esteem and adoption of mankind.

By what means is this object attainable? Evidently by one of two only. Either the existence of the same passion or interest in a majority at the same time, must be prevented; or the majority, having such co-existent passion or interest, must be rendered, by their number and local situation, unable to concert and carry into effect schemes of oppression. If the impulse and the opportunity be suffered to coincide, we well know that neither moral nor religious motives can be relied on as an adequate control. They are not found to be such on the injustice and violence of individuals, and lose their efficacy in proportion to the number combined together; that is, in proportion as their efficacy becomes needful.

From this view of the subject, it may be concluded, that a pure Democracy, by which I mean, a Society, consisting of a small number of citizens, who assemble and administer the Government in person, can admit of no cure for the mischiefs of faction. A common passion or interest will, in almost every case, be felt by a majority of the whole; a communication and concert results from the form of Government itself; and there is nothing to check the inducements to sacrifice the weaker party, or an obnoxious individual. Hence it is, that such Democracies have ever been spectacles of turbulence and contention; have ever been found incompatible with personal security, or the rights of property; and have in general been as short in their lives, as they have been violent in their deaths. Theoretic politicians, who have patronized this species of Government, have erroneously supposed, that by reducing mankind to a perfect equality in their political rights, they would, at the same time, be perfectly equalized and assimilated in their possessions, their opinions, and their passions.

A republic, by which I mean a government in which the scheme of representation takes place, opens a different prospect, and promises the cure for which we are seeking. Let us examine the points in which it varies from pure democracy, and we shall comprehend both the nature of the cure and the efficacy which it must derive from the union.

The two great points of difference, between a democracy and a republic, are, first, the delegation of the government, in the latter, to a small number of citizens, elected by the rest; secondly, the greater number of citizens, and greater sphere of country, over which the latter may be extended.

The effect of the first difference is, on the one hand, to refine and enlarge the public views, by passing them through the medium of a chosen body of citizens, whose wisdom may best discern the true interest of their country, and whose patriotism and love of justice, will be least likely to sacrifice it to temporary or partial considerations. Under such a regulation, it may well happen, that the public voice, pronounced by the representatives of the people, will be more consonant to the public good, than if pronounced by the people themselves, convened for the purpose. On the other hand the effect may be inverted. Men of factious tempers, of local prejudices, or of sinister designs, may by intrigue, by corruption, or by other means, first obtain the suffrages, and then betray the interest of the people. The question resulting is, whether small or extensive republics are most favorable to the election of proper guardians of the public weal, and it is clearly decided in favor of the latter by two obvious considerations.

In the first place, it is to be remarked that, however small the republic may be, the representatives must be raised to a certain number, in order to guard against the cabals of a few; and that however large it may be, they must be limited to a certain number, in order to guard against the confusion of a multitude. Hence, the number of representatives in the two cases not being in proportion to that of the constituents, and being proportionally greatest in the small republic, it follows, that if the proportion of fit characters be not less in the large than in the small republic, the former will present a greater option, and consequently a greater probability of a fit choice.

In the next place, as each Representative will be chosen by a greater number of citizens in the large than in the small Republic, it will be more difficult for unworthy candidates to practise with success the vicious arts, by which elections are too often carried; and the suffrages of the people being more free, will be more likely to center on men who possess the most attractive merit, and the most diffusive and established characters.

It must be confessed, that in this, as in most other cases, there is a mean, on both sides of which inconveniences will be found to lie. By enlarging too much the number of electors, you render the representative too little acquainted with all their local circumstances and lesser interests; as by reducing it too much, you render him unduly attached to these, and too little fit to comprehend and pursue great and national objects. The Federal Constitution forms a happy combination in this respect; the great and aggregate interests being referred to the national, the local and particular, to the state legislatures.

The other point of difference is, the greater number of citizens and extent of territory which may be brought within the compass of Republican, than of Democratic Government; and it is this circumstance principally which renders factious combinations less to be dreaded in the former, than in the latter. The smaller the society, the fewer probably will be the distinct parties and interests composing it; the fewer the distinct parties and interests, the more frequently will a majority be found of the same party; and the smaller the number of individuals composing a majority, and the smaller the compass within which they are placed, the more easily will they concert and execute their plans of oppression. Extend the sphere, and you take in a greater variety of parties and interests; you make it less probable that a majority of the whole will have a common motive to invade the rights of other citizens; or if such a common motive exists, it will be more difficult for all who feel it to discover their own strength, and to act in unison with each other. Besides other impediments, it may be remarked, that where there is a consciousness of unjust or dishonorable purposes, communication is always checked by distrust, in proportion to the number whose concurrence is necessary.

Hence it clearly appears, that the same advantage, which a Republic has over a Democracy, in controlling the effects of faction, is enjoyed by a large over a small Republic—is enjoyed by the Union over the States composing it. Does this advantage consist in the substitution of Representatives, whose enlightened views and virtuous sentiments render them superior to local prejudices, and to schemes of injustice? It will not be denied, that the Representation of the Union will be most likely to possess these requisite endowments. Does it consist in the greater security afforded by a greater variety of parties, against the event of any one party being able to outnumber and oppress the rest? In an equal degree does the increased variety of parties, comprised within the Union, increase this security? Does it, in fine, consist in the greater obstacles opposed to the concert and accomplishment of the secret wishes of an unjust and interested majority? Here, again, the extent of the Union gives it the most palpable advantage.

The influence of factious leaders may kindle a flame within their particular States, but will be unable to spread a general conflagration through the other States: a religious sect, may degenerate into a political faction in a part of the Confederacy but the variety of sects dispersed over the entire face of it, must secure the national Councils against any danger from that source: a rage for paper money, for an abolition of debts, for an equal division of property, or for any other improper or wicked project, will be less apt to pervade the whole body of the Union, than a particular member of it; in the same proportion as such a malady is more likely to taint a particular county or district, than an entire State.

In the extent and proper structure of the Union, therefore, we behold a Republican remedy for the diseases most incident to Republican Government. And according to the degree of pleasure and pride, we feel in being Republicans, ought to be our zeal in cherishing the spirit, and supporting the character of Federalists.

PUBLIUS

Appendix

D

Federalist No. 51

James Madison

6 February 1788

To the People of the State of New York.

To what expedient then shall we finally resort for maintaining in practice the necessary partition of power among the several departments, as laid down in the constitution? The only answer that can be given is, that as all these exterior provisions are found to be inadequate, the defect must be supplied, by so contriving the interior structure of the government, as that its several constituent parts may, by their mutual relations, be the means of keeping each other in their proper places. Without presuming to undertake a full development of this important idea, I will hazard a few general observations, which may perhaps place it in a clearer light, and enable us to form a more correct judgment of the principles and structure of the government planned by the convention.

In order to lay a due foundation for that separate and distinct exercise of the different powers of government, which to a certain extent, is admitted on all hands to be essential to the preservation of liberty, it is evident that each department should have a will of its own; and consequently should be so constituted, that the members of each should have as little agency as possible in the appointment of the members of the others. Were this principle rigorously adhered to, it would require that all the appointments for the supreme executive, legislative, and judiciary magistracies, should be drawn from the same fountain of authority, the people, through channels, having no communication whatever with one another. Perhaps such a plan of constructing the several departments would be less difficult in practice than it may in contemplation appear. Some difficulties however, and some additional expense, would attend the execution of it. Some deviations therefore from the principle must be admitted. In the constitution of the judiciary department in particular, it might be inexpedient to insist rigorously on the principle; first, because peculiar qualifications being essential in the members, the primary consideration ought to be to select that mode of choice, which best secures these qualifications; secondly, because the permanent tenure by which the appointments are held in that department, must soon destroy all sense of dependence on the authority conferring them.

It is equally evident that the members of each department should be as little dependent as possible on those of the others, for the emoluments annexed to their offices. Were the executive magistrate, or the judges, not independent of the legislature in this particular, their independence in every other would be merely nominal.

But the great security against a gradual concentration of the several powers in the same department, consists in giving to those who administer each department, the necessary constitutional means, and personal motives, to resist encroachments of the others. The provision for defense must in this, as in all other cases, be made commensurate to the danger of attack. Ambition must be made to counteract ambition. The interest of the man must be connected with the constitutional right of the place. It may be a reflection on human nature, that such devices should be necessary to control the abuses of government. But what is government itself but the greatest of all reflections on human nature? If men were angels, no government would be necessary. If angels were to govern men, neither external nor internal controls on government would be necessary. In framing a government which is to be administered by men over men, the great difficulty lies in this: You must first enable the government to control the governed; and in the next place, oblige it to control itself. A dependence on the people is no doubt the primary control on the government; but experience has taught mankind the necessity of auxiliary precautions.

This policy of supplying by opposite and rival interests, the defect of better motives, might be traced through the whole system of human affairs, private as well as public. We see it particularly displayed in all the subordinate distributions of power; where the constant aim is to divide and arrange the several offices in such a manner as that each may be a check on the other; that the private interest of every individual, may be a sentinel over the public rights. These inventions of prudence cannot be less requisite in the distribution of the supreme powers of the state.

But it is not possible to give to each department an equal power of self defense. In republican government the legislative authority, necessarily, predominates. The remedy for this inconveniency is, to divide the legislature into different branches; and to render them by different modes of election, and different principles of action, as little connected with each other, as the nature of their common functions, and their common dependence on the society, will admit. It may even be necessary to guard against dangerous encroachments by still further precautions. As the weight of the legislative authority requires that it should be thus divided, the weakness of the executive may require, on the other hand, that it should be fortified. An absolute negative, on the legislature, appears at first view to be the natural defense with which the executive magistrate should be armed. But perhaps it would be neither altogether safe, nor alone sufficient. On ordinary occasions, it might not be exerted with the requisite firmness; and on extraordinary occasions, it might be perfidiously abused. May not this defect of an absolute negative be supplied, by some qualified connection between this weaker department, and the weaker branch of the stronger department, by which the latter may be led to support the constitutional rights of the former, without being too much detached from the rights of its own department?

If the principles on which these observations are founded be just, as I persuade myself they are, and they be applied as a criterion, to the several state constitutions, and to the federal constitution, it will be found, that if the latter does not perfectly correspond with them, the former are infinitely less able to bear such a test.

There are moreover two considerations particularly applicable to the federal system of America, which place that system in a very interesting point of view.

First. In a single republic, all the power surrendered by the people, is submitted to the administration of a single government; and usurpations are guarded against by a division of the government into distinct and separate departments. In the compound republic of America, the power surrendered by the people, is first divided between two distinct governments, and then the portion allotted to each, subdivided among distinct and separate departments. Hence a double security arises to the rights of the people. The different governments will control each other; at the same time that each will be controlled by itself.

Second. It is of great importance in a republic, not only to guard the society against the oppression of its rulers; but to guard one part of the society against the injustice of the other part. Different interests necessarily exist in different classes of citizens. If a majority be united by a common interest, the rights of the minority will be insecure. There are but two methods of providing against this evil: The one by creating a will in the community independent of the majority, that is, of the society itself, the other by comprehending in the society so many separate descriptions of citizens, as will render an unjust combination of a majority of the whole, very improbable, if not impracticable. The first method prevails in all governments possessing an hereditary or self appointed authority. This at best is but a precarious security; because a power independent of the society may as well espouse the unjust views of the major, as the rightful interests, of the minor party, and may possibly be turned against both parties. The second method will be exemplified in the federal republic of the United States. While all authority in it will be derived from and dependent on the society, the society itself will be broken into so many parts, interests and classes of citizens, that the rights of individuals or of the minority, will be in little danger from interested combinations of the majority. In a free government, the security for civil rights must be the same as for religious rights. It consists in the one case in the multiplicity of interests, and in the other, in the multiplicity of sects. The degree of security in both cases will depend on the number of interests and sects; and this may be presumed to depend on the extent of country and number of people comprehended under the same government. This view of the subject must particularly recommend a proper federal system to all the sincere and considerate friends of republican government: Since it shows that in exact proportion as the territory of the union may be formed into more circumscribed confederacies or states, oppressive combinations of a majority will be facilitated, the best security under the republican form, for the rights of every class of citizens, will be diminished; and consequently, the stability and independence of some member of the government, the only other security, must be proportionally increased. Justice is the end of government. It is the end of civil society. It ever has been, and ever will be pursued, until it be obtained, or until liberty be lost in the pursuit. In a society under the forms of which the stronger faction can readily unite and oppress the weaker, anarchy may as truly be said to reign, as in a state of nature where the weaker individual is not secured against the violence of the stronger. And as in the latter state even the stronger individuals are prompted by the uncertainty of their condition, to submit to a government which may protect the weak as well as themselves: So in the former state, will the more powerful factions or parties be gradually induced by a like motive, to wish for a government which will protect all parties, the weaker as well as the more powerful. It can be little doubted, that if the state of Rhode Island was separated from the confederacy, and left to itself, the insecurity of rights under the popular form of government within such narrow limits, would be displayed by such reiterated oppressions of factious majorities, that some power altogether independent of the people would soon be called for by the voice of the very factions whose misrule had proved the necessity of it. In the extended republic of the United States, and among the great variety of interests, parties and sects which it embraces, a coalition of a majority of the whole society could seldom take place on any other principles than those of justice and the general good; and there being thus less danger to a minor from the will of the major party, there must be less pretext also, to provide for the security of the former, by introducing into the government a will not dependent on the latter; or in other words, a will independent of the society itself. It is no less certain than it is important, notwithstanding the contrary opinions which have been entertained, that the larger the society, provided it lie within a practicable sphere, the more duly capable it will be of self government. And happily for the *republican cause,* the practicable sphere may be carried to a very great extent, by a judicious modification and mixture of the *federal principle.*

PUBLIUS

Appendix E

Antifederalists and the Constitution

[Antifederalists opposed ratification of the Constitution because they feared it would create a strong national government that would trample the rights of individual citizens. In the following selection, George Mason, a leading Antifederalist who participated in the Constitutional Convention but who refused to sign the final document, systematically details his objections to the Constitution. Like most Antifederalists, Mason concentrates his criticisms on the risks of giving too much power to the national government. James Madison, a leading Federalist, responded to Mason's objections in a letter to George Washington.]

George Mason, "Objections to the Constitution"

Circulated early October 1787, published in full in the Virginia Journal *(Alexandria), November 22, 1787*

Objections to the Constitution of Government formed by the Convention.

There is no declaration of rights; and the laws of the general government being paramount to the laws and constitutions of the several States, the declarations of rights in the separate States are no security. Nor are the people secured even in the enjoyment of the benefits of the common law, which stands here upon no other foundation than its having been adopted by the respective acts forming the constitutions of the several States.

In the House of Representatives there is not the substance, but the shadow only of representation; which can never produce proper information in the Legislature, or inspire confidence in the people; the laws will therefore be generally made by men little concerned in, and unacquainted with their effects and consequences.

The Senate have the power of altering all money-bills, and of originating appropriations of money, and the salaries of the officers of their own appointment in conjunction with the President of the United States; although they are not the representatives of the people, or amenable to them.

These with their other great powers (viz. their power in the appointment of ambassadors and other public officers, in making treaties, and in trying all impeachments) their influence upon and connection with the supreme executive from these causes, their duration of office, and their being a constant existing body almost continually sitting, joined with their being one complete branch of the Legislature, will destroy any balance in the government, and enable them to accomplish what usurpations they please upon the rights and liberties of the people.

The judiciary of the United States is so constructed and extended as to absorb and destroy the judiciaries of the several States; thereby rendering law as tedious, intricate and expensive, and justice as unattainable by a great part of the community, as in England, and enabling the rich to oppress and ruin the poor.

The President of the United States has no constitutional council (a thing unknown in any safe and regular government) he will therefore be unsupported by proper information and advice; and will be generally directed by minions and favorites—or he will become a tool to the Senate—or a Council of State will grow out of the principal officers of the great departments; the worst and most dangerous of all ingredients for such a council in a free country; for they may be induced to join in any dangerous or oppressive measures, to shelter themselves, and prevent an inquiry into their own misconduct in office; whereas had a constitutional council been formed (as was proposed) of six member, viz. two from the eastern, two from the middle, and two from the southern States, to be appointed by vote of the States in the House of Representatives, with the same duration and rotation in office as the Senate, the Executive would always have had safe and proper information and advice, the President of such a council might have acted as Vice-President of the United States, pro tempore, upon any vacancy or disability of the chief Magistrate; and long continued sessions of the Senate would in a great measure have been prevented.

From this fatal defect of a constitutional council has arisen the improper power of the Senate, in the appointment of public officers, and the alarming dependance and connection between that branch of the Legislature and the supreme Executive.

Hence also sprung that unneccessary and dangerous officer the Vice-President; who for want of other employment is made President of the Senate; thereby dangerously blending the executive and legislative powers; besides always giving to some one of the States an unnecessary and unjust preminence over the others.

The President of the United States has the unrestrained power of granting pardons for treason; which may be sometimes exercised to screen from punishment those whom he had secretly instigated to commit the crime, and thereby prevent a discovery of his own guilt.

By declaring all treaties supreme laws of the land, the Executive and the Senate have, in many cases, an exclusive power of legislation; which might have been avoided by proper distinctions with respect to treaties, and requiring the assent of the House of Representatives, where it could be done with safety.

By requiring only a majority to make all commercial and navigation laws, the five southern States (whose produce and circumstances are totally different from that of the eight northern and eastern States) will be ruined; for such rigid and premature regulations may be made, as will enable the merchants of the northern and eastern States not only to demand an exorbitant freight, but to monopolize the purchase of the commodities at their own price, for many years: To the great injury of the landed interest, and impoverishment of the people: And the danger is the greater, as the gain on one side will be in proportion to the loss on the other. Whereas requiring two-thirds of the members present in both houses would have produced mutual moderation, promoted the general interest and removed an insuperable objection to the adoption of the government.

Under their own construction of the general clause at the end of the enumerated powers, the Congress may grant monopolies in trade and commerce, constitute new crimes, inflict unusual and severe punishments, and extend their power as far as they shall think proper; so that the State Legislatures have no security for the powers now presumed to remain to them; or the people for their rights.

There is no declaration of any kind for preserving the liberty of the press, the trial by jury in civil causes; nor against the danger of standing armies in time of peace.

The State Legislatures are restrained from laying export duties on their own produce.

The general Legislature is restrained from prohibiting the further importation of slaves for twenty odd years; though such importations render the United States weaker, and more vulnerable, and less capable of defence.

Both the general Legislature and the State Legislatures are expressly prohibited making ex post facto laws; though there never was nor can be a Legislature but must and will make such laws, when necessity and the public safety require them, which will hereafter be a breach of all the constitutions in the Union, and afford precedents for other innovations.

This government will commence in a moderate aristocracy; it is at present impossible to foresee whether it will, in its operation, produce a monarchy, or a corrupt oppressive aristocracy; it will most probably vibrate some years between the two, and then terminate between the one and the other.

James Madison to George Washington, "A 'Prolix' Comment on Mason's 'Objections' "

New York, October 18, 1787

I have been this day honoured with your favor of the 10th instant, under the same cover with which is a copy of Col. Mason's objections to the Work of the Convention. As he persists in the temper which produced his dissent it is no small satisfaction to find him reduced to such distress for a proper gloss on it; for no other consideration surely could have led him to dwell on an objection which he acknowledged to have been in some degree removed by the Convention themselves—on the paltry right of the Senate to propose alterations in money bills—on the appointment of the vice President—President of the Senate instead of making the President of the Senate the vice President, which seemed to be the alternative—and on the *possibility,* that the Congress may misconstrue their powers & betray their trust so far as to grant monopolies in trade &c. If I do not forget too some of his other reasons were either not at all or very faintly urged at the time when alone they ought to have been urged; such as the power of the Senate in the case of treaties & of impeachments; and their duration in office. With respect to the latter point I recollect well that he more than once disclaimed opposition to it. My memory fails me also if he did not acquiesce in if not vote for, the term allowed for the further importation of slaves; and the prohibition of duties on exports by the States. What he means by the dangerous tendency of the Judiciary I am at some loss to comprehend. It never was intended, nor can it be supposed that in ordinary cases the inferior tribunals will not have final jurisdiction in order to prevent the evils of which he complains. The great mass of suits in every State lie between Citizen & Citizen, and relate to matters not of federal cognizance. Notwithstanding the stress laid on the necessity of a Council to the President I strongly suspect, though I was a friend to the thing, that if such an one as Col. Mason proposed, had been established, and the power of the Senate in appointments to offices transferred to it, that as great a clamour would have been heard from some quarters which in general echo his Objections. What can he mean by saying that the Common law is not secured by the new Constitution, though it has been adopted by the State Constitutions. The Common law is nothing more than the unwritten law, and is left by all the Constitutions equally liable to legislative alterations. I am not sure that any notice is particularly taken of it in the Constitutions of the States. If there is, nothing more is provided than a general declaration that it shall continue along with other branches of law to be in force till legally changed. The Constitution of Virga. drawn up by Col. Mason himself, is absolutely silent on the subject. An *ordinance* passed during the same Session, declared the Common law as heretofore & all Statutes of prior date to the 4 of James I. to be still the law of the land, merely to obviate pretexts that the separation from G. Britain threw us into a State of nature, and abolished all civil rights and obligations. Since the Revolution every State has made great inroads & with great propriety in many instances on this *monarchical* code. The "revisal of the laws" by a Com̃itte of wch. Col. Mason was a member, though not an acting one, abounds with such innovations. The abolition of the *right of primogeniture,* which I am sure Col. Mason does not disapprove, falls under this head. What could the Convention have done? If they had in general terms declared the Common law to be in force, they would have broken in upon the legal Code of every State in the most material points: they would have done more, they would have brought over from G. B. a thousand heterogeneous & antirepublican doctrines, and even the *ecclesiastical Hierarchy itself,* for that is a part of the Common law. If they had undertaken a discrimination, they must have formed a digest of laws, instead of a Constitution. This objection surely was not brought forward in the Convention, or it wd. have been placed in such a light that a repetition of it out of doors would scarcely have been hazarded. Were it allowed the weight which Col. M. may suppose it deserves, it would remain to be decided whether it be candid to arraign the Convention for omissions which were never suggested to them—or prudent to vindicate the dissent by reasons which either were not previously thought of, or must have been willfully concealed—But I am running into a comment as prolix, as it is out of place.

I find by a letter from the Chancellor (Mr. Pendleton) that he views the act of the Convention in its true light, and gives it his unequivocal approbation. His support will have great effect. The accounts we have here of some other respectable characters vary considerably. Much will depend on Mr. Henry, and I am glad to find by your letter that his favorable decision on the subject may yet be hoped for.—The Newspapers here begin to teem with vehement & virulent calumniations of the proposed Govt. As they are chiefly borrowed from the Pennsylvania papers, you see them of course. The reports however from different quarters continue to be rather flattering.

Appendix F

Letter from Birmingham Jail

April 16, 1963
Birmingham, Alabama

My Dear Fellow Clergymen:

While confined here in the Birmingham city jail, I came across your recent statement calling my present activities "unwise and untimely." Seldom do I pause to answer criticism of my work and ideas. If I sought to answer all the criticisms that cross my desk, my secretaries would have little time for anything other than such correspondence in the course of the day, and I would have no time for constructive work. But since I feel that you are men of genuine good will and that your criticisms are sincerely set forth, I want to try to answer your statement in what I hope will be patient and reasonable terms.

I think I should indicate why I am here in Birmingham, since you have been influenced by the view which argues against "outsiders coming in." I have the honor of serving as president of the Southern Christian Leadership Conference, an organization operating in every southern state, with headquarters in Atlanta, Georgia. We have some eighty-five affiliated organizations across the South, and one of them is the Alabama Christian Movement for Human Rights. Frequently, we share staff, educational, and financial resources with our affiliates. Several months ago the affiliate here in Birmingham asked us to be on call to engage in a nonviolent direct-action program if such were deemed necessary. We readily consented, and when the hour came we lived up to our promise. So I, along with several members of my staff, am here because I was invited here. I am here because I have organizational ties here.

But more basically, I am in Birmingham because injustice is here. Just as the prophets of the eighth century B.C. left their villages and carried their "thus saith the Lord" far beyond the boundaries of their home towns, and just as the Apostle Paul left his village of Tarsus and carried the gospel of Jesus Christ to the far corners of the Greco-Roman world, so am I compelled to carry the gospel of freedom beyond my own home town. Like Paul, I must constantly respond to the Macedonian call for aid.

Moreover, I am cognizant of the interrelatedness of all communities and states. I cannot sit idly by in Atlanta and not be concerned about what happens in Birmingham. Injustice anywhere is a threat to justice everywhere. We are caught in an inescapable network of mutuality, tied in a single garment of destiny. Whatever affects one directly, affects all indirectly. Never again can we afford to live with the narrow, provincial "outside agitator" idea. Anyone who lives in the United States can never be considered an outsider anywhere within its bounds.

You deplore the demonstrations taking place in Birmingham. But your statement, I am sorry to say, fails to express a similar concern for the conditions that brought about the demonstrations. I am sure that none of you would want to rest content with the superficial kind of social analysis that deals merely with effects and does not grapple with underlying causes. It is unfortunate that demonstrations are taking place in Birmingham, but it is even more unfortunate that the city's white power structure left the Negro community with no alternative.

In any nonviolent campaign there are four basic steps: collection of the facts to determine whether injustices exist; negotiation; self-purification; and direct action. We have gone through all these steps in Birmingham. There can be no gainsaying the fact that racial injustice engulfs this community. Birmingham is probably the most thoroughly segregated city in the United States. Its ugly record of brutality is widely known. Negroes have experienced grossly unjust treatment in the courts. There have been more unsolved bombings of Negro homes and churches in Birmingham than in any other city in the nation. These are the hard, brutal facts of the case. On the basis of these conditions, Negro leaders sought to negotiate with the city fathers. But the latter consistently refused to engage in good-faith negotiation.

Then, last September, came the opportunity to talk with leaders of Birmingham's economic community. In the course of the negotiations, certain promises were made by the merchants—for example, to remove the stores' humiliating racial signs. On the basis of these promises, the Reverend Fred Shuttlesworth and the leaders of the Alabama Christian Movement for Human Rights agreed to a moratorium on all demonstrations. As the weeks and months went by, we realized that we were the victims of a broken promise. A few signs, briefly removed, returned; the others remained.

As in so many past experiences, our hopes had been blasted, and the shadow of deep disappointment settled upon us. We had no alternative except to prepare for direct action, whereby we would present our very bodies as a means of laying our case before the conscience of the local and the national community. Mindful of the difficulties involved, we decided to undertake a process of self-purification. We began a series of workshops on nonviolence, and we repeatedly asked ourselves: "Are you able to accept blows without retaliation?" "Are you able to endure the ordeal of jail?" We decided to schedule our direct-action program for the Easter season, realizing that except for Christmas, this is the main shopping period of the year. Knowing that a strong economic-withdrawal program would be the by-product of direct action, we felt that this would be the best time to bring pressure to bear on the merchants for the needed change.

Then it occurred to us that Birmingham's mayoral election was coming up in March, and we speedily decided to postpone action until after election day. When we discovered that the Commissioner of Public Safety, Eugene "Bull" Connor, had piled up enough votes to be in the run-off, we decided again to postpone action until the day after the run-off so that the demonstrations could not be used to cloud the issues. Like many others, we waited to see Mr. Connor defeated, and to this end we endured postponement after postponement. Having aided in this community need, we felt that our direct-action program could be delayed no longer.

You may well ask, "Why direct action? Why sit-ins, marches, and so forth? Isn't negotiation a better path?" You are quite right in calling for negotiation. Indeed, this is the very purpose of direct action. Nonviolent direct action seeks to create such a crisis and foster such a tension that a community which has constantly refused to negotiate is forced to confront the issue. It seeks so to dramatize the issue that it can no longer be ignored. My citing the creation of tensions as part of the work of the nonviolent-resister may sound rather shocking. But I must confess that I am not afraid of the word "tension." I have earnestly opposed violent tension, but there is a type of constructive, nonviolent tension which is necessary for growth. Just as Socrates felt that it was necessary to create a tension in the mind so that individuals could rise from the bondage of myths and half-truths to the unfettered realm of creative analysis and objective appraisal, so must we see the need for nonviolent gadflies to create the kind of tension in society that will help men rise from the dark depths of prejudice and racism to the majestic heights of understanding and brotherhood.

The purpose of our direct-action program is to create a situation so crisis-packed that it will inevitably open the door to negotiation. I therefore concur with you in your call for negotiation. Too long has our beloved Southland been bogged down in a tragic effort to live in monologue rather than dialogue.

One of the basic points in your statement is that the action that I and my associates have taken in Birmingham is untimely. Some have asked, "Why didn't you give the new city administration time to act?" The only answer that I can give to this query is that the new Birmingham administration must be prodded about as much as the outgoing one, before it will act. We are sadly mistaken if we feel that the election of Albert Boutwell as mayor will bring the millenium to Birmingham. While Mr. Boutwell is a much more gentle person than Mr. Connor, they are both segregationists, dedicated to maintenance of the status quo. I have hoped that Mr. Boutwell will be reasonable enough to see the futility of massive resistance to desegregation. But he will not see this without pressure from devotees of civil rights. My friends, I must say to you that we have not made a single gain in civil rights without determined legal and nonviolent pressure. Lamentably, it is an historical fact that privileged groups seldom give up their privileges voluntarily. Individuals may see the moral light and voluntarily give up their unjust posture; but, as Reinhold Niebuhr has reminded us, groups tend to be more immoral than individuals.

We know through painful experience that freedom is never voluntarily given by the oppressor; it must be demanded by the oppressed. Frankly, I have yet to engage in a direct-action campaign that was "well-timed" in view of those who have not suffered unduly from the disease of segregation. For years now I have heard the word "Wait!" It rings in the ear of every Negro with piercing familiarity. This "Wait" has almost always meant "Never." We must come to see, with one of our distinguished jurists, that "justice too long delayed is justice denied."

We have waited for more than 340 years for our constitutional and God-given rights. The nations of Asia and Africa are moving with jetlike speed toward gaining political independence, but we still creep at horse-and-buggy pace toward gaining a cup of coffee at a lunch counter. Perhaps it is easy for those who have never felt the stinging darts of segregation to say, "Wait." But when you have seen vicious mobs lynch your mothers and fathers at will and drown your sisters and brothers at whim; when you have seen hate-filled policemen curse, kick, and even kill your black brothers and sisters; when you see the vast majority of your twenty million Negro brothers smothering in an airtight cage of poverty in the midst of an affluent society; when you suddenly find your tongue twisted and your speech stammering as you seek to explain to your six-year-old daughter why she can't go to the public amusement park that has just been advertised on television, and see tears welling up in her eyes when she is told that Funtown is closed to colored children, and see ominous clouds of inferiority beginning to form in her little mental sky, and see her beginning to distort her personality by developing an unconscious bitterness toward white people; when you have to concoct an answer for a five-year-old son who is asking, "Daddy, why do white people treat colored people so mean?"; when you take a cross-country drive and find it necessary to sleep night after night in the uncomfortable corners of your automobile because no motel will accept you; when you are humiliated day in and day out by nagging signs reading "white" and "colored;" when your first name becomes "nigger," your middle name becomes "boy" (however old you are) and your last name becomes "John," and your wife and mother are never given the respected title "Mrs."; when you are harried by day and haunted by night by the fact that you are a Negro, living constantly at tiptoe stance, never quite knowing what to expect next, and are plagued with inner fears and outer resentments; when you are forever fighting a degenerating sense of "nobodiness"—then you will understand why we find it difficult to wait. There comes a time when the cup of endurance runs over, and men are no longer willing to be plunged into the abyss of despair. I hope, sirs, you can understand our legitimate and unavoidable impatience.

You express a great deal of anxiety over our willingness to break laws. This is certainly a legitimate concern. Since we so diligently urge people to obey the Supreme Court's decision of 1954 outlawing segregation in the public schools, at first glance it may seem rather paradoxical for us consciously to break laws. One may well ask: "How can you advocate breaking some laws and obeying others?" The answer lies in the fact that there are two types of laws: just and unjust. I would be the first to advocate obeying just laws. One has not only a legal but a moral responsibility to obey just laws. Conversely, one has a moral responsibility to disobey unjust laws. I would agree with St. Augustine that "an unjust law is no law at all."

Now, what is the difference between the two? How does one determine whether a law is just or unjust? A just law is a man-made code that squares with the moral law or the law of God. An unjust law is a code that is out of harmony with the moral law. To put it in the terms of St. Thomas Aquinas: An unjust law is a human law that is not rooted in eternal law and natural law. Any law that uplifts human personality is just. Any law that degrades human personality is unjust. All segregation statutes are unjust because segregation distorts the soul and damages the personality. It gives the segregator a false sense of superiority and the segregated a false sense of inferiority. Segregation, to use the terminology of the Jewish philosopher Martin Buber, substitutes an "I-it" relationship for an "I-thou" relationship and ends up relegating persons to the status of things. Hence segregation is not only politically, economically, and sociologically unsound, it is morally wrong and sinful. Paul Tillich has said that sin is separation. Is not segregation an existential expression of man's tragic separation, his awful estrangement, his terrible sinfulness? Thus it is that I can urge men to obey the 1954 decision of the Supreme Court, for it is morally right; and I can urge them to disobey segregation ordinances, for they are morally wrong.

Let us consider a more concrete example of just and unjust laws. An unjust law is a code that a numerical or power majority group compels a minority group to obey but does not make binding on itself. This is *difference* made legal. By the same token, a just law is a code that a majority compels a minority to follow and that it is willing to follow itself. This is *sameness* made legal.

Let me give another explanation. A law is unjust if it is inflicted on a minority that, as a result of being denied the right to vote, had no part in enacting or devising the law. Who can say that the legislature of Alabama which set up that state's segregation laws was democratically elected? Throughout Alabama all sorts of devious methods are used to prevent Negroes from becoming registered voters, and there are some counties in which, even though Negroes constitute a majority of the population, not a single Negro is registered. Can any law enacted under such circumstances be considered democratically structured?

Sometimes a law is just on its face and unjust in its application. For instance, I have been arrested on a charge of parading without a permit. Now, there is nothing wrong in having an ordinance which requires a permit for a parade. But such an ordinance becomes unjust when it is used to maintain segregation and to deny citizens the First-Amendment privilege of peaceful assembly and protest.

I hope you are able to see the distinction I am trying to point out. In no sense do I advocate evading or defying the law, as would the rabid segregationist. That would lead to anarchy. One who breaks an unjust law must do so openly, lovingly, and with a willingness to accept the penalty. I submit that an individual who breaks a law that conscience tells him is unjust, and who willingly accepts the penalty of imprisonment in order to arouse the conscience of the community over its injustice, is in reality expressing the highest respect for law.

Of course, there is nothing new about this kind of civil disobedience. It was evidenced sublimely in the refusal of Shadrach, Meshach, and Abednego to obey the laws of Nebuchadnezzar, on the ground that a higher moral law was at stake. It was practiced superbly by the early Christians, who were willing to face hungry lions and the excruciating pain of chopping blocks rather than submit to certain unjust laws of the Roman Empire. To a degree, academic freedom is a reality today because Socrates practiced civil disobedience. In our own nation, the Boston Tea Party represented a massive act of civil disobedience.

We should never forget that everything Adolf Hitler did in Germany was "legal" and everything the Hungarian freedom fighters did in Hungary was "illegal." It was "illegal" to aid and comfort a Jew in Hitler's Germany. Even so, I am sure that, had I lived in Germany at the time, I would have aided and comforted my Jewish brothers. If today I lived in a Communist country where certain principles dear to the Christian faith are suppressed, I would openly advocate disobeying that country's anti-religious laws.

I must make two honest confessions to you, my Christian and Jewish brothers. First, I must confess that over the past few years I have been gravely disappointed with the white moderate. I have almost reached the regrettable conclusion that the Negro's great stumbling block in his stride toward freedom is not the White Citizen's Counciler or the Ku Klux Klanner, but the white moderate, who is more devoted to "order" than to justice; who prefers a negative peace which is the absence of tension to a positive peace which is the presence of justice; who constantly says, "I agree with you in the goal you seek, but I cannot agree with your methods of direct action"; who paternalistically believes he can set the timetable for another man's freedom; who lives by a mythical concept of time and who constantly advises the Negro to wait for a "more convenient season." Shallow understanding from people of good will is more frustrating than absolute misunderstanding from people of ill will. Lukewarm acceptance is much more bewildering than outright rejection.

I had hoped that the white moderate would understand that law and order exist for the purpose of establishing justice and that when they fail in this purpose they become the dangerously structured dams that block the flow of social progress. I had hoped that the white moderate would understand that the present tension in the South is a necessary phase of the transition from an obnoxious negative peace, in which the Negro passively accepted his unjust plight, to a substantive and positive peace, in which all men will respect the dignity and worth of human personality. Actually, we who engage in nonviolent direct action are not the creators of tension. We merely bring to the surface the hidden tension that is already alive. We bring it out in the open, where it can be seen and dealt with. Like a boil that can never be cured so long as it is covered up but must be opened with all its ugliness to the natural medicines of air and light, injustice must be exposed, with all the tension its exposure creates, to the light of human conscience and the air of national opinion, before it can be cured.

In your statement you assert that our actions, even though peaceful, must be condemned because they precipitate violence. But is this a logical assertion? Isn't this like condemning a robbed man because his possession of money precipitated the evil act of robbery? Isn't this like condemning Socrates because his unswerving commitment to truth and his philosophical inquiries precipitated the act by the misguided populace in which they made him drink hemlock? Isn't this like condemning Jesus because his unique God-consciousness and never-ceasing devotion to God's will precipitated the evil act of crucifixion? We must come to see that, as the federal courts have consistently affirmed, it is wrong to urge an individual to cease his efforts to gain his basic constitutional rights because the quest may precipitate violence. Society must protect the robbed and punish the robber.

I had also hoped that the white moderate would reject the myth concerning time in relation to the struggle for freedom. I have just received a letter from a white brother in Texas. He writes: "All Christians know that the colored people will receive equal rights eventually, but it is possible that you are in too great a religious hurry. It has taken Christianity almost two thousand years to accomplish what it has. The teachings of Christ take time to come to earth." Such an attitude stems from a tragic misconception of time, from the strangely irrational notion that there is something in the very flow of time that will inevitably cure all ills. Actually, time itself is neutral; it can be used either destructively or constructively. More and more I feel that the people of ill will have used time much more effectively than have the people of good will. We will have to repent in this generation not merely for the hateful words and actions of the bad people, but for the appalling silence of the good people. Human progress never rolls in on wheels of inevitability; it comes through the tireless efforts of men willing to be co-workers with God, and without this hard work, time itself becomes an ally of the forces of stagnation. We must use time creatively, in the knowledge that the time is always ripe to do right. Now is the time to make real the promise of democracy and transform our pending national elegy into a creative psalm of brotherhood. Now is the time to lift our national policy from the quicksand of racial injustice to the solid rock of human dignity.

You speak of our activity in Birmingham as extreme. At first I was rather disappointed that fellow clergymen would see my nonviolent efforts as those of an extremist. I began thinking about the fact that I stand in the middle of two opposing forces in the Negro community. One is a force of complacency, made up in part of Negroes who, as a result of long years of oppression, are so drained of self-respect and a sense of "somebodiness" that they have adjusted to segregation; and in part of a few middle-class Negroes who, because of a degree of academic and economic security and because in some ways they profit by segregation, have become insensitive to the problems of the masses. The other force is one of bitterness and hatred, and it comes perilously close to advocating violence. It is expressed in the various black nationalist groups that are springing up across the nation, the largest and best-known being Elijah Muhammad's Muslim movement. Nourished by the Negro's frustration over the continued existence of racial discrimination, this movement is made up of people who have lost faith in America, who have absolutely repudiated Christianity, and who have concluded that the white man is an incorrigible "devil."

I have tried to stand between these two forces, saying that we need emulate neither the "do-nothingism" of the complacent nor the hatred and despair of the black nationalist. For there is the more excellent way of love and nonviolent protest. I am grateful to God that, through the influence of the Negro church, the way of nonviolence became an integral part of our struggle.

If this philosophy had not emerged, by now many streets of the South would, I am convinced, be flowing with blood. And I am further convinced that if our white brothers dismiss as "rabble-rousers" and "outside agitators" those of us who employ nonviolent direct action, and if they refuse to support our nonviolent efforts, millions of Negroes will, out of frustration and despair, seek solace and security in black-nationalist ideologies—a development that would inevitably lead to a frightening racial nightmare.

Oppressed people cannot remain oppressed forever. The yearning for freedom eventually manifests itself, and that is what has happened to the American Negro. Something within has reminded him of his birthright of freedom, and something without has reminded him that it can be gained. Consciously or unconsciously, he has been caught up by the *Zeitgeist,* and with his black brothers of Africa and his brown and yellow brothers of Asia, South America, and the Caribbean, the United States Negro is moving with a sense of great urgency toward the promised land of racial justice. If one recognizes this vital urge that has engulfed the Negro community, one should readily understand why public demonstrations are taking place. The Negro has many pent-up resentments and latent frustrations, and he must release them. So let him march; let him make prayer pilgrimages to the city hall; let him go on freedom rides—and try to understand why he must do so. If his repressed emotions are not released in nonviolent ways, they will seek expression through violence; this is not a threat but a fact of history. So I have not said to my people, "Get rid of your discontent." Rather, I have tried to say that this normal and healthy discontent can be channeled into the creative outlet of nonviolent direct action. And now this approach is being termed extremist.

But though I was initially disappointed at being categorized as an extremist, as I continued to think about the matter I gradually gained a measure of satisfaction from the label. Was not Jesus an extremist for love: "Love your enemies, bless them that curse you, do good to them that hate you, and pray for them which despitefully use you, and persecute you." Was not Amos an extremist for justice: "Let justice roll down like waters and righteousness like an ever-flowing stream." Was not Paul an extremist for the Christian gospel: "I bear in my body the marks of the Lord Jesus." Was not Martin Luther an extremist: "Here I stand; I cannot do otherwise, so help me God." And John Bunyan: "I will stay in jail to the end of my days before I make a butchery of my conscience." And Abraham Lincoln: "This nation cannot survive half slave and half free." And Thomas Jefferson: "We hold these truths to be self-evident, that all men are created equal. . . ." So the question is not whether we will be extremists, but what kind of extremists we will be. Will we be extremists for hate or for love? Will we be extremists for the preservation of injustice or for the extension of justice? In that dramatic scene on Calvary's hill three men were crucified. We must never forget that all three were crucified for the same crime—the crime of extremism. Two were extremists for immorality, and thus fell below their environment. The other, Jesus Christ, was an extremist for love, truth, and goodness, and thereby rose above his environment. Perhaps the South, the nation, and the world are in dire need of creative extremists.

I had hoped that the white moderate would see this need. Perhaps I was too optimistic; perhaps I expected too much. I suppose I should have realized that few members of the oppressor race can understand the deep groans and passionate yearnings of the oppressed race, and still fewer have the vision to see that injustice must be rooted out by strong, persistent, and determined action. I am thankful, however, that some of our white brothers in the South have grasped the meaning of this social revolution and committed themselves to it. They are still all too few in quantity, but they are big in quality. Some—such as Ralph McGill, Lillian Smith, Harry Golden, James McBride Dabbs, Ann Braden, and Sarah Patton Boyle—have written about our struggle in eloquent and prophetic terms. Others have marched with us down nameless streets of the South. They have languished in filthy, roach-infested jails, suffering the abuse and brutality of policemen who view them as "dirty nigger-lovers." Unlike so many of their moderate brothers and sisters, they have recognized the urgency of the moment and sensed the need for powerful "action" antidotes to combat the disease of segregation.

Let me take note of my other major disappointment. I have been so greatly disappointed with the white church and its leadership. Of course, there are some notable exceptions. I am not unmindful of the fact that each of you has taken some significant stands on this issue. I commend you, Reverend Stallings, for your Christian stand on this past Sunday, in welcoming Negroes to your worship service on a nonsegregated basis. I commend the Catholic leaders of this state for integrating Spring Hill College several years ago.

But despite these notable exceptions, I must honestly reiterate that I have been disappointed with the church. I do not say this as one of those negative critics who can always find something wrong with the church. I say this as a minister of the gospel, who loves the church; who was nurtured in its bosom; who has been sustained by its spiritual blessings and who will remain true to it as long as the cord of life shall lengthen.

When I was suddenly catapulted into the leadership of the bus protest in Montgomery, Alabama, a few years ago, I felt we would be supported by the white church. I felt that the white ministers, priests, and rabbis of the South would be among our strongest allies. Instead, some have been outright opponents, refusing to understand the freedom movement and misrepresenting its leaders; all too many others have been more cautious than courageous and have remained silent behind the anesthetizing security of stained-glass windows.

In spite of my shattered dreams, I came to Birmingham with the hope that the white religious leadership of this community would see the justice of our cause and, with deep moral concern, would serve as the channel through which our just grievances could reach the power structure. I had hoped that each of you would understand. But again I have been disappointed.

I have heard numerous southern religious leaders admonish their worshipers to comply with a desegregation decision because it is the law, but I have longed to hear white ministers declare: "Follow this decree because integration is morally right and because the Negro is your brother." In the midst of blatant injustices inflicted upon the Negro, I have watched white churchmen stand on the sideline and mouth pious irrelevancies and sanctimonious trivialities. In the midst of a mighty struggle to rid our nation of racial and economic injustice, I have heard many ministers say: "Those are social issues, with which the gospel has no real concern." And I have watched many churches commit themselves to a completely otherworldly religion which makes a strange, un-Biblical distinction between body and soul, between the sacred and the secular.

I have traveled the length and breadth of Alabama, Mississippi, and all the other southern states. On sweltering summer days and crisp autumn mornings I have looked at the South's beautiful churches with their lofty spires pointing heavenward. I have beheld the impressive outlines of her massive religious-education buildings. Over and over I have found myself asking: "What kind of people worship here? Who is their God?" Where were their voices when the lips of Governor Barnett dripped with words of interposition and nullification? Where were they when Governor Wallace gave a clarion call for defiance and hatred? Where were their voices of support when bruised and weary Negro men and women decided to rise from the dark dungeons of complacency to the bright hills of creative protest?"

Yes, these questions are still in my mind. In deep disappointment I have wept over the laxity of the church. But be assured that my tears have been tears of love. Yes, I love the church. How could I do otherwise? I am in the rather unique position of being the son, the grandson, and the great-grandson of preachers. Yes, I see the church as the body of Christ. But, oh! How we have blemished and scarred that body through social neglect and through fear of being nonconformists.

There was a time when the church was very powerful—in the time when the early Christians rejoiced at being deemed worthy to suffer for what they believed. In those days the church was not merely a thermometer that recorded the ideas and principles of popular opinion; it was a thermostat that transformed the mores of society. Whenever the early Christians entered a town, the people in power became disturbed and immediately sought to convict the Christians for being "disturbers of the peace" and "outside agitators." But the Christians pressed on, in the conviction that they were "a colony of heaven," called to obey God rather than man. Small in number, they were big in commitment. They were too God-intoxicated to be "astronomically intimidated." By their effort and example they brought an end to such ancient evils as infanticide and gladiatorial contests.

Things are different now. So often the contemporary church is a weak, ineffectual voice with an uncertain sound. So often it is an archdefender of the status quo. Far from being disturbed by the presence of the church, the power structure of the average community is consoled by the church's silent—and often even vocal—sanction of things as they are.

But the judgment of God is upon the church as never before. If today's church does not recapture the sacrificial spirit of the early church, it will lose its authenticity, forfeit the loyalty of millions, and be dismissed as an irrelevant social club with no meaning for the twentieth century. Every day I meet young people whose disappointment with the church has turned into outright disgust.

Perhaps I have once again been too optimistic. Is organized religion too inextricably bound to the status quo to save our nation and the world? Perhaps I must turn my faith to the inner spiritual church, the church within the church, as the true *ekklesia* and the hope of the world. But again I am thankful to God that some noble souls from the ranks of organized religion have broken loose from the paralyzing chains of conformity and joined as active partners in the struggle for freedom. They have left their secure congregations and walked the streets of Albany, Georgia, with us. They have gone down the highways of the South on tortuous rides for freedom. Yes, they have gone to jail with us. Some have been dismissed from their churches, have lost the support of their bishops and fellow ministers. But they have acted in the faith that right defeated is stronger than evil triumphant. Their witness has been the spiritual salt that has preserved the true meaning of the gospel in these troubled times. They have carved a tunnel of hope through the dark mountain of disappointment.

I hope the church as a whole will meet the challenge of this decisive hour. But even if the church does not come to the aid of justice, I have no despair about the future. I have no fear about the outcome of our struggle in Birmingham, even if our motives are at present misunderstood. We will reach the goal of freedom in Birmingham and all over the nation, because the goal of America is freedom. Abused and scorned though we may be, our destiny is tied up with America's destiny. Before the pilgrims landed at Plymouth, we were here. For more than two centuries our forebears labored in this country without wages; they made cotton king; they built the homes of their masters while suffering gross injustice and shameful humiliation—and yet out of a bottomless vitality they continued to thrive and develop. If the inexpressible cruelties of slavery could not stop us, the opposition we now face will surely fail. We will win our freedom because the sacred heritage of our nation and the eternal will of God are embodied in our echoing demands.

Before closing I feel impelled to mention one other point in your statement that has troubled me profoundly. You warmly commended the Birmingham police force for keeping "order" and "preventing violence." I doubt that you would have so warmly commended the police force if you had seen its dogs sinking their teeth into unarmed, nonviolent Negroes. I doubt that you would so quickly commend the policemen if you were to observe their ugly and inhumane treatment of Negroes here in the city jail; if you were to watch them push and curse old Negro women and young Negro girls; if you were to see them slap and kick old Negro men and young boys; if you were to observe them, as they did on two occasions, refuse to give us food because we wanted to sing our grace together. I cannot join you in your praise of the Birmingham police department.

It is true that the police have exercised a degree of discipline in handling the demonstrators. In this sense they have conducted themselves rather "nonviolently" in public. But for what purpose? To preserve the evil system of segregation. Over the past few years I have consistently preached that nonviolence demands that the means we use must be as pure as the ends we seek. I have tried to make clear that it is wrong to use immoral means to attain moral ends. But now I must affirm that it is just as wrong, or perhaps even more so, to use moral means to preserve immoral ends. Perhaps Mr. Connor and his policemen have been rather nonviolent in public, as was Chief Pritchett in Albany, Georgia, but they have used the moral means of nonviolence to maintain the immoral end of racial injustice. As T. S. Elliot has said, "The last temptation is the greatest treason: To do the right deed for the wrong reason."

I wish you had commended the Negro sit-inners and demonstrators of Birmingham for their sublime courage, their willingness to suffer, and their amazing discipline in the midst of great provocation. One day the South will recognize its real heroes. They will be the James Merediths, with the noble sense of purpose that enables them to face jeering and hostile mobs, and with the agonizing loneliness that characterizes the life of the pioneer. They will be old, oppressed, battered Negro women, symbolized in a seventy-two-year-old woman in Montgomery, Alabama, who rose up with a sense of dignity and with her people decided not to ride segregated buses, and who responded with ungrammatical profundity to one who inquired about her weariness: "My feets is tired, but my soul is at rest." They will be the young high school and college students, the young ministers of the gospel and a host of their elders, courageously and nonviolently sitting in at lunch counters and willingly going to jail for conscience' sake. One day the South will know that when these disinherited children of God sat down at lunch counters, they were in reality standing up for what is best in the American dream and for the most sacred values in our Judaeo-Christian heritage, thereby bringing our nation back to those great wells of democracy which were dug deep by the founding fathers in their formulation of the Constitution and the Declaration of Independence.

Never before have I written so long a letter. I'm afraid it is much too long to take your precious time. I can assure you that it would have been much shorter if I had been writing from a comfortable desk, but what else can one do when he is alone in a narrow jail cell, other than write long letters, think long thoughts, and pray long prayers?

If I have said anything in this letter that overstates the truth and indicates an unreasonable impatience, I beg you to forgive me. If I have said anything that understates the truth and indicates my having a patience that allows me to settle for anything less than brotherhood, I beg God to forgive me.

I hope this letter finds you strong in faith. I also hope that circumstances will soon make it possible for me to meet each of you, not as an integrationist or a civil-rights leader but as a fellow clergyman and a Christian brother. Let us all hope that the dark clouds of racial prejudice will soon pass away and the deep fog of misunderstanding will be lifted from our fear-drenched communities, and in some not too distant tomorrow the radiant stars of love and brotherhood will shine over our great nation with all their scintillating beauty.

Yours for the Cause of Peace and Brotherhood,
Martin Luther King, Jr.

APPENDIX

G

RACE AND THE U.S. CONSTITUTION

[Race has been a fundamental issue in American politics since the founding of the Republic. As the following excerpts from the Supreme Court's rulings in four landmark cases show, our understanding of the civil rights guaranteed by the Constitution has changed dramatically over the past two centuries.]

DRED SCOTT v. SANDFORD

19 How. 393; 15 L. Ed. 691 (1857)

[Dred Scott was an African-American slave who moved with his owner from Missouri, a slave state, first to Illinois, a free state, and then to the Wisconsin territory, where slavery was illegal under the terms of the Missouri Compromise of 1820. In 1846, Scott asked a state court in Missouri to grant him his freedom on the ground that he had lived for two years in a free state and a free territory. Scott initially won his case, but the judgment was overturned on appeal and eventually made its way to the Supreme Court. In 1857, the Court's southern majority ruled against Scott, arguing that the Missouri Compromise was unconstitutional because Congress had no power to ban slavery in federal territories. As the following excerpt shows, the Court went even further and argued that African Americans descended from slaves were not American citizens and thus had no right to sue in court.]

MR. CHIEF JUSTICE TANEY delivered the opinion of the Court:

. . . .

The question is simply this: Can a Negro, whose ancestors were imported into this country, and sold as slaves, become a member of the political community formed and brought into existence by the Constitution of the United States, and as such become entitled to all the rights, and privileges, and immunities, guaranteed by that instrument to the citizen? One of which rights is the privilege of suing in a court of the United States in the cases specified in the Constitution. . . .

The words "people of the United States" and "citizens" are synonymous terms, and mean the same thing. They both describe the political body who, according to our republican institutions, form the sovereignty, and who hold the power and conduct the Government through their representatives. They are what we familiarly call the "sovereign people," and every citizen is one of this people, and a constituent member of this sovereignty. The question before us is, whether the class of persons described in the plea in abatement compose a portion of this people, and are constituent members of this sovereignty? We think they are not, and that they are not included, and were not intended to be included, under the word "citizens" in the Constitution, and can therefore claim none of the rights and privileges which that instrument provides for and secures to citizens of the United States. On the contrary, they were at that time considered as a subordinate and inferior class of beings, who had been subjugated by the dominant race, and, whether emancipated or not, yet remained subject to their authority, and had no rights or privileges but such as those who held the power and the government might choose to grant them. . . .

[A review of] the legislation of the States . . . shows, in a manner not to be mistaken, the inferior and subject condition of that race at the time the Constitution was adopted, and long afterward, throughtout the thirteen States by which that instrument was framed. . . . It cannot be supposed that they intended to secure to them rights, and privileges, and rank, in the new political body throughout the Union, which every one of them denied within the limits of its own dominion. More especially, it cannot be believed that the large slaveholding States regarded them as included in the word citizens, or would have consented to a Constitution which might compel them to receive them in that character from another State. For if they were so received, and entitled to the privileges and immunities of citizens, it would exempt them from the operation of the special laws and from the police regulations which they considered to be necessary for their own safety. It would give to persons of the Negro race, who were recognised as citizens in any one State of the Union, the right to enter every other State whenever they pleased, singly or in companies, without pass or passport, and without obstruction to sojourn there as long as they pleased, to go where they pleased at every hour of the day or night without molestation, unless they committed some violation of law for which a white man would be punished; and it would give them the full liberty of speech in public and in private upon all subjects upon which its own citizens might speak; to hold public meetings upon political affairs, and to keep and carry arms wherever they went. And all of this would be done in the face of the subject race of the same color, both free and slaves, and inevitably producing discontent and insubordination among them, and endangering the peace and safety of the State. . . .

Undoubtedly, a person may be a citizen, that is, a member of the community who form the sovereignty, although he exercises no share of the political power, and is incapacitated from holding particular offices. Women and minors, who form a part of the political family, cannot vote; and when a property qualification is required to vote or hold a particular office, those who have not the necessary qualification cannot vote or hold the office, yet they are citizens.

So, too, a person may be entitled to vote by the law of the State, who is not a citizen even of the State itself. And in some of the States of the Union foreigners not naturalized are allowed to vote. And the State may give the right to free negroes and mulattoes, but that does not make them citizens of the State, and still less of the United States. And the provision in the Constitution giving privileges and immunities in other States does not apply to them. . . .

No one, we presume, supposes that any change in public opinion or feeling, in relation to this unfortunate race, in the civilized nations of Europe or in this country, should induce the court to give to the words of the Constitution a more liberal construction in their favor than they were intended to bear when the instrument was framed and adopted. Such an argument would be altogether inadmissible in any tribunal called on to interpret it. If any of its provisions are deemed unjust, there is a mode prescribed in the instrument itself by which it may be amended; but while it remains unaltered, it must be construed now as it was understood at the time of its adoption. It is not only the same in words, but the same in meaning, and delegates the same powers to the Government, and reserves and secures the same rights and privileges to the citizen; and as long as it continues to exist in its present form, it speaks not only in the same words, but with the same meaning and intent with which it spoke when it came from the hands of its framers, and was voted on and adopted by the people of the United States. Any other rule of construction would abrogate the judicial character of this court, and make it the mere reflex of the popular opinion or passion of the day. This court was not created by the Constitution for such purposes. Higher and graver trusts have been confided to it, and it must not falter in the path of duty. . . .

[T]he court is of opinion, that, . . . Dred Scott was not a citizen of Missouri within the meaning of the Constitution of the United States, and not entitled as such to sue in its courts. . . .

PLESSY v. FERGUSON

163 U.S. 537; 16 Sup. Ct. 1138; 41 L. Ed. 256 (1896)

[In 1890, the Louisiana state legislature followed the lead of several other southern states and passed a law requiring that "all railway companies carrying passengers in their coaches in this State, shall provide equal but separate accommodations for the white, and colored, races." Homer Adolph Plessy, who was one-eighth African American by descent, was arrested for violating the statute. He was tried in the Criminal District Court of New Orleans, where Judge John H. Ferguson found him guilty. In 1896, the Supreme Court upheld Ferguson's verdict, finding that "separate but equal" laws did not violate the Fourteenth Amendment, as Plessy had argued.]

MR. JUSTICE BROWN delivered the opinion of the Court:

The constitutionality of this act is attacked upon the ground that it conflicts both with the Thirteenth Amendment of the Constitution, abolishing slavery, and the Fourteenth Amendment, which prohibits certain restrictive legislation on the part of the States.

1. That it does not conflict with the Thirteenth Amendment, which abolished slavery and involuntary servitude, except as a punishment for crime, is too clear for argument. . . .

A statute which implies merely a legal distinction between the white and colored races—a distinction which is founded in the color of the two races, and which must always exist so long as white men are distinguished from the other race by color—has no tendency to destroy the legal equality of the two races, or reestablish a state of involuntary servitude. Indeed, we do not understand that the Thirteenth Amendment is strenuously relied upon by the plaintiff in error in this connection.

2. By the Fourteenth Amendment, all persons born or naturalized in the United States, and subject to the jurisdiction thereof, are made citizens of the United States and of the State wherein they reside; and the States are forbidden from making or enforcing any law which shall abridge the privileges or immunities of citizens of the United States, or shall deprive any person of life, liberty, or property without due process of law, or deny to any person within their jurisdiction the equal protection of the laws. . . .

The object of the amendment was undoubtedly to enforce the absolute equality of the two races before the law, but in the nature of things it could not have been intended to abolish distinctions based upon color, or to enforce social, as distinguished from political equality, or a commingling of the two races upon terms unsatisfactory to either. Laws permitting, and even requiring, their separation in places where they are liable to be brought into contact do not necessarily imply the inferiority of either race to the other, and have been generally, if not universally, recognized as within the competency of the state legislatures in the exercise of their police power. The most common instance of this is connected with the establishment of separate schools for white and colored children, which has been held to be a valid exercise of the legislative power even by courts of States where the political rights of the colored race have been longest and most earnestly enforced.

It is . . . suggested by the learned counsel for the plaintiff in error that the same argument that will justify the state legislature in requiring railways to provide separate accomodation for the two races will also authorize them to require separate cars to be provided for people whose hair is of a certain color, or who are aliens, or who belong to certain nationalities, or to enact laws requiring colored people to walk upon one side of the street, and white people upon the other, or requiring white men's houses to be painted white, and colored men's black, or their vehicles or business signs to be of different colors, upon the theory that one side of the street is as good as the other, or that a house or vehicle of one color is as good as one of another color. The reply to all this is that every exercise of the police power must be reasonable, and extend only to such laws as are enacted in good faith for the promotion of the public good, and not for the annoyance or oppression of a particular class. . . .

So far, then, as a conflict with the Fourteenth Amendment is concerned, the case reduces itself to the question whether the statute of Louisiana is a reasonable regulation, and with respect to this there must necessarily be a large discretion on the part of the legislature. In determining the question of reasonableness it is at liberty to act with reference to the established usages, customs, and traditions of the people, and with a view to the promotion of their comfort, and the preservation of the public peace and good order. Gauged by this standard, we cannot say that a law which authorizes or even requires the separation of the two races in public conveyances is unreasonable, or more obnoxious to the Fourteenth Amendment than the acts of Congress requiring separate schools for colored children in the District of Columbia, the constitutionality of which does not seem to have been questioned, or the corresponding acts of state legislatures.

We consider the underlying fallacy of the plaintiff's argument to consist in the assumption that the enforced separation of the two races stamps the colored race with a badge of inferiority. If this be so, it is not by reason of anything found in the act, but solely because the colored race chooses to put that construction upon it. The argument necessarily assumes that if, as has been more than once the case, and is not unlikely to be so again, the colored race should become the dominant power in the state legislature, and should enact a law in precisely similar terms, it would thereby relegate the white race to an inferior position. We imagine that the white race, at least, would not acquiesce in this assumption. The argument also assumes that social prejudices may be overcome by legislation, and that equal rights cannot be secured to the Negro except by an enforced commingling of the two races. We cannot accept this proposition. If the two races are to meet upon terms of social equality, it must be the result of natural affinities, a mutual appreciation of each other's merits, and a voluntary consent of individuals. . . . Legislation is powerless to eradicate racial instincts or to abolish distinctions based upon physical differences, and the attempt to do so can only result in accentuating the difficulties of the present situation. If the civil and political rights of both races be equal one cannot be inferior to the other civilly or politically. If one race be inferior to the other socially, the Constitution of the United States cannot put them upon the same plane. . . .

[Justice John Marshall Harlan dissented from the majority's ruling in ***Plessy v. Ferguson.*** *He argued that the "Constitution is color-blind" and requires that all citizens be treated equally under the law.]*

MR. JUSTICE HARLAN, dissenting:

. . . It was said in argument that the statute of Louisiana does not discriminate against either race, but prescribes a rule applicable alike to white and colored citizens. But this argument does not meet the difficulty. Everyone knows that the statute in question had its origin in the purpose, not so much to exclude white persons from railroad cars occupied by blacks, as to exclude colored people from coaches occupied by or assigned to white persons . . . No one would be so wanting in candor as to assert the contrary. The fundamental objection, therefore, to the statute is that it interferes with the personal freedom of citizens . . . If a white man and a black man choose to occupy the same public conveyance on a public highway, it is their right to do so, and no government, proceeding alone on grounds of race, can prevent it without infringing the personal liberty of each.

. . . In view of the Constitution, in the eye of the law, there is in this country no superior, dominant, ruling class of citizens. There is no caste here. Our Constitution is color-blind, and neither knows nor tolerates classes among citizens. In respect of civil rights, all citizens are equal before the law. The humblest is the peer of the most powerful. The law regards man as man, and takes no account of his surroundings or of his color when his civil rights as guaranteed by the supreme law of the land are involved.

. . . The sure guaranty of the peace and security of each race is the clear, distinct, unconditional recognition by our governments, National and State, of every right that inheres in civil freedom, and of the equality before the law of all citizens of the United States without regard to race. State enactments regulating the enjoyment of civil rights upon the basis of race, and cunningly devised to defeat legitimate results of the war, under the pretence of recognizing equality of rights, can have no other result than to render permanent peace impossible, and to keep alive a conflict of races, the continuance of which must do harm to all concerned.

. . . The arbitrary separation of citizens, on the basis of race, while they are on a public highway, is a badge of servitude wholly inconsistent with the civil freedom and the equality before the law established by the Constitution. It cannot be justified upon any legal grounds.

. . . We boast of the freedom enjoyed by our people above all other peoples. But it is difficult to reconcile that boast with a state of the law which, practically, puts the brand of servitude and degradation upon a large class of our fellow-citizens, our equals before the law. The thin disguise of "equal" accommodations for passengers in railroad coaches will not mislead anyone, nor atone for the wrong this day done. . . .

I am of opinion that the statute of Louisiana is inconsistent with the personal liberty of citizens, white and black, in that State, and hostile to both the spirit and letter of the Constitution of the United States. . . .

BROWN et al. v. BOARD OF EDUCATION

347 U.S. 483; 74 Sup. Ct. 693; 98 L. Ed. 591 (1954)

[In 1950, Oliver Brown, a railroad worker in Topeka, Kansas, attempted to enroll his daughter Linda in the third grade at the Sumner School, a public school for whites located only four blocks from his home. When school officials refused to admit Linda because she was African American, Brown sued the Board of Education for the city of Topeka. Brown's lawsuit eventually reached the Supreme Court, where it was considered along with several other cases challenging the constitutionality of segregated public schools. In 1954, a unanimous Court ruled that segregated school systems denied African-American children equal protection under the law, thereby violating the Fourteenth Amendment. The Court's decision in ***Brown et al. v. Board of Education*** *effectively overturned the decision it had reached fifty years earlier in* ***Plessy v. Ferguson.]***

MR. CHIEF JUSTICE WARREN delivered the opinion of the Court:

These cases come to us from the States of Kansas, South Carolina, Virginia, and Delaware. They are premised on different facts and different local conditions, but a common legal question justifies their consideration together in this consolidated opinion.

In each of the cases minors of the Negro race, through their legal representatives, seek the aid of the courts in obtaining admission to the public schools of their community on a nonsegregated basis. In each instance, they had been denied admission to schools attended by white children under laws requiring or permitting segregation according to race. This segregation was alleged to deprive the plaintiffs of the equal protection of the laws under the Fourteenth Amendment. In each of the cases other than the Delaware case, a three-judge federal district court denied relief to the plaintiffs on the so-called "separate but equal" doctrine announced by this Court in *Plessy v. Ferguson*. . . .

The plaintiffs contend that segregated public schools are not "equal" and cannot be made "equal," and that hence they are deprived of the equal protection of the laws. Because of the obvious importance of the question presented, the Court took jurisdiction. Argument was heard in the 1952 Term, and reargument was heard this Term on certain questions propounded by the Court.

Reargument was largely devoted to the circumstances surrounding the adoption of the Fourteenth Amendment in 1868. It covered exhaustively consideration of the Amendment in Congress, ratification by the states, then existing practices in racial segregation, and the view of the proponents and opponents of the Amendment. This discussion and our own investigation convince us that, although these sources cast some light, it is not enough to resolve the problem with which we are faced. At best, they are inconclusive. The most avid proponents of the postwar Amendments undoubtedly intended them to remove all legal distinctions among "all persons born or naturalized in the United States." Their opponents, just as certainly, were antagonistic to both the letter and the spirit of the Amendments and wished them to have the most limited effect. What others in Congress and the state legislatures had in mind cannot be determined with any degree of certainty.

An additional reason for the inclusive nature of the Amendment's history, with respect to segregated schools, is the status of public education at that time. In the South, the movement toward free common schools, supported by general taxation, had not yet taken hold. Education of white children was largely in the hands of private groups. Education of Negroes was almost nonexistent, and practically all of the race were illiterate. In fact, any education of Negroes was forbidden by law in some states. Today, in contrast, many Negroes have achieved outstanding success in the arts and science as well as in the business and professional world. It is true that public education had already advanced further in the North, but the effect of the Amendment on northern states was generally ignored in the congressional debates. Even in the North, the conditions of public education did not approximate those existing today. The curriculum was usually rudimentary; ungraded schools were common in rural areas; the school term was but three months a year in many states; and compulsory school attendance was virtually unknown. As a consequence, it is not surprising that there should be so little in the history of the Fourteenth Amendment relating to its intended effect on public education.

In the first cases in this Court construing the Fourteenth Amendment, decided shortly after its adoption, the Court interpreted it as proscribing all state-imposed discriminations against the Negro race. The doctrine of "separate but equal" did not make its appearance in this Court until 1896 in the case of *Plessy v. Ferguson* . . . involving not education but transportation. American courts have since labored with the doctrine for over half a century . . . in the field of public education. In *Cumming* v. *County Board of Education* . . . and *Gong Lum v. Rice* . . . the validity of the doctrine itself was not challenged. In more recent cases, all on the graduate-school level, inequality was found in that specific benefits enjoyed by white students were denied to Negro students of the same educational qualifications. . . In none of these cases was it necessary to re-examine the doctrine to grant relief to the Negro plaintiff. And in *Sweatt v. Painter* . . . the Court expressly reserved decision on the question whether *Plessy v. Ferguson* should be held inapplicable to public education.

In the instant cases, that question is directly presented. Here, unlike *Sweatt v. Painter,* there are findings below that the Negro and white schools involved have been equalized, or are being equalized, with respect to buildings, curricula, qualifications and salaries of teachers, and other "tangible" factors. Our decision, therefore, cannot turn on merely a comparison of these tangible factors in the Negro and white schools involved in each of the cases. We must look instead to the effect of segregation itself on public education. . .

We come then to the question presented: Does segregation of children in public schools solely on the basis of race, even though the physical facilities and other "tangible" factors may be equal, deprive the children of the minority group of equal educational opportunities? We believe that it does.

. . . [I]n finding [in *Sweatt v. Painter*] that a segregated law school for Negroes could not provide them equal educational opportunities, this Court relied in large part on "those qualities which are incapable of objective measurement but which make for greatness in a law school." In *McLaurin v. Oklahoma State Regents* . . . the Court, in requiring that a Negro admitted to a white graduate school be treated like all other students, again resorted to intangible considerations: ". . . his ability to study, to engage in discussions and exchange views with other students, and, in general, to learn his profession." Such considerations apply with added force to children in grade and high schools. To separate them from others of similar age and qualifications solely because of their race generates a feeling of inferiority as to their status in the community that may affect their hearts and minds in a way unlikely ever to be undone. The effect of this separation on their educational opportunities was well stated by a finding in the Kansas case by a court which nevertheless felt compelled to rule against the Negro plaintiffs:

"Segregation of white and colored children in public schools has a detrimental effect upon the colored children. The impact is greater when it has the sanction of the law; for the policy of separating the races is usually interpreted as denoting the inferiority of the Negro group. A sense of inferiority affects the motivation of a child to learn. Segregation with the sanction of law, therefore, has a tendency to retard the educational and mental development of Negro children and to deprive them of some of the benefits they would receive in a racially integrated school system."

Whatever may have been the extent of psychological knowledge at the time of *Plessy v. Ferguson,* this finding is amply supported by modern authority. Any language in *Plessy v. Ferguson* contrary to this finding is rejected.

We conclude that in the field of public education the doctrine of "separate but equal" has no place. Separate educational facilities are inherently unequal. Therefore, we hold that the plaintiffs and others similarly situated for whom the actions have been brought are, by reason of the segregation complained of, deprived of the equal protection of the laws guaranteed by the Fourteenth Amendment. . . .

BROWN v. BOARD OF EDUCATION [BROWN II—THE IMPLEMENTATION DECISION]

349 U.S. 294; 75 S. Ct. 753; 99 L.Ed. 1083 (1955)

[Although ***Brown et al. v. Board of Education*** *held that segregated public schools violated the Fourteenth Amendment, the case did not address the question of relief, that is, how the nation should desegregate its public schools. Instead, the Supreme Court scheduled further arguments on the question of relief. After hearing new arguments from the original parties to the lawsuit as well as from the Attorney General of the United States and the attorneys general of six states, the Court ruled in 1955 that the federal courts should oversee desegregation efforts. While recognizing that practical considerations made it impossible to end segregation immediately, the Court ruled that desegregation should proceed with "all deliberate speed."]*

MR. CHIEF JUSTICE WARREN delivered the opinion of the Court:

These cases were decided on May 17, 1954. The opinions of that date, declaring the fundamental principle that racial discrimination in public education is unconstitutional, are incorporated herein by reference. All provisions of federal, state, or local law requiring or permitting such discrimination must yield to this principle. There remains for consideration the manner in which relief is to be accorded. . . .

Full implementation of these constitutional principles may require solution of varied local school problems. School authorities have the primary responsibility for elucidating, assessing, and solving these problems; courts will have to consider whether the action of school authorities constitutes good faith implementation of the governing constitutional principles. Because of their proximity to local conditions and the possible need for further hearings, the courts which originally heard these cases can best perform this judicial appraisal. Accordingly, we believe it appropriate to remand the cases to those courts.

In fashioning and effectuating the decrees, the courts will be guided by equitable principles. Traditionally, equity has been characterized by a practical flexibility in shaping its remedies and by a facility for adjusting and reconciling public and private needs. These cases call for the exercise of these traditional attributes of equity power. At stake is the personal interest of the plaintiffs in admission to public schools as soon as practicable on a nondiscriminatory basis. To effectuate this interest may call for elimination of a variety of obstacles in making the transition to school systems operated in accordance with the constitutional principles set forth in our May 17, 1954, decision. Courts of equity may properly take into account the public interest in the elimination of such obstacles in a systematic and effective manner. But it should go without saying that the vitality of these constitutional principles cannot be allowed to yield simply because of disagreement with them.

While giving weight to these public and private considerations, the courts will require that the defendants make a prompt and reasonable start toward full compliance with our May 17, 1954, ruling. Once such a start has been made, the courts may find that additional time is necessary to carry out the ruling in an effective manner. The burden rests upon the defendants to establish that such time is necessary in the public interest and is consistent with good faith compliance at the earliest practicable date. To that end, the courts may consider problems related to administration, arising from the physical condition of the school plant, the school transportation system, personnel, revision of school districts and attendance areas into compact units to achieve a system of determining admission to the public schools on a nonracial basis, and revision of local laws and regulations which may be necessary in solving the foregoing problems. They will also consider the adequacy of any plans the defendants may propose to meet these problems and to effectuate a transition to a racially nondiscriminatory school system. During this period of transition, the courts will retain jurisdiction of these cases.

The [cases are accordingly remanded to the lower courts] to take such proceedings and enter such orders and decrees consistent with this opinion as are necessary and proper to admit to public schools on a racially nondiscriminatory basis with all deliberate speed the parties to these cases. . . .

Appendix H

The Presidents and Vice Presidents of the United States

Year	President and Vice President	Party of President
1789–1797	**George Washington** John Adams	None
1797–1801	**John Adams** Thomas Jefferson	Federalist
1801–1809	**Thomas Jefferson** Aaron Burr (to 1805) George Clinton (to 1809)	Democrat-Republican
1809–1817	**James Madison** George Clinton (to 1813) Elbridge Gerry (to 1817)	Democrat-Republican
1817–1825	**James Monroe** Daniel D. Tompkins	Democrat-Republican
1825–1829	**John Quincy Adams** John C. Calhoun	Democrat-Republican
1829–1837	**Andrew Jackson** John C. Calhoun (to 1833) Martin Van Buren (to 1837)	Democratic
1837–1841	**Martin Van Buren** Richard M. Johnson	Democratic
1841	**William H. Harrison*** John Tyler	Whig
1841–1845	**John Tyler** (VP vacant)	Whig
1845–1849	**James K. Polk** George M. Dallas	Democratic
1849–1850	**Zachary Taylor*** Millard Fillmore	Whig
1850–1853	**Millard Fillmore** (VP vacant)	Whig
1853–1857	**Franklin Pierce** William R. King	Democratic
1857–1861	**James Buchanan** John C. Breckinridge	Democratic
1861–1865	**Abraham Lincoln*** Hannibal Hamlin (to 1865) Andrew Johnson (1865)	Republican
1865–1869	**Andrew Johnson** (VP vacant)	Republican
1869–1877	**Ulysses S. Grant** Schuyler Colfax (to 1873) Henry Wilson (to 1877)	Republican
1877–1881	**Rutherford B. Hayes** William A. Wheeler	Republican
1881	**James A. Garfield*** Chester A. Arthur	Republican
1881–1885	**Chester A. Arthur** (VP vacant)	Republican
1885–1889	**Grover Cleveland** Thomas A. Hendricks	Democratic
1889–1893	**Benjamin Harrison** Levi P. Morton	Republican
1893–1897	**Grover Cleveland** Adlai E. Stevenson	Democratic
1897–1901	**William McKinley*** Garret A. Hobart (to 1901) Theodore Roosevelt (1901)	Republican
1901–1909	**Theodore Roosevelt** (VP vacant, 1901–1905) Charles W. Fairbanks (1905–1909)	Republican
1909–1913	**William Howard Taft** James S. Sherman	Republican
1913–1921	**Woodrow Wilson** Thomas R. Marshall	Democratic
1921–1923	**Warren G. Harding*** Calvin Coolidge	Republican
1923–1929	**Calvin Coolidge** (VP vacant, 1923–1925) Charles G. Dawes (1925–1929)	Republican
1929–1933	**Herbert Hoover** Charles Curtis	Republican
1933–1945	**Franklin D. Roosevelt*** John N. Garner (1933–1941) Henry A. Wallace (1941–1945) Harry S. Truman (1945)	Democratic
1945–1953	**Harry S. Truman** (VP vacant, 1945–1949) Alben W. Barkley (1949–1953)	Democratic
1953–1961	**Dwight D. Eisenhower** Richard M. Nixon	Republican
1961–1963	**John F. Kennedy*** Lyndon B. Johnson	Democratic
1963–1969	**Lyndon B. Johnson** (VP vacant, 1963–1965) Hubert H. Humphrey (1965–1969)	Democratic
1969–1974	**Richard M. Nixon†** Spiro T. Agnew‡ (1969–1973) Gerald R. Ford§ (1973–1974)	Republican
1974–1977	**Gerald R. Ford** Nelson A. Rockefeller§	Republican
1977–1981	**Jimmy Carter** Walter Mondale	Democratic
1981–1989	**Ronald Reagan** George Bush	Republican
1989–1993	**George Bush** J. Danforth Quayle	Republican
1993–	**William J. Clinton** Albert Gore, Jr.	Democratic

*Died in office. †Resigned from the presidency. ‡Resigned from the vice presidency. §Appointed vice president.

Appendix I

Presidential Election Results, 1789–1996

Year	*Candidates*	*Party*	*Popular Vote*	*Electoral Vote*
1789	**George Washington**			69
	John Adams			34
	Others			35
1792	**George Washington**			132
	John Adams			77
	George Clinton			50
	Others			5
1796	**John Adams**	Federalist		71
	Thomas Jefferson	Democrat-Republican		68
	Thomas Pinckney	Federalist		59
	Aaron Burr	Democrat-Republican		30
	Others			48
1800	**Thomas Jefferson**	Democrat-Republican		73
	Aaron Burr	Democrat-Republican		73
	John Adams	Federalist		65
	Charles C. Pinckney	Federalist		64
1804	**Thomas Jefferson**	Democrat-Republican		162
	Charles C. Pinckney	Federalist		14
1808	**James Madison**	Democrat-Republican		122
	Charles C. Pinckney	Federalist		47
	George Clinton	Independent-Republican		6
1812	**James Madison**	Democrat-Republican		128
	DeWitt Clinton	Federalist		89
1816	**James Monroe**	Democrat-Republican		183
	Rufus King	Federalist		34
1820	**James Monroe**	Democrat-Republican		231
	John Quincy Adams	Independent-Republican		1
1824	**John Quincy Adams**	Democrat-Republican	108,740 (30.5%)	84
	Andrew Jackson	Democrat-Republican	153,544 (43.1%)	99
	Henry Clay	Democrat-Republican	47,136 (13.2%)	37
	William H. Crawford	Democrat-Republican	46,618 (13.1%)	41
1828	**Andrew Jackson**	Democratic	647,231 (56.0%)	178
	John Quincy Adams	National Republican	509,097 (44.0%)	83
1832	**Andrew Jackson**	Democratic	687,502 (55.0%)	219
	Henry Clay	National Republican	530,189 (42.4%)	49
	William Wirt	Anti-Masonic		7
	John Floyd	National Republican	33,108 (2.6%)	11
1836	**Martin Van Buren**	Democratic	761,549 (50.9%)	170
	William H. Harrison	Whig	549,567 (36.7%)	73
	Hugh L. White	Whig	145,396 (9.7%)	26
	Daniel Webster	Whig	41,287 (2.7%)	14
1840	**William H. Harrison**	Whig	1,275,017 (53.1%)	234
	Martin Van Buren	Democratic	1,128,702 (46.9%)	60
1844	**James K. Polk**	Democratic	1,337,243 (49.6%)	170
	Henry Clay	Whig	1,299,068 (48.1%)	105
	James G. Birney	Liberty	63,300 (2.3%)	0
1848	**Zachary Taylor**	Whig	1,360,101 (47.4%)	163
	Lewis Cass	Democratic	1,220,544 (42.5%)	127
	Martin Van Buren	Free Soil	291,163 (10.1%)	0

Year	Candidates	Party	Popular Vote	Electoral Vote
1852	**Franklin Pierce**	Democratic	1,601,474 (50.9%)	254
	Winfield Scott	Whig	1,386,578 (44.1%)	42
1856	**James Buchanan**	Democratic	1,838,169 (45.4%)	174
	John C. Fremont	Republican	1,335,264 (33.0%)	114
	Millard Fillmore	American	874,534 (21.6%)	8
1860	**Abraham Lincoln**	Republican	1,865,593 (39.8%)	180
	Stephen A. Douglas	Democratic	1,381,713 (29.5%)	12
	John C. Breckinridge	Democratic	848,356 (18.1%)	72
	John Bell	Constitutional Union	592,906 (12.6%)	79
1864	**Abraham Lincoln**	Republican	2,206,938 (55.0%)	212
	George B. McClellan	Democratic	1,803,787 (45.0%)	21
1868	**Ulysses S. Grant**	Republican	3,013,421 (52.7%)	214
	Horatio Seymour	Democratic	2,706,829 (47.3%)	80
1872	**Ulysses S. Grant**	Republican	3,596,745 (55.6%)	286
	Horace Greeley	Democratic	2,843,446 (43.9%)	66
1876	**Rutherford B. Hayes**	Republican	4,036,571 (48.0%)	185
	Samuel J. Tilden	Democratic	4,284,020 (51.0%)	184
1880	**James A. Garfield**	Republican	4,449,053 (48.3%)	214
	Winfield S. Hancock	Democratic	4,442,035 (48.2%)	155
	James B. Weaver	Greenback-Labor	308,578 (3.4%)	0
1884	**Grover Cleveland**	Democratic	4,874,986 (48.5%)	219
	James G. Blaine	Republican	4,851,931 (48.2%)	182
	Benjamin F. Butler	Greenback-Labor	175,370 (1.8%)	0
1888	**Benjamin Harrison**	Republican	5,444,337 (47.8%)	233
	Grover Cleveland	Democratic	5,540,050 (48.6%)	168
1892	**Grover Cleveland**	Democratic	5,554,414 (46.0%)	277
	Benjamin Harrison	Republican	5,190,802 (43.0%)	145
	James B. Weaver	People's	1,027,329 (8.5%)	22
1896	**William McKinley**	Republican	7,035,638 (50.8%)	271
	William J. Bryan	Democratic; Populist	6,467,946 (46.7%)	176
1900	**William McKinley**	Republican	7,219,530 (51.7%)	292
	William J. Bryan	Democratic; Populist	6,356,734 (45.5%)	155
1904	**Theodore Roosevelt**	Republican	7,628,834 (56.4%)	336
	Alton B. Parker	Democratic	5,084,401 (37.6%)	140
	Eugene V. Debs	Socialist	402,460 (3.0%)	0
1908	**William H. Taft**	Republican	7,679,006 (51.6%)	321
	William J. Bryan	Democratic	6,409,106 (43.1%)	162
	Eugene V. Debs	Socialist	420,820 (2.8%)	0
1912	**Woodrow Wilson**	Democratic	6,286,820 (41.8%)	435
	Theodore Roosevelt	Progressive	4,126,020 (27.4%)	88
	William H. Taft	Republican	3,483,922 (23.2%)	8
	Eugene V. Debs	Socialist	897,011 (6.0%)	0
1916	**Woodrow Wilson**	Democratic	9,129,606 (49.3%)	277
	Charles E. Hughes	Republican	8,538,211 (46.1%)	254
1920	**Warren G. Harding**	Republican	16,152,200 (61.0%)	404
	James M. Cox	Democratic	9,147,353 (34.6%)	127
	Eugene V. Debs	Socialist	919,799 (3.5%)	0
1924	**Calvin Coolidge**	Republican	15,725,016 (54.1%)	382
	John W. Davis	Democratic	8,385,586 (28.8%)	136
	Robert M. La Follette	Progressive	4,822,856 (16.6%)	13
1928	**Herbert C. Hoover**	Republican	21,392,190 (58.2%)	444
	Alfred E. Smith	Democratic	15,016,443 (40.8%)	87
1932	**Franklin D. Roosevelt**	Democratic	22,809,638 (57.3%)	472
	Herbert C. Hoover	Republican	15,758,901 (39.6%)	59
	Norman Thomas	Socialist	881,951 (2.2%)	0
1936	**Franklin D. Roosevelt**	Democratic	27,751,612 (60.7%)	523
	Alfred M. Landon	Republican	16,681,913 (36.4%)	8
	William Lemke	Union	891,858 (1.9%)	0
1940	**Franklin D. Roosevelt**	Democratic	27,243,466 (54.7%)	449
	Wendell L. Wilkie	Republican	22,304,755 (44.8%)	82
1944	**Franklin D. Roosevelt**	Democratic	25,602,505 (52.8%)	432
	Thomas E. Dewey	Republican	22,006,278 (44.5%)	99

Year	*Candidates*	*Party*	*Popular Vote*	*Electoral Vote*
1948	**Harry S. Truman**	Democratic	24,105,812 (49.5%)	303
	Thomas E. Dewey	Republican	21,970,065 (45.1%)	189
	J. Strom Thurmond	States' Rights	1,169,063 (2.4%)	39
	Henry A. Wallace	Progressive	1,157,172 (2.4%)	0
1952	**Dwight D. Eisenhower**	Republican	33,936,234 (55.2%)	442
	Adlai E. Stevenson	Democratic	27,314,992 (44.5%)	89
1956	**Dwight D. Eisenhower**	Republican	35,590,472 (57.4%)	457
	Adlai E. Stevenson	Democratic	26,022,752 (42.0%)	73
1960	**John F. Kennedy**	Democratic	34,227,096 (49.9%)	303
	Richard M. Nixon	Republican	34,108,546 (49.6%)	219
1964	**Lyndon B. Johnson**	Democratic	43,126,233 (61.1%)	486
	Barry M. Goldwater	Republican	27,174,989 (38.5%)	52
1968	**Richard M. Nixon**	Republican	31,783,783 (43.4%)	301
	Hubert H. Humphrey	Democratic	31,271,839 (42.7%)	191
	George C. Wallace	American Independent	9,899,557 (13.5%)	46
1972	**Richard M. Nixon**	Republican	46,632,189 (61.3%)	520
	George McGovern	Democratic	28,422,015 (37.3%)	17
1976	**Jimmy Carter**	Democratic	40,828,587 (50.1%)	297
	Gerald R. Ford	Republican	39,147,613 (48.0%)	240
1980	**Ronald Reagan**	Republican	42,941,145 (50.7%)	489
	Jimmy Carter	Democratic	34,663,037 (41.0%)	49
	John B. Anderson	Independent	5,551,551 (6.6%)	0
1984	**Ronald Reagan**	Republican	53,428,357 (58.8%)	525
	Walter F. Mondale	Democratic	36,930,923 (40.6%)	13
1988	**George Bush**	Republican	48,881,011 (53.4%)	426
	Michael Dukakis	Democratic	41,828,350 (45.6%)	111
1992	**Bill Clinton**	Democratic	44,908,233 (43.0%)	370
	George Bush	Republican	39,102,282 (37.4%)	168
	Ross Perot	Independent	19,741,048 (18.9%)	0
1996	**Bill Clinton**	Democratic	45,628,667 (49.2%)	379
	Robert Dole	Republican	37,869,435 (40.8%)	159
	Ross Perot	Reform	7,874,283 (8.5%)	0

Appendix J

Party Control of the Presidency, Senate, and House of Representatives, 1901–1997

Congress	Years	President	Senate D	Senate R	Senate Other[*]	House D	House R	House Other[*]
57th	1901–1903	McKinley / T. Roosevelt	29	56	3	153	198	5
58th	1903–1905	T. Roosevelt	32	58	—	178	207	—
59th	1905–1907	T. Roosevelt	32	58	—	136	250	—
60th	1907–1909	T. Roosevelt	29	61	—	164	222	—
61st	1909–1911	Taft	32	59	—	172	219	—
62d	1911–1913	Taft	42	49	—	228[‡]	162	1
63d	1913–1915	Wilson	51	44	1	290	127	18
64th	1915–1917	Wilson	56	39	1	231	193	8
65th	1917–1919	Wilson	53	42	1	210	216	9
66th	1919–1921	Wilson	47	48[‡]	1	191	237[‡]	7
67th	1921–1923	Harding	37	59	—	132	300	1
68th	1923–1925	Coolidge	43	51	2	207	225	3
69th	1925–1927	Coolidge	40	54	1	183	247	5
70th	1927–1929	Coolidge	47	48	1	195	237	3
71st	1929–1931	Hoover	39	56	1	163	267	1
72d	1931–1933	Hoover	47	48	1	216[‡]	218	1
73d	1933–1935	F. Roosevelt	59	36	1	313	117	5
74th	1935–1937	F. Roosevelt	69	25	2	322	103	10
75th	1937–1939	F. Roosevelt	75	17	4	333	89	13
76th	1939–1941	F. Roosevelt	69	23	4	262	169	4
77th	1941–1943	F. Roosevelt	66	28	2	267	162	6
78th	1943–1945	F. Roosevelt	57	38	1	222	209	4
79th	1945–1947	Truman	57	38	1	243	190	2
80th	1947–1949	Truman	45	51[‡]	—	188	246[‡]	1
81st	1949–1951	Truman	54	42	—	263	171	1
82d	1951–1953	Truman	48	47	1	234	199	2
83d	1953–1955	Eisenhower	46	48	2	213	221	1
84th	1955–1957	Eisenhower	48[‡]	47	1	232[‡]	203	—
85th	1957–1959	Eisenhower	49[‡]	47	—	234[‡]	201	—
86th[†]	1959–1961	Eisenhower	64[‡]	34	—	283[‡]	154	—
87th	1961–1963	Kennedy	64	36	—	262	175	—
88th	1963–1965	Kennedy / Johnson	67	33	—	258	176	—
89th	1965–1967	Johnson	68	32	—	295	140	—
90th	1967–1969	Johnson	64	36	—	248	187	—
91st	1969–1971	Nixon	58[‡]	42	—	243[‡]	192	—
92d	1971–1973	Nixon	54[‡]	44	2	255[‡]	180	—
93d	1973–1975	Nixon / Ford	56[‡]	42	2	242[‡]	192	—
94th	1975–1977	Ford	61[‡]	37	2	291[‡]	144	—
95th	1977–1979	Carter	61	38	1	292	143	—
96th	1979–1981	Carter	58	41	1	277	158	—
97th	1981–1983	Reagan	46	53	1	243[‡]	192	—
98th	1983–1985	Reagan	46	54	—	268[‡]	167	—
99th	1985–1987	Reagan	47	53	—	253[‡]	182	—
100th	1987–1989	Reagan	55[‡]	45	—	258[‡]	177	—
101st	1989–1991	Bush	55[‡]	45	—	260[‡]	175	—
102d	1991–1993	Bush	56[‡]	44	—	267[‡]	167	1
103d	1993–1995	Clinton	57	43	—	258	176	1
104th	1995–1997	Clinton	47	53[‡]		204	230[‡]	1
105th	1997–1999	Clinton	45	55[‡]	—	207	227[‡]	1

[*]Excludes vacancies at beginning of each session. Party balance immediately following election.

[†]The 437 members of the House in the 86th and 87th Congresses are attributable to the at-large representative given to both Alaska (January 3, 1959) and Hawaii (August 21, 1959) prior to redistricting in 1962.

[‡]Chamber controlled by party other than that of the president.

D = Democrat; R = Republican

Appendix K

Twentieth-Century Justices of the Supreme Court

Name	*Nominated By*	*Service*
John M. Harlan	Hayes	1877–1911
Horace Gray	Arthur	1882–1902
Melville W. Fuller	Cleveland	1888–1910
David J. Brewer	Harrison	1890–1910
Henry B. Brown	Harrison	1890–1906
George Shiras, Jr.	Harrison	1892–1903
Edward D. White	Cleveland	1894–1910
Rufus W. Peckham	Cleveland	1895–1909
Joseph McKenna	McKinley	1898–1925
Oliver W. Holmes	T. Roosevelt	1902–1932
William R. Day	T. Roosevelt	1903–1922
William H. Moody	T. Roosevelt	1906–1910
Horace H. Lurton	Taft	1910–1914
Edward D. White	Taft	1910–1921
Charles E. Hughes	Taft	1910–1916
Willis Van Devanter	Taft	1911–1937
Joseph R. Lamar	Taft	1911–1916
Mahlon Pitney	Taft	1912–1922
James C. McReynolds	Wilson	1914–1941
Louis D. Brandeis	Wilson	1916–1939
John H. Clarke	Wilson	1916–1922
William H. Taft	Harding	1921–1930
George Sutherland	Harding	1922–1938
Pierce Butler	Harding	1922–1939
Edward T. Sanford	Harding	1923–1930
Harlan F. Stone	Coolidge	1925–1941
Charles E. Hughes	Hoover	1930–1941
Owen J. Roberts	Hoover	1930–1945
Benjamin N. Cardozo	Hoover	1932–1938
Hugo L. Black	F. Roosevelt	1937–1971
Stanley F. Reed	F. Roosevelt	1938–1957
Felix Frankfurter	F. Roosevelt	1939–1962
William O. Douglas	F. Roosevelt	1939–1975
Frank Murphy	F. Roosevelt	1940–1949
Harlan F. Stone	F. Roosevelt	1941–1946
James F. Byrnes	F. Roosevelt	1941–1942
Robert H. Jackson	F. Roosevelt	1941–1954
Wiley B. Rutledge	F. Roosevelt	1943–1949
Harold H. Burton	Truman	1945–1958
Fred M. Vinson	Truman	1946–1953
Tom C. Clark	Truman	1949–1967
Sherman Minton	Truman	1949–1956
Earl Warren	Eisenhower	1953–1969
John M. Harlan	Eisenhower	1955–1971
William J. Brennan, Jr.	Eisenhower	1956–1990
Charles E. Whittaker	Eisenhower	1957–1962
Potter Stewart	Eisenhower	1958–1981
Byron R. White	Kennedy	1962–1993

Note: Boldface type indicates service as chief justice.

Name	*Nominated By*	*Service*
Arthur J. Goldberg	Kennedy	1962–1965
Abe Fortas	Johnson	1965–1969
Thurgood Marshall	Johnson	1967–1991
Warren E. Burger	Nixon	1969–1986
Harry A. Blackmun	Nixon	1970–1994
Lewis F. Powell, Jr.	Nixon	1971–1987
William H. Rehnquist	Nixon	1971–1986
John Paul Stevens	Ford	1975–
Sandra Day O'Connor	Reagan	1981–
William H. Rehnquist	Reagan	1986–
Antonin Scalia	Reagan	1986–
Anthony M. Kennedy	Reagan	1988–
David H. Souter	Bush	1990–
Clarence Thomas	Bush	1991–
Ruth Bader Ginsburg	Clinton	1993–
Stephen G. Breyer	Clinton	1994–

Appendix L

Presidential General Election Returns by State, 1996

State	Clinton (Democrat) Vote	%	Dole (Republican) Vote	%	Perot (Reform) Vote	%	Electoral Vote D	R
Alabama	658,431	43%	771,651	50%	92,163	6%	0	9
Alaska	66,508	33	101,234	51	21,536	11	0	3
Arizona	609,761	47	572,847	44	104,287	8	8	0
Arkansas	448,057	54	307,419	37	67,300	8	6	0
California	4,639,935	51	3,412,563	38	667,702	7	54	0
Colorado	670,656	44	691,095	46	99,440	7	0	8
Connecticut	709,149	52	484,638	36	136,723	10	8	0
D.C.	152,031	85	16,637	9	3,479	2	3	0
Delaware	140,209	52	98,906	37	28,693	11	3	0
Florida	2,533,553	48	2,226,099	42	481,225	9	25	0
Georgia	1,045,466	46	1,077,161	47	144,368	6	0	13
Hawaii	205,012	57	113,943	32	27,358	8	4	0
Idaho	163,866	34	253,769	52	61,861	13	0	4
Illinois	2,302,054	54	1,576,534	37	343,942	8	22	0
Indiana	871,033	41	1,010,170	48	218,068	10	0	12
Iowa	615,523	50	489,729	40	102,922	8	7	0
Kansas	383,795	36	577,426	54	91,911	9	0	6
Kentucky	635,804	46	622,339	45	118,768	9	8	0
Louisiana	928,564	52	709,136	40	122,892	7	9	0
Maine	299,894	52	178,683	31	82,773	14	4	0
Maryland	924,284	54	651,682	38	113,684	7	10	0
Massachusetts	1,567,223	62	717,622	28	225,394	9	12	0
Michigan	1,786,702	52	1,332,706	39	302,751	9	18	0
Minnesota	1,087,263	51	746,890	35	250,512	12	10	0
Mississippi	382,621	44	433,439	50	51,258	6	0	7
Missouri	1,023,505	48	889,123	41	216,734	10	11	0
Montana	163,208	41	175,162	44	54,191	14	0	3
Nebraska	231,840	35	355,482	53	76,056	11	0	5
Nevada	196,050	44	187,421	42	41,820	9	4	0
New Hampshire	245,260	50	196,740	40	48,140	10	4	0
New Jersey	1,592,267	53	1,086,374	36	262,265	9	15	0
New Mexico	252,215	49	210,791	41	30,978	6	5	0

Continued

State	Popular Vote: Clinton (Democrat) Vote	%	Dole (Republican) Vote	%	Perot (Reform) Vote	%	Electoral Vote D	R
New York	3,493,548	59	1,852,097	31	479,953	8	33	0
North Carolina	1,094,025	44	1,211,844	49	164,593	7	0	14
North Dakota	106,136	40	124,215	47	32,481	12	0	3
Ohio	2,098,870	47	1,821,580	41	470,188	11	21	0
Oklahoma	488,102	40	582,310	48	130,788	11	0	8
Oregon	318,222	47	249,052	37	71,015	11	7	0
Pennsylvania	2,202,372	49	1,792,493	40	429,248	10	23	0
Rhode Island	217,495	60	96,498	27	39,137	11	4	0
South Carolina	496,146	44	564,979	50	62,733	6	0	8
South Dakota	139,296	43	150,508	46	31,218	10	0	3
Tennessee	905,538	48	860,809	46	105,577	6	11	0
Texas	2,455,735	44	2,731,998	49	377,530	7	0	32
Utah	220,197	33	359,394	54	66,100	10	0	5
Vermont	138,400	54	80,043	31	30,912	12	3	0
Virginia	1,065,737	45	1,117,690	47	158,253	7	0	13
Washington	899,645	51	639,743	36	161,642	9	11	0
West Virginia	320,913	51	230,997	37	70,158	11	5	0
Wisconsin	1,071,385	49	844,540	39	227,223	10	11	0
Wyoming	77,897	37	105,347	50	25,854	12	0	3
Total	**45,341,398**	**49%**	**37,691,548**	**41%**	**7,825,797**	**9%**	**379**	**159**

Source: "The Presidential Vote, State by State," *Wall Street Journal*, 7 November 1996.

Appendix

M

Portrait of the Electorate, 1984–1996

This portrait of Americans at the polls shows how different groups have voted in the last four presidential elections, measuring the ebbs and flows of political alliances that have elected and defeated presidents. The vast size of each sample makes it possible to study the preferences of some groups, such as Jews, Asian Americans, and Hispanic American voters, whose small numbers make them almost invisible in typical national telephone polls.

Percentage of 1996 total vote		*1984*		*1988*		*1992*			*1996*		
		Reagan	*Mondale*	*Bush*	*Dukakis*	*Clinton*	*Bush*	*Perot*	*Clinton*	*Dole*	*Perot*
	Total vote	59	40	53	45	43	38	19	49	41	8
48	Men	62	37	57	41	41	38	21	43	44	10
52	Women	56	44	50	49	45	37	17	54	38	7
83	White	64	35	59	40	39	40	20	43	46	9
10	African American	9	90	12	86	83	10	7	84	12	4
5	Hispanic American	37	62	30	69	61	25	14	72	21	6
1	Asian American	—	—	—	—	31	55	15	43	48	8
17	18–29 years old	59	40	52	47	43	34	22	53	34	10
33	30–44 years old	57	42	54	45	41	38	21	48	41	9
26	45–59 years old	60	40	57	42	41	40	19	49	41	9
24	60 and older	60	39	50	49	50	38	12	48	44	7
35	Republicans	92	7	91	8	10	73	17	13	80	6
26	Independents	63	36	55	43	38	32	30	43	35	17
39	Democrats	25	74	17	82	77	10	13	84	10	5
20	Liberals	28	70	18	81	68	14	18	78	11	7
47	Moderates	53	47	49	50	47	31	21	57	33	9
33	Conservatives	82	17	80	19	18	64	18	20	71	8
23	From the East	53	47	50	49	47	35	18	55	34	9
26	From the Midwest	58	41	52	47	42	37	21	48	41	10
30	From the South	64	36	58	41	41	43	16	46	46	7
20	From the West	61	38	52	46	43	34	23	48	40	8
6	Not a high school graduate	50	50	43	56	54	28	18	59	28	11
24	High school graduate	60	39	50	49	43	36	21	51	35	13
27	Some college education	61	38	57	42	41	37	21	48	40	10
43	College graduate or more	58	41	56	43	44	39	17	47	44	7
26	College graduate	—	—	62	37	39	41	20	44	46	8
17	Post graduate education	—	—	50	48	50	36	14	52	40	5
46	White Protestant	72	27	68	33	33	47	21	36	53	10
29	Catholic	54	45	52	47	44	35	20	53	37	9
3	Jewish	31	67	35	64	80	11	9	78	16	3
23	Union household	46	53	42	57	55	24	21	59	30	9
	Family income is:										
11	Under $15,000	45	55	37	62	58	23	19	59	28	11
23	$15,000–$29,999	57	42	49	50	45	35	20	53	36	9
27	$30,000–$49,999	59	40	56	43	41	38	21	48	40	10
39	Over $50,000	69	30	62	37	39	44	17	44	48	7
18	Over $75,000	—	—	—	—	36	48	16	41	51	7
9	Over $100,000	—	—	65	32	—	—	—	38	54	6
	Family's financial situation is:										
33	Better today	86	14	—	—	24	61	14	66	26	6
45	Same today	50	50	—	—	41	42	17	46	45	8
20	Worse today	15	85	—	—	60	14	25	27	57	13
9	First time voters	61	38	51	47	46	32	22	54	34	11
	Congressional vote:										
49	For the Democratic candidate	23	76	27	72	74	11	15	84	8	7
49	For the Republican candidate	93	7	82	17	10	72	18	15	76	8

APPENDIX

N

AMERICAN POLITICAL PARTIES SINCE 1789

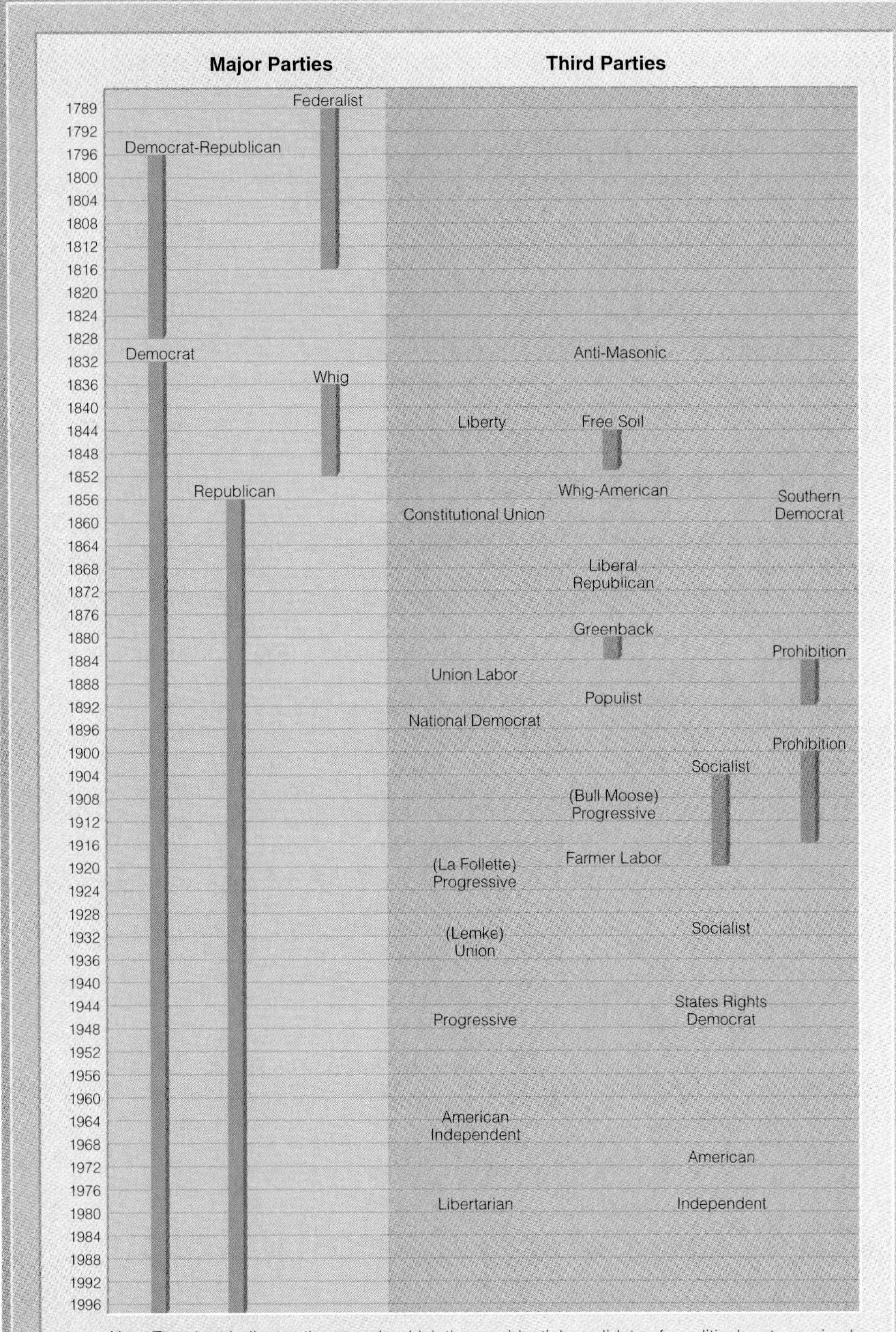

Note: The chart indicates the years in which the presidential candidate of a political party received 1.0 percent or more of the popular vote. Minor parties are not included if the minor party candidate is also the candidate of one of the two major parties (as happened in 1896 when the Populists endorsed William Jennings Bryan, the Democratic candidate). Party candidates sometimes run under different designations in different states (in 1968, George C. Wallace ran for president under at least ten party labels). In such cases, the vote totals for the candidate were aggregated under a single party designation. Sometimes candidates run under no party label, as Ross Perot did in 1992.

Although the Democratic and Republican parties have existed for more than a century, the party system has witnessed the rise and fall of many other parties.

From Harold W. Stanley and Richard G. Niemi, *Vital Statistics on American Politics.*

Appendix O

Contract with America

HOUSE REPUBLICAN
CONTRACT WITH AMERICA
A PROGRAM FOR ACCOUNTABILITY

We've listened to your concerns and we hear you loud and clear. If you give us the majority, on the first day of Congress, a Republican House will:

- Force Congress to live under the same law as every other American
- Cut one out of three Congressional committee staffers
- Cut the Congressional budget

Then, in the first 100 days there will be votes on the following 10 bills:

1. **Balanced budget amendment and the line item veto:** It's time to force the government to live within its means and restore accountability to the budget in Washington.

2. **Stop violent criminals:** Let's get tough with an effective, able and timely death penalty for violent offenders. Let's also reduce crime by building more prisons, making sentences longer and putting more police on the streets.

3. **Welfare reform:** The government should encourage people to work, not to have children out of wedlock.

4. **Protect our kids:** We must strengthen families by giving parents greater control over education, enforcing child support payments, and getting tough on child pornography.

5. **Tax cuts for families:** Let's make it easier to achieve the American Dream: save money, buy a home, and send their kids to college.

6. **Strong national defense:** We need to ensure a strong national defense by restoring the essential parts of our national security funding.

7. **Raise the senior citizens' earning limit:** We can put an end to government age discrimination that discourages seniors from working if they want.

8. **Roll back government regulations:** Let's slash regulations that strangle small business and let's make it easier for people to invest in order to create jobs and increase wages.

9. **Common-sense legal reform:** We can Finally stop excessive legal claims, frivolous lawsuits, and overzealous lawyers.

10. **Congressional term limits:** Let's replace career politicians with citizen legislators. After all, politics shouldn't be a lifetime job.

(Please see reverse side to know if the candidate from your district has signed the Contract as of October 5, 1994.)

If We Break This Contract, Throw Us Out. We Mean It.

Chapter 1, pp. 3–18

1. *Contract With America: The Bold Plan by Rep. Newt Gingrich, Rep. Dick Armey and the House Republicans to Change the Nation*, ed. Ed Gillespie and Bob Schellhas (New York: Times Books/Random House, 1994), 15–59.
2. Jackie Calmes, "Even with New GOP Majorities in Both Houses, Term Limits Face Likely Doom in Next Congress," *Wall Street Journal*, 28 November 1994.
3. "Contract With America," *Gallup Poll Monthly* no. 350, November 1994, 24; "Gallup Short Subjects," *Gallup Poll Monthly* no. 351, December 1994, 32.
4. Holly Idelson, "GOP Internal Divisions Add Obstacles to Proposals," *Congressional Quarterly Weekly Report*" 28 January 1995, 289; Steve Langdon, " 'Contract' Dwarfs Senate GOP's Pledge," *Congressional Quarterly Weekly Report* 25 February 1995, 578.
5. Idelson, "GOP Internal Divisions," 288–89.
6. Quoted in Jennifer Babson, "Limit on Consecutive Terms Heading to House Floor," *Congressional Quarterly Weekly Report*, 4 March 1995, 662.
7. Idelson, "GOP Internal Divisions," 288.
8. Jennifer Babson, "Facing Probable Defeat, GOP Delays Term Limits Debate," *Congressional Quarterly Weekly Report*, 11 March 1995, 732; Babson, "Limit on Consecutive Terms," 663.
9. See James G. Gimpel, *Fulfilling the Contract: The First 100 Days* (Boston: Allyn & Bacon, 1996), chap. 8.
10. Jennifer Babson, "House Rejects Term Limits; GOP Blames Democrats," *Congressional Quarterly Weekly Report*, 1 April 1995, 918.
11. U.S. Term Limits v. Thornton, 514 U.S. —, 131 L Ed 2d 881, 115 S Ct — (1995).
12. See Thomas Galvin, "Limits Score a Perfect 14-for-14, But Court Challenges Loom," *Congressional Quarterly Weekly Report*, 7 November 1992, 3593–94; "Supreme Court Declines Review of State-Level Term Limits," *Congressional Quarterly Weekly Report*, 14 March 1992, 654.
13. Quoted in Calmes, "Even with New GOP Majorities."
14. David Easton, *The Political System: An Inquiry into the State of Political Science*, 2d ed. (New York: Knopf, 1971); Harold Lasswell, *Politics: Who Gets What, When, How* (New York: Whittlesey House, 1936).
15. Robert A. Dahl, *Modern Political Analysis*, 2d ed. (Englewood Cliffs, N.J.: Prentice-Hall, 1970).
16. Gregor Reinhard, "The Origins of the Presidency," in *The American Presidency: A Policy Perspective from Readings and Documents*, ed. David C. Kozak and Kenneth N. Ciboski (Chicago: Nelson-Hall, 1985), 1–13.

Chapter 2, pp. 19–66

1. See, for example, Helen Dewar, "Long on Talk, Short on Legislation," *Washington Post National Weekly Edition*, 8–18 January 1996, 31.
2. David E. Rosenbaum, "Gridlock: When an Irresistible Revolution Meets an Unmovable Constitution," *New York Times*, 20 December 1995.
3. Theodore Draper, "The Constitution Was Made, Not Born," *New York Times Book Review*, 10 October 1993, 3.
4. Samuel Eliot Morrison, *Oxford History of the American People* (New York: Oxford University Press, 1965), 182.
5. Edward S. Corwin, *The President: Office and Powers, 1787–1957*, 4th rev. ed. (New York: New York University Press, 1957), 5–6.
6. John Roche, "The Founding Fathers: A Reform Caucus in Action," *American Political Review* 55 (December 1961): 799–816.
7. Quoted in Draper, "The Constitution Was Made, Not Born," 25.
8. See Calvin C. Jillson, *Constitution Making: Conflict and Consensus in the Federal Convention of 1787* (New York: Agathon Press, 1988), 164–65.
9. John Locke, *Two Treatises of Government* (1630).
10. James Madison, "Federalist No. 10," in Alexander Hamilton, James Madison, and John Jay, *The Federalist Papers*, ed. Garry Wills (New York: Bantam Books, 1982), 45.
11. Charles de Montesquieu, *The Spirit of the Laws* (1734).
12. Richard E. Neustadt, *Presidential Power and the Modern Presidents: The Politics of Leadership from Roosevelt to Reagan* (New York: Free Press, 1990), 29. (Emphasis in the original.)
13. James P. Pfiffner, *The Modern Presidency* (New York: St. Martin's, 1994), 139.
14. Jay Shafritz, *The Dorsey Dictionary of American Government and Politics* (Chicago: Dorsey, 1988), 206.
15. See David Gray Adler, "The Constitution and Presidential Warmaking," *Political Science Quarterly* 103 (Spring 1988): 8–13; Alexander Hamilton, "Federalist No. 69," in Alexander Hamilton, James Madison, and John Jay, *The Federalist Papers*, ed. Garry Wills (New York: Bantam Books, 1982); Louis Henkin, *Foreign Affairs and the Constitution* (Mineola, N.Y.: Foundation Press, 1972), 50–51; Arthur M. Schlesinger, Jr., *The Imperial Presidency* (Boston: Houghton Mifflin, 1989), 6, 61–62.
16. See Ruth Ann Strickland, "The Twenty-seventh Amendment and Constitutional Change by Stealth," *PS: Political Science & Politics* 24 (December 1993): 716–21.
17. Norman J. Ornstein, Thomas E. Mann, and Michael J. Malbin, *Vital Statistics on Congress 1995–1996* (Washington, D.C.: Congressional Quarterly, 1996), 159, 161, 165.
18. McCulloch v. Maryland, 4 Wheat. 316 (1819).
19. Morton Grodzins, "The Federal System," in *Goals for Americans: The Report of the President's Commission on National Goals* (Englewood Cliffs, N.J.: Prentice-Hall, 1960), 265.
20. Ibid.
21. United States v. Lopez, 514 U.S. —, 131 L Ed 2d 626, 115 S Ct (1995). See Aric Press and Bruce Shenitz, "The Limits of Commerce," *U.S. News & World Report*, 8 May 1995.

Chapter 3, pp. 67–92

1. See Malcolm Gladwell, "Fundamental Ignorance about Numbers," *Washington Post National Weekly Edition*, 16–22 October 1995, 7. See also George Gallup, Jr., and Frank Newport, "Americans Ignorant of Basic Census Facts," *Gallup Poll Monthly* no. 294, March 1990, 2. See also the report to the National Election Studies Board of Overseers by Benjamin Highton and Raymond E. Wolfinger, 24 January 1992; Richard Nadeau, Richard G. Niemi, and Jeffrey Levine, "Innumeracy about Minority Populations," *Public Opinion Quarterly* 57 (Fall 1993): 332–47.
2. Gladwell, "Fundamental Ignorance," 7; Nadeau, Niemi, and Levine, "Innumeracy about Minority Populations," 340–43.
3. The numbers reported in this chapter are drawn from U.S. Census figures, as reported in several different sources, including *Statistical Abstract of the United States, 1995*, 115th ed. (Washington, D.C.: U.S. Bureau of the Census, 1995); *Historical Statistics of the United States: Colonial Times to 1970* (Washington, D.C.: U.S. Bureau of the Census, 1975); Harold W. Stanley and Richard G. Niemi, *Vital Statistics on American Politics*, 5th ed. (Washington, D.C.: CQ Press, 1995); *The Universal Almanac 1992* (Kansas City: Andrews and McMeel, 1992); U.S.

Census Bureau, "High School Completion Rates For Young African Americans, Whites Are Similar, Census Bureau Reports," 5 September 1996; U.S. Census Bureau, "Income and Poverty Status of Americans Improve, Health Insurance Coverage Stable, Census Bureau Reports," 26 September 1996; U.S. Census Bureau, "Press Briefing on 1995 Income, Poverty, and Health Insurance Estimates," 26 September 1996.

4. Rhodes Cook, "As Suburban Loyalty Is Tested, Bush Isn't Making the Grade," *Congressional Quarterly Weekly Report,* 26 September 1992, 2967; "Half of U.S. Population Lives in Suburbs," *Des Moines Register,* 27 May 1992.
5. A Yankelovich poll taken in October 1995 revealed a preference for *African American. Black* was the preferred label in a 1995 U.S. Department of Labor survey, and *doesn't matter* was the top choice in a July 1995 Gallup Poll. For reports on the first and third surveys, see "People, Opinions & Polls," *The Public Perspective* 7(February/March 1996): 25. The Labor Department survey is discussed in Asra Q. Nomani, "Work Week," *Wall Street Journal,* 7 November 1995; "Outlook: American Pie," *U.S. News and World Report,* 20 November 1995, 28.
6. Edward G. Carmines and James A. Stimson, *Issue Evolution: Race and the Transformation of American Politics* (Princeton, N.J.: Princeton University Press, 1989), 27–58.
7. Harold W. Stanley and Richard G. Niemi, "Partisanship and Group Support Over Time," in *Controversies in Voting Behavior,* 3d ed., ed. Richard G. Niemi and Herbert F. Weisberg (Washington, D.C.: CQ Press, 1993).
8. See Michael Dawson, *Behind the Mule: Race and Class in African-American Politics* (Princeton, N.J.: Princeton University Press, 1994); Franklin D. Gilliam, Jr., and Kenny J. Whitby, Jr., "Race, Class, and Attitudes Toward Social Welfare Spending: An Ethclass Interpretation," *Social Science Quarterly* 70 (March 1989): 88–100; Byran O. Jackson, Elisabeth R. Gerber, Bruce E. Cain, "Coalitional Prospects in a Multi-Racial Society: African-American Attitudes Toward Other Minority Groups," *Political Research Quarterly* 47(June 1994): 277–94.
9. Data from the Joint Center for Political and Economic Studies, reported in Michael K. Frisby, "Jesse Jackson Ponders Another Presidential Bid, But Decision Hinges on Clinton's Tilt to Right," *Wall Street Journal,* 7 July 1995.
10. See Kim Quaile Hill and Jan Leighley, "Lower-Class Mobilization and Policy Linkage in the U.S. States," *American Journal of Political Science* 39 (February 1995): 75–86.
11. Sam Roberts, "Census Reveals a Surge in Hispanic Population," *New York Times,* 9 October 1994.
12. See the numbers reported in Nomani, "Work Week," and "Outlook: American Pie," 28. See also Rodolfo O. de la Garza, Louis DeSipio, F. Chris Garcia, John Garcia, and Angelo Falcon, *Latino Voices* (Boulder, Colo.: Westview, 1992), 62–64; David Gonzalez, "What's the Problem with 'Hispanic'? Just Ask a 'Latino,'" *New York Times,* 15 November 1992.
13. See James Fay and Kay Lawson, "Is California Going Republican?" and Jeanie R. Stanley, "Party Realignment in Texas," both in *Party Realignment and State Politics,* ed. Maureen Moakley (Columbus: Ohio State University Press, 1992).
14. Bruce Cain and D. Roderick Kiewiet, "Ethnicity and Electoral Choice: Mexican-American Voting Behavior in the California 30th Congressional District," *Social Science Quarterly* 65 (June 1984): 315–27; Bruce E. Cain, D. Roderick Kiewiet, and Carole J. Uhlaner, "The Acquisition of Partisanship by Latinos and Asian Americans," *American Journal of Political Science* 35 (May 1991): 390–422.
15. See "Characteristics of the Latino Vote," *Campaign* 7 (August 1992): 8; de la Garza et al., *Latino Voices,* 127; Christopher L. Warren, "Hispanics," in *Florida's Politics and Government,* 2d ed., ed. Manning J. Dauer (Gainesville: University of Florida Press, 1984).
16. Felicity Barringer, "Immigration Brings New Diversity to Asian Population in the U.S.," *New York Times,* 12 June 1991.
17. Cain, Kiewiet, and Uhlaner, "The Acquisition of Partisanship," 390–422; Fay and Lawson, "Is California Going Republican?" 30–33.
18. Nomani, "Work Week"; "Outlook: American Pie," 28.
19. Geoffrey D. Peterson, "An Initial Examination of Native American Voting Behavior in Presidential Elections," *Native American Quarterly,* forthcoming.
20. See "Ahead, A Mostly Minority America," *U.S. News & World Report,* 30 October 1995, 23.
21. Franklin D. Gilliam, Jr., "Exploring Minority Empowerment: Symbolic Politics, Governing Coalitions and Traces of Political Style in Los Angeles," *American Journal of Political Science* (February 1996): 56–81; Jackson, Gerber, and Cain, "Coalitional Prospects," 277–94; Maria Renee Niles, "Blacks and Latinos: Coalition Or Conflict?" presented at the 1995 annual meeting of the Western Political Science Association, Portland, Ore.
22. William A. Henry III, *In Defense of Elitism* (New York: Doubleday, 1994), 74.
23. See, for example, Everett Carll Ladd, ed., *America at the Polls 1994* (Storrs, Conn.: Roper Center, 1995), 124; "Prop. 187 Heightens Black-Hispanic Tensions," *USA Today,* 4 November 1994.
24. Richard Morin, "Who Wants to Know?" *Washington Post National Weekly Edition,* 28 August–3 September 1995, 36.
25. See the results of a February 1995 Princeton Survey Research Associates poll, in "People, Opinions & Polls," *The Public Perspective* 7(February/March 1996): 25.
26. Richard D. Alba, "Assimilation's Quiet Tide," *The Public Interest* 119 (Spring 1995): 3–18.
27. Daniel Seligman, "Talking Back to the IQ Test, Guess Who's in Love with Lefties, More Casino Wars, and Other Matters," *Fortune,* 16 October 1995, 246.
28. See "The Admissions Process: The Rules, the Situations," *USA Today,* 5 July 1995.
29. "INS: Expired Visas Account for Most Illegal Immigrants," *Iowa City Press-Citizen,* 31 January 1995.
30. de la Garza et al., *Latino Voices,* 97–98.
31. Charles Green, "For 1 in 7, English not Main Tongue," *Des Moines Register,* 28 April 1993.
32. Rick Barry, "Arizona Language Law Goes to High Court," *Tampa Tribune,* 5 February 1996; Jonathan Roos, "Committee Oks Bill Proclaiming English as Iowa's Official Language," *Des Moines Register,* 8 February 1996.
33. Bipartisan Commission on Entitlement and Tax Reform, *Final Report to the President* (Washington, D.C.: U.S. Government Printing Office, 1995), 16; Dorcas R. Hardy and C. Colburn Hardy, "How to Beat the New Social Insecurity," *Bottom Line,* 15 October 1992. See also Eric R. Kingson and Edward D. Berkowitz, *Social Security and Medicare: A Policy Primer* (Westport, Conn.: Auburn House, 1993), 102–7.
34. David Wessel, "As Populations Age, Fiscal Woes Deepen," *Wall Street Journal* 11 September 1995.
35. Richard Morin, "The Face of the Single Mother," *Washington Post National Weekly Edition,* 1–7 May 1995, 34.
36. "Census Totals Low for Gays," *Iowa City Press-Citizen,* 12 April 1993; "Gays Finding '10%' Statistic Questioned," *Iowa City Press-Citizen,* 19 April 1993; Tamar Lewin, "New Sex Survey Finds Little of the Wild Life," *Des Moines Register* 7 October 1994; Boyce Rensberger, "Playing Politics by the Numbers," *Washington Post National Weekly Edition,* 26 April–2 May 1993.
37. "Gays Finding '10%' Statistic Questioned," *Iowa City Press-Citizen.*
38. See the data reported in "Portrait of the Electorate: Who Voted for Whom in the House," *New York Times,* 13 November 1994.
39. Rich Tafel, quoted in "Gingrich's Thoughts on Gays," *Des Moines Register,* 24 November 1994.
40. George Gallup, Jr., "Religion in America: Will the Vitality of Churches Be the Surprise of the Next Century?" *The Public Perspective* 6 (October/November 1995): 1–8.

41. Report to the National Election Studies Board of Overseers by Benjamin Highton and Raymond E. Wolfinger, 24 January 1992.
42. See Eric M. Uslaner, "A Tower of Babel on Foreign Policy," in *Interest Group Politics*, 3d. ed., ed. Allan J. Cigler and Burdett A. Loomis (Washington, D.C.: CQ Press, 1991), 308–12.
43. See the data reported in Barbara Hinkson Craig and David M. O'Brien, *Abortion and American Politics* (Chatham, N.J.: Chatham House, 1993), 258; Laurie Goodstein and Richard Morin, "Love the Messenger, Not His Message," *Washington Post National Weekly Edition*, 9–15 October 1995, 37; James L. Guth, Corwin E. Smidt, Lyman A. Kellstedt, and John C. Green, "The Sources of Antiabortion Attitudes: The Case of Religious Political Activists," in *Understanding the New Politics of Abortion*, ed. Malcolm Goggin (Newbury Park, Calif.: Sage, 1993), 49.
44. A. James Reichley, *Religion in American Public Life* (Washington, D.C.: Brookings Institution, 1985), 267–81.
45. Kenneth D. Wald, "Assessing the Religious Factor in Electoral Behavior," in *Religion in American Politics*, ed. Charles W. Dunn (Washington, D.C.: CQ Press, 1989).
46. Kenneth D. Wald, Dennis E. Owen, and Samuel S. Hill, Jr., "Political Cohesion in Churches," *Journal of Politics* 52 (February 1990): 197–215.
47. Jason De Parle, "Without Fanfare, Blacks March to Greater High School Success," *New York Times*, 9 June 1991; "More Blacks Completing High School Than in 1973," *Wall Street Journal*, 21 November 1994; U.S. Census Bureau, "High School Completion Rates for Young African Americans, Whites Are Similar, Census Bureau Reports," 5 September 1996.
48. "The Numbers Bear Out Our Diversity," *Wall Street Journal*, 15 April 1994.
49. Kenneth Pins, "Census Study Finds a Shrinking Middle Class," *Des Moines Register*, 20 February 1992.
50. Kenneth Pins, "Battleground 1992 Finds U.S. Voters in a Quandary," *Des Moines Register*, 16 January 1992.
51. Quoted in "Middle-Class State of Mind, Gingrich Says," *Iowa City Press-Citizen*, 21 December 1995.
52. Quoted in Al Kamen, "If a Senator Answers, Hang Up," *Washington Post National Weekly Edition*, 30 October–5 November 1995, 18.
53. John E. Schwarz, *America's Hidden Success*, rev. ed. (New York: Norton, 1988).
54. Terry L. Anderson, "How the Government Keeps Indians in Poverty," *Wall Street Journal*, 22 November 1995.
55. Kingson and Berkowitz, *Social Security and Medicare*, 75–81.
56. Stanley and Niemi, *Vital Statistics*, 352.
57. See the discussion on estimates of the number of homeless people in *The Universal Almanac 1992*, 215.
58. Lauran Neergaard, "13.5 Million Have Been Homeless: Study May Debunk Misconceptions," *San Francisco Chronicle*, 28 December 1994.
59. "Homeless People in the Middle—Helped or Harassed," *San Francisco Chronicle*, 15 December 1994.
60. Peverill Squire, Raymond E. Wolfinger, and David P. Glass, "Residential Mobility and Voter Turnout," *American Political Science Review* 81 (March 1987): 45–65. See also Ted G. Jelen, "The Impact of Home Ownership on Whites' Racial Attitudes," *American Politics Quarterly* 18 (April 1990): 208–14; Paul William Kingston, John L. P. Thompson, and Douglas M. Eichar, "The Politics of Homeownership," *American Politics Quarterly* 12 (April 1984): 131–50.
61. "Number of U.S. Farms Is Lowest Since 1850," *Des Moines Register*, 10 November 1994.
62. David Hale, "For New Jobs, Help Small Business," *Wall Street Journal*, 10 August 1992.
63. See, for example, the comparison of benefits by company size in "For Employee Benefits, It Pays to Wear the Union Label," *New York Times*, 16 July 1995.
64. William Ryberg, "Labor Movement on Crest of Big Changes Nationwide," *Des Moines Register*, 3 September 1995; Stanley and Niemi, *Vital Statistics*, 176; "Union Members in 1995," *Bureau of Labor Statistics*, 9 February 1996.
65. June Ellenoff O'Neill, "The Shrinking Pay Gap," *Wall Street Journal*, 7 October 1994.
66. Diana Furchtgott-Roth, "Working Wives Widen 'Income Gap,'" *Wall Street Journal*, 20 June 1995.
67. For examples of somewhat more recent work, see Nelson W. Polsby, *Community Power and Political Theory*, rev. ed. (New Haven: Yale University Press, 1980); Clarence N. Stone, "Systemic Power in Community Decision-Making: A Restatement of Stratification Theory," *American Political Science Review* 74 (December 1980): 978–90.
68. Floyd Hunter, *Community Power Structure* (Chapel Hill: University of North Carolina Press, 1953). In the style of the time, Hunter disguises Atlanta by calling it Regional City.
69. Robert A. Dahl, *Who Governs* (New Haven: Yale University Press, 1960).

Chapter 4, pp. 93–124

1. Linda Greenhouse, "Justices Hear Campus Religion Case," *New York Times*, 2 March 1995.
2. James Gannon, "Virginia College Wakes Up To Church/State Debate," *Iowa City Press Citizen*, 12 November 1994.
3. Rosenberger v. University of Virginia, 63 *U.S.L.W.* 4702 (1995). See also Edward Felsenthal, "Religious Speech Wins Added Protection," *Wall Street Journal*, 30 June 1995; Linda Greenhouse, "Church-State Ties," *New York Times*, 30 June 1995.
4. See Robert Bork, *The Tempting of America* (New York: Simon & Schuster, 1990).
5. Dred Scott v. Sandford, 19 Howard 393 (1857).
6. See the excellent discussion in Thomas G. Walker and Lee Epstein, *The Supreme Court of the United States* (New York: St. Martin's, 1993), 118–20.
7. 5 *Annals of Congress* 734 (6 April 1796).
8. 5 *Annals of Congress* 776 (6 April 1796).
9. Brown et al. v. Board of Education, 347 U.S. 483 (1954).
10. Quoted in *The Supreme Court A to Z* (Washington, D.C.: Congressional Quarterly, 1994), 283.
11. Barron v. the Mayor and City Council of Baltimore, 7 Peters (32 U.S.), (1833). See the discussion in Henry J. Abraham and Barbara A. Perry, *Freedom and the Court: Civil Rights and Liberties in the United States*, 6th ed. (New York: Oxford University Press, 1994), 30–32.
12. See The Slaughterhouse Cases, 16 Wall. (83 U.S.) 36 (1872); Hurtado v. California, 110 U.S. 516 (1884).
13. Chicago, Burlington & Quincy Railroad Co. v. Chicago, 166 U.S. 226 (1897).
14. See Mark A. Graber, *Transforming Free Speech: The Ambiguous Legacy of Civil Libertarianism* (Berkeley: University of California Press, 1991); Gitlow v. New York, 268 U.S. 652 (1925).
15. Richard Hofstadter, *The Idea of a Party System* (Berkeley: University of California Press, 1969), 106–8.
16. Quoted in Edwin Emery, *The Press and America: An Interpretative History of the Mass Media*, 3d ed. (Englewood Cliffs, N.J.: Prentice-Hall, 1972), 123.
17. New York Times Co. v. Sullivan, 376 U.S. 254 (1964).
18. James A. Curry, Richard B. Riley, and Richard M. Battistoni, *Constitutional Government* (St. Paul, Minn.: West, 1989), 444.
19. Schenck v. United States, 249 U.S. 47 (1919).
20. Abrams v. United States, 250 U.S. 16 (1919).
21. Ibid.
22. See Justice Stone's footnote in United States v. Carolene Products Co., 304 U.S. 144 (1938).
23. Dennis v. United States, 341 U.S. 494 (1951).
24. Brandenburg v. Ohio, 395 U.S. 444 (1969).
25. For some evidence, see Thomas R. Marshall, *Public Opinion and the Supreme Court* (Boston: Unwin Hyman, 1989), 173–81; Thomas R. Marshall, "Public Opinion, Representation, and the Modern Supreme Court," *American Politics Quarterly* 16 (July 1988): 296–316.
26. Stromberg v. California, 283 U.S. 359 (1931).
27. United States v. O'Brien, 391 U.S. 367 (1968).
28. Texas v. Johnson, 491 U.S. 397 (1989).
29. R.A.V. v. City of St. Paul, 112 S. Ct. 2538 (1992).

30. Wisconsin v. Todd Mitchell, 61 LW 4575 (1993).
31. See United States v. Cruikshank, 92 U.S. 542 (1875).
32. Hague v. Committee of Industrial Organization, 307 U.S. 496 (1939).
33. Cox v. Louisiana, 379 U.S. 536 (1965).
34. This account draws on Fred W. Friendly and Martha J. H. Elliott, *The Constitution—That Delicate Balance* (New York: Random House, 1984), 81–88.
35. See the discussion in Curry, Riley, and Battistoni, *Constitutional Government,* 477–78.
36. National Association for the Advancement of Colored People v. Alabama ex rel Patterson, 357 U.S. 449 (1958).
37. Near v. Minnesota, 283 U.S. 697 (1931).
38. See New York Times Company v. United States and United States v. The Washington Post Company, 403 U.S. 713 (1971).
39. The sequence of events is covered in Deirdre Carmody, "Magazine Pulls Article Under Order," *New York Times,* 15 September 1995; "High Court Will Not Lift Magazine Ban," *New York Times,* 22 September 1995; Patrick Reilly and Wade Lambert, "Judge's Ruling Clears Business Week To Publish Article on Filing in P&G Suit," *Wall Street Journal,* 4 October 1995.
40. Quoted in Iver Peterson, "Court Voids Restraint on Business Week," *New York Times,* 6 March 1996.
41. See Anthony Lewis, *Make No Law: The Sullivan Case and the First Amendment* (New York: Random House, 1991).
42. New York Times Co. v. Sullivan, 376 U.S. 254 (1964).
43. Chaplinsky v. New Hampshire, 315 U.S. 568 (1942). The Court upheld the Comstock Act in Ex Parte Jackson, 96 U.S. 727 (1878).
44. Roth v. United States, 354 U.S. 476 (1957).
45. See the discussion in Curry, Riley, and Battistoni, *Constitutional Government,* 510–11.
46. Jacobellis v. Ohio, 378 U.S. 194 (1964).
47. Miller v. California, 413 U.S. 15 (1973).
48. See especially Jenkins v. Georgia, 418 U.S. 153 (1974).
49. A. James Reichley, *Religion in American Public Life* (Washington, D.C.: Brookings Institution, 1985), 111.
50. See Everson v. Board of Education, 330 U.S. 1 (1947).
51. Meek v. Pittinger, 421 U.S. 349 (1975); Levitt v. Committee for Public Educ., 413 U.S. 472 (1973); Committee for Public Educ. v. Nyquist, 413 U.S. 756 (1973).
52. Tilton v. Richardson, 403 U.S. 672 (1971); Roemer v. Board of Public Works, 426 U.S. 736 (1976).
53. Engel v. Vitale, 370 U.S. 421 (1962).
54. Abington School District v. Schempp (1963); Murray v. Curlett, 374 U.S. 203 (1963).
55. Wallace v. Jaffe, 472 U.S. 38 (1985); Lee v. Weisman, 112 S. Ct. 2649 (1992).
56. Capitol Square Review Board v. Pinette, 63 U.S.L.W. 4684 (1995).
57. Greenhouse, "Church-State Ties."
58. Lemon v. Kurtzman, 403 U.S. 602 (1971).
59. Reynolds v. United States, 98 U.S. 145 (1878).
60. This movement started with Cantwell v. Connecticut, 310 U.S. 296 (1940).
61. West Virginia State Board of Education v. Barnette, 319 U.S. 624 (1943). This ruling overturned Minersville School District v. Gobitis, 310 U.S. 586 (1940).
62. Wisconsin v. Yoder, 406 U.S. 205 (1972).
63. Church of the Lukumi Babalu Aye Inc. v. Hialeah, Fla., 124 L. Ed. 472 (1993).
64. Employment Division, Department of Human Resources v. Smith, 494 U.S. 872 (1990).
65. Peter Steinfels, "New Law Protects Religious Practices," *New York Times,* 17 November 1993.
66. Gordon Witkin, "The Fight to Bear Arms," *U.S. News & World Report,* 22 May 1995, 29; see also Joan Biskupic, "A Second (Amendment) Look at Bearing Arms," *Washington Post National Weekly Edition,* 15–21 May 1995, 33; James D. Wright, "Public Opinion and Gun Control: A Comparison of Results from Two Recent National Surveys," *Annals of the American Academy of Political and Social Science* 455 (May 1981): 24–39.
67. Todd S. Purdum, "Shifting Debate to the Political Climate, Clinton Condemns 'Promoters of Paranoia,'" *New York Times,* 25 April 1995.
68. Neil A. Lewis, "At the Bar," *New York Times,* 5 May 1995.
69. Quoted in Biskupic, "A Second (Amendment) Look at Bearing Arms," 33.
70. Lee Kennett and James LaVerne Anderson, *The Gun in America: The Origins of a National Dilemma* (Westport, Conn.: Greenwood, 1975).
71. "The Virginia Declaration of Rights," reprinted in *The George Mason Lectures* (Williamsburg, Va.: Colonial Williamsburg Foundation, 1976), 20.
72. Quoted in Witkin, "The Fight to Bear Arms," 30.
73. See John K. Mahon, *The History of the Militia and the National Guard* (New York: Macmillan, 1983), chap. 1.
74. William Cohen and John Kaplan, *Constitutional Law: Civil Liberty and Individual Rights,* 2d ed. (Mineola, N.Y.: Foundation Press, 1982), 779–80; John K. Mahon, *The American Militia: Decade of Decision, 1789–1800* (Gainesville: University of Florida Press, 1960), 12; Robert J. Spitzer, *The Politics of Gun Control* (Chatham, N.J.: Chatham House, 1995), 33–36.
75. Abraham D. Sofaer, *War, Foreign Affairs and the Constitution* (Cambridge, Mass.: Ballinger, 1976), 116.
76. Spitzer, *Politics of Gun Control,* 37.
77. Stephen Skowronek, *Building a New American State* (Cambridge: Cambridge University Press, 1982), 315.
78. United States v. Cruikshank, 92 U.S. 542, 553 (1876).
79. Cohen and Kaplan, *Constitutional Law,* 785.
80. Presser v. Illinois, 116 U.S. 252 (1886).
81. Miller v. Texas, 153 U.S. 535 (1894); Roberston v. Baldwin, 165 U.S. 275 (1897).
82. United States v. Miller, 307 U.S. 174 (1939).
83. Lewis v. United States, 455 U.S. 55 (1980).
84. Quilici v. Village of Morton Grove, 695 F. 2d 261 (1982).
85. See, for example, William Van Alstyne, "The Second Amendment and the Personal Right to Bear Arms," *Duke Law Journal* 43 (April 1994): 1236–55; David I. Caplan, "The Right of the Individual to Bear Arms: A Recent Judicial Trend," *Detroit College of Law Review* 1982 (Winter 1982): 789–823; Stephen P. Halbrook, "To Keep and Bear Their Private Arms: The Adoption of the Second Amendment, 1787–1791," *Northern Kentucky Law Review* 10 (1982): 13–39; Stuart B. Hays, "The Right to Bear Arms, a Study in Judicial Misinterpretation," *William and Mary Law Review* 2 (1960): 381–406; Don B. Kates, "Handgun Prohibition and the Original Meaning of the Second Amendment," *Michigan Law Review* 82 (November 1983): 204–73; Ronald B. Levine and David B. Saxe, "The Second Amendment: The Right to Bear Arms," *Houston Law Review* 7 (September 1969): 1–19; Sanford Levinson, "The Embarrassing Second Amendment," *Yale Law Journal* 99 (December 1989): 637–59.
86. Spitzer, *Politics of Gun Control,* 41.
87. Biskupic, "A Second (Amendment) Look at Bearing Arms," 33.
88. Witkin, "The Fight to Bear Arms," 30.
89. Andrew Kirby, "A Smoking Gun: Relations Between the State and Local State in the Case of Firearms Control," *Policy Studies Journal* 18 (Spring 1990): 739–54.
90. Quoted in Peter Applebome, "Paramilitary Groups Are Presenting Delicate Legal Choices for the States," *New York Times,* 10 May 1995.
91. Wolf v. Colorado, 338 U.S. 25 (1949).
92. Mapp v. Ohio, 367 U.S. 643 (1961).
93. United States v. Ross, 456 U.S. 798 (1982).
94. Harris v. United States, 390 U.S. 294 (1968).
95. Coolidge v. New Hampshire, 403 U.S. 433 (1971).
96. California v. Ciraolo, 476 U.S. 207 (1986).
97. Olmstead v. United States, 277 U.S. 438 (1928).
98. Katz v. United States, 389 U.S. 347 (1967).
99. See Title III of the Omnibus Crime Control and Safe Streets Act of 1968.
100. See Plasencia v. U.S., 921 F2d 1557 (1991).
101. California v. Greenwood, 486 U.S. 35 (1988).

102. See Weeks v. United States, 232 U.S. 383 (1914); Mapp v. Ohio, 367 U.S. 643 (1961).
103. See United States v. Peltier, 422 U.S. 531 (1975); United States v. Leon, 468 U.S. 897 (1984).
104. Arizona v. Evans, 115 S.Ct. 1185 (1995); Linda Greenhouse, "Justices Validate Seizure Based on Error on Warrant," *New York Times,* 2 March 1995.
105. General Accounting Office data reported in Kenneth J. Cooper and John F. Harris, "Admissible Evidence Expanded," *Des Moines Register,* 9 February 1995.
106. Paul G. Cassell, "How Many Criminals Has *Miranda* Set Free?" *Wall Street Journal,* 1 March 1995.
107. Joe Davidson, "Senators Weigh Plan, Backed by Hatch, to End 'Miranda,' Exclusionary Rules," *Wall Street Journal,* 8 March 1995.
108. Brown v. Mississippi, 297 U.S. 278 (1936).
109. Spano v. New York, 360 U.S. 315 (1959).
110. Miranda v. Arizona, 384 U.S. 436 (1966).
111. Nix v. Williams, 467 U.S. 431 (1984).
112. Arizona v. Fulminante, 113 L Ed 2d 302 (1991).
113. New York v. Quarles, 467 U.S. 649 (1984).
114. Cassell, "How Many Criminals Has *Miranda* Set Free?"
115. Davidson, "Senators Weigh Plan, Backed by Hatch."
116. Powell v. Alabama, 287 U.S. 45 (1932).
117. Gideon v. Wainwright, 372, U.S. 335 (1963). This decision explicitly overturned the earlier ruling in Betts v. Brady, 316 U.S. 455 (1942).
118. Argersinger v. Hamlin, 407 U.S. 25 (1972).
119. Duncan v. Louisiana, 391 U.S. 145 (1968).
120. See Williams v. Florida, 399 U.S. 78 (1970); Colgrove v. Battin, 413 U.S. 149 (1973).
121. Apodaca v. Oregon, 406 U.S. 404 (1972).
122. Pointer v. Texas, 380 U.S. 400 (1965).
123. See the excellent discussion of Coy v. Iowa, 487 U.S. 1012 (1988); Maryland v. Craig, 111 LEd 2d 666 (1990), in Ellen Alderman and Caroline Kennedy, *In Our Defense: the Bill of Rights in Action* (New York: Avon Books, 1991).
124. Furman v. Georgia, 408 U.S. 238 (1972).
125. Gregg v. Georgia, 428 U.S. 153 (1976).
126. See Stanford v. Kentucky, 492 U.S. 361 (1989) for executing sixteen-year-olds; Thompson v. Oklahoma, 487 U.S. 815 (1988) on not putting fifteen-year-olds to death. On not imposing the death penalty on the insane, see Ford v. Wainwright, 477 U.S. 399 (1986). On executing the mentally retarded, see Penry v. Lynaugh, 492 U.S. 302 (1989).
127. Griswold v. Connecticut, 381 U.S. 479 (1965).
128. Eisenstadt v. Baird, 405 U.S. 438 (1972).
129. Roe v. Wade, 410 U.S. 113 (1973).
130. Webster v. Reproductive Health Services, 492 U.S. 490 (1989); Hodgson v. Minnesota, 497 U.S. 417 (1990).
131. Planned Parenthood of Southeastern Pennsylvania v. Casey, 112 S. Ct. 2791 (1992).
132. Bowers v. Hardwick, 478 U.S. 186 (1986).
133. Cruzan v. Director, Missouri Department of Health, 497 U.S. 261 (1990).

Chapter 5, pp. 125–166

1. Susan Yoachum and Edward Epstein, "UC Scraps Affirmative Action/ Regents' Vote Gives Wilson Major Victory," *San Francisco Chronicle,* 21 July 1995.
2. Ibid.
3. Ibid.
4. Ibid.; Yumi Wilson and J. L. Pimsleur, "Protests at Vote to Repeal," *San Francisco Chronicle,* 21 July 1995.
5. Minor v. Happersett, 21 Wall 162 (1875).
6. Dred Scott v. Sandford, 19 Howard 393 (1857).
7. William Safire, *Safire's New Political Dictionary* (New York: Random House, 1993), 262.
8. The Slaughterhouse Cases, 68 (1 Wall) 36 (1873).
9. United States v. Cruikshank, 92 U.S. 542 (1876).
10. United States v. Reese, 12 U.S. 214 (1876).
11. *Congress A to Z* (Washington, D.C.: Congressional Quarterly, 1993), 31; Michael Barone, Grant Ujifusa, and Douglas Matthews, *The Almanac of American Politics 1976* (New York: Dutton, 1975), 198.
12. Safire, *Safire's New Political Dictionary,* 377–78.
13. Plessy v. Ferguson, 163 U.S. 537 (1896).
14. Safire, *Safire's New Political Dictionary,* 368.
15. Richard Kluger, *Simple Justice* (New York: Knopf, 1975), 111.
16. Walter LaFeber, *The Cambridge History of American Foreign Relations, Volume II: The American Search for Opportunity, 1865–1913* (New York: Cambridge University Press, 1993), 49.
17. *The Concise Columbia Encyclopedia* (New York: Columbia University Press, 1983), 498.
18. William M. Adler, *Land of Opportunity* (New York: Atlantic Monthly Press, 1995), 176–77.
19. Ibid., 177. The Supreme Court's decision is Moore v. Dempsey, 261 U.S. 86 (1923). See also Richard C. Cortner, *A Mob Intent on Death: The NAACP and the Arkansas Riot Cases* (Middletown, Conn.: Wesleyan University Press, 1988).
20. Guinn v. United States, 238 U.S. 347 (1915).
21. Buchanan v. Warley, 245 U.S. 60 (1917).
22. Missouri ex rel. Gaines v. Canada, 305 U.S. 337 (1938).
23. Smith v. Allwright, 321 U.S. 649 (1944).
24. Clark Clifford, *Counsel to the President: A Memoir* (New York: Anchor Books, 1991), 208–9.
25. Ibid., 210–11.
26. Jules Tygiel, *Baseball's Great Experiment* (New York: Oxford University Press, 1983), 37–43.
27. Ibid., 195–200.
28. Quoted in ibid., 280.
29. Sweatt v. Painter, 339 U.S. 629 (1950).
30. McLaurin v. Oklahoma State Regents, 339 U.S. 637 (1950).
31. Brown v. Board of Education, 347 U.S. 483 (1954).
32. Ibid. For an argument that the *Brown* decision was less important than is commonly thought, see Gerald N. Rosenberg, *The Hollow Hope: Can Courts Bring About Social Change?* (Chicago: University of Chicago Press, 1991).
33. Brown v. Board of Education, 347 U.S. 483 (1954).
34. Quoted in Earl Warren, *The Memoirs of Earl Warren* (Garden City, N.Y.: Doubleday, 1977), 291.
35. Brown v. Board of Education (Brown II), 349 U.S. 294 (1955).
36. See Numan V. Bartley, *The Rise of Massive Resistance* (Baton Rouge: Louisiana State University Press, 1969); Robbins L. Gates, *The Making of Massive Resistance* (Chapel Hill: University of North Carolina Press, 1964); Benjamin Muse, *Virginia's Massive Resistance* (Bloomington: Indiana University Press, 1961); Francis M. Wilhoit, *The Politics of Massive Resistance* (New York: Braziller, 1973).
37. See Taylor Branch, *Parting the Waters: America in the King Years, 1954–63* (New York: Simon & Schuster, 1988), 222–24.
38. Earl Black and Merle Black, *Politics and Society in the South* (Cambridge: Harvard University Press, 1987), 95.
39. Griffin v. County School Board of Prince Edward County, 377 U.S. 218 (1964).
40. Black and Black, *Politics and Society in the South,* 96.
41. See Green v. County School Board, 391 U.S. 430 (1968); Alexander v. Holmes County Board of Education, 396 U.S. 19 (1969).
42. See Arthur M. Schlesinger, Jr., *A Thousand Days: John F. Kennedy in the White House* (New York: Greenwich House, 1983), 940–49; Theodore C. Sorensen, *Kennedy* (New York: Harper & Row, 1965), 483–88.
43. See Stephen Lesher, *George Wallace: American Populist* (Reading, Mass.: Addison-Wesley, 1994), 174, 211–34.
44. Gayle v. Browder, 352 U.S. 903 (1956).
45. "Letter from Birmingham Jail," reprinted in Peverill Squire, James M. Lindsay, Cary R. Covington, and Eric R. A. N. Smith, *Dynamics of Democracy,* 2nd ed. (Madison, Wis.: Brown & Benchmark, 1997), 650.
46. Quoted in Branch, *Parting the Waters,* 271.

47. Ibid., 271–74.
48. Lerone Bennett, Jr., *Before the Mayflower* (Baltimore: Penguin, 1964), 322–23; Godfrey Hodgson, *America in Our Time* (New York: Vintage, 1976), 189–91; Safire, *Safire's New Political Dictionary*, 266–67.
49. C. Vann Woodward, *The Strange Career of Jim Crow*, 3d rev. ed. (New York: Oxford University Press, 1974), 184.
50. Quoted in *The Encyclopedic Dictionary of American Government*, 4th ed. (Guilford, Conn.: Dushkin, 1991), 47.
51. See, for example, Black and Black, *Politics and Society in the South*, 126–51.
52. Quoted in *Bartlett's Familiar Quotations*, 15th ed. (Boston: Little, Brown, 1980), 909.
53. See, e.g., Missouri v. Jenkins, 115 S. Ct. 2038 (1995); David Armor, *Forced Justice: School Desegregation and the Law* (New York: Oxford University Press, 1995).
54. See Steven A. Holmes, "For the Civil Rights Movement, A New Reason for Living," *New York Times*, 9 July 1995; Steven A. Holmes, "In a Southern City, Many Blacks Question the N.A.A.C.P.'s Role," *New York Times*, 9 January 1996.
55. See Malcolm X, *The Autobiography of Macolm X* (New York: Grove Press, 1965).
56. See Glenn C. Loury, *One by One from the Inside Out: Essays and Reviews on Race and Responsibility* (New York: Free Press, 1995); Thomas Sowell, *Race and Culture: A World View* (New York: Basic Books, 1994); Shelby Steele, *The Content of Our Character: A New Vision of Race in America* (New York: St. Martin's, 1990).
57. Steele, *The Content of Our Character*, 174.
58. Howard Fineman and Vern E. Smith, "An Angry 'Charmer,'" *Newsweek*, 30 October 1995, 33.
59. David Maraniss, "A March of Contradictions," *Washington Post National Weekly Edition*, 23–29 October 1995, 8.
60. See Charles McClain, ed., *Asian Indians, Filipinos, Other Asian Communities and the Law* (New York: Garland, 1994); Charles McClain, ed., *Chinese Immigrants and American Law* (New York: Garland, 1994); Charles McClain, ed., *Japanese Immigrants and American Law: The Alien Land Laws and Other Issues* (New York: Garland, 1994).
61. LaFeber, *Cambridge History of American Foreign Relations*, 51–52; Charles J. McClain, *In Search of Equality: The Chinese Struggle Against Discrimination in Nineteenth Century America* (Berkeley: University of California Press, 1994), chap. 6.
62. Page Smith, *Democracy on Trial: The Japanese American Evacuation and Relocation in World War II* (New York: Simon & Schuster, 1995), 48.
63. See Thomas G. Paterson, J. Garry Clifford, and Kenneth J. Hagan, *American Foreign Relations, A History: Since 1895*, 4th ed. (Lexington, Mass.: Heath, 1995), 62.
64. See Thomas A. Bailey, "California, Japan, and the Alien Land Legislation of 1913," *Pacific Historical Review* 1:1 (1932): 36–59; Paolo E. Coletta, " 'The Most Thankless Task': Bryan and the California Alien Land Legislation," *Pacific Historical Review* 36 (May 1967): 163–87; Herbert P. LePore, "Prelude to Prejudice: Hiram Johnson, Woodrow Wilson, and the California Land Law Controversy of 1913," *Southern California Quarterly* 61 (Spring 1979): 99–110.
65. Quoted in Paterson, Clifford, and Hagan, *American Foreign Relations*, 65.
66. Smith, *Democracy on Trial*, 49.
67. Dudley O. McGovney, "The Anti-Japanese Land Laws of California and Ten Other States," *California Law Review* 35 (March 1947): 7–60.
68. Takao Ozawa v. United States, 260 U.S. 178 (1922); see also Yuji Ichioka, "The Early Japanese Immigrant Quest for Citizenship: The Background of the 1922 Ozawa Case," *Amerasia Journal* 4:2 (1977): 1–22.
69. See Roger Daniels, Sandra C. Taylor, and Harry H. L. Kitano, eds., *Japanese Americans: From Relocation to Redress*, 2d ed. (Seattle: University of Washington Press, 1991); Charles McClain, ed., *The Mass Internment of Japanese Americans and the Quest for Legal Redress* (New York: Garland, 1994); Smith, *Democracy on Trial*, esp. chaps. 7–15.
70. Hirabayashi v. United States, 320 U.S. 81 (1943); Korematsu v. United States, 323 U.S. 214 (1944); Ex parte Endo, 323 U.S. 283 (1944).
71. See Roger Daniels, "Redress Achieved, 1983–1990," in Roger Daniels, Sandra C. Taylor, and Harry H. L. Kitano, eds., *Japanese Americans: From Relocation to Redress*, 2d ed. (Seattle: University of Washington Press, 1991).
72. Yick Wo v. Hopkins, 118 U.S. 356 (1886); see also McClain, *In Search of Equality*, chap. 4.
73. Lau v. Nichols, 414 U.S. 563 (1974).
74. Nanette Asimov, "Proposal to Alter Lowell Admissions," *San Francisco Chronicle*, 10 January 1996; "New Admissions Policy Offered for San Francisco's Top School," *New York Times*, 11 January 1996; Lawrence J. Siskind, "A Year Later in San Francisco, the Schools Are Still Segregated," *Wall Street Journal*, 12 July 1995.
75. Guadalupe San Miguel, Jr., "Mexican-American Organizations and the Changing Politics of School Desegregation in Texas, 1945–1980," *Social Science Quarterly* 63 (1982): 701–15.
76. Katzenbach v. Morgan, 384 U.S. 641 (1966).
77. Graham v. Richardson, 403 U.S. 365 (1971); Plyler v. Doe, 457 U.S. 202 (1982).
78. U.S. v. Brignoni-Ponce, 422 U.S. 873 (1975); INS v. Delgado, 466 U.S. 210 (1984); INS v. Lopez-Mendoza, 486 U.S. 1032 (1984).
79. Elk v. Wilkins, 112 U.S. 94 (1884).
80. Vine Deloria, Jr., and Clifford M. Lytle, *American Indians, American Justice* (Austin: University of Texas Press, 1983), 222–25.
81. United States v. Sioux Nation of Indians et al., 448 U.S. 371 (1980). See also Edward Lazarus, *Black Hills/White Justice: The Sioux Nation versus the United States, 1775 to the Present* (New York: HarperCollins, 1991).
82. California v. Cabazon Band of Mission Indians, 480 U.S. 202 (1987).
83. George Johnson, "Indians Take on the U.S. in a 90's Battle for Control," *New York Times*, 11 February 1996.
84. Saint Francis College v. Al-Khazraji, 481 U.S. 604 (1987).
85. Bradwell v. Illinois, 16 Wall. 130 (1873).
86. Muller v. Oregon, 208 U.S. 412 (1908); Radice v. New York, 264 U.S. 292 (1924).
87. Justice Joseph Bradley, quoted in Gerald Gunther, *Constitutional Law: Cases and Materials* (Mineola, N.Y.: Foundation Press, 1975), 766.
88. Declaration of Sentiments, reprinted in Pat Andrews, ed., *Voices of Diversity: Perspectives on American Political Ideals and Institutions* (Guilford, Conn.: Dushkin, 1995), 46–47.
89. Nancy E. McGlen and Karen O'Connor, *Women's Rights: The Struggle for Equality in the Nineteenth and Twentieth Centuries* (New York: Praeger, 1983), 272–74.
90. V. O. Key, Jr., *Politics, Parties, and Pressure Groups*, 5th ed. (New York: Crowell, 1964), 614–15.
91. See Jill Zuckman, "As Family Leave Is Enacted, Some See End to Logjam," *Congressional Quarterly Weekly Report*, 6 February 1993, 267–69.
92. Holly Idelson, "A Tougher Domestic Violence Law," *Congressional Quarterly Weekly Report*, 25 June 1995, 1714.
93. Nina Bernstein, "Civil Rights Lawsuit in a Rape Case Challenges Integrity of a Campus," *New York Times*, 11 February 1996.
94. Reed v. Reed, 404 U.S. 71 (1971).
95. Ibid., 76.
96. Pittsburgh Press v. Pittsburgh Commission on Human Relations, 413 U.S. 376 (1973).
97. Phillips v. Martin-Marietta, 400 U.S. 542 (1971); Cleveland Board of Education v. LaFleur, 413 U.S. 632 (1974); Nashville Gas v. Satty, 434 U.S. 136 (1976).
98. Los Angeles Department of Water and Power v. Manhart, 435 U.S. 702 (1978); Arizona Governing Committee v. Norris, 463 U.S. 1073 (1983).
99. Automobile Workers v. Johnson Controls, 499 U.S. 187 (1991). See also Sally J. Kenney, *For Whose Protection? Reproductive Hazards and Exclusionary Policies in the United States and Britain* (Ann Arbor: University of Michigan Press, 1992).
100. United States v. Virginia et al., 94–1941 (1996).

101. Craig v. Boren, 429 U.S. 190 (1976).
102. Orr v. Orr, 440 U.S. 268 (1979); Mississippi University for Women v. Hogan, 458 U.S. 718 (1982).
103. Rostker v. Goldberg, 453 U.S. 57 (1981).
104. Michael M. v. Superior Court of Sonoma County, 450 U.S. 464 (1981).
105. Kahn v. Shevin, 416 U.S. 351 (1974); Califano v. Webster, 430 U.S. 313 (1977); Heckler v. Mathews, 465 U.S. 728 (1984).
106. Johnson v. Transportation Agency, Santa Clara County, 480 U.S. 616 (1987).
107. Nina Bernstein, "Equal Opportunity Recedes for Most Female Lawyers," *New York Times,* 8 January 1996.
108. Ibid.
109. Ibid.
110. Natalie Angier, "Why Science Loses Women in the Ranks," *New York Times,* 14 May 1995.
111. See Stephanie N. Mehta, "Number of Woman-Owned Businesses Surged 43% in 5 Years Through 1992," *Wall Street Journal,* 29 January 1996; Gail Sheehy, "Angry Men, Resilient Women," *New York Times,* 19 June 1995.
112. "A Closer Look: Women's Progress as Lawyers," *New York Times,* 8 January 1996.
113. Angier, "Why Science Loses Women."
114. Saundra Torry, "Equality Is Elusive at Law Schools," *Washington Post National Weekly Edition,* 26 February–3 March 1996, 35.
115. See Steven A. Holmes, "Programs Based on Race and Sex Are Challenged," *New York Times,* 16 March 1995; Peter T. Kilborn, "For Many in Workforce, 'Glass Ceiling' Still Exists," *New York Times,* 16 March 1995; Peter T. Kilborn, "White Males and Management," *New York Times,* 17 March 1995; Deborah Stead, "Breaking the Glass Ceiling with the Power of Words," *New York Times,* 7 January 1996.
116. Bernstein, "Equal Opportunity Recedes."
117. For a more pessimistic assessment, see Joann S. Lublin, "Women at Top Still Are Distant from CEO Jobs," *Wall Street Journal,* 28 February 1996.
118. Catharine A. MacKinnon, *Only Words* (Cambridge: Harvard University Press, 1993), 22. See also Andrea Dworkin and Catharine A. MacKinnon, *Pornography and Civil Rights: A New Day for Women's Equality* (Minneapolis: Organizing Against Pornography, 1988).
119. Nadine Strossen, *Defending Pornography: Free Speech, Sex, and the Fight for Women's Rights* (New York: Scribner, 1995).
120. See, for example, Christina Hoff Sommers, *Who Stole Feminism: How Women Have Betrayed Women* (New York: Simon & Schuster, 1994); Daphne Patai and Noretta Koertge, *Professing Feminism: Cautionary Tales from the Strange World of Women's Studies* (New York: Basic Books, 1994); Katie Roiphe, *Sex, Fear, and Feminism on Campus* (Boston: Little, Brown, 1993).
121. See, for example, Anita K. Blair, "Separate But Equal," *New York Times,* 20 November 1995; Laura Ingraham, "Enter, Women," *New York Times,* 19 April 1995; Megan Rosenfeld, "Feminist Fatales: This Conservative Women's Group Has Traditionalists Seething," *Washington Post,* 30 November 1995.
122. See Robert A. Katzmann, *Institutional Disability* (Washington, D.C.: Brookings Institution, 1986).
123. Janet Reno and Dick Thornburgh, "ADA—Not a Disabling Mandate," *Wall Street Journal,* 26 July 1995.
124. Ibid.
125. James Bovard, "Get a Whiff of This!" *Wall Street Journal,* 27 December 1995.
126. Massachusetts Board of Retirement v. Muriga, 427 U.S. 307 (1976); Vance v. Bradley, 440 U.S. 93 (1979).
127. Carroll J. Doherty, "Congress Reinforces Gay Ban as Court Assaults Continue," *Congressional Quarterly Weekly Report,* 20 November 1993, 3210–11.
128. Quoted in Deb Price, "Gays: Not Special Rights, Just Equal Rights," *Des Moines Register,* 8 November 1995.
129. Bowers v. Hardwick, 478 U.S. 186 (1986).
130. See Dennis Farney, "Gay Rights Confront Determined Resistance from Some Moderates," *Wall Street Journal,* 7 October 1994.
131. Carroll J. Doherty, "How Initiatives Fared," *Congressional Quarterly Weekly Report,* 7 November 1992, 3595; Thomas Galvin, "States Use Ballot Propositions to Take the Initiative," *Congressional Quarterly Weekly Report,* 31 October 1992, 3506.
132. Ibid.; John Schrag, "In Oregon, the Debate That Will Not Die," *Washington Post National Weekly Edition,* 8–14 January 1996, 20.
133. Romer v. Evans, 64 LW 4353.
134. See David W. Dunlap, "Fearing a Toehold for Gay Marriages, Conservatives Rush to Bar the Door," *New York Times,* 6 March 1996; Melanie Kirkpatrick, "Gay Marriage: Who Should Decide?" *Wall Street Journal,* 13 March 1996.
135. Craig v. Boren, 429 U.S. 190 (1976); Mississippi University for Women v. Hogan, 458 U.S. 718 (1982).
136. Craig v. Boren, 429 U.S. 197 (1976).
137. See, for example, Peter Passell, "Economic Scene," *New York Times,* 11 January 1996; "Short Guys Finish Last," *Economist,* 23 December 1995–5 January 1996, 19–22.
138. Regents of the University of California v. Bakke, 438 U.S. 265 (1978).
139. See United Steelworkers of America v. Weber, 443 U.S. 193 (1979); Sheet Metal Workers v. EEOC, 478 U.S. 421 (1986); Local Number 93, International Association of Firefighters, AFL-CIO, C.L.C. v. City of Cleveland, 478 U.S. 501 (1986).
140. Johnson v. Transportation Agency, Santa Clara County, 480 U.S. 616 (1987).
141. City of Richmond v. J. A. Croson Co., 488 U.S. 469 (1989).
142. Adarand Constructors v. Pena, 115 S. CT. 2097 (1995). See Holly Idelson, "Ruling Rocks Foundation of Affirmative Action," *Congressional Quarterly Weekly Report,* 17 June 1995, 1743–45.
143. Ann Devroy and Kevin Merida, "Drawing the Line on Affirmative Action," *Washington Post National Weekly Edition,* 3–9 July 1995.
144. Quoted in Steven A. Holmes, "White House to Suspend a Program for Minorities," *New York Times,* 8 March 1996.
145. See an excerpt of the list in "Affirmative Action in Action," *Wall Street Journal,* 27 February 1995; Holly Idelson, "A 30-Year Experiment," *Congressional Quarterly Weekly Report,* 3 June 1995, 1579.
146. Idelson, "A 30-Year Experiment," 1579.
147. Quoted in Holmes, "White House to Suspend a Program for Minorities."
148. Udayan Gupta, "Minority Firms Fear More Jobs Will Vanish as Mandates End," *Wall Street Journal,* 12 April 1995.
149. Paul M. Barrett, "Minority Contractors Find Gains Are Eroded by Courtroom Attacks," *Wall Street Journal,* 7 December 1994; Gupta, "Minority Firms Fear More Jobs Will Vanish."
150. Paul M. Barrett, "Federal Preferences for Minority Firms Illustrate Affirmative-Action Dispute," *Wall Street Journal,* 14 March 1995.
151. See Paul M. Barrett and Michael K. Frisby, " 'Place, Not Race' Could Be Next Catch Phrase in Government's Affirmative-Action Programs," *Wall Street Journal,* 19 October 1995.
152. Pamela Burdman, "UC Officials Roll Out Plans on Preferences," *San Francisco Chronicle,* 14 December 1995.

Chapter 6, pp. 169–200

1. *Contract With America: The Bold Plan by Rep. Newt Gingrich, Rep. Dick Armey and the House Republicans to Change the Nation,* ed. Ed Gillespie and Bob Schellhas (New York: Random House, 1994).
2. Quoted in Cici Connolly, "GOP Accentuates the Positive; Hopefuls to Sign Compact," *Congressional Quarterly Weekly Report,* 24 September 1994, 2711.
3. The 104th Congress: A Congressional Quarterly Reader, ed. Roger H. Davidson and Walter J. Oleszek (Washington, D.C.: CQ Press, 1995), 10.
4. Maureen Dowd, "Americans Like GOP Agenda But Split on How to Reach Goals," *New York Times,* 15 December 1994.
5. Times Mirror Center for the People & the Press, "Public Expects GOP Miracles," 8 December 1994, 30.
6. Stephen Earl Bennett and Linda L. M. Bennett, "Out of Sight, Out of Mind: Americans' Knowledge of Party Control of the House of Representatives, 1960–1984," *Political Research Quarterly* 46 (March 1993): 67–80;

Norman R. Luttbeg and Michael M. Gant, "The Failure of Liberal-Conservative Ideology as a Cognitive Structure," *Public Opinion Quarterly* 49 (Spring 1985): 80–93.
7. See Richard Morin, "Foreign Aid: Mired in Misunderstanding," *Washington Post National Weekly Edition*, 20–26 March 1995, 37.
8. Richard Morin, "What Informed Opinion?" *Washington Post National Weekly Edition*, 10–16 April 1995, 36.
9. Robert S. Erikson, Norman R. Luttbeg, and Kent L. Tedin, *American Public Opinion*, 4th ed. (New York: Macmillan, 1991), 1–2.
10. The Pew Research Center for the People & the Press, "A Dull Campaign, Clinton Will Win Say More Than 70% of Voters," 2 August 1996, 31.
11. Giuseppe DiPalma and Herbert McClosky, "Personality and Conformity: The Learning of Political Attitudes," *American Political Science Review* 70 (December 1970): 1054–73.
12. Michael S. Delli Carpini and Scott Keeter, "Stability and Change in the U.S. Public's Knowledge of Politics," *Public Opinion Quarterly* 55 (Winter 1991): 583–612.
13. Maxwell E. McCombs and L. E. Mullins, "Consequences of Education: Media Exposure, Political Interest and Information-Seeking Orientations," *Mass Communication Review* 1 (August 1973): 27–31; Eric R. A. N. Smith, *The Unchanging American Voter* (Berkeley: University of California Press, 1989), 180–86.
14. Ralph Frammolino, "U.S. Adults Lagging in Literacy, Study Finds," *Los Angeles Times*, 9 September 1993.
15. David B. Magleby, *Direct Legislation: Voting on Ballot Propositions in the United States* (Baltimore: Johns Hopkins University Press, 1984).
16. This is the percent scoring 350 or higher on the Prose Literacy Scale. The survey excluded non-English speakers. U.S. National Center for Education Statistics, Department of Education, *Digest of Educational Statistics, 1992*, 399, Table 378.
17. Steven J. Rosenstone and John Mark Hansen, *Mobilization, Participation, and Democracy in America* (New York: Macmillan, 1993), 164–65.
18. Robert C. Luskin, "Explaining Political Sophistication," *Political Behavior* 12 (December 1990): 331–61.
19. See Smith, *The Unchanging American Voter*, 178–80, 196–210.
20. See Paul R. Abramson, *Political Attitudes in America* (San Francisco: Freeman, 1983).
21. Data from the *American National Election Studies* (Ann Arbor, Mich.: Inter-University Consortium for School and Political Research, 1993).
22. The Pew Research Center for the People & the Press, "TV Viewership Declines," 13 May 1996, p. 64.
23. Robert T. Bower, *The Changing Television Audience in America* (New York: Columbia University Press, 1985); Smith, *The Unchanging American Voter*, 180–86.
24. Thomas E. Patterson, *Out of Order* (New York: Vintage, 1993).
25. W. Russell Neuman, Marion R. Just, and Ann N. Crigler, *Common Knowledge: News and the Construction of Political Meaning* (Chicago: University of Chicago Press, 1992), 78–95.
26. Larry M. Bartels, "Message Received: The Political Impact of Media Exposure," *American Political Science Review* 87 (June 1993): 267–85; Xinshu Zhao and Steven H. Chafee, "Campaign Advertisements versus Television News as Sources of Political Issue Information," *Public Opinion Quarterly* 59 (Spring 1995): 41–65.
27. V. O. Key, Jr., *Public Opinion and American Democracy* (New York: Knopf, 1961), 265, 282–85.
28. R. Douglas Arnold, *The Logic of Congressional Action* (New Haven: Yale University Press, 1990), 64–68.
29. Stanley Feldman, "Structure and Consistency in Public Opinion: The Role of Core Beliefs and Values," *American Journal of Political Science* 32 (May 1988): 416–40.
30. John R. Zaller, *The Nature and Origins of Mass Opinion* (New York: Cambridge University Press, 1992).
31. Richard Dawson, Kenneth Prewit, and Karen Dawson, *Political Socialization*, 2d ed. (Boston: Little-Brown, 1977).
32. Christine B. Williams and Daniel R. Minns, "Agent Credibility and Receptivity Influences in Children's Political Learning," *Political Behavior* 8 (1986): 175–200.
33. Sandra K. Schwartz, "Preschoolers and Politics," in *New Directions in Political Socialization*, ed. David C. Schwartz and Sandra K. Schwartz (New York: Free Press, 1975).
34. Paul Allen Beck, "The Role of Agents in Political Socialization," in *Handbook of Political Socialization*, ed. Stanley A. Renshon (New York: Free Press, 1977).
35. Fred I. Greenstein, *Children and Politics* (New Haven: Yale University Press, 1965), 55–84; Robert D. Hess and Judith V. Torney, *The Development of Political Attitudes in Children* (Chicago: Aldine, 1967).
36. M. Kent Jennings and Richard G. Niemi, *The Political Character of Adolescence: The Influence of Families and Schools* (Princeton, N.J.: Princeton University Press, 1974), 39.
37. M. Kent Jennings and Richard G. Niemi, *Generations and Politics: A Panel Study of Young Adults and their Parents* (Princeton, N.J.: Princeton University Press, 1981), 91.
38. Donald Searing, Gerald Wright, and George Rabinowitz, "The Primacy Principle: Attitude Change and Political Socialization," *British Journal of Political Science* 6 (March 1976): 83–113.
39. Richard Merelman, "Democratic Politics and the Culture of American Education," *American Political Science Review* 74 (June 1980): 319–33.
40. Theodore M. Newcomb, *Personality and Social Change* (New York: Holt, Rinehart & Winston, 1943).
41. George Comstock, "Social and Cultural Impact of the Mass Media," in *What's News: The Media in American Society*, ed. Elie Abel (San Francisco: Institute for Contemporary Studies, 1981).
42. Doris A. Graber, *Mass Media and American Politics*, 3d ed. (Washington, D.C.: CQ Press, 1989), 167–76.
43. Rick DuBrow, "Latino Roles Still 'Mired in Stereotypes,'" *Los Angeles Times*, 1 October 1994.
44. Richard C. Vincent, "Clio's Consciousness Raised? Portrayal of Women in Rock Videos, Reexamined," *Journalism Quarterly* 66 (Spring 1989): 155–60.
45. Linda Heath and John Petraitis, "Television Viewing and Fear of Crime: Where Is the Mean World?" *Basic and Applied Social Psychology* 8 (March/June 1987): 97–123.
46. William Mayer, *The Changing American Mind: How and Why American Public Opinion Changed Between 1960 and 1988* (Ann Arbor: University of Michigan Press, 1992), 165.
47. Theodore M. Newcomb, "Persistence and Regression of Changed Attitudes: Long-Range Studies," *Journal of Social Issues* 19 (October 1963): 3–14; see also Duane F. Alwin, Ronald Cohen, and Theodore Newcomb, *Political Attitudes over the Life Span: The Bennington Women After Fifty Years* (Madison: University of Wisconsin Press, 1991).
48. See Herbert McClosky, "Consensus and Ideology in American Politics," *American Political Science Review* (June 1964): 361–82.
49. Kenneth R. Hoover, *Ideology and Political Life* (Monterey, Calif.: Brooks/Cole, 1987), 80–106.
50. This discussion of democracy and capitalism follows that of Herbert McClosky and John Zaller, *The American Ethos: Public Attitudes Toward Capitalism and Democracy* (Cambridge: Harvard University Press, 1984). For an analysis of ideologies focused on the values of equality and freedom, see Kenneth M. Dolbeare and Linda J. Medcalf, *American Ideologies Today* (New York: Random House, 1988).
51. Hoover, *Ideology and Political Life*, 9–28.
52. Ibid., 60–72.
53. Bill Boyarsky, *Ronald Reagan: His Life and Rise to the Presidency* (New York: Random House, 1981), 79; see also James A. Morone, *The Democratic Wish* (New York: Basic Books, 1991), chap. 7.
54. See, for example, Richard Morin, "Medicare Changes Get a Jaundiced Look," *Washington Post National Weekly Edition*, 10–16 July 1995, 37.
55. Jack Citrin, Beth Reingold, Evelyn Walters, and Donald P. Green, "The 'Official English' Movement and the Symbolic Politics of Language in the

United States," *Western Political Quarterly* 43 (September 1990): 535–59; James Crawford, *Hold Your Tongue: Bilingualism and the Politics of "English Only"* (Reading, Mass.: Addison Wesley, 1992).
56. See Joseph R. Gusfield, *Symbolic Crusade: Status Politics and the American Temperance Movement* (Urbana: University of Illinois Press, 1963).
57. Mary Lou Kendrigan, *Gender Differences: Their Impact on Public Policy* (Westport, Conn.: Greenwood, 1991).
58. See "What Women Think about the Feminist Label," *The Public Perspective* 3 (November/December 1991): 92–93.
59. Ethel Klein, *Gender Politics* (Cambridge: Harvard University Press, 1984).
60. Philip E. Converse, "The Nature of Belief Systems in Mass Publics," in *Ideology and Discontent*, ed. David Apter (New York: Free Press, 1964), 211–12.
61. Luttbeg and Gant, "The Failure of Liberal/Conservative Ideology as a Cognitive Structure," 85.
62. Smith, *The Unchanging American Voter*, 171–72.
63. Ibid., 105.
64. Stephen Bennett, "Consistency among the Public's Social Welfare Policy Attitudes," *American Journal of Political Science* 17 (August 1973): 544–70; Norman H. Nie with Kristi Andersen, "Mass Belief Systems Revisited: Political Change and Attitude Structure," *Journal of Politics* 36 (August 1974): 541–91; Gerald Pomper, "From Confusion to Clarity: Issues and American Voters: 1956–1968," *American Political Science Review* 66 (June 1972): 415–28.
65. Thomas Ferguson and Joel Rogers, *Right Turn: The Decline of the Democrats and the Future of American Politics* (New York: Hill and Wang, 1986), 12. For a similar description, see Lloyd A. Free and Hadley Cantril, *The Political Beliefs of Americans: A Study of Public Opinion* (New Brunswick, N.J.: Rutgers University Press, 1967), 37.
66. "Portrait of a Skeptical Public," *Business Week*, 20 November 1995, 138.
67. These data are not shown. See Tom W. Smith, "That Which We Call Welfare by Any Other Name Would Smell Sweeter: An Analysis of the Impact of Question Wording on Response Patterns," *Public Opinion Quarterly* 51 (Spring 1987): 75–83. See also Stanley Feldman and John Zaller, "The Political Culture of Ambivalence: Ideological Responses to the Welfare State," *American Journal of Political Science* 36 (February 1992): 268–307.
68. On spending preferences, see Theodore J. Eismeier, "Public Preferences about Government Spending: Partisan, Social, and Attitudinal Sources of Policy Differences," *Political Behavior* 4 (1982): 133–45; Arthur Sanders, "Rationality, Self-Interest, and Public Attitudes on Public Spending," *Social Science Quarterly* 69 (Summer 1988): 311–34.
69. Richard M. Scammon and Ben J. Wattenberg, *The Real Majority* (New York: Coward, McCann & Geoghegan, 1970), 35–44.
70. Paul M. Sniderman, Richard A. Brody, and Philip E. Tetlock, *Reasoning and Choice: Explorations in Political Psychology* (New York: Cambridge University Press, 1991), chap. 7; Samuel A. Stouffer, *Communism, Conformity and Civil Liberties: A Cross-Section of the Nation Speaks Its Mind* (Garden City, N.Y.: Doubleday, 1955); see also John L. Sullivan, James Piereson, and George E. Marcus, *Political Tolerance and American Democracy* (Chicago: University of Chicago Press, 1982).
71. Paul R. Abramson, *Political Attitudes in America: Formation and Change* (San Francisco: Freeman, 1983), 241–59; see also Howard Schuman, Charlotte Steeh, and Lawrence Bobo, *Racial Attitudes in America: Trends and Interpretations* (Cambridge: Harvard University Press, 1985), 163–92; Paul M. Sniderman, Richard A. Brody, and Philip E. Tetlock, *Reasoning and Choice: Explorations in Political Psychology* (New York: Cambridge University Press, 1991), 120–39; John L. Sullivan, James Piereson, and George F. Marcus, *Political Tolerance and American Democracy* (Chicago: University of Chicago Press, 1982).
72. Thomas Byrne Edsall with Mary D. Edsall, *Chain Reaction: The Impact of Race, Rights, and Taxes on American Politics* (New York: Norton, 1991).
73. David W. Moore, "Americans Today Are Dubious about Affirmative Action," *Gallup Poll Monthly*, no. 354, March 1995, 37.
74. Elizabeth Adell Cook, Ted G. Jelen, and Clyde Wilcox, *Between Two Absolutes: Public Opinion and the Politics of Abortion* (Boulder, Colo.: Westview, 1992); Barbara Hinkson Craig and David M. O'Brien, *Abortion and American Politics* (Chatham, N.J.: Chatham House, 1993).
75. Warren E. Miller and M. Kent Jennings, *Parties in Transition* (New York: Sage, 1986); Benjamin I. Page, Robert Y. Shapiro, Paul W. Gronke, and Robert M. Rosenberg, "Constituency, Party, and Representation in Congress," *Public Opinion Quarterly* 48 (Winter 1984): 741–56; Eric R. A. N. Smith, Richard Herrera, and Cheryl L. Herrera, "The Measurement Characteristics of Congressional Roll-Call Indexes," *Legislative Studies Quarterly* 15 (May 1990): 283–95.
76. See *Gallup Report*, no. 281, February 1989.
77. Benjamin I. Page and Robert Y. Shapiro, *The Rational Public* (Chicago: University of Chicago Press, 1992), 45.
78. Larry M. Bartels, "Constituency Opinion and Congressional Policy Making: The Reagan Defense Buildup," *American Political Science Review* 85 (June 1991): 457–74. See also Arthur Sanders, *Victory* (Armonk, N.Y.: Sharpe, 1992), 48–53.
79. Ronald Brownstein, "Americans Less Willing to Rely on Sanctions," *Los Angeles Times*, 14 January 1991. See also John Mueller, *Policy and Opinion in the Gulf War* (Chicago: University of Chicago Press, 1994), 34–36.
80. "Americans Back Bush Decision Overwhelmingly," *Los Angeles Times*, 19 January 1991. See also Mueller, *Policy and Opinion in the Gulf War*, chap. 4.
81. See Tom W. Smith, "Liberal and Conservative Trends in the United States Since World War II," *Public Opinion Quarterly* 54 (Winter 1990): 479–507, which is the source for the facts in this and the next two paragraphs.
82. Schuman, Steeh, and Bobo, *Racial Attitudes in America*, esp. chap. 3.
83. Jennifer Baggette, Robert Y. Shapiro, and Lawrence R. Jacobs, "The Polls: Social Security: An Update," *Public Opinion Quarterly* 59 (Fall 1995): 420–42.
84. Mayer, *The Changing American Mind*, 111–34.
85. Ibid., 19–22; Mark Warr, "The Polls: Public Opinion on Crime and Punishment," *Public Opinion Quarterly* 59 (Summer 1995): 296–310.
86. Mary Lou Kendrigan, "Progressive Democrats and Support for Women's Issues," in *The Democrats Must Lead*, ed. James MacGregor Burns, William Crotty, Lois Lovelace Duke, and Lawrence D. Longley (Boulder, Colo.: Westview, 1992); Klein, *Gender Politics*, esp. 32–46.
87. Taylor Branch, *Parting the Waters: America in the King Years, 1954–63* (New York: Simon & Schuster, 1988); Dennis Chong, *Collective Action and the Civil Rights Movement* (Chicago: University of Chicago Press, 1991).
88. Alexander Hamilton, James Madison, and John Jay, *The Federalist Papers*, ed. Garry Wills (New York: Bantam Books 1982), nos. 63 and 71.

Chapter 7, pp. 201–230

1. Raymond E. Wolfinger and Steven Rosenstone, *Who Votes?* (New Haven: Yale University Press, 1980), 102.
2. Steven J. Rosenstone and John Mark Hansen, *Mobilization, Participation, and Democracy in America* (New York: Macmillan, 1993), 130–31.
3. Ibid., 136–41.
4. Walter Dean Burnham, "Theory and Voting Research: Some Reflections on Converse's 'Change in the American Electorate,'" *American Political Science Review* 68 (September 1974): 1002–23.
5. Angus Campbell, Philip E. Converse, Warren E. Miller, and Donald E. Stokes, *The American Voter* (Chicago: University of Chicago Press, 1960), 483–89.

6. Paul R. Abramson, John H. Aldrich, and David W. Rohde, *Change and Continuity in the 1992 Elections* (Washington, D.C.: CQ Press, 1994), 109.
7. See Paul R. Abramson, *Political Attitudes in America* (San Francisco: Freeman, 1983).
8. Arthur H. Miller et al., "Group Consciousness and Participation," *American Journal of Political Science* 25 (August 1981): 494–511; Richard D. Shingles, "Black Consciousness and Political Participation: The Missing Link," *American Political Science Review* 75 (March 1981): 76–91.
9. Eric R. A. N. Smith, *The Unchanging American Voter* (Berkeley: University of California Press, 1989), chap. 4.
10. M. Margaret Conway, *Political Participation in the United States,* 2d ed. (Washington, D.C.: CQ Press, 1991), 49–50. The 1994 data are from the University of Michigan's 1994 American National Election Study.
11. Jack Citrin, "The Alienated Voter," *Taxing and Spending* (October 1978): 1–7; Rosenstone and Hansen, *Mobilization, Participation, and Democracy,* 147–50; Stephen D. Shaffer, "A Multivariate Explanation of Decreasing Turnout in Presidential Elections, 1960–1976," *American Journal of Political Science* 25 (February 1981): 68–95.
12. David Glass, Peverill Squire, and Raymond Wolfinger, "Voter Turnout: An International Comparison," *Public Opinion* 6 (December/January 1984): 49–55.
13. Sidney Verba and Norman H. Nie, *Participation in America* (New York: Harper & Row, 1972), chap. 20.
14. Wolfinger and Rosenstone, *Who Votes?,* 77–78.
15. V. O. Key, Jr., *Southern Politics* (New York: Random House, 1949).
16. Michael Ross, "Landmark Voter Bill OKd; GOP Filibuster Fails," *Los Angeles Times,* 12 May 1993.
17. See Richard Sammon, "Deal May Speed Up 'Motor Voter,'" *Congressional Quarterly Weekly Report,* 1 May 1993, 1080; Richard Sammon, "House OKs 'Motor Voter' for Final Senate Vote," *Congressional Quarterly Weekly Report,* 8 May 1993, 1144; Richard Sammon, "Senate Kills Filibuster Threat, Clears 'Motor Voter' Bill," *Congressional Quarterly Weekly Report,* 15 May 1993, 1221; David G. Savage, "High Court Backs Law to Spur Voter Registration," *Los Angeles Times,* 23 January 1996.
18. John Harwood, "In a Surprise for Everyone, Motor-Voter Law Is Providing a Boost for GOP, Not Democrats," *Wall Street Journal,* 11 June 1996.
19. Barbara Vobejda, "Just Under Half of Possible Voters Went to the Polls," *Washington Post,* 7 November 1996; Stephen Knack, "Does 'Motor Voter' Work? Evidence from State-Level Data," *Journal of Politics* 57 (August 1995): 796–811; Staci L. Rhine, "Registration Reform and Turnout Change in the American States," *American Politics Quarterly* 24 (October 1994): 409–26.
20. Rosenstone and Hansen, *Mobilization, Participation, and Democracy,* chap. 6.
21. Timothy Egan, "Oregon's Mail-in Senate Vote Buoys Clinton and Democrats," *New York Times,* 1 February 1996.
22. See, for example, Brad Cain, "U.S. Senate Primary in Oregon a Test of Mail Voting," *Seattle Times,* 8 October 1995.
23. Richard A. Brody, "The Puzzle of Political Participation in America," *The New American Political System,* ed. Anthony King (Washington, D.C.: American Enterprise Institute, 1978), 287–334.
24. See Walter Dean Burnham, "The Changing Shape of the American Political Universe," *American Political Science Review* 59 (March 1965): 7–28; Walter D. Burnham, *Critical Elections and the Mainsprings of American Politics* (New York: Norton, 1970); Burnham, "Theory and Voting Research," 1002–23.
25. See Philip E. Converse, "Change in the American Electorate," in *The Human Meaning of Social Change,* ed. Angus Campbell and Philip E. Converse (New York: Russell Sage Foundation, 1972); Philip E. Converse, "Comment on Burnham's 'Theory and Voting Research,'" *American Political Science Review* 68 (September 1974): 1024–27; Jerrold G. Rusk, "Comment: The American Electoral Universe: Speculation and Evidence," *American Political Science Review* 68 (September 1974): 1028–49.
26. Richard Hofstadter, *The Age of Reform* (New York: Vintage Books, 1955).
27. Frances Fox Piven and Richard A. Cloward, *Why Americans Don't Vote* (New York: Pantheon, 1988), chap. 3.
28. Ibid., chap. 2; Paul Kleppner, *Who Voted? The Dynamics of Electoral Turnout* (New York: Praeger, 1982); Burnham, "Theory and Voting Research," 1002–23.
29. Piven and Cloward, *Why Americans Don't Vote,* chap. 3; Morgan J. Kousser, *The Shaping of Southern Politics: Suffrage Restrictions and the Establishment of the One-Party South* (New Haven: Yale University Press, 1974); C. Vann Woodward, *Origins of the New South: 1877–1913* (Baton Rouge: Louisiana State University Press, 1951).
30. Widespread scientific survey research did not begin until the mid-1930s. George Gallup conduced the best-known early work. See George H. Gallup, *The Gallup Poll: Public Opinion 1935–1971* (New York: Random House, 1972).
31. Ruy A. Teixeira, *The Disappearing American Voter* (Washington, D.C.: Brookings Institution, 1992).
32. Rosenstone and Hansen, *Mobilization, Participation, and Democracy,* chap. 7.
33. Wolfinger and Rosenstone, *Who Votes?,* chap. 4.
34. Stephen Earl Bennett and David Resnick, "The Implications of Nonvoting for Democracy in the United States," *American Journal of Political Science* 34 (August 1990): 771–802; Glenn Mitchell II and Christopher Wlezien, "The Impact of Legal Constraints on Voter Registration, Turnout, and the Composition of the American Electorate," *Political Behavior* 17 (June 1995): 179–202.
35. Benjamin Radcliff, "Turnout and the Democratic Vote," *American Politics Quarterly* 22 (July 1994): 277–96.
36. On European turnout, see Glass, Squire, and Wolfinger, "Voter Turnout," 49–55.
37. See Steven F. Lawson, *In Pursuit of Power: Southern Blacks and Electoral Politics, 1965–1982* (New York: Columbia University Press, 1982).
38. Rosenstone and Hansen, *Mobilization, Participation, and Democracy,* chaps. 5–6.
39. Verba and Nie, *Participation in America,* chap. 4.
40. Jerrold Rusk, "Political Participation in America: A Review Essay," *American Political Science Review* 70 (June 1976): 583–91.
41. Sidney Verba, Kay Lehman Schlozman, and Henry E. Brady, *Voice and Equality: Civic Voluntarism in American Politics* (Cambridge: Harvard University Press, 1995), 51–52.
42. Rosenstone and Hansen, *Mobilization, Participation, and Democracy,* 45.
43. Robert D. Hess and Judith V. Torney, *The Development of Political Attitudes in Children* (Chicago: Aldine, 1967), 96.
44. Quoted in Dan Balz, "A Little Too Social for Suburbia," *Washington Post National Weekly Edition,* 27 May–2 June 1996, 13; see also Bruce E. Keith et al., *The Myth of the Independent Voter* (Berkeley: University of California Press, 1992), chap. 4.
45. See Angus Campbell et al., *The American Voter,* chap. 3; Abramson, *Political Attitudes,* chap. 5.
46. Smith, *The Unchanging American Voter,* chap. 3; John R. Zaller, *The Nature and Origins of Mass Opinion* (New York: Cambridge University Press, 1992).
47. See Sara Fritz and John Broder, "$700,000 Lawsuit Accuses Clinton of Sexual Harassment," *Los Angeles* Times, 7 May 1994; Stephen Labaton, "Ex-Arkansas State Employee Files Suit Accusing Clinton of a Sexual Advance," *New York Times,* 7 May 1994.
48. *The Year in Figures* (Washington, D.C.: Times Mirror Center for the People & the Press, 1995), 8.
49. Gregory B. Markus and Philip E. Converse, "A Dynamic Simultaneous Equation Model of Electoral Choice," *American Political Science Review* 73 (December 1979): 1055–70.
50. "A Closer Look at the Voters," *Washington Post,* 6 November 1996.

51. Susan E. Howell, "Racism, Cynicism, Economics, and David Duke," *American Politics Quarterly* 22 (April 1994): 190–207.
52. Data from the 1994 NORC General Social Survey. See also Howard Schuman, Charlotte Steeh, and Lawrence Bobo, *Racial Attitudes in America* (Cambridge: Harvard University Press, 1985).
53. See also R. Darcy, Susan Welch, and Janet Clark, *Women, Elections, and Representation* (New York: Longman, 1987).
54. See Thomas Byrne Edsall with Mary D. Edsall, *Chain Reaction: The Impact of Race, Rights, and Taxes on American Politics* (New York: Norton, 1991); Nicholas P. Lovrich, Jr., Charles H. Sheldon, and Erik Wasmann, "The Racial Factor in Nonpartisan Judicial Elections: A Research Note," *Western Political Quarterly* 41 (December 1988): 807–16.
55. On the subject of amateurs in politics, see David T. Canon, *Actors, Athletes, and Astronauts: Political Amateurs in the United States Congress* (Chicago: University of Chicago Press, 1990).
56. Abramson, Aldrich, and Rohde, *Change and Continuity in the 1992 Elections*, chap. 7; Morris P. Fiorina, *Retrospective Voting in American National Elections* (New Haven: Yale University Press, 1981).
57. Abramson, Aldrich, and Rohde, *Change and Continuity in the 1992 Elections*, chap. 6.
58. V. O. Key, Jr., *Politics, Parties, and Pressure Groups*, 5th ed. (New York: Crowell, 1964), 568.
59. Michael S. Lewis-Beck and Tom W. Rice, *Forecasting Elections* (Washington, D.C.: CQ Press, 1992).
60. See D. Roderick Kiewiet, *Macroeconomics and Micropolitics* (Chicago: University of Chicago Press, 1983); Donald R. Kinder and D. Roderick Kiewiet, "Economic Discontent and Political Behavior," *American Journal of Political Science* 23 (August 1979): 495–527; Donald R. Kinder and D. Roderick Kiewiet, "Sociotropic Politics: The American Case," *British Journal of Political Science* 11 (April 1981): 129–61. For an alternate view, see Steven J. Rosenstone, John Mark Hansen, and Donald R. Kinder, "Measuring Change in Personal Economic Well-Being," *Public Opinion Quarterly* 50 (Summer 1986): 176–92.
61. "A Closer Look at the Voters."
62. Campbell et al., *The American Voter*, 168–87.
63. Paul R. Abramson, John H. Aldrich, and David W. Rohde, *Change and Continuity in the 1988 Elections*, rev. ed. (Washington, D.C.: CQ Press, 1991), chap. 6; Abramson, Aldrich, and Rohde, *Change and Continuity in the 1992 Elections*, chap. 6.
64. See Edward G. Carmines and James A. Stimson, "Two Faces of Issue Voting," *American Political Science Review* 74 (March 1980): 78–91.
65. See Abramson, Aldrich, and Rohde, *Change and Continuity in the 1988 Elections*, 185–87; William H. Flanigan and Nancy H. Zingale, *Political Behavior of the American Electorate*, 6th ed. (Dubuque, Iowa: Brown, 1988), 132–40.
66. Barbara G. Farah and Ethel Klein, "Public Opinion Trends," in Gerald M. Pomper et al., *The Election of 1988: Reports and Interpretations* (Chatham, N.J.: Chatham House, 1989), 121–25; Ethel Klein, *Gender Politics* (Cambridge: Harvard University Press, 1984), chap. 9; Susan Welch and Lee Sigelman, "A Black Gender Gap?" *Social Science Quarterly* 70 (March 1989): 120–33; Susan Welch and Lee Sigelman, "A Gender Gap among Hispanics? A Comparison with Blacks and Anglos," *Western Political Quarterly* 45 (March 1992): 181–99.

Chapter 8, pp. 231–266

1. Quoted in Jann S. Wenner and William Greider, "The Rolling Stone Interview: President Clinton," *Rolling Stone*, 9 December 1993, 81.
2. Thomas Jefferson, "To John Norvell," in *The Writings of Thomas Jefferson* (New York: G. P. Putnam, 1898), vol. ix, 224.
3. Quoted in Daniel P. Moynihan, "The Presidency & the Press," *Commentary*, March 1971, 41.
4. Quoted in Christopher Hanson, "Media Bashing," *Columbia Journalism Review*, November/December 1992, 52.
5. James Madison, "Letter to W. T. Barry," in *The Writings of James Madison*, vol. 9, 1819–1836, ed. Gaillard Hunt (New York: G. P. Putnam, 1910), 103.
6. Thomas Jefferson, "To Edward Carrington," *Writings*, vol. iv, 360.
7. Among others, see Bernard Berelson, Paul Lazarsfeld, and William McPhee, *Voting* (Chicago: University of Chicago Press, 1954); Leo Bogart, *Press and Public: Who Reads What, When, Where and Why in American Newspapers* (Hillsdale, N.J.: Lawrence Erlbaum Associates, 1981); Paul Lazarsfeld, Bernard Berelson, and Hazel Gaudet, *The People's Choice* (New York: Columbia University Press, 1948); Suzanne Pingree, "Children's Cognitive Processes in Constructing Social Reality," *Journalism Quarterly* 60 (Autumn 1983): 415–22.
8. Laurance Parisot, "Attitudes About the Media: A Five-Country Comparison," *Public Opinion* 10 (January–February 1988): 60; *The Year in Figures* (Washington, D.C.: Times Mirror Center for the People & the Press, 1995), 1.
9. Benjamin I. Page, Robert Y. Shapiro, and Glenn R. Dempsey, "What Moves Public Opinion?" *American Political Science Review* 81 (March 1987): 23–43.
10. See, for example, *Harris Poll 1995*, no. 13, 12 February 1995; *Harris Poll 1995*, no. 21, 29 March 1995; *Harris Poll 1995*, no. 24, 3 April 1995.
11. Shanto Iyengar and Donald R. Kinder, *News That Matters: Television and American Public Opinion* (Chicago: University of Chicago Press, 1987), 33.
12. Ibid., 60.
13. See Daniel Schorr, "Ten Days that Shook the White House," *Columbia Journalism Review*, July/August 1991, 21–23.
14. On the news media and Congress, see Timothy E. Cook, *Making Laws and Making News: Media Strategies in the U.S. House of Representatives* (Washington, D.C.: Brookings Institution, 1989); Stephen Hess, *Live from Capitol Hill! Studies of Congress and the Media* (Washington, D.C.: Brookings Institution, 1991); Stephen Hess, *The Ultimate Insiders: U.S. Senators in the National Media* (Washington, D.C.: Brookings Institution, 1986); Thomas E. Mann and Norman J. Ornstein, eds., *Congress, the Press and the Public* (Washington, D.C.: AEI/ Brookings Institution, 1994).
15. Quoted in Pamela Fessler, "Congress' Record on Saddam: Decade of Talk, Not Action," *Congressional Quarterly Weekly Report*, 27 April 1991, 1068.
16. For discussions of the news media and the presidency, see, among others, Michael Baruch Grossman and Martha Joynt Kumar, *Portraying the President: The White House and the News Media* (Baltimore: Johns Hopkins University Press, 1981); Samuel Kernell, *Going Public: New Strategies of Presidential Leadership*, 2d ed. (Washington, D.C.: CQ Press, 1992); Fred Smoller, *The Six O'Clock Presidency: A Theory of Press Relations in the Age of Television* (New York: Praeger, 1990); John Tebbel and Sarah Miles Watts, *The Press and the Presidency: From George Washington to Ronald Reagan* (New York: Oxford University Press, 1985).
17. Mitchell Stephens, *A History of News: From the Drum to the Satellite* (New York: Penguin Books, 1988), 222.
18. Edwin Emery, *The Press and America: An Interpretative History of the Mass Media*, 3d ed. (Englewood Cliffs, N.J.: Prentice Hall, 1972), 118; Stephens, *A History of News*, 187–88.
19. See Emery, *The Press and America*, chap. 11; Michael Schudson, *Discovering the News: A Social History of American Newspapers* (New York: Basic Books, 1978), chap. 1.
20. Emery, *The Press and America*, 373.
21. *Statistical Abstract of the United States, 1995*, 115th ed. (Washington, D.C.: U.S. Bureau of the Census, 1995), 571, 579.
22. *Statistical Abstract of the United States, 1970*, 91st ed. (Washington, D.C.: U.S. Bureau of the Census, 1970), 499; *Statistical Abstract of the United States, 1995*, 579.
23. Mark Hertsgaard, *On Bended Knee: The Press and the Reagan Presidency* (New York: Schocken Books, 1989), 78.

24. Alex S. Jones, "Rethinking Newspapers," *New York Times*, 1 January 1991; *Statistical Abstract of the United States, 1995*, 61, 571.
25. *Statistical Abstract of the United States, 1986*, 106th ed. (Washington, D.C.: U.S. Bureau of the Census, 1986), 550; *Statistical Abstract of the United States, 1995*, 8, 571.
26. "Hard Numbers," *Columbia Journalism Review*, May/June 1994, 17.
27. Richard Harwood, "Rotten News for Everyone," *Washington Post*, 1 September 1991; Times Mirror Center for the People & the Press, "Did O. J. Do It? Network News Viewing and Newspaper Reading Off," 6 April 1995, 7.
28. *Statistical Abstract of the United States, 1995*, 571.
29. Ken Auletta, *Three Blind Mice: How the TV Networks Lost Their Way* (New York: Random House, 1991).
30. Robert Goldberg and Gerald Jay Goldberg, *Anchors: Brokaw, Jennings, Rather and the Evening News* (New York: Birch Lane Press, 1990), 107.
31. Ernest Leiser, "See It Now: The Decline of Network News," *Washington Journalism Review*, January/February 1988, 49.
32. Mark Robichaux, "Slicing It Thin," *Wall Street Journal*, 9 September 1994.
33. Howard Kurtz, "There's Anger in the Air," *Washington Post National Weekly Edition*, 31 October–6 November 1994, 8.
34. Maureen Groppe, "Tuning in with Voters," *Congressional Quarterly Weekly Report*, 9 April 1994, 854; Rick Wartzman, "Democrats Try to Play Catch-Up on Talk Radio," *Wall Street Journal*, 8 February 1995.
35. Maureen Groppe, "Talk-Radio Hosts Decide to Go Off the Air and on the Ballot," *Congressional Quarterly Weekly Report*, 9 April 1994, 853; *Harris Poll 1995*, no. 19, 20 March 1995.
36. Kurtz, "There's Anger in the Air," 8; Taylor, "Most Americans," 2.
37. Darlene Superville, "Political Radio Shows Gain Popularity Among Many American Social Groups," *Daily Iowan*, 25 September 1995; *Statistical Abstract of the United States, 1995*, 157. See also John H. Fund, "Why Clinton Shouldn't Be Steamed at Talk Radio," *Wall Street Journal*, 7 July 1994; Groppe, "Talk Radio Hosts," 854; Taylor, "Most Americans," 2.
38. "Internet Survey Estimates 9.5 Million Users in U.S.," *Wall Street Journal*, 12 January 1996; Steve Lohr, "Who Uses Internet? 5.8 Million Are Said to Be Linked in U.S.," *New York Times*, 27 September 1995; Times Mirror Center for the People & the Press, "Americans Going Online . . . Explosive Growth, Uncertain Destinations," 16 October 1995.
39. See Graeme Browning, "The Messages of a New Medium," *National Journal*, 21 October 1995, 2617.
40. Edmund L. Andrews, "The 104th Congress: The Internet; Mr. Smith Goes to Cyberspace," *New York Times*, 6 January 1995.
41. Edmund L. Andrews, "The '96 Race on the Internet: Surfer Beware," *New York Times*, 23 October 1995; Edwin Diamond and Gregg Geller, "Will Press Coverage Be Virtual in the On-Line Political World?" *National Journal*, 16 September 1995, p. 2303; Gerald F. Seib, "Presidential Races Are Being Changed by Latest Technology," *Wall Street Journal*, 4 August 1995.
42. Ben H. Bagdikian, *The Media Monopoly*, 3d ed. (Boston: Beacon Press, 1990), 21.
43. Hertsgaard, *On Bended Knee*, 78.
44. William Glaberson, "The Press: Bought and Sold and Gray All Over," *New York Times*, 30 July 1995.
45. See Dan Carney, "Congress Fires Its First Shot in Information Revolution," *Congressional Quarterly Weekly Report*, 3 February 1996, 289–94; Dan Carney, "From Televisions to Telephones . . . Highlights of the New Laws," *Congressional Quarterly Weekly Report*, 3 February 1996, 290–91.
46. "Telecom Vote Signals Competitive Free-for-All: Likely Mergers Herald an Era of Megacarriers," *Wall Street Journal*, 2 February 1996.
47. Ibid.
48. Robichaux, "Slicing It Thin"; *Statistical Abstract of the United States, 1995*, 571.
49. *Statistical Abstract of the United States, 1995*, 576.
50. Doris A. Graber, *Mass Media and American Politics*, 4th ed. (Washington, D.C.: CQ Press, 1994), 39–40.
51. John C. Busterna and Kathleen A. Hansen, "Presidential Endorsement Patterns by Chain-Owned Papers, 1976–1984," *Journalism Quarterly* 67 (Fall 1990): 286–94.
52. Quoted in Robert Kurz, "Congress and the Media: Forces in the Struggle Over Foreign Policy," in *The Media and Foreign Policy*, ed. Simon Serfaty (New York: St. Martin's, 1990), 77.
53. Elie Abel, *Leaking: Who Does It? Who Benefits? At What Cost?* (New York: Priority Press, 1987), 44.
54. Jay Peterzell, "Can the CIA Spook the Press?" *Columbia Journalism Review*, July/August 1986, 18–19.
55. Larry Speakes with Robert Pack, *Speaking Out: The Reagan Presidency from Inside the White House* (New York: Avon Books, 1989), 279.
56. Quoted in Jon Swann, "Jennifer," *Columbia Journalism Review*, November/December 1992, 36.
57. Quoted in Hanson, "Media Bashing," 54.
58. Peter Stoler, *The War Against the Press: Politics, Pressure and Intimidation in the 80's* (New York: Dodd, Mead, 1986), 4–5.
59. Chris Hedges, "The Unilaterals," *Columbia Journalism Review*, May/June 1991, 27–29.
60. Jason DeParle, "17 News Executives Criticize U.S. for 'Censorship' of Gulf Coverage," *New York Times*, 3 July 1991.
61. See W. Lance Bennett and David L. Paletz, eds., *Taken by Storm: The Media, Public Opinion, and U.S. Foreign Policy in the Gulf War* (Chicago: University of Chicago Press, 1994); Hedrick Smith, ed., *The Media and the Gulf War: The Press and Democracy in Wartime* (Washington, D.C.: Seven Locks Press, 1992); *The Media at War: The Press and the Persian Gulf Conflict* (New York: Gannett Foundation, 1991).
62. Paul Farhi, "TV Shows Come and Go, But Licenses Live On," *Washington Post National Weekly Edition*, 23–29 October 1995, p. 18.
63. Anthony Ramirez, "Radio Giant Is Set for a Growth Spurt," *New York Times*, 18 September 1995.
64. Graber, *Mass Media and American Politics*, 114–15.
65. Miami Herald Publishing Co. v. Tornillo, 418 U.S. 241 (1974); Red Lion Broadcasting Co. v. FCC, 395 U.S. 367 (1969).
66. Graber, *Mass Media and American Politics*, 83–86.
67. Sam Donaldson, *Hold On, Mr. President!* (New York: Fawcett Crest, 1987), 6.
68. Edwin Diamond, *The Tin Kazoo* (Cambridge, Mass.: MIT Press, 1975), 94.
69. Peter J. Boyer, "Famine in Ethiopia: The TV Accident that Exploded," *Washington Journalism Review*, January 1985, 20.
70. Timothy Crouse, *The Boys on the Bus* (New York: Ballantine Books, 1974), 7.
71. Cook, *Making Laws and Making News*, 47.
72. Hertsgaard, *On Bended Knee*, 314. See also Nick Kotz, "What the *Times* and *Post* Are Missing," *Washington Monthly*, March 1977, 45–49; Timothy Noah, "The Pentagon Press: Prisoners of Respectability," *Washington Monthly*, September 1983, 44; Speakes, *Speaking Out*, 282.
73. Quoted in Lawrence Weschler, "The Media's One and Only Freedom Story," *Columbia Journalism Review*, March/April 1990, 31.
74. Gerald C. Stone and Elinor Grusin, "Network TV as the Bad News Bearer," *Journalism Quarterly* 61 (Autumn 1984): 517–23; Joseph R. Dominick, "Business Coverage in Network Newscasts," *Journalism Quarterly* 58 (Spring 1981): 179–85.
75. Joe S. Foote and Michael E. Steele, "Degree of Conformity in Lead Stories in Early Evening Network TV Newscasts," *Journalism Quarterly* 63 (Spring 1986): 19–23.
76. Stephens, *A History of the News*, 266–68.
77. See Daniel C. Hallin, "The Media, the War in Vietnam, and Political Support: A Critique of the Thesis of an Oppositional Media," *Journal of Politics* 46 (February 1984): 21.

78. Herbert J. Gans, *Deciding What's News: A Study of CBS Evening News, NBC Nightly News, Newsweek and Time* (New York: Vintage Books, 1980), 31–38.
79. Lewis H. Lapham, "Trained Seals and Sitting Ducks," *Harper's Magazine,* May 1991, 10.
80. Hertsgaard, *On Bended Knee,* 228.
81. Quoted in Stephen Bates, *If No News, Send Rumors: Anecdotes of American Journalism* (New York: Henry Holt, 1989), 61.
82. David Halberstam, *The Powers That Be* (New York: Knopf, 1979), 39.
83. Hertsgaard, *On Bended Knee,* 115.
84. Gans, *Deciding What's News,* 81.
85. See Christopher Georges, "Bad News Bearers," *Washington Monthly,* July/August 1993, 28–34; Todd Gitlin, "Whiplash," *American Journalism Review,* April 1993, 35–36; William Glaberson, "The Capitol Press vs. the President: Fair Coverage or Unreined Adversity?" *New York Times,* 17 June 1993; Tom Rosenstiel, *Strange Bedfellows: How Television and the Presidential Candidates Changed American Politics, 1992* (New York: Hyperion, 1993).
86. Emery, *The Press and America,* 269, 389.
87. See L. Brent Bozell III and Brent H. Baker, eds., *And That's the Way It Isn't: A Reference Guide to Media Bias* (Alexandria, Va.: Media Research Center, 1990); S. Robert Lichter and Stanley Rothman, "Media and Business Elites," *Public Opinion* (October/November 1981): 42–46, 59–60; S. Robert Lichter, Stanley Rothman, and Linda S. Richter, *The Media Elite: America's New "Powerbrokers"* (New York: Adler and Adler, 1986); William Schneider and I. A. Lewis, "Views on the News," *Public Opinion* 8 (August/September 1985): 6–11, 58–59; G. Cleveland Wilhoit and David H. Weaver, *The American Journalist: A Portrait of U.S. News People and Their Work* (Bloomington: Indiana University Press, 1986).
88. Schneider and Lewis, "Views on the News," 6.
89. See Christopher Georges, "Dole Joins in Republican Attacks on the Press, While Party Expands Use of Alternative Media," *Wall Street Journal,* 29 May 1996; Elaine S. Povich, *Partners & Adversaries: The Contentious Connection Between Congress & the Media* (Arlington, Va.: Freedom Forum, 1996).
90. Edward J. Epstein, *News From Nowhere* (New York: Random House, 1973), 137, 207.
91. Busterna and Hansen, "Presidential Endorsement Patterns," 286–94.
92. Elizabeth Kolbert, "Maybe the Media DID Treat Bush a Bit Harshly," *New York Times,* 22 November 1992.
93. Quoted in Graeme Browning, "Too Close for Comfort?" *National Journal,* 3 October 1992, 2247.
94. Gloria Borger, "Cynicism and Tankophobia," *U.S. News & World Report,* 5 June 1995, 34.
95. *The People, the Press, and Their Leaders 1995* (Washington, D.C.: Times Mirror Center for the People & the Press, 1995), 9.
96. Quoted in Borger, "Cynicism," 34.
97. Thomas E. Patterson, *Out of Order* (New York: Vintage, 1994), 245; Larry Sabato, *Feeding Frenzy: How Attack Journalism Has Transformed American Politics* (New York: Free Press, 1991), 207.
98. *The People, the Press,* 112–13.
99. Ben Bradlee, *A Good Life: Newspapering and Other Adventures* (New York: Simon & Schuster, 1995), 406.
100. Peter J. Boyer, *Who Killed CBS? The Undoing of America's Number One News Network* (New York: Random House, 1988), 308.
101. Robert Krolick, "Reuven Frank and Ed Bliss on TV News," *Washington Journalism Review,* July/August 1991, 43; see also Rick Marin with Peter Katel, "Miami's Crime Time Live," *Newsweek,* 20 June 1994, 71–72.
102. Walter Goodman, "Nightly News Looks Beyond the Headlines," *New York Times,* 7 July 1991.
103. Bogart, *Press and Public,* 200–4.
104. See, for example, Robert Entman, *Democracy without Citizens: Media and the Decay of American Politics* (New York: Oxford University Press, 1989), 103–8.
105. Randall Rothenberg, "CNN Wins Much Acclaim, But Will It Win Sponsors?" *New York Times,* 21 January 1991.
106. Harold W. Stanley and Richard G. Niemi, *Vital Statistics on American Politics,* 5th ed. (Washington, D.C.: CQ Press, 1995), 57. See also, Matthew R. Kerbel, *Edited for Television: CNN, ABC, and the 1992 Presidential Campaign* (Boulder, Colo.: Westview, 1994).
107. Jonathan Alter, "How the Media Blew It," *Newsweek,* 21 November 1988, 24.
108. See John Tierney, "Sound Bites Become Smaller Mouthfuls," *New York Times,* 23 January 1992.
109. See, for example, "The Press and Campaign '92: A Self-Assessment," a supplement to the *Columbia Journalism Review,* March/April 1993.
110. Rosentiel, *Strange Bedfellows,* esp. 164–71.
111. Quoted in Elizabeth Kolbert, "Bypassing the Press Helps Candidates; Does It Also Serve the Public Interest?" *New York Times,* 8 November 1992.
112. Quoted in D. D. Guttenplan, "Covering a Runaway Campaign," *Columbia Journalism Review,* November/December 1992, 24.
113. Elizabeth Kolbert, "For Talk Shows, Less News Is Good News," *New York Times,* 28 June 1992.
114. See Timothy M. Phelps and Helen Winternitz, *Capitol Games: Clarence Thomas, Anita Hill, and the Story of a Supreme Court Nomination* (New York: Hyperion, 1992).
115. Martin Linsky, *Impact: How the Press Affects Federal Policymaking* (New York: Norton, 1986), 238.
116. See, for example, "Two Leaks, But by Whom?" *Newsweek,* 27 July 1987, 16.
117. Donald T. Regan, *For the Record: From Wall Street to Washington* (New York: St. Martin's, 1989), 280.
118. Linsky, *Impact,* 238.
119. James J. Kilpatrick, "'Trust-Me' Journalism: An Identifiable Source Is Fed Up," *Washington Journalism Review,* January/February 1988, 43–45; William H. Lewis, "The Cloning of the American Press," *Washington Quarterly* 2 (Spring 1979): 31–38; Roger Morris, "Eight Days in April: The Press Flattens Carter with the Neutron Bomb," *Columbia Journalism Review,* November/December 1978, 25–30.
120. Quoted in Abel, *Leaking,* 27.
121. See Bob Woodward and Carl Bernstein, *All the President's Men* (New York: Simon & Schuster, 1974).

Chapter 9, pp. 267–294

1. Cheryl Lynn Herrera, Richard Herrera, and Eric R. A. N. Smith, "Public Opinion and Congressional Representation," *Public Opinion Quarterly* 56 (Summer 1992): 185–205; Byron E. Shafer and William J. M. Claggett, *The Two Majorities: The Issue Context of Modern American Politics* (Baltimore: Johns Hopkins University Press, 1995), chap. 6.
2. Joseph A. Schlesinger, *Political Parties and the Winning of Office* (Ann Arbor: University of Michigan Press, 1991).
3. Michael Barone, *Our Country: The Shaping of America from Roosevelt to Reagan* (New York: Free Press, 1990), 247–48, 317.
4. E. E. Schattschneider, *Party Government* (New York: Farrar and Rinehart, 1942), 1.
5. G. Bingham Powell, Jr., *Contemporary Democracies* (Cambridge: Harvard University Press, 1982).
6. Herbert McClosky and John Zaller, *The American Ethos: Public Attitudes Toward Capitalism and Democracy* (Cambridge: Harvard University Press, 1984).
7. The spatial model was first elaborated in Anthony Downs, *An Economic Theory of Democracy* (New York: Harper & Row, 1957). For an excellent introduction to contemporary work on the spatial theory, see James M. Enelow and Melvin J. Hinich, *The Spatial Theory of Voting* (New York: Cambridge University Press, 1984).
8. Michael Barone and Grant Ujifusa, *The Almanac of American Politics 1992* (Washington, D.C.: National Journal, 1991), 87–88.
9. Howard Fineman, "Throwing a Mighty Tantrum: The Lure of Third-Party Candidacies," *Newsweek,* 27 April 1992, 28; see also Fred Barnes, "The Spoiler," *The New Republic,* 15 June 1992, 10–11; John B. Judis, "The Executive," *The New Republic,* 15 June 1992, 19–23.

10. See Gerald M. Pomper, "The Presidential Election," in Gerald M. Pomper et al., *The Election of 1992,* (Chatham, N.J.: Chatham House, 1993), 132–56.
11. This is a generic description of a proportional system. The systems of individual nations differ in many details. See Rein Taagepera and Matthew Soberg Shugart, *Seats and Votes: The Effects and Determinants of Electoral Systems* (New Haven: Yale University Press, 1989).
12. Maurice Duverger, *Political Parties* (New York: Wiley, 1959); see also William H. Riker, "The Two-Party System and Duverger's Law: An Essay on the History of Political Science," *American Political Science Review* 76 (December 1982): 753–66.
13. Donald Bruce Johnson and Kirk H. Porter, *National Party Platforms 1840–1972* (Urbana: University of Illinois Press, 1973); see also Gerald M. Pomper with Susan S. Lederman, *Elections in America: Control and Influence in Democratic Politics,* 2d ed. (New York: Longman, 1980).
14. This description of the politics of civil rights is largely taken from Edward G. Carmines and James A. Stimson, *Issue Evolution: Race and the Transformation of American Politics* (Princeton, N.J.: Princeton University Press, 1989), 35–58.
15. John Frederick Martin, *Civil Rights and the Crisis of Liberalism* (New York: St. Martin's, 1979); James A. Morone, *The Democratic Wish: Popular Participation and the Limits of American Government* (New York: Basic Books, 1990).
16. Johnson and Porter, *National Party Platforms,* 542.
17. Ibid., 554.
18. See Tom Wicker, *One of Us: Richard Nixon and the American Dream* (New York: Random House, 1991), 238–42.
19. Taylor Branch, *Parting the Waters: America in the King Years, 1954–1963* (New York: Simon & Schuster, 1988); Dennis Chong, *Collective Action and the Civil Rights Movement* (Chicago: University of Chicago Press, 1991).
20. Arthur M. Schlesinger, Jr., *A Thousand Days: John F. Kennedy in the White House* (Greenwich, Conn.: Fawcett, 1965).
21. Charles Whalen and Barbara Whalen, *The Longest Debate: A Legislative History of the 1964 Civil Rights Act* (New York: New American Library, 1985).
22. James L. Sundquist, *Dynamics of the Party System,* rev. ed. (Washington, D.C.: Brookings Institution, 1983).
23. Hubert H. Humphrey, *The Education of a Private Man* (Minneapolis: University of Minnesota Press, 1991), 203.
24. Wicker, *One of Us,* 336–86
25. Robert Axelrod, "Presidential Election Coalitions in 1984," *American Political Science Review,* 80 (March 1986): 281–84; Earl Black and Merle Black, *Politics and Society in the South* (Cambridge: Harvard University Press, 1987).
26. Everett Carll Ladd, Jr., with Charles D. Hadley, *Transformations of the American Party System,* 2d ed. (New York: Norton, 1978).
27. See, for instance, the 5 December 1988 issue of *The New Republic.*
28. Jon F. Hale, "The Democratic Leadership Council: Institutionalizing a Party Faction," in *The State of the Parties: The Changing Role of Contemporary American Parties,* ed. Daniel M. Shea and John C. Green, (Lanham, Md.: Rowman & Littlefield, 1994); see also Thomas Ferguson and Joel Rogers, *Right Turn: The Decline of the Democrats and the Future of American Politics* (New York: Hill and Wang, 1986), 4–11.
29. For instance, see James MacGregor Burns et al., *The Democrats Must Lead: The Case for a Progressive Democratic Party* (Boulder, Colo.: Westview, 1992); Arthur Sanders, *Victory: How a Progressive Democratic Party Can Win and Govern* (Armonk, N.Y.: Sharpe, 1992).
30. John W. Mashek, "Moderates Rally to Fight GOP's Religious Right," *Santa Barbara News-Press,* 2 January 1993.
31. See Alexander Hamilton, James Madison, and John Jay, *The Federalist Papers,* ed. Garry Wills (New York: Bantam Books, 1982), esp. no. 10.
32. William Nisbet Chambers, *Political Parties in a New Nation* (New York: Oxford University Press, 1963).
33. Lee Benson, *The Concept of Jacksonian Democracy* (Princeton, N.J.: Princeton University Press, 1961).
34. Robert V. Remini, *The Election of Andrew Jackson* (Philadelphia: Lippincott, 1963), 51–120.
35. Richard P. McCormick, *The Presidential Game: The Origins of American Presidential Politics* (New York: Oxford University Press, 1982).
36. Remini, *The Election of Andrew Jackson,* 184–91.
37. Everett Carll Ladd, Jr., *American Political Parties: Social Change and Political Response* (New York: Norton, 1963).
38. Sundquist, *Dynamics of the Party System,* 134–69.
39. Ibid., 170–81; Gabriel Kolko, *The Triumph of Conservatism: A Reinterpretation of American History, 1900–1916* (Chicago: Quadrangle Books, 1963).
40. Steven J. Rosenstone, Roy L. Behr, and Edward H. Lazarus, *Third Parties in America: Citizen Response to Major Party Failure* (Princeton, N.J.: Princeton University Press, 1984), 85–88.
41. Sherman J. Maisel, *Macro-Economics* (New York: Norton, 1982).
42. Arthur M. Schlesinger, Jr., *The Coming of the New Deal* (Boston: Houghton-Mifflin, 1958).
43. Barone, *Our Country,* chap. 12.
44. Kristi Anderson, *The Creation of a Democratic Majority, 1928–1936* (Chicago: University of Chicago Press, 1979); Sundquist, *Dynamics of the Party System,* 198–239.
45. See Walter Dean Burnham, *Critical Elections and the Mainsprings of American Politics* (New York: Norton, 1970).
46. V. O. Key, Jr., "A Theory of Critical Elections," *Journal of Politics* 17 (February 1955): 3–18.
47. Burnham, *Critical Elections and the Mainsprings of American Politics,* esp. 9–10.
48. Sundquist, *Dynamics of the Party System,* 1–49, 298–331.
49. For another insightful theoretical interpretation, see Jerome M. Clubb, William H. Flanigan, and Nancy H. Zingale, *Partisan Realignment: Voters, Parties and Government in American History* (Beverly Hills, Calif.: Sage, 1980).
50. See Martin P. Wattenberg, *The Decline of American Political Parties, 1952–1992* (Cambridge: Harvard University Press, 1994); Martin P. Wattenberg, *The Rise of Candidate-Centered Politics* (Cambridge: Harvard University Press, 1991).
51. See Bruce E. Keith et al., *The Myth of the Independent Voter* (Berkeley: University of California Press, 1992).
52. See Gary C. Jacobson, *The Electoral Origins of Divided Government: Competition in U.S. House Elections, 1946–1988* (Boulder, Colo.: Westview, 1990).
53. Eric R. A. N. Smith and Peverill Squire, "State and National Politics in the Mountain West," in *The Politics of Realignment,* ed. Peter F. Galderisi et al. (Boulder, Colo.: Westview, 1987), 33–54; see also the data on regional voting in Harold W. Stanley and Richard G. Niemi, *Vital Statistics on American Politics,* 5th ed. (Washington, D.C.: CQ Press, 1995), 129.
54. See John E. Chubb and Paul E. Peterson, "Realignment and Institutionalization," and Thomas E. Cavanaugh and James L. Sundquist, "The New Two-Party System," both in *The New Direction in American Politics,* ed. John E. Chubb and Paul E. Peterson (Washington, D.C.: Brookings Institution, 1985).
55. See Alan L. Abramowitz, "The End of the Democratic Era? 1994 and the Future of Congressional Election Research," *Political Research Quarterly* 48 (December 1995): 873–89; Alfred J. Tuchfarber et al., "Interpreting the 1994 Election Results: A Direct Test of Competing Explanations," paper delivered at the annual meeting of the American Association for Public Opinion Research, May 1995.
56. Edward C. Banfield and James Q. Wilson, *City Politics* (New York: Vintage, 1963), 116–21.
57. For a novel use of walking-around money, see Thomas B. Rosenstiel, "Consultant Rivalry Led to Lie, Rollins Says," *Los Angeles Times,* 21 November 1993; " 'Walking-Around Money': A Dubious Tradition," *Newsweek,* 22 November 1993, 33.

58. Paul Allen Beck and Frank J. Sorauf, *Party Politics in America,* 7th ed. (New York: HarperCollins, 1992), 79. For an excellent description of the Daley machine, see Milton Rakove, *Don't Make No Waves . . . Don't Back No Losers* (Bloomington: Indiana University Press, 1975).
59. Austin Ranney, *Curing the Mischiefs of Faction: Party Reform in America* (Berkeley: University of California Press, 1975), 79–80.
60. Jerrold G. Rusk, "The Effect of the Australian Ballot Reform on Split Ticket Voting: 1876–1908," *American Political Science Review* 70 (December 1970): 1220–38; see also Francis Fox Piven and Richard A. Cloward, *Why Americans Don't Vote* (New York: Pantheon Books, 1988), 73–74.
61. Joseph A. Schlesinger, "The New American Political Party," *American Political Science Review* 79 (December 1985): 1152–69.
62. *Bartlett's Familiar Quotations,* 16th ed., ed. Justin Kaplan (Boston: Little, Brown, 1992), 398.
63. Spencer C. Olin, Jr., *California Politics, 1846–1920: The Emerging Corporate State* (San Francisco: Boyd and Fraser, 1981), chap. 5.
64. James Gimpel, "Reform-Resistant and Reform-Adopting Machines: The Electoral Foundations of Urban Politics: 1910–1930," *Political Research Quarterly* 46 (June 1993): 371–82; Raymond E. Wolfinger, *The Politics of Progress* (Englewood Cliffs, N.J.: Prentice-Hall, 1974), 87–92.
65. Richard Hofstadter, *The Age of Reform* (New York: Vintage, 1955).
66. James Q. Wilson, *The Amateur Democrat* (Chicago: University of Chicago Press, 1962).
67. See Robert Agranoff, ed., *The New Style in Election Campaigns* (Boston: Holbrook, 1972).
68. Stephen A. Salmore and Barbara G. Salmore, *Candidates, Parties, and Campaigns: Electoral Politics in America* (Washington, D.C.: CQ Press, 1985), 19–61.
69. Herbert E. Alexander, *Financing Politics: Money, Elections and Political Reform,* 3d ed. (Washington, D.C.: CQ Press, 1984), chap. 7.
70. Herbert E. Alexander, *Financing Politics,* 4th ed. (Washington, D.C.: CQ Press, 1992).
71. Cornelius P. Cotter et al., *Party Organizations in American Politics* (New York: Praeger, 1984), 41–59.
72. Steven J. Rosenstone and John Mark Hansen, *Mobilization, Participation, and Democracy in America* (New York: Macmillan, 1993).
73. John F. Bibby and Thomas M. Holbrook, "Parties and Elections," in *Politics in the American State: A Comparative Analysis,* eds. Virginia Gray and Herbert Jacob (Washington, D.C.: CQ Press, 1996).
74. Cotter et al., *Party Organizations,* 16–17.
75. Robert J. Huckshorn, "The Role Orientations of State Party Chairmen," in *The Party Symbol,* ed. William Crotty (San Francisco: Freeman, 1980), 50–62.
76. Cornelius P. Cotter and Bernard C. Hennessy, *Politics without Power: The National Party Committees* (New York: Atherton, 1964).
77. Larry J. Sabato, *The Party's Just Begun* (Glenview, Ill.: Scott, Foresman/Little, Brown, 1988).
78. See Xandra Kayden and Eddie Mahe, *The Party Goes On* (New York: Basic Books, 1985).
79. Laura Berkowitz and Steve Lilienthal, "A Tale of Two Parties: National Party Committee Policy Initiatives," and Anthony Corrado, "The Politics of Cohesion: The Role of the National Party Committees in the 1992 Election," both in *The State of the Parties: The Changing Role of Contemporary American Parties,* ed. Daniel M. Shea and John C. Green (Lanham, Md.: Rowman & Littlefield, 1994).
80. Diana Dwyre, "Party Strategy and Political Reality: The Distribution of Congressional Campaign Committee Resources," in *The State of the Parties: The Changing Role of Contemporary American Parties,* ed. Daniel M. Shea and John C. Green (Lanham, Md.: Rowman & Littlefield, 1994); Paul S. Herrnson, *Party Campaigning in the 1980s* (Cambridge: Harvard University Press, 1988).

Chapter 10, pp. 295–328

1. Catalina Camia, "Interior Conferees Concur on Mining Moratorium," *Congressional Quarterly Weekly Report,* 24 September 1994, 2677–78; Catalina Camia, "Senate Oks Mining Law Rewrite; Bill Is Backed by Industry," *Congressional Quarterly Weekly Report,* 29 May 1993, 1355; Catalina Camia, "Senators, Conceding Defeat, Drop Mining Law Rewrite," *Congressional Quarterly Weekly Report,* 1 October 1994, 2785–86; Laura Michaelis, "Economic, Ecological Climate Favors Mining Law Overhaul," *Congressional Quarterly Weekly Report,* 20 March 1993, 662–63.
2. Charles McCoy, "Babbit Grudgingly Approves $275 Sale of Land Holding $1 Billion in Minerals," *Wall Street Journal,* 7 September 1995.
3. Jeffrey M. Berry, *The Interest Group Society,* 2d ed. (Glenview, Ill.: Scott, Foresman/Little, Brown, 1989).
4. James Madison, "Federalist No. 10," in *The Federalist Papers,* ed. Garry Wills (New York: Bantam Books, 1982), 42–49.
5. Berry, *The Interest Group Society,* 4.
6. See Graeme Browning, "Colleges at the Trough," *National Journal,* 7 March 1992, 565–69; Eliza Newlin Carney, "Colleges Try a New Course," *National Journal,* 11 December 1993, 2949–50; William H. Honan, "With Money Threatened, Colleges Are Moving on All Lobbying Fronts," *New York Times,* 28 June 1995; Michael Wines, "A New Maxim for Lobbyists: What You Know, Not Whom," *New York Times,* 3 November 1993.
7. See Jack L. Walker, Jr., *Mobilizing Interest Groups in America: Patrons, Professions, and Social Movements* (Ann Arbor: University of Michigan Press, 1991), 20–23.
8. Alexis de Tocqueville, *Democracy in America,* ed. J. P. Mayer (New York: Anchor Books, 1969), 513.
9. Robert H. Salisbury, "Washington Lobbyists: A Collective Portrait," in *Interest Group Politics,* 2d ed., ed. Allan J. Cigler and Burdett A. Loomis (Washington, D.C.: CQ Press, 1986), 148–49; David Segal, "A Nation of Lobbyists," *Washington Post National Weekly Edition,* 17–23 July 1995, 11.
10. Philip A. Mundo, *Interest Groups: Cases and Characteristics* (Chicago: Nelson-Hall, 1992), 9.
11. John T. Tierney and Kay Lehman Schlozman, "Congress and Organized Interests," in *Congressional Politics,* ed. Christopher J. Deering (Chicago: Dorsey Press, 1989), 198.
12. "Portrait of the Electorate," *New York Times,* 10 November 1996.
13. On the agricultural lobby, see William P. Browne, *Private Interests, Public Policy, and American Agriculture* (Lawrence: University of Kansas Press, 1988); John Mark Hansen, *Gaining Access: Congress and the Farm Lobby, 1919–1981* (Chicago: University of Chicago Press, 1991).
14. See Reed McManus, "Down on the Farm Bureau," *Sierra,* November/December 1994, 32–34.
15. "Powerful Doctor's Group Struggles to Keep Members," *Iowa City Press-Citizen,* 1 July 1996.
16. See Jeffrey Berry, *Lobbying for the People: The Political Behavior of Public Interest Groups* (Princeton, N.J.: Princeton University Press, 1977).
17. For evidence on the effectiveness of public relations campaigns, see Robert B. Albritton and Jarol B. Manheim, "News of Rhodesia: The Impact of a Public Relations Campaign," *Journalism Quarterly* 56 (Winter 1983): 622–28; Jarol B. Manheim and Robert B. Albritton, "Changing National Images: International Public Relations and Media Agenda Setting," *American Political Science Review* 78 (September 1984): 641–57.
18. See John R. MacArthur, *Second Front: Censorship and Propaganda in the Gulf War* (New York: Hill and Wang, 1992).
19. See Peter Behr, "NAFTA Creating Odd Alliances," *Washington Post,* 4 September 1993; Bruce Stokes, "A Hard Sell," *National Journal,* 16 October 1993, 2472–76.
20. Keith Schneider, "Environmentalists Fight Each Other Over Trade Accord," *New York Times,* 16 September 1993.
21. See George Anders and Hilary Stout, "Medical Debate: Physicians Are Split by Age and Region on Health Reforms," *Wall Street Journal,* 15 October 1993; Barnaby J. Feder, "Medical Group Battles to Be Heard over Others on Health-Care Changes," *New York Times,* 11 June 1993; "Physician's Group Calls for Cap on Spending," *Iowa City Press-Citizen,* 15 September 1992.

22. Jeffrey Schmalz, "Gay Politics Goes Mainstream," *New York Times Magazine,* 11 October 1992, 21.
23. William Glaberson, "Syracuse's Feline Lobbyists Thwart Proposed Cat Limits," *New York Times,* 9 July 1991.
24. See David B. Truman, *The Governmental Process: Political Interests and Public Opinion* (New York: Knopf, 1951), chap. 3–4.
25. Timothy Noah, "New Single-Issue Pressure Groups Sprout Up on the Right to Support the Republican Agenda," *Wall Street Journal,* 31 May 1995.
26. The classic statement of the collective goods dilemma is Mancur Olson, *The Logic of Collective Action* (Cambridge: Harvard University Press, 1965).
27. Robert H. Salisbury, "An Exchange Theory of Interest Groups," *Midwest Journal of Political Science* 13 (February 1969): 1–32.
28. Glaberson, "Syracuse's Feline Lobbyists."
29. See Jack L. Walker, "The Origins and Maintenance of Interest Groups in America," *American Political Science Review* 77 (June 1983): 397–404.
30. Walker, *Mobilizing Interest Groups,* 31.
31. Walker, "The Origins and Maintenance of Interest Groups," 401.
32. Berry, *Lobbying for the People,* 28.
33. Peter Clark and James Q. Wilson, "Incentive Systems: A Theory of Organizations," *Administrative Science Quarterly* 6 (September 1961): 129–66; Terry M. Moe, *The Organization of Interests: Incentives and the Internal Dynamics of Political Interest Groups* (Chicago: University of Chicago Press, 1980); James Q. Wilson, *Political Organizations* (New York: Basic Books, 1973).
34. Olson, *The Logic of Collective Action,* chap. 1.
35. On the problem of interest group maintenance, see David C. King and Jack L. Walker, Jr., "The Origins and Maintenance of Groups," in Walker, *Mobilizing Interest Groups,* 75–102; Lawrence S. Rothenberg, "Organizational Maintenance and the Retention Decision in Groups," *American Political Science Review* 82 (December 1988): 1129–52.
36. Steven A. Holmes, "For the Civil Rights Movement, A New Reason for Living," *New York Times,* 9 July 1995.
37. Ibid.
38. David C. Morrison, "Sounding a Call to Arms for the 1990s," *National Journal,* 13 November 1993, 2728–30.
39. Kay Lehman Schlozman and John T. Tierney, *Organized Interests and American Democracy* (New York: Harper & Row, 1986).
40. On PAC contributions to state and local elections, see Herbert E. Alexander and Anthony Corrado, *Financing the 1992 Election* (Armonk, N.Y.: Sharpe, 1995), chap. 1; Ruth S. Jones, "Financing State Elections," in *Money and Politics in the United States,* ed. Michael J. Malbin (Chatham, N.J.: Chatham House, 1984); Ruth S. Jones, "State and Federal Legislative Campaigns: Same Song, Different Verse," *Election Politics* 3 (Summer 1986): 8–12; Frank J. Sorauf, *Money in American Elections* (Glenview, Ill.: Scott, Foresman/Little, Brown, 1988), chap. 9.
41. Harold W. Stanley and Richard G. Niemi, *Vital Statistics on American Politics,* 5th ed. (Washington, D.C.: CQ Press, 1995), 164.
42. Federal Election Commission, "PAC Activity in 1994 Elections Remains at 1992 Levels," 31 March 1995, 9.
43. Stanley and Niemi, *Vital Statistics,* 166.
44. See Herbert Alexander, *Financing the 1980 Election* (Lexington, Mass.: Lexington Books, 1983), 130–31; John A. C. Conybeare and Peverill Squire, "Political Action Committees and the Tragedy of the Commons: The Case of Nonconnected PACs," *American Politics Quarterly* 22 (April 1994): 154–74; Larry J. Sabato, *PAC Power: Inside the World of Political Action Committees* (New York: Norton, 1985), 50.
45. Federal Election Commission, "PAC Activity Rebounds in 1991–92 Election Cycle—Unusual Nature of Contests Seen as Reason," 29 April 1993, 3.
46. "Negative or Educational?" *National Journal,* 7 January 1995, 27.
47. Federal Election Commission, "PAC Activity in 1994 Elections," 11.
48. Stanley and Niemi, *Vital Statistics,* 169.
49. "FEC Reports House PAC Funds," *Congressional Quarterly Weekly Report,* 20 March 1993, 696.
50. See Phil Kuntz, "PACs Flip-Flop Again, Sending More Money to Democrats in Congress than Republicans," *Wall Street Journal,* 23 May 1996.
51. For statistical studies of the effect of PAC contributions on congressional voting, see Janet M. Grenzke, "PACs and the Congressional Supermarket: The Currency Is Complex," *American Journal of Political Science* 33 (February 1989): 1–24; John R. Wright, "PACs, Contributions, and Roll Calls," *American Political Science Review* 79 (June 1985): 400–14; John R. Wright, "Contributions, Lobbying, and Committee Voting in the U.S. House of Representatives," *American Political Science Review* 84 (June 1990): 417–38.
52. Quoted in Dan Clawson, Alan Neustadtl, and Denise Scott, *Money Talks: Corporate PACs and Political Influence* (New York: Basic Books, 1992), 90.
53. "Where the PAC Money Goes," *Congressional Quarterly Weekly Report,* 30 May 1992, 1525.
54. See, for example, Richard L. Hall and Frank W. Wayman, "Buying Time: Moneyed Interests and the Mobilization of Bias in Congressional Committees," *American Political Science Review* 84 (September 1990): 797–820; Laura Langbein, "Money and Access: Some Empirical Evidence," *Journal of Politics* 48 (November 1986): 1052–62; Laura Langbein and Mark Lotwis, "The Political Efficacy of Lobbying and Money: Gun Control in the U.S. House, 1986," *Legislative Studies Quarterly* 15 (August 1990): 413–40.
55. Quoted in Clawson, Neustadtl, and Scott, *Money Talks,* 1.
56. Quoted in "Washington Wire," *Wall Street Journal,* 17 February 1995.
57. Quoted in Richard L. Berke, "G.O.P. Seeks Foes' Donors, and Baldly," *New York Times,* 17 June 1995; David Maraniss and Michael Weisskopf, "Cashing In," *Washington Post National Weekly Edition,* 4–10 December 1995, 7.
58. Quoted in Phil Kuntz, "The Money Chase," *Wall Street Journal,* 23 October 1995.
59. Jill Abramson, "Women Are Now Key Players in Lobbying Game, For Big Companies or Heading Their Own Firms," *Wall Street Journal,* 2 August 1995.
60. Salisbury, "Washington Lobbyists," 151–55.
61. Wines, "A New Maxim for Lobbyists."
62. See John R. Wright, *Interest Groups and Congress: Lobbying, Contributions, and Influence* (Boston: Allyn & Bacon, 1996).
63. Bernard Asbell, *The Senate Nobody Knows* (Baltimore: Johns Hopkins University Press, 1981), 370–71.
64. Quoted in Wines, "A New Maximum for Lobbyists."
65. Quoted in Schlozman and Tierney, *Organized Interests,* 85.
66. On the strategic use of information by lobbyists, see Wright, *Interest Groups and Congress,* 4, 95–113.
67. Ibid., 38–49.
68. Jill Abramson and Timothy Noah, "In GOP-Controlled Congress, Lobbyists Remain as Powerful as Ever—and Perhaps More Visible," *Wall Street Journal,* 20 April 1995; Stephen Engelberg, "Business Leaves the Lobby and Sits at Congress's Table, *New York Times,* 31 March 1995.
69. See Mark A. Peterson, "The Presidency and Organized Interests: White House Patterns of Interest Group Liaison," *American Political Science Review* 86 (September 1992): 612–26; John Orman, "The President and Interest Group Access," *Presidential Studies Quarterly* 18 (Fall 1988): 787–91; Joseph A. Pika, "Opening Doors for Kindred Souls: The White House Office of Public Liaison," in *Interest Group Politics,* 3d ed., ed. Allan J. Cigler and Burdett A. Loomis (Washington, D.C.: CQ Press, 1991), 277–78.
70. Wines, "A New Maxim for Lobbyists."
71. On how interest groups decide between inside and outside strategies, see Thomas L. Gais and Jack L. Walker, Jr., "Pathways to Influence in American Politics," in Walker, *Mobilizing Interest Groups,* 103–21.
72. Thomas Galvin, "Prospects Are Poor for Enacting Mining Fees This Year," *Congressional Quarterly Weekly Report,* 2 October 1993, 2637.

73. See, for example, Elizabeth Kolbert, "When a Grass-Roots Drive Actually Isn't," *New York Times,* 26 March 1995; Jane Fritsch, "The Grass Roots, Just A Free Phone Call Away," *New York Times,* 23 June 1995.
74. Fritsch, "The Grass Roots."
75. Kirk Victor, "Astroturf Lobbying Takes a Hit," *National Journal,* 23 September 1995, 2359–60.
76. Betty H. Zisk, *The Politics of Transformation: Local Activism in the Peace and Environmental Movements* (Westport, Conn.: Praeger, 1992), 142.
77. Kim Lane Scheppele and Jack L. Walker, Jr., "The Litigation Strategies of Interest Groups," in Walker, *Mobilizing Interest Groups,* 157–83.
78. Quoted in Bill McAllister, "VA Hospitals Refuse to Sound Retreat," *Washington Post National Weekly Edition,* 29 May–4 June 1995, 31.
79. Quoted in Katherine McCarron, "Holding Lawmakers' Feet to the Fire," *National Journal,* 17 October 1992, 2379.
80. Benjamin A. Holden, "Electric Power Industry Faces Static Among Members," *Wall Street Journal,* 10 June 1996.
81. "Media PAC Contributions, 1992 Election Cycle," *Congressional Quarterly Weekly Report,* 19 September 1992, 2799.
82. Joe B. Wyatt, "Pork Barrel Science," *New York Times,* 12 October 1993.
83. *Harris Poll 1994,* no. 73, 17 November 1994, 3.
84. David Segal, "A Nation of Lobbyists," *Washington Post National Weekly Edition,* 17–23 July 1995, 11.
85. Ibid.
86. Quoted in William Safire, *Safire's Political Dictionary* (New York: Random House, 1978), 384.
87. E. E. Schattschneider, *The Semi-Sovereign People* (New York: Holt, Rinehart and Winston, 1960), 35.
88. Jonathan D. Salant and Richard Sammon, "Senate Bans Lavish Gifts from Interest Groups," *Congressional Quarterly Weekly Report,* 29 July 1995, 2237–38.
89. Jonathan D. Salant, "House Votes to Toughen Gift Restrictions," *Congressional Quarterly Weekly Report,* 18 November 1995, 3516–19.
90. See Adam Clymer, "Congress Passes Bill to Disclose Lobbyists' Roles," *New York Times,* 30 November 1995; Jonathan D. Salant, "Bill Would Open Windows on Lobbying Efforts," *Congressional Quarterly Weekly Report,* 2 December 1995, 3631–33.
91. For discussions of the political gridlock over campaign finance reform, see David S. Cloud, "Rank and File Raise Pressure for Campaign Overhaul," *Congressional Quarterly Weekly Report,* 4 November 1995, 3351; Beth Donovan, "Democrats' Overhaul Bill Dies on Senate Procedural Votes," *Congressional Quarterly Weekly Report,* 1 October 1994, 2757–58; Elizabeth Drew, "Watch 'Em Squirm," *New York Times Magazine,* 14 March 1993; Frank J. Sorauf, *Inside Campaign Finance: Myths and Realities* (New Haven: Yale University Press, 1992), 191–246.
92. United States v. Harris, 347 U.S. 612 (1954).
93. Sorauf, *Inside Campaign Finance,* 200.
94. Ibid.

Chapter 11, pp. 331–380

1. Quoted in Robert Marshall Wells and Karen Foerstel, "Clinton Proposes Increase in Minimum Wage," *Congressional Quarterly Weekly Report,* 4 February 1995, 371.
2. Times Mirror Center for the People & the Press, "Strong Support for Minimum Wage Hike and Preserving Entitlements," 17 February 1995, 16–17.
3. Quoted in "A Call for Debate on the Minimum Wage," *San Francisco Chronicle,* 17 February 1995.
4. George B. Galloway, *History of the House of Representatives* (New York: Crowell, 1961), 1–2.
5. See David Butler and Bruce Cain, *Congressional Redistricting: Comparative and Theoretical Perspectives* (New York: Macmillan, 1992), 17–23.
6. George E. Mowry, *The Era of Theodore Roosevelt and the Birth of Modern America* (New York: Harper & Row Torchbooks, 1958), 80, 264.
7. Elaine K. Swift, "Reconstitutive Change in the U.S. Congress: The Early Senate, 1789–1841," *Legislative Studies Quarterly* 14 (May 1989): 175–203.
8. Nelson W. Polsby, "The Institutionalization of the U.S. House of Representatives," *American Political Science Review* 62 (March 1968): 144–68.
9. H. Douglas Price, "Congress and the Evolution of Legislative 'Professionalism,'" in *Congress in Change,* ed. Norman J. Ornstein (New York: Praeger, 1975), 5.
10. James Sterling Young, *The Washington Community 1800–1828* (New York: Harcourt, Brace & World, 1966), 57.
11. Polsby, "The Institutionalization of the U.S. House of Representatives," 144–68.
12. Samuel Kernell, "Toward Understanding 19th Century Congressional Careers: Ambition, Competition, and Rotation," *American Journal of Political Science* 21 (November 1977): 669–93.
13. Young, *The Washington Community,* 52–53.
14. Nelson W. Polsby, "The Washington Community, 1960–1980," in *The New Congress,* ed. Thomas E. Mann and Norman J. Ornstein (Washington, D.C.: American Enterprise Institute, 1981), 30.
15. David T. Canon, "The Institutionalization of Leadership in the U.S. Congress," *Legislative Studies Quarterly* 14 (August 1989): 415–43.
16. Polsby, "The Institutionalization of the U.S. House of Representatives," 144–68.
17. Nelson W. Polsby, Miriam Gallaher, and Barry Spencer Rundquist, "The Growth of the Seniority System in the U.S. House of Representatives," *American Political Science Review 63* (September 1969): 787–807.
18. Raymond E. Wolfinger and Joan Heifetz Hollinger, "Safe Seats, Seniority, and Power in Congress," in *Readings on Congress,* ed. Raymond E. Wolfinger (Englewood Cliffs, N.J.: Prentice-Hall, 1971).
19. Quoted in Roger H. Davidson and Walter J. Oleszek, *Congress and Its Members,* 3d ed. (Washington, D.C.: CQ Press, 1990), 218.
20. Steven S. Smith, *Call to Order* (Washington, D.C.: Brookings Institution, 1989).
21. Lawrence C. Dodd and Bruce I. Oppenheimer, "Consolidating Power in the House: The Rise of the New Oligarchy," in *Congress Reconsidered,* 4th ed., ed. Lawrence C. Dodd and Bruce I. Oppenheimer (Washington, D.C.: CQ Press, 1989).
22. See Lawrence C. Dodd and Bruce I. Oppenheimer, "Maintaining Order in the House: The Struggle of Institutional Equilibrium," in *Congress Reconsidered,* 5th ed., ed. Lawrence C. Dodd and Bruce I. Oppenheimer (Washington, D.C.: CQ Press, 1993); Paul J. Quirk, "Structure and Performance: An Evaluation," in *The Postreform Congress,* ed. Roger H. Davidson (New York: St. Martin's, 1992).
23. Steven S. Smith and Christopher J. Deering, *Committees in Congress,* 2d ed. (Washington, D.C.: CQ Press, 1990).
24. John R. Hibbing, *Congressional Careers: Contours of Life in the U.S. House of Representatives* (Chapel Hill: University of North Carolina Press, 1991).
25. John B. Gilmour, "Summits and Stalemates: Bipartisan Negotiations in the Postreform Era," in *The Postreform Congress,* ed. Roger H. Davidson (New York: St. Martin's, 1992); Quirk, "Structure and Performance," 311–12.
26. Jackie Koszczuk, "Gingrich Puts More Power into Speaker's Hands," *Congressional Quarterly Weekly Report,* 7 October 1995, 3049–53; David Rogers, "GOP's Rare Year Owes Much to How Gingrich Disciplined the House," *Wall Street Journal,* 18 December 1995.
27. Koszczuk, "Gingrich Puts More Power into Speaker's Hands," 3052.
28. David S. Cloud, "GOP, to Its Own Great Delight, Enacts House Rules Changes," *Congressional Quarterly Weekly Report,* 7 January 1995, 15; Koszczuk, "Gingrich Puts More Power into Speaker's Hands," 3053.
29. See William S. White, *Citadel* (New York: Harper & Row, 1956).
30. Donald R. Matthews, *U.S. Senators and Their World* (New York: Vintage, 1960).
31. James M. Lindsay, *Congress and Nuclear Weapons* (Baltimore: Johns Hopkins University Press, 1991), 29.
32. Barbara Sinclair, *The Transformation of the U.S. Senate* (Baltimore: Johns Hopkins University Press, 1989).

33. Helen Dewar, "The Etiquette of a Revolution," *Washington Post National Weekly Edition*, 26 June–2 July 1995, 12.
34. Walter J. Oleszek, *Congressional Procedures and the Policy Process*, 3d. ed. (Washington, D.C.: CQ Press, 1989), 223.
35. Albert Somit and Andrea Roemmele, "The Victorious Legislative Incumbent as a Threat to Democracy: A Nine Nation Study," *Extension of Remarks*, July 1995, 9–11.
36. Butler and Cain, *Congressional Redistricting*, 24–26; Galloway, *History of the House of Representatives*, 22–25.
37. In Baker v. Carr (369 U.S. 186 1962), the Supreme Court intervened for the first time in a dispute over the way legislative districts were drawn. In a 1963 decision, Gray v. Sanders (372 U.S. 368), the Court established the "one voter, one vote" principle in state judicial elections. A 1964 decision, Wesberry v. Sanders (376 U.S. 1), extended the one voter, one vote principle to U.S. House elections.
38. Davis v. Bandemer, 478 U.S. 109 (1986).
39. Butler and Cain, *Congressional Redistricting*, 11–13.
40. Albert D. Cover and David R. Mayhew, "Congressional Dynamics and the Decline of Competitive Congressional Elections," in *Congress Reconsidered*, 2d ed., ed. Lawrence C. Dodd and Bruce I. Oppenheimer (Washington, D.C.: CQ Press, 1981), 72–73; John A. Ferejohn, "On the Decline of Competition in Congressional Elections," *American Political Science Review* 71 (March 1977): 166–76; Gary C. Jacobson, *The Electoral Origins of Divided Government: Competition in U.S. House Elections, 1946–1988* (Boulder, Colo: Westview, 1990), 94–96.
41. Peverill Squire, "The Partisan Consequences of Congressional Redistricting," *American Politics Quarterly* (April 1995) 23:229–40; Peverill Squire, "The Results of Partisan Redistricting in Seven U.S. States during the 1970s," *Legislative Studies Quarterly* 10 (May 1985): 259–66.
42. Thornburg v. Gingles, 478 U.S. 30 (1986).
43. Kevin A. Hill, "Does the Creation of Majority Black Districts Aid Republicans? An Analysis of the 1992 Congressional Elections in Eight Southern States," *Journal of Politics* 57 (May 1995): 384–401.
44. Shaw v. Reno, 125 L Ed. 2d 511 (1993).
45. Miller v. Johnson, 63 U.S.L.W. 4726 (1995).
46. Bush, Governor of Texas, et al. v. Vera et al., 94–805 (1996); Shaw et al. v. Hunt, Governor of North Carolina, et al., 94–923 (1996).
47. Richard F. Fenno, Jr., *Home Style* (Boston: Little, Brown, 1978). See also Glen R. Parker, *Homeward Bound: Explaining Changes in Congressional Behavior* (Pittsburgh: University of Pittsburgh Press, 1986).
48. David Mayhew, *Congress: The Electoral Connection* (New Haven: Yale University Press, 1974).
49. John Kirsch, "City to Add 5 Buses, Alter Mall Interchange," *Iowa City Press-Citizen*, 31 May 1995.
50. David Rogers, "Budget-Cutting Republicans Repackage Pork as Regulatory Relief for Their Business Allies," *Wall Street Journal*, 22 August 1995.
51. Mayhew, *Congress*, 61–73.
52. Quoted in David Yepsen, "Troopers Are in a Tough Spot," *Des Moines Register*, 4 November 1991.
53. Mayhew, *Congress*, 49–52.
54. See Timothy E. Cook, *Making Laws and Making News: Media Strategies in the U.S. House of Representatives* (Washington, D.C.: Brookings Institution, 1989); Stephen Hess, *Live From Capitol Hill! Studies of Congress and the Media* (Washington, D.C.: Brookings Institution, 1991).
55. See Mary Collins, "News of the Congress by the Congress," in *American Politics*, 2d ed., ed. Allan J. Cigler and Burdett A. Loomis (Boston: Houghton Mifflin, 1992); Teresa Riordan, "Beam Me Up, Scotty," in *American Politics*, ed. Allan J. Cigler and Burdett A. Loomis (Boston: Houghton Mifflin, 1989); Steven Thomma, "Congress' Perks Add Up Quickly," *Des Moines Register*, 20 October 1991.
56. Ceci Connolly, "Leaving Very Little to Chance, Kennedy Pushes His Clout," *Congressional Quarterly Weekly Report*, 17 September 1994, 2593.
57. Diana Evans Yiannakis, "House Members' Communication Styles: Newsletters and Press Releases," *Journal of Politics* 44 (November 1982): 1049–71.
58. Rep. Morris Udall (D-Ariz.), quoted in William Boot, "Hustling the Folks Back Home," *Columbia Journalism Review*, November/December 1987, 24.
59. Christopher Georges, "Rep. Engel Triumphs by Being Dull in D.C. But Active at Home," *Wall Street Journal*, 11 June 1996.
60. Norman J. Ornstein, Thomas E. Mann, and Michael Malbin, *Vital Statistics on Congress, 1995–1996* (Washington, D.C.: CQ Press, 1996), 81, 85.
61. *"Colorado Republican Federal Campaign Committee et al. v. Federal Election Commission,"* 94–489 (1996).
62. Calculated by authors from ibid., 110–11.
63. Quoted in James M. Perry, "Moderate Republicans Look Like a Dying Breed as Standard Bearers Forsake Acrimonious Senate," *Wall Street Journal*, 28 December 1995.
64. John Harwood, "For California Senator, Fund Raising Becomes Overwhelming Burden," *Wall Street Journal*, 2 March 1994.
65. See Lyn Ragsdale, "Do Voters Matter? Democracy in Congressional Elections," in *Congressional Politics*, ed. Christopher J. Deering (Chicago: Dorsey Press, 1989).
66. Kelly D. Patterson and David B. Magleby, "Trends: Public Support for Congress," *Public Opinion Quarterly* 56 (Winter 1992): 539–51; Samuel C. Patterson and Gregory A. Caldeira, "Standing up for Congress: Variations in Public Esteem Since the 1960s," *Legislative Studies Quarterly* 15 (February 1990): 25–47.
67. See "AMA Campaign Aims to Boost Doctor's Image," *Des Moines Register*, 13 August 1991; Robert L. Kahn, Barbara A. Gutek, Eugenia Barton, and Daniel Katz, "Americans Love Their Bureaucrats," in *Bureaucratic Power in National Policy Making*, 4th ed., ed. Francis E. Rourke (Boston: Little, Brown, 1986).
68. Jacobson, *The Electoral Origins of Divided Government*, chap. 4; Peverill Squire, "Challengers in U.S. Senate Elections," *Legislative Studies Quarterly* 14 (November 1989): 531–47.
69. See David T. Canon, *Actors, Athletes, and Astronauts: Political Amateurs in the United States Congress* (Chicago: University of Chicago Press, 1990).
70. See Linda L. Fowler and Robert D. McClure, *Political Ambition: Who Decides to Run for Congress* (New Haven: Yale University Press, 1989).
71. Peverill Squire, "Competition and Uncontested Seats in U.S. House Elections," *Legislative Studies Quarterly* 14 (May 1989): 281–95.
72. Squire, "Challengers," 531–47; Mark C. Westlye, *Senate Elections and Campaign Intensity* (Baltimore: Johns Hopkins University Press, 1991).
73. Mark G. Michaelsen, "My Life as a Congressional Candidate," in *The Quest for National Office*, ed. Stephen J. Wayne and Clyde Wilcox (New York: St. Martin's, 1992).
74. Gary C. Jacobson, *Money in Congressional Elections* (New Haven: Yale University Press, 1980).
75. See Gary C. Jacobson, *The Politics of Congressional Elections*, 3d ed. (New York: HarperCollins, 1992), 57.
76. Susan A. Banducci and Jeffrey A. Karp, "Electoral Consequences of Scandal and Reapportionment in the 1992 House Elections," *American Politics Quarterly* 22 (January 1994): 223–26; Gary C. Jacobson, "Checking Out: The Effects of Bank Overdrafts on the 1992 House Elections," *American Journal of Political Science* 38 (August 1994): 601–24.
77. James E. Campbell, "The Presidential Surge and Its Midterm Decline in Congressional Elections," *Journal of Politics* 53 (May 1991): 477–87.
78. Jacobson, *The Politics of Congressional Elections*, 162–72.
79. Randall L. Calvert and John A. Ferejohn, "Coattail Voting in Recent Presidential Elections," *American Political Science Review* 77 (June 1983): 407–19.
80. Morris P. Fiorina, *Divided Government* (New York: Macmillan, 1992).
81. See Rich Jaroslovsky, "Washington Wire," *Wall Street Journal*, 21 January 1994.

82. R. Michael Alvarez and Matthew M. Schousen, "Policy Moderation or Conflicting Expectations?" *American Politics Quarterly* 21 (October 1993): 410–38; Jacobson, *The Electoral Origins of Divided Government,* 112–20.
83. See Irwin N. Gertzog, *Congressional Women: Their Recruitment, Treatment, and Behavior* (New York: Praeger, 1984), 13–31.
84. Barbara C. Burrell, *A Woman's Place Is in the House: Campaigning for Congress in the Feminist Era* (Ann Arbor: University of Michigan Press, 1994), 131–50.
85. See Carol M. Swain, *Black Faces, Black Interests: The Representation of African Americans in Congress* (Cambridge: Harvard University Press, 1993).
86. Bernard Grofman and Lisa Handley, "Minority Population and Black and Hispanic Congressional Success in the 1970s and 1980s," *American Politics Quarterly* 17 (October 1989): 436–45.
87. See, for example, Rodney E. Hero and Caroline J. Tolbert, "Latinos and Substantive Representation in the U.S. House of Representatives: Direct, Indirect, or Nonexistent?" *American Journal of Political Science* 39 (August 1995): 640–52.
88. See Burrell, *A Woman's Place,* 151–74; Sue Thomas, *How Women Legislate* (New York: Oxford University Press, 1994), chap. 3; Arturo Vega and Juanita M. Firestone, "The Effects of Gender on Congressional Behavior and the Substantive Representation of Women," *Legislative Studies Quarterly* 20 (May 1995): 213–22.
89. David Broder, "A Representative Congress," *Washington Post National Weekly Edition,* 10–16 July 1995.
90. See Louis Fisher, "History of Pay Adjustments for Members of Congress," in *The Rewards of Public Service,* ed. Robert W. Hartman and Arnold R. Weber (Washington, D.C.: Brookings Institution, 1980).
91. Phil Kuntz, "Congressmen Squirm as Their Pensions Come Under Spotlight," *Wall Street Journal,* 26 January 1995.
92. See Thomma, "Congress' Perks Add Up Quickly"; "Congress' Perks," *Des Moines Register,* 3 October 1991.
93. Thomas J. O'Donnell, "Controlling Legislative Time," in *The House at Work,* ed. Joseph Cooper and G. Calvin Mackenzie (Austin: University of Texas Press, 1981); David E. Price, *The Congressional Experience* (Boulder, Colo.: Westview, 1992), 37–39.
94. Rep. Jack Fields of Texas (R-Tex.), quoted in "TX 08: Fields Departs," *The Hotline Weekly,* 18 December 1995.
95. Rep. Fred Grandy (R-Iowa), quoted in Kenneth Pins, "Tired But Not Tongue-Tied, Grandy Leaves Political Life," *Des Moines Register,* 16 October 1994.
96. "Leach's Wife Gets Him Ready to Head Banking Committee," *Iowa City Press-Citizen,* 23 November 1994.
97. Rep. Tim Roemer (D-Ind.), quoted in Phil Duncan, "Routines in the House and Family Values," *Congressional Quarterly Weekly Report,* 21 October 1995, 3238.
98. "No Home Back Home: 100 Congressmen Don't Have Second Residences," *USA Today,* 13 December 1982.
99. Rep. Donald Pease (D-Ohio), quoted in George Will, "Hating Government's Losses," *Iowa City Press-Citizen,* 18 November 1991.
100. Quoted in John L. Moore, *Speaking of Washington* (Washington, D.C.: Congressional Quarterly, 1993), 147.
101. Dennis F. Thompson, *Ethics in Congress: From Individual to Institutional Corruption* (Washington, D.C.: Brookings, 1995), 2.
102. Ibid., 3.
103. Phil Kuntz, "House Vote Bars Members' Acceptance of Almost All Free Meals, Gifts, Trips," *Wall Street Journal,* 17 November 1995.
104. See Jonathan D. Salant, "Faircloth Cleared by Ethics Panel," *Congressional Quarterly Weekly Report,* 4 March 1995, 665; "Senator Seeks Advice on Hogs," *Des Moines Register,* 12 December 1994.
105. Amy Barrett, "How Are You Voting? What Are Your Stocks?" *Business Week,* 28 August 1995, 66–68; Thompson, *Ethics in Congress,* esp. chap. 6.
106. Sarah A. Binder, "Partisanship and Procedural Choice: Institutional Change in the Early Congress, 1789–1823," *Journal of Politics* 57 (November 1995): 1093–1118; John F. Hoadley, "The Emergence of Political Parties in Congress, 1789–1803," *American Political Science Review* 74 (September 1980): 757–79.
107. David W. Rohde, *Parties and Leaders in the Postreform House* (Chicago: University of Chicago Press, 1991), 31–34.
108. See John M. Barry, *The Ambition and the Power* (New York: Penguin, 1989).
109. Jonathan D. Salant, "New Chairmen Swing to the Right; Freshmen Get Choice Posts," *Congressional Quarterly Weekly Report,* 10 December 1995, 3494.
110. Barbara Sinclair, "The Emergence of Strong Leadership in the 1980s House of Representatives," *Journal of Politics* 54 (August 1992): 657–84.
111. Rep. Joe Scarborough (R-Fla.), quoted in "GOP Can't Sell Plan to Return Workers," *Des Moines Register,* 5 January 1996.
112. Donna Cassata, "GOP Leaders Walk a Fine Line to Keep Freshmen on Board," *Congressional Quarterly Weekly Report,* 14 October 1995, 3122–23; Kenneth Pins, "GOP Isn't Afraid to Flex Its Muscle to Ensure Unity," *Des Moines Register,* 1 October 1995; David Rogers, "GOP Disciplines Member of House Over 'Wrong' Vote," *Wall Street Journal,* 12 October 1995.
113. Cassata, "GOP Leaders Walk a Fine Line," 3122.
114. See Mary Alice Nye, "Conservative Coalition Support in the House of Representatives: 1963–1988," *Legislative Studies Quarterly* 17 (May 1993): 255–70.
115. See Charles O. Jones, *The Minority Party in Congress* (Boston: Little, Brown, 1970); Rohde, *Parties and Leaders in the Postreform House,* 127–32.
116. Dodd and Oppenheimer, "Maintaining Order in the House," 60–62.
117. Jennifer Babson, "Democrats Refine the Tactics of Minority Party Power," *Congressional Quarterly Weekly Report,* 15 July 1995, 2037; David S. Cloud with Julianna Grunwald, "Democrats Find Their Footing in Minority Party Trenches," *Congressional Quarterly Weekly Report,* 1 July 1995, 1893–96; Carroll J. Doherty, "Uproar over Democrat's Switch Snarls House Foreign Aid Bill," *Congressional Quarterly Weekly Report,* 1 July 1995, 1936–38.
118. Quoted in Albert R. Hunt, "A Voice for the Minority," *Wall Street Journal,* 15 June 1995.
119. "Senate Firsts," *Senate History* 14 (Fall 1991): 6–7.
120. See Roger H. Davidson, "The Senate: If Everyone Leads, Who Follows?" in *Congress Reconsidered,* 4th ed., ed. Lawrence C. Dodd and Bruce I. Oppenheimer (Washington, D.C.: CQ Press, 1989).
121. James H. Kuklinski and Lee Sigelman, "When Objectivity Is Not Objective: Network Television Coverage of U.S. Senators and the 'Paradox of Objectivity,'" *Journal of Politics* 54 (August 1992): 810–33; Peverill Squire, "Who Gets National News Coverage in the U.S. Senate?" *American Politics Quarterly* 16 (April 1988): 139–56.
122. Norman Ornstein, quoted in Graeme Browning, "Freelancers," *National Journal,* 24 September 1995, 2203.
123. Kenneth A. Shepsle and Barry R. Weingast, "The Institutional Foundations of Committee Power," *American Political Science Review* 81 (March 1987): 85–104; Kenneth A. Shepsle and Barry R. Weingast, "Why Are Congressional Committees Powerful?" *American Political Science Review* 81 (September 1987): 935–45.
124. Keith Krehbiel, *Information and Legislative Organization* (Ann Arbor: University of Michigan Press, 1991), 254–56.
125. Ornstein, Mann, and Malbin, *Vital Statistics on Congress, 1995–1996,* 121.
126. Richard F. Fenno, Jr., *Congressmen in Committees* (Boston: Little, Brown, 1973).
127. Richard L. Hall and Bernard Grofman, "The Committee Assignment Process and the Conditional Nature of Committee Bias," *American Political Science Review* 84 (December 1990): 1149–66.
128. Jonathan D. Salant, "Retrenching House Democrats Seek Solace in Seniority," *Congressional Quarterly Weekly*

Report, 17 December 1994, 3546; September Trevino, "GOP Adds Seats to 4 Panels," *Congressional Quarterly Weekly Report,* 10 June 1995, 1612.

129. Ornstein, Mann, and Malbin, *Vital Statistics on Congress, 1995–1996,* 135–36.
130. Jonathan D. Salant, "LSOs Are No Longer Separate, But Work's Almost Equal," *Congressional Quarterly Weekly Report,* 27 May 1995, 14.
131. Jackie Calmes, "Conservatives Bash GOP Congressional Staffers as Moderates Out of Step with the Revolution," *Wall Street Journal,* 18 July 1995; John H. Fund, "Bob Dole's Dealmaker," *Wall Street Journal,* 7 July 1995.
132. Christine DeGregorio and Kevin Snider, "Leadership Appeal in the U.S. House of Representatives: Comparing Officeholders and Aides," *Legislative Studies Quarterly* 20 (November 1995): 491–511.
133. For an extended discussion of the legislative process, see Walter J. Oleszek, *Congressional Procedures and the Policy Process,* 4th ed. (Washington, D.C.: CQ Press, 1996).
134. Smith, *Call to Order,* 155.
135. Alan Greenblatt, "Two Members, Two Approaches to Competing Demands," *Congressional Quarterly Weekly Report,* 17 June 1995, 1705.
136. C. Lawrence Evans, "Influence in Congressional Committees: Participation, Manipulation, and Anticipation," in *Congressional Politics,* ed. Christopher J. Deering (Chicago: Dorsey Press, 1989); Richard L. Hall, "Committee Decision Making in the Postreform Congress," in *Congress Reconsidered,* 4th ed., ed. Lawrence C. Dodd and Bruce I. Oppenheimer (Washington, D.C.: CQ Press, 1989).
137. Richard L. Hall and C. Lawrence Evans, "The Power of Subcommittees," *Journal of Politics* 52 (May 1990): 335–55.
138. See "Discharge Petitions Get GOP Attention," *Congressional Quarterly Weekly Report,* 2 October 1993, 2618; Phil Kuntz, "Anti-Secrecy Drive Putting Democrats on the Defensive," *Congressional Quarterly Weekly Report,* 11 September 1993, 2369–70.
139. Oleszek, *Congressional Procedures,* 149–50.
140. Sinclair, *The Transformation of the U.S. Senate,* 136.
141. Smith, *Call to Order,* 98–119.
142. Ibid., 202–3; Timothy J. Conlan, Margaret T. Wrightson, and David R. Beam, *Taxing Choices: The Politics of Tax Reform* (Washington, D.C.: CQ Press, 1990), 190–91.
143. George Anthan, "Congress Gives Pizza Firms a Slice of the School Lunch Pie," *Des Moines Register,* 28 November 1991.
144. Brigid Schulte, "Fine Print Is Often Missed," *Des Moines Register,* 27 October 1995.
145. Lindsay, *Congress and Nuclear Weapons,* 140.
146. See R. Douglas Arnold, *The Logic of Congressional Action* (New Haven: Yale University Press, 1990); William T. Bianco, *Trust: Representatives and Constituents* (Ann Arbor: University of Michigan Press, 1994).
147. Mathew D. McCubbins and Thomas Schwartz, "Congressional Oversight Overlooked: Police Patrols versus Fire Alarms," *American Journal of Political Science* 28 (February 1984): 165–79. For evidence on the frequency of police-patrol oversight, see Joel D. Aberbach, *Keeping a Watchful Eye* (Washington, D.C.: Brookings Institution, 1990), 93–104.
148. John A. Ferejohn and Charles R. Shipan, "Congressional Influence on Administrative Agencies: A Case Study of Telecommunications Policy," in *Congress Reconsidered,* 4th ed., ed. Lawrence C. Dodd and Bruce I. Oppenheimer (Washington, D.C.: CQ Press, 1989).
149. Quoted in "Critics Rip Plan to Force Disability Treadmill Tests," *Des Moines Register,* 22 May 1991.
150. See Jennifer Babson, "House Approves Crime Funds, Rejects Peacekeeping Cuts," *Congressional Quarterly Weekly Report,* 2 July 1994, 1809; Joseph E. Broadhus, "The EEOC and the House," *Liberty,* November/December 1994,16–17; Jon Healy, "Airport Funding Measure Heads to President," *Congressional Quarterly Weekly Report,* 13 August 1995, 2330; Jon Healy, "Airport Program Renewal OK'd," *Congressional Quarterly Weekly Report,* 18 June 1995, 1593.
151. Nelson W. Polsby, *Congress and the Presidency,* 4th ed. (Englewood Cliffs, N.J.: Prentice-Hall, 1986), 14.

Chapter 12, pp. 381–424

1. James L. Sundquist, *The Decline and Resurgence of Congress* (Washington, D.C.: Brookings Institution, 1981), chap. 2.
2. See David Gray Adler, "The Constitution and Presidential Warmaking," *Political Science Quarterly* 103 (Spring 1988): 8–13; Alexander Hamilton, "Federalist No. 69," in *The Federalist Papers,* ed. Garry Wills (New York: Bantam Books, 1982); Louis Henkin, *Foreign Affairs and the Constitution* (Mineola, N.Y.: Foundation Press, 1972), 50–51; Arthur M. Schlesinger, Jr., *The Imperial Presidency* (Boston: Houghton Mifflin, 1989), 6, 61–62.
3. Some scholars argue that the president's personality is the single most important determinant of how a presidency works. See, for example, James D. Barber, *The Presidential Character: Predicting Performance in the White House,* 4th ed. (Englewood Cliffs, N.J.: Prentice-Hall, 1992).
4. Wilfred Binkley, *The Powers of the President* (Garden City, N.Y.: Doubleday, Doran, 1937), chap. 2.
5. James Sterling Young, *The Washington Community 1800–1828* (New York: Harcourt, Brace & World, 1966), 160–80.
6. Leonard D. White, *The Jacksonians: A Study in Administrative History, 1829–1861* (New York: Macmillan, 1954), 22–25.
7. Binkley, *The Powers of the President,* 120–30.
8. George B. Galloway with Sidney Wise, *History of the House of Representatives,* 2d ed. (New York: Crowell, 1976), 315–17.
9. Sidney M. Milkis and Michael Nelson, *The American Presidency: Origins and Development, 1776–1993,* 2d ed. (Washington, D.C.: CQ Press, 1994), 248–49.
10. Fred Greenstein, "Change and Continuity in the Modern Presidency," in *The New American Political System,* ed. Anthony King (Washington, D.C.: American Enterprise Institute, 1978), 45–85; Nelson W. Polsby, ed. *The Modern Presidency* (New York: Random House, 1973).
11. William E. Leuchtenburg, *Franklin D. Roosevelt and the New Deal* (New York: Harper & Row, 1963), chap. 3; Nelson W. Polsby, "Some Landmarks in Modern Presidential-Congressional Relations," in *Both Ends of the Avenue,* ed. Anthony King (Washington, D.C.: American Enterprise Institute, 1983).
12. Clinton Rossiter, *The American Presidency* (New York: Harcourt, Brace, 1960), chap. 1.
13. Austin Ranney, *Curing the Mischief of Faction* (Berkeley: University of California Press, 1975), 171–74.
14. Ibid., 68.
15. Ibid., 69.
16. Robert K. Murray, *The 103rd Ballot* (New York: Harper & Row, 1976).
17. Nelson W. Polsby, *Consequences of Party Reform* (New York: Oxford University Press, 1983), 9–16.
18. James Lengle and Byron Shafer, "Primary Rules, Political Power, and Social Change," *American Political Science Review* 70 (March 1976): 25–40.
19. Polsby, *Consequences of Party Reform,* 56.
20. Ibid., 53–54.
21. See the discussion in Nelson W. Polsby, "The Iowa Caucuses in a Front-Loaded System: A Few Historical Lessons," in *The Iowa Caucuses and the Presidential Nominating Process,* ed. Peverill Squire (Boulder, Colo.: Westview, 1989).
22. Michael L. Goldstein, *Guide to the 1996 Presidential Election* (Washington, D.C: CQ Press, 1995), 27.
23. "OK, Phil, Take Off the Snowshoes," *National Journal,* 10 April 1993, 857.
24. "Don't Expect Many Postcards," *National Journal,* 7 August 1993, 1959.
25. Polsby, *Consequences of Party Reform,* 66.
26. Lester G. Seligman and Cary R. Covington, *The Coalitional Presidency* (Chicago: Dorsey Press, 1989), chap. 3.

27. John H. Aldrich, "Presidential Campaigns in Party- and Candidate-Centered Eras," and Mathew D. McCubbins, "Party Decline and Presidential Campaigns in the Television Age," both in *Under the Watchful Eye: Managing Presidential Campaigns in the Television Era,* ed. Mathew D. McCubbins (Washington, D.C.: CQ Press, 1992).
28. For a detailed discussion of the FECA and its amendments, see Nelson W. Polsby and Aaron Wildavsky, *Presidential Elections: Strategies and Structures of American Politics,* 9th ed. (Chatham, N.J.: Chatham House, 1996), chap. 3.
29. Stephen J. Wayne, *The Road to the White House 1996* (New York: St. Martin's, 1996), 34–35.
30. Herbert E. Alexander and Anthony Corrado, *Financing the 1992 Election* (Armonk, N.Y.: Sharpe, 1995), 244; Wayne, *The Road to the White House 1996,* 51.
31. Kathleen Hall Jamieson, *Dirty Politics* (New York: Oxford University Press, 1992), 17–25.
32. Alexander and Corrado, *Financing the 1992 Election,* 110; Federal Election Commission, "Parties' Pre General Reports Show Large Jumps in Financial Activity Over Previous Two Election Cycles," 29 October 1996.
33. Martin Wattenberg, *The Rise of Candidate-Centered Politics: Presidential Elections of the 1980s* (Cambridge: Harvard University Press, 1991).
34. Wayne, *The Road to the White House 1996,* 193.
35. For an excellent discussion of the details and "what ifs" that enshroud the electoral college, see Walter Berns, ed., *After the People Vote: A Guide to the Electoral College,* rev. ed. (Washington, D.C.: American Enterprise Institute, 1992).
36. Norman J. Ornstein, "Three Disputed Elections," in *After the People Vote: A Guide to the Electoral College,* rev. ed., ed. Walter Berns (Washington, D.C.: American Enterprise Institute, 1992).
37. Goldstein, *Guide to the 1996 Presidential Election,* 74.
38. Lyn Ragsdale, *Vital Statistics on the Presidency: Washington to Clinton* (Washington, D.C: CQ Press, 1996), 396.
39. Louis Fisher, *Constitutional Conflicts Between Congress and the President,* 3d ed. (Lawrence: University of Kansas Press, 1991), 86, 93.
40. Louis Fisher, *Presidential Spending Power* (Princeton, N.J.: Princeton University Press, 1975), 107.
41. Robert Pear, "Bush Orders Quicker Expenditure of $9.7 Billion to Aid Economy," *New York Times,* 6 December 1991.
42. Quoted in Louis Fisher, *President and Congress* (Princeton, N.J.: Princeton University Press, 1972), 36.
43. See Fisher, *Constitutional Conflicts Between Congress and the President,* chap. 2–3.
44. Myers v. United States, 272 U.S. 52 (1926); Humphrey's Executor v. United States, 295 U.S. 602 (1935).
45. Schlesinger, *Imperial Presidency,* esp. chap. 5–8.
46. John Hart, *The Presidential Branch* (New York: Pergamon Press, 1987), chap. 2.
47. U.S. Congress, Committee on Post Office and Civil Service, "Presidential Staffing—A Brief Overview," (Washington, D.C.: U.S. Government Printing Office, 1978); Harold W. Stanley and Richard G. Niemi, *Vital Statistics on American Politics,* 5th ed. (Washington, D.C.: CQ Press, 1995), 247–48.
48. Leuchtenburg, *Franklin D. Roosevelt and the New Deal,* 192.
49. Jimmy Carter, *Keeping Faith: Memoirs of a President* (New York: Bantam Books, 1983), 32–33.
50. Kenneth T. Walsh and Bruce B. Auster, "Taking the Offensive," *U.S. News & World Report,* 29 January 1996, 34.
51. Quoted in Paul C. Light, *Vice Presidential Power: Advice and Influence in the White House* (Baltimore: Johns Hopkins University Press, 1984), 13. For a review of some of the most amusing disparagements of the vice presidency, see Paul F. Boller, Jr., *Congressional Anecdotes* (New York: Oxford University Press, 1991), 223–29.
52. Quoted in Milkis and Nelson, *The American Presidency,* 417. Milkis and Nelson observe that Garner actually referred to "a bodily fluid other than spit" (430).
53. Matthew Cooper and Sander Thoenes, "Leave It to Al and Victor," *U.S. News & World Report,* 26 June 1995, 43; Donald G. McNeil, Jr., "Gore Visit Signals New Status for Pretoria," *New York Times,* 4 December 1995.
54. Paul Brace and Barbara Hinckley, *Follow the Leader: Opinion Polls and the Modern Presidents* (New York: Basic Books, 1992).
55. James M. Perry, "Clinton Relies Heavily on White House Pollster to Take Words Right Out of the Public's Mouth," *Wall Street Journal,* 23 March 1994.
56. Alexander George, *Presidential Decisionmaking in Foreign Policy: The Effective Use of Information and Advice* (Boulder, Colo.: Westview, 1980); Richard T. Johnson, "Presidential Style," in *Perspectives on the Presidency,* ed. Aaron Wildavsky (Boston: Little, Brown, 1975).
57. George E. Reedy, *The Twilight of the Presidency* (New York: World Publishing, 1970).
58. Hugh Heclo, "OMB and the Presidency: The Problem of 'Neutral Competence,'" *Public Interest* 38 (Winter 1975): 80–98.
59. Larry Berman, *The Office of Management and Budget and the Presidency, 1921–1979* (Princeton, N.J.: Princeton University Press, 1979).
60. William Greider, "The Education of David Stockman," *Atlantic Monthly,* December 1981, 32.
61. Terry M. Moe, "The Politicized Presidency," in *The New Direction in American Politics,* ed. John E. Chubb and Paul E. Peterson (Washington, D.C.: Brookings Institution, 1985).
62. Richard E. Neustadt, "Presidency and Legislation: Planning the President's Program," *American Political Science Review* 49 (December 1955): 980–1021; Richard E. Neustadt, "Presidency and Legislation: The Growth of Central Clearance," *American Political Science Review* 48 (September 1954): 641–71.
63. Jeffrey K. Tulis, *The Rhetorical Presidency* (Princeton, N.J.: Princeton University Press, 1987), chap. 5.
64. Richard E. Neustadt, "The Presidency at Mid-century," in *The Presidency,* ed. Aaron Wildavsky (Boston: Little, Brown, 1969), 199.
65. David Stoesz, *Small Change: Domestic Policy Under the Clinton Presidency* (White Plains, N.Y.: Longman, 1996), chap. 2.
66. See James P. Pfiffner, *The Strategic Presidency: Hitting the Ground Running* (Chicago: Dorsey Press, 1988).
67. Stephen Hess, *Organizing the Presidency,* 2d ed. (Washington, D.C.: Brookings Institution, 1988).
68. Richard E. Neustadt, *Presidential Power and the Modern President* (New York: Free Press, 1990), chap. 3.
69. Tulis, *The Rhetorical Presidency,* chap. 5.
70. Samuel Kernell, *Going Public: New Strategies of Presidential Leadership,* 2d. ed. (Washington, D.C.: CQ Press, 1992).
71. Barbara Kellerman, *The Political Presidency: Practice of Leadership from Kennedy Through Reagan* (New York: Oxford University Press, 1984); Kernell, *Going Public,* chap. 5.
72. Jon R. Bond and Richard Fleisher, *The President in the Legislative Arena* (Chicago: University of Chicago Press, 1990).
73. Cary R. Covington, J. Mark Wrighton, and Rhonda Kinney, "A 'Presidency-Augmented' Model of Presidential Success on House Roll Call Votes," *American Journal of Political Science* 39 (November 1995): 1001–24.
74. Mark A. Peterson, *Legislating Together: The White House and Capitol Hill from Eisenhower to Reagan* (Cambridge: Harvard University Press, 1990).
75. See Robert Maranto, *Politics and Bureaucracy in the Modern Presidency* (Westport, Conn.: Greenwood, 1993); Richard W. Waterman, *Presidential Influence and the Administrative State* (Knoxville: University of Tennessee Press, 1989).
76. Ronald Randall, "Presidential Power Versus Bureaucratic Intransigence: The Influence of the Nixon Administration on Welfare Policy," *American Political Science Review* 73 (September 1979): 795–810; B. Dan Wood, "Principals, Bureaucrats, and Responsiveness in Clean Air Enforcements," *American Political Science Review* 82 (March 1988): 213–34.
77. Lyn Ragsdale, "The Politics of Presidential Speechmaking, 1949–1980," *American Political Science Review* 78 (December 1984): 971–84.

78. John A. Maltese, *Spin Control: The White House Office of Communications and the Management of Presidential News* (Chapel Hill: University of North Carolina Press, 1992).
79. See Richard W. Waterman, ed., *The Presidency Reconsidered* (Itasca, Ill.: F. E. Peacock, 1993).
80. Jennifer S. Thomas, "A Haitian Chronology," *Congressional Quarterly Weekly Report,* 23 October 1993, 2898.
81. Christine C. Lawrence, "Ban on Homosexuals to End in Two Steps, Frank Says," *Congressional Quarterly Weekly Report,* 23 January 1993, 187.
82. Bond and Fleisher, *The President in the Legislative Arena,* chap. 7.
83. Chuck Alston, "Bush's High Public Standing Held Little Sway on Hill," *Congressional Quarterly Weekly Report,* 28 December 1991, 3751.

Chapter 13, pp. 425–460

1. Christopher H. Foreman, Jr., "The Fast Track: Federal Agencies and the Political Demand for AIDS Drugs," *Brookings Review* 9 (Spring 1991): 30–37.
2. Philip J. Hilts, "F.D.A. Has Cut Its 'Drug Lag,' Report Finds," *New York Times,* 9 November 1995.
3. "FDA's Critics Renew Efforts to Kill Agency," *Des Moines Register,* 30 January 1995.
4. Charles T. Goodsell, *The Case for Bureaucracy,* 2d ed. (Chatham, N.J.: Chatham House, 1985), 2.
5. See Murray Weidenbaum, "The Pentagon Fruitcake Rules," *New York Times,* 5 January 1992.
6. Despite diffuse public hostility toward "the bureaucracy," surveys show that most citizens are pleased with their personal contacts with government agencies. For a synopsis of these surveys, see Goodsell, *The Case for Bureaucracy,* chap. 2.
7. This definition is adapted from George J. Gordon, *Public Administration in America,* 4th ed. (New York: St. Martin's, 1992), 122.
8. Harold Seidman and Robert Gilmour, *Politics, Position, and Power: From the Positive to the Regulatory State,* 4th ed. (New York: Oxford University Press, 1986), 261–65; Shirley Anne Warshaw, *Powersharing: White House-Cabinet Relations in the Modern Presidency* (Albany: SUNY Press).
9. Harold W. Stanley and Richard G. Niemi, *Vital Statistics on American Politics,* 5th ed. (Washington, D.C.: CQ Press, 1995), 245, 252.
10. Linda Lee, "Dagwood, Meet the Mailman," *New York Times,* 6 November 1995.
11. Ann Crittenden, "Quotas for Good Old Boys," *Wall Street Journal,* 14 June 1995. For a list of agencies that use administrative law judges, see A. Lee Fritschler, *Smoking and Politics: Policymaking and the Federal Bureaucracy,* 3d ed. (Washington, D.C.: Brookings Institution, 1983), 93–94.
12. Terry M. Moe, "Control and Feedback in Economic Regulation: The Case of the NLRB," *American Political Science Review* 79 (December 1985): 109–16.
13. Stanley and Niemi, *Vital Statistics on American Politics,* 5th ed., 250.
14. Michael Nelson, "The Irony of American Bureaucracy," in *Bureaucratic Power in National Policy Making,* 4th ed., ed. Francis E. Rourke (Boston: Little, Brown, 1986), 163–87.
15. James Q. Wilson, "The Rise of the Bureaucratic Society," *Public Interest* 41 (Fall 1975): 77–103.
16. William Lilley III and James C. Miller III, "The New 'Social Regulation,'" *Public Interest* 47 (Spring 1977): 49–61.
17. Frederick C. Mosher, *Democracy and the Public Service,* 2d ed. (New York: Oxford University Press, 1982), 58, 60.
18. Jay M. Shafritz, *The Dorsey Dictionary of American Government and Politics* (Chicago: Dorsey, 1988), 511.
19. N. Joseph Cayer, *Managing Human Resources: An Introduction to Public Personnel Administration* (New York: St. Martin's, 1980), 21.
20. *Statistical Abstract of the United States, 1995,* 115th ed. (Washington, D.C.: Bureau of the Census, 1995), 350.
21. Ibid., 351.
22. James W. Fesler and Donald F. Kettl, *The Politics of the Administrative Process* (Chatham, N.J.: Chatham House Publishers, 1991), 118.
23. Mosher, *Democracy and the Public Service,* 6–8; James Q. Wilson, "The Bureaucracy Problem," *Public Interest* 6 (Winter 1967): 3–9.
24. Frank J. Goodnow, *Politics and Administration: A Study in Government* (New York: Russell and Russell, 1900), 17–26; Woodrow Wilson, "The Study of Administration," *Political Science Quarterly* 2 (June 1887): 197–222. Both discussions are reprinted in *Classics of Public Administration,* 3d ed., ed. Jay M. Shafritz and Albert C. Hyde (Pacific Grove, Calif.: Brooks/Cole, 1992).
25. Francis Rourke, *Bureaucracy, Politics, and Public Policy,* 3d ed. (Boston: Little, Brown, 1984), 3.
26. Donna Cassata, "Freshmen 'Have to Get' Commerce," *Congressional Quarterly Weekly Report,* 29 July 1995, 2273; Annie Tin, "House Unveils Plan to Abolish Department of Commerce," *Congressional Quarterly Weekly Report,* 27 May 1995, 1502.
27. Norton E. Long, "Power and Administration," *Public Administration Review* 9 (Autumn 1949): 257.
28. Rourke, *Bureaucracy, Politics, and Public Policy,* chaps. 2–3.
29. "Congressional Cuts," *Congressional Quarterly Weekly Report,* 9 December 1995, 3727; *CQ Almanac 1989* (Washington, D.C.: Congressional Quarterly, 1990), 787.
30. Samuel H. Beer, "Bureaucracies as Constituencies: The Adoption of General Revenue Sharing," in *Bureaucratic Power in National Policy Making,* 4th ed., ed. Francis E. Rourke (Boston: Little, Brown, 1986), 45–56.
31. Rourke, *Bureaucracy, Politics, and Public Policy,* 58.
32. Martha Derthick, "The Art of Cooptation: Advisory Councils in Social Security," in *Bureaucratic Power in National Policy Making,* 4th ed., ed. Francis E. Rourke (Boston: Little, Brown, 1986), 361–79.
33. See, for example, Kenneth Meier, "Measuring Organizational Power: Resources and Autonomy of Government Agencies," *Administration and Society* 12 (November 1980): 357–75.
34. Joel D. Aberbach, *Keeping a Watchful Eye: The Politics of Congressional Oversight* (Washington, D.C.: Brookings Institution, 1990), 132.
35. Steven S. Smith and Christopher J. Deering, *Committees in Congress,* 2d. ed. (Washington, D.C.: CQ Press, 1990), chap. 2.
36. Richard P. Nathan, *The Administrative Presidency* (New York: Macmillan, 1986).
37. Laurie McGinley, "Clinton's Regulators Zero In on Companies with Renewed Fervor," *Wall Street Journal,* 19 October 1994.
38. B. Dan Wood, "Principals, Bureaucrats, and Responsiveness in Clean Air Enforcements," *American Political Science Review* 82 (March 1988): 213–34.
39. John Quarles, *Cleaning Up America: An Insider's View of the Environmental Protection Agency* (Boston: Houghton Mifflin, 1976), chap. 2.
40. Ronald Randall, "Presidential Power Versus Bureaucratic Intransigence: The Influence of the Nixon Administration on Welfare Policy," *American Political Science Review* 73 (September 1979): 795–810.
41. Elizabeth Sanders, "The Presidency and the Bureaucratic State," in *The Presidency and the Political System,* 3d ed., ed. Michael Nelson (Washington, D.C.: CQ Press, 1990), 409–42.
42. Timothy Noah, "Tobacco-Marketing Rules Anger Many Non-Tobacco Industries," *Wall Street Journal,* 17 October 1995.
43. E. E. Schattschneider, *The Semi-Sovereign People* (New York: Holt, Rinehart and Winston, 1961).
44. Philip J. Hilts, "In Debate on Quayle's Competitiveness Council, the Issue Is Control," *New York Times,* 16 December 1991.
45. Steven Lohr, "Administration Balks at New Job Standards on Repetitive Strain," *New York Times,* 12 June 1995.
46. Matthew Holden, Jr., "'Imperialism' in Bureaucracy," *American Political Science Review* 60 (December 1966): 943–61.
47. Graham T. Allison, *Essence of Decision: Explaining the Cuban Missile Crisis* (Boston: Little, Brown, 1971), 121–23.
48. "What's Wrong with the FAA," *U.S. News & World Report,* 26 June 1995, 29–37.

49. See Edward H. Phillips, "NTSB Calls for Stronger Flight Attendant Training," *Aviation Week and Space Review,* 15 June 1992, 32–33; Edward H. Phillips, "NTSB Finds Slack Flight Safety at FAA," *Aviation Week and Space Technology,* 6 December 1993, 22–23; Edward H. Phillips, "NTSB Presses FAA to Order Twin Commander Check," *Aviation Week and Space Technology,* 3 January 1994, 50–51; Edward H. Phillips, "NTSB Recommends FAA Require Child Safety Seats in Aircraft," *Aviation Week and Space Review,* 28 March 1990, 117; Edward H. Phillips, "NTSB Urges FAA to Ground R22/R44 Helicopters," *Aviation Week and Space Technology,* 16 January 1995, 29–32.
50. Margaret Kriz, "Timber!" *National Journal,* 3 February 1996, 252–57.
51. Douglass Cater, *Power in Washington* (New York: Vintage Books, 1964); J. Leiper Freeman, *The Political Process* (New York: Random House, 1965); Arthur Maass, *Muddy Waters: The Army Engineers and the Nation's Rivers* (Cambridge: Harvard University Press, 1951); Daniel McCool, "Subgovernments as Determinants of Political Viability," *Political Science Quarterly* 105 (Summer 1990): 269–93.
52. Morris P. Fiorina, *Congress: Keystone of the Washington Establishment,* 2d ed. (New Haven: Yale University Press, 1989), 37–47.
53. Fritschler, *Smoking and Politics,* 142.
54. Randall B. Ripley and Grace A. Franklin, *Policy Implementation and Bureaucracy,* 2d ed. (Chicago: Dorsey Press, 1986), 40–41.
55. See Theodore J. Lowi, *The End of Liberalism,* 2d ed. (New York: Norton, 1979).
56. Allan J. Cigler and Burdett A. Loomis, "Organized Interests and the Search for Certainty," in *Interest Group Politics,* 3d ed. (Washington, D.C.: CQ Press, 1991), 388–89; Tom L. Gais, Mark A. Peterson, and Jack L. Walker, "Interest Groups, Iron Triangles, and Representative Institutions in American National Government," *British Journal of Political Science* 14 (April 1984): 161–85.
57. Hugh Heclo, "Issue Networks and the Executive Establishment," in *The New American Political System* (Washington, D.C.: American Enterprise Institute, 1978); John P. Heinz, Edward O. Laumann, Robert L. Nelson, and Robert H. Salisbury, *The Hollow Core: Private Interests in National Policy Making* (Cambridge: Harvard University Press, 1993).
58. David M. Ricci, *The Transformation of American Politics* (New Haven: Yale University Press, 1993).
59. Pew Research Center for the People & the Press, "TV News Viewership Declines," 13 May 1996, 62.
60. Quoted in Gwen Ifill, "Billions in Savings Are Seen with Cut in U.S. Government," *New York Times,* 8 September 1993.
61. "The Proposals—and the Road Ahead," *Congressional Quarterly Weekly Report,* 11 September 1993, 2385–89.
62. Steven Greenhouse, "Budget Office Disputes Savings in Gore's Plan," *New York Times,* 17 November 1993; John Healey, "Catching Up With the Gore Plan," *Congressional Quarterly Weekly Report,* 23 October 1993, 2873.
63. On the work of the Grace Commission, see Randall Fitzgerald and Gerald Lipson, *Pork Barrel: The Unexpurgated Grace Commission Story of Congressional Profligacy* (Washington, D.C.: Cato Institute, 1984).
64. Quoted in Ifill, "Billions in Savings Are Seen."
65. See, for example, Beryl A. Radin, "Varieties of Reinvention: Six NPR 'Success Stories'", in *Inside the Reinvention Machine,* ed. Donald F. Kettl and John J. DiIulio, Jr. (Washington, D.C.: Brookings Institution, 1995), chap. 4.
66. Ronald Smothers, "Agriculture Dept. to Shut Down 1,274 Field Offices," *New York Times,* 7 December 1994.
67. Donald F. Kettl, "Building Lasting Reform: Enduring Questions, Missing Answers," in *Inside the Reinvention Machine,* ed. Donald F. Kettl and John J. DiIulio, Jr. (Washington, D.C.: Brookings Institution, 1995) 16–7, 74.
68. Ibid., 22.
69. Quoted in Ifill, "Billions in Savings Are Seen."
70. See Kenneth J. Meier, *Politics and the Bureaucracy: Policymaking in the Fourth Branch of Government,* 2d ed. (Monterey, Calif.: Brooks/Cole, 1987), chap. 5.
71. See Herbert Kaufman, "Administrative Decentralization and Political Power," *Public Administration Review* 29 (January/February 1969): 3–15.

Chapter 14, pp. 461–490

1. Rubin v. Coors Brewing Co., 115 S.Ct. 1585 (1995).
2. Susan L. Hwang and Paul M. Barrett, "Court Allows Alcohol Levels on Beer Labels," *Wall Street Journal,* 20 April 1995.
3. C. Herman Prichett, *The American Constitution* (New York: McGraw-Hill, 1977), 17–18.
4. See Gregory A. Caldeira, "Public Opinion and the U.S. Supreme Court: FDR's Court-packing Plan," *American Political Science Review* 81 (December 1987): 1139–53.
5. See Robert A. Carp and Ronald Stidham, *The Federal Courts,* 2d ed. (Washington, D.C.: CQ Press, 1991), 63; Thomas G. Walker and Lee Epstein, *The Supreme Court of the United States* (Washington, D.C.: CQ Press, 1993), 75.
6. See Robert A. Carp and Ronald Stidham, *Judicial Process in America* (Washington, D.C.: CQ Press, 1993), 47–49; Paul C. Light, *Forging Legislation* (New York: Norton, 1992), 177–78, 226–27.
7. Stanley and Niemi, *Vital Statistics on American Politics,* 5th ed. (Washington, D.C.: Congressional Quarterly, 1995), 284.
8. Ware v. Hylton, 3 Dall. 199 (1796).
9. Marbury v. Madison, 1 Cr. 137 (1803).
10. Robert G. McCloskey, *The American Supreme Court* (Chicago: University of Chicago Press, 1960), 40–44.
11. See the excellent discussion of Mapp v. Ohio in Fred W. Friendly and Martha J. H. Elliot, *The Constitution—That Delicate Balance* (New York: Random House, 1984), 128–42.
12. Kevin T. McGuire and Barbara Plamer, "Issue Fluidity on the U.S. Supreme Court," *American Political Science Review* 89 (September 1995): 691–702.
13. See Donald L. Horowitz, *The Courts and Social Policy* (Washington, D.C.: Brookings Institution, 1977).
14. Texas Monthly v. Bullock, 489 U.S. 1 (1989).
15. Tom Mooney, "Breaks for Bibles," *Liberty,* March/April 1995, 22–25.
16. Oregon v. Mitchell, 400 U.S. 112 (1970).
17. Joseph T. Keenan, *The Constitution of the United States: An Unfolding Story,* 2d ed. (Chicago: Dorsey Press, 1988), 42–43.
18. Peter Steinfels, "New Law Protects Religious Practices," *New York Times,* 17 November 1993.
19. Keenan, *The Constitution of the United States,* 43–49.
20. Steven E. Schier, *A Decade of Deficits* (Albany: State University of New York Press, 1992), 119.
21. Baker v. Carr, 369 U.S. 186 (1962).
22. The survey data are from The Pew Research Center for the People & the Press, "The Times Mirror News Interest Index: 1989–1995," 5. On the notion that opinion on the Supreme Court can be changed, see Valerie J. Hoekstra, "The Supreme Court and Opinion Change: An Experimental Study of the Court's Ability to Change Opinion," *American Politics Quarterly* 23 (January 1995): 109–29.
23. Gregory A. Caldeira, "Neither Purse Nor the Sword: Dynamics of Public Confidence in the U.S. Supreme Court," *American Political Science Review* 80 (December 1986): 1209–26.
24. Michael W. Link, "Tracking Public Mood in the Supreme Court: Cross-Time Analysis of Criminal Procedure and Civil Rights Cases," *Political Research Quarterly* 48 (March 1995): 61–78; William Mishler and Reginald S. Sheehan, "The Supreme Court as a Countermajoritarian Institution? The Impact of Public Opinion on Supreme Court Decisions," *American Political Science Review* 87 (March 1993): 87–101.
25. John L. Moore, *Speaking of Washington* (Washington, D.C.: Congressional Quarterly, 1993), 178.
26. Walker and Epstein, *The Supreme Court of the United States,* 130–31.

27. Gregory A. Caldeira and John R. Wright, "The Discuss List: Agenda Building in the Supreme Court," *Law and Society Review* 24 (1990): 807–36.
28. See Timothy M. Hagle, "Strategic Retirements: A Political Model of Turnover on the United States Supreme Court," *Political Behavior* 15 (March 1993): 25–48; Peverill Squire, "Politics and Personal Factors in Retirement from the United States Supreme Court," *Political Behavior* 10 (1988): 180–90.
29. Gary King, "Presidential Appointments to the Supreme Court," *American Politics Quarterly* 15 (July 1987): 373–86.
30. See the list in Stanley and Niemi, *Vital Statistics on American Politics,* 271.
31. See Charles M. Cameron, Albert D. Cover, and Jeffrey A. Segal, "Senate Voting on Supreme Court Nominees: A Neoinstitutional Model," *American Political Science Review* 84 (June 1990): 525–34; Jeffrey A. Segal, "Senate Confirmation of Supreme Court Justices: Partisan and Institutional Politics," *Journal of Politics* 49 (November 1987): 998–1015.
32. Bob Woodward and Scott Armstrong, *The Brethren* (New York: Avon Books, 1979), 83.
33. See Mark Silverstein and William Haltom, "You Can't Always Get What You Want: Reflections on the Ginsburg and Breyer Nominations," presented at the 1995 annual meeting of the Western Political Science Association, Portland, Ore.
34. Thomas R. Hensley and Christopher E. Smith, "Membership Change and Voting Change: An Analysis of the Rehnquist Court's 1986–1991 Terms," *Political Research Quarterly* 48 (December 1995): 837–56.
35. Woodward and Armstrong, *The Brethren,* 139–40.
36. See, for example, Michael Comisky, "Can Presidents Pack the Supreme Court? A Micro- and Macro- Look at FDR," *Congress and the Presidency* 22 (Spring 1995): 19–33.
37. W. John Moore, "Court Is in Recess," *National Journal,* 30 October 1993, 2587–90.
38. Caldeira and Wright, "The Discuss List," 813.
39. David O'Brien, *Storm Center: The Supreme Court in American Politics,* 3d ed. (New York: Norton, 1993), 247–56.
40. See Walker and Epstein, *The Supreme Court of the United States,* 81–94.
41. Gregory A. Caldeira and John R. Wright, "Organized Interests and Agenda Setting in the U.S. Supreme Court," *American Political Science Review* 82 (December 1988): 1109–27.
42. Gregory A. Caldeira and John R. Wright, "Amici Curiae before the Supreme Court: Who Participates, When, and How Much," *Journal of Politics* 52 (August 1990): 782–806.
43. Walker and Epstein, *The Supreme Court of the United States,* 136–37.
44. The case was Campbell v. Acuff-Rose Music Inc., 114 S.Ct. 1164 (1994). See Moore, "Court Is in Recess," 2587.
45. Kevin T. McGuire and Gregory A. Caldeira, "Lawyers, Organized Interests, and the Law of Obscenity: Agenda Setting in the Supreme Court," *American Political Science Review* 87 (September 1993): 717–26.
46. Quoted in Paul M. Barrett, "Lawyers Arguing Cases Before Supreme Court Find Experience Can Be Less than Appealing," *Wall Street Journal,* 17 January 1994.
47. Barrett, "Lawyers Arguing Cases"; Walker and Epstein, *The Supreme Court of the United States,* 106.
48. Tracey E. George and Lee Epstein, "On the Nature of Supreme Court Decision Making," *American Political Science Review* 86 (June 1992): 323–37.
49. Hubbard v. United States, 115 S.Ct. 1754 (1995); the case that was overturned was United States v. Bramblett 348 U.S. 503 (1955).
50. Jeffrey A. Segal and Albert D. Cover, "Ideological Values and the Votes of the U.S. Supreme Court Justices," *American Political Science Review* 83 (June 1989): 557–65.
51. Earl Warren, *The Memoirs of Earl Warren* (Garden City, N.Y.: Doubleday, 1977), 309–10.
52. See the letter from Chief Justice William Rehnquist in the *Law, Courts, and Judicial Process Section Newsletter* 7 (Fall 1989): 8.
53. O'Brien, *Storm Center,* 306–14.
54. Joan Biskupic, "The Quiet But Critical Fifth Vote," *Washington Post National Weekly Edition,* 19–25 June 1995.
55. McCloskey, *The American Supreme Court,* 185–86.
56. Beverly Blair Cook, "Justice Brennan and the Institutionalization of Dissent Assignment," *Judicature* 79 (July–August 1995): 17–23.
57. Thomas G. Walker, Lee Epstein, and William J. Dixon, "On the Mysterious Demise of Consensual Norms in the United States Supreme Court," *Journal of Politics* 50 (May 1988): 361–89.
58. Paul M. Barrett, "Top Court Showed Sensitivity to Business Last Term, Despite Spotted-Owl Ruling," *Wall Street Journal,* 30 June 1995; Joan Biskupic, "The Supreme Court's Emerging Power Center," *Washington Post National Weekly Edition,* 11–17 July 1994; see also Christopher E. Smith, Joyce A. Baugh, Thomas R. Hensley, "The First-Term Performance of Justice Stephen Breyer," *Judicature* 79 (September–October 1995): 74–79.
59. Reginald S. Sheehan, William Mishler, and Donald R. Songer, "Ideology, Status, and the Differential Success of Direct Parties Before the Supreme Court," *American Political Science Review* 86 (June 1992): 464–71.
60. Ibid., 469.
61. Marc Galanter, "Why the 'Haves' Come out Ahead: Speculations on the Limits of Legal Change," *Law and Society Review* 9 (Fall 1974): 95–160.
62. These data are taken from Stanley and Niemi, *Vital Statistics on American Politics,* 284.
63. Carp and Stidham, *Judicial Process in America,* 45–46, 310–12; Richard Neely, *How Courts Govern America,* (New Haven: Yale University Press, 1981), 204–5.
64. Carp and Stidham, *The Federal Courts,* 102–4.
65. Quoted in Frank Santiago, "Bush Chooses Hansen to Join Appeals Court," *Des Moines Register,* 31 July 1991.
66. See "Imprints on the Bench," *Congressional Quarterly Weekly Report,* 19 January 1991, 173.
67. See Amy Waldman, "Taking a Hard Right," *Washington Monthly,* September 1995, 39–43.
68. Gerard S. Gryski, Gary Zuk, and Deborah J. Barrow, "A Bench that Looks Like America? Representation of African Americans and Latinos on the Federal Courts," *Journal of Politics* 56 (November 1994): 1076–86.
69. *State Court Caseload Statistics, Annual Report, 1992* (Williamsburg, Va.: National Center for State Courts, 1994).
70. Ronald K. L. Collins, Peter J. Galie, and John Kincaid, "State High Courts, State Constitutions, and Individual Rights Litigation Since 1980: A Judicial Survey," *Publius* 16 (1985): 141–61.
71. Greenwood v. California, 486 U.S. 35 (1988).
72. John Kincaid and Robert F. Williams, "The New Judicial Federalism: The States' Lead in Rights Protection," *Journal of State Government* 65 (April/June 1992): 50–52.
73. Lawrence Baum, "Making Judicial Policies in the Political Arena," in *The State of the States,* 2d ed., ed. Carl E. Van Horn (Washington, D.C.: CQ Press, 1993), 164–65.
74. Gregory A. Caldeira, "Legal Precedent: Structures of Communication Between State Supreme Courts," *Social Networks* 10 (1988): 29–55; Gregory A. Caldeira, "The Transmission of Legal Precedent: A Study of State Supreme Courts," *American Political Science Review* 79 (March 1985): 178–93.
75. Richard J. Hardy and Joseph J. Carrier, "Missouri Courts, Judges, and Juries," in *Missouri Government and Politics,* rev. ed., ed. Richard J. Hardy, Richard R. Dohm, and David Leuthold (Columbia: University of Missouri Press, 1995), 173–87.
76. Larry T. Aspin and William K. Hall, "Retention Elections and Judicial Behavior," *Judicature* 77 (May–June 1994): 306–15.
77. William K. Hall and Larry T. Aspin, "What Twenty Years of Judicial Retention Elections Have Told Us," *Judicature* 70 (April–May 1987): 340–47; Robert C. Luskin, Christopher N. Bratcher, Christopher G. Jordan, Tracy K. Renner, and Kris S. Seago, "How Minority Judges Fare in Retention Elections," *Judicature* 77 (May–June 1994): 316–21.
78. Burton M. Atkins and Harry R. Glick, "Formal Judicial Recruitment and State Supreme Court Decisions," *American Politics Quarterly* 2 (October 1974):

427–49; Henry R. Glick, "The Politics of State-Court Reform," in *The Politics of Judicial Reform,* ed. Philip Dubois (Lexington, Mass.: Heath, 1982), 29–31.
79. Barbara Luck Graham, "Judicial Recruitment and Racial Diversity on State Courts: An Overview," *Judicature* 74 (June–July 1990): 28–34.
80. Luskin et al., "How Minority Judges Fare," 316–21.
81. Edwin Chen, "For Judges, the Stakes Are Rising," *Los Angeles Times,* 4 March 1988. See also Marlene Arnold Nicholson and Norman Nicholson, "Funding Judicial Campaigns in Illinois," *Judicature* 77 (May–June 1994): 294–99; Amy E. Young, "Judicial Politics in the States," in *State Government: CQ's Guide to Current Issues and Activities 1991–92,* ed. Thad L. Beyle (Washington, D.C.: CQ Press, 1991); Robert F. Utter, "Justice, Money, and Sleaze," in *State Government: CQ's Guide to Current Issues and Activities 1992–93,* ed. Thad L. Beyle (Washington, D.C.: CQ Press, 1992).

Chapter 15, pp. 493–526

1. William Petroski, "Faster Highways Ahead," *Des Moines Register,* 29 November 1995; "Repeal of Speed Limits, Helmet Laws Criticized," *Des Moines Register,* 29 November 1995.
2. Richard P. Nathan, "The Role of the States in American Federalism," in *The State of the States,* 2d ed., ed. Carl E. Van Horn (Washington, D.C.: CQ Press, 1993), 23–25.
3. Richard P. Nathan, "The Politics of Printouts: The Use of Official Numbers to Allocate Federal Grants-in-aid," in *American Intergovernmental Relations,* 2d ed., ed. Lawrence J. O'Toole, Jr. (Washington, D.C.: CQ Press, 1993).
4. Kenneth Vines, "The Federal Setting in State Politics," in *Politics in the American States,* 3d ed., ed. Herbert Jacobs and Kenneth Vines (Boston: Little, Brown, 1976), 3–48.
5. U.S. Advisory Commission on Intergovernmental Relations, *Significant Features of Fiscal Federalism, Volume 2: Revenues and Expenditures* (Washington, D.C.: U.S. Government Printing Office, 1992), 60.
6. James W. Fesler and Donald F. Kettl, *The Politics of the Administrative Process* (Chatham, N.J.: Chatham House, 1991), 249–52.
7. See David C. Nice, *Federalism: The Politics of Intergovernmental Relations* (New York: St. Martin's, 1987), 51–54.
8. Russell L. Hanson, "Intergovernmental Relations," in *Politics in the American States: A Comparative Analysis,* 5th ed., ed. Virginia Gray, Herbert Jacob, and Robert B. Albritton (Glenview, Ill.: Scott, Foresman/Little, Brown, 1990), 61.
9. Rochelle L. Stanfield, "Much Ado About Counting," *National Journal,* 7 December 1991, 2992.
10. Hanson, "Intergovernmental Relations," 60–62.
11. George V. Voinovich, "Unfunded Federal Mandates and the Need for a New Federalism," *Common Sense* 1 (Winter 1994): 65.
12. David R. Beam and Timothy J. Conlan, "The Growth of Intergovernmental Mandates in an Era of Deregulation and Decentralization," in *American Intergovernmental Relations,* 2d ed., ed. Lawrence J. O'Toole, Jr. (Washington, D.C.: CQ Press, 1993), 325–26.
13. Timothy J. Conlan, James D. Riggle, and Donna E. Schwartz, "Deregulating Federalism? The Politics of Mandate Reform in the 104th Congress," *Publius* 25 (Summer 1995): 23–40.
14. The term *picket fence federalism* was coined in Terry Sanford, *Storm Over the States* (New York: McGraw-Hill, 1967), 80.
15. See Nathan, "The Role of the States in American Federalism," 17–19; Carl E. Van Horn, "The Quiet Revolution," in *The State of the States,* 2d ed., ed. Carl E. Van Horn (Washington, D.C.: CQ Press, 1993).
16. Michael A. Pagano and Ann O'M. Bowman, "The State of Federalism, 1994–1995," *Publius* 25 (Summer 1995): 1–10.
17. See, for example, Colette Fraley, "Scaled-Back Medicaid Savings Plan Emerges from Conference," *Congressional Quarterly Weekly Report,* 18 November 1995, 3539–40.
18. See, for example, Clifford J. Levy, "States Rally Round a Cry for Less," *New York Times,* 11 February 1996.
19. Jim Simon and Barbara A. Serrano, "Fringe Politics Find the Mainstream," *Seattle Times,* 11 June 1995.
20. Rochelle Sharpe, "Federal Education Law Becomes Hot Target of Wary Conservatives," *Wall Street Journal,* 30 August 1995.
21. Francis X. Clines, "Dole, in New Hampshire Capitol, Gets Bugle Call: Reveille, or Taps?" *New York Times,* 14 February 1996.
22. These data are drawn from *The Book of the States 1992–93* (Lexington, Ky.: Council of State Governments, 1992), 20.
23. John J. Carroll and Arthur English, "Traditions of State Constitution Making," in *Politics in the American States and Communities,* ed. Jack R. Van Der Slik, (Boston: Allyn & Bacon, 1996), 26.
24. Ibid., 30.
25. Richard Morin, "They're All Crooks—Whatever Their Names Are," *Washington Post National Weekly Edition,* 29 May 1989.
26. Richard W. Boyd, "The Effects of Primaries and Statewide Races on Voter Turnout," *Journal of Politics* 51 (August 1989): 713–39; Raymond E. Wolfinger and Steven J. Rosenstone, *Who Votes?* (New Haven: Yale University Press, 1980); Gerald C. Wright, Jr., *Electoral Choice in America* (Chapel Hill, N.C.: Institute for Research in Social Science, 1974), 55.
27. Larry Sabato, *Goodbye to Good-Time Charlie* (Lexington, Mass.: Lexington Books, 1978), 21–22.
28. Thad L. Beyle, "Governors," in *Politics in the American States,* 5th ed., ed. Virginia Gray, Herbert Jacob, and Robert B. Albritton (Glenview, Ill.: Scott, Foresman/Little, Brown, 1990), 217–30; Thomas M. Holbrook, "Institutional Strength and Gubernatorial Elections," *American Politics Quarterly* 21 (July 1993): 261–71.
29. Beyle, "Governors," 220–21; Sabato, *Goodbye to Good-Time Charlie,* 3–5, 71–74.
30. Alan Rosenthal, *Governors and Legislators: Contending Powers* (Washington, D.C.: CQ Press, 1990), 14–15.
31. Thad L. Beyle, "Being Governor," in *The State of the States,* 2d ed., ed. Carl E. Van Horn (Washington, D.C.: CQ Press, 1993), 82.
32. Chip Alexander, "Etheridge, Price Oust Republican House Incumbents; Helms and Hunt Are Re-elected," *Raleigh News and Observer,* 6 November 1996.
33. Rosenthal, *Governors and Legislators,* 161.
34. Michael H. McCabe, "Wisconsin's 'Quirky' Veto Power," in *State Government 1992–93,* ed. Thad L. Beyle (Washington, D.C.: CQ Press, 1992).
35. Beyle, "Governors," 224–26; Rosenthal, *Governors and Legislators,* 9–13.
36. Jack R. Van Der Slik and Kent D. Redfield, *Lawmaking in Illinois* (Springfield, Ill.: Sangamon State University, 1986), 165–67.
37. Charles W. Wiggins, "Executive Vetoes and Legislative Overrides in the American States," *Journal of Politics* 42 (November 1980): 1110–17.
38. Peter Eichstaedt, "No, No, Two Hundred Times No," *State Legislatures,* July/August 1995.
39. Thad Beyle, "Governors: The Middlemen and Women in Our Political System," in *Politics in the American States,* 6th ed., ed. Virginia Gray and Herbert Jacob (Washington, D.C.: CQ Press, 1996), 234.
40. Wiggins, "Executive Vetoes and Legislative Overrides," 1110–17.
41. Joseph F. Zimmerman, *The Government and Politics of New York State* (New York: New York University Press, 1981), 200–204.
42. Alan Rosenthal, *Legislative Life* (New York: Harper & Row, 1981), 70.
43. Kim Fridkin Kahn, "Characteristics of Press Coverage in Senate and Gubernatorial Elections: Information Available to Voters," *Legislative Studies Quarterly* 20 (February 1995): 23–35; Peverill Squire, "Changing State Legislative Leadership Careers," in *Changing Patterns in State Legislative Careers,* ed. Gary F. Moncrief and Joel A. Thompson (Ann Arbor: University of Michigan Press, 1992), 179–80; Charles M. Tidmarch, Lisa J. Hyman, and Jill E. Sorkin, "Press Issue Agendas in the 1982 Congressional and Gubernatorial Election Campaigns," *Journal of Politics* 46 (November 1984): 1226–42.

44. E. Lee Bernick and Charles W. Wiggins, "Executive-Legislative Relations: The Governor's Role and Chief Legislator," in *Gubernatorial Leadership as State Policy,* ed. Eric B. Herzik and Brent W. Brown (New York: Greenwood, 1991), 75–76.
45. Richard C. Kearney, "How a 'Weak' Governor Can Be Strong: Dick Riley and Education Reform in South Carolina," in *State Government 1988–89,* ed. Thad L. Beyle (Washington, D.C.: CQ Press, 1988).
46. See Dan Durning, "Education Reform in Arkansas: The Governor's Role in Policy Making," in *Gubernatorial Leadership and State Policy,* ed. Eric B. Herzik and Brent W. Brown (New York: Greenwood Press, 1991).
47. Thad Beyle, "Enhancing Executive Leadership in the States," *State and Local Government Review* 27 (Winter 1995): 18–35.
48. Peverill Squire, "Challenger Profile and Gubernatorial Elections," *Western Political Quarterly* 45 (March 1992): 125–42; Mark E. Tompkins, "The Electoral Fortunes of Gubernatorial Incumbents: 1947–1981," *Journal of Politics* 46 (May 1984): 520–43.
49. Peverill Squire and Christina Fastnow, "Comparing Gubernatorial and Senatorial Elections," *Political Research Quarterly* 47 (September 1994): 703–20.
50. Alan Rosenthal, "The Legislative Institution: Transformed and at Risk," in *The State of the States,* ed. Carl E. Van Horn (Washington, D.C.: CQ Press, 1989).
51. Jack Rodgers, Robert Sittig, and Susan Welch, "The Legislature," in *Nebraska Government and Politics,* ed. Robert D. Miewald (Lincoln: University of Nebraska Press, 1984).
52. Robb Douglas, "Going Nebraska's Way," in *State Government 1993–94,* ed. Thad L. Beyle (Washington, D.C.: CQ Press, 1993); Bob Mercer, "Reforms Mulled For Legislature," *Rapid City (SD) Journal,* 14 August 1996.
53. Peverill Squire, "Legislative Professionalization and Membership Diversity in State Legislatures," *Legislative Studies Quarterly* 17 (February 1992): 69–79.
54. Peverill Squire, "Professionalization and Public Opinion of State Legislatures," *Journal of Politics* 55 (May 1993): 479–91.
55. Rosenthal, *Governors and Legislators,* 202–3.
56. Peverill Squire, "Divided Government and Public Opinion in the States," *State and Local Government Review* 25 (Fall 1993): 150–54.
57. Citizens Conference on State Legislatures, *State Legislatures: An Evaluation of Their Effectiveness* (New York: Praeger, 1971), 24.
58. Harold W. Stanley and Richard G. Niemi, *Vital Statistics on American Politics,* 5th ed. (Washington, D.C.: CQ Press), 372–73.
59. Victoria Van Son, *CQ's State Fact Finder: Rankings Across America* (Washington, D.C.: Congressional Quarterly, 1993), 296–97.
60. Emily Van Dunk and Thomas M. Holbrook, "The 1994 State Legislative Elections," *Extension of Remarks,* December 1994, 10.
61. See the report of a study by the National Women's Political Caucus in Jane Norman, "Women No Less Electable than Men," *Des Moines Register,* 9 September 1994.
62. Alan Ehrenhalt, *The United States of Ambition* (New York: Times Books, 1991), 197–207.
63. "GOP Women Gaining Legislative Seats," *Des Moines Register,* 4 December 1994.
64. See, for example, Albert J. Nelson, *Emerging Influentials in State Legislatures: Women, Blacks, and Hispanics* (New York: Praeger, 1991); Beth Reingold, "Concepts of Representation Among Female and Male State Legislators," *Legislative Studies Quarterly* 17 (November 1992): 509–37; Michelle Saint-Germain, "Do Their Differences Make a Difference? The Impact of Women in Public Policy in the Arizona Legislature," *Social Science Quarterly* 70 (December 1989): 956– 68; Sue Thomas, "The Impact of Women on State Legislative Policies," *Journal of Politics* 53 (November 1991): 958–76; Sue Thomas and Susan Welch, "The Impact of Gender on Activities and Priorities of State Legislators," *Western Political Quarterly* 44 (June 1991): 445–56.
65. Edith J. Barrett, "The Policy Priorities of African American Women in State Legislatures," *Legislative Studies Quarterly* 20 (May 1995): 223–47.
66. Sue Thomas, *How Women Legislate* (New York: Oxford University Press, 1994).
67. Debra L. Dodson, "Women Officeholders: Continuity and Change Across Two Decades," presented at the 1994 annual meeting of the Southern Political Science Association Meeting, Atlanta.
68. Charles S. Hyneman, "Who Makes Our Laws?" *Political Science Quarterly* 55 (December 1940): 556–81; V. O. Key, Jr., *American State Politics* (New York: Knopf, 1956), 258–63; Samuel P. Orth, "Our State Legislatures," *Atlantic Monthly,* December 1904, 728–39; Belle Zeller, ed., *American State Legislatures* (New York: Crowell, 1954), 71.
69. Eric Hirsch, *State Legislators' Occupations 1993 and 1995* (Denver: National Conference of State Legislators, 1996), 11.
70. Ibid.; Rosenthal, "The Legislative Institution," 99.
71. Beth Bazar, *State Legislators' Occupations: A Decade of Change* (Denver: National Conference of State Legislatures, 1987), 4; Rosenthal, "The Legislative Institution," 72.
72. Hirsch, *State Legislators' Occupations,* 42; see also Rosenthal, "The Legislative Institution," 71–72; Peverill Squire, "Career Opportunities and Membership Stability in Legislatures," *Legislative Studies Quarterly* 13 (February 1988): 65–82; Squire, "Legislative Professionalization," 74.
73. David Breaux and Malcolm Jewell, "Winning Big: The Incumbency Advantage in State Legislative Races," in *Changing Patterns in State Legislative Careers,* ed. Gary F. Moncrief and Joel A. Thompson (Ann Arbor: University of Michigan Press, 1992); Gary W. Cox and Scott Morgenstern, "The Increasing Advantage of Incumbency in the U.S. States," *Legislative Studies Quarterly* 18 (November 1993): 495–514; James C. Garand, "Electoral Marginality in State Legislative Elections, 1968–1986," *Legislative Studies Quarterly* 16 (February 1991): 7–28.
74. See, for example, Cox and Morgenstern, "The Increasing Advantage of Incumbency in the U.S. States," 500; Thomas M. Holbrook and Charles M. Tidmarch, "Sophomore Surge in State Legislative Elections, 1968–86," *Legislative Studies Quarterly* 16 (February 1991): 49–63; Ronald E. Weber, Harvey J. Tucker, and Paul Brace, "Vanishing Marginals in State Legislative Elections," *Legislative Studies Quarterly* 16 (February 1991): 29–47.
75. Richard G. Niemi and Laura R. Winsky, "Membership Turnover in U.S. State Legislatures: Trends and Effects of Districting," *Legislative Studies Quarterly* 12 (February 1987): 115–23; Kwang S. Shin and John S. Jackson, III, "Membership Turnover in U.S. State Legislatures: 1931–1976," *Legislative Studies Quarterly* 4 (February 1979): 95–114.
76. National Conference of State Legislatures, "Pre-election Turnover in State Legislatures," 18 October 1996.
77. Squire, "Career Opportunities and Membership Stability," 71.
78. Ibid., 72; Peverill Squire, "Member Career Opportunities and the Internal Organization of Legislatures," *Journal of Politics* 50 (August 1988): 730.
79. Jack M. Treadway, "Adoption of Term Limits for State Legislatures," *Comparative State Politics* 16 (July 1995): 1–3; see also the data in U.S. Term Limits, "Coming to Terms with Term Limits: A Summary of State Term Limits Laws," *Term Limits Outlook Series* 3 (December 1994); U.S. Term Limits, "Louisiana Goes Big for Term Limits," 30 December 1995.
80. Thomas Galvin, "Limits Score a Perfect 14 for 14, But Court Challenges Loom," *Congressional Quarterly Weekly Report,* 7 November 1992, 3593–94; "Supreme Court Declines Review of State-Level Term Limits," *Congressional Quarterly Weekly Report,* 14 March 1992, 654.
81. Margaret Engle, "Initiative Spending Brings Mixed Results," *Capital Eye,* 15 December 1994, 3–4.

82. Jeffrey A. Karp, "Support for Term Limits," *Public Opinion Quarterly* 59 (Fall 1995): 373–91; James D. King, "Term Limits in Wyoming," *Comparative State Politics* 14 (April 1993): 1–18.
83. Karp, "Support for Term Limits."
84. Glenn Sussman, Nicholas Lovrich, Byron W. Daynes, and Jonathan P. West, "Term Limits and State Legislatures," *Extension of Remarks,* July 1994, 3.
85. Rebecca L. Noah, "The Limited Legislature: The Arizona Case," presented at the 1995 annual meeting of the Western Political Science Association, Portland, Ore.
86. Gary F. Moncrief, Joel A. Thompson, Michael Haddon, and Robert Hoyer, "For Whom the Bell Tolls: Term Limits and State Legislatures," *Legislative Studies Quarterly* 17 (February 1992): 37–47; Cynthia Opheim, "The Effect of U.S. State Legislative Term Limits Revisited," *Legislative Studies Quarterly* 19 (February 1994): 49–59.
87. Alan Rosenthal, *The Third House: Lobbyists and Lobbying in the States* (Washington, D.C.: CQ Press, 1993), 3.
88. Ibid., 4.
89. Virginia Gray and David Lowery, "Stability and Change in State Interest Groups Systems, 1975–1990," *State and Local Government Review* 25 (Spring 1993): 87–96.
90. Kenneth G. Hunter, Laura Ann Wilson, and Gregory G. Brunk, "Societal Complexity and Interest-Group Lobbying in the American States," *Journal of Politics* 53 (May 1991): 488–503; Clive S. Thomas and Ronald J. Hrebenar, "Nationalization of Interest Groups and Lobbying in the States," in *Interest Group Politics,* 3d ed., ed. Allan J. Cigler and Burdett A. Loomis (Washington, D.C.: CQ Press, 1991).
91. Clive S. Thomas and Ronald J. Hrebenar, "Understanding Interest Group Power: Lessons from Developments in the American States Since the Mid-1980s," presented at the 1995 annual meeting of the Midwest Political Science Association, Chicago.
92. Virginia Gray and David Lowery, "The Diversity of State Interest Group Systems," *Political Research Quarterly* 46 (March 1993): 81–97.
93. Margery M. Ambrosius and Susan Welch, "State Legislators' Perceptions of Business and Labor Interests," *Legislative Studies Quarterly* 13 (May 1988): 199–209; Gray and Lowery, "The Diversity of State Interest Group Systems," 81–97; Clive S. Thomas and Ronald J. Hrebenar, "Interest Groups in the States," in *Politics in the American States,* 6th ed., ed. Virginia Gray and Herbert Jacob (Washington, D.C.: CQ Press, 1996), 148.
94. Thomas and Hrebenar, "Interest Groups in the States," 148–49.
95. Ehrenhalt, *The United States of Ambition,* 173.
96. David L. Martin, "Alabama," in *Interest Group Politics in the Southern States,* ed. Ronald J. Hrebenar and Clive S. Thomas (Tuscaloosa: University of Alabama Press, 1992).
97. See, for example, the discussion in Tom Loftus, *The Art of Legislative Politics* (Washington, D.C.: CQ Press, 1994), 133–34.
98. William J. Stern, "The Nomenklature of 'State Capitalism,'" *Wall Street Journal,* 19 December 1995.
99. Cynthia Opheim, "Explaining the Differences in State Lobbying Regulations," *Western Political Quarterly* 44 (June 1991): 405–21; Thomas and Hrebenar, "Nationalization of Interest Groups," 64–66.
100. Opheim, "Explaining the Differences in State Lobbying Regulations," 405–21.
101. Frank J. Sorauf, *Money in American Elections* (Glenview, Ill.: Scott Foresman/Little, Brown, 1988), 284–90.
102. The numbers reported on initiatives and referendums are drawn from *The Book of the States 1991–92,* 329.
103. "On Ballot Measures, Big Spenders Take the Initiative," *Los Angeles Times,* 23 March 1992.
104. Arthur Lupia, "Shortcuts Versus Encyclopedias: Information and Voting Behavior in California Insurance Reform Elections," *American Political Science Review* 88 (March 1994): 63–76.
105. David B. Magleby, "Taking the Initiative: Direct Legislation and Direct Democracy in the 1980s," *PS: Political Science & Politics* 21 (Summer 1988): 600–611.
106. Engle, "Initiative Spending Brings Mixed Results," 3.
107. Paula D. McClain, "Arizona 'High Noon': The Recall and Impeachment of Evan Mecham," *PS: Political Science & Politics* 21 (Summer 1988): 628–38.
108. "Abuse of the Recall," *San Francisco Chronicle,* 24 August 1995; "Assemblyman Defeats GOP Recall Attempt," *San Francisco Chronicle,* 23 August 1995; Greg Lucas, "GOP-Backed Recall Succeeds—Horcher Thrown Out," *San Francisco Chronicle,* 18 May 1995; Stephen Schwartz, "Doris Allen Recalled in Orange County," *San Francisco Chronicle,* 29 November 1995.
109. Susan B. Hansen, "The Politics of State Taxing and Spending," in *Politics in the American States,* 5th ed., ed. Virginia Gray, Herbert Jacob, and Robert B. Albritton (Glenview, Ill.: Scott, Foresman/Little, Brown, 1990), 339–40.
110. Richard F. Winters, "The Politics of Taxing and Spending," in *Politics in the American States,* 6th ed., ed. Virginia Gray and Herbert Jacob (Washington, D.C.: CQ Press, 1996), 332.
111. Ibid., 333; Van Son, *CQ's State Fact Finder,* 315.
112. Sylvia Nasar, "Like U.S., State Governments Look to Affluent to Pay More Tax," *New York Times,* 21 March 1993.
113. Russell D. Murphy, "Connecticut: Lowell P. Weicker, Jr., a Maverick in the 'Land of Steady Habits,'" in *Governors and Hard Times,* ed. Thad Beyle (Washington, D.C.: CQ Press, 1992).
114. Bruce Orwall, "Casino Companies Find States Less Willing to Play," *Wall Street Journal,* 28 November 1995.
115. William D. Eggers and John O'Leary, "An Embarrassment of Riches," *Wall Street Journal,* 29 January 1996.
116. Lucinda Harper, "Many Tax Cuts Put Forth by Governors Are Being Erased by State Legislatures," *Wall Street Journal,* 48 April 1995.
117. See *The Book of the States 1991–92,* 49. On state budgeting, see Edward J. Clynch and Thomas P. Lauth, ed., *Governors, Legislatures, and Budgets* (New York: Greenwood Press, 1991).
118. Glenn Abney and Thomas P. Lauth, "Governors and the Line-Item Veto," presented at the 1994 annual meeting of the Southern Political Science Association, Atlanta; Glenn Abney and Thomas P. Lauth, "The Line-Item Veto in the States: An Instrument for Fiscal Restraint or an Instrument of Partisanship?" *Public Administration Review* (May/June 1985): 372–77.
119. Abney and Lauth, "Governors and the Line-Item Veto," 15–16; Pat Thompson and Steven R. Boyd, "Use of the Line-Item Veto in Texas, 1940–1990," *State and Local Government Review* 26 (Winter 1994): 38–45.
120. Rosenthal, *Governors and Legislators,* 132.
121. *Statistical Abstract of the United States, 1995,* 115th ed. (Washington, D.C.: U.S. Bureau of the Census, 1995), 306.
122. Henry J. Raimondo, "State Budgeting in the Nineties," in *The State of the States,* 2d ed., ed. Carl E. Van Horn (Washington, D.C.: CQ Press, 1993), 34–35.
123. Ibid., 32.
124. James C. Clingermayer and B. Dan Wood, "Disentangling Patterns of State Debt Financing," *American Political Science Review* 89 (March 1995): 108–20.
125. Hansen, "The Politics of State Taxing," 338; D. Roderick Kiewiet and Kristin Szakaly, "The Efficacy of Constitutional Restrictions on Borrowing, Taxing, and Spending: An Analysis of State Bonded Indebtedness, 1961–90," presented at the 1992 annual meeting of the American Political Science Association, Chicago.
126. Hansen, "The Politics of State Taxing," 361–63; Raimondo, "State Budgeting in the Nineties," 33.
127. Laurie McGinley, "States' Finances Are Improving, Survey Reports," *Wall Street Journal,* 27 July 1993.
128. Fox Butterfield, "Prison-Building Binge in California Casts Shadow on Higher Education," *New York Times,* 12 April 1995.
129. Wesley G. Skogan, "Crime and Punishment," in *Politics in the American States,* 5th ed., ed. Virginia Gray, Herbert Jacob, and Robert B. Albritton (Glenview, Ill.: Scott, Foresman/Little, Brown, 1990), 386.

130. Robert Albritton, "Social Services: Welfare and Health," in *Politics in the American States,* 5th ed., ed. Virginia Gray, Herbert Jacob, and Robert B. Albritton (Glenview, Ill.: Scott, Foresman/Little, Brown, 1990), 426–27.
131. Frederick Wirt and Samuel Gove, "Education," in *Politics in the American States,* 5th ed., ed. Virginia Gray, Herbert Jacob, and Robert B. Albritton (Glenview, Ill.: Scott, Foresman/Little, Brown, 1990), 451–54.
132. On the forces driving the development of single-purpose or special districts, see Nancy Burns, *The Formation of American Local Governments* (New York: Oxford University Press, 1994).
133. Stanley and Niemi, *Vital Statistics on American Politics,* 291–92.
134. Ann O'M. Bowman and Richard C. Kearney, *State and Local Government,* 2d ed. (Boston: Houghton Mifflin), 312–20.
135. Stanley and Niemi, *Vital Statistics on American Politics,* 369.
136. *Statistical Abstract of the United States, 1995,* 315.
137. Stanley and Niemi, *Vital Statistics on American Politics,* 296.
138. Lawrence Baum, "Making Judicial Policies in the Political Arena," in *The State of the States,* 2d ed., ed. Carl E. Van Horn (Washington, D.C.: CQ Press, 1993), 163–64.
139. U.S. Advisory Commission on Intergovernmental Relations, "Public Attitudes on Government and Taxes," in *American Intergovernmental Relations,* 2d ed., ed. Lawrence J. O'Toole, Jr. (Washington, D.C.: CQ Press, 1993), 109–10.
140. Dennis L. Dresang and James L. Gosling, *Politics, Policy, and Management in the American States* (New York: Longman, 1989), 41–42.
141. Dirk Johnson, "City Services, It's Now 'Indy-a-First-Place,'" *New York Times,* 2 March 1995.
142. Ibid.
143. David Wessell, "The American Way?" *Wall Street Journal,* 2 October 1995.
144. Robert Barro, "The Imperative to Privatize," *Wall Street Journal,* 29 June 1995.
145. U.S. Advisory Commission on Intergovernmental Relations, "Public Attitudes on Government and Taxes," 110–12.
146. See the report of a *Washington Post*-ABC News poll in Richard Morin, "Power to the States," *Washington Post National Weekly Edition,* 27 March–2 April 1995, 37.
147. See the report of a *Wall Street Journal*-NBC News survey in Albert R. Hunt, "Federalism Debate Is as Much About Power as About Principle," *Wall Street Journal,* 19 January 1995.
148. See the data reported in Everett Carll Ladd, Jr., ed., *America at the Polls 1994* (Storrs, Conn.: Roper Center, 1995), 34.

Chapter 16, pp. 527–562

1. Dirk Johnson, "Coast to Coast, Americans Are Denied, Denied, Denied," *New York Times,* 15 November 1996.
2. Adam Clymer, "Treasury Takes Retirement Funds to Avert Default," *New York Times,* 16 November 1995.
3. James D. Savage, *Balanced Budgets and American Politics* (Ithaca, N.Y.: Cornell University Press, 1988).
4. Donald F. Kettl, *Deficit Politics* (New York: Macmillan, 1992), 21–22.
5. Quoted in "Clinton Outlines His Plan to Spur Economy," *Congressional Quarterly Weekly Report,* 20 February 1993, 399.
6. Jeff Shear, "A Necessary Evil?" *National Journal,* 2 March 1996, 505.
7. *Federal Debt and Interest Costs* (Washington, D.C.: Congressional Budget Office, 1993), 19.
8. Paul Masson and Michael Mussa, "Long-Term Tendencies in Budget Deficits and Debt," in *Budget Deficits and Debt: Issues and Options* (Kansas City, Mo.: Federal Reserve Bank of Kansas, 1995), 30.
9. Robert Eisner, "We Don't Need Balanced Budgets," *Wall Street Journal,* 11 January 1995.
10. See, for example, Paul W. McCracken, "Why Deficits Matter," *Wall Street Journal,* 26 December 1995.
11. Calculated by the authors from the *Statistical Abstract of the United States, 1995,* 115th ed. (Washington, D.C.: U.S. Bureau of the Census), 335–37.
12. Barber B. Conable, Jr., *Congress and the Income Tax* (Norman: University of Oklahoma Press, 1989), 34–37; John F. Witte, *The Politics and Development of the Federal Income Tax* (Madison: University of Wisconsin Press, 1985), 67–75. The court case was Pollock v. Farmers' Loan and Trust Co., 157 U.S. 429, 158 U.S. 601 (1895).
13. Brushaber v. Union Pacific Railroad Company, 240 U.S. 1 (1916).
14. Witte, *The Politics and Development of the Federal Income Tax,* 78.
15. Rep. James Monroe Miller, quoted in David Brinkley, "The Long Road to Tax Reform," *Wall Street Journal,* 18 September 1995.
16. "Tax Report," *Wall Street Journal,* 26 October 1994.
17. Kettl, *Deficit Politics,* 61; Viveca Novak and Paul Starobin, "Spreading the Money," *National Journal,* 14 August 1993, 2017.
18. See the Tax Foundation data reported in Gerald F. Seib and Christina Duff, "Kemp Commission to Avoid Endorsing Flat Tax, Likely Fueling Debate Within Republican Party," *Wall Street Journal,* 16 January 1996; House Ways and Means Committee data reported in James K. Glassman, "The Burden of the Rich," *Washington Post National Weekly Edition,* 17–23 July 1995, 5.
19. *Statistical Abstract of the United States, 1980,* 101st ed. (Washington, D.C.: U.S. Bureau of the Census, 1980), 339.
20. Phil Ebersole, "Despite Cuts, Most People Pay More Taxes," *Des Moines Register,* 15 April 1992.
21. R. Kent Weaver, *Automatic Government* (Washington, D.C.: Brookings Institution, 1988), 67–79.
22. David S. Cloud, "New Levies on Gas and the Rich Would Yield $240 Billion," *Congressional Quarterly Weekly Report,* 7 August 1993, 2132–35.
23. "People, Opinions, and Polls," *The Public Perspective* 6 (February/March 1995): 26.
24. Ibid. See also the excellent discussion in Paul Light, *Artful Work* (New York: Random House, 1985), esp. 63.
25. Kettl, *Deficit Politics,* 49.
26. "People, Opinions, and Polls," 26.
27. Robert D. Hershey, Jr., "Misunderstanding Social Security," *New York Times,* 20 August 1995.
28. Kettl, *Deficit Politics,* 50.
29. Peter G. Peterson, *Facing Up: How to Rescue the Economy from Crushing Debt and Restore the American Dream* (New York: Simon & Schuster, 1993), 106 (emphasis in original).
30. Bipartisan Commission on Entitlement and Tax Reform, *Final Report to the President* (Washington, D.C.: U.S. Government Printing Office, 1995), 16; Dorcas R. Hardy and C. Colburn Hardy, "How to Beat the New Social Insecurity," *Bottom Line,* 15 October 1992. See also Eric R. Kingson and Edward D. Berkowitz, *Social Security and Medicare: A Policy Primer* (Westport, Conn.: Auburn House, 1993), 102–7.
31. Kingson and Berkowitz, *Social Security and Medicare: A Policy Primer* (Westport, Conn.: Auburn House, 1993), 131; Peterson, *Facing Up,* 108–9.
32. Peter Passell, "Can Retirees' Safety Net Be Saved?" *New York Times,* 18 February 1996.
33. See, for example, Ann Reilly Dowd, "Needed: A New War on the Deficit," *Fortune,* 14 November 1994, 191–200.
34. "People, Opinions, and Polls," 23.
35. George Hager, "Seven Ways to Cut the Deficit . . . Easier Said than Done," *Congressional Quarterly Weekly Report,* 2 May 1992, 1144–45.
36. Robin Toner, "Clinton's Social Security Test: Selling Sacrifice to the Elderly," *New York Times,* 7 February 1993.
37. Peterson, *Facing Up,* 108–9.
38. Christopher Georges, "Forbes's Proposal to Restructure Social Security Suggests System Is No Longer Political Third Rail," *Wall Street Journal,* 9 February 1996.
39. "Food Stamp Numbers Beginning to Decline, Government Says," *San Francisco Chronicle,* 11 May 1995.
40. See William Safire, *Safire's New Political Dictionary* (New York: Random House, 1993), 596–97.
41. Quoted in Thomas B. Edsall, "He's Not Running for Preacher," *Washington Post National Weekly Edition,* 3–9 July 1995, 12.

42. Quoted in Katharine Q. Seelye, "The Race that Invective Forgot," *New York Times*, 4 November 1994.
43. Christopher Georges, "Playing to Growing Antigovernment Sentiment, Many Candidates Criticize Pork-Barrel Projects," *Wall Street Journal*, 31 October 1994.
44. Robert D. Hershey, Jr., "A Hard Look at Corporate 'Welfare,'" *New York Times*, 7 March 1995.
45. Michael Wines, "Where the Budget Ax Turns Dull," *New York Times*, 30 August 1995.
46. Ibid.
47. Paul E. Peterson, "The New Politics of Deficits," in *The New Direction of American Politics*, ed. John E. Chubb and Paul E. Peterson (Washington, D.C.: Brookings Institution, 1985).
48. Daniel P. Franklin, *Making Ends Meet* (Washington, D.C.: CQ Press, 1993), 37; Norman J. Ornstein, Thomas E. Mann, and Michael J. Malbin, *Vital Statistics on Congress 1995–1996* (Washington, D.C.: Congressional Quarterly, 1996), 186.
49. Christopher B. Wlezien, "The Political Economy of Supplemental Appropriations," *Legislative Studies Quarterly* 18 (February 1993): 51–76; Christopher B. Wlezien, "The President, Congress, and Appropriations, 1951–1985," *American Politics Quarterly* 24 (January 1996): 43–67.
50. Times Mirror Center for the People & the Press, "Public Expects GOP Miracles," 8 December 1994, 34–35.
51. Times Mirror Center for the People & the Press, "Support for Independent Candidate in '96 Up Again," 24 August 1995.
52. Ronald G. Shafer, "Washington Wire," *Wall Street Journal*, 29 July 1994.
53. Richard Morin, "Foreign Aid: Mired in Misunderstanding," *Washington Post National Weekly Edition*, 20–26 March 1995, 37.
54. Ibid.
55. This was contained in a report on a project by the Joyce Foundation. See Mike Feinsilber, "Congressional Members Want Public to Share Blame," *Iowa City Press-Citizen*, 6 April 1992.
56. Our discussion on the evolution of the budgetary process draws heavily on Aaron B. Wildavsky, *The New Politics of the Budgetary Process*, 2d ed. (New York: HarperCollins, 1992).
57. Richard F. Fenno, Jr., *The Power of the Purse* (Boston: Little, Brown, 1966).
58. Speaker of the House Joe Cannon, quoted in ibid., 99.
59. John B. Gilmour, *Reconcilable Differences* (Berkeley: University of California Press, 1990), 28–35; Allen Schick, *Congress and Money* (Washington, D.C.: Urban Institute, 1980), 415–40.
60. See the discussion in Gilmour, *Reconcilable Differences*, chap. 1.
61. See Ornstein, Mann, and Malbin, *Vital Statistics on Congress 1995–1996*, 189. See also James A. Thurber and Samantha L. Durst, "The 1990 Budget Enforcement Act: The Decline of Congressional Accountability," in *Congress Reconsidered*, 5th ed., ed. Lawrence C. Dodd and Bruce I. Oppenheimer (Washington, D.C.: CQ Press, 1993); Joe White, "The Continuing Resolution: A Crazy Way to Govern?" *Brookings Review* 6 (Summer 1988): 28–35. George Hager, "Harmony Born of Pressure Speeds Spending Wrap-Up," *Congressional Quarterly Weekly Report*, 5 October 1996, 2842–44.
62. Steven E. Schier, *A Decade of Deficits* (Albany: State University of New York Press, 1992), 82.
63. Gilmour, *Reconcilable Differences*, 107–30.
64. Joseph White and Aaron B. Wildavsky, *The Deficit and the Public Interest* (Berkeley: University of California Press, 1989), 427.
65. Bowsher v. Synar, 478 U.S. 714 (1986).
66. See Kettl, *Deficit Politics*, 99.
67. Thurber and Durst, "The 1990 Budget Enforcement Act," 375–97.
68. Quoted in Phil Kuntz, "Congressional Democrats Attack GOP over Balanced Budget Amendment," *Wall Street Journal*, 9 January 1995.
69. Rep. George Radanovich (R-Calif.), quoted in Jackie Calmes, "House GOP Freshmen, Unafraid of Sacred Cows, Face Moment of Truth in Balanced-Budget Talks," *Wall Street Journal*, 11 May 1995.
70. David Wessel, "Budget Battle Hides Congressional Victories that Reduce Spending," *Wall Street Journal*, 27 November 1995.
71. Jackie Calmes, "Clinton's Fiscal '97 Budget Reflects Major Shift Toward Ending Deficits and 'Big Government,'" *Wall Street Journal*, 6 February 1996.
72. Christopher Georges, "Budget-Gap Panel, After Eight Months of Study, Fails to Offer Specific Ideas," *Wall Street Journal*, 15 December 1994; Robert Pear, "Panel on U.S. Benefits Overhaul Fails to Agree on Proposal," *New York Times*, 15 December 1994.
73. Bipartisan Commission, *Final Report to the President*, 8–10, 30; Herbert Stein, "A Presidential Budget Message," *Wall Street Journal*, 19 January 1996.
74. Viveca Novak, "Defective Remedy," *National Journal*, 27 March 1993, 750.
75. Glenn Abney and Thomas P. Lauth, "The Line-Item Veto in the States: An Instrument for Fiscal Restraint or an Instrument of Partisanship?" *Public Administration Review* (May/June 1985): 372–77.
76. See, for example, Jackie Koszczuk, "Republicans' Hopes for 1996 Lie in Unfinished Business," *Congressional Quarterly Weekly Report*, 6 January 1996, 25; Andrew Taylor, "Line-Item Veto Compromise Passes Senate Easily, *Congressional Quarterly Weekly Report*, 25 March 1995, 855.
77. See Jerry Gray, "Compromise Bills Approved on Debt and Line-Item Veto," *New York Times*, 29 March 1996; Andrew Taylor, "Congress Hands President a Budgetary Scalpel," *Congressional Quarterly Weekly Report*, 30 March 1996, 864–67; Andrew Taylor, "Republicans Break Logjam On Line-Item Veto Bill," *Congressional Quarterly Weekly Report*, 16 March 1996, 687.
78. Quoted in Adam Clymer, "Legislation Pits Clinton vs. Democrats," *New York Times*, 18 March 1996.
79. Robert Pear, "A Judicial Group Condemns the Planned Line-Item Veto," *New York Times*, 27 March 1996.
80. Jackie Calmes and Paul M. Barrett, "Line-Item Veto Unlikely to Cure Deficits," *Wall Street Journal*, 29 March 1996.
81. Wildavasky, *The New Politics of the Budgetary Process*, 451.
82. David E. Rosenbaum, "Of Line Items and the Veto," *New York Times*, 29 March 1996.
83. Quoted in Taylor, "Congress Hands President a Budgetary Scalpel" 866.
84. See, for example, Richard J. Tofel, "A Boon for the Constitutional Bar," *Wall Street Journal*, 31 January 1995.
85. Albert R. Hunt, "The Balanced Budget Amendment: A Contract with Evasion," *Wall Street Journal*, 12 January 1995.
86. Rachel Wildavsky, "How Fair Are Our Taxes?" *Wall Street Journal*, 10 January 1996.
87. Ibid.
88. Milton Friedman, *Capitalism and Freedom* (Chicago: University of Chicago Press, 1962), 174–76.
89. John E. Berthoud, "State Lessons for the Flat Tax Debate," *Comparative State Politics* 17 (February 1996): 23–29; David E. Rosenbaum, "A Key Point by Forbes Proves Hard to Confirm," *New York Times*, 3 February 1996.
90. Rosenbaum, "A Key Point by Forbes."
91. Alan Murray, "GOP Adherents Study Merits of a Flat Tax," *Wall Street Journal*, 29 January 1996.
92. Rosenbaum, "A Key Point by Forbes."
93. "Tax Report," *Wall Street Journal*, 29 November 1995.
94. R. W. Apple, Jr., "Candidate of the Flat Tax Is a Bit of a Flat Campaigner," *New York Times*, 12 February 1996.
95. Ibid.
96. See Dan Goodgame, "Is This Flat Tax Unfair?" *Time*, 29 January 1996. Clay Chandler, "The Agency They Love to Get Excised About," *Washington Post*, 23 September 1996.
97. Albert R. Hunt, "The Flat-Tax Snow Job," *Wall Street Journal*, 11 January 1996; "Poll Finds Surprising Support for Tax System," *Cedar Rapids Gazette*, 26 February 1996; "The Flat Tax Is Losing Its Appeal Among U.S. Voters, Poll Finds," *Wall Street Journal*, 8 March 1996.
98. Wildavsky, *The New Politics of the Budgetary Process*, 436–40; Kettl, *Deficit Politics*, 76–91.
99. Wildavsky, *The New Politics of the Budgetary Process*, chap. 10.

Chapter 17, pp. 563–602

1. Lyndon Baines Johnson, "Annual Message to Congress on the State of the Union, 8 January 1964," in *Public Papers of the Presidents of the United States: Lyndon B. Johnson, 1963–1964* (Washington, D.C.: U.S. Government Printing Office, 1965), 114.
2. *Contract With America: The Bold Plan by Rep. Newt Gingrich, Rep. Dick Armey and the House Republicans to Change the Nation,* ed. Ed Gillespie and Bob Schellhas (New York: Times Books/Random House, 1994), 65, 67.
3. Ibid., 125.
4. "Prepared Text for the President's State of the Union Message," *New York Times,* 24 January 1996.
5. William J. Barber, *From New Era to New Deal: Herbert Hoover, the Economists, and American Economic Policy, 1921–1933* (New York: Cambridge University Press, 1985); Michael S. Lewis-Beck and Peverill Squire, "The Transformation of the American State: The New Era-New Deal Test," *Journal of Politics* 53 (February 1991): 106–21; Albert U. Romasco, "Herbert Hoover's Policies for Dealing with the Great Depression: The End of the Old Order or the Beginning of the New?" in *The Hoover Presidency,* ed. Martin L. Fausold and George T. Mazuzan (Albany: State University of New York Press, 1974); Herbert Stein, *The Fiscal Revolution in America* (Chicago: University of Chicago Press, 1969).
6. Arthur M. Schlesinger, Jr., *The Coming of the New Deal* (Boston: Houghton Mifflin, 1958).
7. See David Burner, *Herbert Hoover: A Public Life* (New York: Knopf, 1979), 244.
8. Robert Lekachman, *The Age of Keynes* (New York: Vintage, 1966), chap. 5.
9. John Maynard Keynes, *The General Theory of Employment, Interest, and Money* (New York: Harcourt, Brace, 1965).
10. See John T. Woolley, *Monetary Politics: The Federal Reserve and the Politics of Monetary Policy* (Cambridge: Cambridge University Press, 1984), chap. 2.
11. James Livingston, *Origins of the Federal Reserve System: Money, Class, and Corporate Capitalism, 1890–1913* (Ithaca, N.Y.: Cornell University Press, 1986).
12. Milton Friedman, "The Optimum Quantity of Money" in *The Optimum Quantity of Money and Other Essays* (Chicago: Aldine, 1971), 1–50; Milton Friedman and Anna G. Schwartz, *A Monetary History of the United States* (Chicago: University of Chicago Press, 1963); A. Robert Nobay and Harry G. Johnson, "Monetarism: A Historic-Theoretic Perspective," *Journal of Economic Literature* 15 (June 1977): 470–85; Thomas Mayer, ed., *The Structure of Monetarism* (New York: Norton, 1978).
13. Milton Friedman with Rose D. Friedman, *Capitalism and Freedom* (Chicago: University of Chicago Press, 1962), chap. 3.
14. Joseph A. Pechman, *Federal Tax Policy,* 5th ed. (Washington, D.C.: Brookings Institution, 1987), 8.
15. David M. Jones, *The Politics of Money: The Fed Under Alan Greenspan* (New York: New York Institute of Finance, 1991).
16. Robert E. Lucas, Jr., "Expectations and the Neutrality of Money," *Journal of Economic Theory* 4 (April 1972): 103–24; Robert E. Lucas, Jr., "An Equilibrium Model of the Business Cycle," *Journal of Political Economy* 83 (December 1975): 1113–14.
17. James K. Galbraith and William Darity, Jr., *Macroeconomics* (Boston: Houghton Mifflin, 1994), chap. 8–9; Kevin D. Hoover, *The New Classical Macroeconomics* (Cambridge, Mass: Basil Blackwell, 1988).
18. Robert Solow, "On Theories of Unemployment," *American Economic Review* 70 (March 1980): 1–11.
19. James K. Galbraith and William Darity, Jr., *Macroeconomics* (Boston: Houghton Mifflin, 1994), chap. 10; see also Arjo Klamer, *Conversations with Economists: New Classical Economists and Opponents Speak Out on the Current Controversy in Macroeconomics* (Totowa, N.J.: Rowman & Allanheld, 1983).
20. *Statistical Abstract of the United States, 1995,* 115th ed. (Washington, D.C.: U.S. Bureau of the Census, 1995), 475; U.S. Census Bureau, "Poverty in the United States: 1995," 22 September 1996.
21. "Across the Great Divide," *Wall Street Journal,* 2 October 1995; Keith Bradsher, "Widest Gap in Incomes? Research Points to U.S.," *New York Times,* 27 October 1995; Steven A. Holmes, "Income Disparity Between Poorest and Richest Rises," *New York Times,* 20 June 1996; Robert J. Samuelson, "The Wealth Statistic Myth," *Washington Post National Weekly Edition,* 1–7 May 1995, 5.
22. Keith Bradsher, "Gap in Wealth in U.S. Called Widest in West," *New York Times,* 17 April 1995; Samuelson, "The Wealth Statistic Myth," 5; see also Keith Bradsher, "Rich Control More of U.S. Wealth, Study Says, as Debts Grow for Poor," *New York Times,* 22 June 1996.
23. Bradsher, "Rich Control More of U.S. Wealth."
24. See, for example, Michael Novak, "What Wealth Gap?" *Wall Street Journal,* 11 July 1995; Samuelson, "The Wealth Statistic Myth," 5.
25. Quoted in Keith Bradsher, "America's Opportunity Gap," *New York Times,* 4 June 1995.
26. See, for example, Steven Rattner, "GOP Ignores Income Inequality," *Wall Street Journal,* 23 May 1995.
27. See the data cited in Bradsher, "America's Opportunity Gap."
28. George Gilder, *Wealth and Poverty* (New York: Basic Books, 1981); Jude Wanniski, *The Way the World Works* (New York: Basic Books, 1978).
29. See Kevin Philips, *The Politics of Rich and Poor: Wealth and the American Electorate in the Reagan Aftermath* (New York: Random House, 1990).
30. David A. Stockman, *The Triumph of Politics: Why the Reagan Revolution Failed* (New York: Harper & Row, 1986).
31. See, for example, Ira C. Magaziner and Robert B. Reich, *Minding America's Business: The Decline and Rise of the American Economy* (New York: Harcourt, Brace, Jovanovich, 1982); Lester C. Thurow, *The Zero-Sum Solution* (New York: Simon & Schuster, 1985).
32. See Giovanni Dosi, Laura D'Andrea Tyson, and John Zysman, "Trade, Technologies, and Development: A Framework for Discussing Japan," in *Politics and Productivity: How Japan's Development Strategy Works,* ed. Chalmers Johnson, Laura Tyson, and John Zysman, (New York: HarperBusiness, 1989); Chalmers A. Johnson, *MITI and the Japanese Miracle: The Growth of Industrial Policy, 1925–1975* (Stanford, Calif.: Stanford University Press, 1982).
33. See Vic Comello, "Is Sematech a Model for Global Competitiveness?" *Research & Development,* 25 October 1993, 24–26; Peter Grindley, "SEMATECH and Collaborative Research: Lessons in the Design of High-Technology Consortia," *Journal of Policy Analysis and Management* 13 (Fall 1994): 723–58; William J. Spencer, "SEMATECH after Five Years: High-Technology Consortia and U.S. Competitiveness," *California Management Review* 35 (Summer 1993): 9–32.
34. William G. Mayer, *The Changing American Mind: How and Why American Public Opinion Changed Between 1960 and 1988* (Ann Arbor: University of Michigan Press, 1992), 100–102, 482–85.
35. Times Mirror Center for the People & the Press, "Strong Support for Minimum Wage Hike and Preserving Entitlements," 17 February 1995, 1.
36. Benjamin I. Page and Robert Y. Shapiro, *The Rational Public: Fifty Years of Trends in Americans' Policy Preferences* (Chicago: University of Chicago Press, 1992), chap. 4.
37. James W. Fesler and Donald F. Kettl, *The Politics of the Administrative Process* (Chatham, N.J.: Chatham House, 1991), 292–93.
38. Gabriel Kolko, *The Triumph of Capitalism: A Reinterpretation of American History, 1900–1916* (Chicago: Quadrangle Books, 1963).
39. Bryan Gruley and Albert R. Karr, "Telecom Vote Signals Competitive Free-for-All: Bill's Passage Represents Will of Both Parties," *Wall Street Journal,* 2 February 1996; Albert R. Karr, "Cable Rates Are Up An Average of 10.4% This Year," *Wall Street Journal,* 29 August 1996.
40. David P. Baron, *Business and Its Environment* (Englewood Cliffs, N.J.: Prentice-Hall, 1993), 252.

41. George C. Thompson and Gerald P. Brady, *Text, Cases and Materials on Antitrust Fundamentals* (St. Paul: West, 1979).
42. William E. Leuchtenburg, *Franklin Roosevelt and the New Deal, 1932–1940* (New York: Harper & Row, 1963).
43. George J. Gordon and Michael E. Milakovich, *Public Administration in America,* 5th ed. (New York: St. Martin's, 1995), 408.
44. Martha Derthick and Paul J. Quirk, *The Politics of Deregulation* (Washington, D.C.: Brookings Institution, 1985).
45. Bradley Behrman, "Civil Aeronautics Board," in *The Politics of Regulation,* ed. James Q. Wilson (New York: Basic Books, 1980).
46. Larry N. Gerston, Cynthia Fraleigh, and Robert Schwab, *The Deregulated Society* (Pacific Grove, Calif.: Brooks/Cole, 1988).
47. Murray Edelman, *The Symbolic Uses of Politics* (Urbana: University of Illinois Press, 1964); Theodore J. Lowi, *The End of Liberalism* (New York: Norton, 1969), chaps. 3–4; George J. Stigler, "The Theory of Economic Regulation," *Bell Journal of Economics and Management Science* 2 (Spring 1971): 3–21.
48. Gerston, Fraleigh, and Schwab, *The Deregulated Society,* chap. 5.
49. Barry Bearak and Tom Furlong, "Toting Up Blame for S&L Crisis," *Los Angeles Times,* 16 September 1990; Steven Waldman et al., "The S&L Firestorm," *Newsweek,* 23 July 1990, 14–16.
50. William Lilley III and James C. Miller III, "The New 'Social Regulation,'" *Public Interest* 47 (Spring 1977): 49–61.
51. Gordon and Milakovich, *Public Administration in America,* 408–9.
52. Charles Noble, *Liberalism at Work: The Rise and Fall of OSHA* (Philadelphia: Temple University Press, 1986), chap. 3.
53. Al Gore, *Creating a Government that Works Better & Costs Less: Report of the National Performance Review* (New York: Random House, 1993), 62.
54. Wayne B. Gray, *Productivity Versus OSHA and EPA Regulations* (Ann Arbor, Mich.: UMI Research Press, 1986).
55. W. Kip Viscusi, *Risk by Choice: Regulating Health and Safety in the Workplace* (Cambridge: Harvard University Press, 1983).
56. David P. McCaffrey, *OSHA and the Politics of Health Regulation* (New York: Plenum Press, 1982), 168.
57. M. Green and N. Waitzman, *Business at War on the Law: An Analysis of the Benefits of Safety and Health Regulation* (Washington, D.C.: Corporate Accountability Research Group, 1979).
58. Noble, *Liberalism at Work,* 201–205.
59. Ibid., chap. 7.
60. Don J. Lofgren, *Dangerous Premises: An Insider's View of OSHA Enforcement* (Ithaca, N.Y.: ILR Press, 1989).
61. See, for example, Michael Weisskopf and David Maraniss, "Ruling Out OSHA," *Washington Post National Weekly Edition,* 4–10 September 1995, 6–7.
62. Robert Pear, "With or Without a Budget Pact, the G.O.P.'s Fiscal Squeeze Is On," *New York Times,* 1 February 1996.
63. Asra Q. Nomani, "Businesses Find Allies in GOP to Launch Attacks on Federal Job-Safety and Labor Regulations," *Wall Street Journal,* 20 July 1995.
64. Assistant Secretary of Labor for Occupational Safety and Health Joseph A. Dear, quoted in Pear, "With or Without a Budget Pact."
65. Noble, *Liberalism at Work,* 124–26.
66. On the public's attitude toward the environment before the 1960s, see Roderick Nash, *Wilderness and the American Mind* (New Haven: Yale University Press, 1967).
67. Rachel Carson, *Silent Spring* (Boston: Houghton Mifflin, 1962).
68. Marc K. Landy, Marc J. Roberts, and Stephen R. Thomas, *The Environmental Protection Agency,* expanded ed. (New York: Oxford University Press, 1994), chap. 1.
69. See, for instance, the Ralph Nader group's report on the Air Quality Act in John C. Esposito et al., *Vanishing Air* (New York: Grossman, 1970).
70. Tom Wicker, *One of Us: Richard Nixon and the American Dream* (New York: Random House, 1991), 507–18.
71. Walter A. Rosenbaum, *Environmental Politics and Policy,* 2d ed. (Washington, D.C.: CQ Press, 1991), chap. 3.
72. Mayer, *The Changing American Mind,* 102–108.
73. Paul Portney, "Natural Resources and the Environment," in *The Reagan Record,* ed. John L. Palmer and Isabel V. Sawhill (Cambridge, Mass: Ballinger, 1984), 141–75.
74. "Appendix 2: Federal Spending on Natural Resources and the Environment, Selected Fiscal Years, 1980 to 1993," in *Environmental Policy for the 1990s,* 2d ed., ed. Norman J. Vig and Michael E. Kraft (Washington, D.C.: CQ Press, 1994), 403.
75. Christopher J. Bosso, "After the Movement: Environmental Activism in the 1990s," in *Environmental Policy for the 1990s,* 2d ed., ed. Norman J. Vig and Michael E. Kraft (Washington, D.C.: CQ Press, 1994), 31–50; Mayer, *The Changing American Mind,* 102–8.
76. Richard E. Cohen, *Washington at Work: Back Rooms and Clean Air,* 2d ed. (Boston: Allyn & Bacon, 1995).
77. Norman J. Vig, "Presidential Leadership and the Environment: From Reagan and Bush to Clinton," in *Environmental Policy for the 1990s,* 2d ed., ed. Norman J. Vig and Michael E. Kraft (Washington, D.C.: CQ Press, 1994), 71–95.
78. Joan Hamilton, "Babbitt's Retreat," *Sierra,* July/August 1994.
79. Melissa Healy, "Partisan Politics Swamps Environmentalists," *Los Angeles Times,* 17 October 1994.
80. For a discussion of how this logic plays out in Congress, see R. Douglas Arnold, *The Logic of Congressional Action* (New Haven: Yale University Press, 1990), chap. 2.
81. Norman J. Vig and Michael E. Kraft, "Conclusion: The New Environmental Agenda," in *Environmental Policy for the 1990s,* 2d ed., ed. Norman J. Vig and Michael E. Kraft (Washington, D.C.: CQ Press, 1994), 378–85.
82. H. W. Lewis, *Technological Risk* (New York: Norton, 1990), 266–79.
83. Baron, *Business and Its Environment,* 318–31.
84. Vig and Kraft, "Conclusion," 379–80.
85. See Bob Benenson, "Five Days of Clean Water Debate . . . Yields Many Winners, Many Losers," *Congressional Quarterly Weekly Report,* 20 May 1995, 1414–15; Bob Benenson, "Water Bill Wins House Passage, May Not Survive in Senate," *Congressional Quarterly Weekly Report,* 20 May 1995, 1413; "Issue: Clean Water Act," *Congressional Quarterly Weekly Report,* 6 January 1996, 32.
86. Bob Benenson, "EPA Evades Limits, But Not Cuts," *Congressional Quarterly Weekly Report,* 29 July 1995, 2269; Jeffrey L. Katz, "G.O.P. Moderates Join Democrats in House to Keep EPA Intact," *Congressional Quarterly Weekly Report,* 4 November 1995, 3383; Jeffrey L. Katz, "House Revives EPA Restrictions Before Passing VA-HUD Bill," *Congressional Quarterly Weekly Report,* 5 August 1995, 2366–69.
87. Bob Benenson, "House Panel Votes to Restrict Endangered Species Act," *Congressional Quarterly Weekly Report,* 14 October 1995, 3136–37.
88. Pear, "With or Without a Budget Pact."
89. See John Cushman, Jr., "G.O.P. Backing Off from Tough Stand over Environment," *New York Times,* 26 January 1996; John Cushman, Jr., "Moderates Soften G.O.P. Agenda on Environment," *New York Times,* 24 October 1995; Dennis Farney and Timothy Noah, "Down to Earth: Environmental Stands Alienate Some Backers of the GOP's Agenda," *Wall Street Journal,* 5 March 1996; Allan Freedman, "GOP Trying to Find Balance After Early Stumbles," *Congressional Quarterly Weekly Report,* 20 January 1996, 151–53; Allan Freedman, "Republicans Concede Missteps in Effort to Rewrite Rules," *Congressional Quarterly Weekly Report,* 2 December 1995, 3645–47; Margaret Kriz, "The Green Card," *National Journal,* 16 September 1995, 2262–67; Timothy Noah, "GOP's Rollback of the Green Agenda Is Stalled by a Public Seeing Red over Proposed Changes," *Wall Street Journal,* 26 December 1995; Kenneth Pins, "Environmental Reform Sinks into Uncertainty After Splitting the GOP," *Des Moines Register,* 5 February 1996.
90. Quoted in Cushman, "G.O.P. Backing Off from Tough Stand over Environment."
91. Diana M. DiNitto and Thomas R. Dye, *Social Welfare Politics and Public Policy,* 2d ed. (Englewood Cliffs, N.J.: Prentice-Hall, 1987), 189.

92. Charles E. Gilbert, "Welfare Policy," in *Handbook of Political Science*, vol. 6 (Menlo Park, Calif.: Addison-Wesley, 1975), 111–240.
93. Theda Skocpol, *Protecting Soldiers and Mothers: The Political Origins of Social Policy in the United States* (Cambridge: Harvard University Press, 1992), chap. 1.
94. Ibid.
95. Congressional Quarterly, *Congress and the Nation, 1945–1964* (Washington, D.C.: Congressional Quarterly Service, 1965), 1225; Peter Flora and Jens Alber, "Modernization, Democratization and the Development of Welfare States in Western Europe," in *The Development of Welfare States in Europe and America*, ed. Peter Flora and Arnold J. Heidenheimer (New Brunswick, N.J.: Transaction Press, 1981), 37–80.
96. U.S. Bureau of the Census, *Historical Statistics of the United States, Colonial Times to 1970*, bicentennial edition, part 2 (Washington, D.C.: Government Printing Office, 1975), 348–49; *Statistical Abstract of the United States, 1995*, 337, 380.
97. *Statistical Abstract of the United States, 1995*, 337.
98. Iris J. Lav, Edward Lazere, and Robert Greenstein, *The States and the Poor* (Washington, D.C.: Center on Budget and Policy Priorities, 1993).
99. *Statistical Abstract of the United States, 1995*, 387.
100. Ibid.
101. Ibid., 387, 481.
102. "Welfare Rolls," *Congressional Quarterly Weekly Report*, 22 January 1994, 121.
103. Mary Jo Bane, "Household Composition and Poverty," and William Julius Wilson and Kathryn M. Neckerman, "Poverty and Family Structure: The Widening Gap Between Evidence and Public Policy Issues," both in *Fighting Poverty: What Works and What Doesn't*, ed. Sheldon H. Danziger and Daniel H. Weinberg (Cambridge: Harvard University Press, 1986).
104. George T. Martin, Jr., *Social Policy in the Welfare State* (Englewood Cliffs, N.J.: Prentice-Hall, 1990), 68–69; Lav, Lazere, and Greenstein, *The States and the Poor*, 11–33.
105. DiNitto and Dye, *Social Welfare Politics*, 126.
106. Michael Harrington, *The Other America* (Baltimore: Penguin, 1962); see also the influential review of Harrington's book in Dwight McDonald, "Our Invisible Poor," *New Yorker*, 19 January 1963.
107. Michael Barone, *Our Country: The Shaping of America from Roosevelt to Reagan* (New York: Free Press, 1990), chap. 37; Lyndon Baines Johnson, *The Vantage Point: Perspectives of the Presidency 1963–1969* (New York: Popular Library, 1971), chap. 4.
108. Michael B. Katz, *The Undeserving Poor: From the War on Poverty to the War on Welfare* (New York: Pantheon, 1989), chap. 3.
109. Clarke E. Cochran et al., *American Public Policy*, 4th ed. (New York: St. Martin's, 1993), 225.
110. Hugh Heclo, "The Political Foundations of Antipoverty Policy," in *Fighting Poverty: What Works and What Doesn't*, ed. Sheldon H. Danziger and Daniel H. Weinberg (Cambridge: Harvard University Press, 1986), 312–40.
111. Frances Fox Piven and Richard A. Cloward, *Regulating the Poor: The Functions of Public Welfare*, updated ed. (New York: Vintage, 1993), chaps. 9–10; David Stoloff, "The Short Unhappy History of Community Action Programs," in *The Great Society Reader* (New York: Vintage, 1967), 231–39.
112. James A. Morone, *The Democratic Wish* (New York: Basic Books, 1991), chap. 7.
113. Johnson, *Vantage Point*, chap. 9.
114. Lawrence G. Brewster and Michael E. Brown, *The Public Agenda: Issues in American Politics*, 3d ed. (New York: St. Martin's, 1994), 109.
115. See, for example, Erik Eckholm, "Frayed Nerves of People Without Health Coverage," *New York Times*, 11 July 1994; Howard Fineman, "Mediscare," *Newsweek*, 18 September 1995, 38–40; Robert J. Samuelson, "Health Care: How We Got into This Mess," *Newsweek*, 4 October 1993, 30–35.
116. Martin, *Social Policy in the Welfare State*, 35–36.
117. International Monetary Fund, *Government Finance Statistics Yearbook* (Washington, D.C.: International Monetary Fund, 1994), 44.
118. See Joseph White, *Competing Solutions: American Health Care Proposals and International Experience* (Washington, D.C.: Brookings Institution, 1995).
119. Norman J. Ornstein, Thomas E. Mann, and Michael J. Malbin, *Vital Statistics on Congress 1995–1996* (Washington, D.C.: Congressional Quarterly, 1996), 183, 185.
120. Ruth Rosen, "Which of Us Isn't Taking 'Welfare'?" *Los Angeles Times*, 27 January 1995; Steven Waldman, "Benefits 'R' Us," *Newsweek*, 10 August 1992, 56–58.
121. Lawrence R. Jacobs, Robert Y. Shapiro, and Eli C. Shulman, "The Polls: Medical Care in the United States—An Update," *Public Opinion Quarterly* 57 (Fall 1993): 394–427; Robert Y. Shapiro and Tom W. Smith, "The Polls: Social Security," *Public Opinion Quarterly* 9 (Winter 1985): 561–72; Robert Y. Shapiro and John T. Young, "The Polls: Medical Care in the United States," *Public Opinion Quarterly* 50 (Fall 1986): 418–28.
122. For contrasting views, see Charles Murray, *Losing Ground: American Social Policy 1950–1980* (New York: Basic Books, 1984); John E. Schwarz, *America's Hidden Success: A Reassessment of Public Policy from Kennedy to Reagan*, rev. ed. (New York: Norton, 1983).
123. Theodore R. K. Marmor, Jerry L. Mashaw, and Philip L. Harvey, *America's Misunderstood Welfare State* (New York: HarperCollins, 1990), chap. 4.
124. *Statistical Abstract of the United States, 1995*, 480.
125. Ibid., 481; U. S. Census Bureau, "Poverty in the United States: 1995."
126. Merton C. Bernstein and Joan Brodshaug Bernstein, *Social Security: The System That Works* (New York: Basic Books, 1988), 208.
127. *Statistical Abstract of the United States, 1995*, 480.
128. Ibid., 73; National Center for Health Statistics, *Vital Statistics of the United States, 1990, Vol. II, Mortality, Part A* (Washington, D.C.: U.S. Public Health Service, 1994), section 2, p. 1.
129. Maurice MacDonald, *Food Stamps and Income* (New York: Academic Press, 1977); U.S. Senate Committee on Agriculture, *Hunger in America: Ten Years Later* (Washington, D.C.: U.S. Government Printing Office, 1979).
130. Murray, *Losing Ground*, chaps. 12–13.
131. Ronald B. Mincy, "The Underclass: Concept, Controversy, and Evidence," in *Confronting Poverty: Prescriptions for Change*, ed. Sheldon H. Danzinger, Gary D. Sandefur, and Daniel H. Weinberg (New York: Russell Sage Foundation, 1994), chap. 5.
132. Peter G. Peterson, *Facing Up: How to Rescue the Economy from Crushing Debt and Restore the American Dream* (New York: Simon & Schuster, 1993), 108–109.
133. See, for example, ibid.; Bipartisan Commission on Entitlement and Tax Reform, *Final Report to the President* (Washington, D.C.: U.S. Government Printing Office, 1995).
134. Bipartisan Commission, *Final Report*, 16; Dorcas R. Hardy and C. Colburn Hardy, "How to Beat the New Social Insecurity," *Bottom Line*, 15 October 1992.
135. See B. Guy Peters, *American Public Policy: Promise and Performance*, 4th ed. (Chatham, N.J.: Chatham House, 1996), chap. 10.
136. The following discussion draws on Carl P. Chelf, *Controversial Issues in Social Welfare Policy: Government and the Pursuit of Happiness* (Newbury Park, Calif.: Sage, 1992), chaps. 1 and 6.
137. See R. Kent Weaver, Robert Y. Shapiro, and Lawrence R. Jacobs, "The Polls—Trends: Welfare," *Public Opinion Quarterly* 59 (Winter 1994): 606–27.
138. James Allan Davis and Tom W. Smith, *General Social Surveys, 1972–1993: Cumulative Codebook* (Chicago: National Opinion Research Center, 1993), 120. See also Tom W. Smith, "That Which We Call Welfare by Any Other Name Would Smell Sweeter," *Public Opinion Quarterly* 51 (Spring 1987): 75–83.
139. "Welfare: An American Dilemma," *The Public Perspective* 6 (February/March 1995): 39.
140. Ibid., 43; "Reforming Welfare," *The Public Perspective* 4 (September/October 1993): 87.
141. Ronald Brownstein, "Welfare Debate Puts Blame for Poverty Mainly on the Poor," *Los Angeles Times*, 24 March 1995.
142. See, for example, *Contract With America*, 65–77; Lawrence M. Mead, "Jobs for the Welfare Poor: Work

Requirements Can Overcome the Barriers," in *Controversies in American Public Policy,* ed. John A. Hird (New York: St. Martin's, 1995), 37–53.

143. *Statistical Abstract of the United States, 1995,* 483; U.S. Census Bureau, "Poverty in the United States: 1995."
144. Richard A. Cloward and Frances Fox Piven, "Punishing the Poor, Again: The Fraud of Workfare," in *Controversies in American Public Policy,* ed. John A. Hird (New York: St. Martin's, 1995), 54–60.
145. Joel Blau, *The Visible Poor: Homelessness in the United States* (New York: Oxford University Press, 1992), chap. 4; Neil Gilbert, Harry Specht, and Paul Terrell, *Dimensions of Social Work Policy,* 3d ed. (Englewood Cliffs, N.J.: Prentice-Hall, 1993), 101–3; Peter Rossi, *Down and Out in America* (Chicago: University of Chicago Press, 1989), chap. 7.
146. Donna Cassata, "Finale Expected to Be Short, but Not Necessarily Sweet," *Congressional Quarterly Weekly Report,* 31 August 1996, 2418–55; Jeffrey L. Katz, "Welfare: After 60 Years, Most Control Is Passing to States," *Congressional Quarterly Weekly Report,* 3 August 1996, 2190–96.
147. Alan Finder, "Welfare Clients Outnumber Jobs They Might Fill," *New York Times,* 25 August 1996; Jeffrey L. Katz, "After 60 Years, Most Control is Passing to States," *Congressional Quarterly Weekly Report,* 3 August 1996, 2190–96.
148. Brewster and Brown, *The Public Agenda,* 109.
149. *Statistical Abstract of the United States, 1995,* 109.
150. Brewster and Brown, *The Public Agenda,* 101.
151. Ibid., 118.
152. Laurene A. Graig, *Health of Nations: An International Perspective on U.S. Health Care Reform,* 2d ed. (Washington, D.C.: CQ Press, 1993), chap. 1.
153. Bill Clinton, *Health Security: The President's Report to the American People* (Washington, D.C.: U.S. Government Printing Office, 1993).
154. See, for example, Colette Fraley, "GOP Scores on Medicare, But Foes Aren't Done," *Congressional Quarterly Weekly Report,* 18 November 1995, 3535–38; Colette Fraley, "Historic House Medicare Vote Affirms GOP Determination," *Congressional Quarterly Weekly Report,* 21 October 1995, 3206–10; Colette Fraley, "Republicans Outline Medicare Plan . . . To Hit $270 Billion Budget Target," *Congressional Quarterly Weekly Report,* 16 September 1995, 2780–81; Colette Fraley, "Scaled-Back Medicaid Savings Plan Emerges from Conference," *Congressional Quarterly Weekly Report,* 18 November 1995, 3539; Alissa J. Rubin, "Spadework on Medicare Pays Off for GOP," *Congressional Quarterly Weekly Report,* 23 September 1995, 2895–97.
155. See, for example, Colette Fraley, "Democrats Say GOP Surgery on Medicare Goes Too Far," *Congressional Quarterly Weekly Report,* 7 October 1995, 3068–70.

Chapter 18, pp. 603–636

1. "Clinton's Words on Mission to Bosnia: 'The Right Thing to Do,'" *New York Times,* 28 November 1995.
2. Quoted in William Safire, *Lend Me Your Ears: Great Speeches in History* (New York: Norton, 1992), 727.
3. Quoted in Thomas G. Paterson and Dennis Merrill, eds., *Major Problems in American Foreign Relations, Vol. I* (Lexington, Mass.: Heath, 1995), 77. (Emphasis in the original.)
4. Quoted in ibid., 179–80.
5. See Ernest R. May, *The Making of the Monroe Doctrine* (Cambridge: Harvard University Press, 1975); Dexter Perkins, *The Monroe Doctrine, 1823–1826* (Cambridge: Harvard University Press, 1932).
6. Robert H. Ferrell, *American Diplomacy: A History,* 3d ed. (New York: Norton, 1975), 169.
7. Among others, see Walter LaFeber, *The Cambridge History of American Foreign Relations, Volume II: The American Search for Opportunity, 1865–1913* (New York: Cambridge University Press, 1993).
8. Quoted in Ferrell, *American Diplomacy,* 457.
9. See Ralph Stone, *The Irreconcilables: The Fight Against the League of Nations* (Lexington: University of Kentucky Press, 1970); John Chalmers Vinson, *Referendum for Isolation: Defeat of Article Ten of the League of Nations Covenant* (Athens: University of Georgia Press, 1961); William C. Widenor, "The League of Nations Component of the Versailles Treaty," in *The Politics of Arms Control Treaty Ratification,* ed. Michael Krepon and Dan Caldwell (New York: St. Martin's, 1991).
10. Quoted in Ferrell, *American Diplomacy,* 631.
11. On the genesis of the Marshall Plan, see Joseph Marion Jones, *The Fifteen Weeks* (New York: Harcourt, Brace & World, 1955).
12. Steven Greenhouse, "Rich Nations Criticize U.S. on Foreign Aid," *New York Times,* 8 April 1995.
13. Among others, see George C. Herring, *America's Longest War: The United States and Vietnam, 1959–1975,* 3d ed. (New York: Knopf, 1996); Stanley Karnow, *Vietnam, a History* (New York: Viking Penguin, 1991).
14. Herring, *America's Longest War,* 199.
15. Among others, see Bruce W. Jentleson, *With Friends Like These: Reagan, Bush, and Saddam, 1982–1990* (New York: Norton, 1994).
16. See, for example, Anthony Lake, "From Containment to Enlargement," *State Department Dispatch,* 27 September 1993, 658–64; *A National Security Strategy of Engagement and Enlargement,* The White House, February 1995.
17. Albert R. Hunt, "The People's Perspective," *Wall Street Journal,* 24 April 1995. See also John E. Rielly, "The Public Mood at Mid-Decade," *Foreign Policy* 98 (Spring 1995): 76–93.
18. Richard Morin, "Tuned Out, Turned Off," *Washington Post National Weekly Edition,* 5–11 February 1996, 8.
19. The term *two presidencies* was coined in Aaron Wildavsky, "The Two Presidencies," *Transaction* 4 (December 1966): 7–14. Wildavsky's article spawned a long line of research that has variously confirmed, modified and challenged his original findings. Many of these studies are reprinted in Steven A. Shull, ed., *The Two Presidencies: A Quarter Century Assessment* (Chicago: Nelson-Hall, 1991). The relevance of these subsequent studies to the question of how presidential power varies across policy domains is limited, however, because of methodological problems. See James M. Lindsay and Wayne P. Steger, "The 'Two Presidencies' in Future Research: Moving Beyond Roll-Call Analysis," *Congress & the Presidency* 20 (Autumn 1993): 103–17.
20. See Michael J. Glennon, *Constitutional Diplomacy* (Princeton, N.J.: Princeton University Press, 1990); Louis Henkin, *Foreign Affairs and the Constitution* (Mineola, N.Y.: Foundation Press, 1972); Harold Hongju Koh, *The National Security Constitution: Sharing Power After the Iran-Contra Affair* (New Haven: Yale University Press, 1990).
21. See David Gray Adler, "The Constitution and Presidential Warmaking," *Political Science Quarterly* 103 (Spring 1988): 8–13; Alexander Hamilton, "Federalist No. 69," in *The Federalist Papers,* ed. Garry Wills (New York: Bantam Books, 1982), 350; Henkin, *Foreign Affairs and the Constitution,* 50–51; Arthur M. Schlesinger, Jr., *The Imperial Presidency* (Boston: Houghton Mifflin, 1989), 6, 61–62.
22. Alexander Hamilton, "Federalist No. 70," in Alexander Hamilton, James Madison, and John Jay, *The Federalist Papers,* ed. Garry Wills (New York: Bantam Books, 1982), 356.
23. Among others, see Adler, "The Constitution and Presidential Warmaking," 3–17; John Hart Ely, *War and Responsibility: Constitutional Lessons of Vietnam and Its Aftermath* (Princeton, N.J.: Princeton University Press, 1993); Louis Fisher, *Presidential War Power* (Lawrence: University of Kansas Press, 1995); Schlesinger, *Imperial Presidency,* chaps. 6–8; Abraham D. Sofaer, *War, Foreign Affairs, and Constitutional Power: The Origins* (Cambridge, Mass.: Ballinger, 1976); Francis D. Wormuth and Edwin B. Firmage, *To Chain the Dog of War: The War Powers of Congress in History and Law,* 2d ed. (Urbana: University of Illinois Press, 1989).
24. See Gordon Silverstein, "Judicial Enhancement of Executive Power," in

The President, the Congress, and the Making of Foreign Policy, ed. Paul E. Peterson (Norman: University of Oklahoma Press, 1994).

25. Dellums v. Bush, 752 F. Supp. 1141 (D.D.C. 1990). See also Harold Hongju Koh, "Presidential War and Congressional Consent: The Law Professors' Memorandum in Dellums v. Bush," *Stanford Journal of International Law* 27 (Spring 1991): 247–56.
26. See Thomas M. Franck, "Courts and Foreign Policy," *Foreign Policy* 83 (Summer 1991): 66–86; Thomas M. Franck, *Political Questions: Does the Rule of Law Apply to Foreign Affairs?* (Princeton, N.J.: Princeton University Press, 1992); Glennon, *Constitutional Diplomacy,* 314–42; Koh, *National Security Constitution,* 134–49.
27. See James M. Lindsay, *Congress and Nuclear Weapons* (Baltimore: Johns Hopkins University Press, 1991), 116–21, 145–59; Stephen R. Weissman, *A Culture of Deference: Congress's Failure of Leadership in Foreign Policy* (New York: Basic Books, 1995).
28. Among others, see Holbert N. Carroll, *The House of Representatives and Foreign Affairs,* rev. ed. (Boston: Little, Brown, 1966); Samuel P. Huntington, *The Common Defense: Strategic Programs in National Politics* (New York: Columbia University Press, 1961); James A. Robinson, *Congress and Foreign Policy-Making: A Study in Legislative Influence and Initiative,* rev. ed. (Homewood, Ill.: Dorsey Press, 1967); H. Bradford Westerfield, "Congress and Closed Politics in National Security Affairs," *Orbis* 10 (Fall 1966): 737–53.
29. See, for example, Jeremy D. Rosner, *The New Tug-of-War: Congress, the Executive Branch, and National Security* (Washington, D.C.: Carnegie Endowment, 1995).
30. See Cynthia J. Arnson, *Crossroads: Congress, the Reagan Administration, and Central America* (New York: Pantheon, 1989); Philip Brenner and William M. LeoGrande, "Congress and Nicaragua: The Limits of Alternative Policy Making," in *Divided Government: Cooperation and Conflict Between the President and Congress,* ed. James Thurber (Washington, D.C.: CQ Press, 1991); William M. LeoGrande, "The Controversy over Contra Aid, 1981–90: A Historical Narrative," and Robert A. Pastor, "The War Between the Branches: Explaining U.S. Policy Toward Nicaragua, 1979–89," both in *Public Opinion in U.S. Foreign Policy: The Controversy over Contra Aid,* ed. Richard Sobel (Lanham, Md.: Rowman & Littlefield, 1993).
31. See, for example, *The Tower Commission Report: The Full Text of the President's Special Review Board* (New York: Bantam Books and Times Books, 1987); U.S. Congress, House Select Committee to Investigate Covert Arms Transactions with Iran, *Iran-Contra Affair,* 100th Cong., H. Rept. 433, 1987.
32. Vincent A. Auger, "The National Security Council System After the Cold War," in *U.S. Foreign Policy After the Cold War: Processes, Structures, and Policies,* ed. Randall B. Ripley and James M. Lindsay (Pittsburgh, University of Pittsburgh Press, 1997).
33. See I. M. Destler, "National Security Management: What Presidents Have Wrought," *Political Science Quarterly* 95 (Winter 1980/81): 578–80.
34. Seymour M. Hersh, *The Price of Power: Kissinger in the Nixon White House* (New York: Summit Books, 1983); Walter Isaacson, *Kissinger: A Biography* (New York: Simon & Schuster, 1992).
35. See Bert A. Rockman, "America's Departments of State: Irregular and Regular Syndromes of Policymaking," *American Political Science Review* 75 (December 1981): 911–27; Hedrick Smith, *The Power Game: How Washington Works* (New York: Random House, 1988), chaps. 15–16.
36. See Morton H. Halperin, *Bureaucratic Politics and Foreign Policy* (Washington, D.C.: Brookings Institution, 1974), 235–93.
37. Quoted in Marriner S. Eccles, *Beckoning Frontiers* (New York: Knopf, 1951), 336.
38. The classic works on bureaucratic politics are Graham Allison, *Essence of Decision: Explaining the Cuban Missile Crisis* (Boston: Little, Brown, 1971); Halperin, *Bureaucratic Politics and Foreign Policy;* John D. Steinbruner, *The Cybernetic Theory of Decision: New Dimensions of Political Analysis* (Princeton, N.J.: Princeton University Press, 1974).
39. *Statistical Abstract of the United States, 1995,* 115th ed. (Washington D.C.: U.S. Bureau of the Census, 1993), 350; *The United States Government Manual 1994/1995* (Washington, D.C.: U.S. Government Printing Office, 1994), 437.
40. Glen P. Hastedt, *American Foreign Policy,* 2d ed. (Englewood Cliffs, N.J.: Prentice-Hall, 1991), 144.
41. See Barry Rubin, *Secrets of State: The State Department and the Struggle over U.S. Foreign Policy* (New York: Oxford University Press, 1985).
42. See Duncan L. Clarke, "Why State Can't Lead," *Foreign Policy* 66 (Spring 1987): 128–42.
43. See Carroll J. Doherty, "Helms Puts His Own Stamp on Cuts Gore Rejected," *Congressional Quarterly Weekly Report,* 18 February 1995, 540; Carroll J. Doherty, "Senate Slashes Agency Budgets, Confirms 18 Ambassadors," *Congressional Quarterly Weekly Report,* 16 December 1995, 3821–22; Dick Kirschten, "Helms Has Had Quite a Ride," *Congressional Quarterly Weekly Report,* 23 December 1995, 3177; James M. Lindsay, "The State Department Complex After the Cold War," in *U.S. Foreign Policy After the Cold War: Processes, Structures, and Policies,* ed. Randall B. Ripley and James M. Lindsay, (Pittsburgh: University of Pittsburgh Press, 1997).
44. Quoted in Carroll J. Doherty, "GOP Not Giving Up on Agency Cuts," *Congressional Quarterly Weekly Report,* 20 April 1996, 1059.
45. *Statistical Abstract of the United States, 1995,* 350, 364.
46. James Coates and Michael Kilian, *Heavy Losses: The Dangerous Decline of American Defense* (New York: Viking, 1985); Smith, *The Power Game,* chap. 8; Richard A. Stubbing with Richard A. Mendel, *The Defense Game: An Insider Explores the Astonishing Realities of America's Defense Establishment* (New York: Harper & Row, 1986).
47. James Schlesinger, "The Office of the Secretary of Defense," in *Reorganizing the Pentagon: Leadership in War and Peace,* ed. Robert J. Art, Vincent Davis, and Samuel P. Huntington (New York: Pergamon-Brassey's, 1985), 261.
48. See, for example, Paul N. Stockton, "Post-Cold War Change in the Department of Defense," in *U.S. Foreign Policy After the Cold War: Processes, Structures, and Policies,* ed. Randall B. Ripley and James M. Lindsay (Pittsburgh: Pittsburgh University Press, 1997).
49. "An Analysis of the Administration's Future Years Defense Program for 1995 through 1999," *CBO Papers,* January 1995, 19.
50. Ibid., 27.
51. See, for example, Dom M. Snider, "The Coming Defense Train Wreck," *Washington Quarterly* 19 (Winter 1996): 89–101; Dov S. Zakheim, "A Top-Down Plan for the Pentagon," *Orbis* 39 (Spring 1995): 173–87.
52. See, for example, Lawrence J. Korb, "Our Overstuffed Armed Forces," *Foreign Affairs* 74 (November/December 1995): 22–34.
53. Calculated from data in *Statistical Abstract of the United States, 1995,* 356.
54. Korb, "Our Overstuffed Armed Forces," 23.
55. For discussions of the structure of the intelligence community, see Loch Johnson, *Secret Agencies: U.S. Intelligence in a Hostile World* (New Haven: Yale University Press, 1996); Jeffrey T. Richelson, *The U.S. Intelligence Community,* 2d ed. (Cambridge, Mass.: Ballinger, 1989).
56. See Robert M. Gates, "The CIA and American Foreign Policy," *Foreign Affairs* 66 (Winter 1987/88): 215–30; Loch K. Johnson, *America's Secret Power: The CIA in a Democratic Society* (New York: Oxford University Press, 1989); Loch K. Johnson, "Covert Action and Accountability: Decision-Making for America's Secret Foreign Policy," *International Studies Quarterly* 33 (March 1989): 81–109; Frank J. Smist, *Congress Oversees the United States Intelligence Community, 1947–1994,* 2d ed. (Knoxville: University of Tennessee Press, 1994).
57. See James Bamford, *The Puzzle Palace: A Report on NSA, America's Most Secret Agency* (Boston: Houghton Mifflin, 1982).

58. Donna Cassata, "Members Fear Fiscal Crackdown May Sap Spy Agency," *Congressional Quarterly Weekly Report,* 25 November 1995, 1588.
59. Donna Cassata, "Spy Budget Cleared for Clinton; Plan for New Agency Curbed," *Congressional Quarterly Weekly Report,* 23 December 1996, 3894–95.
60. See, for example, Roy Godson, Ernest May, and Gary Schmitt, eds., *U.S. Intelligence at the Crossroads: Agendas for Reform* (Washington, D.C.: Brassey's, 1995); Steven Greenhouse, "The Greening of American Diplomacy," *New York Times,* 9 October 1995; Loch K. Johnson, "Reinventing the CIA: Strategic Intelligence and the End of the Cold War," in *U.S. Foreign Policy After the Cold War: Processes, Structures, and Policies,* ed. Randall B. Ripley and James M. Lindsay (Pittsburgh: University of Pittsburgh Press, 1997).
61. For discussions of Congress's role in making foreign policy, see Cecil V. Crabb, Jr., and Pat M. Holt, *Invitation to Struggle: Congress, the President, and Foreign Policy,* 4th ed. (Washington, D.C.: CQ Press, 1992); Barbara Hinckley, *Less than Meets the Eye: Foreign Policy Making and the Myth of the Assertive Congress* (Chicago: University of Chicago Press, 1994); James M. Lindsay, *Congress and the Politics of U.S. Foreign Policy* (Baltimore: Johns Hopkins University Press, 1994); Thomas E. Mann, ed., *A Question of Balance: The President, the Congress, and Foreign Policy* (Washington, D.C.: Brookings Institution, 1990); Paul E. Peterson, *The President, the Congress, and the Making of Foreign Policy* (Norman: University of Oklahoma Press, 1994); Randall B. Ripley and James M. Lindsay, eds., *Congress Resurgent: Foreign and Defense Policy on Capitol Hill* (Ann Arbor: University of Michigan Press, 1993); Gerard Felix Warburg, *Conflict and Consensus: The Struggle Between Congress and the President over Foreign Policymaking* (New York: Harper & Row, 1989); Weissman, *A Culture of Deference.*
62. Daniel S. Cheever and H. Field Haviland, Jr., *American Foreign Policy and the Separation of Powers* (Cambridge: Harvard University Press, 1952), 48; W. Stull Holt, *Treaties Defeated in the Senate* (Baltimore: Johns Hopkins University Press, 1933), 121; Warburg, *Conflict and Consensus,* 20; Woodrow Wilson, *Congressional Government: A Study in American Politics* (Gloucester, Mass.: Peter Smith, 1973).
63. Quoted in James L. Sundquist, *The Decline and Resurgence of Congress* (Washington, D.C.: Brookings Institution, 1981), 125.
64. See, for example, John Lehman, *Making War: The 200-Year-Old Battle Between the President and Congress over How America Goes to War* (New York: Scribner's, 1992), 214; Mackubin Thomas Owens, "Micromanaging the Defense Budget," *Public Interest* 100 (Summer 1990): 132.
65. On the International Relations and Foreign Relations committees, see James M. McCormick, "Decision Making in the Foreign Affairs and Foreign Relations Committees," in *Congress Resurgent: Foreign and Defense Policy on Capitol Hill,* ed. Randall B. Ripley and James M. Lindsay (Ann Arbor: University of Michigan Press, 1993). On the National Security and Armed Services committees, see Christopher J. Deering, "Decision Making in the Armed Services Committees," in *Congress Resurgent: Foreign and Defense Policy on Capitol Hill,* ed. Randall B. Ripley and James M. Lindsay (Ann Arbor: University of Michigan Press, 1993). On the intelligence committees, see Johnson, "Covert Action and Accountability," 81–109; Frederick M. Kaiser, "Congressional Rules and Conflict Resolution: Access to Information in the House Select Committee on Intelligence," *Congress and the Presidency* 15 (Spring 1988): 49–73. On the Appropriations Committees, see Joseph White, "Decision Making in the Appropriations Subcommittees on Defense and Foreign Operations," in *Congress Resurgent: Foreign and Defense Policy on Capitol Hill,* ed. Randall B. Ripley and James M. Lindsay (Ann Arbor: University of Michigan Press, 1993).
66. See James M. Lindsay, "Congress and Foreign Policy: Why the Hill Matters," *Political Science Quarterly* 107 (Winter 1992–93): 609–26; Lindsay, *Congress and the Politics of U.S. Foreign Policy,* chaps. 4–6; James M. Lindsay and Randall B. Ripley, "How Congress Influences Foreign and Defense Policy," in *Congress Resurgent: Foreign and Defense Policy on Capitol Hill,* ed. Randall B. Ripley and James M. Lindsay (Ann Arbor: University of Michigan Press, 1993), 22–35.
67. For extended legal analyses of the power of the purse, see William C. Banks and Peter Raven-Hansen, *National Security Law and the Power of the Purse* (New York: Oxford University Press, 1994); Kate Stith, "Congress' Power of the Purse," *Yale Law Journal* 97 (June 1988): 1343–96.
68. See Sharyn O'Halloran, "Congress and Foreign Trade Policy," in *Congress Resurgent: Foreign and Defense Policy on Capitol Hill,* ed. Randall B. Ripley and James M. Lindsay (Ann Arbor: University of Michigan Press, 1993).
69. Paul N. Stockton, "Congress and Defense Policy-Making for the Post-Cold War Era," in *Congress Resurgent: Foreign and Defense Policy on Capitol Hill,* ed. Randall B. Ripley and James M. Lindsay (Ann Arbor: University of Michigan Press, 1993).
70. See Norman Ornstein, "Interest Groups, Congress, and American Foreign Policy," in *American Foreign Policy in an Uncertain World,* ed. David P. Forsythe (Lincoln: University of Nebraska Press, 1984); John T. Tierney, "Congressional Activism in Foreign Policy: Its Varied Forms and Stimuli," in *The New Politics of American Foreign Policy,* ed. David A. Deese (New York: St. Martin's, 1994); John T. Tierney, "Interest Group Involvement in Congressional Foreign and Defense Policy," in *Congress Resurgent: Foreign and Defense Policy on Capitol Hill,* ed. Randall B. Ripley and James M. Lindsay (Ann Arbor: University of Michigan Press, 1993).
71. The literature on ethnic lobbies is large. Among others, see Mohammed E. Ahrari, ed., *Ethnic Groups and U.S. Foreign Policy* (New York: Greenwood, 1987); Mitchell Bard, *The Water's Edge and Beyond: Defining the Limits to Domestic Influence on United States Middle East Policy* (New Brunswick, N.J.: Transaction, 1991); David Howard Goldberg, *Foreign Policy and Ethnic Interest Groups* (Westport, Conn.: Greenwood, 1990); F. Chidozie Ogene, *Interest Groups and the Shaping of Foreign Policy: Four Case Studies of United States African Policy* (New York: St. Martin's, 1983); Eric Uslaner, "A Tower of Babel on Foreign Policy?" in *Interest Group Politics,* 3d ed., ed. Allan J. Cigler and Burdett A. Loomis (Washington, D.C.: CQ Press, 1991); Paul Y. Watanabe, *Ethnic Groups, Congress, and American Foreign Policy* (Westport, Conn.: Greenwood, 1984).
72. For an exception to this view, see John H. Aldrich, John L. Sullivan, and Eugene Borgida, "Foreign Affairs and Issue Voting: Do Presidential Candidates 'Waltz Before a Blind Audience?'" *American Political Science Review* 83 (March 1989): 123–42.
73. James M. McCormick and Michael Black, "Ideology and Senate Voting on the Panama Canal Treaty," *Legislative Studies Quarterly* 8 (February 1983): 45–64; George Moffett III, *The Limits of Victory: The Ratification of the Panama Canal Treaties* (Ithaca, N.Y.: Cornell University Press, 1985).
74. See Richard Sobel, "Public Opinion about U.S. Intervention in Nicaragua: A Polling Addendum," in *Public Opinion in U.S. Foreign Policy,* ed. Richard Sobel (Lanham, Md.: Rowman & Littlefield, 1993); Richard Sobel, "Public Opinion about United States Intervention in El Salvador and Nicaragua," *Public Opinion Quarterly* 53 (Spring 1990): 114–28.
75. Holly Idelson, "National Opinion Ambivalent as Winds of War Stir Gulf," *Congressional Quarterly Weekly Report,* 5 January 1991, 14–17; John Mueller, "American Public Opinion and the Gulf War: Some Polling Issues," *Public Opinion Quarterly* 57 (Spring 1993): 87; John Mueller, *Policy and Opinion in the Gulf War* (Chicago: University of Chicago Press, 1994).

76. See, for example, Michael R. Kagay, "Occupation Lifts Clinton's Standing in Poll, but Many Americans Are Skeptical," *New York Times,* 21 September 1994; Richard Morin, "How Do People Really Feel About Bosnia?" *Washington Post National Weekly Edition,* 4–10 December 1995, 34; "Opinion Outlook: Views on National Security," *National Journal,* 30 July 1994, 1822; "Opinion Outlook: Views on National Security," *National Journal,* 25 November 1995, 2945; "Opinion Outlook: Views on National Security," *National Journal,* 23 December 1995, 3174.
77. Gabriel Almond, *The American People and Foreign Policy* (New York: Harcourt, Brace, 1950); Lloyd A. Cantril and Hadley Cantril, *The Political Beliefs of Americans: A Study of Public Opinion* (New York: Clarion Book, 1968); John E. Rielly, ed., *American Public Opinion and U.S. Foreign Policy* (Chicago: Chicago Council on Foreign Relations, 1991).
78. See, for example, "America's Grade on 20th-Century European Wars: F," *New York Times,* 3 December 1995; Gilbert M. Grosvenor, "Superpowers Not So Super in Geography," *National Geographic* 176 (December 1989): 817; Warren E. Leary, "Two Superpowers Failing in Geography," *New York Times,* 9 November 1989.
79. Rielly, "The Public Mood," 77.
80. James M. McCormick, *American Foreign Policy and Process,* 2d ed. (Itasca, Ill.: Peacock, 1992), 485–90.
81. Mark G. McDonough, "Panama Canal Treaty Negotiations (B): Concluding a Treaty," Kennedy School of Government, Harvard University, Case no. C14-79-224, 1979, 11.
82. The classic treatment of the rally-'round-the-flag effect is John E. Mueller, *War, Presidents, and Public Opinion* (New York: Wiley, 1973). For more recent studies of the rally effect, see Bradley Lian and John R. Oneal, "Presidents, the Use of Military Force, and Public Opinion," *Journal of Conflict Resolution* 37 (June 1993): 277–300; Suzanne L. Parker, "Toward an Understanding of 'Rally' Effects: Public Opinion in the Persian Gulf War," *Public Opinion Quarterly* 59 (Winter 1995): 526–46.
83. Mueller, "American Public Opinion and the Gulf War," 80–91; "Opinion Outlook," *National Journal,* 9 February 1991, 356.
84. See Bruce W. Jentleson, "The Pretty Prudent Public: Post Post-Vietnam American Opinion on the Use of Force," *International Studies Quarterly* 36 (March 1992): 49–74.
85. Samuel P. Huntington, "The U.S.—Decline or Renewal?" *Foreign Affairs* 67 (Winter 1988/89): 81.
86. Ibid.
87. See David P. Calleo, *Beyond American Hegemony* (New York: Basic Books, 1987); Paul Kennedy, *The Rise and Fall of the Great Powers: Economic Change and Military Conflict from 1500 to 2000* (New York: Random House, 1987); Walter Russell Mead, *Mortal Splendor* (Boston: Houghton Mifflin, 1987).
88. See, for example, Huntington, "Decline or Renewal," 76–96; Henry R. Nau, *The Myth of America's Decline: Leading the World Economy into the 1990s* (New York: Oxford University Press, 1992); Joseph S. Nye, Jr., *Bound to Lead: The Changing Nature of American Power* (New York: Basic Books, 1990).
89. See Lance T. LeLoup, "The Fiscal Straitjacket: Budgetary Constraints on Congressional Foreign and Defense Policy-Making," in *Congress Resurgent: Foreign and Defense Policy on Capitol Hill,* ed. Randall B. Ripley and James M. Lindsay (Ann Arbor: University of Michigan Press, 1993).
90. "Congressional Cuts," *Congressional Quarterly Weekly Report,* 9 December 1995, 3727; *CQ Almanac 1989* (Washington, D.C.: Congressional Quarterly, 1990), 787.
91. See, for example, Steven Greenhouse, "Foreign Aid: Under Siege in the Budget Wars," *New York Times,* 30 April 1995; Richard Morin, "Foreign Aid: Mired in Misunderstanding," *Washington Post National Weekly Edition,* 20–26 March 1995, 37.
92. John M. Deutch, "The New Nuclear Threat," *Foreign Affairs* 71 (Fall 1992): 120–34; Thomas L. Friedman, "Beyond START II: A New Level of Instability," *New York Times,* 10 January 1993; Kenneth R. Timmerman, "Want to Buy the Bomb? No Problem," *New York Times,* 25 November 1992.
93. The term *intermestic issues* was coined in Bayless Manning, "The Congress, the Executive, and Intermestic Affairs: Three Proposals," *Foreign Affairs* 55 (January 1977): 306–24.
94. Keith Bradsher, "Administration Cuts Flurry of Deals," *New York Times,* 16 November 1993; Keith Bradsher, "Clinton's Shopping List for Votes Has Ring of Grocery Buyer's List," *New York Times,* 17 November 1993.
95. Bruce Stokes, "Who's Standing Tall?" *National Journal,* 21 October 1989, 2568–73.
96. David C. Morrison, "Sorting Out the Gulf War's Bottom Line," *National Journal,* 16 March 1991, 646–47.
97. See National Academy of Sciences, *Policy Implications of Greenhouse Warming* (Washington, D.C.: National Academy Press, 1991).
98. James Brooke, "President, in Rio, Defends His Stand on Environment," *New York Times,* 13 June 1992; Michael Wines, "Bush and Rio," *New York Times,* 11 June 1992; Michael Wines, "Bush Leaves Rio with Shots at Critics, Foreign and Domestic," *New York Times,* 14 June 1992.
99. Pat Towell, "Clinton's Policy Is Battered, But His Powers Are Intact," *Congressional Quarterly Weekly Report,* 23 October 1993, 2896–2901.
100. Donna Cassata, "As U.N. Marks Its 50th Year, Congress Demands Change," *Congressional Quarterly Weekly Report,* 21 October 1995, 3215.
101. See, for example, Bob Benenson, "Free Trade Carries the Day as GATT Easily Passes," *Congressional Quarterly Weekly Report,* 3 December 1994, 3446–50; Alissa J. Rubin, "Dole, Clinton Compromise Greases Wheels for GATT," *Congressional Quarterly Weekly Review,* 26 November 1994, 3405.
102. Keith Bradsher, "U.S. Ban on Mexico Tuna Is Overruled," *New York Times,* 23 August 1991; Tim W. Ferguson, "One Entangling Edible in the GATT Fight," *Wall Street Journal,* 23 November 1993; Ted L. McDorman, "The GATT Consistency of U.S. Fish Import Embargoes to Stop Driftnet Fishing and Save Whales, Dolphins and Turtles," *George Washington Journal of International Law and Economics* 24 (1991): 477–526.
103. Benenson, "Free Trade Carries the Day," 34–50; Rubin, "Dole, Clinton Compromise," 3405.
104. Bhushan Bahree, "WTO Panel Rules Against U.S. in Dispute over Gasoline Norm," *Wall Street Journal,* 18 January 1996; David E. Sanger, "World Trade Group Orders U.S. to Alter Clean Air Act," *New York Times,* 18 January 1986.

GLOSSARY

A

Advice and consent Refers to the provision in Article II of the Constitution that requires the president to gain the Senate's approval of appointees to a variety of government positions.

Advocacy advertising Newspaper, television, and radio advertisements that promote an interest group's political views.

Affirmative action Programs designed to take positive actions to increase the number of women and minorities in jobs and educational programs.

Aid to Families with Dependent Children (AFDC) A public assistance program that provides government aid to low-income families with children.

Americans with Disabilities Act of 1990 An act of Congress that seeks to minimize job discrimination, maximize access to government programs, and ensure access to public accommodations for people with disabilities.

Amicus curiae Literally, friend of the court. A person or group that files a legal brief in a case they are not directly involved in.

***Amicus curiae* brief** Literally, friend of the court. A brief filed with the court by a person or group who is not directly involved in the legal action but who has views on the matter.

Antifederalists The label describing those who opposed adoption of the Constitution. While opponents gave a variety of reasons for rejecting the Constitution, their main concern was that a strong national government would jeopardize individual rights.

Articles of Confederation The document written by the states following their declaration of independence from England and adopted in 1781. It established a system of strong states and a weak national government with a legislative branch but no separate executive or judicial branches and few powers beyond the sphere of foreign relations.

Astroturf lobbying Efforts, usually led by interest groups with deep financial pockets, to create synthetic grass-roots movements by aggressively encouraging voters to contact their elected officials about specific issues.

Attentive publics or **issue publics** People who follow a particular issue closely, are well informed about it, and have strong opinions on it.

Attitude consistency The degree to which a person's political opinions all fall at about the same point on the liberal-conservative dimension.

Attitudes or **opinions** Preferences on specific issues.

Australian ballot A government-printed ballot (as opposed to one distributed by political parties) that allows people to vote in secret.

B

Baby boomers The generation of Americans born between 1946 and 1964.

Bad tendency doctrine The doctrine that speech need only be likely to lead to negative consequences, in Congress's judgment, for it to be illegal.

Balanced budget A federal budget in which spending and revenues are equal.

Bargaining strategy Direct negotiations the White House conducts with other political actors, such as members of Congress and leaders of interest groups, that attempt to reach mutually beneficial agreements.

Bicameral legislature A legislature with two houses—such as the House and the Senate.

Bill of Rights The name given to the first ten amendments of the Constitution. They outline a large number of important individual rights.

Block grants Grants of money from the federal government that state and local governments may spend on any program serving the general purpose of the grant.

Broadcast television Television stations that make their programming available over the airwaves without charge. Most local cable companies include broadcast television channels as part of their basic package of services.

Brown v. Board of Education The landmark 1954 Supreme Court decision holding that separate was not equal and public schools must be desegregated.

Brown v. Board of Education II The 1955 Supreme Court decision that stated that the nation's entrenched system of segregated schools should desegregate with "all deliberate speed."

Budget and Accounting Act of 1921 An act of Congress that created the Bureau of the Budget and allowed the president to review and coordinate the spending proposals of federal agencies and departments.

Budget deficit The amount by which government spending exceeds government revenues in a single year.

Budget surplus The amount by which government revenues exceed government spending in a single year.

Bureaucracy In general usage, the set of government agencies that carries out government policies. The bureaucracy is characterized by formalized structures, specialized duties, a hierarchical system of authority, routine record-keeping, and a permanent staff.

Bureaucrats A term used generally to identify anyone who works within a large, formal organization. More specifically, it refers to career civil service employees of the government.

C

Cabinet An informal designation that refers to the collective body of individuals appointed by the president to head the executive departments. The cabinet can, but rarely does, function as an advisory body to the president.

Cable television Television programming not originally transmitted over the air, as with broadcast television, but rather carried via coaxial or fiber optic cable into the homes of people who pay a monthly fee.

Candidate-centered campaigns Campaigns in which candidates set up campaign organizations, raise money, and campaign independently of other candidates in their party.

Candidate characteristics The candidate's character, personality, experiences, past record, and physical appearance.

Categorical grants-in-aid Grants of money from the federal government to pay for specific state and local government activities under strict federal guidelines.

Caucus/convention system A nomination method in which registered party members attend a party caucus, or meeting, to choose a nominee. In large districts, local caucuses send delegates to represent them at a convention.

Caucus A closed meeting of members of a political party to discuss matters of public policy and political strategy, and in some cases, to select candidates for office.

Central legislative clearance The power the Budget and Accounting Act of 1921 granted to the president to create a package of legislative proposals and budgets for congressional consideration.

Centrist parties Parties close to the political center.

Checks and balances The powers each branch of government can use to block the actions of other branches.

Citizen groups Interest groups, also known as public interest groups, dedicated to promoting a vision of good public policy rather than the economic interests of their members.

Civil disobedience The nonviolent refusal to obey what one perceives to be unjust laws.

Civil liberties The freedoms guaranteed to all Americans in the Bill of Rights (although some are in the body of the Constitution). These liberties include freedom of speech, freedom of religion, and the right to assemble peaceably.

Civil rights The equality of rights for all people regardless of race, sex, ethnicity, religion, and sexual orientation. Civil rights are rooted in the courts' interpretation of the Fourteenth Amendment and in laws that Congress and the state legislatures pass.

Civil Rights Act of 1964 An act of Congress that outlaws racial segregation in public accommodations and employment and prevents tax dollars from going to organizations that discriminate on the basis of race, color, or national origin.

Civil rights movement The mobilization of people to push for racial equality.

Civil service The method by which most government employees have been hired, promoted, and fired since the 1880s. Personnel decisions are based on merit, or the competence of the individual to do the job, rather than the individual's political loyalties.

Classical liberalism A political philosophy, particularly strong in the eighteenth century, that claims that the rights of the individual predate the existence of government and take priority over government policy. This philosophy advocates the protection of individual freedoms from the government.

Clear and present danger standard The doctrine that Congress may limit speech if it causes a clear and present danger to the interests of the country.

Clientele The recipients of the services a government agency's programs provide.

Closing date The last day before the election when one can register to vote—usually described in number of days before Election Day.

Cloture The procedure to stop a filibuster, which requires a supermajority of sixty votes.

Coercive force The ability of a government to compel its citizens to obey its decisions.

Cold War A phrase used to describe the high level of tension and distrust that characterized relations between the Soviet Union and the United States from the late 1940s until the early 1990s.

Collective goods dilemma A dilemma created when people can obtain the benefits of interest group activity without paying any of the costs associated with it. In this situation, the interest group may not form because everyone has an incentive to let someone else pay the costs of group formation.

Concurring opinion A statement from one or more Supreme Court justices agreeing with a decision in a case, but giving an alternative explanation for it.

Conference Committee An *ad hoc* committee of House and Senate members formed to resolve the differences in a bill that passes each body with different provisions.

Congressional Budget and Impoundment Control Act of 1974 An act of Congress that created the new budget process and the Congressional Budget Office and that curtailed the president's power to impound funds.

Congressional Budget Office (CBO) A nonpartisan congressional agency in charge of assisting Congress in reviewing and coordinating budget requests to Congress.

Connecticut Compromise A plan the Connecticut delegation proposed at the Constitutional Convention. This plan sought to manage the dispute between large- and small-population states by creating a two-house legislature with representation in one house based on population and representation in the second house set at two seats per state.

Conservatism The political philosophy that government should play a minimal role in society (except in the area of traditional moral values) with the goal of ensuring all its citizens economic freedom.

Conservative Coalition The Conservative Coalition appears when a majority of southern Democrats votes with a majority of Republicans against a majority of northern Democrats.

Constituent service Favors members of Congress do for constituents—usually in the form of help in dealing with the federal bureaucracy.

Constitutional courts The three-tiered system of federal district courts, courts of appeal (originally circuit courts), and the Supreme Court. Article III of the Constitution provides for the creation of these courts.

Containment A bedrock principle of U.S. foreign policy from the 1940s to the 1980s that emphasized the need to prevent communist countries, especially the Soviet Union, from expanding the territory they controlled.

Continuing resolutions Temporary laws Congress passes to keep the government running when Congress misses the deadline for passing the budget.

Contract With America The ten-point platform that Republican candidates for the House of Representatives campaigned on in 1994.

Corporate welfare Government subsidies or tax breaks of questionable value to private corporations.

Cost-of-living adjustment (COLA) An increase in Social Security or other benefits designed to keep pace with inflation.

Critical elections Elections that disrupt party coalitions and create new ones in a party realignment.

Cross-cutting cleavages Divisions that split society into small groups so that people have different allies and opponents in different policy areas and no group forms a majority on all issues.

D

De facto segregation Segregation that results from the actions of individuals rather than the government.

De jure segregation Government-imposed laws that required African Americans to live and work separately from white Americans.

Democracy A form of government in which the people (defined broadly to include all adults or narrowly to exclude women or slaves, for example) are the ultimate political authority.

Detente A policy the Nixon administration followed to develop more cordial relations with the Soviet Union.

Direct democracy Mechanisms such as the initiative, referendum, and recall—powers that enable voters to use the ballot box to set government policy.

Direct lobbying Trying to influence public policy through direct contact with government officials.

Direct primary An election in which voters and not party leaders directly choose a party's nominees for political office.

Discretionary spending Federal spending on programs that can be controlled through the regular budget process.

Dissenting opinion A statement from one or more Supreme Court justices explaining why they disagree with a decision in a case.

Divided government When the president is of one party and the other party has a majority in at least one house of Congress.

Dual federalism An interpretation of federalism that held that the national government was supreme within those areas specifically assigned to it in the Constitution, and the states were supreme in all other areas of public policy.

Duverger's Law The generalization that if a nation has a single-member, plurality electoral system, it will develop a two-party system.

E

Easy issues Simple issues that allow voters to make quick, emotional decisions without much information.

Economic issues Issues relating to the distribution of income and wealth in society.

Economic regulation Laws and governmental rules that affect the competitive practices of private business.

Electoral college The body of electors, whose composition is determined by the results of the general election, that chooses the president and vice president. To win in the electoral college, candidates must secure a majority of the electoral vote.

Enlargement The policy President Bill Clinton proposed as a substitute for containment. It calls on the United States to promote the emergence of market democracies; that is, countries that combine a free market economic system with a democratic political system.

Entitlement programs Programs, created by legislation, that require the government to pay a benefit directly to any individual who meets the eligibility requirements the law establishes.

Enumerated powers Powers explicitly identified in the text of the Constitution.

Environmental impact statement A document federal agencies must issue that analyzes the environmental impact of any significant actions they plan to take.

Equal Pay Act of 1963 An act of Congress law that banned wage discrimination based on sex, race, religion, and national origin.

Equal-time provision A federal law that stipulates that if a radio or television station gives or sells air time to a candidate for political office, it must provide all candidates for public office with access to the airwaves under the same conditions.

Establishment clause The provision in the First Amendment of the Constitution that "Congress shall make no law respecting an establishment of religion."

Exclusionary rule The doctrine, stemming from the Fourth Amendment, that the government cannot use illegally obtained evidence in court.

Executive agreements International agreements that, unlike treaties, do not require the approval of two-thirds of the Senate to become binding on the United States.

Executive amendment A procedure allowing governors to reject a bill by returning it to the legislature with changes that would make it acceptable; the legislature must agree to the changes for the bill to become law.

Executive order A presidential directive to an agency of the federal government that tells the agency to take some specified action.

Expertise Specialized knowledge acquired through work experience or training and education.

Expressive benefits The feelings of satisfaction people derive from working for an interest group cause they believe is just and right. Also known as purposive benefits.

F

Fairness doctrine A regulation the FCC adopted in 1949 and repealed in 1987. It required broadcasters to provide "reasonable opportunities for the expression of opposing views on controversial issues of public importance."

Federal Communications Commission (FCC) An independent federal agency that regulates interstate and international communication by radio, television, telephone, telegraph, cable, and satellite.

Federal Reserve System An independent regulatory commission that Congress created in 1913 to oversee the nation's money supply.

Federalism A two-tiered form of government in which governments on both levels are sovereign and share authority over the same geographic jurisdiction.

Federalists The label describing those who supported adoption of the Constitution. They believed in the need for a national government stronger than the one provided under the Articles of Confederation.

Feminization of poverty The trend in the United States in which families headed by women account for a growing share of the people who live below the poverty line.

Filibuster The tactic of stalling a bill in the Senate by talking endlessly about the bill in order to win changes in it or kill it.

Fire-alarm oversight Congressional oversight hearings designed to investigate a problem after it has become highly visible.

Fiscal federalism The principle that the federal government should play a major role in financing some of the activities of state and local governments.

Fiscal policy Using the federal government's control over taxes and spending to influence the condition of the national economy.

Flat tax Any income tax system in which taxable income is taxed at the same percentage rate regardless of the taxpayer's income.

Food Stamp program A public assistance program established in 1964 that provides stamps (or coupons) to low-income people to buy food.

Franchise The right to vote.

Franking privilege The right of a member of Congress to send official mail without paying postage.

Free exercise clause The provision in the First Amendment of the Constitution that "Congress shall make no law prohibiting the free exercise" of religion.

Free riders People or groups who benefit from the efforts of others without bearing any of the costs.

Free trade An economic policy that holds that lowering trade barriers will benefit the economies of all the countries involved.

Freedom of Information Act An act of Congress passed in 1966 that created a system through which anyone can petition the government to declassify secret documents.

Frontloading The decision states make to move their primaries and caucuses to earlier dates to increase their impact on the nomination process.

G

Gender gap The difference between men's and women's voting rates for either a Democratic or Republican candidate.

General Agreement on Tariffs and Trade (GATT) An international organization that existed between 1947 and 1995. GATT was used by its member countries to set many of the rules governing world trade. In 1995, it gave way to the World Trade Organization.

General revenue sharing A program giving federal money to state and local governments with no restrictions on how it will be spent.

Gerrymandering Drawing congressional district boundaries to favor one party over the other.

Globalism The idea that the United States should be prepared to use military force around the globe to defend its political and economic interests.

Going public strategy Direct presidential appeals to the public for support. Presidents use public support to pressure other political actors to accept their policies.

Grass-roots lobbying Trying to influence public policy indirectly by mobilizing an interest group's membership and the broader public to contact elected officials.

Great Depression The worst economic crisis in U.S. history, with unemployment rates reaching 25 percent. It began in 1929 and lasted until the start of World War II.

Great Society The economic and social programs Congress enacted during Lyndon Johnson's presidency, from 1963 to 1969.

Gross domestic product (GDP) A measure of a country's total economic output in any given year.

Group consciousness Identification with one's social group (for instance, black consciousness).

H

Hard issues Complicated issues that require voters to have information about the policy and to spend time considering their choices.

Home style The way in which members of Congress present themselves to their constituents in the district.

Horse-race journalism News coverage of elections that focuses on which candidate is leading in the polls rather than on the substantive issues in the campaign.

I

Ideology An elaborate set of interrelated beliefs with overarching, abstract principles that make people's political philosophies coherent.

Impeachment Formally charging a government official with having committed "Treason, Bribery, or other High Crimes and Misdemeanors." Officials convicted of such charges are removed from office.

Implied powers Governmental powers not enumerated in the Constitution; authority the government is assumed to have in order to carry out its enumerated powers.

Incitement standard The doctrine that speech must cause listeners to be likely to commit immediate illegal acts for the speech itself to be illegal.

Independent expenditures Funds raised and spent without contact with the supported candidate.

Industrial policy The policy of seeking to strengthen selected industries by targeting them for governmental aid rather than letting the forces of the free market determine their fates.

Initiative A proposed law or amendment placed on the ballot by citizens, usually through a petition.

Interest group An organized group of people who share some goals and try to influence public policy.

Intermediate scrutiny A legal standard for judging whether a discriminatory law is unconstitutional. Intermediate scrutiny lies somewhere between the rational and strict scrutiny standards. It requires the government to show that a discriminatory law serves important governmental interests and is substantially related to the achievement of those objectives, or a group to show that the law does not meet these two standards.

Intermestic issues Issues such as trade, the environment, and drug trafficking that affect both domestic and foreign interests.

Interstate commerce clause The provision in Article I of the Constitution granting Congress the power to "regulate commerce among the several states."

Iron triangles The alliance of a government agency, congressional committee or subcommittee, and political interest group for the purpose of directing government policy within the agency's jurisdiction to the mutual benefit of the three partners.

Isolationism A foreign policy built on the principle of avoiding formal military and political alliances with other countries.

Issue networks A loose collection of groups or people in and out of government who interact on a policy issue on the basis of their interest and knowledge rather than just on the basis of economic interests.

Issue publics or **attentive publics** People who follow a particular issue closely, are well informed about it, and have strong opinions on it.

J

Jim Crow laws Laws that discriminated against African Americans, usually by enforcing segregation.

Judicial activism The vigorous use of judicial review to overturn laws and make public policy from the federal bench.

Judicial review The doctrine allowing the Supreme Court to review and overturn decisions made by Congress and the president.

K

Keynesian economics An economic theory, based on the work of British economist John Maynard Keynes, that contends that the national government can manage the economy by running budget surpluses and budget deficits.

L

Laissez faire An economic theory, dominant at the start of the twentieth century, that argued that the federal government's only role in the economy was to ensure a stable supply of money.

Lame duck An officeholder whose political power is weakened because his or her term is coming to an end.

Leaks Confidential government information surreptitiously given to journalists.

Left The liberal end of the political spectrum.

Legislative courts Various administrative courts and tribunals that Congress establishes, as Article I of the Constitution provides.

Legitimacy A self-imposed willingness of citizens to respect and obey the decisions of their government.

Libel law Laws governing written or visual publications that unjustly injure a person's reputation.

Liberalism The political philosophy that government should play an expansive role in society (except in the area of personal morality) with the goal of protecting its weaker citizens and ensuring political and social equality for all citizens.

Line-item veto The ability of an executive to delete or veto some provisions of a bill, while allowing the rest of the bill to become law.

Literacy test A test of ability to read and write, used in the South to prevent people from voting.

Lobbying Trying to influence governmental decisions, especially the voting decisions legislators make on proposed legislation.

Lobbyists People who make their living trying to influence public policy.

Lucas critique An economic theory that contends that if people act rationally, then their reactions to changes in government policy will often negate the intent of those changes.

Lynching The unlawful killing, usually by hanging, of a person by a mob.

M

Majority opinion The document announcing and usually explaining the Supreme Court's decision in a case.

Majority tyranny A situation in which the majority uses its advantage in numbers to suppress the rights of the minority.

Mandates Laws Congress passes that require state and local governments to undertake specified actions.

Marbury v. Madison The Supreme Court decision in 1803 that established the principle of judicial review.

Marshall Plan A multibillion-dollar U.S. aid program in the late 1940s and early 1950s that helped Western European countries rebuild their economies in the wake of World War II.

Massive resistance The policy many southern states followed in the wake of the first Brown decision of fiercely resisting desegregation.

Material benefits The actual goods and services that come from belonging to an interest group.

Material scarcity The inability of a society to provide its citizens with all the goods and services they may want or need.

Means test A requirement that people must fall below certain income and wealth requirements to qualify for government benefits.

Median voter hypothesis The theory that the best possible position for a politician who cares only about winning elections is the center—that is, in the position of the median voter.

Medicaid A public assistance program that provides publicly subsidized health care to low-income Americans.

Medicare A social insurance program that provides basic hospital insurance and supplementary insurance for doctors' bills and other health care expenses for people over the age of sixty-five.

Midterm elections The congressional elections that take place midway through a president's four-year term.

Miranda rights The rights against self-incrimination that the Fifth Amendment guarantees. Miranda rights include the right to remain silent during questioning, the right to know that any statements suspects make may be used as evidence against them, and the right to speak to an attorney before questioning.

Missouri Plan/Merit System The system some states use to select judges, appointing them but requiring them to stand for periodic reelection.

Monetary theory An economic theory that contends that a nation's money supply, or the amount of money in circulation, is the primary if not sole determinant of the health of the national economy.

Monroe Doctrine A basic principle of U.S. foreign policy that dates back to a warning President James Monroe issued in 1823 that the United States would resist further European efforts to intervene in the affairs of the Western Hemisphere.

Muckraking An early form of investigative journalism popular at the beginning of the twentieth century.

Multilateralism An approach in which three or more countries cooperate for the purpose of solving some common problem.

N

National debt The total amount of money the federal government owes to pay for accumulated deficits.

National interest The idea that the United States has certain interests in international relations that most Americans agree on.

National supremacy An interpretation of federalism that holds that the national government's laws should take precedence over state law. This idea is based on the provision in Article VI of the Constitution that the national government's laws are the "supreme law of the land."

Necessary and proper clause The provision in Article I of the Constitution that states that Congress possesses whatever additional and unspecified powers it needs to fulfill its responsibilities.

Neo-isolationism The idea that the United States should reduce its role in world affairs and return to a foreign policy similar to the one it pursued before World War II.

Neutral competence The belief that staff members (usually career civil servants) should be able to work competently for any president, regardless of partisan affiliation or policy preferences and without advocating the policies of individual presidents.

New Deal The economic and social programs Congress enacted during Franklin Roosevelt's presidency before World War II.

New Deal coalition The Democratic Party coalition that formed in 1932. It got its name from President Franklin Delano Roosevelt's New Deal policies.

New Jersey Plan A plan for a new national government that the New Jersey delegation proposed at the Constitutional Convention in 1787. Its key feature consisted of giving each state equal representation in the national legislature, regardless of its population.

Non-discretionary spending Federal spending on programs such as Social Security that cannot be controlled through the regular budget process.

North Atlantic Treaty Organization (NATO) A military alliance founded in 1949 for the purpose of defending Western Europe from attack. Members of NATO include the United States, Canada, and fourteen European countries.

O

Objective press A form of journalism that developed in the 1920s and which continues to predominate today. It emphasizes that journalists should strive to keep their opinions out of their coverage of the news.

Obscenity law Laws governing materials whose predominant appeal is to a prurient interest in nudity, sex, or excretion.

Office of Management and Budget (OMB) The agency in charge of assisting the president in reviewing and coordinating budget requests to Congress from federal agencies and departments. Formerly the Bureau of the Budget.

One Hundred Days A benchmark period for assessing a new president's performance, based on the first three months of Franklin Roosevelt's presidency, when he gained passage of more than a dozen major bills as part of his New Deal agenda.

Opinions or **attitudes** Preferences on specific issues.

Original intent The theory that judges should interpret the Constitution by determining what the founders intended when they wrote it.

P

Pack journalism The tendency of journalists to cover stories because other journalists are covering them and to ignore stories that other journalists aren't covering.

Party dealignment A trend in which voter loyalties to the two major parties weaken.

Party identification The psychological feeling of belonging to a particular political party, which influences voting behavior.

Party machine A party organization built on the use of selective, material incentives for participation.

Party platform An official statement of beliefs, values, and policy positions that a national party convention issues.

Party realignment A long-term shift in the electoral balance between the major parties.

Patronage The practice of rewarding partisan supporters with government jobs. Also known as the spoils system.

Patronage job A job given as a reward for loyal party service.

Pentagon Papers A set of secret government documents—leaked to the press in 1971—showing that Presidents Kennedy and Johnson misled the public about U.S. involvement in Vietnam.

Photo opportunities Events that political candidates and government officials stage to allow newspaper photographers and television news crews to take flattering photos.

Picket-fence federalism The tendency of federal, state, and local agencies concerned with the same issues to coordinate their efforts with each other and to be insulated from other government agencies that deal with different issues.

Pluralism The theory that political power is spread widely and that different groups of people exercise power on different issues.

Pocket veto The power of the president to veto a bill passed during the last ten days of a session of Congress simply by failing to sign it.

Police-patrol oversight Congressional oversight hearings designed to take a wide-ranging look for possible problems.

Policy oversight Efforts by Congress to see that the legislation it passes is implemented, that the expected results have come about, and whether new laws are needed.

Policy rule A decision a government institution reaches on a specific political question within its jurisdiction.

Political action committees (PACs) Organizations that solicit contributions from members of interest groups and channel those contributions to election campaigns.

Political agenda The list of issues that people think are important and that government officials are actively debating.

Political cleavages Divisions in society around which parties organize.

Political party A coalition of people seeking to control the government by contesting elections and winning office.

Poll tax Before 1964, the tax that people paid in some states if they chose to vote.

Pool reporting A system the Defense Department instituted in the 1980s for reporting from a combat zone during wartime. With pool reporting, military officials escort small groups of reporters when they interview American troops.

Pork barrel Legislation that appropriates government money for local projects of questionable value that may ingratiate a legislator with his or her constituents.

Prior restraint An act of government preventing publication or broadcast of a story or document.

Privatization Turning government programs over to private companies to run, or selling government assets to the private sector.

Pro-life Favoring the policy of making abortion illegal.

Pro-choice Favoring the policy of allowing women to choose whether to have abortions.

Progressive movement An early twentieth-century political movement that sought to advance the public interest by reducing the power of political parties in the selection of candidates and the administration of government.

Progressive tax A tax system in which those with high incomes pay a higher percentage of their income in taxes than those with low incomes.

Proportional representation system A system in which legislators are elected at large and each party wins legislative seats in proportion to the number of votes it receives.

Prospective issue voting Deciding how to vote on the basis of a candidate's likely future policies.

Public assistance Government programs, such as Medicaid and food stamps that are funded out of general tax revenues and that are designed to provide benefits only to low-income people.

R

Rainy day fund Surplus revenue a state government holds in reserve for budget emergencies and shortfalls.

Rational scrutiny A legal standard for judging whether a discriminatory law is unconstitutional. Rational scrutiny requires the government only to show that a law is reasonable and not arbitrary.

Reapportionment The redistribution of seats in the House of Representatives among the states, which occurs every ten years following the census, so that the size of each state's delegation is proportional to its share of the total population.

Referendum An election held allowing voters to accept or reject a proposed law or amendment passed by a legislative body.

Regressive tax A tax system in which those with high incomes pay a lower percentage of their income in taxes than those with low incomes.

Regulatory policy Laws and government rules targeting private business for the purpose of (1) protecting consumers and other businesses from what the government deems unfair business practices; (2) protecting workers from unsafe or unhealthy working conditions; (3) protecting consumers from unsafe products; and (4) protecting a number of groups from discrimination.

Republicanism A system of government in which the people's selected representatives run the government.

Retrospective issue voting Deciding how to vote on the basis of past policy outcomes.

Revenue neutral A quality of any tax reform plan that will neither increase nor decrease government revenue.

Reverse discrimination Laws and policies that discriminate against whites, especially white males.

Right The conservative end of the political spectrum.

Roe v. Wade A 1973 Supreme Court decision that a woman's right to privacy prevents states from barring her from having an abortion during the first trimester of pregnancy. States can impose reasonable regulations on abortions during the second trimester and can prohibit abortions under most circumstances in the third trimester.

Rule adjudication Determining whether an agency's rules have been violated.

Rule administration The core function of the bureaucracy—to carry out the decisions of Congress, the president, or the courts.

Rule making Formulating the rules for carrying out the programs a bureaucratic agency administers.

Rule of Four The Supreme Court rule that at least four justices must decide that a case merits a review before it goes on the Court's schedule.

Rust Belt The Rust Belt states are the major industrial states of the Northeast and Midwest. For the most part, they have not enjoyed great population or economic growth in the second half of the twentieth century.

S

Select committees Congressional committees that typically are created for only specific lengths of time and that lack authority to report legislation.

Selective benefits Any benefit given to a member of a group but denied to nonmembers.

Selective perception A phenomenon in which people perceive the same event differently because they have different beliefs and personal experiences.

Senatorial courtesy The practice a president follows in choosing a nominee for a district or appeals court judgeship. The president selects a nominee from a list supplied by the senior senator of the president's party from the state or region where the vacancy occurs.

Seniority rule The congressional norm of making the member of the majority party with the longest continuous service on a committee the chair of that committee.

Separate-but-equal standard The now-rejected Supreme Court doctrine that separation of the races was acceptable as long as each race was treated equally.

Separation of powers The principle that each of the three powers of government—legislative, executive, and judicial—should be held by a separate branch of government.

Shays's Rebellion A protest, staged by small farmers from western Massachusetts and led by Daniel Shays, an officer in the American Revolutionary War, against the state's taxes and policy of foreclosing on debtor farmers.

Single-member districts A legislative district in which only one legislator is elected.

Single-member, plurality electoral system A system in which each district elects a single member as its representative; the winner in each district is the candidate who receives a plurality of the vote.

Social insurance Government programs, such as Social Security and Medicare, that require future beneficiaries to make contributions (otherwise known as taxes) and that distribute benefits without regard to the recipient's income.

Social issues Issues based on moral or value judgments.

Social regulation Laws and governmental rules designed to protect Americans from dangers or unfair practices associated with how private businesses produce their products or with the products themselves.

Social Security Act of 1935 The act of Congress that created the Social Security tax (Federal Insurance Contribution Act—FICA) and Social Security programs.

Social welfare policy Government programs that provide goods and services to citizens to improve the quality of their lives.

Socialization The process by which people acquire values and opinions from their societies.

Socioeconomic status Social status as measured by one's education, income, and occupation.

Sociotropic voters People who vote on the basis of their community's economic interests, rather than their personal economic interests.

Soft money Expenditures political parties make during an election for any activity that serves the purpose of increasing voter turnout.

Solidary benefits The emotional and psychological enjoyment that comes from belonging to an interest group whose members share common interests and goals.

Sound bite A short excerpt from a person's speech or conversation that appears on radio or television news.

Sovereignty The power of self-rule.

Spin control The practice of trying to persuade journalists to cover news stories in ways that put policies one likes in the most favorable light.

Spoils system The method used to hire and fire government employees during most of the 1800s. Government employees of the new president's choosing would replace those a previous president had appointed. Government jobs were the "spoils" (or rewards) of the electoral "wars." This system was also known as patronage.

Standing committee A permanent committee in Congress with jurisdiction over a specific policy area. Such a committee has tremendous say over the details of legislation within its jurisdiction.

Stare decisis The doctrine that previous Supreme Court decisions should be allowed to stand.

States' rights An interpretation of federalism that claimed that states possessed the right to accept or reject federal laws.

Strict scrutiny A legal standard for judging whether a discriminatory law is unconstitutional. Strict scrutiny requires the government to show a compelling reason for a discriminatory law.

Structural rules Rules that establish the organization, procedures, and powers of government.

Subcommittees The smaller units of a standing committee that oversee one part of the committee's jurisdiction.

Suffrage The right to vote.

Sun Belt The Sun Belt states are the states in the South, Southwest, and West Coast—areas that have experienced tremendous population and economic growth since 1950.

Supply-side economics An economic theory that argues that if the government cuts taxes, reduces spending, and eliminates regulations, resources will be freed up to fuel the economy to produce even more goods and services.

T

Talk radio Political talk shows on radio. Since the early 1990s, talk radio has emerged as an important force in American politics.

Term limits Laws that limit the number of terms a person may serve in an elected, and in some cases, an appointed office.

Third World A term loosely defined to mean the developing countries in Asia, Africa, and Latin America.

Truman Doctrine A policy, announced by President Truman in 1947, that the United States would oppose communist attempts to overthrow or conquer non-communist countries.

Turnover Change in membership of Congress between elections.

Two presidencies The argument that presidents have much greater influence over the content of foreign policy than the content of domestic policy.

Two-party system A political system in which two major parties dominate.

U

Unilateralism The tendency of the United States to act alone in foreign affairs without consulting other countries.

Unit rule A winner-take-all system which requires that the candidate with the most popular votes receive all of that state's electoral votes.

V

Values Basic principles which lead people to form opinions on specific issues.

Virginia Plan A plan for a new national government that the Virginia delegation proposed at the Constitutional Convention in 1787. It called for a strong, essentially unitary national government, with separate executive and judicial branches, and a two-house legislative branch with representation based on each state's population.

Voter turnout The percentage of people who actually vote.

Voting Rights Act of 1965 An act of Congress that bars states from creating voting and registration practices that discriminate against African Americans and other minorities.

W

Women's movement The mobilization of people to push for equality between the sexes.

World Trade Organization (WTO) The international trade agency that began operation in 1995 as the successor to the General Agreement on Tariffs and Trade.

Writ of certiorari A Supreme Court order for a lower court to send it the records of a case—the first step in reviewing a lower court case.

Y

Yellow journalism A form of journalism, popular at the end of the nineteenth centuy, that emphasized sensational and sometimes lurid news coverage.

PHOTOGRAPHS

Chapter 1

Chapter 1 Opener: p. 3: © Dany Krist/Uniphoto Picture Agency; p. 6: © Bruce Reedy Photography; p. 7: © Richard A. Bloom; p. 9L: Reuters/Bettmann; p. 9R: UPI/Bettmann Newsphotos; p. 10: © Les Stone/Sygma; p. 11: AP/Wide World Photos; p. 13: UPI/Bettmann; p. 15: UPI/Bettmann

Chapter 2

Chapter 2 Opener: p. 19: © Joe Sohm/The Image Works; p. 21: North Wind Picture Archives; p. 23: National Archives; p. 24: The Bettmann Archive; p. 25 and p. 27T: North Wind Picture Archives; p. 27B: Andrew W. Mellon Collection, National Gallery of Art, Washington; p. 28: The Bettmann Archive; p. 29, p. 32, p. 33TR, p. 33MR, and p. 33BR: North Wind Picture Archives; p. 33L: *The Federalist* No. 10 (detail), from *The New-York Packet,* 23 November 1787; p. 38: © Mark C. Burnett/PhotoEdit; p. 39: © Chromosohm Media/The Image Works, Inc.; p. 40: © Jeffrey Markowitz/Sygma; p. 44: UPI/Bettmann; p. 45: UPI/Corbis-Bettmann; p. 48L and p. 48R: North Wind Picture Archives; p. 49 and p. 50: The Bettmann Archive; p. 52: UPI/Bettmann

Chapter 3

Chapter 3 Opener: p. 67: © Jonathan Elderfield/Gamma Liaison Network; p. 69: © Alan Carey/The Image Works, Inc.; p. 70L: James L. Shaffer; p. 70R: © Elizabeth Crews/The Image Works; p. 73: © Bob Daemmrich/The Image Works, Inc.; p. 75: AP/Wide World Photos; p. 82: © Myrleen Ferguson Cate/PhotoEdit; p. 85, p. 91L and p. 91R: AP/Wide World Photos

Chapter 4

Chapter 4 Opener: p. 93: AP/Wide World Photos; p. 95: © Jennifer Ferranti; p. 96, p. 99, and p. 100: The Bettmann Archive; p. 102: © William Greenblatt/Gamma Liaison; p. 110: AP/Wide World Photos/courtesy of *Columbus Dispatch;* p. 106: © Business Week; p. 108: AP/Wide World Photos; p. 111: © Tony Savino/Sygma; p. 114: Courtesy of Federal Bureau of Investigation, Office of Public and Congressional Affairs; p. 120: Collection of Supreme Court of the United States; p. 123: © Chromosohm Media/The Image Works, Inc.

Chapter 5

Chapter 5 Opener: p. 125 © Dan Budnik/Woodfin Camp & Associates; p. 127: © J. Patrick Forden/Sygma; p. 128: North Wind Picture Archives; p. 130: The Bettmann Archive; p. 131 and p. 132: UPI/Bettmann; p. 135: The Bettmann Archive; p. 136, p. 137, and p. 139: UPI/Bettmann; p. 143: © Allan Tannenbaum/Sygma; p. 145: AP/Wide World Photos; p. 147: © J. Pat Carter/Gamma Liaison; p. 149: The Bettmann Archive; p. 150: North Wind Picture Archives; p. 151: © Les Stone/Sygma; p. 154: © Liaison/Gamma Liaison; p. 157: © Cynthia Johnson/Gamma Liaison; p. 159: © Michael Wilhelm; p. 161: © Joe Sohm/The Image Works

Chapter 6

Chapter 6 Opener: p. 169: © Allan Tannenbaum/Sygma; p. 171: AP/Wide World Photos; p. 172: © Bob Daemmrich/The Image Works, Inc.; p. 177: © Bob Daemmrich/The Image Works, Inc.; p. 179: © Don & Pat Valenti/Tony Stone Images; p. 180: AP/Wide World Photos; p. 182L and p. 182R: UPI/Bettmann; p. 184L: © Mark Reinstein/Uniphoto Picture Agency; p. 184R: UPI/Bettmann; p. 185L: AP/Wide World Photos; p. 185R: National Archives

Chapter 7

Chapter 7 Opener: p. 201: AP/Wide World Photos; p. 205L: The Bettmann Archive; p. 205R: © John Ficara/Sygma; p. 206: AP/Wide World Photos; p. 209: UPI/Corbis-Bettmann; p. 210L: UPI/Bettmann; p. 210R: © Bob Daemmrich/The Image Works, Inc.; p. 212: AP/Wide World Photos; p. 217: © Paula Scully/Gamma-Liaison; p. 221TR: © Jean Louis Atlan/Sygma; p. 221BR: Topham/The Image Works; p. 221TL: AP/Wide World Photos; p. 221BL: AP/Wide World Photos; p. 221MT: Corbis-Bettmann; p. 221MB: AP/Wide World Photos; p. 225: © Rob Crandall/The Image Works, Inc.; p. 226TL, p. 226TR, p. 226BL, and p. 226BR: National Archives

Chapter 8

Chapter 8 Opener: p. 231: © 1996 Cable News Network, Inc. All rights reserved; p. 233: © Dirck Halstead/Gamma Liaison; p. 234L: © Capital Cities/ABC, Inc., Eddie Adams, photographer; p. 234R: © Jacques Chenet/Gamma Liaison; p. 237: 1898 *New York Journal;* p. 238: The Bettmann Archive; p. 239: © David Wells/The Image Works, Inc.; p. 242: © Dennis Brack/Black Star; p. 243L: Courtesy of Buchanan for President Web Site; p. 247: © Derek Hudson/Sygma; p. 250: © Les Stone/Sygma; p. 253: AP/Wide World Photos; p. 254: © Wally McNamee/Sygma; p. 259: *New York Daily News* photo; p. 260: AP/Wide World Photos

Chapter 9

Chapter 9 Opener: p. 267: AP/Wide World Photos; p. 269: AP/Wide World Photos; p. 270: UPI/Bettmann Newsphotos; p. 272: © Brad Markel/Gamma-Liaison; p. 280: The Bettmann Archive; p. 286: UPI/Bettmann; p. 287: © Chicago Tribune photo by Michael Budrys; p. 290, p. 291T, and p. 291B: AP/Wide World Photos

Chapter 10

Chapter 10 Opener: p. 295: © Douglas Burrows/Gamma-Liaison; p. 297: Courtesy of Rayrock Mines; p. 299: North Wind Picture Archives; p. 302: © Cynthia Johnson/Gamma-Liaison; p. 306: © The Syracuse Newspapers/photo by Nicholas Lisi; p. 308L and p. 308R: Courtesy of National Rifle Association of America; p. 313: © Dennis Brack/Black Star; p. 314: © Richard A. Bloom; p. 315: © Eddie Adams/Sygma; p. 317: Courtesy of Texas Medical Association; 10.10: © Stuart Franklin/Sygma; p. 318R: © John Eisele; p. 320: © Stephen Crowley/New York Times Pictures

Chapter 11

Chapter 11 Opener: p. 331: © John Lawrence/Tony Stone Images; p. 333L: © Mark Reinstein/Uniphoto Picture Agency; p. 333R: Architect of the Capitol; p. 336L: North Wind Picture Archives; p. 336R: AP/Wide World Photos; p. 337: © Terry Ashe/Gamma-Liaison; p. 341: Ray Lustig photo © 1995, The Washington Post. Reprinted with permission; p. 356: UPI/Bettmann; p. 357: AP/Wide World Photos; p. 360: © David Scull/New York Times Pictures; p. 362: Photo by Harry Baumert, courtesy of *The Des Moines Register;* p. 365: © Terry Ashe/Gamma-Liaison; p. 368: © Richard A. Bloom; p. 372: AP/Wide World Photos; p. 374: © Paul Hosefros/NYT Pictures

Chapter 12

Chapter 12 Opener: p. 381: © Glen Allison/Tony Stone Images; p. 383: North Wind Picture Archives; p. 384: AP/Wide World Photos; p. 387: The Bettmann Archive; p. 388: © Topham/The Image Works; p. 392: North Wind Picture Archives; 12.6A: AP/Wide World Photos; p. 395R: UPI/Bettmann; p. 398: © Clinton-Gore '96 Primary Committee, Inc. and courtesy of Political Communication Center/University of Oklahoma; p. 399: Courtesy of CAMPAIGN Magazine; p. 401T and p. 401B: North Wind Picture Archives; p. 403: White House Photo; p. 408TL: © Jeffrey Markowitz/Sygma; p. 408TR: AFP/Corbis-Bettmann; p. 408B: © Larry Downing/Sygma; p. 409T: UPI/Bettmann; p. 409B: © Cynthia Johnson/Gamma Liaison; p. 413: © Wally McNamee/Sygma; p. 420: © Brad Markel/Gamma Liaison

Chapter 13
Chapter 13 Opener: p. 425: © Robert E. Daemmrich/Tony Stone Images; p. 427: © Paul Conklin/PhotoEdit; p. 430: © Diana Walker/Gamma Liaison Network; p. 432T&B: United States Postal Service Elvis Presley Enterprises, Inc., and estate of Marilyn Monroe; p. 433TL: © Mark Richards/PhotoEdit; p. 433TR: © Holt Confer/Uniphoto Picture Agency; p. 433BL: © Les Moore/Uniphoto Picture Agency; p. 433BR: © Michael Newman/PhotoEdit; p. 438: White House Photo courtesy of USCAR; p. 440: North Wind Picture Archives; p. 442L: © Uniphoto Picture Agency; p. 442R: © John Coletti/Uniphoto Picture Agency; p. 444: © Rodney Mims/Sygma; p. 445: © Ira Wyman/Sygma; p. 446: © *Congressional Quarterly* photo illustration by Patt Chisholm; p. 448L: © Perry Alan Werner/The Image Works, Inc.; p. 448R: © Teresa Zabala/Uniphoto Picture Agency; p. 449: © Larry Downing/Sygma; p. 450: © Paul Conklin/PhotoEdit; p. 452: UPI/Bettmann; p. 456: © James L. Shaffer; p. 458: © Jeffrey Markowitz/Sygma

Chapter 14
Chapter 14 Opener: p. 461: © Ed Elberfeld/Uniphoto Picture Agency; p. 463: *COORS* and *COORS EXTRA GOLD* trademarks and photograph copyright © Coors Brewing Company. Use of these properties has been authorized by Coors; p. 471: AP/Wide World Photos; p. 472: UPI/Bettmann; p. 473: AP/Wide World Photos; p. 478T: © Sygma; p. 478B and p. 479T: © Gamma Liaison; p. 479B: © Arthur Grace/Sygma

Chapter 15
Chapter 15 Opener: p. 493: © Robert Holmes/Corbis Media; p. 494: Wyoming Tribune-Eagle photo; p. 498TL: © David Young-Wolff/PhotoEdit; p. 498BL: © Larry Kolvoord/The Image Works, Inc.; p. 498TR: © David Young-Wolff/PhotoEdit; p. 498BR: © Tony Freeman/PhotoEdit; p. 504: © Tom Horan/Sygma; p. 506: AP/Wide World Photos; p. 509: UPI/Bettmann Newsphotos; p. 512: Los Angeles Times Photo; p. 523: Nancy Andrews photo © 1995, The Washington Post. Reprinted with permission.

Chapter 16
Chapter 16 Opener: p. 527: © Bob Coyle; p. 529: © Tom Horan/Sygma; p. 545: © Don Reina/Sandone & Reina; p. 551: UPI/Bettmann; p. 554: Courtesy of Congressional Budget Office; p. 555: © Richard A. Bloom

Chapter 17
Chapter 17 Opener: p. 563: © Chromosohm Media, Inc./Corbis Media; p. 565 and p. 567: UPI/Bettmann; p. 568: © Robert Visser/Sygma; p. 570: © Michael Springer/Gamma Liaison; p. 576: Courtesy of Intuit; p. 578: © Marty Katz/New York Times Pictures; p. 580: Courtesy of U.S. Department of Labor-OSHA; p. 584: © Galen Rowell/Corbis Media; p. 588: © Kolvoord/The Image Works; p. 589: Courtesy of Social Security Administration; p. 591: © Brooks Kraft/Sygma; p. 595: © Barbara Campbell/Gamma Liaison; p. 598: © Todd Buchanan/New York Times Pictures; p. 599: © Brad Markel/Gamma Liaison

Chapter 18
Chapter 18 Opener: p. 603: © Dirck Halstead/Gamma Liaison; p. 605: © Scott D. Peterson/Gamma Liaison; p. 606: North Wind Picture Archives; p. 607: AP/Wide World Photos; p. 610: © Paul Conklin/PhotoEdit; p. 613: © Wally McNamee/Sygma; p. 614: © Jean Guichard/Sygma; p. 616: © Michael Newman/PhotoEdit; p. 618: © Mark Reinstein/Uniphoto Picture Agency; p. 620L: Courtesy *Foreign Service Journal;* p. 620R: Liz Allan, *Foreign Service Journal;* p. 621: AP/Wide World Photos; p. 623: © Larry Downing/Sygma; p. 626: © Paul Conklin/PhotoEdit; p. 632: © Antonio Ribeiro/Gamma Liaison; p. 633: © Scott Peterson/Gamma Liaison

LINE ART

Bensen Studios, Inc.
3.4, 3.8A-B, 3.9, 4.3, 5.1, 5.2, 7.5, 10.3, 12.10, 14.4, 14.6, 15.3, 15.5, 17.1; text art, page 672

Precision Graphics
2.1, 2.2, 2.3, 2.4, 2.5, 3.1, 3.2, 3.3, 3.6, 3.7, 3.10, 4.1, 4.2, 5.3, 6.1, 6.2, 6.3, 7.1, 7.2, 7.3, 7.4, 8.1, 9.1, 9.2, 9.3, 9.4, 9.5, 10.1, 10.2, 10.4, 10.5, 11.1, 11.2, 11.4, 11.6, 11.7, 11.10, 12.1, 12.2, 12.3, 12.4, 12.5, 12.6, 12.7, 12.8, 12.9, 13.1, 13.2, 13.3, 13.4, 13.5, 13.6, 14.1, 14.2, 14.3, 14.5, 15.1, 15.2, 15.4, 16.1, 16.2, 16.3, 16.4, 16.6, 16.7, 16.8, 16.9, 16.10, 16.11, 18.2, 18.3; text art, page 671

Name Index

A

Abel, Elie, 246
Aberbach, Joel D., 376, 449
Abington School District v. Schempp, 109
Abney, Glenn, 520, 556
Abraham, Henry J., 97
Abramowitz, Alan L., 284
Abramson, Jill, 313, 314
Abramson, Paul R., 175, 192, 204, 205, 222, 223, 225
Abrams v. United States, 100
Abritton, Robert, 521
Adarand Constructors v. Pena, 163
Adler, David Gray, 40, 386, 612, 613
Adler, William M., 133
Adlerman, Ellen, 120
Agranoff, Robert, 289
Ahrari, Mohammed E., 625
Alba, Richard D., 76
Albritton, Robert B., 303
Aldrich, John H., 204, 222, 223, 225, 396, 625
Alexander, Herbert E., 289, 308, 309, 398, 399
Alexander v. Holmes County Board of Education, 137
Allison, Graham T., 452, 619
Almond, Gabriel, 626
Alston, Chuck, 422
Alter, Jonathan, 260
Alvarez, R. Michael, 353
Alwin, Duane F., 180
Ambrosius, Margery M., 512
American National Election Studies, 176
American Political Science Review, 469
Anders, George, 304
Andersen, Kristi, 187
Anderson, James LaVerne, 112
Anderson, Kristi, 281
Anderson, Terry L., 83
Andrews, Edmund L., 243
Andrews, Pat, 149
Angier, Natalie, 155
Anthan, George, 375
Apodaca v. Oregon, 120
Apple, R.W., Jr., 559
Applebome, Peter, 115
Argersinger v. Hamlin, 119
Arizona Governing Committee v. Norris, 153
Arizona v. Evans, 118
Arizona v. Fulminante, 119
Armstrong, Scott, 474, 475
Arnold, R. Douglas, 176, 376, 584
Arnson, Cynthia J., 617
Asbell, Bernard, 313
Asimov, Nanette, 146
Aspin, Larry T., 486
Atkins, Burton M., 486
Auger, Vincent A., 618
Auletta, Ken, 240
Auster, Bruce B., 407
Automobile Workers v. Johnson Controls, 153
Axelrod, Robert, 277

B

Babson, Jennifer, 4, 5, 364, 377
Bagdikian, Ben H., 244
Baggette, Jennifer, 196
Bahree, Bhushan, 633
Bailey, Thomas A., 144
Baker, Brent H., 255
Baker v. Carr, 343, 469
Balz, Dan, 219
Bamford, James, 622
Banducci, Susan A., 352
Bane, Mary Jo, 590
Banfield, Edward C., 285
Banks, William C., 624
Barber, James D., 386
Barber, William J., 565
Bard, Mitchell, 625
Barnes, Fred, 276
Baron, David P., 576, 585
Barone, Michael, 131, 270, 276, 281, 591
Barrett, Amy, 360, 482
Barrett, Edith J., 509
Barrett, Paul M., 164, 462, 477, 557
Barringer, Felicity, 74
Barrow, Deborah J., 485
Barry, John M., 361
Barry, Rick, 78
Bartels, Larry M., 176, 195
Bartlett's Familiar Quotations, 141, 287
Bartley, Numan V., 136
Barton, Eugenia, 351
Barton v. the Mayor and City Council of Baltimore, 97
Bates, Stephen, 253
Battistoni, Richard M., 99, 104, 108
Baugh, Joyce A., 482
Baum, Lawrence, 485, 523
Bazar, Beth, 510
Beam, David R., 372, 499
Bearak, Barry, 577
Beck, Paul Allen, 178, 285
Beer, Samuel H., 448
Behr, Peter, 303
Behr, Roy L., 280
Behrman, Bradley, 577
Benenson, Bob, 585, 632, 633
Bennett, Lerone, Jr., 138
Bennett, Linda L.M., 171
Bennett, Stephen, 171, 187, 215
Bennett, W. Lance, 247
Benson, Lee, 279
Berelson, Bernard, 233
Berke, Richard L., 312
Berkowitz, Edward D., 78, 86, 542
Berkowitz, Laura, 291
Berman, Larry, 413
Bernick, E. Lee, 507
Berns, Walter, 400
Bernstein, Carl, 263
Bernstein, Joan Brodshaug, 594
Bernstein, Merton C., 594
Bernstein, Nina, 152, 154, 155
Berry, Jeffrey M., 296, 301, 306
Berthoud, John E., 559
Beyle, Thad L., 505, 507
Bianco, William T., 376
Bibby, John F., 290
Binder, Sarah A., 360
Binkley, Wilfred, 386, 387
Bipartisan Commission, 556
Bipartisan Commission on Entitlement and Tax Reform, 78, 542, 596
Biskupic, Joan, 112, 115
Black, Earl, 137, 140, 277
Black, Merle, 137, 140, 277
Black, Michael, 625
Blair, Anita K., 156
Blau, Joel, 597
Bobo, Lawrence, 192, 196, 220
Bogart, Leo, 233, 258
Boller, Paul F., Jr., 408
Bond, Jon R., 420, 421
The Book of the States 1991–92, 514, 520
The Book of the States 1992–93, 503
Boot, William, 349
Borger, Gloria, 256, 257
Borgida, Eugene, 625
Bork, Robert, 95
Bosso, Christopher J., 583
Bovard, James, 157
Bower, Robert T., 176
Bowers v. Hardwick, 123, 158
Bowman, Ann O'M., 501, 522
Bowsher v. Synar, 552
Boyarsky, Bill, 185
Boyd, Richard W., 503
Boyd, Steven R., 520
Boyer, Peter J., 250, 258
Bozell, L. Brent, III, 255
Brace, Paul, 410, 510
Bradely, Joseph, 148
Bradlee, Ben, 257
Bradsher, Keith, 571, 572, 630, 633
Bradwell v. Illinois, 148
Brady, Gerald P., 577
Brady, Henry E., 216
Branch, Taylor, 137, 138, 197, 277
Brandenburg v. Ohio, 101
Bratcher, Christopher N., 486
Breaux, David, 510
Brenner, Philip, 617
Brewster, Lawrence G., 592, 597, 599
Brinkley, David, 535
Broadhus, Joseph E., 377
Broder, David, 355
Broder, John, 219
Brody, Richard A., 191, 192, 212
Brooke, James, 632
Brown, Michael E., 592, 597, 599
Browne, William P., 301
Brown et al. v. Board of Education, 96, 135, 136
Browning, Graeme, 242, 256, 296, 364
Brownstein, Ronald, 195, 597
Brown v. Mississippi, 119
Brunk, Gregory G., 511
Brushaber v. Union Pacific Railroad Company, 534
Buchanan v. Warley, 134
Burner, David, 566
Burnham, Walter Dean, 204, 213, 214, 281
Burns, James MacGregor, 196, 278
Burns, Nancy, 522
Burrell, Barbara C., 354, 355
Bush, Governor of Texas, et al. v. Vera et al., 345
Business Week, 188
Busterna, John C., 245, 256
Butler, David, 334, 343, 344
Butterfield, Fox, 521

C

Cain, Brad, 212, 343, 344
Cain, Bruce, 72, 74, 75, 334
Caldeira, Gregory A., 351, 464, 469, 472, 476, 477, 485
California v. Cabazon Band of Mission Indians, 147
California v. Ciraolo, 117
California v. Greenwood, 117
Calleo, David P., 627
Calmes, Jackie, 4, 7, 367, 553, 555, 557
Calvert, Randall L., 353
Cameron, Charles M., 473
Camia, Catalina, 296
Campbell, Angus, 204, 219, 223
Campbell, James E., 352
Campbell v. Acuff-Rose Music Inc., 477
Cannon, Joe, 549
Canon, David T., 221, 335, 352
Cantril, Hadley, 188, 626
Cantril, Lloyd A., 626
Cantwell v. Connecticut, 111
Capitol Square Review Board v. Pinette, 109
Caplan, David I., 114
Carmines, Edward G., 72, 224, 276
Carmody, Deirdre, 106
Carney, Dan, 244
Carney, Eliza Newlin, 296
Carp, Robert A., 464, 483
Carpini, Michael S. Delli, 174
Carrier, Joseph J., 486
Carroll, Holbert N., 615
Carroll, John J., 503

Carson, Rachel, 581
Carter, Jimmy, 407
Cassata, Donna, 362, 363, 446, 597, 623, 632
Cassell, Paul G., 118, 119
Cater, Douglass, 454
Cavanaugh, Thomas E., 283
Cayer, N. Joseph, 440, 441
CBO Papers, 621, 622
Chafee, Steven H., 176
Chambers, William Nisbet, 279
Chaplinsky v. New Hampshire, 108
Cheever, Daniel S., 624
Chelf, Carl P., 596
Chen, Edwin, 486
Chicago, Burlington & Quincy Railroad Co. v. Chicago, 97
Chong, Dennis, 277
Chubb, John E., 283
Church of the Lukumi Babalu Aye Inc. v. Hialeah, Fla., 111
Cigler, Allan J., 456
Citrin, Jack, 186, 205
City of Richmond v. J.A. Croson Co., 163
Claggett, William J.M., 269
Clark, Janet, 221
Clark, Peter, 306
Clarke, Duncan L., 619
Clawson, Dan, 311, 312
Cleveland Board of Education v. LaFleur, 153
Clifford, Clark, 134
Clifford, J. Garry, 144
Clines, Francis X., 502
Clingermayer, James C., 520
Clinton, Bill, 599
Cloud, David S., 325, 340, 364, 540
Cloward, Richard A., 214, 286, 591, 597
Clubb, Jerome M., 282
Clymer, Adam, 325, 528, 557
Clynch, Edward J., 520
Coates, James, 621
Cochran, Clarke E., 591
Cohen, Richard E., 583
Cohen, Ronald, 180
Cohen, William, 113
Coletta, Paolo E., 144
Collins, Mary, 347
Collins, Ronald K.L., 485
Colorado Republican Federal Campaign Committee et al. v. Federal Election Commission, 350
Columbia Journalism Review, 240, 261
Comello, Vic, 574
Comisky, Michael, 475
Comstock, George, 179
Conable, Barber B., Jr., 534
The Concise Columbia Encyclopedia, 133
Congress A to Z, 131
Congressional Quarterly, 589
Congressional Quarterly Weekly Report, 312, 323, 370, 484, 510, 532, 590, 628
Conlan, Timothy J., 499
Connolly, Ceci, 170, 347
Contract with America: The Bold Plan by Rep. Newt Gingrich, Rep. Dick Armey and the House Republicans to Change the Nation, 4, 170, 564, 597
Converse, Philip E., 187, 204, 213, 219
Conway, M. Margaret, 205
Conybeare, John A.C., 309
Cook, Beverly Blair, 481
Cook, Elizabeth Adell, 193
Cook, Rhodes, 69
Cook, Timothy E., 235, 347
Coolidge v. New Hampshire, 117
Cooper, Kenneth J., 118
Cooper, Matthew, 409
Corrado, Anthony, 308, 398, 399
Cortner, Richard C., 133
Corwin, Edward S., 22
Cotter, Cornelius P., 289, 290, 291
Cover, Albert D., 344, 473, 477
Covington, Cary R., 396, 420
Cox, Gary W., 510
Cox v. Louisiana, 104
Coy v. Iowa, 120
Crabb, Cecil V., Jr., 624
Craig, Barbara Hinkson, 81, 193
Craig v. Boren, 154, 160
Crawford, James, 186
Crigler, Ann N., 176
Crittenden, Ann, 433
Crotty, William, 196
Crouse, Timothy, 250
Cruzan v. Director, Missouri Department of Health, 123
Curry, James A., 99, 104, 108
Cushman, John, Jr., 585

D

Dahl, Robert A., 10, 90
Daniels, Roger, 145
Darcy, R., 221
Darity, William, Jr., 570
Davidson, Joe, 118, 119
Davidson, Roger H., 338, 364
Davis, James Allan, 596
Davis v. Bandemer, 344
Dawson, Karen, 177
Dawson, Michael, 72
Dawson, Richard, 177
Daynes, Byron W., 510
Dear, Joseph A., 581
Deering, Christopher J., 339, 449, 624
DeGregorio, Christine, 367
de la Garza, Rodolfo O., 73, 74, 78
Dellums v. Bush, 615
Deloria, Vine, Jr., 146
de Montesquieu, Charles, 35
Dempsey, Glenn R., 234
Dennis v. United States, 100
De Parle, Jason, 81, 247
Derthick, Martha, 577
DeSipio, Louis, 73, 74, 78
Des Moines Register, 86, 351, 376, 426, 509
Destler, I.M., 618
De Tocqueville, Alexis, 299
Deutch, John M., 630
Devroy, Ann, 163
Dewar, Helen, 20, 341
Diamond, Edwin, 243, 249
DiNitto, Diana M., 586, 590
DiPalma, Giuseppe, 174
Dixon, William J., 481
Dodd, Lawrence C., 339, 363, 376, 550
Dodson, Debra L., 509
Doherty, Carroll J., 158, 159, 364, 619
Dolbeare, Kenneth M., 181
Dominick, Joseph R., 251
Donaldson, Sam, 249
Donovan, Beth, 325
Dosi, Giovanni, 574
Douglas, Robb, 508
Dowd, Ann Reilly, 542
Dowd, Maureen, 170
Downs, Anthony, 272
Draper, Theodore, 21, 29
Dred Scott v. Sandford, 95, 129
Dresang, Dennis L., 523
Drew, Elizabeth, 325
DuBrow, Rick, 179
Duff, Christina, 536
Duke, Lois Lovelace, 196
Duncan, Phil, 358
Duncan v. Louisiana, 120
Dunlap, David W., 160
Durning, Dan, 507
Durst, Samantha L., 550, 553
Duverger, Maurice, 276
Dworkin, Andrea, 156
Dwyre, Diana, 292
Dye, Thomas R., 586, 590

E

Easton, David, 9
Ebersole, Phil, 537
Eccles, Marriner S., 619
Eckholm, Erik, 592
Edelman, Murray, 577
Edsall, Mary D., 193, 221
Edsall, Thomas Byrne, 193, 221, 544
Egan, Timothy, 212
Eggers, William D., 520
Ehrenhalt, Alan, 509, 513
Eichar, Douglas M., 86
Eichstaedt, Peter, 507
Eisenstadt v. Baird, 121
Eismeier, Theodore J., 189
Eisner, Robert, 533
Elk v. Wilkins, 146
Elliot, Martha J. H., 468
Elliott, Martha J. H., 104
Ely, John Hart, 613
Emery, Edwin, 99, 236, 255
Employment Division, Department of Human Resources v. Smith, 111
The Encyclopedic Dictionary of American Government, 140
Enelow, James M., 272
Engelberg, Stephen, 314
Engel v. Vitale, 109
Engle, Margaret, 510, 515
English, Arthur, 503
Entman, Robert, 258
Environmental Policy for the 1990s, 583
Epstein, Edward, 126, 256
Epstein, Lee, 95, 464, 471, 476, 477, 481
Erikson, Robert S., 173
Esposito, John C., 581
Evans, C. Lawrence, 370
Everson v. Board of Education, 109

F

Falcon, Angelo, 73, 74, 78
Farah, Barbara G., 227
Farhi, Paul, 248
Farney, Dennis, 158, 585
Fastnow, Christina, 507
Fay, James, 74
Feder, Barnaby J., 304
Federal Debt and Interest Costs, 532
Federal Election Commission, 309
Feinsilber, Mike, 548
Feldman, Stanley, 177, 189
Felsenthal, Edward, 94
Fenno, Richard F., Jr., 346, 366, 549
Ferejohn, John A., 344, 353, 376
Ferguson, Thomas, 188, 278
Ferguson, Tim W., 633
Ferrell, Robert H., 606, 607
Fesler, James W., 441, 497, 575
Fessler, Pamela, 235
Fields, Jack, 358
Finder, Alan, 597
Fineman, Howard, 142, 276, 592
Fiorina, Morris P., 222, 353, 454
Firestone, Juanita M., 355
Firmage, Edwin B., 613
Fisher, Louis, 356, 403, 404, 613
Fitzgerald, Randall, 457
5 Annals of Congress, 95
Flanigan, William H., 225, 282
Fleisher, Richard, 420, 421
Foerstel, Karen, 332
Foote, Joe S., 251
Ford v. Wainwright, 121
Foreman, Christopher H., Jr., 426
Fowler, Linda L., 352
Fraleigh, Cynthia, 577
Fraley, Colette, 501, 600
Frammolino, Ralph, 175
Franck, Thomas M., 615
Franklin, Daniel P., 546
Franklin, Grace A., 456
Free, Lloyd A., 188
Freedman, Allan, 585
Freeman, J. Leiper, 454
Friedman, Milton, 559, 568
Friedman, Rose D., 568
Friedman, Thomas L., 630
Friendly, Fred W., 104, 468
Frisby, Michael K., 73, 164
Fritsch, Jane, 319
Fritschler, A. Lee, 433, 455
Fritz, Sara, 219
Fund, John H., 242, 367
Furchgott-Roth, Diana, 88
Furlong, Tom, 577
Furman v. Georgia, 120

G

Gais, Thomas L., 316, 456
Galanter, Marc, 482
Galbraith, James K., 570
Galie, Peter J., 485
Gallaher, Miriam, 338
Galloway, George B., 332, 388

Gallup, George, Jr., 68, 80, 214
Gallup Poll Monthly, 4
Gallup Report, 194
Galvin, Thomas, 6, 316, 510
Gannon, James, 94
Gans, Herbert J., 253
Gant, Michael M., 171, 187
Garand, James C., 510
Garcia, F. Chris, 73, 74, 78
Garcia, John, 73, 74, 78
Gates, Robbins L., 136
Gates, Robert M., 622
Gaudet, Hazel, 233
Gayle v. Browder, 138
Geller, Gregg, 243
George, Alexander, 410
George, Tracey E., 477
Georges, Christopher, 255, 349, 542, 544, 555
Gerber, Elisabeth R., 72, 75
Gerston, Larry N., 577
Gertzog, Irwin N., 354
Gideon v. Wainwright, 119
Gilbert, Charles E., 588
Gilbert, Neil, 597
Gilder, George, 573
Gilliam, Franklin D., Jr., 72, 75
Gilmour, John B., 339, 549, 551
Gilmour, Robert, 429
Gimpel, James, 5, 288
Gitlin, Todd, 255
Glaberson, William, 244, 255, 304, 305
Gladwell, Malcolm, 68
Glass, David P., 86, 206, 215
Glassman, James K., 536
Glennon, Michael J., 612, 615
Glick, Harry R., 486
Glick, Henry R., 486
Godson, Roy, 623
Goldberg, David Howard, 625
Goldberg, Gerald Jay, 240
Goldberg, Robert, 240
Goldstein, Michael L., 394, 402
Gonzalez, David, 73
Goodgame, Dan, 559
Goodman, Walter, 258
Goodnow, Frank J., 442
Goodsell, Charles T., 427
Goodstein, Laurie, 81
Gordon, George J., 427, 577, 579
Gore, Al, 580
Gosling, James L., 523
Gove, Samuel, 521
Graber, Doris A., 179, 245, 248, 249
Graber, Mark A., 97
Graham, Barbara Luck, 486
Graham v. Richardson, 146
Graig, Laurene A., 599
Gray, Jerry, 557
Gray, Virginia, 511, 512
Gray, Wayne B., 580
Gray v. Sanders, 343
Green, Charles, 78
Green, Donald P., 186
Green, John C., 81
Green, M., 580
Greenblatt, Alan, 369
Greenhouse, Linda, 94, 110, 118
Greenhouse, Steven, 457, 607, 623, 629
Greenstein, Fred I., 178, 388
Greenstein, Robert, 590
Green v. County School Board, 137
Greenwood v. California, 485
Gregg v. Georgia, 120
Greider, William, 232, 413
Grenzke, Janet M., 311
Griffin v. County School Board of Prince Edward County, 137
Grindley, Peter, 574
Griswold v. Connecticut, 121
Grodzins, Morton, 51, 52
Grofman, Bernard, 354, 366
Gronke, Paul W., 193
Groppe, Maureen, 242
Grossman, Michael Baruch, 235
Grosvenor, Gilbert M., 626
Gruley, Bryan, 576
Grunwald, Julianna, 364
Grusin, Elinor, 251
Gryski, Gerard S., 485
Guinn v. United States, 134
Gunther, Gerald, 148
Gupta, Udayan, 164
Gusfield, Joseph R., 186
Gutek, Barbara A., 351
Guth, James L., 81
Guttenplan, D.D., 262

H

Haddon, Michael, 511
Hadley, Charles D., 277
Hagan, Kenneth J., 144
Hager, George, 542
Hagle, Timothy M., 473
Hague v. Committee of Industrial Organization, 104
Halberstam, David, 253
Halbrook, Stephen P., 114
Hale, David, 87
Hale, Jon F., 278
Hall, Richard L., 312, 366, 370
Hall, William K., 486
Hallin, Daniel C., 252
Halperin, Morton H., 619
Haltom, William, 474
Hamilton, Alexander, 40, 197, 279, 386, 612, 613
Hamilton, Joan, 584
Handley, Lisa, 354
Hansen, John Mark, 175, 203, 205, 211, 214, 216, 217, 223, 289, 301
Hansen, Kathleen A., 245, 256
Hansen, Susan B., 517, 520, 521
Hanson, Christopher, 232, 246
Hanson, Russell L., 497, 499
Hardy, C. Colburn, 78, 542
Hardy, Dorcas R., 78, 542
Hardy, Richard J., 486
Harper, Lucinda, 520
Harrington, Michael, 591
Harris, John F., 118
Harris Poll 1994, 324
Harris Poll 1995, 234
Harris v. United States, 117
Hart, John, 405
Harvey, Philip L., 594
Harwood, John, 208, 351
Harwood, Richard, 240
Hastedt, Glen P., 619
Haviland, H. Field, Jr., 624
Hays, Stuart B., 114
Healey, John, 457
Healy, Jon, 377
Heath, Linda, 180
Heckler v. Mathews, 154
Heclo, Hugh, 413, 457, 591
Hedges, Chris, 247
Heinz, John P., 457
Henkin, Louis, 612
Hennessy, Bernard C., 291
Henry, William A., III, 75
Hensley, Thomas R., 475, 482
Hero, Rodney E., 354
Herrera, Cheryl L., 193, 269
Herrera, Richard, 193, 269
Herring, George C., 608
Hersh, Seymour M., 618
Hershey, Robert D., Jr., 542, 545
Hertsgaard, Mark, 239, 244, 250, 253
Hess, Robert D., 178, 217
Hess, Stephen, 235, 347, 417
Hibbing, John R., 339
Highton, Benjamin, 68, 81
Hill, Kevin A., 344
Hill, Kim Quaile, 73
Hill, Samuel S., Jr., 81, 188
Hilts, Philip J., 426, 451
Hinckley, Barbara, 410, 624
Hinds, Michael, 510
Hinich, Melvin J., 272
Hirabayashi v. United States, 145
Hirsch, Eric, 509, 510
Historical Statistics of the United States: Colonial Times to 1970, 69
Hoadley, John F., 360
Hodgson, Godfrey, 138
Hodgson v. Minnesota, 121
Hoekstra, Valerie J., 469
Hofstadter, Richard, 98, 214, 288
Holbrook, Thomas M., 290, 509, 510
Holden, Benjamin A., 322
Holden, Matthew, Jr., 452
Hollinger, Joan Heifetz, 338
Holmes, Steven A., 142, 155, 163, 307, 571
Holt, Pat M., 624
Holt, W. Stull, 624
Honan, William H., 296
Hoover, Kenneth R., 181, 183, 185
Horowitz, Donald L., 468
Howell, Susan E., 220
Hoyer, Robert, 511
Hrebenar, Ronald J., 511, 512, 514
Hubbard v. United States, 477
Huckshorn, Robert J., 291
Humphrey, Hubert H., 277
Hunt, Albert R., 364, 525, 558, 560, 611
Hunter, Floyd, 90
Hunter, Kenneth G., 511
Huntington, Samuel P., 615, 627
Hurtado v. California, 97
Hwang, Susan L., 462
Hyman, Lisa J., 507
Hyneman, Charles S., 509

I

Ichioka, Yuji, 144
Idelson, Holly, 4, 152, 163, 625
Ifill, Gwen, 457
Ingraham, Laura, 156
Ingram, Carl, 208
INS v. Delgado, 146
INS v. Lopez-Mendoza, 146
International Monetary Fund, 593
Iowa City Press-Citizen, 77, 79, 80, 82, 301, 304, 358
Iyengar, Shanto, 235

J

Jackson, Byran O., 72, 75
Jackson, John S., III, 510
Jacobellis v. Ohio, 108
Jacobs, Lawrence R., 196, 594, 596
Jacobson, Gary C., 283, 344, 352, 353
Jamieson, Kathleen Hall, 398
Jaroslovsky, Rich, 353
Jay, John, 197, 279
Jefferson, Thomas, 232, 233
Jelen, Ted G., 86, 193
Jenkins v. Georgia, 108
Jennings, M. Kent, 178, 193
Jentleson, Bruce W., 611, 627
Jewell, Malcolm, 510
Jillson, Calvin C., 30
Johnson, Chalmers A., 574
Johnson, Dirk, 523, 528
Johnson, Donald Bruce, 276, 277
Johnson, George, 148
Johnson, Harry G., 568
Johnson, Loch, 622, 623, 624
Johnson, Lyndon Baines, 564, 591, 592
Johnson, Richard T., 410
Johnson v. Transportation Agency, Santa Clara County, 154, 163
Jones, Alex S., 239
Jones, Charles O., 363
Jones, David M., 569
Jones, Joseph Marion, 607
Jones, Ruth S., 308
Jordan, Christopher G., 486
Judis, John B., 276
Just, Marion R., 176

K

Kagay, Michael R., 625
Kahn, Kim Fridkin, 507
Kahn, Robert L., 351
Kahn v. Shevin, 154
Kaiser, Frederick M., 624
Kalager, Jon K., 220
Kamen, Al, 82
Kaplan, John, 113
Karnow, Stanley, 608
Karp, Jeffrey A., 352, 510
Karr, Albert R., 576
Katel, Peter, 258
Kates, Don B., 114
Katz, Daniel, 351
Katz, Jeffrey L., 585, 597
Katz, Michael B., 591
Katzenbach v. Morgan, 146
Katzmann, Robert A., 156
Katz v. United States, 117
Kaufman, Herbert, 458
Kayden, Xandra, 291
Kearney, Richard C., 507, 522
Keenan, Joseph T., 469
Keeter, Scott, 174
Keith, Bruce E., 219, 283
Kellerman, Barbara, 419

Kellstedt, Lyman A., 81
Kendrigan, Mary Lou, 186, 196
Kennedy, Caroline, 120
Kennedy, Paul, 627
Kennett, Lee, 112
Kenney, Sally J., 153
Kerbel, Matthew R., 258
Kernell, Samuel, 235, 335, 418
Kerthick, Martha, 449
Kettl, Donald F., 441, 458, 497, 530, 536, 541, 552, 575
Key, V.O., Jr., 149, 176, 208, 222, 281, 509
Keynes, John Maynard, 566
Kiewiet, D. Roderick, 74, 223, 520
Kilborn, Peter T., 155
Kilian, Michael, 621
Kilpatrick, James J., 263
Kincaid, John, 485
Kinder, Donald R., 223, 235
King, David C., 307
King, Gary, 473
King, James D., 510
Kingson, Eric R., 78, 86, 542
Kingston, Paul William, 86
Kinney, Rhonda, 420
Kirby, Andrew, 115
Kirkpatrick, Melanie, 160
Kirsch, John, 347
Kirschten, Dick, 619
Kitano, Harry H. L., 145
Klamer, Arjo, 570
Klein, Ethel, 186, 227
Kleppner, Paul, 214
Kluger, Richard, 133
Knack, Stephen, 208
Koertge, Noretta, 156
Koh, Harold Hongju, 615
Kolbert, Elizabeth, 256, 261, 262, 319
Kolko, Gabriel, 280, 576
Korb, Lawrence J., 622
Koszczuk, Jackie, 340, 556
Kotz, Nick, 250
Kousser, Morgan J., 214
Kraft, Michael E., 584, 585
Krehbiel, Keith, 365
Kriz, Margaret, 453, 585
Krolick, Robert, 258
Kuklinski, James H., 364
Kumar, Martha Joynt, 235
Kuntz, Phil, 311, 312, 357, 358, 370, 553
Kurtz, Howard, 242
Kurz, Robert, 245

L

Labaton, Stephen, 219
Ladd, Everett Carll, 75, 525
Ladd, Everett Carll, Jr., 277, 280
LaFeber, Walter, 133, 144, 606
Lake, Anthony, 611
Lambert, Wade, 106
Landy, Marc K., 581
Langbein, Laura, 312
Langdon, Steve, 4
Lapham, Lewis H., 253
Lasswell, Harold, 9
Laumann, Edward O., 457
Lauth, Thomas P., 520, 556
Lau v. Nichols, 145
Lav, Iris J., 590
Lawrence, Christine C., 421
Lawson, Kay, 74
Lazarsfeld, Paul, 233
Lazarus, Edward H., 147, 280
Lazere, Edward, 590
Leary, Warren E., 626
Lederman, Susan S., 276
Lee, Linda, 432
Lee v. Weisman, 109
Lehman, John, 624
Leiser, Ernest, 240
Lekachman, Robert, 566
LeLoup, Lance T., 627
Lemon v. Kurtzman, 110
Lengle, James, 393
LeoGrande, William M., 617
LePore, Herbert P., 144
Lesher, Stephen, 137
Leuchtenburg, William E., 388, 407, 577
Levine, Jeffrey, 68
Levine, Ronald B., 114
Levinson, Sanford, 114
Levitt v. Committee for Public Educ., 109
Levy, Clifford J., 501
Lewin, Tamar, 79
Lewis, Anthony, 107
Lewis, H.W., 584
Lewis, I.A., 255
Lewis, Neil A., 112
Lewis, William H., 263
Lewis-Beck, Michael S., 222, 565
Lewis v. United States, 114
Lian, Bradley, 626
Lichter, S. Robert, 255
Light, Paul C., 408, 464
Lilienthal, Steve, 291
Lilley, William, III, 438, 579
Lindsay, James M., 340, 375, 612, 615, 619, 624
Link, Michael W., 469
Linsky, Martin, 262
Lipson, Gerald, 457
Livingston, James, 568
Local Number 93, International Association of Firefighters, AFL-CIO, C.L.C. v. City of Cleveland, 163
Locke, John, 32
Lofgren, Don J., 580
Loftus, Tom, 513
Lohr, Steve, 242, 452
Long, Norton E., 446
Longley, Lawrence D., 196
Loomis, Burdett A., 456
Los Angeles Department of Water and Power v. Manhart, 153
Los Angeles Times, 515
Lotwis, Mark, 312
Loury, Glenn C., 142
Lovrich, Nicholas, 510
Lovrich, Nicholas P., Jr., 221
Lowery, David, 511, 512
Lowi, Theodore J., 456, 577
Lublin, Joann S., 155
Lucas, Greg, 516
Lucas, Robert E., Jr., 570
Lupia, Arthur, 515
Luskin, Robert C., 175, 486
Luttbeg, Norman R., 171, 173, 187
Lytle, Clifford M., 146

M

Maass, Arthur, 454
McAllister, Bill, 322
MacArthur, John R., 303
McCabe, Michael H., 505
McCaffrey, David P., 580
McCarron, Katherine, 322
McClain, Charles, 143, 144, 145
McClain, Paula D., 515
McCloskey, Robert G., 467, 481
McClosky, Herbert, 174, 180, 181, 272
McClure, Robert D., 352
McCombs, Maxwell E., 175
McCormick, James M., 624, 625, 626
McCormick, Richard P., 279
McCoy, Charles, 296
McCracken, Paul W., 533
McCubbins, Mathew D., 376, 396
McCulloch v. Maryland, 49
MacDonald, Maurice, 595
McDonough, Mark G., 626
McDorman, Ted L., 633
McGinley, Laurie, 450, 521
McGlen, Nancy E., 149
McGovney, Dudley O., 144
McGuire, Kevin T., 468, 477
MacKinnon, Catharine A., 156
McLaurin v. Oklahoma State Regents, 135
McManus, Reed, 301
McNeil, Donald G., Jr., 409
McPhee, William, 233
Madison, James, 33, 197, 232, 279, 296
Magaziner, Ira C., 574
Magleby, David B., 175, 351, 515
Mahe, Eddie, 291
Mahon, John K., 113
Maisel, Sherman J., 281
Malbin, Michael J., 44, 350, 365, 367, 546, 550, 593
Malcolm X, 142
Maltese, John A., 421
Manheim, Jarol B., 303
Mann, Thomas E., 44, 235, 350, 365, 367, 546, 550, 593, 624
Manning, Bayless, 630
Mapp v. Ohio, 117, 118, 468
Maraniss, David, 143, 312, 580
Maranto, Robert, 421
Marbury v. Madison, 467
Marcus, George E., 191
Marcus, George F., 192
Marin, Rick, 258
Markus, Gregory B., 219
Marmor, Theodore R. K., 594
Marshall, Thomas R., 101
Martin, David L., 513
Martin, George T., Jr., 590, 593
Martin, John Frederick, 276
Maryland v. Craig, 120
Mashaw, Jerry L., 594
Mashek, John W., 278
Massachusetts Board of Retirement v. Muriga, 158
Masson, Paul, 532
Matthews, Donald R., 340
Matthews, Douglas, 131
May, Ernest, 605, 623
Mayer, Thomas, 568
Mayer, William, 180, 196, 575
Mayhew, David R., 344, 347
Mead, Lawrence M., 597
Mead, Walter Russell, 627
Medcalf, Linda J., 181
The Media at War: The Press and the Persian Gulf Conflict, 247
Meek v. Pittinger, 109
Mehta, Stephanie N., 155
Meier, Kenneth, 449, 458
Mendel, Richard A., 621
Merelman, Richard, 178
Merida, Kevin, 163
Merrill, Dennis, 605
Miami Herald Publishing Co. v. Tornillo, 248
Michaelis, Laura, 296
Michael M. v. Superior Court, 154
Michaelsen, Mark G., 352
Milakovich, Michael E., 577, 579
Milkis, Sidney M., 388, 409
Miller, Arthur H., 205
Miller, James C., III, 438, 579
Miller, James Monroe, 535
Miller, Warren E., 193, 204
Miller v. California, 108
Miller v. Johnson, 345
Miller v. Texas, 114
Mincy, Ronald B., 595
Minersville School District v. Gobitis, 111
Minns, Daniel R., 177
Minor v. Happersett, 126
Miranda v. Arizona, 119
Mishler, William, 469, 482
Mississippi University for Women v. Hogan, 160
Missouri ex rel. Gaines v. Canada, 134
Missouri v. Jenkins, 142
Mitchell, Glenn, II, 215
Moe, Terry M., 306, 414, 433
Moffett, George, III, 625
Moncrief, Gary F., 511
Mooney, Tom, 468
Moore, David W., 193
Moore, John L., 358, 471
Moore, W. John, 476, 477
Moore v. Dempsey, 133
Morgenstern, Scott, 510
Morin, Richard, 76, 79, 81, 171, 172, 185, 503, 525, 547, 611, 625, 629
Morone, James A., 185, 276, 592
Morris, Roger, 263
Morrison, David C., 307, 631
Morrison, Samuel Eliot, 22
Mosher, Frederick C., 439, 441
Mowry, George E., 334
Moynihan, Daniel P., 232
Mueller, John, 195, 625, 626
Muller v. Oregon, 148
Mullins, L.E., 175
Mundo, Philip A., 300
Murphy, Russell D., 519
Murray, Charles, 594, 595
Murray, Robert K., 391
Murray v. Curlett, 109
Muse, Benjamin, 136
Mussa, Michael, 532
Myers v. United States, 404

N

Nadeau, Richard, 68
Nasar, Sylvia, 519
Nash, Roderick, 581
Nashville Gas v. Satty, 153
Nathan, Richard P., 450, 496, 501
National Academy of Sciences, 631
National Association for the Advancement of Colored People v. Alabama ex rel. Patterson, 105
National Center for Health Statistics, 595
National Journal, 309, 395, 625
Nau, Henry R., 627
Near v. Minnesota, 105
Neckerman, Kathryn M., 590
Neergaard, Lauran, 86
Nelson, Albert J., 509
Nelson, Michael, 388, 409, 434
Nelson, Robert L., 457
Neuman, W. Russell, 176
Neustadt, Richard E., 36, 414, 416, 418
Neustadtl, Alan, 311, 312
Newcomb, Theodore M., 179, 180
Newport, Frank, 68
The New Republic, 278
Newsweek, 262, 285
New York Times, 87, 106, 111, 155, 301, 564, 604, 626
New York Times Company v. United States, 105
New York v. Quarles, 119
Nice, David C., 497
Nicholson, Marlene Arnold, 486
Nicholson, Norman, 486
Nie, Norman H., 187, 207, 216
Niemi, Richard G., 68, 72, 86, 87, 178, 258, 283, 309, 311, 430, 434, 466, 483, 509, 510, 522, 523
Niles, Maria Renee, 75
Nix v. Williams, 119
Noah, Rebecca L., 511
Noah, Timothy, 250, 305, 314, 451, 585
Nobay, A. Robert, 568
Noble, Charles, 579, 580, 581
Nomani, Asra Q., 72, 73, 75, 581
NORC General Social Survey, 220
Norman, Jane, 509
Novak, Michael, 572
Novak, Viveca, 556
Nye, Joseph S., Jr., 627
Nye, Mary Alice, 363

O

O'Brien, David M., 81, 193, 476, 480
O'Connor, Karen, 149
O'Donnell, Thomas J., 357
Ogene, F. Chidozie, 625
O'Halloran, Sharyn, 625
O'Leary, John, 520
Oleszek, Walter J., 338, 341, 368, 371
Olin, Spencer C., Jr., 288
Olmstead v. United States, 117
Olson, Mancur, 305, 307
Omnibus Crime Control and Safe Streets Act of 1968, 117
O'Neal, John R., 626
104th Congress: A Congressional Quarterly Reader, 170
O'Neill, June Ellenoff, 88
Opheim, Cynthia, 511, 514
Oppenheimer, Bruce I., 339, 363, 376, 550
Orman, John, 315
Ornstein, Norman J., 44, 235, 350, 364, 365, 367, 401, 546, 550, 593, 625
Orr v. Orr, 154
Orth, Samuel P., 509
Orwall, Bruce, 520
Owen, Dennis E., 81
Owens, Mackubin Thomas, 624

P

Pack, Robert, 246
Pagano, Michael A., 501
Page, Benjamin I., 193, 195, 234, 575
Paletz, David L., 247
Parisot, Laurance, 233
Parker, Glen R., 346
Parker, Suzanne L., 626
Passell, Peter, 163, 542
Pastor, Robert A., 617
Patai, Daphne, 156
Paterson, Thomas G., 144, 605
Patterson, Kelly D., 351
Patterson, Samuel C., 351
Patterson, Thomas E., 176, 257
Pear, Robert, 404, 555, 557, 581, 585
Pease, Donald, 358
Pechman, Joseph A., 569
Penry v. Lynaugh, 121
People, Opinions, and Polls, 541, 542
The People, the Press, 257
Perry, Barbara A., 97
Perry, James M., 351, 410
Peters, B. Guy, 596
Peterson, Geoffrey D., 75
Peterson, Iver, 106
Peterson, Mark A., 315, 420, 456
Peterson, Paul E., 283, 546, 624
Peterson, Peter G., 542, 596
Peterzell, Jay, 246
Petraitis, John, 180
Petroski, William, 494
Pew Research Center for the People & the Press, 176, 457, 469
Pfiffner, James P., 36, 417
Phelps, Timothy M., 262
Philips, Kevin, 573
Phillips, Edward H., 453
Phillips v. Martin-Marietta, 153
Piereson, James, 191, 192
Pika, Joseph A., 315
Pimsleur, J.L., 126
Pingree, Suzanne, 233
Pins, Kenneth, 82, 358, 362, 585
Pittsburgh Press v. Pittsburgh Commission on Human Relations, 153
Piven, Frances Fox, 214, 286, 591, 597
Plamer, Barbara, 468
Planned Parenthood of Southeastern Pennsylvania v. Casey, 121
Plasencia v. U.S., 117
Plessy v. Ferguson, 131
Plyler v. Doe, 146
Pointer v. Texas, 120
Pollock v. Farmers' Loan and Trust Co., 534
Polsby, Nelson W., 90, 335, 338, 378, 388, 394, 395, 397
Pomper, Gerald, 187, 223, 276
Porter, Kirk H., 276, 277
Portney, Paul, 583
Povich, Elaine S., 255
Powell, G. Bingham, Jr., 271
Powell v. Alabama, 119
Presser v. Illinois, 114
Prewit, Kenneth, 177
Price, David E., 357
Price, Deb, 158
Price, H. Douglas, 335
Prichett, C. Herman, 463
Public Educ. v. Nyquist, 109
The Public Perspective, 72, 76, 186, 540, 541, 596, 597
Purdum, Todd S., 112

Q

Quarles, John, 451
Quilici v. Village of Morton Grove, 114
Quirk, Paul J., 220, 339, 577

R

Rabinowitz, George, 178
Radanovich, George, 553
Radcliff, Benjamin, 215
Radice v. New York, 148
Radin, Beryl A., 458
Ragsdale, Lyn, 351, 403, 421
Raimondo, Henry J., 520
Rakove, Milton, 285
Ramirez, Anthony, 248
Randall, Ronald, 421, 451
Ranney, Austin, 285, 390
Rattner, Steven, 572
R.A.V. v. City of St. Paul, 103
Raven-Hansen, Peter, 624
Redfield, Kent D., 505
Red Lion Broadcasting Co. v. FCC, 248
Reed v. Reed, 153
Reedy, George E., 411
Regan, Donald T., 262
Regents of the University of California v. Bakke, 163
Rehnquist, William, 480
Reich, Robert B., 574
Reichley, A. James, 81, 109
Reilly, John E., 626
Reilly, Patrick, 106
Reingold, Beth, 186, 509
Reinhard, Gregor, 16
Remini, Robert V., 279
Renner, Tracy K., 486
Reno, Janet, 156
Rensberger, Boyce, 79
Resnick, David, 215
Revenues and Expenditures, 497
Reynolds v. United States, 110
Rhine, Staci L., 208
Ricci, David M., 457
Rice, Tom W., 222
Richelson, Jeffrey T., 622
Richter, Linda S., 255
Rielly, John E., 611
Riggle, James D., 499
Riker, William H., 276
Riley, Richard B., 99, 104, 108
Riordan, Teresa, 347
Ripley, Randall B., 456, 624
Roberston v. Baldwin, 114
Roberts, Marc J., 581
Roberts, Sam, 73
Robichaux, Mark, 241, 245
Robinson, James A., 615
Roche, John, 24
Rockman, Bert A., 618
Rodgers, Jack, 508
Roemer, Tim, 358
Roemer v. Board of Public Works, 109
Roemmele, Andrea, 342
Roe v. Wade, 121
Rogers, David, 340, 347, 362
Rogers, Joel, 188, 278
Rohde, David W., 204, 222, 223, 225, 360, 363
Roiphe, Katie, 156
Romasco, Albert U., 565
Romer v. Evans, 159
Roos, Jonathan, 78
Rosen, Ruth, 593
Rosenbaum, David E., 20, 557, 559
Rosenbaum, Walter A., 582
Rosenberg, Gerald N., 136
Rosenberg, Robert M., 193
Rosenberger v. University of Virginia, 94
Rosenfeld, Megan, 156
Rosenstiel, Thomas B., 285
Rosenstiel, Tom, 255
Rosenstone, Steven J., 175, 203, 205, 211, 214, 216, 217, 223, 280, 289
Rosenthal, Alan, 505, 507, 509, 510, 511, 520
Rosentiel, Thomas B., 261
Rosner, Jeremy D., 615
Ross, Michael, 208
Rossi, Peter, 597
Rossiter, Clinton, 389
Rostker v. Goldberg, 154
Rothenberg, Randall, 258
Rothman, Stanley, 255
Roth v. United States, 108
Rourke, Francis, 446, 447
Rubin, Alissa J., 600, 632
Rubin, Barry, 619
Rubin v. Coors Brewing Co., 462
Rundquist, Barry Spencer, 338
Rusk, Jerrold G., 213, 216, 286
Ryberg, William, 87

S

Sabato, Larry J., 257, 291, 309, 504
Safire, William, 129, 131, 133, 324, 544, 604
Saint Francis College v. Al-Khazraji, 148
Saint-Germain, Michelle, 509
Salant, Jonathan D., 325, 360, 361, 366, 367
Salisbury, Robert H., 305, 313, 457
Salmore, Barbara G., 289
Salmore, Stephen A., 289
Sammon, Richard, 208, 325

Samuelson, Robert J., 571, 572, 592
Sanders, Arthur, 189, 195
Sanders, Elizabeth, 451
Sanford, Terry, 500
San Francisco Chronicle, 86, 332, 516, 542
Sanger, David E., 633
San Miguel, Guadalupe, Jr., 146
Santiago, Frank, 484
Savage, David G., 208
Savage, James D., 529
Saxe, David B., 114
Scammon, Richard M., 190
Scarborough, Joe, 362
Schattschneider, E.E., 271, 324, 451
Schenck v. United States, 99
Scheppele, Kim Lane, 320
Schier, Steven E., 469, 551
Schlesinger, Arthur M., Jr., 40, 137, 277, 386, 405, 566, 612, 613
Schlesinger, James, 621
Schlesinger, Joseph A., 269, 287
Schlozman, Kay Lehman, 216, 300, 307, 313
Schmalz, Jeffrey, 304
Schmitt, Gary, 623
Schneider, Keith, 303
Schneider, William, 255
Schorr, Daniel, 235
Schousen, Matthew M., 353
Schrag, John, 159
Schulte, Brigid, 375
Schuman, Howard, 192, 196, 220
Schwab, Robert, 577
Schwartz, Anna G., 568
Schwartz, Donna E., 499
Schwartz, Sandra K., 178
Schwartz, Stephen, 516
Schwartz, Thomas, 376
Schwarz, John E., 83, 594
Scott, Denise, 311, 312
Seago, Kris S., 486
Searing, Donald, 178
Seelye, Katharine Q., 544
Segal, David, 299, 324
Segal, Jeffrey A., 473, 477
Seib, Gerald F., 243, 536
Seidman, Harold, 429
Seligman, Daniel, 76
Seligman, Lester G., 396
Senate History, 364
Serrano, Barbara A., 502
Shafer, Byron, 269, 393
Shafer, Ronald G., 547
Shaffer, Stephen D., 205
Shafritz, Jay, 37, 439
Shapiro, Robert Y., 193, 195, 196, 234, 575, 594, 596
Sharpe, Rochelle, 502
Shaw et al. v. Hunt, Governor of North Carolina, et al., 345
Shaw v. Reno, 345
Shear, Jeff, 532
Sheehan, Reginald S., 469, 482
Sheehy, Gail, 155
Sheet Metal Workers v. EEOC, 163
Shepsle, Kenneth A., 365
Shin, Kwang S., 510
Shingles, Richard D., 205
Shipan, Charles R., 376
Shugart, Matthew Soberg, 276
Shull, Steven A., 612
Shulman, Eli C., 594
Sigelman, Lee, 227, 364
Silverstein, Gordon, 613
Silverstein, Mark, 474
Simon, Jim, 502
Sinclair, Barbara, 341, 362, 371
Siskind, Lawrence J., 146
Sittig, Robert, 508
Skocpol, Theda, 588
Skogan, Wesley G., 521
Skowronek, Stephen, 113
Slaughterhouse Cases, 97, 130
Smidt, Corwin E., 81
Smist, Frank J., 622
Smith, Christopher E., 475, 482
Smith, Eric R.A.N., 175, 187, 193, 205, 219, 269, 283
Smith, Hedrick, 247, 618
Smith, Page, 144
Smith, Steven S., 339, 368, 372, 449
Smith, Tom W., 189, 195, 594, 596
Smith, Vern E., 142
Smith v. Allwright, 134
Smoller, Fred, 235
Smothers, Ronald, 458
Snider, Dom M., 622
Snider, Kevin, 367
Sniderman, Paul M., 191, 192
Sobel, Richard, 625
Sofaer, Abraham D., 113, 613
Solow, Robert, 570
Somit, Albert, 342
Sommers, Christina Hoff, 156
Songer, Donald R., 482
Sorauf, Frank J., 285, 308, 325, 327, 514
Sorensen, Theodore C., 137
Sorkin, Jill E., 507
Sowell, Thomas, 142
Spano v. New York, 119
Speakes, Larry, 246, 250
Specht, Harry, 597
Spencer, William J., 574
Spitzer, Robert J., 113
Squire, Peverill, 86, 206, 215, 283, 309, 344, 352, 364, 473, 507, 508, 509, 510, 565
Stanfield, Rochelle L., 498
Stanford v. Kentucky, 121
Stanley, Harold W., 72, 86, 87, 258, 283, 309, 311, 430, 434, 466, 483, 509, 521, 522, 523
Stanley, Jeanie R., 74
State Court Caseload Statistics, Annual Report, 485
Statistical Abstract of the United States, 69, 238, 239, 240, 242, 520, 523, 534, 536, 571, 590, 594, 595, 597, 599, 619, 621, 622
Stead, Deborah, 155
Steeh, Charlotte, 192, 196, 220
Steele, Michael E., 251
Steele, Shelby, 142
Steger, Wayne P., 612
Stein, Herbert, 565
Steinbruner, John D., 619
Steinfels, Peter, 111, 469
Stephens, Mitchell, 236, 252
Stern, William J., 513
Stidham, Ronald, 464, 483
Stigler, George J., 577
Stimson, James A., 72, 224, 276
Stith, Kate, 624
Stockman, David A., 574
Stockton, Paul N., 621, 625
Stoesz, David, 416
Stokes, Bruce, 303, 631
Stokes, Donald E., 204
Stoler, Peter, 247
Stoloff, David, 591
Stone, Clarence N., 90
Stone, Gerald C., 251
Stone, Ralph, 607
Stouffer, Samuel A., 191
Stout, Hilary, 304
Strickland, Ruth Ann, 42
Stromberg v. California, 101
Strossen, Nadine, 156
Stubbing, Richard A., 621
Sullivan, John L., 191, 192, 625
Sundquist, James L., 277, 280, 281, 283, 385, 624
Superville, Darlene, 242
The Supreme Court A to Z, 96
Sussman, Glenn, 510
Swain, Carol M., 354
Swann, Jon, 246
Sweatt v. Painter, 135
Swift, Elaine K., 335
Szakaly, Kristin, 520

T

Taagepera, Rein, 276
Tafel, Rich, 80
Takao Ozawa v. United States, 144
Taylor, Andrew, 556, 557
Taylor, Sandra C., 145, 242
Tebbel, John, 235
Tedin, Kent L., 173
Teixeira, Ruy A., 214
Term Limits Outlook Series, 510
Terrell, Paul, 597
Tetlock, Philip E., 191, 192
Texas Monthly v. Bullock, 468
Texas v. Johnson, 103
Thoenes, Sander, 409
Thomas, Clive S., 511, 512, 514
Thomas, Jennifer S., 421
Thomas, Stephen R., 581
Thomas, Sue, 355, 509
Thomma, Steven, 347, 357
Thompson, Dennis F., 358
Thompson, George C., 577
Thompson, Joel A., 511
Thompson, John L.P., 86
Thompson v. Oklahoma, 121
Thornburgh, Dick, 156
Thornburg v. Gingles, 344
Thurber, James A., 550, 553
Tidmarch, Charles M., 507, 510
Tierney, John T., 260, 300, 307, 313, 625
Tilton v. Richardson, 109
Times Mirror Center for the People & the Press, 170, 174, 240, 242, 256, 332, 547, 575
Timmerman, Kenneth R., 630
Tin, Annie, 446
Tofel, Richard J., 558
Tolbert, Caroline J., 354
Tompkins, Mark E., 507
Toner, Robin, 542
Torney, Judith V., 178, 217
Torry, Saundra, 155
Towell, Pat, 632
The Tower Commission Report: The Full Text of the President's Special Review Board, 618
Treadway, Jack M., 510
Trevino, September, 366
Truman, David B., 305
Tuchfarber, Alfred J., 284
Tucker, Harvey J., 510
Tulis, Jeffrey K., 415, 418
Tygiel, Jules, 134, 135
Tyson, Laura D'Andrea, 574

U

Udall, Morris, 349
Uhlaner, Carole J., 74
Ujifusa, Grant, 131, 276
U.S. Advisory Commission on Intergovernmental Relations, 497, 523, 524
U.S. Bureau of the Census, 589
U.S. Census Bureau, 69, 81
U.S. Congress, Committee on Post Office and Civil Service, 405
U.S. National Center for Education Statistics, 175
U.S. News & World Report, 75, 453
U.S. Senate Committee on Agriculture, 595
U.S. Term Limits v. Thornton, 6
U.S. v. Brignoni-Ponce, 146
United States v. Carolene Products Co., 100
United States v. Cruikshank, 104, 113, 130
United States v. Harris, 327
United States v. Leon, 118
United States v. Lopez, 53
United States v. Miller, 114
United States v. O'Brien, 101
United States v. Peltier, 118
United States v. Reese, 131
United States v. Ross, 117
United States v. Sioux Nation of Indians et al., 147
United States v. The Washington Post Company, 105
United States v. Virginia et al., 153
United Steelworkers of America v. Weber, 163
The Universal Almanac 1992, 69, 86
USA Today, 77, 358
Uslaner, Eric, 81, 625
Utter, Robert F., 486

V

Van Alstyne, William, 114
Vance v. Bradley, 158
Van Der Slik, Jack R., 505
Van Dunk, Emily, 509
Van Horn, Carl E., 501
Van Son, Victoria, 509, 519
Vega, Arturo, 355
Verba, Sidney, 207, 216

Victor, Kirk, 319
Vig, Norman J., 583, 584, 585
Vincent, Richard C., 180
Vines, Kenneth, 496
Vinson, John Chalmers, 607
Virginia Declaration of Rights, 112
Viscusi, W. Kip, 580
Vital Statistics on American Politics, 69
Voinovich, George V., 499

W

Waitzman, N., 580
Wald, Kenneth D., 81
Waldman, Amy, 484
Waldman, Steven, 577
Walker, Jack L., Jr., 297, 305, 307, 316, 320, 456, 471, 476
Walker, Thomas G., 95, 464, 481
Wallace v. Jaffe, 109
Wall Street Journal, 81, 163, 242, 244, 245, 312, 560, 571
Walsh, Kenneth T., 407
Walters, Evelyn, 186
Wang, 188
Warburg, Gerard Felix, 624
Ware v. Hylton, 466
Warren, Earl, 136, 480
Warshaw, Shirley Anne, 429
Wartzman, Rick, 242
Washington Journalism Review, 263
Washington Post National Weekly Edition, 248
Wasmann, Erik, 221
Waterman, Richard W., 421
Wattenberg, Ben J., 190
Wattenberg, Martin P., 283, 399
Watts, Sarah Miles, 235
Wayman, Frank W., 312
Wayne, Stephen J., 398, 400
Weaver, David H., 255
Weaver, R. Kent, 539, 596
Weber, Ronald E., 510
Webster v. Reproductive Health Services, 121
Weeks v. United States, 118
Weidenbaum, Murray, 427
Weingast, Barry R., 365
Weisskopf, Michael, 312, 580
Weissman, Stephen R., 615
Welch, Susan, 221, 227, 508, 509, 512
Wells, Robert Marshall, 332
Wenner, Jann S., 232
Weschler, Lawrence, 251
Wessel, David, 78, 523, 554
West, Jonathan P., 510
Westerfield, H. Bradford, 615
West Virginia State Board of Education v. Barnette, 111
Whalen, Barbara, 277
Whalen, Charles, 277
White, Joseph, 550, 551, 593, 624
White, Leonard D., 387
White, William S., 340
Wicker, Tom, 277, 581
Widenor, William C., 607
Wiggins, Charles W., 507
Wilcox, Clyde, 193
Wildavsky, Aaron, 397, 548, 551, 557, 560, 612
Wildavsky, Rachel, 558, 559
Wilhoit, Francis M., 136
Wilhoit, G. Cleveland, 255
Will, George, 358
Williams, Christine B., 177
Williams, Robert F., 485
Williams v. Florida, 120
Wilson, James Q., 285, 289, 306, 437, 441
Wilson, Laura Ann, 511
Wilson, William Julius, 590
Wilson, Woodrow, 442, 624
Wilson, Yumi, 126
Wines, Michael, 296, 313, 316, 545, 632
Winsky, Laura R., 510
Winternitz, Helen, 262
Winters, Richard F., 519
Wirt, Frederick, 521
Wisconsin v. Todd Mitchell, 104
Wisconsin v. Yoder, 111
Wise, Sidney, 388
Witkin, Gordon, 112, 113, 115
Witte, John F., 534
Wlezien, Christopher, 215, 546
Wolfinger, Raymond E., 68, 81, 86, 203, 206, 214, 215, 288, 338, 503
Wolf v. Colorado, 117
Wood, B. Dan, 421, 451, 520
Woodward, Bob, 263, 474, 475
Woodward, C. Vann, 139, 214
Wooley, John T., 567
Wormuth, Francis D., 613
Wright, Gerald, 178
Wright, Gerald C., Jr., 503
Wright, James D., 112
Wright, John R., 311, 313, 314, 472, 476
Wrighton, J. Mark, 420
Wrightson, Margaret T., 372
Wyatt, Joe B., 323

Y

The Year in Figures, 219, 233
Yepsen, David, 347
Yiannakis, Diana Evans, 349
Yick Wo v. Hopkins, 145
Yoachum, Susan, 126
Young, Amy E., 486
Young, James Sterling, 335, 387
Young, John T., 594

Z

Zakheim, Dov S., 622
Zaller, John, 177, 181, 189, 219, 272
Zeller, Belle, 509
Zhao, Xinshu, 176
Zimmerman, Joseph F., 507
Zingale, Nancy H., 225, 282
Zisk, Betty H., 320
Zuckman, Jill, 152
Zuk, Gary, 485
Zysman, John, 574

Subject Index

A

Abortion
  Planned Parenthood of Southeastern Pennsylvania v. Casey and, 478–479
  public opinion on, 193–194
  Roe v. Wade and, 121
Accommodating interest groups, 303
Activism. *See also* Political activists
  judicial, 467–468
Administrative discretion, of federal bureaucracy, 447
Advertising, advocacy, 316
Advice and consent, 429
Advocacy advertising, 316
Affirmative action, 160, 162–164
  government hiring and, 443
AFL-CIO, 301
African Americans, 72–73, 128–143
  Brown v. Board of Education decision and, 132, 135–137, 658–660
  Brown v. Board of Education II decision and, 136, 660
  civil rights legislation and, 139–141
  civil rights movement and, 138–139
  continuing fight against discrimination and, 141–143
  early civil rights organizations and, 133–135
  Jim Crow laws and, 130–133
  poverty among, 83–84, 86
  slavery and, 26, 128–129
Age
  of American population, 78
  protection against discrimination on basis of, 157
  voter turnout and, 203
Age Discrimination Act of 1975, 157
Age Discrimination in Employment Act of 1967, 157
Agencies
  of Executive Office of the President. *See* Executive Office of the President (EOP)
  federal. *See* Federal bureaucracy
Agenda
  foreign policy, changing, 629–631
  political. *See* Political agenda
Agricultural interest groups, 301
Agriculture Department, 448
Aid to Families with Dependent Children (AFDC), 439, 451, 586, 590, 594
Air Force, 452
Alien and Sedition Acts of 1798, 98–99
Amendments, to Constitution. *See* Constitution; *specific amendments*
American Bar Association (ABA), 301
American Farm Bureau Federation, 301
American Indian Movement (AIM), 147
American Indians, 75
  discrimination against, 146–148
American Medical Association (AMA), 301
American population, 68–88
  age of, 78
  budget deficits and, 546–548
  changes in, 70–72
  diversity of, 88–89
  education of, 81
  family households and, 78–79
  growth of, 69
  home ownership of, 86
  immigration and, 76–77
  language of, 77–78
  occupation of, 86–88
  political knowledge of. *See* Political knowledge
  presidents' relationships with, 421
  public opinion of. *See* Ideology; Political knowledge; Public opinion
  race and ethnicity of, 72–76. *See also specific specific groups*
  religion of, 80–81
  sexual orientation of, 79–80
  wealth and income of, 82–86
Americans with Disabilities Act of 1990 (ADA), 156–157
Amicus curiae briefs, 320, 476–477
Antifederalists, Constitution and, 28–29, 648–649
Appellate courts, federal, 483
Architectural Barriers Act of 1968, 156
Arms, right to bear, 112–116
Articles of Confederation, 22–23
  text of, 639–642
Asian Americans, 74
  discrimination against, 143–146
Assembly, freedom of, 104–105
Association, freedom of, 104–105
Astroturf lobbying, 319
Attentive publics, 176–177
Attitude consistency, 187
Attitudes. *See* Public opinion; Values and opinions
Australian ballot, 213, 272, 285–286

B

Babbitt, Bruce, 445
Baby boomers, 78
Bad tendency doctrine, 100–102
Balanced budget, 529, 553–556
  balanced budget amendments and, 558
Ballot, Australian, 213, 272
Ballots
  Australian, 213, 272, 285–286
  requirements for being listed on, 272–273
Bargaining strategy, used by presidents, 418
Bias
  in government rules, 14–15
  of interest groups, 307–308
  in news reporting, 251–253, 254–256
Bicameral legislatures, 36, 332–333. *See also* Congress
Bill of Rights, 30–31, 43. *See also* Civil liberties; *specific amendments*
  limits on government powers in, 37
  state government's authority and, 96–97
Bills of attainder, 37
Black Americans. *See* African Americans
Black Codes, 129
Blanket primaries, 270
Block grants, 496
Boggs, Thomas Hale, Jr., 314
Brady Bill of 1993, 115
Broadcast television, 240
Brown, Oliver, 132
Brown v. Board of Education, 132, 135–137, 658–660
Brown v. Board of Education II, 136, 660
Buchanan, Patrick J., 184
Buckley v. Valeo, 398–399
Budget and Accounting Act of 1921, 549
Budgetary process, 548–560
  continuing resolutions and, 550
  flat tax and, 558–560
  line-item veto and, 556–558
  1995 budget battle and, 554–555
  rationality of, 560
  reform in 1970s, 549–551
  reform in 1980s, 551–552
  reform in 1990s, 553
  from Washington to Nixon, 548–549
Budget deficits, 529, 546–548
  Congress and, 546
  presidents and, 546
  public and, 546–548
Budget Enforcement Act of 1990 (BEA), 553
Budgets
  federal. *See* Balanced budget; Budgetary process; Budget deficits; Federal budget
  state, 517–521
Budget surpluses, 529
Burden of proof, 160, 161
Bureaucracy, 426–428. *See also* Federal bureaucracy
  definition of, 427–428
  foreign policy, 618–624
Business interest groups, 300
Business Roundtable, 300
Byrd Rule, 373

C

Cabinet, 429–430
Cable News Network (CNN), 239, 258
Cable television, rise of, 240–241
Cable Television Reregulation Act of 1992, 311–312
Campaigns
  candidate-centered, 289, 399–400
  finance of, 308, 309–312, 325, 350–351, 396–399
  laws governing finance of, 396–399
  media coverage of, 258–262
  voter turnout and, 208, 210–212
Candidate-centered campaigns, 289, 399–400
Candidates
  campaigns of. *See* Campaigns
  characteristics of, voter choice and, 220–221
Capitalism, definition of, 181
Capital punishment, 120–121
Categorical grants-in-aid, 496, 497
Caucus/convention system, 270
Caucuses, congressional, 339, 390
Central Intelligence Agency (CIA), 452, 622
Central legislative clearance, 404
Centrist parties, 271
Checks and balances, 35–36
Chicanos. *See* Hispanic Americans
Chief diplomat, as presidential role, 389
Chief executive, as presidential role, 389
Chief justices, of Supreme Court, 471–472
Chief legislator, as presidential role, 389
Chief of state, as presidential role, 389
Citizen interest groups, 301–302
Citizen referenda, 514
City commission form of government, 522
Civil disobedience, 138
  as interest group strategy, 319–320
Civil liberties, 93–124
  Bill of Rights and. *See* Bill of Rights; *specific amendments*
  civil rights and, 127

constitutional interpretation
and, 94–96
of criminal suspects, 116–121
under First Amendment. *See* First Amendment
privacy as constitutional right and, 121–123
protection against cruel and unusual punishment and, 120–121
protection against search and seizure and, 117–118
Civil rights, 125–165
affirmative action and, 160, 162–164
of African Americans. African Americans
of American Indians, 146–148
of Asian Americans, 143–146
burden of proof and, 160, 161
civil liberties and, 127
early civil rights organizations and, 133–135
of gays and lesbians, 157–159
of Hispanic Americans, 146
of people with age claims, 157
of people with disabilities, 156–157
spatial model of elections applied to, 276–278
of white ethnic groups, 148
of women. *See* Women; Women's movement
Civil Rights Act of 1957, 139, 140
Civil Rights Act of 1960, 139, 140
Civil Rights Act of 1964, 140, 152
Civil Rights Act of 1991, 141
Civil rights movement, 138–139
Civil Service Reform Act of 1978, 441
Civil service system, 287–288, 440–441, 442–443
affirmative action and, 443
veteran's preference and, 442–443
Civil War, national supremacy and, 50–51
Classical economics, 565
Classical liberalism, 183, 185
Clay, Henry, 336
Clayton Antitrust Act of 1914, 577
Clear and present danger standard, 99
Clientele services, of federal bureaucracy, 437
Clientele support, as federal bureaucracy role, 447–448
Clinton, Bill, management style of, 412
Closed primaries, 270
Closing date, for voter registration, 207–208
Cloture, 371
Coalitions, among interest groups, 303
Coercive force, as basis of government's authority, 10–11, 21–22
Cold War
foreign policy during, 608
foreign policy following, 610–611, 627–633
Collective goods dilemma, 305
Colonial experience, Constitution and, 21–22
Command-and-control approach, 584–585
Commander in chief, as presidential role, 389
Commerce Department, 446
Committees, in Congress, 337, 338, 363, 364–367, 368–370, 370, 372
Concurrent majorities, 36
Concurring opinions, of Supreme Court, 481
Confederal government, 22, 47
Conference committees, 372
in Congress, 365
Conflict, 8–11
Constitution as reflection of, 20–31
in environmental protection, 584
within federal bureaucracy, 452–453
government's role in managing, 9–11
among interest groups, 303–304
roots of, 8–9
Congress, 331–379
bicameral structure of, 36, 332–333
budget deficits and, 546
caucuses in, 390
changing attitudes toward service in, 335–336
civil rights legislation enacted by, 139–141
committees in, 337, 338, 364–367, 368–370, 370, 372
constitutional provisions for, 38–39
decision making in. *See* Congressional voting
elections for. *See* Congressional elections
ethics and, 358, 360
federal bureaucracy and, 449–450
federal courts and, 463–464
foreign policy and, 615, 617, 624–625
House of Representatives and. *See* House of Representatives
as job, 355–358
legislative process in. See Legislative process
members of, 353–355, 356–357
party control of (list), 665
party leadership in, 361–364
policy oversight by, 376–377
political parties in, 360–361
presidents' relationships with, 420
representation and, 354, 377–378
Senate and. *See* Senate
staff of, 367
term limits and, 4–8
war power of, 614
Congressional Budget and Impoundment Control Act of 1974, 549–550, 551
Congressional Budget Office (CBO), 549, 554–555
Congressional elections, 341–353
advantages of incumbents in, 346–351
campaign money for, 350–351
challenger's disadvantages in, 351–352
districts versus states and, 345–346
incumbents and, 341–342, 346–351
midterm, 352–353, 417
redistricting and gerrymandering and, 342–345
voter behavior and outcomes of, 352–353
Congressional voting, 372–376
Byrd Rule and, 373
personal versus constituent preferences and, 375–376
voting cues and, 374–375
Congress of Racial Equality (CORE), 138
Connecticut Compromise, 26
Conservatism, 181, 183, 184
Conservative Coalition, 363
Constituent service, 347
Constitution, 19–54
amendment process for, 41–42, 45
Antifederalists and, 648–649
Articles of Confederation and, 22–23
bicameralism and, 36
Bill of Rights and. *See* Bill of Rights
checks and balances and, 35–36
civil liberties and. *See* Bill of Rights; Civil liberties; *specific amendments*
colonial experience and, 21–22
Congress and, 38–39
Constitutional Convention and. *See* Constitutional Convention
core provisions of, 38–42
Eighth Amendment to, 120–121
electoral rules and, 34–35
executive branch and, 39–40
federal bureaucracy and, 434–435
federal courts and, 462–463
federalism and. *See* Federalism
Federalist-Antifederalist controversy over, 28–29
Fifth Amendment to, 118–119
First Amendment to. *See* First Amendment
foreign policy and, 612
Fourth Amendment to, 117–118
individual rights and democratic rule and, 32
individual rights under, 42–43
interstate commerce clause of, 52–53
interstate relations and, 41
judiciary and, 40–41
legislative process and, 43–44, 45
limitation of government action and, 37
majority rule and, 32–37
necessary and proper clause of, 39
Ninth Amendment to, 122
obstacles to amending, 43–44, 45
original intent rule for interpreting, 95–96
political flexibility and, 44, 46
presidency and, 382–386
presidential powers and, 385–386, 403
ratification of, 28–31
Second Amendment to, 112–116
separation of powers and, 35
Sixth Amendment to, 119–120
supremacy of federal law and, 42
Supreme Court rulings on racial cases and, 656–660
text of, 55–66
Twenty-second Amendment to, 13, 385
Constitutional Convention, 23–28
Connecticut Compromise and, 26
New Jersey Plan and, 25–26
presidency alternatives considered at, 384
presidential powers and, 26–28
three-fifths compromise and, 26
Virginia Plan and, 24, 25
Constitutional courts, 464
Constitutional initiatives, 514
Constitutional referenda, 514
Constitutions, of states, 503
Consumer price index (CPI), 540–541
Containment, 608–610
Context of politics, 16
Continuing resolutions, 550
Contract With America, 4, 170
text of, 672
Corporate welfare, 544–546
Cost-of-living adjustments (COLAs), 539
Costs, of local government, 523
Council-manager form of government, 522
Countercyclical programs, 567
Court of Appeals Act of 1891, 464
Courts, 461–488
federal. *See* Federal courts; Supreme Court; Supreme Court decisions
state, 485–486
Criminal suspects' rights, 116–121
Critical elections, 281
Cross-cutting cleavages, 88–89
Cruel and unusual punishment, protection against, 120–121
Cynicism, of news media, 256–257

D

Daley, Richard J., 286–287
Death penalty, 120–121
Decision making, by Supreme Court justices, 477–480
Declaration of Independence, text of, 637–638
De facto segregation, 141–142
Defense Department, 447, 618, 619, 621–622
Deficit spending, rise of, 530–531
De jure segregation, 131–133
Delegate theory of representation, 377
Democracy, 34
definition of, 181
direct. *See* Direct democracy
news media and, 263

Democratic party, 271, 280–281. *See also* Political parties
civil rights and, 276–277
dealignment of, 282–283
formation of, 279
national organization of, 291–292
PAC contributions to, 311
realignment of, 284
Democratic rule, 32
Democrat-Republican party, 279, 390
Demographics. *See also* American population
political knowledge and, 174–175
voter turnout and, 203–204
Detente, 610
Direct democracy, 514–516
recall and, 515–516
referenda and initiatives and, 514–515
Direct initiatives, 514
Direct lobbying, 313
Direct primaries, 270, 286–287
Disabilities, rights of people with, 156–157
Discretionary spending, 543–544
Discrimination. *See also* African Americans; Civil rights; Women
reverse, 162–163
Dissenting opinions, of Supreme Court, 481
District courts, 483
Disturbance theory, 305
Diversity, of American society, 88–89. *See also* Ethnicity; Multiculturalism; Race; *specific groups*
Divided government, 353, 420
Domestic policy. *See also* Economic policy; Economic regulation; Regulation; Regulatory policy; Social regulation; Social welfare policy
foreign policy versus, 611–617
Dred Scott v. Sandford, 95, 129, 467, 656–657
Dual federalism, 51, 495
Duverger's Law, 276

E

Easy issues, 224
Economic constraints, on foreign policy, 627–629
Economic interest groups, 300–301
Economic issues, public opinion on, 190
Economic policy, 564–574
evaluation of, 569–570
fiscal, 566–567
income and wealth distribution and, 571–572
industrial, 574
monetary, 567–569
restraint versus intervention and, 565–566
supply-side economics and, 573–574
Economic regulation, 575–579
evolution of, 576–579
objectives of, 575–576
Edelman, Marian Wright, 315
Education
of American population, 81
as interest group role, 298
values and opinions and, 178–179
voter turnout and, 203
Education campaigns, of interest groups, 316–317
Eighth Amendment, 120–121
Elastic clause, 39
Elections, 34–35
campaigns for. *See* Campaigns
congressional. *See* Congressional elections
Constitutional provisions for, 34–35
critical, 281
geographically defined representation and, 35
gubernatorial, 507
indirect, 34
midterm, 352–353, 417
presidential. *See* Presidential elections
primary. *See* Primary elections
requirements for being listed on ballot and, 272–273
spatial theory of, 272–275, 276–278
of state legislators, 510
terms of office and, 35. *See also* Term limits
Electoral college, 400–402
Electronic media. *See* News media; *specific electronic media*
Emancipation Proclamation, 129
Endangered Species Act of 1973, 585
Enlargement, 611
Entertainment, news coverage as, 257–258, 259
Entitlement programs, 539–544
limiting, 543–544
public opinion on, 196
Social Security. *See* Social Security
Enumerated powers, of presidency, 385–386
Environmental impact statements, 582
Environmental protection, 581–586
evolution of policy and, 581–584
future directions for, 584–586
political conflicts in, 584
Environmental Protection Agency (EPA), 432, 438, 447, 451, 582–583, 585
Equal Employment Opportunity Commission (EEOC), 376–377
Equal Pay Act of 1963, 151
Equal rights, affirmative action and, 160, 162–164
Equal Rights Amendment (ERA), 44, 152
Equal-time provision, 248
Establishment clause, 43, 108–110
Ethics, Congress and, 358, 360
Ethnicity
of American population, 72–76. *See also specific groups*
multiculturalism and, 75–76
voter turnout and, 203
Exclusionary rule, 117–118
Executive agreements, 615, 616
Executive amendment, governors and, 505
Executive branch. *See also* Presidency
constitutional provisions for, 39–40
Executive departments, 428–430
Executive Office of the President (EOP)
functions of agencies of, 409–410
historical development of, 405
key agencies in, 406–409
staff's role in, 413–414
Executive orders, 421–422
Executive power, 27
Expertise, of federal bureaucracy, 448–449
Ex post facto laws, 37
Expressive benefits, of interest groups, 306

F

Factions, 279
Fairness doctrine, news media and, 248
Family, values and opinions and, 177–178
Family and Medical Leave Act of 1993, 152
Family households, of American population, 78–79
Federal aid, 494–498
consequences of, 497–498
dual federalism and, 495
fiscal federalism and, 495–496
forms of, 496
Federal Aviation Administration, 452–453
Federal budget, 527–561. *See also* Balanced budget; Budgetary process; Budget deficits
deficit spending increase and, 530–531
foreign policy and, 627–629
growth of, 529–530
inflation and, 540–541
national debt growth and, 532–534
persistence of deficits and, 546–548
revenue sources and, 534–537. *See also* Taxes
spending and. *See* Government spending
Federal bureaucracy, 425–460
administrative discretion and, 447
agency expertise and, 448–449
civil service system and, 440–441, 442–443
clientele services role of, 437
clientele support for, 447–448
conflicts within, 452–453
congressional constraints on, 449–450
constitutional foundations of, 434–435
definition of, 427–428
evolving role of, 456–457
executive departments in, 428–430
expanding functions of, 436–439
goals of, 445–446
government by gentlemen and, 439
government corporations in, 430, 432
growth of, 435–436
income redistribution role of, 438–439
independent agencies in, 432
independent regulatory commissions in, 430
interest groups and, 451–452
iron triangles and, 454–456
judicial constraints on, 453–454
national maintenance role of, 437
political character of, 442–445
political resources of, 446–449
power differences in, 449
presidential constraints in, 450–451
presidents' relationships with, 421–422
private sector regulation by, 438
reform of, 457–458
rule adjudication by, 433
rule administration by, 432
rule making by, 432–433
spoils system and, 439–440
Federal Communications Commission (FCC), 248, 438
Federal courts, 462–466, 483–485. *See also* Supreme court; Supreme Court decisions
of appeal, 483
Congress and, 463–464
constitutional, 464
Constitution and, 462–463
district, 483
federal bureaucracy and, 453–454
judicial activism of, 467–468
judicial review by, 466–468
legislative, 464
limitations on, 468–469
nomination and confirmation of justices for, 483–485
system of, 464–466
Federal Deposit Insurance Corporation (FDIC), 432
Federal Election Campaign Act of 1971 (FECA), 289, 350, 397–399
1974 amendments to, 397–399
1979 amendments to, 399
Federal Emergency Management Agency (FEMA), 432
Federalism, 37, 46–53, 494–502
changing nature of, 500–502
Civil War and, 50–51
confederal, unitary, and federal governments and, 47
dual, 51, 495

financial aid and, 494–498
fiscal, 51–53, 495–496
mandates and, 499
national supremacy and, 47–49, 50–53
picket-fence, 500
states' rights and, 49–50
Federalist No. 10 (Madison), 33, 296
text of, 643–645
Federalist No. 51 (Madison), text of, 646–647
Federalists, 279
Constitution and, 28–29
Federal Reserve System, 568–569
Federal Savings and Loan Insurance Corporation (FSLIC), 432
Feminization of poverty, 86
Fifth Amendment, 118–119
Filibustering, 371
Financial resources, of interest groups, 322–323
Fire-alarm oversight, 376–377
First Amendment, 97–104
establishment clause of, 43, 108–110
freedom of assembly and association and, 104–105
freedom of religion and, 108–112
freedom of speech and, 97–104
freedom of the press and, 105–108, 245–249
free exercise clause of, 108–109, 110–112
Fiscal federalism, 51–53, 495
Fiscal policy, 566. *See also* Government spending; Taxes
Flat tax, 558–560
Food and Drug Administration (FDA), 426, 451
Food Stamp program, 591
Foreign policy, 603–634
changing agenda for, 629–631
following Cold War, 610–611, 627–633
Congress and, 615, 617
Constitution and, 612
domestic policy versus, 611–617
economic and budgetary constraints on, 627–629
during era of globalism, 607–610
during era of isolationism, 604–607
executive agreements and, 615, 616
making of. *See* Foreign policy making
precedent and, 613, 614
president's influence over, 612–613
Supreme Court rulings affecting, 613, 615, 616
unilateralism versus multilateralism and, 631–633
Foreign policy making, 617–627
Congress' role in, 624–625
Defense Department's role in, 621–622
intelligence community's role in, 622–623
president's role in, 618
public's role in, 625–627
State Department's role in, 619, 620
Foreign Service, 620
Formula grants, 496
Fourth Amendment, 117–118
Franchise, 204. *See also* Voting rights
Franking privilege, 347, 349
Freedom, 181
Freedom of assembly and association, 104–105
Freedom of Information Act of 1966, 246
Freedom of religion, 108–112
establishment clause and, 43, 108–110
free exercise clause and, 108–109, 110–112
Freedom of speech, 97–104
political speech and, 98–101, 102
symbolic speech and, 101, 103–104
Freedom of the press, 105–108, 245–249
for electronic media, 247–249
libel and, 106–108
limits to, 246–247
obscenity and, 108
prior restraint and, 105–106
Free exercise clause, 108–109, 110–112
Free riders, 305
Free trade, 629
Friends, values and opinions and, 177–178
Frontloading, 395

G

Gays, 79–80
gay rights and, 157–159
Gender, voter turnout and, 204
Gender discrimination. *See* Women
Gender gap, 227
General Agreement on Tariffs and Trade (GATT), 629, 632, 633
General revenue sharing, 496
Gerrymandering, 344–345
Gilleo, Margaret, 102
Gingrich, Newt, 336
Globalism, 607–610
Going public strategy, used by presidents, 418–419
Government
conflict management role of, 9–11
divided, 353, 420
federalism and. *See* Federalism
by gentlemen, 439
hiring by. *See* Civil service system; Patronage
limits on powers of, 37
lobbying of, 312–316
media's influence on, 235–236
public opinion on level of, 524–525
Government corporations, 430, 432
Government interest groups, 302–303
Government lobbying, direct, 313
Government rules, 11–16
biased character of, 14–15
changes in, 15–16
policy, 12, 14
structural, 11–12, 13
Government spending, 538–546
changing nature of, 538–539
deficit, rise of, 530–531
discretionary, 543–544
economic management using, 566–567
entitlement programs and, 539–544
non-discretionary, 543
on pork barrel projects, 544–546
for social welfare programs, 593–594
by states, 521
Governors, 503–507
election of, 507
powers of, 505, 507
profile of, 504–505, 506
terms of office of, 503–504
Grace Commission, 457
Gramm, Phil, 184
Gramm-Rudman Act of 1987, 551–552
Grants, 496, 497
Grass-roots lobbying, 317–319
Great Depression, 565–566
fiscal federalism and, 52
Great Society, 52, 437, 590–592
Gross domestic product (GDP), 566
Group consciousness, 205
Groups, 16–17
Gubernatorial elections, 507
Gun control laws, 115–116

H

Habeas corpus, 37
Hard issues, 224
Health, Education, and Welfare Department (HEW), 451, 581
Health care programs, 592
future of, 597, 599–600
Hearst, William Randolph, 238
Henry, Patrick, 28
Hispanic Americans, 73–74
discrimination against, 146
poverty among, 83–84, 86
Home ownership, of American population, 86
Home pages, 243
Home style, 346
Honoraria, 356–357
Horse-race journalism, 258–259
Households, of American population, 78–79
House of Representatives, 333–334, 337–340. *See also* Congress
caucuses in, 339
change during 1970s and 1980s, 338–339
change during 1990s, 340
committees in, 337, 338, 363, 370
during early twentieth century, 337–338
legislative process on floor of, 370–371
majority leadership in, 361–363
minority leadership in, 363–364
during nineteenth century, 337
party control of (list), 665
reapportionment and, 334
seniority rule in, 338
turnover in membership of, 333
Hyde, Henry, on term limits, 7

I

Ideology, 180–187
changes over time, 183, 185
conservative, 181, 183, 184
ideological thinking by public and, 187
liberal, 181–182
molding of, 186–187
news media's bias and, 254–256
sources of, 185–186
Immediate scrutiny, 160, 161
Immigration, 76–77. *See also* Asian Americans; Hispanic Americans
Impeachment, 385
Implied powers, of presidency, 386
Incitement standard, 101
Income
of American population, 82–86
voter turnout and, 203
Income distribution
economic policy and, 571–572
redistribution as federal bureaucracy role, 438–439
Independent agencies, in federal bureaucracy, 432
Independent expenditures, 398–399
Independent regulatory commissions, 430
Individual rights, under Constitution, 32, 42–43
Individuals, 16
Industrial policy, 574
Inflation, 540–541
Inglis, Bob, on term limits, 6
Initiatives, state government and, 514–515
Institutional constraints, on presidency, 417–418
Institutionalized expectations, of presidency, 414–415
Institutions, 17
Intelligence community, foreign policy and, 622–623
Interest groups, 295–328
bias of, 307–308
citizen, 301–302
civil disobedience as strategy of, 319–320
coalitions and divisions among, 303–304
contributions of, 327
definition of, 296–298
economic, 200–201
education campaigns mounted by, 316–317
evaluation of, 323–327
federal bureaucracy and, 451–453
financial resources of, 322–323
formation of, 305–307
government, 302–303
government lobbying by, 312–316

grass-roots lobbying by, 317–319
growth of, 299–300
influence of, 320–323
iron triangles and, 454–456
leadership of, 322
litigation by, 320
maintenance of, 307
membership of, 322
objectives of, 323
obstacles to formation of, 304–305
political action committees, 308–312
political parties versus, 297
public opinion on, 323–325
reform of, 325–327
roles of, 297–298
in state politics, 511–514
inside strategies of, 308–316
outside strategies of, 316–320
Intermestic issues, 630
Internet, growth of, 242–243
Interposition, doctrine of, 49
Interstate commerce clause, 52–53
Interstate Commerce Commission (ICC), 430, 438, 576, 577, 578
Interstate relations, constitutional provisions for, 41
Iron triangles, 454–456
limitations on, 454–455
participants in, 454
political implications of, 455–456
Isolationism, 604–607
Issue networks, 457
Issue publics, 176–177
Issue voting, 221–224
easy and hard issues and, 224
prospective, 222, 223–224
retrospective, 221–223

J

Jackson, Jesse, 182
Jim Crow laws, 130–133
Journalistic conventions. *See* News reporting
Judicial activism, 467–468
Judicial review, 466–468
Judicial scrutiny, 160, 161
Judiciary. *See also* Courts; Federal courts; Supreme Court; Supreme Court decisions
constitutional provisions for, 40–41
Judiciary Act of 1789, 463, 466, 471
Justice Department, 447

K

Kennedy, Anthony, 478–479
Kennedy, Edward M., 182
Keynesian economics, 566–567, 567
King, Angus, 506
King, Martin Luther, Jr., "Letter from Birmingham Jail" of, 650–655
King-of-the-Hill rule, 370–371
Knowledge. *See* Political knowledge
Ku Klux Klan (KKK), 109–110, 131, 133

L

Labor Department, 447–448
Laissez faire, 565
Lame ducks, 503–504
Language, of American population, 77–78
Latino Americans. *See* Hispanic Americans
Laws. *See* Legislation; Legislative process
Leadership
in Congress, 361–364
of interest groups, 322
presidential. *See* Presidency; Presidential powers
Leaks, media's reliance on, 262–263
Learning, lifetime, values and opinions and, 180
Left, 181. *See also* Liberalism
Legislation. *See also* Legislative process
anti-discrimination, 139, 140, 141, 152, 156–157
anti-slavery, 128–129
antitrust, 577
budgetary, 549, 551–553, 556–558
campaign finance, 396–399
civil rights, 139–141, 150–152, 156–157
civil service, 441, 442
elections, 289
environmental, 581–584, 585
ex post facto, 37
federal, supremacy of, 42
gun control, 115–116
Jim Crow laws, 130–133
judicial, 463, 464, 466, 471
lobbying, 326, 327
obscenity, 108
presidential powers and, 403–404
social welfare, 589, 590, 592
state laws, 486
telecommunications, 244, 246, 311–312
voting and elections, 140, 206–208, 209, 344, 350
Legislative courts, 464
Legislative process, 368–372
committee process and, 368–370
in conference committees, 372
constitutional obstacles to, 43–44, 45
on House floor, 370–371
policy initiation and, 368
on Senate floor, 371–372, 373
Legislative referenda, 514
Legislatures. *See also* Congress
bicameral, 36, 332–333
proportional representation system and, 276
single-member, plurality electoral system and, 275
state. *See* State legislatures
Legitimacy, as basis of government's authority, 10–11, 21
Lesbians, 79–80
gay rights and, 157–159
"Letter from Birmingham Jail" (King), 650–655
Libel law, 106–108
Liberalism, 181–182
classical, 32, 183, 185
of news media, 254–256
Lifetime learning, values and opinions and, 180
Line-item veto
gubernatorial, 505, 507
presidential, 556–558
Literacy tests, 208
Litigation. *See also* Courts; Federal courts; Supreme Court; Supreme Court decisions
as interest group strategy, 320
Lobbying
astroturf, 319
of government, 312–316
grass-roots, 317–319
Lobbying Disclosure Act of 1995, 326
Lobbyists, 313
Local governments, 521–525. *See also* Federalism
costs of, 523
federal aid to, 494–498
federal mandates and, 499
forms of, 521–522
picket-fence federalism and, 500
privatization of government services and, 523–524
public opinion on, 524–525
representation and, 522–523
structure of, 522
Local party organizations, 285–290
consequences of reform for, 288–290
reforms affecting machines and, 285–288
Locke, John, 32
Lucas critique, 569–570
Lynching, 133

M

Madison, James, 29
on Constitution, 649
Federalist No. 10 of, 33, 296, 643–645
Federalist No. 51 of, 646–647
Mainstream interest groups, 303
Majority opinions, of Supreme Court, 480–481
Majority tyranny, 32
Management styles, of presidents, 410–413
Mandates, 499
Marburg v. Madison, 466–467
Market incentives, 585
Marshall, John, on federalism, 48
Marshall Plan, 607
Mason, George, on Constitution, 648–649
Massive resistance, 136–137
Material benefits, of interest groups, 306
Material scarcity, conflict resulting from, 8–9
Mayor-council form of government, 522
Means tests, 586
Media. *See* News media
Median voter hypothesis, 273–275
Medicaid, 501, 592, 594
Medicare, 592, 593–594
Medicare Act of 1965, 592
Merit civil service system, 287–288
Merit System, for judicial selection, 486
Middle class, 82
Midterm elections, 352–353, 417
Militias, state, 112–113
Miranda rights, 119
Mission goals, 445–446
Missouri Plan, 486
Monetary theory, 567–569
Money supply, control of, 567–569
Monroe Doctrine, 605–606
Motor Voter Act of 1993, 208
Muckraking, 237
Multiculturalism, 75–76
Multilateralism, 631–632

N

Name recognition, incumbents and, 351
National Aeronautics and Space Administration (NASA), 449
National American Woman Suffrage Association (NAWSA), 150
National Association for the Advancement of Colored People (NAACP), 104–105, 133–134, 135, 307
National Association of Manufacturers (NAM), 300
National debt, 529
consequences of, 533–534
growth of, 532–534
National Environmental Quality Act of 1969 (NEPA), 582
National interest, 611
National maintenance, as federal bureaucracy role, 437
National Organization for Women (NOW), 151
National party organizations, 291–292
National Performance Review (NPR), 457, 458
National Reconnaissance Office, 622–623
National Rifle Association (NRA), 112, 305, 306, 307
National Security Council (NSC), 408, 414, 618
National supremacy, 47–49, 50–53
Civil War and, 50–51
fiscal federalism and, 51–53
National Traffic Safety Board (NTSB), 452–453

National Voter Registration Act of 1993, 208
Native Americans, 75
discrimination against, 146–148
Necessary and proper clause, 39
Neo-isolationism, 611
Neutral competence, 413
New Deal, 52, 566
New Deal coalition, 281
New Jersey Plan, 25–26
News media, 231–264
campaign coverage by, 258–262
cynicism of, 256–257
democracy and, 263
evaluation of, 254–263
freedom of the press and. *See* Freedom of the press
ideological bias of, 254–256
journalistic conventions and, 236–239
news as entertainment and, 257–258, 259
ownership of, 243–245
political agenda and, 234–235
presidential election coverage by, 396
public opinion and, 233–234
readership and viewership and, 238–243
reliance on leaks, 262–263
reporting by. *See* News reporting
values and opinions and, 179–180
Newspapers. *See also* News media
decline of, 239–240
News reporting, 236–239, 249–253
changing rules for, 259
freedom of the press and, 245–249
horse-race journalism and, 258–259
muckraking and, 237
objective press and, 237
pool reporting and, 247
selection of topics for, 249–251
telling of story and, 251–253
yellow journalism and, 236
Ninth Amendment, 122
Nominations
of justices for lower federal courts, 483–485
presidential. *See* Presidential nominations
of Supreme Court justices, 473–474
Non-discretionary spending, 543
North American Free Trade Agreement (NAFTA), 303, 629, 630
North Atlantic Treaty Organization (NATO), 608
Nullification, doctrine of, 49

O

Objective press, 237
Obscenity law, 108
Occupation
of American population, 86–88
voter turnout and, 203
Occupational Safety and Health Administration (OSHA), 438, 452, 579–581
O'Connor, Sandra Day, 472, 478–479
Office of Economic Opportunity (OEO), 591
Office of Management and Budget (OMB), 407–408, 413, 451, 549, 554–555
Office of Public Liaison, 410
Office of the First Lady, 407
Office of the Vice President, 408–409
One Hundred Days, 417
O'Neill, June E., 554–555
Open primaries, 270
Opinion leader, as presidential role, 389
Opinions
public. *See* Public opinion; Values and opinions
of Supreme Court, 480–481
Organized labor, as interest group, 301
Original intent, 95–96

P

Parties. *See* Political parties; *specific parties*
Party dealignment, 282–283
Party identification, voter choice and, 217–220
Party machines, 285–288
Party platforms, 276–278
Party realignments, 281–282
Patronage, 285, 286–288, 439–440
Pendleton Act of 1883, 288
Penny press, 236
Pentagon papers, 105–106
Perception, selective, 234
Photo opportunities, 259–260
Picket-fence federalism, 500
Planned Parenthood of Southeastern Pennsylvania v. Casey, 478–479
Platforms, of political parties, 276–278
Plessy, Homer Adolf, 132
Plessy v. Ferguson, 131, 132, 657–658
Pluralism, 89
Pocket veto, 38, 386
Police-patrol oversight, 376
Policy
abstract symbols versus, 188–190
domestic. *See* Domestic policy; Economic policy; Economic regulation; Social regulation
federal courts' role in making, 466–469
foreign. *See* Foreign policy; Foreign policy making
initiation of, in legislative process, 368
Policy oversight, 376–377
fire-alarm, 376–377
police-patrol, 376
Policy process, 17
Policy rules, 12, 14
Political action committees (PACs), 308–312, 350, 352
Political activists, 215–217
causes of activism and, 215–216
types of, 216–217
Political agenda
building of, as interest group role, 298
media's influence on, 234–235
Political cleavages, 268
Political knowledge, 170–177
distribution in American population, 174–175
issue publics and, 176–177
limitation of, 170–174
sources of, 176
Political participation, 201–229. *See also* Voter turnout
activism and, 215–217
as interest group role, 298
voter choice and. *See* Voter choice
Political parties, 267–293. *See also* specific parties
caucus/convention system and, 270
centrist, 271
in Congress, 360–361
control of presidency and Congress (list), 665
conventions of, 390–391, 392–393
dealignment of, 282–283
description of, 268–269
direct primaries and, 270
Duverger's Law and, 276
fifth system in U.S. (1932–?), 281
first system in U.S. (1796–1824), 279
fourth system in U.S. (1896–1928), 280
functions of, 269–271, 272–273
future of, 283–284
interest groups versus, 297
local organization of, 285–290
machines and, 285–288
multiparty systems and, 275–276
national organization of, 291–292
party identification and, 217–220
platforms of, 276–278
presidential election defeat and, 278
realignments of, 281–282
relationships among party organizations and, 292
second system in U.S. (1828–1856), 279–280
spatial theory of elections and, 272–275, 276–278
state organization of, 290–291
third system in U.S. (1860–1892), 280
timeline of, 671
two-party system and, 271, 275–276
Political power, 89–91
Political speech, freedom of, 98–101, 102
Poll taxes, 208
Pollution prevention, 585
Pool reporting, 247
Popular referenda, 514
Population. *See* American population
Pork barrel programs, 544–546
Poverty, 83–86. *See also* Social welfare policy
feminization of, 86
measurement of, 85
Precedent
foreign policy and, 613, 614
presidential powers and, 404
Prerogative Model, of presidential power, 405
Presidency, 381–423
assessment as institution, 415
budget deficits and, 546
cabinet and, 429–430
conflicting expectations of leadership by, 416
Congress and, 420
congressional elections and, 352–353
constitutional provisions for, 39–40
constitutional rules governing, 382–386
elections for. *See* Presidential elections; Presidential nominations
Executive Office of the President and. *See* Executive Office of the President (EOP)
executive orders and, 421–422
external expectations' influence on, 414–415
federal bureaucracy and, 421–422, 450–451
foreign policy and, 612–613, 618
Franklin Roosevelt's impact on, 388
impeachment and, 385
institutional and political independence of, 383, 385
institutional constraints on, 417–418
lower federal court nominations and, 483–485
party control of (list), 665
powers of. *See* Presidential powers
in practice, 386–388
presidential management styles and, 410–413
relations with public, 421
roles of, 389
strategies for, 418–419
Supreme Court legacies and, 475
Supreme Court nominations and, 473–474
time constraints and, 417
two presidencies and, 612
Presidential elections, 389–402
campaign finance laws and, 396–399
candidate-centered campaigns for, 399–400
consequences for governing, 402

defeat in, 278
electoral college and, 400–402
media coverage of, 396
nominations for. *See* Presidential nominations
primary, 391–396
profile of electorate in 1980–1996 (chart), 670
results of (list), 662–664
returns by state in 1996 election (list), 668–669
Presidential nominations, 390–396
congressional caucuses and, 390
direct primary elections and, 391–396
party conventions and, 390–391, 392–393
Presidential powers, 402–405
Constitutional Convention and, 26–28
enumerated, 385–386
implied, 386
models of, 404–405
shared, 385
sources of, 403–404
Presidents, list of, 661
Press, freedom of, 105–108
Primary elections
blanket, 270
closed, 270
direct, 270, 286–287, 391–396
open, 270
Prior restraint, 105–106
Privacy, right to, 121–123
Privatization, of government services, 523–524
Pro-choice position, 193–194
Professional associations, as interest groups, 301
Program monitoring, as interest group role, 298
Progressive movement, 391
Progressive taxes, 536
Project grants, 496
Pro-life position, 193–194
Proof, burden of, 160, 161
Proportional representation (PR) system, 276
Prospective issue voting, 222, 223–224
Psychological characteristics
political knowledge and, 175
vote turnout and, 204–206
Public assistance programs, 586, 590
future of, 596–597
recipients of benefits and, 598
Public Broadcasting System, 245
Public opinion, 169–198
abstract symbols versus concrete policies and, 188–190
attitude consistency and, 187
causes of change in, 196–197
changes over time, 195–196
on economic issues, 190
foreign policy and, 625–627
ideological thinking and, 187
ideologies and. *See* Ideology
interest group mobilization of, 316–320
on interest groups, 323–325
knowledge about politics and. *See* Political knowledge
media's influence on, 233–234
on social issues, 190, 191–195
Public opinion polls, methods for, 172–173
Punishment, cruel and unusual, protection against, 120–121

Q

Queen-of-the Hill rule, 371

R

Race
of American population, 72–76. *See also specific groups*
multiculturalism and, 75–76
Supreme Court rulings on racial cases and, 656–660
voter turnout and, 203
Radical interest groups, 303
Radio. *See also* News media
freedom of the press and, 247–249
talk, rise of, 241–242
Rainy day funds, 520
Random samples, simple, 172
Rational scrutiny, 160, 161
Reagan, Ronald, management style of, 412
Reaganomics, 573
Reapportionment, 334
Recall, of state officials, 515–516
Reconstruction, 129, 280
Redistricting, congressional elections and, 342–345
Referenda, state government and, 514–515
Regressive taxes, 537
Regulation, 574–586
economic, 575–579
as federal bureaucracy role, 438
social, 575, 579–586
Regulatory commissions, independent, 430
Regulatory policy, 574
Rehnquist, William, 472, 479
Religion
of American population, 80–81
freedom of, 108–112
Representation
Congress and, 354, 377–378
delegate theory of, 377
as interest group role, 298
local government and, 522–523
trustee theory of, 377
Reprogramming authority, 403–404
Republicanism, 34
Republican party, 271, 280–281. *See also* Political parties
civil rights and, 276–277
Contract With America of, 4, 170, 672
dealignment of, 282–283
national organization of, 291–292
PAC contributions to, 311
realignment of, 284
Required reserve ratio, 569
Restricted Model, of presidential power, 404
Retrospective issue voting, 221–223
Revenue neutral taxes, 559
Revenues. *See also* Taxes
of states, 517–520
Revenue sharing, general, 496
Reverse discrimination, 162–163
Right, 183. *See also* Conservatism
Right to bear arms, 112–116
gun control laws and, 115–116
state militias and, 112–113
Supreme Court rulings on, 113–115
Rivlin, Alice, 555
Roe v. Wade, 121
Roosevelt, Franklin Delano, impact on presidency, 388
Rule adjudication, 433
Rule administration, 432
Rule making, 432–433
Rule of Four, 476
Rules. *See also* Government rules
bias in, 14–15
Byrd Rule, 373
constitutional, governing presidency, 382–386
electoral, 34–35
exclusionary, 117–118
original intent, 95–96
policy, 12, 14
seniority, 338
structural, 11–12, 13
two-thirds, 392–393
Rules Committee, 370
Rust Belt, 72

S

Save Abandoned Cats and Kittens Society of Syracuse, 304–305
Scarcity, material, conflict resulting from, 8–9
Schools, values and opinions and, 178–179
Search, protection against, 117–118
Second Amendment, 112–116
Segregation
de facto, 141–142
de jure, 131–133
Seizure, protection against, 117–118
Select committees, in Congress, 365
Selective benefits, of interest groups, 306–307
Selective perception, 234
Senate, 334
advice and consent of, 429
change in, 340–341
confirmation of justices of lower federal courts by, 483
confirmation of Supreme Court justices by, 474
leadership in, 364
legislative process on floor of, 371–372, 373
lower federal court nominations and, 483–485
party control of (list), 665
Senatorial courtesy, 483
Senior Executive Service (SES), 441
Seniority rule, in House, 338
Separate-but-equal standard, 131
Separation of powers, 35
Sex discrimination. *See* Women
Sexual orientation
of American population, 79–80
protection against discrimination on basis of, 157–159
Shakman, Michael, 286–287
Shays's Rebellion, 23
Sherman Antitrust Act of 1890, 577
Simple random samples, 172
Single-issue groups, 302
Single-member, plurality electoral system, 275
Single-member districts, 342–343
Sixth Amendment, 119–120
Slavery
legislation banning, 128–129
three-fifths compromise and, 26
Small Business Administration (SBA), 455–456
Smith, Margaret Chase, 356
Snowe, Olympia, 357
Social characteristics, political knowledge and, 175
Social context, 67–91. *See also* American population
Social groups, voter choice of, 226–228
Social insurance, 586, 589–590. *See also* specific programs
Social issues, public opinion on, 190, 191–195
Socialization, 177. *See also* Values and opinions
Social regulation, 575, 579–586
environmental, 581–586
to protect worker safety and health, 579–581
Social Security, 589–590, 593–594
future of, 595–596
Social Security Act of 1935, 535, 589, 590
Social Security Administration (SSA), 448–449
Social welfare policy, 586–600
concepts and categories of, 586–587
current status of, 593–595
evolution of, 587–592
Food Stamp program and, 591
future of, 595–600
health care and, 592, 597, 599–600
in other advanced industrial countries, 593
other types of governmental spending versus, 593
public assistance programs and, 589–590, 596–597, 598
relative emphasis on various programs and, 593–594
Social Security and, 589–590, 595–596
success of programs and, 594–595
War on Poverty and, 590–592
welfare as private sector and local responsibility and, 588
Socioeconomic status
political knowledge and, 175
voter turnout and, 203
Sociotropic voters, 222–223

Soft money, 399
Solidary benefits, of interest groups, 306
Sound bites, 260
Souter, David, 478–479
Southern Christian Leadership Conference (SCLC), 138, 182
Sovereignty, 632–633
Spatial theory of elections, 272–275, 276–278
Speaker of the House, 361–363
Speech, freedom of, 97–104
Spending, by states, 521
Spin control, 235
Spoils system, 285, 286–288, 439–440
Staff
congressional, 367
of Executive Office of the President, role of, 413–414
Standing committees, in House, 337
Stare decisis, 477
Planned Parenthood of Southeastern Pennsylvania v. Casey and, 478–479
State courts, 485–486
judicial selection for, 485–486
length of service on, 485
organization of, 485
state laws and, 485
State Department, 447, 452, 618, 619, 620
State legislatures, 507–511
elections, turnover, and term limits and, 510–511, 512–513
membership of, 509–510
organization of, 507–508
professionalization of, 508–509
State militias, 112–113
State party organizations, 290–291
States, 502–521. *See also* Federalism
Bill of Rights versus power of, 96–97
budgeting and, 521
constitutions of, 503
direct democracy and, 514–516
federal aid to, 494–498
federal mandates and, 499
governors of, 503–507
House districts versus, 345–346
interest groups and, 511–514
legislatures of. *See* State legislatures
picket-fence federalism and, 500
public opinion on, 524–525
relations among, constitutional provisions for, 41
revenues of, 517–520
spending by, 521
States' rights, 49–50
Stewardship Model, of presidential power, 405
Strict scrutiny, 160, 161
Structural rules, 11–12, 13
Subcommittees, in House, 338
Suffrage, for women, 149–150
Sun Belt, 72
Supermajority, 36
Supply-side economics, 573–574
Supreme Court, 464, 468–482
burden of proof and, 160, 161
career paths of justices on, 470–471, 472
chief justice of, 471–472
hearing of cases by, 475–477
individual decision making by justices on, 477–480
justices of, 470, 666–667
length of service on, 472–473
limitations on, 468–469
litigants winning cases before, 482
nomination and confirmation of appointees to, 473–474
opinions of, 480–481
presidential legacies on, 475
rewards of serving on, 473
rulings on right to bear arms, 113–115
voting patterns of, 481–482
Supreme Court decisions. *See also specific cases*
on criminal suspects' rights, 117, 119–121
on discrimination, 130–133, 135–136, 147–148, 153–154, 159, 162–163
on federalism, 47–49
foreign policy and, 613, 615, 616
on freedom of assembly and association, 104–105
on freedom of religion, 109–111
of freedom of speech, 99–104
on freedom of the press, 105–108
overturn of, 478–479
on racial cases, 656–660
on right to bear arms, 113–115
on term limits, 6–7
on women's rights, 153–154
Survival goals, 445, 446
Symbolic speech, freedom of, 101, 103–104
Symbols, concrete policies versus, 188–190

T

Talk radio, rise of, 241–242
Taney, Roger, on federalism, 48
Taxes, 534–537
economic management using, 566–567
flat, 558–560
historical perspective on, 534–535
income and payroll, 535–537
poll, 208
progressive, 536
regressive, 537
revenue neutral, 559
state, 517–520
Telecommunications Competition and Deregulation Act of 1996, 244
Television. *See also* News media
broadcast, 240
cable, rise of, 240–241
freedom of the press and, 247–249
Temperance movement, 186
Term limits, 4–8
for state legislators, 510–511, 512–513
Twenty-second Amendment and, 13, 385
Terms of office, 35. *See also* Term limits
of governors, 503–504
of presidents, 384
of state court justices, 485
of Supreme Court justices, 472–473
Third World, 608
Three-fifths compromise, 26
Time constraints, of presidents, 417
Trade
free, 629
interstate, 52–53, 430, 438, 576, 577, 578
multilateralism and, 632
NAFTA and, 303, 629, 630
Treasury Department, 431
Treasury securities, 569
Truman Doctrine, 607
Trustee theory of representation, 377
Turner, Ted, 239
Tweed, William Marcy "Boss," 210
Twenty-second Amendment, 13, 385
Two-party system, 271, 275–276
Two presidencies, 612
Two-thirds rule, 392–393

U

Unanimous consent agreements, 372
Unilateralism, 631
Unions, as interest group, 301
Unitary government, 47
Unit rule, 400–401

V

Values and opinions. *See also* Public opinion
conflict resulting from differences in, 9
family and friends' influence on, 177–178
lifetime learning and, 180
media's influence on, 179–180
schools' influence on, 178–179
Van Buren, Martin, 392–393
Velasquez, Willie, 210
Veteran's preference, government hiring and, 442–443
Veto
line-item, 505, 507, 556–558
pocket, 38
presidential, 385–386
Vice presidents
list of, 661
as Senate leaders, 364
Vietnam War, 609–610
Violence Against Women Act of 1994, 152
Virginia Plan, 24, 25
Voodoo economics, 573
Voter choice, 217–228
candidate characteristics and, 220–221
changes over time, 225
issues and, 221–224
median voter hypothesis and, 273–275
party identification and, 217–220
social groups and, 226–228
Voter registration laws, voter turnout and, 206–208, 209
Voters, sociotropic, 222–223
Voter turnout, 202–215
campaign contacts and, 208, 210–212
decline of, 212–214
demographic characteristics of voters and, 203–204
importance of, 214–215
psychological characteristics of voters and, 204–206
registration laws and, 206–208, 209
socioeconomic characteristics of voters and, 203
Voting
congressional. *See* Congressional voting
by Supreme Court justices, 481–482
Voting rights, 203
of African Americans, 140
of women, 149–150
Voting Rights Act of 1965, 140, 209
1982 amendments to, 344

W

War, power to declare, 614
War on Poverty, 590–592
Watt, James, 444–445
Wealth, of American population, 82–86
Wealth policy, economic policy and, 571–572
Welfare. *See* Social welfare policy; *specific programs*
Whig party, 280, 390
Whip, 362
White Americans, 72
discrimination against ethnic groups of, 148
White House Office, 406–407, 410
Women, 148–156
continuing struggle against sex discrimination and, 154–156
federal legislation protecting rights of, 150–152
feminization of poverty and, 86
right to vote and, 149–151
Supreme Court decisions protecting rights of, 153–154
voter choice of, 227
Women's movement
continuing, 154–156
early, 149–150
reemergence of, 150–154
World Trade Organization (WTO), 629, 632–633
World Wide Web, 242–243
Writs of certiorari, 475

Y

Yellow journalism, 236

1880 | 1890 | 1900 | 1910 | 1920 | 1930 | 1940

1881 President James Garfield assassinated by a disgruntled job-seeker

1883 Pendleton Act creates the Civil Service System

1887 Interstate Commerce Commission created, the first independent regulatory commission

1896 *Plessy v. Ferguson* holds "separate but equal" to be constitutional

McKinley-Bryan election; realignment toward Republicans

1897 *Chicago, Burlington, and Quincy Railroad Co. v. Chicago,* first application of Bill of Rights to the states

1898 Spanish-American War; the United States acquires Hawaii and Puerto Rico

1901 Theodore Roosevelt succeeds to presidency following the assassination of William McKinley

1903 Wisconsin becomes first state to use direct primaries for all nominations

1912 Woodrow Wilson elected president

1913 16th Amendment ratified, allowing income taxes

17th Amendment ratified, providing for direct election of senators

1916 Louis Brandeis named first Jewish Supreme Court Justice

1917 United States enters World War I

1918 World War I ends

1919 18th Amendment ratified, beginning Prohibition

Senate rejects the Treaty of Versailles

1920 19th Amendment ratified, giving women the right to vote

1921 Congress passes the Budget and Accounting Act, creating the Bureau of the Budget

1929 Stock Market crashes; the Great Depression begins

1931 *Near v. Minnesota,* restricts use of prior restraint

1932 Franklin D. Roosevelt elected president

1933 Roosevelt initiates New Deal during "First 100 Days"

20th Amendment ratified, moving the beginning of the president's term to January 20

21st Amendment ratified, repealing Prohibition

1935 Social Security system created

1819 *McCulloch v. Maryland* recognizes the implied powers of Congress and establishes the supremacy of national laws over the states

1820 Missouri Compromise enacted

1824 John Quincy Adams elected president by the House of Representatives despite finishing second in the popular vote

1829 "Spoils system" instituted for making federal hiring decisions

1830 Anti-Masonic party holds nation's first party convention

1832 South Carolina passes Ordinance of Nullification in an attempt to establish states' rights

1861 Southern states establish the Confederate States of America

Confederate forces attack Fort Sumter and begin the Civil War

1863 Lincoln announces Emancipation Proclamation

National debt surpasses $1 billion

1865 Civil War ends

Lincoln assassinated

Federal budget first surpasses $1 billion

1876 Rutherford B. Hayes elected president even though Samuel Tilden receives a majority of the popular vote

1820 | 1830 | 1840 | 1850 | 1860 | 1870 | 1880

1833 *Barron v. Baltimore,* Bill of Rights applies only to federal government, not cities and states

1841 William Henry Harrison dies and John Tyler becomes first vice president to assume the presidency

1846-48 Mexican-American War

1857 Dred Scott case

1860 Abraham Lincoln elected president

1866 13th Amendment ratified, abolishing slavery

1867 14th Amendment ratified, granting due process and equal protection

House impeaches President Andrew Johnson; Senate falls one vote short of removing him from office

1870 15th Amendment ratified, granting African Americans the right to vote